Management
Information Systems
Managing the Digital Firm

Second Canadian Edition

Kenneth C. Laudon
New York University

Jane P. Laudon
Azimuth Information Systems

CANADIAN ADAPTATION BY
Mary Elizabeth Brabston
I.H. Asper School of Business
University of Manitoba

PEARSON
Prentice
Hall

Toronto

For
Erica and Elisabeth
—K.C.L. and J.P.L.—

For my parents,
Donald Campbell Brabston and
Mary Jane Coolman Brabston
—M.E.B.—

National Library of Canada Cataloguing in Publication

Laudon, Kenneth C., 1944–

Management information systems : managing the digital firm / Kenneth C. Laudon, Jane P. Laudon; Canadian adaptation by Mary Elizabeth Brabston. — 2nd Canadian ed.

Includes bibliographical references and index.
ISBN 0-13-121352-0

1. Management information systems. 2. Information technology—Management. I. Laudon, Jane Price II. Brabston, Mary Elizabeth, 1948– III. Title.

T58.6.L38 2005   658.4'038   C2004-900278-3

0-13-121352-0

Vice-President, Editorial Director: Michael J. Young

Acquisitions Editor: Laura Paterson Forbes

Marketing Manager: Steve McGill

Developmental Editor: Maurice Esses

Production Editor: Cheryl Jackson

Copy Editor: Rohini Herbert
Proofreader: Mary Teresa Bitti

Production Coordinator: Janette Lush

Page Layout: Joan M. Wilson

Permissions Manager: Susan Wallace-Cox

Art Director: Mary Opper

Cover and Interior Design: Lisa LaPointe

Cover Image: Michael Prince/CORBIS/MagmaPhoto.com

1 2 3 4 5   09 08 07 06 05

Printed and bound in the United States of America.

ABOUT THE AUTHORS

Kenneth C. Laudon is a Professor of Information Systems at New York University's Stern School of Business. He holds a B.A. in Economics from Stanford and a Ph.D. from Columbia University. He has authored eleven books dealing with information systems, organizations, and society. Professor Laudon has also written over forty articles concerned with the social, organizational, and management impacts of information systems, privacy, ethics, and multimedia technology.

Professor Laudon's current research is on the planning and management of large-scale information systems and multimedia information technology. He has received grants from the National Science Foundation to study the evolution of national information systems at the Social Security Administration, the IRS, and the FBI. A part of this research is concerned with computer-related organizational and occupational changes in large organizations, changes in management ideology, changes in public policy, and understanding productivity change in the knowledge sector.

Ken Laudon has testified as an expert before the United States Congress. He has been a researcher and consultant to the Office of Technology Assessment (United States Congress) and to the Office of the President, several executive branch agencies, and Congressional Committees. Professor Laudon also acts as an in-house educator for several consulting firms and as a consultant on systems planning and strategy to several Fortune 500 firms. Ken works with the Concours Group to provide advice to firms developing enterprise systems.

Ken Laudon's hobby is sailing.

Jane Price Laudon is a management consultant in the information systems area and the author of seven books. Her special interests include systems analysis, data management, MIS auditing, software evaluation, and teaching business professionals how to design and use information systems.

Jane received her Ph.D. from Columbia University, her M.A. from Harvard University, and her B.A. from Barnard College. She has taught at Columbia University and the New York University Graduate School of Business. She maintains a lifelong interest in Oriental languages and civilizations.

The Laudons have two daughters, Erica and Elisabeth.

ABOUT THE CANADIAN ADAPTER

Mary Elizabeth Brabston, B.A., M.B.A., Ph.D., is a tenured Assistant Professor of Management Information Systems at the University of Manitoba's I.H. Asper School of Business. Dr. Brabston has also taught at the Copenhagen Business School as a visiting professor. Prior to the Asper School, Dr. Brabston taught at the University of Tennessee at Chattanooga. Dr. Brabston received her doctorate at Florida State University. A native of Alabama in the United States, Dr. Brabston became a Canadian citizen in 2003. Having spent her life working as a banker, political staffer, development officer, and academic, Dr. Brabston brings a comprehensive view to her analysis of how information systems can help organizations achieve their potential—and the challenges associated with doing so. Dr. Brabston's teaching and research interests focus on strategic planning and applications of information systems and information resource management, as well as electronic commerce design, use, and implementation. Her work has appeared in such publications as the *Journal of Computing and Information Technology, Journal of Computer Information Systems, Journal of Information Systems Education,* and *Human Relations.*

BRIEF CONTENTS

CONTENTS

**PART III CREATING AND MANAGING INFORMATION
SYSTEMS 323**

CHAPTER 10 SYSTEMS DEVELOPMENT 324

PREFACE

Management Information Systems: Managing the Digital Firm, Second Canadian Edition, is based on the premise that information systems knowledge is essential for creating competitive firms, managing global corporations, adding business value, and providing useful products and services to customers. This book provides an introduction to management information systems (MIS) that undergraduate and MBA students will find vital to their professional success.

DIGITAL INTEGRATION OF THE ENTERPRISE: THE EMERGING DIGITAL FIRM

The growth of the Internet, the globalization of trade, and the rise of information economies have recast the role of information systems (IS) in business and management. Internet technology is supplying the foundation for new business models, new business processes, and new ways of distributing knowledge. The wave of dot-com failures has not deterred companies from using Internet technology to drive their businesses. Companies are relying on Internet and networking technology to conduct more of their work electronically, seamlessly linking factories, offices, and sales forces around the globe. Leading-edge firms, such as Celestica, Cisco Systems, and Dell Inc., are extending these networks to suppliers, customers, and other groups outside the organization so they can react instantly to customer demands and market shifts. Cisco Systems' corporate managers can use information systems to "virtually close" their books at any time, generating consolidated financial statements based on up-to-the-minute figures on orders, discounts, revenue, product margins, and staffing expenses. Executives can constantly analyze performance at all levels of the organization. Digital integration both within the firm and without, from the warehouse to the executive suite, from suppliers to customers, is changing how we organize and manage a business firm. Ultimately, these changes are leading to fully digital firms where all internal business processes and relationships with customers and suppliers are digitally enabled. In digital firms, information to support business decisions is available any time and anywhere in the organization. Accordingly, we have changed the subtitle of this text to *Managing the Digital Firm*.

NEW COVERAGE IN THE SECOND CANADIAN EDITION

This edition more fully explores the digital integration of the firm and the use of Internet technology to digitally enable business processes for electronic business and electronic commerce. It pays special attention to new applications and technologies that improve firms' relationships with customers and create additional value through closer collaboration with suppliers and other business partners. It also calls attention to the need to demonstrate the business value of information systems in the organization. The following descriptions summarize this new direction.

EXPANDED COVERAGE OF ENTERPRISE APPLICATIONS FOR DIGITAL INTEGRATION

Systems for supply chain management, customer relationship management, knowledge management, and enterprise systems are the major enterprise applications that firms today are using to achieve digital integration. This edition more fully explores how companies are using enterprise applications to coordinate activities, decisions, and knowledge across the enterprise and to create value networks with customers and suppliers.

- Chapters 1 and 2 introduce the four enterprise applications.
- Chapter 2 provides detailed discussions of enterprise systems and systems for supply chain management and customer relationship management.
- Chapter 3 discusses value webs.
- Chapter 4 discusses how the Internet can be used for supply chain management.
- Chapters 6, 9, and 10 expand coverage of the information technology infrastructure for digital integration, including Web services, XML, enterprise application integration software, and Internet tools and services.

- Chapter 11 addresses the security issues raised by enterprise applications.
- Chapter 12 contains a section on the difficulties of implementing enterprise applications.
- Chapter 13 details decision support and executive support applications for customer relationship management, supply chain management, and enterprise-wide decision making.
- Chapter 14 provides an expanded discussion of knowledge management systems.

NEW FOCUS ON THE BUSINESS VALUE OF INFORMATION SYSTEMS

New material in Chapter 1 alerts students to the need to demonstrate how information systems contribute to better management decisions and higher firm profitability. Chapter 6 discusses the total cost of ownership of information technology assets and the question of whether firms should rent hardware, software, and other technologies from technology service providers or own them. Chapter 12 ("Information as a Critical Resource: Information Resource Management") has been reworked to incorporate the most up-to-date research in the MIS field on how to measure the business value of information systems.

NEW LEADING-EDGE TOPICS

In addition to new coverage of enterprise applications and the business value of systems, this edition includes up-to-date treatment of topics such as

- Collaborative commerce (Chapters 2 and 4)
- New Internet business models and private exchanges (Chapter 4)
- Utility computing model (Chapter 6)
- Peer-to-peer and grid computing (Chapter 6)
- Wi-Fi wireless networks (Chapter 8) and Wi-Fi security issues (Chapter 11)
- Web services (Chapter 10)
- Object-oriented modelling (Chapter 10) and Unified Modelling Language (UML) (Chapter 11)
- Business intelligence (Chapter 14)

INCREASED ATTENTION TO ETHICS AND PRIVACY

Chapter 5 provides a fresh, new look at the ethical, legal, and social issues in the digital firm. E-commerce has made privacy and intellectual property protection among the most pressing ethical and social issues today—issues that managers and business professionals cannot afford to ignore.

A TRULY INTERNATIONAL PERSPECTIVE

A new chapter (Chapter 15) is devoted to managing international information systems. Moreover, all chapters of the text are illustrated with real-world examples from over 100 corporations from around the world, including not only Canada but also the United States, Europe, Asia, Latin America, Africa, Australia, and the Middle East.

MORE EMPHASIS ON THE MANAGERIAL PERSPECTIVE

In keeping with the managerial perspective of the book, we have now combined the former chapters on computer hardware and computer software into one chapter (Chapter 6). At the same time, we have now added some discussions of technical material to the Companion Website (see the following section).

SUPPLEMENTAL COVERAGE ON THE COMPANION WEBSITE

In order to shorten the book somewhat, we are presenting some material on the Companion Website (www.pearsoned.ca/laudon) rather than in the text itself. This material falls into two main categories. In most cases, a prominent reference is included in the printed book in the appropriate chapter:

- Some technical material that was previously in the book has now been moved to the Companion Website, in keeping with requests from the majority of faculty members who adopted the first Canadian edition. Our philosophy in determining what, if any, material we would move to the Web was simple. We wanted to retain enough technical material that a student could immediately use what he or she had learned in buying and using a PC and that the material would prove useful, without being overwhelming, to a manager over the long term.

■ Some brand new material has been commissioned for the Companion Website. Concise discussions of such topics as SAS Miner, Encryption, Biometrics, and How to Combat Spam, Bugs, and Spyware extend the material in the printed book.

BOOK OVERVIEW

Part I ("Organizational Foundations of Information Systems and Technology"), consisting of Chapters 1–5, is concerned with the organizational foundations of systems, their strategic role, and the organizational and management changes driving electronic business and the emerging digital firm. This part provides an extensive introduction to real-world systems, focusing on their relationships to organizations, management, business processes, and important ethical, legal, and social issues.

Part II ("Information Technology Infrastructure"), consisting of Chapters 6–9, provides the technical foundation for understanding information systems. It describes the hardware, software, data storage, and telecommunications technologies that comprise the organization's information technology infrastructure. Part II concludes by describing how all of these information technologies work together with the Internet to create a new infrastructure for the digital integration of the enterprise.

Part III ("Creating and Managing Information Systems"), consisting of Chapters 10–12, focuses on the process of developing information systems in organizations. This part describes how companies use new information systems to redesign their organizations and business processes and the role of new technologies such as Web services for rapid application development and digital integration. Part III details technologies, policies, and procedures that must be in place to assure quality, security, and control. Managers must understand the business value of systems and manage systems-related change.

Part IV ("Higher-Level and Global Information Systems"), consisting of Chapters 13–15, describes the role of information systems in capturing and distributing organizational knowledge and in enhancing management decision making across the enterprise. It shows how knowledge management, work group collaboration, and individual and group decision making are supported by knowledge work, group collaboration, artificial intelligence, decision support, and executive support systems. Part IV also details issues in managing international information systems. Numerous examples are drawn from multinational systems and global business environments.

FLEXIBILITY OF CHAPTER ORDER

The chapters in the text are placed in a logical order for a typical introductory MIS class. However, some instructors prefer to teach the material in a different order. Accordingly, we have organized the book in a modular fashion so that most individual chapters stand on their own and do not depend on earlier chapters. For example, Part II on technology could be taught before Part I on organizational issues. Chapter Five on ethics could be taught at the end of the course.

FEATURES OF THE SECOND CANADIAN EDITION

For this second Canadian edition, we have created some new features and enhanced those that we used in the previous edition. Included are many unique features designed to create an active, dynamic learning environment. We have attempted to make the material more accessible, engaging, and meaningful. Thus, throughout the book we have paid more attention to functional business applications. We have also integrated applications of Internet technology throughout the text and the entire learning package. And we have incorporated more active hands-on learning projects and problem solving scenarios.

We have also enhanced our hallmark, integrated framework for analyzing information systems. This framework portrays information systems as being composed of management, organization, and technology elements. We use this model to describe and analyze information systems and information system problems throughout the body of the text and in the special features.

INFORMATION
SYSTEMS
SECURITY,
QUALITY, AND
CONTROL

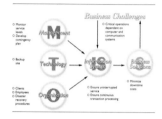

■ **LEARNING OBJECTIVES.** Each chapter opens with a set of learning objectives to help students understand the material effectively. The objectives in this edition have been redesigned to enable students to see more clearly how they can use the knowledge in their jobs. The objectives now list questions, answered in each chapter, in language that both IS professionals and general business managers can easily understand. And the chapter summary shows how the chapter answers those questions. Examples of these new objectives are:

- How can Internet technology support e-business and supply chain management?

- What computer processing and storage capability does our organization need to handle its information and business transactions?

- How should we manage our firm's hardware and software assets?

■ **CHAPTER-OPENING VIGNETTE.** An opening vignette describing a real-world organization establishes the themes and importance of the chapter. The vignette shows how a real-world organization meets a business challenge using information systems.

■ **BUSINESS CHALLENGES DIAGRAM.** A diagram analyzes the opening vignette in terms of the management, organization, and technology model used throughout the text.

■ **MANAGEMENT CHALLENGES.** Following the chapter-opening vignette, each chapter presents several challenges relating to the chapter topic that managers are likely to encounter. These challenges are multifaceted and sometimes pose dilemmas. They make excellent springboards for class discussion. Some of the Management Challenges include finding the right Internet business model, overcoming the organizational obstacles to building a database environment, and measuring system costs and benefits when they are difficult to quantify.

■ **"WINDOW ON" BOXES.** Three types of "Window On" boxes are used throughout the text: Window on Management, Window on Organizations, and Window on Technology. Each chapter contains two "Window On" boxes that present real-world examples illustrating the management, organization, and technology issues in the chapter. Each "Window On" box concludes with a section called "To Think About," containing questions for students to consider in applying chapter concepts to management problem solving. The themes for each type of box include the following:

- **WINDOW ON MANAGEMENT.** Management problems raised by systems and their solutions; management strategies and plans; careers and experiences of managers using systems.

- **WINDOW ON TECHNOLOGY.** Hardware, software, telecommunications, data storage, standards, and systems-development methodologies.

- **WINDOW ON ORGANIZATIONS.** Activities of private and public organizations using information systems; experiences of people working with systems.

■ **MIS IN ACTION: MANAGER'S TOOLKIT.** Each chapter contains a section entitled "MIS in Action: Manager's Toolkit" with a checklist to help students apply chapter concepts to deal with specific business problems, such as how to integrate the Wireless Web into business strategy, how to benefit from customer relationship management, and how to develop a disaster recovery plan. Students will find these sections useful guides when they work on projects for the course and in their future jobs.

■ **REFERENCES TO ADDITIONAL TOPICS.** As mentioned earlier, we have presented some additional topics on the Companion Website to supplement the material in the text. Boxed references to the additional topics are included in the appropriate chapter in the book.

■ **MANAGEMENT WRAP-UP.** Near the end of each chapter, a Management Wrap-Up, with Questions for Discussion, summarizes key issues using the authors' management, organization, and technology framework for analyzing information systems.

- **CHAPTER SUMMARY.** A summary keyed to the learning objectives is provided near the end of each chapter.

- **KEY TERMS.** Key terms are boldfaced where they are defined in the body of the text. They are restated with their definitions in the margins, and they are listed alphabetically with page references near the end of each chapter to facilitate review.

- **REVIEW QUESTIONS.** Review Questions in each chapter provide students with the opportunity to test their comprehension of the chapter material.

- **APPLICATION SOFTWARE EXERCISE.** A new improved Application Software Exercise in each chapter requires students to use application software tools to develop solutions to real-world business problems based on chapter concepts. Required data files and complete instructions are provided on the Companion Website. The exercises have been redesigned so that they require more critical thinking than the exercises in previous editions and so that they are more relevant to the topics in each chapter. The new Application Software Exercises include business problems such as the following:

  - Improving supply chain management (Chapter 2)
  - Analyzing a dot-com business (Chapter 4)
  - Designing a customer database for auto sales (Chapter 12)
  - Capital budgeting for information technology investments (Chapter 12)

- **GROUP PROJECT.** A group project near the end of each chapter encourages students to develop teamwork and oral and written presentation skills. The group projects have been enhanced to make more use of the Internet. For instance, students might be asked to work in small groups to evaluate the Web sites of two competing businesses or to develop a corporate ethics code on privacy that considers e-mail privacy and the monitoring of employees using networks.

- **INTERNET TOOLS.** A set of Internet Tools near the end of each chapter is divided into two sections. One lists additional material on the Companion Website. The other consists of an annotated list of some additional Web sites that students can access to discover more about the topics in the chapter. Some of these Web sites will be useful references for instructors as well. Students may find that they continue to refer to some of these Web sites long after the course is over.

- **CASE STUDY.** Each chapter concludes with a Case Study (with Questions) based on a real-world organization. These cases help students synthesize chapter concepts and apply their knowledge to concrete problems and scenarios. Case studies ask students to analyze how the systems that are being discussed provide value to the firm.

- **MAKE IT YOUR BUSINESS.** At the end of each part of the book, a new "Make IT Your Business" section shows how the topics covered relate to the major functional areas of business: finance and accounting, human resources, manufacturing and production, and sales and marketing. This section also directs students to pages in the chapters on which functional business examples can be found.

- **CANADIAN CASE STUDY.** Each part closes with a more detailed Canadian Case Study (with Questions) based on a real-world organization. A CBC video segment (provided on the Companion Website) illustrates some of the material discussed in the case.

- **REFERENCES.** A list of references is given near the back of the book.

COMPANION WEBSITE (WWW.PEARSONED.CA/LAUDON)

As befits a book on management information systems, we have prepared a robust Companion Website for students and instructors. It provides a wide array of materials for interactive learning and management problem solving, including the following:

- **INTERACTIVE STUDY GUIDE.** An Interactive Study Guide will help students review skills and check their mastery of chapter concepts with a variety of self-test questions. Students can send their answers to an electronic grader and receive instant feedback.

- **ELECTRONIC COMMERCE AND ELECTRONIC BUSINESS PROJECTS.** A Web-based Electronic Commerce or Electronic Business Project is provided for each chapter. Students can use interactive software at various company Web sites and other Web tools to solve specific business problems related to chapter concepts. These projects encourage critical-thinking skills as students explore business resources on the Internet.

- **MANAGEMENT DECISION PROBLEMS.** A Management Decision Problem is also provided for each chapter. Management Decision Problems provide opportunities to apply chapter concepts to additional real-world, management decision making scenarios. These problems can be used for practical group learning or individual learning both in and outside of the classroom.

- **ADDITIONAL TOPICS.** As mentioned earlier, some brand new material along with some technical material formerly in the book has been specially prepared to extend and supplement the text. A prominent reference to each additional topic is included in the appropriate chapter of the book.

- **CBC/PEARSON EDUCATION CANADA VIDEO LIBRARY FOR MIS.** The CBC and Pearson Education Canada have combined their experience in global reporting and academic publishing to create a special set of videos to supplement the textbook. The library consists of five video segments that supplement the part-ending Canadian Case Studies in the book.

- **GLOSSARY.** An electronic Glossary of all the key terms is provided for convenience.

- **DESTINATIONS.** The Companion Website also includes links to all the Websites described at the ends of the chapters in the book.

INSTRUCTOR'S RESOURCE CD-ROM

The Instructor's Resource CD-ROM contains a rich collection of materials to facilitate the teaching of the course. Some of the material presented on the CD-ROM can also be downloaded from a secure password-protected instructor's area of the Companion Website. The CD-ROM includes the following items:

- **INSTRUCTOR'S MANUAL.** The Instructor's Manual provides answers or notes for all questions in the textbook—namely, the questions in the "Windows On" Boxes, the Management Wrap-Up questions, the Review Questions, the Application Software Exercises, the Group Projects, the Case Studies, and the Canadian Case Studies. The Instructor's Manual also features an in-depth lecture outline, teaching objectives, and teaching suggestions.

- **PEARSON TESTGEN.** A comprehensive testbank of various types of questions has been prepared to accompany the new edition. The questions are rated by difficulty level, and the answers are referenced by section. The testbank is presented in a special computerized format known as Pearson TestGen. It enables instructors to view and edit the existing questions, add questions, generate tests, and print the tests in a variety of formats. Powerful search and sort functions make it easy to locate questions and arrange them in any order desired. TestGen also enables instructors to administer tests on a local area network, have the tests graded electronically, and have the results prepared in electronic or printed reports. Issued on a CD-ROM, the Pearson TestGen is compatible with IBM or Macintosh systems.

- **POWERPOINT SLIDES.** Electronic colour slides are available in Microsoft PowerPoint. The slides illuminate and build on key concepts in the text.

- **IMAGE LIBRARY.** The Image Library consists of electronic files of all the figures and tables in the book. These images can easily be imported into Microsoft PowerPoint to create new presentations or to add to existing ones.

ACKNOWLEDGMENTS

The production of any book involves valued contributions from a number of persons. I would like to thank all of my editors for encouragement, insight, and strong support during the production of this edition. Maurice Esses, who edited the first Canadian edition as well, is a truly outstanding editor who guided the development of both editions with a skilled and creative hand. I am also grateful to Steve McGill for his superb marketing work, Kelly Torrance and Laura Paterson Forbes for their role as acquisitions editors in managing this project, Cheryl Jackson for her production editorial work, Rohini Herbert for copy editing, Mary Teresa Bitti and Lu Cormier for proofreading, and Joan Wilson for formatting the book. Thanks also to Janette Lush for coordinating production of the text and Lisa LaPointe for designing the interior and cover of the book.

I would also like to thank the following instructors who provided formal reviews for the second Canadian edition. I am grateful for their efforts and expertise in helping to strengthen the new edition:

David Chan (York University)

Danny Cho (Brock University)

Elizabeth Evans (Nova Scotia Community College)

Len Fertuck (University of Toronto)

Rebecca Grant (University of Victoria)

David Horspool (British Columbia Institute of Technology)

Francisco B. P. Moro (University of Windsor)

Raafat Saade (Concordia University)

Roy Sinn (Langara College)

Carolyn Watters (Dalhousie University)

I would also like to thank my colleagues at the University of Manitoba's I.H. Asper School of Business who offered suggestions and support. It is my hope that this group endeavour contributes to a shared vision and understanding of the MIS field for many Canadian students.

Mary Brabston
I.H. Asper School of Business
University of Manitoba

A Great Way to Learn and Instruct Online

The Pearson Education Canada Companion Website is easy to navigate and is organized to correspond to the chapters in this textbook. Whether you are a student in the classroom or a distance learner you will discover helpful resources for in-depth study and research that empower you in your quest for greater knowledge and maximize your potential for success in the course.

Companion Website

[www.pearsoned.ca/laudon]

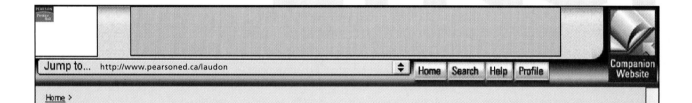

Jump to... | http://www.pearsoned.ca/laudon | ⇕ | Home | Search | Help | Profile

Home >

PH Companion Website

Management Information Systems: Managing the Digital Firm, Second Canadian Edition, by Laudon, Laudon, and Brabston

Student Resources

The modules in this section provide students with tools for learning course material. These modules include:

- Management Decision Problems
- Destinations
- Quizzes
- Electronic Commerce and Business Projects
- Application Software Exercises
- Glossary
- Additional Topics

In the quiz modules students can send answers to the grader and receive instant feedback on their progress through the Results Reporter. Coaching comments and references to the textbook may be available to ensure that students take advantage of all available resources to enhance their learning experience.

Instructor Resources

A link to the protected Instructor's Central site provides instructors with additional teaching tools. Downloadable PowerPoint Presentations, Electronic Transparencies, and an Instructor's Manual are just some of the materials that may be available in this section. Where appropriate, this section will be password protected. To get a password, simply contact your Pearson Education Canada Representative or call Faculty Sales and Services at 1-800-850-5813.

PART I

ORGANIZATIONAL FOUNDATIONS OF INFORMATION SYSTEMS AND TECHNOLOGY

MANAGING THE DIGITAL FIRM: CANADA AND THE WORLD

As a manager, you will need to know how information systems can make businesses more competitive, efficient, and profitable. After reading this chapter, you should be able to answer the following questions:

1. *What is the role of information systems in today's competitive business environment?*

2. *What exactly is an information system? What do managers need to know about information systems?*

3. *How are information systems transforming organizations and management?*

4. *How have the Internet and Internet technology transformed business?*

5. *What are the major management challenges to developing and using information systems?*

Toyota's Grand Vision

Building only cars that customers order and building them in record time have been every auto maker's dream. Now it appears that Toyota Motor Corporation is coming close to making that dream come true. In March 2002, Toyota signed an agreement to purchase $1.2 billion to $1.8 billion in software, hardware, and services from France's Dassault Systems S.A. and IBM to link Toyota's 56 plants in 25 countries and its 1000-plus suppliers. The technology will enable Toyota to model every aspect of car production, including the automobile's look, the parts that make it run, the sequence in which components are assembled, and the design of the factory itself.

Dassault will supply Toyota with its 3-D Product Lifecycle Management suite, which includes design collaboration, product-life-cycle management (PLM), and production-support applications. IBM will supply hardware, services, and additional software to link the PLM system with other systems in the company. The new system will replace Toyota's own internally developed

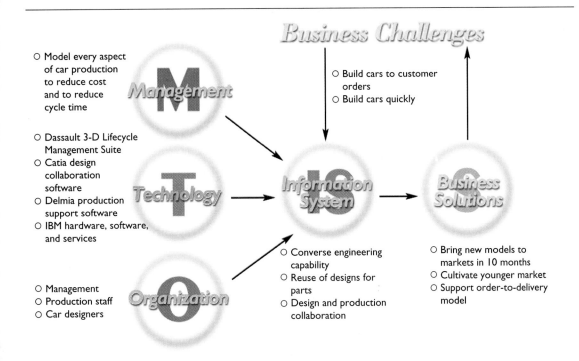

computer-aided design (CAD) and product-data-management systems, which have been highly praised but could not perform the functions Toyota needs to stay ahead of the curve in automobile manufacturing.

Dassault's design-collaboration software, called Catia, will enable Toyota's designers to collaborate with each other and with far-flung suppliers that are also design partners. They will be able to construct 3-D designs on the computer and then test these digital designs for "manufacturability"—determining whether the design of individual parts and assemblies of parts makes them easy to install as the car is being assembled. Toyota will be the first auto manufacturer to test designs for manufacturability on a global basis. Other manufacturers can only use such tools for isolated processes, such as testing the fit of precision parts in a critical assembly.

Toyota also plans to use the Catia tools for converse engineering: Instead of having engineers decide the car's design down to the last detail before sending a design prototype to production, many parts, such as alternators, that do not affect the car's styling will be created later in the process by production engineers. Rather than have concept and design drive manufacturing and other downstream processes, Toyota prefers using manufacturing efficiency to drive concept and design. Catia will also enable Toyota to reuse designs for parts, such as a hood. The car maker's engineers will be able to search a library of existing hood designs, use the software to change the shape and contours of a design, and automatically test the new design for manufacturability. Toyota can then use the hood's current supplier for the new part.

Dassault's production-support software, called Delmia, will let separate engineering teams use design and manufacturability data to create a plan that specifies the order in which parts are to be installed in a car as it moves down a production line. Toyota ultimately hopes to use that plan to digitally model the entire factory environment, specifying what is done at each step in the production process; which tools, supplies, and parts are required; the number of people stationed at each assembly stop; and the tasks they will perform. Toyota has already started using Delmia to model the production line in a few of its plants.

Once the design, production plan, and factory floor strategy fit together, Toyota can transmit the specifications for the new car model to its production and supply chain management systems. Integration of digital design and digital manufacturing will enable Toyota to bring new models to market in 10 months instead of several years. Product-to-market time has become more important as Toyota tries to cultivate a younger market. The average Toyota buyer is now 45 years old, and Toyota would like to attract more young buyers who purchase cars on the basis of the latest fashion trends. Toyota hopes its new design and production support systems will help it quickly turn marketing information about young consumers into cars that can take to the road within weeks.

Toyota's ultimate vision is to be able to use all of these new tools and ways of working to support an order-to-delivery model in which it could build a car to customer specifications and deliver it within days. Toyota used Internet technology to create the Dealer Daily system that links Toyota and Lexus dealers with Toyota's new design and production management system to help dealers work with customers to custom-configure their cars and have them delivered days later.

Sources: Steve Konicki, "Revving Up," *InformationWeek*, April 1, 2002, and "Toyota Paves the Road to Customization," *InformationWeek*, June 3, 2002.

The changes taking place at Toyota Motor Corporation exemplify the transformation of business firms throughout the world as they rebuild themselves as fully digital firms. These digital firms use the Internet and networking technology to make data flow seamlessly among different parts of the organization; streamline the flow of work; and create electronic links with customers, suppliers, and other organizations.

All types of businesses, both large and small, are using information systems, networks, and Internet technology to conduct more of their business electronically, achieving new levels of efficiency, competitiveness, and profitability. This chapter starts our investigation of information systems and organizations by describing information systems from both technical and behavioural perspectives and by surveying the changes they are bringing to organizations and management.

1.1 WHY INFORMATION SYSTEMS?

Today, it is widely recognized that knowledge about information systems is essential for managers because most organizations need information systems to survive and prosper. Information systems can help companies extend their reach to faraway locations, offer new products and services, reshape jobs and work flows, and perhaps profoundly change the way they conduct business.

THE COMPETITIVE BUSINESS ENVIRONMENT AND THE EMERGING DIGITAL FIRM

Four powerful worldwide changes have altered the business environment: (1) the emergence and strengthening of the global economy, (2) the transformation of industrial economies and societies into knowledge- and information-based service economies, (3) the transformation of the business enterprise, and (4) the emergence of the digital firm. These changes in the business environment and climate, summarized in Table 1.1, pose a number of new challenges to business firms and their management.

TABLE 1.1 | THE CHANGING CONTEMPORARY BUSINESS ENVIRONMENT

Globalization

Management and control in a global marketplace

Competition in world markets

Global work groups

Global delivery systems

Transformation of Industrial Economies

Knowledge- and information-based economies

New products and services

Knowledge: a central productive and strategic asset

Time-based competition

Shorter product life

Turbulent environment

Limited employee knowledge base

Transformation of the Enterprise

Flattening

Decentralization

Flexibility

Location independence

Low transaction and coordination costs

Empowerment

Collaborative work and teamwork

Emergence of the Digital Firm

Digitally enabled relationships with customers, suppliers, and employees

Core business processes accomplished via digital networks

Digital management of key corporate assets

Rapid sensing and responding to environmental changes

Emergence of the Global Economy

A growing percentage of the North American economy—and other advanced industrial economies in Europe and Asia—depends on imports and exports. Foreign trade, both imports and exports, accounts for more than 25 percent of the goods and services produced in North America, and even more in such countries as Japan and Germany. Companies are also distributing core business functions in product design, manufacturing, finance, and customer support to locations in other countries where the work can be performed more cost-effectively. The success of firms today and in the future depends on their ability to operate globally.

Today, information systems provide the communication and analytic power that firms need for conducting trade and managing businesses on a global scale. Controlling the far-flung global corporation—communicating with distributors and suppliers, operating 24 hours a day in different national environments, coordinating global work teams, and servicing local and international reporting needs—is a major business challenge that requires powerful information system responses.

Globalization and information technology also bring new threats to domestic business firms: Because of global communication and management systems, customers now can shop in a worldwide marketplace, obtaining price and quality information reliably 24 hours a day. To become competitive participants in international markets, firms need powerful information and communication systems.

Transformation of Industrial Economies

Canada, the United States, Japan, Germany, and other major industrial powers are being transformed from industrial economies to knowledge- and information-based service economies, while manufacturing has been moving to low-wage countries. In a knowledge- and information-based economy, knowledge and information are key ingredients in creating wealth.

The knowledge and information revolution began at the turn of the 20th century and has gradually accelerated. Today, most people no longer work on farms or in factories but, instead, are found in sales, education, healthcare, banks, insurance firms, and law firms; they also provide business services, such as copying, computer programming, or making deliveries. These jobs primarily involve working with, distributing, or creating new knowledge and information. In fact, knowledge and information work now accounts for a significant 60 percent of the North American gross national product and nearly 55 percent of the labour force.

knowledge- and information-intensive products

Products that require a great deal of learning and knowledge to produce.

Knowledge and information are becoming the foundation for many new services and products. **Knowledge- and information-intensive products**, such as computer games, require a great deal of knowledge to produce. Entire new information-based services have sprung up, such as Lexis, Dow Jones News Service, and America Online. Information-based fields employ millions of people. Knowledge is used more intensively in the production of traditional products as well. In the automobile industry, as shown in the chapter-opening description of Toyota, both design and production now rely heavily on knowledge and information technology.

In a knowledge- and information-based economy, information technology and systems take on great importance. Knowledge-based products and services of great economic value, such as credit cards, overnight package delivery, and worldwide reservation systems, are based on new information technologies. Information technology constitutes more than 70 percent of the invested capital in service industries, such as finance, insurance, and real estate.

Across all industries, information and the technology that delivers it have become critical, strategic assets for business firms and their managers (Leonard-Barton, 1995). Information systems are needed to optimize the flow of information and knowledge within the organization and to help management maximize the firm's knowledge resources. Because employees' productivity depends on the quality of the systems serving them, management decisions about information technology are critically important to the firm's prosperity and survival.

Transformation of the Business Enterprise

There has been a transformation in the possibilities for organizing and managing the business enterprise. Some firms have begun to take advantage of these new possibilities. The traditional business firm was, and still is, a hierarchical, centralized, structured arrangement of specialists that typically relied on a fixed set of standard operating procedures to deliver a mass-produced product (or service). The new style of business firm is a flattened (less hierarchical), decentralized, flexible arrangement of generalists who rely on nearly instant information to deliver mass-customized products and services uniquely suited to specific markets or customers.

The traditional management group relied and still relies on formal plans, a rigid division of labour, and formal rules. The new manager relies on informal commitments and networks to establish goals (rather than formal planning), a flexible arrangement of teams and individuals working in task forces, and a customer orientation to achieve coordination among employees. The new manager appeals to the knowledge, learning, and decision making of individual employees to ensure proper operation of the firm. Once again, information technology makes this style of management possible.

The Emerging Digital Firm

digital firm

Organization where nearly all significant business processes and relationships with customers, suppliers, and employees are digitally enabled, and key corporate assets are managed through digital means.

business processes

The unique ways in which organizations coordinate and organize work activities, information, and knowledge to produce a product or service.

Intensive use of information technology in business firms since the mid-1990s, coupled with equally significant organizational redesign, has created the conditions for a new phenomenon in industrial society—the fully digital firm. The **digital firm** can be defined along several dimensions. A digital firm is one where nearly all of the organization's *significant business relationships* with customers, suppliers, and employees are digitally enabled and mediated. *Core business processes* are accomplished through digital networks spanning the entire organization or linking multiple organizations. **Business processes** refer to the unique manner in which work is organized, coordinated, and focused to produce a valuable product or service. Developing a new product, generating and fulfilling an order, and hiring an employee are examples of business processes, and the way organizations accomplish their business processes can be a source of competitive strength. (A detailed discussion of business processes can be found in Chapter 2.) *Key corporate assets*—intellectual property, core competencies, and financial and human assets—are managed through digital means. In a digital firm, any piece of information required to support key business decisions is available at any time from anywhere in the firm. Digital firms *sense and respond* to their environments far more rapidly than traditional firms, giving them more flexibility to survive in turbulent times. Digital firms offer extraordinary opportunities for more global organization and management. By digitally enabling and streamlining their work, digital firms have the potential to achieve unprecedented levels of profitability and competitiveness.

Toyota Motor Corporation is using new software tools and Internet technology to drive its processes for designing and manufacturing automobiles and to integrate them with customers and suppliers. The company is moving toward a digital firm organization.

Digital firms are distinguished from traditional firms by their near total reliance on a set of information technologies to organize and manage. For managers of digital firms, information technology is not simply a useful handmaiden, an enabler, but rather it is the core of the business and a primary management tool.

There are four major systems that help define the digital firm that are described in detail throughout the book. **Supply chain management systems** seek to automate the relationship between suppliers and the firm to optimize the planning, sourcing, manufacturing, and delivery of products and services. **Customer relationship management systems** attempt to develop a coherent, integrated view of all of the relationships a firm maintains with its customers. **Enterprise systems** create an integrated enterprise-wide information system to coordinate key internal processes of the firm, integrating data from manufacturing and distribution, sales, finance, and human resources. Finally, **knowledge management systems** seek to create, capture, store, and disseminate firm expertise and knowledge. Collectively, these four systems represent the areas where corporations are digitally integrating their information flows and making major information system investments. You will learn more about these systems in subsequent chapters, and they receive special attention in Chapters 2 and 14.

A few firms, such as Cisco Systems and Dell Inc., are close to becoming fully digital firms, using the Internet to drive every aspect of their business. In most other companies, a fully digital firm is still more vision than reality, but this vision is driving them toward digital integration. Despite the recent decline in technology investments and Internet-only dot-com businesses, firms are continuing to invest heavily in information systems that integrate internal business processes and build closer links with suppliers and customers. Toyota Motor Corporation, described in the chapter-opening vignette, is moving toward a digital firm organization as it electronically integrates its key business processes with customers and suppliers.

WHAT IS AN INFORMATION SYSTEM?

An **information system** can be defined technically as a set of interrelated components that collect (or retrieve), process, store, and distribute information to support decision making and control in an organization. In addition to supporting decision making, coordination, and control, information systems may also help managers and workers analyze problems, visualize complex subjects, and create new products.

supply chain management systems

Information systems that automate the relationship between a firm and its suppliers in order to optimize the planning, sourcing, manufacturing, and delivery of products and services.

customer relationship management systems

Information systems for creating a coherent, integrated view of all of the relationships a firm maintains with its customers.

enterprise systems

Integrated enterprise-wide information systems that coordinate key internal processes of the firm, integrating data from manufacturing and distribution, finance, sales, and human resources.

knowledge management systems

Systems that support the creation, capture, storage, and dissemination of firm expertise and knowledge.

information system

Interrelated components working together to collect, process, store, and disseminate information to support decision making, coordination, control, analysis, and visualization in an organization.

information

Data that have been shaped into a form that is meaningful and useful to human beings.

data

Streams of raw facts representing events occurring in organizations or the physical environment before they have been organized and arranged into a form that people can understand and use.

input

The capture or collection of raw data from within the organization or from its external environment for processing in an information system.

processing

The conversion, manipulation, and analysis of raw input into a form that is more meaningful to humans.

output

The distribution of processed information to the people who will use it or to the activities for which it will be used.

feedback

Output that is returned to the appropriate members of the organization to help them evaluate or correct input or processing.

Information systems contain information about significant people, places, and things within the organization or in the environment surrounding it. By **information**, we mean data that have been shaped into a form that is meaningful and useful to human beings. **Data**, in contrast, are streams of raw facts representing events occurring in organizations or the physical environment before they have been organized and arranged into a form that people can understand and use.

A brief example contrasting information and data may prove useful. Supermarket checkout counters ring up millions of pieces of data, such as product identification numbers or the cost of each item sold. These pieces of data can be summed and analyzed to provide meaningful information, such as the total number of bottles of dish-washing detergent sold at a particular store, which brands of dish-washing detergent were selling the most rapidly at that store or sales territory, or the total amount spent on that brand of dish-washing detergent at that store or sales region (see Figure 1.1).

Three activities in an information system produce the information that organizations need to make decisions, control operations, analyze problems, and create new products or services. These activities are input, processing, and output (see Figure 1.2). **Input** captures or collects raw data from within the organization or from its external environment. **Processing** converts this raw input into a more meaningful form. **Output** transfers the processed information to the people who will use it or to the activities for which it will be used. Information systems also require **feedback**, which is output that is returned to appropriate members of the organization to help them evaluate or correct the input or processing stage.

In Toyota Motor Corporation's system for transmitting designs to production, the raw input would most likely consist of the part identification number, the part description, the cost of the part, the identification number and name of the part supplier, and perhaps a graphic representation of that component. A computer stores these data and processes them by analyzing how a part's shape and size might change if engineers changed a few specifications, the impact of using that part on the cost of producing a car, and whether it would be easy to assemble in Toyota cars. The system would display graphics showing changes made to the part designs and reports indicating the cost and manufacturability of these parts, which become the system outputs. The system, thus, provides meaningful information, such as what parts are supplied by what manufacturers, the cost of these parts, what designs could be reused, and whether a specific part would fit well in a Toyota car.

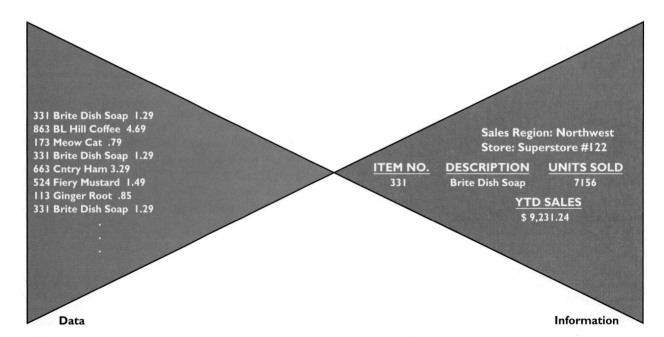

Figure 1.1 Data and information. Raw data from a supermarket checkout counter can be processed and organized in order to produce meaningful information, such as the total unit sales of dish-washing detergent or the total sales revenue from dish-washing detergent for a specific store or sales territory.

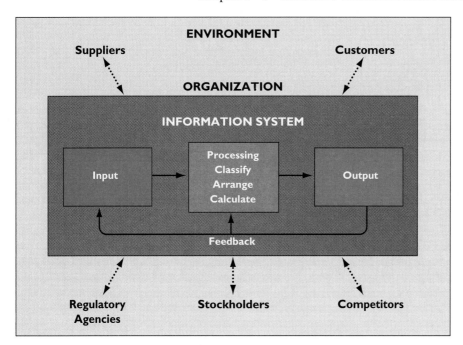

Figure 1.2 Functions of an information system. An information system contains information about an organization and its surrounding environment. Three basic activities—input, processing, and output—produce the information organizations need. Feedback is output returned to appropriate people or activities in the organization to evaluate and refine the input or processing. Environmental factors, such as customers, suppliers, competitors, stockholders, and regulatory agencies, interact with the organization and its information systems.

Our interest in this book is in formal, organizational **computer-based information systems (CBIS)**, such as those designed and used by Toyota Motor Corporation and its customers, suppliers, and employees. **Formal systems** rest on accepted and fixed definitions of data and procedures for collecting, storing, processing, disseminating, and using these data. The formal systems we describe in this text are structured; that is, they operate in conformity with predefined rules that are relatively fixed and not easily changed. For instance, Toyota's systems would require a unique number for identifying each part, a description of that part, the identification of the part supplier, and the cost of the part.

Informal information systems (such as office gossip networks) rely, by contrast, on unstated rules of behaviour. There is no agreement on what is information or on how it will be stored and processed. These informal systems are essential for the life of an organization, but an analysis of their qualities is beyond the scope of this text.

Formal information systems can be either computer based or manual. Manual systems use paper-and-pencil technology. Manual systems serve important needs, but they, too, are not the subject of this text. Computer-based information systems, in contrast, rely on computer hardware and software technology to process and disseminate information. From this point on, when we use the term *information systems,* we are referring to computer-based information systems—formal organizational systems that rely on computer technology. The Window on Technology describes some of the typical technologies used in computer-based information systems today.

Although computer-based information systems use computer technology to process raw data into meaningful information, there is a sharp distinction between a computer and a computer program on the one hand and an information system on the other. Electronic computers and related software programs are the technical foundation, the tools and materials, of modern information systems. Computers provide the equipment for storing and processing information. Computer programs, or software, are sets of operating instructions that direct and control computer processing. Knowing how computers and computer programs work is important in designing solutions to organizational problems, but computers are only part of an information system. A house is an appropriate analogy. Houses are built with hammers, nails, and wood, but these do not make a house. The architecture, design, setting, landscaping, and all of the decisions that lead to the creation of these features are part of the house and are crucial for solving the problem of putting a roof over one's head. Computers and programs are the hammer, nails, and lumber of CBIS, but alone they cannot produce the information a particular organization needs. To understand information systems, one must understand the problems they are designed to solve, their architectural and design elements, and the organizational processes that lead to these solutions.

computer-based information systems (CBIS)

Information systems that rely on computer hardware and software for processing and disseminating information.

formal system

System resting on accepted and fixed definitions of data and procedures, operating with predefined rules.

UPS COMPETES GLOBALLY WITH INFORMATION TECHNOLOGY

United Parcel Service (UPS), the world's largest air and ground package-distribution company, started out in 1907 in a closet-size basement office. Jim Casey and Claude Ryan—two teenagers from Seattle with two bicycles and one telephone—promised the "best service and lowest rates." UPS has used this formula successfully for more than 90 years.

Today, UPS delivers more than 13.6 million parcels and documents each day to the United States and to more than 200 other countries and territories. The firm has been able to maintain its leadership in small-package delivery services in the face of stiff competition from FedEx and Airborne Express by investing heavily in advanced information technology. During the past decade, UPS has poured more than $1 billion a year into technology and systems to boost customer service while keeping costs low and streamlining its overall operations.

Using a handheld computer called a Delivery Information Acquisition Device (DIAD), UPS drivers automatically capture customers' signatures along with pickup, delivery, and time-card information. The drivers then place the DIAD into their truck's vehicle adapter, an information-transmitting device that is connected to the cellular telephone network. (Drivers may also transmit and receive information using an internal radio in the DIAD.) Package tracking information is then transmitted to UPS's main computers in Mahwah, New Jersey, and Alpharetta, Georgia. From there, the information can be accessed worldwide to provide proof of delivery to the customer or respond to customer queries.

Through its automated package tracking system, UPS can monitor packages throughout the delivery process. At various points along the route from sender to receiver, a barcode device scans shipping information on the package label; the information is then fed into the central computer. Customer service representatives can check the status of any package from desktop computers linked to the central computers and are able to respond immediately to inquiries from customers. UPS customers can also access

this information from the company's Web site, using their own computers or wireless devices, such as pagers and cell phones.

Anyone with a package to ship can access the UPS Web site to track packages, check delivery routes, calculate shipping rates, determine time in transit, and schedule a pickup. Businesses anywhere can use the Web site to arrange UPS shipments and bill the shipments to the company's UPS account number or credit card. The data collected at the UPS Web site are transmitted to the UPS central computer and then back to the customer after processing. UPS also provides tools that enable such customers as Cisco Systems to embed UPS functions, such as tracking and cost calculations into their own Web sites so that they can track shipments without visiting the UPS site.

UPS recently created a UPS Supply Chain Solutions division that provides a complete bundle of standardized services to subscribing companies at a fraction of what it would cost to build their own systems and infrastructure. These services include supply chain design and management, freight forwarding, customs brokerage, mail services, multimodal transportation, and financial services in addition to logistic services.

To Think About: What are the inputs, processing, and outputs of UPS's package tracking system? What technologies are used? How are these technologies related to UPS's business strategy? How do they provide value for the customer? What would happen if these technologies were not available?

Sources: Dave Clarke Mora, "UPS CEO Mike Eskew, Thinking at the Speed of Business," *Profit,* May 2002; "Eskew: UPS Targeting Supply Chain," *JoC Online,* May 7, 2002; "UPS Logistics Interview with Tim Geiken, UPS Vice President of E-Commerce Marketing," *eyefortransport,* March 22, 2002, **www.eyefortransport.com**; Brent Adams, "UPS Logistics Provides Variety of Services at Local Center," *Business First,* April 19, 2002; Samuel Greengard, "United Parcel Service: Ahead of Time," *IQ Magazine,* May/June 2001; and Rick Brooks, "Got Mail?" *Wall Street Journal,* June 22, 2001; and Rick Brooks, "Outside the Box," *Wall Street Journal,* E-Commerce section, February 12, 2001.

A BUSINESS PERSPECTIVE ON INFORMATION SYSTEMS

Businesses are not in the business of processing information for its own sake. Instead, they process information in order to improve organizational performance and produce profits. From a business perspective, an information system is an important instrument for creating value for the organization. There are many ways in which information systems can contribute to a firm's value, including increasing the firm's return on its investments (accounting ROI), enhancing the company's strategic position, or increasing the market value of the firm's stock. (More detail on alternative ways to measure the business value of information systems can be found in Chapters 3 and 12). Information processing activities support management decision making, enhance the execution of business processes and, as a result, increase business value. For example, the information system for analyzing supermarket checkout data illustrated in Figure 1.1 can increase firm profitability by helping managers make better decisions about which products to stock and promote in retail supermarkets.

Every business has an *information value chain*, illustrated in Figure 1.3, in which raw information is systematically acquired and then transformed through various stages that add value to that information. Immediately, we can see that the value of an information system to a business as well as the decision to invest in any new information system is, in large part, determined by the extent to which the system will lead to better management decisions, more efficient business processes, and higher firm profitability. Although there are other reasons why systems are developed, their primary purpose is to contribute to corporate value.

The business perspective calls attention to the organizational and managerial natures of information systems. An information system also represents organizational and management solutions, based on information technology, to challenges posed by the environment. To fully understand information systems, a manager must understand the broader organization, management, and information technology dimensions of systems (see Figure 1.4) and their power to provide solutions to challenges and problems in the business environment. We refer to this broader understanding of information systems, which encompasses an understanding of the management and organizational dimensions of systems as well as the technical dimensions of systems as **information systems literacy**. Information systems literacy includes a behavioural as well as a technical approach to studying information systems. **Computer literacy**, in contrast, focuses primarily on knowledge of information technology.

Review the diagram at the beginning of the chapter that reflects this expanded definition of an information system. The diagram shows how Toyota's design collaboration and production support systems and its dealer system solve the business challenges presented by changing

Using a handheld computer called a Delivery Information Acquisition Device (DIAD), UPS drivers automatically capture customers' signatures along with pickup, delivery, and time-card information. UPS information systems use these data to track packages while they are being transported.

information systems literacy

Broad-based understanding of information systems that includes behavioural knowledge about organizations and individuals using information systems as well as technical knowledge about computers.

computer literacy

Knowledge about information technology, focusing on understanding how computer-based technologies work.

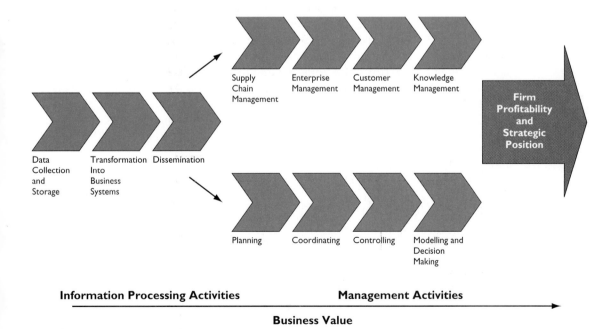

Figure 1.3 The business information value chain. From a business perspective, information systems are part of a series of value-adding activities for acquiring, transforming, and distributing information that managers can use to improve decision making, enhance organizational performance, and ultimately increase firm profitability.

Figure 1.4 Information systems are more than computers. Using information systems effectively requires an understanding of the organization, management, and information technology shaping the systems. All information systems can be described as organizational and management solutions to challenges posed by the environment that will help create value for the firm.

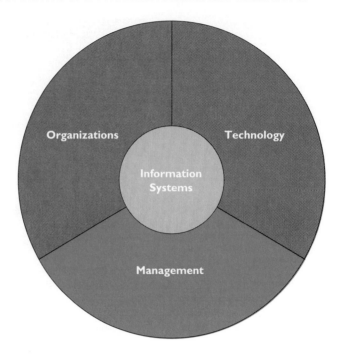

markets and diminishing product-to-market cycles. These systems create value for Toyota by making its product development and production processes more efficient and cost effective. The diagram also illustrates how management, technology, and organizational elements work together to create the systems. Each chapter of this text begins with a diagram similar to this one to help you analyze the chapter opening case. You can use this diagram as a starting point for analyzing any information system or information system problem you encounter. The Manager's Toolkit provides guidelines on how to use this framework for problem solving.

Organizations

Information systems are an integral part of organizations. Indeed, for some companies, such as credit reporting firms, there would be no business without information systems. The key elements of an organization are its people, structure, operating procedures, politics, and culture. We introduce these components of organizations here and describe them in greater detail in Chapter 3. Organizations are composed of different levels and specialties. Their structures reveal a clear-cut division of labour. Experts are employed and trained for different functions. The major **business functions**, or specialized tasks performed by business organizations, consist of sales and marketing, manufacturing, finance, accounting, and human resources (see Table 1.2).

Chapter 2 provides more detail on these business functions and the ways in which they are supported by information systems. Each part of this text now concludes with a *Make IT*

business functions

Specialized tasks performed in a business organization, including manufacturing and production, sales and marketing, finance, accounting, and human resources.

MIS IN ACTION: MANAGER'S TOOLKIT

HOW TO ANALYZE A BUSINESS INFORMATION SYSTEM PROBLEM

Information system problems in the business world represent a combination of management, organization, and technology issues. Here is a six-step process for analyzing a business problem involving information systems.

1. Identify the problem. What kind of problem is it? Is it a management problem, an organizational problem, a technology problem, or a combination of these? What are the management, organization, and technology issues that contributed to the problem?

2. What is the solution to the problem? What are the objectives of this solution? Are several alternative solutions possible? Which is the best alternative, and why?

3. How will this solution provide value for the firm?

4. What technologies could be used to generate the solution?

5. What changes to organizational processes will be required by the solution?

6. What management policy will be required to implement the solution?

TABLE 1.2	MAJOR BUSINESS FUNCTIONS
Function	**Purpose**
Sales and marketing	Selling the organization's products and services
Manufacturing and production	Producing products and services
Finance	Managing the organization's financial assets (cash, stocks, bonds, etc.)
Accounting	Maintaining the organization's financial records (receipts, disbursements, paycheques, etc.); accounting for the flow of funds
Human resources	Attracting, developing, and maintaining the organization's labour force; maintaining employee records

Your Business section showing how the chapter topics in that part relate to each of these functional areas. This section also provides page numbers in each chapter where these functional examples can be found. Icons placed next to these functional business examples in the chapter-opening vignettes, Window On boxes, chapter-ending case studies, and in the body of the chapters will help you identify them.

An organization coordinates work through a structured hierarchy and formal, standard operating procedures. The hierarchy arranges people in a pyramid structure of rising authority and responsibility. The upper levels of the hierarchy consist of managerial, professional, and technical employees, and the lower levels consist of operational personnel.

Standard operating procedures (SOPs) are formal rules that have been developed over a long time for accomplishing tasks. These rules guide employees in a variety of procedures, from writing an invoice to responding to customer complaints. Most procedures are formalized and written down, but others are informal work practices, such as a requirement to return telephone calls from co-workers or customers, that are not formally documented. The firm's business processes, which we defined earlier, are based on its SOPs, and many business processes and SOPs are incorporated into information systems, for example, procedures on how to pay a supplier or how to correct an erroneous bill.

Organizations require many different kinds of skills and people. In addition to managers, **knowledge workers** (such as engineers, architects, or scientists) design products or services and create new knowledge, and **data workers** (such as secretaries, bookkeepers, or clerks) process the organization's paperwork. **Production or service workers** (such as machinists, assemblers, or packers) actually produce the organization's products or services.

Each organization has a unique culture—a fundamental set of assumptions, values, and ways of doing things—that has been accepted by most of its members. Parts of an organization's culture can always be found embedded in its information systems. For instance, United Parcel Service's concern with placing service to the customer first is an aspect of its organizational culture that can be found in the company's package tracking systems.

Different levels and specialties in an organization create different interests and points of view. These views often conflict. Conflict is the basis for organizational politics. Information systems come out of this cauldron of differing perspectives, conflicts, compromises, and agreements that are a natural part of all organizations. In Chapter 3, we examine these features of organizations in greater detail.

Management

Management's job is to make sense out of the many situations faced by organizations, make decisions, and formulate action plans to solve organizational problems. Managers perceive business challenges in the environment; they set the organizational strategy for responding and allocate the human and financial resources to achieve the strategy and coordinate the work. Throughout, they must exercise responsible leadership. The business information systems described in this book reflect the hopes, dreams, and realities of real-world managers.

But managers must do more than manage what already exists. They must also create new products and services and even re-create the organization from time to time. A substantial part

standard operating procedures (SOPs)

Formal rules for accomplishing tasks that have been developed to cope with expected situations.

knowledge workers

Workers, such as engineers or architects, who design products or services and create knowledge for the organization.

data workers

Workers, such as secretaries or bookkeepers, who process the organization's paperwork.

production or service workers

Workers who actually produce the products or services of the organization.

of management responsibility is creative work driven by new knowledge and information. Information technology can play a powerful role in redirecting and redesigning the organization. Chapter 3 describes managers' activities and management decision making in detail.

It is important to note that managerial roles and decisions vary at different levels of the organization. **Senior managers** make long-range strategic decisions about what products and services to produce. **Middle managers** carry out the programs and plans of senior management. **Operational managers** are responsible for monitoring the firm's daily activities. All levels of management are expected to be creative and to develop novel solutions to a broad range of problems. Each level of management has different information needs and information system requirements.

Technology

Information technology is one of many tools managers use to cope with change. **Computer hardware** is the physical equipment used for input, processing, and output activities in an information system. It consists of the following: the computer processing unit; various input, output, and storage devices; and physical media to link these devices together. Chapter 6 describes computer hardware in greater detail.

Computer software consists of the detailed preprogrammed instructions that control and coordinate the computer hardware components in an information system. Chapter 6 explains the importance of computer software in information systems.

Storage technology includes both the physical media for storing data, such as magnetic or optical disks or tapes, and the software governing the organization of data on these physical media. More detail on physical storage media can be found in Chapter 6, while Chapter 7 covers data organization and access methods.

Communications technology, consisting of both physical devices and software, links the various pieces of hardware and transfers data from one physical location to another. Computers and communications equipment can be connected in networks for sharing voice, data, images, sound, or even video. A **network** links two or more computers to share data or such resources as printers. Chapters 8 and 9 provide more details on communications and networking technology and issues.

All of these technologies represent resources that can be shared throughout the organization and constitute the firm's **information technology (IT) infrastructure**. The IT infrastructure provides the foundation or platform on which the firm can build its specific information systems. Each organization must carefully design and manage its IT infrastructure so that it has the set of technology services it needs for the work it wants to accomplish with information systems. Chapters 6 through 9 of this text examine each major technology component of IT infrastructure and show how they all work together to create the technology platform for the organization.

Let us return to UPS's package tracking system discussed in the Window on Technology and identify the organization, management, and technology elements. The organization element anchors the package tracking system in UPS's sales and production functions (the main product of UPS is a service–package delivery). It specifies the required procedures for identifying packages with both sender and recipient information, taking inventory, tracking the packages en route, and providing package status reports for UPS customers and customer service representatives. The system must also provide information to satisfy the needs of managers and workers. UPS drivers need to be trained in both package pickup and delivery procedures and in using the package tracking system so that the drivers can work efficiently and effectively. UPS customers may need some training to use UPS in-house package tracking software or the UPS Web site. UPS's management is responsible for monitoring service levels and costs and for promoting the company's strategy of combining low-cost and superior service. Management decided to use automation to increase the ease of sending a package via UPS and of checking its delivery status, thereby reducing delivery costs and increasing sales revenues. The technology supporting this system consists of handheld computers, barcode scanners, wired and wireless communications networks, desktop computers, UPS's central computer, storage technology for the package delivery data, UPS in-house package tracking software, and software to access the World Wide Web. The result is an information system solution to the business challenge of providing a high level of service with low prices in the face of mounting competition.

---

senior managers

People occupying the topmost hierarchy in an organization who are responsible for making long-range decisions.

middle managers

People in the middle of the organizational hierarchy who are responsible for carrying out the plans and goals of senior management.

operational managers

People who monitor the day-to-day activities of the organization.

computer hardware

Physical equipment used for input, processing, and output activities in an information system.

computer software

Detailed, preprogrammed instructions that control and coordinate the work of computer hardware components in an information system.

storage technology

Physical media and software governing the storage and organization of data for use in an information system.

communications technology

Physical devices and software that link various computer hardware components and transfer data from one physical location to another.

network

The linking of two or more computers to share data or such resources as printers.

information technology (IT) infrastructure

Computer hardware, software, data and storage technology, and networks providing a portfolio of shared information technology resources for the organization.

1.2 CONTEMPORARY APPROACHES TO INFORMATION SYSTEMS

Multiple perspectives on information systems show that the study of information systems is a multidisciplinary field. No single theory or perspective dominates. Figure 1.5 illustrates the major disciplines that contribute problems, issues, and solutions in the study of information systems. In general, the field can be divided into technical and behavioural approaches. Information systems are sociotechnical systems. Though they are composed of machines, devices, and "hard" physical technology, they require substantial social, organizational, and intellectual investments to make them work properly.

TECHNICAL APPROACH

The technical approach to information systems places importance on mathematically based models to study information systems as well as on the physical technology and formal capabilities of these systems. The disciplines that contribute to the technical approach are computer science, management science, and operations research. Computer science is concerned with establishing theories of computability, methods of computation, and methods of efficient data storage and access. Management science emphasizes the development of models for decision-making and management practices. Operations research focuses on mathematical techniques for optimizing selected parameters of organizations, such as transportation, inventory control, and transaction costs.

BEHAVIOURAL APPROACH

An important part of the information systems field is concerned with behavioural issues that arise in the development and long-term maintenance of information systems. Such issues as strategic business integration, design, implementation, utilization, and management cannot be explored usefully with the models used in the technical approach. Other behavioural disciplines contribute important concepts and methods. For instance, sociologists study information systems with an eye toward how groups and organizations shape the development of systems and also how systems affect individuals, groups, and organizations. Psychologists study information systems with an interest in how human decision makers perceive and use formal information. Economists study information systems with an interest in what impact systems have on control and cost structures within the firm and within markets.

The behavioural approach does not ignore technology. Indeed, information systems technology is often the stimulus for a behavioural problem or issue. But the focus of this approach is generally not on technical solutions. Instead, it concentrates on changes in attitudes, management and organizational policy, and behaviour.

APPROACH OF THIS TEXT: SOCIOTECHNICAL SYSTEMS

The study of **management information systems (MIS)** arose in the 1970s to focus on computer-based information systems aimed at managers (Davis and Olson, 1985). MIS combine the theo-

management information systems (MIS)

The study of information systems focusing on their use in business and management.

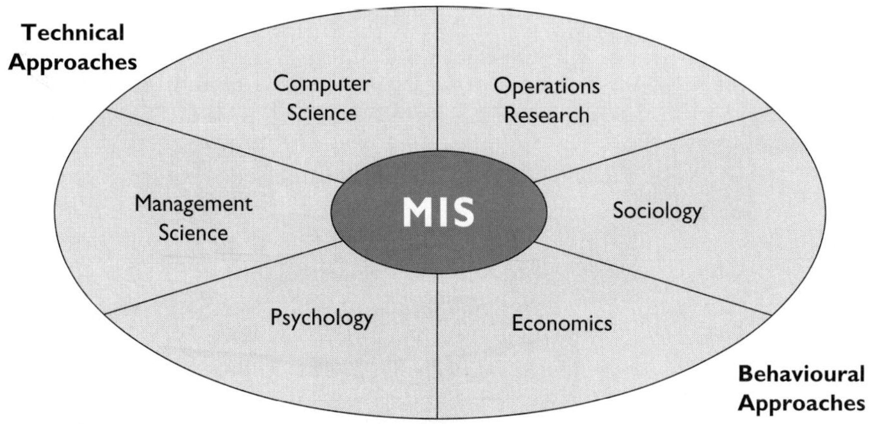

Figure 1.5 Contemporary approaches to information systems. The study of information systems deals with issues and insights contributed from technical and behavioural disciplines.

retical work of computer science, management science, and operations research with a practical orientation toward developing system solutions to real-world problems and managing information technology resources. It also pays attention to behavioural issues surrounding the development, use, and impact of information systems using the fields of sociology, economics, and psychology. The study of information systems has just started to influence other disciplines (Baskerville and Myers, 2002) through such concepts as the information processing view of the firm.

Our experience as academics and practitioners leads us to believe that no single perspective effectively captures the reality of information systems. Problems with systems—and their solutions—are rarely all technical or all behavioural. Our best advice to students is to understand the perspectives of all disciplines. Indeed, the challenge and excitement of the information systems field is that it requires appreciation and tolerance of many different approaches.

Adopting a sociotechnical systems perspective helps avoid a purely technological approach to information systems. For instance, the fact that information technology is rapidly declining in cost and growing in power does not necessarily or easily translate into productivity enhancement or bottom-line profits.

In this book, we stress the need to optimize the system's performance as a whole. Both the technical and the behavioural components need attention. This means that technology must be changed and designed so that it fits organizational and individual needs. At times, the technology may have to be "de-optimized" to accomplish this fit. Organizations and individuals must also be changed through training, learning, and planned organizational change in order to allow the technology to operate and prosper (see, for example, Liker et al., 1987). People and organizations change to take advantage of new information technology. Figure 1.6 illustrates this process of mutual adjustment in a sociotechnical system.

1.3   TOWARD THE DIGITAL FIRM: THE NEW ROLE OF INFORMATION SYSTEMS IN ORGANIZATIONS

Managers cannot ignore information systems because these systems play such a critical role in contemporary organizations. Today's systems directly affect how managers decide, plan, and manage their employees and increasingly shape what, where, when, and how products are produced. Therefore, the responsibility for the systems cannot be delegated to technical decision makers.

THE WIDENING SCOPE OF INFORMATION SYSTEMS

Figure 1.7 illustrates the new relationship between organizations and information systems. There is a growing interdependence between business strategy, rules, and procedures on the one hand, and information systems software, hardware, databases, and telecommunications on the other. A change in any of these components often requires changes in other components. This relationship becomes critical when management plans for the future. What a

Figure 1.6 A sociotechnical perspective on information systems. In a sociotechnical perspective, the performance of a system is optimized when both the technology and the organization mutually adjust to one another until a satisfactory fit is obtained.

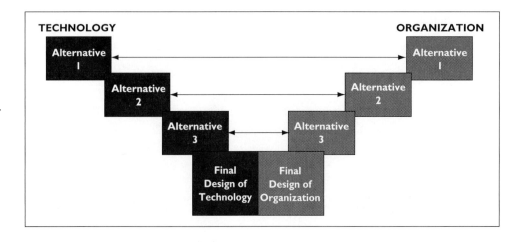

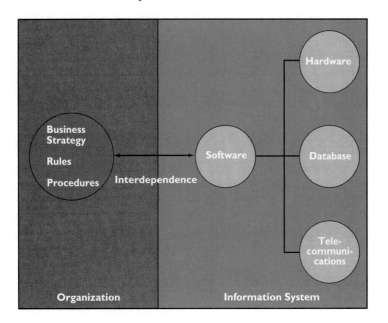

Figure 1.7 The interdependence between organizations and information systems. In contemporary systems, there is a growing interdependence among the organizational business strategy, rules, and procedures and the organization's information systems. Changes in strategy, rules, and procedures increasingly require changes in hardware, software, databases, and telecommunications. Existing systems can act as a constraint on organizations. Often, what the organization would like to do depends on what its systems will permit it to do.

business would like to do in five years often depends on what its systems will be able to do. Increasing market share, becoming the high-quality or low-cost producer, developing new products, and increasing employee productivity depend more and more on the kinds and quality of information systems in the organization.

A second change in the relationship between information systems and organizations results from the growing reach and scope of system projects and applications. Building and managing systems today involves a much larger part of the organization than it did in the past. As firms become more like "digital firms," the system enterprise extends to customers, vendors, and even industry competitors (see Figure 1.8). Where early systems produced largely technical changes that affected only a few people in the firm, contemporary systems have been bringing about managerial changes (who has what information about whom, when, and how often) and institutional "core" changes (what products and services are produced, under what conditions, and by whom). As companies move toward digital firm organizations, nearly all of the firm's managers and employees, as well as customers and vendors, participate in a variety of firm systems, tied together by a digital information web. For instance, what a customer does on a firm's Web site can trigger an employee to make an on-the-spot pricing decision or alert a firm's suppliers to potential "stockout" situations.

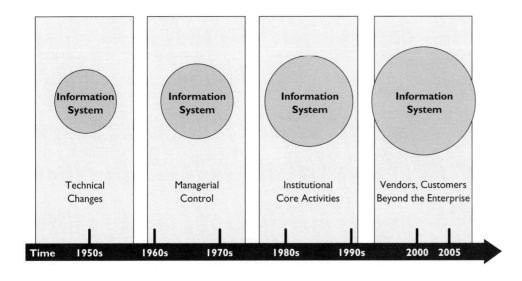

Figure 1.8 The widening scope of information systems. Over time, information systems have come to play a larger role in the life of organizations. Early systems brought about largely technical changes that were relatively easy to accomplish. Later systems affected managerial control and behaviour and subsequently "core" institutional activities. In the digital firm era, information systems extend far beyond the boundaries of the firm to encompass vendors, customers, and even competitors.

THE NETWORK REVOLUTION AND THE INTERNET

The reasons why information systems play such a large role in organizations and affect so many people are the soaring power and the declining cost of computer technology. Computing power, which has been doubling every 18 months, has improved the performance of microprocessors over 25 000 times since their invention 30 years ago. With powerful, easy-to-use software, the computer can crunch numbers, analyze vast pools of data, or simulate complex physical and logical processes with animated drawings, sounds, and even tactile feedback.

The soaring power of computer technology has spawned powerful communication networks that organizations can use to access vast storehouses of information from around the world and to coordinate activities across space and time. These networks are transforming the shape and form of business enterprises, creating the foundation for the digital firm.

The world's largest and most widely used network is the **Internet**. The Internet is a global network of networks that are both commercial and publicly owned. The Internet connects hundreds of thousands of different networks from more than 200 countries around the world. Nearly 600 million people working in science, education, government, and business use the Internet to exchange information or perform business transactions with other organizations around the globe.

The Internet is extremely elastic. If networks are added or removed or failures occur in parts of the system, the rest of the Internet continues to operate. Through special communication and technology standards, any computer can communicate with virtually any other computer linked to the Internet using ordinary telephone lines and satellite technology. Companies and private individuals can use the Internet to exchange business transactions, text messages, graphic images, and even video and sound, whether they are located next door or on the other side of the globe. Table 1.3 describes some of the Internet's capabilities.

The Internet is creating a new "universal" technology platform on which to build all sorts of new products, services, strategies, and organizations. It is reshaping the way information systems are being used in business and daily life. By eliminating many technical, geographic, and cost barriers obstructing the global flow of information, the Internet is inspiring

Internet

Global network of networks that is a collection of hundreds of thousands of private and public networks.

TABLE 1.3

WHAT YOU CAN DO ON THE INTERNET

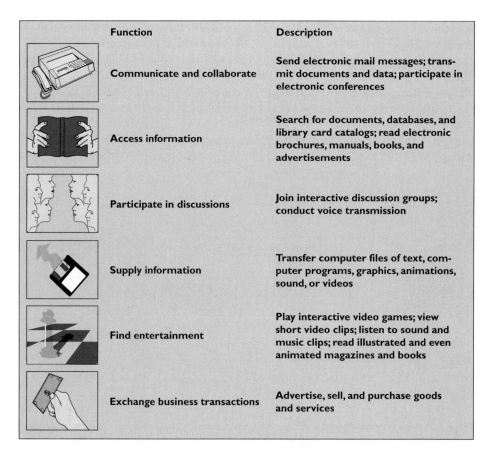

	Function	Description
	Communicate and collaborate	Send electronic mail messages; transmit documents and data; participate in electronic conferences
	Access information	Search for documents, databases, and library card catalogs; read electronic brochures, manuals, books, and advertisements
	Participate in discussions	Join interactive discussion groups; conduct voice transmission
	Supply information	Transfer computer files of text, computer programs, graphics, animations, sound, or videos
	Find entertainment	Play interactive video games; view short video clips; listen to sound and music clips; read illustrated and even animated magazines and books
	Exchange business transactions	Advertise, sell, and purchase goods and services

The Internet. This global network of networks provides a highly flexible platform for information sharing. Digital information can be distributed at almost no cost to millions of people throughout the world.

new uses of information systems and new business models. The Internet provides the primary technology platform for the digital firm.

Because it offers so many new possibilities for doing business, the Internet capability, known as the **World Wide Web**, is of special interest to organizations and managers. The World Wide Web is a system with universally accepted standards for storing, retrieving, formatting, and displaying information in a networked environment. Information is stored and displayed as electronic "pages" that can contain text, graphics, animations, sound, and video. These Web pages can be linked electronically to other Web pages, regardless of where they are located, and viewed by any type of computer. By clicking on highlighted words or buttons on a Web page, you can link to related pages to find additional information, software programs, or still more links to other points on the Web. The Web can serve as the foundation for new kinds of information systems, such as those described in the Window On boxes and the chapter-opening vignette.

All of the Web pages maintained by an organization or individual are called a **Web site**. Businesses are creating Web sites with stylish typography, colourful graphics, push-button interactivity, and often sound and video to disseminate product information widely, to "broadcast" advertising and messages to customers, to collect electronic orders and customer data, and, increasingly, to coordinate far-flung sales forces and organizations on a global scale.

In Chapters 4 and 9, we describe the Web and other Internet capabilities in greater detail. We also discuss relevant features of Internet technology throughout the text because it affects so many aspects of information systems in organizations.

World Wide Web

A system with universally accepted standards for storing, retrieving, formatting, and displaying information in a networked environment.

Web site

All of the World Wide Web pages maintained by an organization or an individual.

NEW OPTIONS FOR ORGANIZATIONAL DESIGN: THE DIGITAL FIRM AND THE COLLABORATIVE ENTERPRISE

The explosive growth in computing power and networks, including the Internet, is turning organizations into networked enterprises, allowing information to be instantly distributed within and beyond the organization. Companies can use this information to improve their internal business processes and to coordinate these business processes with those of other organizations. These new technologies for connectivity and collaboration can be used to redesign and reshape organizations, transforming their structure, scope of operations, reporting and control mechanisms, work practices, work flows, products, and services. The ultimate end product of these new ways of conducting business electronically is the digital firm.

Flattening Organizations and the Changing Management Process

Large, bureaucratic organizations, which primarily developed before the computer age, are often inefficient, slow to change, and less competitive than newly created organizations.

Figure 1.9 Flattening organizations. Information systems can reduce the number of levels in an organization by providing managers with information to supervise larger numbers of workers and by giving lower-level employees more decision-making authority.

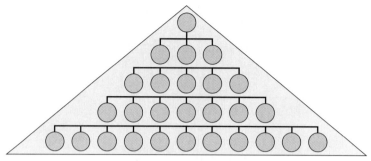

A traditional hierarchical organization with many levels of management

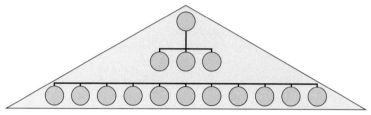

An organization that has been "flattened" by removing layers of management

Some of these large organizations have downsized, reducing the number of employees and the number of levels in their organizational hierarchies. In digital firms, hierarchy and organizational levels do not disappear. Instead, digital firms develop "optimal hierarchies" that balance the decision making load across an organization, resulting in flatter organizations. Flatter organizations have fewer levels of management, with lower-level employees being given greater decision making authority (see Figure 1.9). Those employees are empowered to make more decisions than in the past, they no longer work standard nine-to-five hours, and they no longer necessarily work in an office. Moreover, these employees may be scattered geographically, sometimes working half a world away from the manager.

This means that the management span of control has also been broadened, allowing high-level managers to manage and control more workers spread over greater distances. Many companies have eliminated thousands of middle managers as a result of these changes. AT&T Canada, IBM, and both Ford Motor Canada and General Motors Canada are only a few of the organizations that have eliminated more than 30 000 middle managers in one fell swoop.

Information technology is also recasting the management process by providing powerful new tools for more precise planning, forecasting, and monitoring. For instance, it is now possible for managers to obtain information on organizational performance down to the level of specific transactions from just about anywhere in the organization at any time. Product managers at Frito-Lay Corporation, the world's largest manufacturer of salty snack foods, can know within hours precisely how many bags of Fritos have been sold at its customers' stores on any street in America, how much they were sold for, and what the competition's sales volumes and prices are.

Separating Work from Location

Communications technology has eliminated distance as a factor for many types of work in many situations. Salespersons can spend more time in the field with customers and have more up-to-date information with them while carrying much less paper. Many employees can work remotely from their homes or cars, and companies can reserve space at smaller central offices for meeting clients or other employees. Collaborative teamwork across thousands of kilometres has become a reality as designers work on a new product together even if they are located on different continents. Lockheed Martin Aeronautics developed a real-time system for collaborative product design and engineering based on the Internet, which it uses to coordinate tasks with its partners, such as BAE and Northrup Grumman. Engineers from all three companies work jointly on designs over the Internet. Previously, the company and its partners worked separately on designs, hammering out design differences in lengthy face-to-

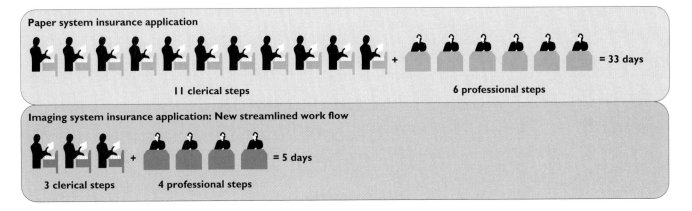

Figure 1.10 Redesigned work flow for insurance underwriting. An application requiring 33 days in a paper system would only take five days using computers, networks, and a streamlined work flow.

face meetings. A drawing that once took 400 hours now takes 125 hours, and the design phase of projects has been cut in half (Konicki, 2001).

Reorganizing Work Flows

Information systems have been progressively replacing manual work procedures with automated work procedures, work flows, and work processes. Electronic work flows have reduced the cost of operations in many companies by displacing paper work and the manual routines that accompany it. Improved work flow management has enabled many corporations not only to cut costs significantly but also to improve customer service at the same time. For instance, insurance companies can reduce processing of applications for new insurance from weeks to days (see Figure 1.10).

Redesigned work flows can have a profound impact on organizational efficiency and can even lead to new organizational structures, products, and services. We discuss the impact of restructured work flows on organizational design in greater detail in Chapters 3 and 10.

Increasing Flexibility of Organizations

Companies can use communications technology to organize in more flexible ways, increasing their ability to sense and respond to changes in the marketplace and to take advantage of new opportunities. Information systems can give both large and small organizations additional flexibility to overcome some of the limitations posed by their size. Table 1.4 describes some of the ways in which information technology can help small companies act

TABLE 1.4	HOW INFORMATION TECHNOLOGY INCREASES ORGANIZATIONAL FLEXIBILITY

Small Companies

Desktop machines, inexpensive computer-aided design (CAD) software, and computer-controlled machine tools provide the precision, speed, and quality of giant manufacturers.

Information immediately accessed by telephone and communications links eliminates the need for research staff and business libraries.

Managers can easily obtain the information they need to manage large numbers of employees in widely scattered locations.

Large Companies

Custom manufacturing systems allow large factories to offer customized products in small quantities.

Massive databases of customer purchasing records can be analyzed so that large companies can know their customers' needs and preferences as easily as local merchants.

Information can be easily distributed down the ranks of the organization to empower lower-level employees and work groups to solve problems.

"big" and help big companies act "small." Small organizations can use information systems to acquire some of the muscle and reach of larger organizations. They can perform coordinating activities, such as processing bids or keeping track of inventory, and many manufacturing tasks with very few managers, clerks, or production workers.

mass customization

The capacity to offer individually tailored products or services on a large scale.

Large organizations can use information technology to achieve some of the agility and responsiveness of small organizations. One aspect of this phenomenon is **mass customization**, the ability to offer individually tailored products or services on a large scale. Information systems can make the production process more flexible so that products can be tailored to each customer's unique set of requirements (Zipkin, 2001). Software and computer networks can be used to link the plant floor tightly with orders, design, and purchasing and to finely control production machines so products can be turned out in greater variety and easily customized with no added cost for small production runs. For example, Levi Strauss has equipped its stores with an option called Original Spin, which allows customers to design jeans to their own specifications, rather than picking the jeans off the rack. Customers enter their measurements into a personal computer, which then transmits the customer's specifications over a network to Levi's plants. The company is able to produce the custom jeans on the same lines used to manufacture its standard items. There are almost no extra production costs because the process does not require additional warehousing, production overruns, and inventories. Lands' End has implemented a similar system for customizing chino slacks and jeans that allows customers to enter their measurements over its Web site.

A related trend is micromarketing, in which information systems can help companies pinpoint tiny target markets for these finely customized products and services—as small as individualized "markets of one." We discuss micromarketing in more detail in Chapters 2, 3, and 13.

Redefining Organizational Boundaries: New Avenues for Collaboration

A key feature of the emerging digital firm is the ability to conduct business across firm boundaries almost as efficiently and effectively as it can conduct business within the firm. Networked information systems allow companies to coordinate with other organizations across great distances. Transactions, such as payments and purchase orders, can be exchanged electronically among different companies, thereby reducing the cost of obtaining products and services from outside the firm. Organizations can also share business data, catalogues, or mail messages through networks. These networked information systems can create new efficiencies and new relationships between an organization, its customers, and suppliers, redefining organizational boundaries.

The chapter-opening vignette described how Toyota is networked to its suppliers, including the Dana Corporation of Toledo, Ohio, a tier-one supplier of chassis, engines, and other major automotive components. Through this electronic link, the Dana Corporation monitors Toyota production and ships components exactly when needed (McDougall, 2001). Toyota and Dana have, thus, become linked business partners with mutually shared responsibilities.

interorganizational systems

Information systems that automate the flow of information across organizational boundaries and link a company to its customers, distributors, or suppliers.

Systems linking a company, such as Toyota, to its customers, distributors, or suppliers are termed **interorganizational systems** because they automate the flow of information across organizational boundaries. Digital firms use interorganizational systems to link not only with their suppliers and customers but also sometimes with their competitors, to create and distribute new products and services without being limited by traditional organizational boundaries or physical locations. For example, Cisco Systems does not manufacture the networking products it sells; it uses other companies, such as Flextronics, for this purpose. Cisco uses the Internet to transmit orders to Flextronics and to monitor the status of orders as they are being shipped. (More detail on Flextronics can be found in the Chapter 3 opening vignette.)

Many of these interorganizational systems are increasingly based on Web technology and provide more intense sharing of knowledge, resources, and business processes than in the past. Firms are using these systems to work jointly with suppliers and other business partners on product design and development and on the scheduling and flow of work in manufacturing, procurement, and distribution. These new levels of interfirm collaboration and coordination can lead to higher levels of efficiency, value to customers, and ultimately significant competitive advantage.

THE DIGITAL FIRM: ELECTRONIC COMMERCE, ELECTRONIC BUSINESS, AND NEW DIGITAL RELATIONSHIPS

The changes we have just described represent new ways of conducting business electronically both inside and outside the firm that can ultimately result in the creation of digital firms. Increasingly, the Internet is providing the underlying technology for these changes. The Internet can link thousands of organizations into a single network, creating the foundation for a vast digital marketplace. A **digital market** is an information system that links together many buyers and sellers to exchange information, products, services, and payments. Through computers and networks, these systems function like electronic intermediaries, with lowered costs for typical marketplace transactions, such as matching buyers and sellers, establishing prices, ordering goods, and paying bills (Bakos, 1998). Buyers and sellers can complete purchase and sale transactions digitally, regardless of their location.

A vast array of goods and services are being advertised, bought, and exchanged worldwide using the Internet as a global marketplace. Companies are furiously creating eye-catching electronic brochures, advertisements, product manuals, and order forms on the World Wide Web. All kinds of products and services are available on the Web, including fresh flowers, books, real estate, musical recordings, electronics, and steaks. Even electronic financial trading has arrived on the Web for stocks, bonds, mutual funds, and other financial instruments. The Window on Organizations describes another type of Web-based financial service—Internet-only banking.

Increasingly, the Web is being used for business-to-business transactions as well. For example, recognising that its legacy system for electronic invoicing posed obstacles to efficiency and expanding business relationships, Crestar Energy, a wholly owned subsidiary of Gulf Canada resources, deployed a flexible Web-based invoicing system that allows vendors to submit invoices and query their status via the Internet. This solution has enabled Crestar to forge new business relationships and strengthen old ones while reducing invoice processing costs and increasing efficiency. At least a portion of Canada's online automotive trade will flow through Covisint, the online B2B marketplace opened by Ford, General Motors, DaimlerChrysler, Renault, and Nissan in 2002. Airlines can use the Boeing Corporation's Web site to order parts electronically and check the status of their orders. Altranet Energy Technologies of Houston, Texas, operates an Internet marketplace called altranet.com where many different energy industry suppliers and buyers can meet any time of day or night to trade natural gas, liquids, and electricity in a spot market for immediate delivery. Participants can select their trading partners, confirm transactions, and obtain credit and insurance.

The global availability of the Internet for the exchange of transactions between buyers and sellers has fuelled the growth of electronic commerce. **Electronic commerce**, also known as **e-commerce**, is the process of buying and selling goods and services electronically with

digital market

A marketplace that is created by computer and communication technologies that link many buyers and sellers.

electronic commerce (e-commerce)

The process of buying and selling goods and services electronically involving transactions using the Internet, networks, and other digital technologies.

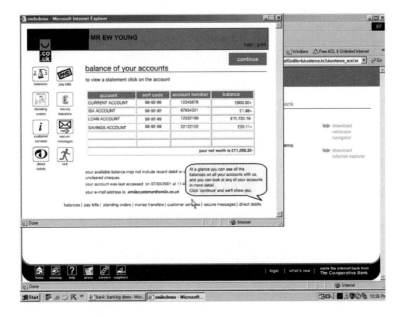

Figure 1.11 Smile.co.uk is an Internet-only bank where customers can view their accounts and perform banking transactions any hour of the day or night. A wide array of banking and financial services are available on the Web.

WHY ARE INTERNET-ONLY BANKS SMILING IN THE UNITED KINGDOM?

Despite the recent collapse of many dot-coms, some Internet businesses are starting to catch on. Internet banking appears to be taking a foothold in the United Kingdom. Four Internet-only banks have collectively captured 5 percent of the total British banking market.

What can these online-only banks offer their customers? Perhaps their most important benefit is that customers use the Web to bank at any hour of the day or night, including weekends and holidays—a service that no physical bricks-and-mortar bank can offer. Customers can also view their current records, determine if a particular cheque has cleared yet, apply for new or additional credit, pay bills (at no cost to them, not even postage), and communicate with the bank. They can ask questions and receive answers, often within 24 hours. With those services, customers can control their own banking, for example, by avoiding overdrafts. Also, the banks' costs are usually much lower, enabling the online banks to lower customer costs and pay higher interest rates. Smile, an Internet-only British bank, says its costs are only 10 percent of the costs of a competing bricks-and-mortar bank, and Smile puts much of its savings into higher interest rates for customer chequing and savings accounts (see Figure 1.11).

However, online-only banks have a few shortcomings. Banking at a physical bank enables customers to make deposits directly, cash cheques, withdraw cash, and even talk with bank staff face-to-face. Today, some online-only banks are allowing their customers to use ATMs to withdraw cash, and in some cases, the bank eats the normal charges when one bank's customer uses another bank's ATM machine. Deposits are normally only made by mail, a drawback for some. Moreover, when customers bank with online-only banks, they cannot talk with their bank staff face-to-face, a personal touch that many bank customers desire. And some transactions, such as mortgages, are complex. Working with actual bankers is considered a necessity by many.

Nonetheless, many still feel positive about Internet banking. "I feel much more in control of my own finances," says Annabelle Watson, a 26-year-old advertising executive and customer of Smile. "In the past, I felt dictated to by my own bank," she points out. She claims her bank has a user-friendly Web site that gives customers the impression they are dealing with an attentive 24-hour bank manager. Smile.com has added a do-it-yourself area to its Web site that contains savings and budget calculators and other tools, and it is considering giving clients access to their accounts through wireless phones.

Bricks-and-mortar banks have their problems, too. Customers appreciate and now often need online banking because of its ease and the ability of customers to bank on their own schedule. In response, many traditional banks have added Internet banking features so that they can offer the best of both worlds. However, their costs quite naturally remain higher than those of online-only banks because of their bricks-and-mortar side. Other traditional banks have started online-only bank subsidiaries, including Cooperative Bank PLC, a well-established British bank that is the founder and parent of Smile.

Internet-only banks have faced very tough times in the United States. For example, one of the largest Internet-only banks, Wingspan, was recently absorbed by its parent, Bank One Corp. The question is, can they survive? Bob Head, the CEO of Smile, is positive about the future of his company. "We believe Internet banking will become the norm for millions of people in the future, and Smile will be successful in the long term because it offers so much more [than traditional banking]." If Smile can keep attracting new customers and improve its service, while established U.K. banks are shifting more of their service to the Internet, they may indeed become a dot-com success story.

To Think About: Do you think Internet-only banking will survive? Why, or why not? What are the organizational and technical problems Internet-only banks face? What are the organizational and technical problems traditional banks with online services face?

Sources: Susannah Rodgers, "Keep on Smiling," *Wall Street Journal,* April 15, 2002; and Andrew Ross Sorkin, "Your Money Where Your Modem Is," *New York Times,* Circuits, May 30, 2002.

---

computerized business transactions using the Internet, networks, and other digital technologies. It also encompasses activities supporting those market transactions, such as advertising, marketing, customer support, delivery, and payment. By replacing manual and paper-based procedures with electronic alternatives and by using information flows in new and dynamic ways, electronic commerce can accelerate ordering, delivery, and payment for goods and services while reducing companies' operating and inventory costs (see Figure 1.12).

The Internet has emerged as the primary technology platform for electronic commerce. Equally importantly, Internet technology is facilitating the management of the rest of the business—publishing employee personnel policies, reviewing account balances and production plans, scheduling plant repairs and maintenance, and revising design documents. Companies are taking advantage of the connectivity and ease of use of Internet technology to create internal corporate networks called **intranets** that are based on Internet technology.

intranet

An internal network based on Internet and World Wide Web technology and standards.

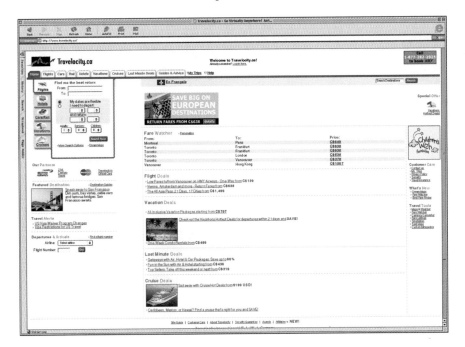

Figure 1.12 Visitors to the Travelocity.ca Web site can find information on airlines, hotels, and vacation packages, and they can make online airline and hotel reservations. The Internet is fuelling the growth of electronic commerce.

The number of these private intranets for organizational communication, collaboration, and coordination is soaring.

The chapter-opening vignette described how Toyota Motor Corporation is allowing its dealers to access portions of its private intranet to help them coordinate customer orders with production and design activities. Private intranets extended to authorized users outside the organization are called **extranets**, and firms use these networks to coordinate their activities with other firms for making purchases, collaborating on design, and other interorganizational work. Chapters 4 and 9 provide more detail on intranet and extranet applications and technology.

It is these broader uses of Internet technology, along with e-commerce, that are driving the move toward digital firms. In this text, we use the term **electronic business**, or **e-business**, to describe the use of Internet and digital technology to execute all of the business processes in the enterprise. E-business includes e-commerce as well as processes for the internal management of the firm and for coordination with suppliers and other business partners.

Figure 1.13 illustrates a digital firm making intensive use of Internet and digital technologies for electronic business. Information can flow seamlessly among different parts of the company and between the company and external entities—its customers, suppliers, and business partners. Organizations will move toward this digital firm vision as they use the Internet, intranets, and extranets to digitally enable their internal business processes and their interorganizational relationships.

E-business can fundamentally change the way organizations perform their work. To use the Internet and other digital technologies successfully for e-business, e-commerce, and the creation of digital firms, organizations may have to redefine their business models, reinvent business processes, change corporate cultures, and create much closer relationships with customers and suppliers. We treat these issues in greater detail in following chapters.

extranet

Private intranet that is accessible to authorized outsiders.

electronic business (e-business)

The use of Internet and digital technology to execute all of the business processes in the enterprise; includes e-commerce as well as processes for the internal management of the firm and for coordination with suppliers and other business partners.

1.4 LEARNING TO USE INFORMATION SYSTEMS: NEW OPPORTUNITIES WITH TECHNOLOGY

Although information systems are creating many exciting opportunities for both businesses and individuals, they are also a source of new problems, issues, and challenges for managers.

Figure 1.13 Electronic business and electronic commerce in the emerging digital firm. Companies can use the Internet, intranets, and extranets for e-commerce transactions with customers and suppliers, for managing internal business processes, and for coordinating with suppliers and other business partners. E-business includes e-commerce as well as the management and coordination of the enterprise.

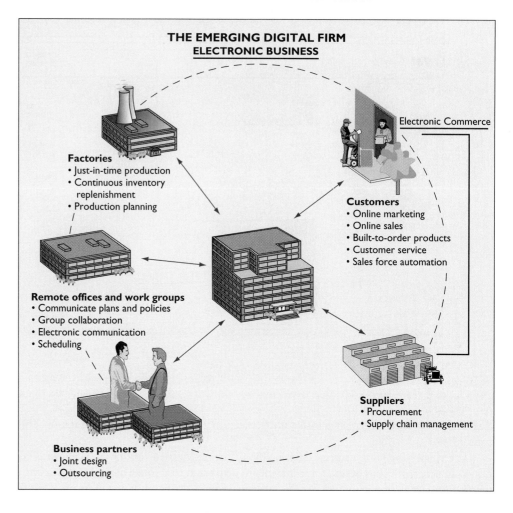

In this course, you will learn about both the challenges and opportunities information systems pose, and you will be able to use information technology to enrich your learning experience.

THE CHALLENGE OF INFORMATION SYSTEMS: KEY MANAGEMENT ISSUES

Although information technology is advancing at a blinding pace, there is nothing easy or mechanical about developing and using information systems. There are five key challenges confronting managers:

1. **The Strategic Business Challenge: Realizing the Digital Firm: How can businesses use information technology to become competitive, effective, and digitally enabled?** Creating a digital firm and obtaining benefits is a long and difficult journey for most organizations. Despite heavy information technology investments, many organizations are not realizing significant business value from their systems, nor are they becoming digitally enabled. The power of computer hardware and software has grown much more rapidly than the ability of organizations to apply and use this technology. To fully benefit from information technology, realize genuine productivity, and take advantage of digital firm capabilities, many organizations actually need to be redesigned. They will have to make fundamental changes in organizational behaviour, develop new business models, and eliminate the inefficiencies of outmoded organizational structures. If organizations merely automate what they are doing today, they are largely missing the potential of information technology.

2. **The Globalization Challenge: How can firms understand the business and system requirements of a global economic environment?** The rapid growth in international

trade and the emergence of a global economy call for information systems that can support both producing and selling goods in many different countries. In the past, each regional office of a multinational corporation focused on solving its own unique information problems. Given the language, cultural, and political differences among countries, this focus frequently resulted in chaos and the failure of central management controls. To develop integrated, multinational information systems, businesses must develop global hardware, software, and communications standards; create cross-cultural accounting and reporting structures (Roche, 1992); and design transnational business processes.

3. **The Information Architecture and Infrastructure Challenge: How can organizations develop an information architecture and information technology infrastructure that can support their goals when business conditions and technologies are changing so rapidly?** Many companies are saddled with expensive and unwieldy information technology platforms that cannot adapt to innovation and change. Their information systems are so complex and brittle that they act as constraints on business strategy and execution. Meeting new business and technology challenges may require redesigning the organization and building a new information architecture and information technology (IT) infrastructure.

Information architecture is the particular form that information technology takes in an organization to achieve selected goals or functions. It is a design for the firm's key business application systems and the specific ways that they are used by each organization. Because managers and employees directly interact with these systems, it is critical for organizational success that the information architecture meet business requirements now and in the future.

It is difficult—if not impossible—to represent the complexity of contemporary information architecture and IT infrastructure in a single diagram as firms move toward digital firm organizations. Figure 1.14, nevertheless, attempts to illustrate the major ele-

information architecture

The particular design that information technology takes in a specific organization to achieve selected goals or functions.

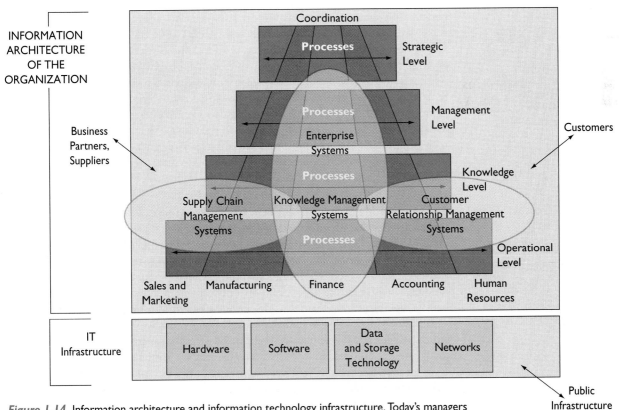

Figure 1.14 Information architecture and information technology infrastructure. Today's managers must know how to arrange and coordinate the various computer technologies and business system applications to meet the information needs of each level of the organization and the needs of the organization as a whole.

ments of information architecture found in today's emerging digital firms. The figure depicts the firm's major vertical business application systems for each of the major functional areas of the business, including sales and marketing, manufacturing, finance, accounting, and human resources. These systems were among the first developed in most organizations. The figure also depicts major horizontal systems automating business processes that cross functional and hierarchical boundaries. These systems are typically developed after major functional systems are in place. Finally, this figure depicts major contemporary information technology investments in enterprise, supply chain management, customer relationship management, and knowledge management systems—key waypoints on the journey toward a truly digital firm. These contemporary systems extend outwards to suppliers and customers and inwards to employee knowledge and expertise, supporting firm-wide processes that span across all organizational units.

The firm's IT infrastructure provides the technology platform for this architecture. Computer hardware, software, data and storage technology, networks, and human resources required to operate the equipment constitute the shared IT resources of the firm and are available to all of its applications. Contemporary IT infrastructures are linked to public infrastructures, such as the Internet. Although this technology platform is typically operated by technical personnel, general management must decide how to allocate the resources it has assigned to hardware, software, data storage, and telecommunications networks to make sound information technology investments (Weill and Broadbent, 1997 and 1998).

Typical questions regarding information architecture and IT infrastructure facing today's managers include the following: Should the corporate sales data and function be distributed to each corporate remote site, or should they be centralized at headquarters? Should the organization develop systems to connect the entire enterprise or maintain separate islands of applications? Should the organization extend its infrastructure outside its boundaries to link to customers or suppliers? There is no one right answer to each of these questions (see Allen and Boynton, 1991). Moreover, business needs are constantly changing, which requires the information technology architecture to be reassessed continually (Feeny and Willcocks, 1998).

Creating the information architecture and IT infrastructure for a digital firm is an especially formidable task. Most companies are crippled by fragmented and incompatible computer hardware, software, telecommunications networks, and information systems that prevent information from flowing freely among different parts of the organization. Although Internet standards are solving some of these connectivity problems, creating data and creating computing platforms that span the enterprise and, increasingly, link the enterprise to external business partners are rarely as seamless as promised. Many organizations are still struggling to integrate their islands of information and technology into a coherent architecture. Chapters 6 through 9 provide more detail on information architecture and IT infrastructure issues.

4. **The Information Systems Investment Challenge: How can organizations determine the business value of information systems?** A major problem raised by the development of powerful, inexpensive computers involves not technology but management and organizations. It is one thing to use information technology to design, produce, deliver, and maintain new products. It is another thing to make money doing it. How can organizations obtain a sizable payoff from their investment in information systems? How can management make sure that information systems contribute to corporate value?

Engineering massive organizational and system changes in the hope of positioning a firm strategically is complicated and expensive. Senior management can be expected to ask these questions: How can we evaluate our information system investments as we do other investments? Are we receiving the kind of return on investment from our systems that we should be? Do our competitors get more? Far too many firms still cannot answer these questions. Their executives are likely to have trouble figuring out how much they actually spend on technology or how to measure the returns on their technology investments. Most companies lack a clearcut decision making process for deciding which technology investments to pursue and for managing those investments (Hartman, 2002).

5. **The Responsibility and Control Challenge: How can organizations ensure that their information systems are used in an ethically and socially responsible manner?** How can we design information systems that people can control and understand? Although information systems have provided enormous benefits and efficiencies, they have also created new problems and challenges of which managers should be aware. Table 1.5 describes some of these problems and challenges.

Many chapters of this text describe scenarios that raise these ethical issues, and Chapter 5 is devoted entirely to this topic. A major management challenge is to make informed decisions that are sensitive to the negative consequences of information systems as well to the positive ones.

Managers will also be faced with ongoing problems of security and control. Information systems are so essential to business, government, and daily life that organizations must take special steps to ensure that they are accurate, reliable, and secure. A firm invites disaster if it uses systems that do not work as intended, that do not deliver information in a form that people can interpret correctly and use, or that have control rooms where controls do not work or where instruments give false signals. Information systems must be designed so that they function as intended and so that humans can control the process.

Managers will need to ask: Can we apply high-quality assurance standards to our information systems as well as to our products and services? We discuss these issues further in Chapter 11. Can we build information systems that respect people's rights of privacy while still pursuing our organization's goals? Should information systems monitor employees? What do we do when an information system designed to increase efficiency and productivity eliminates people's jobs? Chapter 5 addresses these issues.

This text is designed to provide future managers with the knowledge and understanding required to deal with these challenges. To further this objective, each succeeding chapter begins with a Management Challenges box that outlines the key issues of concern to managers.

INTEGRATING TEXT WITH TECHNOLOGY: NEW OPPORTUNITIES FOR LEARNING

In addition to the changes in business and management that we have just described, we believe that information technology creates new opportunities for learning that can make the MIS course more meaningful and exciting. We have provided a Web site to integrate the text with leading-edge technology.

As you read each chapter of the text, you can visit the Companion Website (www.prenhall.com/laudon) and use the Internet for interactive learning and management problem solving. The Internet Connection icon in the chapter directs you to Web sites for which we have provided additional exercises and projects related to the concepts and organizations described in that particular chapter. For each chapter, you will also find an Electronic

| **TABLE 1.5** | **POSITIVE AND NEGATIVE IMPACTS OF INFORMATION SYSTEMS** |

Benefit of Information System	Negative Impact
Information systems can perform calculations or process paperwork much faster than people can.	By automating activities that were previously performed by people, information systems may eliminate jobs.
Information systems can help companies learn more about the purchase patterns and preferences of their customers.	Information systems may allow organizations to collect personal details about people, which violates their privacy.
Information systems provide new efficiencies through such services as automated teller machines (ATMs), telephone systems, or computer-controlled airplanes and air terminals.	Information systems are used in so many aspects of everyday life that system outages can cause shutdowns of businesses or transportation services, paralyzing communities.
Information systems have made possible new medical advances in surgery, radiology, and patient monitoring.	Heavy users of information systems may suffer repetitive stress injury, technostress, and other health problems.
The Internet distributes information instantly to millions of people across the world.	The Internet can be used to distribute illegal copies of software, books, articles, and other intellectual property.

Commerce or Electronic Business project where you can use Web research and interactive software at various company Web sites to solve specific problems. A graded online Interactive Study Guide contains questions to help you review what you have learned and test your mastery of chapter concepts. The Web site for each chapter includes a Management Decision Problem with a real-world decision making scenario for you to analyze. You can also use the Companion Website to find links to additional online case studies, international resources, and technology updates.

New to this edition is a Running Case study based on a simulated company that allows students to learn about a specific business and develop information system solutions for that business. Each chapter of the text contains a Running Case scenario and project where students can apply their analytical skills and chapter concepts. Some of these projects require extensive use of the Web or spreadsheet and database software. A complete description of each Running Case project and required data files can be found on the Companion Website.

Application software exercises require students to use spreadsheet, database, Web browser, and other application software in hands-on projects related to chapter concepts. They have been redesigned for this edition to make them more challenging and relevant to chapter topics. Students can apply the application software skills they have learned in other courses to real-world business problems. You can find these exercises following the Review Questions at the end of each chapter and both the exercises and their data files on the Companion Website.

Longer, more detailed case studies conclude each major part of the text. These case studies require students to apply what they have learned to analyze a real-world situation confronting real-world companies today.

You will find an Internet Tools section toward the end of every chapter to show how you can use the Web to enrich your learning experience.

MANAGEMENT WRAP-UP

Managers are problem solvers who are responsible for analyzing the many challenges confronting organizations and for developing strategies and action plans. Information systems are one of the tools that deliver the information required for solutions. Information systems both reflect management decisions and serve as instruments for changing the management process.

Information systems are rooted in organizations and are an outcome of organizational structure, culture, politics, work flows, and standard operating procedures. They are instruments for organizational change and value creation, making it possible to recast these organizational elements into new business models and redraw organizational boundaries. Advances in information systems are accelerating the trend toward globalized, knowledge-driven economies and flattened, flexible, decentralized organizations that can coordinate with other organizations across great distances.

A network revolution is under way. Information systems technology is no longer limited to computers but consists of an array of technologies that enable computers to be networked together to exchange information across great distances and organizational boundaries. The Internet provides global connectivity and a flexible platform for the seamless flow of information across the enterprise and between the firm and its customers and suppliers.

For Discussion

1. Information systems are too important to be left to computer specialists. Do you agree? Why, or why not?

2. As computers become faster and cheaper and the Internet becomes more widely used, most of the problems we have with information systems will disappear. Do you agree? Why, or why not?

SUMMARY

1. *What is the role of information systems in today's competitive business environment?* Information systems have become essential for helping organizations deal with changes in global economies and the business enterprise. Information systems provide firms with communication and analytic tools for conducting trade and managing businesses on a global scale. Information systems are the foundation of new knowledge-based products and services and help firms manage their knowledge assets. Information systems make it possible for businesses to adopt flatter, more decentralized structures and more flexible arrangements of employees and management. Organizations are trying to become more competitive and efficient by transforming themselves into digital firms where nearly all core business processes and relationships with customers, suppliers, and employees are digitally enabled.

2. *What exactly is an information system? What do managers need to know about information systems?* The purpose of an information system is to collect, store, and disseminate information from an organization's environment and internal operations to support organizational functions and decision making, communication, coordination, control, analysis, and visualization. Information systems transform raw data into useful information through three basic activities: input, processing, and output. From a business perspective, an information system represents an organizational and management solution based on information technology to a challenge posed by the environment. The information system is part of a series of value-adding activities for acquiring, transforming, and distributing information that managers can use to improve decision making, enhance organizational performance, and, ultimately, increase firm profitability.

   Information systems literacy requires an understanding of the organizational and management dimensions of information systems as well as the technical dimensions addressed by computer literacy. Information systems literacy draws on both technical and behavioural approaches to studying information systems. Both perspectives can be combined into a sociotechnical approach to systems.

3. *How are information systems transforming organizations and management?* The kinds of systems developed today are very important for the organization's overall performance, especially in today's highly globalized and information-based economy. Information systems are driving both daily operations and organizational strategy. Powerful computers, software, and networks, including the Internet, have helped organizations become more flexible, eliminate layers of management, separate work from location, coordinate with suppliers and customers, and restructure work flows, giving new powers to both line workers and management. Information technology provides managers with tools for more precise planning, forecasting, and monitoring of the business. To maximize the advantages of information technology, there is a much greater need to plan the organization's information architecture and information technology (IT) infrastructure.

4. *How have the Internet and Internet technology transformed business?* The Internet provides the primary technology infrastructure for electronic commerce, electronic business, and the emerging digital firm. The Internet and other networks have made it possible for businesses to replace manual and paper-based processes with the electronic flows of information. In electronic commerce (e-commerce), businesses can exchange electronic purchase and sale transactions with each other and with individual customers. Electronic business (e-business) uses Internet and other digital technology for organizational communication and coordination, collaboration with business partners, and the management of the firm as well as for electronic commerce transactions. Digital firms use Internet technology intensively to manage their internal processes and relationships with customers, suppliers, and other external entities.

5. *What are the major management challenges to developing and using information systems?* There are five key management challenges in building and using information systems: (1) designing systems that are competitive and efficient; (2) understanding the system requirements of a global business environment; (3) creating an information architecture and IT infrastructure that support the organization's goals; (4) determining the business value of information systems; and (5) designing systems that people can control, understand, and use in a socially and ethically responsible manner.

KEY TERMS

Business functions,   12

Business processes,   6

Communications technology,   14

Computer-based information systems (CBIS),   9

Computer hardware,   14

Computer literacy,   11

Computer software,   14

Customer relationship management systems,   7

Data,   8

Data workers,   13

Digital firm,   6

Digital market,   23

Electronic business (e-business),   25

Electronic commerce (e-commerce),   23

Enterprise systems,   7

Extranet,   25

Feedback,   8

Formal system,   9

REVIEW QUESTIONS

1. Why are information systems essential in business today? Describe four trends in the global business environment that have made information systems so important.

2. Describe the capabilities of a digital firm. Why are digital firms so powerful? What are the four principal systems driving the movement toward digital firms?

3. What is an information system? Distinguish between a computer, a computer program, and an information system. What is the difference between data and information?

4. What activities convert raw data to usable information in information systems? What is their relationship to feedback?

5. What are the functions of an information system from a business perspective? What role do they play in the business information value chain?

6. What is information systems literacy? How does it differ from computer literacy?

7. What are the organization, management, and technology dimensions of information systems?

8. Distinguish between a behavioural approach and a technical approach to information systems in terms of the questions asked and the answers provided. What major disciplines contribute to an understanding of information systems?

9. What is the relationship between an organization and its information systems? How has this relationship changed over time?

10. What are the Internet and the World Wide Web? How have they changed the role played by information systems in organizations?

11. Describe some of the major changes that information systems are bringing to organizations.

12. How are information systems changing the management process?

13. What is the relationship between the network revolution, the digital firm, electronic commerce, and electronic business?

14. What are interorganizational systems? Why are they becoming more important? How have the Internet and Web technology affected these systems?

15. What do we mean by information architecture and information technology infrastructure? Why are they important concerns for managers?

16. What are the key management challenges involved in building, operating, and maintaining information systems today?

APPLICATION SOFTWARE EXERCISE

DATABASE EXERCISE: ADDING VALUE TO INFORMATION FOR MANAGEMENT DECISION MAKING

Effective information systems add value to data to create meaningful information for management decisions that improve business performance. At the Companion Website for Chapter 1, you can find a Store and Regional Sales Database with raw data on weekly store sales of computer equipment in various sales regions. The database includes fields for store identification number, sales region number, item number, item description, unit price, units sold, and the weekly sales period when the sales were made. Develop some reports and queries to make this information more useful to management. Modify the database table, if necessary, to provide all of the information you require. Here are some questions you might consider:

A. Which are the best performing stores and sales regions?

B. What are the best-selling products?

C. Which stores and sales regions are strongest in which products?

D. What are the strongest and weakest selling periods? For which stores? Which sales regions? Which products?

E. How can your company improve sales in the weakest store and sales region? (Answers will vary.)

GROUP PROJECT

In a group with three or four classmates, find a description in a computer or business magazine of an information system used by an organization. Look for information about the company on the Web to gain further insight into the company, and prepare a brief description of the business. Describe the system you have selected in terms of its inputs, processes, and outputs, and in terms of its organization, management, and technology features and the importance of the system to the company. If possible, use electronic presentation software to present your analysis to the class.

 INTERNET TOOLS

COMPANION WEBSITE

At www.pearsoned.ca/laudon, you will find valuable tools to facilitate and enhance your learning of this chapter as well as opportunities to apply your knowledge to realistic situations:

- An Interactive Study Guide of self-test questions that will provide you with immediate feedback.
- Application exercises.
- An Electronic Commerce Project that will use the interactive software at the UPS Web site to help a company calculate and budget for its shipping costs.
- A Management Decision Problem on planning a new Internet business.
- Updates of material in the chapter.

ADDITIONAL SITES OF INTEREST

There are many interesting Web sites to enhance your learning about information systems. You can search the Web yourself, or just try the following sites to add to what you have already learned.

Pearson Education Canada Laudon, Laudon, and Brabston Web site

    www.pearsoned.ca/laudon

    The Web site that supports this text; you should bookmark this site on your computer.

Gartner Group

    www.gartner.com

    A wealth of research information on a wide variety of management information systems topics.

Information Technology Association of Canada

    www.itac.ca

    Web site for professionals that includes Canadian e-commerce case studies and a lot of information on IT careers and job skills.

CASE STUDY: *Gold Medal Information Technology for the Olympics*

Here's a dilemma: How does the European Union's lowest-tech country meet the gargantuan information requirements of the Athens 2004 Olympics?

In 2004, Games organizers must provide a lightning-quick information feed to thousands of reporters and Olympic officials in near-zero response times. That task is being handled by SchlumbergerSema, the information technology systems provider that took over from IBM as Olympic sponsor after the Sydney 2000 Games.

The benchmark for failure has already been set—ironically by the city that beat Athens to the 1996 Olympics. In media circles, Atlanta 1996 is best remembered as the Glitch Games after an information blackout left reporters groping in the dark for competition results. Some critics fear a different kind of blackout in Athens 2004—a real one. "It's true; here you see power outages very often," says Mr. Claude Philipps, Schlumberger summer Olympics Games manager. "[Greek organizers] took this seriously... There is a diesel generator in every venue." Given the enormity of the IT task, this is a risk that Greek organizers cannot afford to take (and money they cannot afford to save).

With an IT project this big, you have to start early. Schlumberger, a $14.3-billion company headquartered in New York, Paris, and The Hague, Netherlands, is overseeing the development and operation of computing systems for the 2004 Summer Olympics in Athens, and when the Games were still 20 months away, the company had already completed half the necessary software applications. The IT giant opened its Athens Integration Test Laboratory in 2002, where it will test these applications and train the nearly 4000 people needed to run them.

Schlumberger's work for the Athens Games is part of an IT contract that it calls the world's largest. The company agreed to handle every detail of IT work for four successive Olympics, a project that began with the 2002 Winter Games in Salt Lake City and will end with the Beijing Summer Games in 2008. "We act as a global integrator, pulling together a team of 10 to 12 technology companies. We provide the key applications. We provide the hardware. And we operate the systems during the Games," says Claude Philipps, chief technology integrator for the 2004 Games, who spoke to *PC Magazine* via phone from his office in Athens.

The task is much larger this time around than in Salt Lake. While the Salt Lake Organizing Committee handed out 89 000 accreditations for 78 sporting events spanning 10 different venues, the Athens 2004 Organizing Committee for the Olympic Games' (ATHOC) will provide 200 000 accreditations for 300 events in 37 venues." Schlumberger calculates that the 2004 Games will require two to three times more "IT power" than the Salt Lake 2002 Winter Games, its first assignment as official sponsor. For Athens, it will obtain and provide 10 000 computers, 450 servers, 2000 fax machines and copiers, and 2000 printers, plus a workforce of nearly 4000 (3500 of whom will be volunteers).

These machines, networked with optical fibre and tied to the Internet, will run two types of applications: Games Management Systems (GMS), which handle organizational tasks including accreditation, accommodations, health services, and transportation; and Info Diffusion Systems (IDS), which provide journalists, officials, public Web sites, sponsors, and television commentators with results, statistics, and other important information related to the events themselves.

The company has already completed the GMS applications, which must be up and running well in advance of the Games. A handful of the IDS tools are finished. Developing them is a much greater challenge. "GMS is an important piece, but the most important piece is the real-time results systems," says Philipps. "If they fail, two to three billion people across the world will not be happy." For the benefit of commentators, the systems must send distances, times, scores, and other results across the network as soon as the data become available. According to Philipps, when a runner crosses the finish line, the person's time will reach commentators' desktops no more than three-tenths of a second later.

In addition to building the applications and laying down all of the hardware needed to run them, including redundant machines, hubs, routers, and networking cable, Schlumberger will spend more than 200 000 hours testing the systems at the Athens Integration Lab. How much will all this cost? About $500 million, which seems reasonable, considering how much the company spent on the Salt Lake Games. Though the Salt Lake project was, at most, half the size of the Athens project, it cost about $450 million. In at least one sense, Schlumberger's Olympian task is very much like any other IT project. It is easier the second time around.

The 1998 Winter Olympics in Nagano, Japan, had just ended, but Dave Busser, the chief information officer of the Salt Lake Organizing Committee (SLOC), was already on the phone to the world's leading technology companies, trying to put together the massive array of computer and telephone equipment needed to run the Salt Lake City Games in 2002. He would need the next four years to get all the right hardware and software in place and tested, drawing on the expertise of 17 different technology companies and spending roughly $450 million.

"It's one of the biggest projects you can imagine," Busser told *PC Magazine*. "And the deadline for getting it all done was absolutely not going to change." Busser and his team did get it done, with the games having few, if any, high-tech mishaps.

Olympic Specs

A wide area high speed network comprising almost 50 000 kilometres of optical fibre spanned the Games' 41 venues. "It was the largest in Utah," Busser continued. "And probably, on any given day, the largest private network in the United States." The network connected over 5000 Gateway desktops and laptops, 500 to 600 servers from Gateway and Sun, myriad printers from Xerox and Kodak, and the requisite timing devices and scoreboards from Seiko.

Then there was the official Web site of the games, which was visited by over 15 million unique users over the course of the games. The site was hosted and operated by MSNBC, with Qwest providing the network access and various peripheral applications. "It was the largest single-event Web site in history," said Busser. And then there was the telephony equipment. The committee relied on 14 000 desk phones, 10 000 mobile phones, and 7000 two-way radios. More than 2300 people were needed to operate all this technology. Half were volunteers, and half were employees of SLOC or the various technology companies supplying equipment.

What was SLOC's massive network of machines used for? Some systems handled organizational duties, tending to everything from transportation around the city to accreditation at the various athletic venues to hotel accommodations. Others systems managed the competitions themselves, keeping track of the athletes' performances and supplying television commentators with up-to-the-minute information. Still other components served as information kiosks for members of the media and visitors to the Games.

The machines installed at the athletic venues were the most important and had to be incredibly fast so that television commentators could have the latest data at their fingertips. "Data had to be delivered almost in real time," said Busser. "We agreed to deliver the result data to the commentators in 300 milliseconds." The infrastructure also had to be reliable. Systems at each venue could tap into a central data centre through the SLOC wide area network but were also designed to operate on their own and have access to backup data. "We could have lost our primary data centre, and the events would still go on. Supporting athletic competition was our first priority."

Failures are always possible, as any IT manager will tell you, but Busser and his team spent weeks and weeks trying to ensure mishaps would be kept to a minimum. "We did over 100 000 hours of testing and conducted two comprehensive technical rehearsals where we actually tested all of our operational procedures," said Busser. "When the real thing started, we didn't have a couple of weeks to work through the bugs. We didn't have that grace period. Everything had to work on day one."

According to Busser, everything did work on day one and continued to work through the Salt Lake City Games. Gateway, which supplied all of the PCs for the Games as well as technical support for those PCs, is in agreement. Schlumberger moved from

Salt Lake City to Athens without a real break. Before Atlanta, IBM had run the Olympics' information technology for years without a glitch. It will be interesting to see if Schlumberger continues to grab the gold for its Olympic performance.

Sources: Cade Metz, "Athens Apps Up and Running," *PC Magazine*, December 23, 2002, available at http://www.pcmag.com/print_article/ 0,3048,a=35110,00.asp, accessed June 8, 2003; Cade Metz, "Olympian Technology Powers the Games," *PC Magazine*, February 22, 2002, available at http://www.pcmag.com/print_article/0,3048,a=23111,00.asp, accessed June 8, 2003; John Hadoulis, "Fixing Games Glitches before They Happen," *Athens News*, April 4, 2003, available at www.invgr.com/ olympics_schlumbergersema_glitches.htm, accessed June 8, 2003; "Olympics Testing Labs Opened," *eWeek*, November 11, 2002, available at www.eweek.com/, accessed June 8, 2003; David Aponovich, "No Medal, But IT Integrator Still Scores at Salt Lake Games," *CIO Update*, February 27, 2002, available at www.cioupdate.com/news/article.php/10493_981721, accessed June 8, 2003.

CASE STUDY QUESTIONS

1. What are the obstacles to implementing the information systems for the Athens Olympic games?
2. How do you think the Internet and the World Wide Web have changed the Olympics? What impact have they had on fans of the Olympics?
3. What features or characteristics does the Olympics infrastructure have to exhibit in order to deliver the data required by Schlumberger?
4. Do you think the Olympics should award long-term contracts, like the Schlumberger contract? Why or why not?

INFORMATION SYSTEMS IN THE ORGANIZATION

As a manager, you will need to understand the role of the various types of information systems in organizations. After completing this chapter, you should be able to answer the following questions:

1. *What are the major types of information systems in a business? What roles do they play?*

2. *Why should managers pay attention to business processes? Why do firms need to integrate their business processes?*

3. *What are the benefits and challenges of using enterprise systems?*

4. *What are the benefits of using information systems to support supply chain management and collaborative commerce?*

5. *What are the benefits of using information systems for customer relationship management and knowledge management?*

Fast-Track Fashions at Zara

In the fast-paced world of fashion retailing, nothing is as important as time to market, not even advertising or labour costs. No company knows that better than Zara, a worldwide women's apparel chain headquartered in La Coruna, Spain, that is now part of the Inditex global retail conglomerate. For decades, apparel companies have farmed out their production to low-wage countries, hoping to benefit from lower labour costs. Zara decided against this because its management believed that the ability to respond quickly to shifts in customer tastes would prove much more efficient and profitable than outsourcing to low-cost contract manufacturers. As Jose Maria Castellano, Inditex CEO, put it succinctly: "The fashion world is in constant flux and is driven not by supply but by customer demand."

By meticulously coordinating the entire production process, Zara can react much more quickly than its competitors to percolating fashion trends. Zara has what many believe is the world's most responsive supply chain. About half the items it sells are made in its own factories; the rest are outsourced. Zara restocks its stores twice a week, delivering both reordered items and completely new styles. Rival apparel chains, in contrast, only receive new designs once or twice a season. Zara's prolific design department likewise outstrips the competition by churning out more than 10 000 fresh new designs each year. No competitor comes close. "It's like you walk into a new store every two weeks," observes Tracy Mullin, president and CEO of the National Retail Federation.

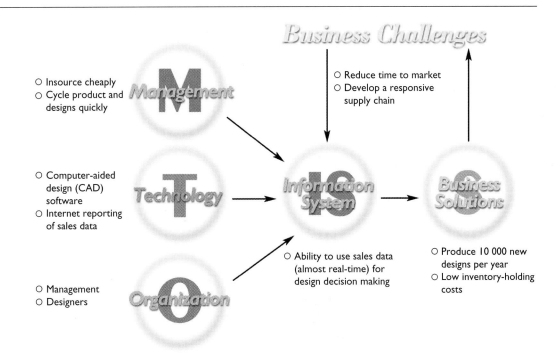

Every working day, the manager of a Zara store reports exactly what has been sold to corporate headquarters via the Internet. This information is quickly relayed to Zara's design department, which can create or alter products in a matter of days. Zara's 200 designers draw the latest fashion ideas on their computers and send them over Zara's intranet to Zara's nearby factories. Within days, the new garments are cut, dyed, stitched, and pressed. In just three weeks, the clothes will be hanging in Zara stores all over the world. Zara's time to market is 12 times faster than its rivals, such as The Gap.

Zara maintains a gigantic 836 000 square metre warehouse in La Coruna that is connected to 14 of its factories through a maze of tunnels, each with a rail hanging from its ceiling. Along these rails, cables transport bunches of clothes on hangers or in suspended racks into the warehouse. Each bundle is supported by a metal bar with a series of tabs coded to indicate exactly where in the warehouse that bundle should be placed. There, the merchandise is sorted, rerouted, and re-sorted until it gets to the staging area of the distribution centre. Every Zara store has its own staging area here to assemble its orders. As soon as a store's order is complete, it is carted directly to a loading dock, and packed with other stores' shipments, in order of delivery. Deliveries to European stores are placed on trucks; shipments outside Europe are sent by plane. The vast majority of items are in the warehouse for only a few hours, and Zara constantly fine-tunes the size and sequence of deliveries to maintain that tight schedule.

Zara's manufacturing costs run 15 to 20 percent higher than those of rivals, but they are more than offset by the advantages of split-second time to market. By responding so quickly to customer tastes, Zara almost never needs to correct merchandise blunders or stage across-the-board inventory write-offs. In 2001, when many clothing chains saw sales and profits slide, Zara's profits climbed 31 percent, and the company has historically maintained steady profit margins that are among the best in the industry. The way Zara runs its business is not confined to retail. For any company that cares about time to market, response to customers, and streamlined business processes, Zara is clearly the company to watch.

Sources: Miguel Helft, "Fashion Fast Forward," *Business 2.0*, May 2002; and "Inditex: A Business Model That Is Tailor-Made," *Barcelona Business*, May 2001.

MANAGEMENT CHALLENGE

Businesses need different types of information systems to support decision making and work activities for various organizational levels and functions. Many may need systems that integrate information and business processes from different functional areas. Zara, for instance, needed information systems that would allow it to precisely coordinate its supply chain. It found a solution in integrating systems and business processes for design, production, and logistics. The opening vignette presents the potential rewards to firms with well-conceived systems linking the entire enterprise. These systems typically require a significant amount of organizational and management change and raise the following management challenges:

1. **Integration.** Although it is necessary to design different systems serving different levels and functions in the firm, more and more firms are finding advantages in integrating systems. However, integrating systems for different organizational levels and functions to freely exchange information can be technologically difficult and costly. Managers need to determine what level of system integration is required and how much it is worth in dollars.

2. **Enlarging the scope of management thinking.** Most managers are trained to manage a product line, a division, or an office. They are rarely trained to optimize the performance of the organization as a whole and often are not given the means to do so. But enterprise systems and industrial networks require managers to take a much larger view of their own behaviour, including other products, divisions, departments, and even outside business firms. Investments in enterprise systems are huge, they must be developed over long periods of time, and they must be guided by a shared vision of the objectives.

In this chapter, we examine the role of the various types of information systems in organizations. First, we look at ways of classifying information systems based on the organizational level they support. Next, we look at systems in terms of the organizational function they serve. We show how systems can support business processes for the major business functions and processes that span more than one function. We then examine enterprise applications—enterprise systems, supply chain management systems, customer relationship management systems, and knowledge management systems—which enable organizations to integrate information from multiple functions and business processes across entire firms and even entire industries.

2.1   MAJOR TYPES OF SYSTEMS IN ORGANIZATIONS

Because there are different interests, specialties, and levels in an organization, there are different kinds of systems. No single system can provide all the information an organization needs. Figure 2.1 illustrates one way to depict the kinds of systems found in an organization. In the illustration, the organization is divided into strategic, management, knowledge, and operational levels and then is further divided into functional areas, such as sales and marketing, manufacturing, finance, accounting, and human resources. Systems are built to serve these different organizational interests (Anthony, 1965).

DIFFERENT KINDS OF SYSTEMS

Four main types of information systems serve different organizational levels: (1) operational-level systems, (2) knowledge-level systems, (3) management-level systems, and (4) strategic-level systems. **Operational-level systems** support operational managers by keeping track of the elementary activities and transactions of the organization, such as sales, receipts, cash deposits, payroll, credit decisions, and the flow of materials in a factory. The principal purpose of systems at this level is to answer routine questions and to track the flow of transactions through the organization. How many parts are in inventory? What happened to Mr. Williams's payment? To answer these kinds of questions, information generally must be easily

operational-level systems

Information systems that monitor the elementary activities and transactions of the organization.

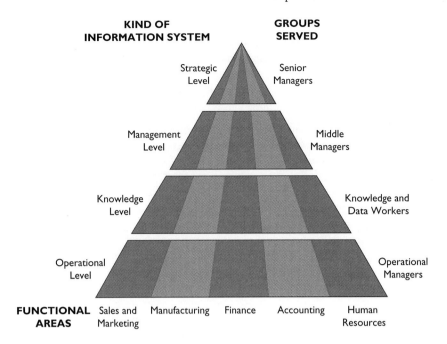

KIND OF
INFORMATION SYSTEM

GROUPS
SERVED

Strategic
Level

Senior
Managers

Management
Level

Middle
Managers

Knowledge
Level

Knowledge and
Data Workers

Operational
Level

Operational
Managers

**FUNCTIONAL
AREAS**   Sales and
Marketing   Manufacturing   Finance   Accounting   Human
Resources

Figure 2.1 Types of information systems. Organizations can be divided into strategic, management, knowledge, and operational levels and into five major functional areas: sales and marketing, manufacturing, finance, accounting, and human resources. Information systems serve each of these levels and functions.

available, current, and accurate. Examples of operational-level systems include a system to record bank deposits from automatic teller machines or one that tracks the number of hours worked each day by employees on a factory floor.

Knowledge-level systems support the organization's knowledge and data workers. The purpose of knowledge-level systems is to help the business firm integrate new knowledge into the business and to help the organization control the flow of paperwork. Knowledge-level systems, especially in the form of workstations and office systems, are among the fastest-growing applications in business today.

Management-level systems serve the monitoring, controlling, decision making, and administrative activities of middle managers. The principal question addressed by such systems is: Are things working well? Management-level systems typically provide periodic reports, rather than instant information, on operations. An example is a relocation control system that reports on the total moving, house hunting, and home financing costs for employees in all company divisions, noting wherever actual costs exceed budgets.

Some management-level systems support nonroutine decision making (Keen and Morton, 1978). They tend to focus on less structured decisions for which information requirements are not always clear. These systems often answer "what-if" questions: What would be the impact on production schedules if we were to double sales in the month of December? What would happen to our return on investment if a factory schedule were delayed for six months? Answers to these questions frequently require new data from outside the organization, as well as data from inside that cannot be easily drawn from existing operational-level systems.

Strategic-level systems help senior management tackle and address strategic issues and long-term trends, both in the firm and in the external environment. Their principal concern is matching changes in the external environment with existing organizational capability. What will employment levels be in five years? What are the long-term industry cost trends, and where does our firm fit in? What products should we be making in five years?

Information systems also serve the major business functions, such as sales and marketing, manufacturing, finance, accounting, and human resources. A typical organization has operational-, management-, knowledge-, and strategic-level systems for each functional area. For example, the sales function generally has a sales system on the operational level to record daily sales figures and to process orders. A knowledge-level system designs promotional displays for the firm's products. A management-level system tracks monthly sales figures by sales territory and reports on territories where sales exceed or fall below anticipated levels. A system to forecast sales trends over a five-year period serves the strategic level. We first describe the specific categories of systems serving each organizational level and their value to the organization.

knowledge-level systems
Information systems that support knowledge and data workers in an organization.

management-level systems
Information systems that support the monitoring, controlling, decision making, and administrative activities of middle managers.

strategic-level systems
Information systems that support the long-range planning activities of senior management.

Our Companion Website for this chapter shows how organizations use these systems for each major business function. At the end of each part of this text, we further discuss how each major business function uses information systems in a section we call *Make IT Your Business.*

SIX MAJOR TYPES OF SYSTEMS

Figure 2.2 shows the specific types of information systems that correspond to each organizational level. The organization has executive support systems (ESS) at the strategic level, management information systems (MIS) and decision support systems (DSS) at the management level, knowledge work systems (KWS) and office systems at the knowledge level, and transaction processing systems (TPS) at the operational level. Systems at each level, in turn, are specialized to serve each of the major functional areas. Thus, the typical systems found in organizations are designed to assist workers or managers at each level and in the functions of sales and marketing, manufacturing, finance, accounting, and human resources.

While we present here one model of categorizing information systems, there are other models, ranging from two types of systems to eight or more types. All of the models incorporate the same basic systems, simply assigning them to different categories. For example, we assign expert systems to decision support systems here, while others may make expert systems a separate category.

Table 2.1 summarizes the features of the six types of information systems. It should be noted that each of the different systems might have components that are used by organizational levels and groups other than their main constituencies. A secretary may find information on an MIS, or a middle manager may need to extract data from a TPS.

Transaction Processing Systems

Transaction processing systems (TPS) are the basic business systems that serve the operational level of the organization. A transaction processing system is a computerized system that performs and records the daily routine transactions necessary to conduct business. Examples are sales order entry, hotel reservations, payroll, employee record keeping, and shipping.

transaction processing systems (TPS)

Computerized systems that perform and record the daily routine transactions necessary to conduct business; they serve the organization's operational level.

Figure 2.2 The six major types of information systems. This figure provides examples of TPS, office systems, KWS, DSS, MIS, and ESS, showing the level of the organization and business function that each supports.

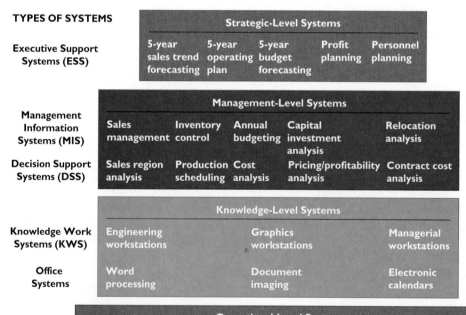

TABLE 2.1	CHARACTERISTICS OF INFORMATION PROCESSING SYSTEMS			
Type of System	Information Inputs	Processing	Information Outputs	Users
ESS	Aggregate data; external, internal	Graphics; simulations; interactive	Projections; responses to queries	Senior managers
DSS	Low-volume data or massive databases optimized for data analysis; analytic models and data analysis tools	Interactive; simulations; analysis	Special reports; decision analyses; responses to queries	Professionals; staff managers
MIS	Summary transaction data; high-volume data; simple models	Routine reports; simple models; low-level analysis	Summary and exception reports	Middle managers
KWS	Design specifications; knowledge base	Modelling; simulations	Models; graphics	Professionals; technical staff
Office systems	Documents; schedules	Document management; scheduling; communication	Documents; schedules; mail	Clerical workers
TPS	Transactions; events	Sorting; listing; merging; updating	Detailed reports; lists; summaries	Operations personnel; supervisors

At the operational level, tasks, resources, and goals are predefined and highly structured. The decision to grant credit to a customer, for instance, is made by a lower-level supervisor according to predefined criteria. All that must be determined is whether the customer meets the criteria.

Figure 2.3 depicts a payroll TPS, which is a typical accounting transaction processing system found in most firms. A payroll system keeps track of the money paid to employees. The master file is composed of discrete pieces of information (such as a name, address, or employee number) called data elements. Data are keyed into the system, updating the data elements. The elements in the master file are combined in different ways to make up reports of interest to management and government agencies and to send paycheques to employees. These TPS can generate other reports by combining existing data elements.

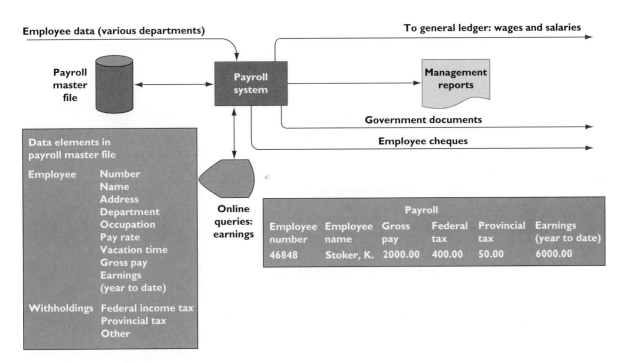

Figure 2.3 A symbolic representation for a payroll TPS.

TYPE OF TPS SYSTEM				
Sales/ marketing systems	Manufacturing/ production systems	Finance/ accounting systems	Human resources systems	Other types (e.g., university)
Major functions of system				
Sales management	Scheduling	Budgeting	Personnel records	Admissions
Market research	Purchasing	General ledger	Benefits	Grade records
Promotion	Shipping/receiving	Billing	Compensation	Course records
Pricing	Engineering	Cost accounting	Labour relations	Alumni
New products	Operations		Training	
Major application systems				
Sales order information system	Machine control systems	General ledger	Payroll	Registration system
Market research system	Purchase order systems	Accounts receivable/payable	Employee records	Student transcript system
Sales commission system	Quality control systems	Funds management systems	Benefit systems	Curriculum class control systems
			Career path systems	Alumni benefactor system

Figure 2.4 Typical applications of TPS. There are five functional categories of TPS: sales/marketing, manufacturing/production, finance/accounting, human resources, and other types of systems specific to a particular industry. Within each of these major functions are subfunctions. For each of these subfunctions (e.g., sales management), there is a major application system.

Other typical TPS applications are identified in Figure 2.4. The figure shows that there are five functional categories of TPS: (1) sales/marketing, (2) manufacturing/production, (3) finance/accounting, (4) human resources, and (5) other types of TPS that are unique to a particular industry. The UPS package tracking system described in Chapter 1 is an example of a manufacturing TPS. UPS sells package delivery services; the TPS system keeps track of all of its package shipment transactions.

Transaction processing systems are often so central to a business that TPS failure for a few hours can spell a firm's demise and perhaps the demise of other firms linked to it. Imagine what would happen to UPS if its package tracking system were not working! What would the airlines do without their computerized reservation systems?

Managers need TPS to monitor the status of internal operations and the firm's relations with the external environment. TPS are also major producers of information for the other types of systems. (For example, the payroll system illustrated here, along with other accounting TPS, supplies data to the company's general ledger system, which is responsible for maintaining records of the firm's income and expenses and for producing reports, such as income statements and balance sheets.)

KNOWLEDGE WORK AND OFFICE SYSTEMS

knowledge work systems (KWS)

Information systems that aid knowledge workers in the creation and integration of new knowledge in the organization.

office systems

Computer systems, such as word processing, electronic mail systems, and scheduling systems, that are designed to increase the productivity of data workers in the office.

Knowledge work systems (KWS) and **office systems** serve the information needs at the knowledge level of the organization. Knowledge work systems aid knowledge workers, while office systems primarily aid data workers (although they are also used extensively by knowledge workers).

As first discussed in Chapter 1, *knowledge workers* are people who hold formal university degrees and who are often members of recognized professions, such as engineers, doctors, lawyers, and scientists. Their jobs consist primarily of creating new information and knowledge. KWS, such as scientific or engineering design workstations, promote the creation of new knowledge and ensure that new knowledge and technical expertise are properly integrated into the business. *Data workers* typically have less formal advanced educational degrees and tend to process, rather than create, information. They consist primarily of secretaries, bookkeepers, filing clerks, or managers, whose jobs are principally to use, manipulate,

Desktop publishing software enables users to control all aspects of the design and layout process for professional-looking documents.

or disseminate information. Office systems are information technology applications designed to increase data workers' productivity by supporting the coordinating and communicating activities of the typical office. Office systems coordinate diverse information workers, geographic units, and functional areas. The systems communicate with customers, suppliers, and other organizations outside the firm and serve as clearinghouses for information and knowledge flows.

Typical office systems handle and manage documents through word processing, desktop publishing, document imaging, and digital filing; scheduling through electronic calendars; and communication through electronic mail, voice mail, or videoconferencing. **Word processing** refers to the software and hardware technology that creates, edits, formats, stores, and prints documents (see Chapter 6). Word processing systems represent the single most common application of information technology to office work, in part because producing documents is what offices are all about. **Desktop publishing** produces professional publishing-quality documents by combining output from word processing software with design elements, graphics, and special layout features. Companies are now starting to publish documents in the form of Web pages for easier access and distribution. We describe Web publishing in more detail in Chapter 14.

Document imaging systems are another widely used knowledge application. Document imaging systems convert paper documents and images into digital form so that they can be stored and accessed by the computer.

Management Information Systems

In Chapter 1, we defined management information systems as the study of information systems in business and management. The term management information systems (MIS) also designates a specific category of information systems serving management-level functions. **Management information systems (MIS)** serve the management level of the organization, providing managers with reports and, in some cases, with online access to the organization's current performance and historical records. Typically, they are oriented almost exclusively to internal, not environmental or external, events. MIS primarily serve the functions of planning, controlling, and decision making at the management level. Generally, they depend on underlying transaction processing systems for their data.

MIS summarize and report on the company's basic operations. The basic transaction data from TPS are compressed and are usually presented in long reports that are produced on a regular schedule. Figure 2.5 shows how a typical MIS transforms transaction level data from inventory, production, and accounting into MIS files that are used to provide managers with reports. Figure 2.6 shows a sample report from this system.

MIS usually serve managers interested in weekly, monthly, and yearly results—not day-to-day activities. MIS generally provide answers to routine questions that have been specified in advance and have a predefined procedure for answering them. For instance, MIS reports

---

word processing

Office system technology that facilitates the creation of documents through computerized text editing, formatting, storing, and printing.

desktop publishing

Technology that produces professional-quality documents combining output from word processors with design, graphics, and special layout features.

document imaging systems

Systems that convert paper documents and images into digital form so that they can be stored and accessed by the computer.

management information systems (MIS)

Information systems at the management level of an organization that serve the functions of planning, controlling, and decision making by providing routine summary and exception reports.

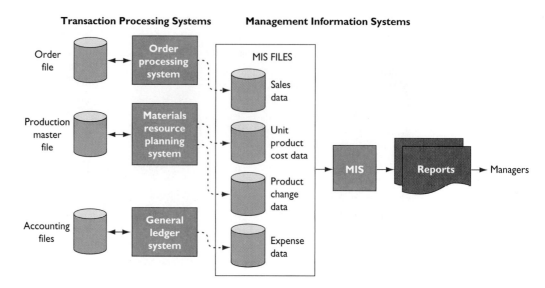

Figure 2.5 How management information systems obtain their data from the organization's TPS. In the system illustrated by this diagram, three TPS supply summarized transaction data at the end of the time period to the MIS reporting system. Managers gain access to the organizational data through the MIS, which provides them with the appropriate reports.

Figure 2.6 A sample report that might be produced by the MIS in Figure 2.5.

Consolidated Consumer Products Corporation
Sales by Product and Sales Region: 2003

PRODUCT CODE	PRODUCT DESCRIPTION	SALES REGION	ACTUAL SALES	PLANNED	ACTUAL VS. PLANNED
4469	Carpet Cleaner	Northeast	4,066,700	4,800,000	0.85
		South	3,778,112	3,750,000	1.01
		Midwest	4,867,001	4,600,000	1.06
		West	4,003,440	4,400,000	0.91
	TOTAL		16,715,253	17,550,000	0.95
5674	Room Freshener	Northeast	3,676,700	3,900,000	0.94
		South	5,608,112	4,700,000	1.19
		Midwest	4,711,001	4,200,000	1.12
		West	4,563,440	4,900,000	0.93
	TOTAL		18,559,253	17,700,000	1.05

might list the total pounds of lettuce used this quarter by a fast-food chain or, as illustrated in Figure 2.6, compare total annual sales figures for specific products to planned targets. These systems are generally not flexible and have little analytical capability. Most MIS use simple routines, such as summaries and comparisons, as opposed to sophisticated mathematical models or statistical techniques.

Decision Support Systems

decision support systems (DSS)

Information systems at the organization's management level that combine data and sophisticated analytical models or data analysis tools to support semi-structured and unstructured decision making.

Decision support systems (DSS) also serve the management level of the organization. DSS help managers make decisions that are unique, rapidly changing, and not easily specified in advance. They address problems where the procedure for arriving at a solution may not be fully predefined in advance. Although DSS use internal information from TPS and MIS, they often bring in information from external sources, such as current stock prices or product prices of competitors. While DSS primarily serve the managerial levels of the firm, they may be used at any level in the organization's hierarchy.

Clearly, by design, DSS have more analytical power than other systems. They are built explicitly with a variety of models to analyze data or they condense large amounts of data into a form in which they can be analyzed by decision makers. DSS are designed so that users can work with them directly; these systems explicitly include user-friendly software. DSS are interactive; the user can change assumptions, ask new questions, and include new data. *Group decision support systems (GDSS)* use computer-mediated communication tools, such as networks, anonymous input and voting, and whiteboards to support groups as they make decisions. We discuss DSS and GDSS in Chapter 13. *Expert systems* provide what appears to be intelligence, with the ability to make decisions and reach conclusions. Expert systems are used in a wide variety of applications, from spell-checking and grammar-checking to tax programs and credit card authorization. We discuss these cutting-edge applications in Chapter 14.

A DSS for assessing patients under long-term care has been implemented in Ontario. Patients receiving healthcare at home or in nursing homes can be assessed using standardized categories developed at the University of Waterloo and the University of Alberta in conjunction with MED e-care Healthcare Solutions, Inc., a Toronto-based software development firm (www.mede-care.com). Patients can be assessed using the new DSS, and their records can be transmitted electronically from one agency to another, as needed, such as when a patient moves from home healthcare to a nursing home. Patients can be assessed repeatedly to determine how they are responding over time. Among the data elements that are assessed in the minimum data set standard categories (MDS) are cognitive abilities, memory, depression, history of falls, pressure ulcers, and incontinence. Using the assessment tools, patient care can be planned before the patient even arrives at the nursing home. MED e-care is also partnering with other Canadian firms, such as Momentum Software, Winnipeg, Manitoba, to provide its MDSsoftware for nursing homes throughout North America. Figure 2.7 illustrates the type of DSS now being developed; interestingly, by using MDS and other standards being developed for patient assessment, many vendors can develop a variety of DSS tools for long-term care applications. (Zeidenberg, 2000) We describe other types of DSS in Chapter 13.

Executive Support Systems

Senior managers use **executive support systems (ESS)** to make decisions. ESS serve the strategic level of the organization. They address nonroutine decisions requiring judgment, evaluation, and insight because there is no agreed-on procedure for arriving at these solutions. ESS create a generalized computing and communications environment, rather than providing any fixed application or specific capability. ESS are designed to incorporate data about external events, such as new tax laws or competitors, but they also draw summarized information from internal MIS and DSS. They filter, compress, and track critical data, emphasizing the reduction of time and effort required to obtain information useful to executives. ESS employ the most advanced graphics software and can deliver graphs and data from many sources immediately to a senior executive's office or to a boardroom.

Unlike the other types of information systems, ESS are not designed primarily to solve specific problems. Instead, ESS provide a generalized computing and telecommunications

executive support systems (ESS)

Information systems at the organization's strategic level designed to address unstructured decision making through advanced graphics and communications.

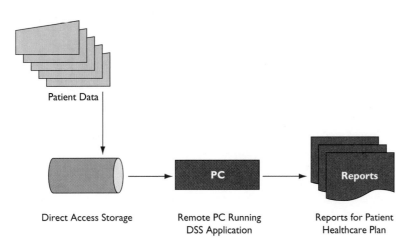

Patient Data

Direct Access Storage

PC

Remote PC Running DSS Application

Reports

Reports for Patient Healthcare Plan

Figure 2.7 DSS for assessing and monitoring patients. It is used daily by healthcare professionals responsible for providing healthcare to patients who require long-term care.

Figure 2.8 Model of a typical executive support system. This system pools data from diverse internal and external sources and makes them available to executives in an easy-to-use form.

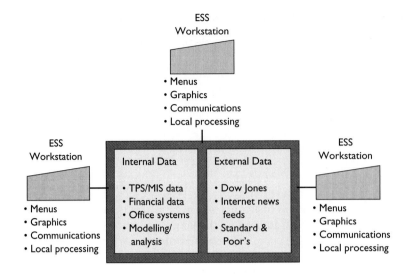

capacity that can be applied to a changing array of problems. Although many DSS are designed to be highly analytical, ESS tend to make less use of analytical models.

Questions ESS assist in answering include the following: What business should we be in? What are the competitors doing? What new acquisitions would protect us from cyclical business swings? Which units should we sell to raise cash for acquisitions (Rockart and Treacy, 1982)? Figure 2.8 illustrates a model of an ESS. It consists of workstations with menus, interactive graphics, and communications capabilities that can access historical and competitive data from internal corporate systems and external databases, such as Dow Jones News/Retrieval or Ipsos-Reid, the Canadian polling firm. Because ESS are designed to be used by senior managers who may have little direct contact or experience with computer-based information systems, they incorporate easy-to-use graphic interfaces. More details on leading-edge applications of DSS and ESS can be found in Chapter 13.

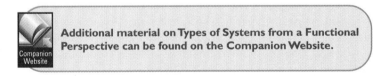

Additional material on **Types of Systems from a Functional Perspective** can be found on the **Companion Website.**

Figure 2.9 Interrelationships among systems. The various types of systems in the organization have interdependencies. TPS are major producers of information that is required by the other systems, which, in turn, produce information for other systems. These different types of systems are only loosely coupled in most organizations.

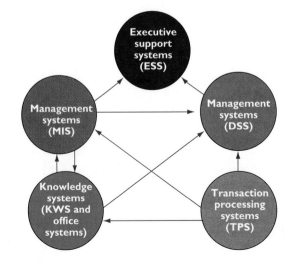

RELATIONSHIP OF SYSTEMS TO ONE ANOTHER

Figure 2.9 illustrates how the systems serving different levels in the organization are related to one another. TPS are typically a major source of data for other systems while ESS are primarily a recipient of data from lower-level systems. The other types of systems may exchange data with each other as well. Data may also be exchanged among systems serving different functional areas. For example, an order captured by a sales system may be transmitted to a manufacturing system as a transaction for producing or delivering the product specified in the order or to an MIS for financial reporting.

It is definitely advantageous to have some measure of integration among these systems so that information can flow easily among different parts of the organization. But integration costs money, and integrating many different systems is extremely time consuming and complex. Each organization must weigh its needs for integrating systems against the difficulties of mounting a large-scale systems integration effort. The discussion of enterprise systems in Section 2.2 treats this issue in greater detail.

2.2 ENTERPRISE APPLICATIONS: ENTERPRISE SYSTEMS AND SYSTEMS FOR SUPPLY CHAIN MANAGEMENT, CUSTOMER RELATIONSHIP MANAGEMENT, AND KNOWLEDGE MANAGEMENT

Electronic commerce, electronic business, and intensifying global competition are forcing firms to focus on speed to market, improving customer service, and more efficient execution. The flow of information and work needs to be orchestrated so that the organization can perform like a well-oiled machine. These changes require powerful new systems that can integrate information from many different functional areas and organizational units and coordinate the firm's activities with those of suppliers and other business partners.

In previous sections of this chapter, you learned that there are many specialized types of systems found in organizations serving different business functions and organizational levels. Many of these systems were developed in isolation from each other and, consequently, could not automatically exchange information. Information needed to support decision making was often "stuck" in these specialized silos of information. Manufacturing units might not know exactly how many and what types of items to produce because their systems could not easily obtain information from systems that processed customer orders. Managers planning Canadian business units could not easily share information with Asian offices or European offices because each had developed their own set of systems. In this environment, operating a "global firm" or even a highly coordinated enterprise within a single country becomes nearly impossible.

One solution is to develop a separate "middleware" software bridge to each of these specialized systems to link them all together (see Chapter 6). This is both an expensive and unsatisfactory solution. Another solution, now more common, is to develop or buy entirely new **enterprise applications** that can coordinate activities, decisions, and knowledge across many different functions, levels, and business units in a firm. Chapter 1 introduced the principal digital firm applications used for this purpose: enterprise systems, supply chain management systems, customer relationship management systems, and knowledge management systems. Each of these enterprise applications integrates a related set of functions and business processes to enhance the performance of the organization as a whole.

Generally, these more contemporary systems take advantage of corporate intranets and Web technologies that enable the efficient transfer of information within the firm and to partner firms. These systems are inherently cross-level, cross-functional, and business process oriented. Review Figure 1.13 in Chapter 1, which shows that the architecture for these enterprise applications encompasses processes spanning the entire organization and, in some cases, extending beyond the organization to customers, suppliers, and other key business partners.

enterprise applications

Systems that can coordinate activities, decisions, and knowledge across many different functions, levels, and business units in a firm. Includes enterprise systems, supply chain management systems, customer relationship management systems, and knowledge management systems.

INTEGRATING FUNCTIONS AND BUSINESS PROCESSES

The new digital firm business environment and the deployment of enterprise applications require companies to think more strategically about their business processes, which we introduced in Chapter 1. *Business processes* refer to the manner in which work is organized, coordinated, and focused to produce a valuable product or service. Business processes are concrete workflows of material, information, and knowledge-sets of activities. Business processes also refer to the unique ways in which organizations coordinate work, information, and knowledge and the ways in which management chooses to coordinate work. A company's business processes can be a source of competitive strength if they enable the company to innovate better or to execute better than its rivals. Business processes can also be a liability if they are based on outdated ways of working that impede organizational responsiveness and efficiency.

Some business processes support the major functional areas of the firm while others are cross-functional. Table 2.2 describes some typical business processes for each of the functional areas.

Many business processes are cross-functional, transcending the boundaries between sales, marketing, manufacturing, and research and development. These cross-functional processes cut across the traditional organizational structure, grouping employees from different functional specialties to complete a piece of work. For example, the order fulfillment process at many companies requires cooperation among the sales function (receiving the order, entering the order), the accounting function (credit checking and billing for the order), and the manufacturing function (assembling and shipping the order). Figure 2.10 illustrates how this cross-functional process might work. Information systems support these cross-functional processes as well as processes for the separate business functions.

Today's firms are finding that they can become more flexible and productive by coordinating their business processes more closely and, in some cases, integrating these processes so that they focus more on efficient management of resources and customer service. Enterprise applications are designed to support organization-wide process coordination and integration. Enterprise systems create an integrated organization-wide platform to coordinate key internal processes of the firm. Information systems for supply chain management (SCM) and customer relationship management (CRM) can help coordinate processes for managing the firm's relationship with its suppliers and customers. Knowledge management systems enable organizations to better manage processes for capturing and applying knowledge and expertise.

ENTERPRISE SYSTEMS

Enterprise systems, which we introduced in Chapter 1, provide a technology platform where organizations can integrate and coordinate their major internal business processes. They address the problem of organizational inefficiencies created by isolated islands of informa-

TABLE 2.2	EXAMPLES OF FUNCTIONAL BUSINESS PROCESSES
Functional Area	**Business Process**
Manufacturing and production	Assembling the product
	Checking for quality
	Producing bills of materials
Sales and marketing	Identifying customers
	Making customers aware of the product
	Selling the product
Finance and accounting	Paying creditors
	Creating financial statements
	Managing cash accounts
Human resources	Hiring employees
	Evaluating employees' job performance
	Enrolling employees in benefits plans

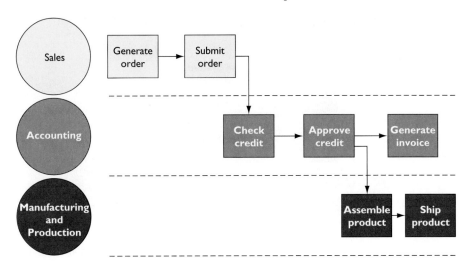

Figure 2.10 The order fulfillment process. Generating and fulfilling an order is a multistep process involving activities performed by the sales, manufacturing and production, and accounting functions.

tion, business processes, and technology. A large organization typically has many different kinds of information systems that support different functions, organizational levels, and business processes. Most of these systems are built around different functions, business units, and business processes that do not "talk" to each other. Managers might have a hard time assembling the data they need for a comprehensive, overall picture of the organization's operations. For instance, sales personnel might not be able to tell at the time they place an order whether the items that were ordered were in inventory; customers might not be able to track their orders; and manufacturing might not be able to communicate easily with finance to plan for new production. This fragmentation of data in many separate systems could, thus, have a negative impact on organizational efficiency and business performance. Figure 2.11 illustrates the traditional arrangement of information systems.

Enterprise systems, also known as enterprise resource planning (ERP) systems solve this problem by providing a single information system for organization-wide coordination of key business processes. Enterprise software models and automates many business processes, such as filling an order or scheduling a shipment, with the goal of integrating information across the company and eliminating complex, expensive links between computer systems in different areas of the business. Information that was previously fragmented in different systems can seamlessly flow throughout the firm so that it can be shared by business processes in manufacturing, accounting, human resources, and other areas of the firm. Discrete business processes

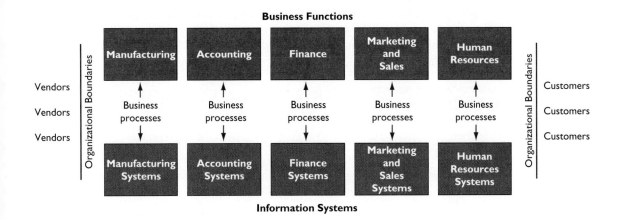

Figure 2.11 Traditional view of systems. In most organizations, separate systems built over a long period of time support discrete business processes and discrete business functions. The organization's systems rarely included vendors and customers.

Figure 2.12 Enterprise systems. Enterprise systems can integrate the key business processes of an entire firm into a single software system that allows information to flow seamlessly throughout the organization. These systems focus primarily on internal processes but may include transactions with customers and vendors.

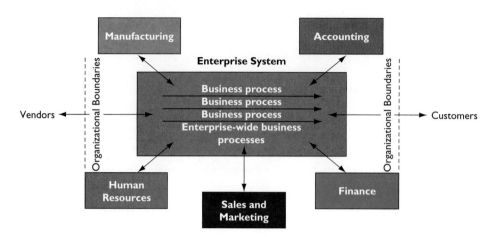

from sales, production, finance, and logistics can be integrated into company-wide business processes that flow across organizational levels and functions. An enterprise-wide technical platform serves all processes and levels. Figure 2.12 illustrates how enterprise systems work.

The enterprise system collects data from various key business processes (see Table 2.3) and stores the data in a single comprehensive data repository where they can be used by other parts of the business. Managers have more precise and timely information for coordinating the daily operations of the business and a firm-wide view of business processes and information flows.

For instance, when a sales representative in Brussels enters a customer order, the data flow automatically to others in the company who need to see them. The factory in Hong Kong receives the order and begins production. The warehouse checks its progress online and schedules the shipment date. The warehouse can check its stock of parts and replenish whatever the factory has depleted. The enterprise system stores production information where it can be accessed by customer service representatives to track the progress of the order through every step of the manufacturing process. Updated sales and production data automatically flow to the accounting department. The system transmits information for calculating the salesperson's commission to the payroll department. The system also automatically recalculates the company's balance sheets, accounts receivable and payable ledgers, cost-centre accounts, and available cash. Corporate headquarters in Winnipeg can view up-to-the-minute data on sales, inventory, and production at every step of the process, as well as updated sales and production forecasts and calculations of product cost and availability.

Enterprise systems have been primarily oriented toward helping companies manage their internal manufacturing, financial, and human resource processes and were not originally designed to support major processes encompassing entities outside the firm. However, enterprise software vendors are starting to enhance their products so that firms can link their enterprise systems with the systems of vendors, suppliers, manufacturers, distributors, and retailers or link their enterprise systems to the systems for supply chain management and customer relationship management.

TABLE 2.3	**BUSINESS PROCESSES SUPPORTED BY ENTERPRISE SYSTEMS**

Manufacturing processes, including inventory management, purchasing, shipping, production planning, production scheduling, material requirements planning, and plant and equipment maintenance

Financial and accounting processes, including accounts payable, accounts receivable, cash management and forecasting, product cost accounting, cost-centre accounting, asset accounting, general ledger, and financial reporting

Sales and marketing processes, including order processing, pricing, shipping, billing, sales management, and sales planning

Human resource processes, including personnel administration, time accounting, payroll, personnel planning and development, benefits accounting, applicant tracking, and travel expense reporting

Benefits and Challenges of Enterprise Systems

Enterprise systems promise to integrate the diverse business processes of a firm into a single, integrated information architecture, but they also present major challenges.

Benefits of Enterprise Systems   Enterprise systems promise to greatly change four dimensions of business: (1) firm structure, (2) management process, (3) technology platform, and (4) business capability. Companies can use enterprise systems to support organizational structures that were not previously possible or to create a more disciplined organizational culture. For example, they might use enterprise systems to integrate the corporation across geographic or business unit boundaries or to create a more uniform organizational culture in which everyone uses similar processes and information. An enterprise-enabled organization does business the same way worldwide, with cross-functional coordination and information flowing freely across business functions.

Information supplied by an enterprise system is structured around cross-functional business processes, and it can improve management reporting and decision making. For example, an enterprise system might help management more easily determine which products are most or least profitable. An enterprise system could potentially supply management with better data about business processes and overall organizational performance.

Enterprise systems promise to provide firms with a single, unified, and all-encompassing information system technology platform that houses data on all the key business processes. The data have common, standardized definitions and formats that are accepted by the entire organization. You will learn more about the importance of standardizing organizational data in Chapter 7.

Enterprise systems can also help create the foundation for a customer- or demand-driven organization. By integrating discrete business processes in sales, production, finance, and logistics, the entire organization can respond more efficiently to customer requests for products or information, forecast new products, and develop and deliver them as demand requires. Manufacturing has better information to produce only what customers have ordered, procure exactly the right amount of components or raw materials to fill actual orders, stage production, and minimize the time that components or finished products are in inventory.

Challenges of Enterprise Systems   Although enterprise systems can improve organizational coordination, efficiency, and decision making, they have proven very difficult and costly to develop. They require not only large technology investments but also fundamental changes in the way the business operates. Companies will need to rework their business processes to make information flow smoothly among them. Employees will have to take on new job functions and responsibilities. Many barriers must be overcome before the benefits of enterprise systems can be realized (Robey, Ross, and Boudreau, 2002). Organizations that do not understand how much change will be required or that are unable to make this change will have problems implementing enterprise systems, or they may not be able to achieve a higher level of functional and business process integration.

Enterprise systems require complex pieces of software and large investments of time, money, and expertise. (A typical large enterprise system installation costs $15 million and may run over $100 million for very large companies implementing full-function systems across many divisions [Hitt, Wu, and Zhou, 2002; O'Leary, 2000]). Enterprise software is deeply intertwined with corporate business processes. It might take a large company three to five years to fully implement all of the organizational and technology changes required by an enterprise system. Because enterprise systems are integrated, it is difficult to make a change in only one part of the business without affecting other parts as well. There is the prospect that the new enterprise systems could eventually prove as brittle and hard to change as the old systems they replaced, binding firms to outdated business processes and systems.

Companies may also fail to achieve strategic benefits from enterprise systems if integrating business processes using the generic models provided by standard ERP software prevents the firm from using unique business processes that had been sources of advantage over competitors. Enterprise systems promote centralized organizational coordination and decision making, which may not be the best way for some firms to operate. There are companies that clearly do not need the level of integration provided by enterprise systems (Davenport, 2000 and 1998). Chapter 12 provides more detail on the organizational and technical challenges to enterprise system implementation.

SUPPLY CHAIN MANAGEMENT AND COLLABORATIVE COMMERCE

supply chain management

Close linkage and coordination of activities involved in buying, making, and moving a product.

supply chain

Network of organizations and business processes for procuring materials, transforming raw materials into intermediate and finished products, and distributing the finished products to customers.

reverse logistics

The return of items from buyers to sellers in a supply chain.

Supply chain management systems are more outward-facing, focusing on helping the firm manage its relationship with suppliers. **Supply chain management** is the close linkage and coordination of activities involved in buying, making, and moving a product. It integrates supplier, manufacturer, distributor, and customer logistics processes to reduce time, redundant effort, and inventory costs. The **supply chain** is a network of organizations and business processes for procuring materials, transforming raw materials into intermediate and finished products, and distributing the finished products to customers. It links suppliers, manufacturing plants, distribution centres, conveyances, retail outlets, people, and information through such processes as procurement, inventory control, distribution, and delivery to supply goods and services from source through consumption. Materials, information, and payments flow through the supply chain in both directions. Goods start out as raw materials and move through logistics and production systems until they reach customers. The supply chain includes **reverse logistics**, in which returned items flow in the reverse direction from the buyer back to the seller.

Figure 2.13 provides a simplified illustration of a supply chain. The *upstream* portion of the supply chain includes the organization's suppliers and their suppliers and the processes for managing relationships with them. The *downstream* portion consists of the organizations and processes for distributing and delivering products to the final customers. The manufacturer also manages internal supply chain processes for transforming the materials, components, and services furnished by suppliers into finished goods and for managing materials and inventory.

The supply chain illustrated in Figure 2.13 has been simplified. Most supply chains, especially those for large manufacturers, such as automakers, are multi-tiered, with many thousands of primary, secondary, and tertiary suppliers. DaimlerChrysler, for instance, has over 20 000 suppliers of parts, packaging, and technology. Its primary suppliers are its principal suppliers, which furnish chassis, engines, and other major automotive components. These suppliers have their own suppliers (secondary suppliers), who, in turn, may have their own sets of suppliers (tertiary suppliers). To manage the supply chain, a company tries to eliminate redundant steps, delays, and the amount of resources tied up along the way (see Figure 2.14).

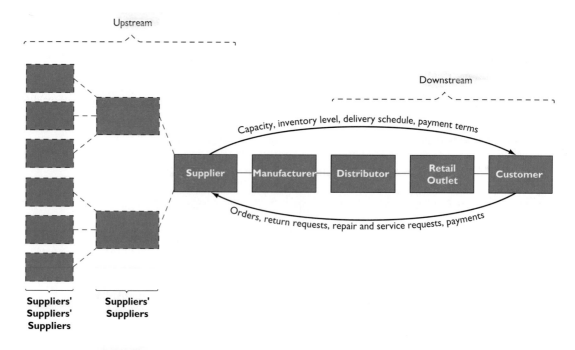

Figure 2.13 A supply chain. This figure illustrates the major entities in the supply chain and the flow of information upstream and downstream to coordinate the activities involved in buying, making, and moving a product. Suppliers transform raw materials into intermediate products or components, and then manufacturers turn them into finished products. The products are shipped to distribution centres and from there to retailers and customers.

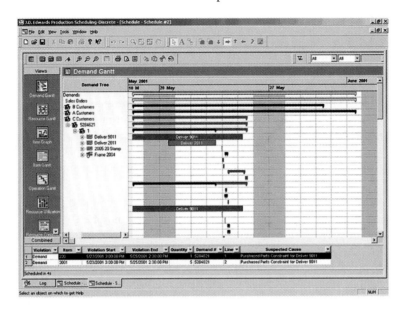

Figure 2.14 J.D. Edwards supply chain management software includes capabilities for production scheduling that can calculate the quantity of each item in production that is needed to meet customer demand and send alerts to suppliers to ship more items when inventory is running too low. This demand Gantt chart shows which customer orders are affected by a missed delivery so that alternative suppliers can be located.

Companies that skillfully manage their supply chains get the right amount of their products from the source to the point of consumption with the least amount of time and the lowest cost. Information systems make supply chain management more efficient by helping companies coordinate, schedule, and control procurement, production, inventory management, and delivery of products and services. Supply chain management systems can be built using intranets, extranets, or special supply chain management software. Table 2.4 describes how companies can benefit from using information systems for supply chain management.

Inefficiencies in the supply chain, such as parts shortages, underutilized plant capacity, excessive finished goods inventory, or runaway transportation costs, are caused by inaccurate or untimely information. For example, manufacturers may keep too many parts in inventory because they do not know exactly when they will receive their next shipment from their suppliers. Suppliers may order too few raw materials because they do not have precise information on demand. These supply chain inefficiencies can waste as much as 25 percent of a company's operating costs.

One recurring problem in supply chain management is the **bullwhip effect**, in which information about the demand for a product gets distorted as it passes from one entity to the next across the supply chain (Lee, Padmanabhan, and Wang, 1997). A slight rise in demand for an item might cause different members in the supply chain—distributors, manufacturers, suppliers, suppliers' suppliers, and suppliers' suppliers' suppliers—to stockpile inventory so that each has enough "just in case." These changes will ripple throughout the supply chain, magnifying what started out as a small change from planned orders and creating excess

bullwhip effect

Large fluctuations in inventories along the supply chain resulting from small unanticipated fluctuations in demand.

TABLE 2.4	HOW INFORMATION SYSTEMS CAN FACILITATE SUPPLY CHAIN MANAGEMENT

Information Systems Can Help Participants in the Supply Chain

Decide when and what to produce, store, and move

Rapidly communicate orders

Track the status of orders

Check inventory availability and monitor inventory levels

Reduce inventory, transportation, and warehousing costs

Track shipments

Plan production based on actual customer demand

Rapidly communicate changes in product design

inventory and increased production, warehousing, and shipping costs. If all members of the supply chain could share dynamic information about inventory levels, schedules, forecasts, and shipments, they would have a more precise idea about how to adjust their sourcing, manufacturing, and distribution plans.

Supply chain management uses systems for supply chain planning (SCP) and supply chain execution (SCE). *Supply chain planning systems* enable the firm to generate demand forecasts for a product and to develop sourcing and manufacturing plans for that product. *Supply chain execution systems* manage the flow of products through distribution centres and warehouses to ensure that products are delivered to the right locations in the most efficient manner. Table 2.5 provides more details on supply chain planning and execution systems.

COLLABORATIVE COMMERCE

Successful supply chain management requires an atmosphere of trust where all the members of the supply chain agree to cooperate and to honour the commitments they have made to each other (Welty and Becerra-Fernandez, 2001). They must be able to work together on the same goal and to redesign some of their business processes so that they can coordinate their activities more easily. In some industries, companies have extended their supply chain management systems to collaborate more closely with customers, suppliers, and other firms in their industry. This is a much broader mission than traditional supply chain management systems, which focused primarily on managing the flow of transactions among organizations. It focuses on using shared systems and business processes to optimize the value of relationships.

Companies are relying on these new collaborative relationships to further improve their planning, production, and distribution of goods and services. The use of digital technologies to enable multiple organizations to collaboratively design, develop, build, move, and manage products through their life cycles is called **collaborative commerce**. Firms can integrate their systems with those of their supply chain partners to coordinate demand forecasting, resource planning, production planning, replenishment, shipping, and warehousing. They can work jointly with suppliers on product design and marketing. Customers can provide feedback for marketers to use to improve product design, support, and service. Equipped with appropri-

collaborative commerce

The use of digital technologies to enable multiple organizations to collaboratively design, develop, build, and manage products through their life cycles.

TABLE 2.5	**SUPPLY CHAIN PLANNING AND EXECUTION SYSTEMS**

Capabilities of Supply Chain Planning Systems

Order planning: Select an order fulfillment plan that best meets the desired level of service to the customer, given existing transportation and manufacturing constraints.

Advanced scheduling and manufacturing planning: Provide detailed coordination of scheduling based on analysis of changing factors, such as customer orders, equipment outages, or supply interruptions. Scheduling modules create job schedules for the manufacturing process and supplier logistics.

Demand planning: Generate demand forecasts from all business units using statistical tools and business forecasting techniques.

Distribution planning: Create operating plans for logistics managers for order fulfillment, based on input from demand and manufacturing planning modules.

Transportation planning: Track and analyze inbound and outbound movement of materials and products to ensure that materials and finished goods are delivered at the right time and place at the minimum cost.

Capabilities of Supply Chain Execution Systems

Order commitments: Allow vendors to quote accurate delivery dates to customers by providing more real-time detailed information on the status of orders from availability of raw materials and inventory to production and shipment status.

Final Production: Organize and schedule final subassemblies required to make each final product.

Replenishment: Coordinate component replenishment work so that warehouses remain stocked with the minimum amount of inventory in the pipeline.

Distribution management: Coordinate the process of transporting goods from the manufacturer to distribution centres to the final customer. Provide online customer access to shipment and delivery data.

Reverse distribution: Track the shipment and accounting for returned goods or remanufactured products.

ate software tools, they can actually help companies design and develop some types of products. For example, LIS Corporation and VLSI Technology provide customers with tools for designing their own specialized computer chips. GE Plastics provides its customers with Web-based tools to help them design better plastic products (Thomke and von Hippel, 2002). A firm engaged in collaborative commerce with its suppliers and customers can achieve new levels of efficiency in reducing product design cycles, minimizing excess inventory, forecasting demand, and keeping partners and customers informed (see Figure 2.15).

One of the most difficult aspects of supply chain management is accurately forecasting demand. If the information going into a demand forecasting system is flawed, or if the forecasters do not properly interpret the data, demand forecasts will be off target. Companies are trying to address this problem by working together with their business partners on **collaborative planning, forecasting, and replenishment (CPFR)**. Companies can collaborate with suppliers and buyers to formulate demand forecasts, develop production plans, and coordinate shipping, warehousing, and stocking activities to ensure that retail and wholesale shelf space is replenished with the right quantities of the right goods.

Another important area of collaboration is joint marketing coordination and product design. Manufacturers can coordinate their internal design and marketing activities with engineers and design companies as well as with their supply chain partners. By involving their suppliers in product design and marketing, manufacturing firms can ensure that the goods produced actually fulfill the claims of marketers. Marketers can channel customer feedback directly to product designers at the firm and its suppliers.

The Window on Management shows how some companies are engaging in collaborative commerce for this purpose. Collaborative commerce makes "closed loop marketing," in which customer feedback drives marketing and production, much closer to realization. Table 2.6 illustrates collaborative commerce applications for other important business processes.

Industrial Networks for Interorganizational Business Processes

Internet technology makes this level of collaboration possible by providing a platform where systems from different companies can seamlessly exchange information. Web-enabled networks for the coordination of transorganizational business processes provide an infrastructure for collaborative commerce activities. These networks are called **private industrial networks**, and they permit firms and their business partners to share product design and development, marketing, inventory, production scheduling, and unstructured communications, such as transmission of graphics, e-mail, and computer-aided design (CAD) drawings. Many of these networks are "owned" and managed by large companies that use them to coordinate purchases, orders, and other activities with their suppliers, distributors, and selected business partners.

For instance, Procter & Gamble (P&G), the world's largest consumer goods company, developed an integrated industry-wide system to coordinate grocery store point-of-sale systems

collaborative planning, forecasting, and replenishment (CPFR)
Collaboration of firms with their suppliers and buyers to formulate demand forecasts, develop production plans, and coordinate shipping, warehousing, and stocking activities.

private industrial networks
Web-enabled networks linking systems of multiple firms in an industry for the coordination of transorganizational business processes.

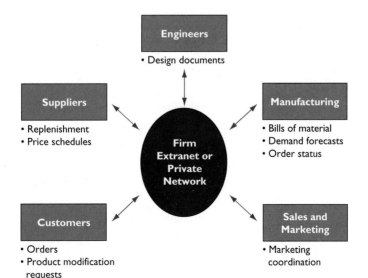

Figure 2.15 Collaborative commerce. Collaborative commerce is a set of digitally enabled collaborative interactions between an enterprise and its business partners and customers. Data and processes that were once considered internal can be shared by the collaborative community.

TABLE 2.6	**HOW BUSINESSES ARE ENGAGING IN COLLABORATIVE COMMERCE**

Business Process	Collaborative Commerce Activities
Product design and development: Companies can work jointly with customers and business partners on designing new products or modifying existing products	Extranet enables customers of Cummins Inc. to access updates on their engine orders. Truck manufacturers can view early prototypes for Cummins' line of engines and ask for modifications. Real-time design collaboration tools let Cummins engineers work with customers' engineers via the Web. A customer council reviews all significant updates to the Cummins site.
Service and support: Companies can share information about service, support, and troubleshooting	American Axle and Manufacturing, which produces automobile driveline systems, chassis components, and forged products, uses the Web to share photos of defective parts that stall its assembly line with suppliers, discuss the problem, and solve it on the spot.
Supply chain coordination: Companies can work closely with suppliers and contract manufacturers, reducing inventory	Hewlett Packard (HP) Laserjet Imaging Systems uses a Web-based workgroup collaboration system to share information with its contract manufacturers, distribution centres, and resellers. The application extracts parts plans entered in HP's ERP system and forwards them to a shared electronic workspace where the plans can be accessed by suppliers. Suppliers can adjust their plans so that their inventory and HP's are coordinated with each other.
Logistics: Companies can reduce logistics costs by coordinating their deliveries to share transportation and shipping facilities	General Mills, Kellogg, Land O' Lakes, and Monsanto use a common system based on Internet technology to share their excess shipping capacity. The system uses a private network to coordinate underutilized shipping capacity of container trucks and railroad cars to reduce participating companies' logistics costs.
Sales support and training: Companies and their distributors can share technical information, conduct training, and provide technical support information	Group Dekko consists of 12 independently operated manufacturing companies that produce such components as wire harnesses, moulded plastic parts, metal stamping for automobiles, and office furniture. The Group uses a common shared data repository, where partner firms share documents about quality standards, graphics, engineering drawings, material bills, pricing, and routing information.
Channel management: Companies and their distributors can collaborate on pricing and share sales leads	Compaq Computer Asia/Pacific uses the Partners Online Web-based system to coordinate pricing with its Asian distributors, where prices are often negotiable. Distributors can enter the pricing requirements of bids to customers into the system so that they can be routed to the salesperson in charge of the account and to the finance department for approval or rejection.

with grocery store warehouses, shippers, its own manufacturing facilities, and its suppliers of raw materials. This single industry-spanning system effectively allows P&G to monitor the movement of all its products from raw materials to customer purchase. P&G uses data collected from point-of-sale terminals to trigger shipments to retailers of items that customers have purchased that need restocking. Electronic links to suppliers enable P&G to order materials from its own suppliers when its inventories are low. The system helps P&G reduce its inventory by allowing the company to produce products as demand occurs at the retail level. P&G is implementing an Ultimate Supply System that uses Internet technology to link retailers and suppliers to its private corporate intranet. By having retailers and suppliers integrate their systems with P&G's systems, P&G hopes to reduce product cycle time by half, inventory costs by $6.7 billion, and systems costs by $7.5 billion.

Similarly, Safeway U.K. has electronic links to suppliers where it can share information about forecasts, shelf space, and inventory in its supermarkets so that suppliers can track demand for their products, adjust production, and adjust the timing and size of deliveries. The suppliers can download Safeway's information into their enterprise systems or production planning systems. Suppliers send Safeway information about product availability, production capacity, and inventory levels.

Although private industrial networks are primarily used today to coordinate the activities of a single firm and its business partners, some can encompass an entire industry, coordinating the business processes for the key players in that industry, including suppliers, transporters, production firms, distributors, and retailers. For example, the Open Access Same-Time Information System (OASIS) Web sites link North American electrical utility companies in regional power pool groups to sell their surplus power to wholesalers and to locate the transmission facilities for moving the power between its source and the customers.

A few industrial networks have been developed to support collaboration among firms in multiple industries. General Mills, Kellogg, Land O' Lakes, and Monsanto now use a shared Internet system to share their excess shipping capacity. The system uses a private network to

THE NEED FOR COLLABORATION

The worldwide grocery industry is fighting for its very existence. Faced with declines in aisle traffic and customer visits, supermarkets and specialty stores are losing market share at a time when convenience-focused consumers are spending larger amounts of money in the food service sector. Supercentres are also pursuing the consumer for their twice-weekly grocery trips. Supercentres—led by Wal-Mart—gained about five million new customers in 2001, nabbing both shopping trips and sales from retail grocery stores (Information Resources, 2002). Other market competitors include convenience stores, mass merchandisers, wholesale clubs, and restaurants.

The increased competitiveness is forcing change on the slow-to-change, traditional grocery industry. One area for innovation is collaboration among grocers and their trading partners. Associations, such as the Grocery Manufacturers of America (GMA), have publicly prompted grocers to speed up adoption of standards and technologies for collaboration.

In June 2002, GMA warned their members that $9 billion in retail sales was in danger of being lost due to out-of-stock inventory in the top 25 product categories alone. GMA urged their members to accurately forecast and order products since the average supermarket holds 32 000 stock keeping units (SKUs).

Wal-Mart introduced collaborative planning, forecasting, and replenishment (CPFR) processes in the early 1990s; CPFR can help grocers, too—even in competing with Wal-Mart! Yet the grocery industry has been slow to change to CPFR processes. Kevin Stadler, Senior Vice-President for Collaborative Business Solutions, of JDA Software Group, feels that the slow rate of CPFR implementation is partially due to the complexity of various CPFR models published by various industry committees. Many CPFR initiatives have not progressed past small tests involving only a few items traded through a few distribution points. But there are exemplars in the grocery industry.

The UK-based Londis Holdings plc, with 2200 independently owned grocery stores, has been celebrated for supply chain efficiencies achieved by its CPFR initiative. Londis collaboratively manages inventory with 20 major consumer goods trading partners. Londis is trying to achieve total synchronization of its supply chain, with the goal to ensure that each store has sufficient stock throughout trading hours.

Londis provides its partners with real-time open access to a single demand forecast via a common information system. Using this system, Londis has improved service levels by 3 percent (averaging 99 percent) and reduced inventory by 10 to 20 percent. Londis' trading partners, including Coca-Cola, Kraft, and Nestlé, can also consolidate their own knowledge.

The Voluntary Interindustry Commerce Standards (VICS) Committee has established nine steps for CPFR. Nearly 100 retail/manufacturing trading pairs are using this simple approach to implement their own CPFR systems. VICS uses four specific functions for CPFR. These are (1) demand collaboration, (2) upfront agreement, (3) long-range execution planning, and (4) order forecast collaboration. Each of these functions builds on the preceding functions, so a trading pair can start with establishing an upfront agreement and gradually implement CPFR. For grocers, traditionally slow to change, a step-by-step process using industry-accepted standards may finally mean the successful implementation of a tool to help them in the war they are fighting against their extra-industry competitors.

To Think About: Why does the retail grocery industry need to implement CPFR? What are the benefits they hope to achieve-in terms of customer satisfaction and efficiencies? Why are grocery stores slower than other types of retail outlets to implement CPFR systems? What are some of the challenges of implementing CPFR systems?

Sources: Based on Kevin Stadler, "ECR: Leveling the Playing Field," *Food Logistics*, September 2002; Information Resources, Inc., available **www.infores.com**, accessed May 30, 2003; Londis Holdings plc, available **www.londis.co.uk**, accessed May 30, 2003.

---

coordinate underutilized shipping capacity of container trucks and railroad cars to reduce participating members' logistics costs.

CUSTOMER RELATIONSHIP MANAGEMENT (CRM)

Instead of treating customers as exploitable sources of income, businesses are now viewing them as long-term assets to be nurtured through customer relationship management. *Customer relationship management (CRM),* which we introduced in Chapter 1, focuses on managing all of the ways that a firm deals with its existing and potential new customers. CRM is both a business and technology discipline that uses information systems to integrate all of the business processes surrounding the firm's interactions with its customers in sales, marketing, and service. The ideal CRM system provides end-to-end customer care from receipt of an order through product delivery and after-sales service and support (see Figure 2.16).

In the past, a firm's processes for sales, service, and marketing were highly compartmentalized and did not share very much essential customer information. Some information on a specific customer might be stored and organized in terms of that person's account with the

Figure 2.16 Siebel Systems provides an integrated suite of customer relationship management applications to help organizations implement customer-driven best practices across their sales, marketing, and customer service. Illustrated here are capabilities for tracking the responses to sales campaigns across all customer contact points: direct mail, telephone, e-mail, the Web, and face-to-face interactions.

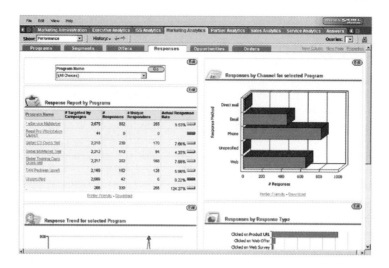

company. Other pieces of information about the same customer might be organized by products that were purchased. There was no way to consolidate all of this information to provide a unified view of a customer across the company. CRM tools try to solve this problem by integrating the firm's customer-related processes and consolidating customer information from multiple channels—retail stores, telephone, e-mail, wireless devices, or the Web—so that the firm can present one cohesive face to the customer (see Figure 2.17).

Good CRM systems consolidate customer data from multiple sources and provide analytical tools for answering such questions as: What is the value of a particular customer to the firm over his or her lifetime? Who are our most loyal customers? (It costs six times more to sell to a new customer than to an existing customer [Kalakota and Robinson, 2001].) Who are our most profitable customers? (Typically 80 to 90 percent of a firm's profits are generated by 10 to 20 percent of its customers.) What do these profitable customers want to buy? Firms can then use the answers to acquire new customers, provide better service and support, customize their offerings more precisely to customer preferences, and provide ongoing value to retain profitable customers. Chapters 3, 4, 9, and 13 provide additional details on customer relationship management applications and technologies. The Window on Organizations shows how some financial services companies have benefited from customer relationship management.

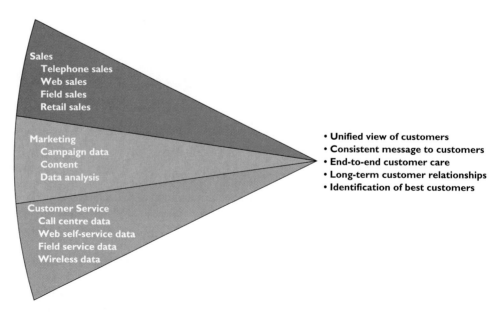

Figure 2.17 Customer relationship management (CRM). Customer relationship management applies technology to look at customers from a multifaceted perspective. CRM uses a set of integrated applications to address all aspects of the customer relationship, including customer service, sales, and marketing.

CUSTOMER RELATIONSHIP MANAGEMENT: A BOON FOR FINANCIAL SERVICES

Competition in the financial services industry is more intense than ever, with banks, brokerage firms, and insurance companies vying for each other's business. To survive, financial service firms need to find better ways of serving their customers—and profiting from them. Meriwest Credit Union, the former IBM San Jose Employees Federal Credit Union, found itself facing a new competitive environment when it reorganized in 1998 from a federally chartered employee credit union to a state-chartered credit union. Meriwest had already expanded beyond IBM to become the employee credit union for about 350 companies, but with the change to a community charter, Meriwest could pitch its services to more than six million people in the San Francisco Bay area who could also be served by traditional banks. Meriwest also needed to increase the number of deposit dollars per customer and loans to its longstanding customers.

The systems Meriwest had been using were not up to the job. Customer service representatives spent excessive amounts of time switching between multiple systems in order to respond to customer inquiries about savings and chequing account balances, loans, mortgages, and credit card bills. Even after all the systems had been polled for this information, service representatives were still left with an incomplete picture of what type of customer they were dealing with because these systems could not easily assemble historical data about each customer's activity.

In 1999, Meriwest implemented Siebel Systems' customer relationship management software to both consolidate customer account information and make it more meaningful. The new customer relationship management system pulled together data from 11 different systems into a common view of the customer

that could be used to offer more services. For example, the CRM system would enable Meriwest to identify customers with high balances who might be interested in a certificate of deposit or customers with college age children or retirement planning needs whom the credit union could service. Customer relationship management, combined with stepped-up advertising and representative training is paying off. At the end of 2001, deposits were up 27 percent over the 1998 level, and loans per customer were up 46 percent.

The insurance industry is also turning to customer relationship management to more effectively market new and existing services in competition with other financial services companies. MetLife implemented DWL's Customer software to consolidate customer data from all of its existing legacy information systems. Any of MetLife's 40 lines of business will be able to update and view customer files and sell other products of interest to specific customers. Australian P&C Direct is trying to ensure that every business unit has a current and consistent view of a customer's data. The company created a data repository that marks all customer records with census data and lifestyle codes so that the sales department can better target customers for cross-selling. For example, the marketing representatives could view all the products a customer has purchased so that, for example, they could sell life insurance policies to customers with health insurance policies.

To Think About: How have customer relationship management systems changed how organizations can service their customers? How have the organizations described here obtained value from CRM systems?

Sources: David F. Carr, "Cozying Up to the Customer," *Baseline,* June 2002; and Jennifer Maselli, "Insurers Look to CRM for Profits," *InformationWeek,* May 6, 2002.

MIS IN ACTION: MANAGER'S TOOLKIT

HOW TO BENEFIT FROM CUSTOMER RELATIONSHIP MANAGEMENT

When setting up CRM systems, managers need to have a clear understanding of the business questions concerning customers that the system should answer. Here are some key questions to ask when gathering customer information:

Customer status: Is the firm interested in information about existing customers, new customers, or both?

Customer identity: Who is this customer? What does he/she want? What is our market strength? What part of our potential market are we not meeting?

Customer value: What is the customer's value to the business? Why is this customer important?

Channels: What channel or channels did the customer use to interact with the company? Were these interactions over the telephone, via e-mail, through the corporate Web site, or through company sales representatives or retail stores? Which channel or channels are the most important?

Nature of interaction: Why did the customer interact with the company? Was it to purchase an item, to secure customer service, or to return merchandise? What is the intended outcome for this interaction?

Metrics: How can the company measure the value of its interaction with the customer? Can it be measured in terms of cost savings, increased revenue, or higher levels of customer satisfaction?

Investing in CRM software alone will not automatically produce better information about customers, and many customer relationship management systems fall short of their objectives. These systems require changes in sales, marketing, and customer service processes to encourage sharing of customer information; support from top management; and a very clear idea of the benefits that could be obtained from consolidating customer data (Ebner et. al., 2002; Goodhue, Wixom, and Watson, 2002). Chapter 12 provides more detail on the challenges of implementing successful CRM systems. The Manager's Toolkit describes some of the customer data issues that managers must address.

KNOWLEDGE MANAGEMENT SYSTEMS IN THE ENTERPRISE

The value of a firm's products and services is based not only on its physical resources but also on intangible knowledge assets. Some firms can perform better than others because they have better knowledge about how to create, produce, and deliver products and services. This firm knowledge is difficult to imitate, it is unique, and it can be leveraged into long-term strategic benefit. *Knowledge management systems*, which we introduced in Chapter 1, collect all relevant knowledge and experience in the firm and make it available wherever and whenever it is needed to support business processes and management decisions. They also link the firm to external sources of knowledge.

Knowledge management systems (KMS) support processes for discovering and codifying knowledge, sharing knowledge, and distributing knowledge, as well as supporting processes for creating new knowledge and integrating it into the organization. This chapter has already described several kinds of systems used in knowledge management, office systems for the distribution of knowledge and information and knowledge work systems to facilitate knowledge creation. Other knowledge management applications help companies map sources of knowledge, create corporate knowledge directories of employees with special areas of expertise, identify and share best practices, and codify the knowledge of experts so that it can be embedded in information systems and used by other members of the organization. Knowledge management systems also include tools for knowledge discovery that enable the organization to recognize patterns and important relationships in large pools of data. Table 2.7 provides examples of knowledge management systems, and Chapters 13 and 14 describe these knowledge management applications in detail.

TABLE 2.7	**KNOWLEDGE MANAGEMENT SYSTEMS IN THE ORGANIZATION**
Organizational Process	**Role of Knowledge Management Systems**
Creating knowledge	Knowledge work systems provide knowledge workers with graphics, analytical, communication, and document management tools as well as access to internal and external sources of data to help them generate new ideas.
Discovering and codifying knowledge	Artificial intelligence systems can elicit and incorporate expertise from human experts or find patterns and relationships in vast quantities of data. Decision support systems analyzing large databases can also be used for knowledge discovery.
Sharing knowledge	Group collaboration systems can help employees access and work simultaneously on the same document from many different locations and coordinate their activities.
Distributing knowledge	Office systems and communication tools can distribute documents and other forms of information among information and knowledge workers and link offices to other business units inside and outside the firm.

MANAGEMENT WRAP-UP

Enterprise applications require management to take a firm-wide view of business processes and information flows. Managers need to determine which business processes should be integrated, the short- and long-term benefits of this integration, and the appropriate level of financial and organizational resources to support this integration.

There are many types of information systems in an organization that support different organizational levels, functions, and business processes. Some of these systems, including the enterprise applications (enterprise systems, supply chain management, customer relationship management, and knowledge management), span more than one function or business process and may be tied to the business processes of other organizations. Systems integrating information from different business functions, business processes, and organizations often require extensive organizational change.

Information systems that support firm- or industry-wide information flows and business processes require major technology investments and planning. Firms must have an information technology (IT) infrastructure that can support firm- or industry-wide computing.

For Discussion

1. Supply chain management is less about managing the physical movement of goods and more about managing information. Discuss the implications of this statement.

2. Adopting an enterprise system is a key business decision as well as a technology decision. Do you agree? Why, or why not? Who should make this decision?

SUMMARY

1. *What are the major types of systems in a business? What roles do they play?* There are six major types of information systems in contemporary organizations. Operational-level systems are transaction processing systems (TPS) that track the flow of the daily routine transactions that are necessary to conduct business. Knowledge-level systems support clerical, managerial, and professional workers. They consist of office systems for increasing data workers' productivity and knowledge work systems for enhancing knowledge workers' productivity. Management-level systems (MIS and DSS) provide the management control level with reports and access to the organization's current performance and historical records. Most MIS reports condense information from TPS and are not highly analytical. Decision support systems (DSS) support management decisions when these decisions are unique, rapidly changing, and not specified easily in advance. Executive support systems (ESS) support the strategic level by providing a generalized computing and communications environment to assist senior management's decision making.

   The various types of systems in the organization exchange data with one another. TPS are a major source of data for other systems, especially MIS and DSS. ESS primarily receive data from lower-level systems.

2. *Why should managers pay attention to business processes? Why do firms need to integrate their business processes?* Business processes refer to the manner in which work is organized, coordinated, and focused to produce a valuable product or service. Managers need to pay attention to business processes because they determine how well the organization can execute their tasks and, thus, are a potential source of strategic success or failure. Although each of the major business functions has its own set of business processes, many other business processes are cross-functional, such as fulfilling an order. Information systems can help organizations achieve efficiencies by automating parts of these processes or by helping organizations rethink and streamline them. Firms can become more flexible and efficient by coordinating their business processes more closely, and, in some cases, integrating these processes so that they are more focused on efficient management of resources and customer service.

3. *What are the benefits and challenges of using enterprise systems?* Enterprise systems create an integrated organization-wide platform to coordinate key internal processes of the firm. Enterprise systems integrate the key business processes in sales, production, finance, logistics, and human resources into a single software system so that

information can flow throughout the organization, improving coordination, efficiency, and decision making. Enterprise systems can help create a more uniform organization in which everyone uses similar processes and information and measures their work in terms of organization-wide performance standards. The coordination of sales, production, finance, and logistics processes provided by enterprise systems helps organizations respond more rapidly to customer demands.

Enterprise systems are very difficult to implement successfully. They require extensive organizational change, use complicated technologies, and require large up-front costs for long-term benefits that are difficult to quantify. Once implemented, enterprise systems are very difficult to change.

4. *What are the benefits of using information systems to support supply chain management and collaborative commerce?* Information systems for supply chain management can help coordinate processes for managing the firm's relationship with its customers. Supply chain management is the close linkage of activities involved in buying, making, and moving products. Information systems make supply chain management more efficient by helping companies coordinate, schedule, and control procurement, production, inventory management, and delivery of products and services to customers.

Collaborative commerce enables multiple organizations to collaboratively design, develop, build, move, and manage products through their life cycles. A firm engaged in collaborative commerce with its suppliers and customers can achieve new efficiencies by reducing product design cycles, minimizing excess inventory, forecasting demand, and keeping partners and customers informed. Private industrial networks are Web-enabled networks that support collaborative commerce activities by providing an infrastructure for transorganizational business processes and information flows.

5. *What are the benefits of using information systems for customer relationship management and knowledge management?* Customer relationship management (CRM) uses information systems to coordinate all of the business processes surrounding the firm's interactions with its customers. CRM systems consolidate customer information from multiple sources—telephone, e-mail, wireless devices, traditional sales and marketing systems, or the Web—so that the firm can obtain a unified view of a customer. CRM systems help businesses identify profitable customers and opportunities for improving customer service. Knowledge management systems enable firms to optimize the creation, sharing, and distribution of knowledge to improve business processes and management decisions.

KEY TERMS

Bullwhip effect, 53

Collaborative commerce, 54

Collaborative planning, forecasting, and replenishment (CPFR), 55

Decision-support systems (DSS), 44

Desktop publishing, 43

Document imaging systems, 43

Enterprise applications, 47

Executive support systems (ESS), 45

Knowledge-level systems, 39

Knowledge work systems (KWS), 42

Management information systems (MIS), 43

Management-level systems, 39

Office systems, 42

Operational-level systems, 38

Private industrial networks, 55

Reverse logistics, 52

Strategic-level systems, 39

Supply chain, 52

Supply chain management, 52

Transaction processing systems (TPS), 40

Word processing, 43

REVIEW QUESTIONS

1. Identify and describe the four levels of the organizational hierarchy. What types of information systems serve each level?

2. List and briefly describe the major types of systems in organizations.

3. What are the five types of TPS in business organizations? What functions do they perform? Give examples of each.

4. Describe the functions performed by knowledge work and office systems and some typical applications of each.

5. What are the characteristics of MIS? How do MIS differ from TPS? From DSS?

6. What are the characteristics of DSS? How do they differ from those of ESS?

7. Describe the relationships among TPS, office systems, KWS, MIS, DSS, and ESS.

8. What is a business process? Give two examples of processes for functional areas of the business and one example of a cross-functional process.

9. Why are organizations trying to integrate their business processes? What are the four key enterprise applications for organization-wide process integration?

10. What are enterprise systems? How do they change the way an organization works?

11. What are the benefits and challenges of implementing enterprise systems?

12. What is supply chain management? What activities does it comprise? Why is it so important to businesses? How do information systems facilitate supply chain management?

13. What is collaborative commerce? How can organizations benefit from it?

14. How can organizations benefit from participating in private industrial networks?

15. What is customer relationship management? Why is it so important to businesses? How do information systems facilitate customer relationship management?

16. What is the role of knowledge management systems in the enterprise? What organizational processes are supported by knowledge management applications?

APPLICATION SOFTWARE EXERCISE

SPREADSHEET EXERCISE: IMPROVING SUPPLY CHAIN MANAGEMENT

You run a company that manufactures aircraft components. You have many competitors that are trying to offer lower prices and better service to customers, and you are trying to determine if you can benefit from better supply chain management. At the Companion Website for Chapter 2, you can find a spreadsheet file that contains a list of all of the items that your firm has ordered from its suppliers over the past three months. The fields on the spreadsheet file include vendor name, vendor identification number, the purchaser's order number, item identification number and item description (for each item ordered from the vendor), the cost per item, number of units of the item ordered, the total cost of each order, the vendors' accounts payable terms, promised shipping date, promised transit time, and actual arrival date for each order.

Prepare a recommendation of how you can use the data in this spreadsheet database to improve your supply chain management. You may wish to look at ways to identify preferred suppliers or other ways of improving the movement and production of your products. Some criteria you might consider include the supplier's track record for on-time deliveries, suppliers offering the best accounts payable terms, and suppliers offering lower pricing when the same item can be provided by multiple suppliers. Use your spreadsheet software to prepare reports and, if appropriate, graphs to support your recommendations.

GROUP PROJECT

With a group of three or four other students, select a business using an industrial network for supply chain management. Use the Web, newspapers, journals, and computer or business magazines to find out more about that organization and its use of information technology and links to other organizations. If possible, use presentation software to present your findings to the class.

 ## INTERNET TOOLS

COMPANION WEBSITE

At www.pearsoned.ca/laudon, you will find valuable tools to facilitate and enhance your learning of this chapter as well as opportunities to apply your knowledge to realistic situations:

■ An interactive Study Guide of self-test questions that will provide you with immediate feedback.

■ Application exercises

■ An Electronic Business Project for logistics planning—please check the U.S. CW—www.prenhall.com/laudon.

■ A Management Decision Problem requiring you to analyze enterprise process integration and its impact on production planning.

■ Additional material on Types of Systems from a Functional Perspective.

■ Updates of material in the chapter.

ADDITIONAL SITES OF INTEREST

There are many interesting sites to enhance your learning about how information systems are categorized and how they support organizations. You can search the Web yourself, or just try the following sites to add to what you have already learned.

Brint
   www.brint.com
   Search for interesting articles on a variety of business and technology topics.

Tech Tutorials
   www.techtutorials.com
   Offers free tutorials on a variety of PC applications.

ComputerWorld and ComputerWorld Canada
   http://www.computerworld.com and
   www.itworldcanada.com/index.cfm/ci_id/598.htm
   The leading computer periodical for IS managers.

Computing Canada
   www.itbusiness.ca
   Canada's leading computer periodical; the site also hosts other Canadian computer-related periodicals.

CASE STUDY   *Ceridian Uses CRM to Target Customers*

Ceridian Canada, Canada's leading provider of payroll and human resource management services, is based in Winnipeg, Manitoba. A unit of American-based Ceridian Corporation, Ceridian Canada serves 38 500 companies across Canada, ranging from small businesses to large corporations. Ceridian Canada was established as an independent business unit in 1998, when Ceridian Corporation consolidated the operations of two recently acquired companies. The company currently operates a nationwide network of branch offices across Canada, with 1300 employees, and pays a total of 2.4 million employees through its services—fully 17 percent of the Canadian workforce.

The Canadian market for payroll processing services has, in recent years, consolidated significantly. Ceridian Canada and Automatic Data Processing Canada (a unit of American-based Automatic Data Processing Corporation) have emerged as the dominant players in a market that once supported nearly half a dozen competitors. As the market has changed, the underlying product line has assumed less importance as a competitive differentiator, reflecting the commodity or "utility" status that characterizes modern payroll service offerings. Quality customer service—already a key strategic competency—has emerged as the industry's pivotal competitive requirement. Payroll providers have addressed the customer service issue on two levels. Not merely content to focus on traditional customer service metrics—including problem resolution timeframes—providers are trying to improve customer satisfaction by offering alternative service delivery channels, such as Web-based self-service. Ceridian Canada faced the challenges common to the result of a merger: unifying a fragmented, often divergent set of business processes. The main one process was customer service.

Cultural factors represented a significant barrier to working out common customer service practices. But structural factors—including a lot of geographic dispersion—made synchronization even harder. Mark Alpern, Vice-President of Customer Care and Quality, says that the traditional "branch-centric" approach to customer interaction made the creation of a consistent set of processes extra problematic. "Under our previous framework, customer information for the Winnipeg branch was held in Winnipeg, the Halifax branch data was held in Halifax, and so on," says Alpern. "There was a lack of consistency in process from branch to branch to the extent that each branch was unique."

Ceridian Canada's disparate information technology (IT) infrastructure—a vestige of its formation—made the problem worse. Beyond fragmented information resources, the company's generic customer service approach, based on account management, also emerged as a troublesome issue. This approach had each account manager responsible for servicing more than 100 customers. But as the company expanded, it became apparent

that continued success would depend on changing this individualized approach to customer service. Customer survey responses proved what Ceridian management had realized: Customers were more and more frustrated with trouble accessing their service representative by phone. By 1999 it had become clear that a fundamental change to Ceridian Canada's approach to customer service was needed.

Moving quickly, the company redesigned its customer service processes around a team-based structure. This permitted various members of an account team to address a client inquiry. There were multiple benefits of this team-based approach for customers, including better access, faster problem resolution, and generally higher satisfaction. But for Ceridian, the move to a team-based customer service model meant more: it necessitated a more flexible, integrated infrastructure for sharing internal data. Alpern explains that the company's "change in philosophy" on customer service required an equally bold initiative on the technology side. "We saw the need to fundamentally change the way we store, access, and use customer information," says Alpern. "This, in turn, required a shift in our infrastructure strategy toward a more centralized, standardized approach."

Ceridian Canada's new vision for customer service and customer data management depended on two crucial technological factors: company-wide customer relations management (CRM) and a single national customer database. Implementing a CRM solution would provide the key portal for account teams servicing customers. Creating a national customer database to replace branch-specific customer information databases would reduce redundancy. Bob Aldridge, Project Director for the CRM initiative, explains that the two major tasks involved completely redefining customer service processes and selecting a CRM platform able to support the company's new vision for customer interaction. "While the redefinition of our internal processes was a task that we were clearly best prepared to perform, we viewed the CRM vendor selection process as an area where we could leverage outside expertise," says Aldridge. IBM Global Services was selected to help them assess the various alternatives."

Ceridian Canada investigated a number of platforms over a nine-month period, finally creating a short-list of three vendors. In late 1999, Ceridian Canada selected Siebel Systems. According to Aldridge, his company chose Siebel's Call Centre and Service solution because of the product's functionality as well as Siebel's top-ranked status in CRM technology innovation. "Although we had developed some very exacting specifications as an outgrowth of our process redesign efforts, the breadth and depth of Siebel's functionality accommodated them easily," says Aldridge. Ceridian gained confidence in its approach toward technology from Siebel's position as a market leader.

Beyond focusing its electronic business initiatives on employees (e.g., using CRM to facilitate team-based customer service), the company has also developed customer-facing Web-based solutions, such as Powerpay, a fully Web-based payroll solution targeted to small businesses. Though Powerpay is a new element of Ceridian's core service portfolio, the company has also leveraged Web technology to expand its customer service delivery channels. The most important initiative in this area has centred on Web-based self-service, which allows Ceridian Canada customers access to various service features via a Web browser. In late 2000, the company investigated the chance to leverage its CRM investments, the most crucial element of which was its national customer database. Ceridian Canada envisioned this as a solution that would offer Web-based access to customer data drawn from the core CRM customer database. Also, as with the CRM initiative it was derived from, the Web self-service plan was designed to improve the quality of customer service through increased convenience. Equally important, the platform was also seen as a scalable, low-cost channel for handling less complex customer inquiries.

Ceridian Canada chose IBM's WebSphere Application Server as the core technology powering the solution and chose IBM Global Services to develop the solution itself. As Aldridge points out, the WebSphere Application Server was selected on the basis of its flexibility and ease of integration with the Siebel platform. "We saw WebSphere as a highly flexible, standards-based infrastructure for building advanced Web applications," says Aldridge. "Its tight fit with Siebel—also a best-of-breed solution—made complete sense for us."

As the project began, the Ceridian Canada/IBM Global Services team faced serious obstacles, many of which were related to people and process issues. The most serious business-level challenge for the CRM solution was managing staff and management employee expectations. A major ongoing challenge for the WebSphere-based self-service solution has been to comprehend fully the impact the solution had on the company's traditional customer service channel. Ceridian Canada believes that a clear understanding of the interplay of online and "offline" customer service channels is crucial to developing a coherent, integrated set of customer service processes.

A major technical challenge that the CRM project threw up was the complexity inherent in the configuration effort; the most important issue was the issue of legacy (older systems) integration. Ceridian Canada's branches had independently developed their own methods of gathering and storing data, Aldridge explained, which led to a wide variety of data formats. The task of transferring data stored in multiple formats on different systems to one standardized database was formidable, illustrating how complex Ceridian's problems initially were.

In January 2000, staff from IBM Global Services' CRM practice began implementing the Siebel CRM solution. Redesigning Ceridian Canada's core customer service processes was a critical early phase. This exercise created the business-process framework around which the IBM team would design the Siebel solution. The IBM team completed the next phase, the design and configuration of the solution, in 2000. Soon after that, the actual solution development and integration effort began. IBM Global Services deployed the Siebel solution on a site-by-site basis, completing the implementation of the first site in August 2000. After the deployment, all of Ceridian Canada's customer service employees gained access to the STAR (Service and Technology Achieving Results) system.

In March 2001, after a two-month development effort, IBM Global Services finished a pilot version of Ceridian Canada's Web self-service application. Development was in two phases, the first being focused on database integration, and the second focused on the solution's user interface component. A limited group of customers has, since that time, used a beta version of the solution. There were two main goals:

1. devise a practical application that customers could test and approve
2. determine how successful the solution was

In the end, Ceridian Canada hopes to offer the solution to all of its customers, though it will phase its use in slowly in order to accurately track its infrastructure needs.

Within the company, employees refer to Ceridian's CRM solution as STAR (Service and Technology Achieving Results). Customer care representatives and managers within the customer service organization use it the most. Ceridian's billing and finance staff also uses STAR, accessing data through workflow from the Customer Care organization. A centralized database comprises the core of the STAR system; it stores payroll account information and interaction records pertaining to customer contact. When a representative is not able to personally deal with a client's problem, the STAR system can create and track service requests. Using this workflow-like capability, the representative can figure out where in the company to direct the query.

Although the STAR system is nominally a CRM platform, customer service representatives can also use it to acquire much data from disparate parts of the company. An example might be a representative using STAR to collect a customer's account and payment history. According to Aldridge, integrating knowledge management features with the STAR system's core CRM functionality will lead to improvements in Ceridian Canada's account teams' effectiveness. "Our strategy is to give as much knowledge to our front-line employees as possible," he says. "By empowering our reps with more information, we're able to dramatically reduce our problem resolution times by minimizing the need to escalate the inquiry to other parts of the company."

STAR has been integrated with Ceridian Canada's core legacy systems, which is one of its strengths. Take the following scenario as an example: Customer Care representatives download billing and tax information to STAR each month. With this done, representatives have access to this data as needed. Ceridian has been able to add value to its CRM platform through integration of the STAR platform with its internal systems. The company has simultaneously leveraged its legacy investments.

Ceridian is justly proud of its Web self-service application. Any of the company's nearly 40 000 clients will be able to access it through a Web browser. Security is based on an Internet security standard, secure sockets layer (SSL). Clients will be able to track the status of service requests online. This service goes well beyond read-only capabilities—it allows clients to proactively program elements of the STAR database. These changes are then reflected by Ceridian's core payroll processing system.

Ceridian Canada's branch users access the STAR system via local area network (LAN); each LAN is connected to the main servers in Winnipeg by a wide area network. In Winnipeg, IBM Netfinity servers host the company's CRM and Web self-service solutions. These servers also have the ability to store the staggering amounts of data generated by the business.

Data, ranging from simple name, address, and contact information to production schedules (e.g., when customers run their payroll) to billing and remittance information (e.g., tax payments to government agencies), is stored in the production database server. This national customer database is the core of the STAR solution. Integration with Ceridian's legacy systems—principally client-server systems—throughout the company's branches, means data flow between STAR and legacy systems is bi-directional.

An IBM Netfinity server within the general architecture of the STAR system will also host Ceridian Canada's Web self-service platform. This system was developed by IBM Global Services, runs IBM WebSphere Application Server, and accesses the STAR database. Alpern suggests that Web-service will leverage WebSphere's ability to deliver targeted content based on user identity. According to Alpern, personalization technology is a key future design element, since it repeatedly brings customers back to Web sites. "WebSphere's robust support for personalization," says Alpern, "will allow us to create an even stronger solution for our customers."

Ceridian Canada most values customer satisfaction and retention. It is in these measures that the company believes it will see the best evidence of the benefits of its recent technological investments. The payroll services industry is highly competitive, and quality of customer service is the main difference between competitors. Given this, the most important metric of a company's health is customer satisfaction. Because of this, Ceridian regularly surveys its clients. Results show that the changes implemented by the company are already paying off, with reported satisfaction levels rising. However, Alpern suggests there's more to come. "We expect our aggregate customer satisfaction levels to increase by 20 percent over the next three years as a direct result of giving our customers what they want," he says. "Faster, better service along with more choice, flexibility, and convenience."

A key benefit of STAR is the infrastructure needed to build large-scale change upon. With STAR in place, Ceridan could can efficiently move to a team-based approach. This is one significant operational benefit from the system's implementation; another is increasing the efficiency of its customer service operation. Ceridian has seen is a substantial, measurable improvement along a number of different performance parameters. Aldridge notes that better processing of inquiries has been one of the most immediate gains. "When we researched our old process, we found that for every customer call coming in, we were making two or more calls internally," he says. "Since deploying STAR, we've already seen significant decreases in the number of internal calls resulting from customer inquiries. Over the next few years, we expect to cut our internal calling volume by no less than half."

Ceridian Canada expects the addition of its Web self-service solution to lead to even further improvements in efficiency and customer satisfaction. However, as Aldridge points out, the dual benefits of cost reduction and cost avoidance may well emerge as the platform's key source of payback. "The key," says Aldridge, "is the solution's ability to suppress customer service costs, even as the company grows at a healthy clip." "The Web self-service solution provides us with a low-cost channel for handling simple inquiries that, nonetheless, take up precious internal resources," notes Aldridge. "The beauty of the Web self-service solution is that it will allow us to grow our customer base while keeping the cost of supporting that base essentially stable. Over the next three years, we expect to avoid 20 percent of the customer service costs that we would have otherwise incurred."

Deploying the system throughout its branches and bringing its 800 customer service representatives online is only a first step. The vision for the future, according to Alpern, is to create a "virtual call centre" with coast-to-coast customer service capability. "We made a conscious choice not to build a traditional, centralized call centre in order to stay close to our customers," he says. "Instead, we wanted to build a more flexible, intelligent solution that combines software and hardware with advanced routing capability. The STAR system is an important element of this vision." In terms of Web-service, Ceridian plans to have a production version of its WebSphere-based solution up and running 12-months hence. The company is cognizant of the potentially huge number of Web self-service users, and has consequently prioritized the performance and capacity of the system's infrastructure. "We are committed to providing high levels of performance to our Web self-service customers," explains Alpern. "Our choice of WebSphere Application Server as the core of our solution ensures that we'll get the best performance and reliability available on the market today."

Web self-service will bring challenges as well as benefits. One of the former challenges will be creating a platform that can deliver top-quality performance to a huge base of clients. This will entail delivering decent service to large and sophisticated users while keeping the service minimal enough to satisfy smaller clients.

Ceridian Canada and epost, Canada Post's electronic commerce initiative, recently signed an agreement to offer e-tax forms and e-payslip solutions to Ceridian's business clients and their respective employees. Businesses that adopt the solution(s) will have the option to deliver their annual T4s and Ceridian payslips to employees via the epost service. Epost began delivering electronic T4s to employees in February 2003, and will deliver e-payslips later in the year.

***Sources*:** "Ceridian Canada: IBM and Siebel Deliver a Leading Edge CRM Solution," IBM Case Study, available www-3.ibm.com/software/success /cssdb.nsf/CS/AKLR-54F57G?OpenDocument&Site=default, November 13, 2001, accessed May 30, 2003; Ceridian Canada Web site, available www.ceridian.ca, accessed May 30, 2003; "Ceridian Canada Takes Customer Service to a New Level," available http://www.crmadvocate.com/ casestudy/siebel/ceridian_61.pdf, accessed May 30, 2003; "Ceridian Canada and epost sign agreement to enable employers," available www. nati.net/m_pressrelease.asp?PressType=Member, accessed May 30, 2002.

CASE STUDY QUESTIONS

1. Why do you think payroll services have become a commodity or utility service? How does this affect the way Ceridian approaches its business?

2. Why did Ceridian ask IBM to help evaluate CRM system vendors? What do you think the benefits were of asking an outsider to help?

3. How did the use of the STAR system integrate Ceridian's databases? What are the benefits of this integration?

4. What do you think are the benefits that Ceridian's clients perceive in the new systems?

5. Did Ceridian need to implement the Web-based self-service initiative? What are the benefits of that initiative for Ceridian's customers? For Ceridian?

6. Review the six types of information systems categorized in this chapter. Categorize each of the systems mentioned in the case as one of those types of systems. Explain your answer.

INFORMATION SYSTEMS, ORGANIZATIONS, MANAGEMENT, AND STRATEGY

Objectives

As a manager, you will need to know how to use information systems strategically and how these systems can help you make better decisions. After completing this chapter, you should be able to answer the following questions:

1. *What do managers need to know about organizations in order to build and use information systems successfully?*

2. *What impact do information systems have on organizations?*

3. *How do information systems support the activities of managers in organizations?*

4. *How can businesses use information systems for competitive advantage?*

5. *Why is it so difficult to develop successful information systems, including systems that promote competitive advantage?*

Flextronics' Strategic Supply Chain

You may not have heard of Flextronics, but you probably use something they have made every day. Singapore-based Flextronics is a contract manufacturer that makes the innards of technology products, such as cell phones, personal computers (PCs), and Internet hardware for such household names as Cisco Systems, Dell Computers, and Ericsson mobile phones. In the fast-paced, hypercompetitive technology industry, profit margins for electronic manufacturing services, such as Flextronics, are razor-thin, amounting to no more than 3 to 5 percent. Yet during the past seven years, Flextronics has been able to move rapidly from a tiny company to a multibillion-dollar global operation. How did Flextronics do it?

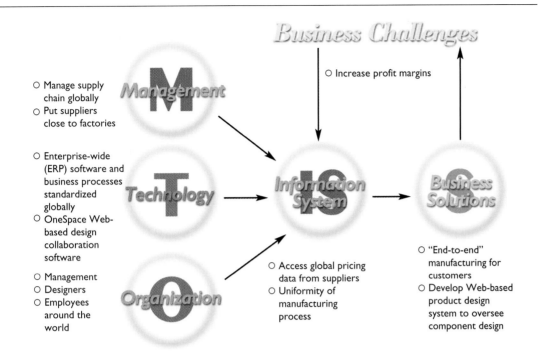

The answer lies in skillful supply chain management. Flextronics continually collects and analyzes its supply chain information to standardize and coordinate the work of its factories around the globe. The company developed a low-cost manufacturing network in China, Singapore, Mexico, and other locations around the world. Flextronics facilities are built like campuses with water, sewer, and computer lines and buildings for suppliers so that they can be close to Flextronics' factories. The campuses are standardized so that they look and perform the same way, regardless of their location. Flextronics, thus, can offer inexpensive manufacturing facilities that are not too far away from its European and North American clients.

Flextronics uses the same enterprise resource planning software in the same configuration in all of its factories so that it can standardize and coordinate their work more precisely. The same business processes for doing manufacturing work are, thus, replicated worldwide. Employees who access Flextronics' global information system can see data pulled together from practically every Flextronics factory on four continents. A parts buyer in Mexico can see what prices a Singapore parts buyer is obtaining for a specific component and use that information to get a price break from suppliers. When someone uses the system to place an order, the system displays a pop-up window that might show where he or she could get a better price on that same item and whether the component could be obtained from a Flextronics factory that is overstocked on that item. Flextronics' 2000 design engineers can work jointly on design specifications from many different locations using OneSpace Web-based collaboration software.

Armed with this powerful software and well-designed business processes, Flextronics is now assuming responsibility for even larger portions of its clients' supply chains. About 85 to 90 percent of Flextronics' revenue comes from its traditional outsourced manufacturing work, where the company makes a part of a product for a client and then ships it to the client for assembly into the finished product. What Flextronics' new strategy will do is enable customers, such as Cisco Systems, to entrust the manufacturing process for entire products to Flextronics. Cisco will focus on product design and marketing, and Flextronics will do the rest. Flextronics can use its new end-to-end manufacturing capabilities for other clients as well. Ericsson, the Swedish cell phone manufacturer, recently contracted to hand over its entire manufacturing process to Flextronics.

Flextronics plans to take over design work for customers as well. In the works is a Web-based product design system that extracts individual component information from a repository of product data and delivers it to designers so they can see each potential component's quality, availability, and supplier history. Flextronics will then be able to use that information for bulk purchases of materials so that they can charge less for manufacturing and, hopefully, win more clients.

Sources: Tzyh Ng, "Inside the No. 1 Tech Outsourcer," *Business Week,* February 19, 2002; Mel Duvall, "Supply Chain: Forecasts on Demand," *CIO Insight,* May 15, 2002; and Christopher Koch, "Yank Your Chain," *Darwin Magazine,* October 2001.

MANAGEMENT CHALLENGES

Flextronics illustrates the interdependence of business environments, organizational culture, management strategy, and the development of information systems. Flextronics developed enterprise systems and global business processes in response to competitive pressures from its surrounding environment, but this systems effort could not succeed without a significant amount of organizational and management change. New information systems have changed the way Flextronics runs its business and makes management decisions. The experience of Flextronics raises the following management challenges:

1. **Sustainability of competitive advantage.** The competitive advantages strategic systems confer do not necessarily last long enough to ensure long-term profitability. Because competitors can retaliate and copy strategic systems, competitive advantage is not always sustainable. Markets, customer expectations, and technology change; globalization has made these changes even more rapid and unpredictable (Eisenhardt, 2002). The Internet can make competitive advantage disappear very quickly, as virtually all companies can use this technology (Porter, 2001; Yoffie and Cusumano, 1999). Classic strategic systems, such as American Airlines' SABRE computerized reservation system, Citibank's automatic teller machine (ATM) system, and FedEx's package tracking system, benefited by being the first in their industries. Then, rival systems emerged. Information systems alone cannot provide an enduring business advantage. Systems originally intended to be strategic frequently become tools for survival, required by every firm to stay in business, or they may inhibit organizations from making the strategic changes essential for future success (Eardley, Avison, and Powell, 1997).

2. **Fitting technology to the organization (or vice versa).** On the one hand, it is important to align information technology to the business plan, to the firm's business processes, and to senior management's strategic business plans. Information technology is, after all, supposed to be the servant of the organization. On the other hand, these business plans, processes, and management strategy all may be very outdated or incompatible with the envisioned technology. In these instances, managers will need to change the organization to fit the technology or adjust both the organization and the technology to achieve an optimal "fit."

 This chapter explores the relationships between organizations, management, information systems, and business strategy. We introduce the features of organizations that you will need to understand when you design, develop, and operate information systems. We also scrutinize the role of the manager and the management decision-making process, identifying areas where information systems can enhance managerial effectiveness. We conclude by examining the problems that firms face from competition and the ways in which information systems can provide competitive advantage.

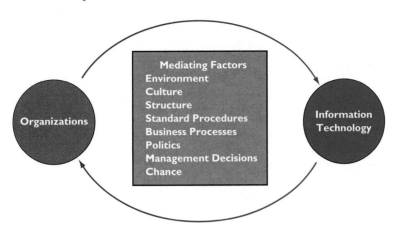

Figure 3.1 The two-way relationship between organizations and information technology. This complex two-way relationship is mediated by many factors, not the least of which are the decisions made—or not made—by managers. Other factors mediating the relationship include organizational culture, bureaucracy, politics, business fashion, and pure chance.

3.1 ORGANIZATIONS AND INFORMATION SYSTEMS

Information systems and organizations influence one another. Information systems must be aligned with the organization to provide information that is needed by important groups within the organization. At the same time, the organization must be aware of and be open to the influences of information systems in order to benefit from new technologies.

The interaction between information technology and organizations is very complex and is influenced by a great many mediating factors, including the organization's structure, standard operating procedures, politics, culture, surrounding environment, and management decisions (see Figure 3.1). Managers must be aware that information systems can markedly alter life in the organization. They cannot successfully design new systems or understand existing systems without understanding organizations. Managers do decide what systems will be developed, what they will do, how they will be implemented, and so forth. Sometimes, however, the outcomes are the result of pure chance and of both good and bad luck.

WHAT IS AN ORGANIZATION?

An **organization** is a stable, formal social structure that takes resources from the environment and processes them to produce outputs. This technical definition focuses on three elements of an organization. (1) *Capital and labour* are primary production factors provided by the environment. (2) The *organization* (the firm) transforms these inputs into products and services in a production function. (3) The *products and services* are consumed by environments in return for supply inputs (see Figure 3.2). An organization is more stable in terms of

organization (technical definition)

A stable, formal, social structure that takes resources from the environment and processes them to produce outputs.

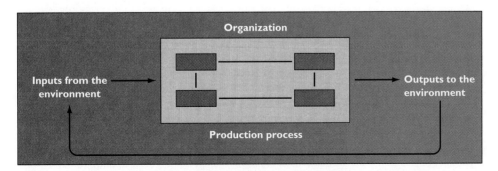

Figure 3.2 The technical microeconomic definition of the organization. In the microeconomic definition of organizations, capital and labour (the primary production factors provided by the environment) are transformed by the firm through the production process into products and services (outputs to the environment). The products and services are consumed by the environment, which supplies additional capital and labour as inputs in the feedback loop.

longevity and routineness than an informal group (such as a group of friends that meets every Friday for lunch). Organizations are formal legal entities that have internal rules and procedures and must abide by laws. Organizations are also social structures because they are a collection of social elements, much as a machine has a structure—a particular arrangement of valves, cams, shafts, and other parts.

This definition of organizations is powerful and simple, but it is not very descriptive or even predictive of real-world organizations. A more realistic behavioural definition of an **organization** is that it is a collection of rights, privileges, obligations, and responsibilities that are delicately balanced over a period of time through conflict and conflict resolution (see Figure 3.3). In this behavioural view of the firm, people who work in organizations develop customary ways of working; they gain attachments to existing relationships; and they make arrangements with subordinates and superiors about how work will be done, how much work will be done, and under what conditions. Most of these arrangements and feelings are not discussed in any formal rule book.

How do these definitions of organizations relate to information system technology? A technical view of organizations encourages us to focus on the way inputs are combined into outputs when technology changes are introduced into the company. The firm is seen as infinitely malleable, with capital and labour substituting for each other quite easily. But the more realistic behavioural definition of an organization suggests that developing new information systems or updating old ones involves much more than a technical rearrangement of machines or workers—that some information systems change the organizational balance of rights, privileges, obligations, responsibilities, and feelings that have been established over a long period of time.

Technological change requires changes in who owns and controls information, who has the right to access and update that information, and who makes decisions about whom, when, and how. For instance, Flextronics is using enterprise systems to provide buyers with more information on parts purchases so that they can make better purchasing decisions. This more complex view forces us to look at the way work is designed and the procedures used to achieve outputs.

The technical and behavioural definitions of organizations are not contradictory. Indeed, they complement each other: The technical definition tells us how thousands of firms in competitive markets combine capital, labour, and information technology, while the behavioural model takes us inside the individual firm to see how that technology affects the organization's inner workings. Section 3.2 describes how each of these definitions of organizations can help explain the relationships between information systems and organizations.

Some features of organizations are common to all organizations; others distinguish one organization from another. Let us look first at the features common to all organizations.

COMMON FEATURES OF ORGANIZATIONS

You might think that, besides being Canadian, the Hudson's Bay Company, Air Canada, and the Royal Canadian Mounted Police don't have much in common, but they do. In some respects, all modern organizations are alike because they share the characteristics that are

organization (behavioural definition)

A collection of rights, privileges, obligations, and responsibilities that are delicately balanced over a period of time through conflict and conflict resolution.

Figure 3.3 The behavioural view of organizations. The behavioural view of organizations emphasizes group relationships, values, and structures.

TABLE 3.1	**STRUCTURAL CHARACTERISTICS OF ALL ORGANIZATIONS**

Clear division of labour

Hierarchy

Explicit rules and procedures

Impartial judgments

Technical qualifications for positions

Maximum organizational efficiency

listed in Table 3.1. A German sociologist, Max Weber, was the first to describe these "ideal-typical" characteristics of organizations in 1911. He called organizations **bureaucracies** that have certain "structural" features.

According to Weber, all modern bureaucracies have a clear-cut division of labour and specialization. Organizations arrange specialists in a hierarchy of authority in which everyone is accountable to someone, and authority is limited to specific actions. Authority and action are further limited by abstract rules or procedures (standard operating procedures, or SOPs) that are interpreted and applied to specific cases. These rules create a system of impartial and universal decision making; everyone is treated equally. Organizations try to hire and promote employees on the basis of technical qualifications and professionalism (not personal connections). The organization is devoted to the principle of efficiency—maximizing output using limited inputs.

According to Weber, bureaucracies are prevalent because they are the most efficient form of organization. Other scholars have supplemented Weber's definition, identifying additional features of organizations. All organizations develop standard operating procedures, politics, and cultures.

bureaucracy

Formal organization with a clear-cut division of labour, abstract rules and procedures, and impartial decision making that uses technical qualifications and professionalism as a basis for promoting employees.

Standard Operating Procedures

Organizations that survive over time become very efficient, producing a limited number of products and services by following standard routines. These standard routines become codified into reasonably precise rules, procedures, and practices called **standard operating procedures (SOPs)** that are developed to cope with virtually all expected situations. Some of these rules and procedures are written, formal procedures. Most are "rules of thumb" to be followed in specific situations. Business processes are based on SOPs.

These standard operating procedures have a great deal to do with the efficiency that modern organizations attain. For instance, in the assembly of a car, managers and workers develop complex standard procedures to handle thousands of motions in a precise fashion, permitting the finished product to roll off the assembly line. Any change in SOPs requires an enormous organizational effort. Indeed, the organization may need to halt the entire production process before the old SOPs can be retired.

Difficulty in changing standard operating procedures is one reason Detroit automakers have been slow to adopt Japanese mass-production methods. For many years, North American automakers followed Henry Ford's mass-production principles. Ford believed that the cheapest way to build a car was to churn out the largest number of autos by having workers repeatedly perform a simple task. By contrast, Japanese automakers have emphasized "lean production" methods whereby a smaller number of workers, each performing several tasks, can produce cars with less inventory, less investment, and fewer mistakes. Workers have multiple job responsibilities and are encouraged to stop production in order to correct a problem.

standard operating procedures (SOPs)

Precise rules, procedures, and practices developed by organizations to cope with virtually all expected situations.

Organizational Politics

People in organizations occupy different positions with different specialties, concerns, and perspectives. As a result, they naturally have divergent viewpoints about how resources, rewards, and punishments should be distributed. These differences matter to both managers and employees, and they result in political struggle, competition, and conflict within every organization. Political resistance is one of the great difficulties of bringing about organizational change—especially the development of new information systems. Virtually all information systems that bring about significant changes in goals, procedures, productivity, and personnel are politically charged and will elicit serious political opposition.

Organizational Culture

All organizations have bedrock, unassailable, unquestioned (by the members) assumptions that define their goals and products. **Organizational culture** is this set of fundamental assumptions about what products the organization should produce, how it should produce them, where, and for whom. Generally, these cultural assumptions are taken totally for granted and are rarely publicly announced or spoken about (Schein, 1985).

You can see organizational culture at work by looking around your university or college. Some bedrock assumptions of university life are that professors know more than students, the reason students attend college is to learn, and classes follow a regular schedule. Organizational culture is a powerful unifying force that restrains political conflict and promotes common understanding, agreement on procedures, and common practices. If we all share the same basic cultural assumptions, then agreement on other matters is more likely.

At the same time, organizational culture is a powerful restraint on change, especially technological change. Most organizations will do almost anything to avoid making changes in these basic assumptions. Any technological change that threatens commonly held cultural assumptions usually meets with a great deal of resistance. However, there are times when the only sensible way for a firm to move forward is to employ a new technology that directly opposes an existing organizational culture. When this occurs, the technology is often stalled while the culture slowly adjusts.

UNIQUE FEATURES OF ORGANIZATIONS

Although all organizations do have common characteristics, no two organizations are identical. Organizations have different structures, goals, constituencies, leadership styles, tasks, and surrounding environments.

Different Organizational Types

One important way in which organizations differ is in their structures or shapes. The differences among organizational structures are characterized in many ways. Mintzberg's classification, described in Table 3.2, identifies five basic kinds of organizations (Mintzberg, 1979).

organizational culture

The set of fundamental assumptions about what products the organization should produce, how and where it should produce them, and for whom they should be produced.

TABLE 3.2   ORGANIZATIONAL STRUCTURES

Organizational Type	Description	Example
Entrepreneurial structure	Young, small firm in a fast-changing environment. It has a simple structure and is managed by an entrepreneur serving as its single chief executive officer.	Small start-up business
Machine bureaucracy	Large bureaucracy existing in a slowly changing environment, producing standard products. It is dominated by a centralized management team and centralized decision making.	Midsize manufacturing firm
Divisionalized bureaucracy	Combination of multiple machine bureaucracies, each producing a different product or service, all topped by one central headquarters.	Great West Life Assurance Company
Professional bureaucracy	Knowledge-based organization where goods and services depend on the expertise and knowledge of professionals. Dominated by department heads with weak centralized authority.	Law firms, school systems
Adhocracy	"Task force" organization that must respond to rapidly changing environments. Consists of large groups of specialists organized into short-lived multidisciplinary teams and has weak central management.	Consulting firms, such as the Rand Corporation or Toronto's Research Infosource.

Organizations and Environments

Organizations reside in environments from which they draw resources and to which they supply goods and services. Organizations and environments have a reciprocal relationship. On the one hand, organizations are open to, and dependent on, the social and physical environments that surround them. Without financial and human resources—people willing to work reliably and consistently for a set wage or revenue from customers—organizations could not exist. Organizations must respond to legislative and other requirements imposed by government, as well as to the actions of customers and competitors. On the other hand, organizations can influence their environments. Organizations form alliances with others to influence the political process; they advertise to influence customer acceptance of their products.

Figure 3.4 shows that information systems play an important role in helping organizations perceive changes in their environments and also in helping organizations act on their environments. Information systems are key instruments for *environmental scanning*, helping managers identify external changes that might require an organizational response.

Environments generally change much faster than do organizations. The main reasons for organizational failure are inability to adapt to a rapidly changing environment and lack of resources—particularly among young firms—to sustain even short periods of troubled times (Freeman et al., 1983). New technologies, new products, and changing public tastes and values (many of which result in new government regulations) put strains on any organization's culture, politics, and people. Most organizations do not cope well with large environmental shifts. The inertia built into an organization's standard operating procedures, the political conflict raised by changes to the existing order, and the threat to closely held cultural values typically inhibit organizations from making significant changes. It is not surprising that only 10 percent of the Fortune 500 companies in 1919 still exist today.

Other Differences among Organizations

Organizations have different shapes or structures for many other reasons also. They differ in their ultimate goals and the types of power used to achieve them. Some organizations have coercive goals (e.g., prisons); others have utilitarian goals (e.g., businesses). Still others have normative goals (e.g., universities, religious groups). Organizations also serve different groups or have different constituencies, some primarily benefiting their members, others benefiting clients, stockholders, or the public. The nature of leadership differs greatly from one organization to another—some organizations may be more democratic or authoritarian than others. Another way organizations differ is by the tasks they perform and the technology they use. Some organizations perform primarily routine tasks that could be reduced to formal rules that require little judgment (such as manufacturing auto parts), while others (such as consulting firms) work primarily with nonroutine tasks.

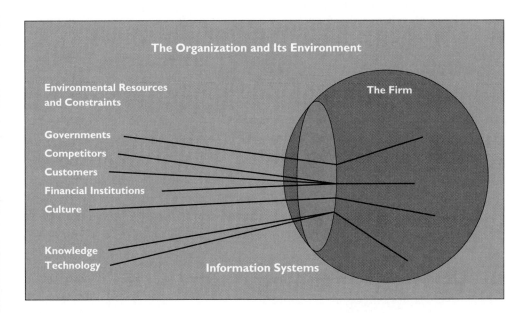

Figure 3.4 Environments and organizations have a reciprocal relationship. Environments shape what organizations can do, but organizations can influence their environments and decide to change environments altogether. Information technology plays a critical role in helping organizations perceive environmental changes and in helping organizations act on their environments.

TABLE 3.3	A SUMMARY OF SALIENT FEATURES OF ORGANIZATIONS

Common Features	Unique Features
Formal structure	Organizational type
Standard operating procedures (SOPs)	Environments
Politics	Goals
Culture	Power
	Constituencies
	Function
	Leadership
	Tasks
	Technology
	Business processes

As you can see in Table 3.3, the list of unique features of organizations is longer than the common features list. Information systems will have different impacts on different types of organizations. Different organizations in different circumstances will experience different effects from the same technology. The Window on Organizations shows, for example, how unique environments, culture, and organizational characteristics have affected Internet use and electronic commerce in South Korea and the Middle East. Only by close analysis of a specific organization can a manager effectively design and manage information systems.

3.2   THE CHANGING ROLE OF INFORMATION SYSTEMS IN ORGANIZATIONS

Information systems have become integral, online, interactive tools deeply involved in the minute-to-minute operations and decision making of large organizations. We now describe the changing role of systems in organizations and how it has been shaped by the interaction of organizations and information technology.

INFORMATION TECHNOLOGY INFRASTRUCTURE AND INFORMATION TECHNOLOGY SERVICES

information systems department

The formal organizational unit that is responsible for the information systems function in the organization.

programmers

Highly trained technical specialists who write computer software instructions.

systems analysts

Specialists who translate business problems and requirements into information requirements and systems, acting as a liaison between the information systems department and the rest of the organization.

information systems managers

Leaders of the various specialists in the information systems department.

One way that organizations can influence how information technology will be used is through decisions about the technical and organizational configuration of systems. Previous chapters described the ever-widening role of information systems in organizations. Supporting this widening role have been changes in information technology (IT) infrastructure, which we defined in Chapter 1. Each organization determines exactly how its infrastructure will be configured. Chapters 6 through 9 detail the various technology alternatives that organizations can use to design their infrastructures.

Another way that organizations have affected information technology is through decisions about who will design, develop, and maintain the organization's IT infrastructure. These decisions determine how information technology services will be delivered.

The formal organizational unit or function responsible for technology services is called the **information systems department**. The information systems department is responsible for maintaining the hardware, software, data storage, and networks that comprise the firm's IT infrastructure.

The information systems department consists of specialists, such as programmers, systems analysts, project leaders, and information systems managers (see Figure 3.5). **Programmers** are highly trained technical specialists who write the software instructions for the computer. **Systems analysts** constitute the principal liaison between the information systems groups and the rest of the organization. It is the systems analyst's job to translate business problems and requirements into information requirements and systems. **Information systems managers** are

E-COMMERCE—SOUTH KOREAN AND MIDDLE EASTERN STYLE

Why is e-commerce not spreading relatively equally throughout the world? In some countries, its use is exploding, while in other countries, few people have turned to the Internet despite its growing value and importance. Let us compare South Korea at one end of the spectrum with the Arab Middle Eastern countries at the other end.

E-commerce, including commerce using wireless mobile devices, is growing rapidly in South Korea, a country with only 11 million households. According to the research firm eMarketer, Korean retail e-commerce revenue was $3.69 billion in 2001 and is expected to reach almost $16 billion in 2004. That research also predicts that in 2004 business-to-business e-commerce will rise to over $14 billion. To understand why the growth is so rapid, we need to examine the country's economic and cultural environments.

Part of the answer is that per capita, South Korea has the highest online penetration in the world. Nearly half of all South Koreans use the Internet, and about 95 percent of them are online at least once a week. In fact, the country has a higher high-speed network penetration than any other country, and by 2001, over 59 percent of South Koreans were using mobile phones. South Korean Internet users spend twice as much time online as do people in the United States. One key factor is that the cost of these technologies is not too high for most Koreans. Another factor is that the Korean government has played a major role in the growing commitment to these technologies. Several government organizations, such as the Ministry of Commerce, Industry, and Energy, the Fair Trade Commission, and the Ministry of Culture and Tourism are all working to advance the use of these technologies.

One challenge for Korean e-commerce is that Korean citizens use the Internet mostly for communication and information. Only about 12.3 percent of them are shopping online. The main problem is their fear that the Internet lacks security. (According to the Australian Institute of Criminology, approximately 5 to 10 percent of online transactions in Asia involve fraud.) To address this problem, the government has developed a highly secure digital-signature system, and it is also promoting the use of electronic money and credit cards.

Compare this with the Middle East. With an Arab population of about 270 million, only 4.22 million go online. Moreover, of the 20 most used sites in the Arab world, only Kunoozy.com is purely for e-commerce, and it ranks 19th in popularity. According to Stephane Jais, the Middle East and Africa sales manager for DoubleClick, an Internet advertising firm, "There aren't a lot of e-commerce sites in the Middle East. Moreover," she says, "the few commercial sites that do exist are small with only about 1000 visitors daily. And most of their sales are for Arabs who are living abroad." Why the difference?

Cost is definitely the major reason. In 2000, for example, the gross domestic product (GDP) in Jordan was $5,250, while the average PC cost was about $3,750 and 30 hours of Internet usage per month cost about $2,100. In the same year, only 2.2 out of 100 Egyptians owned a PC, while in Syria, that number was only 1.43. In comparison, the per capita ownership in North America is 58.5 per 100. Even the Internet cafés in the Middle East are few and small, with only one or two computers in the back rooms of grocery stores. These are mainly used for communication.

Online shopping is difficult for other reasons. Very few Middle Easterners have credit cards, and credit cards are vital for online retail shopping. Moreover, tariffs are as high as 100 percent, making foreign products too expensive. In addition, the common approach to shopping in that part of the world is haggling over price, a pleasure to many residents in those countries.

To Think About: What organizational factors describe why South Korea and the Arab Middle East have had such different experiences in adopting e-commerce? How would a company's management, organization, and technology have to change to either purchase or sell goods in South Korea or in the Middle East?

Sources: David Rosenberg, "No Sale," *Wall Street Journal*, April 15, 2002; Mark Resch, "South Korea," *IQ Magazine*, January/February 2002; and Jessica Schneider Davis, "Safe Business in Asia," *IQ Magazine*, July/August 2002.

---

leaders of teams of programmers and analysts, project managers, physical facility managers, telecommunications managers, and heads of office system groups. They are also managers of computer operations and data entry staff. Also, external specialists, such as hardware vendors and manufacturers, software firms, and consultants, frequently participate in the day-to-day operations and long-term planning of information systems.

In many companies, the information systems department is headed by a **chief information officer (CIO)**. The CIO is a senior manager who oversees the use of information technology in the firm.

End users are representatives of departments outside of the information systems group for whom applications are developed. They play an increasingly large role in the design and development of information systems.

chief information officer (CIO)

Senior manager in charge of the information systems function in the firm.

end users

Representatives of departments outside the information systems group for whom applications are developed.

Figure 3.5 Information technology services. Many types of specialists and groups are responsible for the design and management of the organization's information technology (IT) infrastructure.

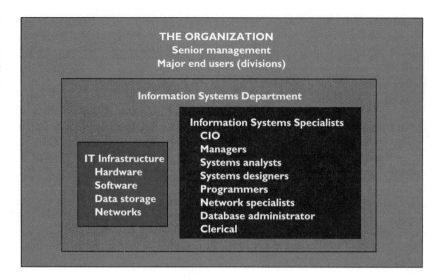

In the early years, the information systems group was composed mostly of programmers, who performed very highly specialized but limited technical functions. Today, a growing proportion of staff members are systems analysts and network specialists, with the information systems department acting as a powerful change agent in the organization. The information systems department suggests new business strategies and new information-based products and services and coordinates both the development of the technology and the planned changes in the organization.

In the past, firms generally developed their own software and managed their own computing facilities. Today, many firms are turning to external vendors to provide these services (see Chapters 6, 9, and 10) and using their information systems departments to manage these service providers.

HOW INFORMATION SYSTEMS AFFECT ORGANIZATIONS

How have changes in information technology affected organizations? To find answers, we draw on research and theory based on both economic and behavioural approaches.

Economic Theories

From an economic standpoint, information technology can be viewed as a factor of production that can be freely substituted for capital and labour. As the cost of information technology falls, it is substituted for labour, which historically has been a rising cost. Hence, information technology should result in a decline in the number of middle managers and clerical workers as information technology substitutes for their labour.

transaction cost theory

Economic theory stating that firms grow larger because they can conduct marketplace transactions internally more cheaply than they can with external firms in the marketplace.

Information technology also helps firms contract in size because it can reduce transaction costs—the costs incurred when a firm buys on the marketplace what it cannot make itself. According to **transaction cost theory**, firms and individuals seek to economize on transaction costs, much as they do on production costs. Using markets is expensive (Williamson, 1985; Coase, 1937) because of such costs as locating and communicating with distant suppliers, monitoring contract compliance, buying insurance, obtaining information on products, and so forth. Traditionally, firms have tried to reduce transaction costs by getting bigger, hiring more employees, or buying their own suppliers and distributors, as General Motors used to do.

Information technology, especially the use of networks, can help firms lower the cost of market participation (transaction costs), making it worthwhile for firms to contract with external suppliers instead of using internal sources. For example, by using computer links to external suppliers, DaimlerChrysler Corporation can achieve economies by obtaining more than 70 percent of its parts from the outside. Information systems make it possible for such companies as Cisco Systems and Dell Computer to outsource their production to contract manufacturers, such as Flextronics, instead of making their products themselves. Figure 3.6

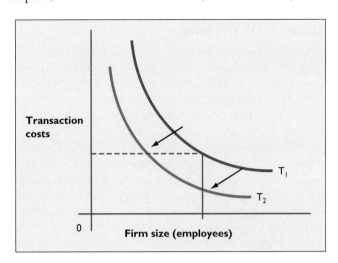

Figure 3.6 The transaction cost theory of the impact of information technology on the organization. Firms traditionally grew in size in order to reduce transaction costs. Information technology potentially reduces the costs for a given size, shifting the transaction cost curve inward, opening up the possibility of revenue growth without increasing size or even revenue growth accompanied by shrinking size.

shows that as transaction costs decrease, firm size (the number of employees) should shrink because it becomes easier and cheaper for the firm to contract for the purchase of goods and services in the marketplace, rather than to make the product or service itself. Firm size can stay constant or contract even if the company increases its revenues. (For example, General Electric reduced its workforce from about 400 000 people in the early 1980s to about 230 000 while increasing revenues 150 percent.)

Information technology also can reduce internal management costs. According to **agency theory**, the firm is viewed as a "nexus of contracts" among self-interested individuals, rather than as a unified, profit-maximizing entity (Jensen and Meckling, 1976). A principal (owner) employs "agents" (employees) to perform work on his or her behalf. However, agents need constant supervision and management because otherwise, they will tend to pursue their own interests, rather than those of the owners. As firms grow in size and scope, agency costs or coordination costs rise because owners must expend more and more effort supervising and managing employees.

agency theory

Economic theory that views the firm as a nexus of contracts among self-interested individuals who must be supervised and managed.

Information technology, by reducing the costs of acquiring and analyzing information, permits organizations to reduce agency costs because it becomes easier for managers to oversee a greater number of employees. Figure 3.7 shows that by reducing overall management costs, information technology allows firms to increase revenues while shrinking the number of middle management and clerical workers. We have seen examples in earlier chapters where information technology expanded the power and scope of small organizations by allowing them to perform coordinating activities, such as processing orders or keeping track of inventory, with very few clerks and managers.

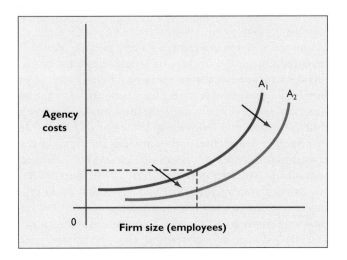

Figure 3.7 The agency cost theory of the impact of information technology on the organization. As firms grow in size and complexity, traditionally, they experience rising agency costs. Information technology shifts the agency cost curve down and to the right, allowing firms to increase size while lowering agency costs.

Behavioural Theories

Although economic theories try to explain how large numbers of firms act in the marketplace, behavioural theories from sociology, psychology, and political science are more useful for describing the behaviour of individual firms. Behavioural research has found little evidence that information systems automatically transform organizations, although the systems may be instrumental in accomplishing this goal once senior management decides to pursue this end.

Behavioural researchers have theorized that information technology could change the hierarchy of decision making in organizations by lowering the costs of information acquisition and broadening the distribution of information (Malone, 1997). Information technology could bring information directly from operating units to senior managers, thereby eliminating middle managers and their clerical support workers. Information technology could permit senior managers to contact lower-level operating units directly by using networked telecommunications and computers, eliminating middle management intermediaries. Information technology could also distribute information directly to lower-level workers, who could then make their own decisions on the basis of their own knowledge and information without any management intervention. However, some research suggests that computerization increases the information given to middle managers, empowering them to make more important decisions than in the past, thus reducing the need for large numbers of lower-level workers (Shore, 1983).

In post-industrial societies, authority increasingly relies on knowledge and competence and not merely on formal positions. Hence, the shape of organizations should "flatten" because professional workers tend to be self-managing; decision making should become more decentralized as knowledge and information become more widespread throughout the organization (Drucker, 1988). Information technology may encourage "task force" networked organizations in which groups of professionals come together, face-to-face or electronically, for short periods of time to accomplish a specific task (e.g., designing a new automobile); once the task is accomplished, the individuals join other task forces. More firms may operate as **virtual organizations**, where work no longer is tied to geographic locations. Virtual organizations use networks to link people, assets, and ideas. They can ally with suppliers, customers, and sometimes even competitors to create and distribute new products and services without being limited by traditional organizational boundaries or physical locations. For example, Calyx and Corolla is a networked virtual organization selling fresh flowers directly to customers, bypassing traditional florists. The firm takes orders via telephone or from its Web site and transmits them to grower farms, which ship them in FedEx vans directly to customers.

Who makes sure that self-managed teams do not head off in the wrong direction? Who decides which person works on what team and for how long? How can managers evaluate the performance of someone who is constantly rotating from team to team? How do people know where their careers are headed? New approaches for evaluating, organizing, and informing workers are required; not all companies can make virtual work effective (Davenport and Pearlson, 1998).

No one knows the answers to these questions, and it is not clear that all modern organizations will undergo this transformation. General Motors, for example, may have many self-managed knowledge workers in certain divisions, but it still will have a manufacturing division structured as a large, traditional bureaucracy. In general, the shape of organizations historically changes with the business cycle and with the latest management fashions. When times are good and profits are high, firms hire large numbers of supervisory personnel; when times are tough, they let go many of these same people (Mintzberg, 1979).

Another behavioural approach views information systems as the outcome of political competition between organizational groups for influence over the organization's policies, procedures, and resources (Laudon, 1974; Keen, 1981; Kling, 1980; Laudon, 1986). Information systems inevitably become bound up in organizational politics because they influence access to a key resource, namely, information. Information systems can affect who does what to whom, when, where, and how in an organization. Because information systems potentially change an organization's structure, culture, politics, and work, there is often considerable resistance to them when they are introduced.

virtual organization

Organization using networks to link people, assets, and ideas to create and distribute products and services without being limited to traditional organizational boundaries or physical locations.

There are several ways to visualize organizational resistance. Leavitt (1965) used a diamond shape to illustrate the interrelated and mutually adjusting character of technology and organization (see Figure 3.8). Here, changes in technology are absorbed, deflected, and defeated by organizational task arrangements, structures, and people. In this model, the only way to bring about change is to change the technology, tasks, structure, and people simultaneously. Other authors have spoken about the need to "unfreeze" organizations before introducing an innovation, quickly implementing it, and "refreezing" or institutionalizing the change (Kolb, 1970; Alter and Ginzberg, 1978). (See Chapter 12 for further discussion of change management.)

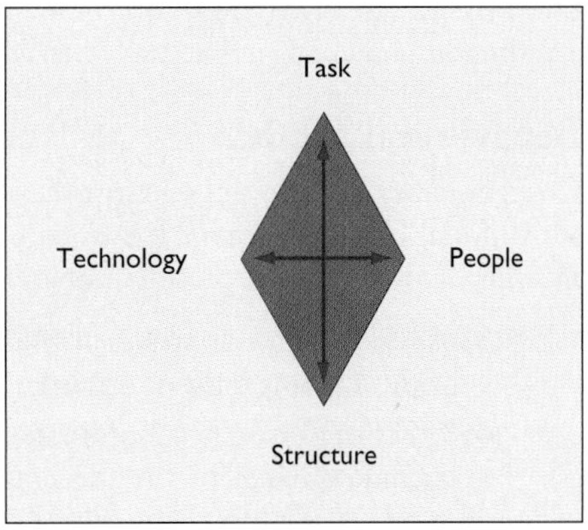

Figure 3.8 Organizational resistance and the mutually adjusting relationship between technology and the organization. Implementing information systems has consequences for task arrangements, structures, and people. According to this model, in order to implement change, all four components must be changed simultaneously.
Source: Leavitt, 1965.

THE INTERNET AND ORGANIZATIONS

The Internet, especially the World Wide Web, is beginning to have an important impact on the relationships between firms and external entities, and even on the organization of business processes inside a firm. The Internet increases the accessibility, storage, and distribution of information and knowledge for organizations. In essence, the Internet is capable of dramatically lowering the transaction and agency costs facing most organizations. For instance, brokerage firms and banks in Toronto can now "deliver" their internal operations procedures manuals to their employees at distant locations by posting them on their corporate Web sites, saving millions of dollars in distribution costs. A global sales force can receive nearly instant price product information updates via the Web or instructions from management via e-mail. Vendors of some large retailers can access retailers' internal Web sites directly for up-to-the-minute sales information and initiate replenishment orders instantly.

Businesses are rapidly rebuilding some of their core business processes based on Internet technology and making this technology a key component of their information technology (IT) infrastructures. If prior networking is any guide, one result will be simpler business processes, fewer employees, and much flatter organizations than in the past.

3.3 MANAGERS, DECISION MAKING, AND INFORMATION SYSTEMS

To determine how information systems can benefit managers, we must first examine what managers do and what information they need for decision making and other functions. We must also understand how decisions are made and what kinds of decisions can be supported by formal information systems.

THE ROLE OF MANAGERS IN ORGANIZATIONS

Managers play a key role in organizations. Their responsibilities range from making decisions to writing reports, attending meetings, and arranging birthday parties. We can better understand managerial functions and roles by examining classical and contemporary models of managerial behaviour.

Classical Descriptions of Management

The **classical model of management**, which describes what managers do, was largely unquestioned for the more than 70 years since the 1920s. Henri Fayol and other early writers first described the five classical functions of managers as planning, organizing, coordinating, deciding, and controlling. This description of management activities dominated management thought for a long time, and it is still popular today.

But these terms actually describe formal managerial functions and are unsatisfactory as a description of what managers actually do. The terms do not address what managers do when

classical model of management

Traditional description of management that focused on its formal functions of planning, organizing, coordinating, deciding, and controlling.

they plan, decide things, and control the work of others. We need a more fine-grained understanding of how managers actually behave.

Behavioural Models

Contemporary behavioural scientists have observed that managers do not behave as the classical model of management led us to believe. Kotter (1982), for example, describes the morning activities of the president of an investment management firm.

> 7:35 A.M. Richardson arrives at work, unpacks her briefcase, gets some coffee, and begins making a list of activities for the day.
>
> 7:45 A.M. Bradshaw (a subordinate) and Richardson converse about a number of topics and exchange pictures recently taken on summer vacations.
>
> 8:00 A.M. They talk about a schedule of priorities for the day.
>
> 8:20 A.M. Wilson (a subordinate) and Richardson talk about some personnel problems, cracking jokes in the process.
>
> 8:45 A.M. Richardson's secretary arrives, and they discuss her new apartment and arrangements for a meeting later in the morning.
>
> 8:55 A.M. Richardson goes to a morning meeting run by one of her subordinates. Thirty people are there, and Richardson reads during the meeting.
>
> 11:05 A.M. Richardson and her subordinates return to the office and discuss a difficult problem. They try to define the problem and outline possible alternatives. She lets the discussion roam away from and back to the topic again and again. Finally, they agree on the next step.

In this example, it is difficult to determine which activities constitute Richardson's planning, coordinating, and decision making. **Behavioural models** state that the actual behaviour of managers appears to be less systematic, more informal, less reflective, more reactive, less well organized, and much less serious than the classical model of management would indicate.

Observers find that managerial behaviour actually has five attributes that differ greatly from the classical description: First, managers perform a great deal of work at an unrelenting pace; studies have found that managers engage in more than 600 different activities each day with no break in pace. Second, managerial activities are fragmented; most activities last for less than nine minutes, and only 10 percent of the activities exceed one hour in duration. Third, managers prefer speculation, hearsay, and gossip; they want current, specific, ad hoc information (printed information often will be too old). Fourth, they prefer oral forms of communication to written forms because oral media provide greater flexibility, require less effort, and bring a faster response. Fifth, managers give high priority to maintaining a diverse and complex web of contacts that acts as an informal information system and helps them execute their personal agendas and short- and long-term goals.

Analyzing managers' day-to-day behaviour, Mintzberg found that it could be classified into 10 **managerial roles**. Managerial roles are expectations of the activities that managers should perform in an organization. Mintzberg found that these managerial roles fell into three categories: interpersonal, informational, and decisional.

Interpersonal Roles.   Managers act as figureheads for the organization when they represent their companies to the outside world and perform symbolic duties, such as giving out employee awards. Managers act as leaders, attempting to motivate, counsel, and support subordinates. Managers also act as liaisons between various organizational levels; within each of these levels, they serve as liaisons among the members of the management team. Managers provide time and favours, which they expect to be returned.

Informational Roles.   Managers act as the nerve centres of their organization, receiving the most concrete, up-to-date information and redistributing it to those who need to be aware of it. Managers are, therefore, information disseminators and spokespersons for their organizations.

Decisional Roles.   Managers make decisions. They act as entrepreneurs by initiating new kinds of activities; they handle disturbances arising in the organization; they allocate resources

---

behavioural models

Descriptions of management based on behavioural scientists' observations of what managers actually do in their jobs.

managerial roles

Expectations of the activities that managers should perform in an organization.

interpersonal roles

Mintzberg's classification for managerial roles where managers act as figureheads and leaders for the organization.

informational roles

Mintzberg's classification for managerial roles where managers act as the nerve centres of their organizations, receiving and disseminating critical information.

decisional roles

Mintzberg's classification for managerial roles where managers initiate activities, handle disturbances, allocate resources, and negotiate conflicts.

TABLE 3.4	MANAGERIAL ROLES AND SUPPORTING INFORMATION SYSTEMS

Role	Behaviour	Support Systems
Interpersonal Roles		
Figurehead	→	None exist
Leader	----Interpersonal--→	None exist
Liaison	→	Electronic communication systems
Informational Roles		
Nerve centre	→	Management information systems, ESS
Disseminator	--Information--→	Mail, office systems
Spokesperson	processing →	Office and professional systems, workstations
Decisional Roles		
Entrepreneur	Decision--→	None exist
Disturbance handler	making--→	None exist
Resource allocator	→	DSS systems
Negotiator	→	None exist

Source: Kenneth C. Laudon and Jane P. Laudon; and Mintzberg, 1971.

to staff members who need them; and they negotiate conflicts and mediate between conflicting groups in the organization.

Table 3.4, based on Mintzberg's role classifications, is one view of where systems can and cannot help managers. The table shows that information systems do not yet contribute to some important areas of management life. These areas will provide great opportunities for future systems efforts.

MANAGERS AND DECISION MAKING

Decision making is often a manager's most challenging role. Information systems have helped managers communicate and distribute information; however, they have provided only limited assistance, to date, for management decision making. Because decision making is an area that system designers have sought most of all to affect (with mixed success), we now turn our attention to this issue.

The Process of Decision Making

A corporate chief executive learns how to use a computer. Some senior managers lack computer knowledge or experience and require systems that are extremely easy to use.

strategic decision making

Determining the long-term objectives, resources, and policies of an organization.

management control

Monitoring how efficiently and effectively resources are used and how well operational units are performing.

operational control

Deciding how to carry out specific tasks specified by upper and middle management and establishing criteria for completion and resource allocation.

knowledge-level decision making

Evaluating new ideas for products, services, ways to communicate new knowledge, and ways to distribute information throughout the organization.

Decision making can be classified by organizational level, corresponding to the strategic, management, knowledge, and operational levels of the organization introduced in Chapter 2. **Strategic decision making** determines the long-term objectives, resources, and policies of the organization. Decision making for **management control** is principally concerned with how efficiently and effectively resources are used and how well operational units are performing. **Operational control** decision making determines how to carry out the specific tasks set forth by strategic and middle-management decision makers. **Knowledge-level decision making** deals with evaluating new ideas for products and services, ways to communicate new knowledge, and ways to distribute information throughout the organization.

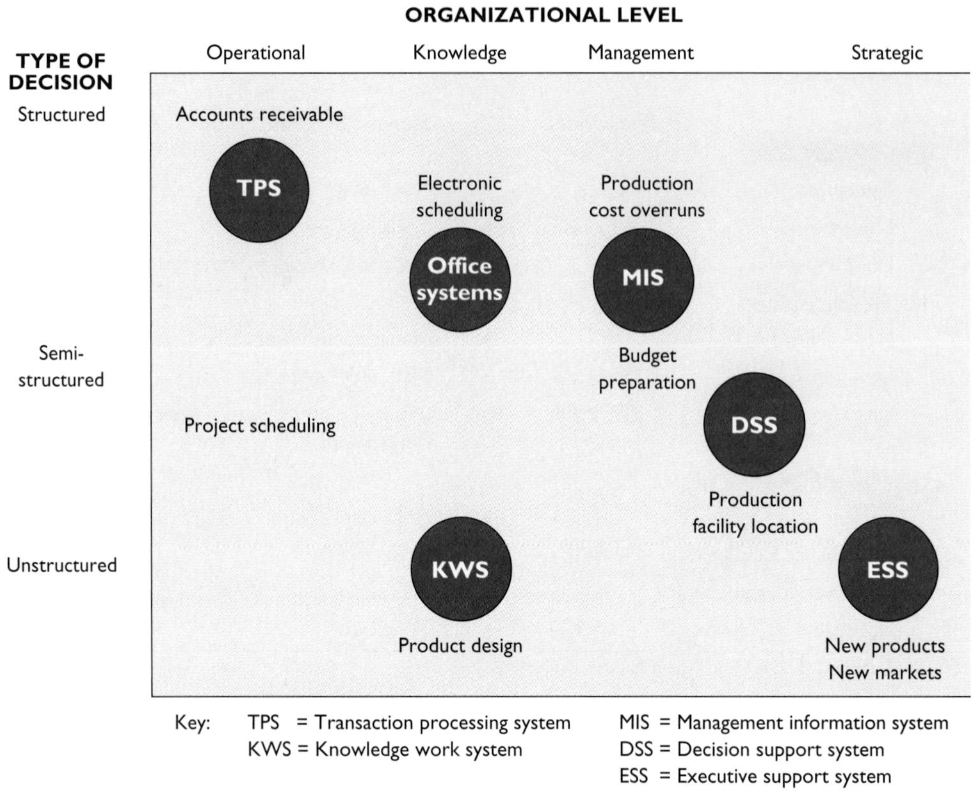

Figure 3.9 Different kinds of information systems at the various organization levels support different types of decisions.

ORGANIZATIONAL LEVEL

	Operational	Knowledge	Management	Strategic

TYPE OF DECISION

Structured — Accounts receivable — **TPS**

Electronic scheduling — **Office systems**

Production cost overruns — **MIS**

Semi-structured — Project scheduling

Budget preparation — **DSS**

Production facility location

Unstructured — **KWS**

Product design

ESS — New products / New markets

Key: TPS = Transaction processing system   MIS = Management information system
        KWS = Knowledge work system   DSS = Decision support system
                                                ESS = Executive support system

unstructured decisions

Nonroutine decisions in which the decision maker must provide judgment, evaluation, and insights into the problem definition; there is no agreed-on procedure for making such decisions.

structured decisions

Decisions that are repetitive, routine, and have a definite procedure for handling them.

intelligence

The first of Simon's four stages of decision making, when the individual collects information to identify problems occurring in the organization.

design

Simon's second stage of decision making, when the individual conceives of possible alternative solutions to a problem.

choice

Simon's third stage of decision making, when the individual selects among the various solution alternatives.

Within each of these levels of decision making, researchers classify decisions as structured and unstructured. **Unstructured decisions** are those in which the decision maker must provide judgment, evaluation, and insights into the problem definition. Each of these decisions is novel, important, and nonroutine, and there is no well-understood or agreed-on procedure for making them (Gorry and Scott-Morton, 1971). **Structured decisions**, by contrast, are repetitive and routine, and they involve a definite procedure for handling them so that they do not have to be treated each time as if they were new. Some decisions are *semistructured*; in these cases, only part of the problem has a clear-cut answer provided by an accepted procedure.

The grid shown in Figure 3.9 combines these two views of decision making. In general, operational control personnel face fairly well structured problems. In contrast, strategic planners tackle highly unstructured problems. Many of the problems knowledge workers encounter are fairly unstructured as well. Nevertheless, each level of the organization contains both structured and unstructured problems.

Stages of Decision Making

Making decisions consists of several different activities. Simon (1960) described four different stages in decision making: intelligence, design, choice, and implementation.

Intelligence consists of identifying and understanding the problems occurring in the organization—why the problem exists, where, and with what effects. Traditional management information systems (MIS) that deliver a wide variety of detailed information can help identify problems, especially if the systems report exceptions.

During solution **design**, the individual designs possible solutions to the problems. Smaller decision support systems (DSS) are ideal in this stage of decision making because they operate on simple models, can be developed quickly, and can be operated with limited data.

Choice consists of choosing among solution alternatives. Here, the decision maker might need a larger DSS to develop more extensive data on a variety of alternatives and complex models or data analysis tools to account for all of the costs, consequences, and opportunities.

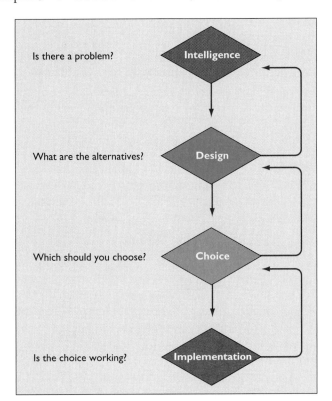

During solution **implementation**, when the decision is put into effect, managers can use a reporting system that delivers routine reports on the progress of a specific solution. Support systems can range from full-blown MIS to much smaller systems, as well as project-planning software operating on personal computers.

In general, the stages of decision making do not necessarily follow a linear path. Think again about the decision you made to attend a specific college. At any point in the decision making process, you may have to loop back to a previous stage (see Figure 3.10). For instance, one can often come up with several designs but may not be certain about whether a specific design meets the requirements for the particular problem. This situation requires additional intelligence work. Alternatively, one can be in the process of implementing a decision, only to discover that it is not working. In such a case, one is forced to repeat the design or choice stage.

Models of Decision Making

A number of models attempt to describe how people make decisions. Some of these models focus on individual decision making, while others focus on decision making in groups.

Individual models of decision making assume that human beings are in some sense rational. The **rational model** of human behaviour is premised on the idea that people engage in basically consistent, rational, value-maximizing calculations. According to this model, an individual identifies goals, ranks all possible alternative actions by their contributions to those goals, and chooses the alternative that contributes most to those goals.

Critics of the rational model explain that, in fact, people cannot specify all of the alternatives and that most individuals do not have singular goals and so are unable to rank all alternatives and consequences. Many decisions are so complex that calculating the choice (even if done by computer) is virtually impossible. Instead of searching through all alternatives, people tend to choose the first available alternative that moves them toward their ultimate goal. In making policy decisions, people choose policies most like the previous policy (Lindblom, 1959). Finally, some scholars point out that decision making is a continuous process in which final decisions are always being modified.

Other research has found that humans differ in how they maximize their values and in the frames of reference they use to interpret information and make choices. Tversky and

implementation

Simon's final stage of decision making, when the individual puts the decision into effect and reports on the progress of the solution.

rational model

Model of human behaviour based on the belief that people, organizations, and nations engage in basically consistent, value-maximizing calculations.

Kahneman showed that humans have built-in biases that can distort decision making. People can be manipulated into choosing alternatives that they might otherwise reject simply by changing the frame of reference (Tversky and Kahneman, 1981).

cognitive style

Underlying personality dispositions toward the treatment of information, selection of alternatives, and evaluation of consequences.

Cognitive style describes underlying personality dispositions toward the treatment of information, the selection of alternatives, and the evaluation of consequences. **Systematic decision makers** approach a problem by structuring it in terms of some formal method. They evaluate and gather information in terms of their structured method. **Intuitive decision makers** approach a problem with multiple methods, using trial and error to find a solution. They tend not to structure information gathering or evaluation (McKenney and Keen, 1974). Neither style is considered superior to the other, and each may be advantageous in certain decision situations. While structured problems with clearcut issues can be best handled by "thinking first" in logical steps, others requiring novel, creative solutions may be best solved through a flash of intuition or by trying out several courses of action to see what works (Mintzberg and Westley, 2001).

systematic decision makers

Cognitive style that describes people who approach a problem by structuring it in terms of some formal method.

intuitive decision makers

Cognitive style that describes people who approach a problem with multiple methods in an unstructured manner, using trial and error to find a solution.

Decision making often is not performed by a single individual but by entire groups or organizations. **Organizational models of decision making** take into account the structural and political characteristics of an organization. Bureaucratic, political, and even "garbage can" models have been proposed to describe how decision making takes place in organizations.

organizational models of decision making

Models of decision making that take into account the structural and political characteristics of an organization.

According to **bureaucratic models of decision making**, an organization's most important goal is the preservation of the organization itself. The reduction of uncertainty is another major goal. Policy tends to be incremental, only marginally different from the past because radical policy departures involve too much uncertainty. These models depict organizations generally as not "choosing" or "deciding" in a rational sense. Rather, according to bureaucratic models, whatever organizations do is the result of standard operating procedures (SOPs) honed over years of active use.

bureaucratic models of decision making

Models of decision making where decisions are shaped by the organization's standard operating procedures (SOPs).

Organizations rarely change their SOPs because they may have to change personnel and incur risks (who knows if the new techniques work better than the old ones?). Although senior management and leaders are hired to coordinate and lead the organization, they are effectively trapped by the organization's standard solutions. Some organizations do, of course, change; they learn new ways of behaving; and they can be led. But all of these changes require a long time. Look around, and you will find many organizations doing pretty much what they did 10, 20, or even 30 years ago.

political models of decision making

Models of decision making where decisions result from competition and bargaining among the organization's interest groups and key leaders.

In **political models of decision making**, what an organization does is a result of political bargains struck among key leaders and interest groups. Organizations do not come up with "solutions" that are "chosen" to solve some "problem." They come up with compromises that reflect the conflicts, the major stakeholders, the diverse interests, the unequal power, and the confusion that constitute politics.

"garbage can" model

Model of decision making that states that organizations are not rational and that decisions are solutions that become attached to problems for accidental reasons.

A theory of decision making, called the **"garbage can" model**, states that organizations are not rational. Decision making is largely accidental and is the product of a stream of solutions, problems, and situations that are randomly associated. This model could explain why organizations sometimes apply the wrong solutions to the wrong problems. The Exxon Corporation's delayed response to the 1989 Alaska oil spill is an example. Within an hour after the Exxon tanker Valdez ran aground in Alaska's Prince William Sound on March 29, 1989, workers were preparing emergency equipment; however, the aid was not dispatched. Instead of sending out emergency crews, the Alyeska Pipeline Service Company (which was responsible for initially responding to oil spill emergencies) sent the crews home. The first full emergency crew did not arrive at the spill site until at least 14 hours after the shipwreck, by which time the oil had spread beyond effective control. Yet, enough equipment and personnel had been available to respond effectively. Much of the 10 million gallons of oil fouling the Alaska shoreline in the worst tanker spill in American history could have been confined had Alyeska acted more decisively.

IMPLICATIONS FOR THE DESIGN AND UNDERSTANDING OF INFORMATION SYSTEMS

In order to deliver genuine benefits, information systems must be developed with a clear understanding of the organization in which they will reside and exactly how they can contribute to managerial decision making. In our experience, the central organizational factors to consider when planning a new system are as follows:

- The environment in which the organization must function.
- The structure of the organization: hierarchy, specialization, and standard operating procedures.
- The organization's culture and politics.
- The type of organization and its style of leadership.
- The principal interest groups affected by the system and the attitudes of workers who will be using the system.
- The kinds of tasks, decisions, and business processes that the information system is designed to assist.

Systems should be developed to support both group and organizational decision making. Information systems developers should design systems that have the following characteristics:

- They are flexible and provide many options for handling data and evaluating information.
- They are capable of supporting a variety of styles, skills, and knowledge as well as keeping track of many alternatives and consequences.
- They are sensitive to the organization's bureaucratic and political requirements.

3.4 INFORMATION SYSTEMS AND BUSINESS STRATEGY

Certain types of information systems have become especially critical to firms' long-term prosperity and survival. These systems, which are powerful tools for staying ahead of the competition, are called *strategic information systems.*

WHAT IS A STRATEGIC INFORMATION SYSTEM?

Strategic information systems change the goals, operations, products, services, or environmental relationships of organizations to help them gain an edge over competitors. Systems that have these effects may even change the business of organizations. For instance, The Bank of Montreal transformed its core business from traditional banking services, such as customer chequing and savings accounts and loans, to electronic commerce, money management, and financial information services, providing online access to individuals and businesses to handle their financial record keeping, cash management, and investment information and transactions. The Bank of Montreal provides online services that include point-of-sale automobile financing; recruiting and hiring their own employees; consumer financing for small- to medium-sized businesses, permitting the companies' customers to finance purchase of their products and services immediately; and wireless services for cellular phone– and personal digital assistant–using bank customers. The Bank of Montreal also developed the first *virtual bank* in Canada (Ray, 2000; Baroudi, 2000).

Strategic information systems should be distinguished from strategic-level systems for senior managers that focus on long-term, decision making problems. Strategic information systems can be used at all organizational levels and are more far reaching and deep rooted than the other kinds of systems we have described. Strategic information systems profoundly alter the way a firm conducts its business or the very business of the firm itself. As we will see, organizations may need to change their internal operations and relationships with customers and suppliers in order to take advantage of new information technology.

Traditional models of strategy are being modified to accommodate the impact of digital firms and new information flows. Before the emergence of the digital firm, business strategy emphasized competing head-to-head against other firms in the same marketplace. Today, the emphasis is increasingly on exploring, identifying, and occupying new market niches before competitors; understanding the customer value chain better; and learning faster and more deeply than competitors.

strategic information systems

Computer systems at any level of the organization that change goals, operations, products, services, or environmental relationships to help the organization gain a competitive advantage.

There is generally no single all-encompassing strategic system, but, instead, there are a number of systems operating at different levels of strategy—the business, firm, and industry levels. For each level of business strategy, there are strategic uses of systems. And for each level of business strategy, there is an appropriate model used for analysis.

BUSINESS-LEVEL STRATEGY AND THE VALUE CHAIN MODEL

At the business level of strategy, the key question is, "How can we compete effectively in this particular market?" The market might be light bulbs, utility vehicles, or cable television. The most common generic strategies at this level are (1) to become the low-cost producer, (2) to differentiate the product or service, and/or (3) to change the scope of competition by either enlarging the market to include global markets or narrowing the market by focusing on small niches not well served by competitors. Digital firms provide new capabilities for supporting business-level strategy by managing the supply chain, building efficient customer "sense and response" systems, and participating in "value webs" to deliver new products and services to market.

Leveraging Technology in the Value Chain

At the business level, the most common analytical tool is value chain analysis. The **value chain model** highlights specific activities in the business where competitive strategies can be best applied (Porter, 1985) and where information systems are most likely to have a strategic impact. The value chain model identifies specific, critical leverage points where a firm can use information technology most effectively to enhance its competitive position. Exactly where can it obtain the greatest benefit from strategic information systems? What specific activities can be used to create new products and services, enhance market penetration, lock in customers and suppliers, and lower operational costs? The value chain model views the firm as a series or "chain" of basic activities that add a margin of value to a firm's products or services. These activities can be categorized as either primary activities or support activities.

Primary activities are most directly related to the production and distribution of the firm's products and services that create value for the customer. Primary activities include inbound logistics, operations, outbound logistics, sales and marketing, and service. Inbound logistics include receiving and storing materials for distribution to production. Operations transforms inputs into finished products. Outbound logistics entail storing and distributing finished products. Sales and marketing includes promoting and selling the firm's products. The service activity includes maintenance and repair of the firm's goods and services. **Support activities** make the delivery of the primary activities possible and consist of organization infrastructure (administration and management), human resources (employee recruiting, hiring, and training), technology (improving products and the production process), and procurement (purchasing input).

Organizations have competitive advantage when they provide more value to their customers or when they provide the same value to customers at a lower price. An information system could have a strategic impact if it helped the firm provide products or services at a lower cost than its competitors could or if it provided products and services at the same cost as its competitors could but with greater value. The activities that add the most value to products and services depend on the features of each particular firm.

The firm's value chain can be linked to the value chains of its other partners, including suppliers, distributors, and customers. Figure 3.11 illustrates the activities of the firm value chain and the industry value chain, showing examples of strategic information systems that could be developed to make each of the value activities more cost effective. A firm can achieve a strategic advantage by providing value not only through its internal value chain processes but also through powerful, efficient ties to industry value partners.

Digitally enabled networks can be used to purchase supplies and also to closely coordinate production of many independent firms. For instance, the Italian casual wear company Benetton uses subcontractors and independent firms for labour-intensive production processes, such as tailoring, finishing, and ironing, while maintaining control of design, procurement, marketing, and distribution. Benetton uses computer networks to provide independent businesses and foreign production centres with production specifications so

---

value chain model

Model that highlights the primary or support activities that add a margin of value to a firm's products or services and shows where information systems can best be applied to achieve a competitive advantage.

primary activities

Activities most directly related to the production and distribution of a firm's products or services.

support activities

Activities that make the delivery of a firm's primary activities possible; consist of the organization's infrastructure, human resources, technology, and procurement.

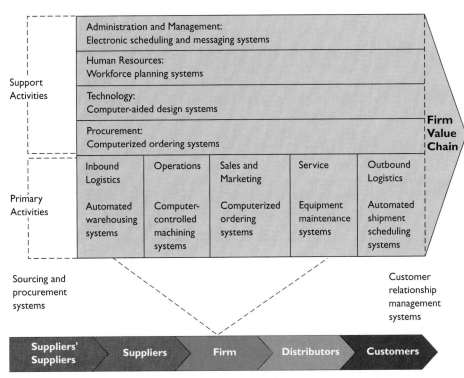

Figure 3.11 The firm value chain and the industry value chain. Illustrated are various examples of strategic information systems for the primary and support activities of a firm and its value partners that would add a margin of value to a firm's products or services.

that they can efficiently produce the items needed by Benetton's retail outlets (Camuffo, Romano and Vinelli, 2001).

Internet technology has made it possible to extend the value chain so that it ties together all of the firm's suppliers, business partners, and customers into a value web. A **value web** is a collection of independent firms that use information technology to coordinate their value chains to collectively produce a product or service for a market. It is more customer driven and operates in less linear fashion than does the traditional value chain. Figure 3.12 shows

value web

Customer-driven network of independent firms that use information technology to coordinate their value chains to collectively produce a product or service for a market.

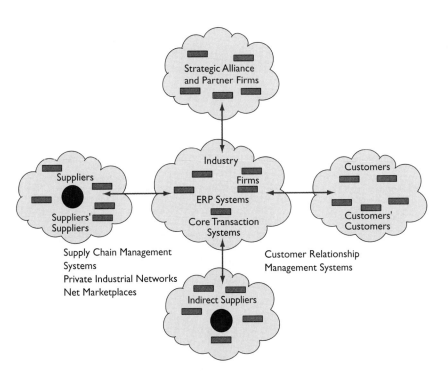

Figure 3.12 The value web. The value web is a networked business ecosystem that can synchronize the value chains of business partners within an industry to rapidly respond to changes in supply and demand.

that this value web functions like a dynamic business ecosystem, synchronizing the business processes of customers, suppliers, and trading partners among different companies in an industry or related industries. These value webs are flexible and adaptive to changes in supply and demand. Relationships can be bundled or unbundled in response to changing market conditions. A company can use its value web to maintain longstanding relationships with many customers over long periods or to respond immediately to individual customer transactions. Firms can accelerate time to market and to customers by optimizing their value web relationships to make quick decisions on who can deliver the required products or services at the right price and to the right location.

Businesses should try to develop strategic information systems for both the internal and external value chain activities that add the most value. A strategic analysis might, for example, identify sales and marketing activities where information systems could provide the greatest boost. The analysis might recommend a system to reduce marketing costs by targeting marketing campaigns more efficiently or by providing information for developing products more finely attuned to a firm's target market. A series of systems, including some linked to systems of other value partners, might be required to create a strategic advantage.

Value chains and value webs are not static. From time to time, they may have to be redesigned to keep pace with changes in the competitive landscape (Fine et al., 2002). Companies may need to reorganize and reshape their structural, financial, and human assets and recast systems to tap new sources of value.

We now show how information technology at the business level helps the firm reduce costs, differentiate products, and serve new markets.

Information System Products and Services

product differentiation

Competitive strategy for creating brand loyalty by developing new and unique products and services that are not easily duplicated by competitors.

Firms can use information systems to create unique new products and services that can be easily distinguished from those of competitors. Strategic information systems for **product differentiation** can prevent the competition from responding in kind so that firms with differentiated products and services no longer have to compete on the basis of cost.

Many of these information technology–based products and services have been created by financial institutions. Citibank developed ATMs and bank debit cards in 1977. Citibank became, at one time, the largest bank in the United States. Citibank ATMs were so successful that its competitors were forced to counterstrike with their own ATM systems. Citibank, Bank of Montreal, and others have continued to innovate by providing online electronic banking services so that customers can do most of their banking transactions with home computers linked to proprietary networks or the Internet. These banks have recently launched new account aggregation services that let customers view all of their accounts, including their credit cards, investments, online travel rewards, and even accounts from competing banks, from a single online source. Some companies, such as ING, have used the Web to set up "virtual banks" offering a full array of banking services without any physical branches. (Customers mail in their deposits and use designated ATMs to obtain cash.)

Computerized reservation systems, such as American Airlines' SABRE system, started out as a powerful source of product differentiation for the airline and travel industries. These traditional reservation systems are now being challenged by new travel services where consumers can make their own airline, hotel, and car reservations directly on the Web, bypassing travel agents and other intermediaries. The Window on Management describes how competitive strategy is changing in this industry.

Manufacturers and retailers are starting to use information systems to create products and services that are custom tailored to fit the precise specifications of individual customers. Dell Computer Corporation sells directly to customers using assemble-to-order manufacturing. Individuals, businesses, and government agencies can buy computers directly from Dell, customized with the exact features and components they need. They can place their orders directly using a toll-free telephone number or Dell's Web site. Once Dell's production control receives an order, it directs an assembly plant to assemble the computer on the basis of the configuration specified by the customer using components from an on-site warehouse (see Figure 3.13). Chapter 1 describes other instances in which information technology is creating customized products and services while retaining the cost efficiencies of mass-production techniques. These assemble-to-order strategies require careful coordination of

DUELLING TRAVEL SITES

Travel is a gigantic business, generating bookings worth $54 billion in 2001 in Canada alone. Travel agents have traditionally been paid by the providers, including airlines, hotels, and car rentals. This cost to providers has risen about 7 percent annually over the last decade so that airlines pay $18 to $25 per ticket, and they are desperate to lower those costs. The Internet has now made it simple for customers to bypass agents and handle travel transactions themselves. In 2000, about 8 percent of all travel reservations in Canada were made using the Internet, and that share could eventually grow to 50 percent or more.

The struggle for the online travel business has taken a new twist with the entry of Henry Silverman of Cendant and Barry Diller of Expedia. They have different visions and different strategies on how to use Internet technology and information systems to build a profitable business.

Silverman built Hospitality Franchise Systems (HFS), the precursor of Cendant, into a powerhouse with interests in lodging (such as Ramada, Travelodge, and Howard Johnson), timeshares (RCI's 60 000 units), and car rentals (Avis). In June 2001, he bought Galileo International, the second largest reservations booking system used by travel agents (after SABRE). Silverman's vision is to transform Galileo from a transaction system into one that could help airlines market their tickets better by using the existing network of travel agents to sell special packaged trips. Galileo could help airlines, hotels, car-rental companies, and tours assemble special deals that the system would broadcast to travel agents. (Cendant-owned or -controlled brands could be emphasized in such promotions.) By expanding the use of Galileo, which receives a transaction fee for each reservation booked on the system, Cendant could expect an earnings growth of 10 percent from this part of its business.

To hedge his bets on the Internet, Silverman also developed his own online travel agency called Trip.com, which he inherited with Galileo, and purchased Cheap Tickets, a top-10 online travel site featuring bargain airline tickets. Silverman's vision includes personalizing these sites so that travellers could sort vacation destinations on the basis of cost, schedule, and even "personality" (sports, family, and so on).

Analysts caution that Silverman is backing the travel agents, which are looking more like "industry dinosaurs," and that Web travel sites, such as Expedia, Orbitz, and Travelocity, all have great headstarts over Cendant. In addition to eliminating travel agent commissions, airlines are trying to cut the transaction fee they pay to reservation systems, such as Galileo, which, they claim, use expensive and out-of-date technology. In 2001, Galileo's share of airline bookings fell to 26 percent, compared with 31 percent in 1998.

Barry Diller has been chairman of Paramount Pictures and a founder of the Fox Broadcasting TV network and the Home Shopping Network (HSN). Using HSN as a base, he obtained majority ownership of cable television and film studio companies, as well as Ticketmaster, Hotels.com (a hotel room broker), CitySearch.com, and Match.com (a dating service). Early in 2002, he purchased a controlling stake in Expedia, the number-one online travel site from Microsoft. Diller's vision is an online emporium where travellers will be able to fulfill all their travel arrangement needs. Diller believes he can use the Internet and other media to package travel in ways that traditional travel agencies and booking systems cannot. Moreover, he plans to use Expedia to create a 24-hour TV channel dedicated to selling travel packages based on his properties. Consumers will be able to book a flight, a hotel room, or tickets to a game, obtain restaurant reservations, and even make a date, all at the same time using his Web site or a toll-free telephone number.

To Think About: Describe the problems traditional and online travel agents face, and then describe the Cendant and Expedia strategies. Which of the two companies do you think is most likely to succeed? Why?

Sources: Motoko Rich and Julia Angwin, "Two Tycoons Make Unlikely Bets on the Turbulent Travel Industry," *Wall Street Journal*, May 3, 2002; Saul Hansell, "For Cendant's Travel Business, Ride Is Bumpier than Expected," *New York Times*, July 8, 2002; and Motoko Rich, "Trip.com Starts Tough Trek to Top Spot in Online Travel," *Wall Street Journal*, April 29, 2002.

customer requirements with production and flexible processes throughout the firm's value chain (Holweg and Pil, 2001).

Systems to Focus on Market Niche

Businesses can create new market niches by identifying a specific target for a product or service that it can serve in a superior manner. Through **focused differentiation**, the firm can provide a specialized product or service for this narrow target market better than its competitors can.

An information system can give companies a competitive advantage by producing data for finely tuned sales and marketing techniques. These systems treat existing information as a resource that the organization can "mine" to increase profitability and market penetration. Information systems enable companies to finely analyze customer buying patterns, tastes, and preferences so that they efficiently pitch advertising and marketing campaigns to smaller and smaller target markets.

focused differentiation

Competitive strategy for developing new market niches for specialized products or services where a business can compete in the target area better than its competitors can.

Figure 3.13 At Dell Canada's Web site, customers can select the options they want and order their computer custom built to these specifications. Dell's assemble-to-order system is a major source of competitive advantage.

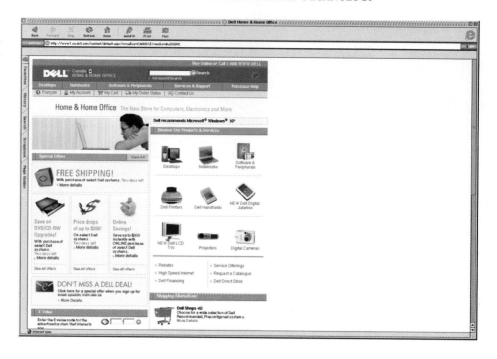

The data come from a range of sources: credit card transactions, demographic data, purchase data from checkout counter scanners at supermarkets and retail stores, and data collected when people access and interact with Web sites. Sophisticated software tools can find patterns in these large pools of data and infer rules from them that can be used to guide decision making. Analysis of the data can drive one-to-one marketing, where personal messages can be created on the basis of individualized preferences.

For example, Hudson's Bay Company continually analyzes purchase data from its credit card users to target these customers with special promotions. The company might mail to customers who purchase a television a maintenance contract form and a coupon for a reduced price on a DVD player. Yahoo.com captures and analyzes data generated when people visit its Web site. It uses this information to target users with personalized content and advertising geared to their interests, such as auto purchases or personal finance. The Canadian Imperial Bank of Commerce (CIBC) analyzes its customer account data to identify its most profitable customers so that it can offer them special services. The level of fine-grained customization provided by these data analysis systems parallels that for mass customization described in Chapter 1. More examples of customer data analysis can be found in Chapters 7 and 14.

The cost of acquiring a new customer has been estimated to be five times that of retaining an existing customer. By carefully examining transactions of customer purchases and activities, firms can identify profitable customers and win more of their business. Likewise, companies can use these data to identify nonprofitable customers. Companies that skillfully use customer data will focus on identifying their most valued customers and use data from a variety of sources to understand their needs (Reinartz and Kumar, 2002; Davenport, Harris, and Kohli, 2001; Clemons and Weber, 1994).

Supply Chain Management and Efficient Customer Response Systems

Digital firms have the capabilities to go far beyond traditional strategic systems for taking advantage of digital links with other organizations. A powerful business-level strategy available to digital firms involves linking the value chains of vendors and suppliers to the firm's value chain. Integration of value chains can be carried further by linking the customer's value chain to the firm's value chain in an "efficient customer response system." Firms using systems to link with customers and suppliers can reduce their inventory costs while responding rapidly to customer demands.

By keeping prices low and shelves well stocked using a legendary inventory replenishment system, Wal-Mart has become the leading retail business in the United States. Wal-Mart's "continuous replenishment system" sends orders for new merchandise directly to suppliers as soon as consumers pay for their purchases at the cash register. Point-of-sale terminals record the bar code of each item passing the checkout counter and send a purchase transaction directly to a central computer at Wal-Mart headquarters. The computer collects the orders from all Wal-Mart stores and transmits them to suppliers. Suppliers can also access Wal-Mart's sales and inventory data using Web technology. Because the system can replenish inventory with lightning speed, Wal-Mart does not need to spend much money on maintaining large inventories of goods in its own warehouses. The system also allows Wal-Mart to adjust purchases of store items to meet customer demands. Competitors, such as Sears, have been

Wal-Mart's continuous inventory replenishment system uses sales data captured at the checkout counter to transmit orders to restock merchandise directly to its suppliers. The system enables Wal-Mart to keep costs low while fine-tuning its merchandise to meet customer demands.

spending 24.9 percent of sales on overhead. But by using systems to keep operating costs low, Wal-Mart pays only 16.6 percent of sales revenue for overhead. (Operating costs average 20.7 percent of sales in the retail industry.)

Wal-Mart's continuous replenishment system is an example of efficient supply chain management, which we introduced in Chapter 2. Supply chain management systems can not only lower inventory costs, but they can also deliver the product or service more rapidly to the customer. Supply chain management can, thus, be used to create **efficient customer response systems** that respond to customer demands more efficiently. An efficient customer response system directly links consumer behaviour back to distribution, production, and supply chains. Wal-Mart's continuous replenishment system provides this type of efficient customer response. Dell Computer Corporation's assemble-to-order system, described earlier, is another example of an efficient customer response system.

The convenience and ease of using these information systems raise **switching costs** (the cost of switching from one product to a competing product), which discourages customers from going to competitors. For example, Source Medical is the Canadian arm of Allegiance Corporation, which began as American Health Corporation and later became Baxter International, eventually becoming Allegiance Corporation, a division of Cardinal Health. Baxter's original "stockless inventory" and ordering system, still in use by Allegiance and Source Medical, uses supply chain management to create an efficient customer response system. Participating hospitals become unwilling to switch to another supplier because of the system's convenience and low cost. Source Medical is the largest hospital supplier in Canada. When hospitals want to place an order, they do not need to call a salesperson or send a purchase order—they simply use a PC with Internet access on-site to order from the full Source Medical supply catalogue. The system generates shipping, billing, invoicing, and inventory information, and the online response provides customers with an estimated delivery date. With nine regional customer-facing distribution warehouses from Vancouver to St. John's, along with local warehousing closer to their customers, Source Medical can make daily deliveries of its products, often within hours of receiving an order.

Source Medical delivery personnel no longer drop off their cartons at loading docks to be placed in hospital storerooms. Instead, they deliver orders directly to the hospital corridors, dropping them at nursing stations, operating rooms, and supply closets. This has created in effect a "stockless inventory," with Source Medical serving as the hospitals' warehouse.

Figure 3.14 compares stockless inventory with the just-in-time supply method and traditional inventory practices. While just-in-time supply allows customers to reduce their inventories by ordering only enough material for a few days' inventory, stockless inventory allows them to eliminate their inventories entirely. All inventory responsibilities shift to the distributor, which manages the supply flow. The stockless inventory is a powerful instrument for "locking in" customers, thus giving the supplier a decided competitive advantage.

efficient customer response system

System that directly links consumer behaviour back to distribution, production, and supply chains.

switching costs

The expense a customer or company incurs in lost time and resources when changing from one supplier or system to a competing supplier or system.

BAXTER   **CUSTOMERS**

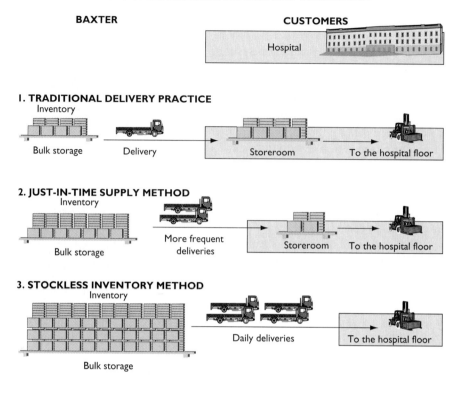

Figure 3.14 Stockless inventory compared with traditional and just-in-time supply methods. The just-in-time supply method reduces inventory requirements of the customer, while stockless inventory allows the customer to eliminate inventories entirely. Deliveries are made daily, sometimes directly to the departments that need the supplies.

Information systems can also raise switching costs by making product support, service, and other interactions with customers more convenient and reliable (Vandenbosch and Dawar, 2002; Chen and Hitt, 2002).

Supply chain management and efficient customer response systems are two examples of how emerging digital firms can engage in business strategies not available to traditional firms. Both types of systems require network-based information technology infrastructure investment and software competence to make customer and supply chain data flow seamlessly among different organizations. Both types of strategies have greatly enhanced the efficiency of individual firms and the Canadian economy as a whole by moving toward a *demand-pull production system,* and away from the *traditional supply-push economic system,* in which factories were managed on the basis of 12-month official plans, rather than on near-instantaneous customer purchase information. Figure 3.15 illustrates the relationships between supply chain management, efficient customer response, and the various business-level strategies.

FIRM-LEVEL STRATEGY AND INFORMATION TECHNOLOGY

A business firm is typically a collection of businesses. Often, the firm is organized financially as a collection of strategic business units, and the returns to the firm are directly tied to strategic business unit performance. Information systems can improve the overall performance of these business units by promoting synergies and core competencies. The idea driving synergies is that when some units can be used as inputs to other units, or two organizations can pool markets and expertise, these relationships can lower costs and generate profits. Recent mergers, such as those of Air Canada and Canadian Airlines, Rogers and Cantel, and the Toronto Dominion Bank and Canada Trust, occurred precisely for this purpose. One use of information technology in these synergy situations is to tie together the operations of disparate business units so that they can act as a whole. These systems should lower retailing costs, increase customer access to new financial products, and speed up the process of marketing new instruments (see Figure 3.15).

Enhancing Core Competencies

A second concept for firm-level strategy involves the notion of "core competency." The argument is that the performance of all business units can increase insofar as these business units

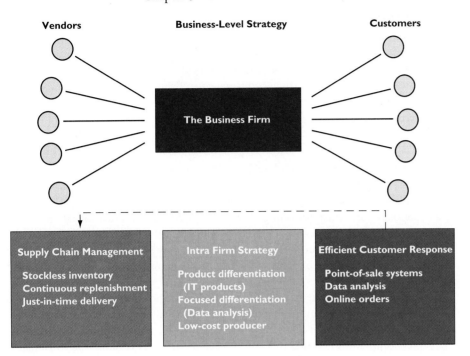

Figure 3.15 Business-level strategy. Efficient customer response and supply chain management systems are often interrelated, helping firms "lock in" customers and suppliers while lowering operating costs. Other types of systems can be used to support product differentiation, focused differentiation, and low-cost producer strategies.

develop or create a central core of competencies. A **core competency** is an activity at which a firm is a world-class leader. Core competencies may involve being the world's best miniature parts designer, the best package delivery service, or the best thin-film manufacturer. In general, a core competency relies on knowledge that is gained over many years of experience and a first-class research organization or simply key people who follow the literature and stay abreast of new external knowledge.

core competency

Activity at which a firm excels as a world-class leader.

Any information system that encourages the sharing of knowledge across business units enhances competency. These systems might encourage or enhance existing competencies and help employees become aware of new external knowledge; these systems might also help a business leverage existing competencies to related markets.

INDUSTRY-LEVEL STRATEGY AND INFORMATION SYSTEMS: COMPETITIVE FORCES AND NETWORK ECONOMICS

Firms together comprise an industry, such as the automotive, telephone, television broadcasting, and forest products industries, to name a few. The key strategic question at this level of analysis is, "How and when should we compete with, as opposed to cooperate with, others in the industry?" While most strategic analyses emphasize competition, a great deal of money can be made by cooperating with other firms in the same industry or firms in related industries. For instance, firms can cooperate to develop industry standards in a number of areas; they can cooperate by working together to build customer awareness and by working collectively with suppliers to lower costs (Shapiro and Varian, 1999). The three principal concepts for analyzing strategy at the industry level are information partnerships, the competitive forces model, and network economics.

Information Partnerships

Firms can form information partnerships and even link their information systems to achieve unique synergies. In an **information partnership**, both companies can join forces without actually merging by sharing information (Konsynski and McFarlan, 1990). Air Canada has an arrangement with Canadian Imperial Bank of Commerce (CIBC) to award one mile in its frequent flyer program for every dollar spent using a CIBC Aerogold credit card. Air Canada benefits from increased customer loyalty, and CIBC gains new credit card subscriptions and a highly creditworthy customer base for cross-marketing. Air Canada has also allied with

information partnership

Cooperative alliance formed between two or more corporations for the purpose of sharing information to gain strategic advantage.

Primus Canada, awarding five frequent flyer miles for each dollar of long-distance billing when a customer spends over $15 a month.

These partnerships help firms gain access to new customers, creating new opportunities for cross-selling and targeting products. Companies that have been traditional competitors may find these alliances to be mutually advantageous. Baxter Healthcare International offers its customers medical supplies from competitors as well as office supplies through its electronic ordering channel.

The Competitive Forces Model

competitive forces model

Model used to describe the interaction of external influences, specifically threats and opportunities, that affect an organization's strategy and ability to compete.

In Porter's **competitive forces model**, which is illustrated in Figure 3.16, a firm faces a number of external threats and opportunities: the threat of new entrants into its market, the pressure from substitute products or services, the bargaining power of customers, the bargaining power of suppliers, and the positioning of traditional industry competitors (Porter, 1985).

Competitive advantage can be achieved by enhancing the firm's ability to deal with customers, suppliers, substitute products and services, and new entrants to its market, which, in turn, may change the balance of power between a firm and other competitors in the industry in the firm's favour.

How can information systems be used to achieve strategic advantage at the industry level? By working with other firms, industry participants can use information technology to develop industry-wide standards for exchanging information or business transactions electronically (see Chapters 6, 8, and 9), which force all market participants to subscribe to similar standards. Earlier, we described how firms can benefit from value webs with complementary firms in the industry. These efforts increase efficiency at the industry level as well as the business level, making product substitution less likely and perhaps raising entry costs, thus discouraging new entrants. Also, industry members can build industry-wide, information technology-supported consortia, symposia, and communications networks to coordinate activities concerning government agencies, foreign competition, and competing industries.

An example of this type of industry-level cooperation can be found in Covisint, an electronic marketplace shared by the major automobile manufacturers for procurement of auto parts. Although General Motors, Ford, and DaimlerChrysler aggressively compete on such factors as design, service, quality, and price, they can raise the industry's productivity by working together to create an integrated supply chain. Covisint enables all manufacturers and suppliers to trade on a single Internet site, sparing manufacturers the cost of setting up their own Web-based marketplaces.

In the digital firm era, the competitive forces model needs modification. The traditional Porter model assumes a relatively static industry environment; relatively clearcut industry boundaries; and a relatively stable set of suppliers, substitutes, and customers. Instead of participating in a single industry, today's firms are much more aware that they participate in "industry sets"—multiple related industries that consumers can choose from to obtain a

Figure 3.16 Porter's competitive forces model. There are various forces that affect an organization's ability to compete and, therefore, greatly influence a firm's business strategy. There are threats from new market entrants and from substitute products and services. Customers and suppliers wield bargaining power. Traditional competitors constantly adapt their strategies to maintain their market positioning.

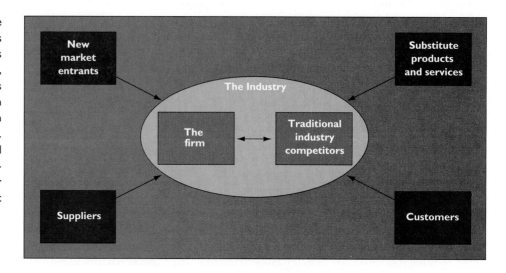

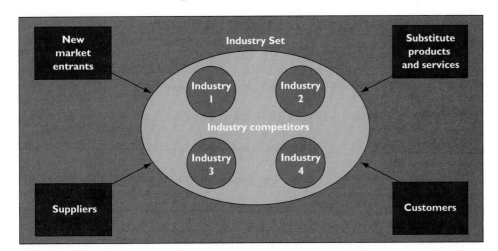

Figure 3.17 The new competitive forces model. The digital firm era requires a more dynamic view of the boundaries between firms, customers, and suppliers, with competition occurring among industry sets.

product or service (see Figure 3.17). For instance, automobile companies compete against other automobile companies in the "auto industry," but they also compete against many other industries in the "transportation industry set," such as railway, air, and bus transportation companies. Success or failure for a single auto company may depend on the success or failure of various other industries. Colleges may think they are in competition with other traditional colleges, but in fact, they are in competition with electronic distance learning universities, publishing companies that have created online college courses, and private training firms that offer technical certificates—all of which are members of a much larger "education industry set." In the digital firm era, we can expect greater emphasis on building strategies to compete and cooperate with other members of a firm's industry set.

Nevertheless, the competitive forces model remains a valid model for analyzing strategy, even considering the impact of the Internet. Internet technology has affected industry structure by providing technologies that make it easier for rivals to compete on price alone and for new competitors to enter the market. Profits have also been dampened because the Internet dramatically increases the information available to customers for comparison shopping, thus raising their bargaining power. Although the Internet can provide benefits, such as new channels to customers and new operating efficiencies, firms cannot achieve competitive advantage unless they have carefully integrated Internet initiatives into their overall strategy and operations. In the age of the Internet, the traditional competitive forces are still at work, but competitive rivalry has become much more intense (Porter, 2001).

Network Economics

A third strategic concept useful at the industry level is **network economics**. In traditional economics—the economics of factories and agriculture—production experiences diminishing returns. The more any given resource is applied to production, the lower the marginal gain in output, until a point is reached where the additional inputs produce no additional outputs. This is the law of diminishing returns, and it is the foundation for most of modern economics.

In some situations, the law of diminishing returns does not work. For instance, in a network, the marginal costs of adding another participant are about zero, while the marginal gain can be much larger. The larger the number of subscribers in a telephone system or the Internet, the greater is the value to all participants. It is no more expensive to operate a television station with 1000 subscribers than with 10 million subscribers. And the value of a community of people grows with size, while the cost of adding new members is inconsequential.

From this network economics perspective, information technology can be strategically useful. Internet sites can be used by firms to build "communities of users"—like-minded customers who want to share their experiences. This can build customer loyalty and enjoyment and build unique ties to customers. Canoe.ca and iVillage, an online community for women, are examples. Both businesses are based on networks of millions of users, and both companies have used the Web and Internet communication tools to build communities.

network economics
Model of strategic systems at the industry level based on the concept of a network where adding another participant entails zero marginal costs but can create much larger marginal gain.

GEOGRAPHICALLY BASED INTERNATIONAL STRATEGIES

Many countries, regions, provinces, or even cities and towns are developing and implementing strategic initiatives using advanced information technology to "grow" their area. We are aware of American technology centres, such as Silicon Valley in Northern California, the area in Massachusetts around the Massachusetts Institute of Technology, and the Research Triangle in North Carolina. But Canada has technology centres, too, fostered and supported by local governments. The following are just a few examples from Canada and abroad that illustrate this dynamic approach to community renewal.

The City of Winnipeg, Manitoba, is trying to build an "information corridor" in the older part of the city known as the Exchange District. Already, several buildings in the District house multiple Internet or multimedia companies. CanWest Global, headquartered in Winnipeg, recently announced that it was bringing its call centre with 1200 employees and a wealth of technology to Winnipeg and locating in the Exchange District. Many call centres, such as Royal Bank and Faneuil Marketing, call Winnipeg home.

Despite the emergence of a Silicon Valley North in the Ottawa region and other e-business clusters in Toronto and Waterloo in Ontario and in Montreal, Calgary, and Vancouver, there are few other successful cluster activities in the rest of Canada because the linkages among universities, business, and the financial community are generally not as strong or as focused as is the case with their American counterparts. Factors which create tight linkages—directed research, the cross-pollination among university faculty, business management, and technology staff, and active early-stage venture capitalists—are too infrequent and subscale to drive new business creation. Moreover, Canadian Internet startups in all geographic locations face a set of common challenges in gaining access to financing and in attracting and retaining information technology talent.

Nonetheless, Vancouver has created a niche for the computer graphics industry, along with many other high-tech companies, according to George Hunter, Executive Director of the British Columbia Technology Industries Association. Hunter also feels that Kelowna and Victoria have thriving software industries. Ottawa's advanced technology industry created the area known as Silicon Valley North, with a broad range of emerging firms, including multimillion-dollar players, such as Nortel Networks, Newbridge Networks Corporation (bought in 2000 by Alcatel S.A.) and Corel Corporation. Today, Ottawa is home to a number of industry giants, such as JDS Uniphase, Mitel Corporation, Cognos Inc., GSI Lumonics Inc., EDS Systemhouse, JetForm Corporation, Simware Inc., and more.

Other countries are also taking major strategic information technology initiatives to attract business to their shores—or deserts. Dubai Internet City is the first complete Information Technology and Telecommunications centre in the world to have been built inside a free-trade zone. "I had a vision to transform the old economy by making Dubai a hub for the new economy," Dubai's Crown Prince Mohammad bin Rashid said. Dubai Internet City offers modern, ready-to-operate, fully serviced office space with cutting-edge technology and both wired and wireless networks. Dubai Internet City allows 100 percent foreign ownership of companies, and laws relating to partnerships with local sponsors have been relaxed. Sales, company earnings, and private income are exempt from any form of taxation. Companies can also take land on a renewable lease of up to 50 years and build their own offices. Dubai Internet City's infrastructure uses Sun Microsystems' server platforms, iPlanet software, Lucent cabling, and Cisco components. Siemens was project integrator. Dubai Internet City is the biggest information technology building in the Middle East and has the largest-generation Internet Protocol telephony system in the world.

The Malaysian government built a Multimedia SuperCorridor outside the capital city of Kuala Lumpur to serve as the springboard for the information technology industry. It appears that its vision lacked the infrastructure and partnerships with local and national business to achieve the success of its neighbour, Singapore. Spurred by its role as a transportation centre in Asia, Singapore has become one of the world's most competitive air, sea, and telecommunications hubs. Years ago, Singapore's government committed to educating its populace on advancing information technologies; their educational commitment spurred development in this area so that their infrastructure is as robust and fast as that found in

North America. Promoting its Free Trade Zone also signalled the world that Singapore was open for information technology business.

Here in Canada, a federal initiative known as CANARIE is Canada's advanced Internet development agency—it is roughly analogous to the Internet2 effort in the United States. Two of its main projects are CA*Net2 and CA*Net3. Headquartered in Ottawa, CANARIE has already succeeded in enhancing Canadian R&D Internet speeds by a factor of almost one million since its inception in 1993. More information on CA*Net2 and CA*Net3 initiatives can be found in Chapter 9.

USING SYSTEMS FOR COMPETITIVE ADVANTAGE: MANAGEMENT ISSUES

Strategic information systems often change the organization as well as its products, services, and operating procedures, driving the organization into new behaviour patterns. Using technology for strategic benefit requires careful planning and management. Managers interested in using information systems for competitive advantage will need to perform a strategic systems analysis. The Manager's Toolkit describes some of the issues this analysis will have to address.

Managing Strategic Transitions

Adopting the kinds of strategic systems described in this chapter generally requires changes in business goals, relationships with customers and suppliers, internal operations, and information architecture. These sociotechnical changes, affecting both social and technical elements of the organization, can be considered **strategic transitions**—a movement between levels of sociotechnical systems.

These changes often entail blurring of organizational boundaries, both external and internal. Suppliers and customers must become intimately linked and may share each other's responsibilities. For instance, in Baxter International's and Source Medical's stockless inventory systems, these companies have assumed responsibility for managing their customers' inventories (Johnston and Vitale, 1988). Managers will need to devise new business processes for coordinating their firms' activities with those of customers, suppliers, and other organizations. The organizational change requirements surrounding new information systems are so important that they merit attention throughout this text. Chapters 10 and 12 examine organizational change issues in great detail.

strategic transitions

A movement from one level of sociotechnical system to another is often required when adopting strategic systems that demand changes in the social and technical elements of an organization.

MIS IN ACTION: MANAGER'S TOOLKIT

IDENTIFYING OPPORTUNITIES FOR STRATEGIC INFORMATION SYSTEMS

Managers are expected to identify the types of systems that would provide a strategic advantage to their firms. Here are some key questions to ask:

1. Examine the structure of the industry to which the firm belongs.

   ■ What are some of the competitive forces at work in the industry? Are there new entrants to the industry? What is the relative power of suppliers, customers, and substitute products and services over prices?

   ■ Is the basis of competition quality, price, or brand?

   ■ What are the direction and nature of change within the industry? From where are the momentum and change coming?

   ■ How does the industry currently use information technology? Is the organization behind or ahead of the industry in its application of information systems?

2. Examine business, firm, and industry value chains.

   ■ How does the company create value for the customer? Through lower prices and transaction costs or higher quality? Are there any places in the value chain where the business could create more value for customers and additional profit for the company?

   ■ Does the firm understand and manage its business processes using the best practices available? Is it taking maximum advantage of supply chain management, customer relationship management, and enterprise systems?

   ■ Does the firm leverage its core competencies?

   ■ Are the industry supply chain and customer base changing in ways that benefit or harm the firm?

   ■ Could the firm benefit from strategic partnerships and value webs?

   ■ Where in the value chain would information systems provide the greatest value to the firm?

SUSTAINING COMPETITIVE ADVANTAGE

A firm achieving a competitive advantage typically has "first mover" advantages. While the risks and costs associated with achieving a competitive advantage can be formidable, the first-mover advantages can enable the business to beat its competition. These first-mover advantages include enhancing customer and brand loyalty, having one's name forever associated with a product (much like snowmobiles have been called "SkiDoos" for years), and simply becoming the "go to" company, as Wal-Mart did.

Once a competitive advantage is achieved, it is only rarely sustained over the long term. While the business that is leapfrogging ahead of its competition has considerable first-mover advantages, other firms observe what the competitive advantage is and how it was achieved. They then determine how to copy that core competency, to do even better, perhaps by adding bells and whistles to a product or service, and they can almost always do it cheaper, since most of the research and development work has already been done by the first company.

Nevertheless, the first-mover company must continually seek to maintain its competitive advantage. It must commit itself to the concept of **strategic intent**, constantly looking for additional ways to achieve a competitive advantage, even when it already has that advantage (Hamel and Pralahad, 1989). Frequently, this means looking for new strategic information system opportunities or ways to enhance existing strategic information systems.

strategic intent

The concept of constantly looking for additional ways to achieve a competitive advantage, even when one already has that advantage.

MANAGEMENT WRAP-UP

Information technology provides tools for managers to carry out both their traditional and newer roles, allowing them to monitor, plan, and forecast with more precision and speed than ever before and to respond more rapidly to the changing business environment. Finding ways to use information technology to achieve competitive advantage at the business, firm, and industry levels is a key management responsibility. In addition to identifying the business processes, core competencies, and relationships with others in the industry that can be enhanced with information technology, managers need to oversee the sociotechnical changes required to implement strategic systems.

Each organization has a unique constellation of information systems that result from its interaction with information technology. Contemporary information technology can lead to major organizational changes and efficiencies by reducing transaction and agency costs and can also be a source of competitive advantage. Developing meaningful strategic systems generally requires extensive changes in organizational structure, culture, and business processes that often encounter resistance.

Information technology offers new ways of organizing work and using information that can promote organizational survival and prosperity. Technology can be used to differentiate existing products, create new products and services, nurture core competencies, and reduce operational costs. Selecting an appropriate technology for the firm's competitive strategy is a key decision. Maintaining a competitive advantage is also key to a firm's competitive strategy.

For Discussion

1. It has been said that there is no such thing as a sustainable strategic advantage. Do you agree? Why, or why not?

2. It has been said that the advantage that leading-edge retailers, such as Dell and Wal-Mart, have over their competition is not technology; rather it is their management. Do you agree? Why, or why not?

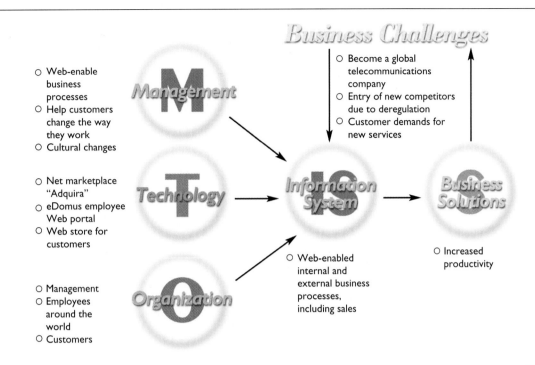

Union has removed Telefonica's near-monopolistic position, opening the marketplace to many new competitors, especially in the areas of services and long distance. Customers are demanding new services, such as high-capacity communication services, media, and the Internet, which can supplement telecommunications companies' traditional sources of revenue.

Telefonica thinks it can meet its objectives by moving both its internal and external business processes to the Web. In addition to improving its own efficiency and productivity, Telefonica hopes to leverage its expertise to help customers use Internet technology to change the way they work as well. The business processes that Telefonica is moving to the Internet span its entire value chain, from purchasing, to production to distribution. The business processes include applications for online procurement and sales to customers as well as internal finance and human resources applications.

Telefonica and its partners have created a Net marketplace called Adquira to purchase indirect goods and services, including communications and office equipment, fixtures and fittings, travel, financial and insurance products, maintenance and repairs, and cleaning services. The Adquira platform offers three alternative technologies for businesses. Large companies can use an Internet procurement tool called Adquira Comprador to integrate procurement processes. Adquira Marketplace is an electronic Net marketplace, where companies of any size can request bids for various products and make purchases. Adquira Subastas offers capabilities for buyers and suppliers to use complex auctions to buy and sell various goods and services.

The 75-year old Telefonica had firmly established business processes. Cultural changes were required to make its electronic commerce and electronic business initiatives effective. People had to change the way they were doing their jobs and handling customer service. The company's CEO and top management communicated the importance of the Internet to the entire company, making it very clear that they fully backed the e-transformation process. Cisco Systems, which supplies much of Telefonica's networking and Internet technology, worked with Telefonica to identify the business processes where electronic commerce and electronic business could have the greatest impact.

Ideally, Telefonica would like to increase productivity by 25 percent in the next three to four years and has started to see results. Its eDomus employee information portal, with 27 000 page views per day, produced $20 million in savings the first year. The Telefonica Online Web site has also proved very successful as a new channel for selling products and services to customers.

Sources: Kay Watanabe, "Internet Transformation," *IQ Magazine*, July/August 2002; "Company Profiles: Adquira, Spain" www.line56.com, accessed July 20, 2002; and www.telefonica.com accessed July 20, 2002.

MANAGEMENT CHALLENGES

Like Telefonica S.A., many companies are starting to use the Internet to communicate with both their customers and suppliers, creating new digital electronic commerce networks that bypass traditional distribution channels. Companies are using Internet technology to streamline their internal business processes as well. Digitally enabling business processes and relationships with other organizations can help companies achieve new levels of competitiveness and efficiency, but they raise the following management challenges:

1. **Digitally enabling the enterprise requires a complete change of mindset.** Digital firms require new organizational designs and management processes. To use Internet and other digital technology for organizational coordination, collaboration, and electronic commerce successfully, companies must examine and perhaps redesign entire business processes, rather than trying to graft new technology on existing business practices. Companies must consider a different organizational structure, changes in organizational culture, a different support structure for information systems, different procedures for managing employees and networked processing functions, and perhaps a different business strategy.

2. **Finding a successful Internet business model.** Companies have raced to put up Web sites in the hope of increasing earnings through electronic commerce. However, many electronic commerce sites have yet to turn a profit or to make a tangible difference in firms' sales and marketing efforts. Cost savings or access to new markets promised by the Web may not materialize. Companies need to think carefully about whether they can create a genuinely workable business model on the Internet and how the Internet relates to their overall business strategy. Internet technology alone is not a substitute for an effective business strategy (Rangan and Adner, 2001; Willcocks and Plant, 2001).

Internet technology is creating a universal technology platform for buying and selling goods and for driving important business processes inside the firm. It has inspired new ways of organizing and managing that are transforming businesses and the use of information systems in everyday life. In addition to bringing many new benefits and opportunities, electronic business and electronic commerce are creating new sets of management challenges. We describe these challenges so that organizations can understand the management, organization, and technology issues that must be addressed to benefit from digital integration.

4.1 ELECTRONIC BUSINESS, ELECTRONIC COMMERCE, AND THE EMERGING DIGITAL FIRM

Throughout this edition, we emphasize the benefits of integrating information across the enterprise, creating an information technology infrastructure in which information can flow seamlessly from one part of the organization to another and from the organization to its

SUMMARY

1. *What do managers need to know about organizations in order to build and use information systems successfully?* Managers need to understand certain essential features of organizations in order to build and use information systems successfully. All modern organizations are hierarchical, specialized, and impartial. They use explicit standard operating procedures to maximize efficiency. All organizations have their own cultures and politics arising from differences in interest groups. Organizations differ in goals, groups served, social roles, leadership styles, incentives, surrounding environments, and types of tasks performed. These differences create varying types of organizational structures, and they also help explain differences in organizations' use of information systems.

2. *What impact do information systems have on organizations?* Information systems and the organizations in which they are used interact with and influence each other. The introduction of a new information system will affect organizational structure, goals, work design, values, competition between interest groups, decision making, and day-to-day behaviour. At the same time, information systems must be designed to serve the needs of important organizational groups and will be shaped by the organization's structure, tasks, goals, culture, politics, and management. Information technology can reduce transaction and agency costs, and these changes have been amplified in organizations using the Internet. The information systems department is the formal organizational unit that is responsible for the organization's information systems function. Organizational characteristics and managerial decisions determine the role this group will actually play.

3. *How do information systems support the activities of managers in organizations?* There are several different models of what managers actually do in organizations that show how information systems can be used for managerial support. Early classical models of managerial activities stressed the functions of planning, organizing, coordinating, deciding, and controlling. Contemporary research looking at the actual behaviour of managers has found that managers' real activities are highly fragmented, variegated, and brief in duration, with managers moving rapidly and intensely from one issue to another.

The nature and level of decision making are important factors in building information systems for managers. Decisions can be structured, semistructured, or unstructured, with structured decisions clustering at the operational level of the organization and unstructured decisions at the strategic planning level. Decision making can also take place at the individual or group level. Individual models of decision making assume that human beings can rationally choose alternatives and consequences on the basis of the priority of their objectives and goals. Organizational models of decision making illustrate that real decision making in organizations takes place in arenas where many psychological, political, and bureaucratic forces are at work.

Information systems have been most helpful to managers by providing support for their roles in disseminating information, providing liaison between organizational levels, and allocating resources. However, some managerial roles cannot be supported by information systems, and information systems are less successful at supporting unstructured decisions.

4. *How can businesses use information systems for competitive advantage?* Businesses can use strategic information systems to gain an edge over competitors. These systems change organizational goals, business processes, products, services, or environmental relationships. Information systems can be used to support strategy at the business, firm, and industry level. At the business level of strategy, information systems can be used to help firms become the low-cost producers, differentiate products and services, or serve new markets. Information systems can also be used to "lock in" customers and suppliers using efficient customer response and supply chain management applications. Value chain analysis is useful at the business level to highlight specific activities in the business where information systems are most likely to have a strategic impact.

At the firm level, information systems can be used to achieve new efficiencies or to enhance services by tying together the operations of disparate business units so that they can function as a whole or by promoting the sharing of knowledge across business units. At the industry level, systems can promote competitive advantage by facilitating cooperation with other firms in the industry and by creating consortiums or communities for sharing information, exchanging transactions, or coordinating activities. The competitive forces model, information partnerships, and network economics are useful concepts for identifying strategic opportunities for systems at the industry level.

5. *Why is it so difficult to develop successful information systems, including systems that promote competitive advantage?* Information systems are closely intertwined with an organization's structure, culture, and business processes. New systems disrupt established patterns of work and power relationships, so there is often considerable resistance to them when they are introduced.

Implementing strategic systems often requires extensive organizational change and a transition from one sociotechnical level to another. These changes are called *strategic transitions* and are often difficult and painful to achieve. Moreover, not all strategic systems are profitable, and they can be expensive to build. Many strategic information systems are easily copied by other firms so that strategic advantage is not always sustainable.

KEY TERMS

Agency theory,   79

Behavioural models,   82

Bureaucracy,   73

Bureaucratic models of decision making,   86

Chief information officer (CIO),   77

Choice,   84

Classical model of management,   81

Cognitive style,   86

Competitive forces model,   96

Core competency,   95

Decisional roles,   82

Design,   84

Efficient customer response system,   93

End users,   77

Focused differentiation,   91

"Garbage can" model,   86

Implementation,   85

Information partnership,   95

Information systems department,   76

Information systems managers,   76

Informational roles,   82

Intelligence,   84

Interpersonal roles,   82

Intuitive decision makers,   86

Knowledge-level decision making,   83

Management control,   83

Managerial roles,   82

Network economics,   97

Operational control,   83

Organization (behavioural definition),   72

Organization (technical definition),   71

Organizational culture,   74

Organizational models of decision making,   86

Political models of decision making,   86

Primary activities,   88

Product differentiation,   90

Programmers,   76

Rational model,   85

Standard operating procedures (SOPs),   73

Strategic decision making,   83

Strategic information systems,   87

Strategic intent,   100

Strategic transitions,   99

Structured decisions,   84

Support activities,   88

Switching costs,   93

Systematic decision makers,   86

Systems analysts,   76

Transaction cost theory,   78

Unstructured decisions,   84

Value chain model,   88

Value web,   89

Virtual organization,   80

REVIEW QUESTIONS

1. What is an organization? Compare the technical definition of organizations with the behavioural definition.

2. What features do all organizations have in common? In what ways can organizations differ?

3. How are information technology services delivered in organizations? Describe the role played by programmers, systems analysts, information systems managers, and the chief information officer (CIO).

4. Describe the major economic theories that help explain how information systems affect organizations.

5. Describe the major behavioural theories that help explain how information systems affect organizations.

6. Why is there considerable organizational resistance to the introduction of information systems?

7. Compare the descriptions of managerial behaviour in the classical and behavioural models.

8. What specific managerial roles can information systems support? Where are information systems particularly strong in supporting managers, and where are they weak?

9. What are the four stages of decision making described by Simon?

10. Compare individual and organizational models of decision making.

11. What is the impact of the Internet on organizations and the process of management?

12. What is a strategic information system? What is the difference between a strategic information system and a strategic-level system?

13. Describe appropriate models for analyzing strategy at the business level and the types of strategies and information systems that can be used to compete at this level.

14. Describe appropriate models for analyzing strategy at the firm level and the types of strategies and information systems that can be used to compete at this level.

15. How can the competitive forces model, information partnerships, and network economics be used to identify strategies at the industry level?

16. How have the value chain and competitive forces models changed as a result of the Internet and the emergence of digital firms?

17. Why are strategic information systems difficult to develop? Why are competitive advantages hard to maintain?

APPLICATION SOFTWARE EXERCISE

DATABASE EXERCISE: USING A DATABASE FOR STRATEGIC BUSINESS DEVELOPMENT

The Presidents' Inn is a small three-storey hotel on the shores of the Atlantic Ocean in St. John's, Newfoundland, a popular Canadian vacation spot. Ten rooms overlook side streets, 10 rooms have bay windows that offer limited views of the ocean, and the remaining 10 rooms in the front of the hotel face the ocean. Room rates are based on room location, length of stay, and number of guests per room. Room rates are the same for one to four guests. Fifth and sixth guests must pay an additional $20 charge each per day. Guests staying for seven days or more receive a 10-percent discount on their daily room rates.

Business has grown steadily over the past 10 years. Now totally renovated, the hotel uses a romantic-weekend package to attract couples, a vacation package to attract young families, and a weekday discount package to attract business travellers. The owners currently use a manual reservation and bookkeeping system, which has caused many problems. Sometimes, two different families have been booked in the same room at the same time. Management does not have immediate data about the hotel's daily operations and income.

Use the information provided in this description and in the database tables on the Companion Website for Chapter 3 to develop reports that would provide information to help management make the business more competitive and prof-itable. The database and related queries should be designed to make it easy to identify information, such as the average length of stay per room type, the average number of visitors per room type, and the base income per room (i.e., length of visit multiplied by the daily rate) during a specified period of time.

After identifying the above information, write a brief report describing what your database information tells you about your current business situation. For example, what is your strongest customer base? What specific business strategies might you pursue to increase room occupancy and revenue? How could the database be improved to provide better information for strategic decisions?

GROUP PROJECT

With a group of three or four students, select a company described in *The Financial Post, The Globe and Mail, Canadian Business,* or another business publication. Visit the company's Web site to find out additional information about that company and to see how the firm is using the Web. On the basis of this information, analyze the business. Include a description of the organization's features, such as important business processes, culture, structure, and environment, as well as its business strategy. Suggest strategic information systems appropriate for that particular business, including those based on Internet technology, if appropriate. If possible, use electronic presentation software to present your findings to the class.

 INTERNET TOOLS

COMPANION WEBSITE

The Internet Tools for this chapter will take you to the NetBank Web site where you can see how one company used the Internet to create an entirely new type of business. You can complete an exercise for analyzing this Web site's capabilities and its strategic benefits.

At www.pearsoned.ca/laudon, you will find valuable tools to facilitate and enhance your learning of this chapter as well as opportunities to apply your knowledge to realistic situations:

- An Interactive Study Guide of self-test questions that will provide you with immediate feedback.
- Application exercises.
- An Electronic Commerce Project on competitive auto pricing and sales on the Web—please check U.S. CW— www.prenhall.com/laudon.
- A Management Decision Problem, where you can analyze customer acquisition costs.
- Updates of material on the chapter.

ADDITIONAL SITES OF INTEREST

There are many interesting Web sites to enhance your learning about how information systems affect organizations and how they can be used to support an organization's strategy. You can search the Web yourself, or just try the following sites to add to what you have already learned.

Harvard Business Review
   www.hbr.com
   A must-read for business majors. Includes articles on a variety of business issues, including strategic information systems.

Source Medical
   www.sourcemedical.com
   The Canadian spinoff of Baxter Healthcare's medical products distribution operation maintains a well-organized Web site for the casual viewer. The customers access part of Source Medical's Web site that is not available to the general public to find out what they need to know about Canada's largest medical products distributor.

Knowledge Management Magazine article about the "attention economy"
   http://www.kmmagazine.com/xq/asp/sid.0/articleid. 258E7641-A0F4-47A3-AC635C00E2BC8478/qx/ display.htm
   Tom Davenport, a leading management scholar, proposes a new way to add or lose value in an organization—the ability to manage attention.

Case Study: *What Happened to Kmart?*

On January 22, 2002, Kmart filed for Chapter 11 bankruptcy protection. It was the largest retailer ever to do so, and this shocked many people. Kmart had made retail history when its founder, the Kresge "five and dime store" chain, invented the concept of the discount store. S.S. Kresge founded the Kresge chain in 1899, and by 1929, there were 19 Kresge stores operating in Canada. The first Kmart was established in Detroit, Michigan, in 1962, the same year Wal-Mart opened its first store in Rogers, Arkansas. By the end of 1963, Kmart had 63 stores converted from Kresge's.

In the years following the founding of Kmart and Wal-Mart, however, Wal-Mart expanded quickly by following a strategy of everyday low prices. Wal-Mart used information technology (IT) to track sales in all of its stores and to replenish its fastest-selling products. Wal-Mart demonstrated its willingness to spend needed funds on IT by installing registers with bar-code scanners in each store during the late 1970s and early 1980s, which fed the sales data into the back-end store computers. The result was Wal-Mart sales data were always current, and store managers knew what was selling well and what was not. In time, many orders were routed straight from the Wal-Mart store to the appropriate supplier, and the delivery went from that supplier directly to the store. Wal-Mart recently developed an extranet to work closely with key suppliers on such matters as how to increase sales on specific products. Many analysts believe Wal-Mart has the most sophisticated supply chain system in the industry.

By 1983, with its cutting-edge information systems, Wal-Mart was already spending only two cents per dollar getting goods to its stores, while Kmart was spending five cents. From that differential alone, Wal-Mart could sell the same product at a price 3 percent lower than Kmart's, an important saving to many shoppers. In 1990, Wal-Mart passed Kmart as the largest discount chain with annual sales of US $32.6 billion for Kmart's US $32.3 billion. Wal-Mart was well on its way to becoming the world's largest retailer. In December 2001, Target, Kmart's other major competitor, passed Kmart as the second largest discount chain. Target had prospered by emphasizing its merchandising, distinguishing itself as a low-cost source of quality and style.

Kmart, in contrast, used a promotions-driven business model, drumming up business by advertising "blue-light" specials using circulars inserted into local newspapers. In an attempt to stay ahead of Wal-Mart, Kmart started investing $1 billion to modernize its information systems in 1987. According to David Carlson, then Kmart's CIO, the company developed capabilities to collect the necessary data, but it did not use them to forecast demand, relying instead on management's judgments. Carlson notes that Kmart's suppliers promoted as many of their products as they could sell, rather than helping Kmart to focus on the better-selling items, as was Wal-Mart's approach. Beginning in 1984, Kmart began diversifying its businesses by acquiring Waldenbooks, Payless Drugstores, Sports Authority, and OfficeMax. It also opened its first Super Kmart Center, a much larger store that now included groceries.

Kmart continued to lose ground to competitors, while it gained the image of being old fashioned, outdated, and frumpy. It had a reputation of being a run-down place to shop with an inferior selection of products. Many of its shelves were empty, while its prices were too high. Its image was that it offered poor customer service and did not care about competition. By 1994, Kmart was on the verge of bankruptcy. It sold off its newer businesses to concentrate on its discount stores, and in 1997, it inaugurated the very popular Martha Stewart product lines for the home.

In 1999, Kmart began developing BlueLight.com, a Web site designed to sell a few items in order to draw customers to physical stores and to polish its image. In May 2000, watching its hemorrhaging continue, the company hired Charles Conaway, the former CVS drugstore chain president, as Kmart's chairman and CEO.

Conaway pledged to turn the company around within two years and said his goal was to make Kmart the primary destination for mothers looking for low-priced clothing, housewares, and packaged food for their families. He announced plans to restructure Kmart to increase the productivity of Kmart stores, inventories, and information systems. He closed 72 stores, reducing staff by 5000. He even announced Kmart would spend about US $1.4 billion for IT over two years versus only US $263 million during the previous two years. However, in August 2001, Kmart announced a second quarter loss of US $22 million, and Conaway blamed pricing pressure, particularly from Wal-Mart. Kmart reduced prices on 30 000 of its 70 000 items and cut down on advertising circulars. Consumer habits are hard to change, and Kmart sales took a big hit.

Sales at Wal-Mart and Target grew in 2001, while those at Kmart continued to decline. Conaway said he had not found a formula to distinguish his company from his competitors. Since Conaway had taken over, Kmart had increased the percentage of items in stock to 86 percent, compared with 73 percent two to three years earlier. In a conference with Wall Street analysts, Conaway said that Kmart was "doing a phenomenal job of reinventing" its supply chain, which would be visible to all in a year's time.

Despite Kmart's continuing falling sales and rising losses, Conaway again mandated price cuts, this time on 50 000 products. When Fleming Companies, now Kmart's sole grocery supplier, suspended shipments to Kmart because of Kmart's failure to meet its weekly payment of $78 million, the company realized it could no longer meet all of its financial obligations. Kmart had to declare Chapter 11 bankruptcy.

Kmart had clearly exhibited many problems. For instance, former Kmart CIO Dave Carlson said he had tried to unify Kmart's two separate computer systems in its distribution system, but he was turned down because the project was considered to be too expensive. When Conaway was first hired, he wanted to find new ways to bring customers into the stores, so he cut back on Kmart's primary method of Sunday circulars but offered no clear alternative strategy. In 2000, central planners were still allocating 60 percent of Kmart's goods to specific stores. Conaway tried to address this problem, but by December 2001, 40 percent of its goods were still being allocated by central planning, rather than by local stores. Also, Kmart continued to expand the variety of its products, rather than focusing on fast-selling items, as did Wal-Mart. Shipping was such a problem that in December 2000, being limited to only 900 trucks per day, Kmart was forced to choose between shipping toothpaste and shipping Christmas trees. Warehousing was also an obvious problem since 15 000 truck-trailers were parked behind its stores holding excess inventory because they had no more storage space. Conaway did successfully eliminate this problem within a few months, thereby also reducing the "shrink" (stolen product) rate. Many analysts and observers, including Conaway, believed supply chain management was Kmart's most serious problem, particularly when compared with Wal-Mart. Kmart's promotions-driven business model created sharp spikes and drops in demand for products and has been much more difficult to support with supply chain management systems than everyday low pricing models, such as Wal-Mart's. Indications of supply chain troubles were everywhere. Outdated technology at the distribution centres resulted in supplies often sitting on pallets for 24 or more hours until they were recorded in the central tracking system. The shelves displaying popular products were often empty, and to reorder them from regional distribution centres, store merchandisers first had to hand-sift through previous purchasing receipts. Kmart's inventory turnover rate was very low. In the year 2000, Kmart's was an anemic 3.6, while Wal-Mart's was 7.3 and Target's was 6.3. Gary Buzek, the president of IHL Consulting Group, estimated that Kmart could add $1.9 billion in profit just by matching its competitors' turnover rates.

Conaway moved ahead quickly. In July, he selected i2 Technologies of Dallas, Texas, to work with Kmart in a project to rebuild its supply chain systems. i2 had been a highly successful vendor of supply chain software, although principally for manufacturers, while Kmart's new software had to be designed for its retail business. The project was to improve Kmart's management of sales forecasting, inventory sourcing, logistics, and reporting. i2 planned to use the Kmart project to create templates for sale to the retail industry in general and then customize them specifically for Kmart. The project would connect these new systems to appropriate in-store technology, such as bar-code scanners at cash registers. It would also include micromerchandising, which enables individual stores to select their own merchandise according to the needs and demands of their local community. i2 claimed its software would track the ability of key suppliers to supply their products. It would also analyze Kmart's needs and execute the required orders, schedule shipments, and record the delivery of products. i2 claimed its software would reduce excess inventory in stores and distribution centres, thus lowering costs and enabling Kmart to lower prices. Sales would then grow and profits increase. Conaway stated Kmart's supply chain would become the best in the retail business, although Lora Cecere, a Gartner analyst, did question the ability to succeed in implementing such a gigantic, complex project.

Katrina Roche, i2's chief marketing officer, stated, "i2 excels at sales, but its execution isn't always flawless." Supply chain

management software for manufacturing still accounted for 90 percent of i2's business, and it had only recent limited experience in the retail sector. One major roadblock was that manufacturers use a relatively small number of stock-keeping units (SKUs) that must be handled by supply chain management software. Unfortunately, Kmart had over 70 000 SKUs in its 2,100 stores, meaning the system must deal with 147 million possible pairings, and this number is increased by inserting many distribution centres and time periods involved. The i2 software was simply not designed to handle such huge data sets. Yet, advanced planning software is fundamental to supply chain management, and the problem could only be solved by Kmart purchasing more hardware, an expensive solution for a company facing Kmart's financial problems.

The i2 project was organized with a team of 500 working in an isolated location. It included over 100 personnel from Deloitte Consulting who were to customize i2's existing software, making it able to track the movement of goods to Kmart's more than 2,100 stores. Conaway announced that the first applications would go live in early 2001, followed by a "rapid, methodical rollout" of several dozen business releases with a total of 93 distinct improvements, all by August 2002.

In February 2001, several suppliers, including Pharmavite Corp. of Northridge, California, and Bell Sports Corp. of Irving, Texas, said they were seeing improved inventory management in the last three months. Also, Kmart announced a $200-million program to purchase and install new point-of-sale terminal cash registers from IBM to improve customer service with faster checkout technologies.

In June 2001, Kmart began installing new warehouse management software called PkMS, from Manhattan Associates. Its goal was to move products more quickly through Kmart's distribution centres to the stores, thereby cutting costs while getting the product on the shelves before it has sold out. The software was installed at corporate headquarters and in all distribution centres. Using it, workers who pick, pack, and ship products to the stores use bar code scanners to locate each item and to track the flow of the goods. A spokesperson said Kmart would save $15 million a year by increasing productivity and lowering labour costs. Management hoped it might also increase sales. The result was that Kmart could track 30 SKUs at the beginning of the third quarter (2001), 119 000 in late November, and 500 000 three months later. However, Buzek believed the information would be useless because management just did not believe in the system. In September, the company announced a $148 million write-off of its previous warehouse management system because it was so extensively modified that it could no longer work well and cost too much to maintain. Observers and analysts claim the write-off included abandoning some of i2's software. Kmart also wrote off $65 million for two outdated distribution centres, replacing them with two newer ones purchased from Toys 'R' Us.

In December 2001, word came out that the i2 project had fallen way behind. John West, i2's chief technology officer until late in 2001, said the software worked but the project had stalled because of Kmart's "operational issues." One member of the i2 users group said, "If the data's not right, it's not that it doesn't work; it's just that you won't get the answer you want." Interestingly, when i2 had problems with Nike, it again blamed its customer and not itself. According to Karen Peterson, a Gartner analyst, Kmart originally did not understand the complex difficulties of the project. Another observer, Jim Dion, president of Chicago retail consulting firm Dionco Inc., said that with the project's difficulty in connecting its point-of-sale and inventory systems to its distribution systems, Kmart was still sending many of its orders on paper. Also in December, Kmart indicated it was now trying to modernize 800 of its stores at a cost of around $1 billion and that money was competing with funds needed to modernize its supply chain. During the Christmas 2001 selling period, Kmart moved fewer products off its shelves than it had in 2000.

When Kmart was forced to declare bankruptcy, it did indicate some plans for survival. Conaway announced that the company would use Chapter 11 bankruptcy protection to break store leases in 284 stores in 40 states and then close them. In June 2002, Kmart changed the name of its Web site from BlueLight.com to Kmart.com to attract a younger audience and help focus on Kmart stores and sales promotions. (BlueLight had never become a profitable Web business.) Kmart.com will also see an expanded variety of name brand products, such as Pentax cameras and Disney apparel. Management believes Kmart.com also meshes better than BlueLight.com with the company's current "Stuff of Life" campaign, which is trying to position the chain as a family-friendly budget-minded store. Emphasizing exclusive brands, such as Martha Stewart Everyday and Joe Boxer, may help Kmart distinguish itself from its rivals. Conaway believes Kmart should be able to emerge from Chapter 11 in 2003.

The question is, will Kmart truly be able to bounce back? What will it take to keep going? The company still does not have a low enough cost structure to compete with Wal-Mart's low prices, nor does it have the trendy image of Target. What can Kmart do to become the shopping destination of choice?

Kmart in Canada

Like its Kresge parent stores, Kmart Canada developed its own following and competed with Zellers, Canadian Tire, and, of course, Wal-Mart. Wal-Mart entered the Canadian market by buying the bankrupt Woolco stores. Wal-Mart, Zellers, and Kmart competed head to head in the Canadian market for years. By 1997, Wal-Mart Canada was selling almost as much as Zellers and Kmart Canada combined. Wal-Mart Canada was growing at a rate of 29 percent, while Zellers growth was only 1.4 percent, and Kmart was losing 6 percent. In March 1997, Wal-Mart Canada passed Zellers to rank as Canada's largest department store. Wal-Mart's share of the discount department store group was 56 percent in 1999.

In 1997, Kmart sold Kmart Canada to an investor group which included York Management Services, Inc., Capital d'Amerique CDPQ Inc. (a wholly-owned subsidiary of Caisse de depot et placement du Quebec), and Cherokee Ventures Canada Inc. George Heller, former president of Bata Industries North America and Europe, was appointed president and CEO

by the new owners. For the sale, Kmart Corporation received about $185 million and kept a 12.5 percent equity interest in Kmart Canada.

At the time of the purchase, Kmart Canada secured a new $135 million revolving line of credit from Congress Financial Corporation. "We are committed to rebuilding Kmart Canada into a strong, national retail business," said Heller, who brought to Kmart Canada more than 25 years of experience in retail management. "Our goal is to create a profitable business through customer service, the support of our associates, strengthened information and technology systems, and investment in Kmart Canada's presence and vitality," Heller said at the time.

Soon after the takeover by the investor group, Hudson's Bay offered to buy Kmart Canada for $265 million, a 300-percent return for the investor group. The Kmart acquisition made Hudson's Bay, an old-line Canadian firm, the largest owner of discount stores in Canada. It leapt from the middle of the pack to being even bigger than Wal-Mart! Hudson's Bay merged Kmart Canada with its 112 stores into their 298 Zellers stores, hoping to make Zellers a strong competitor against Wal-Mart. By the time Kmart merged with Zellers, there were 112 Kmart Canada stores with annual sales of over $1.2 billion and more than 12,600 full- and part-time employees. Hudson's Bay estimated that the merger would close 40 Kmart Canada stores, relocate the others or move Zellers into them, and attempt to offset the loss of most of the 4000 to 6000 employees from the merged Zellers/Kmart Canada by finding them new jobs in their other specialty format stores. As a result of these changes, Zellers now operates in 17 new markets.

Heller is now president of Zellers. Today, Zellers has 350 stores across Canada. Heller is now President and CEO of the entire Hudson's Bay Company, which includes not only Zellers but also Home Outfitters and hbc.com, their electronic-commerce unit. Today, Zellers is facing the same kind of competition that Kmart Canada did from Wal-Mart. The Bay has worked hard to achieve synergy from their various companies by combining credit cards from Zellers and Home Outfitters with the Bay card and by merging their loyalty card memberships and points. Using a Bay credit card and HBC loyalty card, shoppers can charge purchases at any of the three types of stores and receive loyalty points, a significant improvement over the past when one customer could have three credit cards for these stores and three loyalty accounts with insufficient points in any one account. Added together, customers now perceive they receive more value by being able to combine points from purchases at all three stores.

But is that enough to stave off the Wal-Mart competition? Can Zellers become the shoppers' discount department store of choice?

Sources: Mitchell Pacelle and Amy Merrick, "Kmart Gets Pressure from Two Investors to Hurry a Rebound," *Wall Street Journal,* September 12, 2002; Jenny Strasburg, "Kmart Turns Off BlueLight.Com," *San Francisco Chronicle,* June 20, 2002; Amy Merrick, "Kmart Renames Its Web Site, Turned Off by BlueLight.com," *Wall Street Journal,* June 20, 2002; Michael Levy and Dhruv Grewal, "So Long, Kmart Shoppers," *Wall Street Journal,* January 28, 2002; Constance L. Hays, "Kmart to Close 284 Stores; 22 000 Jobs Will Be Cut," *New York Times,* March 9, 2002; Kim Girard, "Kmart:

SCM Gone Wrong," *Baseline*, January 23, 2002, www.baselinemag.com; "Kmart Corporation to Close 284 Under-Performing Stores Based on Financial Objectives Review," Kmart Corporation, March 8, 2002; Carol Sliwa, "IT No Bargain for Troubled Kmart," *itworld.ca*, March 1, 2002; Carol Sliwa, "IT Difficulties Help Take Kmart Down," *ComputerWorld*, January 28, 2002; Steve Konicki, "Now in Bankruptcy, Kmart Struggled with Supply Chain," *InformationWeek*, January 28, 2002, www.informationweek.com; Carol Sliwa, "Beyond IT: Business Strategy Was a Problem, Too," *ComputerWorld*, January 25, 2002; Peter Abell, "Kmart Declares Chapter 11," *AMR Research,* January 23, 2002, www.amrresearch.com; Edward Cone, "Commentary: Blame Enough to Go Around at Kmart," *Baseline*, January 23, 2002, www.baselinemag.com; "Kmart Files Chapter 11," *ABCNEWS.com*, November 22, 2002, www.abcnews.go.com; Stephanie Strom and Leslie Kaufman, "Kmart is on Verge of Filing a Claim for Bankruptcy," *New York Times*, January 22, 2002; David F. Carr and Edward Cone, "Code Blue," *Baseline*, December 10, 2001, www.baselinemag.com; Ted Kemp, "Kmart Calls Supply Chain to Rescue," *InternetWeek*, December 7, 2001, www.internetweek.com; Constance L. Hays, "Slow Lane to Kmart's Recovery; Consumers Turn Frugal and Many Suppliers Discontent," *New York Times*, November 8, 2001; Constance L. Hays and Leslie Kaufman, "Some Suppliers Say Kmart Has Pressed for Deals," *New York Times*, October 25, 2001; Alorie Gilbert, "i2 Forecasts Slow Growth, Losses," *Information Week*, April 19, 2001; "Dog of the Day: i2 Technologies," *Forbes*, February 27, 2001; Jack McCarthy, "Managing through Reorganization," *InfoWorld*, July 20, 2001; Todd R. Weiss, "Kmart to Spend $270 Million on New Technology for its Stores," *ComputerWorld*, February 15, 2001; Marc L. Songini, "Pharmavite to Launch Collaborative System with Kmart," *ComputerWorld*, February 5, 2001; Chris Nolan, "Attention Kmart Shoppers," *Smart Business,* February 1, 2001; "Canada's Oldest Retailer Establishes Zellers Headquarters in Brampton," *BramFacts*, available www.city.brampton.on.ca, accessed June 4, 2003; Ed Strapagiel, "In the Year 5 A.W.: 5 Years After Wal-Mart," available www.kubas.com, accessed June 4, 2003; Susan Thorne, "U.S. Retail Execs Migrate to Canada," available www.icsc.org/srch/sct/, accessed June 5, 2003; Paula Moore, "Kmart Owners Couldn't Pass Up a Deal," *Denver Business Journal*, February 23, 1998; "Investor Group Acquires Kmart Canada; New President and CEO Appointed," June 16, 1997, available www.kmart.com/corp/story/pressrelease/, accessed June 5, 2003; "A Look at Kmart's History," *The Miami Herald*, January 14, 2003, available www.miami.com/mld/miamiherald/4745342.htm, accessed. June 5, 2003.

CASE STUDY QUESTIONS

1. Evaluate Kmart using the value chain and competitive forces models. What was Kmart's business model and business strategy?

2. What was the relationship of information systems to Kmart's business processes and business strategy? How well did its systems support its strategy?

3. What management, organization, and technology factors contributed to Kmart's problems?

4. How important was supply chain management in contributing to Kmart's problems? Evaluate Conaway's decision to use i2 software to improve Kmart's supply chain management.

5. Were those blaming software for the collapse of Kmart correct? Explain your answer.

6. It has been said that "Wal-Mart uses its IT strategically, and it fully integrates it into its operating model." Does this statement apply to Kmart? Explain your response.

7. List the problems Conaway faced when he took over Kmart, and then describe the short- and long-range policies you would have followed had you been in his place.

8. Do you think that Zellers can compete effectively with Wal-Mart in Canada? Explain your answer.

4

THE DIGITAL FIRM: ELECTRONIC BUSINESS AND ELECTRONIC COMMERCE

Objectives

As a manager, you will want to know how your firm can benefit from conducting business electronically using Internet technology. After reading this chapter, you should be able to answer the following questions:

1. *How has Internet technology changed value propositions and business models?*

2. *What is electronic commerce? How has electronic commerce changed consumer retailing and business-to-business transactions?*

3. *What are the principal payment systems for electronic commerce?*

4. *How can Internet technology facilitate management and coordination of internal business processes and supply chain management?*

5. *What are the major managerial and organizational challenges posed by electronic business and electronic commerce?*

Telefonica S.A. Goes Digital

Telefonica S.A. is the leading provider of telecommunications services in the Spanish- and Portuguese-speaking world, serving more than 500 million people. It is also the largest multinational company in Spain, with related telecommunications businesses in over 40 other countries.

Telefonica wants to become one of the top service providers in the world within the next four years, but reaching this goal will not be easy. Telecommunications deregulation in the European

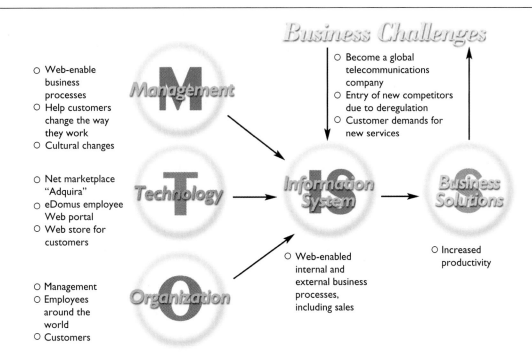

Union has removed Telefonica's near-monopolistic position, opening the marketplace to many new competitors, especially in the areas of services and long distance. Customers are demanding new services, such as high-capacity communication services, media, and the Internet, which can supplement telecommunications companies' traditional sources of revenue.

Telefonica thinks it can meet its objectives by moving both its internal and external business processes to the Web. In addition to improving its own efficiency and productivity, Telefonica hopes to leverage its expertise to help customers use Internet technology to change the way they work as well. The business processes that Telefonica is moving to the Internet span its entire value chain, from purchasing, to production to distribution. The business processes include applications for online procurement and sales to customers as well as internal finance and human resources applications.

Telefonica and its partners have created a Net marketplace called Adquira to purchase indirect goods and services, including communications and office equipment, fixtures and fittings, travel, financial and insurance products, maintenance and repairs, and cleaning services. The Adquira platform offers three alternative technologies for businesses. Large companies can use an Internet procurement tool called Adquira Comprador to integrate procurement processes. Adquira Marketplace is an electronic Net marketplace, where companies of any size can request bids for various products and make purchases. Adquira Subastas offers capabilities for buyers and suppliers to use complex auctions to buy and sell various goods and services.

The 75-year old Telefonica had firmly established business processes. Cultural changes were required to make its electronic commerce and electronic business initiatives effective. People had to change the way they were doing their jobs and handling customer service. The company's CEO and top management communicated the importance of the Internet to the entire company, making it very clear that they fully backed the e-transformation process. Cisco Systems, which supplies much of Telefonica's networking and Internet technology, worked with Telefonica to identify the business processes where electronic commerce and electronic business could have the greatest impact.

Ideally, Telefonica would like to increase productivity by 25 percent in the next three to four years and has started to see results. Its eDomus employee information portal, with 27 000 page views per day, produced $20 million in savings the first year. The Telefonica Online Web site has also proved very successful as a new channel for selling products and services to customers.

Sources: Kay Watanabe, "Internet Transformation," *IQ Magazine*, July/August 2002; "Company Profiles: Adquira, Spain" www.line56.com, accessed July 20, 2002; and www.telefonica.com accessed July 20, 2002.

MANAGEMENT CHALLENGES

Like Telefonica S.A., many companies are starting to use the Internet to communicate with both their customers and suppliers, creating new digital electronic commerce networks that bypass traditional distribution channels. Companies are using Internet technology to streamline their internal business processes as well. Digitally enabling business processes and relationships with other organizations can help companies achieve new levels of competitiveness and efficiency, but they raise the following management challenges:

1. **Digitally enabling the enterprise requires a complete change of mind-set.** Digital firms require new organizational designs and management processes. To use Internet and other digital technology for organizational coordination, collaboration, and electronic commerce successfully, companies must examine and perhaps redesign entire business processes, rather than trying to graft new technology on existing business practices. Companies must consider a different organizational structure, changes in organizational culture, a different support structure for information systems, different procedures for managing employees and networked processing functions, and perhaps a different business strategy.

2. **Finding a successful Internet business model.** Companies have raced to put up Web sites in the hope of increasing earnings through electronic commerce. However, many electronic commerce sites have yet to turn a profit or to make a tangible difference in firms' sales and marketing efforts. Cost savings or access to new markets promised by the Web may not materialize. Companies need to think carefully about whether they can create a genuinely workable business model on the Internet and how the Internet relates to their overall business strategy. Internet technology alone is not a substitute for an effective business strategy (Rangan and Adner, 2001; Willcocks and Plant, 2001).

Internet technology is creating a universal technology platform for buying and selling goods and for driving important business processes inside the firm. It has inspired new ways of organizing and managing that are transforming businesses and the use of information systems in everyday life. In addition to bringing many new benefits and opportunities, electronic business and electronic commerce are creating new sets of management challenges. We describe these challenges so that organizations can understand the management, organization, and technology issues that must be addressed to benefit from digital integration.

4.1 ELECTRONIC BUSINESS, ELECTRONIC COMMERCE, AND THE EMERGING DIGITAL FIRM

Throughout this edition, we emphasize the benefits of integrating information across the enterprise, creating an information technology infrastructure in which information can flow seamlessly from one part of the organization to another and from the organization to its customers, suppliers, and business partners. The emerging digital firm requires this level of information integration, and companies increasingly depend on this type of infrastructure today to remain efficient and competitive. Internet technology has emerged as the key enabling technology for this digital integration.

INTERNET TECHNOLOGY AND THE DIGITAL FIRM

For a number of years, companies used proprietary systems to integrate information from their internal systems and to link to their customers and trading partners. These systems were expensive and based on technology standards that only a few could follow. The Internet is rapidly becoming the infrastructure of choice for electronic commerce because it offers businesses an even easier way to link with other businesses and individuals at a very low cost. It provides a universal and easy-to-use set of technologies and technology standards that can be adopted by all organizations, no matter what computer system or information technology platform the organizations are using.

Trading partners can directly communicate with each other, bypassing intermediaries and inefficient multilayered procedures. Web sites are available to consumers 24 hours a day. Some information-based products, such as software, music, and videos, can actually be physically distributed via the Internet. Vendors of other types of products and services can use the Internet to distribute the information surrounding their wares, such as product pricing, options, availability, and delivery time. The Internet can replace existing distribution channels or extend them, creating outlets for attracting and serving customers who otherwise would not patronize the company. For example, Web-based discount brokerages have attracted new customers who could not afford paying the high commissions and fees charged by conventional brokerage and financial services firms.

Companies can use Internet technology to radically reduce their transaction costs. Chapter 3 introduced the concept of transaction costs, which include the costs of searching for buyers and sellers, collecting information on products, negotiating terms, writing and enforcing contracts, and transporting merchandise. Information on buyers, sellers, and prices for many products is immediately available on the Web. For example, manually processing a single customer order can cost $15. Using a Web-based system, the cost drops to $.80 per transaction. Table 4.1 provides other examples of transaction cost reductions from the Internet or Internet technology. Handling transactions electronically can reduce transaction costs and delivery time for some goods, especially those that are purely digital (such as software, text products, images, or videos) because these products can be distributed over the Internet as electronic versions.

Moreover, Internet technology is providing the infrastructure for running the entire business because its technology and technology standards can also be used to make information flow seamlessly from one part of the organization to another. Internet technology provides a much lower cost and easier-to-use alternative for coordination activities than proprietary networks. Managers can use e-mail and other Internet communication capabilities to oversee

TABLE 4.1	HOW THE INTERNET REDUCES TRANSACTION COSTS	
Transaction	Traditional	Internet
Chequing bank account balance	$1.08	$.13
Answering a customer question	$10–$45	Answering an e-mail query: $1–$5
		Web self-service: $.10–$.20
Trading 100 shares of stock	$100	$9.95
Correcting an employee record	$128	$2.32
Processing an expense report	$36, 22 days	$4–$8, 72 hours
Sending an advertising brochure	$.75–$10	$0–$.25
Paying a bill	$2.22–$3.32	$.65–$1.10

larger numbers of employees, to manage many tasks and subtasks in projects, and to coordinate the work of multiple teams working in different parts of the world. Internet standards can be used to link disparate systems, such as ordering and logistics tracking, which previously could not communicate with each other. The Internet also reduces other agency costs, such as the cost to coordinate activities of the firm with suppliers and other external business partners. The low-cost connectivity and universal standards provided by Internet technology are the driving force behind the explosion of electronic business and the emergence of the digital firm.

NEW BUSINESS MODELS AND VALUE PROPOSITIONS

The Internet has introduced major changes in the way companies conduct business. It has created a dramatic drop in the cost of developing, sending, and storing information while making that information more widely available. Millions of people can exchange massive amounts of information directly, instantly, and for free.

In the past, information about products and services was usually tightly bundled with the physical value chain for those products and services. If a consumer wanted to find out about the features, price, and availability of a refrigerator or an automobile, for instance, that person had to visit a retail store that sold those products. The cost of comparison shopping was very high because people had to physically travel from store to store.

The Internet has changed that relationship. When people are connected electronically, information about products and services can flow on its own directly and instantly to consumers. The traditional link between the flow of the product and the flow of product-related information can be broken. Information is not limited to traditional physical methods of delivery. Customers can find out about products on their own on the Web and buy directly from product suppliers instead of using intermediaries, such as retail stores.

business model

An abstraction of what an enterprise is and how the enterprise delivers a product or service, showing how the enterprise creates wealth.

The unbundling of information from traditional value chain channels is having a disruptive effect on old business models and is creating new business models as well. A **business model** describes how the enterprise produces, delivers, and sells a product or service, showing how the enterprise delivers value to customers and how it creates wealth (Magretta, 2002). Some of the traditional channels for exchanging product information have become unnecessary or uneconomical, and business models based on the coupling of information with products and services may no longer be necessary.

For example, in pre-Internet retailing days, people who wanted to purchase books had to go to a physical bookstore in order to learn what titles were available, the books' contents, and prices. The bookstore had a monopoly on this information. When Amazon.com opened as an online bookstore, it provided visitors to its Web site with a vast electronic catalogue containing close to three million titles, along with tables of contents, reviews, and other information about those titles. People could order books directly from their desktop computers. Amazon.com was able to sell books at a lower cost because it did not have to pay rent, employee salaries, warehousing, and other overhead expenses to maintain physical retail bookstores. (Amazon.com had almost no inventory costs because it relied on book distributors to stock most of its books.) Traditional booksellers who maintained physical storefronts were threatened. Selling books and other goods directly to consumers online without using physical storefronts represents a new business model. Publishers are now challenging this business model by selling digital electronic books directly to consumers without any intermediaries at all.

Financial service business models underwent a similar revolution. In the past, people wishing to purchase stocks or bonds had to pay high commissions to full-service brokers, such as Merrill Lynch. Individual investors relied on these firms both to execute their trading transactions and to provide them with investment information. It was difficult for individual investors to obtain stock quotes, charts, investment news, historical data, investment advice, and other financial information on their own. This information can be found now in abundance on the Web, and investors can use financial Web sites to place their own trades directly for very small transaction fees. The unbundling of financial information from trading has sharply reduced the need for full-service retail brokers.

The Changing Economics of Information

The Internet and the Web have vastly increased the total amount and quality of information available to all market participants, consumers and merchants alike. Customers benefit from lower **search costs**—the effort to find suitable products and to find all the suppliers, prices, and delivery terms for a specific product anywhere in the world (Bakos, 1998). Merchants also benefit because they can use the same technology to find out much more about consumers and to provide more accurate and detailed information to target their marketing and sales efforts.

The Internet shrinks information asymmetry, making it easier for consumers to find out the variety of prices in a market and to discover the actual costs merchants pay for products. An **information asymmetry** exists when one party in a transaction has more information that is important for the transaction than the other party. That information can determine relative bargaining power. For example, until auto retailing sites appeared on the Web, there was a pronounced information asymmetry between auto dealers and customers. Only the auto dealers knew the manufacturers' prices, and it was difficult for consumers to shop around for the best price. Auto dealers' profit margins depended on this asymmetry of information. Now, consumers have access to a legion of Web sites providing competitive pricing information, and the majority of auto buyers use the Internet to shop around for the best deal. Thus, the Web has reduced the information asymmetry surrounding an auto purchase. The Internet has also helped businesses seeking to purchase from other businesses to reduce information asymmetries and locate better prices and terms (see Figure 4.1).

Before the Internet, businesses had to make tradeoffs between the richness and reach of their information. **Richness** refers to the depth and detail of information—the amount of information the business can supply to the customer as well as information the business collects about the customer. **Reach** refers to how many people a business can connect with and how many products it can offer those people. Rich communication occurs, for example, when a sales representative meets with a customer, sharing information that is very specific to that interaction. This type of interaction is very expensive for a business because it can only take place with a small audience. Newspaper and television ads could reach millions of people quite inexpensively, but the information they provide is much more limited. It used to be prohibitively expensive for traditional businesses to have both richness and reach. Few, if any, companies could afford to provide highly detailed, customized information to a large mass audience. The Internet has transformed richness–reach relationships (see Figure 4.2). Using

search costs

The time and money spent locating a suitable product and determining the best price for that product.

information asymmetry

Situation where the relative bargaining power of two parties in a transaction is determined by one party in the transaction possessing more information essential to the transaction than the other party.

richness

Measure of the depth and detail of information that a business can supply to the customer as well as information the business collects about the customer.

reach

Measure of how many people a business can connect with and how many products it can offer those people.

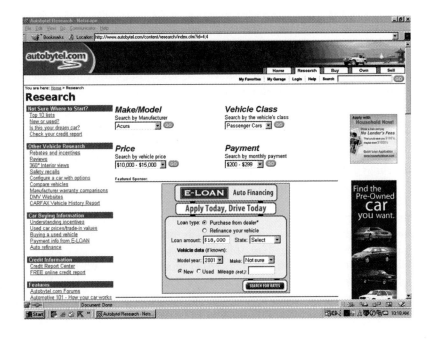

Figure 4.1 Visitors to Autobytel.com can research the price, availability, and features of most models of new and used cars and find the best prices and terms for auto purchases. The Internet can reduce search costs and information asymmetry.

Figure 4.2 The changing economics of information. In the past, companies have had to trade off between the richness and reach of their information. Internet connectivity and universal standards for information-sharing radically lower the cost of providing rich, detailed information to large numbers of people, reducing the tradeoff.

Source: Reprinted by permission of Harvard Business School Press. From: *Blown to Bits: How the New Economics of Information Transforms Strategy* by Philip B. Evans and Thomas Wurster. Boston, MA, 2000, p. 31. Copyright © 2000 by the President of Fellows of Harvard College; all rights reserved.

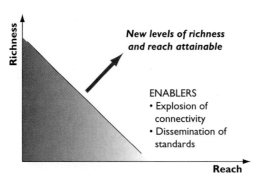

the Internet and Web multimedia capabilities, companies can quickly and inexpensively provide detailed product information and detailed information specific to each customer to very large numbers of people simultaneously (Evans and Wurster, 2000).

Internet-enabled relationships between richness and reach are changing internal operations as well. Organizations can now exchange rich, detailed information among large numbers of people, making it easier for management to coordinate more jobs and tasks. In the past, management's span of control had to be much narrower because rich communication could only be channelled among a few people at a time using cumbersome manual paper-based processes. Digitally enabled business processes have become new sources of organizational efficiency, reducing operating costs while improving the accuracy and timeliness of customer service.

Internet Business Models

The Internet can help companies create and capture profit in new ways by adding extra value to existing products and services or providing the foundation for new products and services. Table 4.2 describes some of the most important Internet business models that have emerged. All, in one way or another, add value: They provide the customer with a new product or service; they provide additional information or service along with a traditional product or service; or they provide a product or service at much lower cost than traditional means.

Some of these new business models take advantage of the Internet's rich communication capabilities. eBay is an online auction forum, using e-mail and other interactive features of the Web. People can make online bids for items, such as computer equipment, antiques and collectibles, wine, jewellery, rock-concert tickets, and electronics, that are posted by sellers from around the world. The system accepts bids for items entered on the Internet, evaluates the bids, and notifies the highest bidder. eBay collects a small commission on each listing and sale. eBay is one of many Web sites that has a Canadian version as well as the original American version. For example, linking to www.ebay.ca takes you to an auction site for Canadians, where you can specify that you only want to look at items for sale in Canada.

Business-to-business auctions are proliferating as well. GoIndustry, for instance, features Web-based auction services for business-to-business sales of used heavy industrial equipment and machinery. Online bidding, also known as **dynamic pricing**, is expected to grow rapidly because buyers and sellers can interact so easily through the Internet to determine what an item is worth at any particular moment.

The Internet has created online communities, where people with similar interests can exchange ideas from many different locations. Some of these virtual communities are providing the foundation for new businesses. Tripod, Geocities, and FortuneCity (which started out in the United Kingdom) provide communities for people wishing to communicate with others about arts, careers, health and fitness, sports, business, travel, and many other interests. Members can post their own personal Web pages, participate in online discussion groups, and join online "clubs" with other like-minded people. A major source of revenue for these communities is providing ways for corporate clients to target customers, including the placement of banner ads and pop-up ads on their Web sites. A **banner ad** is a graphic display on a Web page used for advertising. The banner is linked to the advertiser's Web site so that a person clicking on the banner will be transported to a Web page with more information about the advertiser. **Pop-up ads** work in the opposite manner. They automatically open up when a user accesses a specific Web site, and the user must click on the ad to make it disappear.

Even traditional retailing businesses are enhancing their Web sites with chat, message boards, and community-building features as a means of encouraging customers to spend

dynamic pricing

Pricing of items based on real-time interactions between buyers and sellers that determine what an item is worth at any particular moment.

banner ad

A graphic display on a Web page used for advertising. The banner is linked to the advertiser's Web site so that a person clicking on it will be transported to the advertiser's Web site.

pop-up ad

Ad that opens automatically and does not disappear until the user clicks on it.

TABLE 4.2	**INTERNET BUSINESS MODELS**	
Category	Description	Examples
Virtual storefront	Sells physical products directly to consumers or to individual businesses.	Chapters.Indigo.ca EPM.com
Information broker	Provides product, pricing, and availability information to individuals and businesses. Generates revenue from advertising or from directing buyers to sellers.	Edmunds.com Kbb.com, Insweb.com, ehealthinsurance.com IndustrialMall.com
Transaction broker	Saves users money and time by processing online sales transactions, generating a fee each time a transaction occurs. Also provides information on rates and terms.	BayStreet.ca TDWaterhouse.com
Online marketplace	Provides a digital environment where buyers and sellers can meet, search for products, display products, and establish prices for those products. Can provide online auctions or reverse auctions where buyers submit bids to multiple sellers to purchase at a buyer-specified price as well as negotiated or fixed pricing. Can serve consumers or B2B e-commerce, generating revenue from transaction fees.	eBay.ca Priceline.com ChemConnect.com Pantellos.com
Content provider	Creates revenue by providing digital content, such as digital news, music, photos, or video, over the Web. The customer may pay to access the content, or revenue may be generated by selling advertising space.	FinancialPost.com Yahoo.ca Canada.com
Online service provider	Provides online service for individuals and businesses. Generates revenue from subscription or transaction fees, from advertising, or from collecting marketing information from users.	@Backup.com Xdrive.com Employease.com Salesforce.com
Virtual community	Provides online meeting place where people with similar interests can communicate and find useful information.	Kidshelp.sympatico.ca FROGnet (a list server for French speaking researchers in non–French-speaking countries)
Portal	Provides initial point of entry to the Web along with specialized content and other services.	iVillage.com WeShopCanada.com Canoe.ca MSN.ca

more time, return more frequently, and hopefully make more purchases online. Many retail Web sites have seen their sales increase after they added these features.

The Web's information resources are so vast and rich that special business models called **portals** have emerged to help individuals and organizations locate information more efficiently. A portal is a Web site or other service that provides an initial point of entry to the Web or to internal company data. Yahoo! is an example. It provides a directory of information on the Internet along with news, sports, weather, telephone directories, maps, games, shopping, e-mail, and other services. There are also specialized portals to help users with specific interests. For example, StarMedia is a portal customized for Latin American Internet users. (Companies are also building their own internal portals to provide employees with streamlined access to corporate information resources—see Chapter 14.)

Yahoo! and other portals and Web content sites often combine content and applications from many different sources and service providers. Other Internet business models use syndication as well to provide additional value. For example, E*TRADE, the discount Web trading site, purchases most of its content from outsiders sources, such as Reuters (news), Bridge Information Systems (quotes), and BidCharts.com (charts). Online **syndicators** that aggregate content or applications from multiple sources, package them for distribution, and resell them to third-party Web sites have emerged as another variant of the online content

portal

Web site or other service that provides an initial point of entry to the Web or to internal company data.

syndicator

Business aggregating content or applications from multiple sources, packaging them for distribution, and reselling them to third-party Web sites.

Figure 4.3 iVillage is an Internet business based on an online community for women sharing similar interests, such as diet and fitness, parenting, pregnancy, home and garden, and food. The company generates revenue from advertising banners on its Web pages.

provider business model (Werbach, 2000). The Web makes it much easier for companies to aggregate, repackage, and distribute information and information-based services.

Chapter 6 describes application service providers, such as Employease.com or Salesforce.com, that feature software that runs over the Web. They provide online services to subscribing businesses. Other online service providers offer services to individual consumers, such as remote storage of data at Xdrive.com. Service providers generate revenue through subscription fees or from advertising (see Figure 4.3).

Most of the business models described in Table 4.2 are called **pure-play** business models because they are based purely on the Internet. These firms did not have an existing bricks-and-mortar business when they designed their Internet business. However, many existing retail firms, such as L. L. Bean, Office Depot, Recreational Equipment, Inc. (REI), or *The Wall Street Journal* have developed Web sites as extensions of their traditional bricks-and-mortar businesses. These businesses represent a hybrid **clicks-and-mortar** business model.

pure-play

Business models based purely on the Internet.

clicks-and-mortar

Business model where the Web site is an extension of a traditional bricks-and-mortar business.

4.2   ELECTRONIC COMMERCE

Although most commercial transactions still take place through conventional channels, rising numbers of consumers and businesses are using the Internet for electronic commerce (e-commerce). Projections show that by 2006, total e-commerce spending by consumers and businesses could surpass $7.5 trillion.

CATEGORIES OF ELECTRONIC COMMERCE

There are many ways in which e-commerce transactions can be classified. One is by looking at the nature of the participants in the e-commerce transaction. The three major e-commerce categories are business-to-consumer (B2C), business-to-business (B2B), and consumer-to-consumer (C2C) e-commerce.

business-to-consumer (B2C) e-commerce

Electronic retailing of products and services directly to individual consumers.

business-to-business (B2B) e-commerce

Electronic sales of goods and services among businesses.

consumer-to-consumer (C2C) e-commerce

Consumers selling goods and services electronically to other consumers.

- **Business-to-consumer (B2C) e-commerce** involves retailing products and services to individual shoppers. Chapters.Indigo.ca, which sells books, software, and music to individual consumers, is an example of B2C e-commerce.

- **Business-to-business (B2B) e-commerce** involves sales of goods and services among businesses. Milpro.com, Milacron Inc.'s Web site for selling cutting tools, grinding wheels, and metal working fluids to more than 100 000 small machining businesses, is an example of B2B e-commerce.

- **Consumer-to-consumer (C2C) e-commerce** involves consumers selling directly to consumers. For example, eBay, the giant Web auction site, allows people to sell their goods to other consumers by auctioning the merchandise off to the highest bidder.

Another way of classifying e-commerce transactions is in terms of the participants' physical connection to the Web. Until recently, almost all e-commerce transactions took place over wired networks. Now, cell phones and other wireless handheld digital appliances are Internet enabled so that they can be used to send e-mail or access Web sites. Companies are rushing to offer new sets of Web-based products and services that can be accessed by these wireless devices. For example, in the United Kingdom, customers of Virgin Mobile can use their cell phones to browse Virgin's Web site and purchase compact discs, wine, TV sets, and washing machines. Subscribers to Japan's NTT DoCoMo Internet cell phone service can send and receive e-mail, tap into online news, purchase airplane tickets, trade stocks, and browse through restaurant guides, linking to Web sites that have been redesigned to fit on tiny screens. The use of handheld wireless devices for purchasing goods and services has been termed **mobile commerce** or **m-commerce.** Both business-to-business and business-to-consumer e-commerce transactions can take place using m-commerce technology. Chapter 9 discusses m-commerce and wireless Web technology in detail.

mobile commerce (m-commerce)

The use of wireless devices, such as cell phones or handheld digital information appliances, to conduct both business-to-consumer and business-to-business e-commerce transactions over the Internet.

CUSTOMER-CENTRED RETAILING

Despite the many failures of dot-com retail companies since mid-2000, online retailing continues to grow at a brisk pace. The Internet provides companies with new channels of communication and interaction that can create closer yet more cost-effective relationships with customers in sales, marketing, and customer support. Companies can use the Web to provide ongoing information, service, and support, creating positive interactions with customers that can serve as the foundation for long-term relationships and repeat purchases.

Direct Sales over the Web

Manufacturers can sell their products and services directly to retail customers, bypassing such intermediaries as distributors or retail outlets. Eliminating intermediaries in the distribution channel can significantly lower purchase transaction costs. Operators of virtual storefronts, such as Amazon.com or EPM.com, do not have large expenditures for rent, sales staff, and the other operations associated with a traditional retail store. Airlines can sell tickets directly to passengers through their own Web sites or through travel sites, such as Travelocity.com, without paying commissions to travel agents.

To pay for all the steps in a traditional distribution channel, a product may have to be priced as high as 135 percent of its original manufacturing cost (Mougayar, 1998). Figure 4.4 illustrates how much savings can result from eliminating each of these layers in the distribution process. By selling directly to consumers or reducing the number of intermediaries, companies can achieve higher profits while charging lower prices. The removal of organizations or business process layers responsible for intermediary steps in a value chain is called **disintermediation.**

disintermediation

The removal of organizations or business process layers responsible for certain intermediary steps in a value chain.

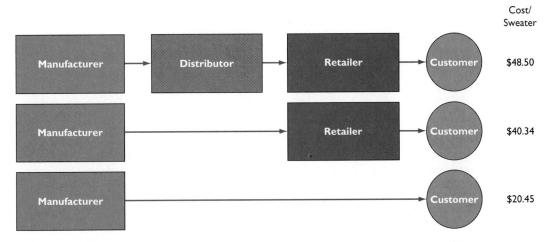

Figure 4.4 The benefits of disintermediation to the consumer. The typical distribution channel has several intermediary layers, each of which adds to the final cost of a product, such as a sweater. Removing layers lowers the final cost to the consumer.

The Internet is accelerating disintermediation in some industries and creating opportunities for new types of intermediaries in others. In certain industries, distributors with warehouses of goods or intermediaries, such as real estate agents, may be replaced by new "service hubs" specializing in helping Internet users reduce search costs, tailor offerings more precisely to their needs, obtain assurances about quality, handle product complexity, or preserve anonymity while conducting online transactions (Anderson and Anderson, 2002; Gallaugher, 2002; Hagel, III, and Singer, 1999). The information brokers listed in Table 4.2 are examples of one type of service where these intermediaries can provide value. The process of shifting the intermediary function in a value chain to a new source is called **reintermediation.**

reintermediation

The shifting of the intermediary role in a value chain to a new source.

Interactive Marketing and Personalization

Marketers can use the interactive features of Web pages to hold consumers' attention or to capture detailed information about their tastes and interests for one-to-one marketing (see Chapter 3). Web sites have become a bountiful source of detailed information about customer behaviour, preferences, needs, and buying patterns that companies can use to tailor promotions, products, services, and pricing. Some customer information may be obtained by asking visitors to "register" online and provide information about themselves, but many companies are also collecting customer information by using software tools that track the activities of Web site visitors. Companies can use special Web site auditing software capable of tracking the number of times visitors request Web pages, the Web pages of greatest interest to visitors after they have entered the sites, and the path visitors followed as they clicked from Web page to Web page. They can analyze this information about customer interests and behaviour to develop more precise profiles of existing and potential customers.

For instance, TravelWeb.com, a Web site offering electronic information on more than 16 000 hotels in 138 countries and online reservation capability, tracks the origin of each user and the screens and the Web page links he or she uses to learn about customer preferences. The Hyatt hotel chain found that Japanese users are most interested in the resort's golf facilities—valuable information in shaping market strategies and for developing hospitality-related products.

Communications and product offerings can be tailored precisely to individual customers. Firms can create unique personalized Web pages that display content or ads for products or services of special interest to each user, improving the customer's experience and creating additional value (see Figure 4.5). By using **Web personalization** technology to modify the Web pages presented to each customer, marketers can achieve the benefits of using individual salespeople at dramatically lower costs. Personalization can also help firms form lasting relationships with customers by providing individualized content, information, and services. Here are some examples:

Web personalization

The tailoring of Web content directly to a specific user.

- Amazon.com retains information on each customer's purchases. When a customer returns to the Amazon.com Web site, that person will be greeted with a Web page recommending books on the basis of that person's purchase history or past purchases of other buyers with similar histories.
- American Airlines is using personalization to reduce its cost structure by encouraging customers to manage their frequent flyer accounts and purchase tickets through its Web site instead of through a travel agent. American Airlines can create individual "travel agencies" for its customers on the Web, informing them that if they take one more domestic flight this year, they can achieve platinum frequent flyer status next year. American Airlines expects to sell $500 million worth of tickets from its Web site.
- Dell Inc. allows users to create their own personal "Dell sites," where Dell can offer them special prices and deals based on the information they provide about their interests and computing requirements. Users can buy exactly what they want without having to call a representative, hunt down the products available, and try to work out deals.

Many other Web sites are using personalization technologies to deliver Web pages with content and banner ads geared to the specific interests of the visitor (see Figure 4.6). Chapters 5, 9, and 14 describe additional technologies that gather the information on Web site visitors to make this type of personalized advertising and customer interaction possible. They also describe how companies are trying to combine Web visitor data with customer data from other sources, such as offline purchases, customer service records, or product registrations to create detailed profiles of individuals. Critics worry that companies gathering so much personal information on Web site visitors pose a threat to individual privacy, especially when much of this information is gathered without the customer's knowledge. Chapter 5 provides a detailed discussion of Web site privacy issues raised by these practices.

The cost of customer surveys and focus groups is very high. Learning how customers feel or what they think about one's products or services through visits to Web sites is much cheaper. Web sites providing product information also lower costs by shortening the sales cycle and reducing the amount of time sales staff must spend in customer education. The Web shifts more marketing and selling activities to the customer because customers fill out their own online order forms. By using the Web to provide vendors with more precise information about

Figure 4.5 Web site personalization. Firms can create unique personalized Web pages that display content or ads for products or services of special interest to individual users, improving the customer experience and creating additional value.

their preferences and suggestions for improving products and services, customers are being transformed from passive buyers to active participants in creating value (Prahalad and Ramaswamy, 2000). The Window on Management shows how companies have benefited from using customers and customer communities on the Web to test and improve products and services.

M-Commerce and Next-Generation Marketing

Within the next few years, the Web will be accessible from almost anywhere, as consumers turn to wireless telephones, handheld digital appliances, interactive television, and other information appliances to link to the Internet. Chapter 9 discusses m-commerce and new wireless Internet devices in greater detail. Travellers can access the Internet in automobiles,

Figure 4.6 Web sites can tailor their content to the specific interests of individual visitors. Bluefly.com personalizes its Web pages to display other items the visitor has viewed.

MOHAWKS TAKE LEAD ON INTERNET SERVICE

Just five years ago, the Mohawk Council of Kahnawake would never have dreamed that it would become a powerhouse driving the Internet. "It was an amazing combination of things," said Grand Chief Joseph Tokwiro Norton. "In fact, an official from the state of New York started it all—that was the beginning of a very fruitful partnership. Now, Mohawk Internet Technologies (MIT) is a major player in the e-business."

Kahnawake is located on the south shore of the St. Lawrence River, 14 kilometres south of downtown Montreal. Additionally, the Mohawks of Kahnawake claim ownership of the Seigneurie de Sault St-Louis, a 1680 seigniorial grant which includes the current Reserve as well as 99 square kilometres of additional land on the Reserve's eastern border, presently alienated from the Mohawks and occupied by a number of non-Indian municipalities. The Mohawk Territory of Kahnawake is governed by a Band Council called the Mohawk Council of Kahnawake (MCK). The Council is composed of a Grand Chief and 11 Chiefs elected by a plurality of votes in a biennial general election. Administrative and financial responsibility for the operations of the community is vested in the MCK.

Kahnawake has reassumed authority over programs and services in a number of jurisdictional areas. This includes control in whole or in part in the following sectors: justice (Court of Kahnawake and the Kahnawake Peacekeepers), education, social services, health, and economic development. Institutions in all of these sectors have been created by MCK directive or grass root initiative. Most are governed by a board or committee of community members representing a cross-section of the population.

The Mohawks of Kahnawake have one of the highest per-family annual incomes of any Native community in Canada. The Mohawks have traditionally engaged in mobile employment, most notably high steel construction occupations. They have recently refocused their efforts on expanding the development of the local economy through initiatives to integrate with key regional industry sectors, notably high technology, aerospace, and trade and tourism.

Mohawk Internet Technologies (MIT) is a unique business initiative of the Mohawk Council of Kahnawake (MCK) and its business partners. Keeping with the historic tradition of the North American trading post, MIT serves as one of the predominant electronic business (e-business) centres on the Internet. MIT is not a bank, casino, or online store but, rather, the Internet service provider for numerous e-businesses that enjoy fast, reliable Internet access in a free-enterprise environment specifically geared toward cross-business alliances and development. MIT wanted to create a technology park that would include other value-added services required by e-businesses, such as common office spaces for call centres, phone services, and support for electronic security. The core of the business is server hosting. "Keeping in mind business objectives while setting up this whole infrastructure was the key factor in order to create services that not only work but also exceed customer expectations," said Jean-Guy Quenneville, MIT's Director of Engineering.

Kahnawake was uniquely positioned to develop a world-class Internet Service Provider (ISP). First, there is underground fibre-optic cable running through the community. Second, an abandoned mattress factory provided the perfect space to set up the 1,115-square-metre electronic business centre. And third, Kahnawake is next door to Montreal, with its full fleet of transportation and telecommunications services. Kahnawake is now home to MIT's world-class co-location server park.

"When that New York official approached us," Norton explains, "we immediately saw the possibilities. Other business partners soon jumped on board." With an investment of $4 million, Mohawk Internet Technologies (MIT) provides Internet services to some of the world's most visible businesses. "I can't name names," says Norton, "because some of our business customers are competitors. Complete confidentiality and security is key. But I can say that you'd immediately recognize most of these major financial, health, and educational institutions."

MIT prides itself on providing a full slate of services for big business, including common infrastructure and technical services, such as a Network Operations Centre and a Customer Support Centre. These are designed to monitor network performance, answer customer queries, and respond to service interruptions. Hosting and access, consulting and support, and MIT affiliate programs and services are also available.

What sets MIT apart from other co-location ISPs? "It's definitely our advanced technology," emphasizes Norton, "as well as our unique combination of services." The facility boasts state-of-the-art server room facilities, with superior network infrastructure, raised flooring, air conditioning, and a clean-room environment. "In this business, security is paramount, so we offer 24/7 physical security, including multiple cameras, intrusion alarm systems, and regular security patrols."

"Our vision," continues Norton, "is to be a modern-day trading post of the Internet—a central location where our business partners and e-customers join together in an environment specifically geared toward cross-business alliances and development." E-customers buy, sell, or trade their products and services through MIT. And the Kahnawake community benefits, too—more than half of its approximately 200 employees come from the community itself. "We're opening ourselves to the world," says Norton. Recently, e-businesses from Australia, the United States, and Europe have chosen MIT as their ISP.

To Think About: How did Mohawk Internet Technologies become such big business for the Mohawk Council of Kahnawake? Do you think they can fulfill their vision of being a modern day trading post on the Internet? Why or why not?

Sources: Karin Lynch, "Powering the Internet through Partnership," *Circles of Light,* available **http://www.ainc-inac.gc.ca/nr/nwltr/col/2001/may0101_e.html**; accessed June 6, 2003; Mohawk Internet Technologies Web site, **www.mohawk.ca,** accessed June 6, 2003; Jean-Guy Quenneville, "Matching Technology with Business Objectives," ITX Awards Submission, 2000.

Target	Platform	When	Content and Service
Traveler	Computer-equipped car 	Whenever car is moving	Provide maps, driving directions, weather reports, ads for nearby restaurants and hotels.
Parent	Cell phone 	During school days	Notify about school-related closings: Hello, Caroline. Your children's school is closing early. Press 1 for closure reason. Press 2 for weather reports. Press 3 for traffic reports
Stockbroker	Pager 	During trading days. Notify if unusually high trading volume.	Summary portfolio analysis showing changes in positions for each holding.

Figure 4.7 Customer personalization with the ubiquitous Internet. Companies can use mobile wireless devices to deliver new value-added services directly to customers at any time and place, extending personalization and deepening their relationships.

airports, hotels, and train stations. Mobile commerce will provide businesses with additional channels for reaching customers and with new opportunities for personalization. Location tracking software in some of these devices will enable businesses to track users' movements and supply information, advertisements, and other services, such as local weather reports or directions to the nearest restaurant, while they are on the go. Instead of focusing on how to bring a customer to a Web site, marketing strategies will shift to finding ways of bringing the message directly to the customer at the point of need (Kenny and Marshall, 2000). Figure 4.7 illustrates how personalization can be extended via the ubiquitous Internet and m-commerce.

Customer Self-Service

The Web and other network technologies are inspiring new approaches to customer service and support. Many companies are using their Web sites and e-mail to answer customer questions or to provide customers with helpful information. The Web provides a medium through which customers can interact with the company, at the customers' convenience, and find information that previously required a human customer-support expert. Automated self-service or other Web-based responses to customer questions cost a fraction of the price of using a live customer service representative on the telephone.

Companies are realizing substantial cost savings from Web-based customer self-service applications. Air Canada, Westjet, Northwest, and other major airlines have created Web sites where customers can review flight departure and arrival times, seating charts, and airport logistics; check frequent-flyer miles; and purchase tickets online. Yamaha Corporation of America has reduced customer calls concerning questions or problems by allowing customers to access technical solutions information from the service and support area of its Web site. If they cannot find answers on their own, customers can send e-mails to an actual technician. Chapter 1 described how customers of UPS can use its Web site to track shipments, calculate shipping costs, determine time in transit, and arrange for a package pickup. FedEx and other package delivery firms provide similar Web-based services.

New software products are even integrating the Web with customer call centres, where customer service problems have been traditionally handled over the telephone. A **call centre**

call centre

An organizational department responsible for handling customer service issues by telephone and other channels.

is an organizational department responsible for handling customer service issues by telephone and other channels. For example, visitors can click on a "push-to-talk" link on the Lands' End Web site that lets a user request a phone call. The user enters his or her telephone number, and a call-centre system directs a customer service representative to place a voice telephone call to the user's phone. Some systems also let the customer interact with a service representative on the Web while talking on the phone at the same time.

BUSINESS-TO-BUSINESS ELECTRONIC COMMERCE: NEW EFFICIENCIES AND RELATIONSHIPS

For a number of years, companies have used proprietary systems for business-to-business (B2B) e-commerce. Now they are turning to the Web and Internet technology. By eliminating inefficient paper-based processes for locating suppliers, ordering supplies, or delivering goods and by providing more opportunities for finding the lowest-priced products and services, business-to-business Web sites can save participants anywhere from 5 to 45 percent.

For business-to-business e-commerce, companies can sell to other businesses using their own Web sites as electronic storefronts, or they can execute purchase and sale transactions through private industrial networks or Net marketplaces. We introduced *private industrial networks* in Chapter 2. Private industrial networks focus on continuous business process coordination between companies for collaborative commerce and supply chain management. A private industrial network typically consists of a large firm using an extranet to link to its suppliers and other key business partners (see Figure 4.8). The network is owned by the buyer, and it permits the firm and its designated suppliers, distributors, and other business partners to share product design and development, marketing, production scheduling, inventory management, and unstructured communication, including graphics and e-mail. Another term for a private industrial network is a **private exchange**. Private exchanges are currently the fastest-growing type of B2B commerce.

Net marketplaces, which are sometimes called *e-hubs*, provide a single digital marketplace based on Internet technology for many different buyers and sellers (see Figure 4.9). They are industry-owned or operate as independent intermediaries between buyers and sellers. Net marketplaces are more transaction oriented (and less relationship-oriented) than private industrial networks, generating revenue from purchase and sale transactions and other services provided to clients. Participants in Net marketplaces can establish prices through online negotiations, auctions, or requests for quotations, or they can use fixed prices.

There are many different types of Net marketplaces and ways of classifying them. Some Net marketplaces sell direct goods and some sell indirect goods. *Direct goods* are goods used in a production process, such as sheet steel for auto body production. *Indirect goods* are all other goods not directly involved in the production process, such as office supplies or products for maintenance and repair. Some Net marketplaces support contractual purchasing based on long-term relationships with designated suppliers, and others support short-term spot purchasing, where goods are purchased based on immediate needs, often from many different suppliers. Some Net marketplaces serve vertical markets for specific industries, such

private exchange
Another term for a private industrial network.

Net marketplace
A single digital marketplace based on Internet technology linking many buyers to many sellers.

Figure 4.8 A private industrial network. A private industrial network, also known as a private exchange, links a firm to its suppliers, distributors, and other key business partners for efficient supply chain management and other collaborative commerce activities.

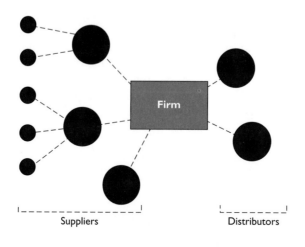

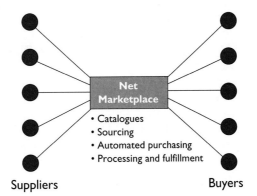

Figure 4.9 A Net marketplace. Net marketplaces are online marketplaces where multiple buyers can purchase from multiple sellers.

as automobiles, telecommunications, or machine tools, while others serve horizontal markets for goods and services that can be found in many different industries, such as office equipment or transportation.

W. W. Grainger serves the horizontal market for sourcing MRO (maintenance, repair, and operations) products used in many different industries. Its Web site provides a single source from which customers can make spot purchases of indirect goods from many different suppliers. Grainger.com features online versions of Grainger's three-kilogram paper catalogue plus access to parts and supplies from other sources and capabilities for electronic ordering and payment. Most of this site is open to the public. Customers benefit from lower search costs, lower transaction costs, wide selection, and lower prices, while Grainger earns revenue by charging a markup on the products it distributes.

Ariba and CommerceOne are independently owned, third-party intermediaries that bundle extensive e-commerce services with Net marketplaces for long-term contractual purchasing of both indirect and direct goods. They provide both buyers and sellers with software systems and services to run Net marketplaces, aggregating hundreds of catalogues into a single marketplace and customizing procurement and sales processes to work with their systems. For buyers, Ariba and CommerceOne automate sourcing, contract management, purchase orders, requisitions, business rules enforcement, and payment. For sellers, these Net marketplaces provide services for catalogue creation and content management, order management, invoicing, and settlement. For example, Federal Express uses Ariba's e-procurement system for $12 million in purchases. Employees use Ariba to order from more than 32 MRO suppliers and catalogues. The system automatically invokes FedEx's business rules for purchasing to route, review, and approve requisitions electronically. By using this Net marketplace, FedEx has reduced the cost of processing purchases by 75 percent and the prices paid for MRO supplies by 12 percent, and it has cut parts delivery time from an average of seven days to two days.

Covisint is an example of an industry-owned Net marketplace serving the vertical market for automobile manufacturing. It brings a small number of prechosen buyers in contact with thousands of preselected suppliers and provides value-added software services for procurement, transaction management, and payment. Industry-owned Net marketplaces focus on long-term contract purchasing relationships and on providing common networks and computing platforms for reducing supply chain inefficiencies. Buyer firms can benefit from competitive pricing among alternative suppliers, and suppliers can benefit by having stable long-term selling relationships with large firms. The ultimate goal of some industry-owned Net marketplaces is the unification of an entire industry supply chain. The Window on Organizations provides more detail on the challenges facing Covisint as it struggles to become a viable business model.

Exchanges are third-party Net marketplaces that can connect thousands of suppliers and buyers for spot purchasing. Many exchanges provide vertical markets for a single industry, such as food, electronics, or industrial equipment, and they primarily deal with direct inputs. For example, Altra Market Place operates an online exchange for spot purchases in the energy industry. Suppliers use the exchange to sell natural gas, liquids, and power to small utilities and energy distributors.

Exchanges proliferated during the early years of e-commerce, but many have failed. Suppliers were reluctant to participate because the exchanges encouraged competitive bidding

exchange

Third-party Net marketplace that is primarily transaction oriented and that connects many buyers and suppliers for spot purchasing.

COVISINT: THE VISION AND THE REALITY

When Covisint was first announced in early 2000 as a giant Net marketplace for the automotive industry, hopes ran high. General Motors, Ford, DaimlerChrysler, Renault, and Nissan, who helped found Covisint, were counting on it to squeeze excess costs out of the process of purchasing auto parts and equipment. (The Big-3 American automakers spend about $360 billion each year on direct and indirect supplies.) Lower prices would be achieved by requiring suppliers to bid for orders together over the Covisint Web site and by reducing the cost of each purchase order transaction from $150 to $15 or $30. Covisint includes an analysis tool to help the manufacturers rank competition from suppliers by using such attributes as quality, price, and delivery date. The automobile producers believed they could save billions every year, trimming costs by $1,800 to $4,500 per car. Even though these companies were rivals, they believed they could realize additional savings by sharing one common industry Net marketplace, rather than bearing the costs of setting up their own procurement platforms. Covisint could also provide savings to suppliers by providing a low-cost point of entry for trading with manufacturers.

Eventually, Covisint would link automakers to the entire supply chain, providing online global communication for demand forecasting, capacity planning, and logistics that would make it possible to build automobiles to order. Participating automobile manufacturers would be able to view their supply chains as components moved through the system, with purchase orders, supplier shipment dates, and production schedules displayed on the Covisint Web site. Covisint could help reduce the time it takes to develop a new automobile from 42 months to 12 to 18 months by providing collaborative software tools for car designers, engineers, parts manufacturers, and materials suppliers to share design documents and schedules.

That was the initial vision for Covisint. The reality has turned out to be less far reaching. Auto industry suppliers have been reluctant to participate fully in Covisint. Many first-tier suppliers—the largest in the industry—have already built their own private networks to be used with the lower-tier suppliers who sell parts to them. The tier I suppliers fear they could lose money and control over their own supply chains if Covisint becomes a single point of entry for transactions among all suppliers in the entire auto industry. Suppliers also worry that bidding for orders with competitors on an industry-wide exchange will turn their products into commodities—that they will lose the benefit of loyalty to their brands.

On June 28, 2002, Covisint announced it was scaling back operations and installing a new team of top managers. The restructuring eliminated Covisint's core supply chain management business, leaving Covisint with auctions and some procurement functions as its principal sources of revenue. Automakers will still be able to use Covisint to manage contracts with suppliers and to request proposals to build specific parts. Covisint will continue to target small suppliers which do not connect directly to automakers' private procurement networks.

To Think About: What are the strengths and weaknesses of Covisint's business model? How could it provide value to its users? Why has it been so difficult for Covisint to realize its original vision?

Sources: Anton Gonsalves and Steve Konicki, "Change at the Top for Covisint," *Information Week*, July 1, 2002; "English Resigns Covisint CEO Post as Auto-Parts Exchange Restructures," *Wall Street Journal*, June 28, 2002; Christopher Koch, "Motorcity Shakeup," *Darwin Magazine*, January 2002; Ruhan Memishi, "Covisint's Starts and Stops," *InternetWorld*, January 1, 2001; Bill Robinson, "Covisint: Driving the Automotive Industry," *IQ Magazine*, January/February 2001; Richard Brown, "GM Spends $98 Billion via Covisint," *Line56*, August 21, 2001; and Chuck Moozakis, "Big Auto Suppliers to Wield Tech Clout," *InternetWeek*, August 13, 2001.

---

that drove prices down and did not offer any long-term relationships with buyers or services to make lowering prices worthwhile. Many essential direct purchases are not conducted on a spot basis, requiring contracts and consideration of such issues as delivery timing, customization, and quality of products (Laudon, 2002; Wise and Morrison, 2000). The early exchanges primarily performed relatively simple transactions and could not handle these complexities as well as the more sophisticated B2B Net marketplaces we previously described (Andrew, Blackburn, and Sirkin, 2000).

ELECTRONIC COMMERCE PAYMENT SYSTEMS

electronic payment system

The use of digital technologies, such as credit cards, smart cards, and Internet-based payment systems, to pay for products and services electronically.

Special **electronic payment systems** have been developed to handle ways of paying for goods electronically on the Internet. Electronic payment systems for the Internet include systems for credit card payments, digital cash, digital wallets, accumulated balance digital payment systems, stored value payment systems, peer-to-peer payment systems, electronic cheques, and electronic billing presentment and payment systems.

Credit cards account for 95 percent of online payments in North America and about 50 percent of all online transactions outside of North America. The more sophisticated e-commerce software (see Chapter 9) has capabilities for processing credit card purchases on the Web. Businesses can also contract with services that extend the functionality of existing credit card payment systems. **Digital credit card payment systems** extend the functionality of credit cards so that they can be used for online shopping payments. They make credit cards safer and more convenient for merchants and consumers by providing mechanisms for authenticating the validity of the purchaser's credit card and arranging for the bank that issued the credit card to deposit money for the amount of the purchase in the seller's bank account. Chapter 11 describes the technologies for secure credit card processing in more detail.

Digital wallets make paying for purchases over the Web more efficient by eliminating the need for shoppers to repeatedly enter their addresses and credit card information each time they buy something. A **digital wallet** securely stores credit card and owner identification information and provides that information at an e-commerce site's "checkout counter." The electronic wallet enters the shopper's name, credit card number, and shipping information automatically when invoked to complete the purchase. Amazon.com's 1-Click shopping, which enables a consumer to automatically fill in shipping and credit card information by clicking one button, uses electronic wallet technology. Gator, Yahoo Wallet, and America Online's Quick Checkout are other digital wallet systems.

Micropayment systems have been developed for purchases of less than $10, such as downloads of individual articles or music clips, that would be too small for conventional credit card payments. Accumulated balance digital payment systems or stored value payment systems are useful for such purposes. **Accumulated balance digital payment systems** allow users to make micropayments and purchases on the Web, accumulating a debit balance that they must pay periodically on their credit card or telephone bills. Qpass, for instance, collects all of a consumer's small purchases for monthly billing on a credit card. *The New York Times* uses Qpass to bill consumers wishing to access articles on *The Times'* Web site. Trivnet lets consumers charge small purchases to their monthly telephone bill. Paystone Canada lets customers "load funds" to their Paystone account from their bank accounts in Canada and the United States. Paystone's customers can then purchase from any online merchants displaying the Paystone logo by charging their purchases to their Paystone accounts.

Stored value payment systems enable consumers to make instant online payments to merchants and other individuals on the basis of value stored in a digital account. Online value systems rely on the value stored in a consumer's bank, chequing, or credit card account, and some of these systems require the use of a digital wallet. Smart cards are another type of stored value system used for micropayments. A **smart card** is a plastic card the size of a credit card that stores digital information. The smart card can store health records, identification data, or telephone numbers, or it can serve as an "electronic purse" in place of cash. The Mondex and American Express Blue smart cards contain electronic cash and can be used to transfer funds to merchants in physical storefronts and to merchants on the Internet. Both are contact smart cards that require use of special card reading devices whenever the cards need to transfer cash to either an online or an offline merchant. (Internet users must attach a smart card reader to their PCs to use the card. To pay for a Web purchase, the user would swipe the smart card through the card reader.)

Digital cash (also known as electronic cash, or e-cash) can also be used for micropayments or larger purchases. **Digital cash** is currency represented in electronic form that moves outside the normal network of money (paper currency, coins, cheques, credit cards). Users are supplied with client software and can exchange money with another e-cash user over the Internet or with a retailer accepting e-cash. eCoin.net is an example of a digital cash service. In addition to facilitating micropayments, digital cash can be useful for people who do not have credit cards and wish to make Web purchases.

New Web-based **peer-to-peer payment systems** have sprung up to serve people who want to send money to vendors or individuals who are not set up to accept credit card payments. The party sending money uses his or her credit card to create an account with the designated payment at a Web site dedicated to peer-to-peer payments. The recipient "picks up" the payment by visiting the Web site and supplying information about where to send the payment (a bank account or a physical address.) PayPal is a popular peer-to-peer payment system.

digital credit card payment systems

Secure services for credit card payments on the Internet that protect information transmitted among users, merchant sites, and processing banks.

digital wallet

Software that stores credit card and owner identification information and provides these data automatically during e-commerce purchase transactions.

micropayment

Payment for a very small sum of money, often less than $10.

accumulated balance digital payment systems

Systems enabling users to make micropayments and purchases on the Web, accumulating a debit balance on their credit card or telephone bills.

stored value payment systems

Systems enabling consumers to make instant online payments to merchants and other individuals on the basis of value stored in a digital account.

smart card

A credit-card-sized plastic card that stores digital information and that can be used for electronic payments in place of cash.

digital cash

Currency represented in electronic form that moves outside the normal network of money.

peer-to-peer payment system

Electronic payment system for people who want to send money to vendors or individuals who are not set up to accept credit card payments.

digital chequing

Systems that extend the functionality of existing chequing accounts so that they can be used for online shopping payments.

electronic billing presentment and payment systems

Systems used for paying routine monthly bills that allow users to view their bills electronically and pay them through electronic fund transfers from banks or credit card accounts.

Digital chequing payment systems, such as CHEXpedite and Western Union MoneyZap, extend the functionality of existing chequing accounts so that they can be used for online shopping payments. Digital cheques are less expensive than credit cards and much faster than traditional paper-based chequing. These cheques are encrypted with a digital signature that can be verified and used for payments in electronic commerce. Electronic cheque systems are useful in business-to-business electronic commerce.

Electronic billing presentment and payment systems are used for paying routine monthly bills (see Figure 4.10). They allow users to view their bills electronically and pay them through electronic fund transfers from bank or credit card accounts. These services support payment for online and physical store purchases of goods or services after the purchase has taken place. They notify purchasers about bills that are due, present the bills, and process the payments. Some of these services, such as CheckFree, consolidate subscribers' bills from various sources so that they can all be paid at one time. Canada Post offers epost, a Web-based service for bill presentation. Customers add vendors, such as their utility companies or The Bay, to their epost account, and their bills are sent to them electronically, rather than by hard copy through Canada Post. Customers can use epost to pay their bills or access their online banking accounts directly from the epost site. Table 4.3 summarizes the features of these payment systems.

The process of paying for products and services purchased on the Internet is complex and merits additional discussion. We discuss electronic commerce security in detail in Chapter 11. Figure 4.11 provides an overview of the key information flows in electronic commerce.

4.3 ELECTRONIC BUSINESS AND THE DIGITAL FIRM

Businesses are finding that some of the greatest benefits of Internet technology come from applications that lower agency and coordination costs. Although companies have used internal networks for many years to manage and coordinate their business processes, intranets are quickly becoming the technology of choice for electronic business.

HOW INTRANETS SUPPORT ELECTRONIC BUSINESS

Intranets are inexpensive, scalable to expand or contract as needs change, and accessible from most computing platforms. While most companies, particularly the larger ones, must support a multiplicity of computer platforms that cannot communicate with each other,

Figure 4.10 PayPal is a peer-to-peer payment system, which enables users to pay anyone with an e-mail address or to send a personal or group bill online.

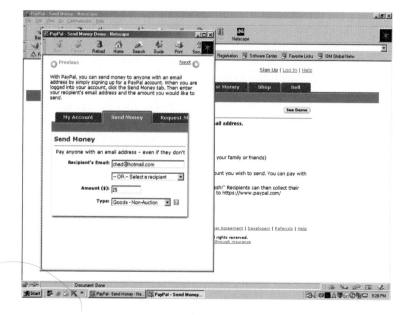

TABLE 4.3   EXAMPLES OF ELECTRONIC PAYMENT SYSTEMS FOR E-COMMERCE

Payment System	Description	Commercial Example
Digital credit card payment	Secure services for credit card payments on the Internet protect information transmitted among users, merchant sites, and processing banks	CyberSource IC Verify
Digital wallet	Software that stores credit card and other information to facilitate payment for goods on the Web	Gator AOL Quick Checkout
Accumulated balance payment system	Accumulates micropayment purchases as a debit balance that must be paid periodically on credit card or telephone bills	Qpass Trivnet
Digital cash	Enables consumers to make instant payments to merchants based on value stored in a systems digital account	Paystone Canada Mondex smart card American Express Blue smart card
Peer-to-peer payment systems	Digital currency that can be used for micropayments or larger purchases	eCoin.net
	Sends money using the Web to individuals or vendors who are not set up to accept credit card payments	PayPal
Digital chequing	Electronic cheque with a secure digital signature	Western Union MoneyZap CHEXpedite
Electronic billing presentment and payment	Supports electronic payment for online and physical store purchases of goods or presentment and services after the purchase has taken place	CheckFree epost.ca

intranets provide instant connectivity, uniting all computers into a single, virtually seamless, network system. Web software presents a uniform interface, which can be used to integrate many different processes and systems throughout the company. Companies can connect their intranets to internal company transaction systems, enabling employees to take actions central to a company's operations.

Intranets can help organizations create a richer, more responsive information environment. Internal corporate applications based on the Web page model can be made interactive using a variety of media, text, audio, and video. A principal use of intranets has been to create online repositories of information that can be updated as often as required. Product catalogues, employee handbooks, telephone directories, or benefits information can be revised immediately as changes occur. This "event-driven" publishing allows organizations to

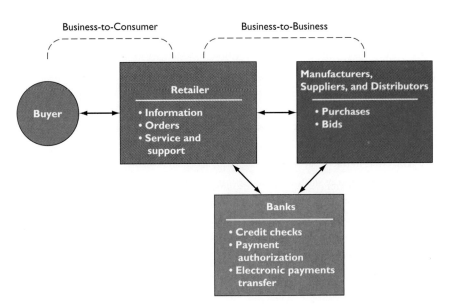

Figure 4.11 Electronic commerce information flows. Individuals can purchase goods and services electronically from online retailers, which, in turn, can use electronic commerce technologies to link directly to their suppliers or distributors. Electronic payment systems are used in both business-to-consumer and business-to-business e-commerce.

respond more rapidly to changing conditions than traditional paper-based publishing, which requires a rigid production schedule. Made available via intranets, documents always can be up to date, eliminating paper, printing, and distribution costs. For instance, Sun Healthcare, a chain of nursing and long-term care facilities headquartered in Albuquerque, New Mexico, saved $600 000 in printing and mailing costs when it put its corporate newsletter on an intranet. The newsletter is distributed to 69 000 employees in 49 states. Glaxo Wellcome of Mississauga, Ontario, decided to move from a portfolio of two or three "blockbuster" drugs to a roster of 30 or more mid-range new drugs. In order to manage the change, its information technology specialists developed an intranet-based relationship management capability for its marketing and sales departments, a system with information sharing as its underlying theme. Research and strategic planning have been streamlined and enhanced to reduce costs by $3 million and have cut the time for a drug to be added to the company's repertoire from 12 months to less than nine. Conservative studies of returns on investment (ROIs) from intranets show ROIs of 23 to 85 percent, and some companies have reported ROIs of more than 1000 percent. More information on the business value of intranets can be found in Chapter 12. Table 4.4 summarizes the organizational benefits of intranets.

INTRANETS AND GROUP COLLABORATION

Intranets provide a rich set of tools for creating collaborative environments in which members of an organization can exchange ideas, share information, and work together on common projects and assignments, regardless of their physical locations. For example, Noranda Inc., a large Canadian mining company, uses an intranet to keep track of its mineral exploration research in a dozen offices in North and South America, Australia, and Europe.

Some companies are using intranets to create enterprise collaboration environments linking diverse groups, projects, and activities throughout the organization. For example, the Mitre Corporation, which conducts research and development work for the United States federal government, set up a collaborative environment called Mitre Information Infrastructure for sharing personnel, planning, and project information. The intranet includes a corporate directory with names, telephone numbers, and résumés of Mitre employees; a Lessons Learned Library with best practices and lessons learned from 10 years of Mitre projects; and capabilities for filing human resources reports, such as time sheets, service requests, and property inventory and tracking forms. Chapter 14 provides a detailed discussion of intranets in collaborative work.

INTRANET APPLICATIONS FOR ELECTRONIC BUSINESS

Intranets are springing up in all the major functional areas of businesses, allowing organizations to manage more business processes electronically. Figure 4.12 illustrates some of the intranet applications that have been developed for finance and accounting, human resources, sales and marketing, and manufacturing and production.

TABLE 4.4	ORGANIZATIONAL BENEFITS OF INTRANETS

Connectivity: accessible from most computing platforms

Can be tied to internal corporate systems and core transaction databases

Can create interactive applications with text, audio, and video

Scalable to larger or smaller computing platforms as requirements change

Easy-to-use, universal Web interface

Low startup costs

Richer, more responsive information environment

Reduced information distribution costs

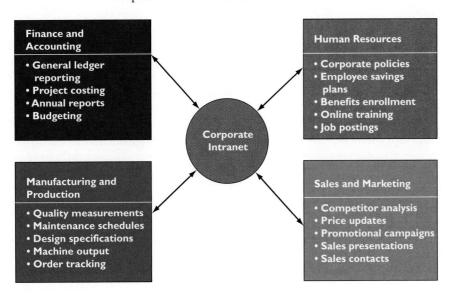

Figure 4.12 Functional applications of intranets. Intranet applications have been developed for each of the major functional areas of the business.

Finance and Accounting

Many organizations have extensive transaction processing systems (TPS) that collect operational data on financial and accounting activities, but their traditional management reporting systems, such as general ledger systems and spreadsheets, often cannot bring this detailed information together for decision making and performance measurement. Intranets can be very valuable for finance and accounting because they can provide an integrated view of financial and accounting information online in an easy-to-use format. Table 4.5 provides some examples.

TABLE 4.5	INTRANETS IN FINANCE AND ACCOUNTING
Organization	**Intranet Application**
Gulf Canada Resources (**www.gulf.ca**)	Intranet-based corporate budgeting system helps Gulf improve its cash flow forecasting and its ability to integrate acquisitions quickly. Users are able to check field-level production figures against forecast numbers to help them react to underperforming or overperforming recovery sites and to add or subtract capital, where needed.
Maple Leaf Sports & Entertainment (MLSEL) (**www.torontomapleleafs.com**)	Intranet-based accounting system capable of streamlining all of its venues, services, and products while maintaining high performance. Using Great Plains eEnterprise software, MLSEL has achieved a seamless integration of all of its data, enhanced performance, ease of reporting, and scalability while combining 170 000 general ledger accounts. The new system creates customized reports for a diverse group of users.
Cisco Systems	Sales and related financial data are updated three times daily, and net income, margin, order, and expense numbers are made instantly available to managers over an intranet. The company can close its books within 24 hours after the end of each quarter.
British Standards Institution (BSI)	Web-based reporting system using software from Crystal Decisions allows the finance department to monitor uninvoiced income or outstanding debt each day.
Bell Canada	By using software and Web-based training techniques, Bell Canada provides its managers with basic financial training before introducing them to more complex shareholder value concepts. Managers are able to gain far more knowledge and benefit from shareholder value learning because they now understand basic finance. With the online Finance Series, the company has been able to provide in half a day the same learning that would take two days in a traditional classroom environment.

Human Resources

Principal responsibilities of human resources departments include keeping employees informed of company issues and providing information about employees' personnel records and benefits. Human resources can use intranets for online publishing of corporate policy manuals, job postings and internal job transfers, company telephone directories, and training classes. Employees can use an intranet to enroll in healthcare plans, employee savings, and other benefit plans if the intranet is linked to the firm's human resources or benefits system, or to take online competency tests. Human resources departments can rapidly deliver information about upcoming events or company developments to employees using newsgroups or e-mail broadcasts (see Figure 4.13). Table 4.6 lists examples of how intranets are used in the area of human resources.

Sales and Marketing

Earlier, we described how the Internet and the Web can be used for selling to individual customers and to other businesses. Internet technology also can be applied to the internal management of the sales and marketing functions. One of the most popular applications for corporate intranets is to oversee and coordinate the activities of the sales force. Sales staff can dial in for updates on pricing, promotions, rebates, or customers, or to obtain information about competitors. They can access presentations and sales documents and customize them for customers. Table 4.7 describes examples of these applications.

MANUFACTURING AND PRODUCTION

In manufacturing, information management issues are highly complex, involving massive inventories and volatile costs, capturing and integrating real-time production data flows, and changing relationships with suppliers. The manufacturing function typically uses multiple types of data, including graphics as well as text, which are scattered in many disparate systems. Manufacturing information is often very time sensitive and difficult to retrieve because files must be continuously updated. Developing intranets that integrate manufacturing data under a uniform user interface is more complicated than in other functional areas.

Despite these difficulties, companies are launching intranet applications for manufacturing. Intranets coordinating the flow of information between lathes, controllers, inventory systems, and other components of a production system can make manufacturing information more accessible to different parts of the organization, increasing precision and lowering costs. Table 4.8 describes some of these uses.

Figure 4.13 Benefits.com enables human resources professionals to administer employee benefits programs and manage employee data over a corporate intranet.

TABLE 4.6	**INTRANETS IN HUMAN RESOURCES**
Organization	**Intranet Application**
Henan Electric Power Transmission and Transformation Co. (China)	Company-wide intranet posts a centralized calendar of corporate events. When planning large meetings and events, employees can download standardized registration forms and process them online.
TransCanada Pipelines	Employees process their timesheets and expense reports and manage their own healthcare plan and pension accounts using an intranet.
CIBC	Web-enabled StaffSmart coordinates staffing needs at more than 1200 branches via the corporate intranet. Using the intranet, the bank allocates employees to different branches at varying days or times to meet fluctuating demand.
TD Canada Trust	The bank's People Development site has three major segments: Know Yourself, Know TD, and Taking Action. Within these three modules, employees across Canada can assess their skills, interests, and values; write a development plan; access competency information; learn more about the bank's business units and goals; link to online course registration; and study a host of online tools and tips.
E*TRADE	Uses Icarian Workforce software on the corporate intranet to automate the entire job applicant tracking process. The software automatically takes in applicant information from such sources as online headhunters and online job posting sites, tracking all applicants from requisition through interviewing. The data are integrated with the corporate human resources system.

TABLE 4.7	**INTRANETS IN SALES AND MARKETING**
Organization	**Intranet Application**
SwissAir	Marketing intranet provides reports, tools, and design guidelines to help the company's marketing staff in 150 cities exchange minutes and presentations about upcoming marketing campaigns and develop themes and promotions.
American Express	Uses a Web-based sales management system by Salesnet to help its North American sales team (which sells gift cheques and incentive cards to corporate clients) distribute and track qualified sales leads. More than 50 members of the sales team can access the system using wireless devices.
Xerox Canada	Using NetXpert, a Web-based application, Xerox executives and senior managers can access all demographic data on national accounts via the Xerox intranet. This includes such information as total revenue, installed equipment, sales cycles, business year-to-date, as well as other customer contact information—names of senior management personnel, location of offices, and so on.
Rogers AT&T (**www.rogers.com**)	Using a BackWeb application, the intranet can "pop up" a box or flash on the employee's display screen, displaying information in text, audio, video, or multimedia format. The intranet can also send employees information at crucial times, such as pushing new deals for cell phones or special offers to call centre employees before they can even take the next customer call.
Yesmail.com	E-mail marketing company set up a sales intranet for sharing tools and documents about contacts, sales leads, and prospects, and used Web conferencing technologies to train remote sales staff. The application includes a methodology to measure the company's progress in different stages of the sales process.

SUPPLY CHAIN MANAGEMENT AND COLLABORATIVE COMMERCE

Intranets can also be used to simplify and integrate business processes spanning more than one functional area. These cross-functional processes can be coordinated electronically, increasing organizational efficiency and responsiveness, and they can also be coordinated with the business processes of other companies. Internet technology has proved especially useful for supply chain management and collaborative commerce.

TABLE 4.8	INTRANETS IN MANUFACTURING AND PRODUCTION

Organization	Intranet Application
Noranda Inc.	Intranet for its Magnola magnesium production facility in Quebec monitors plant operations remotely using a virtual control panel and video cameras.
Sony Corporation	Intranet delivers financial information to manufacturing personnel so that workers can monitor the production line's profit-and-loss performance and adapt performance accordingly. The intranet also provides data on quality measurements, such as defects and rejects, as well as maintenance and training schedules.
TransCanada Pipelines	Managers can schedule plant maintenance using an online system linked to procurement software that automatically secures needed parts from inventory or generates purchase orders.
Mobility Canada	A custom-designed Lotus Notes/Domino application routes documents through a customizable workflow profile—which means the approval process never gets overlooked. The document, which could be authored anywhere in the country, must receive a digital signature from approvers listed in a profile before being automatically published on the Web. An archive date can be set to pull the document from the Web and any links pointing to it are removed automatically. This simplifies the creation and management of the WWW content. The Web pages are created by the owners of the information, rather than by a dedicated HTML editor. This gives the business area greater control and responsibility over information destined for the public, and HTML bottlenecks are eliminated because Domino does the coding.
Rockwell International	Intranet improves process and quality of manufactured circuit boards and controllers by establishing home pages for its Milwaukee plant's computer-controlled machine tools that are updated every 60 seconds. Quality control managers can check the status of a machine by calling up its home page to learn how many pieces the machine output that day, what percentage of an order that output represents, and what tolerances the machine is adhering to.

Chapter 2 introduced the concept of supply chain management, which integrates procurement, production, and logistics processes to supply goods and services from their source to final delivery to the customer. In the pre-Internet environment, supply chain coordination was hampered by the difficulties of making information flow smoothly among many different kinds of systems servicing different parts of the supply chain, such as purchasing, materials management, manufacturing, and distribution. Enterprise systems could supply some of this integration for internal business processes, but these systems are difficult and costly to develop.

Some of this integration can be supplied more inexpensively using Internet technology. Firms can use intranets to improve coordination among their internal supply chain processes, and they can use extranets to coordinate supply chain processes shared with their business partners. *Extranets*, which we introduced in Chapter 1, are private intranets extended to authorized users outside the company. Many of the private industrial networks discussed in this chapter and in Chapter 2, are based on extranets for streamlining supply chain management.

Using Internet technology, all members of the supply chain can instantly communicate with each other, using up-to-date information to adjust purchasing, logistics, manufacturing, packaging, and schedules. A manager can use a Web interface to tap into suppliers' systems to see if inventory and production capabilities match demand for the manufacturer's products. Business partners can use Web-based supply chain management tools to collaborate online on forecasts. Sales representatives can tap into suppliers' production schedules and logistics information to monitor customers' order status. As extended supply chains start sharing production, scheduling, inventory, forecasting, and logistics information online instead of by phone or fax, companies can respond more accurately to changing customer demands. Manufacturers can communicate up-to-the-minute information to suppliers so that they can postpone their products' final configuration and delivery until the last moment. The low cost of providing this information with Web-based tools, instead of costly proprietary systems, encourages companies to share critical business information with a greater number of suppliers. Table 4.9 provides examples of Web-based supply chain management applications.

TABLE 4.9	EXAMPLES OF WEB-BASED SUPPLY CHAIN MANAGEMENT APPLICATIONS
Organization	**Supply Chain Management Application**
Celestica	Toronto-based electronics manufacturing services provider has an extranet for its 1000 suppliers, which use it to pull production planning information from Celestica's supply chain systems. When Celestica gets demand forecast data from one of its large customers, suppliers can view the data through Celestica's corporate portal and let Celestica know how quickly they can deliver the required materials.
Hudson's Bay Company	HBC.net (intranet) and HBC.biz (extranet) for B2B relationships were launched in 2000. This e-business transformation made HBC a complete e-business and affects everything from store operations to administration and supply chain management. The extranet allows suppliers to log on daily to existing sales systems and gather details on how much of their product has been sold and reduces people, equipment, and management costs while improving service. HBC.com is the Bay's B2C e-commerce site that collects data on customers to be used in improving marketing and sales efforts.
Bombardier Aerospace (**www.bombardier.com**)	Business Aircraft Customer Support's extranet for its clients includes a number of communication tools for them as well as a proprietary Part Ordering tool (with over 20 000 parts) that allows its clients to order plane parts online. Using its extranet, Bombardier's technicians not only learn specifically how to repair or overhaul a certain item but also can order the necessary parts online.
Nabisco and Wegman's Food Markets	Created a joint Web-based forecast to maximize the profitability of shelf space for Nabisco Planter's products. The forecast initiated replenishment orders; refined the established forecasting–replenishment plan to drive sourcing, production, and transportation plans; and monitored execution against these plans. After this system was implemented, Planters' sales increased by 54 percent, while stock availability rose from 92.8 to 96.6 percent.
DaimlerChrysler Corporation	The Supplier Partner Information Network (SPIN) allows 3500 of DaimlerChrysler's 12 000 suppliers to access portions of its intranet, where they can get the most current data on design changes, parts shortages, packaging information, and invoice tracking. DaimlerChrysler can use the information from SPIN to reassign workers so that shortages do not hold up assembly lines. DaimlerChrysler believes SPIN has reduced the time to complete various business processes by 25 to 50 percent.

As more and more companies embrace the Internet and e-commerce, they are re-examining how they move products to customers. Order fulfillment can be the most expensive—and sometimes the most critical—operation in e-commerce. The Internet has introduced new ways of managing warehousing, shipping, and packaging based on access to supply chain information that can give companies an edge in delivering goods and services at a reasonable cost. Companies can use information flows from the supply chain to postpone delivery decisions until they have the most up-to-date and complete information on what the customer wants so that products can be delivered in the most direct and cost-effective way (Lee and Whang, 2001).

Internet-based supply chain management applications are clearly changing the way businesses work internally and with each other. In addition to reducing costs, these supply chain management systems provide more responsive customer service, allowing the workings of the business to be driven more by customer demand. Earlier supply chain management systems were driven by production master schedules based on forecasts or best guesses of demand for products. With new flows of information made possible by Web-based tools, supply chain management can follow a demand-driven model.

Internet technology has given a great boost to collaborative product development that is more customer driven as well. The development of a new product usually involves collaboration among different departments in a single firm and, increasingly, among several different organizations. Internet technology provides communication and collaboration tools to connect designers, engineers, marketing, and manufacturing employees. Companies can work internally or with their business partners more efficiently to bring products more rapidly to market, from their initial design and engineering to marketing and sales. Internet-based tools also help companies work with contract manufacturers to build these new products. Customer feedback from Web sites or online communities can be fed into product design.

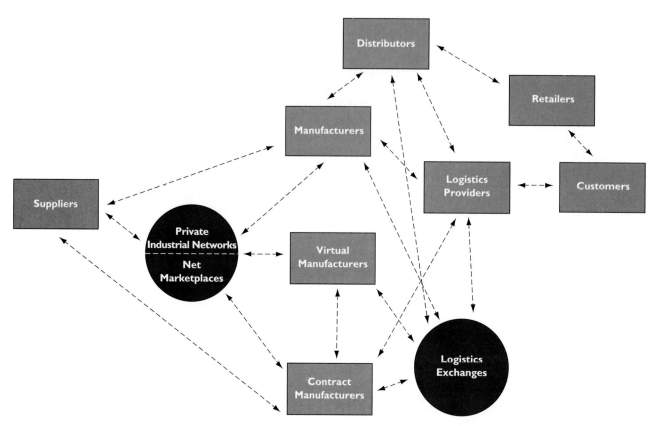

Figure 4.14 The future Internet-driven supply chain. The future Internet-driven supply chain operates like a digital logistics nervous system. It provides multidirectional communication among firms, networks of firms, and e-marketplaces so that entire networks of supply chain partners can immediately adjust inventories, orders, and capacities.

Ultimately, the Internet could create a "digital logistics nervous system" throughout the supply chain. The system would permit simultaneous, multidirectional communication of information about participants' inventories, orders, and capacities and would work to optimize the activities of individual firms and groups of firms interacting in e-commerce marketplaces (see Figure 4.14). As more digital firms evolve, this future "digital logistics nervous system" will come closer to being realized.

4.4 MANAGEMENT CHALLENGES AND OPPORTUNITIES

Although digitally enabling the enterprise with Internet technology offers organizations a wealth of new opportunities and ways of doing business, it also presents managers with a series of challenges. Many new Internet business models have yet to prove enduring sources of profit. Web-enabling business processes for electronic commerce and electronic business requires far-reaching organizational change. The legal environment for electronic commerce has not yet solidified, and companies pursuing electronic commerce must be vigilant about establishing trust, security, and consumer privacy.

UNPROVEN BUSINESS MODELS

Not all companies make money on the Web. Hundreds of retail dot-com firms, including MyKidsBenefit.com, Webvan.com, WinePlanet.com.au, Garden.com, Chinese Books Cyberstore, Productopia.com, and Pets.com, have closed their doors. Fleetscape.com, M-Xchange.com, Industrial Vortex.com, and other exchanges have shut down also. The consulting firm Booz Allen & Hamilton Inc. estimated there were 1734 online marketplaces in 2000, and only 407 are expected to remain by 2004 (Meehan, 2002). Dot-com stock prices collapsed after many of these companies failed to generate enough revenue to sustain their costly marketing campaigns, infrastructures, and staff salaries, losing money on every sale they made. Business models built around the Internet are new and largely unproven.

Doing business over the Internet is not necessarily more efficient or cost effective than traditional business methods. Virtual retailers may not need to pay for costly storefronts and retail workers, but they require heavy outlays for warehousing, customer service call centres, and customer acquisition. Challenges also confront businesses that are trying to use the Web to supplement or enhance a traditional business model. Businesses that are unclear about their online strategy—and its relationship to their overall business strategy—can waste thousands and even millions of dollars building and maintaining a Web site that fails to deliver the desired results (Pinker, Seidmann, and Foster, 2002). Even successful Web sites can incur very high costs. For example, The Bay, the flagship chain of Hudson's Bay Company's department stores, has brick-and-mortar retail stores and a profitable Web site. It has hefty payroll expenditures to pay for the skilled technical staff supporting the Web site and additional shipping expenses to make sure Web orders are delivered to customers in a timely fashion. Hudson's Bay spends $40 million annually on upgrading and remodelling its Web site.

BUSINESS PROCESS CHANGE REQUIREMENTS

Even if a company has a viable business model, it can fail if it is badly managed or its business model is poorly executed. E-commerce and e-business require careful orchestration of the firm's divisions, production sites, and sales offices, as well as closer relationships with customers, suppliers, and other business partners in its network of value creation. Essential business processes must be redesigned and more closely integrated, especially those for supply chain management. In addition to integrating processes inside the firm, supply chain management requires aligning the business practices and behaviours of a number of different companies participating in the supply chain. Companies will need well-defined policies and procedures for sharing data with other organizations, including specifications for the type, format, level of precision, and security of the data to be exchanged (Barua, Konana, Whinston, and Yin, 2001). Traditional boundaries between departments and divisions and between companies and suppliers can be an impediment to collaboration and relationship building. The digitally enabled enterprise must transform the way it conducts business on many levels to act rapidly and with precision.

Channel Conflicts

Using the Web for online sales and marketing may create **channel conflict** with the firm's traditional channels, especially for less information-intensive products that require physical intermediaries to reach buyers. A company's sales force and distributors may fear that their revenues will drop as customers make purchases directly from the Web or that they will be displaced by this new channel.

Channel conflict is an especially troublesome issue in business-to-business e-commerce, where customers buy directly from manufacturers via the Web instead of through distributors or sales representatives. Milacron Inc. operates one of heavy industry's most extensive Web sites for selling machine tools to contract manufacturers. To minimize negative repercussions from channel conflict, Milacron is paying full commissions to its representatives for online sales made in their territory, even if the sales reps do not personally work on the sale or meet the buyer. Other companies are devising other solutions, such as offering only a portion of their full product line on the Web. Using alternative channels created by the Internet requires very careful planning and management.

LEGAL ISSUES

Laws governing e-commerce are still being formulated. Legislatures, courts, and international agreements are just starting to settle such questions as the legality and force of e-mail contracts, the role of electronic signatures, and the application of copyright laws to electronically copied documents. Moreover, the Internet is global, and it is used by individuals and organizations in hundreds of different countries. If a product were offered for sale in Thailand via a server in Singapore and the purchaser lived in Hungary, whose laws would apply? The legal and regulatory environment for e-commerce has not been fully established.

channel conflict
Competition between two or more different distribution channels used to sell the products or services of the same company.

TRUST, SECURITY, AND PRIVACY

E-commerce cannot flourish unless there is an atmosphere of trust among buyers, sellers, and other partners involved in online transactions. Since online relationships are more impersonal than those in "bricks-and-mortar" commerce, many consumers remain hesitant to make purchases over the Web from unfamiliar vendors. Consumers also worry about the security and confidentiality of the credit card and other personal data that they supply over the Internet (Bhattacherjee, 2002; McKnight, Choudhury, and Kacmar, 2002). The technological and institutional framework for e-commerce cannot yet dispel consumer perceptions of risk and uncertainty.

Internet-based systems are even more vulnerable to penetration by outsiders than are private networks because the Internet was designed to be open to everyone. Any information, including e-mail, passes through many computer systems on the Internet before it reaches its destination. It can be monitored, captured, and stored at any of these points along the route. Hackers, vandals, and computer criminals have exploited Internet weaknesses to break into computer systems, causing harm by stealing passwords, obtaining sensitive information, electronic eavesdropping, or "jamming" corporate Web sites to make them inaccessible. We explore Internet security, computer crime, and technology for secure electronic payments in greater detail in Chapters 5 and 11.

4.5   STATUS OF CANADIAN ELECTRONIC COMMERCE

Commercial use of the Internet was begun in the United States and rapidly spread to other parts of the world. As a close trading partner, Canada began e-commerce shortly after the United States but was slower to embrace this new trading method. While a higher percentage of Canadians use the Internet than do Americans, the percentage of e-commerce use per capita or per business is lower in Canada than the United States. What e-commerce trends are there in Canada? What barriers are there to conducting e-commerce in Canada? How are taxation issues addressed? Is another country deliberately cannibalizing Canadian e-commerce sales?

CURRENT STATISTICS ON CANADIAN AND INTERNATIONAL E-COMMERCE

In an April 2003 report, Statistics Canada reported that the total value of private sector sales over the Internet soared in 2002, rising 27.2 percent from 2001, to $13.7 billion after an increase of 46 percent in 2001. However, e-commerce sales still accounted for only a small fraction of total operating revenues. Only 7.5 percent of private sector businesses selling goods reported selling online in 2002, down from 10 percent in 1999, but marginally up from 6.7 percent in 2001. Canadian businesses received $13.2 billion in customer orders over the Internet in 2002, up 28.4 percent from 2001, which showed an increase of 84.1 percent in online sales.

In contrast, public sector sales over the Internet totalled $325 million, down 7.8 percent from 2001. Despite the decline in the value of orders received, the proportion of public sector institutions selling goods and services online rose from 12.8 percent in 2001 to 14.2 percent in 2002.

In spite of the overall growth, e-commerce sales still accounted for only 0.6 percent of total private sector operating revenue in 2002, up from 0.5 percent in 2001 and from 0.2 percent in 1999. Canada's e-commerce is still volatile. Among businesses responding to the survey in both 2001 and 2002, 43 percent that sold online in 2001 stopped doing so in 2002. In 2002, seven firms stopped selling over the Internet for every 10 that started.

Measured by value, Canadian e-commerce sales were highest in wholesale trade, followed by manufacturing, transportation and warehousing, and retail trade. Sales in these industries accounted for 70 percent of all Internet sales in 2002. Overall, 27 percent of Canadian sales over the Internet were to consumers. The dollar value of B2C sales rose 58.5 percent to $3.7 billion in 2002, while B2B sales reached $9.7 billion, an increase of 19.8 percent. Large businesses are still the big players in Canadian e-commerce. Enterprises with more than 500 employees were responsible for 41 percent of Internet sales, slightly up from 40 percent in 2001.

While one-third of businesses have a Web site, three-quarters of all firms use the Internet for some purpose, and one-third of all businesses make online purchases. Even more interesting is that nearly 100 percent of public sector organizations used the Internet, with almost

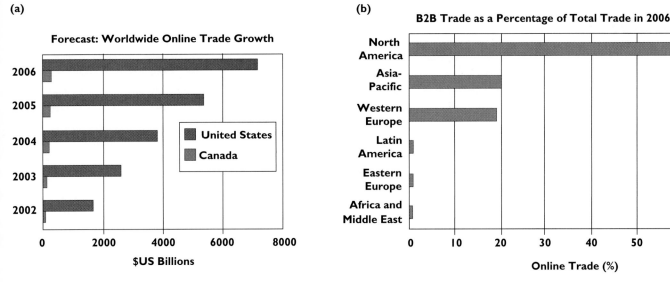

Figure 4.15 Global e-commerce growth

Source: From Industry Canada's E-Commerce Statistics and Sources. Website http://strategis.ic.gc.ca/ epic/internet/inecom-come.nsf/ vwGeneratedInterE/h_qy00010e.html.

88 percent having a Web site, and 77 percent using an intranet, up from 85 percent and 52 percent in 2002, respectively. The Case Study on Canada's Government Online initiative discusses this in further detail.

Interestingly, American e-commerce in 2002 totalled about $76 billion for the private sector alone. Figure 4.15 and Tables 4.10 and 4.11 provide a clearer view of the global growth of e-commerce. Recent studies show the trend for worldwide e-commerce continuing to grow by more than 50% per year. As Figure 4.15 shows, Canada's Strategis reports that worldwide online trade should grow to almost $4 trillion US and by 2006 is forecast to be close to $8 trillion US. Figure 4.15b looks at regional breakdowns for B2B online trading compared to total trading in 2006. This reveals that B2B trade in North America will account for almost 60% of online trade while in the Asia-Pacific and Western European regions, B2B trade only makes up 20% of online trading. B2B trading in other regions is forecast to remain at a minimal level through 2006. Table 4.10 shows the differences in Internet access between English- and non-English speaking peoples. The statistics reveal that although English-speaking peoples only make up 8 percent of the world's population, they make up 35 percent of those with Internet access. Interestingly, this is down from 45 percent just two years before. Table 4.11 reveals that North America will have 51 percent of the world's e-commerce, the Asia/Pacific region 24.3 percent, and Europe 22.6 percent, while Latin America will have only 1.2 percent. Finally, Table 4.11 reveals the proportion of Web content provided in various languages. Today, almost 69 percent of Web content is provided in English, even though only 45 percent of the world's online population is English speaking, and only 8 percent of the world's total population is English speaking (see Figure 4.16).

TABLE 4.10   GLOBAL INTERNET ACCESS

	Percentage of Internet Access (M)	World Online Population	Total Population (M)
English	238.5	35.2%	508
Non-English	439.8	64.8%	5822
European Languages (non-English)	238.1	35.1%	1218
Asian Languages	201.7	29.7%	263
TOTAL WORLD	648.7		940

Source: Adapted from Global Reach, www.glreach.com/globstats, accessed November 22, 2001.

Figure 4.16 An interesting view of global e-commerce projected for 2004 ranked by regions.

Source: Forrester Research, reprinted by Global Reach, http://glreach.com/ eng/ed/art/2004.ecommerce.php3, accessed June 7, 2003.

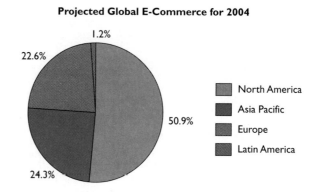

E-COMMERCE BUSINESS SALES TO CANADIANS BY AMERICAN FIRMS

Several studies have shown that Canadian consumers and businesses conduct a significant amount of their electronic purchases with American firms. Many of these American firms, such as Amazon.com, established early pre-eminence in the online marketplace and are difficult for any similar firm located anywhere in the world to compete with. Were it not for e-commerce, those sales would have taken place with Canadian companies. These lost sales are significant and could result in the restructuring of entire industries and the demise of some Canadian companies. Considering the North American Free Trade Act (NAFTA) and other trade agreements between Canada and other countries, there is little that can be done at present to prevent the Canadian sales going to other countries, primarily the United States. There is little, if any, reason to believe that non-Canadian firms are deliberately cannibalizing Canadian sales, any more than there is reason to believe that Canadian firms engaged in foreign trade are deliberately cannibalizing the sales in those countries. But many American companies have Canadian Web sites, open for e-commerce, such as Yahoo.ca and Travelocity.ca; other firms, such as IBM and Microsoft, have purchased the domain names for Canadian versions of their Web sites and route those addresses to a Canadian area of the dot-com URL, for example, www.ibm.ca routes the user immediately to www.ibm.com/ca. These companies are certainly attempting to serve the Canadian market.

Not all of the impacts of the Internet and e-commerce are positive, and not all of these globally positive impacts are beneficial to individual countries. Canada, unfortunately, is not an exception to the potential for the negative impacts of lost sales. What other barriers are there to Canadian e-commerce?

BARRIERS TO E-COMMERCE IN CANADA

Among businesses that did not buy or sell over the Net, 56 percent said they believed their goods or services did not lend themselves to Internet transactions. Thirty-six percent preferred to maintain their current business model. Fourteen percent felt that security was a concern, and 12 percent said the cost of development and maintenance was too high. Finally, 10 percent of

TABLE 4.11	WEB CONTENT BY LANGUAGE			
English	68.4%	Russian	1.9%
Japanese	5.9%	Italian	1.6%
German	5.8%	Portuguese	1.4%
Chinese	3.9%	Korean	1.3%
French	3.0%	Other	4.6%
Spanish	2.4%	Total Web pages:	313 B

Source: Vilaweb.com, as quoted by eMarketer.

non–e-commerce businesses said there was a lack of skilled employees, while 9.6 percent said that their customers are not ready to buy online. Canada is a country with a much larger percentage of small- and medium-sized businesses (SMEs) than is the United States. The SMEs typically do not have the expertise or staff to transform the nature of their business into e-commerce. With such a large rural, widely dispersed population, Canada's broadband access is also a barrier to e-commerce among that portion of Canadians who live in outlying areas.

The Boston Consulting Group (Canada) report mentioned above, titled *Fast Forward: Accelerating Canada's Leadership in the Internet Economy*, was the result of meetings of the Canadian E-Business Roundtable, whose membership includes Gaylen Duncan, the CEO of the Information Technology Association of Canada, and Nancy Hughes Anthony, the President and CEO of the Canadian Chamber of Commerce. The study maintains that—in spite of its warnings—Canada is poised to lead the Internet economy, given its sophisticated infrastructure, highly connected population, early Internet policy initiatives, and skilled workforce, but warns that Canada has not yet embraced its opportunities to lead.

The report warns of several significant barriers to becoming a major global player in e-commerce. These barriers include a lack of urgency among Canadian business leaders to make the Internet a strategic priority, a growing shortage of skilled information technology talent to fill critical positions, a false sense of security in Canadian retail circles that have been sheltered from American competition, to date, by the high costs of cross-border shipping, currency conversion, and taxes. Another constraint is that investment decisions in Canada are based largely on traditional return on investment (ROI) models which may not be appropriate for this type of investment decision.

Canadian businesses must leverage the broad reach of the Internet to move into larger markets or to establish themselves in promising new niche markets. This is problematic, since many small- and medium-sized businesses (SMEs) lack managers with e-business expertise or the in-house information technology staff to handle technical challenges. The most recent edition of the Roundtable's report (*Fast Forward 3.0*, released in 2002) shows that most of these barriers are gradually being eroded, save for the failure of SMEs to take advantage of their opportunity to conduct e-commerce. Even more troubling is the conservative investor culture in Canada. The Canadian investor environment is far less dynamic than is the American one because the venture capital market is dominated by passive and semipublic investors. Labour-sponsored, government, or hybrid funding agencies—none of which is permitted to take a large ownership stake in the companies in which it invests—make up over 60 percent of the Canadian venture capital pool. In contrast, only 1 percent of American funds are managed by nonprivate investors.

Despite the emergence of Silicon Valley North in the Ottawa region and other e-business clusters in Toronto and Waterloo in Ontario, Montreal in Quebec, Calgary in Alberta, and Vancouver in British Columbia, there are few other successful cluster activities in the rest of Canada because the linkages among universities, businesses, and the financial community are generally not as strong or as focused as with their American counterparts. Canadian Internet startups in all geographic areas face a set of common challenges in gaining access to financing and in attracting and retaining information technology talent.

The report also criticized the lack of emphasis Canadian universities place on entrepreneurship and new business creation. The Roundtable made a series of recommendations involving the development of a national e-business strategy. These recommendations include the following:

- Put all levels of government services completely online. (See the Case Study at the end of this chapter for progress in this area.)

- Offer financial incentives to businesses to get wired.

- Lower business and legacy taxes. (Federal business taxes were lowered from 28 to 21 percent within the last five years for sectors currently facing the highest tax rates—including high-tech industries.)

- Restructure current tax and securities regulations that create barriers to early-stage capital formulation on a large scale.

The Roundtable has identified six priority areas for accelerating Canada's e-business leadership.

1. Establish Canada's brand in e-business.
2. Accelerate the transformation of existing business.
3. Foster e-business creation and growth.
4. Expand the e-business talent pool (initiatives in both the homegrown labour market and reforming immigration laws are helping in this area).
5. Make putting government services online a priority (again, see this chapter's Case Study).
6. Build Canada's e-business leadership profile internationally.

The risks of inertia in these initiatives, according to the report, are forfeiting first-mover advantages, competing at a scale disadvantage, getting shut out of traditional supply relationships, and missing global market opportunities. Finally, the Roundtable identified five opportunities for Canada to lead in e-business.

1. **Network Infrastructure**: Canada's historic investments in leading-edge research in network technologies are evident today in the quality and breadth of its Internet backbone. Canada also has a growing number of innovative new technology companies supplying the Internet. The continued growth of these companies and their progeny will establish Canada as an important source of technologies that will accelerate the performance of Internet networks around the world.
2. **Multimedia North**: As broadband capacity grows, the demand for animation and Web-based graphics will expand exponentially. Canada is well positioned to be a leading multimedia supplier. Canada's animation and design schools are renowned internationally and feed a growing multimedia industry.
3. **Global Customer Care Centres**: The Internet has created a new type of call centre that integrates online and telephone solutions for customer service. Given the rapid decline in telecommunications costs, global call centres are now feasible—if they can be staffed by sophisticated response teams with higher-order technical, language, and service skills. Other countries, such as Ireland, are Canada's competition in this arena.
4. **Remote Service Provider**: Canada's experience in remote delivery of healthcare and educational services is promising for extending existing services to global markets and for developing new programs and services that can be delivered over the Web. Canada already ranks second globally in the development of remote learning programs with over 1800 online courses in place.
5. **Web Tools Developer**: Many niche markets are still open to new dot-com companies that Web-enhance the offerings of leading global Internet players. Canadian companies are already creating and commercializing a variety of Web tools, such as navigation tools, site performance enhancers and testers, new search technologies, and new payment solutions.

If the Canadian government, businesses, educational institutions, and people can focus on these issues, Canada can take its place at the head of the e-commerce movement and help lead the world in the latest *industrial revolution*.

E-Commerce Taxation Issues

If borders are meaningless in the Internet economy, buyers and sellers can be anywhere. For governments that have long defined their consumer taxation powers along geographical lines, this is a scary premise. With Canadians making an estimated $3 billion in online purchases in 2000, lost tax revenue is a problem that will only grow with time.

The problem is this. In the old economy, you paid tax on a purchase—say, a CD—at the store where you bought the product because it was assumed you would use it in the same tax jurisdiction. The music store then remitted that tax to the appropriate governments. But things get tricky the moment you order that CD online from another jurisdiction or, worse still, download it as a digital file directly to your home computer. Who collects the tax? Who remits it? Should there be any tax at all?

In Canada, online orders coming from another country are supposed to be taxed just like traditional mail order items: Canadian Customs should hold them at the border until you pay the tax. But that seldom happens in reality. As for digital downloads? How does Canadian Customs monitor these sales?

The Web provides an unprecedented ability to learn about and target customers. But the same capability can also undermine individual privacy. Companies collecting detailed customer information over the Web will need to balance their desire to profit from the information with the need to safeguard individual privacy.

Digitally enabling the enterprise with Internet technology requires careful management planning. The Manager's Toolkit lists some important questions managers should ask when exploring the use of the Internet for electronic commerce and electronic business.

MIS IN ACTION: MANAGER'S TOOLKIT

DIGITALLY ENABLING THE ENTERPRISE: TOP QUESTIONS TO ASK

Managers need to understand precisely how Internet technology will benefit their company and the challenges they face when implementing electronic commerce and electronic business applications. Here are some key questions to ask:

1. How much digital integration does our business need to remain competitive? How can the digital integration provided by Internet technology change our business model? Should we change our business model?

2. How can we measure the success of digitally enabling the enterprise? Will the benefits outweigh the costs?

3. How will business processes have to be changed to use Internet technology seriously for e-commerce or e-business? How much process integration is required?

4. How will we have to recast our relationships with customers, suppliers, and other business partners to take advantage of digitally enabled business processes?

5. Do we have the appropriate information technology infrastructure for digitally enabling our business? What technical skills and employee training will be required to use Internet technology? How can we integrate Internet applications with existing applications and data?

6. How can we make sure our intranet is secure from entry by outsiders? How secure is the electronic payment system we are using for e-commerce?

7. Are we doing enough to protect the privacy of the customers we reach electronically?

MANAGEMENT WRAP-UP

Managers need to carefully review their strategy and business models to determine how to maximize the benefits of Internet technology. They should anticipate making organizational changes to take advantage of this technology, including new business processes, new relationships with the firm's value chain partners and customers, and even new business designs. Determining how and where to digitally enable the enterprise with Internet technology is a key management decision.

The Internet can dramatically reduce transaction and agency costs and is fuelling new business models. By using the Internet and other networks for e-commerce, organizations can exchange purchase and sale transactions directly with customers and suppliers, eliminating inefficient intermediaries. Organizational processes can be streamlined by using the Internet and intranets to make communication and coordination more efficient. To take advantage of these opportunities, organizational processes must be redesigned.

Internet technology has created a universal computing platform that has become the primary infrastructure for e-business, e-commerce, and the emerging digital firm. Web-based applications integrating voice, data, video, and audio are providing new products, services, and tools for communicating with employees and customers. Intranets enable companies to make information flow between disparate systems, business processes, and parts of the organization.

For Discussion

1. How does the Internet change consumer and supplier relationships?

2. The Internet may not make corporations obsolete, but they will have to change their business models. Do you agree? Why, or why not?

SUMMARY

1. *How has Internet technology changed value propositions and business models?* The Internet is rapidly becoming the infrastructure of choice for e-commerce and e-business because it provides a universal and easy-to-use set of technologies and technology standards that can be adopted by all organizations, no matter what computer system or information technology platform they are using. Internet technology provides a lower-cost and easier-to-use alternative for coordination activities than do proprietary networks. Companies can use Internet technology to radically reduce their transaction costs.

   The Internet radically reduces the cost of creating, sending, and storing information about products and services while making that information more widely available. Customers can find out about products on their own on the Web and buy directly from product suppliers instead of using intermediaries, such as retail stores. This unbundling of information from traditional value chain channels is having a disruptive effect on old business models, and it is creating new business models as well.

   The Internet shrinks information asymmetry and has transformed the relationships between information richness and reach. The Internet can help companies create and capture profit in new ways by adding extra value to existing products and services or by providing the foundation for new products and services. Many different business models for e-commerce on the Internet have emerged, including virtual storefronts, information brokers, transaction brokers, online marketplaces, content providers, online service providers, virtual communities, and portals.

2. *What is electronic commerce? How has electronic commerce changed consumer retailing and business-to-business transactions?* E-commerce is the process of buying and selling goods electronically with computerized business transactions using the Internet or other digital network technology. It includes marketing, customer support, delivery, and payment. The three major types of e-commerce are business-to-consumer (B2C), business-to-business (B2B), and consumer-to-consumer (C2C). Another way of classifying e-commerce transactions is in terms of the participants' physical connection to the Web. Conventional e-commerce transactions, which take place over wired networks, can be distinguished from mobile or m-commerce, the purchase of goods and services using handheld wireless devices.

   The Internet provides a universally available set of technologies for electronic commerce that can be used to create new channels for marketing, sales, and customer support, and to eliminate intermediaries in buy and sell transactions. Interactive capabilities on the Web can be used to build closer relationships with customers in mar-

keting and customer support. Firms can use various Web personalization technologies to deliver Web pages with content geared to the specific interests of each user, including technologies to deliver personalized information and ads through m-commerce channels. Companies can also reduce costs and improve customer service by using Web sites to provide helpful information as well as e-mail and even telephone access to customer service representatives.

   B2B e-commerce generates efficiencies by enabling companies to electronically locate suppliers, solicit bids, place orders, and track shipments in transit. Businesses can use their own Web sites to sell to other businesses or use Net marketplaces or private industrial networks.

3. *What are the principal payment systems for electronic commerce?* The principal electronic payment systems for e-commerce are credit card systems, digital wallets, accumulated balance digital payment systems, stored value systems, digital cash, peer-to-peer payment systems, electronic cheques, and electronic billing presentment and payment systems. Accumulated balance systems, stored value systems (including smart cards), and digital cash are useful for small micropayments.

4. *How can Internet technology facilitate management and coordination of internal business processes and supply chain management?* Private, internal corporate networks called intranets can be created using Internet standards. Extranets are private intranets that are extended to selected organizations or individuals outside the firm. Intranets and extranets are the underpinnings of electronic business by providing a low-cost technology that can run on almost any computing platform. Organizations can use intranets to create collaboration environments for coordinating work and information sharing, and they can use intranets to make information flow between different functional areas of the firm. Intranets also provide a low-cost alternative for improving coordination among organizations' internal supply chain processes. Extranets can be used to coordinate supply chain processes shared with external organizations.

5. *What are the major managerial and organizational challenges posed by electronic business and electronic commerce?* Many new business models based on the Internet have not yet found proven ways to generate profits or reduce costs. Digitally enabling a firm for electronic commerce and electronic business requires far-reaching organizational change, including redesign of business processes; recasting relationships with customers, suppliers, and other business partners; and new roles for employees. Channel conflicts may erupt as the firm turns to the Internet as an alternative outlet for sales. Security, privacy, and legal issues pose additional e-commerce challenges.

KEY TERMS

Accumulated balance digital
  payment systems, 125

Banner ad, 114

Business model, 112

Business-to-business (B2B)
  e-commerce, 116

Business-to-consumer (B2C)
  e-commerce, 116

Call centre, 121

Channel conflict, 135

Clicks-and-mortar, 116

Consumer-to-consumer (C2C)
  e-commerce, 116

Digital cash, 125

Digital chequing, 126

Digital credit card payment
  systems, 125

Digital wallet, 125

Disintermediation, 117

Dynamic pricing, 114

Electronic billing presentment
  and payment systems, 126

Electronic payment system,
  124

Exchange, 123

Information asymmetry, 113

Micropayment, 125

Mobile commerce
  (m-commerce), 117

Net marketplace, 122

Peer-to-peer payment system,
  125

Pop-up ads, 114

Portal, 115

Private exchange, 122

Pure-play, 116

Reach, 113

Reintermediation, 118

Richness, 113

Search costs, 113

Smart card, 125

Stored value payment systems,
  125

Syndicator, 115

Web personalization, 118

REVIEW QUESTIONS

1. What are the advantages of using the Internet as the infrastructure for e-commerce and e-business?

2. How is the Internet changing the economics of information and business models?

3. Name and describe six Internet business models for e-commerce. Distinguish between a pure-play Internet business model and a clicks-and-mortar business model.

4. Name and describe the various categories of e-commerce.

5. How can the Internet facilitate sales and marketing to individual customers? Describe the role played by Web personalization.

6. How can the Internet help provide customer service?

7. How can Internet technology support business-to-business e-commerce?

8. What are Net marketplaces? Why do they represent an important business model for B2B e-commerce? How do they differ from private industrial networks?

9. Name and describe the principal electronic payment systems used on the Internet.

10. Why are intranets so useful for e-business?

11. How can intranets support organizational collaboration?

12. Describe the uses of intranets for e-business in sales and marketing, human resources, finance and accounting, and manufacturing.

13. How can companies use Internet technology for supply chain management?

14. Describe the management challenges posed by e-commerce and e-business on the Internet.

15. What is channel conflict? Why is it a growing problem in e-commerce?

APPLICATION SOFTWARE EXERCISE

SPREADSHEET EXERCISE: ANALYZING A DOT-COM BUSINESS

Pick one e-commerce company on the Internet, such as Ashford.com, *The Financial Post*, Buy.com, Yahoo.ca, or Priceline.com. Study the Web pages that describe the company and explain its purpose and structure. Look for articles at such Web sites as Sedar.com, GlobeInvestor.com, or strategis.ic.gc.ca that comment upon the company. Use a Web search engine to find out about the company's Web site; press releases, reviews, and company annual reports can be helpful here. Create a simplified spreadsheet of the company's balance sheets and income statements for the past three years.

Is the company a dot-com success, borderline business, or failure? What information is the basis of your decision? Why? When answering these questions, pay special attention to the company's three-year trends in revenues, costs of sales, gross margins, operating expenses, and net margins. The Companion Website provides definitions of these terms and how they are calculated. Prepare an overhead presentation (minimum of five slides), including appropriate spreadsheets or charts, and present your work to your professor and/or classmates. If the company is successful, what additional business strategies could it pursue to become even more successful? If the company is a borderline or failing business, what specific business strategies (if any) could make it more successful?

GROUP PROJECT

Form a group with three or four of your classmates. Select two businesses that are competitors in the same industry and that use their Web sites for e-commerce. Visit their Web sites. You might compare, for example, the Web sites for virtual banking created by Bank of Montreal and RBC (Royal Bank), or the Internet trading Web sites of E*TRADE and BayStreet.ca. Prepare an evaluation of each business's Web site in terms of its functions, user-friendliness, and how well it supports the company's business strategy. Which Web site does a better job? Why? Can you make some recommendations to improve these Web sites?

 # INTERNET TOOLS

COMPANION WEBSITE

The Internet Tools for this chapter will take you to several Web sites where you can complete an exercise to evaluate several virtual storefront businesses.

At www.pearsoned.ca/laudon, you will find valuable tools to facilitate and enhance your learning of this chapter as well as opportunities to apply your knowledge to realistic situations.

- An Interactive Study Guide of self-test questions that will provide you with immediate feedback.
- Application exercises
- An Electronic Commerce project where you can build an electronic commerce storefront—please check the U.S. CW—www.prenhall.com/laudon.
- A Management Decision Problem on measuring the effectiveness of Web advertising.
- Updates of material in the chapter

ADDITIONAL SITES OF INTEREST

There are many interesting Web sites to enhance your learning about e-commerce and e-business. You can search the Web yourself, or just try the following sites to add to what you have already learned.

Ecommerce Times
> **www.ecommercetimes.com**
>
> The latest on e-commerce technologies, business models, and companies

Internet Week
> **www.internetweek.com**
>
> A weekly publication of the latest happenings on the Internet

Chapters.Indigo.ca
> **www.chapters.indigo.ca**
>
> Canada's alternative to Amazon.com

CASE STUDY: *Government Online: Canada's E-Government Initiative*

The Canadian government is on top when it comes to developing e-government service, according to a recent study conducted by Accenture. The study, *e-Government Leadership: Engaging the Customer,* explores the status of 22 e-governments across the globe, from Canada and the United States to Singapore and Australia. This is the third year in a row Canada has assumed the number one position.

Graeme Gordon, Accenture Canada's e-government partner in Ottawa, says he is not surprised to see Canada leading the survey. "E-government isn't just about offering services online, which a lot of countries still focus on," Gordon said. "E-government is more about transforming government services to provide more effective and more efficient services and also coming to the realization that those services have to be customer-centric."

The study ranked 22 countries by researching the sophistication of the online services being offered. Various researchers conducted online tests of the government Web sites to survey the services being offered. Such factors as publication of information, electronic interaction, and transaction quality between government and customers were all considered as part of the overall Web site. Accenture also conducted interviews with 143 executive representatives within governments.

Once the research was complete, each GOL (Government On-Line) was categorized into a plateau, or level of online maturity. The first plateau is the lowest overall maturity, which means the government has a little more than just an online presence. This year, Canada's GOL just moved into the fifth and highest plateau—which is overall service transformation. "A lot of work is going on within departments to try to better understand what customers want," Gordon said.

The percentage of Canadian citizens accessing government services or products online is among the highest in the world, according to the second Government Online Study published by a London market research company. Forty-eight per cent of Canadians have used the Internet to access e-government services in the last 12 months, according to the survey by Taylor Nelson Sofres. As a result, the nation ranked seventh out of 31 countries in terms of the highest level of e-government usage among citizens. Sweden (57%), Norway (56%), Singapore (53%), Denmark (53%), Faroe Islands (52%), and Finland (49%) rounded out the top six.

The study, which was published in November, also showed that Canadians most often use e-government services to obtain information. And while the government in Canada has not experienced a significant increase in the number of people reached through online services, more people are downloading information and standardized forms. Twenty-seven per cent of Canadians consider it safe to use the Internet to provide government with personal information, the study showed.

On a worldwide scale, 30 percent of citizens said they had accessed government services online, compared with 26 percent a year ago. Countries showing the highest increases include Australia, Turkey, the Netherlands, and the United States. Countries with the lowest level of use were Japan and the United Kingdom, each with 13 percent of the population. The study, which polled almost 29 000 people, was conducted to examine the impact of the Internet on governments both nationally and globally.

The ongoing modernization of service delivery systems by governments has two main objectives: (1) to improve service to citizens and, (2) in an environment where cost savings continues to be a priority for most jurisdictions, to ensure that government remains efficient and competitive in the delivery of those services.

If these modernized systems are to last beyond the project development and pilot stage, governments need to ensure that they meet citizens' needs and are developed around the principles of good governance. Regarding the former, many studies tell us what citizens, as users of government services, expect in the area of service delivery. *Citizens First* and *Citizens First 2000,* both sponsored by a number of federal departments and provincial governments, provide solid data on the desire of citizens for timely service, staff competence, service that goes the extra mile, fairness, and an appropriate outcome. *Citizens First* reported that 42 percent of respondents expect governments to provide a higher standard of service than the private sector. Regarding e-delivery, *Citizens First 2000* indicates that the e-channel's capacity to link different programs and jurisdictions and to complete a service transaction quickly means that as a channel, it has the potential to help governments meet specific citizen expectations regarding fast, efficient, and seamless service delivery. In a similar vein, a soon- to-be-released study, sponsored by the Institute of Public Administration of Canada (IPAC), shows that citizens and businesses expect governments to make more use of the Internet in delivering services.

As for governance, governments have been experimenting with new forms of service delivery, including collaborative arrangements with departments, other jurisdictions, and the private and not-for-profit sectors to improve the efficiency of service delivery. In some cases, these arrangements are designed to eliminate duplication and overlap. The creation of gateways and service clusters on the Government of Canada Web site, for example, is more than just an improved series of access opportunities for users; it is expected to lead to efficiencies behind the scenes as departments and eventually jurisdictions use interoperable systems. In other cases, it is believed that a partner can deliver a program better than government: the use of private sector agents, especially in remote areas, can both improve service and cut costs. Sometimes, a partnership can be used to integrate systems and, thus, improve service. The Nova Scotia Business Registry, a partnership among Service Nova Scotia and Municipal Relations, the Workmen's Compensation Board of Nova Scotia, and the Canada Customs and Revenue Agency, is an example.

No matter what the reason for the new arrangement, or the form it takes, governments have to ensure that appropriate accountability and reporting procedures are in place and that there is a shared understanding between all stakeholders regarding the outcomes. As noted, the principles of improved citizen service and good governance are guiding governments as they improve the delivery of services, including e-services, to citizens. The question is, should they guide governments as they improve delivery of administrative services internally to public servants? Financial systems, personnel systems, and, more recently, purchasing services are highly automated, with many jurisdictions on their second or third generation of back-office systems. As the focus turns toward providing services and tools via e-systems internally to public servants, is it important to use the same user-centric emphasis and good governance principles that are applied to the improved delivery of services to the public?

The answer has to be "Yes."

At the end of the day, public servants are users, too. Thus, in designing e-systems for administration in the public sector, one goal should be to improve service to the user. Presumably, the data which provide information regarding the needs of citizens as users could apply to public servant users as well. For example, it can be assumed that public sector users will expect their e-service delivery systems to provide timely and efficient information and tools.

Many of these internal changes involve collaboration between sectors and departments as they integrate existing business systems. This process involves considerable organizational change, and for the change to be sustained, issues related to good governance must be considered. If they are not, the long-term success of the initiative may be at risk.

Put differently, governments are fairly good at setting up shared arrangements in order to undertake specific projects. One example is the Ontario Government of Canada project called the lost wallet Web site (http://canadians-canadiens. gc.ca/wallet/wallet_e.html). One of the lessons arising from the lost wallet project was that more emphasis should have been placed on the long-term governance of the project.

One way to protect the long-term sustainability of e-projects—whether for internal or external users—is to pay attention to the expected outcomes and impacts. Is there clarity and agreement on what these outcomes are? In collaborative arrangements or partnerships, it is important that each partner and stakeholder agree not only on what the long-range outcomes are, but what their contribution to the arrangement will be. This will have implications for accountability and reporting.

Outcomes are not the same as outputs. An output might refer to a specific application of an integrated financial system. Determining outcomes moves the reference point into the realm of behavioural and organizational changes: for example, one outcome of a two-department, integrated financial system might be to promote a culture of collaboration and to nurture horizontal management skills among the public servants in those departments. Another might be to encourage public servants to make greater use of e-systems when accessing these products and services.

The creation of a shared outcome is one thing; the evaluation of it is quite another. Evaluation of outcomes can be difficult for a number of reasons. First of all, since outcomes are usually long-term in nature, they are often difficult to maintain in government and may change. Second, there is often uncertainty about causality when measuring an outcome: for example, in the case noted above, if, in fact, a culture of collaboration and horizontal management does not develop among the public servants of the two departments, would it prove that the integrated financial system was a failure? Might there not have been other factors at play, such as outdated departmental rules and regulations?

In spite of these challenges, the setting of shared outcomes and their measurement are important steps in ensuring the long-term sustainability of arrangements, such as those that arise from public sector e-systems for administration. The stakes can be high since shared e-systems typically involve large investments as well as multiple partners and stakeholders, including politicians, managers, developers (often from the private sector) and, of course, users. By agreeing on the outcomes and the role that each player has in ensuring them, the chances of misunderstanding and project failure can be minimized.

And still, in spite of Canada's high standing in terms of the percentage of Canadian citizens accessing government services or products online, it can be difficult—and frustrating—for Canadians to find what they want from government online.

If you build it, they will come. That may have worked for a baseball diamond in a cornfield as it did in the movie *Field of Dreams*, but when it comes to online government services, the Canadian government should probably let citizens and businesses know about them and entice them to use these services.

Canada's government portal, **www.gc.ca**, has received kudos both in a variety of e-government studies and from other countries, which look to it as a model for their own sites. It has three gateways—services for Canadians, services for non-Canadians, and services for businesses. But people do not seem to be taking full advantage of those services.

BusinessGateway.ca, the portal for Canadian businesses, files its business information and applications under 10 different sections, but Jaime Pitfield, Director General for government online at Industry Canada in Ottawa, said businesses mostly use just four sections: Business Start Up, Tax, Regulations, and Financing.

The lesser-used areas are: Business Statistics and Analysis, E-Business, Human Resources Management, Exporting/Importing, Innovation/Research and Development/Technology, and Selling to Government/Tenders.

Pitfield said the government has not really focused on marketing BusinessGateway.ca: "We have to be more creative in how we get the URL out there." He added that 70 percent of visitors to BusinessGateway.ca are first-time users, and he admitted they need to improve on that statistic. According to Pitfield, the majority of businesses using the portal are small businesses, with 50 percent of users having 10 or fewer employees. "I think the reason is that big business is more sophisticated in terms of dealing with government," he said.

The Canadian government has promised that by 2005 (it was recently pushed back a year), through the GOL initiative, Canadians will have electronic access to all federal programs and services. The guiding principles for Canada's government site and online initiatives boil down two areas: (1) organizing services and information around the needs and expectations of citizens, and (2) taking a whole government approach, incorporating services from all levels of government and public sector departments. In terms of service organization, the government is looking to make services accessible to all, easy to use, less time consuming, and less costly to use.

Mark Groleau, controller of -Fluke Transportation Group and Fox 40 International, based in Hamilton, Ontario, said the government portal was very easy to use. He has used the tax section of BusinessGateway.ca to look up tax bulletins and to access forms, which are all indexed on the site and can be printed or, in some cases, e-mailed directly. "It's just as good as if I went to a post office or government office and picked up the forms there." The tax area is linked directly to the CCRA, and Groleau said he used both those sites frequently. "I think what they've done is excellent, but I wonder how many people know it exists?" He added that when compared with the government sites he has used in the United States, Canada's site is much more customer friendly.

That assertion is in agreement with the results of a recent Accenture study. The 2002 report, *Realizing the Vision,* looked at 23 countries and measured the online government services available in each, how the services had changed since 2001 and highlighted emerging trends in e-government. Canada was ranked first, trailed closely by Singapore and the United States.

The study found that of the 64 online services the Canadian government offers, 32 achieved the maximum CRM (customer relationship management) score. The key to this, it states, is that Canada deploys services that are based on user research and attuned to user needs. Pitfield said focus groups and testing procedures are used to determine the needs of each service before it can be brought online by the Canadian government.

Graeme Gordon, partner responsible for e-government practice at Accenture in Ottawa, said Canada maintained its lead this year, even though there were only four new services being offered online at the time. "Canada retained its lead from last year because it's very citizen centred. It did very well in the CRM area. Where it fell down was in the introduction of new services."

"In fact, if you look at the progress Canada made between this year and last year—out of the 23 countries, Canada was 15th in terms of introduction of new services," Gordon said. However, he said it is very clear that Canada is seen as a leader in the global e-government market.

Brian Nutt, the Chief Operationg Officer (COO) of PureEdge Solutions Inc. in Victoria, said that to him as an informed and tech-savvy taxpayer, all government online initiatives seem like a good thing. However, the degree to which GOL will affect the majority of people still remains to be seen. "How quickly can these initiatives impact the traditionally nonconnected citizenry? Government online has to be an enhancement to existing services. There is always going to be a cross section of people who are happier with faxes or mail," Nutt said.

As for taking a "whole of government approach," the Canadian government's Web site states that government wants a centrally coordinated system to achieve progress across the entire government. Collaboration across departments and agencies and across jurisdictions involving not-for-profit and private sectors is also considered imperative.

Currently, Canada's privacy laws make it hard for different departments, provinces, and municipalities to talk to each other openly. Pitfield said open communication and exchange of information is better on the business side of things. "On the individual level, we cannot share information," he said.

However, he added that that kind of easy flow of information and tying in federal and provincial applications are something people want most. According to Pitfield, government has released Version 2 of its portal, and one of the top priorities is working with the provinces. "In focus testing, the groups said, 'Thank you for putting all these forms online, but where are the provincial forms?' So, Version 2 incorporates provincial forms," Pitfield said.

Gaylen Duncan, President of the Information Technology Association of Canada (ITAC) in Ottawa, said Canada is losing ground and users because of privacy and data integration issues. "We lost our privacy long ago. We should merge those files: but we're doing okay compared to a lot of other countries."

Nutt said it would be nice to just have to submit updates, such as an address change, to one Web site and have it automatically be spread throughout all levels of government. "One of the best ways to be more responsive is to get collaboration beyond government boundaries," adding that people have to be more willing to have their information shared.

Gordon agreed that privacy and security are major barriers to the successful implementation of government online services. "How do you deal with it, though? I don't think anyone has the silver bullet for that right now," he said. "It's an opportunity to break down some of the walls, but at the same time do it in such a way that it maintains citizens' comfort levels with the privacy of their data."

Vivienne Jupp, managing partner for global e-government services at Accenture, said as online initiatives mature, they are seeing strategies that recognize barriers. "One of the most serious challenges governments face now is building electronic bridges between agencies at the federal level, but also with their counterparts at the regional, provincial, and local levels," she said.

As it stands now, each province has a link to its own government site off of gc.ca, as do all the ministries and depart-

ments, but visitors are still required to enter information more than once. Pitfield said they are working on a program for Canadian businesses, which will ask for "tombstone" information and carry that through the business gateway, so soon businesses will only have to enter their information once.

Norman Betts, minister of Business New Brunswick, said that beyond data collaboration, GOL has still become a good thing for citizens and businesses. "It has allowed us to not only streamline and be cost efficient in the delivery of government services—and not only to do it conveniently and reduce red tape and all of those things—but to push some of the physical end of the delivery that is required to sustain rural areas," Betts said.

Sources: Victoria Berry, "Governing Online Services," *ComputerWorld Canada*, June 14, 2002, available http://www.itworldcanada.com/index.cfm/highlight_keywords/Governing%20Online%20Services/ci_id/41071.htm, accessed June 7, 2003; "The Canadian Government Is on Top," *CIO Canada Governments Review*, May 1, 2003; "Study: Canadians Utilizing E-Government," *CIO Canada Governments Review*, December 1, 2002; Toby Fyfe, "E-Government on the Inside... Looks a Lot Like the Outside," *CIO Canada Governments Review*, April 1, 2002; Graeme Gordon, "Following the Leader," *CIO Canada Governments Review*, June 1, 2002.

CASE STUDY QUESTIONS

1. Who is in charge of the Government On-Line initiative? Should there be just one person? Should that information be easy to find? To whom or to which department do all of these GOL initiatives report?

2. Of the three "portals" to Canadians, non-Canadians, and businesses, which one do you think should be the top priority? Can all three be a top priority?

3. How does the issues of privacy and security enter into putting government online? How do you think government can "work around" these problems?

4. How do you think government should communicate to its citizens what content they have put online and where it is located?

5. Go online and look at www.businessgateway.ca. What do you think of this Web site? Does it give first-time users a user-friendly way to navigate to information they need? How could it be improved?

SOCIAL, LEGAL, AND ETHICAL ISSUES IN THE INFORMATION AGE

One of your managerial responsibilities is to make informed decisions that reflect an understanding of the ethical and social issues as well as the business issues surrounding the use of information systems. After reading this chapter, you should be able to answer the following questions:

1. *What ethical, social, and political issues are raised by information systems?*

2. *Are there specific principles for conduct that can be used to guide decisions about ethical dilemmas?*

3. *Why does contemporary information technology pose challenges to the protection of individual privacy and intellectual property?*

4. *How have information systems affected everyday life?*

5. *How can organizations develop corporate policies for ethical conduct?*

BT Cellnet Tests the Waters for Spamming

In the United Kingdom, sending short text messages on mobile phones has skyrocketed, especially among teenagers and young adults. This is a demographic group that advertisers are anxious to reach. BT Cellnet, an operator of mobile phone services, is experimenting with using its text messaging service as a marketing channel. When users sign up for their services, mobile phone carriers obtain a great deal of demographic data, which marketers could use to target their

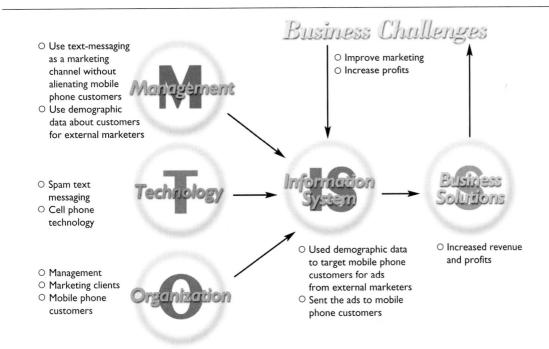

advertisements more precisely to different age and income groups. On the whole, British mobile service operators have been protective of their customers and aggressive against beaming unsolicited electronic messages to them. But the potential revenue stream from using these unsolicited messages, also known as *spam,* to market goods and services is so alluring that some carriers are quietly starting to test the waters.

Working with Enpocket—a spinoff of Engage, an American enterprise marketing software firm—BT Cellnet started testing ads beamed as short text messages to its mobile phone users. One portion of its initial target group consisted of 3000 customers who agreed beforehand to have advertising messages sent to them in exchange for a chance to win a £1000 (Cdn $2250) prize. The other portion of the group consisted of 1000 customers who were beamed messages even though they did not explicitly sign up for the program but were told how to stop the messages if they wished.

The use of spam in mobile commerce (m-commerce) has been criticized by privacy advocates and others concerned with ethical business practices. Many people resent being sent electronic advertisements unless they have voluntarily signed up to receive them. The cost and "nuisance factor" for unsolicited mobile phone messages is far greater than for unsolicited postal mail. Unlike postal junk mail, the cost of electronic spam is generally borne by its recipients, who are charged for both sending and receiving short text messages. But one person's spam is another person's business model, and some electronic pitches provide benefits. Alastair Tempest, Director-General of the European Direct Marketing Association, points out that direct marketing is much more targeted than unsolicited spam and that a ban on spam would hamper "legitimate" marketing.

Sources: Brian McDonough, "BT Cellnet Tests the Water for Mobile Ads," *mBusiness,* February 2002; and Brandon Mitchener, "All Spam, All the Time," *Wall Street Journal,* October 29, 2001.

MANAGEMENT CHALLENGES

Technology can be a double-edged sword. It can be the source of many benefits. One great achievement of contemporary computer systems is the ease with which digital information can be analyzed, transmitted, and shared among many people. But at the same time, this powerful capability creates new opportunities for breaking the law or taking benefits away from others. Balancing the convenience and privacy implications of using m-commerce technology to track consumers and send unsolicited e-mail is one of the compelling ethical issues raised by contemporary information systems. As you read this chapter, you should be aware of the following management challenges:

1. **Understanding the ethical and moral risks of new technology.** Rapid technological change means that the choices facing individuals also rapidly change, and the balance of risk and reward and the probabilities of apprehension for wrongful acts change as well. Protecting individual privacy has become a serious ethical issue. In this environment, it will be important for management to conduct an ethical and social impact analysis of new technologies. One might take each of the moral dimensions described in this chapter and briefly speculate on how a new technology will impact each dimension. There may not always be right answers for how to behave but there should be management awareness of the ethical and moral risks of new technology.

2. **Establishing corporate ethics policies that include information systems issues.** As managers, you will be responsible for developing, enforcing, and explaining corporate ethics policies. Historically, corporate management has paid much more attention to financial integrity and personnel policies than to the information systems area. But from what you will know after reading this chapter, it is clear your corporation should have an ethics policy in the information systems area covering such issues as privacy, property, accountability, system quality, and quality of life. The challenge will be in educating non–information system managers to the need for these policies as well as educating your workforce.

The Internet and electronic commerce have awakened new interest in the ethical and social impacts of information systems. Internet and digital firm technologies that make it easier than ever to assemble, integrate, and distribute information have unleashed new concerns about appropriate use of customer information, the protection of personal privacy, and the protection of intellectual property. These issues have moved to the forefront of social and political debate in Canada and many other countries.

Although protecting personal privacy and intellectual property on the Internet are now in the spotlight, there are other pressing ethical issues raised by the widespread use of information systems. They include establishing accountability for the consequences of information systems, setting standards to safeguard system quality that protect the safety of the individual and society, and preserving values and institutions considered essential to the quality of life in an information society. This chapter describes these issues and suggests guidelines for dealing with these questions, with special attention to the ethical challenges posed by the Internet.

5.1 UNDERSTANDING ETHICAL AND SOCIAL ISSUES RELATED TO SYSTEMS

ethics

Principles of right and wrong that can be used by individuals acting as free moral agents to make choices to guide their behaviour.

Ethics refers to the principles of right and wrong that individuals, acting as free moral agents, use to make choices to guide their behaviour. Information technology and information systems raise new ethical questions for both individuals and societies because they create opportunities for intense social change and, thus, threaten existing distributions of power, money, rights, and obligations. Like other technologies, such as steam engines, electricity, telephone, automobiles, and radio, information technology can be used to achieve social progress, but it can also be used to commit crimes and threaten cherished social values. The development of information technology will produce benefits for many and costs for others. When using information systems, it is essential to ask: What is the ethical and socially responsible course of action?

A MODEL FOR THINKING ABOUT ETHICAL, SOCIAL, AND POLITICAL ISSUES

Ethical, social, and political issues are closely linked. The ethical dilemma you may face as a manager of information systems typically is reflected in social and political debate. One way to think about these relationships is given in Figure 5.1. Imagine society as a more or less calm pond on a summer day, a delicate ecosystem in partial equilibrium with individuals and with social and political institutions. Individuals know how to act in this pond because social institutions (family, education, organizations) have developed well-honed rules of behaviour, and these are backed by laws developed in the political sector that prescribe behaviour and promise sanctions for violations. Now, toss a rock into the centre of the pond. But imagine that instead of a rock, the disturbing force is a powerful shock of new information technology and systems hitting a society more or less at rest. What happens? Ripples, of course.

Suddenly, individual actors are confronted with new situations often not covered by the old rules. Social institutions cannot respond overnight to these ripples; it may take years to develop etiquette, expectations, social responsibility, "politically correct" attitudes, or approved rules. Political institutions also require time before developing new laws and often require the demonstration of real harm before they act. In the meantime, you may have to act. You may be forced to act in a legal "grey area."

We can use this model to illustrate the dynamics that connect ethical, social, and political issues. This model is also useful for identifying the main moral dimensions of the "information society," which cut across various levels of action—individual, social, and political.

MORAL DIMENSIONS OF THE INFORMATION AGE

The major ethical, social, and political issues raised by information systems include the following moral dimensions:

▪ *Information rights and obligations*: What **information rights** do individuals and organizations possess with respect to information about themselves? What can they protect? What obligations do individuals and organizations have concerning this information?

information rights

The rights that individuals and organizations have with respect to information that pertains to themselves.

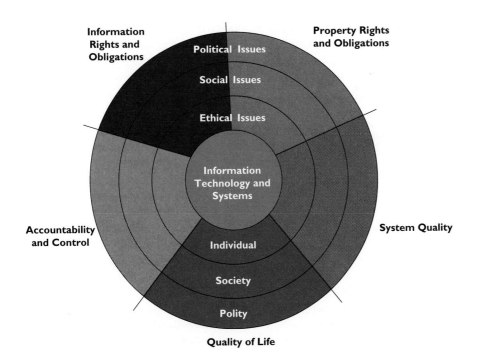

Figure 5.1 The relationship among ethical, social, and political issues in an information society. The introduction of new information technology has a ripple effect, raising new ethical, social, and political issues that must be dealt with on the individual, social, and political levels. These issues have five moral dimensions: information rights and obligations, property rights and obligations, accountability and control, system quality, and quality of life.

▮ *Property rights*: How will traditional intellectual property rights be protected in a digital society in which tracing and accounting for ownership is difficult and ignoring these property rights is so easy?

▮ *Accountability and control*: Who can and will be held accountable and liable for the harm done to individual and collective information and property rights?

▮ *System quality*: What standards of data and system quality should we demand to protect individual rights and the safety of society?

▮ *Quality of life*: What values should be preserved in an information- and knowledge-based society? What institutions should we protect from violation? What cultural values and practices are supported by the new information technology?

We explore these moral dimensions in detail in Section 5.3.

KEY TECHNOLOGY TRENDS THAT RAISE ETHICAL ISSUES

Ethical issues long preceded information technology; they are the abiding concerns of free societies everywhere. Nevertheless, information technology has heightened ethical concerns, put stress on existing social arrangements, and made existing laws obsolete or severely crippled. There are four key technological trends responsible for these ethical stresses, and they are summarized in Table 5.1.

Advances in data storage techniques and rapidly declining storage costs have been responsible for the multiplying databases on individuals—employees, customers, and potential customers—maintained by private and public organizations. These advances in data storage have made the routine violation of individual privacy both cheap and effective. Already massive data storage systems are cheap enough for regional and even local retailing firms to use in identifying customers.

Advances in data analysis techniques for large pools of data are a third technological trend that heightens ethical concerns because they enable companies to find out much more detailed personal information about individuals. With contemporary information technology, companies can assemble and combine the myriad pieces of information on an individual stored by computers much more easily than in the past. Think of all the ways you generate computer information about yourself—credit card purchases, telephone calls, magazine subscriptions, video rentals, mail-order purchases, banking records, and local, state, and federal government records (including court and police records). Put together and mined properly, this information could reveal not only your credit information but also your driving habits, your tastes, your associations, and your political interests.

Companies with products to sell purchase relevant information from these sources to more finely target their marketing campaigns. Chapters 3 and 7 describe how companies can analyze large pools of data from multiple sources to rapidly identify buying patterns of customers and suggest individual responses. The use of computers to combine data from multi-

TABLE 5.1	TECHNOLOGY TRENDS THAT RAISE ETHICAL ISSUES	

Trend	Impact
Computing power doubles every 18 months	More organizations depend on computer systems for critical operations
Rapidly declining data storage costs	Organizations can easily maintain detailed databases on individuals
Data analysis advances	Companies can analyze vast quantities of data gathered on individuals to develop detailed profiles of individual behaviour
Networking advances and the Internet	Copying data from one location to another and accessing personal data from remote locations are much easier.

ple sources and create electronic dossiers of detailed information on individuals is called **profiling**. For example, hundreds of Web sites allow DoubleClick www.doubleclick.net, an Internet advertising broker, to track the activities of their visitors in exchange for revenue from advertisements based on visitor information DoubleClick gathers. DoubleClick uses this information to create a profile of each online visitor, adding more detail to the profile as the visitor accesses an associated DoubleClick site. Over time, DoubleClick can create a detailed dossier of a person's spending and computing habits on the Web that can be sold to companies to help them target their Web ads more precisely.

A new data analysis technology called **non-obvious relationship awareness (NORA)** has given both government and private sectors even more powerful profiling capabilities. NORA can take information about people from many disparate sources, such as employment applications, telephone records, customer listings, and "wanted" lists, and correlate relationships to find obscure hidden connections that might help identify criminals or terrorists (see Figure 5.2). NORA technology can scan data and extract information as the data are being generated so that it could, for example, instantly identify a man at an airline ticket counter who shares a phone number with a known terrorist before that person boards an airplane. The technology could prove a valuable tool for homeland security but does have significant privacy implications.

Last, advances in networking, including the Internet, promise to greatly reduce the costs of moving and accessing large quantities of data and open the possibility of mining large pools of data remotely using small desktop machines, permitting an invasion of privacy on a scale and precision previously unimaginable.

The development of global digital-superhighway communication networks widely available to individuals and businesses poses many ethical and social concerns. Who will account for the flow of information over these networks? Will you be able to trace information collected about you? What will these networks do to the traditional relationships among family, work, and leisure? How will traditional job designs be altered when millions of "employees" become subcontractors using mobile offices which they themselves must pay for?

profiling

The use of computers to combine data from multiple sources and create electronic dossiers of detailed information on individuals.

non-obvious relationship awareness (NORA)

Technology that can find obscure hidden connections between people or other entities by analyzing information from many different sources to correlate relationships.

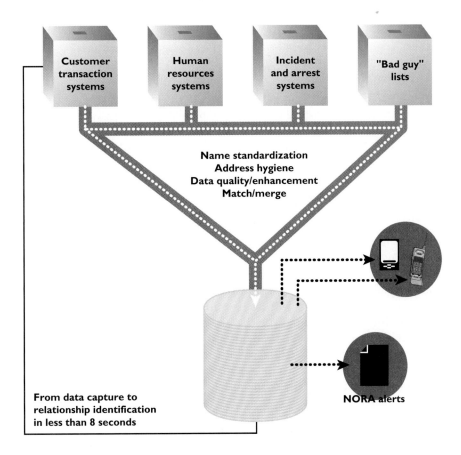

Figure 5.2 Non-Obvious Relationship Awareness (NORA). NORA technology can take information about people from disparate sources and find obscure, non-obvious relationships. It might discover, for example, that an applicant for a job at a casino shares a telephone number with a known criminal and issue an alert to the hiring manager.

Credit card purchases can make personal information available to market researchers, telephone marketers, and direct mail companies. Advances in information technology facilitate the invasion of privacy.

In the next section, we consider some ethical principles and analytical techniques for dealing with these kinds of ethical and social concerns.

5.2 ETHICS IN AN INFORMATION SOCIETY

Ethics is a concern of humans who have freedom of choice. Ethics is about individual choice: When faced with alternative courses of action, what is the correct ethical choice? What are the main features of "ethical choice?

BASIC CONCEPTS: RESPONSIBILITY, ACCOUNTABILITY, AND LIABILITY

responsibility

Accepting the potential costs, duties, and obligations for the decisions one makes.

accountability

The mechanisms for assessing responsibility for decisions made and actions taken.

liability

The existence of laws that permit individuals to recover the damages done to them by other actors, systems, or organizations.

due process

A process in which laws are well known and understood and there is an ability to appeal to higher authorities to ensure that laws are applied correctly.

Ethical choices are decisions made by individuals who are responsible for the consequences of their actions. **Responsibility** is a key element of ethical action. Responsibility means that you accept the potential costs, duties, and obligations for the decisions you make. **Accountability** is a feature of systems and social institutions. It means that mechanisms are in place to determine who took responsible action, who is responsible. Systems and institutions in which it is impossible to find out who took what action are inherently incapable of ethical analysis or ethical action. Liability extends the concept of responsibility further to the area of the law. **Liability** is a feature of political systems in which a body of laws is in place that permits individuals to recover the damages done to them by other actors, systems, or organizations. **Due process** is a related feature of law-governed societies and is a process in which laws are known and understood, and there is an ability to appeal to higher authorities to ensure that the laws are applied correctly.

These basic concepts form the underpinning of an ethical analysis of information systems and those who manage them. First, as discussed in Chapter 3, information technologies are filtered through social institutions, organizations, and individuals. Systems do not have "impacts" by themselves. Whatever information system impacts exist are products of institutional, organizational, and individual actions and behaviours. Second, responsibility for the consequences of technology falls clearly on the institutions, organizations, and individual managers who choose to use the technology. Using information technology in a "socially responsible" manner means that you can and will be held accountable for the consequences of your actions. Third, in an ethical political society, individuals and others can recover damages done to them through a set of laws characterized by due process. The Manager's Toolkit provides some guidelines for performing an ethical analysis.

MIS IN ACTION: MANAGER'S TOOLKIT

HOW TO CONDUCT AN ETHICAL ANALYSIS

When confronted with a situation that presents ethical issues, how should you analyze and reason about the situation? Here is a five-step process to guide your decision making:

1. *Identify and clearly describe the facts.* Find out who did what to whom, and where, when, and how. In many instances, you will be surprised at the errors in the initially reported facts, and often, you will find that simply getting the facts straight helps define the solution. It also helps to get the opposing parties involved in an ethical dilemma to agree on the facts.

2. *Define the conflict or dilemma, and identify the higher-order values involved.* Ethical, social, and political issues always reference higher values. The parties to a dispute all claim to be pursuing higher values (e.g., freedom, privacy, protection of property, or the free enterprise system). Typically, an ethical issue involves a dilemma: two diametrically opposed courses of action that support worthwhile values. For example, the chapter-opening vignette and the Window

on Organizations illustrate two competing values: the need for companies to use marketing to become more profitable and the need to protect individual privacy.

3. *Identify the stakeholders.* Every ethical, social, and political issue has stakeholders: players in the game who have an interest in the outcome, who have invested in the situation, and who usually have vocal opinions. Find out the identity of these groups and what they want. This will be useful later when designing a solution.

4. *Identify the options that you can reasonably take.* You may find that none of the options satisfy all the interests involved but that some options do a better job than others. Sometimes, arriving at a "good" or ethical solution may not always be a "balancing" of consequences to stakeholders.

5. *Identify the potential consequences of your options.* Some options may be ethically correct, but disastrous from other points of view. Other options may work in this one instance but not in other similar instances. Always ask yourself, "What if I choose this option consistently over time?"

CANDIDATE ETHICAL PRINCIPLES

Once your analysis is complete, what ethical principles or rules should you use to make a decision? What higher-order values should inform your judgment? Although you are the only one who can decide which among many ethical principles you will follow and how you will prioritize them, it is helpful to consider some ethical principles with deep roots in many cultures that have survived throughout recorded history.

1. Do unto others as you would have them do unto you (the Golden Rule). Putting yourself in the place of others and thinking of yourself as the object of the decision can help you think about "fairness" in decision making.

2. If an action is not right for everyone to take, then it is not right for anyone (**Immanuel Kant's categorical imperative**). Ask yourself, "If everyone did this, could the organization, or society, survive?"

3. If an action cannot be taken repeatedly, then it is not right to take at all (**Descartes' rule of change**). This is the slippery-slope rule: An action may bring about a small change now that is acceptable, but if repeated, would bring unacceptable changes in the long run. In the vernacular, it might be stated as, "Once started down a slippery slope, you may not be able to stop."

4. Take the action that achieves the higher or greater value (**utilitarian principle**). This rule assumes you can prioritize values in a rank order and understand the consequences of various courses of action.

5. Take the action that produces the least harm or the least potential cost (**risk aversion principle**). Some actions have extremely high failure costs of very low probability (e.g., building a nuclear generating facility in an urban area) or extremely high failure costs of moderate probability (speeding and automobile accidents). Avoid these high-failure-cost actions, paying greater attention obviously to the high failure cost potential of moderate to high probability.

6. Assume that virtually all tangible and intangible objects are owned by someone else unless there is a specific declaration otherwise. (This is the **ethical "no free lunch" rule**.) If something someone else has created is useful to you, it has value, and you should assume the creator wants compensation for this work.

Immanuel Kant's categorical imperative

A principle that states that if an action is not right for everyone to take, it is not right for anyone.

Descartes' rule of change

A principle that states that if an action cannot be taken repeatedly, then it is not right to be taken at any time.

utilitarian principle

A principle that assumes that one can put values in rank order and understand the consequences of various courses of action.

risk aversion principle

A principle that states that one should take the action that produces the least harm or incurs the least cost.

ethical "no free lunch" rule

An assumption that all tangible and intangible objects are owned by someone else unless there is a specific declaration otherwise and that the creator wants compensation for this work.

Although these ethical rules cannot be guides to action, actions that do not easily pass these rules deserve some very close scrutiny and a great deal of caution. The appearance of unethical behaviour may do as much harm to you and your company as actual unethical behaviour.

PROFESSIONAL CODES OF CONDUCT

When groups of people claim to be professionals, they take on special rights and obligations because of their special claims to knowledge, wisdom, and respect. Professional codes of conduct are promulgated by associations of professionals, such as the Canadian Medical Association (CMA), the Canadian Bar Association (CBA), the Association of Information Technology Professionals (AITP), the Canadian Information Processing Society (CIPS), and the Association of Computing Machinery (ACM). These professional groups take responsibility for the partial regulation of their professions by determining entrance qualifications and competence. Codes of ethics are promises by professions to regulate themselves in the general interests of society. For example, avoiding harm to others, honouring property rights (including intellectual property), and respecting privacy are among the General Moral Imperatives of the ACM's Code of Ethics and Professional Conduct (ACM, 1993).

SOME REAL-WORLD ETHICAL DILEMMAS

Information systems have created new ethical dilemmas in which one set of interests is pitted against another. For example, many of the large telephone companies in Canada are using information technology to reduce the sizes of their workforces. Voice recognition software reduces the need for human operators by allowing computers to recognize a customer's responses to a series of computerized questions.

Many companies monitor what their employees are doing on the Internet to prevent them from wasting company resources on nonbusiness activities. Computer Associates International fired at least 10 employees at its Herndon office in December 2000 for sending sexually explicit e-mail. Xerox Corporation fired 40 workers in 1999 for spending too much of their work time surfing the Web. A Mississauga, Ontario, engineer was fired from his job for sending pictures of Cindy Crawford in a bathing suit over e-mail (See Chapter 9). Firms believe they have the right to monitor employee e-mail and Web use because they own the facilities, intend their use to be for business purposes only, and create the facility for a business purpose (see the Window on Management in Chapter 8).

In each instance, you can find competing values at work, with groups lined on either side of a debate. A company may argue, for example, that it has the right to use information systems to increase productivity and reduce the size of its workforce to lower costs and stay in business. Employees displaced by information systems may argue that employers have some responsibility for their welfare. Business owners might feel obligated to monitor employee e-mail and Internet use to minimize drains on productivity (Urbaczewski and Jessup, 2002). Employees might believe they should be able to use the Internet for short personal tasks in place of the telephone (see Figure 5.3). A close analysis of the facts can sometimes produce compromised solutions that give each side "half a loaf." Try to apply some of the principles of ethical analysis described to each of these cases. What is the right thing to do?

5.3   THE MORAL DIMENSIONS OF INFORMATION SYSTEMS

In this section, we take a closer look at the five moral dimensions of information systems first described in Figure 5.1. In each dimension, we identify the ethical, social, and political levels of analysis and use real-world examples to illustrate the values involved, the stakeholders, and the options chosen.

INFORMATION RIGHTS: PRIVACY AND FREEDOM IN THE INTERNET AGE

privacy

The claim of individuals to be left alone, free from surveillance or interference from other individuals, organizations, or the state.

Privacy is the claim of individuals to be left alone, free from surveillance or interference from other individuals or organizations, including the state. Claims to privacy are also involved at

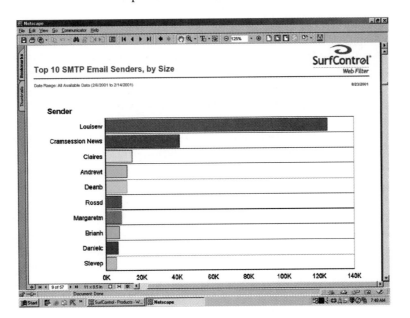

Figure 5.3 SurfControl offers tools for tracking Web and e-mail activity and for filtering unauthorized e-mail and Web site content. The benefits of monitoring employee e-mail and Internet use should be balanced with the need to respect employee privacy.

the workplace. Millions of employees are subject to electronic and other forms of high-tech surveillance (Ball, 2001). Information technology and systems threaten individual claims to privacy by making the invasion of privacy cheap, profitable, and effective.

A description of Canadian and American privacy laws is given below. In terms of international trade, organizations need to follow the privacy laws of the countries of their trading partners. For this reason, we have chosen to highlight American privacy laws as the United States is Canada's most significant trading partner. We also highlight European privacy protection laws. While these laws are similar, there are some interesting differences.

The claim to privacy is protected in the Canadian, American, and German charters or constitutions in a variety of ways, and in other countries through various statutes. In Canada, the claim to privacy is protected primarily by the right to be secure against unreasonable search or seizure found in the Charter of Rights and Freedoms. In addition, on April 13, 2000, Parliament passed the ***Personal Information Protection and Electronic Documents Act (PIPEDA)***, Canada's modern privacy law. The *PIPEDA* establishes the following principles to govern the collection, use, and disclosure of personal information: accountability, identifying the purposes for the collection of personal information, obtaining consent, limiting collection, limiting use, disclosure and retention, ensuring accuracy, providing adequate security, making information management policies readily available, providing individuals with access to information about themselves, and giving individuals the right to challenge an organization's compliance with these principles.

The *PIPEDA* further provides for the Privacy Commissioner to receive complaints concerning contraventions of the principles, conduct investigations, and attempt to resolve such complaints. Unresolved disputes relating to certain matters can be taken to the Federal Court for resolution. The law's provisions are being phased in from January 1, 2001, to January 1, 2004. This act complements the 1983 *Privacy Act,* which imposes rules on how federal government departments and agencies collect, use, and disclose personal information.

Every Canadian province and territory has enacted legislation parallel to the federal *Privacy Act* and the *Access to Information Act.* These laws prevent the unnecessary distribution of one's personal information and guarantee access to unrestricted government information.

As in the federal jurisdiction, the laws apply only to information held by the public sector. "Public sector" organizations under the privacy laws include public or private companies that are regulated by the government, such as financial institutions, air transportation companies, and broadcast media. Quebec is the only province with a privacy law governing the private sector. Other than in Quebec, there are no laws in Canada that regulate what private businesses can do with your personal information. This means that there is nothing to prevent a private company from distributing your personal information to other businesses. At

Personal Information Protection and Electronic Documents Act (PIPEDA)

Canada's modern privacy law that established Canada's fair information principles governing the collection, use, and disclosure of personal information.

present, Quebec is the only province with privacy laws for the private sector that meet European Union (EU) standards. That is significant for international trade, which increasingly focuses on information, not hard products. Interestingly, the United States does not meet the EU standards either.

Due process has become a key concept in defining privacy. Due process requires that a set of rules or laws exist that clearly define how information about individuals will be treated and what appeal mechanisms are available. Perhaps the best statement of due process in record keeping is given by the *Canadian Standards Association's Model Privacy Code*. Published in March 1996, the Code establishes 10 basic principles for all organizations that collect or use personal information. Retailers, direct marketers, financial institutions, telecommunications companies, product manufacturers, service providers, schools, universities, hospitals, personnel departments, and government agencies are potential users.

By choosing to adopt the Code, organizations demonstrate that they are following fair, nationally accepted principles. The Code is also an important resource for consumers, employees, patients, and other "data subjects," says Professor Jim Savary, former Vice-President of Policy and Issues at the Consumers' Association of Canada. "The Code is a vehicle for challenging an organization's behaviour. You can refer to these principles if you are uneasy about the information you are asked to supply or how it will be used."

The 10 practices in the Code are:

1. Accountability
2. Identifying purposes
3. Consent
4. Limiting collection
5. Limiting use, disclosure, and retention
6. Accuracy
7. Safeguards
8. Openness
9. Individual access
10. Challenging compliance

Fair Information Practices (FIP)

A set of principles, originally set forth in 1973, that governs the collection and use of information about individuals and forms the basis of most North American and European privacy laws.

Most North American and European privacy laws are based on a regime called Fair Information Practices (FIP), first set forth in a report written in 1973 by an American government advisory committee (U.S. Department of Health, Education, and Welfare, 1973). **Fair Information Practices (FIP)** is a set of principles governing the collection and use of information about individuals. Fair Information Practices preceded, but are similar to, the *Model Privacy Code* in Canada. The five Fair Information Practices principles are listed in Table 5.2.

FIP principles are based on the notion of a "mutuality of interest" between the record holder and the individual. The individual has an interest in engaging in a transaction, and the record keeper—usually a business or government agency—requires information about

TABLE 5.2	**PRINCIPLES OF FAIR INFORMATION PRACTICES**

1. There should be no personal record systems whose existence is secret.

2. Individuals have rights of access, inspection, review, and amendment to systems that contain information about them.

3. There must be no use of personal information for purposes other than those for which it was gathered without prior consent.

4. Managers of systems are responsible and can be held accountable and liable for the damage done by systems for their reliability and security.

5. Governments have the right to intervene in the information relationships among private parties.

TABLE 5.3 **FEDERAL PRIVACY LAWS IN THE UNITED STATES**

1. **General Federal Privacy Laws**

    Freedom of Information Act, 1968 as Amended (5 USC 552)

    Privacy Act of 1974 as Amended (5 USC 552a)

    Electronic Communications Privacy Act of 1986

    Computer Matching and Privacy Protection Act of 1988

    Computer Security Act of 1987

    Federal Managers Financial Integrity Act of 1982

2. **Privacy Laws Affecting Private Institutions**

    Fair Credit Reporting Act of 1970

    Family Educational Rights and Privacy Act of 1978

    Right to Financial Privacy Act of 1978

    Privacy Protection Act of 1980

    Cable Communications Policy Act of 1984

    Electronic Communications Privacy Act of 1986

    Video Privacy Protection Act of 1988

    Communications Privacy and Consumer Empowerment Act of 1997

    Data Privacy Act of 1997

    Consumer Internet Privacy Protection Act of 1999

the individual to support the transaction. Once gathered, the individual maintains an interest in the record, and the record may not be used to support other activities without the individual's consent.

Fair Information Practices form the basis of 16 American statutes (see Table 5.3) that set forth the conditions for handling information about individuals in such areas as credit reporting, education, financial records, newspaper records, cable communications, electronic communications, and even video rentals. Knowledge of these laws is important to any organization engaging in trade with American organizations. The American *Privacy Act* of 1974 is the most important of these laws, regulating the federal government's collection, use, and disclosure of information. Most federal privacy laws apply only to the federal government. Only credit, banking, cable, and video rental industries have been regulated by American privacy law.

In the United States, privacy law is enforced by individuals who must sue agencies or companies in court to recover damages. European countries and Canada define privacy in a similar manner to that in the United States, but they have chosen to enforce their privacy laws by creating privacy commissions or data protection agencies to pursue complaints brought by citizens.

The European Directive on Data Protection

In Europe, privacy protection is much more stringent than in North America. Unlike North America, European countries do not allow businesses to use personally identifiable information without consumers' prior consent. On October 25, 1998, the European Commission's Directive on Data Protection came into effect, broadening privacy protection in the EU nations. The directive requires companies to inform people when they collect information about them and disclose how it will be stored and used. Customers must provide their informed consent before any company can legally use data about them, and they have the right to access that information, correct it, and request that no further data be collected. **Informed consent** can be defined as consent given with knowledge of all the facts needed to make a rational decision. EU member nations must translate these principles into their own laws and cannot transfer personal data to such countries as Canada that do not have similar privacy protection regulations.

informed consent

Consent given with knowledge of all the facts needed to make a rational decision.

Figure 5.4 How cookies can identify Web visitors. Cookies are written by a Web site on a visitor's hard drive. When the visitor returns to that Web site, the Web server requests the ID number from the cookie and uses it to access the data stored by that server on that visitor. The Web site can then use these data to display personalized information.

cookie

Tiny file deposited on a computer hard drive when an individual visits certain Web sites; used to identify the visitor and track visits to the Web site.

Cookies? I Didn't Order Any Cookies

Here is how a cookie works:

1. A user opens a Web browser and selects a Web site to visit.

2. The user's computer sends a request for information to the computer running the Web site.

3. The Web site computer, called a server, sends the information that allows the user's computer to display the Web site. It also sends a cookie —a data file that contains information like an encrypted user ID and information about when the user visited and what the user did on the site.

www

4. The user's computer receives the cookie and places it in a file on the hard drive.

5. Whenever the user goes back to the Web site, the server running the site retrieves the cookie to help it identify the user.

www

The *PIPEDA*, passed by Parliament in 1999, places Canada in accord with the European Directive on Data Protection, permitting Canadians to continue to do business with European companies. The *PIPEDA* requires consent from consumers before a company can collect or distribute information about them.

Internet Challenges to Privacy

Internet technology has posed new challenges to the protection of individual privacy. Information sent over this vast network of networks may pass through many different computer systems before it reaches its final destination. Each of these systems is capable of monitoring, capturing, and storing communications that pass through it.

It is possible to record many online activities, including which online newsgroups or files a person has accessed, which Web sites and Web pages he or she has visited, and what items that person has inspected or purchased over the Web. Much of this monitoring and tracking of Web site visitors occurs in the background without the visitor's knowledge. Tools to monitor visits to the World Wide Web have become popular because they help organizations determine who is visiting their Web sites and how to better target their offerings. (Some firms also monitor their employees' Internet use to see how they are using company network resources.) Web retailers now have access to software that lets them watch the online shopping behaviour of individuals and groups while they are visiting a Web site and making purchases. The commercial demand for this personal information is enormous.

Web sites can learn the identity of their visitors if the visitors voluntarily register at the site to purchase a product or service or to obtain a free service, such as information. Web sites can also capture information about visitors without their knowledge using "cookie" technology. **Cookies** are tiny files deposited on a computer hard drive when a user visits certain Web sites. Cookies identify the visitor's Web browser software and track visits to the Web site. When the visitor returns to a site that has deposited a cookie, the Web site software will search the visitor's computer, find the cookie, and "know" what that person has done in the past. It may also update the cookie, depending on the activity during the visit. In this way, the site can customize its contents for each visitor's interests. For example, if you purchase a book on the Amazon.com Web site and return later from the same browser, the site will welcome you by name and recommend other books of interest on the basis of your past purchases. DoubleClick, introduced earlier in this chapter, uses cookies to build its dossiers with details of online purchases and to examine the behaviour of Web site visitors. Figure 5.4 illustrates how cookies work.

Web sites using "cookie" technology cannot directly obtain visitors' names and addresses. However, if a person has registered at a site, that information can be combined with cookie data to identify the visitor. Web site owners can also combine the data they have gathered from "cookies" and other Web site monitoring tools with personal data from other sources, such as offline data collected from surveys or paper catalogue purchases, to develop very detailed profiles of their visitors. (See Figure 5.5.)

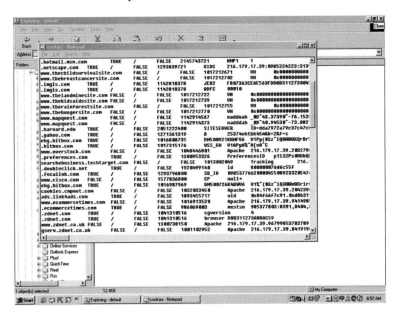

Figure 5.5 Cookies are tiny files deposited on a computer hard drive when users visit certain Web sites. Although cookies can provide valuable marketing information, the practice of collecting Web site visitor data raises worries about protecting individual privacy.

The Internet is inspiring even more subtle and surreptitious tools for surveillance (Bennett, 2001). **Web bugs** (sometimes called *invisible.GIFs* or *clear.GIFS*) are tiny graphic files embedded in e-mail messages and Web pages that are designed to monitor who is reading the e-mail message or Web page. They transmit information about the user and the page being viewed to a monitoring computer. Because Web bugs are very tiny, colourless, and virtually invisible, they can be difficult for unsophisticated Internet users to detect. Marketers use these Web bugs as another tool to monitor online behaviour and can develop detailed consumer profiles by combining Web bug data with data from other sources.

Canada has allowed businesses to gather transaction information generated in the marketplace and then use that information for other marketing purposes without obtaining the informed consent of the individual whose information is being used. Canadian e-commerce sites are largely content to publish statements on their Web sites informing visitors about how their information will be used. Some have added *opt-out* selection boxes to these information policy statements. An **opt-out** model of informed consent permits the collection of personal information until the consumer specifically requests that the data *not* be collected. Privacy advocates would like to see wider use of an **opt-in** model of informed consent in which a business is prohibited from collecting any personal information unless the consumer takes specific action to approve information collection and use.

The online industry has preferred self-regulation to privacy legislation for protecting consumers. In 1998, the online industry formed the Online Privacy Alliance to encourage self-regulation to develop a set of privacy guidelines for its members. The group is promoting the use of online "seals," such as that of TRUSTe, certifying Web sites adhering to certain privacy principles. Members of the advertising network industry, including DoubleClick, Adforce, Avenue A, and 24/7 Media, have created an additional industry association called the Network Advertising Initiative (NAI, www.networkadvertising.org) to develop its own privacy policies to help consumers opt out of advertising network programs and provide consumer redress from abuses. In general, however, most Internet businesses do little to protect the privacy of their customers, and consumers do not do as much as they should to protect themselves (see the Window on Organizations).

Web bugs

Tiny graphic files embedded in e-mail messages and Web pages that are designed to monitor online Internet user behaviour.

opt-out

Model of informed consent permitting the collection of personal information until the consumer specifically requests that the data not be collected.

opt-in

Model of informed consent prohibiting an organization from collecting any personal information unless the individual takes specific action to approve information collection and use.

Technical Solutions

In addition to legislation, new technologies are being developed to protect user privacy during interactions with Web sites. Many of these tools are used for encrypting e-mail, for making e-mail or Web surfing activities appear anonymous, or for preventing user computers from accepting "cookies." Table 5.4 describes some of these tools.

Interest is now growing in tools to help users determine the kind of personal data that can be extracted by Web sites. The Platform for Privacy Preferences, known as P3P, enables

PRIVACY FOR SALE

Jupiter Research, an online consulting company, published a report on June 3, 2002, that concluded that most Internet businesses do very little to protect the privacy of individuals who use the Net, nor do their customers. Rob Leathern, the author of the report, said, "If you make it easy for customers to exercise their privacy rights, they will do it." But, the report concludes, most customers will not protect their own privacy if it is difficult, and neither will the corporations.

For Internet companies, the cause appears to be easy to understand. Profits are difficult to achieve on the Internet, and so companies want to collect information about visitors to their sites, including such information as names, e-mail addresses, postal addresses, and even telephone numbers for the purpose of increasing their own sales and selling that data to other companies. Several studies have found that only 50 percent of the companies surveyed had privacy policies, even though most have Web sites. Of the companies that do post privacy policies on their Web sites, more than half do not monitor their sites to make sure they adhere to these policies.

Yahoo!, the giant Internet portal, is one of many examples. It has informed its registered users that it can send them e-mail advertisements and make telemarketing calls to them, even though some of them had previously chosen not to receive any marketing from Yahoo! Yahoo! claimed it had not loosened its privacy policy but only made it more explicit and that it would focus primarily on selling its own services, rather than those of its advertisers. "What Yahoo! has done is unconscionable," said Seth Godin, formerly Yahoo!'s vice-president for direct marketing. He continued, "They would be better off sending offers to a million people who said they want to receive a coupon each day," rather than to 10 million, most of whom did not want to receive them. Mark Rotenberg, Executive Director of the Electronic Privacy Information Center (EPIC), explained, "People thought they were going to get e-mail solicitations. They didn't expect that their dealings with Yahoo! would cause them to receive phone calls."

America Online, the largest Internet service provider, has rented its subscribers list to others for a long time and also calls users to promote its services. CNET's ZDNet rents (but does not sell) its list to mailing-list brokers. One such broker, Direct Media of Greenwich, Connecticut, enables businesses to use its list of nearly three million names at a cost of $125 per thousand for a single mailing. Advertisers typically pay for the right to use each name on the list for a single mailing or telephone call, but they do not own the information outright.

The Jupiter Research report found a similar problem with consumers. About 70 percent of online customers claim they are concerned about online privacy, but only 40 percent say they even read the privacy statements on Web sites. At the same time, 82 percent of online users admit they would give personal information when shopping at new Web sites if they were offered a chance to win $100. Only one-third of one percent of Yahoo! users abandoned Yahoo! after it announced its new privacy policy. Several companies, such as Zero-Knowledge Systems and SafeWeb, have offered products that enable users to surf the Web anonymously, but consumers have been reluctant to pay for these technologies. A few companies, such as Hewlett-Packard, install this software on the new computers they sell. Other companies also purchase the software so they can maintain privacy in their communications with their own remote employees. But consumers remain unwilling to purchase this software.

To Think About: Apply the guidelines for ethical analysis to the failure to protect the privacy of individuals. On the basis of this analysis, what legal or business steps do you think should be taken to better protect the privacy of customers using the Internet?

Sources: Bob Tedeschi, "Privacy Is Common Issue Online," *New York Times*, June 3, 2002; Saul Hansell, "Seeking Profits, Internet Companies Alter Privacy Policy," *New York Times*, April 11, 2002; "The Big Yahoo! Privacy Storm That Wasn't," *Wall Street Journal*, May 13, 2002; Rick Whiting, "Making Privacy Work,"*Information-Week*, August 19, 2002; and Jane Black, "Faceless Snoopers Have the Upper Hand," *BusinessWeek Online*, June 5, 2002, **www.businessweek.com**.

P3P

Industry standard designed to give users more control over personal information gathered on the Web sites they visit; stands for Platform for Privacy Preferences.

automatic communication of privacy policies between an electronic commerce (e-commerce) site and its visitors. **P3P** provides a standard for communicating a Web site's privacy policy to Internet users and for comparing that policy to the user's preferences or to other standards, such as the U.S. Federal Trade Commission's new FIP guidelines or the European Directive on Data Protection. Users can use P3P to select the level of privacy they wish to maintain when interacting with the Web site (see Figure 5.6).

The P3P standard allows Web sites to publish privacy policies in a form that computers can understand. Once codified according to P3P rules, the privacy policy becomes part of the software for individual Web pages. Users of recent versions of Microsoft Internet Explorer Web browsing software can access and read the P3P site's privacy policy and a list of all cookies coming from the site. Internet Explorer lets users adjust their computers to screen out all cookies or let in selected cookies based on specific levels of privacy. For example, the "medium" level accepts cookies from "first-party" host sites that have opt-in or opt-out policies but rejects third-party cookies that use personally identifiable information without an opt-in policy.

TABLE 5.4 **PRIVACY PROTECTION TOOLS**

Privacy Protection Function	Description	Example
Managing cookies	Block or limit cookies from being placed on the user's computer	Microsoft Internet Explorer 5 and 6 CookieCrusher
Blocking ads	Control ads that pop up based on user profiles and prevent ads from collecting or sending information	BHO Cop AdSubtract
Encrypting e-mail or data	Scramble e-mail or data so that they cannot be read	Pretty Good Privacy (PGP)
Anonymizers	Allow users to surf the Web without being identified or to send anonymous e-mail	Anonymizer.com

However, P3P only works with Web sites of members of the World Wide Web Consortium who have translated their Web site privacy policies into P3P format. The technology will display cookies from Web sites that are not part of the consortium, but users will not be able to obtain sender information or privacy statements. Many users may also need to be educated about interpreting company privacy statements and P3P levels of privacy.

Ethical Issues

The ethical privacy issue in this information age is as follows: Under what conditions should I (you) invade the privacy of others? What legitimates intruding into others' lives through unobtrusive surveillance, through market research, or by whatever means? Do we have to inform people that we are eavesdropping? Do we have to inform people that we are using credit history information for employment screening purposes?

Social Issues

The social issue of privacy concerns the development of "expectations of privacy" or privacy norms, as well as public attitudes. In what areas of life should we as a society encourage people to think they are in "private territory" as opposed to public view? For instance, should we as a society encourage people to develop expectations of privacy when using electronic mail, cellular telephones, bulletin boards, the postal system, the workplace, or the street? Should expectations of privacy be extended to criminal conspirators? (See Figure 5.7.)

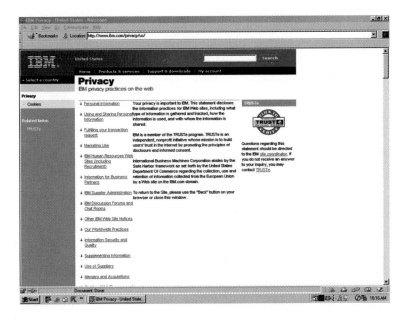

Figure 5.6 Web sites are starting to post their privacy policies for visitors to review. The TRUSTe seal designates Web sites that have agreed to adhere to TRUSTe's established privacy principles of disclosure, choice, access, and security.

Figure 5.7 Recent versions of Microsoft's Internet Explorer Web browsing software support the P3P system for establishing Web site visitor privacy preferences. Users can adjust P3P settings to the level of privacy protection they desire when accessing a Web site.

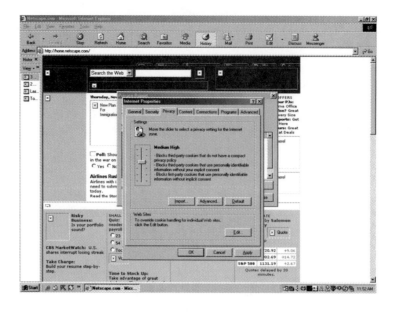

Political Issues

The political issue of privacy concerns the development of statutes that govern the relations between record keepers and individuals. Should we permit the Canadian Security Intelligence Service (CSIS) to monitor e-mail at will in order to apprehend suspected criminals and terrorists? To what extent should e-commerce sites and other businesses be allowed to maintain personal data about individuals?

PROPERTY RIGHTS: INTELLECTUAL PROPERTY

intellectual property

Intangible property created by individuals or corporations that is subject to protections under trade secret, copyright, and patent law.

Contemporary information systems have severely challenged existing laws and social practices that protect private intellectual property. **Intellectual property** is considered to be intangible property created by individuals or corporations. Information technology has made it difficult to protect intellectual property because computerized information can be so easily copied or distributed on networks. Intellectual property is subject to a variety of protections under three different legal traditions: trade secret, copyright, and patent law.

Trade Secrets

trade secret

Any intellectual work or product used for a business purpose that can be classified as belonging to that individual or business, provided it is not based on information in the public domain.

Any intellectual work product—a formula, device, pattern, or compilation of data—used for a business purpose can be classified as a **trade secret**, provided it is not based on information in the public domain. Trade secret law has arisen out of the broad "duty of good faith" and the principle of equity that whoever "has received information in confidence shall not take unfair advantage of it."

The Supreme Court of Canada has stated that the test for whether there has been a breach of confidence consists of three elements:

1. The information conveyed must be confidential (that is, it must not be public knowledge).
2. The information must have been communicated in confidence.
3. The information must have been misused by the party to whom it was communicated.

As trade secret law in Canada is a matter of provincial jurisdiction, the drafting and interpretation of agreements that contain trade secret provisions must be carried out by a lawyer in the province that governs the agreement in question. Similarly, the assessment of whether a breach of confidence has occurred must be carried out by a lawyer in the province that governs the obligation of confidence. In general, trade secret laws grant a monopoly on the ideas behind a work product, but it can be a very tenuous monopoly.

Software that contains novel or unique elements, procedures, or compilations can be included as a trade secret. Trade secret law protects the actual ideas in a work product, not only their manifestation. To make this claim, the creator or owner must take care to bind employees and customers with nondisclosure agreements and to prevent the secret from falling into the public domain.

The limitation of trade secret protection is that although virtually all software programs of any complexity contain unique elements of some sort, it is difficult to prevent the ideas in the work from falling into the public domain when the software is widely distributed.

Copyright

Copyright is a statutory grant that protects creators of intellectual property from having their work copied by others for any purpose for a period of at least 50 years. The Copyright Office registers copyrights and enforces copyright law in Canada. Parliament has extended copyright protection to books, periodicals, lectures, dramas, musical compositions, maps, drawings, artwork of any kind, and motion pictures. The intent behind copyright laws has been to encourage creativity and authorship by ensuring that creative people receive the financial and other benefits of their work. Most industrial nations have their own copyright laws, and there are several international conventions and bilateral agreements through which nations coordinate and enforce their laws.

Copyright law in Canada is one of the principal means of protecting computer software in Canada. Canadian copyright law is governed by the *Copyright Act*, which protects original literary, artistic, musical, and dramatic works. Computer software is protected in Canada as a literary work. Canadian copyright comes into existence automatically, and in the case of software, it comes into existence at the time the software was created and continues until the end of the calendar year in which the *author* of the software dies (regardless of whether the author has sold or assigned the copyright in the software or not) and continues for an additional period of 50 years following the end of that calendar year.

"Moral" rights are also protected under Canadian copyright law. Moral rights in Canada include the right of the author of a piece of software to be associated with the software by name or pseudonym, and the right to remain anonymous. They also include the author's right to the integrity of the software (that is, the author's right to stop the software from being distorted, mutilated or modified, to the prejudice of the author's honour or reputation, or from being used in association with a product, service, cause or institution).

Moral rights remain with the *author* of a piece of software, even where the software, or the copyright in the software, has been sold or assigned, regardless of whether the author created the software in the employ of someone else or created it under contract, or otherwise.

Copyright protection is clearcut: It protects against copying of entire programs or their parts. Damages and relief are readily obtained for infringement. The drawback to copyright protection is that the underlying ideas behind a work are not protected, only their manifestation in a work. A competitor can use your software, understand how it works, and develop new software that follows the same concepts without infringing on a copyright.

"Look and feel" copyright infringement lawsuits are precisely about the distinction between an idea and its expression. Most of this type of copyright infringement has occurred in the United States. For instance, in the early 1990s, Apple Computer sued Microsoft Corporation and Hewlett-Packard Inc. for infringement of the *expression* of Apple's Macintosh interface. Among other claims, Apple claimed that the defendants copied the expression of overlapping windows. The defendants counterclaimed that the idea of overlapping windows can only be expressed in a single way and, therefore, was not protectable under the "merger" doctrine of copyright law. When ideas and their expression merge, the expression cannot be copyrighted. In general, courts appear to be following the reasoning of a 1989 American case—*Brown Bag Software* vs. *Symantec Corp.*—in which the court dissected the elements of software alleged to be infringing. The court found that similar concepts, functions, general functional features (e.g., drop-down menus), or colours are protected by copyright law (*Brown Bag* vs. *Symantec Corp.*, 1992).

Patents

A **patent** grants the owner an exclusive monopoly on the ideas behind an invention for 17 to 20 years. The intent behind patent law is to ensure that inventors of new machines, devices, or methods receive the full financial and other rewards of their labour and yet still make widespread use of the invention possible by providing detailed diagrams for those wishing to

copyright
A statutory grant that protects creators of intellectual property against copying by others for any purpose for a period of at least 50 years.

patent
A legal document that grants the owner an exclusive monopoly on the ideas behind an invention for 17 to 20 years; designed to ensure that inventors of new machines or methods are rewarded for their labour while making widespread use of their inventions.

use the idea under license from the patent's owner. The granting of a patent is determined by the Patent Office and relies on court rulings.

The key concepts in patent law are originality, novelty, and invention. The Canadian Patent Office does not accept applications for software patents because software is considered to fall under Canadian copyright law. In the United States, the U.S. Patent Office did not routinely issue patents on software until a 1981 Supreme Court decision that held that computer programs could be a part of a patentable process. Since that time, hundreds of American software patents have been granted, and thousands await consideration.

The strength of patent protection is that it grants a monopoly on the underlying concepts and ideas of software. The difficulty is passing stringent criteria of non-obviousness (e.g., the work must reflect some special understanding and contribution), originality, and novelty as well as years of waiting to receive protection.

Challenges to Intellectual Property Rights

Contemporary information technologies, especially software, pose a severe challenge to existing intellectual property regimes and, therefore, create significant ethical, social, and political issues. Digital media differ from books, periodicals, and other media in terms of ease of replication; ease of transmission; ease of alteration; difficulty classifying a software work as a program, book, or even music; compactness—making theft easy; and difficulties in establishing uniqueness. In 2001, about 25 percent of business software programs in North America were illegally copied, and the global software piracy rate jumped from 37 percent in 2000 to 40 percent, costing the industry about $11 billion. Likewise, global sales of illegally copied music CDs jumped 50 percent in 2001 (Associated Press, 2002; Mariano, 2002).

The proliferation of electronic networks, including the Internet, has made it even more difficult to protect intellectual property. Before the use of networks became widespread, copies of software, books, magazine articles, or films had to be stored on physical media, such as paper, computer disks, or videotape, creating some hurdles to distribution. Using networks, information can be more widely reproduced and distributed.

The Internet was designed to transmit information, including copyrighted information, freely around the world. With the World Wide Web in particular, one can easily copy and distribute virtually anything to thousands and even millions of people around the world, even if they are using different types of computer systems. Information can be illicitly copied from one place and distributed through other systems and networks, even though these parties do not willingly participate in the infringement.

Individuals have been illegally copying and distributing digitized MP3 music files, based on the MPEG-1 Audio Layer-3 (MP3) standard, on the Internet. Napster provided software and services that enabled users to locate and share digital music files, including those protected by copyright. In July 2000, a federal district court in San Francisco ruled that Napster had to stop listing all copyrighted files without permission on its central index, and the company was forced to declare bankruptcy. Major entertainment industry groups subsequently filed suit to block illegal file sharing on other Web sites, such as Madster, Grokster, Kazaa, and Morpheus. However, other software and services for file trading over the Web, such as Gnutella, cannot be so easily regulated, so copyrighted music continues to be traded for free.

The manner in which information is obtained and presented on the Web further challenges intellectual property protections (Okerson, 1996). Web pages can be constructed from bits of text, graphics, sound, or video that may come from many different sources. Each item may belong to a different entity, creating complicated issues of ownership and compensation (see Figure 5.8). Web sites can also use a capability called **framing** to let one site construct an on-screen border around content obtained by linking to another Web site. The first site's border and logo stay on screen, making the content of the new Web site appear to be "offered" by the previous Web site.

Mechanisms are being developed to sell and distribute books, articles, and other intellectual property on the Internet, and some copyright protection is being provided by the U.S. *Digital Millennium Copyright Act (DMCA)* of 1998. The *Digital Millennium Copyright Act* was enacted to bring the United States in compliance with the World Intellectual Property Organization (WIPO) treaty. The *DMCA* prevents the unauthorized circumvention of technological protection measures and clarifies the liability of Internet service providers. The *DMCA* makes it illegal to circumvent technology-based protections of copyrighted materials.

framing

Displaying content including the content of another Web site inside one's own Web site within a frame or a window.

Digital Millennium Copyright Act (DMCA)

Adjusts American copyright laws to the Internet age by making it illegal to make, distribute, or use devices that circumvent technology-based protections of copyrighted materials.

LOGO
Web site publisher

TEXTUAL CONTENT
writer or newspaper
publisher

ARTICLE EXCERPT
writer or newspaper
publisher

BUSINESS
stock exchanges,
wire service, or
database publisher

PHOTOGRAPH
freelance photographer,
wire service, photo
agency, photo library, or
newspaper publisher

COLUMN
writer, syndication
service, or newspaper
publisher

Figure 5.8 Who Owns the Pieces? Anatomy of a Web page. Web pages are often constructed with elements from many different sources, clouding issues of ownership and intellectual property protection.

Internet service providers (ISPs) are required to "take down" sites of copyright infringers that they are hosting once they are notified of the problem. The 1998 act went further than the WIPO treaty required by including the making of copies of computer programs for computer maintenance, allowing the making of digital works for preservation purposes, and providing federal protection for industrial design in vessel hulls. Database protection was left out at the last moment because it was a very contentious item.

What effect did the *DCMA* have on Canadian copyright legislation? The *DMCA* set the agenda for copyright discussions in Canada on the following:

- Technological tampering—"devices" or "conduct"
- ISP liability
- Library provisions to be examined
- Database protection

The Speech from the Throne in the fall of 2002 looked to establish policy which would bring Canada into alignment with WIPO and which would also look at some other long-term aims of copyright legislation in Canada. Compliance with WIPO would include short-term goals of technological measures protection and digital rights management as well as the liability of the Internet service provider when copyright is infringed upon by its users. The government also plans to look at the blank recording levy that is currently in place and to examine the fair-use part of the *Act* and whether it could or should be expanded. In the medium term, Canadian lawmakers will be looking at the duration of copyright and whether it should be increased to life plus 70 years as has just taken place in the United States. And finally, in the longer term, protection of native folklore and oral histories will be examined.

Ethical Issues

The central ethical issue concerns the protection of intellectual property, such as software, digital books, digital music, or digitized video. Should I (you) copy for my own use a piece of software or other digital content material protected by trade secret, copyright, and/or patent law? Is there continued value in protecting intellectual property when it can be so easily copied and distributed over the Internet?

Social Issues

There are several property-related social issues raised by new information technology. Most experts agree that current intellectual property laws are breaking down in the information age. The vast majority of Americans report in surveys that they routinely violate some minor laws—everything from speeding to taking paper clips from work to copying books and software. The ease with which software and digital contents can be copied and the difficulty in finding and prosecuting the perpetrators contribute to making us a society of lawbreakers. These routine thefts threaten to significantly reduce the speed with which new information technologies can and will be introduced and, thus, threaten further advances in productivity and social well being.

Political Issues

The main property-related political issue concerns the creation of new property protection measures to protect investments made by creators of new software, digital books, and digital entertainment. Microsoft and 1400 other software and information content firms are represented by the Software and Information Industry Association (SIIA), which lobbies for new laws and enforcement of existing laws to protect intellectual property around the world. (SIIA was formed on January 1, 1999, from the merger of the Software Publishers Association [SPA] and the Information Industry Association [IIA]). The SIIA runs an anti-piracy hotline for individuals to report piracy activities and educational programs to help organizations combat software piracy; it has also published guidelines for employee use of software. At the SIIA Web site (www.siia.net), there is a "Canadian Section" with its own board of Canadian executives and online forms for reporting piracy. The SIIA has developed model Employee Usage Guidelines for software, described in Table 5.5.

Allied against SIIA are a host of groups and millions of individuals who believe that antipiracy laws cannot be enforced in the digital age and that software should be free or be paid for on a voluntary basis (shareware software). According to these groups, the greater social benefit results from the free distribution of software.

ACCOUNTABILITY, LIABILITY, AND CONTROL

Along with privacy and property laws, new information technologies are challenging existing liability law and social practices for holding individuals and institutions accountable. If a person is injured by a machine controlled, in part, by software, who should be held accountable and, therefore, held liable? Should a public bulletin board or an electronic service, such as America Online, permit the transmission of pornographic or offensive material (as broadcasters), or should they be held harmless against any liability for what users transmit (as is true of common carriers, such as the telephone system)? What about the Internet? If you outsource your information processing, can you hold the external vendor liable for injuries done to your customers? Some real-world examples may shed light on these questions.

Examples of Recent Liability Problems

In November 1998, a railway backhoe operator accidentally cut AT&T Canada's fibre cable along the railway line between Toronto and Windsor, crashing computers, knocking out phone lines, and generally disrupting communications in southern Ontario. The main branch of the Bank of Nova Scotia could not use its computers.

On November 28, 2000, a double failure in Sprint Canada's network shut down trading on Vancouver's Canadian Venture Exchange for more than two hours. Three hundred thousand Rogers@Home cable customers were left without service recently when a rodent chewed through cables that were exposed during routine repairs.

In 1998, fires struck twice in communication "closets" in Toronto, disrupting long-distance and Internet service to millions of Canadians—in particular, interestingly enough, in Western Canada. Who is liable for any economic harm caused to individuals or businesses that could not access their full account balances from the Bank of Nova Scotia or make stock trades when these long-distance and Internet services were out?

In April 1990, a computer system at Shell Pipeline Corporation failed to detect a human operator error. As a result, 93 000 barrels of crude oil were shipped to the wrong trader. The

TABLE 5.5	EMPLOYEE USAGE GUIDELINES FOR [ORGANIZATION]

Purpose Software will be used only in accordance with its license agreement. Unless otherwise provided in the license, any duplication of copyrighted software, except for backup and archival purposes by software manager or designated department, is a violation of copyright law. In addition to violating copyright law, unauthorized duplication of software is contrary to [organization's] standards of conduct. The following points are to be followed to comply with software license agreements:

1. All users must use all software in accordance with its license agreements and the [organization's] software policy. All users acknowledge that they do not own this software or its related documentation and, unless expressly authorized by the software publisher, may not make additional copies except for archival purposes.

2. [Organization] will not tolerate the use of any unauthorized copies of software or fonts in our organization. Any person illegally reproducing software can be subject to civil and criminal penalties, including fines and imprisonment. All users must not condone illegal copying of software under any circumstances and anyone who makes, uses, or otherwise acquires unauthorized software will be appropriately disciplined.

3. No user will give software or fonts to any outsiders including clients, customers, and others. Under no circumstances will software be used within [organization] that has been brought in from any unauthorized location under [organization's] policy, including, but not limited to, the Internet, the home, friends, and colleagues.

4. Any user who determines that there may be a misuse of software within the organization will notify the Certified Software Manager, department manager, or legal counsel.

5. All software used by the organization on organization-owned computers will be purchased through appropriate procedures.

I have read [organization's] software code of ethics. I am fully aware of our software compliance policies and agree to abide by them. I understand that violation of any above policies may result in my termination.

_____

EMPLOYEE SIGNATURE

_____

DATE

Published by the SPA Anti-Piracy. You are given permission to duplicate and modify this policy statement so long as attribution to the original document comes from SPA Anti-Piracy.

---

error cost $2 million because the trader sold the oil that should not have been delivered to him. A court ruled later that Shell Pipeline was liable for the loss of the oil because the error was due to a human operator who entered erroneous information into the system. Shell was held liable for not developing a system that would prevent the possibility of misdeliveries (King, 1992). Whom would you have held liable—Shell Pipeline? The trader for not being more careful about deliveries? The human operator who made the error?

These cases point out the difficulties faced by information systems executives who ultimately are responsible for the harm done by systems developed by their staffs. In general, insofar as computer software is part of a machine, and the machine injures someone physically or economically, the producer of the software and the operator can be held liable for damages. Insofar as the software acts more like a book, storing and displaying information, courts have been reluctant to hold authors, publishers, and booksellers liable for the contents (the exception being instances of fraud or defamation), and hence courts have been wary of holding software authors liable for "booklike" software.

In general, it is very difficult (if not impossible) to hold software producers liable for their software products when those products are considered like books, regardless of the physical or economic harm that results. Historically, print publishers, books, and periodicals have not been held liable because of fears that liability claims would interfere with First Amendment rights guaranteeing freedom of expression.

What about "software as service?" Automatic teller machines (ATMs) are a service provided to bank customers. Should this service fail, customers will be inconvenienced and perhaps harmed economically if they cannot access their funds in a timely manner. Should liability protections be extended to software publishers and operators of defective financial, accounting, simulation, or marketing systems?

Software is very different from books. Software users may develop expectations of infallibility about software; software is less easily inspected than a book and more difficult to compare with other software products for quality; software claims actually to perform a task, rather than describe a task like a book; and people come to depend on services essentially based on software. Given the centrality of software to everyday life, the chances are excellent that liability law will extend its reach to include software even when it merely provides an information service.

Between 1985 and 1987, six patients were crippled or died after receiving oncology treatments from a Therac-25 radiation machine produced by Atomic Energy of Canada Limited (AECL) (then a Canadian crown corporation, now privatized) and a French corporation, Compagnie Generale de Radiologie (CGR). One of the patients who died was treated in Ontario. The massive radiation doses were caused by "glitches" in the software code: not one or two "bugs," but several coding errors caused the Therac-25 to deliver massive radiation doses whenever certain "keying" operations were performed. Who is responsible for these injuries and deaths? Who is liable? The programmer who wrote the code? AECL and CGR that sold the machine with its accompanying software and should have tested the code? The medical facility where the radiation treatments were provided? The technicians who delivered the treatments?

Telephone systems have not been held liable for the messages transmitted because they are regulated "common carriers." In return for their right to provide telephone service, they must provide access to all, at reasonable rates, and achieve acceptable reliability. But broadcasters and cable television systems are subject to a wide variety of federal and local constraints on content and facilities. Organizations can be held liable for offensive content on their Web sites; and online services, such as Microsoft Network (MSN) or America Online, might be held liable for postings by their users.

Ethical Issues

The central liability-related ethical issue raised by new information technologies is whether individuals and organizations that create, produce, and sell systems (both hardware and software) are morally responsible for the consequences of the uses of these systems (see Johnson and Mulvey, 1995). If so, under what conditions? What liabilities (and responsibilities) should the user assume, and what should the provider assume?

Social Issues

The central liability-related social issue concerns the expectations that society should allow to develop around service-providing information systems. Should individuals (and organizations) be encouraged to develop their own backup devices to cover likely or easily anticipated system failures, or should organizations be held strictly liable for the system services they provide? If organizations are held strictly liable, what impact will this have on the development of new system services? Can society permit networks and bulletin boards to post libellous, inaccurate, and misleading information that will harm many persons? Or should information service companies become self-regulating and self-censoring?

Political Issues

The leading liability-related political issue is the debate between information providers of all kinds (from software developers to network service providers), who want to be relieved of liability as much as possible (thereby maximizing their profits), and service users—individuals, organizations, and communities—who want organizations to be held responsible for providing high-quality system services (thereby maximizing the quality of service). Service providers argue they will withdraw from the marketplace if they are held liable, while service users argue that only by holding providers liable can they guarantee a high level of service and compensate injured parties. Should legislation impose liability or restrict liability on service providers? This fundamental cleavage is at the heart of numerous political and judicial conflicts.

SYSTEM QUALITY: DATA QUALITY AND SYSTEM ERRORS

The debate over liability and accountability for unintentional consequences of system use raises a related but independent moral dimension: What is an acceptable, technologically feasible level of system quality? (See Chapter 11.) At what point should system managers say, "Stop testing, we've done all we can to perfect this software. Ship it!" Individuals and organizations may be held responsible for avoidable and foreseeable consequences, which they have a duty to perceive and correct. And the grey area is that some system errors are foreseeable and correctable only at very great expense, an expense so great that pursuing this level of perfection is not feasible economically; no one could then afford the product. For example, although software companies try to debug their products before releasing them to the marketplace, they knowingly ship products with bugs because the time and cost of fixing all minor errors would prevent these products from ever being released (Rigdon, 1995). What if the product was not offered on the marketplace? Would social welfare as a whole not advance and perhaps even decline? Carrying this further, just what is the responsibility of a producer of computer services? Should it withdraw the product that can never be perfect, warn the user, or forget about the risk ("let the buyer beware")?

Three principal sources of poor system performance are software bugs and errors, hardware or facility failures caused by natural or other causes, and poor quality of input data. Chapter 11 discusses why zero defects in software code of any complexity cannot be achieved and why the seriousness of remaining bugs cannot be estimated. Hence, there is a technological barrier to perfect software, and users must be aware of the potential for catastrophic failure. The software industry has not yet arrived at testing standards for producing software of acceptable but not perfect performance (Collins et al., 1994).

Although software bugs and facility catastrophe are likely to be widely reported in the press, by far the most common source of business system failure is data quality. Few companies routinely measure the quality of their data, but studies of individual organizations report data error rates ranging from 0.5 to 30 percent (Redman, 1998).

Ethical Issues

The central quality-related ethical issue that information systems raise is: At what point should I (or you) release software or services for consumption by others? At what point can you conclude that your software or service achieves an economically and technologically adequate level of quality? What are you obliged to know about the quality of your software, its procedures for testing, and its operational characteristics?

Social Issues

The leading quality-related social issue once again deals with expectations: As a society, do we want to encourage people to believe that systems are infallible, that data errors are impossible? Do we, instead, want a society where people are openly skeptical and questioning of the output of machines, where people are at least informed of the risk? By heightening awareness of system failure, do we inhibit the development of all systems, which, in the end, contribute to social well being?

Political Issues

The leading quality-related political issue concerns the laws of responsibility and accountability. The Standards Council of Canada sets Canadian standards, including the international ISO 9000 and ISO 14000 standards. Many of these standards relate to computing and information systems, but penalties for failure to abide by the standards are unclear or nonexistent. Should industry associations be encouraged to develop industry-wide standards of quality? Or should Parliament wait for the marketplace to punish poor system quality, recognizing that this will not work in some instances (e.g., if all retail grocers maintain poor quality systems, then customers have no alternatives)?

QUALITY OF LIFE: EQUITY, ACCESS, AND BOUNDARIES

The negative social costs of introducing information technologies and systems are beginning to mount along with the power of the technology. Many of these negative social consequences are not violations of individual rights, nor are they property crimes. Nevertheless, these negative consequences can be extremely harmful to individuals, societies, and political institutions. Computers and information technologies potentially can destroy valuable elements of our culture and society, even while they bring us benefits. If there is a balance of good and bad consequences of using information systems, whom do we hold responsible for the bad consequences? Next, we briefly examine some of the negative social consequences of systems, considering individual, social, and political responses.

Balancing Power: Centre versus Periphery

An early fear of the computer age was that huge, centralized computers would concentrate power at corporate headquarters and in the nation's capital, resulting in a Big Brother society, as was suggested in George Orwell's novel *1984*. The shift toward highly decentralized computing, coupled with an ideology of "empowerment" of thousands of workers and the decentralization of decision making to lower organizational levels, have reduced fears of power centralization in institutions. Yet, much of the "empowerment" described in popular business magazines is trivial. Lower-level employees may be empowered to make minor decisions, but the key policy decisions may be as centralized as in the past.

Rapidity of Change: Reduced Response Time to Competition

Information systems have helped create much more efficient national and international markets. The more efficient global marketplace has reduced the normal social buffers that permitted businesses many years to adjust to competition. "Time-based competition" has an ugly side: The business you work for may not have enough time to respond to global competitors and may be wiped out in a year, along with your job. We stand the risk of developing a "just-in-time society" with "just-in-time jobs, workplaces, families, and vacations".

Maintaining Boundaries: Family, Work, and Leisure

Parts of this book were written on trains, planes, as well as on family "vacations" and during what otherwise might have been "family" time. The danger of ubiquitous computing, telecommuting, nomad computing, and the "do anything anywhere" computing environment is that it might actually come true. If so, the traditional boundaries that separate work from family and just plain leisure will be weakened. Although authors have traditionally worked just about anywhere (typewriters have been portable for nearly a century), the advent of information systems, coupled with the growth of knowledge work occupations, means that more and more people will be working when traditionally they would have been playing or communicating with family and friends. The "work umbrella" now extends far beyond the eight-hour day.

Weakening traditional institutions poses clearcut dangers. Families and friends historically have provided powerful support mechanisms for individuals, and they act as balance points in a society by preserving "private life," providing a place for one to collect one's thoughts, to think in ways different from those of one's employer, and to dream.

Dependence and Vulnerability

Today, our businesses, governments, schools, and private associations, such as churches, are incredibly dependent on information systems and are, therefore, highly vulnerable if these systems should fail. With computer systems now as ubiquitous as the telephone system, it is startling to realize that there are no regulatory or standard-setting forces in place similar to telephone, electrical, radio, television, or other public-utility technologies. The absence of standards and the criticality of some system applications will probably elicit demands for national standards and perhaps regulatory oversight.

Computer Crime and Abuse

Many new technologies in the industrial era have created new opportunities for committing crimes. Technologies, including computers, create new valuable items to steal, new ways to steal them, and new ways to harm others. **Computer crime** is the commission of illegal acts through the use of a computer or against a computer system. Computers or computer systems can be the objects of crime (destroying a company's computer centre or a company's computer files) as well as the instruments of crime (stealing computer lists by illegally gaining access to a computer system using a home computer). Simply accessing a computer system without authorization, with intent to do harm or even by accident, is now a federal crime. **Computer abuse** is the commission of acts involving a computer that may not be illegal but are considered unethical.

The Canadian government has been very aggressive in implementing computer crime legislation. There are basically two sections in the *Canadian Criminal Code*, Sections 342.1 and 430, that define computer crime. Section 342.1 is itself divided into two parts. The first part deals with most of the items that would traditionally be considered computer crime. It defines unlawful entry into systems and interception of transmissions as well as mandating a harsh 10-year prison sentence for violation of these laws. The second part defines data or computer programs, to give written documentation as to what kind of materials would qualify under the statute. Section 430 defines the actual destruction, alteration, and interruption of data or data transmission as criminal acts. It does not set specific sentences, but it can be assumed that they would be similar in nature to Section 342.1. Other related codes that more generally refer to the misuse of telecommunications include Section 184, the unlawful interception of telecommunications; Section 326, theft of telecommunications; and Section 327, possession of a device to intercept telecommunications.

The item, however, that truly distinguishes the Canadian government from other governments that try to enforce computer crime laws is the clear definition of a jurisdictional boundary for computer crime. All sections pertaining to such events fall under the mandate of the Royal Canadian Mountain Police (RCMP), specifically the Information Technology Security Branch (ITSB). In consultation with the Treasury Board Secretariat (TSB) and the Communications Security Establishment (CSE), the ITSB is responsible for information technology security for the whole country. The ITSB's primary role is to educate the government on security matters by running seminars, printing documents, and providing consultation; however, they are also required to work with local law enforcement officials to crack down on computer crime.

The ITSB is composed of three branches. (1) The Security Evaluation and Inspection Team's (SEIT) primary function is to set up, secure, and be a consulting organization for any computers and networks set up by the government of Canada. (2) The Computer Investigative Support Unit (CISU) is the legal branch of the RCMP. It provides legal counsel, acquires warrants, and directs the prosecution of computer criminals. (3) The Counter Technical Intrusion Unit (CTIU) is responsible for performing periodic sweeps of governmental computer systems, assisting local police, and performing technical evaluations in cases of communication thefts.

No one knows the magnitude of the computer crime problem—how many systems are invaded, how many people engage in the practice, or what the total economic damage is, but this problem is estimated to cost more than $2 billion in North America alone. Many companies are reluctant to report computer crimes because they may involve employees. The most economically damaging kinds of computer crime are the introduction of viruses, theft of services, and disruption of computer systems. "Hacker" is the pejorative term for a person who uses computers in illegal or abusive ways. Hacker attacks are on the rise, posing new threats to organizations linked to the Internet (see Chapter 11).

Although some people enjoy the convenience of working at home, the "do anything anywhere" computing environment can blur the traditional boundaries between work and family time.

computer crime

The commission of illegal acts through the use of a computer or against a computer system.

computer abuse

The commission of acts involving a computer that may not be illegal but are considered unethical.

Computer viruses (see Chapter 11) have increased exponentially during the past decade. More than 20 000 viruses have been documented, many causing huge losses because of lost data or crippled computers. Although many firms now use antivirus software, the proliferation of computer networks will increase the probability of infections.

Following are some illustrative computer crimes:

- On January 17, 2002, Stewart Richardson, an online dealer in collectible figurines, with glowing reviews in his eBay feedback record, abruptly closed shop and left for parts unknown after withdrawing over $330 000 from his bank account. The money came from payments for items he auctioned off in early January. The people who had paid for these items never received them because many of these items never existed (Wingfield, 2002).

- Michael Whitt Ventimiglia, a former information technology worker at GTE Corporation, pleaded guilty to the charge of unintentionally damaging protected computers on May 15, 2000, at a Verizon Communications network support centre in Tampa, Florida. Ventimiglia used his ability to gain access to GTE's secure computers and began erasing data on the computers, entering a command that prevented anyone from stopping the destruction. Ventimiglia's actions caused damage amounting to more than $300 000 (Sullivan, 2001).

- An 11-member group of hackers, dubbed "The Phonemasters" by the Federal Bureau of Investigation (FBI), gained access to telephone networks of companies, including British Telecommunications, AT&T Corporation, MCI Communications Corporation, Southwestern Bell, and Sprint. They were able to access credit-reporting databases belonging to Equifax and TRW Inc., as well as databases owned by LexisNexis and Dunn & Bradstreet information services. Members of the ring sold credit reports, criminal records, and other data they pilfered from the databases, causing losses amounting to $2.7 million. The FBI apprehended group members Calvin Cantrell, Corey Lindsley, and John Bosanac, and they were sentenced to jail terms of two to four years in a federal prison. Other members remain at large (Simons, 1999).

Traditionally, employees—insiders—have been the source of the most injurious computer crimes because they have the knowledge, access, and, frequently, a job-related motive to commit such crimes. However, the Internet's ease of use and accessibility have created new opportunities for computer crime and abuse by outsiders. Auction fraud is currently the most prevalent form of computer crime on the Internet.

Most Canadian laws related to computer crime come under consumer law, contract law, and the *Criminal Code of Canada*. In the United States, Congress passed the *Computer Fraud and Abuse Act* in 1986. This *Act* makes it illegal to access a computer system without authorization. Nonetheless, in Canada and elsewhere, new technologies make new laws necessary. The *PIPEDA*, the Canadian privacy law, was only introduced in 1997 to remedy the onslaught of privacy concerns associated with the Internet and newer data-mining applications. The final provisions of the *PIPEDA* do not go into force until 2004.

spamming

The practice of sending unsolicited e-mail and other electronic communications.

One widespread form of abuse is **spamming**, in which organizations or individuals send out thousands and even hundreds of thousands of unsolicited e-mail and electronic messages. This practice has been growing because it only costs a few cents to send thousands of messages advertising one's wares to Internet users. Some American state laws prohibit or restrict spamming, but it is largely unregulated. No provincial laws have thus far been enacted regarding spamming. (Parliament is slowly considering legislation to outlaw false labelling of e-mail solicitations.) On May 30, 2002, the European Parliament passed a ban on unsolicited commercial messaging. Electronic marketing can only be targeted to people who have given prior consent. Table 5.6 describes other practices where the Internet has been used for illegal or malicious purposes.

Employment: Trickle-Down Technology and Re-engineering Job Loss

Re-engineering work (see Chapter 10) is typically hailed in the information systems community as a major benefit of new information technology. It is much less frequently noted that redesigning business processes could potentially cause millions of middle-level managers and clerical workers to lose their jobs. One economist has pointed out the possibility that we will

TABLE 5.6	INTERNET CRIME AND ABUSE

Problem	Description
Spamming	Marketers send out unsolicited mass e-mail to recipients who have not requested this information.
Hacking	Hackers exploit weaknesses in Web site security to obtain access to proprietary data such as customer information and passwords. They may use "Trojan horses" posing as legitimate software to obtain information from the host computer.
Jamming	Jammers use software routines to tie up the computer hosting a Web site so that legitimate visitors can't access the site.
Malicious software	Cyber vandals use data flowing through the Internet to transmit computer viruses, which can disable computers that they "infect" (see Chapter 14).
Sniffing	Sniffing, a form of electronic eavesdropping, involves placing a piece of software to intercept information passing from a user to the computer hosting a Web site. This information can include credit card numbers and other confidential data.
Spoofing	Spoofers fraudulently misrepresent themselves as other organizations, setting up false Web sites where they can collect confidential information from unsuspecting visitors to the site.

create a society run by a small "high-tech elite of corporate professionals...in a nation of the permanently unemployed" (Rifkin, 1993).

Other economists are much more sanguine about potential job losses. They believe relieving bright, educated workers from re-engineered jobs will result in these workers moving to better jobs in fast-growth industries. Left out of this equation are blue-collar workers, and older, less well educated middle managers. It is not clear that these groups can be retrained easily for high-quality (high-paying) jobs. Careful planning and sensitivity to employee needs can help companies redesign work to minimize job losses.

Equity and Access: Increasing Racial and Social Class Cleavages

Does everyone have an equal opportunity to participate in the digital age? Will the social, economic, and cultural gaps that exist in North America and other societies be reduced by information systems technology? Or will the cleavages be increased, permitting the "better off" to become even better off relative to others?

These questions have not yet been fully answered because the impact of information technology on various groups in society has not been thoroughly studied. What is known is that information, knowledge, computers, and access to these resources through educational institutions and public libraries are inequitably distributed along ethnic and social class lines, as are many other information resources. Several studies have found that certain ethnic and income groups in North America are less likely to have computers or Internet access, even though computer ownership and Internet access have soared in the past five years. Higher-income families in each ethnic group are more likely to have home computers and Internet access than lower-income families in the same group (U.S. Department of Commerce, 1998; Rainie and Packel, 2001). A similar **digital divide** exists in North American schools, with schools in high-poverty areas much less likely to have computers, high-quality educational technology programs, or Internet access available for their students. Left uncorrected, the "digital divide" could lead to a society of information haves, computer literate and skilled, versus a large group of information have-nots, computer illiterate and unskilled.

Public interest groups want to narrow this "digital divide" by making digital information services, including the Internet, available to "virtually everyone" just as basic telephone service is now. The Window on Management describes how the Canadian province of Alberta is addressing this problem.

digital divide

Large disparities in access to computers and the Internet among different social groups and different locations.

ALBERTA NARROWS ITS DIGITAL DIVIDE

Internet access is increasing worldwide, but its cost can exacerbate cleavages between urban and rural areas as well as among different social classes and ethnic groups. The people in Canada's province of Alberta have seriously tried to address this problem.

Alberta is a province of immense size. However, its population is relatively small, with only three million people, and very spread out. Although the province has a flourishing technology industry, its economy depends heavily on agriculture, energy, and tourism. Alberta's digital divide is substantial, with most rural Alberta businesses having no access to high-speed Internet services. Until recently, those who did get access paid much higher prices than those in urban areas. Grant Chaney, Chief Technology Officer for SuperNet, explained, "We were seeing a growing gap between urban and rural Alberta. We wanted to make sure that our own digital divide was being addressed." He added "Alberta has a pretty diverse geography and a lot of population in rural areas."

Making Internet access available to all homes in the rural areas with over 4,500 facilities in over 400 communities was clearly difficult due to the limited financial means of most residents. The rates were simply not competitive. For example, the few rural-based businesses that used an Internet service provider (ISP) paid up to several thousand dollars per month. The Alberta government realized that all of its residents needed reliable, up-to-date information from their hospitals, libraries, schools, and government offices and that the only way to provide inexpensive and widespread access to this information would be through stable high-speed networks connected to the Internet.

Recognition of the problem led to the establishment of a project dubbed SuperNet. Alberta described its project's purpose this way. "Currently, only about 30 communities in Alberta have some access to affordable high-speed residential Internet services. Alberta SuperNet will give 422 communities that access at significantly lower rates than even slow-speed service, which may or may not be currently available."

The Alberta government decided it must offer rural access to SuperNet at prices that were competitive with the Edmonton and Calgary urban areas. This meant that SuperNet must offer the rural ISPs access to the Internet at much lower rates than were currently available. Then, the ISPs, in turn, would pass the savings on to their customers.

Besides rural access, SuperNet has another positive result in that it gives business to the companies building and supplying the system. In addition to spurring economic activity, SuperNet is expected to promote better education and medical care. Rural areas would be able to access a comprehensive pharmaceutical information network, real-time health records transfer, and telemedicine applications. Specialists could use the network's video capabilities to help rural doctors diagnose patients with unfamiliar symptoms. Children in remote classrooms would be able to take classes that are unavailable at their local schools and learn from teachers in other parts of the province.

To Think About: Evaluate the SuperNet approach to narrowing the digital divide. Could this approach be used in other provinces, states, and countries? Explain your answer. Suggest other ways governments might help solve the digital divide problem.

Sources: G Patrick Pawling, "The Alberta Connection: Government and Private Industry Are Working Together," *IQ Magazine*, January/February 2002; and "Alberta SuperNet," **http://www3.gov.ab.ca/innsci/supernet/inside.html**.

Health Risks: RSI, CVS, and Technostress

repetitive stress injury (RSI)

Occupational disease that occurs when muscle groups are forced through repetitive actions with high-impact loads or thousands of repetitions with low-impact loads.

carpal tunnel syndrome (CTS)

Type of RSI in which pressure on the median nerve through the wrist's bony carpal tunnel structure produces pain.

The most important occupational disease today is **repetitive stress injury (RSI)**. RSI occurs when muscle groups are forced through repetitive actions often with high-impact loads (such as tennis) or tens of thousands of repetitions under low-impact loads (such as working at a computer keyboard).

The single largest source of RSI is the computer keyboard. About 50 million Americans use computers at work. The most common kind of computer-related RSI is **carpal tunnel syndrome (CTS)**, in which pressure on the median nerve through the wrist's bony structure, called the carpal tunnel, produces pain. The pressure is caused by constant repetition of keystrokes: In a single shift, a data entry clerk may perform 23 000 keystrokes. Symptoms of carpal tunnel syndrome include numbness, shooting pain, inability to grasp objects, and tingling. Millions of workers have been diagnosed with carpal tunnel syndrome.

RSI is avoidable. Designing workstations for a neutral wrist position (using a wrist rest to support the wrist), proper monitor stands, and footrests all contribute to proper posture and reduced RSI. New, ergonomically correct keyboards are also an option, although their effectiveness has yet to be clearly established. These measures should be backed by frequent

Repetitive stress injury (RSI) is the leading occupational disease today. The single largest cause of RSI is computer keyboard work.

rest breaks, rotation of employees to different jobs, and movement toward voice or scanner data entry.

RSI is not the only occupational illness caused by computers. Back and neck pain, leg stress, and foot pain also result from poor ergonomic designs of workstations. **Computer vision syndrome (CVS)** refers to any eyestrain condition related to computer monitors. Its symptoms, usually temporary, include headaches, blurred vision, and dry and irritated eyes.

The newest computer-related malady is **technostress**, which is stress induced by computer use. Its symptoms include aggravation, hostility toward humans, impatience, and fatigue. The problem according to experts is that humans working continuously on computers come to expect other humans and human institutions to behave like computers, providing instant response, attentiveness, and an absence of emotion. Computer-intense workers are aggravated when put on hold during phone calls and become incensed or alarmed when their PCs take a few seconds longer to perform a task. Technostress is thought to be related to the high levels of job turnover in the computer industry, high levels of early retirement from computer-intense occupations, and elevated levels of drug and alcohol abuse.

The incidence of technostress is not known but is thought to be in the millions in North America and growing rapidly. Computer-related jobs now top the list of stressful occupations, based on health statistics in several industrialized countries.

To date, the role of radiation from computer monitors in occupational disease has not been proved. These video display terminals (VDTs) emit nonionizing electric and magnetic fields at low frequencies. These rays enter the body and have unknown effects on enzymes, molecules, chromosomes, and cell membranes. Long-term studies are investigating the relationship between low-level electromagnetic fields and birth defects, low birth weight, stress, and other diseases. All manufacturers have reduced display screen emissions since the early 1980s, and European countries, such as Sweden, have instituted stiff radiation emission standards.

The computer has become a part of our lives—personally as well as socially, culturally, and politically. It is unlikely that the issues and our choices will become easier as information technology continues to transform our world. The growth of the Internet and the information economy suggests that all the ethical and social issues we have described will be intensified further in the first digital century.

computer vision syndrome (CVS)

Eyestrain condition related to computer monitor use; symptoms include headaches, blurred vision, and dry and irritated eyes.

technostress

Stress induced by computer use; symptoms include aggravation, hostility toward humans, impatience, and enervation.

Management Actions: A Corporate Code of Ethics

Some corporations, including FedEx, IBM, American Express, and Merck & Co, have developed far-reaching corporate information systems codes of ethics. Most firms, however, have not developed these codes of ethics, leaving their employees in the dark about expected correct behaviour. There is some dispute concerning a general code of ethics versus a specific information systems code of ethics. There is a recent movement to ensure that all employees are aware of these codes; many companies require their employees to sign a statement affirming that they have read, understood, and "accepted" the code. Frequently, these companies issue annual updates to ensure that employees have not forgotten their ethical responsibilities. As managers, you should strive to develop an information systems–specific set of ethical standards for each of the five moral dimensions:

- *Information rights and obligations.* A code should cover such topics as employee e-mail and Internet privacy, workplace monitoring, treatment of corporate information, and policies on customer information.

- *Property rights and obligations.* A code should cover such topics as software licenses, ownership of firm data and facilities, ownership of software created by employees on company hardware, and software copyrights. Specific guidelines for contractual relationships with third parties should be covered as well.

- *Accountability and control.* The code should specify a single individual responsible for all information systems, and others who are responsible for individual rights, the protection of property rights, system quality, and quality of life (e.g., job design, ergonomics, employee satisfaction) should report to this individual. Responsibilities for control of systems, audits, and management should be clearly defined. The potential liabilities of systems officers and the corporation should be detailed in a separate document.

- *System quality.* The code should describe the general levels of data quality and system error that can be tolerated with detailed specifications left to specific projects. The code should require that all systems attempt to estimate data quality and system error probabilities.

- *Quality of life.* The code should state that the purpose of systems is to improve the quality of life for customers and for employees by achieving high levels of product quality, customer service, employee satisfaction, and human dignity through proper ergonomics, job and workflow design, and human resource development.

Management Wrap-Up

Managers are ethical rule makers for their organizations. They are charged with creating the policies and procedures to establish ethical conduct, including the ethical use of information systems. Managers are also responsible for identifying, analyzing, and resolving the ethical dilemmas that invariably crop up as they balance conflicting needs and interests.

Rapid changes fuelled by information technology are creating new situations where existing laws or rules of conduct may not be relevant. New "grey areas" are emerging, in which ethical standards have not yet been codified into law. A new system of ethics for the Information Age is required to guide individual and organizational choices and actions.

Information technology is introducing changes that create new ethical issues for societies to debate and resolve. Increasing computing power, storage, and networking capabilities, including the Internet, can expand the reach of individual and organizational actions and magnify their impact. The ease and anonymity with which information can be communicated, copied, and manipulated in online environments are challenging traditional rules of right and wrong behaviour.

For Discussion

1. Should producers of software-based services, such as ATMs, be held liable for economic injuries suffered when their systems fail?

2. Should companies be responsible for unemployment caused by their information systems? Why, or why not?

SUMMARY

1. *What ethical, social, and political issues are raised by information systems?* Information technology has raised new possibilities for behaviour for which laws and rules of acceptable conduct have not yet been developed. The main ethical, social, and political issues raised by information systems centre around information rights and obligations, property rights, accountability and control, system quality, and quality of life.

   Ethical, social, and political issues are closely related. Ethical issues involve individuals who must choose a course of action, often in a situation in which two or more ethical principles are in conflict (a dilemma). Social issues spring from ethical issues as societies develop expectations in individuals about the correct course of action. Political issues spring from social conflict and have to do largely with laws that prescribe behaviour and seek to use the law to create situations in which individuals behave correctly.

2. *Are there specific principles for conduct that can be used to guide decisions about ethical dilemmas?* Six ethical principles are available to judge conduct. These principles are derived independently from several cultural, religious, and intellectual traditions and comprise the Golden Rule, Immanuel Kant's categorical imperative, Descartes' rule of change, the utilitarian principle, the risk aversion principle, and the ethical "no free lunch" rule. These principles should be used in conjunction with an ethical analysis to guide decision making. The ethical analysis involves identifying the facts, values, stakeholders, options, and consequences of actions. Once completed, one can consider what ethical principle to apply to a situation to arrive at a judgment.

3. *Why does contemporary information technology pose challenges to the protection of individual privacy and intellectual property?* Contemporary information technology, including Internet technology, challenges traditional regimens for protecting individual privacy and intellectual property. Data storage and data analysis technology allows companies to easily gather personal data about individuals from many different sources and analyze these data to create detailed electronic profiles about individuals and their behaviour. Data flowing over the Internet can be monitored at many points. The activities of Web site visitors can be closely tracked using "cookies" and other Web monitoring tools. Not all Web sites have strong privacy protection policies, and they do not always allow for informed consent regarding the use of personal information. The online industry prefers self-regulation to the government tightening privacy protection legislation.

   Traditional copyright laws are insufficient to protect software piracy becuse digital material can be so easily copied. Internet technology also makes intellectual property even more difficult to protect because digital material can be so easily copied and transmitted to many different locations simultaneously over the Net. Web pages can be easily constructed by using pieces of content from other Web sites without permission.

4. *How have information systems affected everyday life?* Although computer systems have been sources of efficiency and wealth, they have some negative impacts. Errors in large computer systems are impossible to eradicate totally. Computer errors can cause serious harm to individuals and organizations, and existing laws and social practices are often unable to establish liability and accountability for these problems. Less serious errors are often attributable to poor data quality, which can cause disruptions and losses for businesses. Jobs can be lost when workers are replaced by computers or tasks become unnecessary in re-engineered business processes. The ability to own and use a computer may be exacerbating socioeconomic disparities among different racial groups and social classes. Widespread use of computers increases opportunities for computer crime and computer abuse. Computers can also create health problems, such as repetitive stress injury, computer vision syndrome, and technostress.

5. *How can organizations develop corporate polices for ethical conduct?* For each of the five moral dimensions of information systems, corporations should develop an ethics policy statement to assist individuals and to encourage the correct decisions. The following are the policy areas. *Individual information rights:* Spell out corporate privacy and due process policies. *Property rights:* Clarify how the corporation will treat property rights of software owners. *Accountability and control:* Clarify who is responsible and accountable for corporate information. *System quality:* Identify methodologies and quality standards to be achieved. *Quality of life:* Identify corporate policies on family, computer crime, decision making, vulnerability, job loss, and health risks.

KEY TERMS

Accountability,   154
Carpal tunnel syndrome (CTS),   176
Computer abuse,   173
Computer crime,   173
Computer vision syndrome (CVS),   177
Cookie,   160
Copyright,   165
Descartes' rule of change,   155
Digital divide,   175
Digital Millennium Copyright Act (DMCA),   166
Due process,   154
Ethical "no free lunch" rule,   155
Ethics,   150

Fair Information Practices
  (FIP), 158
Framing, 166
Immanuel Kant's categorical
  imperative, 155
Information rights, 151
Informed consent, 159
Intellectual property, 164

Liability, 154
Non-obvious relationship
  awareness (NORA), 153
Opt-in, 161
Opt-out, 161
P3P, 162
Patent, 165

*Personal Information
Protection and Electronic
Documents Act (PIPEDA)*,
157
Privacy, 156
Profiling, 153
Repetitive stress injury (RSI),
  176

Responsibility, 154
Risk aversion principle, 155
Spamming, 174
Technostress, 177
Trade secret, 164
Utilitarian principle, 155
Web bugs, 161

REVIEW QUESTIONS

1. In what ways are ethical, social, and political issues connected? Give some examples.

2. What are the key technological trends that heighten ethical concerns?

3. What are the differences among responsibility, accountability, and liability?

4. What are the five steps in an ethical analysis?

5. Identify and describe six ethical principles.

6. What is a professional code of conduct?

7. What are meant by "privacy" and "fair information practices"?

8. How is the Internet challenging the protection of individual privacy?

9. What role can informed consent, legislation, industry self-regulation, and technology tools play in protecting individual privacy of Internet users?

10. What are the three different regimes that protect intellectual property rights? What challenges to intellectual property rights are posed by the Internet?

11. Why is it so difficult to hold software services liable for failure or injury?

12. What is the most common cause of system quality problems?

13. Name and describe four "quality of life" impacts of computers and information systems.

14. What is technostress, and how would you identify it?

15. Name three management actions that could reduce RSI injuries.

APPLICATION SOFTWARE EXERCISE

**WORD PROCESSING AND WEB PAGE
DEVELOPMENT TOOL EXERCISE:
CREATING A SIMPLE WEB SITE**

Build a simple Web site of your own design for a business using the Web page creation function of Microsoft Word, Microsoft FrontPage, Macromedia Dreamweaver, or a Web page development tool of your choice. Your Web site should include a home page with a description of your business and at least one picture or graphic. From the home page, you must be able to link to a second Web page and, from there, link to a third Web page. Make the home page long enough so that when you arrive at the bottom of the page, you can no longer see the top. There you

must include a link back to the top. Also include a link to one of the secondary Web pages. On that secondary page, include a link to the top of that page, and a link back to the top of the home page. Also include a link to the third page, which should contain a link to its own top and a link back to the top of the home page. Finally, on one of the secondary pages, include another picture or graphic, and on the other page, include an object that you create using Microsoft Excel or other spreadsheet software. The Companion Website for Chapter 5 includes instructions for completing this project. If you have tested all the functions and they all are now working to your satisfaction, save the pages you have created for submission to your instructor.

GROUP PROJECT

With three or four of your classmates, develop a corporate ethics code on privacy that addresses both employee privacy and the privacy of customers and users of the corporate Web site. Be sure to consider e-mail privacy and employer monitoring of work-

sites, as well as corporate use of information about employees concerning their off-job behaviour (e.g., lifestyle, home arrangements, and so forth). If possible, use electronic presentation software to present your ethics code to the class.

INTERNET TOOLS

COMPANION WEBSITE

The Internet Connection for this chapter will direct you to a series of Web sites where you can learn more about the privacy issues raised by the use of the Internet and the Web. You can complete an exercise to analyze the privacy implications of existing technologies for tracking Web site visitors.

At www.pearsoned.ca/laudon, you will find valuable tools to facilitate and enhance your learning of this chapter as well as opportunities to apply your knowledge to realistic situations:

- An Interactive Study Guide to test your knowledge of the topics in this chapter, and get instant feedback where you need more practice.
- Application exercises
- An Electronic Commerce project that uses the interactive software at the Google Groups Web site to explore the use of Internet discussion groups for targeted marketing.
- A Management Decision Problem where you can analyze whether employees are spending too much personal time on the Web and address the ethical implications of monitoring their Web usage.
- Updates of material in the chapter.

ADDITIONAL SITES OF INTEREST

There are many interesting Web sites to enhance your learning about social, legal, and ethical issues involved in managing information technology. You can search the Web yourself, or just try the following sites to add to what you have already learned.

Electronic Privacy Information Center
  www.epic.org
    A wealth of information on privacy issues.

Standards Council of Canada
  www.scc.ca
    Research any standard that has been adopted in Canada by this standards regulating body.

Business Ethics: Corporate Social Responsibility Report
  www.business-ethics.com
    Magazine devoted to business ethics issues.

CASE STUDY: *Are You Really Secure?*

George Edwards thought his company's security measures were top-notch until the day a third-party assessor came in to test the steps ProPharm had taken to protect itself from attacks.

When the person sent by IBM Corp. walked unimpeded into ProPharm's Markham (Ontario) offices, there was a quick realization that not even basic physical security had been taken into account, said Edwards, a vice-president at the company, which supplies computer technology to pharmacies. And when the assessor asked who the chief security officer was, Edwards was once again at a loss.

"We were thinking we're pretty good," he said.

Edwards was speaking during a seminar held in Ottawa, where the results of an Ipsos-Reid study on Canadian CEOs' attitudes toward security were announced. He said that the outside evaluation showed the company that there were many areas in which security could be improved.

ProPharm's once ill-conceived approach to security is not that different from other Canadian companies. For most, security is only a secondary concern, said David Saffran, a senior vice-president and managing director at Ipsos-Reid.

In a survey of 250 CEOs, protecting the company from malicious attacks ranked fourth in a list of priorities behind reducing the company's overall expenses, maintaining and building revenues, and hiring qualified staff.

This lukewarm approach to security could come at a cost. According to RCMP statistics, cybercrime is up 65 percent from last year. And a large number of hacking events go unreported each year, as companies are afraid of going public with such information, said Sgt. Charles Richer, a team leader with the RCMP's technological crime unit in Ottawa.

Cyberattacks have become more sophisticated since the days of Mafia Boy, Richer said, referring to the Canadian teenager who managed to shut down several high-profile American Web sites in 2000. Though unable to go into details of the cases he has investigated, Richer said in one denial of service attack, a company was losing $100 000 a day.

Theft of data is happening at a disturbing rate, he said. Smart card cloning through reverse engineering is also possible if there is not enough security. "We're investigating things that could have been prevented," Richer said. Although individual viruses are not as common as they once were, more worms are starting to appear, he added. Many of the crimes are internally generated. Often, the attack is generated from within the network, or the victim knows the perpetrator.

Often, people are the weakest link. "Human issues are at the heart of the matter," Richer said, which is why it is essential to train and communicate with employees.

The Ipsos-Reid study also found that 46 percent of CEOs reported being hit with a widespread infection by malicious software, and 20 percent admitted to being hit by an external hacker in the past year. "To combat such attacks, it is important to get an outside assessment of your security system while it is still in the design phase," Edwards said. ProPharm was forced to undergo such an assessment in order to comply with the Ontario government's requirements.

As a supplier to pharmacies, the company is more aware of the importance of protecting confidential information than most companies, but this is something all organizations have to worry about, Edwards said. Among the measures that IBM recommended to ProPharm was the creation of a "poison pill" for the Linux boxes at pharmacies. If a box is stolen and then used to connect to the ProPharm network through which insurance claims are validated, then not only will the connection be severed, but the computer will be sent a command to commit suicide.

Once the system was in place, ProPharm then had a third party test it through ethical hacking. "You shouldn't proofread your own work," Edwards said.

But many companies want to live in a world where employees would never think of causing intentional damage. "We're a happy family," to quote 1970s punk rockers the Ramones, is often the corporate thinking. Problem is, few companies really are.

Very few people join companies with the intention to steal. Like it or not, the disgruntled employee is a product of the environment.

Rene Hamel, KPMG Toronto's vice-president of forensic technology services and an ex-RCMP investigator, knows a few things about the criminal mind. He said corporate Canada, for the most part, does not spend enough time trying to understand information technology culture. And though he does not condone the actions of internal hackers, he understands how they can be created and, more importantly, how dangerous they can be if they turn on a company.

"IT employees—you've got to treat them well," Hamel said.

Although he does not blame the victim, Simon Perry, vice-president of security solutions with Islandia, (New York)-based Computer Associates International, said he was not about to let corporations completely off the hook. "Organizations are happy to paint themselves as victims of us versus them, but they don't want…to admit that, due to their core governance, they have turned one of us into one of them," he said.

Often, a company's only recourse is to fire the employee, since going to the courts means media scrutiny and the acknowledgement that there was a bad apple within and that internal security was an afterthought. So, it is necessary to create an environment where motive and information technology access have been reduced to help minimize the possibility of an internal hack.

"Policy is important because without policy there is no establishment of repercussion," said Adel Melek, partner with Deloitte & Touche in Toronto and national leader of the security services practice. Often, employees do not know exactly what is and is not acceptable corporate policy, he said.

Ches Somers, another Toronto-based ex-RCMP officer and associate managing director of investigations with risk consulting company Kroll Inc., likes the idea of an annual review of corporate policy so that it is not forgotten.

Policies vary from company to company. Some will forbid any personal Web and e-mail use, while others will go so far as to outline what exactly constitutes a "crime." Sometimes, it is even necessary to spell out what should be obvious, such as "no hacking password files or sending corporate takeover strategies to friends."

It is important to be specific so that employees cannot use the "I didn't know" defence, Melek said.

Admittedly, corporate policy will probably only stop the fence-sitter, but it is necessary to have a policy as a starting point. Also, the more employees know and understand the repercussions of their actions, the less likely it is they will go ahead with them.

Even before companies look to anti-hacking technology, they must first change their corporate strategies to reflect the need to compartmentalize data. Companies often have too many people with access to too much information. It can prove to be a motivating factor for illicit activities—if a product developer learns the true value of an invention from marketing, will he or she be more or less prone to bolt with the information as a result? The answer is often the former. This is backed by the fact that the number-one insider job is the theft of proprietary information.

"You have multi-billion-dollar companies that are still being run like mom and pop shops," said Peter Vakof, vice-president with dispute analysis and investigations at PricewaterhouseCoopers in Toronto. "There is no person at any company who needs access to everything," Perry said.

The Royal Bank follows this thinking. Though Peter Cullen is the bank's chief privacy officer, a c-level executive, he has no access to customer information. The military learned long ago that requiring two people to launch nuclear missiles dramatically reduces the possibility of a rogue launch. To date, this thinking has proven successful. In companies which require a lot of people to be kept in the loop, requiring multiple users to change, copy, or delete certain corporate data increases security.

Bruce Schneier, CTO of Counterpane, likes to recount one of his company's internal hacker war stories. A disgruntled employee with a major American airline was attempting to access the corporate Human Resources system. Schneier admits that it is difficult to catch a one-time insider job that is mistake-free, but this individual was not a pro. Within minutes of detecting the hack, Counterpane was on the phone with the airline, giving them the exact geographic location of the penetration attempt. They caught the hacker red-handed in front of the keyboard at an office in Mexico City.

For companies with the money and the need, 24/7 internal network monitoring is essential. But to do so, the monitors (actual people, not machines) need to really understand the network and its peculiarities. Technology probably will not catch something suspicious unless those monitoring the system understand it well enough to pick out vague abnormalities. The problem? The average company does not pay enough attention to its networks, Schneier said.

Though Schneier's story seems like the actions of information technology secret agents, had the airline not been able to catch the hacker in the act, dealing with the intrusion may have been problematic. In fact, for a company to dismiss an employee, unless there is a confession, the hacker has to be caught in the act. There are too many stolen user names and passwords for guilt to be established solely on the basis of who the system said penetrated the network.

Were a defence lawyer able to prove the corporate password file was insecure, or a sniffer could be placed on the internal network (to monitor keystrokes and steal passwords), a company might find itself apologizing and paying compensation to someone of uncertain innocence. This is one of the reasons Hamel always wants the hacker caught in front of the keyboard committing the crime before he suggests a company go further with its investigation.

"For an investigator, at the end of the day, it doesn't matter which file you have recovered, it doesn't matter what electronic evidence you've got, you have to put that person in front of the keyboard."

Hamel's years with the RCMP taught him that despite their best efforts, criminals eventually become complacent. But for one-time hacks by skilled hackers, do not expect to catch them in the act. Since not every company can afford to monitor all systems 24/7, it is necessary, as an absolute minimum, that all companies audit their systems access on a regular basis.

There are those who push the biometrics solution so that employees cannot disavow access gained using their name. But this is overkill, Perry said. "Internally, user IDs and passwords are just as strong as digital certificates and biometrics for 99 per cent of the company."

But the threats to corporate information security do not have to come from inside or from hackers seeking a thrill. A few months after September 11, 2001, the U.S. FBI released a warning to corporate America and, by extension, corporate Canada, stating that there was an increased risk of major cyber attacks in the next 12 months. In late 2001, the Canadian Department of National Defence's Office of Critical Infrastructure Protection and Emergency Preparedness (OCIPEP) issued a similar advisory, saying that Al-Qaida terrorists could launch a cyber attack on Canadian interests. Nothing unusual was reported following either warning.

Are the warnings legitimate, a well-intentioned reminder, or a demonstration of a firm grasp of the obvious?

The simple fact is that companies are getting hacked around the clock. So, why the periodic dire warnings from government agencies? Part of the theory is that hackers have changed their stripes. No longer does our greatest concern come from the usual suspects: script kiddies, disgruntled employees, and a few indignant security gurus bent on teaching the corporate world a lesson. Call it a post-9/11 wake-up call.

"The same kind of people who were fully prepared to fly airplanes into large buildings, killing both themselves and thousands of people, could also be willing to take down and destroy companies' whole IT systems—not for gain, not for bragging rights, but for pure destructive purpose," said

Andrew Bartels, research leader for industry perspectives on information technology with research firm Giga Information Group Inc. "Prior to two or three years ago, the idea of a cyber attack of this magnitude was viewed as so remote as to not even worry about."

And lack of expertise is not a barrier to those with malicious intent. There are some very smart hackers for hire out there, especially due to economic problems in Eastern Europe, where so many are unemployed, observed Chris Anderson, partner in the security and technologies solutions practice with consulting firm Ernst and Young in Mississauga, Ontario. Additionally, with the tools freely available on the Internet, hackers do not have to be that good to get through most of the defences they find.

Richard Reiner is the CEO of Toronto-based security firm FSC Internet Corporation. Reiner said his company sees about 50 000 hack attempts a day. Some days, it spikes two or three times higher. Reiner does not want to speculate on the probability of an attack occurring, but he said if he were to guess, an attack would come in the form of a co-ordinated strike on several levels. Insiders who are perceived as cooperating with a rogue nation would be the most bang for the buck," he said. "But that is purely hypothetical."

"If it were to happen, a large-scale cyber attack would probably not damage the overall fabric of the Internet, since it is pretty hard to take down," said Simon Perry, Vice-President, Security Solutions, at Computer Associates International. "The target might be key infrastructure businesses at the commercial level in conjunction with a physical attack," he said, acknowledging that he too was making no more than an educated guess.

So, how good are Canadian corporate defences? Are they prepared if a massive cyber attack comes their way? "No, they are not," was the simple answer of Computer Associates' Perry. "Most companies don't have anywhere near best-practice security." FSC Internet's Reiner was even less optimistic. "There are perhaps 10 companies in this country that have effective, mature information-security management programs."

The general consensus is that the majority of Canadian companies are not prepared for a large-scale cyber attack. Hacking anecdotes support this notion. Reiner related the story of a very large Canadian business in the early stages of deploying some Internet-facing systems destined to do the majority of its customer transactions. The first generation of the system was moved very quickly into production, a common enough occurrence in information technology deployments, and it was hacked almost immediately. "[The hackers] put some money into their pockets that belonged to others and also got hold of customer information," he said.

Another company was about to open a major e-business initiative for the first time. It spent millions on security and, prior to opening the system to the Internet, asked FSC to test its effectiveness. "It was zero. Fifteen minutes after starting the test we had control of their environment," he said. "But kudos to them for realizing the system should be tested."

Sources: Poonam Khanna, "Mounties Claim Cybercrime Up 65 Percent This Year," *ComputerWorld Canada*, November 15, 2002, available www.itworld.ca, accessed June 8, 2003; Chris Conrath, "Hacking from the Inside," *Network World Canada*, available www.itworld.ca, accessed June 8, 2003; Chris Conrath, "Are We Ready for the Big One?" *CIO Canada*, October 1, 2002, available www.itworld.ca, accessed June 8, 2003.

CASE STUDY QUESTIONS

1. How much money should a company spend on securing its information systems from hackers? Explain your answer.

2. Who do you think are more likely to hack into a company's information systems: current employees, ex-employees, or outsiders? Why?

3. Do you think there is a credible hacking threat from terrorists? How could you anticipate this?

4. Why do companies leave themselves open for hacking attempts? How could they prevent them?

5. Is it ethical to hack? Is it ethical to use tools that are freely available on the Web to hack? What should be the punishment for hackers?

6. Do you think Canadian laws are up to date enough to deal with hacking? Explain your answer.

Make IT Your Business

As we discussed in Chapter 2, information systems of all types support all of the functional areas of a business. At the end of each part of the text, we discuss some of the ways in which information systems described in that part support four of the major functional areas: finance and accounting, sales and marketing, manufacturing and production, and human resources.

Finance and Accounting

Finance and accounting systems help firms keep track of their assets and fund flows. They can help firms maximize returns on their financial assets and investments and maintain financial records. Companies can use the Internet to obtain data on interest rates, market conditions, and other factors to help them monitor and plan their investments. Firms that have embarked on ambitious programs to integrate their systems can use corporate intranets to obtain company-wide views of their firm's financial performance.

Enterprise systems can integrate financial information with production and sales information so that the impact of sales and manufacturing transactions can be immediately reflected on the firm's balance sheets, accounts receivable and payable ledgers, and reports of cash flows. Management can use enterprise systems to obtain up-to-the-minute reports of the firm's overall financial performance.

The Internet has also opened up new avenues for businesses to make and receive payments electronically and has provided the financial industry with new products and channels to customers. Poor data quality and software errors can have a devastating impact on the firm's financial and accounting systems because errors in these systems can easily lead to huge losses. Financial and accounting systems are prime targets for computer crime, as are the specialized financial systems of financial and banking institutions. One growing area of computer crime is securities fraud over the Internet. You can find examples of finance and accounting applications on pages 24, 59, and 129.

Human Resources

Human resources systems help businesses develop staffing requirements; identify potential new employees; maintain employee records; track employee training, skills, and job performance; and help managers develop appropriate plans for employee compensation and career development. Enterprise systems can help businesses coordinate their staffing levels with sales and production activities and financial resources.

Networked systems also make it possible to create work groups outside traditional places of work. Employees from many different locations can use information systems to work together on virtual teams. Understanding human resource issues is essential for successful system implementation because people need to adjust to the organizational change created by introducing a new information system.

Many companies are installing self-service human resources (HR) systems on intranets to deliver HR-related services, such as enrolling in insurance and medical plans, maintaining employee savings plans, and applying for company jobs. Companies can realize productivity and publishing savings by using Web technology to deliver interactive employee training and HR policy manuals and company directories. HR staff members can use intranets to access employee records from the firm's basic HR transaction systems.

Developing and enforcing a corporate ethics policy and procedures that balance the need to run the business responsibly and efficiently with the need to safeguard employee privacy, health, and well being have become important responsibilities of the human resources function. You can find examples of human resources applications on page 131.

Manufacturing and Production

Manufacturing and production systems solve problems related to the planning, development, and delivery of products and services, and control the flow of production. Supply chain management (SCM) systems provide information to coordinate sourcing and procurement, production scheduling, order fulfillment, inventory management, product development, warehousing, and customer service. When these processes are coordinated among supply chain members, goods can move smoothly and on time from suppliers to manufacturers to customers. Information systems can be used to streamline manufacturing and production processes so that they require fewer steps and less human intervention. By taking advantage of more precise flows of information, firms can tighten coordination of production and distribution, lowering transaction and agency costs.

Collaborative commerce can promote further supply chain and product development efficiencies by facilitating collaborative interactions between the firm and its suppliers, customers, and other business partners. Internet technology creates a common platform for communication and data exchange that can be used to integrate manufacturing and production data from disparate systems inside the firm. Large manufacturers can use software and networks for mass customization, whereas small manufacturers can use desktop computers with computer-aided design software and computer-controlled machines to output products with the precision and speed of larger firms.

Knowledge management systems provide tools and information to help engineers, designers, and product development staff innovate and design new products. You can find examples of manufacturing and production applications on pages 2–4, 10, 36–37, 68–70, 104–107, 124, 132, and 133.

Sales and Marketing

Information systems help businesses promote products, contact customers, track sales, and provide ongoing service and support. They can also be used to analyze the performance of the firm's sales staff. Today, customer relationship management (CRM) systems are especially useful for consolidating customer data from different sources so that the firm can coordinate its interactions with customers and provide better long-term customer relationships. Systems can be used to analyze vast pools of data for highly targeted marketing campaigns, and they can also generate unique new products and services that the organization can sell.

Efficient customer response systems can improve sales by tightly coordinating production and distribution with customer orders. The Internet has reduced consumer search costs and transaction costs, making it much easier to comparison shop and find the right combination of trust, fulfillment, customer service, and price to meet consumers' needs. Internet technologies can help differentiate products by using personalization, customization techniques, and community marketing techniques.

The Internet has broadened the scope of marketing communications by making it easier for firms to reach large numbers of people. The Internet has also increased the richness of marketing communications by combining text, video, and audio content into rich messages and providing capabilities for users to interactively control the experience. Personalized messages can be delivered at very low cost to individuals and groups.

The customer information that is required to create a personalized Web experience raises serious privacy concerns, because contemporary information technology makes it so easy for businesses to monitor online behaviour and assemble highly detailed profiles of individual consumers. You can find examples of sales and marketing applications on pages 59, 64–67, 77, 91–92, 104–107, 108–110, 117–122, 131, 148–149, 162.

E-MAIL WITH TEETH: INAPPROPRIATE E-MAIL CAN TAKE A BITE OUT OF YOUR ASSETS

We secure our hardware, software, and data to prevent unethical people from misusing or stealing them. But sometimes, by ensuring that we can keep data, such as e-mail messages, we leave our organizations open to misinterpretation, bad publicity, and lawsuits that favour our competition.

Throughout history, the installation of security measures has lagged significantly behind the discovery of a threat. Unfortunately, it usually takes a major event to precipitate widespread adoption of protective measures. One example is the Microsoft antitrust trial. One of the more scary aspects of this case, for all of us, was the way the Justice Department foraged through Microsoft's e-mail archives. It used any e-mail that was sent that could be interpreted as incriminating against Microsoft.

Microsoft had been seeking to make deals with companies, such as Apple, Hewlett-Packard, and Intel to keep them from supporting Java. In theory, Java could allow computer users to run Web browsers, word processors, and numerous other applications without the need for Windows, a concept that, Chairman and CEO Bill Gates said, "scares the hell out of me," according to an e-mail Sun Microsystems, the maker of Java, subpoenaed from Microsoft.

According to another Microsoft e-mail, the overall strategy, which at times sparked internal division among Microsoft executives, included letting "the Java (developer tools) space fragment so that 'write once, run anywhere' does not happen," referring to Sun's slogan for Java. According to Microsoft internal e-mail, executives were also concerned about some of Intel's Java projects and explored ways to get the chipmaker to scale them back. Intel did in fact drop the development of its JMedia player, ostensibly due to "changing Java market conditions."

Earlier, in 1989, Gates e-mailed his staff: "You never sent me a response on the question of what things an app (application) would do that make it run with MSDOS and not run with DR-DOS. Is there (sic) feature they have that might get in our way?" Two years later, Microsoft programmers and executives exchanged e-mails that discussed putting code in a beta version of Windows 3.1 which would cause an error message to be displayed when the software ran on top of DR-DOS, then marketed by Novell. Debate among the staff was hot. "I hate this whole thing. I think it's totally rude, reinforces the image that

users have of us as the evil ones, etc.," wrote one employee. The code never appeared in a commercial version of Windows 3.1.

"If you're going to kill someone there isn't much reason to get all worked up about it and angry," a Microsoft executive wrote in an e-mail discussing how Microsoft should compete against Novell. "Any discussions beforehand are a waste of time. We need to smile at Novell while we pull the trigger." One way Microsoft sought to gain an advantage, e-mail suggests, was by charging computer sellers for every machine sold, whether or not they contained Microsoft software. A Microsoft employee in one e-mail acknowledged that by getting Hyundai Electronics to sign such "per processor" licenses—so named because sellers were charged based on the number of CPUs they sold—DR-DOS and its then maker, Digital Research, were put at a severe disadvantage. Digital Research "is still alive," the employee wrote. "We are pushing [Hyundai] to sign the amendment on processor based license. This will block out DR once signed."

Perhaps even worse, Gates wrote (or co-wrote) a book, titled *Business @ the Speed of Thought*. In it, he stated: "I read all the e-mail that employees send me, and I pass items on to people for action." Gates actions as documented in this book contrast harshly with remarks he made in connection with the Microsoft antitrust trial. In pretrial testimony, Gates frequently asserted that he could not remember sending or receiving e-mails bearing his name, especially when they appeared to contradict key statements made in his defence.

Asked, for instance, if he explored ways to encourage Apple Computer to "undermine" Sun Microsystems' Java, Gates said he could not remember using those words and doubted he had any involvement in discussions with Apple over Java. Government attorneys then showed Gates a 1997 e-mail he had sent to Microsoft subordinates, asking directly: "Do we have a clear plan on what we want Apple to do to undermine Sun?" Gates claimed he did not remember sending the e-mail. But he did admit that it appeared to be legitimately an e-mail he had sent.

As recently as during the antitrust trial, Gates could not resist sending e-mails that should have been destroyed. The new e-mails detail efforts by Gates to get makers of handheld computing devices to embrace a scaled-down version of Windows. In one e-mail, Gates suggested that Microsoft should change some of its desktop software so that some new features "run only on our PDAs" (personal digital assistants). Gates argued that might make a manufacturer of PDAs or mobile phones choose a Microsoft operating system over another system. In a second e-mail to some of his top executives, Gates was upset that cellular telephone manufacturer Nokia had joined a consortium called Symbian PLC to develop technology for the so-called smart mobile phones. Gates complained that Symbian would promote Java. Gates said: "Using Sun is just declaring war on us... If either of these things are the case, then these guys are really at (war) with us and we should do the most extreme things we can. This may mean not working with them in some of the other areas."

Yet, for all the bad results that Microsoft's e-mails had for the antitrust trial, not all were admitted. One in particular was disallowed by the second judge to hear the case. She disallowed an e-mailed memorandum from Microsoft Senior Vice-President Joachim Kempin calling for Microsoft to take retaliatory action against computer makers who did not cooperate by not supporting Linux operating systems. Judge Colleen Kollar-Kotelly said that admitting the e-mail would prejudice Microsoft's defence.

Perhaps more than any other case, the Microsoft trial has established an obvious connection between e-mail and legal liability. The fallout of this is fear in the corporate sector—because it is now clear that the contents of an e-mail are actionable in a court of law. Who among us has not sent an e-mail that, taken out of context, could be considered dubious?

People memorialize things in e-mail that they would never, ever say on company letterhead. As coverage of the Microsoft trial pointed out in graphic detail, the executives at Microsoft incriminated themselves vigorously with the comments they made in e-mail. Others have had similar problems with their e-mails, too.

When Netscape's Jim Barksdale took the stand in the Microsoft antitrust case in 1998, he was in for a surprise. As cross-examination began on his previous testimony, an e-mail was introduced into evidence. It was to Microsoft from Netscape founder Jim Clark, and in it Clark offered Microsoft an equity stake in the company he started. Browser software wasn't Netscape's main business, Clark had written. His company was focusing instead on server software.

But it is not just what executives and other employees say in their e-mails about the company's business and in pursuit of business that can hurt the company. Employee abuse of e-mail is becoming a costly liability issue for corporations around the world. After managers at Morgan Stanley & Co. (now Morgan Stanley Dean Witter & Co.) were said to have sent an e-mail that read, "My parole officer tel me if I miss disappointment they gonna send me back to da big house," African American employees filed suit. The U.S. *Civil Rights Act* of 1964 prohibits discrimination based on gender or race, and interpretations of the Act can require an employer to provide a workplace free of discrimination and harassment. Morgan Stanley then faced a $60-million race discrimination suit.

A suit against R.R. Donnelly involved 165 racial, ethnic, and sexual jokes sent via e-mail. Chevron recently paid out $2.2 million

for sexual harassment charges after employees received an e-mail joke listing "25 reasons why beer is better than women." In *Faragher v. City of Boca Raton* and *Burlington Industries Inc. v. Ellerth*, the American courts made employers liable for the wrongful action of supervisors, even if the employers were unaware of specific actions. This means that if companies do not take additional steps to actively prevent sexual harassment they will be opening themselves up to larger damage awards.

In 2002 alone, according to the International Computer Security Association (ICSA), employee security breaches increased by 35 percent, and the leak of proprietary information increased by 58 percent. Much of this was via e-mail. The U.S. Equal Employment Opportunity Commission reported that discrimination claims have escalated by 50 percent, from 10 532 in 1992 to 15 889 in 1998, again largely due to e-mails that reeked of discrimination.

According to an online survey by World Research, 40 percent of respondents receive "heavy to very heavy" amounts of junk e-mail everyday. According to the Society for Human Resource Management (SHRM), 22 percent of its members responding to a random survey have received employee complaints about inappropriate or offensive e-mail. Also, according to the SHRM, slightly more than half of their members (52%) had written e-mail policies, and of these, only a quarter are actually enforcing them—which can be as expensive as not having a policy at all.

According to Earl Crum of the ISCA (International Computer Security Association), "Internet misuse is becoming a huge drain on corporate productivity. Corporations are losing tens of thousands of dollars in wasted time, as well as the hard costs for providing access to the Internet for so many computers."

While employees surf the Internet, day-trade, instant message their friends, enter chat rooms to meet new friends, and even look at pornography or sexually explicit material and hate sites, companies are losing money due to loss of productivity and the potential impact on employee morale of some of these uses, not to mention the potential for lawsuits due to harassment, discrimination, or plain stupidity. But what is a company to do in the face of this changing and dynamic technology? And won't any corporate actions infringe on employee privacy?

While you may not want the perception among employees that their every move is being watched, companies have the right to monitor their employees' computer activity, including e-mail, instant messaging, and Web surfing. The same is true for voice mail. A variety of companies have sprung up to help their client companies deal with these issues. Some of these companies offer classes, some companies go through all of a client's electronic files, including e-mail, identifying potential problems. Some offer software designed to stop, monitor, or track employee surfing.

A well-known Canadian entity that uses Web monitoring is Canada Customs and Revenue Agency (CCRA). It monitors Internet use by its 25 000 employees using Websense software. The CCRA has specific parameters in mind for its monitoring software: it needed to automate the agency's Internet access policy, in other words barring access to off-limits Web material but also allowing specific users to bypass the software's decision-making intelligence. CCRA customs inspectors, for example, needed to have access to some sites that would generally be considered inappropriate.

The Message Is Clear

The odds are stacked against companies when it comes to corporate e-mail use. E-mail continues to be one of the most widely deployed desktop applications. Judges' rulings have put the burden of proof on companies—not employees. Finally, the costs and negative publicity of an e-mail–based lawsuit can be astronomical.

The problem for business owners now is that any e-mail message sent by any employee, whether appropriate or misguided, whether public or private, may now be interpreted legally as the company's official corporate policy. Water cooler conversations (or at least their e-mail equivalents) are now gospel.

Companies have found themselves with legal trouble due to the contents of their corporate e-mail archives for some time now. But the fallout of the Microsoft antitrust case is a trumpet heralding the importance of content security. Interestingly enough, as of the writing of this text, Microsoft still does not have a policy on the appropriate use of e-mail.

CASE STUDY QUESTIONS

1. Why does Microsoft still not have a policy on e-mail use? Do you think it will develop one? When? Should it develop one?

2. Should corporations be held liable for their employees' e-mails and the content thereof? When should they not be held liable?

3. Should companies be able to monitor their employees' e-mails and Internet activity? When is this appropriate?

4. Develop a policy on e-mail use for a business and present it in class.

SOURCES

Dan Goodin, "Microsoft's Holy War on Java," *CNET News* (September 23, 1998), available http://news.com/2009-1001_3-215854.html, accessed July 18, 2003; "Faceoff: Microsoft Anti-Trust Trial Opens," *Net4TV Voice* (October 25, 1998), available http://net4tv.com/voice/Story.cfm?storyID=250, accessed July 18, 2003; Dan Goodin, "Microsoft Emails Focus on DR-DOS Threat," *CNET News* (April 28, 1999), available http://news.com/2100-1001-225129.html, accessed July 18, 2003; Dan Goodin, "Friend or Foe: Gates's Book Backs Email," *CNET News* (March 15, 1999), available http://news.com/2009-1001_3-223043.html, accessed July 18, 2003; "Judge Disallows Email Memo in Anti-Trust Case," (June 3, 2002), available www.theage.com.au, accessed July 18, 2003; Dan Orzech, "Under IT's Radar, Instant Messaging Invades Corporate Desktops," *CIO Update* (July 11, 2003), available www.cioupdate.com/trends/article.php/2234191, accessed July 18, 2003; "WebSense in Use at Canada Customs and Revenue Agency," available www.websense.com/products/why/casestudies/ccra.cfm, accessed July 18, 2003; Victor Woodward, "It's the Email, Stupid!" *Domino Power Magazine* (December 1998), available www.dominopower.com/issuesprint/issue199812/legal.html.

VIDEO RESOURCE

"E-Mail Alert," *Venture* 851 (October 27, 2002).

INFORMATION TECHNOLOGY INFRASTRUCTURE

HARDWARE AND SOFTWARE

Objectives

As a manager, you will face many decisions about purchasing and using hardware and software to improve the performance of your firm. After completing this chapter, you should be able to answer the following questions:

1. *What computer processing and storage capability does our organization need to manage its information and conduct business transactions?*

2. *What arrangement of computers and computer processing would best benefit our organization?*

3. *What kinds of software do we need to run our business? What criteria should we use to select our software?*

4. *How do we stay current on new software? How do we know that it would benefit our organization?*

5. *How should we acquire and manage the firm's hardware and software?*

Navigation Canada Manages Canadian Airspace

In 1996, Navigation Canada (NavCan, **www.navcan.ca**) was founded to manage air traffic over 38 million square kilometres of Canadian airspace. On September 11, 2001, thousands of aircraft flying over North America or to North America were rerouted to the nearest airport to reduce the threat of airborne terrorism. Navigation Canada handled 239 international aircraft that were over oceans and diverted about 1500 aircraft that were in Canadian airspace—without incidence.

About two dozen countries have shed direct state control of air navigation over the last 16 years. NavCan has the best radical performance improvement of them all—32 percent improvement in performance efficiency, 33 percent lower charges to airlines, and 14 percent fewer managerial and administrative staff.

All of this would not have been possible without significant improvements in NavCan's hardware and software assets. When NavCan was founded, it used outdated Digital Equipment Corporation VAX cluster computers that required air traffic controllers to hunt for information on six different systems. Starting in 1996, NavCan took full advantage of its new autonomy. Using user fees from airlines and passengers to fund these initiatives, NavCan is on its way to spending

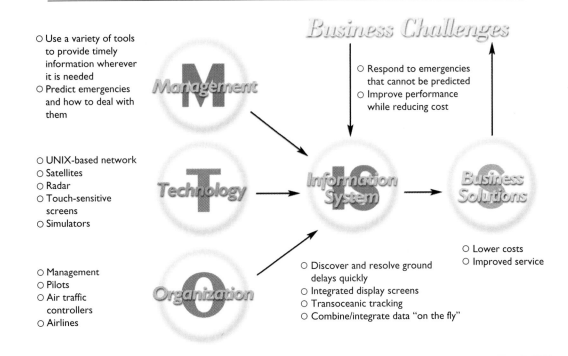

Business Challenges

○ Use a variety of tools to provide timely information wherever it is needed
○ Predict emergencies and how to deal with them

Management

○ Respond to emergencies that cannot be predicted
○ Improve performance while reducing cost

○ UNIX-based network
○ Satellites
○ Radar
○ Touch-sensitive screens
○ Simulators

Technology

Information System

Business Solutions

○ Lower costs
○ Improved service

○ Management
○ Pilots
○ Air traffic controllers
○ Airlines

Organization

○ Discover and resolve ground delays quickly
○ Integrated display screens
○ Transoceanic tracking
○ Combine/integrate data "on the fly"

$1 billion over a 10-year period to ensure the safety of Canadian airways. New technology increased landing efficiency by as much as 30 percent, saving airports the cost of new runways. Enhanced radar, working with upgraded computer hardware, will save airlines $170 million in the next 14 years by letting them fly at more fuel-efficient altitudes with less rerouting. New software permits controllers to discover and resolve ground delays quickly.

NavCan is a leader in the area of software development. Its Gander Automated Air Traffic System (GAATS) uses satellites, not radar, to track transoceanic air traffic. NavCan's Integrated Information Display System/Extended Computer Display System (IIDS/EXCDS) allows management of electronic flight data online. Its Canadian Automated Air Traffic System (CAATS) allows an air traffic controller to access automated real-time flight data processing and position reports for radar and non-radar airplanes on a sole monitor.

NavCan is even installing Web-based information kiosks for pilots in airports. These will offer pilots a wide range of information and capabilities, including detailed and interpretive briefings, printable graphics from distant flight information centres, and eventually, the ability to file flight plans via the Web.

It is evident that NavCan also maintains up-to-date hardware. NavCan's architecture is based on UNIX-compatible servers and workstations. NavCan is constantly updating its infrastructure to support not only its sophisticated software applications, but also the addition of new radar sites and control tower enhancements. In keeping with these advancements, NavCan also maintains a state-of-the-art training facility, including simulators that allow students to train in "real-time" situations.

Sources: "Nav Canada's Striking Success," Frontier Centre for Public Policy, September 18, 2002, available www.fcpp.org; "Technology and Innovation Solutions," Navigation Canada, available www.navcanada.ca/navcanada.asp; Joel Baglole, "Canada's New Automated System Simplifies Transoceanic Air Traffic," *The Wall Street Journal*, May 9, 2002, available http://webreprints.djreprints.com).

MANAGEMENT CHALLENGES

Navigation Canada found that its efficiency and effectiveness were hampered by outdated technology. NavCan found it could offer improved service by using the right hardware and software. In order to select appropriate technology, NavCan's management had to understand the capabilities of computer hardware and software technologies, how to select hardware and software to meet current and future business requirements, and the financial and business rationale for their hardware and software investments. The new software applications represent an important technology asset. Computer hardware and software technologies can improve organizational performance, but they raise the following management challenges:

1. **The centralization versus decentralization debate.** A longstanding issue among information system managers and chief executive officers (CEOs) has been the question of how much to centralize or distribute computing resources. Should processing power and data be distributed to departments and divisions, or should they be concentrated at a single location using a large centrally based computer? Should organizations deliver application software to users over networks from a central location or allow users to maintain software and data on their own desktop computers? Client-server computing facilitates decentralization, but network computers and mainframes support centralization. Which is the best for the organization? Each organization will have a different answer based on its own needs. Managers need to make sure that the computing model they select is compatible with organizational goals (Schuff and St. Louis, 2001).

2. **The application backlog.** Advances in computer software have not kept pace with computer hardware. Developing software has become a major occupation for organizations. A great deal of software must be intricately designed and implemented. Moreover, the software itself is only one component of a complete information system that must be carefully designed and coordinated with organizational strategy, tactics, politics, and culture, as well as hardware components. The "software crisis" is actually part of a larger systems analysis, design, and implementation issue, which will be treated in detail later. Despite major gains from fourth-generation programming languages, personal desktop software tools, object-oriented programming, and software tools for the Web, many businesses continue to face a backlog in developing the information systems they need, or they may not be able to develop them at all.

Although managers and business professionals do not need to be computer technology experts, they should have a basic understanding of the role of hardware and software in the organization's information technology (IT) infrastructure so that they can make technology decisions that promote organizational performance and productivity. This chapter surveys the capabilities of computer hardware and software and highlights the major issues in managing the firm's hardware and software.

6.1 COMPUTER HARDWARE AND INFORMATION TECHNOLOGY INFRASTRUCTURE

infrastructure

Physical hardware required to interconnect computers and users; includes hardware, software (e.g., operating systems), data, and networking technologies.

Computer hardware, which we defined in Chapter 1, provides the underlying physical foundation for the firm's IT infrastructure. **Infrastructure** is the physical hardware used to interconnect computers and users. It includes not only the hardware and software components we will discuss in this chapter, but also software, data, and networking technologies. All infrastructure components require computer hardware for their storage or operation.

THE COMPUTER SYSTEM

computer

Physical device that takes data as an input, transforms the data by executing stored instructions, and outputs information to one or more devices.

A **computer** is a physical device that receives data from users as input, processes the data according to stored instructions, and outputs the processed information. A contemporary computer system consists of a central processing unit, primary storage, secondary storage, input devices, output devices, and communications devices (see Figure 6.1).

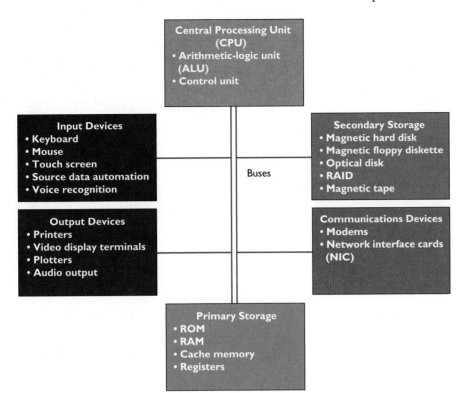

Figure 6.1 Hardware components of a computer system. A contemporary computer system is composed of six major components. The central processing unit manipulates data and controls the other parts of the computer system; primary storage temporarily stores data and program instructions during processing; secondary storage stores data and instructions permanently; input devices convert data and instructions from their input form for processing in the computer; output devices present data in a form that people can understand; and communications devices control the transfer of information to and from different computers on communications networks.

The central processing unit manipulates data into a more useful form and controls the other parts of the computer system. Primary storage temporarily stores data and program instructions, while secondary storage devices (magnetic and optical disks, magnetic tape) store data and programs even when the computer is not turned on. Input devices, such as a keyboard or mouse, convert data and instructions into electronic form for input into the computer. Output devices, such as printers and video display terminals, convert electronic data produced by the computer system and display them in a form that people can understand. Communications devices provide connections between the computer and communications networks. Buses are circuitry paths for transmitting data and signals among the parts of the computer system.

In order for information to flow through a computer system and be in a form suitable for processing, all symbols, pictures, or words must be reduced to a string of binary digits. A binary digit is called a **bit** and represents either a 0 or a 1. In the computer, the presence of an electronic or magnetic signal means 1, and its absence signifies 0. Digital computers operate directly with binary digits, either singly or strung together to form bytes. A string of eight bits that the computer stores as a unit is called a **byte**. Each byte can be used to store a decimal number, a symbol, a character, or part of a picture (see Figure 6.2).

The CPU and Primary Storage

The **central processing unit (CPU)** is the part of the computer system where the manipulation of symbols, numbers, and characters occurs, and it controls the other parts of the computer system (see Figure 6.3). Located near the CPU is **primary storage** (sometimes called primary or main memory), where data and program instructions are stored temporarily during processing while the computer is on. Buses provide pathways for transmitting data and signals between the CPU, primary storage, and the other devices in the computer system. The characteristics of the CPU and primary storage are very important in determining a computer's speed and capabilities.

Figure 6.3 also shows that the CPU consists of an arithmetic-logic unit and a control unit. The **arithmetic-logic unit (ALU)** performs the computer's principal logic and arithmetic operations. It adds, subtracts, multiplies, and divides, determining whether a number is positive, negative, or zero. In addition to performing arithmetic functions, an ALU must

bit

A binary digit representing the smallest unit of data in a computer system. It can only have one of two states, representing 0 or 1.

byte

A string of bits, usually eight, used to store one number or character in a computer system.

central processing unit (CPU)

Area of the computer system that manipulates symbols, numbers, and characters and controls the other parts of the computer system.

primary storage

Part of the computer that temporarily stores program instructions and data being used by the instructions.

arithmetic-logic unit (ALU)

Component of the CPU that performs the computer's principal logic and arithmetic operations.

Figure 6.2 Bits and bytes. Bits are represented by either a 0 or 1. A string of eight bits constitutes a byte, which represents a character or number. Illustrated here is a byte representing the letter "A" using the ASCII binary coding standard. ASCII stands for American Standard Code for Information Interchange; it is the main coding system used by PCs.

be able to determine when one quantity is greater than or less than another and when two quantities are or are not equal. The ALU can perform logic operations on letters and other characters as well as numbers.

control unit

Component of the CPU that controls and coordinates the other parts of the computer system.

The **control unit** coordinates and controls the other parts of the computer system. It reads a stored program, one instruction at a time, and directs other components of the computer system to perform the program's required tasks. The series of operations required to process a single machine instruction is called the **machine cycle.**

machine cycle

Series of operations required to process a single machine instruction.

Primary storage has three functions. It stores all or part of the software program that is being executed. Primary storage also stores the operating system programs that manage the operation of the computer (see Section 6.3). Finally, the primary storage area holds data that the program is using. Internal primary storage is often called **RAM, or random access memory**. It is called RAM because it can directly access any randomly chosen location in the same amount of time.

RAM (random access memory)

Primary storage of data or program instructions that can directly access any randomly chosen location in RAM in the same amount of time.

Primary memory is divided into storage locations called *bytes*. Each location contains a set of eight binary switches or devices, each of which can store one bit of information. The set of eight bits found in each storage location is sufficient to store one letter, one digit, or one special symbol (such as $). Each byte has a unique address, similar to a mailbox, indicating where it is located in RAM. The computer can remember where the data in all of the bytes are located simply by keeping track of these addresses. Computer storage capacity is measured in bytes. Table 6.1 lists the primary measures of computer storage capacity and processing speed.

Primary storage is composed of *semiconductors*, which are integrated circuits made by printing thousands and even millions of tiny transistors on small silicon chips. There are several different kinds of semiconductor memory used in primary storage. RAM is used for short-term storage of data or program instructions. RAM is *volatile*. Its contents will be lost when the computer's electric supply is disrupted by a power outage or when the computer is turned off. **ROM, or read-only memory**, can only be read from; it cannot be written to and is nonvolatile; its contents are present even when the computer is turned off. ROM chips come from the manufacturer with programs already burned in, or stored, although some ROM chips can be updated electronically. ROM is used in general-purpose computers to store important or frequently used programs.

ROM (read-only memory)

Semiconductor memory chips that contain program instructions. These chips can only be read from; they cannot be written to.

Figure 6.3 The CPU and primary storage. The CPU contains an arithmetic-logic unit and a control unit. Data and instructions are stored in unique addresses in primary storage that the CPU can access during processing. The data bus, address bus, and control bus transmit signals among the CPU, primary storage, and other devices in the computer system.

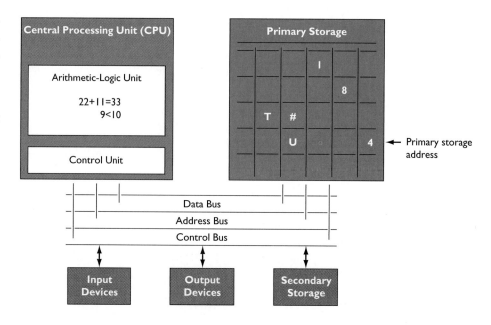

TABLE 6.1	KEY MEASURES OF COMPUTER STORAGE CAPACITY AND PROCESSING SPEED	

Time	Abbreviation	Seconds
Millisecond	ms	1/1 000
Microsecond	mus	1/1 000 000
Nanosecond	ns	1/1 000 000 000
Picosecond	ps	1/1 000 000 000 000

Storage Capacity	Abbreviation	Number of Bytes
Byte	B	1*
Kilobyte	KB	1 000**
Megabyte	MB	1 000 000
Gigabyte	GB	1 000 000 000
Terabyte	TB	1 000 000 000 000

* String of eight bits
** Actually 1024 bytes

COMPUTER PROCESSING

The processing capability of the CPU plays a large role in determining the amount of work that a computer system can accomplish.

Microprocessors and Processing Power

Contemporary CPUs use semiconductor chips called **microprocessors**, which integrate all of the memory, logic, and control circuits for an entire CPU onto a single chip. The speed and performance of a computer's microprocessors help determine a computer's processing power and are based on the number of bits that can be processed at one time (*word length),* the amount of data that can be moved among the CPU, primary storage, and other devices (data bus width), and cycle speed, measured in **megahertz**. (Megahertz is abbreviated MHz and stands for millions of cycles per second).

Microprocessors can be made faster by using **reduced instruction set computing (RISC)** in their design. Conventional chips, based on complex instruction set computing, have several hundred or more instructions hard-wired into their circuitry, and they may take several cycles to execute a single instruction. If the seldom-used instructions are eliminated, the remaining instructions can execute much faster. RISC computers have only the most frequently used instructions embedded in them. A CPU with RISC can execute most instructions in a single machine cycle and sometimes multiple instructions at the same time. RISC technology is often used in scientific and workstation computing. A variety of faster chips with additional features, such as security or lower power requirements, are being developed by chip manufacturers, such as IBM, Intel, and Advanced Micro Devices (AMD).

Parallel Processing

Processing can also be speeded up by linking several processors to work simultaneously on the same task. Figure 6.4 compares parallel processing to serial processing used in conventional computers. In **parallel processing**, multiple processing units (CPUs) break down a problem into smaller parts and work on it simultaneously. Getting a group of processors to attack the same problem at once requires both rethinking the problems and special software that can divide problems among different processors in the most efficient way possible, providing the needed data, and reassembling the many subtasks to reach an appropriate solution.

Massively parallel computers have huge networks of processor chips interwoven in complex and flexible ways to tackle large computing problems. As opposed to parallel processing, where small numbers of powerful but expensive specialized chips are linked together, massively parallel machines link hundreds or even thousands of inexpensive, commonly used chips to break problems into many small pieces and solve them.

microprocessor
Very large scale integrated circuit technology that integrates the computer's memory, logic, and control on a single chip.

megahertz
A measure of cycle speed, or the pacing of events in a computer; one megahertz equals one million cycles per second.

reduced instruction set computing (RISC)
Technology used to enhance the speed of microprocessors by embedding only the most frequently used instructions on a chip.

parallel processing
Type of processing in which more than one instruction can be processed at a time by breaking down a problem into smaller parts and processing them simultaneously with multiple processors.

massively parallel computers
Computers that use hundreds or thousands of processing chips to tackle large computing problems simultaneously.

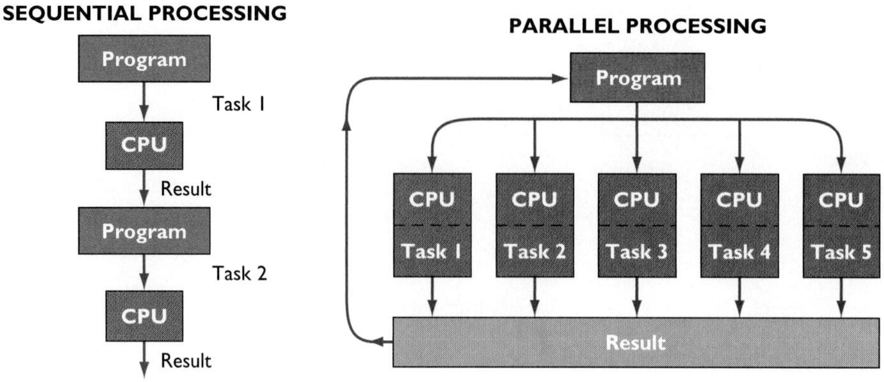

Figure 6.4 Sequential and parallel processing. During sequential processing, each task is assigned to one CPU that processes one instruction at a time. In parallel processing, multiple tasks are assigned to multiple processing units to expedite the result.

SEQUENTIAL PROCESSING

Program

Task I

CPU

Result

Program

Task 2

CPU

Result

PARALLEL PROCESSING

Program

CPU	CPU	CPU	CPU	CPU
Task I	Task 2	Task 3	Task 4	Task 5

Result

STORAGE, INPUT, AND OUTPUT TECHNOLOGIES

The capabilities of computer systems depend not only on the speed and capacity of the CPU but also on the speed, capacity, and design of storage, input, and output technologies. Storage, input, and output devices are called *peripheral devices* because they are outside the main computer system unit.

Secondary Storage Technology

Electronic commerce (e-commerce) and electronic business (e-business) have made storage a strategic technology. Although e-commerce and e-business are reducing manual processes, data of all types must be stored electronically and available whenever needed. Most of the information used by a computer application is stored on secondary storage devices located outside of the primary storage area. **Secondary storage** is used for relatively long-term storage of data outside the CPU. Secondary storage is *nonvolatile* and retains data even when the computer is turned off. The most important secondary storage technologies are magnetic disk, optical disk, and magnetic tape.

Magnetic Disk   The most widely used secondary storage medium today is the **magnetic disk**. There are two kinds of magnetic disks: floppy disks (used in personal computers [PCs]) and **hard disks** (used on large commercial disk drives and PCs). Large mainframe or midrange computer systems have multiple hard-disk drives because they require immense disk storage capacity in the gigabyte and terabyte range. PCs also use **floppy disks,** which are removable and portable, with lower storage capacities and access rates than hard disks. Removable disk drives are popular backup storage alternatives for PC systems. Magnetic disks on both large and small computers permit direct access to individual records so that data stored on the disk can be directly accessed, regardless of the order in which the data were originally recorded.

Disk drive performance can be further enhanced by using a disk technology called **RAID (Redundant Array of Independent Disks)**. RAID devices package more than a hundred disk drives, a controller chip, and specialized software into a single large unit. Traditional disk drives deliver data from the disk drive along a single path, but RAID systems deliver data over multiple paths simultaneously, improving disk access time and reliability. For most RAID systems, data on a failed disk can be restored automatically without the computer system having to be shut down.

Optical Disks   Optical disks, also called compact discs or laser optical discs, use laser technology to store massive quantities of data in a highly compact form. They are available for both PCs and large computers. The most common optical disk system used with PCs is called **CD-ROM (compact disc read-only memory)**. A 4.75-inch compact disc for PCs can store up to 660 megabytes, nearly 300 times more than a high-density floppy disk. Optical disks are most appropriate for applications where enormous quantities of unchanging data must be stored compactly for easy retrieval or for applications combining text, sound, and images.

CD-ROM is read-only storage. No new data can be written to it; it can only be read. *WORM (write once/read many)* and *CD-R (compact disc-recordable)* optical disk systems allow

secondary storage

Relatively long term, nonvolatile storage of data outside the CPU and primary storage.

magnetic disk

A secondary storage medium in which data are stored by means of magnetized spots on a hard or floppy disk.

hard disk

Magnetic disk resembling a metallic platter; used in large computer systems and in most PCs.

floppy disk

Removable magnetic disk storage primarily used with PCs.

RAID (Redundant Array of Independent Disks)

Disk storage technology to boost disk performance by packaging more than 100 smaller disk drives with a controller chip and specialized software in a single large unit to deliver data over multiple paths simultaneously.

CD-ROM (compact disc read-only memory)

Read-only optical disk storage used for imaging, reference, and other applications with massive amounts of unchanging data and for multimedia.

Secondary storage devices, such as floppy disks, optical disks, and hard disks, are used to store large quantities of data outside the CPU and primary storage. They provide direct access to data for easy retrieval.

users to record data only once on an optical disk. Once written, the data cannot be erased but can be read indefinitely. **CD-RW (CD-ReWritable)** technology has been developed to allow users to create rewritable optical disks for applications requiring large volumes of storage where the information is occasionally updated.

Digital video discs (DVDs), also called digital versatile discs, are optical disks the same size as CD-ROMs but of even higher capacity. They can hold a minimum of 4.7 gigabytes of data, enough to store a full-length, high-quality motion picture. DVDs are initially being used to store movies and multimedia applications using large amounts of video and graphics, but they may replace CD-ROMs because they can store large amounts of digitized text, graphics, audio, and video data. Once read-only, writable, and re-writable DVD drives and media are now available.

Magnetic Tape   **Magnetic tape** is an older storage technology that still is employed for secondary storage of large quantities of data that are needed rapidly but not instantly. Magnetic tape is very inexpensive and relatively stable. However, it stores data sequentially and is relatively slow compared with the speed of other secondary storage media. In order to find an individual record stored on magnetic tape, such as an employment record, the tape must be read from the beginning up to the location of the desired record. Typical applications are backing up applications and data or processing payroll every payroll period. Magnetic tape is not widely used today.

Storage Networking   To meet the escalating demand for data-intensive graphics, Web transactions, and other digital firm applications, the amount of data that companies need to store is doubling every 12 to 18 months. Companies are turning to new kinds of storage infrastructures to deal with the complexity and cost of skyrocketing storage requirements.

Large companies have many different storage resources—disk drives, tape backup drives, RAID, and other devices that may be scattered in many different locations. This arrangement is expensive to manage and makes it difficult to access data across the enterprise. Storage networks enable firms to manage all of their storage resources centrally by providing an overall storage plan for all the storage devices in the enterprise.

There are alternative storage networking arrangements. In *direct-attached storage*, storage devices are connected directly to individual server computers and must be accessed through each server, which can create bottlenecks. **Network-attached storage (NAS)** overcomes this problem by attaching high-speed RAID storage devices to a network so that the devices in the network can access this storage through a specialized server dedicated to file service and storage. **Storage-area networks (SANs)** go one step further by placing multiple storage devices on a separate high-speed network dedicated to storage purposes. The SAN creates a large central pool of storage that can be shared by multiple servers so that users can rapidly share data across the SAN. The SAN connects different kinds of storage devices, such as tape libraries and disk arrays. SAN storage devices are located on their own network and are connected using a high-transmission technology, such as Fibre Channel. The network moves data among pools of servers and storage devices, creating an enterprise-wide infrastructure for data storage. Figure 6.5 illustrates how a SAN works.

SANs can be expensive and difficult to manage, but they are very useful for companies that need to share information across applications and computing platforms. SANs can help these companies consolidate their storage resources and provide rapid data access for widely distributed users.

CD-RW (CD-ReWritable)

Optical disk storage that can be rewritten many times by users.

digital video disc (DVD)

High-capacity optical storage medium that can store full-length motion pictures and large amounts of data.

magnetic tape

Inexpensive, older secondary-storage medium in which large volumes of information are stored sequentially by means of magnetized and nonmagnetized spots on tape.

network-attached storage (NAS)

Attaching high-speed RAID storage devices to a network so that the devices in the network can access these storage devices through a specialized server dedicated to file service and storage.

storage area network (SAN)

A high-speed network dedicated to storage that connects different kinds of storage devices, such as tape libraries and disk arrays, so that they can be shared by multiple servers across the enterprise.

Figure 6.5 A storage area network (SAN). A typical SAN consists of a server, storage devices, and networking devices and is used strictly for storage. The SAN stores data on many different types of storage devices, providing data to the enterprise. The SAN supports communication between any server and the storage units as well as between different storage devices in the network.

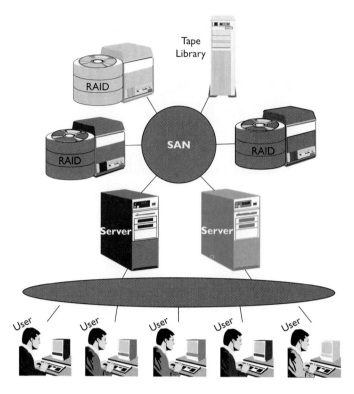

The growth of storage needs has forced businesses to view storage as though it were a utility; as with electricity or water, they want to pay only for the storage they use. These businesses have *outsourced* their data storage to online **storage service providers (SSP)** that rent out storage space to subscribers on the Web.

Input and Output Devices

Human beings interact with computer systems largely through input and output devices. Input devices gather data and convert them into electronic form for use by the computer, whereas output devices display data after they have been processed. Table 6.2 describes the principal input and output devices.

The principal input devices consist of keyboards, pointing devices (such as a computer mouse and touch screens), and *source data automation* technologies (optical and magnetic ink character recognition, pen-based input, digital scanners, audio input, and sensors), which capture data in computer-readable form at the time and place they are created. They also include **radio-frequency identification (RFID)** devices that use tiny tags incorporating embedded microchips containing information about an item and its location to transmit signals over a short distance to special RFID readers. The information is then transferred to a processing device. RFID is especially useful for tracking the location of items as they move through the supply chain. The principal output devices are display screens, sometimes called monitors, cathode ray tube terminals (CRTs), or video display terminals (VDTs), printers, and audio output.

Connections to the Central Computer Unit

All *peripheral* devices (located outside the central computer unit) must be connected in some way to the central computer unit, usually through a **port**. Ports determine which devices can be used on the basis of their connectors and *drivers* (software that manages the interface between the peripheral device and the central computer unit), as well as which cables can be used for the connection.

There are many different kinds of ports. Most keyboards and computer mice use a *PS/2* port, while display screens use a video display port found on the graphics adapter card in the central computer unit. Microphone and headset/speaker ports are found on sound cards. Other ports can be used by a variety of devices. A **serial port** sends a signal along the cable

storage service provider (SSP)

A third-party provider that rents out storage space to subscribers over the Web, allowing customers to store and access their data without having to purchase and maintain their own storage technology.

radio-frequency identification (RFID)

Devices using tiny tags with embedded microchips containing information on an item and its location that is transmitted to special RFID readers.

port

A connection to the central computer unit.

serial port

A connection that only sends one bit at a time along the cable between the peripheral device and the central computer unit.

TABLE 6.2   INPUT AND OUTPUT DEVICES

Input Device	Description
Keyboard	Principal method of data entry for text and numerical data.
Computer mouse	Handheld device with point-and-click capabilities that is usually connected to the computer by a cable. The computer user can move the mouse around on a desktop to control the cursor's position on a computer display screen, pushing a button to select a command. Trackballs and touch pads often are used in place of the mouse as pointing devices on laptop PCs.
Touch screen	Allows users to enter limited amounts of data by touching the surface of a sensitized video display screen with a finger or a pointer. Often found in information kiosks in retail stores, restaurants, and shopping malls.
Optical character recognition	Devices that can translate specially designed marks, characters, and codes into digital form. The most widely used optical code is the bar code, which is used in point-of-sale systems in supermarkets and retail stores. The codes can include time, date, and location data in addition to identification data.
Magnetic ink character	Used primarily in cheque processing for the banking industry. Characters on the bottom of a cheque recognition (MICR) identify the bank, chequing account, and cheque number and are preprinted using a special magnetic ink. A MICR reader translates these characters into digital form for the computer.
Pen-based input	Handwriting-recognition devices, such as pen-based tablets, notebooks, and notepads, convert the motion made by an electronic stylus pressing on a touch-sensitive tablet screen into digital form.
Digital scanner	Translates images, such as pictures or documents, into digital form and are an essential component of image-processing systems.
Audio input	Voice input devices that convert spoken words into digital form for processing by the computer. Microphones, tape cassette players, and other audio devices can serve as input devices for music and other sounds.
Sensors	Devices that collect data directly from the environment for input into a computer system. For instance, today's farmers can use sensors to monitor the moisture of the soil in their fields to help them with irrigation.
Radio frequency (RFID)	Use of tags incorporating microchips to transmit information about items and their location to special identification RFID readers. Useful for tracking the location of items as they move through the supply chain.

Output Device	Description
Display screen monitor	Cathode ray tubes (CRTs) use an electronic gun that shoots a beam of electrons illuminating tiny points on the display screen. Laptop computers use flat panel displays (frequently called liquid crystal display, or LCD), which are less bulky than the more typical cathode ray tube (CRT) monitors. Microsoft recently unveiled a "smart display monitor," which can be disconnected from the central computer unit and used elsewhere in the building as though it were a tablet PC, except that the actual computing hardware is still in the central computer unit.
Printers	Produce a printed hard copy of information output. They include impact printers (such as dot matrix printers) and nonimpact printers (laser, inkjet, and thermal transfer printers).
Audio output	Voice output devices convert digital output data back into intelligible speech. Other audio output, such as music, can be delivered by speakers connected to the computer.

one bit at a time, while a **parallel port** sends the signal multiple bits at a time, much faster than the serial connection.

Recent technology has speeded up port connections. **Firewire**, also known as IEEE1394, is available on all newer Apple computers and is now becoming available on PCs as well; it can transfer data much faster than can older ports. **Universal serial bus (USB)** ports are available on most computers today. USB technology permits up to 127 devices to be "daisy-chained" through only one USB port by use of USB hubs. USB ports and hubs can also provide power to peripheral devices, adding convenience as well as speed. Finally, *wireless ports* permit laptops and handheld computers to be *synchronized* with desktop computers without using cables. They can also connect computers on a network as we will see in Chapter 8.

Batch and Online Input and Processing

The manner in which data are input into the computer affects how the data can be processed. Information systems collect and process information in one of two ways: through

parallel port

A connection that sends multiple bits at a time along the cable between the peripheral device and the central computer unit.

firewire

A port that provides a high speed connection between a peripheral device and the central computer unit.

universal serial bus (USB)

A high-speed port capable of daisy-chaining USB devices through a USB hub to connect numerous peripheral devices to the central computer unit.

batch processing

A method of collecting and processing data in which transactions are accumulated and stored until a specified time when it is convenient or necessary to process them as a group.

online processing

A method of collecting and processing data in which transactions are entered directly into the computer system and processed immediately.

multimedia

The integration of two or more types of media, such as text, graphics, sound, voice, full-motion video, or animation, into a computer-based application.

batch or online processing. In **batch processing**, transactions, such as payroll time cards, are accumulated and stored in a group or batch until the time when, because of some reporting cycle, it is efficient or necessary to process them. Batch processing is found primarily in older systems where users need only occasional reports. In **online processing**, the user enters transactions into a device (such as a data entry keyboard or bar code reader) that is directly connected to the computer system. The transactions usually are processed immediately. Most processing today is online processing.

Figure 6.6 compares batch and online processing. Batch systems often use tape as a storage medium, whereas online processing systems use disk storage, which permits immediate access to specific records. In batch systems, transactions are accumulated in a *transaction file,* which contains all the transactions for a particular time period. Periodically, this file is used to update a *master file,* which contains permanent information on entities. (An example is a payroll master file with employee earnings and deduction data. It is updated with weekly time-card transactions.) Adding the transaction data to the existing master file creates a new master file. In online processing, transactions are entered immediately into the system using a keyboard, pointing device, or source data automation, and the system usually responds immediately. The master file is updated continually.

Interactive Multimedia

The processing, input, output, and storage technologies we have just described can be used to create **multimedia** applications that integrate sound and full-motion video or animation with graphics and text into a computer-based application. Multimedia is becoming the foundation of new consumer products and services, such as electronic books and newspapers, electronic classroom-presentation technologies, full-motion videoconferencing, imaging, graphics design tools, and video and voice mail. PCs today come with built-in multimedia capabilities, including high-resolution colour display screens, CD-ROM or DVD drives to store video, audio, and graphic data, and stereo speakers for amplifying audio output.

Interactive Web pages replete with graphics, sound, animation, and full-motion video have made multimedia popular on the Internet. For example, visitors to the Canadian Broadcasting Corporation (CBC)'s interactive Web site can access news stories from the

Figure 6.6 A comparison of batch and online processing. In batch processing, transactions are accumulated and stored in a group. Because batches are processed at regular intervals, such as daily, weekly, or monthly, information in the system will not always be up to date. In online processing, transactions are input immediately and usually processed immediately. Information in the system is generally up to date. A typical online application is an airline reservation system.

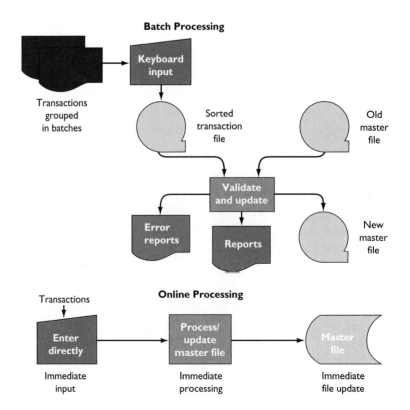

CBC, photos, on-air transcripts, video clips, and audio clips. The video and audio clips are made available using **streaming technology**, which allows audio and video data to be processed as a steady and continuous stream as they are downloaded from the Web.

Multimedia Web sites are also being used to sell digital products, such as digitized music clips. A compression standard known as **MP3** (also called **MPEG3**, which stands for Motion Picture Experts Group, audio layer 3) can compress audio files down to one-tenth or one-twelfth of their original size with virtually no loss in quality. Visitors to such Web sites as MP3.com can download MP3 music clips over the Internet and play them on their own computers.

Multimedia combines text, graphics, sound, and video into a computer-based experience that permits two-way communication. Many organizations use this technology for interactive training.

6.2 CATEGORIES OF COMPUTER SYSTEMS

Contemporary computers can be categorized as mainframes, midrange computers, PCs, workstations, and supercomputers. Managers need to understand the capabilities of each of these types of computers and why some types are more appropriate for certain processing work than others.

CLASSIFYING COMPUTERS

A **personal computer (PC)**, which is sometimes referred to as a *microcomputer*, is a computer that can be placed on a desktop or carried from room to room. Smaller laptop PCs are often used as portable desktops on the road. PCs are used as personal machines as well as in business. Handheld computers as well as newer pen-based PCs fall into this category. PCs are constantly evolving. For example, the latest generation of tablet PCs recognizes handwriting and handles multimedia much better than previous generations of PCs could. A **workstation** also fits on a desktop but has more powerful mathematical and graphics-processing capabilities than has a PC and can perform more complicated tasks in the same amount of time. Workstations are used for scientific, engineering, or design work that requires powerful graphics or computational capabilities.

A **midrange computer** is more powerful, more expensive, and larger than a PC but is capable of supporting the computing needs of smaller organizations or of managing networks of other computers. Midrange computers can be **minicomputers**, which are used in systems for universities, factories, or research laboratories, or they can be **servers**, which are used for managing internal company networks or Web sites. Server computers are specifically optimized to support a computer network, enabling users to share files, software, peripheral devices (such as printers), or other network resources. Servers have large memory and disk-storage capacity, high-speed communications capabilities, and powerful CPUs.

Servers have become important components of firms' IT infrastructures because they provide the hardware platform for e-commerce. By adding special software, they can be customized to deliver Web pages, process purchase and sale transactions, or exchange data with systems inside the company. Organizations with heavy e-commerce requirements and massive Web sites are running their Web and e-commerce applications on multiple servers in **server farms** in computing centres run by commercial vendors, such as IBM.

A **mainframe** is the largest computer, a powerhouse with massive memory and extremely rapid processing power. It is used for very large business, scientific, or military applications where a computer must handle massive amounts of data or many complicated processes.

A **supercomputer** is a highly sophisticated and powerful computer that is used for tasks requiring extremely rapid and complex calculations with hundreds of thousands of variable factors. Supercomputers use parallel processors and traditionally have been used in scientific and military work, such as classified weapons research and weather forecasting, which use complex mathematical models. They are now starting to be used in business for the manipulation of vast quantities of data.

streaming technology

Technology for transferring data so that they can be processed as a steady and continuous stream.

MP3 (MPEG3)

Compression standard that can compress audio files for transfer over the Internet with virtually no loss in quality.

personal computer (PC)

Small desktop or portable computer.

workstation

Desktop computer with powerful graphics and mathematical capabilities and the ability to perform several complicated tasks at once.

midrange computer

Middle-size computer that is capable of supporting the computing needs of smaller organizations or of managing networks of other computers.

minicomputer

Middle-range computer used in systems for universities, factories, or research laboratories.

server

Computer specifically optimized to provide software and other resources to other computers over a network.

server farm

Large group of servers maintained by a commercial vendor and made available to subscribers for e-commerce and other activities requiring heavy use of servers.

mainframe

Largest category of computer; used for major business processing.

supercomputer

Highly sophisticated and powerful computer that can perform very complex computations extremely rapidly.

COMPUTER NETWORKS AND CLIENT-SERVER COMPUTING

Today, stand-alone computers have been replaced by computers in networks for most processing tasks. The use of multiple computers linked by a communications network for processing is called **distributed processing**. In contrast, with **centralized processing**, in which all processing is accomplished by one large central computer, distributed processing distributes the processing work among PCs, midrange computers, and mainframes linked together.

One widely used form of distributed processing is **client-server computing**. Client-server computing splits processing between "clients" and "servers." Both are on the network, but each machine is assigned functions it is best suited to perform. The **client** is the user point-of-entry for the required function and is normally a desktop computer, workstation, or laptop computer. The user generally interacts directly only with the client portion of the application, often to input data or retrieve data for further analysis. The *server* provides the client with services. The server could be anything from a mainframe to a desktop computer, but specialized server computers are often used in this role. Servers store and process shared data and also perform backend functions not visible to users, such as managing network activities. Figure 6.7 illustrates the client-server computing concept. Computing on the Internet uses the client-server model (see Chapter 9).

The exact division of tasks between the client and the server depends on the requirements of each application, including its processing needs, the number of users, and the available resources. For example, client tasks for a large corporate payroll might include inputting data (such as enrolling new employees and recording hours worked), submitting data queries to the server, analyzing the retrieved data, and displaying results on the screen or on a printer. The server portion fetches the entered data and processes the payroll. It controls access so that only authorized users can view or update the data.

In some firms, client-server networks with PCs have actually replaced mainframes and minicomputers. The process of transferring applications from large computers to smaller ones is called **downsizing**. Downsizing can potentially reduce computing costs because memory and processing power on a PC cost a fraction of the cost of their equivalent on a mainframe. The decision to downsize involves many factors in addition to the cost of computer hardware, including the need for new software, training, and perhaps new organizational procedures (see the discussion of total cost of ownership in Section 6.4).

NETWORK COMPUTERS AND PEER-TO-PEER COMPUTING

In one form of client-server computing, client processing and storage capabilities are so minimal that the bulk of computer processing occurs on the server. The term *thin client* is sometimes used to refer to the client in this arrangement. Thin clients, called **network computers (NCs)**, have minimal memory, storage, and processing power and are designed to work on networks. NC users download whatever software or data they need from a central computer over the Internet or their organization's internal network. The central computer also saves information for the user and makes it available for later retrieval, effectively eliminating the need for secondary storage devices, such as hard disks, floppy disks, CD-ROMs, and their drives.

---

distributed processing

The distribution of computer processing work among multiple computers linked by a communications network.

centralized processing

Processing that is accomplished by one large central computer.

client-server computing

A model for computing that splits processing between "clients" and "servers" on a network, assigning functions to the machine most able to perform the function.

client

The user point-of-entry for the required function in client-server computing. Normally, a desktop computer, workstation, or laptop computer.

downsizing

The process of transferring applications from large computers to smaller ones.

network computer (NC)

Simplified desktop computer that does not store software programs or data locally. Users download whatever software or data they need from a central computer over the Internet or their organization's own internal network.

Figure 6.7 Client-server computing. In client-server computing, computer processing is split between client machines and server machines linked by a network. Users interface with the client machines.

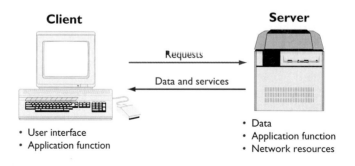

Client

- User interface
- Application function

Requests →
← Data and services

Server

- Data
- Application function
- Network resources

NCs are less expensive to purchase than PCs with local processing and storage and can be administered and updated from a central network server. Software does not have to be purchased, installed, and upgraded for each user because software is delivered and maintained from one central point. Network computers and centralized software distribution thus increase management control over the organization's computing function.

However, PC prices have fallen so much that units can be purchased for almost the same cost as NCs. If a network failure occurs, hundreds or thousands of employees would not be able to use their computers, whereas people could keep working if they had full-function PCs. Companies should closely examine how NCs could fit into their IT infrastructure.

Peer-to-Peer Computing

Another form of distributed processing, called **peer-to-peer computing**, puts processing power back on users' desktops, linking these computers so that they can share processing tasks. Individual PCs, workstations, or other computers can share data, disk space, and even processing power for a variety of tasks when they are linked in a network, including the Internet. The peer-to-peer computing model stands in contrast to the network computing model because processing power resides only on individual desktops and these computers work together without a server or any central controlling authority. One way to view peer-to-peer computing is that each computer acts as both its own client and server.

> **peer-to-peer computing**
> Form of distributed processing that links computers via the Internet or private networks so that they can share processing tasks.

It has been estimated that most companies—and individuals—use less than 25 percent of their processing and storage capacity. Peer-to-peer computing taps the unused disk space or processing power on PC or workstation networks for large computing tasks that previously could only be performed by large expensive server computers or even supercomputers. One form of peer-to-peer computing called **grid computing** uses special software to reclaim unused computing cycles on desktop computers and harness them into a "virtual supercomputer." This platform breaks down problems into small pieces that can run on many separate machines. For example, hundreds of engineers at Pratt & Whitney use grid computing to perform complex computations that simulate airflow through jet engines and test stress on materials, running their jobs on a computational "grid" consisting of 8000 computer chips inside 5000 workstations in three different cities (Ricadela, 2002).

> **grid computing**
> Applying the computational resources of many computers in the network to a single large and complex problem.

Each form of computer processing can provide benefits, depending on the business needs of the organization. Peer-to-peer computing is especially useful for research and design collaboration work, while network computing may be appropriate for firms with a highly centralized IT infrastructure and *high-availability computing*, in which the networks are up 99.99 percent of the time.

6.3 TYPES OF SOFTWARE

To play a useful role in the firm's IT infrastructure, computer hardware requires computer software. Chapter 1 defined computer *software* as the detailed instructions that control the operation of a computer system. Selecting appropriate software for the organization is a key management decision.

A software **program** is a series of statements or instructions to the computer. The process of writing or coding programs is termed *programming*, and individuals who specialize in this task are called *programmers*.

> **program**
> A series of statements or instructions to the computer.

There are two major types of software: system software and application software. Each kind performs a different function. **System software** is a set of generalized programs that manage the computer's resources, such as the central processor, communications links, and peripheral devices. Programmers who write system software are called *system programmers*.

> **system software**
> Generalized programs that manage the computer's resources, such as the central processor, communications links, and peripheral devices.

Application software describes the programs that are written for or by users to apply the computer to a specific task. Software for processing an order or generating a mailing list is application software. Programmers who write application software are called *application programmers*.

> **application software**
> Programs written for a specific application to perform functions specified by end users.

The types of software are interrelated and can be thought of as a set of nested boxes, each of which must interact closely with the other boxes surrounding it. Figure 6.8 illustrates this

Figure 6.8 The major types of software. The relationship between system software, application software, and users can be illustrated by a series of nested boxes. System software—consisting of operating systems, language translators, and utility programs—controls access to the hardware. Application software, such as programming languages and "fourth-generation" languages, must work through the system software to operate. The user interacts primarily with the application software.

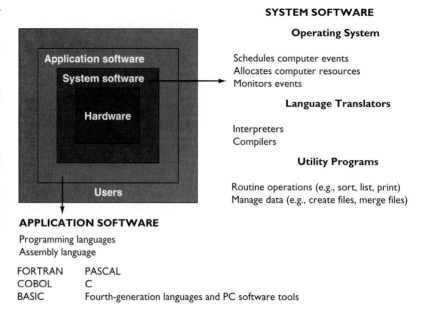

SYSTEM SOFTWARE

Operating System

Schedules computer events
Allocates computer resources
Monitors events

Language Translators

Interpreters
Compilers

Utility Programs

Routine operations (e.g., sort, list, print)
Manage data (e.g., create files, merge files)

APPLICATION SOFTWARE

Programming languages
Assembly language

FORTRAN	PASCAL
COBOL	C
BASIC	Fourth-generation languages and PC software tools

relationship. The system software surrounds and controls access to the hardware. Application software must work through the system software in order to operate. End users work primarily with application software. Each type of software must be specially designed for a specific machine to ensure its compatibility.

System Software and PC Operating Systems

System software coordinates the various parts of the computer system and mediates between application software and computer hardware. The system software that manages and controls the computer's activities is called the **operating system**. Other system software consists of computer language translation programs that convert programming languages into machine language that can be understood by the computer and utility programs that perform common processing tasks.

The operating system is the computer system's chief manager. The operating system allocates and assigns system resources, schedules the use of computer resources and computer jobs, and monitors computer system activities. The operating system provides locations in primary memory for data and programs and controls the input and output devices, such as printers, terminals, and telecommunication links. The operating system also coordinates the scheduling of work in various areas of the computer so that different parts of different jobs can be worked on at the same time. Finally, the operating system keeps track of each computer job and may also keep track of who is using the system, of what programs have been run, and of any unauthorized attempts to access the system. Operating system capabilities, such as multiprogramming, virtual storage, time sharing, and multiprocessing, enable the computer to handle many different tasks and users at the same time. Table 6.3 describes these capabilities. Keep in mind, while we will discuss PC operating systems in detail here, that operating systems also work on midrange computers, mainframes, and supercomputers. Every computer must have an operating system.

Language Translation and Utility Software

System software may include special language translator programs that translate high-level language programs written in programming languages, such as COBOL, FORTRAN, or C, into machine language that the computer can execute. The program in the high-level language before translation into machine language is called **source code**. A **compiler** translates source code into *machine code* called **object code**, which is linked to other object code modules and then executed by the computer. Some programming languages, such as BASIC, do not use a compiler but instead use an *interpreter,* which translates each source code statement one at a time into machine code and then executes it.

---

operating system

The system software that manages and controls the activities of the computer.

source code

Program instructions written in a high-level programming language that must be translated into machine language to be executed by the computer.

compiler

Special system software that translates a high-level language into machine language for execution by the computer.

object code

Program instructions that have been translated into machine language so that they can be executed by the computer.

TABLE 6.3   OPERATING SYSTEM CAPABILITIES

Operating System Capability	Description
Multiprogramming	Permits multiple programs to share a computer system's resources at any one time through concurrent use of the CPU. Only one program is actually using the CPU at any given moment, but the input/output needs of other programs can be serviced at the same time.
Virtual Storage	Handles programs more efficiently by breaking down the programs into tiny sections that are read into memory only when needed. The rest of each program is stored on disk until it is required. Virtual storage allows very large programs to be executed by small machines or a large number of programs to be executed concurrently by a single machine.
Time Sharing	Allows many users to share computer processing resources simultaneously by allocating each a tiny slice of computer time to perform computing tasks and by transferring processing from user to user. This arrangement permits many users to be connected to a CPU simultaneously, with each receiving only a tiny amount of CPU time.
Multiprocessing	Links together two or more CPUs to work in parallel in a single computer system. The operating system can assign multiple CPUs to execute different instructions from the same program or from different programs simultaneously, dividing the work between the CPUs.

System software includes *utility programs* for routine, repetitive tasks, such as copying, clearing primary storage, computing a square root, or sorting. Utility programs can be shared by all users of a computer system and can be used in many different information system applications when requested. Keep in mind that software written for one operating system will probably not run on a different operating system. For example, many programs written for Apple Computers will not run on Windows-based computers and vice versa. This is true for mainframes and other types of computers as well.

PC Operating Systems and Graphical User Interfaces

Like any other software, PC software is based on specific operating systems and computer hardware. Software written for one PC operating system generally cannot run on another. Table 6.4 compares the leading PC operating systems: Windows XP, Windows 98, Windows Me, Windows 2000, Windows 2003 server edition, Windows CE/Pocket PC, Palm, UNIX, Linux, OS/2, the Macintosh operating system, and DOS.

Additional material on specific operating systems can be found on the **Companion Website.**

When a user interacts with a computer, the interaction is controlled by an operating system. A user communicates with an operating system through the user interface of that operating system. Contemporary PC operating systems use a **graphical user interface (GUI),** often called a GUI (pronounced gooey), which makes extensive use of icons, buttons, bars, and boxes to perform tasks. It has become the dominant model for the user interface of PC operating systems and for many types of application software.

Microsoft's Windows family of operating systems and Apple's operating systems provide streamlined GUIs that arrange icons to provide instant access to common tasks. They can perform multiple programming tasks simultaneously and have powerful networking capabilities, including the capability to integrate fax, e-mail, and scheduling programs. They include tools for group collaboration, accessing information from the Internet, and creating and storing Web pages.

The operating system Linux is an example of **open-source software**, which provides all computer users with free access to its program code, so they can modify the code to fix errors

graphical user interface (GUI)

The part of an operating system users interact with that uses icons and a computer mouse to issue commands and make selections.

open-source software

Software that provides free access to its program code, allowing users to modify the program code to make improvements or fix errors.

TABLE 6.4	LEADING PC OPERATING SYSTEMS

Operating System	Features
Windows XP	Reliable, robust operating system for powerful PCs with versions for both home and corporate users. Features support of the Internet, multimedia, and group collaboration, along with powerful networking, security, and corporate management capabilities.
Windows 98/Me	Earlier versions of the Windows operating system for home users. Can be integrated with the information resources of the Web.
Windows 2000	Operating system for PCs, workstations, and network servers. Supports multitasking, multiprocessing, intensive networking, and Internet services for corporate computing.
Windows 2003 server edition	Most recent Windows operating system for servers; formerly known as Windows.Net server.
Windows CE and Pocket PC	Pared-down versions of the Windows operating system, including its graphical user interface, for small handheld computers, personal digital assistants, and wireless communication devices.
Palm OS	Operating system for palm-compatible handheld computers and devices.
UNIX	Used for powerful PCs, workstations, and network servers. Supports multitasking, multiuser processing, and networking. Is portable to different categories of computers.
Linux	Free, reliable alternative to UNIX and Windows 2000 that runs on many different types of computer hardware and can be modified by software developers; may be packaged with additional software and support by a vendor.
OS/2	Robust 32-bit operating system for powerful IBM or IBM-compatible PCs with Intel microprocessors. Used for complex, memory-intensive applications or those that require networking, multitasking, or large programs.
Mac OS	Operating system for the Macintosh computer, featuring multitasking, powerful multimedia and networking capabilities, and a mouse-driven graphical user interface. Supports connecting to and publishing on the Internet.
DOS	16-bit operating system for older PCs based on the IBM PC standard. Does not support multitasking and limits the size of a program in memory to 640K.

or to make improvements. Open-source software, such as Linux, is not owned by any company or individual. A global network of programmers and users manages and modifies the software, usually without being paid to do so. Linux is similar to UNIX, another open-source operating system. Several leading vendors now offer Linux for a small fee. Why would anyone pay for something that is free? The Linux vendors offer support for the system so that if users have a problem, they have someone to call and ask about the problem. Like its cousin, UNIX, Linux is very stable and secure, making it appropriate for running Web sites and other 24/7 systems. While neither UNIX nor Linux, the two leading open-source operating systems, offers a GUI, vendors have developed these user-friendly interfaces to be used with UNIX and Linux to give them more of a "Windows" feel. The Window on Technology describes why the business use of Linux is growing.

PROGRAMMING LANGUAGES AND CONTEMPORARY SOFTWARE TOOLS

Application software is primarily concerned with accomplishing the tasks of end users. Many different languages and software tools can be used to develop application software. Managers should understand which software tools and programming languages are appropriate for their organization's objectives.

Application Programming Languages for Business

machine language

A programming language consisting of the 1s and 0s of binary code.

The first generation of computer languages consisted of **machine language**, which required the programmer to write all program instructions in the 0s and 1s of binary code and to specify storage locations for every instruction and item of data used. Programming in machine

CAN LINUX GO MAINSTREAM?

When Mark's Work Wearhouse Ltd. decided to install a new point-of-sale (POS) system, they decided to use a Linux-based solution from Retek Inc. Mark's joined a number of large retailers, including Home Depot, Wal-Mart, and Benetton, that are implementing large Linux-based applications. Mark's had used older equipment, a 5250-emulation green screen (monochromatic monitor) running off an AS/400, but they wanted technology with staying power. They decided to look for Java-based solutions and chose the same software that Moore's, another Canadian men's clothing business, used. According to Harry Levy, vice-president of POS solutions at Retek, "Retek's fit-client architecture (based on Linux) allows the ability to deploy support centrally from the retailer's headquarters to each store."

Businesses using Linux used to be a tiny minority, but their ranks are swelling. The Dreamworks motion picture studio clustered a series of Linux servers to program the complex graphics for the successful film *Shrek*. Similarly, Boeing's Phantom Works group has customized its server software to perform aircraft design tasks that previously required a supercomputer. Western Geco, the world's largest seismic services company, based in Sussex, in the United Kingdom, is building clusters of Dell PC servers running Linux for the computer-intensive processing required by its research work. Since Linux is rooted in UNIX, many of the tools the company used in its UNIX environment port to Linux very easily.

The financial services industry has been willing to adopt Linux for mission-critical applications because they are less dependent on proprietary applications and operating systems than other industries. They tend to build more of their own applications in-house and that gives them greater flexibility to implement new technologies. Credit Suisse First Boston converted a major worldwide financial trading system called Agora to Linux. Agora performs thousands of complex transactions, and CS First Boston has been able to consolidate its processing operations from 20 RISC servers to a smaller number of servers with Intel processors. Sun Microsystems of Canada recently opened the Sun Linux Competency Centre in Belleville, Ontario, in partnership with Beonix Technology. Anthony Wright, a business development consultant in Markham, Ontario, said, "I think Linux is here to stay. Companies are looking for ways to cut costs. We're going to be able to bring customers to the facility and show them the technology and see how it works and the benefits."

Hardware companies, such as IBM, Hewlett-Packard, Dell, Sun, and Compaq, are offering versions of their computers preloaded with Linux and are spending a significant amount of research dollars to make Linux easier and more effective to use. Oracle, SAP, Veritas, BEA Systems, and other leading software firms are marketing versions of their products that operate on Linux.

The area of greatest success for Linux has been as a server operating system. The International Data Corporation (IDC) calls Linux the fastest growing server operating system, expanding at a compounded annual rate near 30 percent. Linux is rapidly becoming the de facto operating system for server-appliances targeted at small business and home office users who want to easily network a few machines. The fact that Linux is freeware makes it extremely attractive to such users. China recently announced it was adopting Linux as the mainstream operating system for its server computers, and the governments of the United Kingdom and Germany have endorsed Linux.

Linux is also showing promise in software applications embedded in such devices as cell phones or set-top cable television boxes. Linux is very economical in its use of computing resources, which are very limited in such devices.

One key area where Linux has yet to have an impact is desktop software. Some analysts believe that big corporations will still opt for Microsoft Windows and Microsoft Office because they present a complete "soup-to-nuts" set of software tools for PC productivity. However, Microsoft recently changed its Office licensing policy, replacing fees for one-time upgrades with long-term "software maintenance" contracts that made its desktop productivity software even more expensive for businesses to own. Desktop productivity tools that run on Linux, such as Sun's StarOffice, are much less expensive than Office and are becoming more competitive. A recent study by research firm IDC concluded that running Windows was as much as 22 percent cheaper than Linux in some scenarios, such as print and file serving. So, there are no clear decisions to be made about the use of Linus. Each decision is based on the specifics of the computing situation.

To Think About: Should a company select Linux as an operating system for its major business applications? What are the business as well as the technology issues that should be addressed when making that decision?

Sources: Don Clark, "Microsoft Faces New Challenge with Linux's Rising Popularity," *Wall Street Journal*, September 12, 2002; Alex Salkever, "Giant Steps for a Software Upstart," *BusinessWeek online*, May 16, 2002, **www.businessweek.com**; Jim Middlemiss, "IT Challenge: Can Linux Be Trusted?" *Wall Street & Technology*, March 2002; "Vendors Spur Linux On," *InformationWeek*, February 11, 2002; John Pallatto, "Linux Scoring Wins on Enterprise," *Internet World*, June 1, 2002; Michael MacMillan, "For Linux, It's Only Begun," *ComputerWorld Canada*, January 24, 2003; Bernice Couto, "Mark's Sizes Up Linux POS," *Computing Canada*, January 31, 2003; Ryan B. Patrick, "Sun, Beonix Open Linux Facility," *IT World Canada*, January 13, 2003, (**www.itworld.ca**); and John Pallato "Linux Finds Favor on Beijing Servers as Cheaper Option," *Wall Street Journal*, August 8, 2002.

language was a very slow, labour-intensive process. As computer hardware improved and processing speed and memory size increased, programming languages became progressively easier for humans to understand and use. A second-generation language (also called assembly language) is extremely structured and tells the computer exactly what steps to take. This generation requires an assembler (similar to a compiler or interpreter) to translate it to machine code. From the mid-1950s to the mid-1970s, high-level programming languages (also called third-generation or 3G languages) emerged, allowing programs to be written with regular words using sentence-like statements.

For business applications, the most important languages have been COBOL, C, C++, and Visual Basic. **COBOL (Common Business Oriented Language)** was developed in the early 1960s for processing large data files with alphanumeric characters (mixed alphabetic and numeric data) and for performing repetitive tasks, such as payroll. It is not well suited for complex, mathematical calculations but remains useful for many business processing and reporting tasks. **C** is a powerful and efficient language developed in the early 1970s that combines machine portability with tight control and efficient use of computer resources. C is used primarily by professional programmers to create operating systems and application software, especially for PCs, and it can work on a variety of different computers. **C++** is a newer version of C that is object-oriented. (See the discussion of object-oriented programming later in this section). It has all the capabilities of C plus additional features for working with software objects. C++ is used for developing application software. **Visual Basic** is a widely used visual programming tool and environment for creating applications that run on Microsoft Windows. With Visual Basic, users develop programs by using a GUI to choose and modify sections of code written in BASIC.

COBOL (Common Business Oriented Language)

Major programming language for business applications because it can process large data files with alphanumeric characters.

C

A powerful programming language with tight control and efficiency of execution. C is portable across different microprocessors and is used primarily with PCs.

C++

Object-oriented version of the C programming language.

Visual Basic

Visual programming tool for creating applications running on Windows.

Additional material on application programming languages can be found on the **Companion Website**.

Fourth-Generation Languages

fourth-generation language

A programming language that can be employed directly by end users or less-skilled programmers to develop computer applications more rapidly than conventional programming languages.

natural language

Programming language that is very close to human language.

query language

Software tool that provides immediate online answers to requests for information that are not predefined.

Fourth-generation languages consist of a variety of software tools that enable end users to develop software applications with minimal or no technical assistance or that enhance professional programmers' productivity. Fourth-generation languages tend to be nonprocedural, or less procedural, than conventional programming languages. Procedural languages require specification of the sequence of steps, or procedures, that tell the computer what to do and how to do it. Nonprocedural languages need only specify what has to be accomplished, rather than provide details about how to carry out the task. Some of these nonprocedural languages are **natural languages** that enable users to communicate with the computer using conversational commands resembling human speech.

Table 6.5 shows that there are seven categories of fourth-generation languages: (1) PC software tools, (2) query languages, (3) report generators, (4) graphics languages, (5) application generators, (6) application software packages, and (7) very high-level programming languages. The table shows the tools ordered in terms of ease of use by nonprogramming end users. End users are most likely to work with PC software tools and query languages. **Query languages** are software tools that provide immediate online answers to requests for information that are not predefined, such as "Who are the highest-performing sales representatives?" Query languages are often tied to data management software (discussed later in this section) and to database management systems (see Chapter 7.)

Contemporary Tools for Software Development

The need for businesses to fashion systems that are flexible or that can run over the Internet has stimulated approaches to software development based on object-oriented programming tools and new programming languages, such as Java, hypertext markup language (HTML), and eXtensible Markup Language (XML).

TABLE 6.5	CATEGORIES OF FOURTH-GENERATION LANGUAGES		
Fourth-Generation Tool	**Description**	**Example**	**Oriented toward end users**
PC software tools	General-purpose application software packages for PCs.	WordPerfect Internet Explorer Microsoft Access	
Query languages	Languages for retrieving data stored in databases or files. Capable of supporting requests for information that are not predefined.	SQL	
Report generators	Extract data from files or databases to create customized reports in a wide range of formats not routinely produced by an information system. Generally provide more control over the way data are formatted, organized, and displayed than query languages.	RPG III	
Graphics languages	Retrieve data from files or databases and display them in graphic format. Some graphics software can perform arithmetic or logical operations on data as well.	SAS Graph Systat	
Application generators	Contain preprogrammed modules that can generate entire applications, including Web sites, greatly speeding development. A user can specify what needs to be done, and the application generator will create the appropriate program code for input, validation, update, processing, and reporting.	FOCUS PowerBuilder Microsoft FrontPage	
Application software packages	Software programs sold or leased by commercial vendors that eliminate the need for custom-written, in-house software.	PeopleSoft HRMS SAP R/3	
Very high-level programming languages	Generate program code with fewer instructions than conventional languages, such as COBOL or FORTRAN. Designed primarily as productivity tools for professional programmers.	APL Nomad2	**Oriented toward IS professionals**

Object-Oriented Programming Traditional software development methods have treated data and procedures as independent components. A separate programming procedure must be written every time someone wants to take an action on a particular piece of data. The procedures act on data that the program passes to them.

Object-oriented programming combines data and the specific procedures that operate on those data into one object. The object combines data and program code. Instead of passing data to procedures, programs send a message for an object to perform a procedure that is already embedded in it. (Procedures are termed *methods* in object-oriented languages.) The same message may be sent to many different objects, but each will implement that message differently. For example, an object-oriented financial application might have Customer objects sending debit and credit messages to Account objects. The Account objects in turn might maintain Cash-on-Hand, Accounts-Payable, and Accounts-Receivable objects.

An object's data are encapsulated from other parts of the system, so each object is an independent software building block that can be used in many different systems without changing the program code. Thus, object-oriented programming is expected to reduce the time and cost of writing software by producing reusable program code or software "chips" that can be reused in other related systems. Future software development can draw on a library of reusable objects, and productivity gains from object-oriented technology can be magnified if objects are stored in reusable software libraries and explicitly designed for reuse (Fayad and Cline, 1996). However, these benefits are unlikely to be realized unless organizations develop appropriate standards and procedures for reuse (Kim and Stohr, 1998).

Object-oriented programming is based on the concepts of *class* and *inheritance*. Program code is not written separately for every object but for classes, or general categories, of similar objects. Objects belonging to a certain class have the features of that class. Classes of objects, in turn, can inherit all the structure and behaviours of a more general class and then add variables and behaviours unique to each object. New classes of objects are created by choosing an existing class and specifying how the new class differs from the existing class, instead of starting from scratch each time.

object-oriented programming

An approach to software development that combines data and procedures into a single object.

We can see how class and inheritance work in Figure 6.9, which illustrates the relationships among classes concerning employees and how they are paid. Employee is the common ancestor, or superclass, for the other three classes. Salaried, Hourly, and Temporary are subclasses of Employee. The class name is in the top compartment, the attributes for each class are in the middle portion of each box, and the list of operations is in the bottom portion of each box. The features that are shared by all employees—ID (identification number), Name, Address, Date Hired, Position, and Pay—are stored in the Employee superclass, while each subclass stores features that are specific to that particular type of employee. Specific to Hourly employees, for example, are their Hourly Rate and Overtime Rate. A solid line from the subclass to the superclass pointing to the superclass is a generalization path showing that the subclasses Salaried, Hourly, and Temporary have common features that can be generalized into the superclass Employee.

Object-oriented programming has spawned a new programming technology known as **visual programming**. With visual programming, programmers do not write codes. Rather, they use a mouse to select and move around programming objects, copying an object from a library into a specific location in a program, or drawing a line to connect two or more objects.

Java **Java** is a platform-independent, object-oriented programming language developed by Sun Microsystems. Java software is designed to run on any computer or computing device, regardless of the specific microprocessor or operating system it uses. A Macintosh PC, an IBM PC running Windows, a Sun server running UNIX, and even a smart cellular phone or personal digital assistant can share the same Java application.

Java can be used to create miniature programs called *applets* designed to reside on centralized network servers. The network delivers only the applets required for a specific function. With Java applets residing on a network, a user downloads only the software functions and data that he or she needs to perform a particular task, such as analyzing revenue from one sales territory. The user does not need to maintain large software programs or data files on his or her desktop machine. When the user is finished with processing, the data can be saved through the network.

Java is also a very robust language that can handle text, data, graphics, sound, and video, all within one program, if needed. Java applets are often used to provide interactive capabilities for Web pages. For example, Java applets can be used to create animated cartoons or real-time news tickers for a Web site or to add a capability to a Web page to calculate a loan payment schedule online in response to financial data input by the user.

visual programming

The construction of software programs by selecting and arranging programming objects, rather than by writing program codes.

Java

Platform-independent programming language that delivers only the software functionality needed for a particular task, such as a small applet downloaded from a network. Java can run on any computer and any operating system.

Figure 6.9 Class and inheritance. This figure illustrates how classes inherit the common features of their superclass.

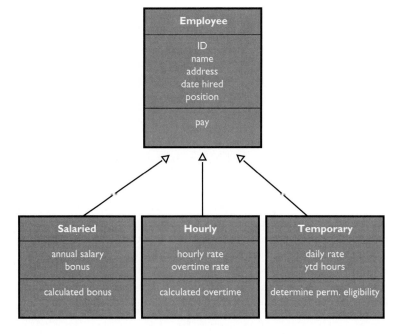

Companies are starting to develop more extensive Java applications running over the Internet or over their private networks because Java applications can potentially run in Windows, UNIX, IBM mainframe, Macintosh, and other environments without having to be rewritten for each computing platform. Java can let PC users manipulate data on networked systems using Web browsers, reducing the need to write specialized software.

Despite these benefits, Java has not yet fulfilled its early promise to revolutionize software development and use. Programs written in current versions of Java tend to run more slowly than "native" programs, although high-performance versions of Java are under development (Pancake and Lengauer, 2001). Vendors, such as Microsoft, are supporting alternative versions of Java that include subtle differences that affect Java's performance in different pieces of hardware and operating systems.

Hypertext Markup Language and eXtensible Markup Language **Hypertext markup language (HTML)** is a page description language for creating hypertext or hypermedia documents, such as Web pages. (See the discussions of hypermedia in Chapter 7 and of Web pages in Chapter 9.) HTML uses instructions called tags to specify how text, graphics, video, and sound are placed on a document and to create dynamic links to other documents and objects stored in the same or remote computers. Using these links, a user need only point at a highlighted key word or graphic, click on it, and immediately be transported to another document. Note that markup languages are not programming languages per se. They instruct computers as to how to display or categorize data, rather than how to manipulate the data (e.g., performing calculations, sorting alphabetically, and so on).

HTML programs can be custom written, but they also can be created using the HTML authoring capabilities of Web browsers or of popular word processing, spreadsheet, data management, and presentation graphics software packages. HTML editors, such as Microsoft FrontPage, Macromedia Dreamweaver, and Adobe GoLive, are more powerful HTML authoring tool programs for creating Web pages.

XML, which stands for **eXtensible Markup Language**, is a new specification originally designed to improve the usefulness of Web documents. While HTML only determines how text and images should be displayed in a Web document, XML describes what the data in these documents mean so that the data can be used in computer programs. In XML, a number is not simply a number; the XML tag specifies whether the number represents a price, a date, or a ZIP code. Table 6.6 illustrates the differences between HTML and XML. Note that the HTML tags simply show how the data will look on the Web page, while the XML tags would permit a visitor to search multiple sites for information, for example, on automobiles in a certain price or body type category.

hypertext markup language (HTML)

Page description language for creating Web pages and other hypermedia documents.

XML (eXtensible Markup Language)

General-purpose language that describes the structure of a document and supports links to multiple documents, allowing data to be manipulated by the computer. Used for both Web and non-Web applications.

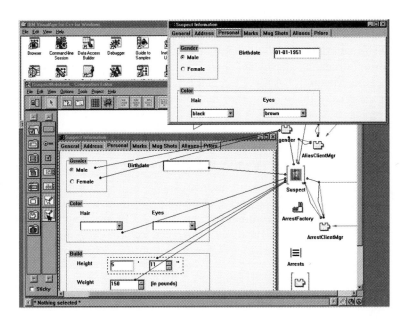

With visual programming tools, such as IBM's Visual Age Generator, working software programs can be created by drawing, pointing, and clicking instead of writing program code.

TABLE 6.6	COMPARISON OF HTML AND XML	
Plain English	HTML	XML
Subcompact	Automobile	AUTOMOBILETYPE="Subcompact"
4 passenger	4 passenger	PASSENGER UNIT="PASS" 4
$19,000	$19,000	PRICE CURRENCY="CDN" $19,000

By tagging selected elements of the content of documents for their meanings, XML makes it possible for computers to automatically manipulate and interpret their data and perform operations on the data without human intervention. Web browsers and computer programs, such as order processing or enterprise resource planning (ERP) software, can follow programmed rules for applying and displaying the data. XML provides a standard format for data exchange.

XML is important for Web-based applications. The key to XML is the setting of standards (or vocabulary) that enable both sending and receiving parties to describe data the same way. Each standard is contained in an XML Document Type Definition (DTD), usually simply called a dictionary. For example, RosettaNet is an XML dictionary developed by 34 leading companies within the PC industry. It defines all properties of a personal computer, such as modems, display screens, and cache memory. As a result, the entire PC industry is now able to speak the same language. The entire supply chain of the industry can now easily be linked without requiring business partners or customers to use a particular programming language, application, or operating system to exchange data. Companies can also use XML to access and manipulate their own internal data without high software development costs.

XHTML (eXtensible Hypertext Markup Language) is a hybrid language combining features of HTML and XML that has been recommended as a replacement for HTML by the World Wide Web Consortium (which works with businesses and governments to create Web standards). XHTML reformulates HTML with XML document-type definitions, giving it additional flexibility and the ability to create Web pages that can be read by many different computing platforms and .Net display devices.

XBRL (eXtensible Business Reporting Language), an extension of XML, is designed to make the preparation of financial statements and reports in a consistent format easier. XBRL will automate the time-consuming task of extracting and combining reporting data for various reports from the same data source.

.Net A business strategy from Microsoft, ***.Net*** is aimed at the convergence of personal computing with the Web. It is intended to provide users with a seamlessly interoperable and Web-enabled interface for applications and computing devices. .Net is an open standard platform for building, deploying, operating, and integrating XML Web services (see Chapter 9). Because Microsoft has had a difficult time getting the public to understand its .Net strategy at the time of this writing, they may be in the process of scrapping that terminology while keeping the strategy itself.

APPLICATION SOFTWARE PACKAGES AND PRODUCTIVITY SOFTWARE

Much of the software used in businesses today is not custom-programmed but consists of application software packages and desktop productivity tools. A **software package** is a prewritten, precoded, commercially available set of programs that eliminates the need for individuals or organizations to write their own software programs for certain functions. There are software packages for system software, but most packaged software is application software.

XHTML (eXtensible Hypertext Markup Language)

Hybrid of HTML and XML that provides more flexibility than HTML.

XBRL (eXtensible Business Reporting Language)

A reporting language developed to make it easier to prepare financial statements and reports in a consistent format.

.Net

(pronounced dot-Net) A business strategy from Microsoft that is aimed at the convergence of personal computing with the Web.

software package

A prewritten, precoded, commercially available set of programs that eliminates the need to write software programs for certain functions.

Additional material on productivity software packages can be found on the **Companion Website.**

Software packages that run on mainframes and larger computers usually require professional programmers for their installation and support. However, there are also application software packages developed explicitly for end users. Productivity software packages for word processing, spreadsheet, data management, presentation graphics, integrated software packages, e-mail, Web browsers, and groupware are the most widely used software tools among business and consumer users.

Integrated Software Packages and Software Suites

Integrated software packages combine the functions of the most important PC software packages, such as word processing, spreadsheets, presentation graphics, and data management. This integration provides a more general-purpose software tool and eliminates redundant data entry and data maintenance. For example, a break-even analysis spreadsheet could be reformatted into a polished report with word processing software without separately keying the data into both programs. Although integrated packages can do many things well, they generally do not have the same power and depth as have single-purpose packages.

Integrated software packages should be distinguished from *software suites*, which are full-featured versions of application software sold as a unit. Microsoft Office is an example of a software suite. MS Office contains Word (word processing software), Excel (spreadsheet software), Access (data management software), PowerPoint (presentation graphics software), and Outlook (a set of tools for e-mail, scheduling, and contact management). **Office 2000** and **Office XP** contain additional capabilities to support collaborative work on the Web, including the ability to manage multiple comments and revisions from several reviewers in a single document and the ability to automatically notify others about changes to documents. Documents created with Office tools can be viewed with a Web browser and published on

integrated software package

A software package that provides two or more applications, such as word processing and spreadsheets, providing for easy transfer of data between them.

Office 2000 and Office XP

Integrated software suites with capabilities for supporting collaborative work on the Web or incorporating information from the Web into documents.

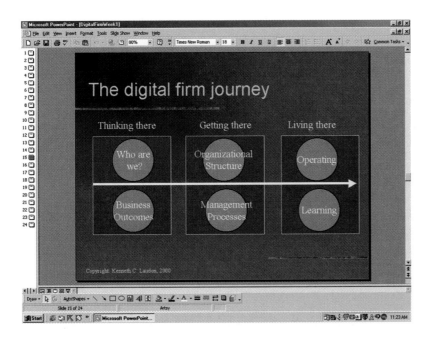

Users can create professional-looking electronic presentations incorporating text, diagrams, and other multimedia elements using presentation graphics software. This slide was created using Microsoft PowerPoint.

the Web. Office XP users can automatically refresh their documents with information from the Web, such as stock quotes and news flashes, and manage multiple e-mail accounts from a single view. *OpenOffice* (which can be downloaded over the Internet) and Sun Microsystems' *StarOffice* are low-cost alternatives to Microsoft Office tools that can run on Linux.

E-mail Software

electronic mail (e-mail)

The computer-to-computer exchange of messages.

Electronic mail (e-mail) is used for the computer-to-computer exchange of messages and is an important tool for communication and collaborative work. A user can send notes or lengthier documents to a recipient on the same network or a different network. Many organizations operate their own e-mail systems, but most communications companies, such as MCI Communications Corporation and American Telephone and Telegraph (AT&T), offer these services, along with commercial online information services, such as America Online and public networks on the Internet.

Web browsers and PC software suites have e-mail capabilities, but specialized e-mail software packages are also available for use on the Internet. In addition to providing electronic messaging, e-mail software has capabilities for routing messages to multiple recipients, message forwarding, and attaching text or multimedia files to messages.

Web Browsers

Web browser

An easy-to-use software tool for accessing the World Wide Web and the Internet.

Web browsers are easy-to-use software tools for displaying Web pages and for accessing the Web and other Internet resources. Web browser software features a point-and-click GUI that can be used to access and display information stored on computers at other Internet sites. Browsers can display or present graphics, audio, and video information as well as traditional text, and they allow you to click on-screen buttons or highlighted words to link to related Web sites. Web browsers have become the primary interface for accessing the Internet or for using networked systems based on Internet technology. You can see examples of Web browser software by looking at the illustrations of Web pages in each chapter of this text.

The two leading commercial Web browsers are Microsoft's Internet Explorer and Netscape. They include capabilities for using e-mail, file transfer, online discussion groups, and bulletin boards, along with other Internet services. Newer versions of these browsers contain support for Web publishing and workgroup computing. (See the following discussion of groupware.)

Groupware

groupware

Software that provides functions and services that support the collaborative activities of work groups.

Groupware provides functions and services to support the collaborative activities of work groups. Groupware includes software for group writing and commenting, information-

Groupware facilitates collaboration by enabling members of a group to work collectively on documents, schedule meetings, and discuss activities, events, and issues. Illustrated here is OpenText's Livelink Meeting Zone, which enables users to set up online meetings to brainstorm new ideas, take notes, create tasks, and share documents.

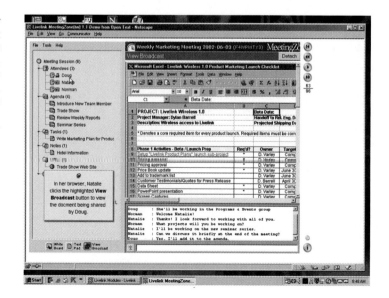

sharing, electronic meetings, scheduling, and e-mail and a network to connect the members of the group as they work on their own desktop computers, often in widely scattered locations. Any group member can review the ideas of others at any time and add to them, or individuals can post a document for others to comment on or edit. Leading commercial groupware products include Lotus Notes and OpenText's Livelink. Groove is a new groupware tool based on peer-to-peer technology, which enables people to work directly with other people over the Internet without going through a central server. Microsoft Internet Explorer and Netscape Web browser software include groupware functions, such as e-mail, electronic scheduling and calendaring, audio and data conferencing, and electronic discussion groups and databases (see Chapter 9). Microsoft's Office 2000 and Office XP software suites also include groupware features using Web technology.

SOFTWARE FOR ENTERPRISE INTEGRATION

Chapters 2 and 3 discussed the growing organizational need to integrate functions and business processes to improve organizational control, coordination, and responsiveness by allowing data and information to flow freely between different parts of the organization. Poorly integrated applications can create costly inefficiencies or slowed down customer service that become competitive liabilities. Alternative software solutions are available to promote enterprise integration.

One alternative, which we introduced in Chapter 2, is to replace isolated systems that cannot communicate with each other with an enterprise system. **Enterprise software** consists of a set of interdependent modules for such applications as sales and distribution, financial accounting, investment management, materials management, production planning, plant maintenance, and human resources that allow data to be used by multiple functions and business processes for more precise organizational coordination and control. The modules can communicate with each other directly or by sharing a common repository of data. Contemporary enterprise systems use a client-server computing architecture. Major enterprise software vendors include SAP, Oracle, PeopleSoft, and Baan. These vendors are now enhancing their products to provide more capabilities for supply chain management and exchange of data with other enterprises.

Individual companies can implement all of the enterprise software modules offered by a vendor or select only the modules of interest to them. They can also configure the software they select to support the way they do business. For example, they could configure the software to track revenue by product line, geographical unit, or distribution channel. However, the enterprise software may not be able to support some companies' unique business processes and often requires firms to change the way they work. Chapter 12 describes the challenges of implementing enterprise software in greater detail.

Most firms cannot jettison all of their existing systems and create enterprise-wide integration from scratch. Many existing legacy mainframe applications are essential to daily operations and very risky to change, but they can be made more useful if their information and business logic can be integrated with other applications (Noffsinger, Niedbalski, Blanks, and Emmart, 1998). One way to integrate various legacy applications is to use special software called **middleware** to create an interface, or bridge, between two different systems. Middleware is software that connects two otherwise separate applications, allowing them to communicate with each other and to pass data between them (see Figure 6.10). Middleware may consist of custom software written in-house or a software package.

There are many different types of middleware. One important use of middleware is to link client and server machines in client-server computing and increasingly to link a Web server to data stored on another computer. A **Web server** is the software for locating and

enterprise software

Set of integrated modules for such applications as sales and distribution, financial accounting, investment management, materials management, production planning, plant maintenance, and human resources that allow data to be used by multiple functions and business processes.

middleware

Software that connects two disparate applications, allowing them to communicate with each other and to exchange data.

Web server

Software that manages requests for Web pages on the computer where they are stored and that delivers the page to the user's computer.

Figure 6.10 Middleware. Middleware is software that functions as a translation layer between two disparate applications so that they can work together.

managing stored Web pages. It locates the Web pages requested by a user on the computer where they are stored and delivers the Web pages to the user's computer. Middleware allows users to request data (such as an order) from the actual transaction system (such as an order processing system) housing the data using forms displayed on a Web browser, and it enables the Web server to return dynamic Web pages based on information users request.

enterprise application integration software

Software that ties together multiple applications to support enterprise integration.

Instead of custom-writing middleware to connect one application to another, companies can now purchase **enterprise application integration software** to connect disparate applications or application clusters. There are a variety of commercial enterprise application integration software products, many featuring business process integration tools to link applications together through business process modelling. The software allows system developers to model their business processes graphically and define the rules that applications should follow to make these processes work. The software then generates the underlying program instructions, governed by the rules of the business processes, to link existing applications to each other so they can exchange data via messages. (An example of these rules might be "When an order has been placed, the order application should tell the accounting system to send an invoice and should tell shipping to send the order to the customer.") Because the enterprise application integration software is largely independent of the individual applications it connects, the organization can change its business processes and grow without requiring changes to the applications. A few enterprise application integration tools allow multiple businesses to integrate their systems into an extended supply chain.

6.4 MANAGING HARDWARE AND SOFTWARE ASSETS

Selection and use of computer hardware and software technology can have a profound impact on business performance. The sociotechnical approach implies that organizations must first consider the needs of the business and only then consider how hardware and software can support these needs.

Computer hardware and software, thus, represent important organizational assets that must be properly managed. We now describe the most important issues in managing hardware and software technology assets: understanding trends in hardware and software as well as the new technology requirements for e-commerce and the digital firm, determining the total cost of ownership (TCO) of technology assets, and determining whether to own and maintain technology assets or to use external technology service providers for the firm's IT infrastructure.

TRENDS IN HARDWARE AND SOFTWARE

Computer technology changes at an incredibly fast rate. Gordon Moore, who founded Intel Corporation, said that computing power doubles approximately every 18 months (known as Moore's Law); incidentally, this means that the price of certain technologies is cut in half about every 18 months, too. Other computing technologies keep up with this pace of change as well. Managers today must stay current on trends in hardware and software and in how computing technology can be used. The following are just two of the trends that are shaping the future of computing.

Microminiaturization and Nanotechnology

The development of so-called superchips and smaller and smaller devices, such as USB hard drives, smart cards, and flash-memory-based storage cards, are all the result of successful efforts to reduce the size of circuitry and other components of the computer. A few of these developments are listed in Table 6.7.

Any-Platform Movement

Microsoft's .Net approach to computing may or may not be the solution to attempts to reach cross-platform nirvana, but .Net does draw attention to the growing need for cross-platform utilization of resources. Users want to be able to access their e-mail and files from wherever

TABLE 6.7	RECENT NANOTECHNOLOGY DEVELOPMENTS IN COMPUTING

Development	Description
Thin polarizing film by Optiva	Can reduce the thickness of liquid crystal displays by 20 to 40 percent and cut costs
Nano solar cells	Could make solar power a widely used electricity alternative
Soft lithography	Could be used in the manufacture of optical computing components and chips requiring nanometre precision

they are. Current developments include *pocket* or *palm* editions of applications, such as word processing or even SAP. But what is needed is the ability to *synchronize* all locations and platforms an individual uses so that they are the same or so that the data and files on each machine can be accessed from any other type of device. Developments in this area are just beginning but hold promise for the future.

HARDWARE REQUIREMENTS FOR E-COMMERCE AND THE DIGITAL FIRM

E-commerce and e-business are placing heavy new demands on hardware technology because organizations are replacing so many manual and paper-based processes with electronic ones. Much larger processing and storage resources are required to process and store the escalating number of digital transactions flowing between different parts of the firm and between the firm and its customers and suppliers. Many people using a Web site simultaneously place great strains on a computer system as does hosting large numbers of interactive Web pages with data-intensive graphics or video. An *n-tier* architecture is used for e-commerce. Typically, the number of tiers is three, resulting in a three-tier architecture. The visitor's browser is the first tier, the backend database the visitor is trying to access over the Internet is the third tier, and the server's *middleware* makes the translation between HTML requests and SQL requests of the database (see Chapter 7 for more discussion on this topic).

Capacity Planning and Scalability

Managers and information systems specialists now need to pay more attention to hardware capacity planning and scalability than they did in the past. **Capacity planning** is the process of predicting when a computer hardware system becomes saturated. It considers such factors as the maximum number of users that the system can accommodate at one time, the impact of existing and future software applications, and performance measures, such as minimum response time for processing business transactions. Capacity planning ensures that the firm has enough computing power for its current and future needs. For example, the Nasdaq Stock Market performs ongoing capacity planning to identify peaks in the volume of stock trading transactions and to ensure it has enough computing capacity to handle large surges in volume when trading is very heavy.

capacity planning
The process of predicting when a computer hardware system becomes saturated to ensure that adequate computing resources are available and that the firm has enough computing power for its current and future needs.

Although capacity planning is performed by information system specialists, input from business managers is essential. Business managers need to determine acceptable levels of computer response time and availability for the firm's mission-critical systems to maintain the level of business performance they expect. New applications, mergers and acquisitions, and changes in business volume will all impact computer workload and must be taken into account when planning hardware capacity.

Scalability refers to the ability of a computer, product, or system to expand to serve a larger number of users without breaking down. E-commerce and e-business both call for scalable IT infrastructures that have the capacity to grow with the business as the size of a Web site and the number of visitors increase. Organizations must make sure they have sufficient computer processing, storage, and network resources to handle surging volumes of digital transactions and to make data immediately available online.

scalability
The ability of a computer, product, or system to expand to serve a larger number of users without breaking down.

TOTAL COST OF OWNERSHIP (TCO) OF TECHNOLOGY ASSETS

total cost of ownership (TCO)

Designates the total cost of owning technology resources, including initial purchase costs, the cost of hardware and software upgrades, maintenance, technical support, and training.

The purchase and maintenance of computer hardware and software is but one of a series of cost components that managers must consider when selecting and managing hardware and software technology assets. The actual cost of owning technology resources includes the original cost of acquiring and installing computers and software; ongoing administration costs for hardware and software upgrades, maintenance, technical support, and training; and even utility and real estate costs for running and housing the technology. The **total cost of ownership (TCO)** model can be used to analyze these direct and indirect costs to help firms determine the actual cost of technology implementations.

When all of these cost components are considered, the TCO for a PC might run up to three times the original purchase price of the equipment. "Hidden costs" for support staff and additional network management frequently make distributed client-server architectures more expensive than centralized mainframe architectures.

Hardware and software acquisition costs account for only about 20 percent of TCO, so managers must pay close attention to administration costs to understand the full cost of the firm's hardware and software. It is possible to reduce some of these administration costs through better management. It has been estimated that businesses spent $130 billion in the last two years on unnecessary technology expenditures (Phillips, 2002). Many large firms are saddled with redundant, incompatible hardware and software because their departments and divisions have been allowed to make their own technology purchases. Their information technology infrastructures have become excessively unwieldy and expensive to administer.

These firms could reduce their TCO through greater centralization and standardization of their hardware and software resources (see the Window on Management). Companies could reduce the size of the information systems staff required to support their infrastructure if the firm minimized the number of different computer models and pieces of software that employees are allowed to use. In a centralized infrastructure, systems can be administered from a central location, and troubleshooting can be performed from that location (David, Schuff, and St. Louis, 2002). The Manager's Toolkit describes the most important TCO components to help you to perform a TCO analysis.

RENT OR BUILD DECISIONS: USING TECHNOLOGY SERVICE PROVIDERS

Some of the most important questions facing managers are: How should we acquire and maintain our technology assets? Should we develop and run them ourselves or lease them from outside sources? In the past, most companies built and ran their own computer facilities and developed their own software. Today, more and more companies are obtaining their hardware and software from external service vendors. Online services for storage and for running application software have become especially attractive options for many firms.

It is important to understand the financial and other implications of these decisions. Buying hardware outright requires the immediate outlay of capital and either in-house support or contracted support from the vendor or the manufacturer at an additional expense; the hardware can become obsolete in a short period of time, and the firm still owns the hardware. Renting requires smaller payments, usually monthly, but it typically does not include much in the way of service or support. Leasing is longer term than renting and usually more expensive than renting as well; however, leasing usually includes service and support and permits an organization to replace hardware more quickly than does an outright purchase. These decisions are contingent on the specifics of the applications being supported and the technical and market environments of the firm, the industry, and the country.

Most software is "leased." The reason for this, as seen in the chapter on Ethics, is so that the software publisher can maintain copyright, preventing those who "lease" the software from copying it as they could if they owned it outright. A wide variety of options are available, including developing software in-house, purchasing a generally available package, purchasing or leasing custom-developed software, or using an application service provider. Chapter 10 describes various ways to develop or acquire software.

CANADIAN PACIFIC MOVES INFORMATION AS WELL AS FREIGHT

Canadian Pacific Railway operates more than 25 000 kilometres of rail in North America, generating over $4 billion in revenue with over 20 000 employees. A wholly owned subsidiary of Canadian Pacific Limited, CPR's fleet consists of 1615 locomotives and 54 000 rail cars. More than 52 percent of the company's revenue comes from traffic moving within Canada, 30 percent from traffic between Canada and the United States, and 18 percent from traffic moving within the continental United States.

With the beginning of the 21st century, however, CPR needs to improve its free flow of information and workgroup projects. CPR has chosen a Microsoft software solution to enable the virtually seamless transfer of Web-based mail and files, and establish collaboration and workflow services for more than 9000 employees across Canada and the United States.

In 1995, CPR moved its headquarters to Calgary, where it conducts 80 percent of its business. At the same time, CPR created an Eastern-based subsidiary, the St. Lawrence and Hudson Railway, headquartered in Montreal, serving the eastern half of Canada and the northeast United States. At that time, CPR knew it needed to expand e-business to better serve its customers, employees, vendors, and suppliers.

"CP Rail was using a 15-year-old messaging system for in-house communication," said Allen Borak, Vice-President of Information Services for Canadian Pacific Rail Limited, CPR's parent company. "The result was that we had a very limited ability to share documents and information among our employees. Retrieval of information was also difficult, and there was a lack of consistency because we had two levels of information—shared information and information stored on individual personal computers." Divisions had to rely on fax or regular mail to move information. But the upgrading job was not a simple one.

CPR had to find an integrated solution for more than 450 individual locations, with a similar look and feel for all applications, and improved accessibility through a single URL. Deployment would also be a tremendous challenge, involving conversion and migration of files, training, and support. CPR wanted their solution to support new initiatives, such as wireless computing.

Gary Stedman, Information Systems Strategist for CPR Limited, said that CPR chose Microsoft Exchange 2000 and Windows 2000 operating system through what he called an ib4e approach (infrastructure before e-business)—CPR would develop and deliver an e-business system in a way that would avoid system conflicts, allow users to become familiar with the GUI, and reduce potential incompatibility among applications.

The ib4e program has two major concepts. First is creating a technical infrastructure to support Internet, communication, and collaborative initiatives through a standards-based approach to ensure a uniform set of applications across the organization. Then, ib4e builds a services infrastructure to support planned information technology growth.

CPR's first ib4e initative was the creation of a standardized Web-mail system using Microsoft Exchange 2000. CPR now plans to develop a networking structure and directory services infrastructure based on Internet standards and to provide data management technologies over a Web-based storage system.

The new system already has 9000 employees on e-mail. CPR employees have a common browser-based interface into their applications and can use Microsoft Office for their productivity tools. Today, CPR has a single place to store its corporate data—its corporate intranet—and a reduced total cost of ownership. More recent CPR initiatives include use of the .Net environment to create its portal architecture, using object-oriented development and the implementation of a document library using Microsoft Exchange. As it moves ahead, CPR will expand its e-business initiatives to ensure improved results.

To Think About: What is the benefit of having a common look and feel across all desktops? What are some of the training challenges in deploying the new computing platform? What are some of the benefits of using a single supplier like Microsoft? What are some of the disadvantages of using a single supplier?

Sources: Based on "Canadian Pacific Railway Speeds Information across Continent," *Microsoft Canada Case Studies,* available **www.microsoft. com/canada/casestudies,** June 2002; "Canadian Pacific Looks to ASP Management Tool," ASP.net, available **www.asp.net/customers,** accessed March 7, 2003; "Enterprise Application Development," Quadrus, available **www.quadrus.com/clients,** accessed March 7, 2003.

Online Storage Service Providers

Some companies are using storage service providers (SSPs) to replace or supplement their own in-house storage infrastructure. A storage service provider (SSP) is a third-party provider that rents out storage space to subscribers over the Web (see Figure 6.11). Storage service providers sell storage as a pay-per-use utility, allowing customers to store their data on remote

MIS IN ACTION: Manager's Toolkit

HOW TO CALCULATE THE TOTAL COST OF OWNERSHIP (TCO) OF TECHNOLOGY ASSETS

In order to determine the total cost of ownership (TCO) of an organization's technology assets, you will need to calculate the cost of the following components:

Hardware acquisition: Purchase price of computer hardware, including computers, terminals, storage, printers

Software acquisition: Purchase or license of software for each user

Installation: Cost to install computers and software

Training: Cost to provide training to information system specialists and end users

Support: Cost to provide ongoing technical support, help desks, and so forth

Maintenance: Cost to upgrade the hardware and software

Infrastructure: Cost to acquire, maintain, and support related infrastructure, such as networks and specialized equipment (including storage backup units)

Downtime: Lost productivity if hardware or software failures cause the system to be unavailable for processing and user tasks

Space and energy: Real estate and utility costs for housing and providing power for the technology

---

computers accessed via networks without having to purchase and maintain their own storage infrastructure and hire storage support staff. To be successful, SSPs must offer very high availability and reliability and also must keep up with the latest technology. SSPs are responsible for monitoring the stored data and for managing their own capacity, response time, and reliability.

Application Service Providers (ASPs)

Section 6.2 described hardware capabilities for providing data and software programs to desktop computers and over networks. It is clear that software will be increasingly delivered and used over networks. Online application service providers (ASPs) are springing up to provide these software services over the Web and over private networks. An **application service provider (ASP)** is a business that delivers and manages applications and computer services from remote computer centres to multiple users via the Internet or a private network. Instead

application service provider (ASP)

Company providing software that can be rented by other companies over the Web or a private network.

Figure 6.11 How managed storage works. By enlisting the services of a storage service provider (SSP), companies do not have to maintain their own storage infrastructure on their premises. They can rent storage technology and management services from a vendor and access their data stored by the vendor over a network.

Source: How Managed Storage Works from COMPUTERWORLD, October 15, 2001. Copyright © 2001. Reprinted by permission of Reprint Management Service.

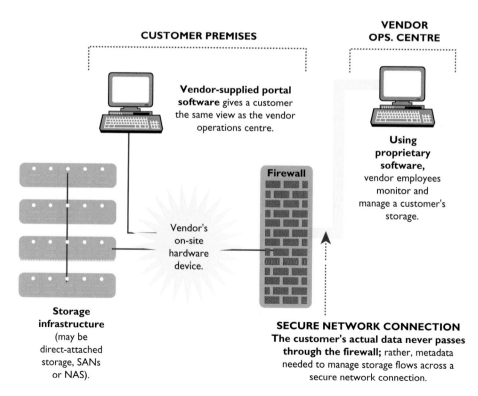

of buying and installing software programs, subscribing companies can rent the same functions from these services. Users pay for the use of this software either on a subscription or per transaction basis. The ASP's solution combines packaged software applications and all of the related hardware, system software, network, and other infrastructure services that the customer would have to purchase, integrate, and manage on its own. The ASP customer interacts with a single entity instead of an array of technologies and service vendors.

The "timesharing" services of the 1970s, which ran such applications as payroll on their computers for other companies, were an earlier version of this type of application hosting. But today's ASPs run a wider array of applications than these earlier services did and deliver many of these software services over the Web. Using Web-based services, servers perform the bulk of the processing, and the only essential program needed by users is their Web browser. Large and medium-sized businesses are using ASPs for enterprise systems, sales force automation, or financial management, and small businesses are using them for such functions as invoicing, tax calculations, electronic calendars, and accounting.

Companies are turning to this "software service" model as an alternative to developing their own software. Some companies will find it much easier to "rent" software from another firm and avoid the expense and difficulty of installing, operating, and maintaining complex systems, such as ERP. The ASP contracts guarantee a level of service and support to make sure that the software is available and working at all times. Today's Internet-driven business environment is changing so rapidly that getting a system up and running in three months instead of six could mean the difference between success and failure. Application service providers also enable small and medium-sized companies to use applications that they otherwise could not afford.

Companies considering the software service model need to carefully assess application service provider costs and benefits, weighing all management, organizational, and technology issues. In some cases, the cost of renting software can add up to more than purchasing and maintaining the application in-house. Yet, there may be benefits to paying more for software through an ASP if this decision allows the company to focus on core business issues instead of technology challenges. More detail on application service providers can be found in Chapter 10.

Other Types of Service Providers

Other types of specialized service providers provide additional resources for helping organizations manage their technology assets. *Management service providers* can be enlisted to manage combinations of applications, networks, storage, and security as well as to provide Web site and systems performance monitoring. *Business continuity service providers* offer disaster recovery and continuous Web availability services to help firms continue essential operations when their systems malfunction (see Chapter 11). Table 6.8 provides examples of the major types of technology service providers.

TABLE 6.8	EXAMPLES OF TECHNOLOGY SERVICE PROVIDERS		
Type of Service Provider	**Description**	**Example**
Storage service provider	Provides online access over networks to storage devices and storage area network technology.	IBM Managed Storage Services (MSS)
Application service	Uses centrally managed facilities to host and manage access to package applications delivered over networks on a subscription basis.	Corio Inc. offers a suite of hosted provider enterprise application software.
Management service provider	Manages combinations of applications, networks, systems, storage, and security as well as providing Web site and systems performance monitoring to subscribers over the Internet.	Totality, Seven Space/ Nuclio
Business continuity service provider	Defines and documents procedures for planning and recovering from system malfunctions that threaten vital business operations.	Comdisco disaster recovery, rapid recovery, and continuous Web availability services.

Utility Computing

Many of the service providers we have just described lease information technology services using fixed price contracts. IBM is championing a **utility computing** model in which companies pay only for the products and services they use, much as they would pay for electricity. In this "pay as you go" model of computing, which is sometimes called on-demand computing or usage-based pricing, customers would pay more or less for server capacity and storage depending on how much of these resources they actually used during a specified time period. IBM offers a full range of usage-based services, including server capacity, storage space, software applications, and Web hosting. Other vendors, including Compaq, Hewlett-Packard, and Electronic Data Systems (EDS) also offer some utility computing services.

Wireless Computing

While wireless computing is a major trend in hardware and software, we will wait until Chapter 8 for a more complete discussion of wireless and mobile technologies.

MANAGEMENT WRAP-UP

Managers should know how to select and manage the organization's hardware and software assets in the firm's IT infrastructure. General managers should understand the costs and capabilities of various hardware and software technologies and the advantages and disadvantages of building and owning these assets or of renting them from outside the organization.

Hardware and software can either enhance or impede organizational performance. Hardware and software selection should be based on organizational and business needs, considering how well the technology meshes with the organization's culture and structure, as well as organizational information-processing requirements. Hardware and software services provided by outside vendors should fit into organizational computing plans.

A range of hardware and software technologies is available to organizations. Organizations have many computer processing options to choose from, including mainframes, workstations, PCs, servers, and network computers, and many different ways of configuring hardware components to create systems. Firms can also select among alternative operating systems and application software tools. Key technology decisions include the appropriateness of the hardware or software for the problem to be addressed and compatibility with other components of the firm's IT infrastructure.

For Discussion

1. Why is selecting computer hardware and software for the organization an important management decision? What management, organization, and technology issues should be considered when selecting computer hardware?

2. Should organizations use application service providers (ASPs) and storage service providers (SSPs) for all their software and storage needs? Why, or why not? What management, organization, and technology factors should be considered when making this decision?

SUMMARY

1. *What computer processing and storage capability does our organization need to manage its information and conduct business transactions?* Managers need to understand the alternative hardware technologies available for processing and storing information so that they can select the right technologies for their business. Modern computer systems have seven major components: a central processing unit (CPU), primary storage, input devices, output devices, secondary storage, connections to the central computer unit, and communications devices. All of these components need to work together to process information for the organization.

2. *What arrangement of computers and computer processing would best benefit our organization?* Managers should understand the capabilities of various categories of computers and arrangements of computer processing. The type of computer and the arrangement of processing power that should be used by the business depend on the nature of the organization and its problems. Computers are categorized as PCs, workstations, midrange computers, mainframes, and supercomputers. Because of continuing advances in microprocessor technology, the distinctions among these types of computers are constantly changing.

   Computers can be networked together to distribute processing among different machines. In the client-server model, processing is split between "clients" and "servers" connected via a network. The exact division of tasks between client and server depends on the application. While network computers help organizations maintain central control over computing, peer-to-peer computing puts processing power back on users' desktops, linking individual PCs, workstations, or other computers through the Internet or private networks to share data, disk space, and processing power for a variety of tasks.

3. *What kinds of software do we need to run our business? What criteria should we use to select software?* Managers should understand the capabilities of various types of software so they can select software that provides the greatest benefit for their firms. There are two major types of software: system software and application software. Multiprogramming, multiprocessing, virtual storage, and time sharing are operating system capabilities that enable computer system resources to be used more efficiently. Other system software includes computer language translation programs that convert programming languages into machine language and utility programs that perform common processing tasks. PC operating systems have developed sophisticated capabilities, such as multitasking and support for multiple users on networks. PC operating systems and many kinds of application software now use graphical user interfaces.

   The general trend in software is toward user-friendly, high-level languages that both increase professional programmer productivity and make it possible for end users to work directly with information systems. The principal programming languages used in business include COBOL, C, C++, and Visual Basic. Each is designed to solve specific types of problems. Enterprise software, middleware, and enterprise application integration software are all software tools for promoting enterprise-wide integration of business processes and information system applications.

   Software selection should be based on such criteria as efficiency, compatibility with the organization's technology platform, vendor support, and whether the software tool is appropriate for the problems and tasks of the organization.

4. *How do we stay current on new software? How do we know that it will benefit our organization?* Object-oriented programming tools and new programming languages, such as Java, Hypertext Markup Language (HTML), and eXtensible Markup Language (XML) can help firms create software more rapidly and efficiently and produce applications based on the Internet or data in Web sites.

   How should we acquire and manage the firm's hardware and software? Hardware and software are both major organizational assets that must be carefully managed. E-commerce and e-business have put new strategic emphasis on technologies that can store vast quantities of transaction data and make them immediately available online. Managers and information systems specialists need to pay special attention to hardware capacity planning and scalability to ensure that the firm has enough computing power for its current and future needs.

   They also need to balance the costs and benefits of owning and maintaining their own hardware and software or renting these assets from external service providers, such as online storage and application service providers. In the utility computing model, subscribers would only pay for the software and hardware services they actually use during a specified time period. Calculating the total cost of ownership (TCO) of the organization's technology assets can help provide managers with the information they need to manage these assets and decide whether to rent or own these assets.

KEY TERMS

Application service provider (ASP), 220

Application software, 203

Arithmetic-logic unit (ALU), 193

Batch processing, 200

Bit, 193

Byte, 193

C, 208

C++, 208

Capacity planning, 217

CD-ROM (compact disk read-only memory), 196

CD-RW (CD-ReWritable), 197

Central processing unit (CPU), 193

Centralized processing, 202

Client, 202

Client-server computing, 202

COBOL (Common Business Oriented Language), 208

Compiler, 204

Computer, 192

Control unit, 194

Digital video disc (DVD), 197

Distributed processing, 202

Downsizing, 202

Electronic mail (e-mail), 214

Enterprise application integration software, 216

Enterprise software, 215

Firewire, 199

Floppy disk, 196

Fourth-generation language, 208

Graphical user interface (GUI), 205

Grid computing, 203

Groupware, 214

Hard disk, 196

Hypertext markup language (HTML), 211

Infrastructure, 192

Integrated software package, 213

Java, 210

Machine cycle, 194

Machine language, 206

Magnetic disk, 196

Magnetic tape, 197

Mainframe, 201

Massively parallel computers, 195

Megahertz, 195

Microprocessor, 195

Middleware, 215

Midrange computer, 201

Minicomputer, 201

MP3 (MPEG3), 201

Multimedia, 200

Natural language, 208

.Net, 212

Network-attached storage (NAS), 197

Network computer (NC), 202

Object code, 204

Object-oriented programming, 209

Office 2000 and Office XP, 213

Online processing, 200

Open-source software, 205

Operating system, 204

Parallel port, 199

Parallel processing, 195

Peer-to-peer computing, 203

Personal computer (PC), 201

Port, 198

Primary storage, 193

Program, 203

Query language, 208

Radio-frequency identification (RFID), 198

RAID (Redundant Array of Independent Disks), 196

RAM (random access memory), 194

Reduced instruction set computing (RISC), 195

ROM (read-only memory), 194

Scalability, 217

Secondary storage, 196

Serial port, 198

Server, 201

Server farm, 201

Software package, 212

Source code, 204

Storage area network (SAN), 197

Storage service provider (SSP), 198

Streaming technology, 201

Supercomputer, 201

System software, 203

Total cost of ownership (TCO), 218

Universal serial bus (USB), 199

Utility computing, 222

Visual Basic, 208

Visual programming, 210

Web browser, 214

Web server, 215

Workstation, 201

XBRL (eXtensible Business Reporting Language), 212

XHTML (eXtensible Hypertext Markup Language), 212

XML (eXtensible Markup Language), 211

REVIEW QUESTIONS

1. What are the components of a contemporary computer system?

2. Name the major components of the CPU and the function of each.

3. Distinguish between serial, parallel, and massively parallel processing.

4. List the most important secondary storage media. What are the strengths and limitations of each?

5. List and describe the major computer input and output devices and types of ports.

6. What is the difference between batch and online processing? Diagram the difference.

7. What is multimedia? What technologies are involved in multimedia?

8. What is the difference between a mainframe, a minicomputer, a server, and a PC? Between a PC and a workstation?

9. Compare the client-server, network computer, and peer-to-peer models of computing.

10. What are the major types of software? How do they differ in terms of users and uses?

11. What is the operating system of a computer? What does it do? What roles do multiprogramming, virtual storage, time sharing, and multiprocessing play in the operation of an information system?

12. List and describe the major PC operating systems.

13. List and describe the major application programming languages for business. How do they differ from fourth-generation languages?

14. What is object-oriented programming? How does it differ from conventional software development?

15. What are Java, HTML, XBRL, and XML? Compare their capabilities. Why are they important?

16. Name and describe the most important PC productivity software tools.

17. Name and describe the kinds of software that can be used for enterprise integration.

18. List and describe the principal issues in managing hardware and software assets.

APPLICATION SOFTWARE EXERCISE

SPREADSHEET EXERCISE: EVALUATING COMPUTER HARDWARE AND SOFTWARE OPTIONS

You have been asked to obtain pricing information on hardware and software for an office of 30 people. Using the Internet, get pricing for 30 PC desktop systems (monitor, computer, and keyboard) manufactured by IBM, Dell, and Compaq as listed at their respective corporate Web sites. (For the purposes of this exercise, ignore the fact that desktop systems usually come with preloaded software packages.) Also, get pricing on 15 monochrome desktop printers manufactured by Hewlett-Packard and Brother. Each desktop system must satisfy the minimum specifications shown in Table 1 below.

Each desktop printer must satisfy the minimum specifications shown in Table 2 below.

After obtaining pricing on the desktop systems and printers, obtain pricing on 30 copies of Microsoft's Office XP, Corel's WordPerfect Office 2002, and IBM's Lotus SmartSuite application packages and on 30 copies of Microsoft Windows XP Professional edition. The application software suite packages come in various versions, so be sure that each package contains programs for word processing, spreadsheet analysis, database analysis, graphics preparation, and e-mail.

Prepare a spreadsheet showing your research results for the desktop systems, for the printers, and for the software. Use your spreadsheet software to determine the desktop system, printer, and software combination that will offer both the best performance and pricing per worker. Since every two workers will share one printer (15 printers/30 systems), assume only half a printer cost per worker in the second spreadsheet. In both spreadsheets, assume that your company will take the standard warranty and servicing contract offered by each product's manufacturer.

TABLE 1	MINIMUM DESKTOP SPECIFICATIONS
Processor speed	1.8GHz
Hard drive	40GB
RAM	256MB
CD-ROM speed	48X
Monitor (diagonal measurement)	17 inches

TABLE 2	MINIMUM MONO-CHROME PRINTER SPECIFICATIONS
Print speed (pages per minute)	12
Print quality	600 × 600
Network ready?	Yes
Maximum price/unit	$1000

GROUP PROJECT

With three or four of your classmates, obtain a copy of OpenOffice www.openoffice.org, which is downloadable for free, or find a low-cost copy of Sun StarOffice and compare its capabilities to the Microsoft Office suite of desktop productivity tools. Evaluate their functions, ease of use, and compatibility with models of computer hardware and operating systems. Which would you purchase for your personal use? For a business? Justify your decision. If possible, use electronic presentation software to present your findings to the class.

INTERNET TOOLS

COMPANION WEBSITE

The Internet Connection for this chapter will direct you to a series of Web sites where you can complete an exercise to survey the products and services of major computer hardware vendors and the use of Web sites in the computer hardware industry.

At www.pearsoned.ca/laudon, you will find invaluable tools to facilitate and enhance your learning of this chapter as well as opportunities to apply your knowledge to realistic situations:

■ An Interactive Study Guide of self-test questions that will provide you with immediate feedback.
■ Application exercises.
■ An Electronic Business Project for salesforce budgeting.
■ A Management Decision Problem on capacity planning for electronic commerce.
■ Additional material on operating systems; application programming languages; productivity software; and integrated software packages.
■ Updates of material in the chapter.

ADDITIONAL SITES OF INTEREST

There are many interesting Web sites to enhance your learning about hardware and software. You can search the Web yourself or just try the following sites to add to what you have already learned.

Tom's Hardware

www.tomshardware.com

The latest news on hardware testing and comparison of one brand of a particular piece of hardware against other brands.

Whatis.com

www.whatis.com

An up-to-date combination dictionary and encylopaedia of hardware, software, and applications.

Dell Canada

www.dell.ca

See how to purchase a personal computer online from Dell Computer's Canadian Web site.

Informit

www.informit.com

For the real "techie" in the class—an excellent Web site for staying up to date with the latest developments about hardware.

Microsoft Canada

www.microsoft.ca

The Canadian arm of the largest software publisher in the world.

IBM Canada

www.ibm.ca

The Canadian arm of the largest mainframe software publisher in the world.

Red Hat Corporation

www.redhat.com

Linux vendor offering software and support for this open-source operating system.

CASE STUDY: *Direct Wines Ages Wine, Not IT*

As the British population consumes increasing amounts of wine, suppliers are fighting hard to increase their share of the retail market. Reading, England–based Direct Wines Ltd., specializes in quality wines from smaller producers and has grown into the world's largest mail order supplier of wines. In 1969, Tony Laithwaite (founder of Direct Wines Ltd.) started importing and retailing French wines. The *Sunday Times* ran a story in 1973 about some of the dodgy practices of the British wine trade, and Laithwaite wrote a letter to the editor distancing his business from other less reputable retailers. His letter drew a huge response from readers, and the newspaper established the *Sunday Times* Wine Club with Laithwaite's help. Today, Direct Wines ships more than 30 million bottles of wine through Laithwaite's (www.laithwaites.co.uk) and *The Sunday Times* Wine Club (www.stwc.co.uk). Direct Wines 2002 revenues were over $400 million.

The key to Direct Wines' success is efficient fulfillment—getting the right product to the right customer at the right time. "Customer service is our most critical success factor," said

Michael Bennett, IT director at Direct Wines. "Even the best products in the world count for very little unless customer orders are fulfilled promptly and accurately." But with over 700 employees, the 31-year old company was finding it hard to coordinate all of the activities along its supply chain through customer order fulfillment. Its supply chain encompasses the wine distributors from whom it buys the wine it offers for sale, its warehouses and distribution centres, transportation facilities and equipment, right to its customers' doors. For example, Direct Wines would order wines from a supplier using computers, record the purchase, arrival, and storage of the wine in its warehouse; record the order of the wine from the customer, bill the customer, and ship to the customer—all using its computer systems. If those computers could "talk" to each other, sharing data, then most of these steps would be processed by computers with little human intervention or chance for human error. In addition, inventory statistics, accounts payable, and accounts receivable could be kept current, and reports on exceptions prepared automatically for management.

Until recently, Direct Wines used different systems to manage different parts of its business. These disparate systems were hard to maintain and upgrade. As is typical, no one decision could be made; rather, many decisions were required to update Direct Wines' IT and systems. Customer data would be housed in one system, vendor data in another, inventory data in still another, and so on. Recognizing the need to update its systems, Direct Wines decided to integrate its information systems.

First, the decision was made to move to SAP's R/3 enterprise-wide system. SAP is the world's leading vendor of enterprise-wide systems (see Chapter 2). SAP software permits data to move from purchasing to receiving to inventory to factory floor to warehousing to distribution, ordering, and billing with almost no human intervention. This is not only more efficient; it is also more accurate, since the potential for human error is reduced. For more about SAP, see the part-ending case for Part IV. Direct Wines then decided to run the new SAP system on Hewlett-Packard's UNIX platform. Hewlett-Packard used a variety of hardware servers tape libraries, and switches (see Chapter 8 on telecommunications) to standardize Direct Wines' hardware.

The increased storage requirements of the new SAP R/3 enterprise-wide system led Direct Wines to implement a storage area network as well, again utilizing the Hewlett-Packard platform. Hewlett-Packard partnered with Prestige Systems, another Direct Wines solutions provider, to design and implement the storage area network (SAN) on Hewlett-Packard's SAN hardware. Finally, Direct Wines decided to implement SAP R/3 using Oracle as the database to be used by SAP R/3. Oracle is the leading enterprisewide database management software in the world (see Chapter 7 for more discussion on databases).

SAP's systems use what SAP calls "best practices" for operation. This means that SAP has mapped the best practices of its leading customers and has developed SAP to work the way these companies operate. Implementing SAP R/3, therefore, meant that Direct Wines had to change some of its business processes so that the new system could integrate data among all the processes. The SAP R/3 implementation was expected to result in more consolidated information that would help Direct Wines relate supply to demand and fulfill customer orders more quickly and more effectively. Better planning and improved inventory management should result in fewer substitutions and should reduce inventory by 10 percent. Direct Wines gets a competitive advantage from being able to fill their orders efficiently and without substitution. The new SAP R/3 system should help them attain this goal.

Sources: "Direct Wines Limited," Hoovers Online, available www.hoovers.com/free/co/factsheet.xhtml?ID=102549, accessed July 21, 2003; "Direct Wines," SPSS Inc., available www.spss.com/success/template_view.cfm?Story_ID=66, accessed July 21, 2003; "Direct Wines—A Case Study," QAS UK Customer Case Studies, available www.qas.com/uk/customers/casestudy.asp?Organisation=DirectWines, accessed July 21, 2003.

CASE STUDY QUESTIONS

1. What problems do you think Direct Wines experienced from using a variety of different systems and platforms?
2. How did hardware fit in with and support Direct Wines' strategy? Do the changes in hardware and software at Direct Wines mean that the role of information technology changed?
3. Why did Direct Wines choose to standardize their platform? What were the main strengths of the new platform?
4. Why did Direct Wines decide to implement SAP R/3? What changes do you think Direct Wines would have to make while implementing SAP R/3?
5. What benefits would Direct Wines achieve from use of a storage area network?
6. What business and technology issues did Direct Wines face when making these changes?

MANAGING DATA RESOURCES

As a manager, you will want to know how to organize your company's data so that they can be easily accessed and utilized. After reading this chapter, you should be able to answer the following questions:

1. *Why do businesses have trouble finding the information they need in their information systems?*

2. *How does a database management system help businesses improve the organization of their information?*

3. *How do the principal types of database models affect the way businesses can access and use information?*

4. *What are the managerial and organizational requirements of a database environment?*

5. *What new tools and technologies can make databases more accessible and useful?*

Singapore's Tourism Board Learns to Manage Its Data

The Singapore Tourism Board (STB) collects, stores, and analyzes data on visitors to Singapore. Mainframe computers capture and process visitor arrival data to generate monthly and annual reports. As Singapore became increasingly popular as a global business and tourist destination, the Tourism Board's information systems department could not keep up with the Singapore government's demand for more accurate and timely statistical information. The Tourism Board was using outdated data management and storage systems in which data were stored in disparate files and formats that were not integrated. It was difficult and time consuming to consolidate the data from so many disparate sources. End users could not easily generate ad hoc reports in their preferred formats.

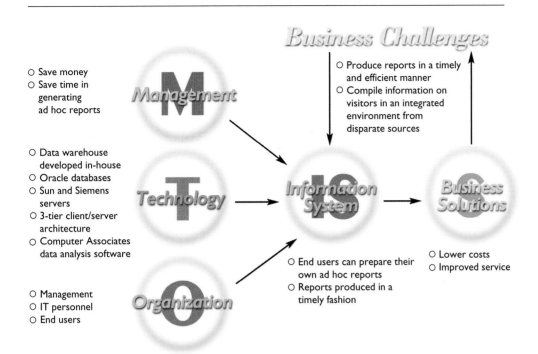

○ Save money
○ Save time in generating ad hoc reports

Management

Business Challenges

○ Produce reports in a timely and efficient manner
○ Compile information on visitors in an integrated environment from disparate sources

○ Data warehouse developed in-house
○ Oracle databases
○ Sun and Siemens servers
○ 3-tier client/server architecture
○ Computer Associates data analysis software

Technology

Information System

Business Solutions

○ Lower costs
○ Improved service

○ Management
○ IT personnel
○ End users

Organization

○ End users can prepare their own ad hoc reports
○ Reports produced in a timely fashion

Patrick Lau Chen Chai, the Chief Information Officer for STB, initiated a project to create a powerful central repository for tourism data that could be used for all key statistical systems as well as the other needs of the Board and the industry. With the endorsement of senior management, Lau's group built a data warehouse called AIMS (Automated Information Management System), which is based on Oracle databases running on Sun and Siemens server computers. The system uses a three-tier client-server architecture so that processing power can be equally distributed among user PCs, the application server, and the database server. To analyze the data in the warehouse, Lau selected tools from Computer Associates, including InfoPump (now Advantage Data Pump), InfoBea-con (now known as Clever Path), InfoReports, and Clever Path analysis software. Clever Path is a set of tools, among which is an online analytical tool to analyze and present the data in a multidimensional format that allows the Tourism Board to generate the required information in different dimensions.

AIMS went live in April 1999. The warehouse has enabled STB to produce its reports much more efficiently and quickly, saving STB a total of 550 person-days that used to be spent producing reports and a total of 546 person-days that used to be spent servicing ad hoc information requests from various departments of the Board. Now, STB can get information on visitors within three days of their arrival in Singapore.

Sources: Winston Raj, "Constructing Potato Head," *CIO Asia*, January 2002 and www.stb.com.sg.

MANAGEMENT CHALLENGES

The Singapore Tourism Board's experience illustrates how much the effective use of information depends on how data are stored, organized, and accessed. Proper delivery of information depends not only on the capabilities of hardware and software but also on the organization's ability to manage data as an important resource. The Tourism Board's inability to assemble visitor data led to inefficient reporting processes that impaired organizational performance. It has been very difficult for organizations to manage their data effectively. Two challenges stand out.

1. **Organizational obstacles to a database environment.** Implementing a database requires widespread organizational change in the role of information (and information managers), the allocation of power at senior levels, the ownership and sharing of information, and patterns of organizational agreement. A database management system (DBMS) challenges the existing power arrangements in an organization and, for that reason, often generates political resistance. In a traditional file environment, each department constructed files and programs to fulfill its specific needs. Now, with a database, files and programs must be built that take into account the full organization's interest in data. Although the organization has spent the money on hardware and software for a database environment, it may not reap the benefits it should if it is unwilling to make the requisite organizational changes.

2. **Integrating data and ensuring data quality.** Moving to a database environment can be a costly long-term process. In addition to the cost of DBMS software, related hardware, and data modelling, organizations should anticipate heavy expenditures for integrating, merging, and standardizing their data so that the data can reside in a database that can serve the entire company. Firms often must spend considerable time merging, cleaning, and standardizing the data that will populate their databases to eliminate inconsistencies, redundancies, and errors that typically arise when overlapping data are stored and maintained by different systems in different functional areas.

This chapter examines the managerial and organizational requirements as well as the technologies for managing data as a resource. Organizations need to manage their data assets very carefully to make sure that the data can be easily accessed and used by managers and employees across the organization. First, we describe the typical challenges facing businesses trying to access information using traditional file management technologies. Then, we describe the technology of database management systems, which can overcome many of the drawbacks of traditional file management and provide the firm-wide integration of information required for digital firm applications. We include a discussion of the managerial and organizational requirements for successfully implementing a database environment.

7.1   ORGANIZING DATA IN A TRADITIONAL FILE ENVIRONMENT

An effective information system provides users with timely, accurate, and relevant information. This information is stored in computer files. When the files are properly arranged and maintained, users can easily access and retrieve the information they need. Well-managed, carefully arranged files make it easy to obtain data for business decisions, whereas poorly managed files lead to chaos in information processing, high costs, poor performance, and little, if any, flexibility. Despite the use of excellent hardware and software, many organizations have inefficient information systems because of poor file management. In this section, we describe the traditional methods that organizations have used to arrange data in computer files. We also discuss the problems with these methods.

FILE ORGANIZATION TERMS AND CONCEPTS

A computer system organizes data in a hierarchy that starts with bits and bytes and progresses to fields, records, files, and databases (see Figure 7.1). A *bit* represents the smallest unit of

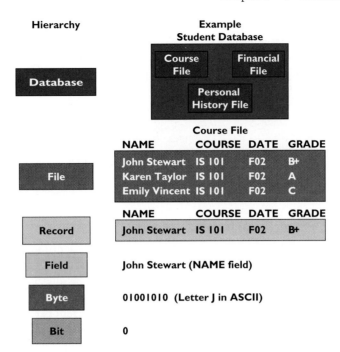

Figure 7.1 The data hierarchy. A computer system organizes data in a hierarchy that starts with the bit, which represents either a 0 or a 1. Bits can be grouped to form a byte to represent one character, number, or symbol. Bytes can be grouped to form a field, and related fields can be grouped to form a record. Related records can be collected to form a file, and related files can be organized into a database.

data a computer can handle. A group of bits, called a *byte,* represents a single character, which can be a letter, a number, or another symbol. A grouping of characters into a word, a group of words, or a complete number (such as a person's name or age) is called a **field**. A group of related fields, such as the student's name, the course taken, the date, and the grade, comprises a **record**; a group of records of the same type is called a **file**. For instance, the student records in Figure 7.1 could constitute a course file. A group of related files makes up a **database**. The student course file illustrated in Figure 7.1 could be grouped with files on students' personal histories and financial backgrounds to create a student database.

A record describes an entity. An **entity** is a person, place, thing, or event on which we maintain information. An order is a typical entity in a sales order file, which maintains information on a firm's sales orders. Each characteristic or quality describing a particular entity is called an **attribute**. For example, order number, order date, order amount, item number, and item quantity would each be an attribute of the entity order. The specific values that these attributes can have can be found in the fields of the record describing the entity order (see Figure 7.2).

Every record in a file should contain at least one field that uniquely identifies instances of that record so that the record can be retrieved, updated, or sorted. This identifier field is called a **key field**. An example of a key field is the order number for the order record illustrated in Figure 7.2 or an employee number or social insurance number for a personnel record (containing employee data such as the employee's name, age, address, job title, and so forth).

PROBLEMS WITH THE TRADITIONAL FILE ENVIRONMENT

In most organizations, systems tended to grow independently and not according to some grand plan. Each functional area tended to develop systems in isolation from other functional areas. Accounting, finance, manufacturing, human resources, and sales and marketing all developed their own systems and data files. Figure 7.3 illustrates the traditional approach to information processing.

Each application, of course, required its own files and its own computer program to operate. For example, the human resources functional area might have had a personnel master file, a payroll file, a medical insurance file, a pension file, a mailing list file, and so forth until tens, perhaps hundreds, of files and programs existed. In the company as a whole, this process led to multiple master files created, maintained, and operated by separate divisions or departments. As this process goes on for five or 10 years, the organization is saddled with hundreds of programs and applications, with no one knowing what they do, what data they use, and who is using the data. The resulting problems are data redundancy, program-data dependence, inflexibility, poor data security, and inability to share data among applications.

field

A grouping of characters into a word, a group of words, or a complete number, such as a person's name or age.

record

A group of related fields.

file

A group of records of the same type.

database

A group of related files.

entity

A person, place, thing, or event about which information must be kept.

attribute

A piece of information describing a particular entity.

key field

A field in a record that uniquely identifies instances of that record so that it can be retrieved, updated, or sorted.

Figure 7.2 Entities and attributes. This record describes the entity called ORDER and its attributes. The order number, order date, item number, quantity, and amount for this particular order are the fields for this record. Order number is the key field because each order is assigned a unique identification number.

Entity = ORDER
Attributes

Order number	Order date	Item number	Quantity	Amount
4340	02/08/03	1583	2	17.40

fields

key field

Data Redundancy and Confusion

data redundancy

The presence of duplicate data in multiple data files.

Data redundancy is the presence of duplicate data in multiple data files. Data redundancy occurs when different divisions, functional areas, and groups in an organization independently collect the same piece of information. Because it is collected and maintained in so many different places, the same data item, such as employee, fiscal year, or product identification code may have different meanings in different parts of the organization. Different systems might use different names for the same item. For instance, the sales, inventory, and manufacturing systems of a clothing retailer might use different codes to represent clothing size. One system might represent clothing size as "extra large," while another might use the code XL for the same purpose. The resulting confusion would make it difficult for companies to create customer relationship management, supply chain management, or enterprise systems that integrate data from different sources.

Program-Data Dependence

program-data dependence

The close relationship between data stored in files and the software programs that update and maintain those files. Any change in data organization or format requires a change in all the programs associated with those files.

Program-data dependence is the tight relationship between data stored in files and the specific programs required to update and maintain those files. Every traditional computer program has to describe the location and nature of the data with which it works. In a traditional file environment, any change in data requires a change in all programs that access the data. Changes, for instance, in tax rates or postal code length or structure require changes in programs. These programming changes may cost millions of dollars to implement in programs that require the revised data.

Figure 7.3 Traditional file processing. The use of a traditional approach to file processing encourages each functional area in a corporation to develop specialized applications. Each application requires a unique data file that is likely to be a subset of the master file. Having these subsets of the master file leads to data redundancy, processing inflexibility, and wasted storage resources.

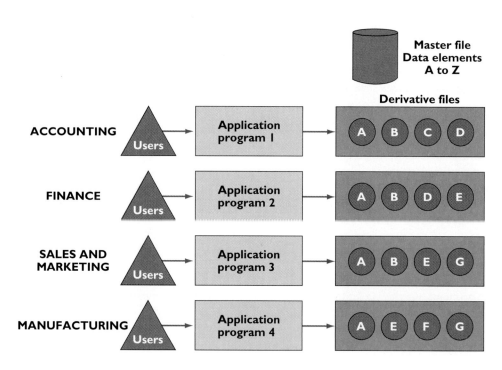

Lack of Flexibility

A traditional file system can deliver routine scheduled reports after extensive programming efforts, but it cannot deliver ad hoc reports or respond to unanticipated information requirements in a timely fashion. The information required by ad hoc requests is somewhere in the system but is too expensive to retrieve. Several programmers would have to work for weeks to put together the required data items in a new file.

Poor Security

Because there is little control or management of data, access to and dissemination of information may be out of control. Management may have no way of knowing who is accessing or even making changes to the organization's data.

Lack of Data Sharing and Availability

The lack of control over access to data in this confused environment does not make it easy for people to obtain information. Because pieces of information in different files and different parts of the organization cannot be combined or integrated, it is virtually impossible for information to be shared or accessed in a timely manner. Information cannot flow freely across different functional areas or different parts of the organization.

7.2 THE DATABASE APPROACH TO DATA MANAGEMENT

Database technology can cut through many of the problems that a traditional file organization creates. A more rigorous definition of a **database** is a collection of data organized to serve many applications efficiently by centralizing the data and minimizing redundant data. Rather than storing data in separate files for each application, data are stored physically to appear to users as being stored in only one location. A single database services multiple applications. For example, instead of a corporation storing employee data in separate information systems and separate files for personnel, payroll, and benefits, the corporation could create a single common human resources database. Figure 7.4 illustrates the database concept.

DATABASE MANAGEMENT SYSTEMS

A **database management system (DBMS)** is simply the software that permits an organization to centralize data, manage them efficiently, and provide access to the stored data by

database (rigorous definition)

A collection of data organized to service many applications at the same time by storing and managing data so that they appear to be in one location.

database management system (DBMS)

Special software to create and maintain a database and enable individual business applications to extract the data they need without having to create separate files or data definitions in their computer programs.

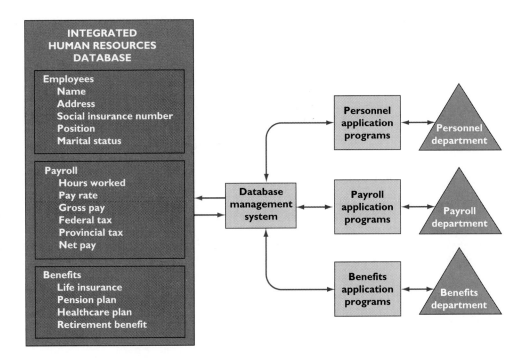

Figure 7.4 The contemporary database environment. A single human resources database serves multiple applications and also allows a corporation to easily draw together all the information for various applications. The database management system acts as the interface between the application programs and the data.

application programs. The DBMS acts as an interface between application programs and the physical data files. When the application program calls for a data item, such as gross pay, the DBMS finds this item in the database and presents it to the application program. Using traditional data files, the programmer would have to specify the size and format of each data element used in the program and then tell the computer where they were located. A DBMS eliminates most of the data definition statements found in traditional programs.

The DBMS relieves the programmer or end user from the task of understanding where and how the data are actually stored by separating the logical and physical views of the data. The **logical view** presents data as they would be perceived by end users or business specialists, while the **physical view** shows how data are actually organized and structured on physical storage media. There is only one physical view of the data, but there can be many different logical views. The database management software makes the physical database available for different logical views needed for various application programs. For example, an employee retirement benefits program might use a logical view of the human resources database illustrated in Figure 7.4 that requires only the employee's name, address, social insurance number, pension plan, and retirement benefits data.

A database management system has three components:

1.   A data definition language
2.   A data manipulation language
3.   A data dictionary

The **data definition language** is the formal language programmers use to specify the content and structure of the database. The data definition language defines each data element as it appears in the database before that data element is translated into the forms required by application programs.

Most DBMS have a specialized language called a **data manipulation language** that is used in conjunction with some conventional application programming languages to manipulate the data in the database. This language contains commands that permit end users and programming specialists to extract data from the database to satisfy information requests and develop applications. The most prominent data manipulation language today is **Structured Query Language, or SQL**. End users and information systems specialists can use SQL as an interactive query language to access data from databases, and SQL commands can be embedded in application programs written in conventional programming languages.

The third element of a DBMS is a **data dictionary**. This is an automated or manual file that stores definitions of data elements and data characteristics, such as usage, physical representation, ownership (who in the organization is responsible for maintaining the data), authorization, and security. Many data dictionaries can produce lists and reports of data use, groupings, program locations, and so on. Figure 7.5 illustrates a sample data dictionary report that shows the size, format, meaning, and uses of a data element in a human resources database. A **data element** represents a field. In addition to listing the standard name (AMT-PAY-BASE), the dictionary lists the names that reference this element in specific systems and identifies the individuals, business functions, programs, and reports that use this data element.

By creating an inventory of data contained in the database, the data dictionary serves as an important data management tool. For instance, business users can consult the dictionary to find out exactly what pieces of data are maintained for the sales or marketing function or even to determine all the information maintained by the entire enterprise. The dictionary could supply business users with the name, format, and specifications required to access data for reports. Technical staff could use the dictionary to determine what data elements and files must be changed if a program is changed.

Most data dictionaries are entirely passive; they simply report. More advanced types are active; changes in the dictionary can be automatically used by related programs. For instance, to change postal codes from six to eight characters, one could simply enter the change in the dictionary without having to modify all application programs using postal codes.

In an ideal database environment, the data in the database are defined only once and used for all applications whose data reside in the database, thereby eliminating data redundancy and inconsistency. Application programs, which are written using a combination of

logical view

A representation of data as they would appear to an application programmer or end user.

physical view

The representation of data as they would actually be organized on physical storage media.

data definition language

The component of a database management system that defines each data element as it appears in the database.

data manipulation language

A language associated with a database management system that end users and programmers use to manipulate data in the database.

Structured Query Language (SQL)

The standard data manipulation language for relational database management systems.

data dictionary

An automated or manual tool for storing and organizing information about the data maintained in a database.

data element

A field.

NAME: AMT-PAY-BASE
FOCUS NAME: BASEPAY
PC NAME: SALARY

DESCRIPTION: EMPLOYEE'S ANNUAL SALARY

SIZE: 9 BYTES
TYPE: N (NUMERIC)
DATE CHANGED: 01/01/95
OWNERSHIP: COMPENSATION
UPDATE SECURITY: SITE PERSONNEL
ACCESS SECURITY: MANAGER, COMPENSATION PLANNING AND RESEARCH
                 MANAGER, JOB EVALUATION SYSTEMS
                 MANAGER, HUMAN RESOURCES PLANNING
                 MANAGER, SITE EQUAL OPPORTUNITY AFFAIRS
                 MANAGER, SITE BENEFITS
                 MANAGER, CLAIMS PAYING SYSTEMS
                 MANAGER, QUALIFIED PLANS
                 MANAGER, SITE EMPLOYMENT/EEO
BUSINESS FUNCTIONS USED BY: COMPENSATION
                 HR PLANNING
                 EMPLOYMENT
                 INSURANCE
                 PENSION

PROGRAMS USING: PI01000
                PI02000
                PI03000
                PI04000
                PI05000

REPORTS USING: REPORT 124 (SALARY INCREASE TRACKING REPORT)
               REPORT 448 (GROUP INSURANCE AUDIT REPORT)
               REPORT 452 (SALARY REVIEW LISTING)
               PENSION REFERENCE LISTING

Figure 7.5 Sample data dictionary report. The sample data dictionary report for a human resources database provides helpful information, such as the size of the data element, which programs and reports use it, and which group in the organization is the owner responsible for maintaining it. The report also shows some of the other names that the organization uses for this piece of data.

the data manipulation language of the DBMS and a conventional programming language, request data elements from the database. Data elements called for by the application programs are found and delivered by the DBMS. The programmer does not have to specify in detail how or where the data are to be found.

A DBMS can reduce program-data dependence along with program development and maintenance costs. Access and availability of information can be increased because users and programmers can perform ad hoc queries of data in the database. The DBMS allows the organization to centrally manage data, their use, and security. The Window on Management illustrates some of these benefits.

TYPES OF DATABASES

Contemporary DBMS use different database models to keep track of entities, attributes, and relationships. Each model has certain processing advantages and certain business advantages.

Relational DBMS

The most popular type of DBMS today for PCs as well as for larger computers and mainframes is the **relational DBMS**. The relational data model represents all data in the database as simple two-dimensional tables called *relations*. The tables appear similar to flat files, but the information in more than one file can be easily extracted and combined. Sometimes, the tables are referred to as *files*.

Figure 7.6 shows a supplier table, a part table, and an order table. In each table, the rows are unique records, and the columns are fields. Another term for a row or record in a relation is a **tuple**. Often, a user needs information from a number of relations to produce a report. Here is the strength of the relational model: It can relate data in any one file or table to data in another file or table as long as both tables share a common data element.

relational DBMS
A type of logical database model that treats data as if they were stored in two-dimensional tables. It can relate data stored in one table to data in another as long as the two tables share a common data element.

tuple
A row or record in a relational database.

A Database Shows the World Awash in Stolen Nuclear Material

The September 11, 2001, terrorist attacks in New York City and Washington, D.C. heightened fears about weapons-grade nuclear material that may have fallen into the wrong hands. In March 2002, Lyudmila Zaitseva, a visiting fellow at Stanford University's Institute for International Studies, observed, "We can only guess by the routes where the [missing nuclear] material is going. We can't be sure if it is Iraq, Iran, North Korea, Al Qaeda, or Hezbollah."

The problem began over 10 years ago with the collapse of the Soviet Union. Since that time, those with knowledge about this issue have expressed fear that the nuclear material has not been well protected or even accounted for. No one even knew just what material was missing, much less where that material was. In recent months, the Strategic Security Project at Stanford University (nicknamed the Database on Nuclear Smuggling, Theft, and Orphan Radiation Sources) began to collect data on what nuclear material was missing and what has happened to it. "It blows the mind, the lack of information," stated George Bunn, an experienced arms control negotiator. "What we're trying to say is: 'What are the facts?'"

The data about stolen radioactive material come from two existing unclassified databases and additional data from sources ranging from government agencies to local media reports. The Strategic Security Project evaluated each entry for accuracy and probability. The data are being stored in a database where DBMS security features can be used to limit access to only approved researchers. The database contains data on illicitly obtained weapons-grade nuclear material as well as scientific and medical material that may have been lost, misplaced, or simply thrown away but could, nevertheless, pose health and security threats. Members of the Stanford group have begun informing appropriate government agencies of the existence of the database and are offering access to the data to approved organizations.

By assembling all the data about lost, misplaced, or stolen nuclear material into a single database, analysts have a more comprehensive and precise picture of how serious a problem wayward nuclear material poses. According to Zaitseva, at least 40 kilograms of weapons-usable uranium and plutonium have been stolen from poorly protected nuclear facilities in the former Soviet Union. Most of this material was subsequently retrieved, but two kilograms of highly enriched uranium stolen from a reactor remains missing. One of several fuel rods that disappeared from a research reactor in the Congo was found to have later resurfaced in Italy, reportedly in the hands of the Mafia, but the other rods still cannot be accounted for.

"This is a smart step," said Michael Levi, the director of the Strategic Security Project. "Knowing what's out there is the first step to bringing it back in." Research to this point has discovered where some of the critical material was initially transported, but we do not know where any of it ended up. Research is continuing, and the information is being securely guarded in the tightly protected DBMS.

Think About: What are the advantages of using a database to track stolen or lost nuclear material? How can such data be better managed using a DBMS?

Source: Andrew Quinn, "Data Show World Awash in Stolen Nuclear Material," *Reuters*, March 6, 2002; and "Fears Over Missing Nuclear Material," *BBC News*, March 7, 2002.

Figure 7.6 The relational data model. Each table is a relation, and each row or record is a tuple. Each column corresponds to a field. These relations can easily be combined and extracted to access data and produce reports, provided that any two share a common data element. In this example, the ORDER file shares the data element "Part_Number" with the PART file. The PART and SUPPLIER files share the data element "Supplier_Number."

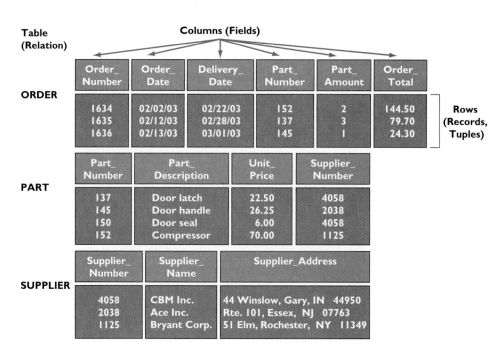

To demonstrate, suppose we wanted to find in the relational database in Figure 7.6 the names and addresses of suppliers who could provide us with part number 137 or part number 152. We would need information from two tables: the supplier table and the part table. Note that these two files have a shared data element: Supplier_Number.

In a relational database, three basic operations, shown in Figure 7.7, are used to develop useful sets of data: select, project, and join. The *select* operation creates a subset consisting of all of the records in the file that meet stated criteria. In other words, Select creates a subset of rows that meet certain criteria. In our example, we want to select records (rows) from the part table where the part number equals 137 or 152. The *join* operation combines relational tables to provide the user with more information than is available in individual tables. In our example, we want to join the now-shortened part table (only parts numbered 137 or 152 will be presented) and the supplier table into a single new result table.

The *project* operation creates a subset consisting of columns in a table, permitting the user to create new tables (also called *views*) that contain only the information required. In our example, we want to extract from the new result table only the following columns: Part_Number, Supplier_Number, Supplier_Name, and Supplier_Address (see Figure 7.7).

Leading mainframe relational DBMS include IBM's DB2 and Oracle from the Oracle Corporation. DB2, Oracle, and Microsoft SQL Server are used as DBMS for midrange computers. Microsoft Access is a PC-based relational DBMS, and Oracle Lite is a DBMS for small handheld computing devices.

Hierarchical and Network DBMS

One can still find older systems that are based on a hierarchical or network data model. The **hierarchical DBMS** presents data to users in a treelike structure. Within each record, data elements are organized into pieces of records called *segments*. To the user, each record looks like an organization chart with one top-level segment called the *root*. An upper segment is connected logically to a lower segment in a parent-child relationship. A parent segment can have more than one child, but a child can have only one parent.

Figure 7.8 shows a hierarchical structure that might be used for a human resources database. The root segment is Employee, which contains basic employee information, such as name, address, and identification number. Immediately below it are three child segments: Compensation (containing salary and promotion data), Job Assignments (containing data about job positions and departments), and Benefits (containing data about beneficiaries and benefit options). The Compensation segment has two children below it: Performance Ratings (containing data about employees' job performance evaluations) and Salary History (containing historical data about employees' past salaries). Below the Benefits segment are child segments for Pension, Life Insurance, and Health Care, containing data about these benefit plans.

While hierarchical structures depict one-to-many relationships (one parent to many children), *network DBMS* depict data logically as many-to-many relationships. In other words, parents can have multiple children, and a child can have more than one parent. Hierarchical and network DBMS are considered outdated and are no longer used for building new database applications. They are much less flexible than relational DBMS and do not support ad hoc, English language–like inquiries for information. All paths for accessing data must be specified in advance and cannot be changed without a major programming effort. For instance, if you queried the human resources database illustrated in Figure 7.8 to find out the names of the employees with the job title of administrative assistant, you would discover that there is no way that the system could find the answer in a reasonable amount of time. This path through the data was not specified in advance.

Relational DBMS, in contrast, have much more flexibility in providing data for ad hoc queries, combining information from different sources, and providing capability to add new data and records without disturbing existing programs and applications. However, these systems can be slowed down if they require many accesses to the data stored on disk to carry out the select, join, and project commands. Selecting one part number from among millions, one record at a time, can take a long time. Of course, the database can be tuned to speed up prespecified queries.

Hierarchical DBMS can still be found in large legacy systems that require intensive high-volume transaction processing. A **legacy system** is a system that has been in existence

hierarchical DBMS
Older logical database model that organizes data in a treelike structure. A record is subdivided into segments that are connected to each other in one-to-many parent-child relationships.

legacy system
A system that has been in existence for a long time and that continues to be used to avoid the high cost of replacing or redesigning it.

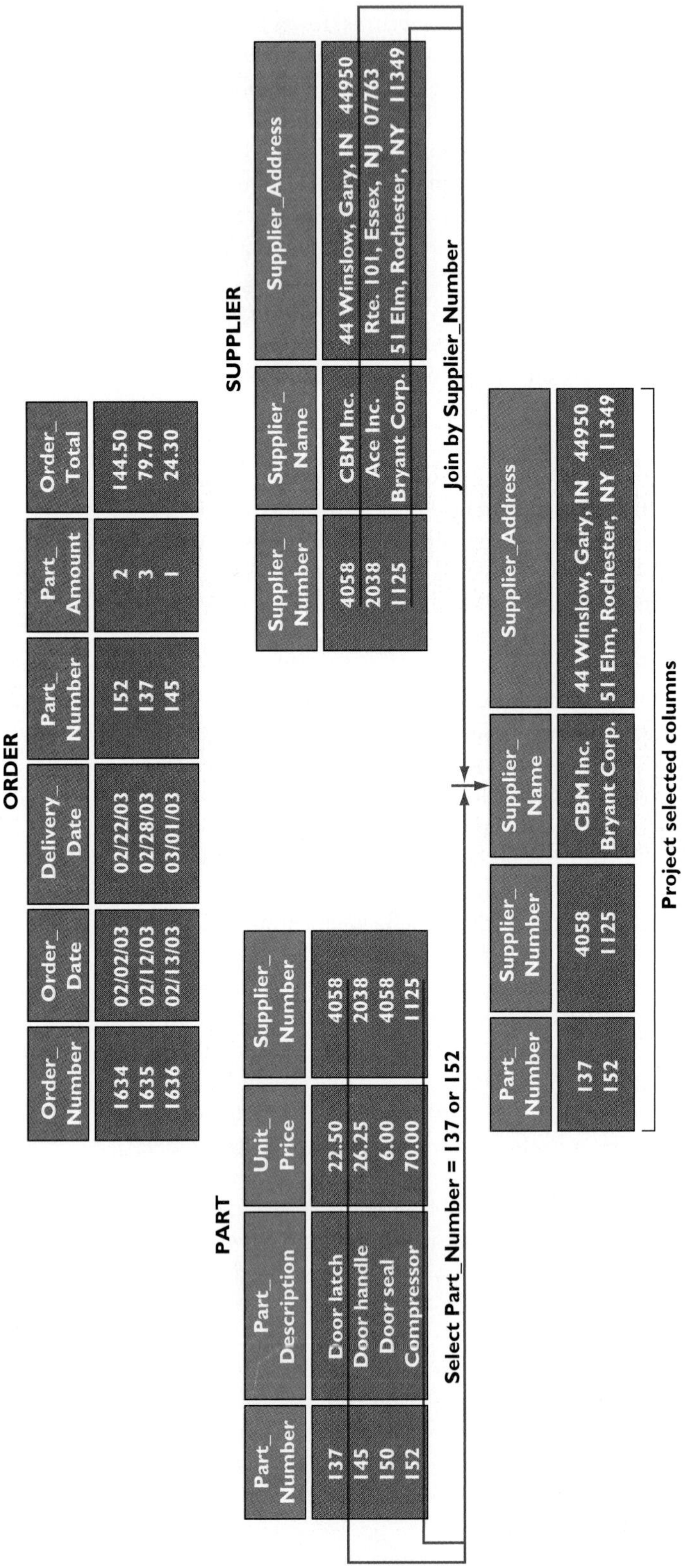

ORDER

Order_Number	Order_Date	Delivery_Date	Part_Number	Part_Amount	Order_Total
1634	02/02/03	02/22/03	152	2	144.50
1635	02/12/03	02/28/03	137	3	79.70
1636	02/13/03	03/01/03	145	1	24.30

PART

Part_Number	Part_Description	Unit_Price	Supplier_Number
137	Door latch	22.50	4058
145	Door handle	26.25	2038
150	Door seal	6.00	4058
152	Compressor	70.00	1125

Select Part_Number = 137 or 152

SUPPLIER

Supplier_Number	Supplier_Name	Supplier_Address
4058	CBM Inc.	44 Winslow, Gary, IN 44950
2038	Ace Inc.	Rte. 101, Essex, NJ 07763
1125	Bryant Corp.	51 Elm, Rochester, NY 11349

Join by Supplier_Number

Part_Number	Supplier_Number	Supplier_Name	Supplier_Address
137	4058	CBM Inc.	44 Winslow, Gary, IN 44950
152	1125	Bryant Corp.	51 Elm, Rochester, NY 11349

Project selected columns

Figure 7.7 The three basic operations of a relational DBMS. The select, project, and join operations allow data from two different tables to be combined and only selected attributes to be displayed.

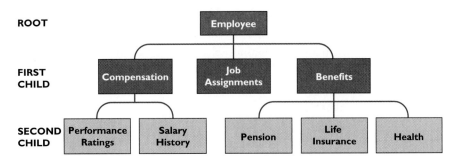

ROOT

FIRST CHILD

SECOND CHILD

Figure 7.8 A hierarchical database for a human resources system. The hierarchical database model looks like an organizational chart or a family tree. It has a single root segment (Employee) connected to lower level segments (Compensation, Job Assignments, and Benefits). Each subordinate segment, in turn, may connect to other subordinate segments. Here, Compensation connects to Performance Ratings and Salary History. Benefits connects to Pension, Life Insurance, and Health Care. Each subordinate segment is the child of the segment directly above it.

for a long time and that continues to be used to avoid the high cost of replacing or redesigning it. Banks, insurance companies, and other high-volume users continue to use reliable hierarchical DBMS, such as IBM's IMS (Information Management System), which was first developed in 1969. As relational products acquire more muscle, firms will shift away completely from hierarchical DBMS, but this will happen over a long period of time.

Object-Oriented Databases

Conventional database management systems were designed for homogeneous data that can be easily structured into predefined data fields and records organized in rows or tables. But many applications today and in the future will require databases that can store and retrieve not only structured numbers and characters, but also drawings, images, photographs, voice, and full-motion video. Conventional DBMS are not well suited to handling graphics-based or multimedia applications. For instance, design data in a computer-aided design (CAD) database consist of complex relationships among many types of data. Manipulating these kinds of data in a relational system requires extensive programming to translate these complex data structures into tables and rows. An **object-oriented DBMS**, however, stores the data and procedures as objects that can be automatically retrieved and shared.

Object-oriented database management systems (OODBMS) are becoming popular because they can be used to manage the various multimedia components or Java applets used in Web applications, which typically integrate pieces of information from a variety of sources. OODBMS are also useful for storing data types, such as recursive data. (An example would be parts within parts as found in manufacturing applications.) Finance and trading applications often use OODBMS because they require data models that must be easy to change to respond to new economic conditions.

Although object-oriented databases can store more complex types of information than relational DBMS, they are relatively slow compared with relational DBMS for processing large numbers of transactions. Hybrid **object-relational DBMS** systems are now available to provide capabilities of both object-oriented and relational DBMS. A hybrid approach can be accomplished in three different ways: by using tools that offer object-oriented access to relational DBMS, by using object-oriented extensions to existing relational DBMS, or by using a hybrid object-relational database management system.

object-oriented DBMS

An approach to data management that stores both data and the procedures acting on the data as objects that can be automatically retrieved and shared; the objects can contain multimedia.

object-relational DBMS

A database management system that combines the capabilities of a relational DBMS and the capabilities of an object-oriented DBMS.

QUERYING DATABASES: ELEMENTS OF SQL

SQL is the principal data manipulation language for relational DBMS and a major tool for querying, reading, and updating a relational database. There are versions of SQL that can run on almost any operating system and computer so that computers are able to exchange data by passing SQL commands to each other. End users and information systems specialists can use SQL as an interactive query language to access data from databases, and SQL commands can also be embedded in application programs written in COBOL, C, and other programming languages.

We now describe the most important basic SQL commands. Convention calls for certain SQL reserved words with special meanings, such as SELECT and FROM, to be capitalized and for SQL statements to be written in multiple lines. Most SQL statements to retrieve data contain the following three clauses:

SELECT   Lists the columns from tables that the user would like to see in a result table

FROM   Identifies the tables or views from which the columns will be selected

WHERE   Includes conditions for selecting specific rows (records) within a single table and conditions for joining multiple tables

The SELECT Statement

The SELECT statement is used to query data from a relational table for specific information. The general form for a SELECT statement that retrieves specified columns for all of the rows in the table is:

SELECT Column_Name, Column_Name,...
FROM Table_Name;

The columns to be obtained are listed after the keyword SELECT and the table to be used is listed after the keyword FROM. Note that column and table names do not have spaces and must be typed as one word or with an underscore and that the statement ends with a semicolon. Review Figure 7.6. Suppose you wanted to see the Part_Number, Part_Description, and Unit_Price for each part in the PART table. You would specify:

SELECT Part_Number, Part_Description, Unit_Price
FROM PART;

Figure 7.9 illustrates the results of your projection.

Conditional Selection

The WHERE clause is used to specify that only certain rows of the table are displayed, based on the criteria described in that WHERE clause. Suppose, for example, you wanted to see the same data, but only for parts in the PART table with unit prices less than $25.00. You would specify:

SELECT Part_Number, Part_Description, Unit_Price
FROM PART
WHERE Unit_Price < 25.00;

Your query would return the results illustrated in Figure 7.10.

Joining Two Tables

Suppose we wanted to obtain information on the names, identification numbers, and addresses of suppliers for each part in the database. We could do this by joining the PART table with the SUPPLIER table and then extracting the required information. The query would look like this:

Figure 7.9 The results of using the SELECT statement to select only the columns Part_Number, Part_Description, and Unit_Price from all rows in the PART table.

Part_ Number	Part_ Description	Unit_ Price
137	Door latch	22.50
145	Door handle	26.25
150	Door seal	6.00
152	Compressor	70.00

Figure 7.10 The results of using a conditional selection to select only parts that meet the condition of having unit prices less than $25.

Part_ Number	Part_ Description	Unit_ Price
137	Door latch	22.50
150	Door seal	6.00

Part_Number	Supplier_Number	Supplier_Name	Supplier_Address
137	4058	CBM Inc.	44 Winslow, Gary, IN 44950
145	2038	Ace Inc.	Rte. 101, Essex, NJ 07763
150	4058	CBM Inc.	44 Winslow, Gary, IN 44950
152	1125	Bryant Corp.	51 Elm, Rochester, NY 11349

Figure 7.11 A projection from joining the PART and SUPPLIER tables.

SELECT PART.Part_Number, SUPPLIER.Supplier_Number,
    SUPPLIER.Supplier_Name, SUPPLIER.Supplier_Address
FROM PART, SUPPLIER
WHERE PART.Supplier_Number = SUPPLIER.Supplier_Number;

The results would look like Figure 7.11. And if we only wanted to see the name, address, and supplier numbers for the suppliers of part numbers 137 or 152, the query would be: S

SELECT PART.Part_Number, SUPPLIER.Supplier_Number,
    SUPPLIER.Supplier_Name, SUPPLIER.Supplier_Address
FROM PART, SUPPLIER
WHERE PART.Supplier_Number = SUPPLIER.Supplier_Number AND
    Part_Number = 137 OR Part_Number = 152;

The results would look like the result of the join operation depicted in Figure 7.7. Note that several conditions can be expressed in the WHERE clause.

7.3 CREATING A DATABASE ENVIRONMENT

In order to create a database environment, one must understand the relationships among the data, the type of data that will be maintained in the database, how the data will be used, and how the organization will need to change to manage data from a company-wide perspective. Increasingly, database design will also have to consider how the organization can share some of its data with its business partners (Jukic, Jukic, and Parameswaran, 2002). We now describe important database design principles and the management and organizational requirements of a database environment.

DESIGNING DATABASES

To create a database, one must go through two design exercises: a conceptual design and a physical design. The conceptual, or logical, design of a database is an abstract model of the database from a business perspective, while the physical design shows how the database is actually arranged on direct access storage devices. Logical design requires a detailed description of the business information needs of the actual end users of the database. Ideally, database design will be part of an overall organizational data planning effort (see Chapter 10).

The conceptual database design describes how the data elements in the database are to be grouped. The design process identifies relationships among data elements and the most efficient way of grouping data elements together to meet information requirements. The process also identifies redundant data elements and the groupings of data elements required for specific application programs. Groups of data are organized, refined, and streamlined until an overall logical view of the relationships among all the data elements in the database emerges.

Database designers document the conceptual data model with an **entity-relationship (ER) diagram**, illustrated in Figure 7.12. The boxes represent entities, and the diamonds represent relationships. The 1 or M on either side of the diamond represents the relationship among entities as either one-to-one, one-to-many, or many-to-many. Figure 7.12 shows that the entity ORDER can have more than one PART, and a PART can only have one SUPPLIER. Many parts can be provided by the same supplier. The attributes for each entity are listed next to the entity, and the key field is underlined.

entity-relationship (ER) diagram

A methodology for documenting databases illustrating the relationship between various entities in the database.

Figure 7.12 An entity-relationship (ER) diagram. This diagram shows the relationships among the entities ORDER, PART, and SUPPLIER that were used to develop the relational database illustrated in Figure 7.6. Observe the notation in the ER diagram. A I means that a part can relate to I order, while the M means that the order may have many parts.

normalization

The process of creating small stable data structures from complex groups of data when designing a relational database.

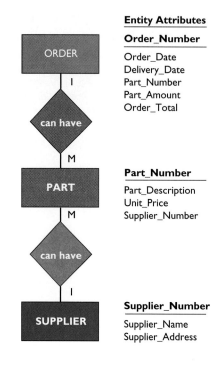

Entity Attributes

Order_Number

Order_Date
Delivery_Date
Part_Number
Part_Amount
Order_Total

Part_Number

Part_Description
Unit_Price
Supplier_Number

Supplier_Number

Supplier_Name
Supplier_Address

To use a relational database model effectively, complex groupings of data must be streamlined to eliminate redundant data elements and awkward many-to-many relationships. The process of creating small, stable data structures from complex groups of data is called **normalization**. Figures 7.13 and 7.14 illustrate this process. In the particular business modelled here, an order can have more than one part, but each part is provided by only one supplier. If we built a relation called ORDER with all the fields included here, we would have to repeat the name, description, and price of each part on the order and the name and address of each part vendor. This relation contains what are called *repeating groups* because there can be many parts and suppliers for each order, and it actually describes multiple entities—parts and suppliers as well as orders. A more efficient way to arrange the data is to break down ORDER into smaller relations, each of which describes a single entity. If we go step by step and normalize the relation ORDER, we emerge with the relations illustrated in Figure 7.14.

If a database has been carefully considered, with a clear understanding of business information needs and usage, the database model will most likely be in some normalized form. Many real-world databases are not fully normalized because this may not be the most sensible way to meet business information requirements. Note that the relational database illustrated in Figure 7.6 is not fully normalized because there could be more than one part for each order. The designers chose to not use the four relations described in Figure 7.14 because most of the orders handled by this particular business are only for one part. The designers might have felt that for this particular business, it was inefficient to maintain four different tables.

Figure 7.13 An unnormalized relation for ORDER. In an unnormalized relation, there are repeating groups. For example, there can be many parts and suppliers for each order. There is only a one-to-one correspondence among Order_Number and Order_Date, Order_Total, and Delivery_Date.

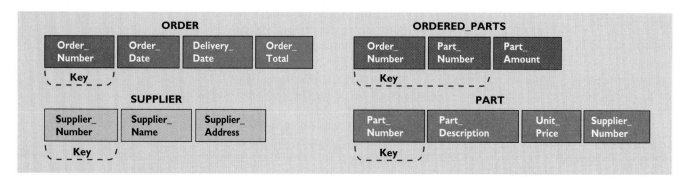

Figure 7.14 A normalized relation for ORDER. After normalization, the original relation ORDER has been broken down into four smaller relations. The relation ORDER is left with only three attributes, and the relation ORDERED_PARTS has a combined, or concatenated, key consisting of Order_Number and Part_Number.

DISTRIBUTING DATABASES

Database design also considers how the data are to be distributed. Information systems can be designed with a centralized database that is used by a single central processor or by multiple processors in a client-server network. Alternatively, the database can be distributed. A **distributed database** is one that is stored in more than one physical location. Parts of the database are stored physically in one location, and other parts are stored and maintained in other locations. There are two main ways of distributing a database (see Figure 7.15). The central database can be partitioned (see Figure 7.15a) so that each remote processor has the necessary data to serve its local area. Changes in local files can be justified with the central database on a batch basis, often at night. Another strategy is to replicate the central database (Figure 7.15b) at all remote locations. For example, Lufthansa Airlines replaced its centralized mainframe database with a replicated database to make information more immediately available to flight dispatchers. Any change made to Lufthansa's Frankfurt DBMS is automatically replicated in New York and Hong Kong. This strategy also requires updating of the central database during "off" hours.

Distributed systems reduce the vulnerability of a single, massive central site. They increase service and responsiveness to local users and often can run on smaller, less expensive computers. Distributed systems, however, are dependent on high-quality telecommunications lines, which themselves are vulnerable. Moreover, local databases can sometimes depart from central data standards and definitions, and they pose security problems by widely distributing access to sensitive data. Database designers need to weigh these factors in their decisions.

MANAGEMENT REQUIREMENTS FOR DBMS

Much more is required for the development of DBMS than simply selecting a logical database model. A database is an organizational discipline or a method, rather than a tool or technology. It requires organizational and conceptual change. Without management support and understanding, database efforts fail. The critical elements in a database environment are (1) data administration, (2) data planning and modelling methodology, (3) database technology and management, and (4) users. This environment is depicted in Figure 7.16.

Data Administration

Database systems require the organization to recognize the strategic role of information and to begin actively to manage and plan for information as a corporate resource. This means that the organization must develop a **data administration** function with the power to define information requirements for the entire company and with direct access to senior management. The chief information officer (CIO) or vice-president of information becomes the primary advocate for database systems in the organization.

Data administration is responsible for the specific policies and procedures through which data can be managed as an organizational resource. These responsibilities include developing

distributed database
A database that is stored in more than one physical location. Parts or copies of the database are physically stored in one location, and other parts or copies are stored and maintained in other locations.

data administration
A special organizational function for managing the organization's data resources, concerned with information policy, data planning, maintenance of data dictionaries, and data quality standards.

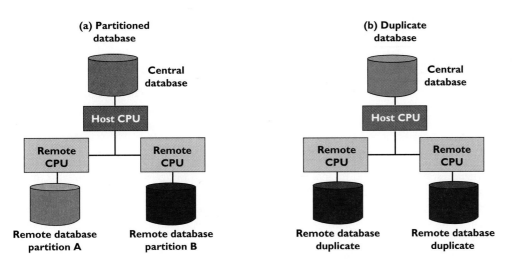

Figure 7.15 Distributed databases. There are alternative ways of distributing a database. The central database can be partitioned (a) so that each remote processor has the necessary data to serve its own local needs. The central database also can be duplicated (b) at all remote locations.

Figure 7.16 Key organizational elements in the database environment. For a database management system to flourish in any organization, data administration functions and data planning and modelling methodologies must be coordinated with database technology and management. Resources must be devoted to train end users to use databases properly.

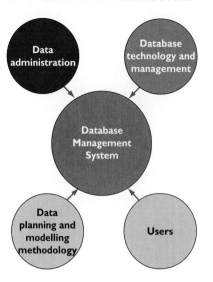

information policy

Formal rules governing the maintenance, distribution, and use of information in an organization.

information policy, planning for data, overseeing logical database design and data dictionary development, and monitoring how information system specialists and end-user groups use data.

The fundamental principle of data administration is that all data are the property of the organization as a whole. Data cannot belong exclusively to any one business area or organizational unit. All data are to be made available to any group that requires them to fulfill its mission. An organization needs to formulate an **information policy** that specifies its rules for sharing, disseminating, acquiring, standardizing, classifying, and inventorying information throughout the organization. Information policy lays out specific procedures and accountabilities, specifying which organizational units share what information, where specific information can be distributed, and who has responsibility for updating and maintaining specific information. Although data administration is a very important organizational function, it has proved very challenging to implement.

Data Planning and Modelling Methodology

The organizational interests served by the DBMS are much broader than those in the traditional file environment; therefore, the organization requires enterprise-wide planning for data. Enterprise analysis, which addresses the information requirements of the entire organization (as opposed to the requirements of individual applications), is needed to develop databases. The purpose of enterprise analysis is to identify the key entities, attributes, and relationships that constitute the organization's data. These techniques are described in greater detail in Chapter 10.

Database Technology, Management, and Users

Databases require new software and staff specially trained in DBMS techniques, as well as new data management structures. Most corporations develop a database design and management group within the corporate information system division that is responsible for defining and organizing the structure and content of their databases and maintaining their databases. In close cooperation with users, the design group establishes the physical database, the logical relations among elements, and the access rules and procedures. The functions it performs are called **database administration.**

A database serves a wider community of users than traditional systems. Relational systems with fourth-generation query languages permit employees who are not computer specialists to access and query large databases. In addition, users include trained computer specialists. To optimize access for nonspecialists, more resources must be devoted to training end users.

database administration

Refers to the more technical and operational aspects of managing data, including physical database design and maintenance.

7.4 DATABASE TRENDS

Organizations are installing powerful data analysis tools and data warehouses to make better use of the information stored in their databases and are taking advantage of database technology linked to the World Wide Web. We now explore these developments.

MULTIDIMENSIONAL DATA ANALYSIS

Sometimes, managers need to analyze data in ways that traditional database models cannot represent. For example, a company selling four different products-nuts, bolts, washers, and screws—in the east, west, and central regions might want to know actual sales by product for each region and might also want to compare them with projected sales. This analysis requires a multidimensional view of data.

To provide this type of information, organizations can use either a specialized multidimensional database or a tool that creates multidimensional views of data in relational databases.

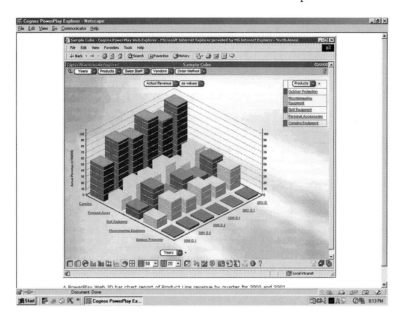

Figure 7.17 Online analytical processing (OLAP) gives users quick, unlimited views of multiple relationships in large quantities of data. This report from Cognos' PowerPlay application shows revenue for multiple product lines by quarter for 2000 and 2001.

Multidimensional analysis enables users to view the same data in different ways using multiple dimensions. Each aspect of information—product, pricing, cost, region, or time period—represents a different dimension. So, a product manager could use a multidimensional data analysis tool to learn how many washers were sold in the east in June, how that compares with the previous month and the previous June, and how it compares with the sales forecast. Another term for multidimensional data analysis is **online analytical processing (OLAP)** (see Figure 7.17).

online analytical processing (OLAP)

Capability for manipulating and analyzing large volumes of data from multiple perspectives.

Figure 7.18 shows a multidimensional model that could be created to represent products, regions, actual sales, and projected sales. A matrix of actual sales can be stacked on top of a matrix of projected sales to form a cube with six faces. If you rotate the cube 90 degrees one way, the face showing will be product versus actual and projected sales. If you rotate the cube 90 degrees again, you can see region versus actual and projected sales. If you rotate 180 degrees from the original view, you can see projected sales and product versus region. Cubes can be nested within cubes to build complex views of data.

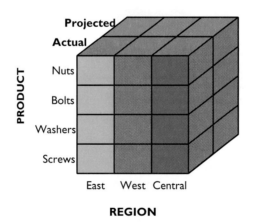

Figure 7.18 Multidimensional data model. The view that is showing is product versus region. If you rotate the cube 90 degrees, the face that will be showing is product versus actual and projected sales. If you rotate the cube 90 degrees again, you can see region versus actual and projected sales. Other views are possible. The ability to rotate the data cube is the main technique for multidimensional reporting. It is sometimes called "slice and dice."

DATA WAREHOUSES AND DATAMINING

Decision makers need concise, reliable information about current operations, trends, and changes. What has been immediately available at most firms is current data only (historical data were available through special information systems reports that took a long time to produce). Data often are fragmented in separate operational systems, such as sales or payroll, so that different managers make decisions from incomplete knowledge bases. Users and information systems specialists may have to spend inordinate amounts of time locating and gathering data (Watson and Haley, 1998). Data warehousing addresses this problem by integrating key operational data from around the company in a form that is consistent, reliable, and easily available for reporting.

What Is a Data Warehouse?

A **data warehouse** is a database that stores current and historical data of potential interest to managers throughout the company. Usually, this involves massive amounts of data. The data originate in many core operational systems and external sources, including Web site transactions, each with different data models. They may include legacy systems, relational or object-oriented DBMS

data warehouse

A database, with reporting and query tools, that stores current and historical data extracted from various operational systems and consolidated for management reporting and analysis.

applications, and systems based on HTML or XML documents. The data from these diverse applications are copied into the data warehouse database as often as needed—hourly, daily, weekly, or monthly. The data are standardized into a common data model and consolidated so that they can be used across the enterprise for management analysis and decision making. The data are available for anyone with authorization to access as needed but cannot be altered.

Figure 7.19 illustrates the data warehouse concept. The data warehouse must be carefully designed by both business and technical specialists to make sure it can provide the right information for critical business decisions. The firm may need to change its business processes to benefit from the information in the warehouse (Cooper, Watson, Wixom, and Goodhue, 2000). The Manager's Toolkit describes how to conduct a business analysis that addresses these issues.

Companies can build enterprise-wide data warehouses where a central data warehouse serves the entire organization, or they can create smaller, decentralized warehouses called data marts. A **data mart** is a subset of a data warehouse, in which a summarized or highly focused portion of the organization's data is placed in a separate database for a specific population of users. For example, a company might develop marketing and sales data marts to deal with customer information. A data mart typically focuses on a single subject area or line of

data mart

A small data warehouse containing only a portion of the organization's data for a specified function or population of users.

Figure 7.19 Components of a data warehouse. A data warehouse extracts current and historical data from operational systems inside the organization. These data are combined with data from external sources and reorganized into a central database designed for management reporting and analysis. The information directory provides users with information about the data available in the warehouse.

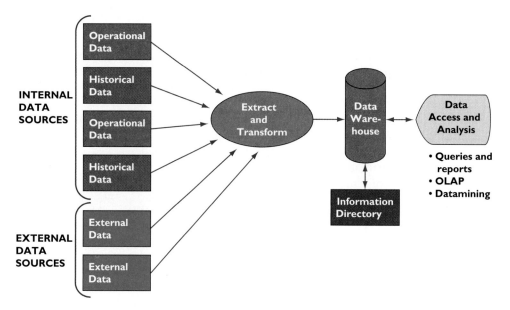

MIS IN ACTION: MANAGER'S TOOLKIT

HOW TO MAKE A DATA WAREHOUSE SERVE THE BUSINESS
The first steps in building a data warehouse involve conducting a thorough business analysis of the information requirements that could be satisfied by a data warehouse. Here are some of the questions managers should ask:

1. *Users:* Who are the primary users of the data warehouse? What levels of the organization and business functions do they represent?
2. *Ownership:* What organizational group or groups own the data? Who is responsible for maintaining the data? Who is authorized to access the data?
3. *Information requirements:* What types of reports should the data warehouse provide? What pieces of data are used in these reports? Do these reports require the data to be detailed or summarized?
4. *Data sources:* What are the sources of data required by the reports? Which pieces come from internal TPS and other systems? Which come from sources outside the company? How can the company obtain the data for these reports?

5. *Currency:* How often do the data in the warehouse need to be updated? How long should historical data in the warehouse be maintained?
6. *Data standards:* Applications that were designed to support different functions or organizational units may use the same term in different ways. These discrepancies must be identified so that each data element is defined and used the same way in the data warehouse system. Does everyone agree on how each piece of data is defined and used?
7. *Quality expectations:* What level of accuracy and completeness of the data in the warehouse is sufficient to meet business needs?
8. *Benefits:* Precisely what are the business benefits of building this data warehouse? To what extent can these benefits be quantified? Are the benefits greater than the costs? (See Chapter 12)
9. *Business process change:* Does the company need to change its business processes in order to use the information from the data warehouse effectively? How much change is required?

business, so it usually can be constructed more rapidly and at lower cost than an enterprise-wide data warehouse. However, complexity, costs, and management problems will arise if an organization creates too many data marts.

Datamining

A data warehouse system provides a range of ad hoc and standardized query tools, analytical tools, and graphical reporting facilities, including tools for OLAP and datamining. **Datamining** uses a variety of techniques to find hidden patterns and relationships in large pools of data and infer rules from them that can be used to predict future behaviour and to guide decision making (Fayyad et al., 2002; Hirji, 2001). Datamining is often used to provide information for targeted marketing where personalized or individualized messages can be created on the basis of individual preferences. There are many other datamining applications in both business and scientific work. These systems can perform high-level analyses of patterns or trends, but they can also drill into more detail where needed. Table 7.1 describes how some organizations are benefiting from datamining, and Chapters 13 and 14 provide more detail on how datamining is being used to guide business decision making.

> **datamining**
> Analysis of large pools of data to find patterns and rules that can be used to guide decision making and predict future behaviour.

Datamining is a tool that is both powerful and profitable, but it poses challenges to the protection of individual privacy. Datamining technology can combine information from many diverse sources to create a detailed "data image" about each of us—our income, our driving habits, our hobbies, our families, and our political interests. The question of whether companies should be allowed to collect this amount of detailed information about individuals is explored in Chapter 5.

 Additional material on datamining (prepared by Francisco B.P. Moro at the University of Windsor) can be found on the Companion Website at www.pearsoned.ca/laudon.

Benefits of Data Warehouses

Data warehouses not only offer improved information, but they also make it easy for decision makers to obtain it. They even include the ability to model and remodel the data. It has been estimated that 70 percent of the world's business information resides on mainframe databases, many of which are for older legacy systems. Many of these legacy systems are critical production applications that support the company's core business processes. As long as these systems can efficiently process the necessary volume of transactions to keep the company running, firms are reluctant to replace them to avoid disrupting critical business functions and high system replacement costs. Many of these legacy systems use hierarchical DBMS or even older non-database files, where information is difficult for users to access. Data warehouses enable decision makers to access data as often as they need to, without affecting the performance of the underlying operational systems. Many organizations are making access to their data warehouses even easier by using Web technology.

TABLE 7.1	**HOW BUSINESSES ARE USING DATAMINING**
Organization	**Datamining Application**
Disco S.A.	Argentine supermarket chain uses datamining to analyze purchasing patterns of more than 1.5 million customers who participate in a frequent-buyer program in over 200 stores.
Bank of Montreal	Analyzes delivery costs and helps to pinpoint inefficiencies so that the bank can support additional channels of electronic delivery while lowering costs.
WorkCover Authority	The New South Wales, Australia, authority, which manages workplace injury management and workers' compensation programs, uses data mining to identify employees making inaccurate insurance premium payments and to cut down on illegitimate insurance claims.
Royal Bank of Canada	Analyzes the financial performance of the company's portfolio of products.
Toronto Police Services	Permits police staff to search for and share information on the road or at the station.

Figure 7.20 A hypermedia database. In a hypermedia database, the user can choose his or her own path to move from node to node. Each node can contain text, graphics, sound, full-motion video, or executable programs.

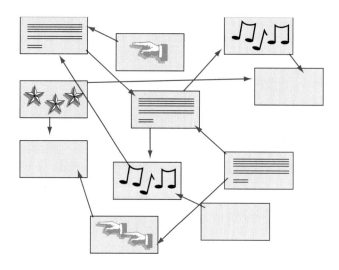

Databases and the Web

Database technology plays an important role in making organizations' information resources available on the World Wide Web. We now explore the role of hypermedia databases on the Web and the growing use of Web sites to access information stored in conventional databases inside the firm.

The Web and Hypermedia Databases

Web sites store information as interconnected pages containing text, sound, video, and graphics using a hypermedia database. The **hypermedia database** approach to information management stores chunks of information in the form of nodes connected by links that the user specifies (see Figure 7.20). The nodes can contain text, graphics, sound, full-motion video, hypermedia links to Web sites, or executable computer programs. Searching for information does not have to follow a predetermined organization scheme. Instead, one can branch instantly to related information in any kind of relationship the Web site author has established. The relationship between records is less structured than in a traditional DBMS.

The hypermedia database approach enables users to access topics in a Web site in whatever order they wish. For instance, from the Web page from Environment Canada illustrated in Figure 7.21, one can branch to other Web pages by clicking on the topics highlighted in blue above the Canadian map or by clicking on HOME, Topics, Publications, What's New, or Weather at the top of the page. We provide more detail on these and other features of Web sites in Chapter 9.

Linking Internal Databases to the Web

Middleware and other software products have been developed to help users gain access to organizations' legacy data via the Web. Refer to our brief discussion of n-tier architecture in Chapter 6. Middleware is the second tier in a three-tier architecture that permits a user using one system and type of database to obtain data from a different type of system or database. For example, a customer with a Web browser might want to search an online retailer's database for pricing information. Figure 7.22 illustrates how that customer might access the retailer's internal databases via the Web. The user would access the retailer's Web site over the Internet using Web browser software on his or her client PC. The user's Web browser software would request data from the organization's databases, using the Web server to transmit the request. Because many backend databases cannot interpret commands written in HTML, the Web server would pass these requests for data to special middleware software that would translate the requests into SQL so that they could be processed by the DBMS working with the database. In a client-server environment, the DBMS often resides on a special dedicated computer called a **database server**. The DBMS receives the SQL requests and provides the required

---

hypermedia database

An approach to data management that organizes data as a network of nodes linked in any pattern the user specifies; the nodes can contain text, graphics, sound, full-motion video, or executable programs.

---

database server

A computer in a client-server environment that is responsible for running a DBMS to process SQL statements and perform database management tasks.

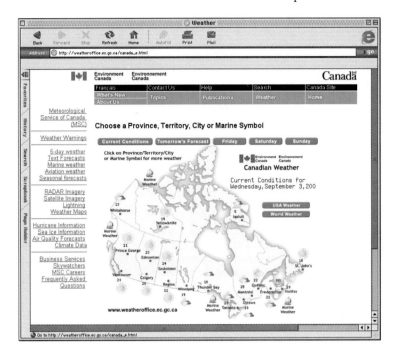

Figure 7.21 From Environment Canada's home Web page, you can branch to other Web pages by clicking on the topics highlighted in blue or by clicking on the options listed on the right side of the Canadian map. Web sites store information as interconnected pages containing text, sound, graphics, and video using a hypermedia approach to data management.

data. The middleware would transfer information from the organization's internal database back to the Web server for delivery in the form of a Web page to the user.

Figure 7.22 shows that the software working between the Web server and the DBMS could be an application server, a custom program, or a series of software scripts. An **application server** is a software program that handles all application operations, including transaction processing and data access, between browser-based computers and a company's backend business applications or databases. The application server takes requests from the Web server, runs the business logic to process transactions on the basis of those requests, and provides connectivity to the organization's backend systems or databases. *Common Gateway Interface (CGI)* is a specification for transferring information between a Web server and a program designed to accept and return data. The program could be written in any programming language, including C, Perl, Java, and Visual Basic.

There are a number of advantages to using the Web to access an organization's internal databases. Web browser software is extremely easy to use, requiring much less training than even user-friendly database query tools. The Web interface requires no changes to the internal database. Companies leverage their investments in older systems because it costs much less to add a Web interface in front of a legacy system than to redesign and rebuild the system to improve user access (see Figure 7.23).

Accessing corporate databases via the Web is creating new efficiencies and opportunities, in some cases even changing the way business is being done. Some companies have created new businesses based on access to large databases via the Web. Others are using Web technology to provide employees with integrated firm-wide views of information. The major enterprise system

application server

Software that handles all application operations between browser-based computers and a company's backend business applications or databases.

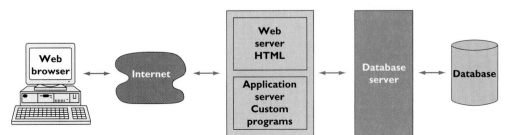

Figure 7.22 Linking internal databases to the Web. Users can access an organization's internal databases through the Web using their desktop PCs and Web browser software.

Figure 7.23 Statistics Canada's Web site (**www.statcan.ca**) links to a huge archival database of statistics, publications, and lists and links to other statistical databases, such as the U.S. Census Bureau. More and more organizations are using the Web to provide an interface to internal databases.

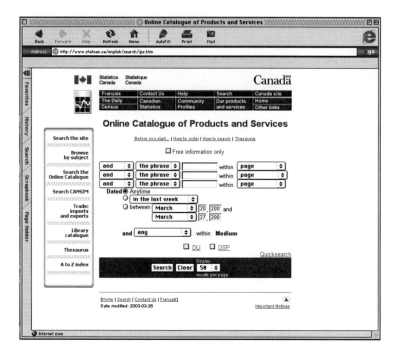

vendors have enhanced their software so that users can access enterprise data through a Web interface. Table 7.2 describes some of these applications of Web-enabled databases.

Database technology has provided many organizational benefits, but it allows businesses and government agencies to maintain large databases with detailed personal information that pose a threat to individual privacy. The Window on Organizations describes some privacy issues raised by public motor vehicle databases that are used by businesses for marketing and other purposes.

TABLE 7.2   EXAMPLES OF WEB-ENABLED DATABASES

Organization	Use of Web-Enabled Database
Thomas Register Advanced Order Online (http://www.thomasregister.com)	Web site links to Thomas' database of more than 170 000 companies, 400 000 products, thousands of product catalogues, and millions of CAD drawings searchable by product, part number, or brand name. Visitors can search for products, view a company's catalogue, request price quotes, make purchases online using a credit card or company purchasing card, and track orders.
IGo.com	Web site is linked to a giant relational database housing information about batteries and peripherals for computers and other portable electronic devices. Visitors can immediately find online information about each electronic device and the batteries and parts it uses and place orders for these parts over the Web.
Mount Sinai Hospital's Micro Web (http://microbiology.mtsinai.on.ca/search.shtml)	Toronto hospital's Microbiology Department's Web site links to a database, which catalogues a variety of data about many bacteria and viruses. Visitors can search the database for statistics about the incidence of viruses and see the latest news about current outbreaks.
Strategis Canada (http://strategis.ic.gc.ca)	Industry Canada's business database portal links to statistics and information about a wide variety of Canadian companies based on criteria selected by the user, such as Aboriginal businesses, aftermarket exporters, or sporting and recreational goods companies.

PUBLIC DATABASES FOR SALE: BOON TO BUSINESS OR THREAT TO PRIVACY?

If you look under the legal age for drinking or smoking, you may have used your driver's licence to prove your age before buying cigarettes or liquor or to see some movies. However, you probably do not realize that all the information contained on your licence can be used by others without your approval. Your licence may carry your birth date, name, address, an identification number, driving restrictions, gender, eye colour, height, and social insurance number. Most licences even include your photograph. Scanners can now be used to check that data. Bars and liquor stores can scan your licence to verify your age. Hospitals can scan that information for their records, while airports and government buildings can scan drivers' licences or passports to identify suspected terrorists or criminals. Many of those scanners not only check the needed data but also store that data on a database, where it becomes useful for other purposes.

The National Law Enforcement Telecommunications System, an American system that can be accessed by Interpol and Canadian police authorities, can be searched for drivers' licence data by the licence number in all provinces and by name and date of birth in Ontario, British Columbia, Quebec, and Alberta. As Paul Barclay, the owner of The Rack, a popular Boston bar that scans licences, says, "It's not just an ID check. It's a tool." For example, police departments sometimes call bars to find out if someone on their lists is at their establishments. Bars may use the data to give special treatment to repeat customers. Some users of these scanners sell their information to companies for use in marketing.

In a different industry, Experian, a unit of London-based Great Universal Stores (GUS) PLC, is one of the largest credit reporting agencies in North America. Experian Automotive united with AutoCheck, LLC, to create the biggest and most sweeping vehicle report system now obtainable. It offers original equipment manufacturers (OEMs), dealers, consumers, and marketing agencies expansive serious damage history data. Experian Automotive Auto History vehicle history reports will be replaced by this new entity, AutoCheck by Experian Automotive (SM).

AutoCheck has a significant edge over its competitors: it's the only such service that gets many different sources of information on vehicles, so it can offer excellent damage history information. Because of this, AutoCheck has discovered many vehicles with a history of damage that were not found by state or provincial reporting requirements. According to AutoCheck vice-president Steve DeMedicis, the company does over 900 000 vehicle history reports every month. This makes it the biggest purveyor of its sort.

Experian's database of 65 terabytes of data is the 10th largest in the world. Experian receives data in 175 different for-

mats from a wide variety of sources. Experian transforms all of the data into a DB2 format, using UTI Extract software from Evolutionary Technologies. The database processes millions of transactions per month. For a per-query fee, Experian can make available on the Web the ownership history for any vehicle bought or sold in Canada or the United States. The company's clients can access the database via the Internet (www.autocheck.com), where they can discover a vehicle's history and value. To gather a variety of information, including vehicle specifications, odometer problems, and potential fraud, clients need only type in a vehicle identification number (VIN).

Close to 400 vehicle auctions in North America use Experian's AutoCheck; this includes 95 percent of independent vehicle auctions. AutoCheck has been playing this role in the used vehicle re-sale industry for over a decade. Their vehicle history reports entail a full and complete measure, helping buoy general public confidence in used car sales. The company examines over 240 000 VINs each week.

Even census data can affect the way you will be treated when you apply for a mortgage. Information on the costs of running a home is used by Canada Mortgage and Housing Corporation in their mortgage insurance program and by banks that can access the census data in their mortgage practices to fine-tune lending criteria and rate policies.

Privacy advocates worry that the unregulated use of public databases allows personal information to be used in ways that the owners have not authorized. The *Personal Information Protection and Electronic Documents Act* of Canada has loopholes regarding publicly available data that could permit driver's licence data to be used for marketing, tracking, or sales purposes—without the knowledge or consent of the driver. Some experts feel that if a person gives his or her driver's licence number when filling out a form, there is an assumption that the data can then be used for any purpose the owner of the form (a vendor, retailer, and so on) wishes. On the form, there may even be a statement to that effect, usually in very fine print. Simply by filling out and turning in the form, the person has given permission for his or her data to be used.

To Think About: Considering these examples along with your own views on regulating the use of public databases, argue in support of the unregulated use of these databases, and then argue in support of those who believe their unregulated use is a violation of an individual's privacy.

Sources: Pimm Fox, "Extracting Dollars from Data," *ComputerWorld*, April 15, 2002; Jennifer B. Lee, "Welcome to the Database Lounge," *New York Times*, March 21, 2002; "The Canadian Interface," available **www.nlets.org/canada.htm**, accessed March 28, 2003; "Experian Automotive, AutoCheck Join Forces," available **www.creditcollectionsworld.com/industry/011702_1.htm**, January 17, 2002.

MANAGEMENT WRAP-UP

Selecting an appropriate data model and data management technology for the organization is a key management decision. Managers will need to evaluate the costs and benefits of implementing a database environment and the capabilities of various DBMS or file management technologies. Management should ascertain that organizational databases are designed to meet management information objectives and the organization's business needs.

The organization's data model should reflect its key business processes and decision-making requirements. Data planning should be performed to make sure that the organization's data model delivers information efficiently for its business processes and enhances organizational performance. Designing a database is an organizational endeavour.

Multiple database and file management options are available for organizing and storing information. Key technology decisions should consider the efficiency of accessing information, flexibility in organizing information, the type of information to be stored and arranged, compatibility with the organization's data model, and compatibility with the organization's hardware and operating systems.

For Discussion

1. It has been said that you do not need database management software to create a database environment. Discuss this view.

2. To what extent should end users be involved in the selection of a database management system and database design?

SUMMARY

1. *Why do businesses have trouble finding the information they need in their information systems?* A computer system organizes data in a hierarchy that starts with bits and bytes and progresses to fields, records, files, and databases. Traditional file management techniques make it difficult for organizations to keep track of all of the pieces of data they use in a systematic way or to organize these data so that they can be easily accessed. Different functional areas and groups were allowed to develop their own files independently. Over time, this traditional file environment creates such problems as data redundancy and inconsistency, program-data dependence, inflexibility, poor security, and lack of data sharing and availability.

2. *How does a database management system help businesses improve the organization of their information?* A database management system (DBMS) consists of software that permits centralization of data and data management so that businesses have a single consistent source for all of their their data needs. A single database services multiple applications. A DBMS includes a data definition language, a data manipulation language, and data dictionary capability. The most important feature of the DBMS is its ability to separate the logical and physical views of data.

The user works with a logical view of data. The DBMS retrieves information so that the user does not have to be concerned with its physical location.

3. *How do the principal types of database models affect the way businesses can access and use their information?* The principal types of databases today are relational DBMS and object-oriented DBMS. Relational DBMS are very flexible for supporting ad-hoc requests for information and for combining information from different sources. This flexibility was not possible with the older hierarchical database models. Object-oriented DBMS can store graphics and other types of data in addition to conventional text data to support multimedia applications. Organizations should use the DBMS that is best suited to their needs.

Designing a database requires both a logical design and a physical design. Databases should be normalized to create small, stable data structures. Database design also considers whether a complete database or portions of the database can be distributed to more than one location to increase responsiveness and reduce vulnerability and costs through replicated or partitioned databases.

4. *What are the management and organizational requirements of a database environment?* Developing a database environment

requires much more than selecting database technology. It requires a formal information policy governing the maintenance, distribution, and use of information in the organization. The organization must also develop a data administration function and a data planning methodology. There is political resistance in organizations to many key database concepts, especially to sharing of information that has been controlled exclusively by one organizational group, so database administration is also needed to overcome this type of resistance.

5. *What new tools and technologies can make databases more accessible and useful?* There are powerful tools available to analyze the information in databases and to take advantage of the information resources on the World Wide Web. Multidimensional data analysis, also known as online analytical processing (OLAP), can represent relationships among data as a multidimensional structure, which can be visualized as cubes of data and cubes within cubes of data, allowing for more sophisticated data analysis. Data can be more conveniently analyzed across the enterprise by using a data warehouse and by datamining to find patterns and rules that can be used to predict future behaviour and to guide decision making. Hypermedia databases allow data to be stored in nodes linked together in any pattern the Web author establishes and are used for storing information at Web sites. Conventional databases can be linked to the Web to facilitate user access to an organization's internal data.

KEY TERMS

Application server, 249	Database, 231	Field, 231	Online analytical processing (OLAP), 245
Attribute, 231	Database (rigorous definition), 233	File, 231	Physical view, 234
Data administration, 243	Database administration, 244	Hierarchical DBMS, 237	Program-data dependence, 232
Data definition language, 234	Database management system (DBMS), 233	Hypermedia database, 248	Record, 231
Data dictionary, 234	Database server, 248	Information policy, 244	Relational DBMS, 235
Data element, 234	Datamining, 247	Key field, 231	Structured Query Language (SQL), 234
Data manipulation language, 234	Distributed database, 243	Legacy system, 237	Tuple, 235
Data mart, 246	Entity, 231	Logical view, 234	
Data redundancy, 232	Entity-relationship (ER) diagram, 241	Normalization, 242	
Data warehouse, 245		Object-oriented DBMS, 239	
		Object-relational DBMS, 239	

REVIEW QUESTIONS

1. Why is file management important for overall system performance?

2. List and describe each of the components in the data hierarchy.

3. Define and explain the significance of entities, attributes, and key fields.

4. List and describe some of the problems of the traditional file environment.

5. Define the terms database and database management system.

6. Name and briefly describe the three components of a DBMS.

7. What is the difference between logical and physical views of data?

8. List some benefits of a DBMS.

9. Describe the principal types of databases and the advantages and disadvantages of each.

10. Name and describe the three most important SQL commands.

11. What is normalization? How is it related to the features of a well-designed relational database?

12. What is a distributed database, and what are the two main ways of distributing data?

13. What are the four key organizational elements of a database environment? Describe each briefly.

14. Describe the capabilities of online analytical processing (OLAP) and datamining.

15. What is a data warehouse? How can it benefit organizations?

16. What is a hypermedia database? How does it differ from a traditional database? How is it used for the Web?

17. How can users access information from a company's internal databases via the Web?

APPLICATION SOFTWARE EXERCISE

DATABASE EXERCISE: BUILDING A RELATIONAL DATABASE FOR A SMALL BUSINESS

Sylvester's Bike Shop, located in Vancouver, British Columbia, sells road, mountain, hybrid, leisure, and children's bicycles. Currently, Sylvester's purchases bikes from three suppliers but plans to add new suppliers in the near future. This rapidly growing business needs a database management system to manage its information.

Initially, the database should house information about suppliers and products. The database will contain two tables: a supplier table and a product table. The reorder level refers to the number of items in inventory that triggers a decision to order more items to prevent a stockout. (In other words, if the number of units of a particular product in inventory falls below the reorder level, the item should be reordered.) The user should be able to perform several queries and produce several managerial reports on the basis of the data contained in the two tables.

Using the information found in the tables on our Web site for Chapter 7, build a simple relational database for Sylvester's. Once you have built the database, perform the following activities.

1. Prepare a report that identifies the five most expensive bicycles. The report should list the bicycles in descending order from most expensive to least expensive, the quantity on hand for each, and the markup percentage for each.

2. Prepare a report that lists each supplier, its products, quantity on hand, and associated reorder levels. The report should be sorted alphabetically by supplier. Within each supplier category, the products should be sorted alphabetically.

3. Prepare a report listing only the bicycles that are low in stock and need to be reordered. The report should provide supplier information for the items identified.

4. Write a brief description of how the database could be enhanced to further improve management of the business. What tables or fields should be added? What additional reports would be useful?

GROUP PROJECT

Review Figure 7.4, which provides an overview of a human resources database. Some additional information that might be maintained in such a database are an employee's date of hire, date of termination, number of children, date of birth, educational level, gender code, year-to-date gross pay and net pay, amount of life insurance coverage, life insurance plan payroll-deduction amount, and pension plan payroll-deduction amount.

Form a group with three or four of your classmates. Prepare two sample reports using the data in the database that might be of interest to either the employer or the employee. What pieces of information should be included in each report? In addition, prepare a data dictionary entry for one of the data elements in the database similar to the entry illustrated in Figure 7.5.

Your group's analysis should determine what business functions use this data element, which function has the primary responsibility for maintaining the data element, and which positions in the organization can access that data element. If possible, use electronic presentation software to present your findings to the class.

 ## INTERNET TOOLS

COMPANION WEBSITE

The Internet Connection for this chapter will direct you to a series of Web sites where you can complete an exercise to evaluate various commercial database management system products.

At www.pearsoned.ca/laudon, you will find valuable tools to facilitate and enhance your learning of this chapter as well as opportunities to apply your knowledge to realistic situations:

- An Interactive Study Guide of self-test questions that will provide you with immediate feedback.
- Application exercises.
- An Electronic Commerce Project for setting up a business in Australia that requires searches of online databases.

- A Management Decision Problem on developing company-wide data standards.
- Updates of material in the chapter.
- Additional material on datamining (prepared by Francisco B.P. Moro at the University of Windsor) can be found on the Companion Website at www.pearsoned.ca/laudon.

ADDITIONAL SITES OF INTEREST

There are many interesting Web sites to enhance your learning about database software. You can search the Web yourself or just try the following sites to add to what you have already learned.

Oracle Corporation
www.oracle.ca

The Canadian arm of one of the world's major database/ERP companies.

Microsoft Office
www.Microsoft.com/office/access

Home Web site of MS Access, the most popular desktop database software.

IBM's DB2
http://www-3.ibm.com/software/data/

Publisher of DB2, the most popular mainframe database software.

CASE STUDY: *Cognos Gives Businesses Intelligence*

Cognos is a market leader in business intelligence (BI) and performance planning software for enterprises. Cognos products cover corporate performance management, or enterprise planning, scorecarding, and business intelligence.

Founded in 1969 in Ottawa, Cognos employs more than 2900 people and has more than 22 000 customers in over 135 countries. Cognos' customers are involved in just about every industry, including automotive, banking, insurance, energy, natural resources, government, healthcare, manufacturing, and pharmaceuticals. Cognos' BI software is used by 80 percent of the Fortune 1000 companies.

What are the results of using Cognos? Shell Oil saved an estimated $210 million by focusing on customer profitability and retention. Restaurant franchise Red Robin saves $15 000 weekly—just in Alfredo sauce. Sesame Street Workshop knows just how many Elmo dolls it will sell. All of this happens because these companies have access to business intelligence by using Cognos data analysis tools.

These tools can only be as effective as the data management platforms from which they draw their information and to which they provide vital added value. An effective BI solution must be supported by a robust, reliable, flexible database that can make information easily accessible, available, and secure. That simple fact, says Rupert Bonham-Carter, director of data warehousing alliances at Cognos, is the reason that Cognos integrates its BI solutions with DB2 data management software from IBM.

DB2 is the leader in database management systems for enterprises. A product of IBM, DB2 has been around for a long time. Originally designed for IBM mainframe architectures, DB2 is now available for almost every platform, including Windows-based PCs. Cognos uses the data to develop business intelligence solutions. They support DB2 because that is what their customers require. The DB2 Universal Database is reliable, robust, and provides unsurpassed performance, according to Bonham-Carter. "By supporting the DB2 data management software family, we have succeeded in attracting and retaining a huge customer base, thereby increasing our sales and revenues and consolidating our market share."

Cognos also supports other platforms, such as leading ERP systems by J.D. Edwards and SAP, many of which run on DB2. Cognos is constantly looking for technology partners, such as

Microsoft, Hewlett-Packard, and Onyx Software, to expand its platform base, thereby expanding its customer base. A typical Cognos-DB2 solution includes components from the Cognos Series 7 suite, which brings together a broad range of BI capabilities, all of which rely on Cognos' ability to datamine:

- Managed reporting—enabling report creation from any data source, for consistent, fact-based decision making
- Analysis—online analytical processing (OLAP), enabling users to explore large volumes of summarized data in a variety of formats, with subsecond response times
- Ad hoc query—enabling novice and experienced users to directly access corporate data resources for real-time data exploration
- Scorecarding—establishing metrics that measure how well the organization is achieving its strategy and using those metrics for information and management decision making
- Visualization—allowing users to view and analyze complex data in graphical formats, including dashboard-style layouts, geographical maps, simple pie or bar graphs, or 3-D graphs with navigational capabilities
- Event detection—automatically delivering time-critical BI to decision makers through e-mail and wireless technologies, enabling them to focus quickly on what needs immediate attention
- Extraction, Transformation, and Load (ETL)—enabling decision makers to extract and unite data from disparate sources and deliver coordinated business intelligence across the organization

Cognos software "slices and dices" data into multidimensional views that permit managers to visualize exactly what is going on in their data, to transform that data from raw data to information and then to knowledge that can be used for decision making. This is datamining at its purest. It is Cognos' ability to bring together data from various sources in various formats and to integrate it into a unified whole picture that enables organizations to transform their raw data into a holistic view of the organization.

Cognos components are integrated with IBM DB2 Warehouse Manager, which automates all the functionality needed to set up and manage a data warehouse. DB2 Warehouse

Manager extracts data from a variety of sources, transforms it, populates the data warehouse, and stores metadata in an Information Catalogue.

Examples of successful customers include the following:

■ AutoZone, a Fortune 500 company and leading national auto parts chain, needed a BI system that could handle the constant addition of new stores and customers and manage data residing in DB2 Universal Database, all the way down to the transaction level. The Cognos and IBM solution has enabled Autozone not only to manage its explosive growth but also to leverage the information from each store in order to provide better service and products and to increase profits.

■ Mexx, a $500-million fashion house based in Voorschoten, The Netherlands, needed to streamline its supply-chain administration and enable more effective decision making. The company implemented a retail information management system powered by DB2 Universal Database, using Cognos Impromptu and PowerPlay for analysis and reporting. Mexx users have quickly realized the business value in the IBM-Cognos solution's consistent, accurate presentation of data.

■ Mother Parkers is a supplier of tea and coffee to North American vending distributors, restaurants, airlines, and supermarket chains, with annual sales exceeding $200 million. To augment its enterprise resource planning (ERP) system with drill-down and ad hoc reporting capabilities that would integrate seamlessly with its IBM AS/400 (now eServer iSeries) environment, Mother Parkers implemented Cognos Impromptu and PowerPlay as part of a BI system based on DB2. The solution is saving time and money, extending the value of the company's ERP system and creating new financial reporting capabilities that are making the company's decision makers more productive.

In Canada alone, Cognos has supported the following governmental efforts:

■ The City of Ottawa People Services Department uses Cognos BI software to better understand and measure performance of the provincially funded Employment and Financial Assistance Programs that it manages. City workers can now make better, more informed decisions without having to consult with information technology personnel, thereby also reducing the demand on the information technology personnel.

■ The Department of Foreign Affairs and International Trade Canada uses Cognos BI software to leverage its existing SAP and PeopleSoft ERP systems to enable worldwide staff to understand and better manage departmental resources in terms of comptrollership modernization, implementing results-based performance measurement, and creating a comprehensive reporting framework.

■ Cognos' Dashboard software enables Human Resources Development Canada (HRDC) to provide managers and executives with access to trailing and leading indicators, enabling them to better understand HRDC's performance,

clients, and services. The Dashboard is a graphic representation of key indicators needed by managers. It makes seeing the indicators easier and makes it easy to connect to the data behind the indicators.

■ Many of the improvements that Navigation Canada implemented (discussed in the opening of Chapter 6) were achieved through the integration of data and data access made possible by Cognos software.

Cognos has also supported the following organizations in Canada:

■ Telus Mobility uses Cognos software to support its enterprise reporting and customer relationship management needs.

■ Future Shop, a Canadian computer and electronics retailer, uses Cognos business intelligence to get one consistent view of data across the organization.

■ The Société des Alcools du Québec (SAQ) is one of the largest retail networks in Quebec, handling commerce of all alcoholic beverages in the province; the Société use Cognos software to create reports and perform sophisticated analysis on the rich business information housed in their J.D. Edwards ERP solution.

■ Canadian Blood Services uses Cognos to track and analyze donor information nationwide and bolster CBS donor recruiting and retention programs.

Sources: Rick Whiting, "Cognos Metrics Manager Now in Series 7," *Asia Computer Weekly*, October 21, 2002; "Industry Leading Technology Vendors Endorse Cognos Metrics Manager," available www.cognos.com.jp/news/releases/2002/1007_2.html, accessed March 29, 2003; Rodney Brown, "Cognos Called Up by U.S. Army Reserve Command to Monitor Operational Readiness," *Mass High Tech*, March 18, 2003; "Cognos Teams with Giuliani Group," *Ottawa Business Journal*, March 10, 2003; "Company Overview," Cognos home page, available www.cognos.com, accessed March 29, 2003; "Cognos Shows Its Intelligence with DB2 Data Management Software," IBM Case Study, available www-3.ibm.com/software/success.

CASE STUDY QUESTIONS

1. What sort of data do you think Cognos can integrate and combine using its BI software?
2. Why would an organization want to use Cognos software? How would it know it was worth the expense?
3. What companies in your own province that are not mentioned above do you think could make use of Cognos BI software? For what purposes?
4. Why do organizations have their data scattered in so many different databases and so many different formats?
5. Would having all of a company's data in one database and in one format eliminate the need for BI software like that offered by Cognos? Why, or why not?
6. Are there any ethical problems that might arise from the use of Cognos BI software? If so, what are they?

TELECOMMUNICATIONS AND NETWORKS

At many points in your career, you will need to make decisions about how to use telecommunications technology and services in your business. After reading this chapter, you should be able to answer these questions:

1. *What technologies are used in telecommunications systems?*
2. *What telecommunications transmission media should our organization use?*
3. *How should our organization design its networks?*
4. *What alternative network services are available to our organization?*
5. *What telecommunications applications can be used for electronic business and electronic commerce?*

New College Campus Means a New Network

Winnipeg's Red River College is nearing completion of a new facility, named the Princess Street Campus. Given the ubiquitous nature of technology today, and the fact that the campus will specialize in state-of-the-art IT programs, it is only fitting that the college has chosen to go beyond simply teaching the technology to immersing itself in it. Students in programs such as computer analyst/programmer, information systems technology, electronics technology, and digital multimedia will learn in an environment that incorporates new technologies into the very walls around them. Red River desired real reliability and lots of bandwidth for high-end applications, and they wanted a network enabled for data, voice, and video. The cable plant provided the foundation for this.

The fastest and most expensive cable in existence is optical fibre, and Red River came up with a unique backbone concept by starting with the idea that in every possible case optical fibre should be close to the end user. This meant running fibre to every podium in every classroom. Each building has a wiring closet from which the fibre optic cable runs to each room. From there, the fastest inexpensive cable (Category 6 copper wire) fans out to each desk. Classroom instructors also have a wide variety of multimedia technology at their fingertips, including switches,

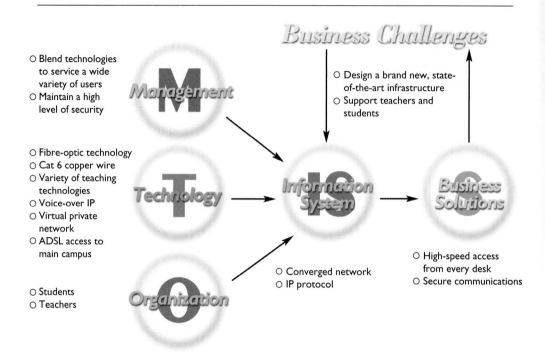

○ Blend technologies
  to service a wide
  variety of users
○ Maintain a high
  level of security

○ Fibre-optic technology
○ Cat 6 copper wire
○ Variety of teaching
  technologies
○ Voice-over IP
○ Virtual private
  network
○ ADSL access to
  main campus

○ Students
○ Teachers

○ Design a brand new, state-
  of-the-art infrastructure
○ Support teachers and
  students

○ Converged network
○ IP protocol

○ High-speed access
  from every desk
○ Secure communications

overhead projector controls, videocassette recorders, visual presenters, videodiscs, and network connections. Some classrooms are expected to have extra heavy use of bandwidth, and in these cases every desk is fully connected by fibre optic cable.

Red River's needs and ideas led the network designers at Cisco to concentrate on optimizing the following areas: quality of service (reliability, accessibility), high bandwidth (fast speed), load balancing (so that all computers are relatively equally used), and reliability. The actual cable plant and network is being installed by Manitoba Telecommunications Systems. The idea is to create a converged network that uses the same wiring to run data, voice, and video. It will utilize the Internet Protocol in a network architecture consisting of three levels: access, distribution, and core. These three tiers will be both physically and logically autonomous. This means that a problem in one layer will not affect the other layers. This type of network has a high level of redundancy in network hardware, which allows for very good reliability. Already implemented on the converged network are staff voice-over IP (VoIP), a cheap long-distance telephone methodology, and data access, with more applications in the pipeline. Unified messaging supports voice mail, and the college plans to implement VoIP for student desktops. Chapter 9 discusses VoIP technology.

In any such setting, security is a concern. Addressing this issue is the use of VPN (virtual private network) encryption, as well as redundant firewalls and extra security for confidential data, such as student records, accessed by students and for between-campus communication.

Red River's main campus is across town, and connectivity to Princess Street is a 100-MB/s link, providing quality of service and class of service, both based on speed and reliability, for voice with separation of data streams. This link to the main campus provides Internet access for the Princess Street Campus using ADSL (asymmetric digital subscriber line), a high speed telephone wire transmission methodology. Bandwidth possibilities being considered for the future include the use of dark fibre, which is unused optical fibre that has been laid but not yet connected, xDSL, another telephone transmission methodology, and CaNet4, the future faster version of the Internet in Canada. Red River hopes that this infrastructure will last a minimum of 15 years with minimal upgrade costs.

Sources: Mark Bishop and Walter Browning, "Warning: Princess Street High-Tech Talk," *Red River College Publication*, January 2003; "Building the Future for You Today," D.H. Neill Design Services, available www.dhneill.com, accessed March 30, 2003; and www.rrc.mb.ca.

MANAGEMENT CHALLENGES

Red River College, like many organizations all over the world, has found ways to benefit from communications technology to enhance its mission and to communicate more efficiently. It would be virtually impossible to conduct business today without using communications technology, and applications of networks and communications technology for electronic business and electronic commerce are multiplying. However, incorporating communications technology into today's applications and information technology infrastructure raises several management challenges:

1. **Managing LANs.** Although local area networks (LANs) can be flexible and inexpensive ways of delivering computing power to new areas of the organization, they must be carefully administered and monitored. LANs are especially vulnerable to network disruption, loss of essential data, and access by unauthorized users (see Chapter 11). Dealing with these problems requires special technical expertise that may be in short supply.

2. **Managing bandwidth.** Networks are the foundation of electronic commerce and the digital economy. Without network infrastructures that offer fast, reliable access, companies would lose many online customers and jeopardize relationships with suppliers and business partners as well. Although telecommunication transmission costs are rapidly dropping, total network transmission capacity (bandwidth) requirements are growing at a rate of more than 40 percent each year. If more people use networks or the firm implements data-intensive applications that require high-capacity transmission, a firm's network costs can easily spiral upward. Balancing the need to ensure network reliability and availability against mushrooming network costs is a central management concern.

Most of the information systems we use today require networks and communications technology. Companies, large and small from all over the world, are using networked systems and the Internet to locate suppliers and buyers, to negotiate contracts with them, and to service their trades. Applications of networks are multiplying in research, organizational coordination, and control. Networked systems are fundamental to electronic commerce and electronic business.

Today's computing tasks are so closely tied to networks that some believe "the network is the computer." This chapter describes the components of telecommunications systems, showing how they can be arranged to create various types of networks and network-based applications that can increase an organization's efficiency and competitiveness.

8.1 COMPONENTS AND FUNCTIONS OF A TELECOMMUNICATIONS SYSTEM

telecommunications

The communication of information by electronic means, usually over some distance.

Telecommunications is the communication of information by electronic means, usually over some distance. Previously, telecommunications meant voice transmission over telephone lines. Today, a great deal of telecommunications transmission is digital data transmission, using computers to transmit data from one location to another. Deregulation of the telecommunications industry and technology advances have led to an explosion of telecommunications products and services that can create the foundation for a digital business environment. Managers will continually be faced with decisions about selecting telecommunications technologies and services to enhance the performance of their firm and how best to incorporate them into their information systems and business processes.

TELECOMMUNICATIONS SYSTEM COMPONENTS

telecommunications system

A collection of compatible hardware and software arranged to communicate information from one location to another.

A **telecommunications system** is a collection of compatible hardware and software arranged to communicate information from one location to another. Figure 8.1 illustrates the components of a large traditional telecommunications system, where processing power is concentrated at a central computer. Telecommunications systems can transmit text, graphic images, voice, or video information. This section describes the major components of telecommunications systems. Subsequent sections describe how the components can be arranged into various types of networks.

The following are essential components of a telecommunications system:

1. Computers to process information.
2. Terminals or any input/output devices that send or receive data.
3. Communications channels, the links by which data or voice are transmitted between sending and receiving devices in a network. Communications channels use various communications media, such as telephone lines, coaxial cable, fibre-optic cable, and wireless transmission.
4. Communications processors, such as modems, multiplexers, controllers, and front-end processors, which provide support functions for data transmission and reception.
5. Communications software, which controls input and output activities and manages other functions of the communications network.

Figure 8.1 Components of a telecommunications system. This figure illustrates some of the hardware components that would be found in a traditional large telecommunications system. They include computers, terminals, communications channels, and communications processors, such as modems, multiplexers, and a front-end processor. Special communications software controls input and output activities and manages other functions of the communications system.

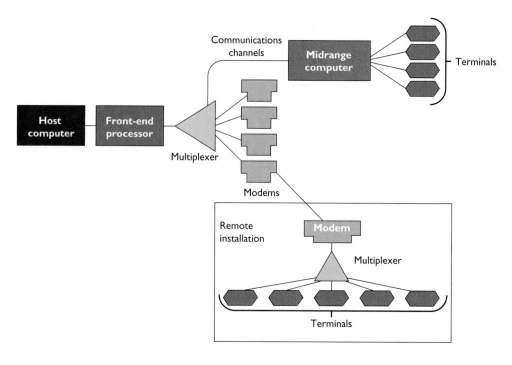

FUNCTIONS OF TELECOMMUNICATIONS SYSTEMS

In order to send and receive information from one place to another, a telecommunications system must perform a number of separate functions. The system transmits information, establishes the interface between the sender and the receiver, routes messages along the most efficient paths, performs elementary processing of the information to ensure that the right message gets to the right receiver, performs editorial tasks on the data (such as checking for transmission errors and rearranging the format), and converts messages from one speed (say, the speed of a computer) into the speed of a communications line or from one format to another. Finally, the telecommunications system controls the flow of information.

A telecommunications network typically contains diverse hardware and software components that need to work together to transmit information. Different components in a network can communicate by adhering to a common set of rules that enable them to "talk" to each other. This set of rules and procedures governing transmission between two points in a network is called a **protocol**. Each device in a network must be able to interpret the other device's protocol. The principal functions of protocols in a telecommunications network are to identify each device in the communication path, to secure the attention of the other device, to verify correct receipt of the transmitted message, to verify that a message requires retransmission because it cannot be correctly interpreted, and to perform recovery when errors occur.

protocol
A set of rules and procedures that govern transmission between the components in a network.

TYPES OF SIGNALS: ANALOG AND DIGITAL

Information travels through a telecommunications system in the form of electromagnetic signals. Signals are represented in two ways: analog and digital signals. An **analog signal** is represented by a continuous waveform that passes through a communications medium. Analog signals are used to handle voice communications and to reflect variations in pitch.

A **digital signal** is a discrete, rather than a continuous, waveform. It transmits data coded into two discrete states: 1-bits and 0-bits, which are represented as on–off electrical pulses. Most computers communicate with digital signals as do many local telephone companies and some larger networks. However, if a traditional telephone network is set up to process analog signals, a digital signal cannot be processed without some alterations. All digital signals must be translated into analog signals before they can be transmitted in an analog system. The device that performs this translation is called a **modem** (Modem is an abbreviation for MOdulation/DEModulation). A modem translates a computer's digital signals into analog form for transmission over ordinary telephone lines, or it translates analog signals back into digital form for reception by a computer (see Figure 8.2).

analog signal
A continuous waveform that passes through a communications medium; used for voice communications.

digital signal
A discrete waveform that transmits data coded into two discrete states as 1-bits and 0-bits, which are represented as on–off electrical pulses; used for data communications.

modem
A device for translating digital signals into analog signals and vice versa.

COMMUNICATIONS CHANNELS

Communications **channels** are the means by which data are transmitted from one device in a network to another. A channel can use different kinds of telecommunications transmission media: twisted wire, coaxial cable, fibre optics, terrestrial microwave, satellite, and other wireless transmission. Each has advantages and limitations. High-speed transmission media are more expensive in general, but they can handle higher volumes, which reduces the cost per bit. For instance, the cost per bit of data can be lower via satellite link than via leased telephone line if a firm uses the satellite link 100 percent of the time. There is also a wide range of speeds possible for any given medium, depending on the software and hardware configuration.

channels
The means by which data or voice are transmitted from one device to another in a network.

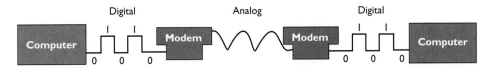

Figure 8.2 Functions of the modem. A modem is a device that translates digital signals from a computer into analog form so that they can be transmitted over analog telephone lines. The modem is also used to translate analog signals back into digital form for the receiving computer.

Twisted Wire

Twisted wire consists of strands of copper wire twisted in pairs and is an older transmission medium. Many of the telephone systems in buildings had twisted wires installed for analog communication, but they can be used for digital communication as well. Although it is low in cost and is already in place, twisted wire can be relatively slow for transmitting data, and high-speed transmission causes interference called *cross-talk*. There are limits to the amount of data that a twisted wire channel can carry, but new software and hardware have raised the twisted-wire transmission capacity to make it useful for local- and wide-area computer networks as well as telephone systems.

Coaxial Cable

Coaxial cable, like that used for cable television, consists of thickly insulated copper wire, which can transmit a larger volume of data than twisted wire. It is often used in place of twisted wire for important links in a telecommunications network because it is a faster, more interference-free transmission medium, with speeds of up to 200 megabits per second. However, coaxial cable is thick, is hard to wire in many buildings, and cannot support analog phone conversations. It must be moved when computers and other devices are moved.

Fibre Optics and Optical Networks

Fibre-optic cable consists of strands of clear-glass fibre, each less than the thickness of a human hair, which are bound into cables. Data are transformed into pulses of light, which are sent through the fibre-optic cable by a laser device at a rate from 500 kilobits to several trillion bits per second. Fibre-optic cable is considerably faster, lighter, and more durable than wire media and is well suited to systems requiring transfers of large volumes of data. However, fibre-optic cable is more difficult to work with, more expensive, and harder to install.

Until recently, fibre-optic cable has been used primarily as the high-speed network **backbone**, while twisted wire and coaxial cable have been used to connect the backbone to individual businesses and households. A backbone is the part of a network that handles the major traffic. It acts as the primary path for traffic flowing to or from other networks. Now, telecommunications carriers are working on bringing fibre all the way into the basements of buildings so that they can provide a variety of new services to businesses and, eventually, to residential customers. These **optical networks** can transmit all types of traffic—voice, data, and video—over fibre cables and provide the massive transmission capacity needed for new types of services and software. Using optical networks, on-demand video, software downloads, and high-quality digital audio can be accessed using set-top boxes and other information appliances without any degradation in quality or any delays.

Currently, fibre-optic networks are slowed down by the need to convert electrical data to optics (light waves) to send the data over a fibre line and then reconvert it. The long-term

goal is to create pure optical networks in which light packets shuttle digital data at tremendous speed without ever converting them to electrical signals. Many new optical technologies are in development for this purpose. Next-generation optical networks will also boost capacity by using **dense wavelength division multiplexing (DWDM)**. DWDM boosts transmission capacity by using many different colours of light, or wavelengths, to carry separate streams of data over the same fibre strand at the same time. DWDM combines up to 160 wavelengths per strand and can transmit up to 6.4 terabits per second over a single fibre. This technology will enable communications service providers to add bandwidth to an existing

Margin glossary

twisted wire

A transmission medium consisting of pairs of twisted copper wires; used to transmit analog phone conversations but can be used for data transmission.

coaxial cable

A transmission medium consisting of thickly insulated copper wire; can transmit large volumes of data quickly.

fibre-optic cable

A fast, light, and durable transmission medium consisting of thin strands of clear-glass fibre bound into cables. Data are transmitted as light pulses.

backbone

Part of a network handling the major traffic and providing the primary path for traffic flowing to or from other networks.

optical network

High-speed networking technologies for transmitting data in the form of light pulses.

Fibre-optic cable can transmit data that have been transformed into pulses of light at speeds up to six terabits per second. Fibre-optic technology is used in high-capacity optical networks.

dense wavelength division multiplexing (DWDM)

Technology for boosting transmission capacity of optical fibre by using many different wavelengths to carry separate streams of data over the same fibre strand at the same time.

fibre-optic network without having to lay more fibre-optic cable. Before wavelength division multiplexing, optical networks could only use a single wavelength per strand.

Wireless Transmission

Wireless transmission that sends signals through air or space without being tied to a physical line has become an increasingly popular alternative to tethered transmission channels, such as twisted wire, coaxial cable, and fibre optics. Today, common technologies for wireless data transmission include microwave transmission and communication satellites; implementations of wireless technologies include pagers, cellular telephones, personal communication services (PCS), smart phones, personal digital assistants (PDAs), and mobile data networks. Additional technologies, I-mode and wireless access protocol, are covered in Chapter 9.

The wireless transmission medium is the electromagnetic spectrum, illustrated in Figure 8.3. Some types of wireless transmission, such as microwave or infrared, by nature occupy specific spectrum frequency ranges (measured in megahertz). Other types of wireless transmissions are actually functional uses, such as cellular telephones and paging devices, that have been assigned a specific range of frequencies by national regulatory agencies and international agreements. Each frequency range has its own strengths and limitations, and these have helped determine the specific function or data communications niche assigned to it.

Microwave systems, both terrestrial and celestial, transmit high-frequency radio signals through the atmosphere and are widely used for high-volume, long-distance, point-to-point communication. Microwave signals follow a straight line and do not bend with the curvature of the earth; therefore, long-distance terrestrial transmission systems require that transmission stations be positioned about 60 kilometres apart, adding to the expense of microwave transmission.

This problem can be solved by bouncing microwave signals off communication **satellites**, enabling them to serve as relay stations for microwave signals transmitted from terrestrial stations. Communication satellites are cost effective for transmitting large quantities of data over very long distances. Satellites are typically used for communications in large, geographically dispersed organizations that would be difficult to tie together through cabling media or terrestrial microwave. For instance, Canadian Forces operating in Afghanistan in 2002 set up satellite communications in the headquarters base in Kandahar, thus linking by satellite multiple bases, which comprised that mission.

Conventional communication satellites move in stationary orbits approximately 35 400 kilometres above the earth. A newer satellite medium, the low-orbit satellite, is beginning to

microwave

A high-volume, long-distance, point-to-point transmission in which high-frequency radio signals are transmitted through the atmosphere from one terrestrial transmission station to another.

satellite

The transmission of data using orbiting satellites that serve as relay stations for transmitting microwave signals over very long distances.

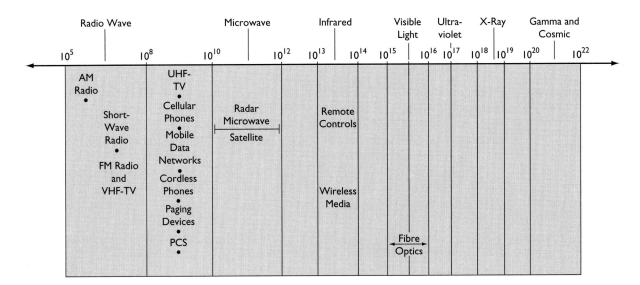

Figure 8.3 Frequency ranges for communications media and devices. Each telecommunications transmission medium or device occupies a different frequency range, measured in megahertz, on the electromagnetic spectrum.

be deployed. These satellites travel much closer to the earth and are able to pick up signals from weak transmitters. They also consume less power and cost less to launch than conventional satellites. With these wireless networks, businesspeople will be able to travel virtually anywhere in the world and have access to full communication capabilities, including video-conferencing and multimedia-rich Internet access.

Wireless transmission technologies are being implemented in situations requiring remote access to corporate systems and mobile computing power. **Paging systems**, which have been used for several decades, originally simply emitted beeps when the user received a message, requiring the user to telephone an office to learn about the message. Today, a paging device can send and receive short alphanumeric messages that the user reads on the pager's screen. Paging is useful for communicating with mobile workers, such as repair crews; one-way paging also can provide an inexpensive way of communicating with workers in offices. For example, Computer Associates distributes two-way pagers with its Computer Associates (CA) Unicenter software, which allows computer network operators to monitor and respond to problems.

Cellular telephones (cell phones) work by using radio waves to communicate with radio antennas (towers) placed within adjacent geographic areas called *cells*. A telephone message is transmitted to the local cell by the cellular telephone and then is handed off from antenna to antenna—cell to cell—until it reaches the cell of its destination, where it is transmitted to the receiving telephone. As a cellular signal travels from one cell into another, a computer that monitors signals from the cells switches the conversation to a radio channel assigned to the next cell. The radio antenna cells normally cover 13-kilometre hexagonal areas, although their radius is smaller in densely populated localities.

Older cellular systems are analog, and newer cellular systems are digital. Digital cell phones are more secure than analog cell phones. A new generation of wireless transmission, known as third generation or 3G, brings wireless transmission speeds up to 2 Mbps, which allows for high-quality wireless audio and video. Because 3G, also known as broadband wireless, requires major changes in wireless infrastructure, it has not reached very many areas yet and will be much more expensive than regular cellular communication. **Personal communication services (PCS)** are a popular type of digital cellular service. PCS are entirely digital. They can transmit both voice and data and operate in a higher frequency range than analog cellular telephones. PCS cells are much smaller and more closely spaced than analog cells and can accommodate higher traffic demands.

Newer models of digital cellular phones can handle voice mail, e-mail, and faxes; save addresses; access a private corporate network; access information from the Internet; and provide wireless voice transmission. These **smart phones** are being equipped with Web browser software that lets digital cellular phones or other wireless devices access Web pages formatted to send text or other information that is suitable for tiny screens. Some smart phone models offer larger screens and keypads to make Internet access easier.

Personal digital assistants (PDA) are small handheld computers, frequently capable of entirely digital communications transmission. They may have built-in wireless telecommunications capabilities as well as work-organization software. A well-known example is the Palm Tungsten W handheld organizer. It can display, compose, send, and receive e-mail messages and can provide access to the Internet. The handheld device includes such applications as an electronic scheduler, address book, and expense tracker and can accept data entered with a special stylus through an onscreen writing pad.

Wireless networks explicitly designed for two-way transmission of data files are called **mobile data networks**. These radio-based networks transmit data to and from handheld computers. One type of mobile data network is based on a series of radio towers constructed specifically to transmit text and data. For example, the Cornwall Community Police Service uses xwave's remote office and dispatch system (ROADS), an application designed to interface to local dispatch systems, to provide messaging between police cars and to access databases, such as the provincial motor vehicle registry, and the Canadian Police Information Centre (CPIC).

Wireless networks and transmission devices can be more expensive, slower, and more error prone than transmission over wired networks, although the major digital cellular networks are upgrading the speed of their services. Transmission capacity and energy supply in

paging system

A wireless transmission technology in which the pager beeps when the user receives a message; used to transmit short alphanumeric messages.

cellular telephone (cell phone)

A device that transmits voice or data, using radio waves to communicate with radio antennas placed within adjacent geographic areas called cells.

personal communication services (PCS)

A wireless cellular technology that uses lower power and higher frequency radio waves than does cellular technology and so can be used with smaller-sized telephones.

smart phone

Wireless phone with voice, text, and Internet capabilities.

personal digital assistants (PDA)

Small, pen-based, handheld computers, frequently with built-in wireless telecommunications capable of entirely digital communications transmission.

mobile data networks

Wireless networks that enable two-way transmission of data files cheaply and efficiently.

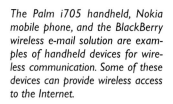
The Palm i705 handheld, Nokia mobile phone, and the BlackBerry wireless e-mail solution are examples of handheld devices for wireless communication. Some of these devices can provide wireless access to the Internet.

wireless devices require careful management in terms of both hardware and software. Security and privacy will be more difficult to maintain because wireless transmission can be easily intercepted (see Chapter 11).

Data cannot be transmitted seamlessly among different wireless networks if they use incompatible standards. For example, digital cellular service in Canada is provided by different operators using one of several competing digital cellular technologies—CDMA (Code Division Multiple Access), GSM (Global System for Mobile Communications), and TDMA (Time Division Multiple Access)—that do not interoperate with each other. Many digital cellular handsets that use one of these technologies cannot operate in other countries outside North America, which operate at different frequencies with still another set of standards. We provide a detailed discussion of these standards and other standards for networking in Chapter 9.

Transmission Speed

The total amount of information that can be transmitted through any telecommunications channel is measured in bits per second (bps). Digital transmission speed has also been measured by the baud rate. A **baud** is a binary event representing a signal change from positive to negative and vice versa. The baud rate is not always the same as the bit rate. At higher speeds, a single signal change can transmit more than one bit at a time, so the bit rate generally will surpass the baud rate.

> **baud**
>
> A change in signal from positive to negative and vice versa that is used as a measure of transmission speed.

One signal change, or cycle, is required to transmit one or several bits per second; therefore, the transmission capacity of each type of telecommunications medium is a function of its frequency. The number of cycles per second that can be sent through that medium is measured in hertz (see Chapter 6). The range of frequencies that can be accommodated on a particular telecommunications channel is called its **bandwidth**. The bandwidth is the difference between the highest and lowest frequencies that can be accommodated on a single channel. The greater the range of frequencies, the greater are the bandwidth and the channel's transmission capacity. Table 8.1 compares the transmission speed and relative costs of the major types of transmissions media.

> **bandwidth**
>
> The capacity of a communications channel as measured by the difference between the highest and lowest frequencies that can be transmitted by that channel.

COMMUNICATIONS PROCESSORS AND SOFTWARE

Communications processors, such as front-end processors, concentrators, controllers, multiplexers, and modems, support data transmission and reception in a telecommunications network. In large computer systems, such as those from IBM, the **front-end processor** is a

> **front-end processor**
>
> A special purpose computer dedicated to managing communications for the host computer in a network.

TABLE 8.1	TYPICAL SPEEDS AND COSTS OF TELECOMMUNICATIONS TRANSMISSION MEDIA		
Medium		**Speed**	**Cost**
Twisted wire		Up to 100 Mbps	Low
Microwave		Up to 200+ Mbps	
Satellite		Up to 200+ Mbps	
Coaxial cable		Up to 200 Mbps	
Fibre-optic cable		Up to 6+ Tbps	High

Mbps = megabits per second

Gbps = gigabits per second

Tbps = terabits per second

special purpose computer dedicated to communications management and is attached to the main, or host, computer. The front-end processor performs communications processing, such as error control, formatting, editing, controlling, routing, and speed and signal conversion.

A **concentrator** is a programmable telecommunications computer that collects and temporarily stores messages from terminals until enough messages are ready to be sent economically. The concentrator bursts signals to the host computer.

A **controller** is a specialized computer that supervises communications traffic between the central processing unit (CPU) and peripheral devices, such as terminals and printers. The controller manages messages from these devices and communicates them to the CPU. It also routes output from the CPU to the appropriate peripheral device.

A **multiplexer** is a device that enables a single communications channel to carry data transmissions from multiple sources simultaneously. The multiplexer divides the communications channel so that it can be shared by multiple transmission devices. The multiplexer may divide a high-speed channel into multiple channels of slower speed or may assign each transmission source a very small slice of time for using the high-speed channel.

Special telecommunications software residing in the host computer, front-end processor, and other processors in the network is required to control and support network activities. This software is responsible for such functions as network control, access control, transmission control, error detection/correction, and security. More detail on security software can be found in Chapter 11.

8.2 COMMUNICATIONS NETWORKS

A number of different ways exist to organize telecommunications components to form a network and hence provide multiple ways of classifying networks. Networks can be classified by the way their components are connected, called **topology**. Networks also can be classified by their geographic scope and the type of services provided. This section describes different networks and the management and technical requirements of creating networks that link entire enterprises.

NETWORK TOPOLOGIES

As illustrated in Figures 8.4 to 8.6, the three most common topologies are the star, bus, and ring topologies.

The Star Network

The **star network** (see Figure 8.4) consists of a central host computer connected to a number of smaller computers or terminals. This topology is useful for applications where some processing must be centralized and some can be performed locally. One problem with the star network is its vulnerability. All communication between points in the network must pass

---

concentrator

Telecommunications computer that collects and temporarily stores messages from terminals for batch transmission to the host computer.

controller

A specialized computer that supervises communications traffic between the CPU and the peripheral devices in a telecommunications system.

multiplexer

A device that enables a single communications channel to carry data transmissions from multiple sources simultaneously.

topology

The way in which the components of a network are connected.

star network

A network topology in which all computers and other devices are connected to a central host computer. All communications between network devices must pass through the host computer.

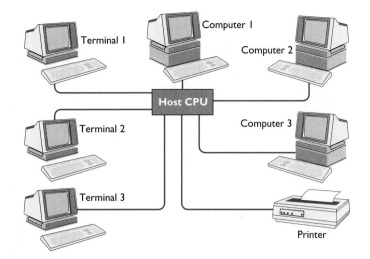

Figure 8.4 A star network topology. In a star network configuration, a central host computer acts as a traffic controller for all other components of the network. All communication among the smaller computers, terminals, and printers must first pass through the central computer.

through the central computer. Because the central computer is the traffic controller for the other computers and terminals in the network, communication in the network will come to a standstill if the host computer stops functioning.

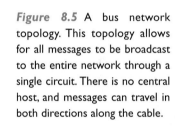

Figure 8.5 A bus network topology. This topology allows for all messages to be broadcast to the entire network through a single circuit. There is no central host, and messages can travel in both directions along the cable.

The Bus Network

The **bus network** (see Figure 8.6) links a number of computers by a single circuit made of twisted wire, coaxial cable, or fibre-optic cable. All of the signals are broadcast in both directions to the entire network, with special software to identify which components receive each message (there is no central host computer to control the network). If one of the computers in the network fails, none of the other components in the network is affected, but if the main bus line goes down, the network goes down. However, the channel in a bus network can handle only one message at a time, so performance can degrade if there is a high volume of network traffic. When two computers transmit messages simultaneously, a "collision" occurs, and the messages are re-sent automatically.

bus network

Network topology linking a number of computers by a single circuit with all messages broadcast to the entire network.

The Ring Network

Like the bus network, the **ring network** (see Figure 8.6) does not rely on a central host computer and will not necessarily break down if one of the component computers malfunctions. Each computer in the network can communicate directly with any other computer, and each processes its own applications independently. However, in a ring topology, the connecting wire, cable, or optical fibre forms a closed loop. Data are passed along the ring from one computer to another and always flow in one direction. Both ring and bus topologies are used in local area networks (LANs), which are discussed in the next section.

ring network

A network topology in which all computers are linked by a closed loop in a manner that passes data in one direction from one computer to another.

PRIVATE BRANCH EXCHANGES, LOCAL AREA NETWORKS (LANS), AND WIDE AREA NETWORKS (WANS)

Networks may be classified by geographic scope into local networks and WANs. WANs encompass a relatively wide geographic area, from several miles to thousands of miles, whereas local networks link local resources, such as computers and terminals, within a department or the building of a firm. Local networks consist of private branch exchanges and local area networks.

Figure 8.6 A ring network topology. In a ring network configuration, messages are transmitted from computer to computer, flowing in a single direction through a closed loop. Each computer operates independently so that if one fails, communication through the network is not interrupted.

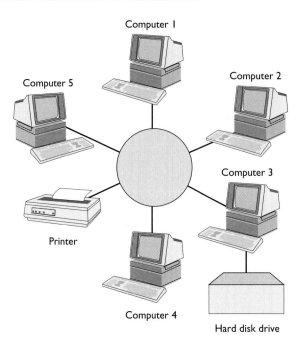

Computer 1

Computer 2

Computer 5

Computer 3

Printer

Computer 4

Hard disk drive

Private Branch Exchanges

private branch exchange (PBX)

A central switching system that handles a firm's voice and digital communications.

A **private branch exchange (PBX)** is a special-purpose computer designed for handling and switching office telephone calls at a company site. It can belong to the company or to a telecommunications provider. Today's PBXs can carry voice and data to create local networks. PBXs can store, transfer, hold, and redial telephone calls, and they also can be used to switch digital information among computers and office devices. Using a PBX, you can write a letter on a personal computer (PC) in your office, send it to the printer, then dial up the local copying machine and have multiple copies of your letter created.

The advantage of digital PBXs over other local networking options is that they do not require special wiring. A PC connected to a network by telephone can be plugged or unplugged anywhere in a building, using the existing telephone lines. Commercial vendors support PBXs, so the organization does not need special expertise to manage them.

The geographic scope of PBXs is limited, usually to 100 metres, although the PBX can be connected to other PBX networks or to packet-switched networks (see the discussion of packet switching in this section) to encompass a larger geographic area. The primary disadvantages of PBXs are that they are limited to telephone lines and they cannot easily handle very large volumes of data.

Local Area Networks

local area network (LAN)

A telecommunications network that requires its own dedicated channels and that encompasses a limited distance, usually one building or several buildings in close proximity.

A **local area network (LAN)** encompasses a limited distance, usually one building or several buildings in close proximity. Most LANs connect devices located within a 610-metre radius, and they have been widely used to link PCs. LANs require their own communications channels and are often controlled and operated by end-user groups or departments in a firm.

LANs generally have higher transmission capacities than PBXs, using bus, star, or ring topologies and a high bandwidth. They are recommended for applications transmitting high volumes of data and other functions requiring high transmission speeds, including video transmissions and graphics. LANs are often used to connect PCs in an office to shared printers and other resources or to link computers and computer-controlled machines in factories.

Figure 8.7 illustrates one model of a LAN. The server acts as a librarian, storing programs and data files for network users. The server determines who gets access to what and in what sequence. Servers may be powerful PCs with large hard-disk capacity, workstations, minicomputers, or mainframes, although specialized computers are available for this purpose.

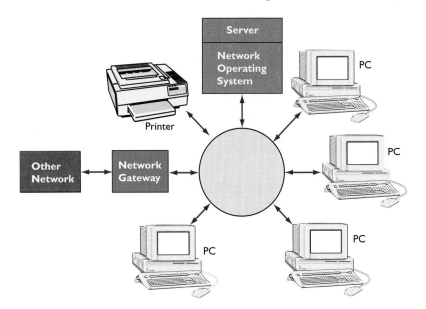

Figure 8.7 A local area network (LAN). A typical local area network connects computers and peripheral devices that are located close to each other, often in the same building.

The network gateway connects the LAN to public networks, such as the telephone network, or to other corporate networks so that the LAN can exchange information with networks external to it. A **gateway** is generally a communications processor that can connect dissimilar networks by translating from one set of protocols to another. A **router** is used to route packets of data through several connected LANs or to a WAN.

LAN technology consists of cabling (twisted wire, coaxial, or fibre-optic cable) or wireless technology that links individual computer devices, network interface cards (which are special adapters serving as interfaces to the cable), and software to control LAN activities. The LAN **network interface card (NIC)** specifies the data transmission rate, the size of message units, the addressing information attached to each message, and network topology (Ethernet uses a bus topology, for example).

LAN capabilities also are defined by the **network operating system (NOS)**. The network operating system can reside on every computer in the network, or it can reside on a single designated server for all the applications on the network. The NOS routes and manages communications on the network and coordinates network resources. Novell NetWare, Microsoft Windows Server 2003, the server versions of Windows 2000, and IBM's OS/2 Warp Server are popular network operating systems.

LANs may take the form of client-server networks, in which the server provides data and application programs to "client" computers on the network (see the Chapter 6 discussion of client-server computing), or they may use a peer-to-peer architecture. A **peer-to-peer** network means that all computers have equivalent responsibilities and capabilities. No computer acts as the server only. The various computers on the network can exchange data by direct access and can share peripheral devices without going through a separate server.

Wired LANs require new wiring each time the LAN is moved. One way to solve this problem is to create a wireless LAN. Wireless LANs have become easier to create and maintain and are starting to provide flexible, low-cost networking for firms and work groups. The **802.11b** network standard (also known as 802.11 High Rate or **Wi-Fi**) can be used to create wireless LANs in homes and offices. Wi-Fi stands for Wireless Fidelity and can transmit up to 11 megabits per second in the 2.4-GHz frequency range within approximately a 100-metre range. Wi-Fi can also provide high-speed Internet access to specially outfitted PCs within a few hundred feet of a Wi-Fi access point or transmitter. Wi-Fi "hot spots" are springing up in hotels, airport lounges, libraries, and college dorms to provide mobile access to the Internet. Starbucks, the international coffeehouse franchise organization, is beginning to offer "hot spots" from T-Mobile for customers to log on. Businesses are using Wi-Fi networks to create low-cost wireless LANs and to provide Internet access from conference rooms and temporary workstations.

gateway

A communications processor that connects dissimilar networks by providing the translation from one set of protocols to another.

router

Device that forwards packets of data from one LAN or WAN to another.

network interface card (NIC)

A device that connects the computer to the network transmission medium and specifies the data transfer rate, the size of message units, the addressing information attached to each message, and network topology.

network operating system (NOS)

Special software that routes and manages communications on the network and coordinates network resources.

peer-to-peer

Network architecture that permits computers on a network to exchange data and share peripheral devices.

802.11b (Wi-Fi)

Standard for high-speed wireless LANs that can transmit up to 11 Mbps within a 100-metre area, providing a low-cost flexible technology for connecting work groups and providing mobile Internet access.

The cost of a Wi-Fi network runs less than $300 per installation, much less than a stationary LAN. Most high-end laptop computers are now Wi-Fi enabled, and special adapters can be purchased to equip other PCs with Wi-Fi capabilities. A simple wireless network can be created by linking several computers that are equipped with Wi-Fi adapters and a wireless access point—a radio receiver/transmitter and antenna that links to a wired network, router, or hub. Access points can be mounted indoors on ceilings or outdoors on poles or towers. These wireless LANs have a range of several hundred feet, although the range can be extended by mounting antennae on towers or by adding access points, with users roaming among them as they would in a cellular phone system. There are a few drawbacks to this technology, however. Wi-Fi networks are susceptible to interference from nearby systems operating in the same spectrum, and there is no way to control additional new devices in the same area that might cause interference. Chapter 11 provides more detail on Wi-Fi security issues.

Bluetooth
Standard for wireless personal area networks that can transmit up to 720 Kbps within a 10-metre to 100-metre area.

Bluetooth is another wireless networking standard that is useful primarily for creating small *personal area networks* linking up to eight devices within a 10-metre area using low-power radio-based communication. Newer Bluetooth technologies can transmit up to 100 metres. Wireless phones, pagers, computers, printers, and computing devices can communicate with each other and even operate each other without direct user intervention. (For example, a person could highlight a telephone number on a wireless Palm PDA and automatically activate a call on a digital phone.) Bluetooth can transmit up to 720 Kbps in the 2.4-GHz band. Bluetooth technologies are being used in the financial services area to "unwire" brokers and money managers from their telephones, even in the office. With a Bluetooth headset, the user can continue a conversation with a client as he or she walks to the vending machine for coffee or to a colleague's office for advice—all without being tethered to their desk by the traditional wired telephone headset.

Wide Area Networks

wide area network (WAN)
Telecommunications network that spans a large geographical distance; may consist of a variety of cable, satellite, and microwave technologies.

switched lines
Telephone lines that a person can access from a terminal to transmit data to another computer, the call being routed or switched through paths to the designated destination.

dedicated lines
Telephone lines that are continuously available for transmission by a lessee. Typically conditioned to transmit data at high speeds for high-volume applications.

Wide area networks (WANs) span broad geographical distances, ranging from several kilometres to entire continents. WANs may consist of a combination of switched and dedicated lines, microwave, and satellite communications. **Switched lines** are telephone lines that a person can access from his or her terminal to transmit data to another computer, the call being routed or switched through paths to the designated destination. **Dedicated lines**, or nonswitched lines, are continuously available for transmission, and the lessee typically pays a flat rate for total access to the line. The lines can be leased or purchased from common carriers or private communications media vendors. Most existing WANs are switched.

Individual business firms may maintain their own WANs. The firm is responsible for telecommunications content and management. However, private WANs are expensive to maintain, or firms may not have the resources or skills to manage their own WANs. In these instances, companies may choose to use commercial network services to communicate over vast distances.

NETWORK SERVICES AND BROADBAND TECHNOLOGIES

In addition to topology and geographic scope, networks can be classified by the types of service they provide.

Value-Added Networks

value-added network (VAN)
Private, multipath, data-only, third-party-managed network that multiple organizations use on a subscription basis.

Value-added networks are an alternative to firms designing and managing their own networks. **Value-added networks (VANs)** are private, third-party-managed networks that offer data transmission and network services to subscribing firms. Subscribers pay only for the amount of data they transmit plus a subscription fee. Customers do not have to invest in network equipment and software and may achieve savings in line charges and transmission costs because the costs of using the network are shared among many users.

Many companies are now using the Internet to transmit their data because it is less expensive than using VANs. In response, today's value-added networks are providing extra services for secure e-mail management and data transmission, management reporting, and electronic document interchange translation (see the discussion of electronic document interchange in Section 8.3).

Other Network Services

Traditional analog telephone service is based on circuit switching, where a direct connection must be maintained between two nodes in a network for the duration of the transmission session. **Packet switching** is a basic switching technique that can be used to achieve economies and higher speeds in long-distance transmission. VANs and the Internet use packet switching. Packet switching breaks up a lengthy block of data into small, fixed bundles called packets. There are many different packet sizes, some of them variable, depending on the communications standard being used. (The X.25 packet switching standard uses packets of 128 bytes each.) Packets include information for directing the packet to the right address and for checking transmission errors along with the data. Data are gathered from many users, divided into small packets, and transmitted via various communications channels. Each packet travels independently through the network. Packets of data originating at one source can be routed through different paths in the network before being reassembled into the original message when they reach their destination. Figure 8.8 illustrates how packet switching works.

Frame relay is a shared network service that is faster and less expensive than packet switching and can achieve transmission speeds up to 1.544 Mbps. Frame relay packages data into frames that are similar to packets, but it does not perform error correction. It works well on reliable lines that do not require frequent retransmissions because of error.

Most corporations today use separate networks for voice, private-line services, and data, each of which is supported by a different technology. A service called **asynchronous transfer mode (ATM)** may overcome some of these problems because it can seamlessly and dynamically switch voice, data, images, and video between users. ATM also promises to tie LANs and WANs together more easily. ATM technology parcels information into uniform cells, each with 53 groups of eight bytes, eliminating the need for protocol conversion. It can pass data between computers from different vendors and permits data to be transmitted at any speed the network handles. ATM can transmit up to 10 gigabits per second.

Integrated Services Digital Network (ISDN) is an international standard for dial-up network access that integrates voice, data, image, and video services in a single link. There are two levels of ISDN service: Basic Rate ISDN and Primary Rate ISDN. Each uses a group of B (bearer) channels to carry voice or data along with a D (delta) channel for signalling and control information. Basic Rate ISDN can transmit data at a rate of 128 kilobits per second on an existing local telephone line. Organizations and individuals requiring the ability to provide simultaneous voice or data transmission over one physical line might choose this service. Primary Rate ISDN offers transmission capacities in the megabit range and is designed for users of high-volume telecommunications services.

packet switching

Technology that breaks blocks of data into fixed bundles and routes them in the most economical way through any available communications channel.

frame relay

A shared network service technology that packages data into bundles for transmission but does not use error-correction routines; cheaper and faster than packet switching.

asynchronous transfer mode (ATM)

A networking technology that parcels information into 53 groups of eight-byte cells, allowing data to be transmitted between computers from different vendors.

Integrated Services Digital Network (ISDN)

International standard for transmitting voice, video, image, and data to support a wide range of services over public telephone lines.

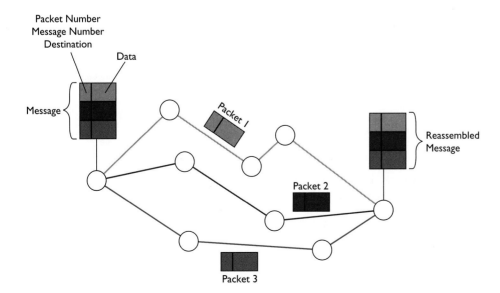

Figure 8.8 Packet-switched networks and packet communications. Data are grouped into small packets, which are transmitted independently via various communications channels and reassembled at their final destination.

digital subscriber line (DSL)

A group of technologies providing high-capacity transmission over existing copper telephone lines.

cable modem

Modem designed to operate over cable TV lines to provide high-speed access to the Web or corporate intranets.

T1 line

A dedicated telephone connection comprising 24 channels that can support a data transmission rate of 1.544 Mbps. Each channel can be configured to carry voice or data traffic.

broadband

High-speed transmission technology; also designates a single communications medium that can carry multiple channels of data simultaneously.

converged network

Network with technology to enable voice, video, and data to run over a single network.

unified messaging

System combining voice messages, e-mail, and fax so that they can all be obtained from a single system.

Other high-capacity services include digital subscriber line (DSL) technologies, cable modems, and T1 lines. Like ISDN, **digital subscriber line (DSL)** technologies also operate over existing copper telephone lines to carry voice, data, and video, but they have higher transmission capacities than ISDN. There are several categories of DSL. Asymmetric digital subscriber line (ADSL) supports a transmission rate of 1.5 to 9 megabits per second when receiving data and up to 640 Kbps when sending data. Symmetric digital subscriber line (SDSL) supports the same transmission rate for sending and receiving data of up to 3 Mbps. **Cable modems** are modems designed to operate over cable TV lines. They can provide high-speed access to the Web or corporate intranets of up to 4 Mbps. However, cable modems use a shared line so that transmission will slow down if there are a large number of local users sharing the cable line. A cable modem at present has stronger capabilities for receiving data than for sending data. A **T1 line** is a dedicated telephone connection comprising 24 channels that can support a data transmission rate of 1.544 Mbps. Each of these 64-Kbps channels can be configured to carry voice or data traffic. These services often are used for high-capacity Internet connections. Table 8.2 summarizes these network services.

High-speed transmission technologies are sometimes referred to as **broadband**. The term broadband is also used to designate transmission media that can carry multiple channels simultaneously over a single communications medium.

NETWORK CONVERGENCE

Most companies maintain separate networks for voice, data, and video, but products are now available to create **converged networks**, which can deliver voice, data, and video in a single network infrastructure. These multiservice networks can potentially reduce networking costs by eliminating the need to provide support services and personnel for each different type of network. Multiservice networks can be attractive solutions for companies running multimedia applications, such as video collaboration, voice-data call centres, distance learning (see the following section), or **unified messaging**, or for firms with high costs for voice services. Unified messaging systems combine voice mail, e-mail, and faxes so that they can all be obtained from one system.

8.3 ELECTRONIC BUSINESS AND ELECTRONIC COMMERCE TECHNOLOGIES

Baxter Healthcare International, described in Chapter 3, realized the strategic significance of telecommunications. The company placed its own computer terminals in hospital supply

TABLE 8.2	NETWORK SERVICES

Service	Description	Bandwidth
X.25	Packet-switching standard that parcels data into packets of 128 bytes	Up to 1.544 Mbps
Frame relay	Packages data into frames for high-speed transmission over reliable lines but does not use error-correction routines	Up to 1.544 Mbps
ATM (asynchronous transfer mode)	Parcels data into uniform cells to allow high-capacity transmission of voice, data, images, and video between different types of computers	25 Mbps–10 Gbps
ISDN	Digital dial-up network access standard that can integrate voice, data, and video services	Basic Rate ISDN: 128 Kbps; Primary Rate ISDN: 1.5 Mbps
DSL (digital subscriber line)	Series of technologies for high-capacity transmission over copper wires	ADSL—up to 9 Mbps for receiving and up to 640 Kbps for sending data; SDSL—up to 3 Mbps for both sending and receiving
T1	Dedicated telephone connection with 24 channels for high-capacity transmission	1.544 Mbps
Cable modem	Service for high-speed transmission of data over cable TV lines that are shared by many users	Up to 4 Mbps

rooms. Customers could dial up a local VAN and send their orders directly to the company. Other companies today are achieving strategic benefits by developing electronic commerce and electronic business applications based on networking technologies.

Electronic mail (e-mail), groupware, voice mail, facsimile (fax) machines, digital information services, teleconferencing, dataconferencing, videoconferencing, and electronic data interchange are key applications for electronic commerce and electronic business because they provide network-based capabilities for communication, coordination, and speeding up the flow of purchase and sale transactions.

ELECTRONIC MAIL AND GROUPWARE

We described the capabilities of electronic mail, or e-mail, in Chapter 6. E-mail eliminates costly long-distance telephone charges, expediting communication between different parts of an organization. Nestlé SA, the Swiss-based multinational food corporation, installed an electronic-mail system to connect its 60 000 employees in 80 countries. Nestlé's European units can use the e-mail system to share information about production schedules and inventory levels to ship excess products from one country to another.

Many organizations operate their own internal e-mail systems, but communications companies, such as AT&T, offer these services as do commercial online information services, such as America Online and public networks on the Internet (see Chapter 9). Employee use of e-mail and the Internet has become an important management issue, as described in the Window on Management, which examines whether monitoring employees using e-mail, the Internet, and other network facilities is ethical.

Although e-mail has become a valuable tool for communication, groupware provides additional capabilities for supporting enterprise-wide communication and collaborative work. Individuals, teams, and work groups at different locations in the organization can use groupware to participate in discussion forums and to work on shared documents and projects. More details on the use of groupware for collaborative work can be found in Chapters 6 and 13.

VOICE MAIL AND FAX

A **voice mail** system digitizes the sender's spoken message, transmits it over a network, and stores the message on disk for later retrieval. When the recipient is ready to listen, the messages are reconverted to audio form. Various store-and-forward capabilities notify recipients that messages are waiting. Recipients have the option of saving these messages for future use, deleting them, or routing them to other parties.

Facsimile (fax) machines can transmit documents containing both text and graphics over ordinary telephone lines. A sending fax machine scans and digitizes the document image. The digitized document is transmitted over a network and reproduced in hard copy form by a receiving fax machine. The process results in a duplicate, or facsimile, of the original.

TELECONFERENCING, DATACONFERENCING, AND VIDEOCONFERENCING

People can meet electronically, even though they are hundreds or thousands of kilometres apart, by using teleconferencing, dataconferencing, or videoconferencing. **Teleconferencing** allows a group of people to confer simultaneously via telephone or via e-mail group communication software. Teleconferencing that includes the ability of two or more people at distant locations to work on the same document or data simultaneously is called **dataconferencing**. With dataconferencing, users at distant locations are able to edit and modify data (text, such as word processing documents; numeric, such as spreadsheets; and graphic) files. Teleconferencing in which participants see each other over video screens is termed *video teleconferencing*, or **videoconferencing**.

These forms of electronic conferencing are growing in popularity because they save travel time and cost. Legal firms might use videoconferencing to take depositions and to convene meetings among lawyers in different branch offices. Videoconferencing can help companies promote remote collaboration from different locations or fill in personnel expertise gaps. Electronic conferencing is useful for supporting telecommuting, enabling home workers to

voice mail
A system for digitizing a spoken message and transmitting it over a network.

facsimile (fax)
A machine that digitizes and transmits documents with both text and graphics over telephone lines.

teleconferencing
The ability to confer with a group of people simultaneously using the telephone or electronic-mail group communication software.

dataconferencing
Teleconferencing in which two or more users are able to edit and modify data files simultaneously.

videoconferencing
Teleconferencing in which participants see each other over video screens.

MONITORING EMPLOYEES ON NETWORKS: UNETHICAL OR GOOD BUSINESS?

E-mail usage has exploded as hundreds of millions of people the world over turn to it for speedy, convenient, and inexpensive business and personal communications. Not surprisingly, the use of e-mail for personal reasons at the workplace has also grown as has use of the Web for personal purposes. A number of studies have concluded that at least 25 percent of employees' online time is spent on non-work-related Web surfing.

Many companies are starting to monitor their employees' use of e-mail and the Internet. A study by the American Management Association concluded that more than 75 percent of large American companies are recording and reviewing employee communications and activities on the job, including e-mail, Internet connections, and computer files. Although Canadian companies have the legal right to monitor employee Internet and e-mail activities, is this type of monitoring unethical, or is it simply good business? Managers worry about the loss of time and employee productivity when employees are focusing on personal, rather than company, business. If personal traffic on company networks is too high, it can also clog the company's network so that work cannot be performed. Some employees at Xerox had sent so much junk and pornographic e-mail while on the job that the company's e-mail system shut down. Too much time on personal business, Internet or not, can mean lost revenue or overcharges to clients. Some employees may be charging clients for time they spend trading stocks over the Web or pursuing other personal business.

When employees use e-mail or the Web with employer facilities, anything they do, including anything illegal, carries the company's name. Therefore, the employer can be traced and held liable. Management's fear is that racist, sexually explicit, or other potentially offensive material could result in adverse publicity and even lawsuits. Even if a company is found not to be liable, responding to lawsuits will cost the company tens of thousands of dollars at a minimum. Companies also fear leakage of trade secrets through e-mail.

Some companies employ a zero-tolerance policy and try to ban all personal activities on corporate networks. Others block employee access to specific Web sites or limit personal time on the Web by using software that allows them to track the Web sites their employees visit, the amount of time they spend at these sites, and the files they download. New Web monitoring software tools even allow employees to see how their activities are being monitored. Fatline Inc.'s FastTracker includes an "employee view" for workers to see what is being recorded about them. Some firms have fired employees who have stepped out of bounds. No solution is problem free, but many consultants believe that companies should have a written corporate policy on employee e-mail and Internet use. The policy should include explicit ground rules that state, by position or level, under what circumstances employees can use company facilities for e-mail or Internet use. The policy should also inform employees if these activities are being monitored and explain why. The rules may need to be tailored to the specific organization because different companies may need to access different Web materials as part of their business. For example, although some companies may exclude anyone from visiting sites that have explicit sexual material, law firm or hospital employees may require access, while investment firms will need to allow many of their employees access to other investment sites.

To Think About: Should managers monitor employee e-mail and Internet usage? Why, or why not? Should Canadian businesses follow the American trend and monitor employees in the workplace? Describe an effective e-mail and Web use policy for a company.

Source: Sandra Swanson, "Employers Take a Closer Look," *Information-Week,* July 15, 2002; Laura Hunt, "E-mail Monitoring: Why You Should Pry," *SearchEbusiness.com,* April 16, 2002; Brett Glass, "Are You Being Watched?" *PC Magazine,* April 2002; Lou Hirsch, "The Boss Is Watching: Monitoring on the Rise," *NewsFactor Network,* June 29, 2001; Stephen Shankland, "Study: Web, E-Mail Monitoring Spreads," *CNET News,* July 8, 2001; and "U.S. Web Use Mostly at Work," Reuters, April 6, 2000.

meet with or collaborate with their counterparts working in the office or elsewhere. The Window on Organizations describes how these technologies can improve medical care throughout the world.

Videoconferencing usually has required special videoconference rooms and equipment that used to be very expensive. Falling prices for room-based videoconferencing and the availability of inexpensive PC-based, desktop videoconferencing systems have reduced videoconferencing costs so that more organizations can benefit from this technology.

Organizations

Desktop videoconferencing systems typically provide "windows" for users to see each other and capabilities for participants to work on the same document from different locations. Most desktop systems provide audio capabilities for two-way, real-time conversations and a *whiteboard*. The whiteboard is a shared drawing program that lets multiple users collaborate on projects by modifying images and text online. There are software products, such as

CLOSING THE HEALTHCARE GAP WITH VIDEOCONFERENCING

In advanced countries, many people live in underserviced areas, but they still need access to adequate healthcare. In Canada, several different programs, most run by hospitals or funded by provincial governments, are beginning to provide advanced healthcare to outlying areas through the use of advanced networking capabilities.

Until recently, if you lived in remote parts of Central British Columbia or the Yukon Territory, getting an X-ray was sometimes a bit different than it is for most Canadians. The difference? Time. Sure there were local X-ray machines, but in many cases, the general practitioners available to the communities could not provide specialized diagnoses. So the X-rays were couriered to radiologists in major referral hospitals, usually in BC's lower mainland. This took time, and in extreme cases, put patients at extra risk. But that has changed with access to a new "telehealth" network. The data network uses Picture Archiving Communications System (PACS), which allows staff at a number of remote hospitals and treatment centres the ability to consult instantly with medical colleagues elsewhere in BC.

Another medical use of videoconferencing was recently seen 8000 km away from Vancouver when four Maritime neurosurgeons collaborated in performing surgery, removing a patient's brain tumour in a Saint John, New Brunswick, operating theatre. The interesting part was that two of those four surgeons weren't there—they were 400 km away, operating a robotic arm from Halifax, Nova Scotia, and watching the results on a monitor. The operation showed the worth of establishing a telerobotic neurosurgery in the region. The aim is to export the specialized knowledge that exists in Halifax to rural parts of the region, instead of forcing patients—often desperately ill—to travel to the city. The telesurgery team worked with a Socrates Robotic Tele-Collaboration System. Costing half a million dollars, the system allows the surgeons in Halifax to control a robotic arm that manipulated a powerful endoscope with a miniature camera.

With two-way video and audio, all four doctors were fully engaged and informed.

The Canada Health Infostructure Partnerships Program (CHIPP) supports collaboration, innovation, and renewal in healthcare delivery through the use of information and communication technologies. Investing primarily in telehealth and electronic health records model projects, CHIPP helps improve accessibility and quality of care for all Canadians. Recently, CHIPP, funded by the Government of Canada, contributed $900 000 to the primary-care telemedicine and distance nursing network in Abitibi-Témiscamingue to improve service delivery to people living in rural and First Nations communities in that region. The funds will create an information network to allow live consultations between physicians from urban communities and a nurse and patient at a rural health centre. This reduces patient and medical personnel travel in a very large geographical area (20 000 km^2).

The Bell Canada Telemedicine Centre, located at Centenary Health Centre, permits health professionals to provide education and service to over 200 000 children. The Centre contains equipment and technology to help diagnose patients through live connections to such centres as the Toronto Hospital for Sick Children. Medical professionals can read X-rays, watch monitors, and hear heartbeats using the Centre's technology.

To Think About: What are the benefits of videoconferencing in medicine? How has videoconferencing changed the way medicine is practised?

Sources: "Canada Health Infostructure Partnerships Program Project: Central BC-Yukon Telemedicine Initiative," available **www.hc-sc.gc.ca/ohih-bsi**, accessed July 31, 2002; Donalee Moulton, "Surgeons in Halifax, patient in Saint John," *Canadian Medical Association Journal*, available **www.cmaj.ca/cgi/content/full/167/11/1282-a**, accessed November 26, 2002; "Anne McLellan Announces Funding for Primary Care Telemedicine and Distance Nursing Network," available **www.hcsc.gc.ca/english/media/releases/2002/2002_05.htm**, accessed February 4, 2002; "Connecting Kids With Care, available **www.bell.ca/en/about/bic/community/telemedicine_Canada.asp**, accessed March 30, 2003.

With PC desktop videoconferencing systems, users can see each other and simultanously work on the same document. Organizations are using videoconferencing to improve coordination and save travel time and costs.

TABLE 8.3	COMMERCIAL DIGITAL INFORMATION SERVICES

Provider	Type of Service
America Online	General interest/business information
Microsoft Network	General interest/business information
Dow Jones News Retrieval	Business/financial information
Dialog	Business/scientific/technical information
LexisNexis	News/business/legal information

Microsoft NetMeeting (a feature of the Windows operating system) and CU-SeeMe (available in both shareware and commercial versions), that provide low-cost tools for desktop videoconferencing over the Internet.

DIGITAL INFORMATION SERVICES, DISTANCE LEARNING, AND E-LEARNING

Powerful and far-reaching digital electronic services enable networked PC and workstation users to obtain information from outside the firm instantly without leaving their desks. Stock prices, periodicals, competitor data, industrial supplies catalogues, legal research, news articles, reference works, and weather forecasts are some of the information that can be accessed online. Many of these services provide capabilities for e-mail, electronic bulletin boards, online discussion groups, shopping, and travel reservations as well as Internet access. Table 8.3 describes the leading commercial digital information services. The following chapter describes how organizations can access even more information resources using the Internet. (See Figure 8.9.)

distance learning

Education or training delivered over a distance to individuals in one or more locations.

Organizations can also use communications technology to run distance learning programs where they can train employees in remote locations without requiring the employees to be physically present in a classroom. **Distance learning** is education or training delivered over

Figure 8.9 America Online gives subscribers access to extensive information resources, including news reports, weather, education, financial services, and information on the Web. Companies and individuals can use their digital information services to obtain information instantly from their desktops.

a distance to individuals in one or more locations. Although distance learning can be accomplished with print-based materials, the distance learning experience is now increasingly based on information technology, with videoconferencing, satellite or cable television, or interactive multimedia, including the Web. The term **e-learning** is increasingly being used to describe instruction using purely digital technology, such as CD-ROMs, the Internet, or private networks. Some distance learning programs use *synchronous communication,* where teacher and student are present at the same time during the instruction, even if they are in different places. Other programs use *asynchronous communication,* where teacher and student do not have person-to-person interaction at the same time or place. For example, students might access a Web site to obtain their course materials and communicate with their instructors via e-mail. (See Figure 8.10.)

e-learning

Instruction delivered through purely digital technology, such as CD-ROMs, the Internet, or private networks.

ELECTRONIC DATA INTERCHANGE

Electronic data interchange (EDI) is a key technology for electronic commerce because it allows the computer-to-computer exchange between two organizations of standard transaction documents, such as invoices, bills of lading, or purchase orders. EDI lowers transaction costs because transactions can be automatically transmitted from one information system to another through a telecommunications network, eliminating the printing and handling of paper at one end and the inputting of data at the other. EDI also may provide strategic benefits by helping a firm lock in customers, making it easier for customers or distributors to order from them, rather than from competitors. EDI can curb inventory costs by minimizing the amount of time that components are in inventory. Also, data entry costs are reduced, and errors to entering data multiple times are greatly reduced.

EDI differs from e-mail in that it transmits an actual structured transaction (with distinct fields, such as the transaction date, transaction amount, sender's name, and recipient's name) as opposed to an unstructured text message, such as a letter. Figure 8.11 illustrates how EDI works.

Organizations can most fully benefit from EDI when they integrate the data supplied by EDI with applications, such as accounts payable, inventory control, shipping, and production planning, and when they have carefully planned for the organizational changes surrounding new business processes (Premkumar, Ramamurthy, and Nilakanta, 1994).

electronic data interchange (EDI)

The direct computer-to-computer exchange between two organizations of standard business transaction documents.

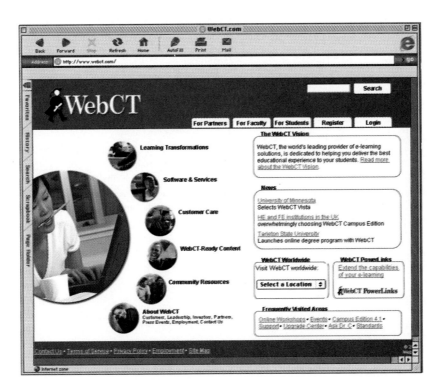

Figure 8.10 Instructors can use WebCT Web-based software to provide their students with course materials and a dedicated academic resource centre on the Web. Such tools can be used to support distance learning.

Figure 8.11 Electronic data interchange (EDI). Companies can use EDI to automate electronic commerce transactions. Purchase orders and payments can be transmitted directly from the customer's computer to the seller's computer. The seller can transmit shipping notices, price changes, and invoices electronically back to the customer.

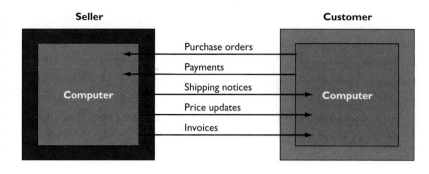

Management support and training in the new technology are essential (Raymond and Bergeron, 1996). Companies must also standardize the form of the transactions they use with other firms and comply with legal requirements for verifying that the transactions are authentic. Many organizations prefer to use private networks for EDI transactions but are increasingly turning to the Internet for this purpose (see Chapters 4 and 9). See Chapter 4 for ways in which extranets are being used for EDI.

Regardless of how an organization approaches its telecommunications needs and environment, management must proactively plan for the future and for implementation of the telecommunications and networking environment. The Manager's Toolkit for this chapter addresses this important issue.

MIS IN ACTION: MANAGER'S TOOLKIT

DEVELOPING A BUSINESS-DRIVEN TELECOMMUNICATIONS PLAN

Throughout your career, you may be asked to find ways to use telecommunications technology to enhance your firm's competitive position. Here are the steps you need to take to develop a strategic telecommunications plan.

1. Determine the role of telecommunications in your firm's strategy. If your firm's long-range business plan requires increasing the scale and scope of operations, creating new products or services, or lowering operational costs, consider whether new telecommunications applications and services could promote these objectives.

2. Assess your firm's existing voice, data, and video communications capabilities. Are they sufficient to meet future business goals? What areas need improvement?

3. If additional telecommunications capabilities are required, establish the scope of these capabilities. You will need to consider the following:

   ◼ *Distance*: Are future communications needs primarily local or long distance?

   ◼ *Services*: What range of telecommunications services are needed? Do they include e-mail, EDI, Web access, voice mail, videoconferencing, graphics transmission, and internally generated transactions? Do these services need to be integrated?

   ◼ *Points of access*: How many different locations and users in the organization require access to new communications services and capabilities?

   ◼ *Utilization*: What frequency and volume of communications does your firm anticipate?

   ◼ *Cost*: How much do the proposed telecommunications technology options cost? Which cost components are fixed? Which are variable?

   ◼ *Security*: What level of security and reliability do the proposed networks have to maintain?

   ◼ *Connectivity*: How much time, money, and effort would be required to make sure that all of the disparate components of a network or multiple networks can communicate with each other (see Chapter 9)?

MANAGEMENT WRAP-UP

Managers need to be continually involved in telecommunications decisions because so many important business processes are based on telecommunications and networks. Management should identify the business opportunities linked to telecommunications technology and establish the business criteria for selecting the firm's telecommunications platform.

Telecommunications technology enables organizations to reduce transaction and coordination costs, promoting electronic commerce and electronic business. The organization's telecommunications infrastructure should support its business processes and business strategy.

Communications technology is intertwined with all the other information technologies and deeply embedded in contemporary information systems. Networks are becoming more pervasive and powerful, with capabilities to transmit voice, data, and video over long distances. Many alternative network designs, transmission technologies, and network services are available to organizations.

For Discussion

1. Network design is a key business decision as well as a technology decision. Why?

2. If you were an international company with global operations, what criteria would you use to determine whether to use a VAN service or a private WAN?

SUMMARY

1. *What technologies are used in telecommunications systems?* A telecommunications system consists of devices that create a network for communication from one location to another by electronic means. The essential components of a telecommunications system are computers, terminals, other input/output devices, communications channels, communications processors (such as modems, multiplexers, controllers, concentrators, and front-end processors), and telecommunications software. Data are transmitted throughout a telecommunications network using either analog signals or digital signals. A modem is a device that translates analog signals to digital signals and vice versa. Different components of a telecommunications network can communicate with each other using a common set of rules called protocols.

2. *What telecommunications transmission media should our organization use?* The capacity of a telecommunications channel is determined by the range of frequencies it can accommodate. The higher the range of frequencies, called bandwidth, the higher is the capacity (measured in bits per second, bps). The principal transmission media are twisted copper telephone wire, coaxial copper cable, fibre-optic cable, and wireless transmission using microwave, satellite, low-frequency radio waves, or infrared waves. The choice of transmission medium depends on the distance and volume of communication required by the organization and its financial resources.

3. *How should our organization design its networks?* Network design should be based on the organization's information requirements and the distance required for transmission. The three common network topologies are the star, bus, and ring networks. Local area networks (LANs) and private branch exchanges (PBXs) are used to link offices and buildings in close proximity. PBXs are limited to existing telephone lines and low transmission speeds. Conventional LANs require special wiring, but technology, such as 802.11b (Wi-Fi), can be used to construct low-cost, high-speed wireless LANs. Wide area networks (WANs) span a broad geographical distance and are private networks that may be independently managed.

4. *What alternative network services are available to our organization?* A number of services are available to organizations for network management and Internet access. Value-added networks (VANs) sell wide area networking services to companies that do not want to build or maintain their own private networks.

   Integrated Services Digital Network (ISDN) is an international standard for high-speed dial-up network access that integrates voice, data, image, and video services in a single link.

   Firms have the option of using frame relay, asynchronous transfer mode (ATM), digital subscriber line, cable modem, and T1 lines for high transmission capacity.

Digital subscriber line (DSL) technologies, cable modems, and T1 lines are often used for high-capacity Internet connections.

5. *What telecommunications applications can be used for electronic business and electronic commerce?* The principal telecommunications applications for electronic commerce and electronic business are e-mail, voice mail, fax, digital information services, distance learning, teleconferencing, dataconferencing, videoconferencing, electronic data interchange (EDI), and groupware. EDI is the computer-to-computer exchange between two organizations of standard transaction documents, such as invoices, bills of lading, and purchase orders.

KEY TERMS

802.11b (Wi-Fi),   269

Analog signal,   261

Asynchronous transfer mode (ATM),   271

Backbone,   262

Bandwidth,   265

Baud,   265

Bluetooth,   270

Broadband,   272

Bus network,   267

Cable modem,   272

Cellular telephone (cell phone),   264

Channels,   261

Coaxial cable,   262

Concentrator,   266

Controller,   266

Converged network,   272

Dataconferencing,   273

Dedicated lines,   270

Dense wavelength division multiplexing (DWDM),   262

Digital signal,   261

Digital subscriber line (DSL),   272

Distance learning,   276

E-learning,   277

Electronic data interchange (EDI),   277

Facsimile (fax),   273

Fibre-optic cable,   262

Frame relay,   271

Front-end processor,   265

Gateway,   269

Integrated Services Digital Network (ISDN),   271

Local area network (LAN),   268

Microwave,   263

Mobile data networks,   264

Modem,   261

Multiplexer,   266

Network interface card (NIC),   269

Network operating system (NOS),   269

Optical network,   262

Packet switching,   271

Paging system,   264

Peer-to-peer,   269

Personal communication services (PCS),   264

Personal digital assistants (PDA),   264

Private branch exchange (PBX),   268

Protocol,   261

Ring network,   267

Router,   269

Satellite,   263

Smart phone,   264

Star network,   266

Switched lines,   270

T1 line,   272

Telecommunications,   260

Telecommunications system,   260

Teleconferencing,   273

Topology,   266

Twisted wire,   262

Unified messaging,   272

Value-added network (VAN),   270

Videoconferencing,   273

Voice mail,   273

Wide area network (WAN),   270

REVIEW QUESTIONS

1. Why has telecommunications technology become such an important issue for managers and organizations?

2. What is a telecommunications system? What are the principal functions of all telecommunications systems?

3. Name and briefly describe each of the components of a telecommunications system.

4. Distinguish between analog and digital signals.

5. Name the different types of telecommunications transmission media and compare them in terms of speed and cost.

6. Name and describe the technologies used for wireless transmission.

7. What are optical networks? Why are they becoming important?

8. What is the relationship between bandwidth and a channel's transmission capacity?

9. Name and briefly describe the different kinds of communications processors.

10. Name and briefly describe the three principal network topologies.

11. Distinguish between a PBX and a LAN.

12. What are the components of a typical LAN? What are the functions of each component? Describe the technologies for wireless LANs.

13. List and describe the various network services.

14. Distinguish between a WAN and a VAN.

15. Define the following: modem, baud, protocol, converged network, and broadband.

16. Name and describe the telecommunications applications that can support electronic commerce and electronic business.

APPLICATION SOFTWARE EXERCISE

You can find a spreadsheet exercise on Analyzing Telecommunications Costs at our Companion Website for Chapter 8.

GROUP PROJECT

With a group of two or three of your fellow students, describe in detail the ways that telecommunications technology can provide a firm with competitive advantage. Use the companies described in Chapter 3 or other chapters you have read thus far to illustrate the points you make, or select examples of other companies using telecommunications from business or computer magazines. If possible, use electronic presentation software to present your findings to the class.

 INTERNET TOOLS

COMPANION WEBSITE

The Companion Website for this chapter will take you to the Rosenbluth Travel Web site where you can complete an exercise to analyze how Rosenbluth International uses the Web and communications technology in its daily operations.

At www.pearsoned.ca/laudon, you will find valuable tools to facilitate and enhance your learning of this chapter as well as opportunities to apply your knowledge to realistic situations:

- An Interactive Study Guide of self-test questions that will provide you with immediate feedback.
- Application exercises.
- An Electronic Business Project to compare and evaluate the supply chain management services of Schneider National and J.B. Hunt.
- A Management Decision Problem on selecting an Internet connection service.
- Updates of material in the chapter.

ADDITIONAL SITES OF INTEREST

There are many interesting Web sites to enhance your learning about telecommunications and networks. You can search the Web yourself or just try the following sites to add to what you have already learned.

World Wide Web Consortium

www.w3.org

One of the World Wide Web coordinating bodies. Find out what the Web may be like in the future.

Canadian Laws

www.laws.justice.gc.ca

Parliament's site to search for laws that have been passed or bills that have been submitted to Parliament. See what Parliament may be planning for regulating telecommunications in Canada.

Search Networking

www.searchnetworking.com

A terrific site to find answers to questions about telecommunications.

CASE STUDY: *Wired or Wireless Where You Least Expect It*

Years ago—or was it only months ago?—an employee or even a business owner or executive could take a holiday and never have to report in for weeks at a time. Long weeks at the beach or even in a foreign country without contact with the office are now a thing of the past. Today, you can be in touch with your workplace from almost anywhere in the world—even while on an airplane—from your own computer.

Business travel accounts for a large portion of Canadian travel expenditures, which means hotel guests often tote laptops along with their luggage. Hotels are doing their part to provide good workspace and business-oriented amenities. Hotels that do not offer Internet access from their hotel rooms (frequently for an added charge) offer business centres, where guests can log on from the hotel's computers.

One example is Starwood Hotels and Resorts Worldwide, which runs Sheraton Hotels (**www.starwoodhotels.com**). Starwood is chasing the tech-savvy traveller with what it calls "smart rooms" in many of it its Sheraton Hotels. These rooms include computers, fax machines, and printers, and are ready for the wired traveller to work out of with no fuss. Starwood has taken the concept a step further as well—from the hotel suite to the restaurant table. At its Sheraton Centre Toronto Hotel restaurant, patrons can choose to be seated at a "Table for One," which is wired for Web access and designed with space for a laptop and paperwork. In New York, the Sheraton offers guests use of Cisco Internet Mobile office that provides Cisco Long-Reach Ethernet Web connectivity from hotel rooms.

What if you are just walking around on your business trip or vacation and decide to stop at McDonald's? There, too, you may not be able to escape the Internet. A number of the fast food giant's outlets in and around New York offer free wireless Internet access with the purchase of an Extra Value meal. McDonald's plans to expand this program to many more outlets in major American cities. Can Toronto and Vancouver be far behind?

Cometa Networks is the wireless LAN hot spot company behind the McDonald's technology. Founded by AT&T, IBM, and Intel, Cometa Networks is positioned as a wholesaler to service providers. IBM Global Services is taking care of security access and much of the backend integration in the McDonald's pilot. According to Norm Korey, vice-president of wireless services for IBM Global Services, it's nothing more than delivery on the promise of Wi-Fi technology in a public environment. He adds that McDonald's pricing plan may change, depending on how the pilot program plays out. The suggestion is that once the free hour of Internet access ends, another hour will cost US$3. And it goes without saying that the longer the customer remains in the restaurant, the more food they're likely to buy.

McDonald's foray into providing Internet access comes as Intel launches a new product called the Centrino chipset. This unit includes an 802.11b wireless LAN (WLAN) module, and Intel wants customers to want to work in public hot spots to support their new product. Intel is paying for an advertising campaign pushing public hot spots at hundreds of Borders Book and Music locations around the US; these services are provided by T-Mobile, which is also providing the services behind the WLAN hot spots in Starbucks' coffee shops.

As you board your next flight, be sure to ask if the plane offers Internet access and computer plug-in services. Today, airlines are starting to make electrical power available at the passenger seat. Most computer or office supply stores now sell power adapters for your computer's power supply to plug into the airplane's outlet. Not only can you plug in to work on your laptop, you can even access the Internet on some aircrafts.

Lufthansa is testing in-flight broadband Internet service for e-mailing and Web surfing. Of course, this service is only for first- or business-class passengers. Still, it may portend the future for tourist class as well. (In fact, Lufthansa is planning on permitting economy-class passengers to connect wirelessly.) British Airways has done the same thing, and Japan Airlines and Scandinavian Airlines (SAS) plan to do likewise. If things go as envisioned, Lufthansa hopes to equip its long-haul jets with FlyNet service. The cost for a passenger to fly connected? Estimated at up to US$35 per flight for unlimited use. Lufthansa is trying it out on its Washington-to-Frankfurt flight for three months; passengers can log on for free using their own laptops. According to the airline, no special software is necessary, and there are twenty-odd laptops on each plane for passengers who left theirs on the ground. (But don't expect the loaners after the test period is over.)

Lufthansa is using a system it got from Boeing: there are ports throughout the planes which are connected via an on-board server and routers to several antennae, which in turn up-link to satellites and from there the Internet. Lufthansa is also testing wireless on-board access. Connexion by Boeing, a unit of The Boeing Company, will provide the satellite-based data communications service in the air. Vodafone Group will provide the WLAN service on the ground.

The in-flight broadband service will offer speeds of up to 20 Mbps to the aircraft and 1 Mbps from the aircraft, although the speeds can vary due to weather and other factors, according to Terrance Scott, a Connexion spokesperson.

"At the very minimum, customers should have ISDN speeds of 64 Kbps, but most of the time speeds will be much higher," said Hoffmann.

"The WLAN service will be available at speeds up to 11 Mbps," he said.

Boeing's system maintains constant contact (unlike slower systems on other airlines, such as Continental Airlines, that connect only periodically), so the connection is about as fast as a cable modem at home.

"Our aim is to offer broadband connectivity to passengers on all our long-haul flights outside of Europe and in our many lounges around the world," he said. "We expect substantial demand for the service," said airline spokesperson Bernd Hoffmann.

But what does one do while waiting at the airport? Lufthansa is also providing wireless Internet access in more than 50 of its airport lounges. The service will be free during the three-month trial period.

Sources: "Hot Wired Hotels," *IQ Magazine,* July/August 2002; "Surf at 9000 Meters?" *Time Canada,* March 2003; Carmen Nobel, "McDonald's Adds WLAN Access to Its Menu," *eWeek,* March 11, 2003; "Notebooks and Accessories: Lufthansa Net Access Takes Flight," *Mobile Computing e-newsletter,* January 16, 2003; John Blau, "Lufthansa Readies Broadband in Flight," *PC World,* December 10, 2002.

CASE STUDY QUESTIONS

1. Why would Lufthansa—and other airlines—want to offer Internet services to passengers? Why would Boeing, a company that makes airplanes, develop and sell the Connexion service? Are these companies following their organizational strategies?

2. What do you think of the idea of offering service for free during the trial period and then charging for it? Have you seen this with other products and services? Is it a good business model for a startup product or service?

3. Do you think it will come to be expected that hotels will offer high-speed Internet access in their hotel rooms? Do you think there should be a charge for Internet access?

4. What happens to the typical employee who wishes to be on vacation but whose boss can insist on the employee checking his or her e-mail, since it is relatively convenient to do so? Should businesses issue policies mandating that vacation time is time away from contact with the company, or should they take advantage of this new connectivity?

CHAPTER

THE INTERNET AND ITS INFRASTRUCTURE

Objectives

As a manager, you will need to know how to maximize the benefits of Internet technology in your firm's information technology infrastructure. After reading this chapter, you should be able to answer the following questions:

1. *What is the new information technology (IT) infrastructure for business? Why is connectivity so important in this infrastructure?*

2. *How does the Internet work? What are its major capabilities?*

3. *How can organizations benefit from using the World Wide Web and Web technology? How can businesses benefit from the Wireless Web?*

4. *What are the principal technologies for supporting electronic commerce and electronic business?*

5. *What management problems are raised by the new information technology IT infrastructure? How can businesses solve these problems?*

Web Services Taking Off? Or Just More Hype?

Even a company like Microsoft Canada has trouble integrating its "islands of data" in its legacy systems. According to Rick Devenuti, Chief Information Officer (CIO) of Microsoft USA, Web services have enabled Microsoft to pull together data from three or four sources, such as their sales force automation system (by Siebel), their customer support data (by Clarify), and their own data warehouse. According to Denuti, the initial impetus for the project was users trying to access Siebel information. "If you wanted to look at current Siebel information, you needed to be connected to a Siebel server and go through the Siebel process. The request (from our internal business clients) was, 'Why can't we do that with a browser?'"

Denuti said, "I think everybody is aware of the power that XML and Web services can provide to the underlying data that the company has ... Many of the peers I talk to don't spend nearly as

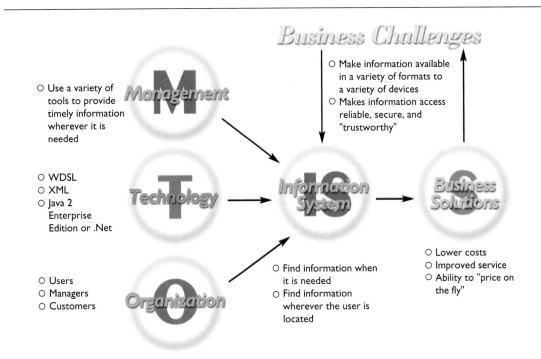

much time around information—how we use it and how we move it around. That's what Web services enable us to do. The term infostructure really resonates with me. That's the task we have. We've got lots of data, lots of business intelligence—how do we get it to the right person at the right time, and can Web services help?" Yet, Denuti acknowledges that there are still hurdles for Web service technology to overcome, particularly reliability, security, and trustworthiness around privacy.

As you can see from Denuti's comments, the latest trend in Internet technologies, called Web services, is to make everything available to anyone who has been given authorization to access the data, information, software, or service being provided over the Internet. Web services (sometimes called application services) are services (usually including some combination of programming and data, but possibly including human resources as well) that are made available from a business's Web server for Web users or other Web-connected programs. Providers of Web services are generally known as application service providers. Web services range from such major services as storage management and customer relationship management (CRM) down to much more limited services, such as the furnishing of a stock quote and the checking of bids for an auction item. The acceleration of the creation and availability of these services is a major Web trend.

Some services can communicate with other services, and this exchange of procedures and data is generally enabled by a class of software known as *middleware*. Services previously possible only with the older standardized service known as *electronic data interchange (EDI)* increasingly are likely to become Web services. Besides the standardization and wide availability to users and businesses of the Internet itself, Web services are also increasingly enabled by the use of eXtensible Markup Language (XML) as a means of standardizing data formats and exchanging data. XML is the foundation for the Web Services Description Language (WSDL).

As Web services proliferate, concerns include the overall demands on network bandwidth and, for any particular service, the effect on performance as demands for that service rise. A number of new products have emerged that enable software developers to create or modify existing applications that can be "published" (made known and potentially accessible) as Web services.

In spite of Microsoft's enthusiasm for Web services, 73 percent of Canadian FP (*Financial Post*) 500 enterprises do not currently have a Web services implementation plan in place even though 54 percent feel that Web services will be somewhat or very important to their organizations in the next three years. As usual, vendors are not making it easy for companies to make their decisions. Sun Microsystems has created one Web services platform based on its open-source Java 2 Enterprise Edition (J2EE), while Microsoft offers .Net, its universal platform technology approach. J2EE is cheap, since it is open source, but it is not easy to use. Microsoft's technology, while costing a lot more, is relatively easy to use. While many companies, such as IBM and Borland Software, are supporting the J2EE environment, Microsoft's approach understands many programming languages, such as Visual Basic and C++, so developers can work in the language of their choice.

RadioShack Canada Ltd., Canada's oldest national electronics retailer with more than 900 stores, has been doing business for 30 years from its Barrie, Ontario, headquarters. Recently, RadioShack Canada partnered with Hewlett-Packard and Microsoft Canada. Presenting all of the content on its Web site in both English and French, a requirement for Canadian businesses, places double demands on its electronic commerce computing infrastructure, according to Vice-President of Information Systems Margo Weeks. RadioShack meets this challenge with ProLiant servers running Microsoft Commerce Server 2002 and other Microsoft software.

"Before upgrading to Microsoft Commerce Server 2002, we had to maintain two separate sites, which amounted to twice the work," explains Weeks. "Due to the multilingual support of Microsoft Commerce Server 2002, we consolidated our Web sites to produce a single implementation with dual-language variants. We are now 50 percent more productive, which is invaluable given the small size of our IT team." In addition to Microsoft Commerce Server 2002, Weeks deployed other components of the Microsoft .Net Web Services framework. Weeks says her team is already employing an extensive menu of tools, including Microsoft .Net Passport, Microsoft Visual Studio .Net, Microsoft Visual Basic .Net, and Microsoft ASP .Net, C#, and Biztalk software. These tools work within the Web services framework to make the plethora of data on RadioShack Canada's Web site available to users from a variety of platforms. The Web site will soon offer RadioShack Canada additional customer-centric features, such as user profiling and business analytics. This will allow RadioShack staff to use analytics to quickly scrutinize very large data sets and to link and analyze complex data over the Web. "This is important to us because it will keep us at the forefront of rapidly determining and providing what our customers want. We can package services and products that fulfill customer needs as quickly as they arise. It allows us to be as responsive as a small company, but with the benefits and resources of a large company."

David Wilkins, a senior technology analyst with Ontario's Ministry of Health and Long-Term Care, had this to say about Web services. "It's basically transferring data around a network. 'Web services' is just a fancy word for what we've already been doing."

Sources: David Carey, "Putting Web Services to Work," *CIO Canada,* December 1, 2002; Ryan B. Patrick, "Portals Key to E-Commerce Growth: Report," *Computerworld Canada,* June 28, 2002; Stefan Dubowski, "Comdex Attendees Ask: Whither Web Services?" *ITWorld Canada,* available www.itworld.ca, accessed July 15, 2002; "RadioShack Canada Ltd.," Customer Case Study, available http://h18006.www1.hp.com/storage/casestudies/radioshackca.html, accessed April 7, 2003.

MANAGEMENT CHALLENGES

Many organizations are extending their information technology infrastructures to include mobile computing devices, access to the Internet, and electronic links to other organizations. Electronic commerce, electronic business, and the emerging digital firm require a new IT infrastructure that can integrate information from a variety of sources and applications. However, using Internet technology and this new IT infrastructure to digitally enable the firm raises the following management challenges:

1. **Taking a broader perspective on infrastructure development.** Electronic business and electronic commerce require an IT infrastructure that can coordinate commerce-related transactions and operational activities across business processes and perhaps link the firm to others in its industry. The new IT infrastructure for the digitally enabled firm connects the whole enterprise and links with other infrastructures, including those of other organizations and the public Internet. Management can no longer think in terms of isolated networks and applications or technologies confined to organizational boundaries.

2. **Selecting technologies for the new IT infrastructure.** Internet technology, XML, and Java can only provide limited connectivity and application integration. Many firms have major applications where disparate hardware, software, and network components must be coordinated through other means. Without additional equipment, expense, and management overhead, networks based on one standard may not be able to be linked to those based on another. Integrating business applications requires software tools that can support the firm's business processes and data structures, and these may not always provide the level of application integration desired. Networks that meet today's requirements may lack the connectivity for domestic or global expansion in the future. Managers may have trouble choosing the right set of technologies for the firm's IT infrastructure.

M̲ost of the information systems we use today require networks and communications technology. Large and small companies all over the world are using networking systems and the Internet to locate suppliers and buyers, to negotiate contracts with them, and to service their needs. Applications of networks are multiplying in research, organizational coordination, and control. Networked systems are fundamental to electronic commerce and electronic business.

Today's computing tasks are so closely tied to networks that some believe "the network is the computer." This chapter describes the components of telecommunications systems, showing how they can be arranged to create various types of networks and network-based applications that can increase an organization's efficiency and competitiveness.

9.1 THE NEW IT INFRASTRUCTURE FOR THE DIGITAL FIRM

Today's firms can use the information technologies we have described in previous chapters to create an IT infrastructure capable of coordinating the activities of entire firms and even entire industries. By enabling companies to radically reduce their agency and transaction costs, this new IT infrastructure provides a broad platform for electronic commerce, electronic business, and the emerging digital firm. This new IT infrastructure is based on powerful networks and Internet technology.

ENTERPRISE NETWORKING AND INTERNETWORKING

Figure 9.1 illustrates the new IT infrastructure, which uses a mixture of computer hardware supplied by different vendors. Large, complex databases that need central storage are found on mainframes or specialized servers, while smaller databases and parts of large databases are

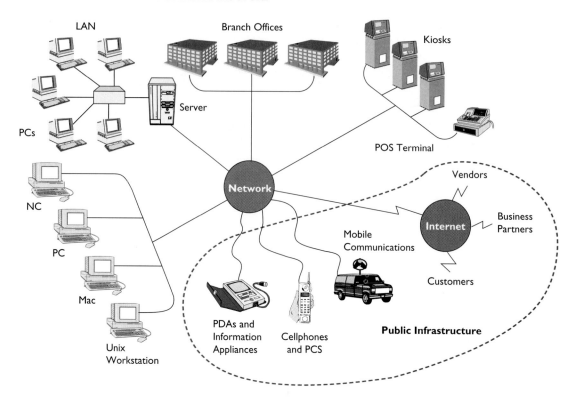

Figure 9.1 The new information technology infrastructure. The new IT infrastructure links desktop workstations, network computers, local area networks (LANs), and server computers in an enterprise network so that information can flow freely throughout different parts of the organization. The enterprise network may also be linked to kiosks, point-of-sale (POS) terminals, PDAs, digital cell phones and personal communications systems (PCS), and other mobile computing devices as well as to the Internet-using public infrastructures. Customers, suppliers, and business partners may also be linked to the organization through this new IT infrastructure.

loaded on personal computers (PCs) and workstations. Client-server computing often is used to distribute more processing power to the desktop. The desktop itself has been extended to a larger workspace that includes programmable cell phones, personal digital applications (PDAs), pagers, and other mobile computing devices. This new IT infrastructure also incorporates public infrastructures, such as the telephone system, the Internet, and public network services. Internet technology plays a pivotal role in this new infrastructure as the principal communication channel with customers, employees, vendors, and distributors.

In the past, firms generally developed their own software and their own computing facilities. As today's firms move toward this new infrastructure, their information systems departments are changing their roles to managers of software packages and software and networking services provided by outside vendors.

Through enterprise networking and internetworking, information flows smoothly between all of these devices within the organization and between the organization and its external environment. In **enterprise networking**, the organization's hardware, software, network, and data resources are arranged to put more computing power on the desktop and to create a company-wide network linking many smaller networks. The system is a network. In fact, for all but the smallest organizations, the system is composed of multiple networks. A high-capacity backbone network connects many LANs and devices.

The backbone may be connected to the networks of other organizations outside the firm, to the Internet, to the networks of public telecommunications service providers, or to other public networks. The linking of separate networks, each of which retains its own identity, into an interconnected network is called **internetworking.**

enterprise networking

An arrangement of the organization's hardware, software, network, and data resources to put more computing power on the desktop and create a company-wide network linking many smaller networks.

internetworking

The linking of separate networks, each of which retains its own identity, into an interconnected network.

STANDARDS AND CONNECTIVITY FOR DIGITAL INTEGRATION

The new IT infrastructure is most likely to increase productivity and competitive advantage when digitized information can move seamlessly through the organization's web of electronic networks, connecting different kinds of machines, people, sensors, databases, functional divisions, departments, and work groups. This ability of computers and computer-based devices to communicate with one another and "share" information in a meaningful way without human intervention is called **connectivity**. Internet technology, XML, and Java software provide some of this connectivity, but these technologies cannot be used as a foundation for all of the organization's information systems. Most organizations still use proprietary networks. They need to develop their own connectivity solutions to make different kinds of hardware, software, and communications systems work together.

Achieving connectivity requires standards for networking, operating systems, and user interfaces. Open systems promote connectivity because they enable disparate equipment and services to work together. **Open systems** are built on public, nonproprietary operating systems, user interfaces, application standards, and networking protocols. In open systems, software can operate on different hardware platforms and, in that sense, can be "portable." Java software, described in Chapter 6, can create an open system environment. The UNIX operating system supports open systems because it can operate on many different kinds of computer hardware. However, there are different versions of UNIX, and no one version has been accepted as an open systems standard. Linux also supports open systems.

Models of Connectivity for Networks

There are different models for achieving connectivity in telecommunications networks. The **Transmission Control Protocol/Internet Protocol (TCP/IP)** model was developed by the U.S. Department of Defense in 1972 and is used in the Internet. Its purpose was to help scientists link disparate computers. Figure 9.2 shows that TCP/IP has a five-layer reference model.

1. *Application:* Provides end-user functionality by translating the messages into the user-host software for screen presentation.

2. *Transmission Control Protocol (TCP):* Performs transport, breaking application data from the end user down into TCP packets called *datagrams.* Each packet consists of a header with the address of the sending host computer, information for putting the data back together, and information for making sure the packets do not become corrupted.

connectivity

A measure of how well computers and computer-based devices communicate and share information with one another without human intervention.

open systems

Software systems that can operate on different hardware platforms because they are built on public nonproprietary operating systems, user interfaces, application standards, and networking protocols.

Transmission Control Protocol/Internet Protocol (TCP/IP)

U.S. Department of Defense reference model for linking different types of computers and networks; used in the Internet.

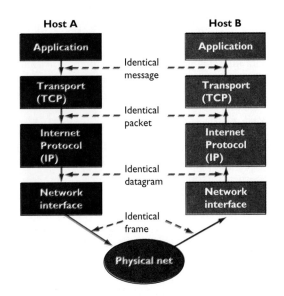

Figure 9.2 The Transmission Control Protocol/Internet Protocol (TCP/IP) reference model. This figure illustrates the five layers of the TCP/IP reference model for communications.

3. *Internet Protocol (IP):* The Internet Protocol receives datagrams from TCP and breaks the packets down further. An IP packet contains a header with address information and carries TCP information and data. IP routes the individual datagrams from the sender to the recipient. IP packets are not very reliable, but the TCP level can keep resending them until the correct IP packets get through.

4. *Network interface:* Handles addressing issues, usually in the operating system, as well as the interface between the initiating computer and the network.

5. *Physical net:* Defines basic electrical-transmission characteristic for sending the actual signal along communications networks.

Two computers using TCP/IP would be able to communicate, even if they were based on different hardware and software platforms. Data sent from one computer to the other would pass downward through all five layers, starting with the sending computer's application layer and passing through the physical net. After the data reached the recipient host computer, they would travel up the layers. The TCP level would assemble the data into a format the receiving host computer could use. If the receiving computer found a damaged packet, it would ask the sending computer to retransmit it. This process would be reversed when the receiving computer responded.

The Internet Protocol that routes the datagrams has recently been updated from version 4 (IPv4) to version 6 (IPv6). The current Internet Protocol, IP Version 4 (IPv4) has been the lingua franca of the Internet for nearly 20 years but has many limitations. The biggest limitation is the physical maximum of just over four billion IPv4 addresses. IPv4 uses a 32-bit address space, which can represent only 4 294 967 296 addresses (2^{32})—and that is not enough to assign to the growing number of machines being added to the Internet. Furthermore, the future will bring new kinds of devices that have their own IP addresses—not just new network appliances but credit cards and more. By contrast, the physical limit of IPv6 addresses is well into the trillions, and shortages will not happen. IPv6 uses 128-bit addressing. IPv6 also includes the capabilities of IPv4. Any server that can support IPv6 packets can also support IPv4 packets. IPv6 is also supposed to address several security problems associated with IPv4.

**Open Systems
Interconnection (OSI)**

International reference model for linking different types of computers and networks.

The **Open Systems Interconnection (OSI)** model is an alternative model developed by the International Standards Organization for linking different types of computers and networks. It was designed to support global networks with large volumes of transaction processing. Like TCP/IP, OSI enables a computer connected to a network to communicate with any other computer on the same network or a different network, regardless of who the manufacturer of the computer was, by establishing communication rules that permit the exchange of information between dissimilar systems. OSI divides the telecommunications process into seven layers.

Other connectivity-promoting standards have been developed for graphical user interfaces (GUIs), electronic mail (e-mail), packet switching, wireless networks, and electronic data interchange (EDI) (see Chapter 8). Any manager wishing to achieve some measure of connectivity in his or her organization should try to use these standards when designing networks, purchasing hardware and software, or developing information system applications.

The Importance of Business Standards

Even if firms adopt the technologies we have just described, they may not be able to solve their connectivity problems. Information cannot flow seamlessly from one system to another or from one organization to another unless all interconnected applications use the same standards for representing data. Even if a firm has company-wide data standards, companies within the same industry may not be able to exchange data if their product descriptions do not correspond to those of other firms. This is one reason why manufacturers have not been able to achieve the level of interorganizational coordination of supply chain processes that they wish even though they have spent $1 billion on information technology since 1999 to make their supply chains more collaborative. Industry-wide standards for describing product data are starting to address this problem, as described in the Window on Organizations.

TECHNOLOGY AND BUSINESS STANDARDS WORK HAND-IN-HAND

Supply chain management systems, private exchanges and Net marketplaces enable companies to automate procurement of goods and services, but a surprising number of firms cannot fully benefit from their connectivity. About 30 percent of the data exchanged between suppliers and retailers does not match up, costing the consumer goods industry $40 billion each year. Orders placed electronically or manually on the basis of erroneous or inconsistent information cannot be fulfilled and must be placed over and over again until the information has been corrected and synchronized.

In the consumer goods business, identification numbers and product configurations change so frequently that manufacturers and retailers have an extremely hard time keeping product information up to date, especially if they order using paper, phone, and fax. "If a customer makes a one-digit error in the code for a product, they may repeatedly place orders for the product to be replenished and not receive it until they [or we] get on the phone and straighten that out," explains Milan Turk, P&G's Director of Customer E-business.

Proctor & Gamble (P&G) produces 60 000 items, and its record on each item contains many fields, including product identification number, description, and package size. Most retail customers use their own codes to maintain this information. When P&G changes existing products, it changes many fields, including identification numbers and product configurations, and it then notifies retailers of these new codes. Turk says it can currently take up to five weeks to distribute product data to retailers using conventional EDI, telephone, fax, or paper documents.

What is needed is a common product-description language, and one has been developed for the retail industry. The Uniform Code Council Inc. of Lawrence, Kansas, a standards organization, has developed UCCnet Global Registry, a central product information registry and data synchronization hub, to standardize product names and description codes so that wholesalers and retailers can use the same data. The registry contains 62 data fields per product, such as manufacturer, part number, price, and package size, providing a common language for companies to talk about an item. UCCnet matches product data from across the industry in a single searchable database.

The Electronic Commerce Council of Canada sponsors ECCNet, Canada's UCCNet equivalent, by linking ECCnet to UCCnet, ensuring a standardized, synchronized Internet-based trading environment for participants on both sides of the border. In December 2002, 10 major retailers and distributors, members of the Canadian Council of Grocery Distributors (CCGD), notified their vendors that product listing through ECCnet has been added as an amendment to their standard terms and conditions of trade, as outlined in their vendor agreement.

Over 3000 vendors were notified that A. de la Chevrotière Ltée., Colemans Group of Companies, Commisso's Grocery Distributors Ltd., Co-op Atlantic, Federated Co-operatives, The Great Atlantic & Pacific Companies of Canada Limited, Loblaw Companies Limited, Metro Inc., Sobeys Inc., and Thrifty Foods Ltd. will not accept new product listings without prior data loading into ECCnet, effective January 1, 2003.

The benefits for large consumer goods suppliers and retailers are very clear. Once both manufacturers, such as P&G, and its retail customers use the UCC data registry, the process of providing updated product information could take hours or minutes instead of days or weeks. One potential sticking point: Companies may have to redesign and rebuild their databases to conform with the UCCnet data standards, which is an expensive proposition for small companies.

To Think About: What are the organizational benefits of using ECCNet? What management, organization, and technology issues must be addressed in order to participate in UCCNet and ECCNet?

Sources: Steve Konicki, "Shopping for Savings," *InformationWeek,* July 1, 2002; Michael Meehan, "Big Retailers Push Data Ties," *Computerworld,* June 10, 2002; Brian Sullivan and Michael Meehan, "UCCnet Standard Could Squeeze Small Retail Suppliers," *Computerworld,* June 6, 2002; Brian Sullivan and Michael Meehan "UCCnet's Promise: Synchronized Product Data," *Computerworld,* June 10, 2002; "Major Grocery Retailers and Distributors Make Product Listing through ECCnet a Standard Term and Condition of Trade," December 18, 2002, available **www.eccc.org**, accessed April 7, 2003.

9.2   THE INTERNET: INFORMATION TECHNOLOGY INFRASTRUCTURE FOR THE DIGITAL FIRM

The Internet is perhaps the most well-known, and the largest, implementation of internetworking, linking hundreds of thousands of individual networks all over the world. The Internet has a range of capabilities that organizations are using to exchange information internally or to communicate externally with other organizations. Internet technology provides the primary infrastructure for electronic commerce, electronic business, and the emerging digital firm.

WHAT IS THE INTERNET?

The Internet began as a U.S. Department of Defense network to link scientists and university professors around the world. Even today, individuals cannot connect directly to the Net, although anyone with a computer, a modem, and the willingness to pay a small monthly usage fee can access it through an Internet service provider. An **Internet service provider (ISP)** is a commercial organization with a permanent connection to the Internet that sells temporary connections to subscribers. Individuals can also access the Internet through popular online services, such as America Online and Microsoft Network (MSN).

No one owns the Internet, and it has no formal management organization. As a creation of the Defense Department for sharing research data, the lack of centralization was deliberate to make it less vulnerable to wartime or terrorist attacks. To join the Internet, an existing network needs only to pay a small registration fee and agree to certain standards based on the TCP/IP reference model. Costs are low. Each organization, of course, pays for its own networks and its own telephone bills, but those costs usually exist independent of the Internet. There are regional Internet companies to which member networks forward all transmissions. These Internet companies route and forward all traffic, and the cost is still only that of a local telephone call. The result is that the costs of e-mail and other Internet connections tend to be far lower than equivalent voice, postal, or overnight courier delivery, making the Internet a very inexpensive communications medium. It is also a very fast method of communication, with messages arriving anywhere in the world in a matter of seconds, or a minute or two at most. We now briefly describe the most important Internet capabilities.

INTERNET TECHNOLOGY AND SERVICES

The Internet is based on client-server technology. Individuals using the Internet control what they do through client applications, such as Web browser software. All the data, including e-mail messages and Web pages, are stored on servers. A client uses the Internet to request information from a particular Web server on a distant computer, and the server sends the requested information back to the client via the Internet.

Client platforms today include not only PCs and other computers but also a wide array of handheld devices and information appliances, some of which can even provide wireless Internet access. An **information appliance** is a device, such as an Internet-enabled cell phone or a TV Internet receiver for Web access and e-mail, that has been customized to perform a few specialized computing tasks well with minimal user effort. Table 9.1 lists

Internet service provider (ISP)
A commercial organization, with a permanent connection to the Internet, that sells temporary connections to subscribers.

information appliance
Device that has been customized to perform a few specialized computing tasks well with minimal user effort.

TABLE 9.1   EXAMPLES OF INTERNET CLIENT PLATFORMS

Device	Description	Example
PC	General purpose computing platform that can perform many different tasks, but can be complex to use	Dell, Compaq, IBM PCs
Net PC	Network computer with minimal local storage and processing capability; designed to use software and services delivered over networks and the Internet	Sun Ray
Smart Phone	Has a small screen and keyboard for browsing the Web and exchanging e-mail in addition to providing voice communication	Nokia 8390
Video Game Console	Video game console with a modem, keyboard, and capabilities to function as a Web access terminal	Microsoft Xbox, Sega Dreamcast
PDA	Wireless handheld personal digital assistant with e-mail and Internet service	Tungsten W
Wireless E-Mail Handheld	Tablet with keyboard that provides text e-mail capabilities; requires linking to an e-mail service	RIM's BlackBerry
TV Internet Receiver	Provides Web surfing and e-mail capabilities using a television set, receiver, and a wireless keyboard	MSNTV

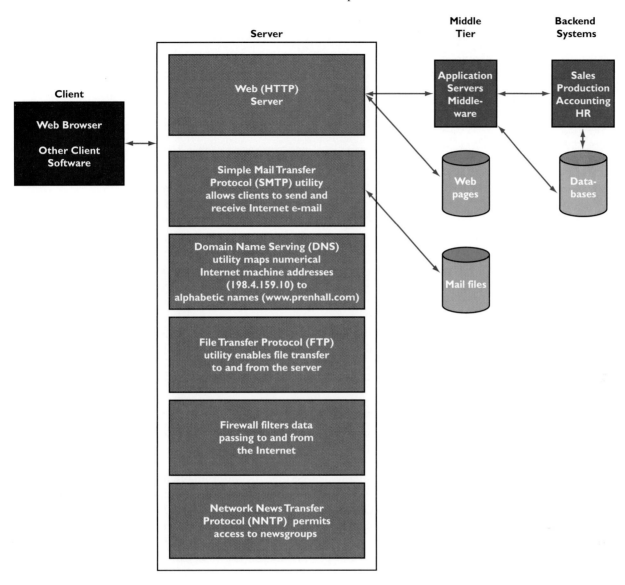

Figure 9.3 Client-server computing on the Internet. Client computers running Web browser and other software can access an array of services on servers via the Internet. These services may all run on a single server or on multiple specialized servers.

examples of some of these client platforms, most of which were described in Chapters 6 and 8. Experts believe that the role of the PC or the desktop computer as the Internet client is diminishing as people turn to these easy-to-use specialized information appliances to connect to the Internet. (See Figure 9.3.)

Servers dedicated to the Internet or even to specific Internet services are the heart of the information on the Net. Each Internet service is implemented by one or more software programs. All of the services may run on a single server computer, or different services may be allocated to different machines. There may be only one disk storing the data for these services, or there may be multiple disks for each type, depending on the amount of information being stored.

Web server software receives requests for Web pages from the client and accesses the Web pages from the disk where they are stored. Web servers can also access other information from an organization's internal information system applications and their associated databases and return that information to the client in the form of Web pages, if desired. Specialized middleware, including application servers, is used to manage the interactions between the Web server and the organization's internal information systems for processing orders, tracking inventory, maintaining product catalogues, and other electronic commerce

TABLE 9.2	MAJOR INTERNET SERVICES
Capability	**Functions Supported**
E-mail	Person-to-person messaging; document sharing
Usenet newsgroups	Discussion groups on electronic bulletin boards
LISTSERVs	Discussion groups using e-mail mailing list servers
Chatting	Interactive conversations
Telnet	Log on to one computer system and do work on another
FTP	Transfer files from computer to computer
World Wide Web	Retrieve, format, and display information (including text, audio, graphics, and video) using hypertext links

functions. For example, if a customer filled out an online form on a Web page to order a product, such as a light fixture, the middleware would translate the request on the Web page into commands that could be used by the company's internal order processing system and customer database.

The most important Internet services for businesses include e-mail, Usenet newsgroups, LISTSERVs, chatting, Telnet, File Transfer Protocol (FTP), and the World Wide Web. They can be used to retrieve and offer information. Table 9.2 lists these capabilities and describes the functions they support.

Communication on the Internet

The Internet provides an array of capabilities for electronic communication that can help companies reduce their communication costs.

Electronic Mail   The Internet has become the most important e-mail system in the world because it connects so many people worldwide, creating a productivity gain that observers have compared with Gutenberg's development of movable type in the 15th century. Organizations use it to facilitate communication between employees and offices and to communicate with customers and suppliers. Researchers use this facility to share ideas and information, even documents and graphic images. Businesses now treat e-mail as an essential communication and collaboration tool.

Figure 9.4 illustrates the components of an Internet e-mail address. The portion of the address to the left of the @ symbol in an e-mail address is the name or identifier of the specific individual or organization. To the right of the @ symbol is the domain name. The **domain name** is the name that identifies a unique node on the Internet. The domain name corresponds to a unique four-byte numeric **Internet Protocol (IP) address** for each computer connected to the Internet. (For example, the domain name www.pearsoned.ca has the IP address 198.4.159.10.) A **Domain Name System (DNS)** maps domain names to their IP addresses.

domain name

The name identifying a unique node on the Internet.

Internet Protocol (IP) address

Four-byte numeric address indicating a unique computer location on the Internet.

Domain Name System (DNS)

A hierarchical system of servers maintaining databases enabling the conversion of domain names to their IP addresses.

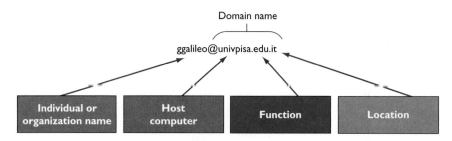

Figure 9.4 Analysis of an Internet address. In English, the e-mail address of physicist and astronomer Galileo Galilei would be translated as "G. Galileo, University of Pisa, educational institution, Italy." The domain name to the right of the @ symbol contains a country indicator, a function indicator, and the location of the host computer.

The domain name contains subdomains separated by a period. The domain that is farthest to the right is the top-level domain, and each domain to the left helps further define the domain by network, department, and even specific computer. The top-level domain name may be either a country indicator or a function indicator, such as *com* for a commercial organization or *gov* for a government institution. Most e-mail addresses end with a country indicator except those in the United States, which ordinarily do not use one. In Figure 9.4, *it*, the top-level domain, is a country indicator, indicating that the address is in Italy. *Edu* indicates that the address is an educational institution; *univpisa* (in this case, University of Pisa) indicates the specific location of the host computer.

In Canada, the Canadian Internet Registration Authority (CIRA) (www.cira.ca) is responsible for registering all domain names with the top domain name of .ca. Non-.ca addresses (e.g., .org, .com) can be registered through a variety of Web sites, but the Canadian top domain names can only be registered through CIRA-certified registrars. In June 2003, there were 346 808 .ca names registered through CIRA.

Usenet Newsgroups (Forums) **Usenet** newsgroups are worldwide discussion groups, in which people share information and ideas on a defined topic, such as radiology or rock bands. Discussion takes place on large electronic bulletin boards, where anyone can post messages for others to read. Many thousands of groups exist discussing almost all conceivable topics. Each Usenet site is financed and administered independently.

LISTSERV A second type of public forum, **LISTSERV**, also known as a list server, allows discussions or messaging to be conducted through predefined groups but uses e-mail mailing list servers instead of bulletin boards for communications. Subscribers receive all messages sent through the LISTSERV by e-mail, whereas newsgroup users must visit the newsgroup to access messages there. If you find a LISTSERV topic you are interested in, you may subscribe to the LISTSERV. From then on, through your e-mail, you will receive all messages sent by others concerning that topic. You can, in turn, send a message to your LISTSERV, and it will automatically be broadcast to the other subscribers. Tens of thousands of LISTSERV groups exist.

Chatting **Chatting** allows two or more people who are simultaneously connected to the Internet to hold live, interactive conversations. Chat groups are divided into channels, and each is assigned its own topic of conversation. The first generation of chat tools was for written conversations, in which participants type their remarks using their keyboard and read responses on their computer screen. Systems featuring voice chat capabilities, such as those offered by Yahoo! Chat, are now becoming popular.

A new enhancement to chat service called **instant messaging** even allows participants to create their own private chat channels. The instant messaging system alerts a person whenever someone on his or her private list is online so that the person can initiate a chat session with that particular individual. There are a number of competing instant messaging systems for consumers, including Yahoo! Messenger, MSN Messenger, and AOL Instant Messenger. Some of these systems can provide voice-based instant messages so that a user can click on a "talk" button and have an online conversation with another person. Companies concerned with security are building proprietary instant messaging systems using such tools as Lotus Sametime.

Chatting and instant messaging can be effective business tools if people who can benefit from interactive conversations set an appointed time to "meet" and "talk" on a particular topic. For instance, Totality, a San Francisco Web-service company, uses instant messaging to help team members collaborate more efficiently while working to keep clients' Web sites running smoothly (Bhattacharjee, 2002). Many online retailers are enhancing their Web sites with chat services to attract visitors, to encourage repeat purchases, and to improve customer service.

Telnet **Telnet** allows someone to be on one computer system while doing work on another. Telnet is a protocol that establishes an error-free, rapid link between two computers, allowing you, for example, to log on to your business computer from a remote computer when you are on the road or working from your home. You can also log in and use third-party

Usenet

Forums in which people share information and ideas on a defined topic through large electronic bulletin boards, where anyone can post messages on the topic for others to see and to which others can respond.

LISTSERV

Online groups using e-mail broadcast from mailing list servers for discussions or messaging.

chatting

Live, interactive conversations over a public network.

instant messaging

Chat service that allows participants to create their own private chat channels so that a person can be alerted whenever someone on his or her private list is online to initiate a chat session with that particular individual.

Telnet

Network tool that allows someone to log on to one computer system while doing work on another.

computers that have been made accessible to the public, for example, to peruse the catalogue of the National Library of Canada. Telnet will use the computer address you supply to locate the computer you want to reach and connect you to it.

Internet telephony

Two-way voice transmission over the Internet using the Internet Protocol's packet-switched connections.

voice-over IP (VoIP)

Voice transmission using the Internet Protocol (IP).

Internet Telephony Hardware and software have been developed for **Internet telephony**, allowing companies to use the Internet for telephone voice transmission. (Internet telephony products sometimes are called IP telephony products.) IP telephony uses the IP to deliver voice information in digital form using packet switching, avoiding the tolls charged by the circuit-switched telephone network (see Figure 9.5). IP telephony calls can be made and received with a desktop computer equipped with a microphone and speakers or with a standard telephone or cell phone. This technology is known as **voice-over IP** (abbreviated **VoIP**). New high-bandwidth networks will eliminate many of the early sound quality problems of this technology and enable the integration of voice with other Internet services.

Companies with multiple sites worldwide that are connected through a private or public IP network or that have seasonally variable demand for voice services are the most likely to benefit initially from this technology (Varshney, Snow, McGivern, and Howard, 2002). Firms can also lower their network management costs by consolidating voice and data into a single communications infrastructure (see the Window on Technology). Businesses can use this technology for applications using video, such as Internet conference calls or Web sites that allow users to reach an actual customer service representative by clicking on a link on a Web page.

virtual private network (VPN)

A secure connection between two points across the Internet to transmit data. Provides a low-cost alternative to a private network.

Virtual Private Networks Internet technology can also reduce communication costs by allowing companies to create virtual private networks as low-cost alternatives to private WANs. A **virtual private network (VPN)** is a secure connection between two points across the Internet, enabling private communications to travel securely over the public infrastructure. VPN services are available through ISPs. The VPN provides many features of a private network at a much lower cost than using private leased telephone lines or frame-relay connections. Companies can save on long-distance communication costs because workers can access remote locations for the cost of making a local call to an ISP.

There are several competing protocols used to protect data transmitted over the public Internet, including Point-to-Point Tunnelling Protocol (PPTP). In a process called tunnelling, packets of data are encrypted and wrapped inside IP packets so that non-IP data can travel through the Internet. By adding this "wrapper" around a network message to hide its content, organizations can create a private connection that travels through the public Internet.

Information Retrieval and Sharing on the Internet

Information retrieval is a second basic Internet function (see below discussion on information retrieval, i.e., information search, on the Web). Many hundreds of library catalogues are available online through the Internet, including those of such giants as the National Library of Canada, the University of Manitoba, and McGill University. In addition, users are able to search many thousands of databases that have been opened to the public by corporations,

Figure 9.5 How IP telephony works. An IP phone call digitizes and breaks up a voice message into data packets that may travel along different routes before being reassembled at their final destination. A server nearest the call's destination, called a gateway, arranges the packets in the proper order and directs them to the telephone number of the receiver or the IP address of the receiving computer.

Source: David G. Wallace, "Using the Internet to Cut Phone Calls Down to Size," *New York Times*, July 19, 2001.

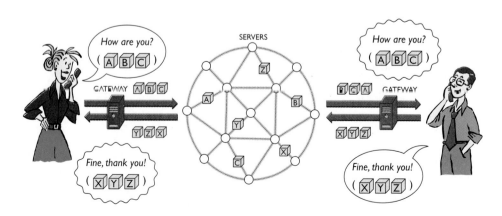

SPORTS SOCCER SCORES WITH VoIP

The perturbed management at Sports Soccer found its staff spending too much time dealing with technology, rather than on selling sports equipment. This 126-store sports retail chain in the United Kingdom and Belgium had immense communications problems, starting with telephone bills that surpassed £250 000 (approximately $553 000) each year because of the multiple telephone lines at most stores. In addition, customers were often frustrated when they had to wait an average of 24 seconds for a simple credit card approval, even for purchases as small as a T-shirt. Inventory replenishment was usually delayed because clogged transmission lines required each store to wait until late afternoon to transmit its daily store sales information via modems, leaving warehouse staff with insufficient time to finish their work. Headquarters also depended on closed circuit TV to transmit and receive important information to and from each store, further clogging corporate and store communication. To make matters worse, Sports Soccer is a growing corporation. What would adding more sites do to all of these vital communications?

After exploring various alternatives, the company settled on a wide area network (WAN) based on Cisco Systems' Architecture for Voice, Video, and Integrated Data (AVVID). This solution centralizes management of voice, data, and closed-circuit TV so that store employees are freed up to concentrate on customers. The new system also has adequate bandwidth to carry the traffic required.

The company installed Cisco's CallManager software to set up two redundant configurations in two separate headquarter buildings connected to two separate phone lines through different phone exchanges. Should one fail, the system could switch to the other. Once the basic network infrastructure had been built, 500 IP telephones were installed in Sports Soccer's head office and all its stores and automatically assigned appropriate local telephone numbers. The company decided to compress all voice calls to save bandwidth, an act that did not degrade the voices because of the high quality of the system.

The new system has reduced credit card transmission approval time to an acceptable average of eight seconds and has solved the stock replenishment problem. With adequate bandwidth, the central system is able to collect sales information in real time so that the central warehouse system can pick items that need replenishment throughout the day and ship them to individual stores in time for store openings the next day. The new system can also monitor such information as price changes occurring at checkout counters. If any bandwidth-hungry video has to be transmitted over the WAN, Cisco's AVVID software enables the company to set priorities for the transmission of different types of IP traffic and applications. That way, the company can assign top priority to credit card transactions so that customer service is not degraded when the network is transmitting video. Sports Soccer's information technology director John Ashley reported that using the VoIP network cost less than half of the the cost of other alternative solutions the company had considered, such as installing PBX systems in every store.

Sports Soccer appears to be no exception. According to researchers, companies can lower their network management costs by consolidating voice and data into a single communications infrastructure while saving 50 percent or more on international voice and fax calls over an IP telephony network. The savings are especially clear for companies that make a large number of high-cost calls to the developing nations. For example, higher education has proved to be a large segment of the convergence market for Cisco, says Brantz Myers, National Solutions Manager for Cisco Canada in Toronto. "Most of the colleges in Canada have become IP telephony customers," Myers says. "That is really driven by a couple of things. One thing is the cost associated with multiple networks. They are really cost-conscious, but they also have good IP networks. It wasn't a big deal for them to add telephony to their networks. This was just another application of the IP network."

To Think About: What are the business benefits of using VoIP? What management, technology, and organization issues did Sports Soccer have to address when implementing this technology? Why would colleges and universities move to VoIP?

Sources: Rhonda Raider, "VoIP Bargain for Retailer," *Packet Magazine*, First Quarter 2002; Rhonda Raider "Redialing Internet Telephony," *BusinessWeek Online*, May 1, 2002; Carly Suppa, "VoIP Makes the Grade," *NetworkWorld Canada*, September 6, 2002.

---

governments, and nonprofit organizations. Individuals can gather information on almost any conceivable topic stored in these databases and libraries. Many computer users all over the world use the Internet to locate and download some of the free, high-quality computer software made available by developers.

File Transfer Protocol **File transfer protocol (FTP)** is used to access a remote computer and retrieve files from it. FTP is a quick and easy method if you know the remote computer site where the file is stored. After you have logged on to the remote computer, you can move around directories that have been made accessible for you and use FTP to search for the file(s) you want to retrieve. Once located, FTP makes transfer of the file to your own computer very easy.

file transfer protocol (FTP)

Tool for retrieving and transferring files from a remote computer.

During the recent SARS outbreak, the Internet was used by millions of people to find and share information about the disease. Some just wanted information. A search using a large Web-based search engine (see discussion below) turned up more than 400 000 entries related to SARS. Doctors and researchers seeking a cure for SARS communicated by e-mail and shared data over the Web. Authorities posted travel and outbreak bulletins on the Web and sent updates by e-mail. For example, the University of Manitoba sent an e-mail to all of its faculty and staff advising them about travel outside Canada. The e-mail was linked to the University's Web site for travel alerts and updates.

NEXT-GENERATION NETWORKS AND INTERNET2

The public Internet was not originally designed to handle massive quantities of data flowing through hundreds of thousands of networks. Experimental national research networks (NRNs) are developing high-speed next generation networks to address this problem. These private networks do not replace the public Internet but do provide test beds for leading-edge technology for research institutions, universities, and corporations that may eventually migrate to the public Internet. These technologies will make it possible for companies to distribute video, audio, three-dimensional simulations, or life-size video teleconferencing that are too data-intensive for today's public Internet without any degradation in performance. Table 9.3 describes the activities of some of these national research networks.

Internet2

Research network with new protocols and transmission speeds that provides an infrastructure for supporting high-bandwidth Internet applications.

In the United States, **Internet2** and Next Generation Internet (NGI) are NRN consortia representing more than 200 universities, private businesses, and government agencies working on a new robust high-bandwidth version of the Internet. The Internet infrastructure is based on a series of interconnected *gigapops*, which are regional high-speed points-of-presence that serve as aggregation points for traffic from participating institutions. These gigapops, in turn, are connected to backbone networks with bandwidths exceeding 2.5 gigabits per second (Gbps). Internet2 connection speeds are in the hundreds of megabits per second range (Mbps), with at least 100 Mbps connections to servers and at least 10 Mbps to the desktop.

In Canada, CANARIE is the equivalent of Internet2, working on similar projects. CANARIE has a working relationship with the American group. CANARIE's mission is to accelerate Canada's advanced Internet development and use by facilitating the widespread adoption of faster, more efficient networks and by enabling the next generation of advanced products, applications, and services to run on them. Headquartered in Ottawa, Ontario, CANARIE employs 33 full-time staff dedicated to the research and implementation of advanced networks and applications that will stimulate economic growth and increase Canada's international competitiveness. CANARIE has already succeeded in enhancing Canadian R&D Internet speeds by a factor of almost one million since its inception in 1993. The organization has also funded numerous advanced Internet applications projects.

In February 1998, the Canadian federal government announced a $55-million commitment to CANARIE to build a national optical R&D Internet network, CA*net 3. A consortium led by Bell Canada was selected as the provider of the core network.

| TABLE 9.3 | EXAMPLES OF NATIONAL RESEARCH NETWORKS |

National Research Network	Activities
6NET	European research network that is the world's largest test bed for Internet protocol version 6 (IPv6), which greatly increases the number of available IP addresses and Internet security.
Welsh Video Network	Runs across the SuperJANET network run by the United Kingdom Education and Research Networking Association and supports high-speed videoconferencing and other digital video for 80 universities and research facilities.
Asia Pacific Advanced Network	Pan-Asian network based in Japan that connects the national research networks of Australia, Hong Kong, Korea, the Philippines, Thailand, China, and Malaysia along with NRNs in Europe, Latin America, and North America.
CANARIE	Canadian project managing the CA*Net2 and CA*Net3 national research networks for developing leading edge Internet capabilities.

The CA*net 3 network will eventually operate at up to 40 Gigabits per second (Gbps) or 250 times the speed of the current CA*net 2 backbone and roughly 750 000 times the speed of the original CA*net. **CA*net 3** is based on Dense Wave Division Multiplexing (DWDM) technology, which expands the information carrying capacity of individual optical fibres by multiplexing a number of wavelengths of laser light. The wavelengths will be connected directly to high performance network routers, which will be the only electrical switching devices on the network.

This direct connection between the DWDM equipment and the routers leads to the definition of the network as an "optical Internet." While other advanced optical networks are still based on synchronous optical network technology (SONET), which is basically designed to carry voice traffic first and Internet traffic second, CA*net 3 was built from the ground up to carry Internet traffic. Ca*net 4, carrying up to eight times the traffic of Ca*net 3 was begun in summer of 2002.

These research groups are developing protocols for permitting different quality-of-service levels. Today's Internet transmissions are "best effort"—packets of data arrive when they arrive without any regard to the priority of their contents. Different types of packets could be assigned different levels of priority as they travel over the network. For example, packets for such applications as videoconferencing, which need to arrive simultaneously without any break in service, would receive higher priority than e-mail messages, which do not have to be delivered instantaneously.

The existing Internet is being enhanced to provide higher transmission speed, different levels of service, and increased security, but the transition to next generation Internet technology will occur slowly (Weiser, 2001).

9.3   THE WORLD WIDE WEB

The World Wide Web (the Web) is at the heart of the explosion in the business use of the Internet. The Web is a system with universally accepted standards for storing, retrieving, formatting, and displaying information using a client-server architecture. The Web combines text, hypermedia, graphics, and sound. It can handle all types of digital communication while making it easy to link resources that are half-a-world apart. The Web uses graphical user interfaces for easy viewing. It is based on a standard hypertext language called Hypertext Markup Language (HTML), which formats documents and incorporates dynamic links to other documents and pictures stored in the same or remote computers (see our discussion in Chapter 6.) Using these links, the user need only point at a highlighted key word or graphic, click on it, and immediately be transported to another document, probably on another computer somewhere else in the world. Users are free to jump from place to place following their own logic and interest.

Web browser software is programmed according to HypertextTransport Protocol (HTTP) standards (see below). The standards are universally accepted, so anyone using a browser can access any of millions of Web sites. Browsers use hypertext's point-and-click ability to navigate or *surf*—move from site to site on the Web—to another desired site. The browser also includes an arrow or back button to enable the user to retrace his or her steps, navigating back, site by site.

Those who offer information through the Web must establish a **home page**—a text and graphical screen display that usually welcomes the user and describes the organization that has established the page. For most organizations, the home page will lead the user to other pages, with all the pages of a company being known as a Web site. For a corporation to establish a presence on the Web, therefore, it must set up a Web site of one or more pages. Most Web pages offer a way to contact the organization or individual. The person in charge of an organization's Web site is called a **Webmaster.**

To access a Web site, the user must specify a **uniform resource locator (URL)**, which points to the address of a specific resource on the Web. For instance, the URL for Pearson Education Canada, the publisher of this text, is http://www.pearsoned.ca. **Hypertext Transport Protocol (HTTP)** is the communications standard used to transfer pages on the Web. *http* defines how messages are formatted and transmitted and what actions Web servers and browsers should take in response to various commands. *Pearsoned.ca* is the domain name identifying the Web server storing the Web pages.

CA*net 3

Canadian equivalent of Internet2, designed to carry high-speed transmission over a government-funded backbone throughout Canada.

home page

A World Wide Web text and graphical screen display that welcomes the user and explains the organization that has established the page.

Webmaster

The person in charge of an organization's Web site.

uniform resource locator (URL)

The address of a specific resource on the Internet.

Hypertext Transport Protocol (HTTP)

The communications standard used to transfer pages on the Web. Defines how messages are formatted and transmitted.

SEARCHING FOR INFORMATION ON THE WEB

Locating information on the Web is a critical function; billions of Web pages are in existence, and this number will quickly double. No comprehensive catalogue of Web sites exists. The principal methods of locating information on the Web are Web site directories, search engines, and broadcast or "push" technology.

Several companies have created directories of Web sites and their addresses, providing search tools for finding information. Yahoo! is an example. People or organizations submit sites of interest, which then are classified. To search the directory, you enter one or more key words and then see displayed a list of categories and sites with those key words in the title.

Other search tools do not require Web sites to be preclassified and will search Web pages on their own automatically. Such tools, called **search engines**, can find Web sites that may be little known. They contain software that looks for Web pages containing one or more of the search terms; then they display matches ranked by a method that usually involves the location and frequency of the search terms. (Some search engine sites use human experts to help with the ranking.) These search engines create indexes of the Web pages they visit. The search engine software then locates Web pages of interest by searching through these indexes. Some search engines are more comprehensive or current than others, depending on how their components are tuned, and some also classify Web sites by subject categories. Google uses special software that indexes and ranks sites on the basis of relevance, measured by the number of users who access them and the number of outside links to a particular page. Specialized search engines are also available to help users locate specific types of information easily. For example, PubMed specializes in searches for articles in medical journals. Some Web sites for locating information, such as Yahoo!, Canoe, and Canada.com, have become so popular and easy to use that they also serve as portals for the Internet (see Chapter 4). (See Figure 9.6.)

There are two ways of identifying Web pages to be tracked by search engines. One is to have Web page owners register their URLs with search engine sites. The other is to use software agents, known as spiders, bots, and Web crawlers, to traverse the Web and identify the Web pages for indexing. Chapter 14 details the capabilities of software agents with built-in intelligence, which can also help users search the Internet for shopping information. **Shopping bots** can help people interested in making a purchase filter and retrieve information about products of interest, evaluate competing products according to criteria they have established, and negotiate with vendors for price and delivery terms (Maes, Guttman, and Moukas, 1999). Many of

search engine

A tool for locating specific sites or information on the Internet.

shopping bot

Software with varying levels of built-in intelligence to help electronic commerce shoppers locate and evaluate products or services they might wish to purchase.

Figure 9.6 AltaVista provides a powerful search engine for accessing Web information resources, including images, video, and audio files as well as text. Users can search for sites of interest by entering key words or by exploring the categories.

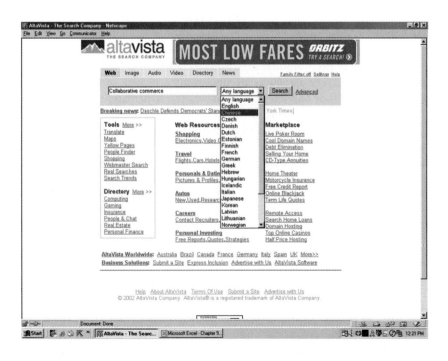

	EXAMPLES OF ELECTRONIC COMMERCE AGENTS
TABLE 9.4	

Agent	Description
MySimon	Real-time shopping bot that searches more than 1000 affiliated and unaffiliated merchants in 90 categories.
BestBookBuys.com	Shopping bot searches 26 online bookstores to help users find the lowest prices for titles they specify.
Bottom Dollar	Bot simultaneously queries many online retailers to obtain the best prices for products specified by the user.
Valuefind	Bot searches for the best deal from retail vendors, auctions, and classified ads. Users can limit the search to a specific price range and to certain Web sites.

these shopping agents search the Web for pricing and availability of products specified by the user and return a list of sites that sell the item along with pricing information and a purchase link. Use of shopping bots does not appear to have piqued the interest of Canadian companies. Canadians wanting to use shopping bots will have to use the American shopping bot applications until a Canadian business begins offering this service. (See Figure 9.7.) Table 9.4 compares various types of electronic commerce agents.

Broadcast and "Push" Technology

Instead of spending hours surfing the Web, users can have the information they are interested in delivered automatically to their desktops through **"push" technology**. A computer broadcasts information of interest directly to the user, rather than having the user "pull" content from Web sites. Push technology automatically sends the user the information, while the user must pull information from the Web through information searches and by deliberately accessing specific Web sites. (See Figure 9.8.)

Special client software allows the user to specify the categories of information he or she wants to receive, such as news, sports, financial data, and so forth, and how often this information should be updated. After finding the kind of information requested, push server programs serve it to the push client. The streams of information distributed through push technology are known as *channels*. Microsoft's Internet Explorer, Netscape Communicator, and Avantgo include push tools that automatically download Web pages, inform the user of updated content, and create channels of user-specified sites. Avantgo is for use on handheld computers. If the user has subscribed through Avantgo to a series of Web sites, each time the

"push" technology

Method of obtaining relevant information on networks by having a computer broadcast information directly to the user on the basis of prespecified interests.

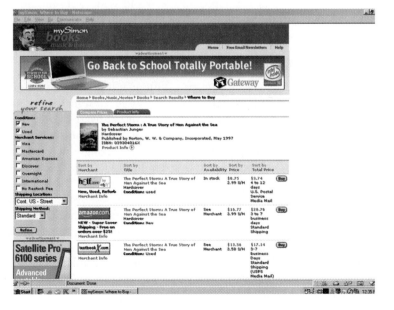

Figure 9.7 MySimon features a shopping bot that can search Internet retailers for price and availability of products specified by the user. Displayed here are the results of a search of prices and sources for a popular book.

Figure 9.8 MicroStrategy's Narrowcast Server uses "push" technology to automatically deliver information on topics of interest to users via the Web, e-mail, pagers, or mobile phones.

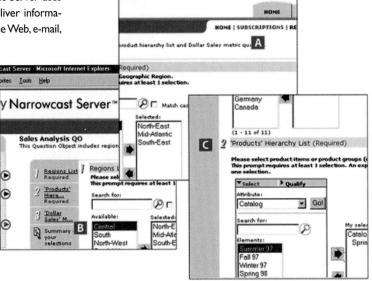

user synchronizes his or her handheld device online, the most recent copies of those Web pages are downloaded to the handheld device. The user can then access those pages as needed. For example, a user could read local restaurant reviews when out of town on vacation and decide where to eat on the basis of the reviews found on the Web page that Avantgo had pushed to the handheld device. Using push technology to transmit information to a select group of individuals is one example of **multicasting**. (LISTSERVs sending e-mail to members of specific mailing lists is another.)

Online marketplaces and exchanges can use push services to alert buyers to price changes and special deals. Companies are using internal push channels to broadcast important information, such as price updates or information about new competitor products, on their own private networks.

multicasting

Broadcasting data to a selected group of recipients.

INTRANETS AND EXTRANETS

Organizations can use Internet networking standards and Web technology to create private networks called *intranets*. We introduced intranets in Chapter 1, explaining that an intranet is an internal organizational network that can provide access to data across the enterprise. An intranet uses the existing company network infrastructure along with Internet connectivity standards and software developed for the World Wide Web. Intranets can create networked applications that can run on many different kinds of computers throughout the organization, including mobile handheld computers and wireless remote access devices.

Intranet Technology

firewall

Hardware and software placed between an organization's internal network and an external network to prevent outsiders from invading private networks.

Although the Web is open to anyone, an intranet is private and is protected from public visits by **firewalls**—security systems with specialized software to prevent outsiders from invading private networks. The firewall consists of hardware and software placed between an organization's internal network and an external network, including the Internet. The firewall is programmed to intercept each message packet passing between the two networks, examine its characteristics, and reject unauthorized messages or access attempts. We provide more detail on firewalls in Chapter 11.

Intranets require no special hardware and can run over any existing network infrastructure. Intranet software technology is the same as that of the World Wide Web. Intranets use HTML to program Web pages and to establish dynamic, point-and-click hypertext links to other pages. The Web browser and Web server software used for intranets are the same as those on the Web. A simple intranet can be created by linking a client computer with a Web browser to a computer with Web server software via a TCP/IP network. A firewall keeps unwanted visitors out.

Extranets

Some firms are allowing people and organizations outside the firm to have limited access to their internal intranets. Private intranets that are extended to authorized users outside the company are called *extranets*, which we also introduced in Chapter 1. For example, authorized buyers could link to a portion of a company's intranet from the public Internet to obtain information about the cost and features of its products. The company can use firewalls to ensure that access to its internal data is limited and remains secure; firewalls can also authenticate users, making sure that only authorized people can access the site.

Extranets are especially useful for linking organizations with suppliers, customers, or business partners. They often are used for collaborating with other companies for supply chain management, product design and development, or training efforts. Private industrial networks are based on extranets. Figure 9.9 illustrates one way that an extranet might be set up.

THE WIRELESS WEB

Chapter 8 described how wireless LAN technology can be used to access the Internet from an untethered PC or handheld computing device. This is one aspect of the wireless Web, but users can only access the Web if they are in range of their wireless networks. The term **Wireless Web** is more often applied to technologies that allow Internet-enabled cell phones, PDAs, and other wireless computing devices to access digital information from the Internet from any location. Mobile Internet access from wireless devices will not replace Internet access through PCs, but it will enable millions of people to obtain Web information services wherever they go. Businesses will increasingly incorporate wireless Internet access into their information technology infrastructures so that employees can access information wherever they are and make decisions instantly without being tethered to a desk or computer.

Ontario Patient Transfer hopes to show how business processes using this wireless technology can become more efficient. Ontario Patient Transfer operates a fleet of ambulances and patient transport vehicles through three branch locations, travelling Ontario-wide and into the United States on-call from regional hospitals. Ontario Patient Transfer employs paramedics, registered nurses, RPNs, EFR-Ds, EMAs, and EMR-Ds for neonatal infant and patient transfer and offers services for on-site medical servicesfor special/sporting events in southern Ontario.

Ontario Patient Transfer will use Nextair's hosted mdispatch™ business solution and has licensed Nextair's AIRIX enabled wireless handheld device applications for its fleet for scheduling, monitoring, and tracking of patient transfer requests to/from hospitals, clinics, diagnostic/treatment centres and nursing homes.

Rick Van Kleef, president of Ontario Patient Transfer said "On-time reliability, customer service, and the need to fulfill contract obligations require complete real-time monitoring of pickup, delivery, and status updates of all fleet and patient transfer activities. As our staff is accustomed to hospital settings where mobile data and device radio modems must be shut off, added to the fact that our staff encounter geographic regions and building settings which do not allow for wireless data coverage, AIRIX allows the mdispatch handheld application to have 100-percent up-time operation. This is a key benefit we did not see with other solutions."

Wireless Web

Technologies enabling users to access digital information from the Internet using wireless mobile computing devices.

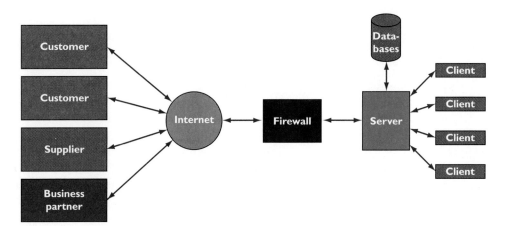

Figure 9.9 Model of an extranet. In this model of an extranet, selected customers, suppliers, and business partners can access a company's private intranet from the public Internet. A firewall allows access only to authorized outsiders.

Figure 9.10 Kyocera's smart phone can be used for wireless e-mail and Web surfing as well as for voice communication. Shown here is a Web page that has been specially formatted for small display screens on handheld mobile devices.

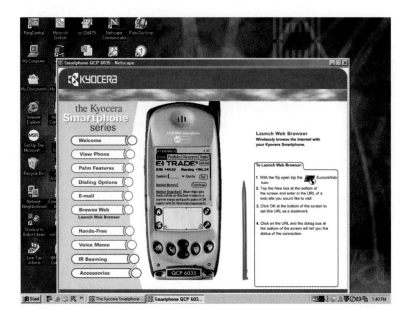

Web content is being reformatted for wireless devices, and new content and services are being developed specifically for those devices. Specialized portals can steer users of Web-enabled wireless devices to the information they are most likely to need. It should be noted that the much slower speeds of wireless technologies, compared with the wired environment, inhibit the use of the Wireless Web. In particular, graphic images are slow to download. Graphic images are also difficult to display on the much smaller display screens usually associated with the Wireless Web.

Chapter 4 introduced *mobile commerce* (*m-commerce*)—the use of the Internet for purchasing goods and services as well as for transmitting messages using handheld wireless devices. Table 9.5 describes what are likely to be the most popular categories of m-commerce services and applications. Location-based applications are of special interest because they take advantage of the unique capabilities of mobile technology. Whenever a user is connected to the Internet via a wireless device (cell phone, PDA, laptop), the transmission technology can be leveraged to determine that person's location and beam location-specific services or product information. For example, drivers could use this capability to obtain local weather data and traffic information along with alternative route suggestions and descriptions of nearby restaurants.

Although m-commerce is just starting up in Canada, millions of users in Japan and Scandinavia already use cell phones to purchase goods, trade files, exchange short text messages, and obtain updated weather and sports reports.

Wireless Web Standards There are a plethora of standards governing every area of wireless communications. The two main standards for the Wireless Web are Wireless Application Protocol (WAP) and i-mode (see Figure 9.11).

TABLE 9.5	**M-COMMERCE SERVICES AND APPLICATIONS**
Type of M-Commerce Service	Applications
Information-based services	Instant messaging, e-mail, or searching for a movie or restaurant using a cell phone or handheld PDA
Transaction-based services	Purchasing stocks, concert tickets, music, or games; searching for the best price of an item using a cell phone and buying it in a physical store or on the Web
Personalized services	Services that anticipate what you want based on your location or data profile, such as updated airline flight information or beaming coupons for nearby restaurants

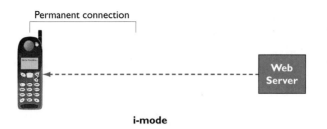

Permanent connection

i-mode

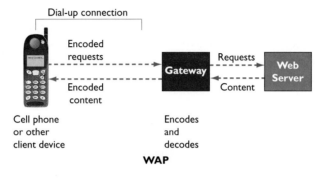

Dial-up connection

Encoded requests

Requests

Encoded content

Content

Cell phone or other client device

Encodes and decodes

WAP

Figure 9.11 WAP versus i-mode. WAP and i-mode are two competing standards for accessing information from the Wireless Web.

Wireless Application Protocol (WAP) is a system of protocols and technologies that lets cell phones and other wireless devices with tiny display screens, low-bandwidth connections, and minimal memory access Web-based information and services. WAP uses **WML (Wireless Markup Language)**, which is based on XML (see Chapter 6) and optimized for tiny displays. A person with a WAP-compliant phone uses the built-in microbrowser to make a request in WML. A **microbrowser** is an Internet browser with a small file size that can work with the low-memory constraints of handheld wireless devices and the low bandwidth of wireless networks. The request is passed to a WAP gateway, which retrieves the information from an Internet server in either standard HTML format or WML. The gateway translates HTML content back into WML so that it can be received by the WAP client. The complexity of the translation process can affect the speed of information delivery. WAP supports most wireless network standards and operating systems for handheld computing devices, such as PalmOS and Windows CE/Pocket PC.

I-mode is a rival standard developed by Japan's NTT DoCoMo mobile phone network; it is widely used in Japan and is being introduced to Europe. I-mode uses compact HTML to deliver content, making it easier for businesses to convert their HTML Web sites to mobile service. I-mode uses packet switching, which allows users to be constantly connected to the network and content providers to broadcast relevant information to users. (WAP users have to dial in to see if a site has changed.) I-mode can handle colour graphics not available on WAP handsets, although WAP is being modified to handle colour graphics.

M-Commerce Challenges

Rollout of m-commerce services has not been as rapid in the United States as in Japan and Europe. There are a number of reasons for this, all stemming from the newness of the technology. Eventually, most of these challenges should be resolved. Keyboards and screens on cell phones are tiny and awkward to use. The data transfer speeds on existing wireless networks are very slow, ranging from 9.6 to 14.4 Kbps, compared with 56 Kbps for a dial-up connection to the Internet via a PC. Each second waiting for data to download costs the customer money. Most Internet-enabled phones have minimal memory and limited power supplies. Web content for wireless devices is primarily in the form of text with very little graphics. Not enough Web sites have reconfigured their services to display only the few lines of text that can be accommodated by cell phone screens.

Unlike Europe, North American wireless networks are based on several incompatible technologies. (Europe uses the GSM standard, while wireless carriers in North America primarily

Wireless Application Protocol (WAP)

System of protocols and technologies that lets cell phones and other wireless devices with tiny displays, low-bandwidth connections, and minimal memory access Web-based information and services.

WML (Wireless Markup Language)

Markup language for Wireless Web sites, based on XML and optimized for tiny displays.

microbrowser

Web browser software with a small file size that can work with low-memory constraints, tiny screens of handheld wireless devices, and low bandwidth of wireless networks.

i-mode

Standard developed by Japan's NTT DoCoMo mobile phone network for enabling cell phones to receive Web-based content and services.

use CDMA or TDMA standards—although GSM use in North America is growing.) For the Wireless Web to take off, more Web sites need to be designed specifically for wireless devices that are more Web friendly.

Some of the limitations of m-commerce may be overcome by using voice recognition and personalization technology. **Voice portals** accept voice commands for accessing information from the Web. Voice portals offer customers a combination of content and services, with users accessing the content by speaking into a telephone. The user can orally request information, such as stock quotes, weather reports, airlines schedules, or news stories. For example, TellMe provides direct access to the Web using voice commands so that users can contact taxis, hotels, and friends as well as obtain weather reports, ski reports, and traffic information. Sophisticated voice recognition software processes the requests, which are translated back into speech for the customer. Personalization technology can organize and filter Web content so that only the information of greatest relevance to users appears on wireless display screens (Billsus et al., 2002).

M-commerce will also benefit from faster wireless networks. Cellular network providers are speeding up their services, preparing new versions of the three main digital standards to double their speed. Third-generation (3G) mobile communication networks will offer transmission speeds ranging from several hundred Kbps to 2 Mbps, depending on the nature of the application. Faster wireless networks will make it possible to stream high-quality video and audio to mobile devices along with new services.

Businesses will need to review all of these issues when determining the role of Wireless Web technology in their business strategy. The Manager's Toolkit provides questions to guide management analysis.

9.4 SUPPORT TECHNOLOGY FOR ELECTRONIC COMMERCE AND ELECTRONIC BUSINESS

Businesses seriously pursuing electronic commerce and electronic business need special tools for maintaining their Web sites. These tools include Web server and electronic commerce server software, customer tracking and personalization tools, Web content management tools, and Web site performance monitoring tools.

WEB SERVERS AND ELECTRONIC COMMERCE SERVERS

In Chapter 6, we introduced Web servers as the software necessary to run Web sites, intranets, and extranets. The core capabilities of Web server software revolve around locating and managing stored Web pages. Web server software locates the Web pages requested by client computers by translating the URL Web address into the physical file address for the

---

voice portal

Portal that can accept voice commands for accessing information from the Web.

MIS IN ACTION: MANAGER'S TOOLKIT

HOW TO INTEGRATE THE WIRELESS WEB INTO BUSINESS STRATEGY

Some businesses will benefit from incorporating the Wireless Web into their business strategy; others may not. Before investing heavily in Wireless Web technology and m-commerce, here are some key questions to ask:

1. *Wireless value proposition:* Does adopting wireless technology enhance the company's existing business model? Can using wireless technology produce substantial gains in sales, customer loyalty, or customer service?

2. *User benefits:* Does using the wireless technology provide a valuable service to the user? How valuable is this service? Does it save customers or employees substantial amounts of time?

3. *Rationale for switching:* Does the wireless technology create a product, service, or business process improvement that is so compelling that it will be enthusiastically adopted? How willing would users be to give up working at their desktops to use the new mobile technology?

4. *Business process change:* What business processes will change as a result of using wireless technology? What jobs and work practices will be affected? Will these changes be easy to make? Will employees require additional training in order to use the new technology? Will business processes of customers and suppliers have to change as well as those of the firm?

requested Web page. The Web server then sends the requested pages to the client. Many Web servers also include tools for authenticating users; support for FTP, search engines, and indexing programs; and capabilities for capturing Web site visitor information in log files. (Each request to the server for a file is recorded as an entry in the Web server log and is called a **hit**.) Apache HTTP Server and Microsoft's Internet Information Services (IIS) are currently the most popular Web servers. Management will have to examine carefully the servers available in order to determine which server offers the functionality that best fits the needs of its site.

Web server computers range in size from small desktop PCs to mainframes, depending on the size of the Web sites. The Web server computer must be large enough to handle the Web server software and the projected traffic of the particular site.

Servers differ in the number of simultaneous users they can handle, how quickly they can service their requests, and the technologies they support in Web applications. Server scalability is a major issue if a company is looking forward to rapid growth.

Specialized **electronic commerce server software** provides functions essential for electronic commerce Web sites, often running on computers dedicated to this purpose. Functions the software must perform for both business-to-consumer and business-to-business electronic commerce include the following:

- Setting up electronic storefronts and electronic catalogues to display product and pricing information.
- Designing electronic shopping carts so customers can collect and pay for the items they wish to purchase.
- Making shipping arrangements.
- Linking to electronic payment processing systems.
- Displaying product availability and tracking shipments.
- Connecting to back-office systems, where necessary.

Systems designed for small business-to-consumer (B2C) electronic commerce usually include wizards and templates to aid in the setting up of the storefronts and catalogues. However, high-end B2C and B2B systems, such as Microsoft's Commerce Server and IBM's WebSphere Commerce Suite, require the help of information technology professionals for installation and support.

CUSTOMER TRACKING AND PERSONALIZATION TOOLS

Customer tracking and personalization tools have several main goals:

- Collecting and storing data on the behaviour of online customers and combining that data with data already stored in the company's back-office systems.
- Analyzing the data in order to better understand the behaviour of online customers.
- Identifying customer preferences and trends.

Chapter 4 described some of the benefits of personalizing Web sites to deliver content specific to each user. Online personalization systems often use **clickstream tracking** tools to collect data on customer activities at Web sites and store them in a log. The tools record the site that users last visited before coming to your Web site and where these users go when they leave your site. They also record the specific pages visited on your site, the time spent on each page of the site, the types of pages visited, and what the visitors purchased. Web sites can also populate databases with explicit data gained when visitors fill out registration forms on the site or purchase products.

Collaborative filtering software tracks users' movements on a Web site, comparing the information it gains about a user's behaviour against data about other customers with similar interests to predict what the user would like to see next. The software then makes recommendations to users on the basis of their assumed interests. For example, Amazon.ca uses collaborative filtering software to prepare personalized book recommendations: "Customers who bought this book also shopped for these items...."

Segmentation and rules-based systems use business rules to deliver certain types of information based on a user's profile, classifying users into smaller groups or segments on the basis

hit

An entry into a Web server's log file generated by each request to the server for a file.

electronic commerce server software

Software that provides functions essential for running electronic commerce Web sites, such as setting up electronic catalogues and storefronts, and mechanisms for processing customer purchases.

clickstream tracking

Tracking data about customer activities at Web sites and storing them in a log.

collaborative filtering

Tracking users' movements on a Web site, comparing the information gleaned about a user's behaviour against data about other customers with similar interests to predict what the user would like to see next.

of these rules. The software uses demographic, geographic, income, or other information to divide, or segment, large populations into smaller groups for targeted content. Broadvision's electronic commerce system for offering personalized content to Web site visitors is a rules-based product.

Data collected from Web site visitors can be stored in databases or data warehouses where the data can be more easily analyzed to unearth customer preferences and trends. Some of these databases combine clickstream data with data from back-office systems and relevant external data to gain a fuller understanding of each customer. Chapter 13 provides additional detail on Web customer data analysis.

WEB CONTENT MANAGEMENT TOOLS

Web content management tools are needed because many companies have Web sites with thousands or hundreds of thousands of pages to manage, a task too great for a Webmaster. Web content management software has emerged to assist the Webmaster and other authorized staff in the collection, assembly, and management of content on a Web site, intranet, or extranet.

The materials on Web sites are often very complex and include many forms of data, such as documents, graphics, and sound. Often, the content must be dynamic, and parts of it must be capable of changing, depending on such circumstances as the identification of the visitor, the day of the month, the price of a product, or the requests of the visitor. **Dynamic page generation** tools store the contents of Web pages as objects in a database, rather than as static HTML documents. When a user requests a Web page, the contents of the page are fetched from the database. Web content management tools help users organize and modify this material when needed and ensure that only those responsible for the specific content are able to update or change it. Often, the browser requests in HTML a response that requires a database to be accessed. The **common gateway interface (CGI)** is a standard way for a Web server to pass a Web user's request to an application program and to receive data back to forward to the user. CGI is used to translate the HTML request into the language of the database. (CGI is also used when users fill out a form online; the CGI translates the HTML form data so that it can be added to the backend database.) Also *Active Server Pages,* a standard developed by Microsoft, and *Java Server Pages,* a standard developed by Sun Microsystems, can be used to furnish dynamic page content. Both these standards embed scripts in their Web pages, which execute to create the page content when the user views the page.

WEB SITE PERFORMANCE MONITORING TOOLS

Most Web sites are plagued by such problems as slow performance, major outages, content errors, broken links between Web pages, transaction failures, and slow-loading pages. To address these problems, companies can use their own **Web site performance monitoring tools** or rely on Web site performance monitoring services.

Web site performance monitoring tools measure the response times of specific transactions, such as inquiries, checking out purchases, or authorizing credit through a credit card. They can pinpoint the location of bottlenecks that slow down a Web site, such as at the Web or application server, a specific database, or a network router. Some tools test the site's scalability through stressing the site by creating many test site visitors. Some tools also identify the causes for slow page loading speeds, such as too many banners, too many dense graphics files, or disk-space problems. (See Figure 9.12.)

WEB HOSTING SERVICES

Companies that lack the financial or technical resources to operate their own Web sites or electronic commerce services can use Web hosting services. A **Web hosting service** maintains a large Web server or series of servers and provides fee-paying subscribers with space to maintain their Web sites. The subscribing companies may create their own Web pages or have the hosting service or a Web design firm create them. Some services offer *co-location,* in which the firm actually purchases and owns the server computer housing its Web site but locates the server in the physical facility of the hosting service.

Web content management tools

Software to facilitate the collection, assembly, and management of content on a Web site, intranet, or extranet.

Dynamic page generation

Technology for storing the contents of Web pages as objects in a database where they can be accessed and assembled to create constantly changing Web pages.

common gateway interface (CGI)

A standard way for a Web server to pass a Web user's request to an application program and to receive data back to be forwarded to the user.

Web site performance monitoring tools

Software tools for monitoring the time to download Web pages and perform Web transactions, identifying broken links between Web pages, and pinpointing other Web site problems and bottlenecks.

Web hosting service

Company with large Web server computers to maintain the Web sites of fee-paying subscribers.

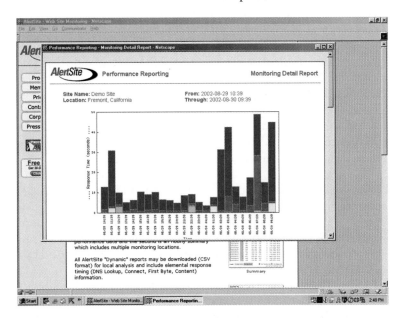

Figure 9.12 The AlertSite Web Site Monitoring System monitors Web sites and other Internet-connected devices to ensure that they are performing optimally. Displayed here is one of its reports showing hourly changes in Web site response time (in seconds).

Companies can also use specialized electronic commerce application service providers to set up and operate their electronic commerce sites or intranets. Such companies as FreeMerchant.com, Yahoo! Store, and ClearOption.com provide low-cost electronic commerce sites to small businesses with very simple electronic commerce requirements that can use a predefined template for displaying and selling their wares.

Web hosting services offer solutions to small companies that do not have the resources to operate their own Web sites or to companies that still are experimenting with electronic commerce. These services cost much less than running one's own Web site, and the hosting services have technical staff who can design, develop, manage, and support the site.

Many large companies use Web hosting services because they offer highly experienced technical staff and servers in multiple global locations, and backup server capacity to ensure 100-percent Web site availability. Such companies as IBM Global Services, Electronic Data Systems (EDS) Corporation, and CGI provide fully managed Web hosting services. High-end managed hosting can range from $50 000 to $1 million per month.

9.5 MANAGEMENT ISSUES AND DECISIONS

An information technology infrastructure for digitally enabling the enterprise requires coordinating many different types of computing and networking technologies, public and private infrastructures, and organizational processes. Careful management and planning are essential.

THE CHALLENGE OF MANAGING THE NEW IT INFRASTRUCTURE

Implementing enterprise networking and the new IT infrastructure has created problems as well as opportunities for organizations. Managers need to address these problems to create an IT infrastructure for digitally enabling their firms.

Electronic commerce and electronic business are forcing companies to reassess their information technology infrastructures in order to remain competitive. Many organizations are saddled with a maze of old legacy applications, hardware, and networks that do not talk to each other. In order to support enterprise-wide business processes that can smoothly link to customers or suppliers via the Internet, they must rebuild their information architectures and IT infrastructures. Five problems stand out: (1) loss of management control over information systems, (2) connectivity and application integration challenges, (3) the need for organizational change, (4) the hidden costs of enterprise computing, and (5) the difficulty of ensuring infrastructure scalability, reliability, and security.

Loss of Management Control

Managing information systems technology and corporate data are proving much more diffi-cult in a distributed environment because of the lack of a single, central point where neces-sary management can be found. Distributed client-server networks, new mobile wireless networks, and Internet computing have empowered end users to become independent sources of computing power that are capable of collecting, storing, and disseminating data and software. Data and software no longer are confined to the mainframe and under the management of the traditional information systems department but reside instead on many different computing platforms throughout the organization.

An enterprise-wide IT infrastructure requires that the business know where all of its data are located and ensure that the same piece of information, such as a product number, is used consistently throughout the organization (see Chapter 7). These data may not always be in a standard format or may reside on incompatible computing platforms. However, observers worry that excess centralization and management of information resources will reduce users' ability to define their own information needs. The dilemma posed by enterprise networking and the new IT infrastructure is one of central management control versus end-user creativ-ity and productivity.

Connectivity and Application Integration Challenges

We have already described the connectivity problems created by incompatible networks and stan-dards, including connectivity problems for wireless networks. Digital firm organizations depend on enterprise-wide integration of their business processes and applications so that they can obtain their information from any point in the value chain. An order from a Web site should be able to trigger events automatically in the organization's accounting, inventory, and distribution applica-tions to speed the product swiftly to the customer. This end-to-end process and application inte-gration is extremely difficult to achieve and beyond the reach of many firms.

Organizational Change Requirements

Enterprise-wide computing is an opportunity to re-engineer the organization into a more effective unit, but it will only create problems or chaos if the underlying organizational issues are not fully addressed. Behind antiquated legacy infrastructures are old ways of doing busi-ness, which must also be changed to work effectively in a new enterprise-wide IT infrastruc-ture. Infrastructure and architecture for a business that can respond to rapidly changing marketplace demands and industry changes require changes in corporate culture and organi-zational structure that are not easy to make. It took several years of hard work and large financial investments for IBM to Web-enable its business processes and convince disparate business units to adopt a "One IBM" mindset where everyone uses common tools. Sun Microsystems, the networking technology giant, experienced a painful two-year conversion of its own information systems to make them run on its own networks (Kanter, 2001).

Hidden Costs of Enterprise Computing

Many companies have found that the savings they expected from distributed client-server computing did not materialize because of unexpected costs. Hardware-acquisition savings resulting from downsizing often are offset by high annual operating costs for additional labour and time required for network and system management. Considerable time must be spent on such tasks as network maintenance; data backup; technical problem solving; and hardware, software, and software-update installations. Gains in productivity and efficiency from equipping employees with wireless mobile computing devices must be balanced against increased costs associated with integrating these devices into the firm's IT infrastructure and providing technical support.

Scalability, Reliability, and Security

Companies seeking to digitally enable their businesses require robust IT infrastructures provid-ing plentiful bandwidth and storage capacity for transmitting and maintaining all of the data generated by electronic commerce and electronic business transactions. Network infrastructures need not only to be able to handle current electronic business and electronic commerce demands but also to be able to scale rapidly to meet future demands while providing high levels of performance and availability for mission-critical applications.

Enterprise networking is highly sensitive to different versions of operating systems and network management software, with some applications requiring specific versions of each. It is difficult to make all of the components of large, heterogeneous networks work together as smoothly as management envisions. **Downtime**—periods of time in which the system is not operational—remains much more frequent in distributed systems than in established mainframe systems and should be considered carefully before taking essential applications off a mainframe.

downtime
Period of time in which an information system is not operational.

Security is of paramount importance in firms with extensive networking and electronic transactions with individuals or other businesses outside organizational boundaries. Networks present end users, hackers, and thieves with many points of access and opportunities to steal or modify data in networks. Systems linked to the Internet are even more vulnerable because the Internet was designed to be open to everyone. Wireless computing devices linked to corporate applications create new areas of vulnerability. We discuss these issues in greater detail in Chapter 11.

SOME SOLUTIONS

Organizations can meet the challenges posed by the new IT infrastructure by planning for and managing business and organizational changes; increasing end-user training; asserting data administration disciplines; and considering connectivity, application integration, bandwidth, and cost controls in their technology planning.

Managing the Change

To gain the full benefit of any new technology, organizations must carefully plan for and manage the change. Business processes may need to be re-engineered to accompany infrastructure changes (see Chapter 10). For example, equipping the sales force with wireless handheld devices for entering orders in the field provides an opportunity for management to review the sales process to see if redundant order entry activities or a separate order entry staff can be eliminated. Management must address the organizational issues that arise from shifts in staffing, function, power, and organizational culture attendant to a new IT infrastructure.

Education and Training

A well-developed training program can help end users overcome problems resulting from the lack of management support and understanding of networked computing (Westin et al., 1985; Bikson et al., 1985). Technical specialists will need training in Web site, wireless, and client-server development and network support methods.

Data Administration Disciplines

The role of data administration (see Chapter 7) becomes even more important when networks link many different applications, business areas, and computing devices. Organizations must systematically identify where their data are located, which group is responsible for maintaining each piece of data, and which individuals and groups are allowed to access and use that data. They need to develop specific policies and procedures to ensure that their data are accurate, available only to authorized users, and properly backed up.

Planning for Connectivity and Application Integration

Senior management must take a long-term view of the firm's IT infrastructure and information architecture, making sure they can support the required level of process and information integration for current and future needs. Infrastructure planning should consider how much connectivity would be required to digitally enable core strategic business processes. To what extent should network services be standardized throughout the organization? Will the firm be communicating with customers and suppliers using different technology platforms? How should wireless mobile computing networks be integrated with the rest of the firm?

Although some connectivity problems can be solved by using intranets or the Internet, the firm will need to establish enterprise-wide standards for other systems and applications. Management can establish policies to keep networks and telecommunications services as homogeneous as possible, setting standards for data, voice, e-mail, and videoconferencing services along with hardware, software, and network operating systems.

An enterprise-wide architecture for integrated business applications and processes cannot be created through piecemeal changes. It represents a long-term endeavour that should be supported by top management and coordinated with the firm's strategic plans.

MANAGEMENT WRAP-UP

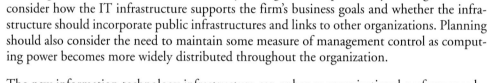

Planning the firm's IT infrastructure is a key management responsibility. Managers need to consider how the IT infrastructure supports the firm's business goals and whether the infrastructure should incorporate public infrastructures and links to other organizations. Planning should also consider the need to maintain some measure of management control as computing power becomes more widely distributed throughout the organization.

The new information technology infrastructure can enhance organizational performance by making information flow more smoothly between different parts of the organization and between the organization and its customers, suppliers, and other value partners. Organizations can use Internet technology and tools to reduce communication and coordination costs, create interactive products and services, and accelerate the distribution of knowledge.

Internet technology is providing the connectivity for the new information technology infrastructure and the emerging digital firm using the TCP/IP reference model and other standards for retrieving, formatting, and displaying information. Key technology decisions should consider the capabilities of Internet, electronic commerce, and new wireless technologies along with connectivity, scalability, reliability, and requirements for application integration.

For Discussion

1. It has been said that developing an IT infrastructure for electronic commerce and electronic business is, above all, a business decision, as opposed to a technical decision. Discuss.

2. A fully integrated IT infrastructure is essential for business success. Do you agree? Why, or why not?

SUMMARY

1. *What is the new information technology (IT) infrastructure for business? Why is connectivity so important in this infrastructure?* The new IT infrastructure uses a mixture of computer hardware supplied by different vendors, including mainframes, PCs, and servers, which are networked to each other. More processing power is available on the desktop through client-server computing and mobile personal information devices that provide remote access to the desktop from outside the organization. The new IT infrastructure also incorporates public infrastructures, such as the telephone system, the Internet, and public network services.

Connectivity is a measure of how well computers and computer-based devices can communicate with one another and "share" information in a meaningful way without human intervention. It is essential in enterprise networking in the new IT infrastructure, where different hardware, software, and network components must work together to transfer information seamlessly from one part of the organization to another. TCP/IP and OSI are important reference models for achieving connectivity in networks. UNIX is an operating system standard that can be used to create open systems as can the Linux operating system. Connectivity also can be achieved by using Internet technology, XML, and Java.

2. *How does the Internet work? What are its major capabilities?* The Internet is a worldwide network of networks that uses the client-server model of computing and the TCP/IP network reference model. Using the Internet, any computer (or computing appliance) can communicate with any other computer connected to the Internet throughout the world. The Internet has no central management. The Internet is used for communications, including e-mail, public forums on thousands of topics, and live, interactive conversations. It also is used for information retrieval from hundreds of libraries and thousands of corporate, government, and nonprofit databases. It has developed into an effective way for individuals and organizations to offer information and products through a Web of graphical user interfaces and easy-to-use links worldwide. Major Internet capabilities include e-mail, Usenet, LISTSERV, chatting, Telnet, FTP, and the World Wide Web.

Many organizations use Internet e-mail, chat, and Usenet services to reduce communications costs when they must manage organizational activities or communicate with employees. Firms are also starting to realize economies by using Internet telephony. Internet technology can also reduce communication costs by allowing companies to create virtual private networks as low-cost alternatives to private WANs.

3. *How can organizations benefit from using the World Wide Web and Web technology? How can businesses benefit from the Wireless Web?* The World Wide Web provides a universal set of standards for storing, retrieving, and displaying information in a client-server environment, enabling users to link to information resources housed in many different computer systems around the world. Web pages featuring text, graphics, video, and sound can be used to create new products and services and closer relationships with customers. Web site directories, search engines, and "push" technology can help users locate the information they need on the Web. Web technologies and Internet networking standards provide the connectivity and interfaces for intranets and extranets that can be accessed by many different kinds of computers both inside and outside the organization.

Wireless Web technologies enable Internet-enabled cell phones, PDAs, and other wireless computing devices to access digital information from the Internet from any location. Employees of businesses equipped with wireless Internet connections can access Web information from any location and make decisions instantly without being tethered to a desk or computer. Wireless Web applications, especially those that are location based, also represent a source of new products, services, and revenue. However, Wireless Web applications have not yet been widely adopted because keyboards and display screens on cell phones are tiny and awkward to use, and data transfer speeds on existing wireless networks are still quite slow.

4. *What are the principal technologies for supporting electronic commerce and electronic business?* Businesses need a series of software tools for maintaining a Web site. Web server software locates and manages Web pages stored on Web server computers. Electronic commerce server software provides capabilities for setting up electronic storefronts and arranging for payments and shipping. Customer tracking and personalization tools collect, store, and analyze data on Web site visitors. Content management tools facilitate the collection, assembly, and management of Web site content. Web site performance monitoring tools monitor the speed of Web site transactions and identify Web site performance problems. Businesses can use an external vendor's Web hosting service as an alternative to maintaining their own Web sites.

5. *What management problems are raised by the new information technology (IT) infrastructure? How can businesses solve these problems?* Problems posed by the new IT infrastructure include loss of management control over systems; the need to carefully manage organizational change; connectivity and application integration challenges; the difficulty of ensuring network scalability, reliability, and security; and controlling the hidden costs of enterprise computing.

Solutions include planning for and managing the business and organizational changes associated with enterprise-wide computing; increasing end-user training; asserting data administration disciplines; and considering connectivity, application integration, bandwidth, and cost controls when planning the IT infrastructure.

KEY TERMS

CA*net 3,   299

Chatting,   295

Clickstream tracking,   307

Collaborative filtering,   307

Common gateway interface (CGI),   308

Connectivity,   289

Domain name,   294

Domain Name System (DNS),   294

Downtime,   311

Dynamic page generation,   308

Electronic commerce server software,   307

Enterprise networking,   288

File Transfer Protocol (FTP),   297

Firewall,   302

Hit,   307

Home page,   299

Hypertext Transport Protocol (HTTP),   299

I-mode,   305

Information appliance,   292

Instant messaging,   295

Internet Protocol (IP) address,   294

Internet Service Provider (ISP),   292

Internet telephony,   296

Internet2,   298

Internetworking,   288

LISTSERV,   295

Microbrowser,   305

Multicasting,   302

Open systems,   289

Open Systems Interconnection (OSI),   290

"Push" technology,   301

Search engine,   300

Shopping bot,   300

Telnet,   295

Transmission Control Protocol/Internet Protocol (TCP/IP),   289

Uniform resource locator (URL),   299

Usenet,   295

Review Questions

1. What are the features of the new information technology infrastructure?

2. Why is connectivity so important for the digital firm? List and describe the major connectivity standards for networking and the Internet.

3. What is the Internet? List and describe alternative ways of accessing the Internet.

4. List and describe the principal Internet capabilities.

5. Describe the capabilities of next generation networks, including CA*net 3? How do they differ from those of the existing public Internet? What benefits can they provide?

6. Why is the World Wide Web so useful for individuals and businesses?

7. Define and describe the following: home page, uniform resource locator (URL), Internet telephony, virtual private network (VPN), and voice portal.

8. List and describe alternative ways of locating information on the Web.

9. What are intranets and extranets? How do they differ from the Web?

10. What is the Wireless Web? How does it differ from the conventional Web?

11. List and describe the types of m-commerce services and applications supported by the Wireless Web.

12. Compare the WAP and i-mode Wireless Web standards.

13. List and describe the principal technologies for supporting electronic commerce and electronic business.

14. Under what conditions should firms consider Web hosting services?

15. Describe five problems posed by the new IT infrastructure.

16. Describe some solutions to the problems posed by the new IT infrastructure.

Application Software Exercise

SPREADSHEET EXERCISE: ANALYZING WEB SITE VISITORS

Your firm, Marina Clothiers, makes casual pants, shirts, and other clothes for both men and women. Your firm has been attempting to increase the number of online customers by placing advertising banners for your Web site at other Web sites. When users click on these banner ads, they are automatically transported to your Web site. Data from your advertising campaign are summarized in the weekly Marketing Trends Report (MTR) produced by your Web site analysis software, which appears on the Companion Website for Chapter 9.

■ *Visitors* are the number of people who visited your Web site by clicking on a banner ad for your site that was placed on an affiliated Web site.

■ *Shoppers* are the number of visitors referred by banner ads who reached a page in your Web site designated as a shopping page.

■ *Attempted buyers* are the number of potential buyers referred by banner ads who reached a Web page designated as a page for summarizing and paying for purchases.

■ *Buyers* are the number of buyers referred by banner ads who actually placed an order from your Web site.

■ *Source* indicates the specific Web site from which visitors came to your Web site.

In trying to increase the number of online customers, you must determine your Web site's success in converting visitors to actual buyers. You must also look at the abandonment rate—the percentage of attempted buyers who abandoned your Web site just as they were about to make a purchase. Low conversion rates and high abandonment rates are indicators that a Web site is not very effective. You also must identify likely Web site partners for a new advertising campaign. Use the MTR with your spreadsheet software to answer the questions below. Include a graphics presentation to support your findings:

■ What are the total numbers of visitors, shoppers, attempted buyers, and buyers at your Web site?

■ Which sources provided the highest conversion rate to buyers at your Web site—that is, the percentage of visitors from a previous site who become buyers on your site? What is the average conversion rate for your Web site?

■ Which sources provided the highest abandonment rate at your Web site—that is the percentage of attempted buyers who abandoned their shopping cart at your Web site before completing a purchase? What is the average abandonment rate for your Web site?

■ On which Web sites (or types of Web sites) should your firm purchase more banner ads?

GROUP PROJECT

Form a group with three or four of your classmates. Prepare evaluations of the wireless Internet capabilities of a Palm and a PocketPC handheld computing device. Your analysis should consider the purchase cost of each device, any additional software required to make it Internet enabled, the cost of wireless Internet services, and what Internet services are available for each device. You should also consider other capabilities of each device, including the ability to integrate with existing corporate or PC applications. Which device would you select? What criteria would you use to guide your selection? If possible, use electronic presentation software to present your findings to the class.

 INTERNET TOOLS

COMPANION WEBSITE

The Companion Website for this chapter will take you to a series of Web sites where you can evaluate tools for providing Wireless Web access.

At www.pearsoned.ca/laudon, you will find valuable tools to facilitate and enhance your learning of this chapter as well as opportunities to apply your knowledge to realistic situations:

■ An Interactive Study Guide of self-test questions that will provide you with immediate feedback.

■ Application exercises.

■ An Electronic Commerce Project where you can evaluate various Web search engines for business research.

■ A Management Decision Problem on reducing agency costs.

■ Updates of material in this chapter.

ADDITIONAL SITES OF INTEREST

There are many interesting Web sites to enhance your learning about the Internet and the new IT infrastructure. You can search the Web yourself or just try the following sites to add to what you have already learned.

Coast Software
www.coast.ca
Canadian company specializing in Web management tools for the enterprise.

ICQ.com
www.icq.com
The most popular chat software company.

Google
www.google.com
The most popular search engine; you can download Google buttons and a Google toolbar to help you search the Web without accessing Google's interface site first.

Wired News
www.wired.com/news
News about a host of Internet technologies.

DoCoMo
www.nttdocomo.com
Information about i-mode and Japan's NTT DoCoMo company and network.

CASE STUDY: *Wireless Web Helps Monitor Hard-to-Access Well Sites*

Originally named Amoco Canada, British Petroleum (BP) has operated in this country for more than half a century under the names BP Canada Energy Company and Castrol brand. Although BP is involved with Natural Gas Liquids (NGL), Gas and Power marketing, Integrated Supply and Trading (IST), Chemicals, Crude Oil Supply, and Air BP, the company's main business is upstream Exploration and Production.

Once an oil producer, BP Canada's main current exposure to oil is as a significant buyer for US refineries—it is in the top three Canadian oil marketers and traders. Central Alberta

Midstream (CAMS) is an entity that manages natural gas wells in Alberta. CAMS is a partnership between BP and Chevron Texaco, the former being the majority owner. BP Canada Energy Company is the country's largest natural gas value chain company. Headquartered in Calgary, the company's exposure to natural gas and its derivatives includes exploration, development, production, processing, marketing, and trading. It operates in six provinces and two territories.

A key player in Canadian natural gas production, BP Canada's wells inject nearly 750 million cubic feet a day into the pipeline system, largely in Canada's western provinces. The company also has landholdings in the arctic—it's the largest onshore landholder in the Mackenzie Delta—and the Maritimes.

BP Canada is also heavily involved in the country's natural gas liquids (NGL) industry. Trading about 200 000 barrels of NGLs a day puts it near the top of the heap in Canadian NGL marketing. Its assets include the Cochin, Canada's largest and longest NGL pipeline, and the Empress plant, one of North America's biggest gas processing facilities. Other NGL assets are pipelines, storage, gathering, fractionation, and processing facilities in western and eastern Canada, as well as terminals throughout the country.

In terms of marketing and trading natural gas, BP Canada's role is significant in the industry. Gas and Power Canada markets natural gas to both Canada and the United States. BP Canada has 1500 employees as well as about 200 contractors on the payroll, the vast majority of whom are Canadians.

Maximum production of a gas well entails constant production. Various factors can cause downtime or a halt to flow. These include liquids accumulating in the wellbore, liquids freezing in lines, or a wide variety of human errors. For efficient production, these problems need to be rapidly noticed, isolated, and fixed.

Traditionally, keeping a gas well operating smoothly meant hands-on operation. In other words, a worker who keeps tabs on equipment must visit a well frequently. The traditional approach works fine for wells that are in close proximity to one another and can be accessed easily. However, gas wells are often found far from civilization. When a well is located off the beaten track, deep in a mountain range or surrounded by thick woods, a daily visit by the operator is neither efficient nor practical.

Recently, BP Canada addressed this problem by installing a Wireless Web to remotely monitor and control well sites in an inaccessible area so that it could produce gas at a maximum rate at a low operating cost. The range of capabilities that the BP Wireless Web handles is called SCADA (supervisory control and data acquisition).

Traditional SCADA systems have existed for some time. They assist gas producers in maintaining decent production rates at reasonable costs. These SCADA systems allow distant field offices control and operation capabilities over remote well sites. SCADA systems also provide accurate, timely production data that can be integrated into corporate production accounting systems.

But traditional SCADA systems are often expensive, causing gas producers, such as BP Canada, to seek better solutions based on upfront capital costs, ongoing operating costs, system reliability, outsourcing, security, and overall system performance. A further consideration is that gas-producing companies may not be the best at building and operating their own telecommunication infrastructure. Traditional SCADA systems require a host computer system and a radio network to be put in place for each remote well site.

BP elected to use a new system that eliminated the host. Instead of a radio network, they used a wireless Internet connection and a remote terminal unit (RTU). The RTU will operate with a Web browser. The new SCADA system is similar to the traditional host-based SCADA systems in that it uses a traditional three-in-one multivariable flow transmitter at the instru-

ment level. Yet significant changes can be found at the RTU level. The RTU generally obtains measurements from the transmitter and does gas flow computations, downloads production data according to American Petroleum Institute guidelines, governs input–output points, and performs complicated operations on the data gathered.

None of this is dissimilar from traditional RTUs and SCADA systems. But what makes this system unique is that each RTU is enabled as an autonomous server on the Web, instead of being a pawn of the host computer. From any browser, a remote operator with Web access can click a given URL, type a password, and pull up its respective RTU. Since many of these well sites are quite small, BP's Web-based SCADA doesn't need much in the way of bandwidth, memory, or processing power. Given the Web-based access, other qualified people can also view the real-time data. This is a significant improvement over traditional SCADA systems as on many occasions a variety of individuals may need to observe remote operations, be they an engineer in Calgary, a minority business partner in Toronto, or an IT contractor in Vancouver.

BP Canada discovered that their remote well sites all had good wireless Web coverage. Their local ISP cellular phone service provider, Telus Mobility of Calgary, uses cellular digital packet data technology to deliver this service for BP Canada.

For BP Canada, a Web-based well site provides for viewing and control functions from a field office, home office, or even a mobile office. Handheld PCs, PDAs, and laptops can all be used to connect to Web-based SCADA.

In addition, operators need to be alerted when there is a problem at the well site, such as no-flow. Using BP Canada's new system, when the flow rate drops below the preconfigured low-flow threshold, the RTU generates an "alarm e-mail" that informs the operator of the abnormal condition. BP's operators all carry alphanumeric pagers or cell phones that support text messaging. From the RTU, the message moves via e-mail to a server in a proximate field office, then becomes an MS Outlook e-mail that bounces to the pager-cell phone ID numbers. Each such alarm carries a characteristic well site signifier, which means alarms are directed to the correct operator. Since the system uses user-friendly MS Outlook as the interface, even non–tech savvy operators are able to configure and govern it. This means they needn't call on IT help in case of vacation or employee illness. In addition to alarm e-mails, each well site's RTU sends a daily e-mail with standard production data at a user-defined time.

BP Canada is also using the Internet to manage its Gas Order Trading System (GOTS). GOTS connects the company's trading parters at Web speed so they can respond to daily fluctuations in the marketplace faster than their competitors. GOTS is a distributed client-server application, written in Microsoft Visual Basic with Web-based components, which permit the company to plug any information related to its trading partners or the business process into a standardized system for a single point of access to the data. For example, employees used to receive order quantity changes by telephone and fax machine. Now they receive customer requested quantity changes through a secure Active Server Page (ASP page), and they can process the change in seconds. The Web application can also provide instant confirmation of scheduled quantities. A side benefit of using the Web for applications such as this is that employees require less training since they are already proficient with browser software. Prior to GOTS, BP Canada was constrained by the volume of data and the speed of data processing. Today, with so much of the process automated, they can handle more data faster.

Sources: Robert Cottingham, "Wireless Web Accesses Well Site SCADA," *Oil and Gas Journal,* December 10, 2001, available http://proquest. umi.com; ".Net Enterprise Servers Solution Built by Quilogy Accelerates 800% Business Growth," Microsoft Case Study, available www.microsoft. com/resources/casestudies, accessed April 10, 2003; BP Canada Web site, www.bp.com/in_your_area/transition_page.asp?id-13, accessed April 10, 2003.

CASE STUDY QUESTIONS

1. Compare using the Wireless Web versus a wired connection for remotely controlling well sites. Why would BP Canada choose a wireless channel, rather than a wired one?
2. Using the competitive forces model, how does the GOTS system give BP Canada a competitive advantage?
3. Using the value chain model, how does the Web-based SCADA provide a competitive advantage?
4. How important is it that operators can determine when and where they receive daily and alarm e-mails? Can you foresee any problems with this method?

Make IT Your Business

Finance and Accounting

Many application software packages for individuals as well as for large businesses support financial processes, such as corporate accounting, tax calculations, payroll processing, or investment planning. Calculating the total cost of ownership (TCO) of technology assets usually requires models and expertise supplied by finance and accounting.

Wireless Web technology has been the source of new financial services. Individual investors and investment professionals can use their mobile phones to obtain stock quotes and financial market news, to make stock trades, and to review their portfolios. Wireless Web and Internet technology are also making it possible to speed up fund flows by providing capabilities for immediate billing and invoicing. Database management software and data warehouses have enabled these firms to organize their data more flexibly so that they can view information by customer, financial product, or other criteria. Financial firms are also intensive users of datamining for analyzing credit risk, for packaging services for targeted customers, or for identifying profitable customers.

Many companies use electronic data interchange (EDI) to transfer payments to suppliers and invoices to large corporate customers. Banks maintain networks to link their automated teller machines (ATMs) and branch offices to central computers that keep track of deposit, withdrawal, and funds transfer transactions occurring at remote locations. Financial services firms today depend on networked systems to provide their managers and clients with instant access to account information. These firms are heavy users of online digital information services, such as Dow Jones, to obtain data on firms' financial positions and on financial markets.

You can find examples of finance and accounting applications on page 207.

Human Resources

Because hardware and software technologies are changing very rapidly, providing many new productivity tools to employees and powerful software packages and services for the human resources department, employees will need frequent retraining in order to use these tools effectively. Companies typically maintain human resources databases enabling them to maintain data on employees, benefits plans, and training programs and to provide reports to the government concerning compliance with health, safety, and equal employment opportunity regulations. Since these human resources databases contain sensitive information, such as salaries, job performance evaluations, and medical history, companies must be very careful about distributing this information.

Companies can use intranets to publish employee bulletins, policy manuals, directories, and other human resources documents. Employees can use telephone-based systems, the Web, or private corporate networks to review their employment records or to make changes to their benefits plans. Managers can use e-mail and videoconferencing to communicate with employees and work teams. Input from human resource specialists is essential when developing a corporate policy for employee use of networks and computing resources. You can find examples of human resources applications on pages 274 and 275.

Manufacturing and Production

Many manufacturing applications are based on client-server networks, which use networked computers to control the flow of work on the factory floor. Handheld computers and bar code scanners are widely used to track items in inventory and to track package shipments. XML provides a set of standards through which all participants in a supply chain can exchange data with each other without high expenditures for specialized translation programs and middleware.

Extranets are especially useful for collaborative commerce and supply chain management and are the primary platform for private industrial networks. They are often used for providing product availability, pricing, and shipment data; for exchanging purchase orders and invoices; and for joint product development activities with other companies. Companies maintain large databases of finished goods, raw materials in inventory, and goods in transit that can be used for supply chain management. The manufacturing process makes use of numerous databases on suppliers, jobs in progress, product components, product quality, and costs.

Computers and computer-controlled machines on the factory floor are often linked in LANs. In companies with advanced manufacturing systems, each step in the manufacturing process uses networks to transmit data to the next step. Data from orders triggers transactions that can be transmitted via networks directly to manufacturing scheduling systems, to supply chain management systems, to the assembly line, and to systems for warehousing and delivery. You can find examples of manufacturing and production applications on pages 190–191, 219, 226–227, 236, 291, 297, 303, and 315–317.

Sales and Marketing

Sales and marketing have benefited from hardware and software technologies that provide customers and sales staff with rapid access to information, responses to customer questions, and order taking. Web browser software provides an easy-to-use interface for accessing product information or placing orders over the Web, while e-mail software is a quick and inexpensive tool for answering customer queries. Web sites can be enhanced with Java applets that allow users to perform calculations or view interactive product demonstrations on Web sites using standard Web browser software. The Web is an especially powerful medium for sales and marketing because it provides capabilities for personalization and interacting with customers that cannot be found in other channels. Companies can engage in ongoing dialogues with customers using e-mail, chat, and electronic discussion groups to solidify their customer relationships.

Wireless Web technology provides new information and location-based services for companies to sell, which could provide major new sources of revenue. By querying customer databases, analysts can identify customers most interested in specific products or highly profitable customers. They can target specialized products and promotions on the basis of these detailed customer profiles. You can find examples of sales and marketing applications on pages 216–217, 228–229, 252, 255–256, 282–283, 284–286, and 297.

BIOMETRICS, TRANSPORTATION, AND PASSPORTS: CANADIAN STYLE

Post September 11, 2001, everyone is reconsidering the claims to anonymity or privacy versus the urgent need for security. A case can be made that insistence upon anonymity is unacceptable in an age of terror and that insistence upon privacy has to be judged according to circumstance and treated with discretion and respect.

The crux of the issue has to do with *personal* circumstance. Boarding planes or trains, conducting financial transactions, driving vehicles, entering the country as a visitor or immigrant, or working for a federal agency are privileged activities, but engaging in any of these activities potentially opens the door to terror and the public has a right to protection against terror. Therefore, according to this logic, no one who enjoys these privileges can insist upon anonymity or total privacy.

But balance and reciprocity are essential. In return for giving up anonymity and total privacy in order to engage in privileged activities, every person ought to be accorded notice, justification, and transparency. Should submitting to this type of identification take a long time with many obstacles, or can it be made simple, short, and relatively sweet?

This is where biometrics enters the picture—or takes the picture. A biometric system is essentially a pattern recognition system which makes personal identification possible by determining the authenticity of a specific physiological or behavioural characteristic possessed by the user.

This method of identification is preferred over traditional methods involving passwords and personal identification numbers (PINs) for various reasons:

1. The person to be identified is required to be physically present at the point-of-identification.
2. Identification based on biometric techniques obviates the need to remember a password or carry a token.

With the increased use of computers as vehicles of information technology, it is necessary to restrict access to sensitive/personal data. By replacing PINs, biometric techniques can potentially prevent unauthorized access to or fraudulent use of ATMs, cellular phones, smart cards, desktop PCs, workstations, computer networks, and workspaces, such as airports and offices.

PINs and passwords may be forgotten, and token-based methods of identification, such as passports and driver's licenses, may be forged, stolen, or lost. Therefore, biometric systems of identification can be both more convenient and more secure.

In information technology, biometrics usually refers to technologies for measuring and analyzing human body characteristics, such as fingerprints, eye retinas and irises, voice patterns, facial patterns, and hand measurements, especially for authentication purposes. Increasingly, face pattern matchers and body scanners are emerging as replacements for computer passwords.

Fingerprint and other biometric devices consist of a reader or scanning device, software that converts the scanned information into digital form, and, wherever the data is to be analyzed, a database that stores the biometric data for comparison with previous records. When converting the biometric input, the software identifies specific points of data as *match points*. The match points are then processed using an algorithm into a value that can be compared with biometric data scanned when a user tries to gain access.

Fingerprint, facial, or other biometric data can be placed on a smart card. Users can then present both the smart card and their fingerprints or faces to merchants, banks, or telephones for an extra degree of authentication. IBM, Microsoft, Novell, and others are developing a standard, called BioAPI, which will allow different manufacturers' biometric software to interact. One technical suggestion to assuage those with privacy concerns is to encrypt biometric data when it is gathered and discard the original data to prevent identity theft.

The BioAPI Consortium (for Biometrics Application Program Interface) was formed to develop a widely available and widely accepted API that will serve for various biometric technologies. The intent is to:

- Work with industry biometric solution developers, software developers, and system integrators to leverage existing standards to facilitate easy adoption and implementation.
- Develop an OS operating-system-independent standard.
- Make the API biometric independent.
- Support a broad range of applications.

Unification efforts have resulted in a single industry standard for Biometrics. Vendors are now announcing products that are designed for BioAPI compliance. The BioAPI standard is open platform and open system, meaning that it operates on any type of computer and with any type of operating system. The BioAPI standard also applies to all forms of biometric measurement—faces, irises, retinas, hands, and fingerprints.

Even without smart cards, it is possible to use biometric data for a variety of purposes. The CIBC and Royal Bank are conducting trials for their Internet banking services to permit customers to log on to their Internet services by using a fingerprint scanner. The database containing the biometric data is on the bank's Web server. The fingerprint data are sent from the customer's PC to the bank's biometric database, where the fingerprint is authenticated. Then, the bank's server authenticates the customer—just as it would if the customer had entered a password—and the customer can begin banking activities. Many customers forget their passwords; this biometrics would resolve that problem. ING Direct Canada is conducting a trial using a mouse with a built-in fingerprint scanner for the same purpose. Credit Union Central of British Columbia (CUC) has deployed 1200 fingerprint readers to dozens of B.C. credit unions to enhance security for wire transfers.

In the aftermath of 9/11, security measures at every airport in the world have increased, requiring passengers to arrive twice the time in advance of their flights. The use of biometrics could enable the entire process to be speeded up. Passengers could sign up for a program that will enable them to be issued a smart card with their biometric data on the card *and* authorization to avoid the lengthy delays. This program is being discussed at the highest levels of government in both Canada and the United States. Passengers who had passed the original screening to receive the card are termed "registered" or "trusted" travellers. Once they had been authenticated at the airport, they would proceed to a dedicated security line and bypass extensive checking.

In Canada, Thunder Bay International Airport is the first Canadian airport to deploy facial-recognition technology, now used only for authenticating airport personnel. Authorized users will swipe their "proximity" cards, which are verified in less than one second. An optical turnstile will be installed, addressing the possibility of two people squeezing into one turnstile revolution. According to Ed Schmidtke, the commercial manager of the airport, "The number one challenge we face today is the sudden increase in human resources and expense to provide enhanced security and clearance of all airport personnel. This project will be successful if we can provide a turnkey access control system that reduces the need for manpower and provides a solution that is both reliable and affordable."

Transport Minister David Collenette has assigned to the Canadian Air Transport Security Authority (CATSA) responsibility to implement an enhanced restricted area pass system for Canadian airports and to screen non-passengers who enter these restricted areas. The new system will use biometrics to identify and authorize individuals to enter these areas. The new pass system will include the use of centralized databases supporting the issuance, verification, cancellation, and tracking of restricted area

passes. CATSA will have to work with multiple stakeholders, such as vendors, labour groups, and airport authorities, to develop and implement the new system.

On another front, G-8 countries have agreed to work on developing and implementing new biometric-based technologies to prevent forgeries of passports and other travel documents to fight crime and terrorism. In May 2003, the G-8 ministers announced the establishment of a high-level working group on biometric technologies to be co-chaired by the United States and France. The ultimate objective of this initiative is to develop a common framework and standards to ensure technical interoperability and reliability. This is a tall order, considering the differences in the countries' laws, infrastructures, and cultures.

The U.S. Department of Homeland Security (DHS) has proposed a border-control system using biometric technology to authenticate the identity of visitors and immigrants entering the United States. DHS expects to deploy this system by the end of 2003 at a cost of US \$400 million. DHS hopes that the system will help authorities confirm the identities of foreign visitors, check them for possible criminal histories, and track their movements more closely. The system should track two biometric identifiers and then check the identifiers against terrorist and criminal watch lists. Fingerprints and photographs will be used at first; later, as the technology is perfected, scans of irises or facial features should be added. Eventually, plans call for the system to integrate with the Student Exchange Visitor System, operated by universities to track foreign students. The data can also be analyzed for visa violations and other irregularities.

Through the Standards Council of Canada, Canadians are participating in the work of committees developing biometrics standards under the auspices of the International Organization for Standardization (ISO) and the International Electrotechnical Commission (IEC). Most of this work is taking place in the subcommittee on personal identification cards and related devices of the ISO and IEC's joint technical committee on information technology (ISO/IEC JTC 1/SC 17).

Since 1999, SC 17 has been working on a variety of biometrics related issues, including:

- how to use the technology for personal identification;
- how to store biometric data on identification cards with chips ("smart cards");
- how to adopt existing standards from outside ISO and IEC; and
- specific requirements for cards and card-reading devices.

The committee's work is helping to ensure that biometrics technology will be applied throughout the world in a consistent and effective fashion. For example, several SC 17 working groups are developing standards to allow consistent use of biometric technology at border crossings throughout the world. This is expected to significantly enhance travel safety and provide countries with better control of their borders.

Joel Shaw, convenor of the working group on machine-readable travel documents (WG3), says the goal of the work is to strengthen security at borders by positively identifying travellers to address the increased concern over terrorism. The process is complex and challenging. The evolution from the traditional passport to one with biometric features has to be done so that all countries can eventually use the required machinery and will be willing to participate. "The working group task force has been at the table in all the discussion regarding biometric technologies," said Mr. Shaw. "Governments have established requirements and the ISO/IEC working group must create standards to meet those needs."

Canada's Passport Office plans to implement an automated facial recognition system in the near future. This system would speed up the customs and immigration processes while increasing accuracy of those systems. The Passport Office is currently in the proposal stage of this project. While this will help with Canadian nationals, it does little to help with the screening of foreign nationals.

Toward that end, the Royal Canadian Mounted Police (RCMP) and Government Services Canada intend to provide a Canada-wide security network for use at airports and border patrol sites. The LiveScan project, part of Canada's larger effort to streamline national security, will provide airports, seaports, border patrol crossings, and other selected law enforcement agencies with the biometric technology they need to protect Canada from potential threats to national security. The integrated network will be designed to enable officials throughout Canada to quickly and easily identify individuals entering our borders by use of a rapid fingerprint search against the established RCMP National AFIS database as well as other shared records repositories. The new system will also support the seamless exchange of fingerprint data between the RCMP and the U.S. Federal Bureau of Investigation (FBI).

CASE STUDY QUESTIONS

1. What are the implications of having a variety of groups, such as the BioAPI Consortium and the SC-17 Group, work on biometric standards? Will this help or hurt the use of biometrics?

2. Canada recently adopted the use of a digitized photograph and other technologies for its passports. How does this affect the likelihood that Canada will adopt the use of biometrics in issuing its passports?

3. What biometric measurement do you think is superior to other measurements, in terms of convenience, accuracy,

cost, and security? Do different measurements offer differing degrees of these factors?

4. Which measurements do you think should be used for various purposes? For example, should the biometric for obtaining and using a passport be different from the one used to access a computer, board a flight, or bank online?

5. Discuss the privacy implications of obtaining and storing biometric data. How could this data be used for purposes the individual whose data was collected did not intend? Could this be harmful to the individual? What steps can be taken to ensure that individual privacy is maintained while using the biometric data for its intended purpose?

SOURCES

Paul Pelletier, "Canada's Passport Office Pursues Facial Recognition," available http://technologyreports.net/security/innovator/?articleID=1107, accessed July 15, 2003; "Canadian Airports and Border Patrol Sites Adopt Fingerprint Biometric," available www.findbiometrics.com/Pages/airport_articles/airports_2.html, accessed July 15, 2003,; Dan Verton, "Feds Plan Biometrics for Border Control," *ComputerWorld*, May 26, 2003; "Biometrics in Banking," available www.bankersonline.com, accessed July 15, 2003; "Transport Minister Announces Further Enhancements to Aviation Security," *Transport Canada*, November 5, 2002, available www.tc.gc.ca/majorissues/transportationsecurity/menu.htm, accessed July 15, 2003; "G-8 Countries Urge Use of Biometrics in Fight Against Terrorism," U.S. Department of State International Information Programs, May 5, 2003, available http://usinfo.state.gov/topical/pol/terror/tests/03050800.htm, accessed July 15, 2003; Verrick French, "In the Age of Terror, When Is It Wrong to Require Positive Identification?" November 25, 2002, available http://technologyreports.net/securityinnovator/index.html?articleID=1101, accessed July 15, 2003; "Thunder Bay Becomes First Canadian Airport to Use Facial Recognition," available www.findbiometrics.com/Pages/airport_articles/airports_3.html, accessed July 15, 2003; "An Overview of Biometrics," Biometrics Research at Michigan State University, available http://biometrics.cse.msu.edu/info.html, accessed July 15, 2003; Chris Conrath, "BC Credit Unions Deploy Biometric Security," *IT Focus*, August 1, 2002, available www.itworldcanada.com, accessed July 10, 2003.

VIDEO RESOURCE

"Biometrics," *MarketPlace* (October 31, 2001).

PART III

CREATING AND MANAGING INFORMATION SYSTEMS

CHAPTER

SYSTEMS DEVELOPMENT

During your career, you will undoubtedly be looking for ways to use new information systems to improve the performance of your firm. You may be asked to help your organization develop a new information system. After reading this chapter, you should be able to answer the following questions:

Objectives

1. *How could developing a new system change the way an organization works?*

2. *How can a company make sure that the new information systems it develops fit its business plan?*

3. *What are the steps required to develop a new information system?*

4. *What alternative methods for developing information systems are available?*

5. *Are there any techniques or systems development approaches to help us develop electronic commerce (e-commerce) and electronic business (e-business) applications more rapidly?*

Using Technology to Win the Insurance Game

When faced with competitors that dwarf you in size and power, victory may depend on leapfrogging their technology curve. This is particularly true in the highly competitive insurance industry.

Family Insurance Solutions Inc. of Vancouver is a managing general agency, a wholesaler intermediary between insurance brokers and an insurance company. Family sells all lines of personal insurance, including auto and property. The majority shareholder of Family is the Economical Mutual Insurance Company, which provides the insurance coverage for Family's clients. Canada-based Economical is one of the largest property and casualty insurers in Canada, with assets approaching $2 billion.

Ian James, Family's Director of Information Technology, explains that the company is growing rapidly. According to James, all of Family's processes are fully automated in a very traditional paper-based world. "Our technology is a very important differentiator of what we bring to the broker community."

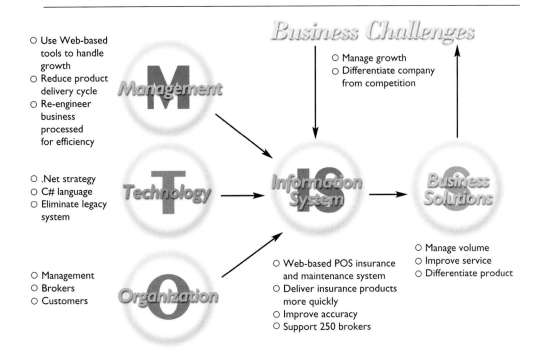

Given this situation, Family elected to create a Web-based point-of-sale (POS) insurance and maintenance system; this would streamline connectivity among its 250 brokers and credit unions throughout the province. The POS application is designed to deal with as much as $75 million in transactions or more. Family has contracted with Calgary-based Pangea Systems Inc. to develop the new POS system. Deployment of the new system is expected to take at least 12 months. According to James, Family currently has a two-tier client-server architecture; the 250 locations connect to Family through a virtual private network (VPN) into a gateway and a database server. One of the main reasons for developing the POS system is maintainability. James says, "That existing system is a legacy system that's grown over a long period of time. There's a real lack of modularity. Everything's sequential and the scope of our testing effort is broad. We tend to have very extended product delivery cycles." And when you are competing with the provincial Goliath insurance monopoly, Insurance Corporation of British Columbia, time-to-market is a real issue, as is operational efficiency.

James says that Family's rapid growth means the system must support large transaction growth. The existing system is working relatively well, but performance is slowly but surely becoming strained. Family is already automated, so reliability is a key concern. If the system goes down, all of the broker clients go down, too. Just three years ago, Family's servers went down, and brokers were unable to issue or service policies for almost a full day. James is determined that will not happen again.

Family plans for the system to be user friendly and easy to use, requiring little training. At the time of this writing, Family has completed the planning phase of systems development and is currently working on confirming that the design will fit its business needs. The company has documented all the requirements of the existing system and is enhancing functionality. After the current phase is completed, Family will enter prototyping to ensure appropriate usability of the system. Because Family is a Microsoft shop, they are using the .Net approach, primarily using the C# language. "It's a less painful transition for developers who having been using C++ for the last number of years," says James. They may also be able to salvage some existing code.

According to Pangea's executive vice-president, Paul Morgan, Family has blended business process re-engineering aspects with their systems development. By modifying their processes while developing their systems, Family should be able to maximize efficiency while providing even better, more accurate service to their customers.

Sources: Gary Hilson, "Composing POS in the Key of C#," *Computing Canada*, April 25, 2003, available www.itbusiness.ca, accessed May 4, 2003; Suzanne Wintrob, "Operating under a Shadow: World in Crisis: Handle Both Data and Human Resources with Care," *The National Post*, February 17, 2003, available www.nationalpost.com, accessed May 4, 2003; Family Insurance Solutions Inc. home page, available www.familyins.com, accessed May 4, 2003.

MANAGEMENT CHALLENGES

Family Insurance's POS system illustrates the many factors at work in the development of a new information system. Developing the new system entailed analyzing the company's problems and constraints with its existing information systems, assessing people's information needs, selecting appropriate technology, and redesigning business processes and jobs. Management still must monitor the systems development effort and evaluate its benefits and costs. The new information system represents a process of planned organizational change. However, developing information systems, especially those on a large scale, presents many challenges. Here are some challenges to consider:

1. **Major risks and uncertainties in systems development.** Information systems development has major risks and uncertainties that make it difficult for the systems to achieve their goals. One problem is the difficulty of establishing information requirements, both for individual end users and for the organization as a whole. The requirements may be too complex or subject to change. Another problem is that the time and cost factors to develop an information system are very difficult to analyze, especially in large projects. A third problem is the difficulty of managing the organizational change associated with a new system. Although developing a new information system is a process of planned organizational change, this does not mean that change can always be planned or controlled. Individuals and groups in organizations have varying interests, and they may resist changes in procedures, job relationships, and technologies. Although this chapter describes some ways of dealing with these risks and uncertainties, the issues remain major management challenges.

2. **Determining where new systems and business processes can have the greatest strategic impact.** One of the most important strategic decisions that a firm can make is not deciding how to use computers to improve business processes but, instead, understanding what business processes need improvement. When systems are used to strengthen the wrong business model or business processes, the business can become more efficient at doing what it should not do (Hammer, 2002). As a result, the firm becomes vulnerable to competitors who may have discovered the right business model. Considerable time and cost can also be spent improving business processes that have little impact on overall firm performance and revenue. Managers need to determine what business processes are the most important to focus on when applying new information technology and how improving these processes will help the firm execute its strategy.

This chapter describes how new information systems are conceived, developed, and implemented, with special attention to the issues of organizational design, business process re-engineering, and total quality management. It describes the core systems development activities and how to ensure that new systems are linked to the organization's business plan and information requirements. This chapter also examines alternative approaches for developing systems.

10.1 SYSTEMS AS PLANNED ORGANIZATIONAL CHANGE

This text has emphasized that an information system is a sociotechnical entity, an arrangement of both technical and social elements. The introduction of a new information system involves much more than new hardware and software. It also includes changes in jobs, skills, management, and organization. In the sociotechnical philosophy, one cannot install new technology without considering the people who must work with it (Bostrom and Heinen, 1977). When we design a new information system, we are redesigning the organization.

One important thing to know about developing a new information system is that this process is one kind of planned organizational change. System developers must understand how a system will affect the organization as a whole, focusing particularly on organizational conflict and changes in the locus of decision making. Developers must also consider how the nature of work groups will change under the new system. Systems can be technical successes but organizational failures because of a failure in the social and political process of developing the system. Analysts and designers are responsible for ensuring that key members of the organization participate in the design process and are permitted to influence the system's ultimate shape.

LINKING INFORMATION SYSTEMS TO THE BUSINESS PLAN

Deciding which new systems to develop should be an essential component of the organizational planning process. Organizations need to develop an information systems plan that supports their overall business plan and in which strategic systems are incorporated into top-level planning. Once specific projects have been selected within the overall context of a strategic plan for the business and the systems area, an **information systems plan** can be developed. The plan serves as a road map indicating the direction of systems development, the rationale, the current situation, the management strategy, the implementation plan, and the budget (see the Manager's Toolkit).

information systems plan

A road map indicating the direction of systems development: the rationale, the current situation, the management strategy, the implementation plan, and the budget.

ESTABLISHING ORGANIZATIONAL INFORMATION REQUIREMENTS

In order to develop an effective information systems plan, the organization must have a clear understanding of both its long- and short-term information requirements. Two principal methodologies for establishing the essential information requirements of the organization as a whole are enterprise analysis and critical success factors.

Enterprise Analysis (Business Systems Planning)

Enterprise analysis (also called *business systems planning*) argues that the firm's information requirements can only be understood by looking at the entire organization in terms of organizational units, functions, processes, and data elements. Enterprise analysis can help identify the key entities and attributes of the organization's data.

enterprise analysis

An analysis of organization-wide information requirements that examines the entire organization in terms of organizational units, functions, processes, and data elements; helps identify the key entities and attributes in the organization's data.

The central method used in the enterprise analysis approach is to take a large sample of managers and ask them how they use information, where they get the information, what their environments are like, what their objectives are, how they make decisions, and what their data needs are. The results of this large survey of managers are aggregated into subunits, functions, processes, and data matrices. Data elements are organized into logical application groups—groups of data elements that support related sets of organizational processes. The weakness of enterprise analysis is that it produces an enormous amount of data that is expensive to collect and difficult to analyze. Most of the interviews are conducted with senior or middle managers, but there is little effort to collect information from clerical workers and supervisory managers. Moreover, the questions frequently focus not on management's critical objectives and where information is needed but, rather, on the existing information that is used. The result is a tendency to automate whatever exists. But in many instances, entirely new approaches to how business is conducted are needed, and these needs are not addressed.

The plan contains a statement of corporate goals and specifies how information technology supports the attainment of those goals. The report shows how general goals will be achieved

MIS IN ACTION: MANAGER'S TOOLKIT

HOW TO DEVELOP AN INFORMATION SYSTEMS PLAN

A good information systems plan should address the following topics:

1. Purpose of the Plan
   - Overview of plan contents
   - Changes in firm's current situation
   - Organization's strategic plan
   - Current business organization and future organization
   - Key business processes
   - Management strategy

2. Strategic Business Plan
   - Current situation
   - Current business organization
   - Changing environments
   - Major goals of the business plan

3. Current Systems
   - Major systems supporting business functions and processes
   - Current infrastructure capabilities
   - Hardware
   - Software
   - Databases
   - Telecommunications and the Internet
   - Difficulties meeting business requirements
   - Anticipated future demands

4. New Developments
   - New system projects
   - Project descriptions

   - Business rationale
   - New infrastructure capabilities required
   - Hardware
   - Software
   - Databases
   - Telecommunications and the Internet

5. Management Strategy
   - Acquisition plans
   - Milestones and timing
   - Organizational re-alignment
   - Internal reorganization
   - Management controls
   - Major training initiatives
   - Personnel strategy

6. Implementation Plan
   - Anticipated difficulties in implementation
   - Progress reports

7. Budget Requirements
   - Requirements
   - Potential savings
   - Financing
   - Acquisition cycle

---

by specific systems projects. It lays out specific target dates and milestones that can be used later to evaluate the plan's progress in terms of how many objectives were actually attained in the time frame specified in the plan. The plan indicates the key management decisions concerning hardware acquisition; telecommunications; centralization/decentralization of authority, data, and hardware; and required organizational change. Organizational changes are usually described, including management and employee training requirements; recruiting efforts; changes in business processes; and changes in authority, structure, or management practice.

Strategic Analysis or Critical Success Factors

critical success factors (CSFs)

A small number of easily identifiable operational goals shaped by the industry, the firm, the manager, and the broader environment that are believed to assure the success of an organization; used to determine the information requirements of an organization.

The strategic analysis or critical success factors approach argues that an organization's information requirements are determined by a small number of **critical success factors (CSFs)** of managers. If these goals can be attained, the firm's or organization's success is assured (Rockart, 1979; Rockart and Treacy, 1982). CSFs are shaped by the industry, the firm, the manager, and the broader environment. An important premise of the strategic analysis approach is that there are a small number of objectives that managers can easily identify and on which information systems can focus.

The principal method used in CSF analysis is personal interviews—three or four—with a number of top managers to identify their goals and the resulting CSFs. These personal CSFs are aggregated to develop a picture of the firm's CSFs. Then, systems are developed to deliver information on these CSFs. (See Table 10.1 for an example of CSFs. For the method of developing CSFs in an organization, see Figure 10.1.)

The strength of the CSF method is that it produces a smaller data set to analyze than does enterprise analysis. Only top managers are interviewed, and the questions focus on a small number of CSFs, rather than a broad inquiry into what information is used or needed. The CSF method takes into account the changing environment which organizations and managers must deal with. This method explicitly asks managers to look at the environment and consider

TABLE 10.1   CRITICAL SUCCESS FACTORS AND ORGANIZATIONAL GOALS

Example	Goals	CSF
Profit concern	Earnings/share	Automotive industry
	Return on investment	Styling
	Market share	Quality dealer system
	New product	Cost control
		Energy standards
Nonprofit	Excellent healthcare	Regional integration with other hospitals
	Meeting government regulations	Improved monitoring of regulations
	Future health needs	Efficient use of resources

Source: Rockart (1979).

how their analysis of it shapes their information needs. It is especially suitable for top management and for the development of decision support systems (DSS) and executive support systems (ESS). Unlike enterprise analysis, the CSF method focuses organizational attention on how information should be handled.

The method's primary weakness is that the aggregation process and the analysis of the data are art forms. There is no particularly rigorous way in which individual CSFs can be aggregated into a clear company pattern. Second, there is often confusion among interviewees (and interviewers) between *individual* and *organizational* CSFs. They are not necessarily the same. What can be critical to a manager may not be important for the organization. Moreover, this method is clearly biased toward top managers because they are the ones (generally the only ones) interviewed.

SYSTEMS DEVELOPMENT AND ORGANIZATIONAL CHANGE

New information systems can be powerful instruments for organizational change, enabling organizations to redesign their structure, scope, power relationships, workflows, products, and services. Table 10.2 describes some of the ways that information technology is being used to transform organizations and business processes.

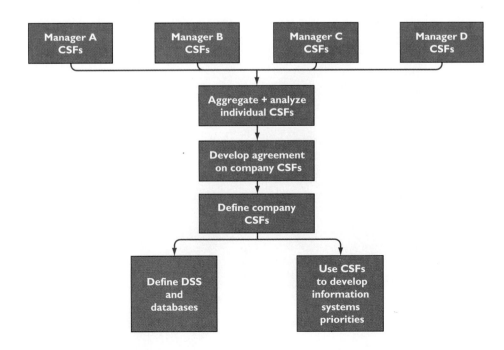

Figure 10.1 Using CSFs to develop systems. The CSF approach relies on interviews with key managers to identify their CSFs. Individual CSFs are aggregated to develop CSFs for the entire firm. Systems can then be developed to deliver information on these CSFs.

TABLE 10.2	HOW INFORMATION TECHNOLOGY CAN TRANSFORM ORGANIZATIONS	
Information Technology	**Organizational Change**	
Global networks	International division of labour: The operations of a firm and its business processes are no longer determined by location; the global reach of firms is extended; costs of global coordination decline. Transaction costs decline.	
Enterprise networks	Collaborative work and teamwork: The organization of work can now be coordinated across divisional boundaries; the costs of management (agency costs) decline. Multiple tasks can be worked on simultaneously from different locations.	
Distributed computing	Empowerment: Individuals and work groups now have the information and knowledge to act. Business processes can be streamlined. Management costs decline. Hierarchy and centralization decline.	
Portable computing	Virtual organizations: Work is no longer tied to physical location. Knowledge and information can be delivered anywhere they are needed, anytime. Work becomes portable.	
Multimedia, graphical interfaces	Accessibility: Everyone in the organization—even senior executives—can access information and knowledge. Organizational costs decline as workflows move from paper to digital image, documents, and voice. Complex knowledge objects can be stored and represented as objects containing graphics, audio, video, or text.	

The Spectrum of Organizational Change

Information technology can promote various degrees of organizational change, ranging from incremental to far-reaching. Figure 10.2 shows four kinds of structural organizational change that are enabled by information technology: (1) automation, (2) rationalization, (3) re-engineering, and (4) paradigm shifts. Each carries different rewards and risks.

The most common form of information technology–enabled organizational change is **automation**. The first applications of information technology involved assisting employees with performing their tasks more efficiently and effectively. Calculating paycheques and payroll registers, giving bank tellers instant access to customer deposit records, and developing a nationwide network of airline reservation terminals for airline reservation agents are all examples of early automation.

A deeper form of organizational change—one that follows quickly from early automation—is **rationalization of procedures**. Automation frequently reveals new bottlenecks in production and makes the existing arrangement of procedures and structures painfully

automation

Using the computer to speed up the performance of existing tasks.

rationalization of procedures

The streamlining of standard operating procedures, eliminating obvious bottlenecks, so that automation makes operating procedures more efficient.

Figure 10.2 Organizational change carries risks and rewards. The most common forms of organizational change are automation and rationalization. These relatively slow moving and slow changing strategies present modest returns but little risk. Faster and more comprehensive change—like re-engineering and paradigm shifts—carries high rewards but offers substantial chances of failure.

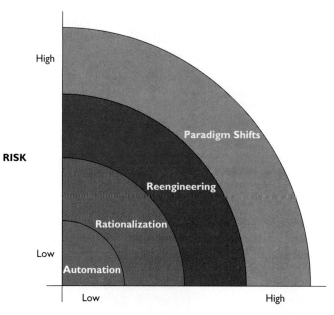

cumbersome. Rationalization of procedures is the streamlining of standard operating procedures, eliminating obvious bottlenecks, so that automation can make operating procedures more efficient. For example, Family Insurance's new POS system described in the chapter-opening vignette is effective not only because it uses computer technology but also because its design will allow the organization to operate more efficiently. The procedures of Family Insurance, or any organization, must be rationally structured to achieve this result. Without a certain amount of rationalization in Family's organization, its computer technology will be useless.

A more powerful type of organizational change is **business process re-engineering**, in which business processes are analyzed, simplified, and redesigned. Using information technology, organizations can rethink and streamline their business processes to improve speed, service, and quality. Business process re-engineering reorganizes workflows, combining steps to cut waste and eliminating repetitive, paper-intensive tasks (sometimes the new design eliminates jobs as well). It is much more ambitious than rationalization of procedures, requiring a new vision of how the process is to be organized.

A widely cited example of business process re-engineering is Ford Motor Company's *invoiceless processing*. Ford employed more than 500 people in its North American Accounts Payable organization. The accounts payable clerks spent most of their time resolving discrepancies between purchase orders, receiving documents, and invoices. Ford re-engineered its accounts payable process, instituting a system wherein the purchasing department enters a purchase order into an online database that can be checked by the receiving department when the ordered items arrive. If the received goods match the purchase order, the system automatically generates a cheque for accounts payable to send to the vendor. There is no need for vendors to send invoices. After re-engineering, Ford was able to reduce head count in accounts payable by 75 percent and produce more accurate financial information (Hammer and Champy, 1993).

Rationalizing procedures and redesigning business processes are limited to specific parts of a business. New information systems can ultimately affect the design of the entire organization by transforming how the organization carries out its business or even the nature of the business itself. For instance, Allegiance Healthcare's stockless inventory system (described in Chapter 3) transformed Allegiance into a working partner with hospitals and into a manager of its customers' supplies. This more radical form of business change is called a **paradigm shift**. A paradigm shift involves rethinking the nature of the business and the nature of the organization itself.

Paradigm shifts and re-engineering often fail because extensive organizational change is so difficult to orchestrate (see Chapter 13). Why then do so many corporations entertain such radical change? Because the rewards are equally high (see Figure 10.2). In many instances, firms seeking paradigm shifts and pursuing re-engineering strategies achieve stunning, order-of-magnitude increases in their returns on investment (or productivity). Some of these success stories, and some failure stories, are included throughout this book.

> **business process re-engineering**
>
> The radical redesign of business processes, combining steps to cut waste and eliminating repetitive, paper-intensive tasks in order to improve cost, quality, and service, and to maximize the benefits of information technology.

> **paradigm shift**
>
> Radical reconceptualization of the nature of the business and the nature of the organization.

10.2 BUSINESS PROCESS RE-ENGINEERING AND PROCESS IMPROVEMENT

Many companies today are focusing on developing new information systems that will improve their business processes. Some of these system projects represent radical restructuring of business processes, while others entail more incremental change.

BUSINESS PROCESS RE-ENGINEERING

If organizations rethink and radically redesign their business processes before applying computing power, they can potentially obtain very large payoffs from their investments in information technology. The home mortgage industry is a leading example of how major corporations have implemented business process re-engineering. The application process for a home mortgage took about six to eight weeks and cost about $3000. The goal of many mortgage banks has been to lower that cost to $1000 and the time to obtain a mortgage to about one week. Leading Canadian mortgage banks have redesigned the mortgage application process. Today, most applicants can have a mortgage preapproved within a couple of days.

The mortgage application process is divided into three stages: origination, servicing, and secondary marketing. Figure 10.3 illustrates how business process redesign has been used in each of these stages.

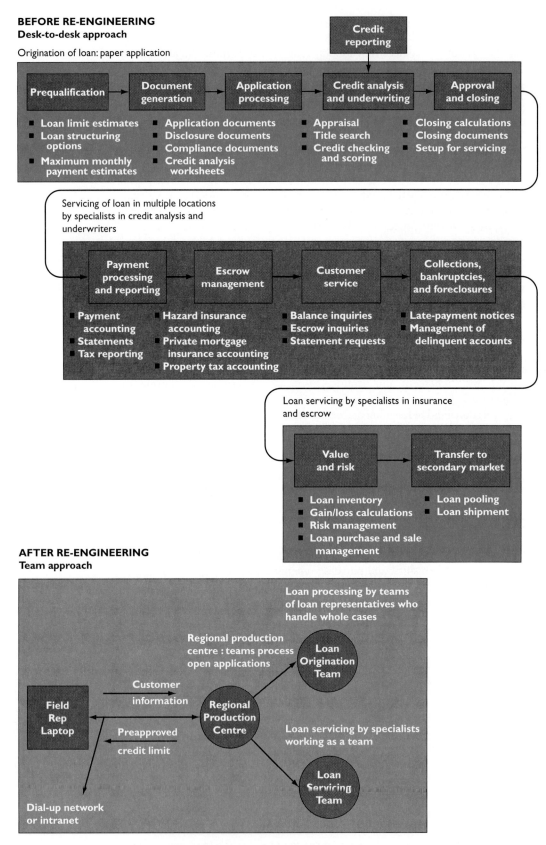

Figure 10.3 Redesigning mortgage processing. By redesigning their mortgage processing systems and the mortgage application process, mortgage banks can reduce the costs of processing the average mortgage from $3000 to $1000, and reduce the time of approval from six weeks to one week or less. Some banks are even preapproving mortgages and locking interest rates on the same day the customer applies.

In the past, a mortgage applicant filled out a paper loan application. The bank entered the application into its computer system. Specialists, such as credit analysts and underwriters from perhaps eight different departments, accessed and evaluated the application individually. If the loan application was approved, the closing was scheduled. After the closing, bank specialists dealing with insurance or funds in escrow serviced the loan. This "desk-to-desk" assembly-line approach might take up to 17 days.

Leading banks have replaced the sequential desk-to-desk approach with a speedier "work cell" or team approach. Now, loan originators in the field enter the mortgage application directly into laptop computers. The software checks the application transaction to make sure that all of the information is correct and complete. The loan originators transmit the loan applications using a dial-up network to regional production centres. Instead of working on the application individually, the credit analysts, loan underwriters, and other specialists convene electronically, working as a team to approve the mortgage. Some banks provide customers with a nearly instant credit lock-in of a guaranteed mortgage so that they can find a house that meets their budget immediately. This type of preapproval of a credit line is truly a radical re-engineering of the traditional business process.

After closing, another team of specialists sets up the loan for servicing. The entire loan application process can take as little as two days. Loan information is easier to access than before, when the loan application could be in eight or nine different departments. Loan originators also can dial into the bank's network to obtain information on mortgage loan costs or to check the status of a loan for the customer.

By redesigning their approach to mortgage processing, mortgage banks have achieved remarkable efficiencies. They have not focused on redesigning a single business process but instead they have re-examined the entire set of logically connected processes required to obtain a mortgage. Instead of automating the previous method of mortgage processing, the banks have completely rethought the entire mortgage application process.

Workflow Management

To streamline the paperwork in the mortgage application process, banks have turned to workflow and document management software. By using this software to store and process documents electronically, organizations can redesign their workflows so that documents can be worked on simultaneously or moved more easily and efficiently from one location to another. The process of streamlining business procedures so that documents can be moved easily and efficiently is called **workflow management**. Workflow and document management software automates processes, such as routing documents to different locations, securing approvals, scheduling, and generating reports. Two or more people can work simultaneously on the same document, allowing much quicker completion time. Work need not be delayed because a file is out or a document is in transit. And with a properly designed indexing system, users will be able to retrieve files in many different ways, on the basis of the content of the document.

workflow management

The process of streamlining business procedures so that documents can be moved easily and efficiently from one location to another.

STEPS IN EFFECTIVE RE-ENGINEERING

To re-engineer effectively, senior management needs to develop a broad strategic vision that calls for redesigned business processes. For example, Mitsubishi Heavy Industries management looked for breakthroughs to lower costs and accelerate product development that would enable the firm to regain world market leadership in shipbuilding. The company redesigned its entire production process to replace expensive labour-intensive tasks with robotic machines and computer-aided design (CAD) tools. Companies should identify a few core business processes to be redesigned, focusing on those with the greatest potential payback and strategic value (Davenport and Short, 1990).

Management must understand and measure the performance of existing processes as a baseline. If, for example, the objective of process redesign is to reduce time and cost in developing a new product or filling an order, the organization needs to measure the time and cost consumed by the unchanged process.

The conventional method of designing systems establishes the information requirements of a business function or process and then determines how they can be supported by information technology. However, information technology can create new design options for various processes because it can be used to challenge longstanding assumptions about work arrangements that used to inhibit organizations. For example, the mortgage processing application we have just described shows that it is no longer necessary for people to be in the same physical location in order to work together on a document. Using networks and document management technology, they can access and work on the same document from many different locations. Information technology should be allowed to influence process design from the start.

Following these steps does not automatically guarantee that re-engineering will always be successful. The organization's information technology (IT) infrastructure should have capabilities to support business process changes that span boundaries between functions, business units, or firms (Broadbent, Weill, and St. Clair, 1999). The majority of re-engineering projects do not achieve breakthrough gains in business performance. A re-engineered business process or a new information system inevitably affects jobs, skill requirements, workflows, and reporting relationships. Fear of these changes breeds resistance, confusion, and even conscious efforts to undermine the change effort. Managing change is neither simple nor intuitive.

The scope of re-engineering projects has widened, adding to their complexity. Today's digital firm environment involves much closer coordination of a firm's business processes with those of customers, suppliers, and other business partners than in the past. Organizations are required to make business process changes that span organizational boundaries and stand to derive substantial benefits from re-engineering inefficient interorganizational processes. These interorganizational processes, such as those for supply chain management, not only need to be streamlined but also coordinated and integrated with those of other business partners. In such cases, re-engineering will involve many companies working together to jointly redesign their shared processes. Re-engineering expert James Champy calls the joint redesign of interorganizational business processes *X-engineering*, and it will be even more challenging to implement successfully than re-engineering processes for a single company. We examine the organizational change issues surrounding re-engineering more carefully in Chapter 12.

PROCESS IMPROVEMENT: TOTAL QUALITY MANAGEMENT (TQM) AND SIX SIGMA

total quality management (TQM)

A concept that makes quality control a responsibility to be shared by all people in an organization.

In addition to increasing organizational efficiency, companies are also changing their business processes to improve the quality in their products, services, and operations. Many are using the concept of **total quality management (TQM)** to make quality the responsibility of all people and functions within an organization. TQM holds that the achievement of quality control is an end in itself. Everyone is expected to contribute to the overall improvement of quality—the engineer who avoids design errors, the production worker who spots defects, the sales representative who presents the product properly to potential customers, and even the secretary who avoids typing mistakes. TQM derives from quality management concepts developed by American quality experts, such as W. Edwards Deming and Joseph Juran, but it was popularized by the Japanese. Another quality concept that is being widely implemented today is six sigma. **Six sigma** is a specific measure of quality, representing 3.4 defects per million opportunities. Most companies cannot achieve this level of quality but use six sigma as a goal in order to implement a set of methodologies and techniques for improving quality and reducing costs. Studies have repeatedly shown that the earlier in the business cycle a problem is eliminated, the less it costs the company. Thus, quality improvements can not only raise the level of product and service quality, but they can also lower costs.

six sigma

A specific measure of quality, representing 3.4 defects per million opportunities; used to designate a set of methodologies and techniques for improving quality and reducing costs.

How Information Systems Support Quality Improvements

TQM and six sigma are considered to be more incremental than business process re-engineering (BPR). TQM typically focuses on making a series of continuous improvements, rather than dramatic bursts of change. Six sigma uses statistical analysis tools to detect flaws in the execution of an existing process and make minor adjustments. Sometimes, however, processes may have to be fully re-engineered to achieve a specified level of quality. Information systems can help firms achieve their quality goals by helping them simplify products or processes, meet benchmarking standards, make improvements on the basis of customer demands, reduce cycle time, and increase the quality and precision of design and production.

Simplifying the Product or the Production Process The fewer the number of steps in a process, the less time and fewer opportunities there are for an error to occur. Ten years ago, 1-800-FLOWERS, a multimillion-dollar telephone- and Web-based floral service with a global reach, was a much smaller company that spent too much on advertising because it could not retain its customers. It had poor service, inconsistent quality, and a cumbersome manual order taking process. Telephone representatives had to write the order, obtain credit card approval, determine which participating florist was closest to the delivery location, select a floral arrangement, and forward the order to the florist. Each step in the manual process increased the chance of human error, and the whole process took at least half an hour. Owners Jim and Chris McCann installed a new computer system that downloads orders taken at tele-centres into a central computer and electronically transmits them to local florists. Orders are now more accurate and arrive at the florist within one to two minutes (Gill, 1998).

Benchmarking Many companies have been effective in achieving quality by setting strict standards for products, services, and other activities and then measuring performance against those standards. This procedure is called **benchmarking**. Companies may use external industry standards, standards set by other companies, internally developed high standards, or some combination of the three. Sears Canada used benchmarking to field more than 24 million calls a year and 110 000 e-mails from customers, 60 percent of which were generated by catalogue sales. By focusing on industry standards, Sears Canada was named number one for customer satisfaction—91 percent of Sears customers who used a contact centre said they were satisfied with the experience. Canadian Tire and Bank of Montreal have similar award-winning centres, all of which participate in industry benchmarking efforts.

benchmarking

Setting strict standards for products, services, or activities and measuring organizational performance against those standards.

Use Customer Demands as a Guide to Improving Products and Services Improving customer service—making customer service the number-one priority—will improve the quality of the product itself. The Mac Call Center focuses on its clients, which are companies selling products through their catalogues. By using call duration management techniques, The Mac Call Center reduced inquiry time for one client by 20 percent with a 93-percent resolution rate, resulting in savings for both the client and the call centre.

Delta Airlines developed information systems to improve service to customers when they are checking in or connecting flights. Improving customer service is one way that information systems can support Total Quality Management (TQM).

Reduce Cycle Time Reducing the amount of time from the beginning of a process to its end (cycle time) usually results in fewer steps. Shorter cycles mean that errors are often caught earlier in production (or logistics or design or whatever the function), often before the process is complete, eliminating many hidden costs. Iomega Corporation in Roy, Utah, a manufacturer of disk drives, was spending $20 million a year to fix defective drives at the end of its 28-day production cycle. Re-engineering the production process allowed the firm to reduce cycle time to a day and a half, eliminating this problem and winning the prestigious Shingo Prize for Excellence in American Manufacturing.

Improve the Quality and Precision of the Design CAD software has made dramatic quality improvements possible in a wide range of businesses from aircraft manufacturing to production of razor blades. Alan R. Burns, head of the Airboss Company in Perth, Australia, used CAD to invent and design a new modular tire made up of a series of replaceable modules or segments so that if one segment were damaged, only that segment, not the whole tire, would need replacing. Burns established quality performance measurements for key tire characteristics, such as load, temperature, speed, wear life, and traction. He entered these data into a CAD software package, which he used to design the modules. Using the software, he was able iteratively to design and test until he was satisfied with the results. He did not need to develop an actual working model until the iterative design process was almost complete. Because of the speed and accuracy of the CAD software, this product was of much higher quality than would have been possible through manual design and testing.

Increase the Precision of Production For many products, one key way to achieve quality is to make the production process more precise, thereby decreasing the amount of variation from one part to another. GE Medical Systems performed a rigorous quality analysis to improve the reliability and durability of its Lightspeed diagnostic scanners. It broke the processes of designing and producing the scanner into many distinct steps and established optimum specifications for each component part. By understanding these processes precisely, engineers learned that a few simple changes would significantly improve the product's reliability and durability (Deutsch, 1998).

10.3 OVERVIEW OF SYSTEMS DEVELOPMENT

Whatever their scope and objectives, new information systems are an outgrowth of a process of organizational problem solving. A new information system is developed as a solution to some type of problem or set of problems the organization perceives it is facing. The problem may be one where managers and employees realize that the organization is not performing as well as expected, or it may come from the realization that the organization should take advantage of new opportunities to perform more successfully.

systems development

The activities that go into producing an information systems solution to an organizational problem or opportunity.

The activities that go into producing an information system solution to an organizational problem or opportunity are called **systems development**. Systems development is a structured kind of problem solving with distinct activities. These activities consist of systems analysis, systems design, programming, testing, conversion, and production and maintenance.

Figure 10.4 illustrates the systems development process. The systems development activities depicted here usually take place in sequential order. But some of the activities may need to be repeated, and some may be taking place simultaneously, depending on the approach to systems development that is being employed (see Section 10.4). Note also that each activity involves interaction with the organization. Members of the organization participate in these activities, and the systems development process creates organizational changes.

SYSTEMS ANALYSIS

systems analysis

The analysis of a problem that the organization will try to solve with an information system.

Systems analysis is the analysis of the problem that the organization will try to solve with an information system. It consists of defining the problem, identifying its causes, specifying the solution, and identifying the information requirements that must be met by a systems solution.

The systems analyst creates a road map of the existing organization and systems, identifying the primary owners and users of data in the organization. These stakeholders have a direct interest in the information affected by the new system. In addition to these organizational aspects, the analyst also briefly describes the existing hardware and software that serve the organization.

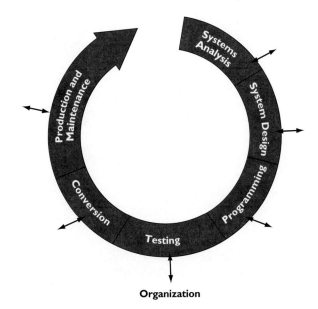

Organization

Figure 10.4 The systems development process. Each of the core systems development activities entails interaction with the organization. From this organizational analysis, the systems analyst details the problems of existing systems. The analyst can identify problem areas and the objectives that a solution would achieve by examining documents, work papers, and procedures; observing systems operations; and interviewing key users of the systems. Often, the solution requires developing a new information system or improving an existing one.

Systems analysis includes a **feasibility study** to determine whether that solution is feasible or achievable from financial, technical, and organizational standpoints. The feasibility study determines whether the proposed system is a good investment, whether the technology needed for the system is available and can be handled by the firm's information systems specialists, and whether the organization can handle the changes introduced by the system.

Normally, the systems analysis process will identify several alternative solutions that the organization can pursue. The feasibility of each is then assessed. A written systems proposal describes the costs and benefits and advantages and disadvantages of each alternative. It is up to management to determine which mix of costs, benefits, technical features, and organizational impacts represents the most desirable alternative.

feasibility study

As part of the systems analysis process, the way to determine whether the solution is achievable, given the organization's resources and constraints.

Establishing Information Requirements

Perhaps the most challenging task of the systems analyst is to define the specific information requirements that must be met by the systems solution selected. At the most basic level, the **information requirements** of a new system involve identifying who needs what information, where, when, and how. Requirements analysis carefully defines the objectives of the new or modified system and develops a detailed description of the functions that the new system must perform. Faulty requirements analysis is a leading cause of systems failure and high systems development costs (see Chapter 11). A system designed around the wrong set of requirements will either have to be discarded because of poor performance or will need to undergo major modifications. Section 10.4 describes alternative approaches to eliciting requirements that help minimize this problem.

In many instances, developing a new system creates an opportunity to redefine how the organization conducts its daily business. Some problems do not require an information systems solution but, instead, need an adjustment in management, additional training, or refinement of existing organizational procedures. If the problem is information related, systems analysis may still be required to diagnose the problem and arrive at the proper solution.

information requirements

A detailed statement of the information needs that a new system must satisfy; identifies who needs what information, and when, where, and how the information is needed.

SYSTEMS DESIGN

Systems analysis describes what a system should do to meet information requirements, and **systems design** shows how the system will fulfill this objective. The design of an information system is the overall plan or model for that system. Like the blueprint of a building or house, it consists of all the specifications that give the system its form and structure.

The systems designer details the systems specifications that will deliver the functions identified during systems analysis. These specifications should address all of the managerial, organizational, and technological components of the systems solution. Table 10.3 lists the types of specifications that would be produced during systems design.

systems design

Details how a system will meet the information requirements as determined by the systems analysis.

Developing successful information systems requires close cooperation among end users and information systems specialists throughout the systems development process.

Like houses or buildings, information systems may have many possible designs. Each design represents a unique blend of technical and organizational components. What makes one design superior to others is the ease and efficiency with which it fulfills user requirements within a specific set of technical, organizational, financial, and time constraints.

TABLE 10.3   DESIGN SPECIFICATIONS

Output

Medium
Content
Timing

Input

Origins
Flow
Data entry

User interface

Simplicity
Efficiency
Logic
Feedback
Errors

Database design

Logical data model
Volume and speed requirements
File organization and design
Record specifications

Processing

Computations
Program modules
Required reports
Timing of outputs

Manual procedures

What activities
Who performs them
When
How
Where

Controls

Input controls (characters, limit, reasonableness)
Processing controls (consistency, record counts)
Output controls (totals, samples of output)
Procedural controls (passwords, special forms)

Security

Access controls
Catastrophe plans
Audit trails

Documentation

Operations documentation
Systems documents
User documentation

Conversion

Transfer files
Initiate new procedures
Select testing method
Cut over to new system

Training

Select training techniques
Develop training modules
Identify training facilities

Organizational changes

Task redesign
Job design
Process design
Organization structure design
Reporting relationships

The Role of End Users

User information requirements drive the entire systems development effort. Users must have sufficient control over the design process to ensure that the system reflects their business priorities and information needs and not the biases of the technical staff (Hunton and Beeler, 1997). Working on design increases users' understanding and acceptance of the system, reducing problems caused by power transfers, intergroup conflict, and unfamiliarity with new systems functions and procedures. As we describe in Chapter 12, insufficient user involvement in the design effort is a major cause of systems failure. However, some systems require more user participation in design than others, and Section 10.4 shows how alternative systems development methods address the user participation issue.

COMPLETING THE SYSTEMS DEVELOPMENT PROCESS

The remaining steps in the systems development process translate the solution specifications established during systems analysis and design into a fully operational information system. These concluding steps consist of programming, testing, conversion, production, and maintenance.

Programming

During the **programming** stage, systems specifications that were prepared during the design stage are translated into program codes. On the basis of detailed design documents for files, transaction and report layouts, and other design details, specifications for each program in the system are prepared. Organizations write the software programs themselves or purchase application software packages for this purpose.

programming
The process of translating the systems specifications prepared during the design stage into program codes.

Testing

Exhaustive and thorough **testing** must be conducted to ascertain whether the system produces the right results. Testing answers the question: "Will the system produce the desired results under known conditions?"

The amount of time needed to answer this question has been traditionally underrated in systems project planning (see Chapter 12). Testing is time consuming: Test data must be carefully prepared, results reviewed, and corrections made in the system. In some instances, parts of the system may have to be redesigned. The risks of glossing over this step are enormous.

Testing an information system can be broken down into three types of activities: unit testing, systems testing, and acceptance testing. **Unit testing**, or program testing, consists of testing each program separately in the system. It is widely believed that the purpose of unit testing is to guarantee that programs are error free, but this goal is realistically impossible. Testing should be viewed instead as a means of locating errors in programs, focusing on finding all the ways to make a program fail. Once pinpointed, problems can be corrected.

Systems testing tests the functioning of the information system as a whole. It tries to determine if discrete modules will function together as planned and whether discrepancies exist between the way the system actually works and the way it was conceived. Among the areas examined are performance time, capacity for file storage and handling peak loads, recovery and restart capabilities, and manual procedures.

Acceptance testing provides the final certification that the system is ready to be used in a production setting. Systems tests are evaluated by users and reviewed by management. When all parties are satisfied that the new system meets their standards, the system is formally accepted for installation in a process known as *signing off*.

The systems development team works with users to devise a systematic test plan. The **test plan** includes all of the preparations for the series of tests we have just described.

Figure 10.5 shows an example of a test plan. The general condition being tested is a record change. The documentation consists of a series of test-plan screens maintained on a database (perhaps a personal computer (PC) database) that is ideally suited to this kind of application.

testing
The exhaustive and thorough process that determines whether the system produces the desired results under known conditions.

unit testing
The process of testing each program separately in the system. Sometimes called program testing.

systems testing
Tests the functioning of the information system as a whole in order to determine if discrete modules will function together as planned.

acceptance testing
Provides the final certification that the system is ready to be used in a production setting.

test plan
Prepared by the development team in conjunction with the users; it includes all of the preparations for the series of tests to be performed on the system.

Figure 10.5 A sample test plan to test a record change. When developing a test plan, it is imperative to include the various conditions to be tested, the requirements for each condition tested, and the expected results. Test plans require input from both end users and information systems specialists.

Procedure	Address and Maintenance "Record Change Series"		Test Series 2		
Prepared By:		Date:	Version:		
Test Ref.	Condition Tested	Special Requirements	Expected Results	Output On	Next Screen
2.0	Change records				
2.1	Change existing record	Key field	Not allowed		
2.2	Change nonexistent record	Other fields	"Invalid key" message		
2.3	Change deleted record	Deleted record must be available	"Deleted" message		
2.4	Make second record	Change 2.1 above	OK if valid	Transaction file	V45
2.5	Insert record		OK if valid	Transaction file	V45
2.6	Abort during change	Abort 2.5	No change	Transaction file	V45

conversion

The process of changing from the old system to the new system.

parallel conversion strategy

A safe and conservative conversion approach where both the old system and its potential replacement are run together for a time until everyone is assured that the new one functions correctly.

direct cutover

A risky conversion approach whereby the new system completely replaces the old one on an appointed day.

pilot study

A strategy to introduce the new system to a limited area of the organization until it is proven to be fully functional; only then can the conversion to the new system across the entire organization take place.

phased approach

Introduces the new system in stages either by functions or by organizational units.

documentation

Descriptions of how an information system works from both a technical and an end-user standpoint.

production

The stage after the new system is installed and the conversion is complete; during this time the system is reviewed by users and technical specialists to determine how well it has met its original goals.

Conversion

Conversion is the process of changing from the old system to the new system. Four main conversion strategies can be employed: the parallel strategy, the direct cutover strategy, the pilot study strategy, and the phased approach strategy.

In a **parallel conversion strategy**, both the old system and its potential replacement are run together for a time until everyone is assured that the new one functions correctly. This is the safest conversion approach because in the event of errors or processing disruptions, the old system can still be used as a backup. However, this approach is very expensive, and additional staff or resources may be required to run the extra system.

The **direct cutover** strategy replaces the old system entirely with the new system on an appointed day. At first glance, this strategy seems less costly than the parallel conversion strategy. However, it is a very risky approach that can potentially be more costly than parallel conversion if serious problems with the new system are found. There is no other system to fall back on. Dislocations, disruptions, and the cost of corrections may be enormous.

The **pilot study** strategy introduces the new system only to a limited area of the organization, such as a single department or operating unit. When the pilot conversion is completed and working smoothly, the system is installed throughout the rest of the organization, either simultaneously or in stages.

The **phased approach** strategy introduces the new system in stages, either by functions or by organizational units. If, for example, the system is introduced by functions, a new payroll system might begin with hourly workers who are paid weekly, followed six months later by adding salaried employees (who are paid monthly) to the system. If the system is introduced by organizational units, corporate headquarters might be converted first, followed by outlying operating units four months later.

Moving from an old system to a new one requires that end users be trained to use the new system. Detailed **documentation** showing how the system works from both technical and end-user standpoints is finalized during conversion time for use in training and everyday operations. Lack of proper training and documentation contributes to system failure, so this portion of the systems development process is very important. The Window on Management shows how Scotiabank used outsourcing, to IBM and Symcor, to handle their implementation of several key information technology functions, including domestic computer operations, automatic teller machines, and desktop computers.

Production and Maintenance

After the new system is installed and the conversion is complete, the system is said to be in **production**. During this stage, the system will be reviewed by both users and technical specialists to determine how well it has met its original objectives and to decide whether any revisions or modifications are in order. In some instances, a formal

SCOTIABANK OUTSOURCES WITH IBM

Scotiabank outsourced several key information technology functions of the bank to IBM that nets IBM about $900 million over the seven-year contract. This is the first outsourcing agreement of its kind for a major Canadian bank. Scotiabank, including its affiliates, employs 52 000 worldwide and has more than 2000 branches and offices in more than 50 countries. The bank has two primary data centres in the Toronto area, where mainframes and servers are located.

Under the agreement, IBM Canada's Global Services Group will manage Scotiabank's domestic computer operations, including data centres, branches, automated banking machines, and desktop computers for 24 000 employees. About 450 Toronto-based bank employees are affected; all of those will be offered equivalent positions with IBM.

"We looked to IBM because of their global expertise, innovative technology services and solutions, and their capability to provide absolute security and privacy of customer data," said Peggy Mulligan, Executive Vice-President, Systems and Operations, of Scotiabank. "Another key factor in our decision was IBM's commitment to providing both a diverse workplace and meaningful career opportunities for our affected employees." The bank decided to outsource key information technology functions because "we really want to focus on our core business, which is delivering financial services," Mulligan said.

Scotiabank Chairman and CEO Peter Godsoe, addressing the House of Commons Standing Committee on Finance, said: "Canadian banks are large enough to invest and to grow in Canada, and we've learned about outsourcing arrangements to acquire scale where necessary. Scotiabank has partnered with IBM to manage several key IT functions and with Symcor to manage all of our cheque and bill processing services."

This contact provides a competitive advantage for both Scotiabank and IBM. The bank will leverage IBM's technology strengths, specifically through partnership in a joint Rapid Application Centre and the deployment of a robust iTeam. At the same time, the partnership will strengthen IBM's presence in the banking industry.

The contract is one of the largest deals thus far for IBM Canada Global Services, according to Rick Horton, General Manager of that group. IBM particularly liked the arrangement because it will gain information technology professionals with financial services experience. According to Horton, many of the 450 employees moving to IBM will still work on the Scotiabank project.

Prior to reaching the agreement, the bank had spent months reviewing leading global service providers to ensure that the highest levels of service would be achieved and that employee career needs were addressed. Scotiabank hired Technology Partners International (TPI) to assist in the review process. TPI's business is to assist their clients in the evaluation, negotiation, and management of sourcing transactions.

But Scotiabank did not stop with the IBM outsourcing contract. Sanchez Computer Associates Inc. signed a software license agreement with Scotiabank to utilize the Sanchez integrated banking platform to process its mortgage loan portfolio.

Scotiabank will use the Sanchez Profile®, Sanchez Xpress™, and Sanchez WebCSR™ products to support mortgage processing, mortgage business integration, and front-end interfaces across the bank's 1000 domestic branches and four call centres. This allows Scotiabank to evaluate future integration of its other legacy banking systems.

To Think About: What issues would Scotiabank have considered during its due diligence review? What prompted Scotiabank to outsource some of its key information technology functions? Did Scotiabank outsource any strategic information technology functions?

Sources: Juleka Dash, "Cost Cutting May Spur IT Outsourcing," *ComputerWorld*, April 26, 2001, available **www.computerworld.com/printthis/2001/0,4814,59661,00. html**, accessed July 30, 2003; Nancy Weil, "Scotiabank Hires IBM in Major Outsourcing Deal," *ITWorld*, available **www.itworld.com/Man/2707/IWD010327hnbankibm/ pfindex.html**, accessed July 30, 2003; Nancy Weil, "Scotiabank Picks IBM Canada for $578 Million Outsourcing Deal," *ComputerWorld*, March 27, 2001, available **www.computerworld.com/printthis/2001/0,4814,59028,00.html**, accessed July 30, 2003; "IBM Canada Announces $900 Million Outsourcing Agreement with Scotiabank," available **www.ibm.com/news/ca/032601_Scotiabank.html**, July 30, 2003; "Scotiabank Selects Sanchez Banking Solution," available **www.sanchez.com/ news/nr_020715.htm**, accessed July 30, 2003.

---

postimplementation audit document will be prepared. After the system has been fine-tuned, it will need to be maintained while it is in production in order to correct errors, meet requirements, or improve processing efficiency. Changes in hardware, software, documentation, or procedures to a production system in order to correct errors, meet new requirements, or improve processing efficiency are termed **maintenance.**

Studies of maintenance have examined the amount of time required for various maintenance tasks. Approximately 20 percent of maintenance time is devoted to debugging or correcting emergency production problems; another 20 percent is concerned with changes in data, files, reports, hardware, or systems software. But 60 percent of all maintenance work consists of making user enhancements, improving documentation, and recoding systems components for greater processing efficiency. The amount of work in the third category of maintenance problems could be reduced significantly through better systems analysis and design practices. Table 10.4 summarizes the systems development activities.

postimplementation audit

Formal review process conducted after a system has been placed in production to determine how well the system has met its original objectives.

maintenance

Changes in hardware, software, documentation, or procedures to a production system to correct errors, meet new requirements, or improve processing efficiency.

TABLE 10.4   SYSTEMS DEVELOPMENT

Core Activity	Description
Systems analysis	Identify problem(s)
	Specify solution
	Establish information requirements
Systems design	Create design specifications
Programming	Translate design specifications into program code
Testing	Unit test
	Systems test
	Acceptance test
Conversion	Plan conversion
	Prepare documentation
	Train users and technical staff
Production and maintenance	Operate the system
	Evaluate the system
	Modify the system

10.4 ALTERNATIVE SYSTEMS DEVELOPMENT APPROACHES

Systems differ in terms of their size and technological complexity and in terms of the organizational problems they are meant to solve. Because there are different kinds of systems, a number of methods have been created to develop systems. This section describes these alternative methods: the traditional systems development life cycle, prototyping, application software packages, end-user development, and outsourcing.

TRADITIONAL SYSTEMS DEVELOPMENT LIFE CYCLE

**systems development
life cycle**

A traditional methodology for
developing an information system that partitions the systems
development process into formal stages that must be completed sequentially with a very
formal division of labour
between end users and information systems specialists.

The **systems development life cycle** is the oldest method for developing information systems and is still used today for medium or large complex systems projects. The life cycle methodology is a phased approach to developing a system, dividing systems development into formal stages. There are different opinions among systems development specialists on how to partition the systems-development stages, but they roughly correspond to the stages of systems development that we have just described. The systems development life cycle methodology maintains a very formal division of labour between end users and information systems specialists. Technical specialists, such as systems analysts and programmers, are responsible for much of the systems analysis, design, and implementation work; end users are limited to providing information requirements and reviewing the technical staff's work. The life cycle also emphasizes formal specifications and paper work, so many documents are generated during the course of a systems project.

The systems development life cycle is still used for developing large complex systems which require a rigorous and formal requirements analysis, predefined specifications, and tight controls over the systems-development process. However, the systems development life cycle approach can be costly, time consuming, and inflexible. Although systems developers can go back and forth among stages in the life cycle, the systems development life cycle is predominantly a "waterfall" approach, in which tasks in one stage are completed before work for the next stage begins. Activities can be repeated, but volumes of new documents must be generated and steps retraced if requirements and specifications need to be revised. This encourages freezing of specifications relatively early in the development process. The life cycle approach is also not suitable for many small desktop systems, which tend to be less structured and more individualized.

PROTOTYPING

Prototyping consists of developing an experimental system rapidly and inexpensively for end users to evaluate. By interacting with the prototype, users can get a better idea of their information requirements. The prototype endorsed by the users can be used as a template to create the final system.

The **prototype** is a working version of an information system or part of the system, but it is meant to be only a preliminary model. Once operational, the prototype will be further refined until it conforms precisely to users' requirements. Once the design has been finalized, the prototype can be converted to a polished production system.

The process of developing a preliminary design, trying it out, refining it, and trying again has been called an *iterative* process of systems development because the steps required to develop a system can be repeated over and over again. Prototyping is more explicitly iterative than the conventional life cycle, and it actively promotes systems design changes. It has been said that prototyping replaces unplanned rework with planned iteration, with each version more accurately reflecting users' requirements.

Steps in Prototyping

Figure 10.6 shows a four-step model of the prototyping process, which consists of the following:

Step 1: *Identify the user's basic requirements.* The systems designer (usually an information systems specialist) works with the user only long enough to capture his or her basic information needs.

Step 2: *Develop an initial prototype.* The systems designer creates a working prototype quickly, using fourth-generation software, interactive multimedia, or computer-aided software engineering (CASE) tools described in Chapter 11.

Step 3: *Use the prototype.* The user is encouraged to work with the system in order to determine how well the prototype meets his or her needs and to make suggestions for improving the prototype.

Step 4: *Revise and enhance the prototype.* The systems developer notes all changes the user requests and refines the prototype accordingly. After the prototype has been revised, the cycle returns to step 3. Steps 3 and 4 are repeated until the user is satisfied.

prototyping
The process of developing an experimental system quickly and inexpensively for demonstration and evaluation so that users can better determine information requirements.

prototype
The preliminary working version of an information system for demonstration and evaluation purposes.

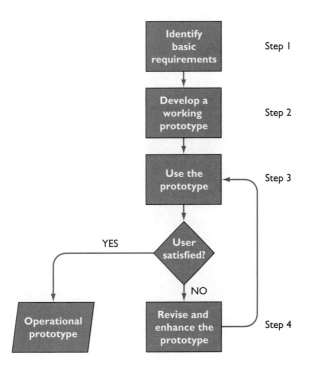

Figure 10.6 The prototyping process. The process of developing a prototype can be broken down into four steps. Because a prototype can be developed quickly and inexpensively, system developers can go through several iterations, repeating steps 3 and 4, to refine and enhance the prototype before arriving at the final operational one.

When no more iterations are required, the approved prototype then becomes an operational prototype that furnishes the final specifications for the application. Sometimes, the prototype itself is adopted as the production version of the system.

Advantages and Disadvantages of Prototyping

Prototyping is most useful when there is some uncertainty about requirements or design solutions. Prototyping is especially useful in designing an information system's **end-user interface** (the part of the system that end users interact with, such as online display and data-entry screens, reports, or Web pages). Because prototyping encourages intense end-user involvement throughout the systems development process (Cerveny et al., 1986), it is more likely to produce systems that fulfill user requirements.

However, rapid prototyping can gloss over essential steps in systems development. If the completed prototype works reasonably well, management may not see the need for reprogramming, redesign, or full documentation and testing to develop a polished production system. Some of these hastily constructed systems may not easily accommodate large quantities of data or a large number of users in a secure production environment.

APPLICATION SOFTWARE PACKAGES

Information systems can be developed using software from **application software packages**, which we introduced in Chapter 6. There are many applications that are common to all business organizations—for example, payroll, accounts receivable, general ledger, or inventory control. For these universal functions with standard processes that do not change a great deal over time, a generic system will fulfill the requirements of many organizations.

If a software package can fulfill most of an organization's requirements, the company does not have to write its own software. The company can save time and money by using the prewritten, predesigned, pretested software programs from the package. Package vendors supply much of the ongoing maintenance and support for the system, including enhancements to keep the system in line with ongoing technical and business developments.

If an organization has unique requirements that the package does not address, many packages include capabilities for customization. **Customization** features allow a software package to be modified to meet an organization's unique requirements without destroying the integrity of the package software. If a great deal of customization is required, additional programming and customization work may become so expensive and time consuming that they eliminate many of the advantages of software packages. Figure 10.7 shows how package costs in relation to total implementation costs rise with the degree of customization. The initial purchase price of the package can be deceptive because of these hidden implementation costs. If the vendor releases new versions of the package, the overall costs of customization will be magnified because these changes will need to be synchronized with future versions of the software.

end-user interface

The part of an information system through which the end user interacts with the system, such as online screens and commands.

application software package

A set of prewritten, precoded, pretested application software programs that are commercially available for sale or lease.

customization

The modification of a software package to meet an organization's unique requirements without destroying the package software's integrity.

Figure 10.7 The effects of customizing a software package on total implementation costs. As the modifications to a software package rise, so does the cost of implementing the package. Savings promised by the package can be whittled away by excessive changes.

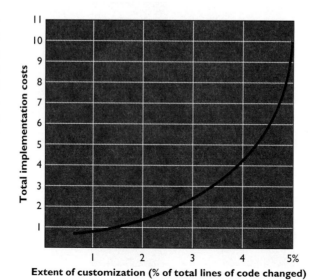

Extent of customization (% of total lines of code changed)

Selecting Software Packages

When a system is developed using an application software package, systems analysis will include a package evaluation effort. The most important evaluation criteria are the functions provided by the package, flexibility, user-friendliness, hardware and software resource requirements, database requirements, installation and maintenance effort, documentation, vendor quality, customization needed, and cost. The package evaluation process often is based on a **Request for Proposal (RFP)**, which is a detailed list of questions submitted to packaged software vendors.

When a software package solution is selected, the organization no longer has total control over the system design process. Instead of tailoring the system design specifications directly to user requirements, the design effort will consist of trying to mould user requirements to conform to the features of the package. If the organization's requirements conflict with the way the package works and the package cannot be customized, the organization will have to adapt to the package and change its procedures. Even if the organization's business processes seem compatible with those supported by a software package, the package may be too constraining if these business processes are continually changing (Prahalad and Krishnan, 2002). A new company just being set up could adopt the business processes and information flows provided by the package as its own business processes, but organizations that have been in existence for some time may not be able to easily change the way they work to conform to the package.

END-USER DEVELOPMENT

Some types of information systems can be developed by end users with little or no formal assistance from technical specialists. This phenomenon is called **end-user development**. Using fourth-generation languages, graphics languages, and PC software tools, end users can access data, create reports, and develop entire information systems on their own, with little or no help from professional systems analysts or programmers. Many of these end-user developed systems can be created much more rapidly than with the traditional systems development life cycle. Figure 10.8 illustrates the concept of end-user development.

Benefits and Limitations of End-User Development

Many organizations have reported gains in application development productivity by using fourth-generation tools that in a few cases have reached 300 to 500 percent. Allowing users to specify their own business needs improves requirements gathering and often leads to a higher level of user involvement and satisfaction with the system. However, fourth-generation

Request for Proposal (RFP)

A detailed list of questions submitted to vendors of software or other services to determine how well the vendor's product can meet the organization's specific requirements.

end-user development

The development of information systems by end users with little or no formal assistance from technical specialists.

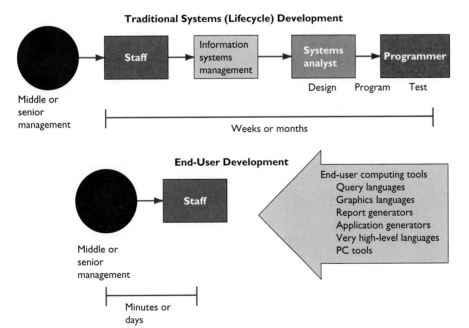

Figure 10.8 End-user versus systems development life cycle development. End users can access computerized information directly or develop information systems, with little or no formal technical assistance. On the whole, end-user-developed systems can be completed more rapidly than those developed through the conventional systems development life cycle.

Source: From *Application Development Without Programmers,* by James Martin, © 1982. Reprinted by permission of Prentice Hall Inc., Upper Saddle River, NJ.

tools still cannot replace conventional tools for some business applications because they cannot easily handle the processing of large numbers of transactions or applications with extensive procedural logic and updating requirements.

End-user computing also poses organizational risks because it occurs outside of traditional mechanisms for information system management and control. When systems are created rapidly, without a formal development methodology, testing and documentation may be inadequate. Control over data can be lost in systems outside the traditional information systems department (see Chapter 7).

Managing End-User Development

To help organizations maximize the benefits of end-user applications development, management should control the development of end-user applications by requiring cost justification of end-user information system projects and by establishing hardware, software, and quality standards for user-developed applications. (See Figure 10.9.)

When end-user computing first became popular, organizations used information centres to promote standards for hardware and software so that end users would not introduce many disparate and incompatible technologies into the firm (Fuller and Swanson, 1992). **Information centres** are special facilities housing hardware, software, and technical specialists to supply end users with tools, training, and expert advice so that they can create information system applications on their own or increase their productivity. The role of information centres is diminishing as end-users become more computer literate, but organizations still need to closely monitor and manage end-user development.

OUTSOURCING

If a firm does not want to use its internal resources to develop or operate information systems, it can hire an external organization that specializes in providing these services to do the work. The process of turning over an organization's computer centre operations, telecommunications networks, or applications development to external vendors is called **outsourcing**. The application service providers (ASPs) described in Chapter 6 are one form of outsourcing. Subscribing companies would use the software and computer hardware provided by the ASP as the technical platform for their systems. In another form of outsourcing, a company would hire an external vendor to design and create the software for its system, but that company would operate the system on its own computers.

Outsourcing has become popular because some organizations perceive it as more cost effective than maintaining their own computer centre or information systems staff. The provider of outsourcing services benefits from economies of scale (the same knowledge,

information centre

A special facility within an organization that provides training and support for end-user computing.

outsourcing

The practice of contracting computer centre operations, telecommunications networks, or applications development to external vendors.

Figure 10.9 Microsoft Front Page is a development tool with many features that can be employed by end users to create Web pages and Web sites without writing program codes.

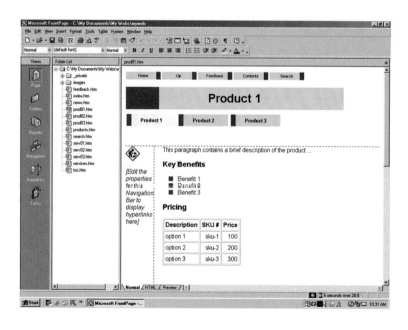

skills, and capacity can be shared with many different customers) and is likely to charge competitive prices for information systems services. Outsourcing allows a company with fluctuating needs for computer processing to pay for only what it uses, rather than to develop its own computer centre, which would be underutilized when there is no peak load. Some firms outsource because their internal information systems staff cannot keep pace with technological changes or innovative business practices or because they want to free up scarce and costly talent for activities with higher payback.

A company can outsource some of the more advanced technologies it would like to implement. For example, the Boyd Group, a Winnipeg-based operator and consolidator of automotive collision repair centres, contracted with Relizon Canada to maintain all of its documents, including storing documents at its Winnipeg business service centre and printing and distributing brochures to Boyd's 66 autobody repair shops in North America. In addition, Relizon will look for opportunities to introduce advanced technologies, such as electronic order forms that should result in even more efficiencies and cost savings.

Not all organizations benefit from outsourcing, and the disadvantages of outsourcing can create serious problems for organizations if they are not well understood and managed (Earl, 1996). Many firms underestimate the costs for identifying and evaluating vendors of information technology services, for transitioning to a new vendor, and for monitoring vendors to make sure they are fulfilling their contractual obligations. These "hidden costs" can easily undercut anticipated benefits from outsourcing (Barthelemy, 2001). When a firm allocates the responsibility for developing and operating its information systems to another organization, it can lose control over its information systems function. If the organization lacks the expertise to negotiate a sound contract, the firm's dependence on the vendor could result in high costs or loss of control over technological direction (Lacity, Willcocks, and Feeny, 1996). Firms should be especially cautious when using outsourcers to develop or to operate applications that give them some type of competitive advantage.

Table 10.5 compares the advantages and disadvantages of each of the systems development alternatives.

10.5 APPLICATION DEVELOPMENT FOR THE DIGITAL FIRM

Electronic commerce (e-commerce), electronic business (e-business), and the emerging digital firm pose new challenges for systems development. Technologies and business conditions are changing so rapidly that agility and scalability have become critical success factors and primary goals of systems design. Businesses need software components that can be added, modified, replaced, or reconfigured to enable them to respond rapidly to new opportunities. Systems must be scalable to accommodate growing numbers of users and to deliver data over multiple platforms—client-server networks, desktop computers with Web browsers, cell phones, and other mobile devices. E-commerce and e-business systems may also need to be designed so that they can run in hosted environments as well as on the company's own hardware and software platforms. To remain competitive, some firms feel pressured to design, develop, test, and deploy Internet or intranet applications in a matter of weeks or months (Earl and Khan, 2001).

Older development methods were based on a much more static view of systems. In the past, systems development would be based on a formal design document with functional specifications that was handed off to a development team. Alternatively, applications might be loosely designed and iteratively developed with multiple passes going to users for review and revision. These development processes often took months or years and were ill suited to the pace and profile of Internet or intranet projects. Traditional methods did not adequately address the new features of Internet-based applications, which might have multiple tiers of clients and servers with different operating systems linked to transaction processing systems, as well as business processes that had to be coordinated with those of customers or suppliers.

In the digital firm environment, organizations need to be able to add, change, and retire their technology capabilities very rapidly. Companies are adopting shorter, more informal development processes for many of their e-commerce and e-business applications, processes that provide fast solutions that do not disrupt their core transaction processing systems and organizational databases. They are relying more heavily on fast-cycle techniques, such as joint

TABLE 10.5	COMPARISON OF SYSTEMS-DEVELOPMENT APPROACHES		
Approach	**Features**	**Advantages**	**Disadvantages**
Systems development life cycle	Sequential step-by-step formal process Written specification and approvals Limited role of users	Necessary for large complex systems and projects	Slow and expensive Discourages changes Massive paperwork to manage
Protoptyping	Requirements specified dynamically with experimental system Rapid, informal, and iterative process Users continually interact with the prototype	Rapid and relatively inexpensive Useful when requirements are uncertain or when end-user interface is very important Promotes user participation	Inappropriate for large, complex systems Can gloss over steps in analysis, documentation, and testing May not meet the organization's unique requirements
Applications software package	Commercial software eliminates need for internally developed software programs	Design, programming, installation, and maintenance work are reduced Can save time and cost when developing common business applications Reduces need for internal information systems resources	May not perform many business functions well Extensive customization raises development costs
End-user development	Systems created by end users using fourth-generation software tools Rapid and informal Minimal role of information systems specialists	Users control systems development Saves development time and cost Reduces application backlog	Can lead to proliferation of uncontrolled information systems and data Systems do not always meet quality assurance standards
Outsourcing	Systems developed and sometimes operated by external vendor	Can reduce or control costs Can produce system when internal resources are not available or technically deficient	Loss of control over the information systems function Dependence on the technical direction and prosperity of external vendors

application design (JAD), prototypes, and reusable standardized software components that can be assembled into a complete set of services for e-commerce and e-business.

OBJECT-ORIENTED DEVELOPMENT

Object-oriented development provides an approach that is believed to be well suited for developing systems that can respond to rapidly changing business environments, including Web applications. Chapter 6 introduced *object-oriented programming*, which combines data and the actions that can be performed on the data into a single object. **Object-oriented development** uses the object as the basic unit of systems analysis and design. The system is modelled as a collection of objects and the relationships between them. (Review Figure 6.10 in Chapter 6.) Data encapsulated in an object can only be accessed and modified by the operations or *methods* associated with that object. Since processing logic resides within objects, rather that in software programs, objects must collaborate with each other to make the system work. This systems development approach contrasts with the traditional structured development approach we described earlier, which models a system by separating data and the processes that act on the data.

The phases of object-oriented development (see Figure 10.10) are similar to those of conventional systems development, consisting of analysis, design, and implementation. However, object-oriented development is more iterative and incremental than traditional

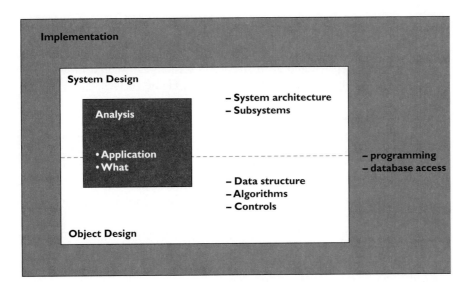

Figure 10.10 Object-oriented development. Object-oriented development consists of progressively developing a system modelled as a series of interrelated objects. The development process is iterative, blending together analysis and design activities.

Source: Modern Systems Analysis and Design, 3rd Edition by Jeffrey A. Hoffer, Joey F. George, and Joseph S. Valacich, copyright 2002. Reprinted by permission of Prentice Hall Inc., Upper Saddle River, NJ.

structured development. During analysis, system developers document the functional requirements of the system, specifying its most important properties and what the proposed system must do. Interactions between the system and its users are analyzed to identify objects, which include both data and processes. The object-oriented design phases describe how the objects will behave and how they will interact with one other. Similar objects are grouped together to form a class, and classes are grouped into hierarchies where a subclass inherits the attributes and methods from its superclass. Chapter 11 provides additional detail on the tools used for object-oriented analysis and design.

The information system is implemented by translating the design into program code, reusing classes that are already available in a library of reusable software objects and adding new ones created during the object-oriented design phase. Implementation may also involve the creation of an object-oriented database. The resulting system must be thoroughly tested and evaluated.

Since objects are reusable, object-oriented development could potentially reduce the time and cost of writing software because organizations could reuse software objects that have already been created as building blocks for other applications. New systems could be created by using some existing objects, changing others, and adding a few new objects.

Object-oriented frameworks have been developed to provide reusable, semicomplete applications that the organization can further customize into finished applications (Fayad and Schmidt, 1997). However, information systems specialists must learn a completely new way of modelling a system (Sircar, Nerur, and Mahapatra, 2001), and object-oriented models of systems are not always more usable than process-oriented models (Agarwal, De, Sinha, and Tanniru, 2000). The benefits from object reuse deteriorate when the object must be modified for the new application (Irwin, 2002). Conversion to an object-oriented approach may require large-scale organizational investments, which management must balance against the anticipated payoffs.

RAPID APPLICATION DEVELOPMENT (RAD)

Object-oriented software tools, reusable software, prototyping, and fourth-generation tools are helping systems developers create working systems much more rapidly than they could using traditional systems development methods and software tools. The term **rapid application development (RAD)** is used to describe this process of creating workable systems in a very short period of time. RAD can include the use of visual programming and other tools for developing graphical user interfaces, iterative prototyping of key system elements, the automation of program codes generation, and close teamwork among end users and information systems specialists. Simple systems often can be assembled from predeveloped components. The process does not have to be sequential, and key parts of development can occur simultaneously.

rapid application development (RAD)

Process for developing systems in a very short time period by using prototyping, fourth-generation tools, and close teamwork among users and systems specialists.

joint application design (JAD)

Process to accelerate the generation of information requirements by having end users and information systems specialists work together in intensive interactive design sessions.

Web services

Software components deliverable over the Internet that enable one application to communicate with another with no translation required using a standard "plug and play" architecture.

SOAP (Simple Object Access Protocol)

Set of rules that allows Web services applications to pass data and instructions to one another.

WSDL (Web Services Description Language)

Common framework for describing the tasks performed by a Web service so that it can be used by other applications.

UDDI (Universal Description, Discovery, and Integration)

Allows a Web service to be listed in a directory of Web services so that it can be easily located by other organizations and systems.

Sometimes, **joint application design (JAD)** is used to accelerate the generation of information requirements and to develop the initial systems design. JAD brings end users and information systems specialists together in an interactive session to discuss the system's design. Properly prepared and facilitated, JAD sessions can significantly speed the design phase while involving users at an intense level. (See Figure 10.11.)

WEB SERVICES

We have already described how firms are basing portions of their IT infrastructure on services supplied by external vendors. Increasingly, new information systems applications will be developed using Web services. **Web services** are software components deliverable over the Internet that enable one application to communicate with another with no translation required. By allowing applications to communicate and share data—regardless of operating system, programming language, or client device—Web services can provide significant cost savings over traditional in-house systems while opening up new opportunities for collaboration with other companies (Patel and Saigal, 2002; Hagel and Brown, 2001). IBM has included Web services tools in its WebSphere e-business software, and Microsoft has incorporated Web services tools in its .Net platform. (See Figure 10.12.)

Web services use an open "plug and play" architecture, rather than a proprietary architecture. This architecture has three layers (see Figure 10.13). The first consists of software standards and communication protocols, such as XML, SOAP, WSDL, and UDDI, that allow information to be exchanged easily among different applications. *XML (eXtensible Markup Language)*, introduced in Chapter 6, provides a standard description of data in Web pages and databases that makes it easier to exchange data among disparate applications and systems. Web services communicate through XML messages over standard Web protocols. **SOAP**, which stands for **Simple Object Access Protocol**, is a set of rules that allows applications to pass data and instructions to one another. **WSDL** stands for **Web Services Description Language**, which is a common framework for describing the tasks performed by a Web service so that it can be used by other applications. **UDDI**, standing for **Universal Description, Discovery, and Integration**, allows a Web service to be listed in a directory of Web services so that it can be easily located. Companies discover and locate Web services through this directory, much as they would locate services in the Yellow Pages of a telephone book. Using these standards and protocols, a software application can connect freely to other applications without custom programming for each different application with which it wants to communicate. Everyone shares the same standards.

The middle layer of Web services consists of a service grid to create environments essential for carrying out critical business activities. The middle layer provides a set of shared utilities, such as security, third-party billing, and payment that are used for critical business functions

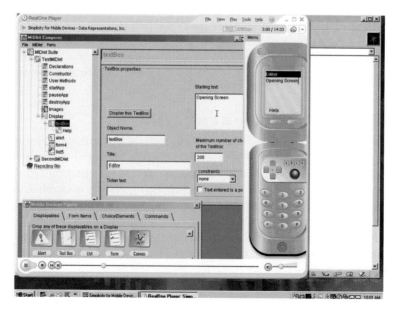

Figure 10.11 Simplicity for Mobile Devices is a cross-platform RAD tool for rapid creation of applications for cell phones and other mobile devices. Rapid application development (RAD) tools enable companies to create rapid system solutions without extensive programming.

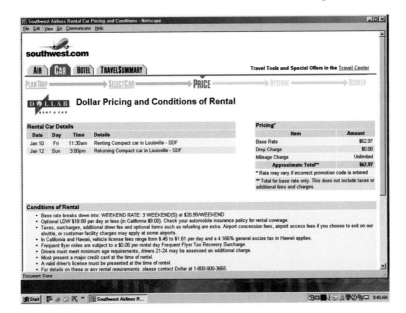

Figure 10.12 Visitors to the Southwestair.com Web site can make on-line reservations for Dollar Rent A Car directly from Southwest's Web site. Both companies use Web services to link their information systems.

and transactions over the Internet. The service grid also includes utilities for transporting messages and identifying available services.

The third layer consists of application services, such as credit card processing or production scheduling, that automate specific business functions. Some application services will be proprietary to a particular company, and others will be shared among all companies. A company may also develop its own application services and then sell them to other companies on a subscription basis. For instance, Citibank developed and markets CitiConnect, an XML-based payment processing service that plugs into existing business-to-business (B2B) Net marketplaces.

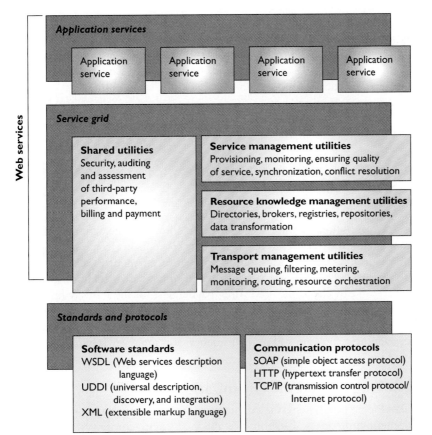

Figure 10.13 The Web Services Architecture. The architecture for Web services has three layers. The most fundamental layer consists of software standards and communication protocols that make it possible for diverse systems to communicate electronically. The middle layer is a service grid where special utilities provide important services and tools. The third layer consists of application services that support common business processes, such as supply chain management or marketing.
Source: from "Your Next IT Strategy" by John Hagel, III, and John Seeley Brown, *Harvard Business Review*, October 2001. Reprinted by permission.

THE LURE OF WEB SERVICES

Singapore Exchange Ltd (SGX) is Asia Pacific's first demutualized, integrated securities and derivatives exchange. SGX provides a diverse array of securities and derivative products and financial market information to its global network of broker members. "We are not directly connected to the investors themselves," says Daniel Tan, SGX's Executive Vice-President and head of its information technology (IT) division. Instead, his company supplies time-sensitive investment information to brokers, who then pass it on to appropriate customers equipped with MSN Messenger, a communication tool bundled with the latest version of Windows, often used for chatting. To be successful in its business, SGX had to spend millions of dollars to develop the security that such a system requires. In addition, the company originally might have had to spend millions more to develop the Internet connections necessary to communicate with all of its customers' systems. Instead, Tan turned to Web Services, enabling SGX to make those connections at a much lower cost.

Web Services provides a set of standards that enable companies to communicate with each other without having to significantly modify their current software programs. In earlier times, one or both of the parties would have to write or rewrite their systems so they could communicate. Web Services use XML for the common language in their communication. Bill Burnham, a Softbank Venture Capital partner, explains the system this way: "Rather than think about individual Web sites, think about the Web holistically, where people create software by linking different applications across the Web." Thus, the Web has expanded way beyond just being a compilation of HTML (hypertext markup language) pages from which people can collect information.

SGX's move to Microsoft.Net Web services technology and establishing connections with its clients took only three months, leaving all of its own systems almost unchanged. Tan says, "I do not have to invest in building the different delivery channels [required to communicate with each one of my customers]."

SGX can reach customers without knowing whether they are using pagers or mobile phones. Information from the SGX Web site goes through several layers to reach the investors, allowing customers to continue operating the way they did before SGX turned to .Net.

SembCorp Logistics also turned to .Net to provide customized services for its customers. SembCorp is Asia's leading integrated logistics services provider, focusing on offshore logistics and supply chain management. It is developing a global logistics network and system to support customers around the globe. Customers can use its Web site to check inventory and to track their shipments. The logistics industry deals with a wide spectrum of customers. Using Web services allowed SembCorp to reduce the complexity involved in linking to customers using different technology platforms without worrying about the delivery mechanism. According to SembCorp's Chief Technology Officer Ng Han Kim, "With .Net, we can lower integration costs for the customer, and we can put more functionalities and features into our services on the Web," thereby attracting more customers to subscribe to the company's logistics services. SembCorp chose Microsoft .Net over Sun's Java because it had committed so much money and resources to developing its Web services platform. SembCorp will take longer to implement Web services than SGX because its .Net applications will penetrate more deeply into the firm's IT infrastructure. SembCorp must streamline and modularize processes involving networks, applications, and backend servers.

To Think About: What are the benefits of using Web services technology? How can they provide value to firms? What management, organization, and technology issues must be addressed when implementing Web services?

Sources: Winston Raj, "The Joys & Pains of.Net," *CIO-Asia*, May 2002; Singapore Exchange Ltd, accessed August 31, 2002, **www.ses.com.sg**; www. **SembCorp Logistics Online**, accessed August 31, 2002; **www.semblog.com**; Sari Kalin, "The Essential Guide to Web Services," *Darwin Magazine*, January 2002.

Organizations can use Web services to automate interactions with each other and they can also use Web services to obtain software components from other organizations to accomplish specific tasks, such as billing services or payment processing (see the Window on Technology). They can use Web services to connect their traditional applications to outside services one by one as the need arises, paying only for the software functionality they need at the moment. Web services promise substantial savings in systems integration costs by reducing the cost of developing separate interfaces among systems. However, Web services and development tools are still in their infancy, and some key standards remain undeveloped or have not yet been agreed on.

Looking Beyond the Organization

Developing new systems for a digital firm environment requires more than innovative development approaches. E-commerce and e-business require systems planning and systems analysis based on a broader view of the organization, one that encompasses business processes extended beyond firm boundaries (Fingar, 2000). Firms can no longer execute their business and systems plans alone because they need to forge new electronic relationships with suppliers, distributors, and customers. Their business processes often need to be integrated with customer and supplier business processes.

MANAGEMENT WRAP-UP

Selection of a systems-development approach can have a big impact on the time, cost, and end product of systems development. Managers should be aware of the strengths and weaknesses of each systems-development approach and the types of problems for which each is best suited.

Organizational needs should drive the selection of a systems-development approach. The impact of application software packages and of outsourcing should be carefully evaluated before they are selected because these approaches give organizations less control over the systems-development process.

Various software tools are available to support the systems-development process. Key technology decisions should be based on the organization's familiarity with the technology and its compatibility with the organization's information requirements, IT infrastructure, and information architecture.

For Discussion

1. Why is selecting a systems development approach an important business decision? Who should participate in the selection process?

2. Some have said that the best way to reduce systems development costs is to use application software packages or fourth-generation tools. Do you agree? Why, or why not?

SUMMARY

1. *How could developing a new system change the way an organization works?* Developing a new information system is a form of planned organizational change that involves many different people in the organization. Because information systems are sociotechnical entities, a change in information systems involves changes in work, management, and the organization. Four kinds of technology-enabled change are (1) automation, (2) rationalization of procedures, (3) business re-engineering, and (4) paradigm shift, with far-reaching changes carrying the greatest risks and rewards. Many organizations are attempting business process re-engineering to redesign workflows and business processes in the hope of achieving dramatic productivity breakthroughs. Information systems can also be used to support total quality management (TQM), six sigma, and other initiatives for incremental process improvement.

2. *How can a company make sure that the new information systems it develops fit its business plan?* Organizations should develop information systems plans that describe how information technology supports the attainment of their business goals. The plans indicate the direction of systems

development, the rationale, implementation strategy, and budget. Enterprise analysis and critical success factors (CSFs) can be used to elicit organization-wide information requirements that must be addressed by the plans.

3. *What are the steps required to develop a new information system?* The core activities in systems development are systems analysis, systems design, programming, testing, conversion, production, and maintenance. Systems analysis is the study and analysis of problems of existing systems and the identification of requirements for their solutions. Systems design provides the specifications for an information system solution, showing how its technical and organizational components fit together.

4. *What alternative methods for developing information systems are available?* There are a number of alternative methods for developing information systems, each suited to different types of problems. The oldest method for developing systems is the systems development life cycle, which requires that information systems be developed in formal stages. Prototyping consists of developing an experimental system rapidly and inexpensively for end users to interact

with and evaluate. Developing an information system using an application software package eliminates the need for writing software programs when developing the information system. End-user development is the development of information systems by end users, either alone or with minimal assistance from information systems specialists. End-user-developed systems can be created rapidly and informally using fourth-generation software tools. Outsourcing consists of using an external vendor to develop (or operate) a firm's information systems. The work is done by the vendor, rather than by the organization's internal information systems staff.

5. *Are there any techniques or systems development approaches to help us develop e-commerce and e-business applications more rapidly?* Businesses today are often required to develop e-commerce and e-business applications very rapidly in order to remain competitive. They are relying more heavily on rapid application design, joint application design (JAD), and reusable software components to speed up the systems development process. Object-oriented software development is expected to reduce the time and cost of writing software and of making maintenance changes because it models a system as a series of reusable objects that combine both data and procedures. Rapid application development (RAD) uses object-oriented software, visual programming, prototyping, and fourth-generation tools for very rapid creation of systems. Web services will enable organizations to develop and enhance systems by obtaining the functionality they need as software application components delivered over the Internet. Web services provide a common set of standards that allows organizations to link their systems regardless of their technology platform through a standard "plug and play" architecture.

KEY TERMS

Acceptance testing, 339

Application software package, 344

Automation, 330

Benchmarking, 335

Business process re-engineering, 331

Conversion, 340

Critical success factors (CSFs), 328

Customization, 344

Direct cutover, 340

Documentation, 340

End-user development, 345

End-user interface, 344

Enterprise analysis, 327

Feasibility study, 337

Information centre, 346

Information requirements, 337

Information systems plan, 327

Joint application design (JAD), 350

Maintenance, 341

Object-oriented development, 348

Outsourcing, 346

Paradigm shift, 331

Parallel conversion strategy, 340

Phased approach, 340

Pilot study, 340

Postimplementation audit, 341

Production, 340

Programming, 339

Prototype, 343

Prototyping, 343

Rapid application development (RAD), 349

Rationalization of procedures, 330

Request for Proposal (RFP), 345

Six sigma, 334

SOAP (Simple Object Access Protocol), 350

Systems analysis, 336

Systems design, 337

Systems development, 336

Systems development life cycle, 342

Systems testing, 339

Test plan, 339

Testing, 339

Total quality management (TQM), 334

UDDI (Universal Description, Discovery and Integration), 350

Unit testing, 339

Web services, 350

Workflow management, 333

WSDL (Web Services Description Language), 350

REVIEW QUESTIONS

1. Why can an information system be considered a planned organizational change?

2. What are the major categories of an information systems plan?

3. How can enterprise analysis and critical success factors be used to establish organization-wide information system requirements?

4. Describe each of the four kinds of organizational change that can be promoted with information technology.

5. What is business process re-engineering? What steps are required to make it effective?

6. What is the difference between systems analysis and systems design? What activities are involved in each?

7. What are information requirements? Why are they difficult to determine correctly?

8. Why is the testing stage of systems development so important? Name and describe the three stages of testing for an information system.

9. What role do programming, conversion, production, and maintenance play in systems development?

10. What is the traditional systems development life cycle? Describe each of its steps and its advantages and disadvantages for systems development.

11. What do we mean by information system prototyping? What are its benefits and limitations? List and describe the steps in the prototyping process.

12. What is an application software package? What are the advantages and disadvantages of developing information systems based on software packages?

13. What do we mean by end-user development? What are its advantages and disadvantages? Name some policies and procedures for managing end-user development.

14. What is outsourcing? Under what circumstances should outsourcing be used for developing information systems?

15. What is the difference between object-oriented development and traditional systems development? What are the advantages of using object-oriented software development in developing systems?

16. What is rapid application development (RAD)? How can it help system developers?

17. What are Web services? How can they help firms develop and enhance their information systems?

APPLICATION SOFTWARE EXERCISE

DATABASE EXERCISE: DESIGNING A CUSTOMER SYSTEM FOR AUTO SALES

Ace Auto Dealers specializes in selling new vehicles from Subaru. The company advertises in local newspapers and is also listed as an authorized dealer on the Subaru Web site and the major Web sites for auto buyers. The company benefits from good local word-of-mouth reputation and name recognition and is a leading source for Subaru vehicles in the Prince Edward Island area.

When a prospective customer enters the showroom, he or she is greeted by an Ace sales representative. The sales representative manually fills out a form with such information as the prospective customer's name, address, telephone number, date of visit, and model and make of vehicle in which he or she is interested. The representative also asks where the prospective buyer heard about Ace—whether it was from a newspaper ad, the Web, or word of mouth and this information is also noted on the form.

If the customer decides to purchase an auto, the dealer fills out a bill of sale form, listing the vehicle identification number, vehicle make and model, colour, options selected, base price, total price, and date of the sale along with the purchaser's name, address, and telephone number. This form also shows the amount of the total purchase price that was financed. Both forms are filed in manual folders—one for sales prospects and another for actual purchases.

Ace does not feel it knows enough about its customers. It cannot easily identify repeat customers at its dealership or customers who have purchased a Subaru in the past from another dealer. It cannot easily determine which prospective buyers have made auto purchases or the percentage of those who have been converted into buyers. Nor can it identify which customer touchpoints have produced the greatest number of sales leads or actual sales so it can focus its advertising and marketing more on the channels that generate the most revenue. Are purchasers coming from newspaper ads, from word of mouth, or from the Web? Additionally, the firm cannot tell whether its customers are more interested in no-frills cars or ones with luxury options.

Prepare a systems analysis report detailing Ace's problem and a systems solution that can be implemented using PC database management software. Then, use database software to develop a simple systems solution. Your systems analysis report should include the following:

1. Description of the problem and its organizational and business impact.
2. Proposed solution, solution objectives, and solution feasibility.
3. Costs and benefits of the solution you have selected. The company has a PC with Internet access and the full suite of Microsoft Office desktop productivity tools.
4. Information requirements to be addressed by the solution.
5. Management, organization, and technology issues to be addressed by the solution, including changes in business processes.

On the basis of the requirements you have identified, design the database and populate it with at least 20 records per table. Print out the database design. Then, use the system you have created to generate queries and reports that would be of most interest to management. Create several prototype data input forms for the system and review them with your instructor. Then, revise the prototypes.

GROUP PROJECT

With three or four of your classmates, select a system described in this text that uses the Web. Examples might include the WestJet site in this chapter, the RadioShack Canada Web site in Chapter 9, or the Direct Wines Web site in Chapter 6. Review the Web site for the system you select. Use what you have learned from the Web site and the description in this book to prepare a report describing some of the design specifications for the system you select. Present your findings to the class.

INTERNET TOOLS

COMPANION WEBSITE

The Companion Website for this chapter will direct you to the SAP Web site where you can complete an exercise to evaluate the capabilities of this major multinational software package and learn more about enterprise systems.

At **www.pearsoned.ca/laudon**, you will find valuable tools to facilitate and enhance your learning of this chapter as well as opportunities to apply your knowledge to realistic situations:

▮ An Interactive Study Guide of self-test questions that will provide you with immediate feedback.
▮ Application exercises.
▮ An Electronic Business Project to redesign business processes to participate in a Net marketplace.
▮ A Management Decision Problem on using a scoring model to evaluate alternative enterprise-wide or enterprise resource planning (ERP) systems.
▮ Updates of material in this chapter.

ADDITIONAL SITES OF INTEREST

There are many interesting Web sites to enhance your learning about systems development. You can search the Web yourself or just try the following sites to add to what you have already learned.

Sybase
> **www.sybase.com**
>
> Sybase has products that can be used in RAD and JAD development.

EDS Canada
> **www.eds.com/canada/ca_about.shtml**
>
> One of the largest outsourcing firms in Canada, EDS Canada is the result of the merger of Canada's SHL Systemhouse and the United States' EDS.

Affinity Systems
> **www.affsys.com**
>
> Toronto-based outsourcer of software development solutions.

CASE STUDY: *Albertans Get ASP Solution for HealthCare*

Alberta Wellnet is the parent organization for a variety of province-wide and regional initiatives to create an integrated health information network. Alberta Wellnet's primary goal is to better the delivery of health services to Albertans by improving access to health information by healthcare providers. According to their vision, "Alberta Wellnet has a single vision and a simple purpose: To enable health service providers to share health information within a secure network environment that will help them to make better decisions about healthcare."

This vision includes upgrading health system management and accountability by creating efficient practice management systems. This will allow doctors to improve patient care, practice management, and professional development; reduce the effort and resources required in the office to manage systems and data; and allow physicians to take advantage of Alberta Wellnet's services.

There are many challenges for doctors who manage their own electronic office systems. It takes time and money to implement and administer these systems—and this time is in short enough supply when it comes to attending patients. There's also the question of specialization. Doctors are specialized in medical arts, not information systems. Having to face difficult decisions in a foreign field increases the obstacles to the adoption of automated practice management systems. The result is that most physicians still operate in a paper-based environment.

Alberta Wellnet became an innovator in the medical industry by tackling these issues. "As a visionary group, Alberta Wellnet had the foresight to realize that the industry trend is moving toward an application service provider (ASP) delivery model, especially for remote geographies. It is definitely a technology whose time has come," says Doug Campbell, project sponsor and solution architect for Alberta Wellnet. ASPs deploy, host, and manage access to applications from a centrally managed facility on a contractual basis. ASPs are then responsible for administering and managing these applications.

Because of physicians' resource restraints and limited staff, an ASP delivery model was perfect, as it "provides an end-to-end managed solution for physicians, which eliminates many of the technological barriers at clinics. It allows physicians to concentrate on what they're best at—patient care." According to Campbell, "It also replaces the costly one-time investment in technology with an affordable monthly subscription fee."

Alberta Wellnet launched a Microsoft software-based ASP pilot project at the Meadowlark Clinic in Edmonton and the Taber Health Clinic, in the small town of Taber, near Calgary. The project delivers office automation software and support services over a high-speed Internet connection, including electronic clinical charting, billing and scheduling, and professional resource applications hosted and managed from a central location in Calgary. The project's first goal was to demonstrate the scalability and reliability of the Microsoft platform for handling mission-critical applications within an ASP delivery model in both urban and rural environments. The second goal involved proving to doctors that this model had real value.

The Microsoft platform was chosen because Alberta Wellnet thought it would work well for everything from desktops to servers running Windows 2000 Advanced Server operating system, SQL Server 7.0, and Microsoft Exchange Server 2000.

"Scalability and reliability were crucial, given our goal for a province-wide rollout to 5000 physicians and their administrative staff," says Campbell. "Microsoft provided a scalable architecture that can easily and remotely handle large numbers of concurrent users, saving both time and money."

Further savings were ensured thanks to the user-friendly aspects of the Microsoft platform. It provided a single point for solution administration, hosting, and management, which allowed organizations to focus their energy on their own business, not information systems management. Another important issue was privacy related to personal health information. Alberta Wellnet was confident that the Microsoft ASP solution would provide comparable security to a local area network, even while allowing authorized dissemination of private medical information.

The pilot phase saw two different groups of applications. One of them provided a professional reference tool application and the interface for the integrated solution. The other provided billing, scheduling, and clinical charting applications. The solution was hosted and integrated through network connections between the server farm in Calgary and the two clinic sites, and provided 32 computers plus thin client units and printers to the clinics.

Microsoft Consulting Services (MCS) played an important role, providing team leadership, developing the original architecture and combined networking and third-party applications needed to create a solution that positioned Alberta Wellnet as a pioneer in healthcare innovation.

The timesaving benefits of an ASP delivery model are apparent in the speed with which the pilot was developed. Only four months after planning began, the pilot was in operation. At this time, the two clinics continue to run the technology, and Alberta Wellnet now expects province-wide use due to the positive results from the pilot project.

It was agreed that trying to have all clinic staff participate in all aspects of the pilot would be a recipe for trouble, given the steep learning curve. Only 30 percent of the doctors in Taber used the solution's full functionality. There was no attempt to convert extent and archived patient data; instead only new data are processed electronically.

There are clear advantages to the solution for patient care. "Physicians have told us that the speed with which the software executes is better than if it had been on a local server," says Campbell. This is important for point-of-care solutions, such as clinical charting, ensuring efficient and knowledgeable care provision during examination. Data can be searched efficiently, which means doctors can review clinical histories and billing without wading through stacks of paper or searching outdated databases. There is also a plan underway that will allow doctors to share patient information using the instant messaging features of Microsoft Exchange 2000.

Doctors like the user-friendly aspects of the ASP-based solution. "The remote manageability of Microsoft's products frees up physicians from system and database maintenance tasks, allowing them to focus on providing quality patient care," says Campbell. To add new users, all it takes is a phone call, which in terms of cost compares favorably to calling in a consultant or hiring an onsite administrator. Doctors gave the system top marks in terms of manageability right down to the desktop; support staff in Calgary can see remote physicians' desktops and walk through problems with them. The Windows-based platform allowed the pilot project to meet each of its goals and offered some extras, including home access and electronic lab results.

But Alberta Wellnet is not through with outsourcing. They recently contracted with QHR Software Group Inc. for the health authorities and their affiliates in Alberta to purchase human resource and payroll software applications over a three-year period. The contract is the result of the Administrative Solutions Common Opportunity Initiative in which Alberta Wellnet issued an RFP for human resource, payroll, staff scheduling, and financial software applications on behalf of several Alberta health authorities.

Alberta Wellnet is also in the second year of a pilot conversion of their Pharmaceutical Information Network (PIN), which links patients, physicians, pharmacies, and other healthcare professionals to improve pharmaceutical services, such as prescription writing and fulfillment, as well as notices of possible drug interactions.

Sources: Susan Ruttan, "Patient Medication Records to Go Online for Doctors: Plan Part of Electronic Health Record," *Edmonton Journal*, March 3, 2003; Alberta Wellnet Web site, available www.albertawellnet.org, accessed May 4, 2003; "Alberta Wellnet: A Microsoft Case Study," available www.microsoft.com/canada/casestudies, accessed May 4, 2003; "Pharmacy/PIN," Western Health Information Collaborative, available www.whic.org/public/profiles/pin.html, accessed July 30, 2003.

CASE STUDY QUESTIONS

1. Analyze the Internet and the World Wide Web as a source of opportunities for Alberta Wellnet.
2. What additional Web-based systems not mentioned in the case do you think Alberta Wellnet could implement?
3. Do you think using the pilot conversion strategy helped Alberta Wellnet? How?
4. Was the ASP model a good way to implement the practice management application? Would a different model, such as in-house development, have worked as well? Why, or why not?
5. What are the management, organization, and technology issues that Alberta Wellnet needed to consider in implementing its ASP solution? The Pharmaceutical Information Network? The human resources and payroll systems? Are these all the same issues for each system?

CHAPTER

INFORMATION SYSTEMS SECURITY, QUALITY, AND CONTROL

Objectives

As a manager, you will want to ensure that your firm's systems are reliable and secure. After completing this chapter, you should be able to answer the following questions:

1. *Why are information systems so vulnerable to destruction, error, abuse, and system quality problems?*

2. *What types of controls are available for information systems?*

3. *What special measures must be taken to ensure the reliability, availability, and security of electronic commerce and digital business processes?*

4. *What are the most important software quality assurance techniques?*

5. *Why are auditing information systems and safeguarding data quality so important?*

The World Trade Center Disaster: Who Was Prepared?

On the morning of September 11, 2001, two airplanes commandeered by terrorists crashed into the World Trade Center (WTC), and a third crashed into the Pentagon, taking 3000 lives. All WTC offices were destroyed, and some nearby buildings were badly damaged and immediately evacuated. Phones lines along the east coast of the United States were jammed, making it difficult to make and receive telephone calls. Clients of telecommunications providers, such as AT&T and Verizon, with computers and switching centres in or near the World Trade Center lost services

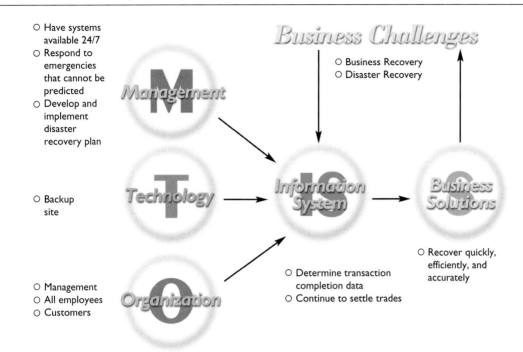

- ○ Have systems available 24/7
- ○ Respond to emergencies that cannot be predicted
- ○ Develop and implement disaster recovery plan

Management

- ○ Backup site

Technology

- ○ Management
- ○ All employees
- ○ Customers

Organization

Business Challenges

- ○ Business Recovery
- ○ Disaster Recovery

Information System

Business Solutions

- ○ Determine transaction completion data
- ○ Continue to settle trades

- ○ Recover quickly, efficiently, and accurately

altogether. Lufthansa Airlines lost telephone services for its passenger sales office in midtown Manhattan and its cargo sales office at Kennedy Airport because it had used AT&T as its primary communications provider and Verizon as the backup. Panicky customers were stalled with busy signals for three days. Lufthansa found another provider to restore phone services within a week, and it is making sure that its primary and backup systems are routed from separate locations in the city.

Merrill Lynch had more than 9000 employees working at the World Trade Center and the World Financial Center nearby. Most were unharmed and were successfully relocated to other places of work. Merrill was able to resume its business later in the day. The firm did not suffer as much as others because it had redundant telecommunications capabilities and a rock-solid disaster recovery plan.

Merrill had carried out an extensive rehearsal of their plan four months earlier, so everyone was prepared on September 11. The plan established priorities for business activities, so the company knew which activities to revive first in the event of a disruption. Then, it "qualified" all of its critical system applications and made sure the technology for restoring those applications was available in the event of a disaster. The plan included procedures for ascertaining the whereabouts of all employees, for collecting information about the damage to the firm's facilities and technology, and for selecting an appropriate response strategy. Predesignated logistics team members had assigned responsibilities for transportation, accommodations, and food. The contingency plan was designed to handle an eight-week absence from Merrill's main facilities.

Within minutes of the World Trade Center attack, Merrill's command centre was operational at one of the company's other Manhattan locations. At the new backup site, the firm was able to figure out each transaction's position when business stopped on September 11. Although the equity markets were closed, Merrill's operations staff was able to settle trades that same evening.

Sources: Juliana Gruenwald, "Communications that Won't Quit," *Fortune/CNET Tech Review,* Winter 2002; John Pallatto, "Contingency Planning," *Internet World,* May 2002; Anthony Guerra, "Recent Run-Through Helps Merrill Deal with Disaster," *Wall Street and Technology,* November 2001; Dennis K. Berman and Calmetta Coleman, "Companies Test System-Backup Plans as They Struggle to Recover Lost Data," *Wall Street Journal,* September 13, 2001.

MANAGEMENT CHALLENGES

The experiences of Lufthansa Airlines and Merrill Lynch during the World Trade Center disaster illustrate the need for organizations to take special measures to protect their information systems and ensure their continued operation. Communication disruptions, use by unauthorized people, software failures, hardware failures, natural disasters, employee errors—and terrorist attacks—can prevent information systems from running properly or running at all. As you read this chapter, you should be aware of the following management challenges:

1. Designing systems that are neither overcontrolled nor undercontrolled.
While security breaches and damage to information systems still come from organizational insiders, security breaches from outside the organization are increasing because firms pursuing electronic commerce are open to outsiders through the Internet. It is difficult for organizations to determine how open or closed they should be to protect themselves. If a system requires too many passwords, authorizations, or levels of security to access information, the system will go unused. Controls that are effective but that do not prevent authorized individuals from using a system are difficult to design.

2. Applying quality assurance standards in large systems projects. This chapter explains why the goal of zero defects in large, complex pieces of software is impossible to achieve. If the seriousness of remaining bugs cannot be ascertained, what constitutes acceptable—if not perfect—software performance? And even if meticulous design and exhaustive testing could eliminate all defects, software projects have time and budget constraints that often prevent management from devoting as much time to thoroughly testing them. Under these circumstances, it would be difficult for managers to define a standard for software quality and then enforce it.

Computer systems play such a critical role in business, government, and daily life that organizations must take special steps to protect their information systems and to ensure that they are accurate, reliable, and secure. This chapter describes how information systems can be controlled and made secure so that they serve the purposes for which they are intended.

11.1 SYSTEM VULNERABILITY AND ABUSE

Before computer automation, data about individuals or organizations were maintained and secured as paper records dispersed in separate business or organizational units. Computer-based information systems concentrate data in computer files that have the potential to be accessed by large numbers of people and by groups outside of the organization. Consequently, automated data are more susceptible to destruction, fraud, error, and misuse.

When computer systems fail to run or work as required, firms that depend heavily on computers experience a serious loss of business function. The longer the computer systems are down, the more serious are the consequences for the firm. Firms that need Web sites to be continuously available online for electronic commerce stand to lose millions of dollars for every business day that the sites are not working. For example, a business might lose over $14 000 for every minute of downtime for its electronic commerce or supply chain management applications (The Standish Group, 2001). Some firms relying on computers to process their critical business transactions might experience a total loss of business function if they lose computer capability for more than a few days.

WHY SYSTEMS ARE VULNERABLE

Large amounts of data stored in electronic form are vulnerable to many more kinds of threats than when they exist in manual form. Table 11.1 lists the most common threats against computerized information systems. These threats can stem from technical, organizational, and environmental factors compounded by poor management decisions.

TABLE 11.1	THREATS TO COMPUTERIZED INFORMATION SYSTEMS

Hardware failure	Fire
Software failure	Electrical problems
Personnel actions	User errors
Terminal access penetration	Program changes
Theft of data, services, equipment	Telecommunications problems

Advances in telecommunications and computer software have magnified these vulnerabilities. Through telecommunications networks, information systems in different locations can be interconnected. The potential for unauthorized access, abuse, or fraud is not limited to a single location but can occur at any access point in the network.

Additionally, more complex and diverse hardware, software, organizational, and personnel arrangements are required for telecommunications networks, creating new areas and opportunities for penetration and manipulation. Wireless networks using radio-based technology are even more vulnerable to penetration because radio frequency bands are easy to scan. Local area networks (LANs) that use the 802.11b (Wi-Fi) standard can be easily penetrated by outsiders armed with laptops, wireless cards, external antennae, and freeware hacking software. Hackers can use these tools to detect unprotected Wi-Fi networks, monitor their traffic, and in some cases, use them to gain access to the Internet or to corporate networks. Although the range of Wi-Fi networks is only a little more than 100 metres, it can be extended up to 400 metres by using external antennae. The Internet poses special problems because it was explicitly designed to be accessed easily by people on different computer systems. The vulnerabilities of telecommunications networks are illustrated in Figure 11.1.

Hackers and Computer Viruses

The explosive growth of Internet use by businesses and individuals has been accompanied by rising reports of Internet security breaches. The main concern comes from unwanted intruders,

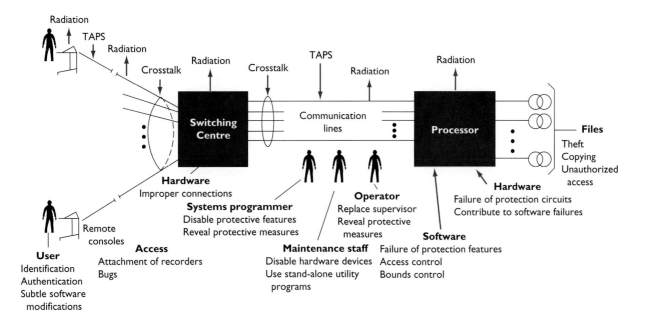

Figure 11.1 Telecommunications network vulnerabilities. Telecommunications networks are highly vulnerable to natural failure of hardware and software and to misuse by programmers, computer operators, maintenance staff, and end users. It is possible to tap communications lines and illegally intercept data. High-speed transmission over twisted wire communications channels causes interference called crosstalk. Radiation can disrupt a network at various points as well.

hacker
_____

A person who gains unauthorized access to a computer network for profit, criminal
mischief, or personal pleasure.

denial of service attack
_____

Flooding a network server or
Web server with false communications or requests for services
in order to crash the network.

computer viruses
_____

Rogue software programs that
are difficult to detect, which
spread rapidly through computer systems, destroying data
or disrupting processing and
memory systems.

or hackers, who use the latest technology and their skills to break into supposedly secure computers or to disable them. A **hacker** is a person who gains unauthorized access to a computer network for profit, criminal mischief, or personal pleasure. For example, confidential financial information from online student loan applications was accessed by a hacker who breached the Manitoba government's main Web site over a period of a week. While inside, the hacker had access to personal financial information from students and their families who completed online application forms for the Manitoba student loan program. The 215 applicants whose data may have been compromised were advised to contact their financial institutions to ensure there was no unauthorized use of the information. There are many more ways that hacker break-ins can harm businesses. Some malicious intruders have planted logic bombs, Trojan horses, and other software that can hide in a system or network until executed at a specified time. (A *Trojan horse* is a software program that appears legitimate but contains a second hidden function that may cause damage.) In **denial of service attacks**, hackers flood a network server or Web server with many thousands of false communications or requests for services in order to crash the network. The network receives so many queries that it cannot keep up with them and is, thus, unavailable to service legitimate requests. The cost of these attacks for businesses is rising at an alarming rate. The Window on Organizations describes the harm created by online theft of credit card numbers.

Serious system disruptions have been caused by hackers propagating **computer viruses**. These are rogue software programs that spread rampantly from system to system, clogging computer memory or destroying programs or data. Many thousands of viruses are known to exist, with 200 or more new viruses created each month. Table 11.2 describes the characteristics of some common viruses.

Many viruses today are spread through the Internet, from files of downloaded software or from files attached to e-mail transmissions. Viruses can also invade computerized information systems from other computer networks as well as from "infected" diskettes from an outside source or infected machines. The potential for massive damage and loss from future computer viruses remains. The Chernobyl, Melissa, and ILOVEYOU viruses caused extensive PC dam-

TABLE 11.2	**EXAMPLES OF COMPUTER VIRUSES**
Virus Name	Description
Concept, Melissa	Macro viruses that exist inside executable programs called macros, which provide functions within such programs as Microsoft Word. Can be spread when Word documents are attached to e-mail. Can copy from one document to another and delete files.
Code Red, Nimda	"Worm" type viruses that arrive attached to e-mail and spread from computer to computer. When launched, they e-mail themselves to computers running Microsoft operating systems and software, slowing Internet traffic as they propagate and circulate.
ILOVEYOU (Love Bug)	Script virus written in script programming language, such as VBScript or JavaScript. Overwrites.jpg and.mp3 files; uses Microsoft Outlook and Internet Relay Chat to spread to other systems.
Monkey	Makes the hard disk look like it has failed because Windows will not run.
Chernobyl	File infecting virus. Erases a computer's hard drive and ROM BIOS (Basic Input/Output System).
Junkie	A "multipartite" virus that can infect files as well as the boot sector of the hard drive (the section of a personal computer [PC] hard drive that the PC first reads when it boots up). May cause memory conflicts.
Form	Makes a clicking sound with each keystroke but only on the 18th day of the month. It may corrupt data on the floppy disks it infects.

WHAT CAN BE DONE ABOUT INTERNET CREDIT CARD THEFT?

The former Soviet Union has spawned a number of organizations that are profiting from electronic commerce. One such organization, headquartered in Odessa, Ukraine, calls itself "the family." It is a global company, buying and selling its products through both Web sites and e-mail, with payment through such online sites as www.WebMoney.ru ("ru" indicates Russia). While its product prices fluctuate, negotiations take place through e-mail. Management is keeping its information and transactions secret, mainly by constantly switching its sites and e-mail addresses. Its customers are global, although most of them are in the former Soviet Union, Eastern Europe, and Asia (primarily Malaysia). The organization is known for rapid, quality service, and it even advertises it products using online banners. Because its products are digital, they are delivered over the Internet. What is different about this company is that it sells stolen credit card numbers. The numbers are purchased from suppliers who are hackers capable of obtaining them by breaking into the computer systems of online merchants.

The problem for the customers of "the family" is that the credit card numbers must be genuine because they are sold to people who will use them to steal products or funds. The seller of the numbers apparently has no way to prove that the numbers it sells are genuine. It is solely based on the seller's reputation; "the family" must rely on its customers' successful use of the numbers. The problem for the rest of us is that the numbers usually are genuine, and so any of us can find an unknown person using our credit cards. Stealing credit card numbers is a large business, and "the family" is but one of a number of organizations engaged in credit card theft. Internet retail merchants face a loss of about $1.4 billion annually, according to a recent survey by Celent Communications, a market research firm. Moreover, online sales using fraudulent credit cards have reached 0.25 percent of total sales using VISA and MasterCard credit cards, while the offline percentage of fraudulent use is only 0.09 percent. The

difference is enormous, with fraudulent online sales topping $2.8 billion annually versus $1.2 billion offline. Richard Power, editorial director of the Computer Security Institute, an association of computer security professionals, says that "the financial losses involved in this kind of theft are underestimated, underreported, and underacknowledged," and he estimates the actual cost worldwide is in the "double-digit billions."

The problem for organizations policing and trying to reduce the fraudulent use of credit cards is that the sellers of credit card numbers use very simple methods to combat detection. The sellers use chat rooms and Web sites to communicate with their customers, but they protect themselves mainly by switching Web site locations, chat rooms, and e-mail addresses very often. The decentralized Internet has become so enormous that it usually takes a huge amount of effort and time to locate an individual or organization that does not want to be found. By the time they are found, they have already moved. Moreover, with its international character, even if they are located, being able to stop them and punish them is exceedingly complex and a very slow process.

In February 2000, The Bank of Nova Scotia revealed that 7000 of its Visa customers were exposed to the American computer security breach that left up to eight million VISA and MasterCard credit card accounts vulnerable to fraud. The total number of Canadian accounts whose information was available to the hackers was 60 000 VISA cardholders and 40 000 MasterCard holders.

To Think About: What management and business problems have been created by credit card theft over the Internet? What measures can be taken to stop this illegal action?

Sources: Matt Richtel, "Credit Card Theft Thrives Online as a Global Market," *New York Times*, May 13, 2002; Tyler Hamilton, "7,000 Visa Clients Exposed to Hacker, Bank Says," *The Winnipeg Free Press*, February 20, 20003; and Mark Baard, "Security Obstacles Plague E-Businesses," *SearchEbusiness*, April 23, 2002, available **http://searchcio.techtarget.com/originalContent/0,289142,sid19_gci818 723,00.html**, accessed July 30, 2003.

---

age worldwide after spreading through infected e mail. Now viruses are spreading to wireless computing devices. Mobile device viruses could pose a serious threat to enterprise computing because so many wireless devices are now linked to corporate information systems. A recent virus was named after Canadian singer Avril Lavigne. A new worm, a form of virus, forces users to visit Lavigne's Web site. The virus searches each PC's hard drive for hypertext markup language (HTML) files that may contain e-mail addresses and then uses its own built-in simple mail transfer protocol (SMTP) engine to send copies of itself to whatever addresses it finds. The virus was released the same week Lavigne was nominated for five Grammy awards.

Organizations can use antivirus software and screening procedures to reduce the chances of infection. **Antivirus software** is designed to check computer systems and disks for the presence of various computer viruses. Often, the software can eliminate the virus from the infected area. However, most antivirus software is only effective against viruses already known when the software is written—to protect their systems, management must continually update their antivirus software. (See Figure 11.2.)

antivirus software

Software designed to detect and often eliminate computer viruses from an information system.

Figure 11.2 Many organizations use antivirus software to check computer systems and disks for the presence of various computer viruses. Symantec's Norton Antivirus software illustrated here identifies viruses that have infected a system and provides tools for eradicating them.

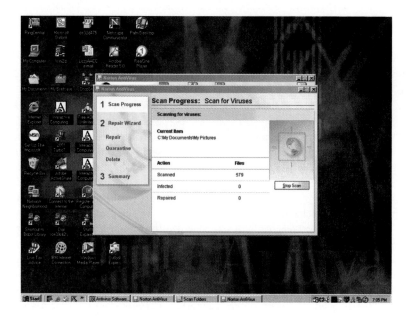

CONCERNS FOR SYSTEM DEVELOPERS AND USERS

The heightened vulnerability of automated data has created special concerns for the builders and users of information systems. These concerns include disaster, security, and administrative error.

Disaster

Computer hardware, programs, data files, and other equipment can be destroyed by fires, power failures, or other disasters. It may take many years and millions of dollars to reconstruct destroyed data files and computer programs, and some may not be replaceable. If an organization needs them to function on a day-to-day basis, it will no longer be able to operate. This is why such companies as National Trust employ elaborate emergency backup facilities. National Trust, a large bank in Ontario, Canada, uses uninterruptable power supply technology provided by International Power Machines (IPM) because electrical power at its Mississauga location fluctuates frequently.

Rather than build their own backup facilities, many firms contract with disaster recovery firms, such as Traxion in Toronto, Ontario, and Comdisco Disaster Recovery Services in Rosemont, Illinois. These disaster recovery firms provide hot sites housing spare computers at locations around the country where subscribing firms can run their critical applications in an emergency. Disaster recovery services offer backup for client-server systems as well as traditional mainframe applications. As firms become increasingly digital and depend on systems that must be constantly available, disaster recovery planning has taken on new importance.

Security

security

Policies, procedures, and technical measures used to prevent unauthorized access, alteration, theft, or physical damage to information systems.

Security refers to the policies, procedures, and technical measures used to prevent unauthorized access, alteration, theft, or physical damage to information systems. Security can be promoted with an array of techniques and tools to safeguard computer hardware, software, communications networks, and data. We have already discussed some disaster protection measures. While the primary focus of security in this chapter is on nonphysical security issues, physical security against theft is also important. Hardware can be fairly easy to steal, with disastrous consequences. In 2003, a computer hard drive containing confidential information about individual Canadians and businesses was stolen and later found. The drive was reported missing from the Regina office of ISM Canada. It contained personal client information on dozens of companies, including 650 000 customers of Investors Group, client information on Saskatchewan's Crown corporations, and tax data on 43 000 Manitoba businesses. Regina police arrested an individual for the theft after they recovered the drive. "Right now, our forensic examiners are looking to confirm if any of the information had indeed been accessed," said Sgt. Rick Bourassa. ISM was still investigating how the drive was taken, in order to prevent this type of breach from being repeated. Other tools and techniques for promoting security will be discussed in subsequent sections.

Errors

Computers also can serve as instruments of error, severely disrupting or destroying an organization's record keeping and operations. For instance, poor software caused the crash of a Mars Polar Lander operated by the U.S. National Aeronautics and Space Administration (NASA) in December 1999. One sensor erroneously detected that the craft's legs had popped out and shut down its rocket engines prematurely, even though another sensor designed to alert the craft when it touched ground did not show this happening. The landing system software had not been programmed to compare the feedback from both sensors (Wessel, 2001). Errors in automated systems can occur at many points in the processing cycle: through data entry, program error, computer operations, and hardware. Figure 11.3 illustrates all of the points in a typical processing cycle where errors can occur.

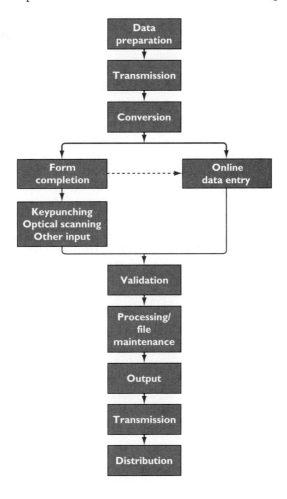

Figure 11.3 Points in the processing cycle where errors can occur. Each of the points illustrated in this figure represents a control point where special automated or manual procedures should be established to reduce the risk of errors during processing.

System Quality Problems: Software and Data

In addition to disasters, viruses, and security breaches, defective software and data also pose a constant threat to information systems, causing untold losses in productivity. An undiscovered error in a company's credit software or erroneous financial data can result in losses of millions of dollars. A hidden software problem in AT&T's long distance system brought down that system, bringing the New York–based financial exchanges to a halt and interfering with billions of dollars worth of business around the country for a number of hours. Modern passenger and commercial vehicles are increasingly dependent on computer programs for critical functions. A hidden software defect in a braking system could result in the loss of lives.

Bugs and Defects

A major problem with software is the presence of hidden **bugs** or program code defects. Studies have shown that it is virtually impossible to eliminate all bugs from large programs. The main source of bugs is the complexity of program code. Even a relatively small program of several hundred lines will contain tens of decisions leading to hundreds or even thousands of different paths. Important programs within most corporations are usually much larger, containing tens of thousands or even millions of lines of code, each with many times the choices and paths of the smaller programs. This type of complexity is difficult to document and design—designers document some reactions wrongly or fail to consider some possibilities. Studies show that about 60 percent of errors discovered during testing are a result of specifications in the design documentation that were missing, ambiguous, in error, or in conflict.

Zero defects, a goal of the total quality management movement, cannot be achieved in larger programs. Complete testing simply is not possible. Fully testing programs that contain thousands of choices and millions of paths would require thousands of years. Eliminating software bugs is an exercise in diminishing returns because it would take proportionately longer testing to detect and eliminate obscure residual bugs (Littlewood and Strigini, 1993). Even

bugs

Program code defects or errors.

with rigorous testing, one could not know for sure that a piece of software was dependable until the product proved itself after much operational use. The message? We cannot eliminate all bugs, and we cannot know with certainty the seriousness of the bugs that do remain.

The Maintenance Nightmare

Another reason that systems are unreliable is that computer software traditionally has been a nightmare to maintain. Maintenance, the process of modifying a system already in use, is the most expensive phase of the systems development process. In most organizations, nearly half of information systems staff time is spent in the maintenance of existing systems.

Why are maintenance costs so high? One major reason is organizational change. The firm may experience large internal changes in structure or leadership, or change may come from the surrounding environment. These organizational changes affect information requirements. Another reason appears to be software complexity, as measured by the number and size of interrelated software programs and subprograms and the complexity of the flow of program logic between them (Banker, Datar, Kemerer, and Zweig, 1993). A third common cause of long-term maintenance problems is faulty systems analysis and design, especially analysis of information requirements. Some studies of large transaction processing systems (TPS) by TRW Inc. (now Northrup Grumman), have found that a majority of system errors—64 percent—result from early analysis errors (Mazzucchelli, 1985).

Figure 11.4 illustrates the cost of correcting errors on the basis of the experience reported by consultants. If errors are detected early, during analysis and design, the cost to the systems development effort is small. But if they are not discovered until after programming, testing, or conversion has been completed, the costs can soar astronomically. A minor logic error, for example, that could take one hour to correct during the analysis and design stage could take 10, 40, and 90 times as long to correct during programming, conversion, and postimplementation, respectively.

Data Quality Problems

The most common source of information systems failure is poor data quality. Data that are inaccurate, untimely, or inconsistent with other sources of information can create serious operational and financial problems for businesses. When faulty data go unnoticed, they can lead to incorrect decisions, product recalls, and even financial losses (Redman, 1998). Companies cannot pursue aggressive marketing and customer relationship management strategies without high-quality data about their customers. Table 11.3 describes examples of data quality problems.

Poor data quality may stem from errors during data input or faulty information system and database design (Wand and Wang, 1996; Strong, Lee, and Wang, 1997). In the following sections, we examine how organizations can deal with data and software quality problems as well as other threats to information systems.

Figure 11.4 The cost of errors over the systems development cycle. The most common, most severe, and most expensive system errors develop in the early design stages. They involve faulty requirements analysis. Errors in program logic or syntax are much less common, less severe, and less costly to repair than design errors.
Source: Alberts, 1976.

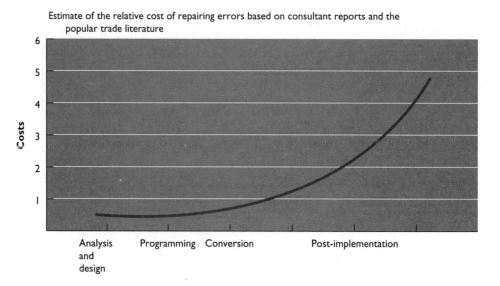

Estimate of the relative cost of repairing errors based on consultant reports and the popular trade literature

TABLE 11.3	EXAMPLES OF DATA QUALITY PROBLEMS

Organization	Data Quality Problem
Royal Bank of Canada	Databases contained "garbage" characters for postal codes because employees did not have the correct client addresses to enter. When the bank tried to target a particular geographical area to promote a popular Christmas loan, a notable percentage of clients came up with the postal code HOHOHO, and the bank could not obtain accurate information for mailings.
Sears Roebuck	Because each of its businesses, including retail, home services, credit, and Web site, had its own information systems with conflicting customer data, Sears could not effectively pursue cross-selling among its customers. Sears needed to develop a massive data warehouse that consolidated and cleansed the data from all of these systems in order to create a single customer list.
Paint Bull	Nearly half the names in its purchased mailing lists of prospective customers were inaccurate or out of date. Paint Bull lost $10 for every promotional package of videos and catalogues that was returned as undeliverable.
FBI	A study of the U.S. FBI's computerized criminal record systems found a total of 54.1 percent of the records in the National Crime Information Center System were inaccurate, ambiguous, or incomplete. The FBI has taken some steps to correct these problems, but computerized criminal history records are used to screen employees in both the public and private sectors. Inaccurate records could unjustly deny people employment.
Supermarkets	Several studies have established that 5 to 12 percent of barcode sales at retail supermarkets are erroneous and that the average ratio of overcharges to undercharges runs 4:1.

Additional material on how to combat spam, bugs, and spyware (prepared by David Chan at York University) can be found on the Companion Website at www.pearsoned.ca/laudon.

11.2 CREATING A CONTROL ENVIRONMENT

To minimize errors, disasters, interruptions of service, computer crimes, and breaches of security, special policies and procedures must be incorporated into the design and implementation of information systems. The combination of manual and automated measures that safeguard information systems and ensure that they perform according to management standards is termed controls. **Controls** consist of all of the methods, policies, and organizational procedures that ensure the safety of the organization's assets, the accuracy and reliability of its accounting records, and operational adherence to management standards.

In the past, the control of information systems was treated as an afterthought, addressed only toward the end of implementation, just before the system was installed. Today, however, organizations are so critically dependent on information systems that vulnerabilities and control issues must be identified as early as possible. The control of an information system must be an integral part of its design. Users and developers of systems must pay close attention to controls throughout the system's life span.

controls

All of the methods, policies, and procedures that ensure protection of the organization's assets, accuracy and reliability of its records, and operational adherence to management standards.

GENERAL CONTROLS AND APPLICATION CONTROLS

Computer systems are controlled by a combination of general controls and application controls. **General controls** govern the design, security, and use of computer programs and the security of data files in general throughout the organization's information technology infrastructure. On the whole, general controls apply to all computerized applications and consist of a combination of hardware, software, and manual procedures that create an overall control environment. **Application controls** are specific controls unique to each computerized application, such as payroll or order processing. They consist of controls applied from the business functional area of a particular system and from programmed procedures.

general controls

Overall controls that establish a framework for controlling the design, security, and use of computer programs throughout an organization.

application controls

Specific controls unique to each computerized application.

General Controls and Data Security

General controls include software controls, physical hardware controls, computer operations controls, data security controls, controls over the systems implementation process, and administrative controls. Table 11.4 describes the function of each of these controls.

TABLE 11.4   GENERAL CONTROLS

Type of General Control	Description
Software controls	Monitor the use of system software and prevent unauthorized access of software programs, system software, and computer programs. System software is an important control area because it performs overall control functions for the programs that directly process data and data files.
Hardware controls	Ensure that computer hardware is physically secure, and check for equipment malfunction. Computer equipment should be specially protected against fires and extremes of temperature and humidity. Organizations that are critically dependent on their computers also must make provisions for backup or continued operation to maintain constant service.
Computer operation controls	Oversee the work of the computer department to ensure that programmed procedures are consistently and correctly applied to the storage and processing of data. They include controls over the setup of computer processing jobs and computer operation, and backup and recovery procedures for processing that ends abnormally.
Data security controls	Ensure that valuable business data files on either disk or tape are not subject to unauthorized access, change, or destruction while they are in use or in storage.
Implementation controls	Audit the systems development process at various points to ensure that the process is properly controlled and managed. The systems development audit looks for the presence of formal reviews by users and management at various stages of development; the level of user involvement at each stage of implementation; and the use of a formal cost-benefit methodology in establishing system feasibility. The audit should look for the use of controls and quality assurance techniques for program development, conversion, and testing and for complete and thorough system, user, and operations documentation.
Administrative controls	Formalized standards, rules, procedures, and control disciplines to ensure that the organization's general and application controls are properly executed and enforced.

data security controls

Controls to ensure that data files on either disk or tape are not subject to unauthorized access, change, or destruction.

administrative controls

Formalized standards, rules, procedures, and disciplines to ensure that the organization's controls are properly executed and enforced.

Although most of these general controls are designed and maintained by information systems specialists, **data security controls** and **administrative controls** require input and oversight from end users and business managers. For example, information systems specialists would be responsible for certain aspects of data security controls, such as making computer terminals available only to authorized users or using system software and application software to create a series of passwords that users would need in order to access systems. Users, however, would specify the business rules for accessing data, such as what positions in the organization have rights to view and update the data.

Figure 11.5 illustrates the security allowed for two sets of users of an online personnel database with sensitive information, such as employees' salaries, benefits, and medical histories. One set of users consists of all employees who perform clerical functions, such as inputting employee data into the system. All individuals with this type of profile can update the system but can neither read nor update sensitive fields, such as salary, medical history, or earnings data. Another profile applies to a divisional manager, who cannot update the system but who can read all of the employee data fields for his or her division, including medical history and salary. These profiles would be established and maintained by a data security system based on access rules supplied by business groups. The data security system illustrated in Figure 11.5 provides very fine-grained security restrictions, such as allowing authorized personnel users to inquire about all employee information, except in confidential fields, such as salary or medical history.

Business users should be responsible for establishing administrative controls, which are formal organizational procedures to make sure that all of the other general and application controls are properly enforced. These controls ensure that job functions are designed to minimize the risk of errors or fraudulent manipulation of the organization's assets. For instance, individuals responsible for operating systems (who typically work in the information systems department) should not also be able to initiate transactions that change the assets held in these systems. Administrative controls should include written policies and procedures establishing formal standards for information systems operations and clearly specified accountabilities and responsibilities. Administrative controls include mechanisms for supervising personnel involved in control procedures to make sure that the controls for an information system perform as intended.

SECURITY PROFILE 1

User: **Personnel Dept. Clerk**

Location: **Division 1**

Employee Identification
Codes with This Profile: 00753, 27834, 37665, 44116

Data Field Restrictions	Type of Access
All employee data for Division 1 only	Read and Update
• Medical history data	None
• Salary	None
• Pensionable earnings	None

SECURITY PROFILE 2

User: **Divisional Personnel Manager**

Location: **Division 1**

Employee Identification
Codes with This Profile: 27321

Data Field Restrictions	Type of Access
All employee data for Division 1 only	Read Only

Figure 11.5 Security profiles for a personnel system. These two examples represent two security profiles or data security patterns that might be found in a personnel system. Depending on the security profile, a user would have certain restrictions on access to various systems, locations, or data in an organization.

Additional material on biometrics (prepared by David Chan at York University) can be found on the Companion Website at www.pearsoned.ca/laudon.

Application Controls

Application controls include both automated and manual procedures that ensure that only authorized data are completely and accurately processed by an application. Application controls can be classified as (1) input controls, (2) processing controls, and (3) output controls.

Input controls check data for accuracy and completeness when they enter the system. There are specific input controls for input authorization, data conversion, data editing, and error handling. **Processing controls** establish that data are complete and accurate during updating. Run control totals, computer matching, and programmed edit checks are used for this purpose. **Output controls** ensure that the results of computer processing are accurate, complete, and properly distributed.

Table 11.5 provides more detailed examples of each type of application control. Not all of the application controls discussed here are used in every information system. Some systems require more of these controls than others, depending on the importance of the data and the nature of the application.

PROTECTING THE DIGITAL FIRM

As companies increasingly rely on digital networks for their revenue and operations, they need to take additional steps to ensure that their systems and applications are always available to support their digital business processes.

High-Availability Computing

In a digital firm environment, information technology (IT) infrastructures must provide a continuous level of service availability across distributed computing platforms. Many factors can disrupt the performance of a Web site, including network failure, heavy Internet traffic, and exhausted server resources. Computer failures, interruptions, and downtime can translate into disgruntled customers, millions of dollars in lost sales, and the inability to perform critical

input controls

The procedures to check data for accuracy and completeness when they enter the system.

processing controls

The routines for establishing that data are complete and accurate during updating.

output controls

Measures that ensure that the results of computer processing are accurate, complete, and properly distributed.

TABLE 11.5   APPLICATION CONTROLS

Name of Control	Type of Application Control	Description
Control totals	Input, Processing	Totals established beforehand for input and processing transactions. These totals can range from a simple document count to totals for quantity fields, such as total sales amount (for a batch of transactions). Computer programs count the totals from transactions input or processed.
Edit checks	Input	Programmed routines that can be performed to edit input data for errors before they are processed. Transactions that do not meet edit criteria will be rejected. For example, data might be checked to make sure they were in the right format (a nine-digit Social Insurance Number should not contain any alphabetic characters).
Computer matching	Input, processing	Matches input data with information held in master or suspense files, with unmatched items noted for investigation. For example, a matching program might match employee time cards with a payroll master file and report missing or duplicate time cards.
Run control totals	Processing, output	Balance the total of transactions processed with total number of transactions input or output.
Report distribution logs	Output	Documentation specifying that authorized recipients have received their reports, cheques, or other critical documents.

online transaction processing

Transaction processing mode in which transactions entered online are immediately processed by the computer.

fault-tolerant computer systems

Systems that contain extra hardware, software, and power supply components that create an environment that provides continuous uninterrupted service.

high-availability computing

Tools and technologies, including backup hardware resources, to enable a system to recover quickly from a crash.

disaster recovery plan

Plan for running the business in the event of a computer outage. Includes organizational procedures as well as backup processing, storage, and database capabilities.

internal transactions. Firms with critical applications requiring online transaction processing, such as those in the airline and financial service industries, have traditionally used fault-tolerant computer systems to ensure 100 percent availability. In **online transaction processing**, transactions entered online are immediately processed by the computer. A high volume of changes to databases, reporting, or requests for information occur each instant. **Fault-tolerant computer systems** contain redundant hardware, software, and power supply components that create an environment that provides continuous, uninterrupted service. Fault-tolerant computers contain extra memory chips, processors, and disk storage devices that can back up a system and keep it running to prevent failure. They can use special software routines or self-checking logic built into their circuitry to detect hardware failures and automatically switch to a backup device. Parts from these computers can be removed and repaired without disruption to the computer system. E-Smart Direct Services, Inc. of Etobicoke, Ontario, a provider of electronic payment processing and authorization services for retailers and financial institutions, needs a technology platform with 100-percent, 24-hour system availability. The company uses fault-tolerant systems from Stratus for this purpose.

Fault tolerance should be distinguished from **high-availability computing**. Both fault tolerance and high-availability computing are designed to maximize application and system availability. Both use backup hardware resources. However, high-availability computing helps firms recover quickly from a crash, while fault tolerance promises continuous availability and the elimination of recovery time altogether. High-availability computing environments are a minimum requirement for firms with heavy electronic commerce processing or that depend on digital networks for their internal operations. High availability computing requires an assortment of tools and technologies to ensure maximum performance of computer systems and networks, including redundant servers, mirroring, load balancing, clustering, storage area networks (see Chapter 6), and a good **disaster recovery plan**. The firm's computing platform must be extremely robust with scalable processing power, storage, and bandwidth.

Disaster recovery planning devises plans for the restoration of computing and communications services after a disruptive event, such as an earthquake, flood, or terrorist attack, has occurred. Business managers and information technology specialists need to work together to determine what kind of plan is necessary and which systems and business functions are most critical to the company. The Manager's Toolkit describes the major elements of a disaster recovery plan.

MIS IN ACTION: MANAGER'S TOOLKIT

HOW TO DEVELOP A DISASTER RECOVERY PLAN
Conduct a business impact analysis to identify the firm's most critical systems and the impact a system outage would have on the business. Managers need to determine the maximum amount of time the business can survive with its systems down and what parts of the business need to be restored first.

■ Assess the risk of particular disasters, such as floods, power outages, or terrorist attacks, occurring at your specific company. (See the discussion of risk assessment in the following section.)

■ Identify the most mission-critical applications, the files they use, and where these files and applications are located.

■ Develop an action plan for handling mission-critical applications, such as using manual processes or running these applications at a disaster recovery service or backup computer system at another location.

■ Outline responsibilities of individual staff members and procedures to follow during a disaster, including how to locate and communicate with employees.

■ Test the disaster recovery plan at least once a year.

■ Use a consistent planning process and methodology so that all business groups understand the ground rules and how disaster planning will be funded.

■ Make sure you have the backing and support of senior management to ensure compliance.

Load balancing distributes large numbers of access requests across multiple servers. The requests are directed to the most available server so that no single device is overwhelmed. If one server starts to get swamped, requests are forwarded to another server with more capacity. **Mirroring** uses a backup server that duplicates all of the processes and transactions of the primary server. If the primary server fails, the backup server can immediately take its place without any interruption in service. However, server mirroring is very expensive because each server must be mirrored by an identical server whose only purpose is to be available in the event of a failure. Clustering is a less expensive technique for ensuring continued availability. High-availability **clustering** links two computers together so that the second computer can act as a backup to the primary computer. If the primary computer fails, the second computer picks up its processing without any pause in the system. (Computers can also be clustered together as a single computing resource to speed up processing.)

Many companies lack the resources to provide a high-availability computing environment on their own. **Management service providers (MSPs)**, which we introduced in Chapter 6, can handle such tasks as management of networks, systems, storage, and security for subscribing clients. Businesses that want to maintain their own networks, servers, desktops, and Web sites but that do not have the resources to monitor them can outsource the work to MSPs.

Internet Security Challenges

High-availability computing also requires a security infrastructure for electronic commerce and electronic business. Large public networks, including the Internet, are more vulnerable because they are virtually open to anyone; and because they are so huge, when abuses do occur, they can have an enormously widespread impact. When the Internet becomes part of the corporate network, the organization's information systems can be vulnerable to actions from outsiders. The architecture of a Web-based application typically includes a Web client, a server, and corporate information systems linked to databases. Each of these components presents security challenges and vulnerabilities, which are illustrated in Figure 11.6 (Joshi, Aref, Ghafoor, and Spafford, 2001).

Computers that are constantly connected to the Internet via cable modem or digital subscriber line (DSL) are more open to penetration by outsiders because they use a fixed Internet address where they can be more easily identified. (With dial-up service, a temporary Internet address is assigned for each session.) A fixed Internet address creates a fixed target for hackers.

Electronic commerce and electronic business require companies to be both more open and more closed at the same time. To benefit from electronic commerce, supply chain management, and other digital business processes, companies need to be open to outsiders, such as customers, suppliers, and trading partners. Corporate systems must also be extended outside the organization so that they can be accessed by employees working with wireless and other mobile computing devices. Yet, these systems must also be closed to hackers and other

load balancing

Distribution of large numbers of requests for access among multiple servers so that no single device is overwhelmed.

mirroring

Duplicating all the processes and transactions of a server on a backup server to prevent any interruption in service if the primary server fails.

clustering

Linking two computers together so that the second computer can act as a backup to the primary computer or speed up processing.

management service provider (MSP)

Company that provides network, systems, storage, and security management for subscribing clients.

Figure 11.6 Internet security challenges. There are security challenges at each of the layers of an Internet computing environment and in the communications between the client and server layers.

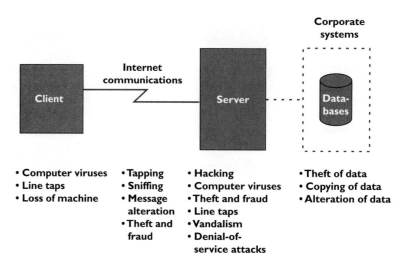

- Computer viruses
- Line taps
- Loss of machine

- Tapping
- Sniffing
- Message alteration
- Theft and fraud

- Hacking
- Computer viruses
- Theft and fraud
- Line taps
- Vandalism
- Denial-of-service attacks

- Theft of data
- Copying of data
- Alteration of data

intruders. The new IT infrastructure requires a new security culture that allows businesses to straddle this fine line. Corporations need to extend their security policies to include procedures for suppliers and other business partners.

Businesses linking to the Internet or transmitting information via intranets and extranets require special security procedures and technologies. Chapter 9 described the use of *firewalls* to prevent unauthorized users from accessing private networks. As growing numbers of businesses expose their networks to Internet traffic, firewalls are becoming a necessity.

A firewall is generally placed between internal LANs and WANs (wide area networks) and external networks, such as the Internet. The firewall controls access to the organization's internal networks by acting like a gatekeeper that examines each user's credentials before he or she can access the network. The firewall identifies names, Internet Protocol (IP) addresses, applications, and other characteristics of incoming traffic. It checks this information against the access rules that have been programmed into the system by the network administrator. The firewall prevents unauthorized communication into and out of the network, allowing the organization to enforce a security policy on traffic flowing between its network and the Internet (Oppliger, 1997).

To create a good firewall, someone must write and maintain the internal rules identifying in very fine detail the people, applications, or addresses that are allowed or rejected. Firewalls can deter, but not completely prevent, network penetration from outsiders and should be viewed as one element in an overall security plan. In order to deal effectively with Internet security, broader corporate policies and procedures, user responsibilities, and security awareness training may be required (Segev, Porra, and Roldan, 1998).

intrusion detection system

Tools to monitor the most vulnerable points in a network to detect and deter unauthorized intruders.

In addition to firewalls, commercial security vendors now provide intrusion detection tools and services to protect against suspicious network traffic. **Intrusion detection systems** feature full-time monitoring tools placed at the most vulnerable points or "hot spots" of corporate networks to continually detect and deter intruders. Scanning software looks for known problems such as bad passwords, checks to see if important files have been removed or modified, and sends warnings of vandalism or system administration errors. Monitoring software examines events as they are happening to identify security attacks in progress. The intrusion detection tool can also be customized to shut down a particularly sensitive part of a network if it receives unauthorized traffic.

Security and Electronic Commerce

Security of electronic communications is a major control issue for companies engaged in electronic commerce. It is essential that commerce-related data of buyers and sellers be kept private when they are transmitted electronically. The data being transmitted also must be protected against being purposefully altered by someone other than the sender, so that, for example, stock market execution orders or product orders accurately represent the wishes of buyers and sellers.

Much online commerce continues to be handled through private electronic data interchange (EDI) networks usually run over value-added networks (VANs). VANs are relatively secure and reliable. However, because they have to be privately maintained and run on high-speed private lines, VANs are expensive, easily costing a company $100 000 per month. They also are inflexible, being connected only to a limited number of sites and companies. As a result, the Internet is emerging as the network technology of choice. EDI transactions on the Internet run from one-half to one-tenth the cost of VAN-based transactions.

Many organizations rely on encryption to protect sensitive information transmitted over the Internet and other networks. **Encryption** is the coding and scrambling of messages to prevent unauthorized access to or understanding of the data being transmitted. A message can be encrypted by applying a secret numerical code called an encryption key so that it is transmitted as a scrambled set of characters. (The key consists of a large group of letters, numbers, and symbols.) In order to be read, the message must be decrypted (unscrambled) with a matching key.

There are several alternative methods of encryption, but "public key" encryption is becoming popular. Public key encryption, illustrated in Figure 11.7, uses two different keys, one private and one public. The keys are mathematically related so that data encrypted with one key only can be decrypted using the other key. To send and receive messages, communicators first create separate pairs of private and public keys. The public key is kept in a directory, and the private key must be kept secret. The sender encrypts a message with the recipient's public key. On receiving the message, the recipient uses his or her private key to decrypt it.

Encryption is especially useful to shield messages on the Internet and other public networks because they are less secure than private networks. Encryption helps protect transmission of payment data, such as credit card information, and addresses the problems of authentication and message integrity. **Authentication** refers to the ability of each party to know that the other parties are who they claim to be. In the nonelectronic world, we use our signatures. (Bank-by-mail systems avoid the need for signatures on cheques they issue to their customers by using well-protected private networks where the source of the request for payment is recorded and can be proven. Microsoft provides an online identification service called Passport for this purpose, authenticating user identification when any Microsoft Web service is accessed.) **Message integrity** is the ability to be certain that the message being sent arrives without being copied or changed.

Digital signatures and digital certificates help with authentication. The Personal Information Protection and Electronic Documents Act (PIPED) of 2000 (also known as Bill C5) has given digital signatures the same legal status as those written on paper. A **digital signature** is a digital code attached to an electronically transmitted message that is used to verify the origins and contents of a message. It provides a way to associate a message with the sender, performing a function similar to a written signature. For an electronic signature to be legally binding in court, someone must be able to verify that the signature actually belongs to whoever sent the data and that the data were not altered after being "signed."

Digital certificates are data files used to establish the identity of people and electronic assets for protection of online transactions (see Figure 11.8). A digital certificate system uses a trusted third party, known as a certificate authority (CA), to validate a user's identity. The

encryption

The coding and scrambling of messages to prevent their being read or accessed without authorization.

authentication

The ability of each party in a transaction to ascertain the identity of the other party.

message integrity

The ability to ascertain that a transmitted message has not been copied or altered.

digital signature

A digital code that can be attached to an electronically transmitted message to uniquely identify its contents and the sender.

digital certificate

An attachment to an electronic message to verify the identity of the sender and to provide the receiver with the means to encode a reply.

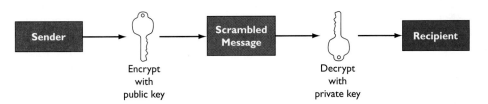

Figure 11.7 Public key encryption. A public key encryption system can be viewed as a series of public and private keys that lock data when they are transmitted and unlock the data when they are received. The sender locates the recipient's public key in a directory and uses it to encrypt a message. The message is sent in encrypted form over the Internet or a private network. When the encrypted message arrives, the recipient uses his or her private key to decrypt the data and read the message.

CA system can be run as a function inside an organization or by an outside company, such as VeriSign Inc. in Mountain View, California. The CA verifies a digital certificate user's identity offline. This information is put into a CA server, which generates an encrypted digital certificate containing owner identification information and a copy of the owner's public key. The certificate authenticates that the public key belongs to the designated owner. The CA makes its own public key available publicly either in print or perhaps on the Internet. The recipient of an encrypted message uses the CA's public key to decode the digital certificate attached to the message, verifies that it was issued by the CA, and then obtains the sender's public key and identification information contained in the certificate. Using this information, the recipient can send an encrypted reply. The digital certificate system would enable, for example, a credit card user and merchant to validate that their digital certificates were issued by an authorized and trusted third party before they exchange data.

SSL (Secure Sockets Layer) and S-HTTP (Secure Hypertext Transport Protocol) are protocols used for secure information transfer over the Internet. They allow client and server computers to manage encryption and decryption activities as they communicate with each other during a secure Web session. Some credit card payment systems use the Secure Sockets Layer (SSL) protocol for encrypting credit card payment data.

Additional material on encryption (prepared by David Chan at York University) can be found on the Companion Website at www.pearsoned.ca/laudon.

Figure 11.8 Digital certificates. Digital certificates can be used to establish the identity of people or electronic assets. They protect online transactions by providing secure, encrypted online communication.

DEVELOPING A CONTROL STRUCTURE: COSTS AND BENEFITS

Information systems can make exhaustive use of all the control mechanisms previously discussed. But controls may be so expensive to develop and so complicated to use that the system is economically or operationally unfeasible. Some form of cost-benefit analysis must be performed to determine which control mechanisms provide the most effective safeguards without sacrificing operational efficiency or being too costly.

One of the criteria that determines how much control is built into a system is the importance of its data. Major financial and accounting systems, for example, such as a payroll system or one that tracks purchases and sales on the stock exchange, must have higher standards of control than a tickler system to track dental patients and remind them that their six-month checkup is due. For instance, Swissair invested in additional hardware and software to increase its network reliability because it was running critical reservation and ticketing applications.

The cost-effectiveness of controls will also be affected by the efficiency, complexity, and expense of each control technique. For example, complete one-for-one checking may be time consuming and operationally impossible for a system that processes hundreds of thousands of utilities payments daily. But it might be possible to use this technique to

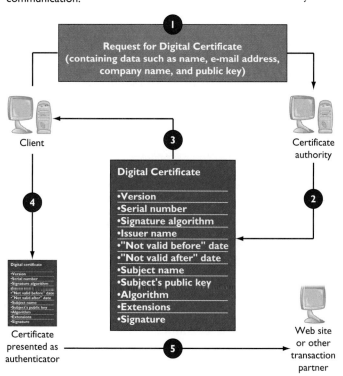

verify only critical data, such as dollar amounts and account numbers, while ignoring names and addresses.

A third consideration is the level of risk if a specific activity or process is not properly controlled. System developers can undertake a **risk assessment**, determining points of vulnerability, the likely frequency of a problem, and the potential damage if it were to occur. For example, if an event is likely to occur no more than once a year, with a maximum of $1000 loss to the organization, it would not be feasible to spend $20 000 on the design and maintenance of a control to protect against that event. However, if that same event could occur at least once a day, with a potential loss of more than $300 000 a year, $100 000 spent on a control might be entirely appropriate.

Table 11.6 shows the results of a risk assessment of three selected areas of an online order processing system. The likelihood of each exposure occurring over a one-year period is expressed as a percentage. The next column shows the highest and lowest possible loss that could be expected each time the exposure occurred and an average loss calculated by adding the highest and lowest figures together and dividing by 2. The expected annual loss for each exposure can be determined by multiplying the average loss by its probability of occurrence.

Table 11.6 illustrates sample results of a risk assessment for an online order processing system that processes 30 000 orders per day. The probability of a power failure occurring in a one-year period is 30 percent. Loss of order transactions while power is down could range from $5000 to $200 000 for each occurrence, depending on how long processing was halted. The probability of embezzlement occurring over a yearly period is about 5 percent, with potential losses ranging from $1000 to $50 000 for each occurrence. User errors have a 98 percent chance of occurring over a yearly period, with losses ranging from $200 to $40 000 for each occurrence. The average loss for each event can be weighted by multiplying it by the probability of its occurrence annually to determine the expected annual loss. Once the risks have been assessed, system developers can concentrate on the control points with the greatest vulnerability and potential loss. In this case, controls should focus on ways to minimize the risk of power failures and user errors. Increasing management awareness of the full range of actions they can take to reduce risks can substantially reduce system losses (Straub and Welke, 1998).

In some situations, organizations may not know the precise probability of threats occurring to their information systems, and they may not be able to quantify the impact of such events. In these instances, management may choose to describe risks and their likely impact in a qualitative manner (Rainer, Snyder, and Carr, 1991).

To decide which controls to use, information systems developers must examine various control techniques in relation to each other and to their relative cost-effectiveness. A control weakness at one point may be offset by a strong control at another. It may not be cost effective to develop tight controls at every point in the processing cycle if the areas of greatest risk are secure or if compensating controls exist elsewhere. The combination of all of the controls developed for a particular application will determine its overall control structure.

risk assessment

Determining the potential frequency of the occurrence of a problem and the potential damage if the problem were to occur; used to determine the cost-benefit ratio of a control.

TABLE 11.6 ONLINE ORDER PROCESSING RISK ASSESSMENT

Exposure	Probability of Occurrence (%)	Loss Range/ Average ($)	Expected Annual Loss ($)
Power failure	30	5000–200 000 (102 500)	30 750
Embezzlement	5	1000–50 000 (25 500)	1275
User error	98	200–40 000 (20 100)	19 698

THE ROLE OF AUDITING IN THE CONTROL PROCESS

MIS audit

Identifies all of the controls that govern individual information systems and assesses their effectiveness.

How does management know that information systems controls are effective? To answer this question, organizations must conduct comprehensive and systematic audits. An **MIS audit** identifies all of the controls that govern individual information systems and assesses their effectiveness. To accomplish this, the auditor must acquire a thorough understanding of operations, physical facilities, telecommunications, control systems, data security objectives, organizational structure, personnel, manual procedures, and individual applications.

The auditor usually interviews key individuals who use and operate a specific information system concerning their activities and procedures. Application controls, overall integrity controls, and control disciplines are examined. The auditor traces the flow of sample transactions through the system and performs tests, using, if appropriate, automated audit software.

The audit lists and ranks all control weaknesses and estimates the probability of their occurrence. It then assesses the financial and organizational impact of each threat. Figure 11.9 is a sample auditor's listing of control weaknesses for a loan system. It includes a section for notifying management of these weaknesses and for management's response. Management is expected to devise a plan for countering significant weaknesses in controls.

11.3 ENSURING SYSTEMS QUALITY

Organizations can improve systems quality by using software quality assurance techniques and by improving the quality of their data.

SOFTWARE QUALITY ASSURANCE METHODOLOGIES AND TOOLS

Solutions to software quality problems include using an appropriate systems development methodology, proper resource allocation during systems development, the use of metrics, and attention to testing.

Structured Methodologies

development methodology

A collection of methods, one or more for every activity within every phase of a development project.

Various tools and development methodologies have been employed to help systems developers document, analyze, design, and implement information systems. A **development methodology** is a collection of methods, one or more for every activity within every phase of

---

Function: Personal Loans _____ Prepared by: _____ J. Ericson _____ Received by: _____ T. Barrow _____
Location: Peoria, Ill. _____ Preparation date: __ June 16, 2003 _____ Review date: _____ June 28, 2003 _____

Nature of Weakness and Impact	Chance for Substantial Error		Effect on Audit Procedures	Notification to Management	
	Yes/No	Justification	Required Amendment	Date of Report	Management Response
Loan repayment records are not reconciled to borrower's records during processing.	Yes	Without a detection control, errors in individual client balances may remain undetected.	Confirm a sample of loans.	5/10/03	Interest Rate Compare Report provides this control.
There are no regular audits of computer-generated data (interest charges).	Yes	Without a regular audit or reasonableness check, widespread miscalculations could result before errors are detected.		5/10/03	Periodic audits of loans will be instituted.
Programs can be put into production libraries to meet target deadlines without final approval from the Standards and Controls group.	No	All programs require management authorization. The Standards and Controls group controls access to all production systems, and assigns such cases to a temporary production status.			

Figure 11.9 Sample auditor's list of control weaknesses. This chart is a sample page from a list of control weaknesses that an auditor might find in a loan system in a local commercial bank. This form helps auditors record and evaluate control weaknesses and shows the results of discussing those weaknesses with management, as well as any corrective actions taken by management.

An auditor interviews key individuals who use and operate a specific information system concerning their activities and procedures. The auditor traces the flow of sample transactions through the system and performs tests using automated audit software.

a systems development project. The primary function of a development methodology is to provide discipline to the entire development process. A good development methodology establishes organization-wide standards for requirements gathering, design, programming, and testing. To produce quality software, organizations must select an appropriate methodology and then enforce its use. The methodology should call for systems requirement and specification documents that are complete, detailed, accurate, and documented in a format the user community can understand before they approve it. Specifications also must include agreed on measures of system quality so that the system can be evaluated objectively while it is being developed and once it is completed.

Structured methodologies have been used to document, analyze, and design information systems since the 1970s. **Structured** refers to the fact that the techniques are performed step by step, with each step building on the previous one. Structured methodologies are top-down, progressing from the highest, most abstract level to the lowest level of detail—from the general to the specific. For example, the highest level of a top-down description of a human resources system would show the main human resources functions: personnel, benefits, compensation, and equal employment opportunity. Each of these would be broken down into the next layer. Benefits, for instance, might include pension, employee savings, healthcare, and insurance. Each of these layers, in turn, would be broken down until the lowest level of detail could be depicted.

The traditional structured methodologies are process oriented, rather than data oriented. Although data descriptions are part of the methods, the methodologies focus on how the data are transformed, rather than on the data themselves. These methodologies are largely linear; each phase must be completed before the next one can begin. Structured methodologies include structured analysis, structured design, and structured programming.

Structured Analysis

Structured analysis is widely used to define system inputs, processes, and outputs. It offers a logical graphic model of information flow, partitioning a system into modules that show manageable levels of detail. It rigorously specifies the processes or transformations that occur within each module and the interfaces that exist between them. Its primary tool is the **data flow diagram (DFD)**, a graphic representation of a system's component processes and the interfaces (flow of data) between them.

structured

Refers to the fact that techniques are carefully performed, step by step, with each step building on a previous one.

structured analysis

A method for defining system inputs, processes, and outputs and for partitioning systems into subsystems or modules that show a logical graphic model of information flow.

data flow diagram

Primary tool for structured analysis that graphically illustrates a system's component processes and the flow of data between them.

Additional material on data flow diagrams can be found on the Companion Website.

Another tool for structured analysis is a data dictionary, which contains information about individual pieces of data and data groupings within a system (see Chapter 7). The data dictionary defines the contents of data flows and data stores so that system developers understand exactly what pieces of data they contain. **Process specifications** describe the transformation occurring within the lowest level of the data flow diagrams. They express the logic for each process.

Structured Design

Structured design encompasses a set of design rules and techniques that promote program clarity and simplicity, thereby reducing the time and effort required for coding, debugging, and maintenance. The main principle of structured design is that a system should be designed from the top down in hierarchical fashion and refined to greater levels of detail. The design should first consider the main function of a program or system, then break this function into subfunctions and decompose each subfunction until the lowest level of detail has been reached. The lowest level modules describe the actual processing that will occur. In this manner, all high-level logic and the design model are developed before detailed program code is written. If structured analysis has been performed, the structured specification document can serve as input to the design process. Our earlier human resources top-down description provides a good overview example of structured design.

As the design is formulated, it is documented in a structure chart. The **structure chart** is a top-down chart, showing each level of design, its relationship to other levels, and its place in the overall design structure. Figure 11.10 shows a high-level structure chart for a payroll system. If a design has too many levels to fit onto one structure chart, it can be broken down further on more detailed structure charts. A structure chart may document one program, one system (a set of programs), or part of one program.

Structured Programming

Structured programming extends the principles governing structured design to the writing of programs to make software programs easier to understand and modify. It is based on the principle of modularization, which follows from top-down analysis and design. Each of the boxes in the structure chart represents a component **module** that is usually directly related to a bottom-level design module. It constitutes a logical unit that performs one or several functions. Ideally, modules should be independent of each other and should have only one entry point and one exit point. They should share data with as few other modules as possible. Each module should be kept to a manageable size. An individual should be able to read and understand the program code for the module and easily keep track of its functions.

Proponents of structured programming have shown that any program can be written using three basic control constructs or instruction patterns: (1) simple sequence, (2) selection, and (3) iteration. These control constructs are illustrated in Figure 11.11.

The **sequence construct** executes statements in the order in which they appear, with control passing unconditionally from one statement to the next. The program will execute statement A and then statement B.

---

process specifications

Describe the logic of the processes occurring within the lowest levels of a data flow diagram.

structured design

Software design discipline encompassing a set of design rules and techniques for designing systems from the top down in hierarchical fashion.

structure chart

System documentation showing each level of design, the relationship among the levels, and the overall place in the design structure; can document one program, one system, or part of one program.

structured programming

Discipline for organizing and coding programs that simplifies the control paths so that the programs can be easily understood and modified; uses the basic control structures and modules that have only one entry point and one exit point.

module

A logical unit of a program that performs one or several functions.

sequence construct

The sequential single steps or actions in the logic of a program that do not depend on the existence of any condition.

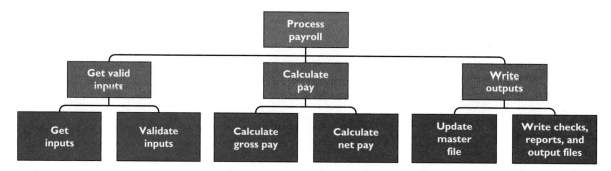

Figure 11.10 High-level structure chart for a payroll system. This structure chart shows the highest or most abstract level of design for a payroll system, providing an overview of the entire system.

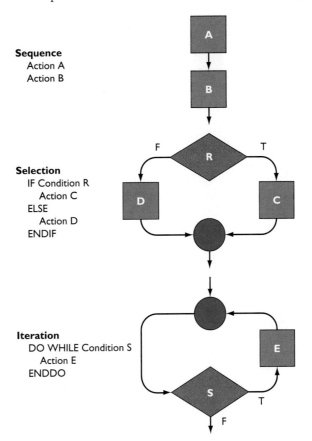

Sequence
    Action A
    Action B

Selection
    IF Condition R
        Action C
    ELSE
        Action D
    ENDIF

Iteration
    DO WHILE Condition S
        Action E
    ENDDO

The **selection construct** tests a condition and executes one of two alternative instructions on the basis of the results of the test. Condition R is tested. If R is true, then statement C is executed. If R is false, then statement D is executed. Control then passes to the next statement. (This is often called "if/then logic.")

The **iteration construct** repeats a segment of code as long as a conditional test remains true. Condition S is tested. If S is true, statement E is executed and control returns to the test of S. If S is false, E is skipped and control passes to the next statement.

Limitations of Traditional Methods

Although traditional methods are valuable, they can be inflexible and time consuming. Completion of structured analysis is required before design can begin, and programming must await the completed deliverables from design. A change in specifications requires that first the analysis documents and then the design documents must be modified before the programs can be changed to reflect the new specification. Structured methodologies are function oriented, focusing on the processes that transform the data. Chapter 10 described how object-oriented development addresses this problem. System developers can also use computer-aided software engineering (CASE) tools to make structured methods more flexible.

Tools and Methodologies for Object-Oriented Development

Chapters 6 and 10 have described how object-oriented development can be used to improve system quality and flexibility. A number of techniques for the analysis and design of object-oriented systems have been developed, but **Unified Modeling Language (UML)** has become the industry standard. UML allows system developers to represent various views of an object-oriented system using various types of graphical diagrams, and the underlying model integrates these views to promote consistency during analysis, design, and implementation.

selection construct

The logic pattern in programming where a stated condition determines which of two alternative actions can be taken.

iteration construct

The logic pattern in programming where certain actions are repeated while a specified condition occurs or until a certain condition is met.

Unified Modeling Language (UML)

Industry standard methodology for analysis and design of an object-oriented software system.

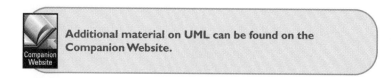

Additional material on UML can be found on the Companion Website.

Computer-Aided Software Engineering

computer-aided software engineering (CASE)

Automation of step-by-step methodologies for software and systems development to reduce the amounts of repetitive work the developer needs to do.

Computer-aided software engineering (CASE) is the automation of step-by-step methodologies for software and systems development to reduce the amount of repetitive work the developer needs to do. Adoption of CASE can free the developer for more creative problem-solving tasks. CASE tools also facilitate the creation of clear documentation and the coordination of team development efforts. Team members can share their work easily by accessing each other's files to review or modify what has been done. Some studies have found that systems developed with CASE and the newer methodologies are more reliable, and they require repairs less often (Dekleva, 1992). Modest productivity benefits can also be achieved if the tools are used properly. Many CASE tools are PC based and have powerful graphical capabilities.

CASE tools provide automated graphics facilities for producing charts and diagrams, screen and report generators, data dictionaries, extensive reporting facilities, analysis and checking tools, code generators, and documentation generators. Most CASE tools are based on one or more of the popular structured methodologies. Some, such as Visible Analyst, illustrated in Figure 11.12, support object-oriented development. In general, CASE tools try to increase productivity and quality through the following capabilities:

- ▪ Enforce a standard development methodology and design discipline.
- ▪ Improve communication between users and technical specialists.
- ▪ Organize and correlate design components and provide rapid access to them via a design repository.
- ▪ Automate tedious and error-prone portions of analysis and design.
- ▪ Automate code generation, testing, and control rollout.

Many CASE tools have been classified in terms of whether they support activities at the front-end or the backend of the systems development process. Front-end CASE tools focus on capturing analysis and design information in the early stages of systems development, while backend CASE tools address coding, testing, and maintenance activities. Backend tools help convert specifications automatically into program code.

Figure 11.12 Visible Analyst is a tool for automating object-oriented analysis and design. Illustrated here are examples of use case and sequence diagrams.

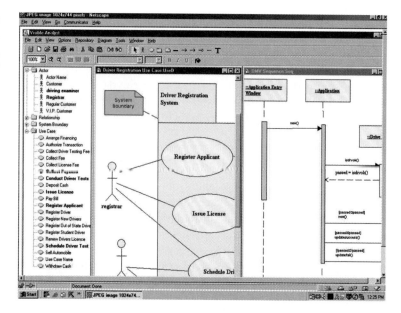

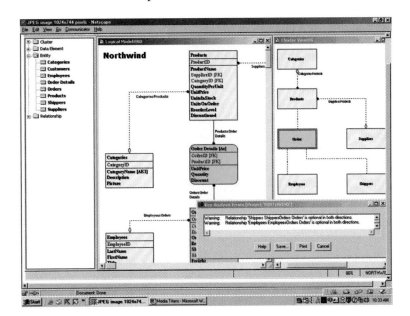

Figure 11.13 CASE tools include capabilities for generating and validating entity-relationship diagrams and data flow diagrams. CASE tools facilitate the creation of clear and accurate design specifications and the coordination of team development efforts.

CASE tools automatically tie data elements to the processes where they are used. If a data flow diagram is changed from one process to another, the elements in the data dictionary would be altered automatically to reflect the change in the diagram. CASE tools also contain features for validating design diagrams and specifications. CASE tools, thus, support iterative design by automating revisions and changes and providing prototyping facilities. (See Figure 11.13.)

A CASE information repository stores all the information defined by the analysts during the project. The repository includes data flow diagrams, structure charts, entity-relationship diagrams, data definitions, process specifications, screen and report formats, notes and comments, and test results. CASE tools now have features to support client-server applications, object-oriented programming, and business process redesign. Methodologies and tool sets are being created to leverage organizational knowledge of business process re-engineering (Nissen, 1998).

To be used effectively, CASE tools require organizational discipline. Every member of a development project must adhere to a common set of naming conventions and standards as well as to a development methodology. The best CASE tools enforce common methods and standards, which may discourage their use in situations where organizational discipline is lacking.

Resource Allocation during Systems Development

Views on **resource allocation** during systems development have changed significantly over the years. Resource allocation determines the way the costs, time, and personnel are assigned to different phases of the project. In earlier times, developers focused on programming, with only about 1 percent of the time and costs of a project being devoted to systems analysis (determining specifications). More time should be spent in specifications and systems analysis, decreasing the proportion of programming time and reducing the need for as much maintenance time. Documenting requirements so that they can be understood from their origin through development, specification, and continuing use can also reduce errors as well as time and costs (Domges and Pohl, 1998). Current literature suggests that about one-quarter of a project's time and cost should be expended in specifications and analysis, with perhaps 50 percent of its resources being allocated to design and programming. Installation and postimplementation ideally should require only one-quarter of the project's resources. Investments in software quality initiatives early in a project are likely to provide the greatest payback (Slaughter, Harter, and Krishnan, 1998).

resource allocation
The determination of how costs, time, and personnel are assigned to different phases of a systems development project.

Software Metrics

Software metrics can play a vital role in increasing system quality. **Software metrics** are objective assessments of the system in the form of quantified measurements. Ongoing use of

software metrics
The objective assessments of the software used in a system in the form of quantified measurements.

metrics allows the information systems department and the user to jointly measure the performance of the system and identify problems as they occur. Examples of software metrics include the number of transactions that can be processed in a specified unit of time, online response time, the number of payroll cheques printed per hour, and the number of known bugs per hundred lines of code.

For metrics to be successful, they must be carefully designed, formal, and objective. They must measure significant aspects of the system. In addition, metrics are of no value unless they are used consistently and unless users agree to the measurements in advance.

Testing

Chapter 10 described the stages of testing required to put an information system in operation—program testing, system testing, and acceptance testing. Early, regular, and thorough testing will contribute significantly to system quality. In general, software testing is often misunderstood. Many view testing as a way to prove the correctness of work they have done. In fact, we know that all sizable software is riddled with errors, and we must test to uncover these errors.

Testing begins at the design phase. Because no coding exists yet, the test normally used is a **walkthrough**—a review of a specification or design document by a small group of people carefully selected on the basis of the skills needed for the particular objectives being tested. Once coding begins, coding walkthroughs also can be used to review program code. However, code must be tested by computer runs. When errors are discovered, the source is found and eliminated through a process called **debugging.**

Electronic commerce and electronic business applications introduce new levels of complexity for testing to ensure high-quality performance and functionality. Behind each large Web site, such as Chapters.Indigo.ca, eBay, or BayStreet.ca, are hundreds of servers, thousands of kilometres of network cable, and hundreds of software programs, creating numerous points of vulnerability. These Web sites must be developed and tested to make sure that they can withstand expected—and unexpected—spikes and peaks in their loads. Both Web site traffic and technical components, such as hardware, software, and networks, must be taken into consideration during application development and during testing.

To test a Web site realistically, companies need to find a way to subject the Web site to the same number of concurrent users as would actually be visiting the site at one time and devise test plans that reflect what these people would actually be doing. For example, a retail electronic commerce site should create a test scenario where there are many visitors just browsing while some are making purchases.

Testing wireless applications poses additional challenges. Many wireless and conventional Web applications are linked to the same backend systems, so the total load on those systems will increase dramatically as wireless users are added. Automated load testing tools that simulate thousands of simultaneous wireless Web and conventional Web browser sessions can help companies measure the impact on system performance.

Many companies delay testing until the end of the application development phase when design decisions have been finalized and most of the software program code has been written. Leaving Web site performance and scalability tests until the end of the application development cycle is extremely risky because these problems often stem from the fundamental workings of the system. To minimize the chance of discovering major structural problems late in the system's development process, companies should perform this testing well before the system is complete. This makes it possible to address performance bottlenecks and other issues in each application level or system component before everything is integrated.

DATA QUALITY AUDITS AND DATA CLEANSING

Information system quality can also be improved by identifying and correcting faulty data, making error detection a more explicit organizational goal (Klein, Goodhue, and Davis, 1997). The analysis of data quality often begins with a **data quality audit**, which is a structured survey of the accuracy and level of completeness of the data in an information system. Data quality audits are accomplished by the following methods:

---

walkthrough

A review of a specification or design document by a small group of people carefully selected on the basis of the skills needed for the particular objectives being tested.

debugging

The process of discovering and eliminating the errors and defects—the bugs—in program code.

data quality audit

A survey and/or sample of files to determine accuracy and completeness of data in an information system.

- Surveying end users for their perceptions of data quality
- Surveying entire data files
- Surveying samples from data files

Unless regular data quality audits are undertaken, organizations have no way of knowing to what extent their information systems contain inaccurate, incomplete, or ambiguous information.

Until recently, many organizations were not giving data quality the priority it deserves (Tayi and Ballou, 1998). Now, electronic commerce and electronic business are forcing more companies to pay attention to data quality because a digitally enabled firm cannot run efficiently without accurate data about customers and business partners. **Data cleansing** has become a core requirement for data warehousing, customer relationship management, and Web-based commerce.

Companies implementing data warehousing often find inconsistencies in customer or employee information as they try to integrate information from different business units. Companies also find mistakes in the data provided by customers or business partners through a Web site. Online Net marketplaces (see Chapter 4) are especially problematic because they use catalogue data from dozens to thousands of suppliers and these data are often in different formats, with different classification schemes for product numbers, product descriptions, and other attributes. Data cleansing tools can be used to correct errors in these data and to integrate these data in a consistent company-wide format (see the Window on Management).

data cleansing

Correcting errors and inconsistencies in data to increase accuracy so that they can be used in a standard company-wide format.

TOYOTA'S DATA SPINS OUT OF CONTROL

The Lexus is Toyota's high-end luxury auto. Lexus owners expect the very best in customer service. When Toyota Motor Sales USA encountered a recurring service problem in 1998, it thought it was giving Lexus owners the gold-plated treatment. The company would contact owners, pick up their vehicles, repair them, and supply owners with loaner cars until the repairs had been completed. Toyota would return the owners' cars fixed, washed, and filled with fuel. Toyota relied on its Corporate Customer Information System to provide the information about this and other service problems. Toyota's call centre in Iowa used the system to handle warranty, roadside assistance, prepaid maintenance, and other service requests.

Data from that system identified Lexus owners with troublesome tires, and Toyota began mailing them cheques for $400 or more to replace troublesome tires. But some of these cheques went to people who did not even own a Lexus, and one was mailed to a Toyota auditor for a vehicle he no longer owned. These mistakes pointed to a massive data quality problem because the Corporate Customer Information System used customer data stored in 15 databases in different parts of the company.

Upon learning of the problem, senior management called for a single centralized customer database that would resolve these discrepancies and shorten the amount of time call centre employees spent accessing customer data. Toyota used Informatica's PowerMart and software tools for data extraction, transforma-

tion, and loading into a central data warehouse capable of storing 250 gigabytes of data. By April 1999, Toyota had built its central customer database and installed the Informatica software. It took an additional six months to get the system in working order. The biggest hurdle was cleansing the data. Toyota's databases had several million records that had to be checked. Some databases had wrong addresses, wrong vehicles, and wrong motors. Toyota had to use the state department's motor vehicle records to check some of the data. In a few instances, the company had to call customers to help them straighten out their records.

The total project cost was over $2.5 million. Toyota believes this is money well spent. Call centre employees can access customer information much more rapidly, so Toyota did not have to increase the size of its staff as the volume of calls went up. Annual vehicle sales have more than doubled, from 750 000 to 1.7 million, and the company trusts that the data in the central database are now accurate enough to support decision making throughout the company.

But the struggle for high data quality never ends. Toyota has continued its data cleansing work, with data from Mexico recently rolled into the system.

To Think About: What management and organizational problems were created by poor data quality at Toyota? What management decisions had to be made to solve this problem?

Sources: Sean Gallagher, "Default Setting" *Baseline*, June 2002; *Informatica* corporate Web site, accessed July 22, 2002, **www.informatica.com**.

MANAGEMENT WRAP-UP

Management is responsible for developing the control structure and quality standards for the organization. Key management decisions include establishing standards for systems accuracy and reliability, determining an appropriate level of control for organizational functions, and establishing a disaster recovery plan.

The characteristics of the organization play a large role in determining its approach to quality assurance and control issues. Some organizations are more quality and control conscious than others. Their cultures and business processes support high standards of quality and performance. Creating high levels of security and quality in information systems may require a process of lengthy organizational change.

A number of technologies and methodologies are available for promoting system quality and security. Such technologies as antivirus and data security software, firewalls, fault-tolerant and high-availability computing technology, and programmed procedures can be used to create a control environment, while software metrics, systems development methodologies, and automated tools for systems development can be used to improve software quality. Organizational discipline is required to use these technologies effectively.

For Discussion

1. It has been said that controls and security should be one of the first areas to be addressed in the design of an information system. Do you agree? Why, or why not?

2. How much software testing is "enough"? What management, organization, and technology issues should you consider in answering this question?

SUMMARY

1. *Why are information systems so vulnerable to destruction, error, abuse, and system quality problems?* With data concentrated into electronic form and many procedures invisible through automation, computerized information systems are vulnerable to destruction, misuse, error, fraud, and hardware or software failures. Online systems and those utilizing the Internet are especially vulnerable because data and files can be immediately and directly accessed through computer terminals or at many points in the network. Hackers can penetrate corporate networks and cause serious system disruptions. Computer viruses can spread rapidly from system to system, clogging computer memory or destroying programs and data. Software presents problems because of the high costs of correcting errors and because software bugs may be impossible to eliminate. Data quality can also severely impact system quality and performance.

2. *What types of controls are available for information systems?* Controls consist of all of the methods, policies, and organizational procedures that ensure the safety of the organization's assets, the accuracy and reliability of its accounting records, and adherence to management standards. There are two main categories of controls: general controls and application controls.

General controls handle the overall design, security, and use of computers, programs, and files for the organization's information technology infrastructure.

Application controls are those unique to specific computerized applications. They focus on the completeness and accuracy of input, updating and maintenance, and the validity of the information in the system.

To determine which controls are required, designers and users of systems must identify all of the control points and control weaknesses and perform risk assessment. They must also perform a cost-benefit analysis of controls and design controls that can effectively safeguard systems without making them unusable.

3. *What special measures must be taken to ensure the reliability, availability, and security of electronic commerce and digital business processes?* Companies require special measures to support electronic commerce and digital business processes. They can use fault-tolerant computer systems or create high-availability computing environments to make sure that their information systems are always available and performing without interruptions. Disaster recovery plans provide procedures and facilities for restoring computing and communication services after they have been disrupted. Firewalls and intrusion detection systems help

safeguard private networks from unauthorized access when organizations use intranets or link to the Internet. Encryption is a widely used technology for securing electronic transmissions over the Internet. Digital certificates provide further protection of electronic transactions by authenticating a user's identity.

4. *What are the most important software quality assurance techniques?* The quality and reliability of software can be improved by using a standard development methodology, software metrics, thorough testing procedures, and by allocating resources to put more emphasis on the analysis and design stages of systems development.

Structured methodologies are used to increase software quality. Structured analysis highlights the flow of data and the processes through which data are transformed; its principal tool is the data flow diagram. Structured design and programming are software design disciplines that produce reliable, well-documented software with a simple, clear structure that is easy for others to understand and maintain. Unified Modeling Language

(UML) provides a standard methodology for modelling an object-oriented system that promotes consistency during analysis, design, and implementation.

Computer-aided software engineering (CASE) automates methodologies for systems development. It promotes standards and improves coordination and consistency during systems development. CASE tools help system developers construct a better model of a system and facilitate revision of design specifications to correct errors.

5. *Why are auditing information systems and safeguarding data quality so important?* Comprehensive and systematic MIS auditing can help organizations to determine the effectiveness of the controls in their information systems. Regular data quality audits should be conducted to help organizations ensure a high level of completeness and accuracy of the data stored in their systems. Data cleansing should also be performed to create consistent and accurate data for company-wide use in electronic commerce and electronic business.

KEY TERMS

Administrative controls, 368

Antivirus software, 363

Application controls, 367

Authentication, 373

Bugs, 365

Clustering, 371

Computer-aided software engineering (CASE), 380

Computer virus, 362

Controls, 367

Data cleansing, 383

Data flow diagram, 377

Data quality audit, 382

Data security controls, 368

Debugging, 382

Denial of service attack, 362

Development methodology, 376

Digital certificate, 373

Digital signature, 373

Disaster recovery plan, 370

Encryption, 373

Fault-tolerant computer system, 370

General controls, 367

Hacker, 362

High-availability computing, 370

Input controls, 369

Intrusion detection system, 372

Iteration construct, 379

Load balancing, 371

Management service provider, 371

Message integrity, 373

Mirroring, 371

MIS audit, 376

Module, 378

Online transaction processing, 370

Output controls, 369

Process specifications, 378

Processing controls, 369

Resource allocation, 381

Risk assessment, 375

Security, 364

Sequence construct, 378

Selection construct, 379

Software metrics, 381

Structure chart, 378

Structured, 377

Structured analysis, 377

Structured design, 378

Structured programming, 378

Unified Modeling Language (UML), 379

Walkthrough, 382

REVIEW QUESTIONS

1. Why are computer systems more vulnerable than manual systems to destruction, fraud, error, and misuse? Name some of the key areas where systems are most vulnerable.

2. Name some features of online information systems that make them difficult to control.

3. How can poor software and data quality affect system performance and reliability? Describe two software quality problems.

4. What are controls? Distinguish between general controls and application controls.

5. Name and describe the principal general and application controls for computerized systems.

6. What is security? List and describe controls that promote security for computer hardware, computer networks, computer software, and computerized data.

7. What special security measures must be taken by organizations linking to the Internet?

8. Distinguish between fault-tolerant and high-availability computing.

9. Describe the role of firewalls, intrusion detection systems, and encryption systems in promoting security.

10. Why are digital signatures and digital certificates important for electronic commerce?

11. What is the function of risk assessment?

12. How does MIS auditing enhance the control process?

13. Name and describe four software quality assurance techniques.

14. What is structured analysis? What is the role of the data flow diagram in structured analysis?

15. How is structured design related to structured programming? How can both promote software quality?

16. How does Unified Modeling Language (UML) support object-oriented analysis and design?

17. Why are data quality audits and data cleansing essential?

APPLICATION SOFTWARE EXERCISE

SPREADSHEET EXERCISE: PERFORMING A SECURITY RISK ASSESSMENT

Winnipeg Paints is a small but highly regarded paint manufacturing company located in Manitoba. The company has a network in place, linking many of its business operations. While the firm feels that its security is adequate, the recent addition of a Web site has been an open invitation to hackers. Management requested a risk assessment. The risk assessment identified several potential exposures; these exposures, associated probabilities, and average losses are summarized in the table that can be found on the Companion Website for Chapter 11. In addition to the potential exposures listed, you should identify at least three other potential threats to Winnipeg Paints, assign probabilities, and estimate a loss range.

Using spreadsheet software and the risk assessment data provided on the Companion Website, calculate the expected annual loss for each exposure. Which control points have the greatest vulnerability? What recommendations would you make to Winnipeg Paints? Prepare a written report that summarizes your findings and recommendations.

GROUP PROJECT

Form a group with two or three other students. Select a system described in one of the chapter-ending cases. Write a description of the system, its functions, and its value to the organization. Then, write a description of both the general and application controls that should be used to protect the organization. If possible, use electronic presentation software to present your findings to the class.

 ## INTERNET TOOLS

COMPANION WEBSITE

The Companion Website for this chapter will take you to a series of Web sites where you can complete an exercise to evaluate various secure electronic payment systems for the Internet.

At www.pearsoned.ca/laudon, you will find valuable tools to facilitate and enhance your learning of this chapter as well as opportunities to apply your knowledge to realistic situations:

- An Interactive Study Guide of self-test questions that will provide you with immediate feedback.
- Application exercises.
- An Electronic Business Project to evaluate security outsourcing services.
- A Management Decision Problem on Analyzing Security Vulnerabilities.
- Additional material on data flow diagrams and UML.
- Additional material on encryption, biometrics, and how to combat spam, bugs, and spyware (prepared by David Chan

at York University) can be found on the Companion Website at www.pearsoned.ca/laudon.

- Updates on material in the chapter.

ADDITIONAL SITES OF INTEREST

There are many interesting Web sites to enhance your learning about information systems security, quality, and control. You can search the Web yourself or just try the following sites to add to what you have already learned.

Information Security Magazine
> **www.infosecuritymag.com**
>
> Up-to-date news and technical briefs on information security issues.

AntiOnline E-Magazine
> **www.antionline.com**
>
> Web magazine for information security officers and others interested in preventing systems security problems.

CompInfo's CASE Tools site
www.compinfo-center.com/apps/case-tools.htm
Learn more about CASE tools through the links provided at this Canadian computer information site.

Microsoft's Visio Web site
www.microsoft.com/office/visio
MS Visio is a leading flowcharting package.

CASE STUDY: *Rogue Currency Trades at Allied Irish Banks: How Could It Happen?*

On February 5, 2002, the financial world was shaken by the revelation of a $1-billion foreign exchange trading loss suffered by Allfirst, a Baltimore bank providing corporate, commercial, correspondent, and retail banking services in the mid-Atlantic states. The bank had been a subsidiary of the Allied Irish Banks PLC (AIB), the largest financial institution in Ireland. The huge loss reminded many of the 1995 Barings Bank scandal, in which a Singapore trader named Nick Leeson had hidden $1.96 billion in losses. Those losses ended with the collapse of Barings. The history of financial market trading is replete with fraudulent traders who were not scrutinized because they were "making so much money," so an Allfirst trader only appeared to be doing the same old thing. One executive in a foreign exchange company observed, "The pressures on people to produce revenues are extraordinary."

The accused foreign exchange trader was John Rusnak, a 37-year-old man with a wife and two children, who lived modestly on a $119 000 salary plus a trader's bonus that never reached $280 000. He had worked for years in the foreign exchange department of Chemical Bank, now J.P. Morgan Chase, and for the past seven years, he had been doing the same thing at Allfirst. The bank's management reported that his huge losses were from unauthorized trades beginning in early 2001, and they were probably from trading in Japanese yen. The yen had declined during the last few months of 2001, and Rusnak apparently expected it to turn and rise against the Euro. Rusnak placed trades to benefit from the expected rise, but the yen fell 11 percent from mid-September to year-end, and Rusnak's losses kept growing. To hide his losses, Rusnak told Allfirst's Treasury Department that he had sold yen currency options to hedge his bets, but in fact, he never had. Rather, he falsified trade confirmations.

In mid-January, to finance his enormous losses, Rusnak began asking for unusually large amounts of money, which triggered an investigation by senior staff members of Allfirst's Treasury Department. Rusnak cooperated, and on Thursday, January 31, Allfirst confronted Rusnak with accusations of having falsified options trades. The next day, he produced 12 paper confirmations to support those trades, but they appeared to be fakes. Allfirst checked on one confirmation by telephoning the Bank of America (BofA) in San Francisco. BofA said that it had not done that trade and proved the BofA logo on the confirmation to be a phony. Rusnak disappeared over the weekend, failed to return phone calls, and did not show up for work on Monday. That day, AIB was informed of the $1-billion loss, and the next day, AIB unwound Rusnak's yen holdings producing a huge Allfirst loss. The following day, the information was released to the public, and the Federal Bureau of Investigation (FBI) moved in.

Allfirst CEO and President, Susan Keating, said, "I am greatly disappointed to learn about these events and that policy and control procedures in place were violated." Allfirst said that Rusnak's upper limit on a trade was only $3.5 million, an impossibly low figure considering the losses he had accumulated. By Thursday, February 7, it became clear that Rusnak had not fled. He hired a lawyer, David Irwin, who said Rusnak had not stolen any of the bank's money and was already cooperating with the FBI. The United States Attorney's office had also been called in to investigate, as were Federal Reserve Bank examiners.

On Friday, AIB said it would install new trading controls as soon as possible to prevent any future trades of this type. It also said management and control of Allfirst Treasury operations would be centralized in Dublin under the direction of the head of AIB's Capital Markets Treasury. AIB also announced it would appoint an external senior expert to lead an internal investigation into the causes of the loss, including violation of internal controls and possible internal and external collusion. The investigation report would state the facts, describe policies and controls and their effectiveness, and make recommendations for improvements. On February 10, Eugene Ludwig, the former head of the U.S. Office of the Comptroller of the Currency, was named to lead the investigation. Two days later, five Allfirst executives were suspended, and 15 executives from Dublin were sent to Baltimore to oversee Allfirst.

Federal agents reported that Rusnak stated he had taken trades, and when losses began to magnify, he began to use a secret strategy to make up for his losses. But his losses "just got deeper." The FBI said, "It isn't looking like he embezzled the $1 billion," although the AIB board said the trades were not authorized by the bank. The FBI found evidence that Rusnak was not trying to steal for himself, but just to recover his immense losses when he had guessed wrong on the direction of the yen. Also, the FBI pointed out that he did not flee and that he cooperated when he was discovered. On the other hand, he did not protect his currency trades with options.

On February 20, after a careful examination of the records, AIB announced that Rusnak's currency trade losses actually began five years earlier in 1997. AIB also said the total loss was now lowered to $967.7 million. AIB also reported the losses were in the bank's proprietary trading account, indicating that the bank had encouraged Rusnak to trade in order to earn profits for the bank. Allfirst was forced to resubmit five years of annual financial statements to the Securities and Exchange Commission (SEC).

On March 11, AIB released the Ludwig report. It concluded that "Mr. Rusnak circumvented the controls that were intended to prevent any such fraud by manipulating the weak control environment in Allfirst's Treasury; notably, he found ways of circumventing changes in control procedures throughout the period of his fraud." The report also said, "Mr. Rusnak took advantage of weak and inexperienced employees in the [Allfirst] Treasury control groups. These employees, by virtue of their inexperience, poor training, poor supervision and, in some cases, laziness, facilitated Mr. Rusnak in circumventing controls." The report even said Rusnak was allowed to trade during his vacation, which was against banking guidelines. However, the report concluded that no one in the bank knowingly conspired with Rusnak. Because of weak controls, six Allfirst employees were dismissed, including Rusnak, David Cronin, Allfirst's Executive Vice-President and Treasurer, Robert Ray, Rusnak's Supervisor, and Jan Palmer, Allfirst's Head of Internal Audit. Keating was neither criticized nor dismissed. Allfirst's Chairman, Frank Bramble, announced his early retirement, claiming it was not related to the scandal.

What went wrong? The industry has a set of best practices for controlling such trades. When a currency trade takes place, if it is for a customer, the trader is required to hedge (buy an option in the opposite direction) to protect against a large loss. Traders normally hedge even if the trade is for the bank or for themselves. When any trade takes place—currency or hedge—both sides must legally confirm the trade, or it will not be valid. Today, that is usually done through a computerized service that can automatically acknowledge and validate both sides of the trade, almost anywhere in the world, within two minutes. If a computerized service is not used, the bank must have a rigourous procedure for approving the counterparty (the other side of a trade) with whom traders are allowed to conduct business. Usually, that will be done by a telephone call to the counterparty.

Workable controls in any financial transaction must include the separation of responsibilities. That is, functions must be separated so that the person making the trade cannot also control or verify the trade. In currency trading (as well as many other types of trading), the organization must separate the duties between a front office or trading desk and the back office, which handles trade accounting and controlling, including enforcing credit limits. All trades must be approved by the back office (today that is mostly done by computer systems). Moreover, traders cannot authorize accounts, set them up, or authorize payments to outside clients.

In 1998, AIB installed software from Misys in the United Kingdom, which could be used to control front and back office work during currency trades. The Misys suite called "Tropics" captures currency trades electronically at the front desk. It also would catch trades that were over the limit. The back office suite called Opics tracks all foreign exchange transactions. Together, the two software packages provide "straight-through processing," enabling trades to be electronically fulfilled on the same day they are executed. This setup catches sham trades, trades beyond approved limits, and trades with nonapproved counterparties. Together, they would automatically generate alerts to the appropriate managers if any rules were broken. AIB also used Crossmar Matching Service, which automatically

electronically confirms both sides of a trade within two minutes. It is used by around 1000 banks, corporations, and fund-management companies.

AIB installed Opics, the back-office software, at Allfirst, but no Tropics front-office software was installed. Therefore, Allfirst did not have straight-through processing, and the information on the trade was given to the back office manually. Allfirst also did not use Crossmar to validate a trade and instead was supposed to rely on telephones.

AIB used risk-management analytics software, in order to evaluate the risk of a trade being considered. Front- and/or back- office systems automatically feed trade data into the software. Once the risk on known trades is calculated, the company can execute countervailing trades in currency options to minimize the risk. AIB installed Askari's RiskBook, which was later acquired by State Street Corp. and renamed TruView. Allfirst did not use RiskBook (TruView), relying instead on Monte Carlo simulation software to calculate a currency trade's risk. Monte Carlo simulations are derived from statistical descriptions of data and try to simulate possible paths that underlying assets could take in the future. Once thousands of paths have been created, a firm can average the value over these paths to determine the most likely outcome. However, Allfirst's 10-K Securities and Exchange filing stated that the company did not take the average but, instead, chose the "tenth worst observation," which minimized the actual amount of risk to which the company was exposed. Moreover, Monte Carlo simulations are typically used for credit risk modelling and not for currency trading. Rusnak seemed to know that Monte Carlo was inadequate, and so he asked his management to purchase RiskBook. He was turned down for budgetary reasons.

According to David Atkinson, a former AIB currency trader, "The controls put in place by AIB's New York office for its own traders were very strong, and I'm amazed that Allfirst didn't have similar measures. If you went a dime over any limit, [AIB's] credit officers would know that. I even got calls on trades that were within the limits if they appeared out of the ordinary."

How did Rusnak bypass the standard safeguards? One issue is the verification of fictitious trades, which should have been found years earlier. Clearly, the back office relied on Rusnak to manually give them information on each trade. Moreover, Rusnak entered his trades using Reuters software on his own computer, and the back-office staff had no access to it, enabling him to give them different information. He used other methods as well. He often gave his fake option trades a one-day expiration date, knowing no one would notice them because Allfirst reports do not list options expiring in one day. In the early days, Rusnak did produce forged confirmation documents for fake trades but ceased that practice in September 1998 when, according to the Ludwig report, he "apparently managed to persuade an individual in the back office not to seek to confirm the purported pairs of options." It further stated: "There was no need for confirmations, he apparently argued, because there was no net transfer of cash. Perhaps this practice suited the convenience of the back-office staffer."

According to the report, "the bogus options were purport-edly with the Tokyo or Singapore branches of major interna-tional financial institutions, and to have made confirming telephone calls would have required the employee to work in the middle of the night." In addition, Larry Smith, the back-office person responsible for verifying Rusnak's trades, told investiga-tors his bosses had told him not to bother verifying trades with banks in Asia. Therefore, the trade confirmations must have come from someone at Allfirst, probably Rusnak himself. Smith said that no action was taken even after he raised his concerns about trade confirmations. Later, after Smith talked with the FBI about these events, he was fired.

To give himself cover, Rusnak sometimes implied that he had a big hedge fund for a client, or he said he was a proprietary trader (trading for his own or the bank's account, not for clients). At other times, he indicated he wanted to trade with other banks that would allow him to bundle all of his trades into a single trade at the end of the day. One trader said this made it easier for him to place false trades that made it look like he was hedging against losses. To Allfirst, it would appear that he made only one trade.

As Rusnak became deeper and deeper in debt, he began to sell deep currency options to raise cash, generating a total of over $420 million in cash in 2001 (but Allfirst had to pay the client when the options expired). These were considered "synthetic loans" to Allfirst, by BofA, which consulted with AIB before approving the deal, making it clear that an AIB executive knew about Rusnak's shenanigans. AIB later denied such consultation had occurred, while BofA refused comment, but Ludwig's report described the event.

The industry's Guidelines for Foreign Exchange Trading Activities were written by foreign exchange executives along with Federal Reserve Bank of New York representatives. It says: "Significant book profits or losses, unusual requests, and trans-actions or patterns of activity inconsistent with a customer's pro-file should be referred to management." Buckley apparently questioned Allfirst's Executive Vice-President and Treasurer David Cronin about the size of Allfirst's currency trading, and Cronin told Buckley to approve the trade. Ludwig's report also said that AIB group Treasurer Patrick Ryan was also informed of a Rusnak position of more than $1 billion yen (around $10 mil-lion), making it clear that AIB knew Rusnak had topped his limit of $2.5 million. The banks that bought his options were BofA, Citibank, Deutsche Bank, and Bank of New York. As the options were exercised, the losses multiplied. This also raised suspicions of external collusion.

On June 6, 2002, a federal grand jury in Baltimore indicted Rusnak on seven counts, including bank fraud and false entry in bank records. He was reported to have been working on a plea agreement and may cooperate with federal prosecutors. On September 26, 2002, Allied Irish Banks announced plans to sell Allfirst Financial to M & T Bank Corporation of Buffalo for $4.34 billion in cash and stock.

Note: All currency values are in Canadian dollars.

Sources: Jonathan Fuerbringer, "Bank Report Says Trader Had Bold Plot," *New York Times*, March 15, 2002; "How Trail of Big Currency Losses Remained Uncovered for 5 Years," *New York Times*, March 5, 2002; "Arcane System Let Currency Trader Hide Losses," *New York Times*, February 19, 2002; "How Much Did a Bank Know about Its Currency Trader's Losses?" *New York Times*, February 16, 2002; "Investigation into Rogue Trades Finds Red Flags but Few Details," *New York Times*, February 11, 2002; "Bank Trader's Losses Total $750 Million," *New York Times*, February 7, 2002; Brian Lavery, "Irish Sells Troubled U.S. Bank but Maintain Some Influence," *New York Times*, September 27, 2002; "6 Fired as Irish Bank Acts on U.S. Trading Loss," *New York Times*, March 15, 2002; "Hidden Currency Losses Go Back 5 Years, Irish Bank Says," *New York Times*, February 21, 2002; "Two Big Questions Await Irish Bank Inquiry," *New York Times*, February 12, 2002; Sean Gallagher, "How Allfirst Trader Fudged Data," *Baseline*, March 11, 2002; "Allfirst Financial: Out of Control," *Baseline*, March 12, 2002; "How Allfirst Gambled on Monte Carlo," *Baseline,* March 12, 2002; Bill Atkinson and Andrew Ratner, "Amid Shareholder Threats, Allied Irish Hold Annual Meeting in Belfast Today," *Baltimore Sun*, May 29, 2002; Conal Walsh, "Fired AIB Man Seeks Cash," *The Observer*, April 28, 2002; Shawn Pogatchnik, "Allied Irish Drops Auditing Firm," *Baltimore Sun*, April 24, 2002; Richard Curran, "AIB Lends 900m to Bail Out Allfirst," *Irish Independent*, April 5, 2002; Craig Karmin and James R. Hagerty, "Allied Irish Trader Lacked Inside Help, Report Indicates," *Wall Street Journal*, March 11, 2002; Alessandra Galloni and Michael R. Sesit, "Lax Controls May Explain Loss at Allied Irish," *Wall Street Journal*, March 8, 2002; Julie Bell and William A. Patalon III, "Investors Sue Officers of Allfirst," *Baltimore Sun*, March 7, 2002; Alessandra Galloni and Michael R. Sesit, "Junior Employee Monitored Risk at Allfirst's Currency-Trading Desk," and "Controls at Allied Irish's Allfirst Likely Failed in Important Ways," *Wall Street Journal*, February 20, 2002; "AIB Suspects Another Employee Aided Rusnak in Trading Fraud," *Wall Street Journal*, February 11, 2002; Oleg Artyukov, "John Rusnak Became Scapegoat," *Pravda*, February 9, 2002; Gary Fields, Erik Portanger, Jathon Sapsford, and Craig Karmin, "As Big Losses Grew, Trader's Solution Backfired," *Wall Street Journal*, February 8, 2002; Rupert Cocke, "Allied Irish Banks to Put in Urgent Trading Controls," *Dow Jones Newswires*, February 8, 2002; Erik Portanger, Michael R. Sesit, and Alessandra Galloni, "Allied Irish Banks Say a Rogue Trader Lost $750 Million in Unauthorized Deals," *Wall Street Journal*, February 7, 2002; Debra Marks, "Biggest Casualty From AIB Fallout Will Be Senior Mgmt," *Wall Street Journal*, February 7, 2002.

CASE STUDY QUESTIONS

1. Briefly describe the Allied Irish and Allfirst problem that suddenly came to light early in February 2002.

2. Describe the control weaknesses at Allfirst and Allied Irish. What management, organization, and technology factors contributed to these weaknesses?

3. Who or what was responsible for the Rusnak trading losses? What role did Allied Irish and Allfirst's systems play? What role did management play?

4. Could information systems have prevented Rusnak from doing what he did? Explain. Could information systems have alerted Allfirst earlier? How?

5. If you were responsible for designing new information sys-tems for AIB and Allfirst, what would you do to solve their control problems?

INFORMATION AS A CRITICAL RESOURCE: INFORMATION RESOURCE MANAGEMENT

CHAPTER 12

Objectives

At many points during your career, you will be involved in projects to build new information systems. You will need to know how to measure the business benefits of these investments and how to make sure that these systems work successfully in your organization. After reading this chapter, you should be able to answer the following questions:

1. *How can our company manage the various components of information resource management and the issues involved with each component?*

2. *How can our company measure the business benefits of our information systems? What models should be used to measure that business value?*

3. *Why do so many systems projects fail? What are the principal reasons for systems failures?*

4. *How should the organizational change surrounding a new system be managed to ensure success?*

5. *What strategies can our organization use to manage the systems implementation process more effectively?*

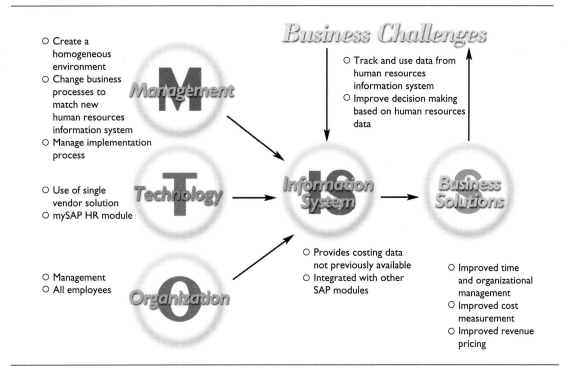

TransAlta Corporation Achieves High ROI on HR System

TransAlta Corp. learned from Gartner Consulting, a major international information technology research company, that they achieved a rate of return of 102 percent over a course of 58 months by implementing mySAP HR. mySAP HR is SAP's latest human resources (HR) information systems module.

The Calgary-based electric generation company first implemented SAP in 1996 and expanded their implementation of mySAP HR in 2001. Mike Williams, senior vice-president of human resources at TransAlta, said that the choice to implement the HR applications was natural, as the company had made the decision to stick with one vendor to facilitate integration. Creating a homogeneous environment was one of the factors that Williams highlighted when discussing the reasons for achieving a successful return on investment (ROI).

"We have a clear policy that says we're going to use one system," Williams said. "A lot of companies run into the trap of multiple systems, letting the latest and greatest flavour of the month creep into the company. We take a different approach to anything we integrate, and SAP is our chosen system. I think it's an important success factor."

James Holincheck, a research director at Gartner Consulting in Stamford, Connecticut, and the analyst who conducted the case study, said that the single vendor solution is not necessarily the right choice for every organization. "There are some benefits to a single vendor solution in terms of integration, but it is not universally required for success either," he said. "What TransAlta did was leverage the technology appropriately to get significant business benefits from it."

In order to make the best use of the applications, Williams admitted that the company changed its processes, rather than customizing the system. "We used the system as designed. I know a lot of companies do custom work so their processes stay whole, but we looked at the system and thought 'If it does it this way, why can't we?'"

Holincheck adds: "You really have to change your business processes with any software solution unless you want to customize the bejesus out of it. By implementing a packaged solution and not altering what you're doing to support it, you're not utilizing the best business practices that are built in," he said.

The third factor that Williams considers to be a contributing factor to the success of the system's integration is that TransAlta took the process one step at a time. "We weren't too ambitious. We started with the basics and then moved onto bigger transactions. We did it one piece at a time, rather than reinvent the world at one go," Williams said.

The study showed that TransAlta would achieve a 10-year savings of $31 million, taking a 10-year useful life period into consideration. Gartner calculated the ROI by evaluating explicit cost-saving or revenue-enhancing benefits associated with related business processes, such as time management and organizational management. Qualitative data was used to examine benefits achieved through mySAP HR, and quantitative data was analyzed for cost and revenue changes achieved after implementing the product.

Sources: Kristy, Pryma, "Alberta Electric Company Standardizes for ROI," available www.itbusiness.ca, accessed May 15, 2003; "Transalta Reports Profits by mySAP Human Resources," available www.sapinfo.net, accessed May 15, 2003.

MANAGEMENT CHALLENGES

One of the principal challenges posed by information systems is ensuring they can deliver genuine business benefits. Organizations need to find ways of measuring the business value of their information systems and ensuring that these systems actually deliver the benefits they promise. There is a very high failure rate among information systems projects because organizations have incorrectly assessed their business value or because firms have failed to manage the organizational change process surrounding the introduction of new technology. The success experienced by TransAlta's mySAP HR project is not as common as managers would like. Successful systems development—even when using a vendor's package, such as mySAP—requires skillful planning and change management, and you should be aware of the following management challenges:

1. **Managing the information systems function as a critical resource**. Organizations today rely on their information systems to stay in business. The proper functioning of these systems—and their contribution to the bottom line—have become critically important to most organizations. Ensuring that appropriate personnel are properly trained, evaluated, and paid; ensuring that systems development projects are well managed; ensuring that proper planning at all levels has been conducted—these are the main issues involved in managing information and information systems as a critical resource for the organization.

2. **Determining benefits and costs of a system when they are difficult to quantify.** Many costs and benefits of information systems are difficult to quantify. Information technology is too deeply embedded into most business processes to be isolated as a variable (Hartman, 2002). The impact of a single technology investment may be difficult to ascertain if it is affected by other interrelated systems and multiple layers of hardware, software, database, and networking technology in the firm's information technology (IT) infrastructure. Managers may have trouble measuring the social costs of implementing new technology in the organization. As the sophistication of systems increases, they produce fewer tangible and more intangible benefits. By definition, there is no solid method for pricing intangible benefits. Organizations could lose important opportunities if they only use strict financial criteria for determining

information systems benefits. However, organizations could make very poor investment decisions if they overestimate the intangible benefits.

3. **Dealing with the complexity of large-scale systems projects.** Large-scale systems, including enterprise systems that affect large numbers of organizational units and staff members, have extensive information requirements and business process changes. These large-scale systems are difficult to oversee, coordinate, and plan for. Implementing these systems, which have multiyear development periods, is especially problematic because the systems are so complex. In addition, there are few reliable techniques for estimating the time and cost to develop large-scale information systems. Guidelines presented in this chapter are helpful but cannot guarantee that a large information system project can be precisely planned with accurate cost figures.

I n this chapter, we examine various ways of measuring the business value provided by information systems, describing both financial and nonfinancial models. We then examine the role of change management in successful system implementation. Finally, we present strategies for reducing the risks in systems projects and improving project management.

12.1 INFORMATION RESOURCE MANAGEMENT

Information resource management (IRM) is the process of managing information systems—including hardware, software, data and databases, telecommunications, people, and the facilities that house these information systems (IS) components—as an asset or resource that is critical to the organization. As recently as 30 years ago, the information systems department was thought of as an "ivory tower" peopled by "pointy-headed geeks" who spoke "technobabble." Running the IS department as though it were any other business function was considered impossible by non-IS managers. What a difference 30 years make!

Today, IS departments are well managed, with personnel regulations and budgets, just like every other department. Like all departments, appropriate, well-thought-out management principles should be used to maximize the value of the IS department. That is the heart of IRM. In the following subsections, we review the basic components of IRM. While we assume that IS managers need to know these components, we also feel strongly that all managers should understand IRM in order to interact effectively and efficiently with the IS department. The IS department is a service provider to other departments and should be held accountable for the level of service provided. Managers who understand the components of IRM can accurately evaluate the level of service the IS department provides to their client departments.

THE INFORMATION SYSTEMS DEPARTMENT

Almost every organization today has a computer. Whether there is only one computer and only one individual who uses it or whether there are thousands of computers located around the world, the duties and functions of the information systems department are vested in one or more individuals. Whether these duties are explicit, as they are in middle- to large-sized organizations, or implicit, as in a "mom-and-pop" shop, these duties must be carried out. The IS department has the following duties and functions:

- Manage computer operations
- Manage systems development and systems development projects
- Manage IS personnel
- Budget for the department and others in the organization who use computers
- Plan for strategic, tactical, and operational level systems and for the IS department's operations
- Justify financial investment in information systems

Figure 12.1 **A typical information systems department structure. Each division has subdivisions to manage the overall departmental responsibilities.**

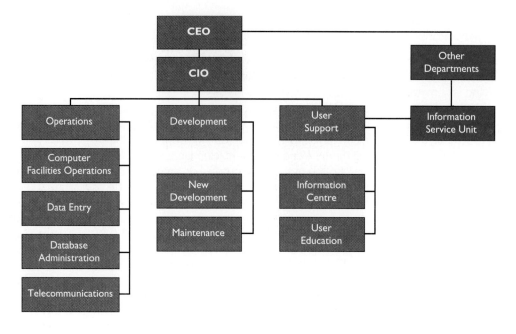

IS departments are structured like other departments; they have managers at all levels and, frequently, division of duties and reporting responsibilities. A typical IS department will have divided its duties into several divisions, such as systems development, telecommunications, electronic commerce/Web, database management, user relations/support, and operations. Each of these divisions might have subdivisions; for example, systems development might have two subdivisions, such as new development and maintenance. Each of the divisions would have a manager to whom those IS staff members assigned to that division would report. Division managers would report to the IS department manager. Figure 12.1 shows a typical IS department structure.

The IS department manager may or may not be the **chief information officer** (CIO). The CIO is the strategic level manager for information systems. As a member of senior management, the CIO is responsible for strategic level IS planning and for ensuring that all IS plans, systems, and operations support the organization's overall strategy. Some organizations have begun calling the CIO a chief technology officer (CTO) or chief knowledge officer (CKO).

In addition to the CIO at the strategic level, the organization may also make use of an MIS (management information system) Steering Committee. The **MIS Steering Committee** sets policy and priorities for the IS department, including approving budgets for major projects and hearing progress reports on those major projects. The MIS Steering Committee is usually composed of the CIO and other members of senior management. In the best-case scenario, the organization's CEO is also a member of the MIS Steering Committee. It is the responsibility of the CIO to represent the IS department on the MIS Steering Committee and to communicate effectively with the committee's membership, "selling" them and other top managers on the IS department's plans and projects.

MANAGING PLANNING, STRATEGY, AND EXTERNAL RELATIONS

Again, like every other department, the IS department should conduct periodic planning at all levels. Strategic IS plans describe from a broad perspective the major strategic information systems that support or will support the organization's strategy. These are long-range plans that have a huge impact on the organization and on the IS department. Tactical IS plans have a shorter focus and concentrate on breaking down the strategic IS plan into more detailed plans that middle-level managers can focus on implementing. Finally, operational-level IS plans detail how the strategic IS plan will be implemented during the coming short term, usually one year. Specific goals and objectives permit measurement of how the IS department is performing in supporting the organization's strategy. Each of these sets of IS plans—strategic, tactical, and operational—should be *aligned* with the organization's strategy and with the organization's strategic, tactical, and operational-level plans (see Figure 12.2).

chief information officer

The strategic-level manager of information systems for an organization.

MIS Steering Committee

A strategic-level committee composed of the CIO and other top managers who set IS policy and prioritize and review major IS projects.

Figure 12.2A Model of Organizational Strategic Vision and Planning

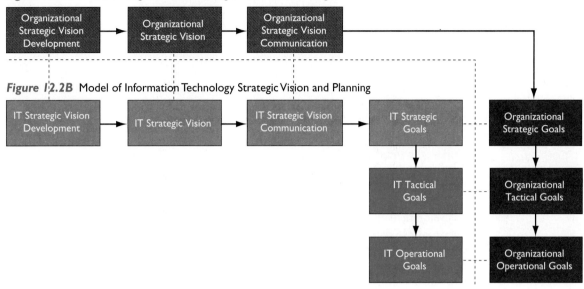

Figure 12.2B Model of Information Technology Strategic Vision and Planning

Figure 12.2 How information systems strategy and planning are aligned with organizational strategy and planning. Figure 12.2A represents the organization's strategy and planning steps and levels while Figure 12.2B represents the IS department's strategy and planning steps and levels. The dashed lines represent alignment between the organizational and IS strategies and plans at all steps and levels.

Source: Mary Brabston, Robert Zmud, and John Carlson, "Strategic Vision for Information Technology," in *Strategic Information Technology: Opportunities for Competitive Advantage,* edited by Raymond Papp, Idea Group Publishing, 2000.

The CIO is responsible for ensuring that these plans are developed and aligned with the organization's plans. The CIO is also the major link to external parties, such as senior-level managers at vendor organizations and strategic partners' CIOs. While many CIOs have been promoted from the ranks of the IS department, because of the communication-intensive nature of the position, many CIOs come from other areas of the organization, such as finance or human resources.

MANAGING SYSTEMS DEVELOPMENT

Systems development has many facets or perspectives. In Chapter 10, we looked at the systems development life cycle and at systems development as organizational change. In this chapter, we look at systems development in terms of managing the implemented system and in terms of personnel assignments to develop systems.

In Chapter 11, we discussed information systems quality, security, and control in detail. These topics are also part of information resource management. Once a system has been implemented, it is the IS department's responsibility to ensure that policies, guidelines, and decisions about the implemented systems are followed. These responsibilities include ensuring that backups are made, that IS audits are conducted when and where appropriate, that appropriate security processes and appropriate controls, such as passwords and locked doors, are maintained and followed. Included in this are network, database, and Web management, which ensure that organizational and department policies are followed in each of these areas and that these parts of the organization's information systems are secure, reliable, available, and accessible, as needed.

In previous chapters, we briefly discussed the role of systems analysts and programmers. IS departments also employ **systems operators** who run the hardware, including loading tape and disk drives, starting and stopping computer "jobs," and ensuring that backups are carried out as dictated by policy. **Data entry operators** enter data in computer-readable format and are managed by database managers. **Network managers** supervise networks, while **Webmasters** handle the organization's Web-based presence. Every organization organizes its IS department and IS components differently. Every organization also calls people who hold

systems operators
IS personnel who actually operate the hardware.

data entry operators
IS personnel who enter data in computer readable format.

network managers
IS personnel who supervise the operations of an organization's networks.

Webmasters
IS personnel who supervise an organization's Web-based presence.

these generic positions by different names. A network manager in one organization may be a local area network (LAN) coordinator in another, but the employee's function is the same.

Many organizations centralize their information systems so that most of the IS components (hardware, software, and so on) are located centrally and managed by a central IS department. In centralized IS departments, most decisions about information systems are made in the IS department. Other organizations choose to decentralize their information systems, permitting organizational departments or divisions to make their own decisions about what information systems to develop or purchase, frequently housing their own networks, hardware, and software. Many of these decentralized organizations also employ extra IS staff who report to the decentralized unit.

Today, the trend is toward information service units and information centres. Figure 12.1 depicts this modern type of IS department structure. An information service unit is an IS group located within a non-IS department, such as marketing. The information service unit is employed by and reports to the IS department; the IS unit handles requests for systems development, training, or assistance from their assigned department, serving as an interface to the IS department. An information centre, also known as user support, is housed in the IS department but handles requests for support, training, assistance, and guidance from other departments. If the marketing department needs to determine whether to upgrade the operating system their desktop computers use, they could call the information centre for advice.

ASSIGNING PERSONNEL TO DEVELOP SYSTEMS

How does an IS manager decide who will be assigned to a particular systems development project? Should an experienced person be assigned to new projects or to maintaining those projects on which he or she has already worked? Should less experienced personnel be assigned to maintenance projects so that they may gain experience?

New systems development is considered to be creative and more desirable than maintenance, which is viewed similarly to semiannual checkups with your dentist. It has to be done, but you would prefer not to have to do it. Every organization handles the assignment of programmers and analysts to individual projects differently. Frequently, rotation is used so that personnel may be assigned to new development for a project and, when that project is completed, move on to a maintenance project. Just as frequently, less experienced IS staff are partnered with more experienced staff on projects, who act as mentors and help them to gain higher levels of expertise.

Finally, the IS department is a service department, providing systems development and other services to other departments. Many businesses have implemented *service level agreements*, in which the IS department signs an agreement with a department for which it is developing a system. The service level agreement specifies milestones and deadlines, the budget, the level of service to be achieved, and other benchmarks. The IS department agrees to these terms and is held accountable by corporate management for meeting these benchmarks.

MANAGING PERSONNEL

We mentioned above that IS staff were formerly viewed as "pointy-headed geeks." Previous generations of hardware and software required a high level of technical knowledge and expertise. Today's systems permit lower levels of technical knowledge, enabling those with a middle level of technical expertise to succeed as programmers and analysts. This trend has opened IS career tracks to non–computer science majors.

While computer science focuses more on the technical side of information systems, the MIS field focuses on the needs of business that can be met by computer-based information systems. Today's IS departments hire both computer science and MIS staff to fulfill their personnel requirements. In addition, yesterday's "pointy-headed geeks" receive education and training in business applications and how to communicate effectively without using "technobabble." More and more, the language of the IS department is "business-ese" instead of 'technobabble.'

Regardless of whether IS staff members came with a computer science or MIS background, like all other organizational employees they must be evaluated periodically. Determining metrics on which to base IS staff evaluation is a difficult task. Should a programmer be evaluated on number of lines of code generated? The code could be inefficient and time consuming to run. Should function points be used instead? Function points define where an actual function has been performed, but some functions are complex, while others are not. Do you evaluate an analyst on how well the assigned user area is satisfied with its analyst? Or how well the analyst works with his or her programming teams? This is not an easy issue. Determining what criteria should be used in evaluating IS staff is a difficult task because each staff member's job presents a different mix of technical and behavioural elements; the variation within the technical or behavioural elements and the mixing of the two, depending on the specific job, makes it difficult to develop and use evaluation criteria over a long period of time. A detailed discussion of this topic is beyond the scope of this text, but IS personnel must be evaluated and counselled on their performance on a periodic basis.

The last 10 years have seen the salaries of IS staff increase rapidly. How does an organization recruit and retain IS staff when they cannot afford to give periodic raises that are as high as the local rate of increase for their classification? Some organizations have taken to giving bonuses based on work done, projects completed, or tenure in the organization. For example, NorthWest Company has on occasion given a "signing bonus" to new employees, accompanied by a retention bonus after one year on the job. Other organizations, such as the City of Winnipeg, have given their IS staff a year-end bonus, up to several thousand dollars, to those employees who have been there for several years. These loyalty bonuses serve to defuse the natural desire of IS staff to "follow the money." How does that fit the company's salary policy?

We hear in Canada about a "brain drain" to the South, in which skilled Canadians are being hired by American companies at inflated salaries. Interestingly, there are experts on each side of the brain-drain issue—those who feel Canada is losing its best and brightest to the United States and those who disagree, arguing that the "brain drain" is only based on almost mythical anecdotal evidence. Regardless of which opinion is correct, the bottom line for IRM is that IS managers must attempt to keep their employees happy. In a time when IS jobs are going unfilled, this makes sense. The slowing economy (particularly following the terrorist attacks on September 11, 2001, in the United States), combined with the recent trend toward dot-com failures, has reduced the number of new IS jobs available. At least in this regard, perhaps the brain drain—if there ever was one—will decrease.

With technology advancing so rapidly, how do IS staff keep their skills up to date? IS departments need to develop policies for staff to receive training and to upgrade their skills. Issues to be addressed by IS training policies are funding and time off to attend seminars, workshops, and courses; eligibility for funding and time off; the number of courses that can be taken in a given period; and the locus of the decision (who decides which courses employees will take) about continuing education.

In addition to keeping employees' skills up to date, providing training opportunities is an excellent way to motivate employees and to retain them. The flip side of the coin is, of course, that the employees will now have advanced skills with which to seek other jobs. Maintaining a challenging, positive environment with a few "perks," such as casual day (now more the norm than an exception) or an onsite day-care service, also helps retain employees.

MANAGING BUDGETS

How can an IS manager know what the budget for the IS department should be for the coming year? A detailed analysis of projects that are ongoing and projects that may come up during the next year is required, along with determining the need to upgrade technologies. The IS department must also examine the potential for extraordinary raises or bonuses for exceptional performance to retain key IS staff in light of the trend in IS salaries. These are not easy calculations. IS projects are notorious for running over budget (see the discussion on change management later in this chapter).

How do you know when you should upgrade hardware or software? What do you do when your most productive and effective analyst comes to you with a job offer that includes a 10-percent increase in salary and requests only a 5-percent raise to stay in your organization? How does that fit within the budget? Every IS organization handles its budgeting issues differently.

Many IS departments receive *revenue* from other departments in the form of *chargebacks*, or internal transfers of funds, to reflect payment for services rendered. Chargebacks for a department can be calculated on the basis of the department's computer usage, the number of nodes the department maintains on the LAN, IS department overhead charges based on the department's size in terms of number of employees or revenues generated, and myriad other ways. It is important that the method of chargeback is well communicated to department heads so that they understand the process and the charges.

Taken together, the topics discussed above comprise the major components of IRM. Being able to justify financial investments in information systems is also part of planning at all levels. The IS department must be able to explain and demonstrate that their budget and systems are worth the organization's financial commitment.

12.2 UNDERSTANDING THE BUSINESS VALUE OF INFORMATION SYSTEMS

Information systems can have several different values for business firms. A consistently strong IT infrastructure can, over the long term, play an important strategic role in the life of the firm. Considered less grandly, information systems can simply facilitate a firm's survival.

It is important also to realize that systems can have value but that the firm may not capture all or even some of the value. Although system projects can result in firm benefits, such as profitability and productivity, some or all of the benefits can go directly to the consumer in the form of lower prices or more reliable services and products (Hitt and Brynjolfsson, 1996). Society can reward firms that enhance consumer surplus by allowing them to survive or by rewarding them with increases in business revenues. But from a management point of view, the challenge is to retain as much of the benefits of systems investments as is feasible in current market conditions.

The worth of systems from a financial perspective essentially revolves around the question of return on invested capital. The value of systems comes down to one question: Does a particular IS investment produce sufficient returns to justify its costs? There are many problems with this approach, not the least of which is how to estimate benefits and count the costs.

TRADITIONAL CAPITAL BUDGETING MODELS

capital budgeting

The process of analyzing and selecting various proposals for capital expenditures.

Capital budgeting models are one of several techniques used to measure the value of investing in long-term capital investment projects. The process of analyzing and selecting various proposals for capital expenditures is called **capital budgeting**. Firms invest in capital projects to expand production to meet anticipated demand or to modernize production equipment to reduce costs. Firms also invest in capital projects for many noneconomic reasons, such as installing pollution control equipment, converting to a human resources database to meet government regulations, or satisfying nonmarket public demands. Information systems are considered long-term capital investment projects.

Six capital budgeting models are typically used to evaluate capital projects:

1. The payback method
2. The accounting rate of return on investment (ROI)
3. The cost-benefit ratio
4. The net present value
5. The profitability index
6. The internal rate of return (IRR)

All capital budgeting methods rely on measures of cash flows into and out of the firm because capital projects generate cash flows into and out of the firm. The investment cost is an immediate cash outflow caused by the purchase of the capital equipment. In subsequent years, the investment may cause additional cash outflows that will be balanced by cash inflows resulting from the investment. Cash inflows take the form of increased sales of more products (for such reasons as new products, higher quality, or increasing market share) or reduced costs in production and operations. The difference between cash outflows and cash inflows is used for calculating the financial worth of an investment. Once the cash flows have been established, several alternative methods are available for comparing different projects and deciding about the investment.

Financial models assume that all relevant alternatives have been examined, that all costs and benefits are known, and that these costs and benefits can be expressed in a common metric—specifically, money. When one has to choose among many complex alternatives, these assumptions are rarely met in the real world although they may be approximated. Table 12.1 lists some of the more common costs and benefits of systems. **Tangible benefits** can be quantified and assigned a monetary value. **Intangible benefits**, such as more efficient customer service or enhanced decision making, cannot be immediately quantified but may lead to quantifiable gains in the long run.

Chapter 6 introduced the concept of total cost of ownership (TCO), which is designed to identify and measure the components of information technology expenditures beyond the initial cost of purchasing and installing hardware and software. However, TCO analysis provides only part of the information needed to evaluate an information technology investment because it does not typically deal with benefits, cost categories, such as complexity costs, and "soft" and strategic factors (discussed later in this section).

Limitations of Financial Models

Many well-known problems emerge when financial analysis is applied to information systems (Dos Santos, 1991). Financial models do not express the risks and uncertainty of their own costs and benefits estimates. Costs and benefits do not occur in the same time frame—costs tend to be upfront and tangible, while benefits tend to be backloaded and intangible. Inflation may affect costs and benefits differently. Technology—especially information technology—can change during the course of the project, causing estimates to vary greatly. Intangible benefits are difficult to quantify. These factors play havoc with financial models.

The difficulties of measuring intangible benefits give financial models an application bias: Transaction and clerical systems that displace labour and save space always produce more measurable, tangible benefits than management information systems, decision support systems, or computer-supported collaborative work systems (see Chapters 13 and 14). Traditional approaches to valuing IS investments tend to assess the profitability of individual system projects for specific business functions. These approaches do not adequately address investments in IT infrastructure, testing new business models, or other enterprise-wide capabilities that could benefit the organization as a whole (Ross and Beath, 2002).

The traditional focus on the financial and technical aspects of an information system tends to overlook the social and organizational dimensions of information systems that may affect the true costs and benefits of the investment. Many companies' information systems

tangible benefits

Benefits that can be quantified and assigned a monetary value; they include lower operational costs and increased cash flows.

intangible benefits

Benefits that are not easily quantified; they include more efficient customer service or enhanced decision making.

TABLE 12.1   COSTS AND BENEFITS OF INFORMATION SYSTEMS

Costs	Intangible Benefits
Hardware	Improved asset utilization
Telecommunications	Improved resource control
Software	Improved organizational planning
Services	Increased organizational flexibility
Personnel	More timely information
Tangible Benefits (cost savings)	More information
Increased productivity	Increased organizational learning
Lower operational costs	Legal requirements attained
Reduced workforce	Enhanced employee goodwill
Lower computer expenses	Increased job satisfaction
Lower outside vendor costs	Improved decision making
Lower clerical and professional costs	Improved operations
Reduced rate of growth in expenses	Higher client satisfaction
Reduced facility costs	Better corporate image

investment decisions do not adequately consider costs from organizational disruptions created by a new system, such as the cost to train end users, the impact that users' learning curve for a new system will have on productivity, or the time managers will need to spend overseeing new systems-related changes. Such benefits as more timely decisions from a new system or enhanced employee learning and expertise may also be overlooked in a traditional financial analysis (Ryan, Harrison, and Schkade, 2002).

There is some reason to believe that investment in information technology requires special consideration in financial modelling. Capital budgeting historically concerned itself with manufacturing equipment and other long-term investments, such as electrical generating facilities and telephone networks. These investments had expected lives of more than one year and up to 25 years. However, information systems differ from manufacturing systems in that their life expectancy is shorter. The very high rate of technological change in computer-based information systems means that most systems are seriously out of date in five to eight years. The high rate of technological obsolescence in budgeting for systems means simply that the payback period must be shorter and the rates of return higher than typical capital projects with much longer useful lives.

Financial models should be used cautiously and the results placed in a broader context of business analysis. Let us look at an example to see how these problems arise and can be handled. The following case study is based on a real-world scenario, but the names have been changed.

CASE EXAMPLE: PRIMROSE, MENDELSON, AND HANSEN

Primrose, Mendelson, and Hansen is a 250-person law partnership in Toronto, with branch offices in London, Los Angeles, and Paris. Founded in 1923, Primrose has excelled in corporate, taxation, environmental, and health laws. Its litigation department is also well known.

The Problem

The firm occupies three floors of a new building. Many partners still have five-year-old PCs on their desktops but rarely use them except to read e-mail. Virtually all business is conducted face-to-face in the office or when partners meet directly with clients on the clients' premises. Most of the law business involves marking up (editing), creating, filing, storing, and sending documents. In addition, the tax, pension, and real estate groups do a considerable amount of spreadsheet work.

With the firm's overall business revenues off 15 percent since 2001, the chair, Edward W. Hansen, III, is hoping to use information systems to cope with the flood of paperwork, enhance service to clients, and slow growth in administrative costs.

First, the firm's income depends on billable hours, and every lawyer is supposed to keep a diary of his or her work for specific clients in 30-minute intervals. Generally, senior lawyers at this firm charge about $500 an hour for their time. Unfortunately, lawyers often forget what they have been working on and must reconstruct their time diaries. The firm hopes that there will be some automated way of tracking billable hours.

Second, much time is spent communicating with clients around the world, with other law firms both in Canada and overseas and with the Primrose branch offices. The fax machine has become the communication medium of choice, generating huge bills and developing lengthy queues. The firm looks forward to using some sort of secure e-mail or even the Internet for communication. Law firms are wary of breaches in the security of confidential client information.

Third, Primrose has no client database! A law firm is a collection of fiefdoms—each lawyer has his or her own clients and keeps the information about them private. This makes it impossible for management to find out who is a client of the firm, who is working on a deal with whom, and so forth. The firm maintains a billing system, but the information in the system is too difficult to search. What Primrose needs is an integrated client management system that will take care of billing, monitor hourly charges, and make client information available to others in the firm. Even overseas offices want to have information on who is taking care of a particular client in other offices.

Fourth, there is no system to track costs. The head of the firm and the department heads who compose the executive committee cannot identify what the costs are, where the money is being spent, who is spending it, and how the firm's resources are being allocated. A decent accounting system that could identify the cash flows and costs a bit more clearly than the firm's existing journal would be a big help.

The Solution

Information systems could obviously have some survival value and perhaps could grant a strategic advantage to Primrose if a system were correctly developed and implemented. We can detail the costs of a new system solution by department and estimated benefits.

The technical solution adopted was the creation of a LAN composed of 300 fully configured Pentium 4 desktop PCs, three Windows.NET servers, and a 10-Mbps (megabit per second) Ethernet LAN on a coaxial cable. The network connects all the lawyers and their secretaries to a single, integrated system, yet permits each lawyer to configure his or her desktop with specialized software and hardware. The older machines were given to charity.

All desktop machines were configured with Windows XP Professional and Office XP software. Lotus Notes was chosen to handle client accounting, document management, group collaboration, and e-mail because it provided an easy-to-use interface and secure links to external networks (including the Internet). The Internet was rejected as an e-mail technology because of its uncertain security. The Primrose LAN is linked to external networks so that the firm can obtain information online from Lexis (a legal database) and several financial database services.

The new system required Primrose to hire a director of systems—a new position for most law firms. Two systems personnel were required to operate the system and train the lawyers. An outside trainer was also hired for a short period.

Figure 12.3 shows the estimated costs and benefits of the system. The system had an actual investment cost of $1 733 100 in the first year (year 0) and a total cost over six years

	Estimated Costs and Benefits 2002–2007											
	A	B	C	D	E	F	G	H	I	J	K	L
1	Year :				0	1	2	3	4	5		
2					2002	2003	2004	2005	2006	2007		
3	**Costs Hardware**											
4		Servers		3@ 20,000	60,000	10,000	10,000	10,000	10,000	10,000		
5		PCs		300@3,000	900,000	10,000	10,000	10,000	10,000	10,000		
6		Network cards		300@100	30,000	0	0	0	0	0		
7		Scanners		6@100	600	500	500	500	500	500		
8												
9	Telecommunications											
10		Routers		10@500	5,000	1,000	1,000	1,000	1,000	1,000		
11		Cabling		150,000	150,000	0	0	0	0	0		
12		Telephone connect costs		50,000	50,000	50,000	50,000	50,000	50,000	50,000		
13												
14	Software											
15		Database		15,000	15,000	15,000	15,000	15,000	15,000	15,000		
16		Network		10,000	10,000	2,000	2,000	2,000	2,000	2,000		
17		Groupware		300@500	150,000	3,000	3,000	3,000	3,000	3,000		
18												
19	Services											
20		Lexis		50,000	50,000	50,000	50,000	50,000	50,000	50,000		
21		Training		300hrs@75/hr	22,500	10,000	10,000	10,000	10,000	10,000		
22		Director of Systems		100,000	100,000	100,000	100,000	100,000	100,000	100,000		
23		Systems Personnel		2@70,000	140,000	140,000	140,000	140,000	140,000	140,000		
24		Trainer		1@50,000	50,000	0	0	0	0	0		
25												
26	**Total Costs**				1,733,100	391,500	391,500	391,500	391,500	391,500	3,690,600	
27	Benefits											
28		1. Billing enhancements			300,000	500,000	600,000	600,000	600,000	500,000		
29		2. Reduced paralegals			50,000	100,000	150,000	150,000	150,000	150,000		
30		3. Reduced clerical			50,000	100,000	100,000	100,000	100,000	100,000		
31		4. Reduced messenger			15,000	30,000	30,000	30,000	30,000	30,000		
32		5. Reduced telecommunications			5,000	10,000	10,000	10,000	10,000	10,000		
33		6. Lawyer efficiencies			120,000	240,000	360,000	360,000	360,000	360,000		
34												
35	**Total Benefits**				540,000	980,000	1,250,000	1,250,000	1,250,000	1,150,000	6,420,000	

Sheet1 / Sheet2 / Sheet3

Figure 12.3 Costs and benefits of the legal information system. This spreadsheet analyzes the basic costs and benefits of implementing an information system for the law firm. The costs for hardware, telecommunications, software, services, and personnel are analyzed over a six-year period.

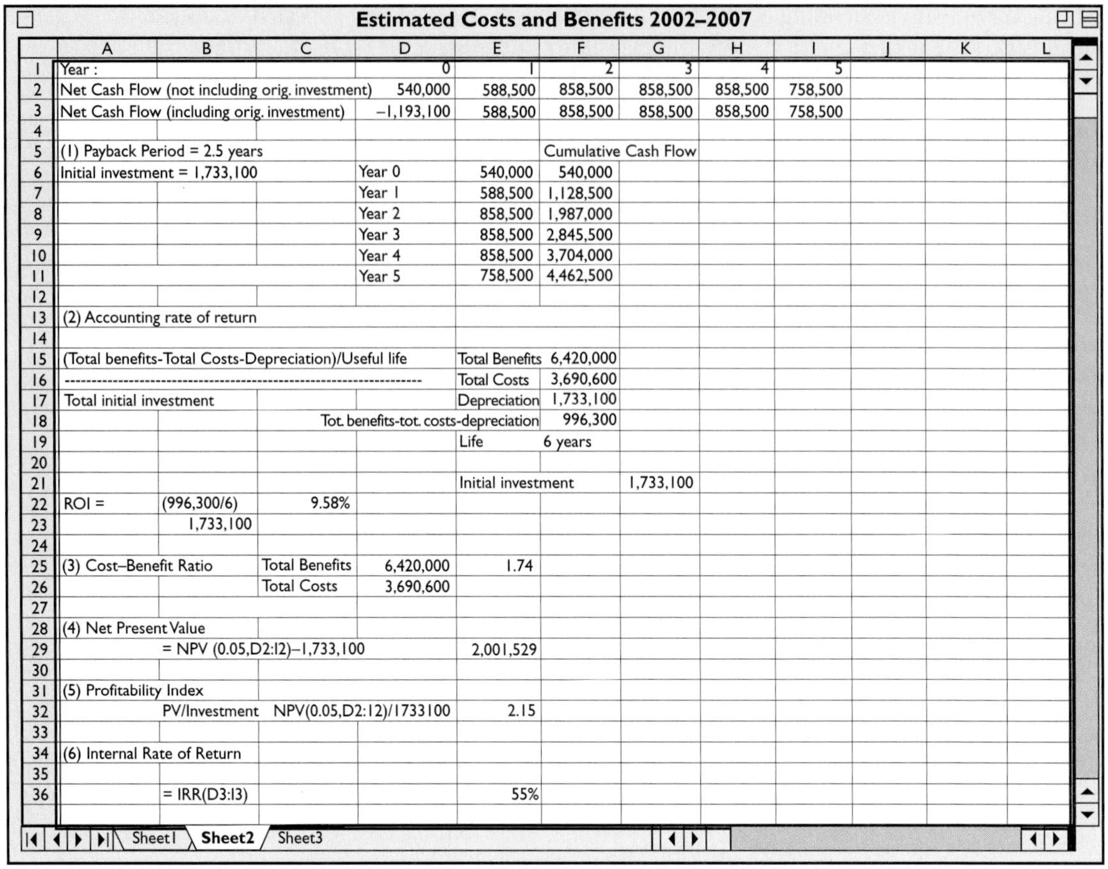

Estimated Costs and Benefits 2002–2007

	A	B	C	D	E	F	G	H	I	J	K	L
1	Year :			0	1	2	3	4	5			
2	Net Cash Flow (not including orig. investment)			540,000	588,500	858,500	858,500	858,500	758,500			
3	Net Cash Flow (including orig. investment)			–1,193,100	588,500	858,500	858,500	858,500	758,500			
4												
5	(1) Payback Period = 2.5 years					Cumulative Cash Flow						
6	Initial investment = 1,733,100			Year 0	540,000	540,000						
7				Year 1	588,500	1,128,500						
8				Year 2	858,500	1,987,000						
9				Year 3	858,500	2,845,500						
10				Year 4	858,500	3,704,000						
11				Year 5	758,500	4,462,500						
12												
13	(2) Accounting rate of return											
14												
15	(Total benefits-Total Costs-Depreciation)/Useful life				Total Benefits	6,420,000						
16	---				Total Costs	3,690,600						
17	Total initial investment				Depreciation	1,733,100						
18			Tot. benefits-tot. costs-depreciation			996,300						
19					Life	6 years						
20												
21					Initial investment		1,733,100					
22	ROI =	(996,300/6)	9.58%									
23		1,733,100										
24												
25	(3) Cost–Benefit Ratio		Total Benefits	6,420,000	1.74							
26			Total Costs	3,690,600								
27												
28	(4) Net Present Value											
29		= NPV (0.05,D2:I2)–1,733,100				2,001,529						
30												
31	(5) Profitability Index											
32		PV/Investment	NPV(0.05,D2:I2)/1733100			2.15						
33												
34	(6) Internal Rate of Return											
35												
36		= IRR(D3:I3)				55%						

Sheet1 **Sheet2** Sheet3

Figure 12.4 Financial models. To determine the financial basis for a project, a series of financial models helps determine the return on invested capital. These calculations include payback period, accounting rate of return (ROI), cost-benefit ratio, net present value, profitability index, and internal rate of return (IRR).

of $3 690 600. The estimated benefits totalled $6 420 000 after six years. Was the investment worthwhile? If so, in what sense? There are financial and nonfinancial answers to these questions. Let us look at the financial models first. They are depicted in Figure 12.4.

The Payback Method

payback method

A measure of the time required to pay back the initial investment on a project.

The **payback method** is quite simple: It is a measure of the time required to pay back the initial investment of a project. The payback period is computed as follows:

$$\frac{\text{Original investment}}{\text{Annual net inflow}} = \text{Number of years to pay back}$$

In the case of Primrose, it will take more than two years to pay back the initial investment. (Because cash flows are uneven, annual cash inflows are summed until they equal the original investment in order to arrive at this number.) The payback method is a popular method because of its simplicity and power as an initial screening method. It is especially good for high-risk projects in which the useful life of a project is difficult to determine. If a project pays for itself in two years, then it matters less how long after two years the system lasts.

The weakness of this measure is caused by its leading virtue, simplicity. The payback method ignores the time value of money, the amount of cash flow after the payback period, the disposal value (usually zero with computer systems), and the profitability of the investment.

Accounting Rate of Return on Investment

Firms make capital investments to earn a satisfactory rate of return. Determining a satisfactory rate of return depends on the cost of borrowing money, but other factors can enter into the equation. These factors include the historic rates of return expected by the firm. In the long run, the desired rate of return must equal or exceed the cost of capital in the marketplace. Otherwise, no one will lend the firm money.

The **accounting rate of return on investment (ROI)** calculates the rate of return from an investment by adjusting the cash inflows produced by the investment for depreciation. It gives an approximation of the accounting income earned by the project.

To find the ROI, first calculate the average net benefit. The formula for the average net benefit is as follows:

$$\frac{\text{(Total benefits} - \text{Total cost} - \text{Depreciation)}}{\text{Useful life}} = \text{Net benefit}$$

This net benefit is divided by the total initial investment to arrive at ROI. The formula is:

$$\frac{\text{Net benefit}}{\text{Total initial investment}} = \text{ROI}$$

In the case of Primrose, the average rate of ROI is 9.58 percent, which could be a good one if the cost of capital (the prime rate) has been hovering around 6 to 8 percent.

The weakness of ROI is that it can ignore the time value of money. Future savings are simply not worth as much in today's dollars as are current savings. However, ROI can be modified (and usually is) so that future benefits and costs are calculated in today's dollars. (The present value function on most spreadsheets will perform this conversion.)

Net Present Value

Evaluating a capital project requires that the cost of an investment (a cash outflow usually in year 0) be compared with the net cash inflows that occur many years later. But these two kinds of inflows are not directly comparable because of the time value of money. Money you have been promised to receive three, four, and five years from now is not worth as much as money received today. Money received in the future has to be discounted by some appropriate percentage rate—usually the prevailing interest rate or sometimes the cost of capital. **Present value** is the value in current dollars of a payment or stream of payments to be received in the future. It can be calculated by using the following formula:

$$\frac{\text{Payment} \times 1 - (1 + 1 \text{ interest})^{-n}}{\text{Interest}} = \text{Present value}$$

Thus, to compare the investment (made in today's dollars) with future savings or earnings, you need to discount the earnings to their present value and then calculate the net present value of the investment. The **net present value** is the amount of money an investment is worth, taking into account its cost, earnings, and the time value of money. The formula for net present value is:

Present value of expected cash flows − Initial investment cost = Net present value

In the case of Primrose, the present value of the stream of benefits is $3 734 629, and the cost (in today's dollars) is $1 733 100, giving a net present value of $2 001 529. In other words, for a $1.7 million investment today, the firm will receive more than $2 million. This is a fairly good rate of ROI and an excellent net present value (NPV).

Cost-Benefit Ratio

A simple method for calculating the returns from a capital expenditure is to calculate the **cost-benefit ratio**, which is the ratio of benefits to costs. The formula is:

$$\frac{\text{Total benefits}}{\text{Total costs}} = \text{Cost} - \text{benefit ratio}$$

In the case of Primrose, the cost-benefit ratio is 1.74, meaning that the benefits are 1.74 times greater than the costs. The cost-benefit ratio can be used to rank several projects for

accounting rate of return on investment (ROI)

Calculation of the rate of return on an investment by adjusting cash inflows produced by the investment for depreciation; approximates the accounting income earned by the investment.

present value

The value, in current dollars, of a payment or stream of payments to be received in the future.

net present value

The amount of money an investment is worth, taking into account its cost, earnings, and the time value of money.

cost-benefit ratio

A method for calculating the returns from a capital expenditure by dividing total benefits by total costs.

comparison. Some firms establish a minimum cost-benefit ratio that must be attained by capital projects. The cost-benefit ratio can, of course, be calculated using present values to account for the time value of money.

Profitability Index

One limitation of net present value is that it provides no measure of profitability. Neither does it provide a way to rank order different possible investments. One simple solution is provided by the profitability index. The **profitability index** is calculated by dividing the present value of the total cash inflow from an investment by the initial cost of the investment. The result can be used to compare the profitability of alternative investments.

$$\frac{\text{Present value of cash inflows}}{\text{Investment}} = \text{Profitability index}$$

In the case of Primrose, the profitability index is 2.15. The project returns more than its cost. Projects can be rank ordered on this index, permitting firms to focus on only the most profitable projects.

Internal Rate of Return

Internal rate of return is a variation of the net present value method. It takes into account the time value of money. **Internal rate of return (IRR)** is defined as the rate of return or profit that an investment is expected to earn. IRR is the discount (interest) rate that will equate the present value of the project's future cash flows to the initial cost of the project (defined here as a negative cash flow in year 0 of $1,193,100). In other words, the value of R (discount rate) is such that Present value − Initial cost = 0. In the case of Primrose, the IRR is 55 percent.

Results of the Capital Budgeting Analysis

Using methods that take into account the time value of money, the Primrose project is cash-flow positive over the time period and returns more benefits than it costs. Against this analysis, one might ask what other investments would be better from an efficiency and effectiveness standpoint? Also, one must ask if all the benefits have been calculated. It may be that this investment is necessary for the survival of the firm or necessary to provide a level of service demanded by its clients. What are other competitors doing? In other words, there may be other intangible and strategic business factors to take into account.

STRATEGIC CONSIDERATIONS

Other methods of selecting and evaluating IS investments involve strategic considerations that are not addressed by traditional capital budgeting methods. When the firm has several alternative investments from which to select, it can employ portfolio analysis and scoring models. It can also apply real options pricing models to information technology investments that are highly uncertain or use a knowledge value-added approach to measure the benefits of changes to business processes. Several of these methods can be used in combination.

Portfolio Analysis

Rather than using capital budgeting, a second way of selecting among alternative projects is to consider the firm as having a portfolio of potential applications. Each application carries risks and benefits. The portfolio can be described as having a certain profile of risk and benefit to the firm (see Figure 12.5). Although there is no ideal profile for all firms, information-intensive industries (e.g., banking or insurance) should have a few high-risk, high-benefit projects to ensure that they stay current with technology. Firms in non-information-intensive industries should focus on high-benefit, low-risk projects.

Risks are not necessarily bad. They are tolerable as long as the benefits are commensurate. Section 12.3 describes the factors that increase the risks of systems projects.

Once strategic analyses have determined the overall direction of systems development, a **portfolio analysis** can be used to select alternatives. Obviously, one can begin by focusing on

profitability index
Used to compare the profitability of alternative investments; it is calculated by dividing the present value of the total cash inflow from an investment by the initial cost of the investment.

internal rate of return (IRR)
The rate of return or profit that an investment is expected to earn.

portfolio analysis
An analysis of the portfolio of potential applications within a firm to determine the risks and benefits, and to select among alternatives for information systems.

systems of high benefit and low risk. These promise early returns and low risks. Second, high-benefit, high-risk systems should be examined; low-benefit, high-risk systems should be totally avoided; and low-benefit, low-risk systems should be re-examined for the possibility of rebuilding and replacing them with more desirable systems having higher benefits.

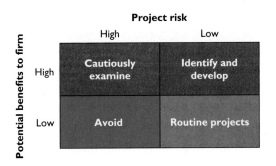

Figure 12.5 A system portfolio. Companies should examine their portfolio of projects in terms of potential benefits and likely risks. Certain kinds of projects should be avoided altogether and others developed rapidly. There is no ideal mix. Companies in different industries have different portfolios.

Scoring Models

A quick and sometimes compelling method for arriving at a decision on alternative systems is a **scoring model**. Scoring models give alternative systems a single score based on the extent to which they meet selected objectives (Matlin, 1989; Buss, 1983).

> **scoring model**
> A quick method for deciding among alternative systems on the basis of a system of weighted ratings for selected objectives.

In Table 12.2, the firm must decide among three alternative office systems: (1) an IBM AS/400 client-server system with proprietary software, (2) a UNIX-based client-server system using an Oracle database, and (3) a Windows client-server system using Windows XP, Windows.NET Server, and Lotus Notes. Column 1 lists the criteria that decision makers may apply to the systems. These criteria are usually the result of lengthy discussions among the decision making group. Often, the most important outcome of a scoring model is not the score but simply agreement on the criteria used to judge a system (Ginzberg, 1979; Nolan, 1982). Column 2 lists the weights that decision makers attach to the decision criteria. The scoring model helps to bring about agreement among participants concerning the rank of the criteria. Columns 3 to 5 use a 1-to-5 scale (lowest to highest) to express the judgments of participants on the relative merits of each system. For example, concerning the percentage of user needs that each system meets, a score of 1 for a system argues that this system, when compared with others being considered, will be low in meeting user needs.

As with all objective techniques, there are many qualitative judgments involved in using the scoring model. This model requires experts who understand the issues and the technology. It is appropriate to cycle through the scoring model several times, changing the criteria and weights, to see how sensitive the outcome is to reasonable changes in criteria. Scoring models are used most commonly to confirm, to rationalize, and to support decisions, rather than as the final arbiters of system selection.

If Primrose had other alternative systems projects to select from, it could have used the portfolio and scoring models as well as financial models to establish the business value of its systems solution.

Primrose did not have a portfolio of applications with which to compare the proposed system. Senior lawyers believed the project was low in risk using well-understood technology.

TABLE 12.2	**SCORING MODEL USED TO CHOOSE AMONG ALTERNATIVE OFFICE SYSTEMS***						
Criterion	Weight	AS/400		UNIX		Windows XP	
Percentage of user needs met	0.40	2	0.8	3	1.2	4	1.6
Cost of the initial purchase	0.20	1	0.2	3	0.6	4	0.8
Financing	0.10	1	0.1	3	0.3	4	0.4
Ease of maintenance	0.10	2	0.2	3	0.3	4	0.4
Chances of success	0.20	3	0.6	4	0.8	4	0.8
Final score			1.9		3.2		4.0
Scale: 1 = low, 5 = high							

*One of the major uses of scoring models is in identifying the criteria of selection and their relative weights. In this instance, an office system based on Windows XP appears preferable.

They believed the rewards were even higher than the financial models stated because the system might enable the firm to expand its business. For instance, the ability to communicate with other law firms, with clients, and with the international staff in remote locations was not even considered in the financial analysis.

Real Options Pricing Models

Some IS projects are highly uncertain. Their future revenue streams are unclear, and their upfront costs are high. Suppose, for instance, that a firm is considering a $20 million investment to upgrade its IT infrastructure. If this infrastructure were available, the organization would have the technology capabilities to respond to future problems and opportunities. Although the costs of this investment can be calculated, not all of the benefits of making this investment can be established in advance. But if the firm waits a few years until the revenue potential becomes more obvious, it might be too late to make the infrastructure investment. In these cases, managers might benefit from using real options pricing models to evaluate information technology investments.

real options pricing models

Models for evaluating information technology investments with uncertain returns by using techniques for valuing financial options.

Real options pricing models (ROPM) use the concept of options valuation borrowed from the financial industry. An option is essentially the right, but not the obligation, to act at some future date. A typical call option, for instance, is a financial option in which a person buys the right (but not the obligation) to purchase an underlying asset (usually a stock) at a definite price (strike price) for a limited period of time. For instance, on January 22, 2002, for $1.50 one could purchase the right (a call option) to buy 100 shares of Wal-Mart common stock at $60 per share in March 2002. If, by March 2002, the price of Wal-Mart stock did not rise above $60, you would not exercise the option, and the value of the option would fall to zero on the strike date. If, however, the price of Wal-Mart common stock rose to, say, $100 per share, you could purchase the stock for the strike price of $60, and retain the profit of $40 per share. The stock option enables the owner to benefit from the upside potential of an opportunity while limiting the downside risk.

ROPM value information systems projects similar to stock options, giving managers the flexibility to make a small capital investment today to create an opportunity in the future. Using ROPM, every information systems project can be treated as an option as long as management has the freedom to cancel, defer, restart, expand, or contract the project. Real options involving investments in capital projects are different from financial options in that they cannot be traded on a market, and they differ in value depending on the firm in which they are used. Thus, an investment in an enterprise system will have very different real option values in different firms because the ability to derive value from even identical enterprise systems depends on firm factors, for example, prior expertise, skilled labour force, market conditions, and other factors. Nevertheless, several scholars have argued that the real options theory can be useful when considering highly uncertain information technology investments, and potentially the same techniques for valuing financial options can be used (Benaroch and Kauffman, 2000; Taudes, Feurstein, and Mild, 2000).

ROPM offer an approach to thinking about information technology projects that takes into account the value of management learning over time and the value of delaying investment. In real options theory, the value of the information technology project (real option) is a function of the value of the underlying information technology asset (present value of expected revenues from the information technology project), the volatility of the value in the underlying asset, the cost of converting the option investment into the underlying asset (the exercise price), the risk free interest rate, and the option time to maturity (length of time the project can be deferred).

The real options model addresses some of the limitations of the discounted cash flow models described earlier, which essentially call for investing in an information technology project only when the value of the discounted cash value of the entire investment is greater than zero. ROPM allow managers to systematically take into account the volatility in the value of information technology projects over time, the optimal timing of the investment, and the changing cost of implementation as technology prices or interest rates rise or fall over time. This model gives managers the flexibility to stage their information technology investment or test the waters with small pilot projects to gain more knowledge about the risks of a project before investing in the entire implementation. Briefly, the ROPM place a value on management learning and the use of an unfolding investment technique (investing in chunks) based on learning over time.

The disadvantages of this model are primarily in estimating all of the key variables, especially the expected cash flows from the underlying asset, and changes in the cost of implementation. Several rule-of-thumb approaches are being developed (McGrath and MacMillan, 2000). ROPM can be useful when there is no experience with a technology, and the future of the technology is highly uncertain.

Knowledge Value-Added Approach

A different approach to traditional capital budgeting is to focus on the knowledge input into a business process as a way of determining the costs and benefits of changes in business processes from new information systems. Any program that uses information technology to change business processes requires knowledge input. The value of the knowledge used to produce improved outputs of the new process can be used as a measure of the value added. Knowledge inputs can be measured in terms of learning time to master a new process, and a return on knowledge can be estimated. This method makes certain assumptions that may not be valid in all situations, especially product design and research and development, where processes do not have predetermined outputs (Housel, El Sawy, Zhong, and Rodgers, 2001).

INFORMATION TECHNOLOGY INVESTMENTS AND PRODUCTIVITY

Information technology now accounts for about 50 percent of total business expenditures on capital equipment in the United States. Whether this investment has translated into genuine productivity gains remains open to debate. Productivity is a measure of the firm's efficiency in converting inputs to outputs. It refers to the amount of capital and labour required to produce a *unit of output*. For over a decade, researchers have been trying to quantify the benefits from information technology investments by analyzing data collected at the economy level, industry level, firm level, and IS application level. The results of these studies have been mixed and the term "productivity paradox" was coined to describe these mixed findings.

Information technology has increased productivity in manufacturing, especially the manufacture of information technology products, as well as in retail. Wal-Mart, which dominates American retailing, has experienced increases in both productivity and profitability over the last decade through managerial innovations and powerful supply chain management systems. Such competitors as Sears, Zeller's, and Costco are trying to emulate these practices. A 2002 study estimated that Wal-Mart's productivity alone accounted for over half of the productivity acceleration in American general merchandise retailing (Johnson, 2002).

However, the extent to which computers have enhanced the productivity of the service sector remains unclear. Some studies show that investment in information technology has not led to any appreciable growth in productivity among office workers. The banking industry, which has been one of the most intensive users of information technology, did not experience any gains in productivity throughout the 1990s (Olazabal, 2002). Corporate downsizing and cost-reduction measures have increased worker efficiency but have not yet led to sustained enhancements signifying genuine productivity gains (Roach, 2000, 1996, and 1988). Cell phones, home fax machines, laptop computers, and information appliances allow the highly paid knowledge workers to get more work done by working longer hours and bringing their work home, but they are not necessarily getting more work done in a specified unit of time.

The contribution of information technology to productivity in information and knowledge industries may be difficult to measure because of the problems of identifying suitable units of output for information work (Panko, 1991). How does one measure the output of a law office? Should one measure productivity by examining the number of forms completed per employee (a measure of physical unit productivity) or by examining the amount of revenue produced per employee (a measure of financial unit productivity) in an information- and knowledge-intensive industry?

Other studies have focused on the value of outputs (essentially revenues), profits, ROI, and stock market capitalization as the ultimate measures of firm efficiency. A number of researchers have found that information technology investments have resulted in increased productivity and better financial performance, including higher stock valuations. (Brynjolfsson and Hitt, 1998 and 1993; Davamanirajan, Mukhopadhyay and Kriebel, 2002; Hitt, Wu and Zhou, 2002; Banker, 2001; Chatterjee, Pacini, and Sambamurthy, 2002; Brynjolfsson and Yang, 2000). Information technology investments were more likely to improve firm performance if they were accompanied by complementary investments in new business processes, organizational structures, and organizational learning that could unleash the potential of the new technology. In addition to this "organizational capital," complementary resources such as up-to-date IT infrastructures have been found to make electronic commerce investments more effective in improving firm performance (Kraemer and Zhu, 2002). Firms that have built appropriate infrastructures—and view their infrastructures as sets of services providing strategic agility—have faster times to market, higher growth rates, and more sales from new products (Weill, Subramani and Broadbent, 2002; Weill and Broadbent, 1998).

In addition to reducing costs, computers may increase the quality of products and services for consumers or may create entirely new products and revenue streams. These intangible benefits are difficult to measure and consequently are not addressed by conventional productivity measures. Moreover, because of competition, the value created by computers may primarily flow to customers, rather than to the company making the investments (Brynjolfsson, 1996). For instance, the investment in ATMs (automatic teller machines) by banks has not resulted in higher profitability for any single bank, although the industry as a whole has prospered and consumers enjoy the benefits without paying higher fees. Productivity may not necessarily increase firm profitability. Hence, the returns of information technology investments should be analyzed within the competitive context of the firm, the industry, and the specific way in which information technology is being applied.

12.3   THE IMPORTANCE OF CHANGE MANAGEMENT IN INFORMATION SYSTEM SUCCESS AND FAILURE

Benefits from information technology investments will be reduced if firms do not consider the costs of organizational change associated with a new system or make these changes effectively (Ryan and Harrison, 2000; Irani and Love, 2000-2001). The introduction or alteration of an information system has a powerful behavioural and organizational impact. It transforms how various individuals and groups perform and interact. Changes in the way that information is defined, accessed, and used to manage the organization's resources often lead to new distributions of authority and power. This internal organizational change breeds resistance and opposition and can lead to the demise of an otherwise good system.

A very large percentage of information systems fail to deliver benefits or to solve the problems for which they were intended because the process of organizational change surrounding systems development was not properly addressed. Successful systems development requires careful change management.

INFORMATION SYSTEM PROBLEM AREAS

The problems causing information **system failure** fall into multiple categories, as illustrated by Figure 12.6. The major problem areas are design, data, cost, and operations.

Design

The actual design of the system may fail to capture essential business requirements or improve organizational performance. Information may not be provided quickly enough to be helpful; it may be in a format that is impossible to digest and use; or it may represent the wrong pieces of data. (See Figure 12.7.)

The way in which nontechnical business users must interact with the system may be excessively complicated and discouraging. A system may be designed with a poor **user interface**. The user interface is the part of the system with which end users interact. For example, an input form

system failure

An information system that either does not perform as expected, is not operational at a specified time, or cannot be used in the way it was intended.

user interface

The part of the information system through which the end user interacts with the system; type of hardware and the series of onscreen commands and responses required for a user to work with the system.

or an online data entry screen may be so poorly arranged that no one wants to enter data. The procedures to request online information retrieval may be so unintelligible that users are too frustrated to make requests. Web sites may discourage visitors from exploring further if Web pages are cluttered and poorly arranged, if users cannot easily find the information they are seeking (see the Window on Organizations), or if it takes too long to access and display the Web page on the user's computer (Palmer, 2002). The Manager's Toolkit provides some guidelines for effective Web page design.

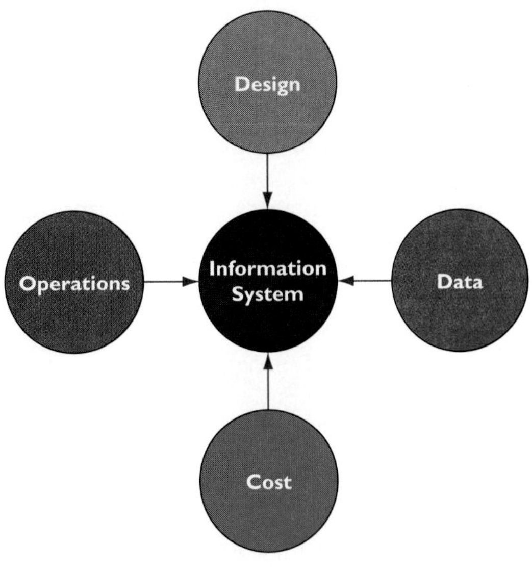

An information system will be judged a failure if its design is not compatible with the structure, culture, and goals of the organization as a whole. Historically, IS design has been preoccupied with technical issues at the expense of organizational concerns. The result has often been information systems that are technically excellent but incompatible with their organization's structure, culture, and goals. Without a close organizational fit, these systems create tensions, instability, and conflict.

Figure 12.6 Information system problem areas. Problems with an information system's design, data, cost, or operations can be evidence of a system failure.

Data

The data in the system may have a high level of inaccuracy or inconsistency. The information in certain fields may be erroneous or ambiguous, or it may not be organized properly for business purposes. Information required for a specific business function may be inaccessible because the data are incomplete.

Cost

Some systems operate quite smoothly, but their cost to implement and run on a production basis may be way over budget. Other system projects may be too costly to complete. In both cases, the excessive expenditures cannot be justified by the demonstrated business value of the information they provide.

Figure 12.7 Before RedEnvelope.com redesigned its Web site, 81 percent of visitors abandoned full shopping carts without completing their purchase, frustrated by inconsistent navigation bars, slow loading Web pages, and a complicated checkout process. The redesigned Web site illustrated here displays navigation bars clearly at the top of each page, loads quickly, and features a streamlined checkout process. After RedEnvelope improved its Web site, sales increased by 95 percent.

IS THE PREMIUM AT INSWEB TOO HIGH FOR USERS?

InsWeb operates an online insurance Web marketplace that enables consumers to shop for a variety of insurance products, including automobile, term life, homeowners, renters, and health insurance. Visitors to the InsWeb site can obtain competing quotes from over 40 well-known and respected insurance companies, including AIG, Allstate, CAN, GE Auto Insurance Program, and Travellers Property Casualty.

InsWeb provides a low-cost channel for insurance companies to acquire new customers who are pre-screened and come from the growing population of technology-oriented consumers who shop online. InsWeb acts as an agent for 11 auto insurers and a conduit of 25 more. The firms that use InsWeb as an agent pay it a commission, while the other firms pay InsWeb a fee for providing leads that usually help them close a deal with customers offline.

The site provides a great deal of useful information, and users can, in theory, use it for one-stop comparison shopping for most of their insurance needs. InsWeb can, for example, show comparative rates on auto insurance and make recommendations on the level of coverage that would be most appropriate, given the policyholder's home and other assets. But making the online application can be tedious and confusing if the multiple-choice options offered as answers to some questions do not correspond to the user's information.

Some business models translate to the Web more easily than others. Some products, such as books or CDs, are relatively straightforward to sell to consumers online. But insurance by nature is a very complex product, requiring users to be armed with a great deal of information in order to understand exactly what they are buying. That is one reason why the insurance business traditionally relied on actual agents to work with customers. How well could InsWeb perform this task?

For health insurance, InsWeb provides some general information but cannot effectively help users compare policies side by side. InsWeb has a tool for this purpose, but it does not provide space for enough information on the policies for which it quotes prices. Users would need to click on each policy individually and read the details to find out important information. InsWeb could make this process more user-friendly by adopting some of the features of other electronic commerce sites offering a large number of similar products. It could have provided a rating system for each policy's coverage or benefits, or it could perhaps include brief comments on the strengths and weaknesses of each policy option. While InsWeb could point users to lower-cost policies, working with the Web site was a great deal of work—perhaps too much work.

To Think About: What organization and technology issues affected the usability of InsWeb's Web site? Why is Web site usability so important in electronic commerce?

Sources: Susan J. Marks, "InsWeb: Too High a Premium?" *BusinessWeek Online*, April 15, 2002; and InsWeb Insurance Online, **www.insweb.com**, accessed July 28, 2003.

Operations

The system does not run well. Information is not provided in a timely and efficient manner because the computer operations that handle information processing break down. Jobs that abort too often lead to excessive reruns and delayed or missed schedules for delivery of information. An online system may be operationally inadequate because the response time is too long.

Some of these problems can be attributed to technical features of information systems, but most stem from organizational factors (Keil, Cule, Lyytinen, and Schmidt, 1998). System developers need to understand these organizational issues and learn how to manage the change associated with a new information system.

CHANGE MANAGEMENT AND THE CONCEPT OF IMPLEMENTATION

implementation

All organizational activities working toward the adoption, management, and routinization of an innovation.

change agent

In the context of implementation, the individual acting as the catalyst during the change process to ensure successful organizational adaptation to a new system or innovation.

To effectively manage the organizational change surrounding the introduction of a new information system, one must examine the process of implementation. **Implementation** refers to all organizational activities working toward the adoption, management, and routinization of an innovation, such as a new information system. In the implementation process, the systems analyst is a **change agent**. The analyst not only develops technical solutions but also redefines the configurations, interactions, job activities, and power relationships of various organizational groups. The analyst is the catalyst for the entire change process and is responsible for ensuring that the changes created by a new system are accepted by all parties involved. The change agent communicates with users, mediates between competing interest groups, and ensures that the organizational adjustment to such changes is complete.

MIS IN ACTION: MANAGER'S TOOLKIT

DESIGNING A USER-FRIENDLY WEB SITE

The design and user-friendliness of a Web site can mean the difference between electronic commerce and electronic business success and failure. Studies have found that poor design is more common than good design and that close to 50 percent of Web shoppers gave up purchasing items online because they could not easily locate the products they wanted on a Web site. Here are the most important factors to consider when designing an effective Web site:

Content: Content should be appropriate to the purpose of the site and its intended audience. Short sentences and paragraphs and bulleted lists should be used so that content can be scanned easily. A search function should be available if the site has large amounts of information.

Page design and layout: Graphics and design convey function and meaning and are an integral part of the user's Web site experience. Page design and layout, including colour, fonts, and images, should be balanced, clean, and uncluttered. Both graphic and text elements should be clearly legible, and pages should be short enough so that users do not have to do a great deal of vertical scrolling. The colours used in the Web site design should be carefully chosen because certain colours convey specific messages. Certain colours also look better offline, rather than online, due to the nature of display screens.

Navigation: Most user interactions with Web sites require navigating hypertext links between Web pages. Web sites should be designed so that users have a clear sense of where they are within the local organization of information. Navigating from page to page should be simple. Users should be able to easily backtrack or return to the home page. Basic navigation links should be present on every page of the Web site.

Accessibility: Users should be able to obtain the information they want with the fewest possible steps in the shortest time. Information on Web sites should be organized to minimize the number of steps through menu pages. Pages should be designed for ease of navigation and readability by those viewers who have limited vision or manual dexterity.

Load factors: Users are frustrated by long delays, so Web pages should load quickly. The loading time for a Web page will be slowed down by large numbers of simultaneous visitors to a Web site and extensive multimedia graphics and dynamic content. Therefore, Web page designs need to be "tuned" to the network access speeds of most users as well as the capabilities of systems where they are hosted.

Standards: The Web site should work with the most popular Web browser software, including Microsoft Internet Explorer and Netscape Navigator and with Macintosh operating systems, as well as computers using the Intel hardware standard and Windows operating systems.

 Additional material on implementation and change models can be found on the Companion Website at www.pearsoned.ca/laudon.

CAUSES OF IMPLEMENTATION SUCCESS AND FAILURE

Implementation outcomes can be largely determined by the following factors:

- The role of users in the implementation process
- The degree of management support for the implementation effort
- The level of complexity and risk of the implementation project
- The quality of management of the implementation process

These are largely behavioural and organizational issues and are illustrated in Figure 12.8.

User Involvement and Influence

User involvement in the design and operation of information systems has several positive results. First, if users are heavily involved in systems design, they have more opportunities to mould the system according to their priorities and business requirements, and more opportunities to control the outcome. Second, they are more likely to react positively to the completed system because they have been active participants in the change process itself. Incorporating the user's knowledge and expertise leads to better solutions.

Thanks to widespread use of the Internet and fourth-generation tools, today's users are assuming more of a leadership role in articulating the adoption, development, and implementation of information technology innovations (Kettinger and Lee, 2002). However, users often take a very narrow and limited view of the problem to be solved and may overlook

Figure 12.8 Factors in information systems success or failure. The implementation outcome can be largely determined by the role of users, the degree of management support, the level of risk and complexity in the implementation project, and the quality of management of the implementation process. Evidence of success or failure can be found in the areas of design, cost, operations, or data of the information system.

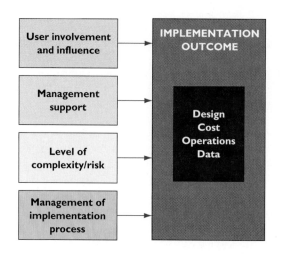

user-designer communications gap

The difference in backgrounds, interests, and priorities that impede communication and problem solving among end users and information systems specialists.

important technology issues or alternative information system solutions. The skills and vision of professional system designers are still required much the same way that the services of an architect are required when building a new house (Markus and Keil, 1994).

The relationship between consultant and client has traditionally been a problem area for IS implementation efforts. Users and information systems specialists tend to have different backgrounds, interests, and priorities. This is referred to as the **user-designer communications gap**. These differences lead to divergent organizational loyalties, approaches to problem solving, and vocabularies. IS specialists, for example, often have a highly technical, or machine, orientation to problem solving. They look for elegant and sophisticated technical solutions in which hardware and software efficiency is optimized at the possible expense of ease of use or organizational effectiveness. Users prefer systems that are oriented to solving business problems or facilitating organizational tasks. Often, the orientations of both groups are so at odds that they appear to speak in different languages. These differences are illustrated in Table 12.3, which depicts the typical concerns of end users and technical specialists (IS designers) regarding the development of a new information system. Communication problems between end users and designers are a major reason why user requirements are not properly incorporated into information systems and why users are driven out of the implementation process.

Systems development projects run a very high risk of failure when there is a pronounced gap between users and technicians and when these groups continue to pursue different goals. Under these conditions, users are often driven out of the implementation process. Because they cannot comprehend what the technicians are saying, users conclude that the entire project is best left in the hands of the IS specialists alone. With so many implementation efforts guided by purely technical considerations, it is no wonder that many systems fail to serve organizational needs.

Management Support and Commitment

If an IS project has the backing and commitment of management at various levels, it is more likely to be perceived positively by both users and the technical information services staff. Both groups will believe that their participation in the development process will receive higher-level attention and priority. They will be recognized and rewarded for the time and

TABLE 12.3	THE USER-DESIGNER COMMUNICATIONS GAP

User Concerns	Designer Concerns
Will the system deliver the information I need for my work?	How much disk storage space will the master file consume?
How quickly can I access the data?	How many lines of program code will it take to perform this function?
How easily can I retrieve the data?	How can we cut down on CPU (central processing unit) time when we run the system?
How much clerical support will I need to enter data into the system?	What is the most efficient way of storing these data?
How will the operation of the system fit into my daily business schedule?	What database management system should we use?

effort they devote to implementation. Management backing also ensures that a systems project will receive sufficient funding and resources to be successful. Furthermore, all the changes in work habits and procedures and any organizational realignments associated with a new system depend on management backing to be enforced effectively. If a manager considers a new system a priority, the system will more likely be treated that way by his or her subordinates (Doll, 1985; Ein-Dor and Segev, 1978).

Level of Complexity and Risk

Systems differ dramatically in their size, scope, level of complexity, and organizational and technical components. Some systems development projects are more likely to fail or suffer delays because they carry a much higher level of risk than others. The level of project risk is influenced by project size, project structure, and the level of technical expertise of the information systems staff and project team.

Project size. The larger the project—as indicated by the dollars spent, the size of the implementation staff, the time allocated for implementation, and the number of organizational units affected—the greater is the risk. Very large-scale system projects have a failure rate that is 50 to 75 percent higher than for other projects because these projects are so complex and difficult to control. The behavioural characteristics of the system—who owns the system and how much it influences business processes—contribute to the complexity of large-scale system projects just as much as technical characteristics, such as the number of lines of program code, length of project, and budget (The Concours Group, 2000; Laudon, 1989; U.S. General Services Administration, 1988).

Project structure. Some projects are more highly structured than others. Their requirements are clear and straightforward, so the outputs and processes can be easily defined. Users know exactly what they want and what the system should do; there is almost no possibility of the users changing their minds. These projects run a much lower risk than those with relatively undefined, fluid, and constantly changing requirements, with outputs that cannot be fixed easily because they are subject to users' changing ideas, or with users who cannot agree on what they want.

Experience with technology. The project risk will rise if the project team and the information system staff lack the required technical expertise. If the team is unfamiliar with the hardware, system software, application software, or database management system, or type of application proposed for the project, it is highly likely that the project will experience technical problems or take more time to complete because of the need to master new skills.

Management of the Implementation Process

The development of a new system must be carefully managed and orchestrated. Often, basic elements of success are forgotten. Training to ensure that end users are comfortable with the new system and fully understand its potential uses is often sacrificed or forgotten in systems development projects. If the budget is strained at the very beginning, toward the end of a project, there will likely be insufficient funds for training and documentation (Bikson et al., 1985).

The conflicts and uncertainties inherent in any implementation effort will be magnified when an implementation project is poorly managed and organized. As illustrated in Figure 12.9, a systems development project without proper management will most likely suffer these consequences:

■ Costs that vastly exceed budgets

■ Unexpected time slippage

■ Technical shortfalls resulting in performance that is significantly below the estimated level

■ Failure to obtain anticipated benefits

Figure 12.9 Consequences of poor project management. Without proper management, a systems development project will take longer to complete and most often will exceed the allocated budget. The resulting information system will most likely be technically inferior and may not be able to demonstrate any benefits to the organization.

man-month

The traditional unit of measurement used by systems designers to estimate the length of time to complete a project; refers to the amount of work a person can be expected to complete in a month.

How badly are projects managed? On average, private sector projects are underestimated by one-half in terms of budget and time required to deliver the complete system promised in the system plan. A very large number of projects are delivered with missing functionality (promised for delivery in later versions). As many as 80 percent of all software projects exceed their budgets, with the "average" software project running 50 percent over budget. Between 30 and 40 percent of all software projects are "runaway" projects that far exceed the original schedule and budget projections and fail to perform as originally specified (Keil, Mann, and Rai, 2000). Why are projects managed so poorly and what can be done about it? Here we discuss some possibilities.

Ignorance and optimism. The techniques for estimating the length of time required to analyze and design systems are poorly developed. Most applications are "first time" (i.e., there is no prior experience in the application area). The larger the scale of systems, the greater is the role of ignorance and optimism. The net result of these factors is that estimates tend to be optimistic, "best case," and wrong. It is assumed that all will go well when, in fact, that rarely happens.

The mythical man-month. The traditional unit of measurement used by systems designers to project costs is the **man-month**. Projects are estimated in terms of how many man-months will be required. However, adding more workers to projects does not necessarily reduce the elapsed time needed to complete a systems project (Brooks, 1974). Unlike cotton picking—when tasks can be rigidly partitioned, communication between participants is not required, and training is unnecessary—developing systems often involves *tasks that are sequentially linked, cannot be performed in isolation, and require extensive communications and training.* Adding labour to software projects where there are many task interdependencies can often slow down delivery as the communication, learning, and coordination costs escalate and detract from the output of participants (Andres and Zmud, 2001-2002). For comparison, imagine what would happen if five amateur spectators were added to one team in a championship professional basketball game? The team composed of five professional basketball players would probably do much better in the short run than the team with five professionals and five amateurs.

Falling behind: Bad news travels slowly upward. Among projects in all fields, slippage in projects, failure, and doubts are often not reported to senior management until it is too late (Smith, Keil, and Depledge, 2001; Keil and Robey, 2001). The CONFIRM project, a very large-scale information systems project to integrate hotel, airline, and rental car reservations, is a classic example. It was sponsored by Hilton Hotels, Budget Rent-A-Car, and Marriott Corporation and developed by AMR Information Services, Inc., a subsidiary of American Airlines Corporation. The project was very ambitious and technically complex, employing a staff of 500. Members of the CONFIRM project management team did not immediately come forward with accurate information when the project started encountering problems coordinating various transaction processing activities. Clients continued to invest in a project that was faltering because they were not informed of its problems with database, decision support, and integration technologies (Oz, 1994).

CHANGE MANAGEMENT CHALLENGES FOR ENTERPRISE APPLICATIONS, BUSINESS PROCESS RE-ENGINEERING (BPR), SUPPLY CHAIN MANAGEMENT, AND CUSTOMER RELATIONSHIP MANAGEMENT

Given the challenges of innovation and implementation, it is not surprising to find a very high failure rate among enterprise system and business process re-engineering (BPR) projects, which typically require extensive organizational change and which may require replacing old technologies and legacy systems that are deeply rooted in many interrelated business processes. A number of studies have indicated that 70 percent of all business process re-engineering projects fail to deliver promised benefits. Likewise, a high percentage of enterprise resource planning projects fail to be fully implemented or to meet the goals of their users even after three years of work.

Many enterprise system and re-engineering projects have been undermined by poor implementation and change management practices that failed to address employees' concerns about change. Dealing with fear and anxiety throughout the organization; overcoming resistance by key managers; changing job functions, career paths, and recruitment practices; and training have posed greater threats to re-engineering than the difficulties companies faced visualizing and designing breakthrough changes to business processes.

Enterprise systems create myriad interconnections among various business processes and data flows to ensure that information in one part of the business can be obtained by any other unit to help people eliminate redundant activities and to make better management decisions. Massive organizational changes are required to make this happen. Information that was previously maintained by different systems and different departments or functional areas must be integrated and made available to the company as a whole. Business processes must be tightly integrated, jobs must be redefined, and new procedures must be created throughout the company. Employees are often unprepared for new procedures and roles (Davenport, 2000 and 1998). New organizational learning is required for organizational members to acquire complex new knowledge about new business rules and business processes and simultaneously "unlearn" what they already know (Robey, Ross, and Boudreau, 2002).

Customer relationship management (CRM) and supply chain management systems are also very difficult to implement successfully. Between 55 percent and 75 percent of CRM projects fail to meet their objectives (McDonnell, 2001; Yu, 2001). Most firms embracing CRM need to transform their focus from a product-centric view to a customer-centric view, which requires some fundamental changes in organizational culture and business processes as well as closer cooperation between the information systems and sales and marketing groups. Supply chain management also requires closer coordination among different functional groups and different organizations as well as extensive business process change.

SYSTEM IMPLICATIONS OF
MERGERS AND ACQUISITIONS

Mergers and acquisitions (M&As) have been proliferating because they are major growth engines for businesses. Potentially, firms can cut costs significantly by merging with competitors, reduce risks by expanding into different industries (e.g., conglomerating), and create larger pools of competitive knowledge and expertise by joining forces with other players. There are also economies of time: A firm can gain market share and expertise very quickly through acquisition, rather than building over the long term.

Although some firms, such as Microsoft and Great West Life, are quite successful in carrying out M&As, research has found that more than 70 percent of all M&As result in a decline in shareholder value and often lead to divestiture at a later time (Lipin and Deogun, 2000; Frank and Sidel, 2002). Many deals suffer from unrealistic expectations about the synergies that could result from merging companies and from poor planning.

Architects of M&As often fail to appreciate the difficulty of integrating the systems of different companies. M&As are deeply affected by the organizational characteristics of the merging companies as well as by their IT infrastructures. Combining the information systems of two different companies usually requires considerable organizational change and complex system projects to manage. If the integration is not properly managed, firms can emerge with a tangled hodgepodge of inherited legacy systems built by aggregating the systems of one firm after another. Without a successful systems integration, the benefits anticipated from the merger cannot be realized, or, worse, the merged entity cannot execute its business processes and loses customers.

When a company targeted for acquisition has been identified, IS managers will need to identify the realistic costs of integration; the estimated benefits of economies in operation, scope, knowledge, and time; and any problematic systems that require major investments to integrate. In addition, IS managers can critically estimate any likely costs and organizational changes required to upgrade the IT infrastructure or make major system improvements to support the merged companies.

12.4 MANAGING IMPLEMENTATION

Not all aspects of the implementation process can be easily controlled or planned. However, the chances for system success can be increased by anticipating potential implementation problems and applying appropriate corrective strategies. Various project management, requirements gathering, and planning methodologies have been developed for specific categories of problems. Strategies have also been devised for ensuring that users play an appropriate role throughout the implementation period and for managing the organizational change process.

CONTROLLING RISK FACTORS

The first step in managing project risk is to identify the nature and level of risk confronting the project (Schmidt, Lyytinen, Keil, and Cule, 2001). Implementers can then adopt a contingency approach to project management, handling each project with the tools, project management methodologies, and organizational linkages geared to its level of risk (Barki, Rivard, and Talbot, 2001; McFarlan, 1981).

Managing Technical Complexity

internal integration tools

Project management technique that ensures that the implementation team operates as a cohesive unit.

Projects with *challenging and complex technology* to master benefit from **internal integration tools**. The success of these projects depends on how well their technical complexity can be managed. Project leaders need both heavy technical and administrative experience. They must be able to anticipate problems and develop smooth working relationships among a predominantly technical team. The team should be under the leadership of a manager with a strong technical and project management background, and team members should be highly experienced. Team meetings should take place frequently. Essential technical skills or expertise not available internally should be secured from outside the organization.

Formal Planning and Control Tools

formal planning tools

Project management technique that structures and sequences tasks, budgeting time, money, and technical resources required to complete the tasks.

formal control tools

Project management technique that helps monitor progress toward completion of a task and fulfillment of goals.

Large projects will benefit from appropriate use of **formal planning** and **formal control tools**. With project management techniques, such as Program Evaluation and Review Technique (PERT) or Gantt charts, a detailed plan can be developed. (PERT lists the specific activities that make up a project, their duration, and the activities that must be completed before a specific activity can start. A Gantt chart, such as that illustrated in Figure 12.10, visually represents the sequence and timing of different tasks in a development project as well as their resource requirements.) Tasks can be defined and resources budgeted.

This project team of professionals is using computing tools to enhance communication, analysis, and decision making.

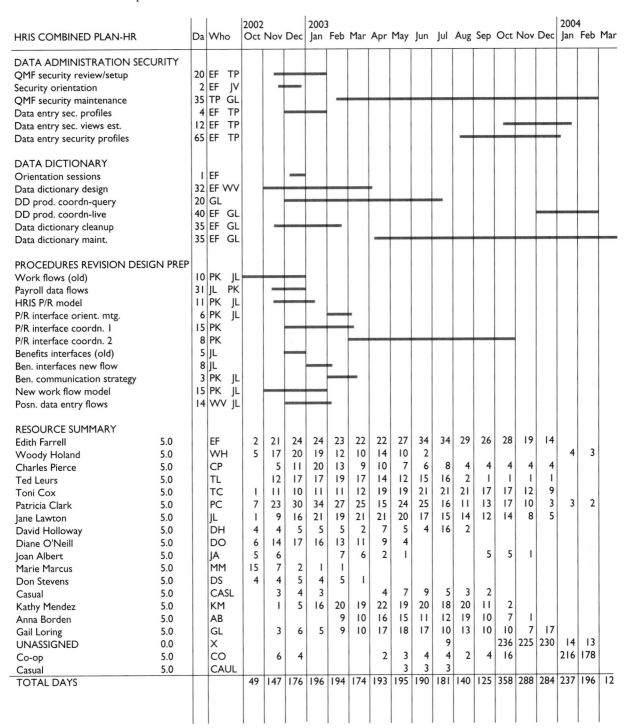

Figure 12.10 Formal planning and control tools help manage IS projects successfully. The Gantt chart in this figure was produced by a commercially available project management software package. It shows the task, person-days, and initials of each responsible person, as well as the start and finish dates for each task. The resource summary provides a manager with the total person-days for each month and for each person working on the project to successfully manage the project. The project described here is a data administration project.

These project management techniques can help managers identify bottlenecks and determine the impact that problems will have on project completion times. They can also help system developers partition implementation into smaller, more manageable segments with defined, measurable business results (Fichman and Moses, 1999). Standard control techniques will successfully chart the progress of the project against budgets and target dates, so deviations from the plan can be spotted.

Increasing User Involvement and Overcoming User Resistance

Projects with relatively *little structure and many undefined requirements* must involve users fully at all stages. Users must be mobilized to support one of many possible design options and to remain committed to a single design. **External integration tools** consist of ways to link the work of the implementation team to users at all organizational levels. For instance, users can become active members of the project team, take on leadership roles, and take charge of installation and training. The implementation team can demonstrate its responsiveness to users, promptly answering questions, incorporating user feedback, and showing their willingness to help (Gefen and Ridings, 2002). Electronic business initiatives which require rapid system responses to emerging opportunities may benefit from using special "organizational architects" with skills and expertise to bridge communication gaps between business users and technology specialists (Sauer and Willcocks, 2002).

Unfortunately, systems development is not an entirely rational process. Users leading design activities have used their positions to further private interests and to gain power, rather than to promote organizational objectives (Franz and Robey, 1984). Users may not always be involved in systems projects in a productive way.

Participation in implementation activities may not be enough to overcome the problem of user resistance. The implementation process demands organizational change. This type of change may be resisted because different users may be affected by the system in different ways. While some users may welcome a new system because it brings changes they perceive as beneficial to them, others may resist these changes because they believe the shifts are detrimental to their interests (Joshi, 1991).

If the use of a system is voluntary, users may choose to avoid it; if use is mandatory, resistance will take the form of increased error rates, disruptions, turnover, and even sabotage. Therefore, the implementation strategy must not only encourage user participation and involvement, it must also address the issue of counterimplementation (Keen, 1981). **Counterimplementation** is a deliberate strategy to thwart the implementation of an information system or an innovation in an organization.

Strategies to overcome user resistance include user participation (to elicit commitment as well as to improve design), user education and training, management edicts and policies, and better incentives for users who cooperate. The new system can be made more user friendly by improving the end-user interface. Users will be more cooperative if organizational problems are solved prior to introducing the new system. The Window on Management shows how Royal Dutch/Shell dealt with user and change management issues.

DESIGNING FOR THE ORGANIZATION

Because the purpose of a new system is to improve the organization's performance, the systems development process must explicitly address the ways in which the organization will change when the new system is installed, including installation of intranets, extranets, and Internet applications. In addition to procedural changes, transformations in job functions, organizational structure, power relationships, and behaviour will all have to be carefully planned. When technology-induced changes produce unforeseen consequences, the organization can benefit by improvising to take advantage of new opportunities. IS specialists, managers, and users should remain open-minded about their roles in the change management process and not adhere to rigid, narrow perceptions (Orlikowski and Hofman, 1997; Markus and Benjamin, 1997). Table 12.4 lists the organizational dimensions that would need to be addressed for planning and implementing many systems.

Although systems analysis and design activities are supposed to include an organizational impact analysis, this area has traditionally been neglected. An **organizational impact analysis** explains how a proposed system will affect organizational structure, attitudes, decision making, and operations. To integrate information systems successfully in the organization, thorough and fully documented organizational impact assessments must be given more attention in the development effort.

external integration tools
Project management technique that links the work of the implementation team to that of users at all organizational levels.

counterimplementation
A deliberate strategy to thwart the implementation of an information system or an innovation in an organization.

organizational impact analysis
Study of the way a proposed system will affect organizational structure, attitudes, decision making, and operations.

Royal Dutch/Shell Masters Change Management

In January 2000, Royal Dutch/Shell Group ordered all of its units to undertake company-wide alterations in its information systems security. The changes included requiring every computer user to change passwords every 35 days (or sooner). In addition Shell's IS groups were ordered to make similar changes in hundreds of servers and networks. The corporate-wide mandate stated that the changes must be completed by the end of June 2000. The project, named Trust Domain, was important to Royal Dutch's ability to protect itself.

Shell Information Technology International (SITI), the company's information technology services division, understood that these changes affected SITI because it not only meant ongoing password updating, but it also meant changing procedures for writing all computer code. In addition, it required making certain every desktop computer had a screen saver operating, and it required changing procedures for employees who dial into SITI's computers so that the systems are secured. SITI was responsible for its 2300 employees adhering to the new security requirements. Janet Jones, a SITI project manager, was assigned the task of managing SITI's change project.

SITI's management had learned from earlier systems projects that even managing relatively minor changes could be difficult. Jones knew that to be successful, any project had to face its organizational impact. She decided the project required a change agent, someone to be responsible for the "people" side of Trust Domain. She first brought in Christy Dillard, who was a change agent specialist Jones had worked with on an earlier project. Dillard then brought on board Anita Bettis, another experienced change agent. Dillard knew her own and Bettis's job focused on tuning in to the morale and reactions of the persons affected by the project, while Jones would maintain responsibility for the technical and project management side. Dillard characterized her and Bettis's task this way: "Lots of people just stick their change agent in an office and leave them there. But you have to embed yourself into the project and the team."

Bettis, Dillard, and Jones analyzed the situation and drew up a document that analyzed the impact of the change on the basis of each employee's job. The document became a foundation for their communications plan and was used when making decisions or attending meetings. Dillard and Jones met every day so that people working on both sides of the project (managing people and managing everything else) were well informed on the project's progress and could air and resolve their differences. They held weekly meetings with a group manager, while the change team met often with focus groups to stay in touch with employee reactions and problems. At weekly department meetings, they held project discussions, giving employees an opportunity to raise questions and objections. The team also identified unofficial leaders at these meetings (those who spoke out the most and had the most impact) so that the project could involve them in helping make the changes actually happen. The project did bump into opposition from those who felt the changes were too little and/or too late and those who believed the project would fail. The change team listened to these complaints and tried to respectfully handle them.

When July 1 arrived, SITI passed an independent audit of the new security measures. However, most departments were ill prepared, and so the deadline was moved to October 1. Jones commented on SITI's success, saying, "Planning a change is like a three-legged stool." "The three legs," she explained, "are technology, process, and people." Her stated position was that a project must "have all three."

To Think About: Why do you think SITI management focused so strongly on the morale of its staff and their criticism of the apparently easy project? Is it important for any information technology project? Explain.

Source: Simone Kaplan, "Quick Change Artists," *CIO Magazine,* March 15, 2002; **www.shell.com**, accessed December 31, 2002.

TABLE 12.4

Organizational Factors in Systems Planning and Implementation

Employee participation and involvement

Job design

Standards and performance monitoring

Ergonomics (including equipment, user interfaces, and the work environment)

Employee grievance resolution procedures

Health and safety

Government regulatory compliance

Allowing for the Human Factor

The quality of information systems should be evaluated in terms of user criteria, rather than the criteria of the IS staff. In addition to such targets as memory size, access rates, and calculation times, systems objectives should include standards for user performance. For example, an objective might be that data entry clerks learn the procedures and codes for four new online data entry screens in a half-day training session.

Areas where users interface with the system should be carefully designed, with sensitivity to ergonomic issues. **Ergonomics** refers to the interaction of people and machines in the work environment. It considers the design of jobs, health issues, and the end-user interface of information systems. The impact of the application system on the work environment and job dimensions must be carefully assessed.

ergonomics

The interaction of people and machines in the work environment, including the design of jobs, health issues, and the end-user interface of information systems.

Sociotechnical Design

Most contemporary systems development approaches tend to treat end users as essential to the systems development process but playing a largely passive role relative to other forces shaping the system, such as the systems designers and management. A different tradition rooted in the European social democratic labour movement assigns users a more active role, one that empowers them to co-determine the role of information systems in the workplace (Clement and Van den Besselaar, 1993).

This tradition of participatory design emphasizes participation by the individuals most affected by the new system. It is closely associated with the concept of sociotechnical design. A **sociotechnical design** plan establishes human objectives for the system that lead to increased job satisfaction. Designers set forth separate sets of technical and social design solutions. The social design plans explore different workgroup structures, allocation of tasks, and the design of individual jobs. The proposed technical solutions are compared with the proposed social solutions. Social and technical solutions that can be combined are proposed as sociotechnical solutions. The alternative that best meets both social and technical objectives is selected for the final design. The resulting sociotechnical design is expected to produce an information system that blends technical efficiency with sensitivity to organizational and human needs, leading to high job satisfaction (Mumford and Weir, 1979). Systems with compatible technical and organizational elements are expected to raise productivity without sacrificing human and social goals.

sociotechnical design

Design to produce information systems that blend technical efficiency with sensitivity to organizational and human needs.

"FOURTH-GENERATION" PROJECT MANAGEMENT

Traditional techniques for managing projects deal with problems of size and complexity by breaking down large projects into subprojects; assigning teams, schedules, and milestones to each; and focusing primarily on project mechanics, rather than business results. These techniques are inadequate for enterprise systems and other large-scale systems projects with extremely complex problems of organizational coordination and change management, complex and sometimes unfamiliar technology, and continually changing business requirements. A new "fourth-generation" of project management techniques is emerging to address these challenges.

In this model, project planning assumes an enterprise-wide focus, driven by the firm's strategic business vision and technology architecture. Project and subproject managers focus on solving problems and meeting challenges as they arise, rather than simply meeting formal project milestones. They emphasize learning as well as planning, seeking ways to adapt to unforeseen uncertainties and chaos that, if properly handled, could provide additional opportunities and benefits (DeMeyer, Loch, and Pich, 2002). It may be useful for organizations to establish a separate program office to manage subprojects, coordinate the entire project effort with other ongoing projects, and coordinate the project with ongoing changes in the firm's business strategy, information technology architecture and infrastructure, and business processes (The Concours Group, 2000).

MANAGEMENT WRAP-UP

Managers must link systems development to the organization's strategy and identify precisely which systems should be changed to achieve large-scale benefits for the organization as a whole. Two principal reasons for system failure are inadequate management support and poor management of the implementation process. Managers should fully understand the level of complexity and risk in new systems projects as well as their potential business value.

Developing an information system is a process of planned organizational change. Many levels of organizational change are possible. Global systems, enterprise systems, supply chain and customer relationship management systems, and business process re-engineering projects are high-risk implementations because they require far-reaching organizational changes that are often resisted by members of the organization. Eliciting user support and maintaining an appropriate level of user involvement at all stages of systems development are essential.

Selecting the right technology for a system solution that fits the problem's constraints and the organization's information technology infrastructure is a key business decision. Systems sometimes fail because the technology is too complex or sophisticated to be easily implemented or because systems developers lack the requisite skills or experience to work with it. Managers and systems developers should be fully aware of the risks and rewards of various technologies as they make their technology selections.

For Discussion

1.   It has been said that when we design an information system we are redesigning the organization. What are the ramifications of this statement?

2.   It has been said that most systems fail because system developers ignore organizational behaviour problems. Why?

SUMMARY

1.   *How can our company manage the various components of information resource management and the issues involved with each component?* The IS department may be structured in any of several ways: centralized as its own department, decentralized within other departments, or with personnel located both centrally and in various information service units and information centres. The CIO and MIS Steering Committee set IS policies and prioritize and review major projects. IS planning takes place at the strategic, tactical, and operational levels and should be aligned with organizational strategy at each level.

    Systems development actually involves a number of IS personnel roles and includes the assignment of staff to various projects, as well as ensuring that security issues are taken care of. IS personnel must be recruited, hired, and retained and must be permitted to keep their skill sets up. Like every other department in an organization, the IS department must set a budget, which is difficult at best, given the trend toward rapidly changing technology and escalating IS personnel salaries.

2.   *How can our company measure the business benefits of our information systems? What models should be used to measure that business value?* There are many different ways in which information systems can provide business value for a firm, including increased profitability and productivity. Some, but not all, of these business benefits can be quantified and measured.

    Capital budgeting models are used to determine whether an investment in information technology produces sufficient returns to justify its costs. The principal capital budgeting models are the payback method, accounting rate of return on investment (ROI), cost-benefit ratio, net present value, profitability index, and internal rate of return (IRR).

Other models for evaluating information system investments involve nonfinancial and strategic considerations. Portfolio analysis and scoring models can be used to evaluate alternative information systems projects. Real options pricing models, which apply the same techniques for valuing financial options to systems investments, can be useful when considering highly uncertain information technology investments.

Although information technology has increased productivity in manufacturing, the extent to which computers have enhanced the productivity of the service sector remains unclear. In addition to reducing costs, computers may increase the quality of products and services for consumers or may create entirely new products and revenue streams. These intangible benefits are difficult to measure and consequently are not addressed by conventional productivity measures.

3. *Why do so many systems projects fail? What are the principal reasons for systems failures?* A very large percentage of information systems fail to deliver benefits or solve the problems for which they were intended because the process of organizational change surrounding systems development was not properly addressed. The principal causes of information systems failure are (1) insufficient or improper user participation in the systems development process, (2) lack of management support, (3) high levels of complexity and risk in the systems development process, and (4) poor management of the implementation process. There is a very high failure rate among business process re-engineering and enterprise system projects because they require extensive organizational change. Customer relationship management and supply chain management system projects, as well as system changes resulting from mergers and acquisitions are also difficult to implement successfully because they usually require fundamental changes to business processes.

4. *How should the organizational change surrounding a new system be managed to ensure success?* Developing an information system is a process of planned organizational change that must be carefully managed. The term implementation refers to the entire process of organizational change surrounding the introduction of a new information system. One can better understand systems success and failure by examining different patterns of implementation. Especially important is the relationship between participants in the implementation process, notably the interactions between system designers and users. Conflicts between the technical orientation of systems designers and the business orientation of end users must be resolved. The success of organizational change can be determined by how well information systems specialists, end users, and decision makers deal with key issues at various stages in implementation.

5. *What strategies can our organization use to manage the systems implementation process more effectively?* Management support and control of the implementation process are essential, as are mechanisms for dealing with the level of risk in each new systems project. Some companies experience organizational resistance to change. Project risk factors can be brought under some control by a contingency approach to project management. The level of risk in a systems development project is determined by three key dimensions: (1) project size, (2) project structure, and (3) experience with technology. The risk level of each project will determine the appropriate mix of external integration tools, internal integration tools, formal planning tools, and formal control tools to be applied.

Appropriate strategies can be used to ensure the correct level of user participation in the systems development process and to minimize user resistance. Information systems design and the entire implementation process should be managed as planned organizational change. Participatory design emphasizes the participation of the individuals most affected by a new system. Sociotechnical design aims for an optimal blend of social and technical design solutions.

KEY TERMS

Accounting rate of return on investment (ROI),   403

Capital budgeting,   398

Change agent,   410

Chief information officer (CIO),   394

Cost-benefit ratio,   403

Counterimplementation,   418

Data entry operator,   395

Ergonomics,   420

External integration tools,   418

Formal control tools,   416

Formal planning tools,   416

Implementation,   410

Intangible benefits,   399

Internal integration tools,   416

Internal rate of return (IRR),   404

Man-month,   414

MIS Steering Committee,   394

Net present value,   403

Network manager,   395

Organizational impact analysis,   418

Payback method,   402

Portfolio analysis,   404

Present value,   403

Profitability index,   404

Real options pricing models,   406

Scoring model,   405

Sociotechnical design,   420

System failure,   408

Systems operator,   395

Tangible benefits,   399

User-designer communications gap,   412

User interface,   408

Webmaster,   395

REVIEW QUESTIONS

1. Name and describe the components involved in information resource management.

2. Compare the role of the CIO with that of the MIS Steering Committee.

3. Name and describe the types or levels of IS planning.

4. Name and describe the various roles IS personnel have in the IS department.

5. Name and describe the principal capital budgeting methods used to evaluate IS projects.

6. What are the limitations of financial models for establishing the value of information systems?

7. Describe how portfolio analysis and scoring models can be used to establish the worth of systems.

8. How can real options pricing models be used to help evaluate information technology investments?

9. Have information systems enhanced productivity in businesses? Explain your answer.

10. Why do developers of new information systems need to address change management?

11. What kinds of problems provide evidence of IS failure?

12. Why is it necessary to understand the concept of implementation when managing the organizational change surrounding a new information system?

13. What are the major causes of implementation success or failure?

14. What is the user-designer communications gap? What kinds of implementation problems can it create?

15. Why is there such a high failure rate among enterprise resource planning (ERP) and business process re-engineering (BPR) projects? Why are customer relationship management and supply chain management systems often difficult to implement?

16. What role do information systems play in the success or failure of mergers and acquisitions?

17. What dimensions influence the level of risk in each systems development project?

18. What project management techniques can be used to control project risk?

19. What strategies can be used to overcome user resistance to systems development projects?

20. What organizational considerations should be addressed by IS design?

APPLICATION SOFTWARE EXERCISE

SPREADSHEET EXERCISE: CAPITAL BUDGETING FOR A NEW CAD SYSTEM

Your company would like to invest in a new computer-aided design (CAD) system, requiring purchases of hardware, software, and networking technology as well as expenditures for installation, training, and support. The Companion Website for Chapter 12 contains tables showing each cost component for the new system as well as annual maintenance costs over a five-year period. You believe the new system will produce annual savings by reducing the amount of labour required to generate designs and design specifications and, thus, increase your firm's annual cash flow. Using the data provided and instructions on the Companion Website for Chapter 12, create a worksheet that calculates the costs and benefits of the investment over a five-year period and analyzes the investment using the six capital budgeting models presented in this chapter. Is this investment worthwhile? Why, or why not?

GROUP PROJECT

Form a group with two or three other students. Write a description of the implementation problems that might be expected for one of the systems described in the Window On boxes or chapter-ending cases in this text. Write an analysis of the steps you would take to solve or prevent these problems. If possible, use electronic presentation software to present your findings to the class.

INTERNET TOOLS

COMPANION WEBSITE

The Companion Website for this chapter will direct you to a series of Web sites where you can complete an exercise to evaluate user interfaces and user-system interactions.

At www.pearsoned.ca/laudon, you will find valuable tools to facilitate and enhance your learning of this chapter as well as opportunities to apply your knowledge to realistic situations:

- An Interactive Study Guide of self-test questions that will provide you with immediate feedback.
- Application exercises.
- An Electronic Commerce Project for buying and financing a home.
- A Management Decision Problem on evaluating ERP Systems using a scoring model.
- Additional material on implementation and change models.
- Updates of material in the chapter.

ADDITIONAL SITES OF INTEREST

There are many interesting Web sites to enhance your learning about information resource management. You can search the Web yourself, or just try the following sites to add to what you have already learned.

International Federation of Accountants
   www.ifac.org
   Full of information of interest to planning and project managers

Project Management Institute
   www.pmi.org

Information for project management professionals
Canadian Risk Management Council
   http://rimscanada.rims.org/Website/ WebsiteDisplay.cfm?WTID=93
   Information about risk management in Canada

Information Resource Management Association of Canada
   www.irmac.ca
   Information related to IRM in Canada

CASE STUDY: *Desjardins Outsources in Canada*

Holding $80 billion in assets and with more than five million individual and corporate members, the Fedération des caisses Desjardins du Québec is Quebec's largest financial institution. Until now Desjardins was relatively unknown to Canadians outside of Quebec. That may change however, with the recent launch of Desjardins' Financial Security Life Assurance Company; a merger of Desjardins-Laurentian Life Assurance (DLLA) and the Imperial Life Assurance Company of Canada. This marks Desjardins' first exposure to the rest of Canada.

The Mouvement des caisses Desjardins is the single largest private employer in Quebec, employing more than 36 000. While its public face is its ubiquitous branch outlets, or *caisses*, clients can also chose from a wide range of financial services, including banking, financing, leasing, securities, investment, insurance, and Visa. It is said that www.desjardins.com sees more traffic than any other financial site in Quebec, with more than 1.5 million hits each month.

André Beauchamp is the Directeur, Direction Transition for Desjardins, and he says that for three consecutive years, the company's internal information systems (IS) ranked with the best in the world, benchmarking at peak performance. Consistent performance measured 360 IMS (mainframe) transactions per second synchronized in two data centers, with a response time of 300 milliseconds. According to Beauchamp, this was the best in North America, and had the direct impact of avoiding line-ups at branches. Having reached this level, the company was loath to slip backwards.

But the organization kept up continual pressure to reduce cost. This posed a problem, as doing so entailed getting more resources for the IS team. Beauchamp explains that this pressure to find efficiencies meant things couldn't continue as they had. "We wanted to stay on top of the mountain," Beauchamp says, but "if you want to be the best, you need money to invest in technology."

The IS team was looking for an added 10 percent in funding to beef up their resources, but the pressure from the organization did not decrease. The opposite occurred, in fact—word came that the team was targeted for budget cuts of 15 percent imminently and another 15 percent in a year or two. The prize riding on this conflict was the team's pride and joy: the superlative performance level they had attained in the competitive world of financial markets.

To resolve the conflict, Desjardins listed their business goals, including improving time-to-market, focusing on strategic utilization of technologies, providing services based on users' capacity to pay, and improving responsiveness to business and competition opportunities/challenges. They also hoped to create a user/payer model at the street or *caisse* level. The solution they came up with was bringing an IT partner into the fold. This would reduce capital investments, investment risks in technologies, and short- and long-term costs.

Their 1999 call for proposals drew responses from a number of IT outsourcing firms eager to demonstrate how they could maximize efficiency while minimizing service disruptions. One consulting firm in particular, CGI Group, Inc., promised immediate cost savings that would not detract from Desjardins' streamlined operations.

In better economic times, companies outsourced their information technology to get access to scarce information technology talent. But in today's declining economy, saving money has risen to the top as one of the primary reasons for outsourcing. Many of the other factors that make outsourcing appealing for some, such as better access to skills and improved time-to-market, remain crucial in recessionary times as well. But at the highest levels of the executive ranks, the question that is increasingly driving outsourcing is: "Can someone else do this for less?"

Canadian outsourcers have won a recent string of contracts, mostly from Canadian insurers seeking to cut costs to help cope with the economic slump. American companies that have been looking offshore also may want to consider the benefits of outsourcing closer to home. These benefits include proximity, cultural similarities, inexpensive labour, and a favourable exchange rate. Another attraction of outsourcing in Canada is that because of the North American Free Trade Agreement (NAFTA), Canadian staff can migrate to the United States as part of outsourcing deals without visa limitations. Another benefit is that Canada's time zones are similar to those in the United States. Still the trend to outsource in Canada is much stronger among Canadian financial companies. For example, both Sun Life Assurance Company of Canada and Manulife Financial Corporation signed outsourcing contracts with IBM.

Fourteen months after Desjardins' initial call for proposals, CGI Group, Inc., got the nod. They in turn introduced Bell/Connexim into the mix. Six months later, in May 2001, Mouvement Desjardins and CGI signed a 10-year, $1.2-billion agreement. CGI would handle data operations management while Desjardins would retain control of its technological orientations.

CGI, a 25-year old company, counts among its clients 20 of the top 25 insurance carriers in the United States and 17 of the top 25 in Canada. CGI's clients include Pilot Insurance Company, the Dominion of Canada General Insurance Company, CGU Group Canada, Ltd., and now Desjardins. CGI is the fourth largest independent information technology services firm in North America, with more than 14 600 professionals. CGI has more than 3000 clients worldwide and more than 60 offices around the world. Outsourcing accounts for 70 percent of CGI's revenue. David Patrick, CGI's senior vice-president of insurance solutions and services, said some customers are completely outsourcing their information technology to CGI while others still maintain some capability in house.

Beauchamp was nearing retirement, and his swan song with Desjardins was being transition manager. He admits that on occasion the work demands were extreme. "It's not easy, but it is worth the trip," he says. "You really have to have an open mind. We play a different dance that we have not played before."

Indeed, if Desjardins had once danced a solitary jig to its own tune, it was now involved in the intricate footwork needed to waltz with three partners, including Bell/Connexim. Choreographing this was no easy task. Part of it entailed two binders bulging with a thousand pages of redesigned processes and transition plans. The schedule for the transition plan had three targets and milestones: six-month, one-year, and two-year.

There is more to the agreement than outlined above. CGI will help Desjardins market its data processing applications to other companies in the financial services industry. The first step will be selling to other credit unions and to the North American financial services industry. CGI's competencies include discovering business solutions with market potential and helping to market them. For Desjardins and CGI, this entails a win-win situation.

CGI's offer also included some business reciprocity where it was to the benefit of both companies, done a on nonexclusive commercial basis and where it was market competitive. For example, if CGI can reduce costs by having its professionals use a Desjardins credit card for their expenses, the potential is there to bring more revenue for Desjardins, Daniel Rocheleau, CGI executive vice-president explains. Other areas of potential reciprocity were identified as using Desjardins Securities for CGI's benefit plan, as well as Desjardins-Laurentian Life Assurance, and Services de paie Desjardins (pay services).

Desjardins managed to offload significant investment risk by selling its information technology assets and data centres to CGI. Because CGI moved their data centre into Desjardins' existing facility, there was no physical move needed, and rollout time was eliminated. Rocheleau explains that "Desjardins was doing things in a very specialized way with highly qualified people you want to keep." Because of this, his company hired about 500 of Desjardins' information technology staff. CGI promised to secure these jobs for at least 12 months and to provide them with comparable working conditions.

Desjardins' network of branches work somewhat as franchises, each being self-owned. For CGI, this means that that the 1800 branches are like having 1800 customers. Each demands focus on its particular and perhaps unique needs. Any modification CGI makes to the whole system must be approved by each branch, which can make for hard slogging.

A workable partnership takes time to mature, explains Rocheleau, which accounts for the lengthy selection process and subsequent transition planning. He points out: "We have to work together 10 years. Are we going to be able to live together (amicably)?"

Given Desjardins' traditional inward focus, no one had ever expected them to outsource, Rocheleau says. When they did, it entailed a seismic shift in the company's culture. This took much time and effort to work out. The way it's turned out, Desjardins uses its financial acumen to work the business relationship with its clients while CGI uses its operational expertise to handle delivery. Add Bell/Connexim's telecommunications expertise to the mix, and today's Desjardins is a very different company than it was five years ago.

An outsourcing partnership like this requires trust, communication, and understanding, Rocheleau stresses. "We have learned how to dance together," he says of Desjardins, CGI, and Bell/Connexim. Certainly the multifaceted and intertwining partnership with transfers of ownership back and forth, reciprocity plans, and commercialization hopes are not unlike an intricate dance. Desjardins is betting on that dance helping them stay at the top of the mountain. The Desjardins customers will be the judge.

Less than a year after the transition, Desjardins surveyed its customers to determine if traditional levels of quality had been retained. The response was positive, and Desjardins plans to do such surveys regularly. "We want to hear everything is the same as before," says Beauchamp. "If customers are seeing no difference, that's good."

Sources: Susan Maclean, "Desjardins Delegates its Data Processing," *ITWorld Canada*, www.itworld.ca, accessed March 1, 2002; Julie Gallagher, "Add Canada to Your Outsourcer Shortlist," *Information Week*, September 9, 2002; Gary Hilson, "CGI Scores IT Hat Trick with Three Insurance Firms," available www.itbusiness.ca, accessed May 2, 2002; Jaikumar Vijayan, "The Outsourcing Boom," *Computerworld*, March 18, 2002, CGI Web site, www.cgi.com, accessed August 1, 2003.

CASE STUDY QUESTIONS

1. Why did Desjardins decide they needed to outsource?
2. What do you think the criteria were that led Desjardins to choose CGI?
3. Summarize the potential problems you think Desjardins faced as it implemented the outsourcing arrangement..
4. If you were a senior manager at Desjardins, what financial measures would you be interested in tracking over the life of the outsourcing contract? Are there other measures or methods you think Desjardins should use in valuing the success of the contract with CGI?
5. What change management initiatives would Desjardins need to take in implementing such a large outsourcing contract? Why?

Make IT Your Business

Finance and Accounting

Many application software packages for individuals as well as for large businesses support financial processes, such as corporate accounting, tax calculations, payroll processing, or investment planning. Calculating the Total Cost of Ownership (TCO) of technology assets usually requires models and expertise supplied by finance and accounting.

Wireless Web technology has been the source of new financial services. Individual investors and investment professionals can use their mobile phones to obtain stock quotes and financial market news, to make stock trades, and to review their portfolios. Wireless Web and Internet technology are also making it possible to speed up fund flows by providing capabilities for immediate billing and invoicing. Database management software and data warehouses have enabled these firms to organize their data more flexibly so that they can view information by customer, financial product, or other criteria. Financial firms are also intensive users of datamining for analyzing credit risk, for packaging services for targeted customers, or for identifying profitable customers.

Many companies use electronic data interchange (EDI) to transfer payments to suppliers and invoices to large corporate customers. Banks maintain networks to link their automated teller machines (ATMs) and branch offices to central computers that keep track of deposit, withdrawal, and funds transfer transactions occurring at remote locations. Financial services firms today depend on networked systems to provide their managers and clients with instant access to account information. These firms are heavy users of online digital information services, such as Dow Jones, to obtain data on firms' financial positions and on financial markets.

You can find examples of finance and accounting applications on pages 314, 352, 356–357, 358–359, 363, 387–389, 410, and 424–425.

Human Resources

Because hardware and software technologies are changing very rapidly, providing many new productivity tools to employees and powerful software package and services for the human resources department, employees will need frequent retraining in order to use these tools effectively. Companies typically maintain human resources databases enabling them to maintain data on employees, benefits plans, and training programs and to provide reports to the government concerning compliance with health, safety, and equal employment opportunity regulations. Since these human resources databases contain sensitive information, such as salaries, job performance evaluations, and medical history, companies must be very careful about distributing this information.

Companies can use intranets to publish employee bulletins, policy manuals, directories, and other human resources documents. Employees can use telephone-based systems, the Web, or private corporate networks to review their employment records or to make changes to their benefits plans. Managers can use e-mail and videoconferencing to communicate with employees and work teams. Input from human resource specialists is essential when developing a corporate policy for employee use of networks and computing resources. You can find examples of human resources applications on pages 391–392 and 419.

Manufacturing and Production

Many manufacturing applications are based on client-server networks, which use networked computers to control the flow of work on the factory floor. Handheld computers and bar code scanners are widely used to track items in inventory and to track package shipments. XML (eXtensible Markup Language) provides a set of standards through which all participants in a supply chain can exchange data with each other without high expenditures for specialized translation programs and middleware.

Extranets are especially useful for collaborative commerce and supply chain management and are the primary platform for private industrial networks. They are often used for providing product availability, pricing, and shipment data; for exchanging purchase orders and invoices; and for joint product development activities with other companies. Companies maintain large databases of finished goods, raw materials in inventory, and goods in transit that can be used for supply chain management. The manufacturing process makes use of numerous databases on suppliers, jobs in progress, product components, product quality, and costs.

Computers and computer-controlled machines on the factory floor are often linked in LANs. In companies with advanced manufacturing systems, each step in the manufacturing process uses networks to transmit data to the next step. Data from orders triggers transactions that can be transmitted via networks directly to manufacturing scheduling systems, to supply chain management systems, to the assembly line, and to systems for warehousing and delivery. You can find examples of manufacturing and production applications on page 405.

Sales and Marketing

Sales and marketing have benefited from hardware and software technologies that provide customers and sales staff with rapid access to information, responses to customer questions, and order-taking. Web browser software provides an easy-to-use interface for accessing product information or placing orders over the Web, while e-mail software is a quick and inexpensive tool for answering customer queries. Web sites can be enhanced with Java applets that allow users to perform calculations or view interactive product demonstrations on Web sites using standard Web browser software. The Web is an especially powerful medium for sales and marketing because it provides capabilities for personalization and interacting with customers that cannot be found in other channels. Companies can engage in ongoing dialogues with customers using e-mail, chat, and electronic discussion groups to solidify their customer relationships.

Wireless Web technology provides new information and location-based services for companies to sell, which could provide major new sources of revenue. By querying customer databases, analysts can identify customers most interested in specific products or highly profitable customers. They can target specialized products and promotions on the basis of these detailed customer profiles. You can find examples of sales and marketing applications on pages 324–326, 383, and 428.

HACKERS, CRACKERS, AND CYBERTERRORISM: WHAT'S AN ORGANIZATION TO DO?

Reducing Internet security risk involves cost, which can lead to reduction of convenience and ease of use. However, a wide variety of systems based on the Internet, including mobile systems, public, private, and personal networks, are under what has been termed "cyberattacks"—illegal attempts to log on to systems for which the *hacker* has not been authorized.

The latest generation of hackers has been termed *crackers*, short for criminal hackers, because their attacks are illegal and frequently wreak large-scale havoc. We will first examine some of these cyberattacks, particularly one type of cyberattack called *denial of service* (DoS), and then its variant *distributed denial of service* (DDoS).

At first glance a DoS attack resembles normal legitimate traffic, which makes it hard to fend off. The difference lies with the intent behind the traffic and with the associated increase in volume. While traffic to a mail server rises and falls according to the myriad of external users, during a DoS attack, a concentrated volley of messages swamps the server and crashes it. Even if the people operating a server know they are being attacked, there is little they can do to deflect the incoming traffic.

DoS attacks can seek to flood a network with traffic or to modify a router's configuration. The goal of both methods is to deny access to legitimate users. The various means of achieving that goal have little in common.

If a DoS attack is noticed in time, a service can be shut down while the organization rides out the attack. That cannot always be done without repercussions, though. For companies whose reputation depends on the reliability and accuracy of their Web-based transactions, a DoS attack can be a major embarrassment and a serious threat to business.

A distributed denial of service (DDoS) attack is slightly different. In this case the attack comes from numerous sites. This increases the difficulty in detection and protection. Blocking a single IP address or network will make little difference, as traffic may be flooding in from thousands of systems. Sometimes viruses infiltrate programs into individual systems that then launch attacks without the system owner even knowing what their computer is engaged in.

A study by researchers at the University of California, San Diego, found that DoS attacks were launched at the rate of 4000 per week in 2001. The study focused on DoS attacks across the Internet for three one-week periods, centring on the number, duration, and focus of the attacks. According to the study's findings, more than 12 000 DoS attacks were launched during those three weeks. A minor proportion of these attacks targeted equipment essential to the operation of the Internet, including routers and name servers.

It was no surprise that well-known sites were targeted, including Amazon.com, AOL.com, and Hotmail.com. But oddly enough DoS attacks hit Romanian computers with almost the same regularity as .com and .net sites. Brazilian computers, in turn, suffered more attacks than .edu and .org computers together. Excepting high profile sites, most victims received fewer than five attacks. Within this group, the majority were hit only once. The study demonstrated that some DoS attacks were aimed at home Internet users; the researchers wondered if this was evidence of DoS use in personal disputes.

The most notorious DDoS attack came from Canada. A teenager from Montreal, whose name has never been released, launched a series of DDoS attacks during a one week period in February of 2000. Mafiaboy, as he was known, downloaded software onto computers around the world that he had hacked into, programming them to bombard the victims' servers with requests for data. The requests were camouflaged so that the receiving servers would perceive them as normal data requests from legitimate visitors. The sheer volume of data overwhelmed the servers, resulting in long delays and crashes. Mafiaboy made himself easy to find: he used an ISP that tracked his activities and made boastful claims in Internet chat rooms. While the boastful claims might be typical of an adolescent, they contained information only the real hacker would know. His victims included CNN, Yahoo!, Amazon, eBay, Dell, eTrade, ZDnet, HMV, and others. These companies lost hundreds of thousands of dollars in lost sales and the resulting loss of customer confidence. Results of a poll by @plan, released one month after the attacks, indicated that the hacker assaults severely damaged consumer confidence in the Internet. Almost 40 percent of American Internet shoppers aged 18 years or older were less likely to make an online purchase in the future. A study released by Information Week Research that same month reported that hacker attacks cost the global economy US $1.6 trillion that year, with the most costly culprit being viruses. Of course, Mafiaboy planted viruses in hundreds of corporate computers to launch his DDos attacks.

DoS attacks can be detected and defeated if the messages have common characteristics, such as all being from the same site or being a common size. In such a case a filter designed to match the pattern can block incoming data. Unfortunately, discovering such a pattern usually means waiting until an attack occurs, by which point the targeted server is already in trouble. New technologies being developed to better detect or even pre-empt DoS attacks include more-sophisticated filters and specially encrypted packet headers that prevent source addresses from being falsified.

Another preventive measure involves placing so-called "choke points" in a system. For instance, a router might have a limit built into it that disallows the sudden flood of messages that entails a DoS attack. Given the diverse nature of DoS attacks, such preventative measures are developing slowly. But Cisco routers have introduced "smart filtering," which is said to be effective.

The Boy Scout model—"be prepared"—is a simple but effective defense against DoS attacks. If backup equipment is in place and working, then an attack on the main server may fail to crash the system. Experts suggest that IT staff practise, prepare, and rehearse before a DoS attack ever happens. This preparation can make all the difference when or if an attack occurs.

In November and December 1999, the National Infrastructure Protection Center (NIPC), a U.S. government agency, received reports that universities and other organizations were detecting the presence of hundreds of Denial of Service agents on their computer networks. Accordingly, the NIPC issued a series of alerts that December to government agencies, industry, and the public about the DDoS threat. In late December 1999, the NIPC determined that a detection tool it had developed for investigative purposes could also be used by network operators to detect the presence of DDoS agents or masters on their operating systems and, thus, would enable them to remove an agent or master and prevent the network from being unwittingly utilized in a DDoS attack. Moreover, at that time, no similar detection tool was available commercially. The NIPC, therefore, decided to take the unusual step of releasing the tool to the Department of Defense, other government agencies, and to the public in an effort to reduce the level of the threat. The first variant of the detection software was made available on the NIPC Web site on December 30, 1999. To maximize the public's awareness of this tool, the NIPC announced its availability in an FBI press release on that same date. Since the first posting of the tool, there have been three later versions that have updated the software and made it applicable across different operating systems.

It was only five weeks after that, however, that Mafiaboy commenced his one-week reign of cyberterror. The original charge used to arrest Mafiaboy was made because of a joint effort between the Federal Bureau of Investigation (FBI) in the United States and the Royal Canadian Mounted Police (RCMP) in Canada. The charge was related to the DDoS attack on CNN in Atlanta, Georgia. It was only four months later that an additional 64 charges were made, 54 of which related to unauthorized access into Internet sites, many of them in the United States. If the companies that were Mafiaboy's victims had downloaded the free NIPC software, they could have prevented their losses.

In June 2002, weatherchannel.com, espn.com, and ABC-NEWS.com suffered DoS attacks which disrupted services to hundreds of thousands of Internet users. In October 2002, the heart of the Internet sustained its largest and most sophisticated attack to date. A DDos attack struck the 13 "root servers" that provide the primary roadmap for almost all Internet communications. The attacks only lasted an hour, and Internet users worldwide were hardly affected. The attack, at its peak, only caused 6 percent of domain name service requests to go unanswered, according to Matrix NetSystems. The DNS system normally responds almost 100 percent of the time.

Chris Morrow, network security engineer for UUNET, said "This is probably the most concerted attack against the Internet infrastructure that we've seen." UUNET is the service provider for two of the world's 13 root servers. A unit of WorldCom Inc., it also handles approximately half of the world's Internet traffic.

DDoS attacks are some of the most common and easiest to perpetrate, but the size and scope of Monday's strike set it apart. Internet Software Consortium Inc. Chairman Paul Vixie said only four or five of the 13 servers were able to withstand the attack and remain available to legitimate Internet traffic throughout the strike. "It was an attack against all 13 servers, which is a little more rare than an attack against any one of us," he said.

Internet addressing giant VeriSign Inc., which operates the most important server from an undisclosed Northern Virginia location, reported no outages. "VeriSign expects that these sort of attacks will happen and VeriSign was prepared," company spokesman Brian O'Shaughnessy said.

Vixie said he was unwilling to compare the attack with others he has witnessed in more than two decades of involvement with Internet architecture but said it was "the largest in recent memory." The root servers, about 10 of which are located in the United States, serve as a sort of master directory for the Internet. The Domain Name System (DNS), which converts complex Internet protocol addressing codes into the words and names that form e-mail and Web addresses, relies on the servers to tell computers around the world how to reach key Internet domains.

At the top of the root server hierarchy is the "A" root server, which every 12 hours generates a critical file that tells the other 12 servers what Internet domains exist and where they can be found. VeriSign manages its servers under contracts with the Commerce Department and the Internet Corporation for Assigned Numbers (ICANN), which manages the DNS. One rung below the root servers in the Internet hierarchy are the servers that house Internet domains, such as dot-com, dot-biz, and dot-info. The DNS is built so that eight or more of the world's 13 root servers must fail before ordinary Internet users start to see slowdowns.

"There are various kinds of attacks all the time on all sorts of infrastructure, and the basic design of the Internet is such that it is designed to withstand those attacks," said Louis Touton, Vice-President of the Internet Corporation for Assigned Names and Numbers (ICANN). "We're not aware of any users that were in any way affected." Obviously the prevalence of attacks does make it important to have increased focus on the need for security and stability of the Internet," he added.

In April 2003, Apache, which makes the popular open-source Web server application, released version 2.0.45 to fix a DoS problem. Apache issued a specific warning for users of OS/2, an IBM operating system, noting that the new patch still had a DoS vulnerability for that operating system. The Apache Software Foundation, which develops the software, rushed the patch out, perhaps to avoid the kind of scenario that occurred the previous June, when a security firm released news of a flaw and gave Apache only a few hours to respond. With nearly 63 percent of the market share, flaws in Apache's software could have astounding affects on Internet use.

Organizations have been caught napping in terms of providing security for their IT infrastructure. Many install software with the default passwords that come with the software, rather than changing the passwords. Any hacker knows to try the default passwords first. Companies do not have solid policies to update their security software on a regular basis, and they do not demand that software vendors plug holes in security before selling the latest edition of their software. Today, insurance companies are starting to demand that companies meet certain requirements regarding securing their IT infrastructure. Police are also becoming more vigilant and aggressive—and more skilled—in tracking down crackers and prosecuting them. What will happen next as crackers, organizations, and police all become more skilled?

CASE STUDY QUESTIONS

1. Do you think what Mafiaboy did was wrong? What should be the penalties for this type of crime?

2. What can companies do to stay alert on these security issues? How do IS professionals stay up to date in terms of their knowledge of security problems and solutions?

3. What should a security plan and policy contain to reduce or eliminate the security problems described in this case?

4. What steps should a company take to avoid DoS attacks? To avoid being hacked? To avoid having data stolen?

5. What steps should software vendors take to avoid the possibility of their software being used for cyberattacks? What can be done to make them take these steps?

SOURCES

"CERT Incident Note IN-2000-04," CERT Coordination Centre, January 15, 2001, available www.cert.org/incident_notes/IN-2000-04.html, accessed July 17, 2003; Sandra Henry-Stockler, "Deconstructing DoS Attacks," *SunWorld*, March 7, 2001, available www.cnn.com/2001/TECH/internet/03/07/dos.attacks.idg/, accessed July 17, 2003; Lori Enos, "'Mafiaboy' Denies New Hacking Charges," *E-Commerce Times*, August 4, 2000, available www.ecommercetimes.com, accessed July 17, 2003; "'Mafiaboy' Hacker Jailed," *BBC News*, September 13, 2001, available http://news.bbc.co.uk/1/hi/sci/tech/1541252.stm, accessed July; "'Mafiaboy' Sentenced to 8 Months," *Wired News*, September 13, 2001, available www.wired.com/news/print/0,1294,46791,00.html, accessed July 17, 2003; "Prison Urged for Mafiaboy," *Wired News*, June 20, 2001, available www.wired.com/news/print/0,1294,44673,00.html, accessed July 17, 2003; "Mafiaboy," National Infrastructure Protection Center, available www.nipc.gov/investigations/mafiaboy.htm, accessed July 17, 2003; James Evans, "Mafiaboy's Story Points to Net Weaknesses," IGD News Service, January 23, 2001, available www.idg.net, accessed July 17, 2003; "Canadian Mafiaboy Charged in DoS Attacks," *E-Commerce Times*, April 19, 2000, available www.ecommercetimes.com/perl/printer/3044/, accessed July 17, 2003; Nick Farrell, "Hackers Cripple U.S. News Sites," *VNU Business Publications*, June 17, 2002, available www.vnunet.com/Print/1132665, accessed July 17, 2003; David McGuire and Brian Krebs, "Attack on Internet Called Largest Ever," *The Washington Post*, October 22, 2002; Robert Lemos, "Assault on Net Servers Fails," *CNET News*, October 22, 2002, available http://news.com.com, accessed July 17, 2003; Sandeep Junnarkar, "Apache Patch to Thwart DoS Attack," *CNET News*, April 3, 2003, available http://news.com.com, accessed July 17, 2003.

VIDEO RESOURCE

"Cyberterror," *The National* (January 21, 2002); "Home Hackers," *The National* (August 26, 2002).

HIGHER-LEVEL AND GLOBAL INFORMATION SYSTEMS

DECISION MAKING IN A DIGITAL AGE

CHAPTER 13

As a manager, you will be asked to make many different kinds of decisions. You will want to know how you can use information systems to improve your decision making, whether you are working alone or in a group. After completing this chapter, you should be able to answer the following questions:

1. *How can information systems help individual managers make better decisions when the problems are nonroutine and constantly changing?*

2. *How can information systems help people working in a group make decisions more efficiently?*

3. *Are there any special systems that can facilitate decision making among senior managers? Exactly what can these systems do to help high-level management?*

4. *What benefits can systems to support management decision making provide for the organization as a whole?*

Objectives

HBC Makes Decisions That Affect Its Customers

Getting the right product to the right customer at the right time to the right channel at the right price is a challenge of enormous complexity when you are Canadian retailer Hudson's Bay Company (HBC). Rob Shields, HBC's Vice-President of CRM and Loyalty and co-Chief Privacy Officer, spearheads the effort to line up more than one million products with the spending of approximately eight million customers. He takes a scientific approach to this monumental task, always calculating costs and measuring results.

"The expression is 'retail is detail,' and this is highly detailed, scientific work," he explains. His focus is "how we get precision working for us—not only to be more efficient with our dollars but more effective; to speak to a lot of people about one thing or one thing to one person."

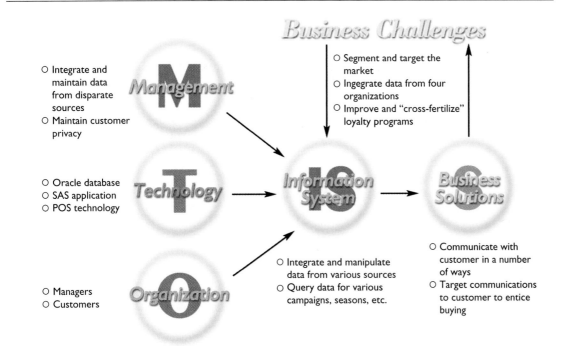

When Shields took on his current role two years ago, HBC had turned its focus on customers to complement the product focus necessary for a retailer. The company redesigned and consolidated its existing multiple loyalty programs and launched its HBC program which it expanded into all its stores. That gave customers one card and four different places to earn points: The Bay, Zellers, Home Outfitters, and HBC.com.

This redesign and launch required constructing a new database which brought together all the aspects of each customer's relationship with HBC. The Oracle database includes the loyalty program database which manages all the loyalty reward points and balances. It also has a database dedicated to the HBC credit card system and another database dedicated to the product inventory system.

An overall hierarchy permits Shields and his team to query, for any given customer, where they shopped, what they purchased, and whether they used a credit card or not.

"In the past, most of the people had only looked at one database for one piece of information, like: how many t-shirts did we sell?" he says. "Now we can say: How many t-shirts did you sell, where did you sell them, what tender were they purchased on, were the loyalty cards used or not, and who [bought them]?"

Shields sees the return on investment (ROI) of their customer relationship management (CRM) capabilities deriving from what you can do with the data—for example, using it to reveal information that will lead to better business decisions. "Oftentimes, we were in the position where we thought we were making the right decision and then we said, 'Have we looked at what customers that will affect?' or 'What will they buy or stop buying as a result of that because it is a destination purchase?' And we have seen that 'Wow, maybe we shouldn't make the decision because we're going to jeopardize a bunch of things.'"

"A more practical, tangible side of the ROI is simply by driving through customer initiatives that have an immediate return," he adds. Shields cites the example of a campaign they ran during the holiday season of 2002. It began with the question: "Do we have anybody who has not shopped with us in the past three to six months?" The database confirmed that a significant population of people had not. A campaign was designed and launched to re-engage customers during the peak season by offering extra loyalty points the next time they shopped at an HBC store. The number of points varied by customer.

HBC uses a number of different vehicles to communicate to customers. Sophisticated direct marketing capabilities permit customer monthly statements that "speak" to customers one to one. Shields says they use SAS Institute's code and develop "very sophisticated business rules and decision trees that basically take all our business objectives for the organization for that point in time."

He stresses that HBC staff never see the individual customer files. "That's the idea of the privacy. [Customers] get a bunch of things offered to [them] that I don't know about. All we do is the macro. On a monthly basis, all our customers go through these business rules and decision trees."

He gives the example of linking an upcoming sale in menswear with customer Joe who has purchased in menswear but not lately or maybe never has. To encourage him to try it out, his statement includes an offer for menswear. HBC recently gained the ability to "speak to customers" through its point-of-sale (POS) contact. Its POS technology, which is a mixture of the NCR Corporation and IBM products, has been upgraded so that a customer making a purchase gets a message on the receipt itself. It may be an offer to earn bonus points in a related department, for example. Shields reports they are always tweaking their CRM initiatives and, more importantly, always measuring them. "If you don't have a solid way of measuring the incremental behavioural change at the customer level, then you shouldn't be doing it," he stresses.

Sources: Susan Maclean, "HBC Captures the CRM Value of Its Data," IT Focus, available www.itworld.com, accessed April 11, 2003; Grant Buckler, "Getting a Grip on CRM," CIO Canada, January 1, 2003; Susan Maclean, "Shoppers Welcome Innovation," November 1, 2002, available www.itworld.ca, accessed April 11, 2003.

MANAGEMENT CHALLENGES

HBC's customer relationship management systems is an example of a decision support system (DSS). These systems have powerful analytic capabilities to support managers during the process of arriving at a decision. Other systems in this category are group decision support systems (GDSS), which support decision making in groups, and executive support systems (ESS), which provide information for making strategic-level decisions. These systems can enhance organizational performance, but they raise the following management challenges:

1. **Building information systems that can actually fulfill executive information requirements.** Even with the use of critical success factors and other information requirements determination methods (see Chapter 10), it may still be difficult to establish information requirements for ESS and DSS serving senior management. Chapter 3 has already described why certain aspects of senior management decision making cannot be supported by information systems because the decisions are too unstructured and fluid. Even if a problem can be addressed by an information system, senior managers may not fully understand their actual information needs. For instance, senior managers may not agree on the firm's critical success factors; or the critical success factors they describe may be inappropriate or may be outdated if the firm is confronting a crisis requiring a major strategic change.

2. **Create meaningful reporting and management decision making processes.** Enterprise systems and data warehouses have made it much easier to supply DSS and ESS with data from many different systems than in the past. The remaining challenge is changing management thinking to use the data that are available to maximum advantage, to develop better reporting categories for measuring firm performance, and to inform new types of decisions. Many managers use the new capabilities in DSS and ESS to obtain the same information as before. Major changes in management thinking will be required to get managers to ask better questions of the data.

Most information systems described throughout this text help people make decisions in one way or another, but DSS, GDSS, and ESS are part of a special category of information systems that are explicitly designed to enhance managerial decision making. Some of these systems represent **business intelligence** applications that focus on gathering, storing, analyzing, and providing access to data from many different sources to help users make better business decisions. By taking advantage of more accurate firm-wide data provided by enterprise systems and the new information technology infrastructure, these systems can support very fine-grained decisions for guiding the firm, coordinating work activities across the enterprise, and responding rapidly to changing markets and customers. Many of these managerial decision making applications are now Web enabled. This chapter describes the characteristics of each of these types of information systems, showing how each enhances the managerial decision making process and ultimately the performance of the organization.

business intelligence

Applications and technologies that focus on gathering, storing, analyzing, and providing access to data from many different sources to help users make better business decisions.

DSS, GDSS, and ESS can support decision making in a number of ways. They can automate certain decision procedures (for example, determining the highest price that can be charged for a product to maintain market share or the right amount of materials to maintain in inventory to maximize efficient customer response and product profitability). They can provide information about different aspects of the decision situation and the decision process, such as what opportunities or problems triggered the decision process, what solution alternatives were generated or explored, and how the decision was reached. Finally, they can stimulate innovation in decision making by helping managers question existing decision procedures or explore different solution designs (Dutta, Wierenga, and Dalebout, 1997). The ability to explore the outcomes of alternative organizational scenarios, use precise firm-wide information, and provide tools to facilitate group decision processes can help managers make decisions that help the firm achieve its strategic objectives (Forgionne and Kohli, 2000).

13.1 DECISION SUPPORT SYSTEMS

As noted in Chapter 2, decision support systems (DSS) assist management decision making by combining data, sophisticated analytical models and tools, and user-friendly software into single powerful systems that can support semistructured or unstructured decision making. DSS provide users with flexible sets of tools and capabilities for analyzing important blocks of data.

MANAGEMENT INFORMATION SYSTEMS AND DECISION SUPPORT SYSTEMS

Some of the earliest applications for supporting management decision making were *management information systems (MIS)*, which we introduced in Chapter 2. MIS primarily provide information on the firm's performance to help managers in monitoring and controlling the business. They typically produce fixed, regularly scheduled reports based on data extracted and summarized from the organization's underlying transaction processing systems (TPS). The format from these reports is often specified in advance. A typical MIS report might show a summary of monthly sales for each of the major sales territories of a company. Sometimes, MIS reports are exception reports, highlighting only exceptional conditions, such as when the sales quotas for a specific territory fall below an anticipated level or employees

TABLE 13.1   EXAMPLES OF MIS APPLICATIONS

Organization	MIS Application
Environment Canada	National Enforcement Management Information System and Intelligence System allows tracking and management of pollution and wildlife enforcement activities and actions relating to legislation enforced by Environment Canada.
Whale Research Lab at the University of Victoria	MIS application catalogues and analyses both cultural and scientific information about resident grey whales in Ahousat First Nations territories off the west coast of Vancouver Island, British Columbia.
California Pizza Kitchen	Inventory Express application "remembers" each restaurant's ordering patterns and compares the amount of ingredients used per menu item to predefined portion measurements established by management. The system identifies restaurants with out-of-line portions and notifies their management so that corrective action can be taken.
PharMark	Extranet MIS identifies patients with drug-use patterns that place them at risk for adverse outcomes.
Black & Veatch	Intranet MIS tracks construction costs for its various projects across the United States.
Taco Bell	TACO (Total Automation of Company Operations) system provides information on food, labour, and period-to-date costs for each restaurant.

have exceeded their spending limit in a dental care plan. Traditional MIS produced primarily hard copy reports. Today, these reports might be available online through an intranet, and many MIS reports can be generated on demand. Table 13.1 provides some examples of MIS applications.

DSS provide new sets of capabilities for nonroutine decisions and user control. MIS provide managers with reports based on routine flows of data and assist in the general control of organizations, while DSS emphasize change, flexibility, and rapid response. With a DSS, there is less of an effort to link users to structured information flows and a correspondingly greater emphasis on models, assumptions, ad hoc queries, and display graphics.

Chapter 3 introduced the distinction between structured, semistructured, and unstructured decisions. Structured problems are repetitive and routine, for which known algorithms provide solutions. Unstructured problems are novel and nonroutine, for which there are no solution algorithms. One can discuss, decide, and ruminate about unstructured problems, but they are not solved in the way that one finds an answer to an equation. Semistructured problems fall between structured and unstructured problems. While MIS primarily address structured problems, DSS support semistructured and unstructured problem analysis. Chapter 3 also introduced Simon's model of decision making, which is composed of four stages: intelligence, design, choice, and implementation. DSS are intended to help design and evaluate alternatives and monitor the adoption or implementation process.

TYPES OF DECISION SUPPORT SYSTEMS

The earliest DSS tended to draw on small subsets of corporate data and were heavily model driven. Recent advances in computer processing and database technology have expanded the definition of a DSS to include systems that can support decision making by analyzing vast quantities of data, including firm-wide data from enterprise systems and transaction data from the Web.

model-driven DSS

Primarily stand-alone system that uses some type of model to perform "what-if" and other kinds of analyses.

Today, there are two basic types of decision support systems: model-driven and data-driven (Dhar and Stein, 1997). **Model-driven DSS** were primarily stand-alone systems isolated from major organizational information systems that used some type of model to

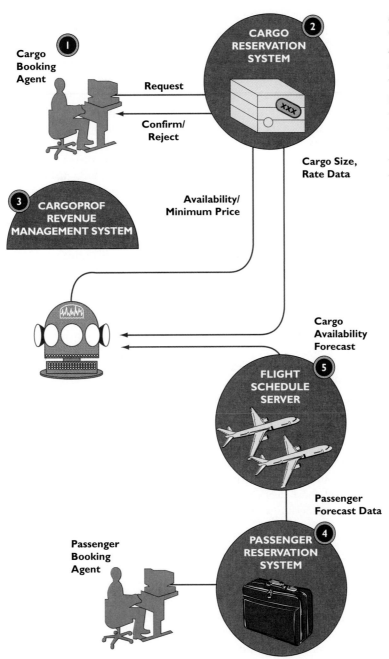

Figure 13.1 Cargo Revenue Optimization at Continental Airlines. When a booking agent (1) requests a cargo reservation, the cargo reservation system (2) passes the shipment details and customer contract rate to CargoProf (3). Meanwhile, the passenger reservation system (4) feeds a passenger forecast to the flight schedule server's cargo capacity forecaster (5), which calculates expected cargo capacity each night for every flight. It passes this capacity data to CargoProf, which calculates for each flight with available cargo space the minimum prices that a booking must meet or exceed in order to be profitable. The cargo reservation system then accepts or rejects the request. Agents with rejected requests can then either try a different day or route to sell the customer into a higher-rate class.

perform "what-if" and other kinds of analyses. These systems were often developed by end-user divisions or groups not under central information system control. Their analysis capabilities were based on a strong theory or model combined with a good user interface that made the model easy to use.

The voyage-estimating DSS described in Chapter 2 and HBC's CRM system described in the chapter-opening vignette are examples of model-driven DSS. Another is Continental Airlines Inc.'s system for cargo revenue optimization. Continental's cargo division developed a software application called CargoProf to maximize revenue from its aircraft freight compartments. The software is a customized package from Manugistics Inc. of Rockville, Maryland, and ensures that Continental sells all available freight space on its carriers at the most profitable price. The system forecasts cargo capacity and sets an optimal value each night on what the carriers need.

Figure 13.1 shows how this system works. Continental booking agents transmit freight order requests for reservations on a given flight. Continental's legacy reservation system captures order data, such as a shipment's weight, dimensions, and contract price, and forwards the data to CargoProf. The CargoProf software checks available capacity in the airplane's bays, taking into account both the size and weight of the cargo, and compares it against a present pricing model. The software then considers several other variables, such as anticipated passenger baggage and extra fuel requirements, based on seasonal factors. CargoProf then analyzes these numbers and either accepts the reservation at the customer's contract price or rejects it if taking on the shipment is not cost effective. If the customer's order is rejected for one flight, CargoProf can check other flights to see if they could profitably carry the cargo. CargoProf can also handle incremental price changes for rush shipments. Users can override CargoProf capacity forecasts on certain flights if, for example, unanticipated head winds require a greater fuel load. By making freight bookings more efficient, CargoProf saved Continental $9 million over a two-year period (Songini, 2002).

The second type of DSS is a **data-driven DSS**. These systems analyze large pools of data found in major organizational systems. They support decision making by allowing users to extract useful information that was previously buried in large quantities of data. Often, data from TPS are collected in data warehouses for this purpose. Online analytical processing (OLAP) and datamining can then be used to analyze the data. Companies are starting to build data-driven DSS to mine customer data gathered from their Web sites as well as data from enterprise systems. WH Smith PLC's system for online sales and profitability analysis described in the Window on Organizations is an example of a data-driven DSS.

Traditional database queries answer such questions as, "How many units of product number 403 were shipped in November 2002?" OLAP, or multidimensional analysis, supports much more complex requests for information, such as, "Compare sales of product 403 relative to plan by quarter and sales region for the past two years." We described OLAP and multidimensional data analysis in Chapter 7. With OLAP and query-oriented data analysis, users need to have a good idea about the information they are looking for.

Datamining, which we introduced in Chapter 7, is more discovery driven. Datamining provides insights into corporate data that cannot be obtained with OLAP by finding hidden patterns and relationships in large databases and inferring rules from them to predict future behaviour. The patterns and rules can then be used to guide decision making and forecast the effect of those decisions. The types of information that can be yielded from datamining include associations, sequences, classifications, clusters, and forecasts.

Associations are occurrences linked to a single event. For instance, a study of supermarket purchasing patterns might reveal that when corn chips are purchased, a cola drink is purchased 65 percent of the time, but when there is a promotion, cola is purchased 85 percent of the time. With this information, managers can make better decisions because they have learned about the profitability of a promotion.

In *sequences*, events are linked over time. One might find, for example, that if a house is purchased, then a new refrigerator will be purchased within two weeks 65 percent of the time, and an oven will be bought within one month of the home purchase 45 percent of the time.

Classification recognizes patterns that describe the group which an item belongs to by examining existing items that have been classified and then inferring a set of rules. For example, such businesses as credit card or telephone companies worry about the loss of steady customers. Classification can help discover the characteristics of customers who are likely to leave and can provide a model to help managers predict who they are so that they can devise special campaigns to retain such customers.

Clustering works in a manner similar to classification when no groups have yet been defined. A datamining tool will discover different groupings within data, such as finding affinity groups for bank cards or partitioning a database into groups of customers on the basis of demographics and types of personal investments.

Although these applications involve predictions, *forecasting* uses predictions in a different way. It uses a series of existing values to forecast what other values will be. For example, forecasting might find patterns in data to help managers estimate the future value of continuous variables, such as sales figures.

data-driven DSS

A system that supports decision making by allowing users to extract and analyze useful information that was previously buried in large databases.

DATA DRIVEN INSIGHTS AT WH SMITH PLC

Window on Organizations
MIS In Action

WH Smith PLC, headquartered in Swindon, England, is the number one book and magazine retailer in the United Kingdom, carrying 60 000 items, such as reading material, stationery, music, computer games, and gifts at its retail outlets and Web site. It runs approximately 530 retail stores, 190 stores in European airports and train stations, more than 500 stores in American airports and hotels, and approximately 20 stores in Australia, Singapore, and Hong Kong combined. In 2001, sales reached $5.66 billion, with a profit of $273 million.

Several years ago, Smith's management saw that the company was running into trouble in that it was not as profitable as it could be. At that time, its corporate executives were "only able to monitor sales and stock at the central office," explained Trevor Dukes, Smith's head of information strategy. He pointed out that "senior store managers were sending us tonnes of paperwork about their stores," more than they could usefully handle. Using paper-based methods, communications were very slow, and information in printed reports was already out of date. Moreover, the stores needed to share information with other stores about what was profitable and what was not and how trends were changing. Stores could not even obtain information about the profitability of individual items. Even directives on promotions and incentives that were sent to the stores were not integrated with the stores' products. Management believed that employees, particularly store and area managers, needed a stronger focus on improving profitability.

Company management initiated a project to provide managers with tools and information to help them make better merchandise and stocking decisions. One major goal was to reduce the immense amount of paper being passed back and forth. Another was to help store managers better understand what was happening within their own stores and within other stores in the company. A third goal was to improve managers' ability to recognize customer buying patterns and to anticipate trends so that they could align their inventory to the trends.

The company adopted a business intelligence software package from MicroStrategy Inc. of McLean, Virginia. The system relies on sales and inventory data from each and every purchase, which are automatically sent to a central data warehouse, where store managers and corporate staff can access this information via the Web. The system contains report templates and wizards, enabling managers to customize the information, as needed, identifying, for example, the highest-margin items, which can then be ranked by sales.

Barrie Stewart, the manager of a store in Dunbartonshire, Scotland, says the new system "allows me to ask several questions, such as: "Is the performance down due to poor display standards, poor stock availability, or incorrect location?" He also asks such questions as whether the product is right for his store and does it earn enough profit for the space it uses. Stewart even shares this information with his employees so, for example, they can display their best-selling products in high visibility locations. He finds that his staff now gives him helpful feedback, including ideas on increasing profit. Stewart even says, "if we see that a high-margin book is selling particularly well in, say, a tourist location, we can add a display at a shop that has high tourist traffic." Dukes points out, "When we see one store selling out of a particular item, we can shift inventory from a store where it isn't selling as well and take advantage of customer demand." The company even has taken the time to train its employees on the system so they can use it themselves.

To Think About: List the ways this DSS helps WH Smith's employees to make decisions. How has it provided value for the firm? Suggest other ways the system can help them make decisions and increase profits.

Sources: Pimm Fox, "Insights Turn into Profits," *ComputerWorld*, February 10, 2002; MicroStrategy Incorporated, "WH Smith PLC Selects Microstrategy to Anchor BI Initiatives," *DSstar*, **www.tge.com/dsstar**, accessed August 15, 2002; and WH Smith PLC corporate Web site, **www.whsmithplc.com**, accessed August 5, 2003.

Datamining, which we discussed in Chapter 7, uses statistical analysis tools as well as neural networks, fuzzy logic, genetic algorithms, or rule-based and other intelligent techniques (described in Chapter 14). It is an important aspect of **knowledge discovery**, which includes selection, preparation, and interpretation of the contents of large databases to identify novel and valuable patterns in the data. (See Figure 13.2.)

As noted in Chapter 3, it is a mistake to think that only individuals in large organizations make decisions. In fact, most decisions are made collectively. Frequently, decisions must be coordinated with several groups before being finalized. In large organizations, decision making is inherently a group process, and a DSS can be designed to facilitate group decision making. (Section 13.2 deals with this issue.)

knowledge discovery

The process of identifying novel and valuable patterns in large volumes of data through the selection, preparation, and evaluation of the contents of large databases.

COMPONENTS OF DSS

Figure 13.3 illustrates the components of a DSS. They include a database of data used for query and analysis, a software system with models, datamining, and other analytical tools and a user interface.

Figure 13.2 Lucent Technologies Visual Insights software can help businesses detect patterns in their data. Each dot in this example represents items purchased at one supermarket, with lines drawn between purchases of individual shoppers. The software shows links between different purchase items, such as cookies and milk.

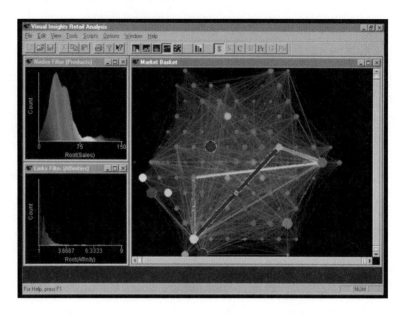

DSS database

A collection of current or historical data from a number of applications or groups. Can be a small PC database or a massive data warehouse.

DSS software system

Collection of software tools that are used for data analysis, such as OLAP tools, datamining tools, or a collection of mathematical and analytical models.

model

An abstract representation that illustrates the components or relationships of a phenomenon.

Figure 13.3 Overview of a decision support system (DSS). The main components of the DSS are the DSS database, the DSS software system, and the user interface. The DSS database may be a small database residing on a personal computer (PC) or a massive data warehouse.

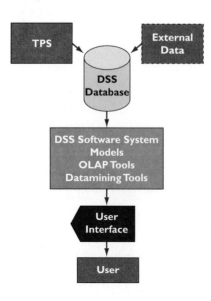

The **DSS database** is a collection of current or historical data from a number of applications or groups. It may be a small database residing on a PC that contains a subset of corporate data that has been downloaded and possibly combined with external data. Alternatively, the DSS database may be a massive data warehouse that is continuously updated by major organizational TPS (including enterprise systems and data generated by Web site transactions.) The data in DSS databases are generally extracts or copies of production databases so that using the DSS does not interfere with critical operational systems.

The **DSS software** contains the software tools that are used for data analysis. It may contain various OLAP tools, datamining tools, or a collection of mathematical and analytical models that can easily be made accessible to the DSS user. A **model** is an abstract representation that illustrates the components or relationships of a phenomenon. A model can be a physical model (such as a model airplane), a mathematical model (such as an equation), or a verbal model (such as a description of a procedure for writing an order). Each decision support system is developed for a specific set of purposes and will make different collections of models available, depending on those purposes.

Perhaps the most common models are libraries of statistical models. Statistical libraries usually contain the full range of expected statistical functions including means, medians, deviations, and scatter plots. The software has the ability to project future outcomes by analyzing a series of data. Statistical modelling software can be used to help establish relationships, such as relating product sales to differences in age, income, or other factors, between communities. Optimization models, often using linear programming, determine optimal resource allocation to maximize or minimize specified variables, such as cost or time. A classic use of optimization models is to determine the proper mix of products within a given market to maximize profits.

Forecasting models are often used to forecast sales. The user of this type of model might supply a range of historical data to project future conditions and the sales that might result from those conditions. The decision maker could vary those future conditions (entering, for example, a rise in raw materials costs or the entry of a new, low-priced competitor in the market) to determine how these new conditions might affect sales. Companies often use this type of software to pre-

Total fixed costs	19000					
Variable cost per unit	3					
Average sales price	17					
Contribution margin	14					
Breakeven point	1357					
		Variable Cost per Unit				
Sales	1357	2	3	4	5	6
Price	14	1583	1727	1900	2111	2375
	15	1462	1583	1727	1900	2111
	16	1357	1462	1583	1727	1900
	17	1267	1357	1462	1583	1727
	18	1188	1267	1357	1462	1583

Figure 13.4 Sensitivity analysis. This table displays the results of a sensitivity analysis of the effect of changing the sales price of a necktie and the cost per unit on the product's breakeven point. It answers the question: "What happens to the breakeven point if the sales price and the cost to make each unit increase or decrease?"

dict the actions of competitors. Model libraries exist for specific functions, such as financial and risk analysis models.

Among the most widely used models are **sensitivity analysis** models that ask "what-if" questions repeatedly to determine the impact of changes in one or more factors on outcomes. "What-if" analysis—working forward from known or assumed conditions—allows the user to vary certain values to test results in order to better predict outcomes if changes occur in those values. "What happens if" we raise the price by 5 percent or increase the advertising budget by $100 000? What happens if we keep the price and advertising budget the same? Desktop spreadsheet software, such as Microsoft Excel or Lotus 1-2-3, is often used for this purpose (see Figure 13.4). Backward sensitivity analysis software is used for goal seeking: If I want to sell one million product units next year, by how much must I reduce the price of the product?

The DSS user interface permits easy interaction between users of the system and the DSS software tools. A graphic, easy-to-use, flexible user interface supports the dialogue between the user and the DSS. The DSS users may be managers or employees with no patience for learning a complex tool, so the interface must be relatively intuitive. Many DSS today are being developed with Web-based interfaces to take advantage of the Web's ease of use, interactivity, and capabilities for personalization and customization. Building successful DSS requires a high level of user participation to make sure the system provides the information managers need. The Manager's Toolkit provides some guidelines for developing DSS solutions.

sensitivity analysis

Models that ask "what-if" questions repeatedly to determine the impact of changes in one or more factors on the outcomes.

DSS Applications and the Digital Firm

There are many ways in which DSS can be used to support decision making. Table 13.2 lists examples of DSS in well-known organizations. Both data-driven and model-driven DSS have become very powerful and sophisticated, providing fine-grained information for decisions that enable a firm to coordinate both internal and external business processes much more precisely. Some of these DSS are helping companies improve supply chain management or customer relationship management. Some take advantage of the company-wide data provided by enterprise systems. DSS today can also harness the interactive capabilities of the Web to provide decision support tools to both employees and customers.

MIS IN ACTION: Manager's Toolkit

HOW TO EVALUATE A DSS PROJECT

If your company is interested in using a DSS to support management decision making, here are some key questions to ask:

1. What kind of problem do you expect this system to solve?
2. Does the solution require the use of models? If so, which ones? What are the variables in the problem?
3. Does the solution require the use of query and data analysis tools? If so, which ones?
4. What data do you need to arrive at a solution? Can all of the data be found from within the company, or do some data come from

external sources? Can you obtain the data automatically from corporate and external databases, or must the data be entered separately? How much effort would be required to assemble the required data for the system?

5. What type of user interface is required? Must users use it to input data as well as to ask questions of the data? Is the interface easy to use?
6. What computer hardware and operating system are required to run this system?
7. How long does it take to get answers from the data? How clear are the results?

TABLE 13.2	EXAMPLES OF DECISION SUPPORT SYSTEMS

Organization	DSS Application
General Accident Insurance	Customer buying patterns and fraud detection
Royal Bank of Canada (RBC)	Customer profiles
Frito-Lay, Inc.	Price, advertising, and promotion selection
Burlington Coat Factory	Store location and inventory mix
Canadian National Railway	Train dispatching and routing
Air Canada	Flight scheduling and passenger demand forecasting

To illustrate the range of capabilities of a DSS, we now describe some successful DSS applications. IBM and San Miguel Corporation's supply chain management systems and Petro-Canada's what-if scenario analysis system are examples of model-driven DSS. Royal Bank of Canada's customer segmentation system and the customer analysis systems used by WH Smith PLC, and Kinki Nippon Tourist are examples of data-driven DSS. We will also examine some applications of geographic information systems (GIS), a special category of DSS for visualizing data geographically.

DSS for Supply Chain Management

Supply chain decisions involve determining "who, what, when, and where" from purchasing and transporting materials and parts through manufacturing products and distributing and delivering those products to customers. Supply chain management systems contain data about inventory, supplier performance, and logistics of materials and finished goods. DSS can draw on this data to help managers examine this complex chain comprehensively and to search among a huge number of alternatives for the combinations that are most efficient and cost effective. The prime management goal might be to reduce overall costs while increasing the speed and accuracy of filling customer orders.

In 1994, IBM Research developed an advanced supply chain optimization and simulation tool called the Asset Management Tool (AMT) to reduce inventory levels, yet maintain enough inventory in the supply chain to respond quickly to customer demands. AMT deals with a range of entities in the supply chain, including targets for inventory and customer service levels, product structure, channel assembly, supplier terms and conditions, and lead-time reduction. Users of AMT can evaluate supply chains in terms of financial tradeoffs associated with various configurations and operational policies.

The IBM Personal Systems Group (PSG) used AMT to reduce supply chain costs to cope with the large volumes, dropping prices, and slim profit margins in the personal computer market. PSG was able to reduce overall pipeline inventory by over 50 percent in 1997 and 1998. The system helped PSG reduce payments made to distributors and resellers to compensate for product price reductions by more than $1.1 billion in 1998. PSG's cycle time from component procurement to product sale was reduced by four to six weeks, bringing reductions of 5 to 7 percent in overall product cost.

IBM's AS/400 midrange computer division used AMT to analyze and quantify the impact of product complexity. Information from the system helped IBM reduce the number of product features, substitute alternative parts, and delay customization. AMT also provided an analysis of the tradeoff between serviceability and inventory in IBM's QuickShip Program, helping the company reduce operational cost by up to 50 percent. IBM has also been able to use AMT to help its business partners improve management of their supply chains. For instance, supply chain analysis helped Piancor, one of IBM's major distributors, identify opportunities for optimizing the product flow between the two companies (Dietrich et al., 2000).

San Miguel Corporation uses DSS for supply chain management to help it distribute more than 300 products, such as beer, liquor, dairy products, and feedgrains to every corner of the Philippine archipelago. A production load allocation system determines the quantity of products to produce for each bottling line and how production output should be assigned to warehouses. It balances ordering, carrying, and stock-out costs while considering frequency of deliveries and minimum order quantities, saving the company $261 000 in inventory costs in one year. The DSS can generate optimal production allocation plans based on either minimizing cost or maximizing profit. San Miguel's system also helps it reassign deliveries and warehouse facilities to counter imbalances in capacity and demand. Managers used information from the system to move more of San Miguel's delivery business to third-party logistics providers so that its own delivery trucks could be used more efficiently. The company found that it could reduce the number of routes serving sales districts in metropolitan Manila alone by 43 percent (del Rosario, 1999).

DSS for Customer Relationship Management

DSS for customer relationship management use datamining to guide decisions about pricing, customer retention, market share, and new revenue streams. These systems typically consolidate customer information from a variety of systems into massive data warehouses and use various analytical tools to "slice it" into tiny segments for one-to-one marketing (see Figure 13.5).

Instead of sending customers the same marketing information, Royal Bank of Canada has developed a DSS for customer segmentation that can tailor messages to very small groups of people and offer them products, services, and prices that are more likely to appeal to them. This DSS consolidates data from various systems in the organization into a data warehouse. The Royal Bank's main customer database is its marketing information file (MIF), which also contains data from every document a customer fills out as well as data from chequing accounts, credit cards, and the Royal Bank's enterprise and billing systems.

By querying the database, analysts can identify customers on the basis of the products they might buy and the likelihood of their changing banks and combine these data with demographic data from external sources. Royal Bank can then identify one or a group of profitable customers who appear to be getting ready to leave the bank. To identify these customers, the bank will look at the customer's bank balance (if it was recently kept low), credit card payments (if they were reduced in amount and perhaps paid later than in the past), and deposits (if they have become sporadic). These signs could indicate a customer recently unemployed, but they could also highlight a profitable customer preparing to switch to another bank. The Royal Bank, using its vast store of data, can quickly learn whether it has profited from this customer's business. It measures profitability by looking at the customer's past ongoing balances, personal use of his or her Royal Bank line of credit, and the car loan and/or mortgage that person holds from the bank. The bank can also deduce from personal data whether the customer is at a stage in life when he or she will need more bank loans and other bank services.

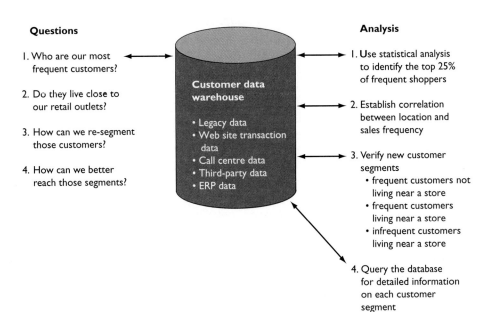

Questions

1. Who are our most frequent customers?

2. Do they live close to our retail outlets?

3. How can we re-segment those customers?

4. How can we better reach those segments?

Customer data warehouse

- Legacy data
- Web site transaction data
- Call centre data
- Third-party data
- ERP data

Analysis

1. Use statistical analysis to identify the top 25% of frequent shoppers

2. Establish correlation between location and sales frequency

3. Verify new customer segments
   - frequent customers not living near a store
   - frequent customers living near a store
   - infrequent customers living near a store

4. Query the database for detailed information on each customer segment

Figure 13.5 DSS for customer analysis and segmentation. This DSS allows companies to segment their customer base with a high level of precision where it can be used to drive a marketing campaign. On the basis of the results of datamining, a firm can develop specific marketing campaigns for each customer segment. For example, it could target frequent customers living near a store with coupons for products of interest and with rewards for frequent shoppers.

Having identified these customer(s), the bank's marketing department might put together a tempting package of banking services at a low price, such as Internet banking, bill payment, unlimited ATM access, and a limited number of branch transactions, all for a fee of $9.95 per month. The bank knows that customers who use these service packages stay with the bank for about three years longer than do those who do not have such a package. If the customer is not satisfied with the specific package, marketing can even tailor a package specifically for that individual. Royal Bank is linking its customer database and legacy systems to the Web so that it can offer customers service packages instantly online as they access their accounts over the Internet. Royal Bank's customer segmentation is so effective that it can achieve a response rate as high as 30 percent to its marketing campaigns, compared with an average of 3 percent for the banking industry (Wilson, 2000 and Radding, 2000).

Kinki Nippon Tourist (KNT), Japan's second largest travel agency, revolutionized Japanese tourism in the early 1980s by providing newspaper advertising and magazines explicitly customized for repeat customers that would allow them to purchase trips over the telephone. (Until KNT opened these new channels, tourists had to arrange their trips through a travel agency). When competitors followed, KNT tried to develop a one-to-one marketing strategy to retain core customers and increase customer loyalty. To store and analyze detailed information on customer preferences, behaviour, and opinions of tours, KNT implemented a massive data warehouse on the basis of a Teradata relational database. The system runs on a WorldMark Massively Parallel Processor and includes data on 1.5 million customers. The data come from telephone calls, conversations with tour operators, and customer questionnaires as well as transactions. Nearly 500 users can access the system directly through individual workstations.

By analyzing the detailed customer data, KNT uncovered new patterns that were previously undetectable in its old legacy systems. For example, it found that customers whose first tour was made by bus were likely to be repeat bus customers. The company can use this finding to target appropriate tours, events, and hospitality to these customers. KNT can also use the data warehouse to determine which newspaper ads work the best for certain tours and which tours are better promoted through direct mail. KNT's call centre operators can use the information from the data warehouse to improve customer service. And KNT uses data from the system to customize its magazines to specific customer segments (NCR, 2001).

Some of these DSS for customer relationship management use data gathered from the Web. Chapter 9 has described how each action a visitor has taken when visiting a particular Web site can be captured on that Web site's log. Companies can mine these data to answer such questions as what customers are purchasing and what promotions are generating the most traffic. The results can help companies tailor marketing programs more effectively, redesign Web sites to optimize traffic, and create personalized buying experiences for Web site visitors. Other DSS combine Web site transaction data with data from enterprise systems.

DSS for Simulating Business Scenarios

We have already described the capabilities of model-driven DSS for performing what-if analyses on problems in specific areas of the firm. DSS with very powerful what-if and modelling capabilities have been developed for modelling entire business scenarios. Model-driven DSS use information from both internal and external sources to help managers tune strategy to a constantly changing array of conditions and variables.

Petro-Canada is one of Canada's largest oil and gas companies with operations spanning the upstream and downstream sectors of the industry. They have fine-tuned their category management processes to support approximately 500 of their convenience sites across Canada. "While we are experts at marketing fuels, convenience retailing is still a new business for us," commented Georges Gasparovics, Petro-Canada's Director of Information Services. "Category management will help us enhance the product and service offering to our guests and maximize non-petroleum revenue opportunities."

According to Gasparovics, JDA Software Group's Open Database Merchanding System (ODBMS) integrated with Win/DSS is integral to their success. "Since establishing and managing pricing structures is a key element to category management, ODBMS helps us implement strategies to better maximize margins and competitively price our products. Win/DSS enables us to collect POS (point-of-sale) information and upload to ODBMS for analysis and decision making."

Data Visualization and Geographic Information Systems

Data from information systems can be made easier for users to digest and act upon by using charts, tables, graphs, maps, digital images, three-dimensional presentations, animations, and other data visualization technologies. By presenting data in graphical form, **data visualization** tools help users see patterns and relationships in large amounts of data that would be difficult to discern if the data were presented as traditional lists of text. Some data visualization tools are interactive, allowing users to manipulate data and see the graphical displays change in response to the changes they make.

Geographic information systems (GIS) are a special category of DSS that use data visualization technology to analyze and display data for planning and decision making in the form of digitized maps. The software can assemble, store, manipulate, and display geographically referenced information, tying data to points, lines, and areas on a map. GIS can, thus, be used to support decisions that require knowledge about the geographic distribution of people or other resources in scientific research, resource management, and development planning. For example, GIS might be used to help state and local governments calculate emergency response times to natural disasters or to help banks identify the best locations for installing new branches or ATM terminals. GIS tools have become affordable even for small businesses, and some can be used on the Web.

GIS have modelling capabilities, allowing managers to change data and automatically revise business scenarios to find better solutions. Parks Canada's geographic information systems (www.parkscanada.pch.gd.ca) are implemented at various administrative levels including headquarters, regional offices, national parks, some heritage canals, and a limited number of historic sites. Current geographic information system applications include wildlife population census, ecological mapping, forest fire research and protection, insect and disease impact assessment, emergency measures preparedness, coastal zone management, eco-tourism development, and land-use planning (see Figure 13.6). The Manitoba Community Newspapers Association's Web site (www.mcna.com) hosts a GIS that tracks 3000 variables to assist media buyers in determining where to place their advertisements. Their data are based on Statistics Canada census data. Sonny's Bar-B-Q, the Gainesville (Florida)–based restaurant chain, used GIS with federal and local census data on median age, household income, total population, and population distribution to help management decide where to open new restaurants. The company's growth plan specifies that it will only expand into regions where barbecue food is very popular but where the number of barbecue restaurants is very small. Sonny's restaurants must also be at least seven miles away from each other.

data visualization

Technology for helping users see patterns and relationships in large amounts of data by presenting the data in graphical form.

geographic information system (GIS)

System with software that can analyze and display data using digitized maps to enhance planning and decision making.

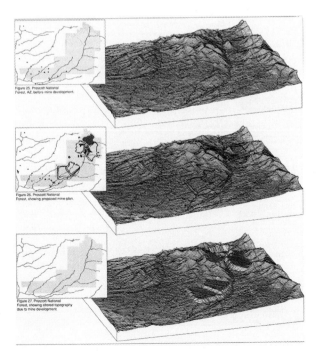

Figure 13.6 The U.S. National Forest service was offered a land swap by a mining company seeking development rights to a mineral deposit in the Prescott National Forest of Arizona. Using a geographic information system (GIS) and a variety of digital maps, the U.S. Geological Survey and the Forest Service created perspective views of the terrain before and after mining. The GIS showed that mining would cause dramatic changes to the topography

Web-Based Customer Decision Support Systems

The growth of electronic commerce has encouraged many companies to develop DSS where customers and employees can take advantage of Internet information resources and Web capabilities for interactivity and personalization. DSS based on the Web and the Internet can support decision making by providing online access to various databases and information pools along with software for data analysis. Some of these DSS are targeted toward management, but many have been developed to attract customers by providing information and tools to assist their decision making as they select products and services. Companies are finding that deciding which products and services to purchase has become increasingly information-intensive. People are now using more information from multiple sources to make purchasing decisions (such as purchasing a car or computer) before they interact with the product or sales staff. **Customer decision support systems (CDSS)** support the decision making process of an existing or potential customer.

People interested in purchasing a product or service can use Internet search engines, intelligent agents, online catalogues, Web directories, newsgroup discussions, e-mail, and other tools to help them locate the information they need to help with their decision. Information brokers, such as Edmunds.com, described in Chapter 4, are also sources of summarized, structured information for specific products or industries and may provide models for evaluating the information. Companies also have developed specific customer Web sites where all the information, models, or other analytical tools for evaluating alternatives are concentrated in one location. Web-based DSS have become especially popular in the financial services area because so many people are trying to manage their own assets and retirement savings. Table 13.3 lists some examples.

customer decision support system (CDSS)

System to support the decision making process of an existing or potential customer.

13.2 Group Decision Support Systems

The DSS we have just described focus primarily on individual decision making. However, so much work is accomplished in groups within organizations that a special category of systems called group decision support systems (GDSS) has been developed to support group and organizational decision making.

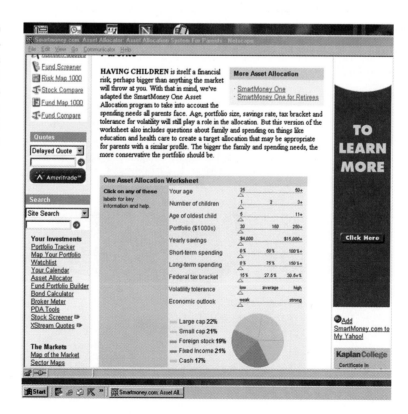

Figure 13.7 SmartMoney.com features online tools to help families with children make decisions about allocating their financial assets. DSS based on the Web can provide information from multiple sources and analytical tools to help potential customers select products and services.

TABLE 13.3	EXAMPLES OF WEB-BASED DSS

DSS	Description
Nikon Optical Canada	Web site allows a wide range of employees, including senior managers, marketing analysts, and sales representatives, to track sales activity of optical lenses purchased by practitioners, distributors, and optical laboratories across the Canadian territories. This enables Nikon to identify profitable customers for future up-sell opportunities, to track margins and areas of profitability, and to more effectively execute marketing campaigns.
Bank of Montreal	Web site enables queries to run against the enterprise-wide database each day and delivers intuitive, drillable reports to senior executives, financial service managers, line-of-business managers, branch employees, and HR personnel. The BMO MIND system also can perform CRM analyses to highlight accounts with low performance rates.
General Electric Plastics	Web site provides a Design Solutions Centre with a Web-based suite of online engineering tools for materials developers in the plastics industry. Visitors can select plastics materials, perform production costs estimates, search for product-specification information, and take online training.
Fidelity Investments	Web site features an online, interactive decision support application to help clients make decisions about investment savings plans and investment portfolio allocations. The application allows visitors to experiment with numerous "what-if" scenarios to design investment savings plans for retirement or a child's college education. If the user enters information about his or her finances, time horizon, and tolerance for risk, the system will suggest appropriate portfolios of mutual funds. The application performs the required number crunching and displays the changing return on investment as the user alters these assumptions.

WHAT IS A GDSS?

A **group decision support system (GDSS)** is an interactive computer-based system to facilitate the solution of unstructured problems by a set of decision makers working together as a group (DeSanctis and Gallupe, 1987). Groupware and Web-based tools for videoconferencing and electronic meetings described earlier in this text can support some group decision processes, but their focus is primarily on communication. GDSS, however, provide tools and technologies geared explicitly toward group decision making and were developed in response to a growing concern over the quality and effectiveness of meetings. The underlying problems in group decision making have been the explosion of decision maker meetings, the increasing duration of those meetings, and the growing number of attendees. Estimates on the amount of a manager's time spent in meetings range from 35 to 70 percent.

group decision support system (GDSS)

An interactive computer-based system to facilitate the solution to unstructured problems by a set of decision makers working together as a group.

Components of GDSS

GDSS make meetings more productive by providing tools to facilitate planning, generating, organizing, and evaluating ideas, establishing priorities, and documenting meeting proceedings for others in the organization. GDSS consist of three basic elements: *hardware, software tools,* and *people. Hardware* refers to the conference facility itself, including the room, the tables, and the chairs. A GDSS facility must be physically laid out in a manner that supports group collaboration. It must also include some electronic hardware, such as electronic display boards, as well as audiovisual, computer, and networking equipment.

Although groupware tools for collaborative work described in Chapter 6 can be used to support group decision making, there are specific GDSS *software tools* for supporting group meetings. These tools were originally developed for meetings in which all participants are in the same room, but they also can be used for networked meetings in which participants are in different locations. Table 13.4 lists the various GDSS software tools.

Together these elements have led to the creation of a range of different kinds of GDSS, from simple electronic boardrooms to elaborate collaboration laboratories. In a collaboration laboratory, individuals work on their own desktop PCs or workstations. Their input is integrated on a file server and is viewable on a common screen at the front of the room; in most systems the integrated input is also viewable on the individual participant's screen.

TABLE 13.4	**GDSS SOFTWARE TOOLS**

Tool	Capability
Electronic questionnaires	Aid the organizers in premeeting planning by identifying issues of concern and by helping to ensure that key planning information is not overlooked.
Electronic brainstorming tools	Allow individuals, simultaneously and anonymously, to contribute ideas on the topics of the meeting.
Idea organizers	Facilitate the organized integration and synthesis of ideas generated during brainstorming.
Questionnaire tools	Support the facilitators and group leaders as they gather information before and during the process of setting priorities.
Tools for voting or setting priorities	Make available a range of methods from simple voting, to ranking in order, to a range of weighted techniques for setting priorities or voting.
Stakeholder identification and analysis tools	Use structured approaches to evaluate the impact of an emerging proposal on the organization and to identify stakeholders and evaluate the potential impact of those stakeholders on the proposed project.
Policy formation tools	Provide structured support for developing agreement on the wording of policy statements.
Group dictionaries	Document group agreement on definitions of words and terms central to the project.
People	Refers not only to the participants but also to a trained facilitator and often to a staff who support the hardware and software.

OVERVIEW OF A GDSS MEETING

In a GDSS electronic meeting, each attendee has a workstation. The workstations are networked and are connected to the facilitator's console, which serves as both the facilitator's workstation and control panel and the meeting's file server. All data that the attendees forward from their workstations to the group are collected and saved on the file server. The facilitator is able to project computer images onto the projection screen at the front of the room. The facilitator also has an overhead projector available. Whiteboards are visible on either side of the projection screen. Many electronic meeting rooms are arranged in a semi-circle and are tiered in legislative style to accommodate a large number of attendees. The facilitator controls the use of tools during the meeting.

Attendees have full control over their own desktop computers. An attendee is able to view the agenda (and other planning documents), look at the integrated screen (or screens as the session progresses), use ordinary desktop PC tools (such as a word processor or a spreadsheet), tap into production data that have been made available, or work on the screen associated with the current meeting step and tool (such as a brainstorming screen). During the

An electronic meeting system provides capabilities for group decision support, such as networked workstations, projection screens, whiteboards, and software tools.

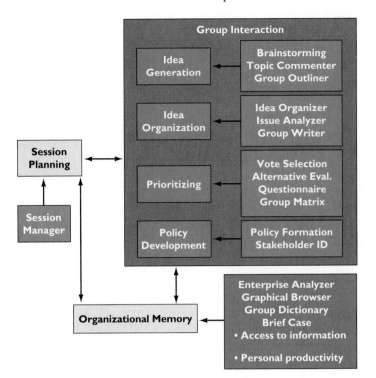

Figure 13.8 Group system tools. The sequence of activities and collaborative support tools used in an electronic meeting system facilitates communication among attendees and generates a full record of the meeting.

Source: From Nunamaker et al., "Electronic Meeting Systems to Support Group Work" in *Communications of the ACM*, July 1991. Reprinted by permission.

meeting, all input to the integrated screens is saved on the file server, and participants' work is kept confidential. When the meeting is completed, a full record of the meeting (both raw material and resultant output) is available to the attendees and can be made available to anyone else with a need for access. Figure 13.8 illustrates the sequence of activities at a typical electronic meeting along with the types of tools used and the output of those tools.

How GDSS Can Enhance Group Decision Making

Studies show that in traditional decision making meetings without GDSS support the optimal meeting size is three to five attendees. Beyond that size, the meeting process begins to break down. Using GDSS software, studies show the meeting size can increase while productivity also increases. One reason for this is that attendees contribute simultaneously, rather than one at a time, which makes more efficient use of meeting time.

A GDSS contributes to a more collaborative atmosphere by guaranteeing contributors' anonymity so that attendees can focus on evaluating the ideas themselves. Attendees can contribute without fear of personally being criticized or of having their ideas rejected because of the identity of the contributor. GDSS software tools follow structured methods for organizing and evaluating ideas and for preserving the results of meetings, allowing nonattendees to locate needed information after the meeting. The documentation of a meeting by one group at one site can also be used as input to another meeting on the same project at another site.

If properly designed and supported, GDSS meetings can increase the number of ideas generated and the quality of decisions while producing the desired results in fewer meetings. However, their outcomes are not necessarily better than face-to-face meetings. GDSS seem most useful for tasks involving idea generation, complex problems, and large groups (Fjermestad and Hiltz, 2000–2001, 1998–1999). One problem with understanding the value of GDSS is their complexity. A GDSS can be configured in an almost infinite variety of ways, and the nature of electronic meeting technology is only one of a number of factors that affect meeting processes and output. The outcome of group meetings depends upon the composition of the group, the manner in which the problem is presented to the group, the facilitator's effectiveness, the organization's culture and environment, the quality of the planning, the cooperation of the attendees, and the appropriateness of tools selected for different types of meetings and decision problems (Hender, Dean, Rodgers, and Nunamaker, 2002; Dennis and Wixom, 2001–2002; Dennis, Wixom, and Vandenberg, 2001).

13.3 EXECUTIVE SUPPORT IN THE ENTERPRISE

We have described how DSS and GDSS help managers make unstructured and semistructured decisions. Executive support systems (ESS), which we introduced in Chapter 2, also help managers with unstructured problems, focusing on the information needs of senior management. Combining data from internal and external sources, ESS create a generalized computing and communications environment that can be focused and applied to a changing array of problems. ESS help senior executives monitor organizational performance, track activities of competitors, spot problems, identify opportunities, and forecast trends.

THE ROLE OF EXECUTIVE SUPPORT SYSTEMS IN THE ORGANIZATION

Contemporary ESS can bring together data from all parts of the organization and allow managers to select, access, and tailor them as needed using easy-to-use desktop analytical tools and online data displays. Use of the systems has migrated down several organizational levels so that the executive and subordinates are able to look at the same data in the same way.

drill down

The ability to move from summary data to lower and lower levels of detail.

Today's systems try to avoid the problem of data overload so common in paper reports because the data can be filtered or viewed in graphical format (if the user so chooses). ESS have the ability to **drill down**, moving from a piece of summary data to lower and lower levels of detail. The ability to drill down is useful not only to senior executives but to employees at lower levels of the organization who need to analyze data. OLAP tools for analyzing large databases provide this capability.

A major challenge of building executive support systems has been to integrate data from systems designed for very different purposes so that senior executives can review organizational performance from a firm-wide perspective. Properly configured and implemented enterprise systems can provide managers with timely, comprehensive, and accurate firm-wide information. ESS based on this data can be considered logical extensions of enterprise system functionality.

External data, including data from the Web, are now more easily available in many ESS as well. Executives need a wide range of external data from current stock market news to competitor information, industry trends, and even projected legislative action. Through their ESS, managers can have access to news services, financial market databases, economic information, and whatever other public data they may require.

Contemporary ESS include tools for modelling and analysis. With only a minimum of experience, most managers find they can use these tools to create graphic comparisons of data by time, region, product, price range, and so on. (While DSS use these tools primarily for modelling and analysis in a fairly narrow range of decision situations, ESS use them primarily to provide status information about organizational performance.)

ESS must be designed so that high-level managers and others can use them without much training. One area that merits special attention is the determination of executive information requirements. ESS need to have some facility for environmental scanning. A key information requirement of managers at the strategic level is the capability to detect signals of problems in the organizational environment that indicate strategic threats and opportunities (Walls et al., 1992).

ESS potentially could give top executives the capability of examining other managers' work without their knowledge, so there may be some resistance to ESS at lower levels of the organization. Implementation of ESS should be carefully managed to neutralize such opposition (see Chapter 12).

BENEFITS OF EXECUTIVE SUPPORT SYSTEMS

Much of the value of ESS is found in their flexibility. These systems put data and tools in the hands of executives without addressing specific problems or imposing solutions. Executives are free to shape the problems as necessary, using the system as an extension of their own thinking processes. These are not decision making systems; they are tools to aid executives in making decisions.

DIGITAL COCKPITS HELP STEER THE ENTERPRISE

Pfizer Canada is a global pharmaceutical company that researches and finds innovative products in the areas of healthcare, animal health, and consumer healthcare.

Pfizer Canada relies on its ability to respond to the fast-paced changes in the pharmaceutical industry and uses a ground-breaking business intelligence infrastructure to nurture this ability.

Pfizer implemented the Pharmaceutical Sales Intelligence (PSI) Factory program to provide a business intelligence infrastructure that would automate the integration of multiple data sources and serve as a single point of access for both reporting and analytical needs. The need arose because too much time was spent retrieving large spreadsheets and manual integration and manipulation of the spreadsheets to obtain the desired business metrics. It was often difficult to maintain and apply data quality controls. The widely different reporting needs of a variety of users, from senior management to sales representatives, increased the report generation workload. Reports were often distributed via the company intranet with significant download times. Pfizer chose Brio Intelligence as the platform for this new initiative. Today, PSI Factory Brio Intelligence dashboards are accessible either online or through compact discs (CDs). For both online and CD modes, the applications are identical. Despite the high volumes of data integrated into each Brio Intelligence dashboard in disconnected mode, performance is almost indistinguishable from their online counterparts.

Data is integrated into the PSI Factory data warehouse on a monthly basis using an automated Extract-Transform-Load process, creating multiple data marts, organized by subject areas; PSI Factory contains almost 500 gigabytes of data.

Custom-developed Brio Intelligence executive information system (EIS) dashboards are then employed to access both kinds of data marts. The Brio software allows PSI Factory to present a consolidated view of both relational and OLAP (multidimensional) data, and the Brio application is integrated with MS Office for reporting requirements.

Data available include daily sales force alignments and activity, sales data from both internal and third-party solutions and prescriber statistical information from third-party sources. EIS dashboards include a dashboard for business planning, highlighting key performance indicators with drill-down option for detailed data by geographical location, highlighting sales trends, market trends, field force activity, and product sales performance; and another for performance evaluation that integrates data from many data marts, highlighting sales growth and percentage of quota met, call frequency, customer reach, and prescription volumes versus competitors.

Almost 100 decision makers use PSI Factory regularly. An additional 500 employees use the output from PSI Factory. Before PSI Factory, it took two person-weeks to integrate and produce reports. These reports now require only two person-days. Integration of the data has also given Pfizer Canada new insights into their business. "The implementation of PSI Factory and Brio Intelligence has provided significant efficiency gains among our analytical resources, and provided our district managers with vital new capabilities," said Sean Kelly, Director of Sales for Pfizer Canada.

To Think About: What are the management benefits of digital dashboards? How do these dashboard systems provide value for the firm? What technical, organization, and management issues do you think Pfizer Canada had to address in developing and installing their digital dashboards?

Sources: Based on "Pfizer Canada Case Study," available **www.brio.com/pdfs/ Pfizer.pdf**, accessed April 11, 2003; Brio Intelligence Corporate Web site, available **www.brio.com**, accessed April 11, 2003.

The most visible benefit of ESS is their ability to analyze, compare, and highlight trends. The easy use of graphics allows the user to look at more data in less time with greater clarity and insight than paper-based systems can provide. In the past, executives obtained the same information by taking up days and weeks of their staffs' valuable time. By using ESS, those staffs and the executives themselves are freed up for the more creative analysis and decision making in their jobs. ESS capabilities for drilling down and highlighting trends also may enhance the quality of analysis and can speed up decision making (Leidner and Elam, 1993–1994).

Some companies are using these systems to monitor key performance indicators for the entire firm and to measure firm performance against changes in the external environment (see the Window on Management). The timeliness and availability of the data result in needed actions being identified and taken earlier. These systems can, thus, help organizations move toward a "sense-and-respond" strategy.

A well-designed ESS could dramatically improve management performance and increase upper management's span of control. Immediate access to so much data allows executives to better monitor activities of the lower units that report to them. That very monitoring ability could allow decision making to be decentralized and to take place at lower operating levels. Executives are often willing to push decision making further down into the organization as long as they can be assured that all is going well. Alternatively, executive support systems based on enterprise-wide data could potentially increase management centralization, enabling senior executives to monitor the performance of subordinates across the company and direct them to take appropriate action when conditions change.

EXECUTIVE SUPPORT SYSTEMS AND THE DIGITAL FIRM

To illustrate the different ways in which an ESS can enhance management decision making, we now describe important types of ESS applications for gathering business intelligence and monitoring corporate performance, including ESS based on enterprise systems.

ESS for Business Intelligence

Today, customer expectations, Internet technology, and new business models can alter the competitive landscape so rapidly that managers need special capabilities for competitive intelligence gathering. ESS can help managers identify changing market conditions, formulate responses, track implementation efforts, and learn from feedback.

BP Sony NV, the Netherlands branch of the multinational electronics giant, wanted more insight from the marketplace to drive its competitive strategy. Until recently, its management reports were based primarily on financial and administrative data that took at least 24 hours to generate. Management wanted to be able to make meaningful decisions based on marketing and sales data as well so that it could respond quickly to marketplace changes. Sony Netherlands constructed a data warehouse and executive information system for this purpose.

The system is now available to 78 users in management, marketing, and sales. They can use the system to help them define strategies, search for opportunities, identify problems, and substantiate actions. Using a drill-down function, they can examine the underlying numbers behind the total result. For instance, while senior management can obtain sales results by business unit or product group, a marketing manager can use the system to look only at the group of products he or she was responsible for. The manager can produce a report to indicate exactly which products are strong or weak performers or to rank dealers by performance. The system is flexible, easy to use, and can provide much of this information to the user online (Information Builders, 2000).

Corset Shop, a highly regarded intimate apparel retailer for more than 37 years, implemented a suite of applications from Montreal's Gemmar Systems International. Corset Shop operates stores under the name Bare Necessities and also operates leased departments coast-to-coast with more than 35 000 stock keeping units (SKUs) of lingerie, sleepwear, loungewear, leg wear, and accessories. Gemmar's Retail-1 ESS gives Corset Shop executives the ability to drill down, look at category, department, or class statistics, rank their best and worst products, and season and age their products and vendors. They can also examine store performance, analyze inventories sell through, refunds, and a host of other types of analysis.

Monitoring Corporate Performance: Balanced Scorecard Systems

Companies have traditionally measured value using financial metrics such as return on investment (ROI), which we describe in Chapter 12. Many firms are now implementing a **balanced scorecard** model that supplements traditional financial measures with measurements from additional perspectives such as customers, internal business processes, and learning and growth. Managers can use balanced scorecard systems to see how well the firm is meeting its strategic goals. The goals and measures for the balanced scorecard vary from company to company. Companies are setting up information systems to populate the scorecard for management.

At Nova Scotia Power, Inc., the balanced scorecard has been linked to many critical systems. For example, the annual business planning and budgeting process is now driven by the

balanced scorecard

Model for analyzing firm performance that supplements traditional financial measures with measurements from additional business perspectives, such as customers, internal business processes, and learning and growth.

balanced scorecard. This new system is called "Strategic Resource Allocation" because it provides the opportunity to display how resource allocation decisions directly influence the achievement of strategy. The balanced scorecard is also linked to the incentive compensation system and has been cascaded throughout the company to ensure goal alignment at every level. Finally, and perhaps most importantly, the balanced scorecard is a powerful communication tool, signalling to everyone in the organization key success measures, and how these measures can influence them.

Amsterdam-based ING Bank, which is part of the ING Group global financial services firm, adopted a balanced scorecard approach when it reorganized itself. Management wanted to shift from a product to a client orientation and develop appropriate performance indicators to measure progress in this new direction. In 1997, the bank built a Web-based balanced scorecard application using SAS tools for data warehousing and statistical analysis to measure progress with 21 indicators. Data to fill out the scorecard, from such sources as financial ledger applications and client retention and market penetration ratios, feed a central data warehouse. The data come from systems running on Lotus Notes, Microsoft Excel spreadsheets, and Oracle and DB2 databases. The data warehouse and balanced scorecard software run on IBM RS/6000 servers. ING initially made the balanced scorecard system available only to midrange executives in sales, but later extended it to 3000 users, including people at nearly every level of its relationship management group. Users regularly check progress with the scorecard. For example, by comparing how many visits they have made to different clients, sales people can make better decisions about how to allocate their time (McCune, 2000).

Enterprise-wide Reporting and Analysis

Enterprise system vendors are now providing capabilities to extend the usefulness of data captured in operational systems to give management a picture of the overall performance of the firm. Some provide reporting of metrics for balanced scorecard analysis as well as more traditional financial and operating metrics. Table 13.5 describes strategic performance management tools for each of the major enterprise system vendors.

Companies can use these new enterprise-reporting capabilities to create measures of firm performance that were not previously available. The head of strategic planning at Dow Chemical led a cross-functional steering team to develop a set of measures and reports based on data from the company's SAP enterprise system. Process experts in different areas of the company defined reporting categories, such as expense management, inventory management, and sales. Dow then developed a data mart for each type of data, amounting to over 20 data marts. The data marts are integrated so that the numbers for the "business results" mart balance with numbers in the expenses and sales marts. Dow also implemented a new set of performance measures based on shareholder value and activity-based costing. **Activity-based costing** is a budgeting and analysis model that identifies all the resources, processes, and

activity-based costing
Model for identifying all the company activities that cause costs to occur while producing a specific product or service so that managers can see which products or services are profitable or losing money and make changes to maximize firm profitability.

TABLE 13.5	STRATEGIC PERFORMANCE MANAGEMENT TOOLS FOR ENTERPRISE SYSTEMS
Enterprise System	**Vendor Description**
SAP	Web-enabled mySAP Strategic Enterprise Management module provides reports giving managers a comprehensive view of firm performance. Features corporate performance metrics, simulation, and planning tools. Managers can model and communicate key performance indicators for a balanced scorecard. Another measurement tool called the Management Cockpit can be used to monitor strategic performance indicators using internal and external benchmarks.
PeopleSoft	Web-enabled Enterprise Performance Management (EPM) features modules for workforce analytics, customer relationship analytics, financial analytics, supply chain analytics, and profitability management for financial services. The Financial Analytics module supports activity-based management and the balanced scorecard.
Oracle	Strategic Enterprise Management includes support for the balanced scorecard, activity-based management, and budgeting. A value-based management module under development will help companies develop and apply new accounting methods for quantifying intellectual capital.

costs, including overhead and operating expenses, required to produce a specific product or service. It focuses on determining firm activities that cause costs to occur, rather than on merely tracking what has been spent. It allows managers to see which products or services are profitable or losing money so that they can determine the changes required to maximize firm profitability. Instead of reporting in terms of product and income, the system can focus on contribution margins and customer accounts, with the ability to calculate the current and lifetime value of each account. The system is used by more than 5000 people, ranging from Dow's CEO to plant floor workers (Davenport, 2000).

Management of Nissan Motor Company of Australia must oversee the activities of 550 people in 23 sites across the Australian continent. The company is primarily involved in Nissan's import and distribution activities for 35 000 automobiles each year. Like other auto-motive companies, Nissan Australia has extensive reporting requirements, including detailed controlling reports for financial accounts and monthly accounts. Managers need detailed reports down to the model level, with controlling reports for each department. When Nissan used an old legacy mainframe system, it would take up to two weeks to create and distribute reports to the company's board of directors.

In 1997, Nissan Australia installed SAP's R/3 enterprise software, serving as a pilot for the rest of the Nissan organization. The company also installed Information Builders' SNAPpack Power Reporter to create custom reports with a Web interface and powerful drill-down capabilities that did not require extensive programming to produce. These reports can be generated immediately and include profit-and-loss reports, gross margin analysis, balance sheets, and wholesale and retail vehicles. Management requests for more profit analysis reports by model, state, and other variables can be easily satisfied (Information Builders, 2000).

MANAGEMENT WRAP-UP

Management is responsible for determining where management support systems can make their greatest contribution to organizational performance and for allocating the resources to build them. Management needs to work closely with system builders to make sure that these systems effectively capture the right set of information requirements and decision processes for guiding the firm.

Management support systems can improve organizational performance by speeding up decision making or improving the quality of management decisions. However, some of these decision processes may not be clearly understood. A management support system will be most effective when system builders have a clear idea of its objectives, the nature of the decisions to be supported, and how the system will actually support decision making.

Systems to support management decision making can be developed with a range of technologies, including the use of large databases, modelling tools, graphics tools, datamining and analysis tools, and electronic meeting technology. Identifying the right technology for the decision or decision process to be supported is a key technology decision.

For Discussion

1.   As a manager or user of information systems, what would you need to know to participate in the design and use of a DSS or an ESS? Why?

2.   If businesses used DSS, GDSS, and ESS more widely, would they make better decisions? Explain.

SUMMARY

1. *How can information systems help individual managers make better decisions when the problems are nonroutine and constantly changing?* A special category of systems called decision support systems (DSS) combines data, sophisticated analytical models and tools, and user-friendly software into a single powerful system that can support semistructured or unstructured decision making. There are two kinds of DSS: model-driven DSS and data-driven DSS. A DSS provides results of model-based or data-driven analysis that help managers design and evaluate alternatives and monitor the progress of the solution that was adopted. The components of a DSS are the DSS database, the DSS software system, and the user interface. The DSS database is a collection of current or historical data from a number of applications or groups that can be used for analysis. The data can come from both internal and external sources, including enterprise systems and the Web. DSS software consists of OLAP and datamining tools or mathematical and analytical models that are used for analyzing the data in the database. The user interface allows users to interact with the DSS software tools directly.

   DSS can help support decisions for supply chain management and customer analysis as well as model alternative business scenarios. DSS targeted toward customers as well as managers are becoming available on the Web. A special category of DSS called geographic information systems (GIS) uses data visualization technology to analyze and display data for planning and decision making with digitized maps.

2. *How can information systems help people working in a group make decisions more efficiently?* People working together in a group can use group decision support systems (GDSS) to help them in the process of arriving at a decision. A GDSS is an interactive computer-based system to facilitate the solution of unstructured problems by a set of decision makers working together as a group, rather than individually. GDSS have hardware, software, and people components. Hardware components consist of the conference room facilities, including seating arrangements and computer and other electronic hardware. Software components include tools for organizing ideas, gathering information, ranking and setting priorities, and documenting meeting sessions. People components include participants, a trained facilitator, and staff to support the hardware and software.

   A GDSS helps decision makers meeting together to arrive at a decision more efficiently and is especially useful for increasing the productivity of meetings larger than four or five people. However, the effectiveness of GDSS is contingent on the composition of the group, the task, appropriate tool selection and meeting support, and the organizational context of the meeting.

3. *Are there any special systems that can facilitate decision making among senior managers? Exactly what can these systems do to help high-level management?* Executive support systems help senior managers with unstructured problems that occur at the strategic level of the organization. ESS provide data from both internal and external sources and provide a generalized computing and communications environment that can be focused and applied to a changing array of problems. These systems can filter out extraneous details for high-level overviews, or they can drill down to provide senior managers with detailed transaction data if required. ESS are starting to take advantage of firm-wide data provided by enterprise systems.

   ESS help senior managers analyze, compare, and highlight trends so that they may more easily monitor organizational performance or identify strategic problems and opportunities. They are very useful for environmental scanning, providing business intelligence to help management detect signals of strategic threats or opportunities from the organization's environment. ESS can increase the span of control of senior management, allowing them to oversee more people with fewer resources.

4. *What benefits can systems to support management decision making provide for the organization as a whole?* DSS, GDSS, and ESS are starting to take advantage of more accurate firm-wide data provided by enterprise systems and the new information technology infrastructure to support very fine-grained decisions for guiding the firm, coordinating work activities across the enterprise, and responding rapidly to changing markets and customers. DSS can be used to guide company-wide decisions in supply chain management, customer relationship management, and planning business scenarios. ESS can be used to monitor company-wide performance using both traditional financial metrics and the balanced scorecard method. The ability to explore the outcomes of alternative organizational scenarios, use precise firm-wide information, and provide tools to facilitate group decision processes can help managers make decisions that help the firm achieve its strategic objectives.

KEY TERMS

- Activity-based costing, 453
- Balanced scorecard, 452
- Business intelligence, 435
- Customer decision support system (CDSS), 446
- Data-driven DSS, 438
- Data visualization, 445
- Drill down, 450
- DSS database, 440
- DSS software system, 440
- Geographic information system (GIS), 445
- Group decision support system (GDSS), 447
- Knowledge discovery, 439
- Model, 440
- Model-driven DSS, 436
- Sensitivity analysis, 441

REVIEW QUESTIONS

1. What is a decision support system (DSS)? How does it differ from a management information system (MIS)?

2. How can a DSS support unstructured or semistructured decision making?

3. What is the difference between a data-driven DSS and a model-driven DSS? Give examples.

4. What are the three basic components of a DSS? Briefly describe each.

5. How can DSS help firms with supply chain management and customer relationship management?

6. What is a geographic information system (GIS)? How does it use data visualization technology? How can it support decision making?

7. What is a customer decision support system? How can the Internet be used for this purpose?

8. What is a group decision support system (GDSS)? How does it differ from a DSS?

9. What underlying problems in group decision making have led to the development of GDSS?

10. Describe the three elements of a GDSS.

11. Name five GDSS software tools.

12. How can GDSS facilitate group decision making?

13. Define and describe the capabilities of an executive support system (ESS).

14. How can the Internet and enterprise systems provide capabilities for executive support systems?

15. What are the benefits of ESS? How do these systems enhance managerial decision making?

APPLICATION SOFTWARE EXERCISE

SPREADSHEET EXERCISE: PERFORMING BREAKEVEN ANALYSIS AND SENSITIVITY ANALYSIS

Selmore Collectible Toy Company (SCTC) makes toy sets consisting of collectible trucks, vans, and cars for the retail market. The firm is developing a new toy set that includes a battery-powered tractor-trailer, complete with cab and trailer, sports car, and motorcycle. Each set sells for $100. Table 1 shows the major components of SCTC's annual fixed costs for the toy set. Each component includes the cost of purchases, depreciation, and operating expenses. Table 2 shows the major components of SCTC's variable costs.

Prepare a spreadsheet to support the decision making needs of SCTC's managers. The spreadsheet should show the fixed costs, variable costs per unit, the contribution margin, and the breakeven point for this product. How many sets does SCTC have to sell before it can start turning a profit? Include a data table to show alternative breakeven points, assuming variations in insurance costs and labour costs. How would increasing the sale price to $125 affect the breakeven point? The Companion Website for Chapter 13 provides more detail on the range of costs to include in your sensitivity analysis and on the calculations required for a simple breakeven analysis.

TABLE 1 SCTC FIXED COSTS

Category	Amount
Land	$ 42 500
Buildings	332 500
Manufacturing machinery	532 000
Office equipment	212 800
Utilities	30 500
Insurance	99 700
Total	**$1 250 000**

TABLE 2 SCTC VARIABLE COSTS

Category	Amount
Labour	$15.00
Advertising	1.00
Shipping & receiving	5.00
Total	**$21.00**

GROUP PROJECT

With three or four of your classmates, identify several groups in your university that could benefit from a GDSS. Design a GDSS for one of those groups, describing its hardware, software, and people elements. Present your findings to the class.

INTERNET TOOLS

COMPANION WEBSITE

The Companion Website for this chapter will take you to a series of Web sites where you can complete an exercise using Web-based DSS.

At www.pearsoned.ca/laudon, you will find valuable tools to facilitate and enhance the learning of this chapter as well as opportunities to apply your knowledge to realistic situations:

- An Interactive Study Guide of self-test questions that will provide you with immediate feedback.

- Application exercises.

- An Electronic Commerce Project that will use the interactive software at the Fidelity Investments Web site for investment portfolio analysis.

- A Management Decision Problem on analyzing a capital budgeting decision.

- Updates of material in the chapter.

ADDITIONAL SITES OF INTEREST

There are many interesting Web sites to enhance your learning about decision support systems. You can search the Web yourself or just try the following sites to add to what you have already learned.

Brio Intelligence
> **www.brio.com**
> Company specializing in digital dashboard applications

Balanced Scorecard.com
> **www.balancedscorecard.com**
> Company specializing in balanced scorecard applications; this site has links to other balanced scorecard information.

Microstrategy
> **www.microstrategy.com**
> Company specializing in business intelligence software, including Web-based DSS

CASE STUDY: *Can DSS Help MasterCard Master the Credit Card Business?*

Credit (charge) cards have been very big business for several decades. In 2001, over $30 trillion in payments for goods and services were charged using credit cards. The cards have made life easier for many people by eliminating the need to carry large amounts of cash for most purchases. Many people also use the cards as a way to borrow money because they need only pay a small percentage of the amount they owe each month, although they are usually charged very high interest rates for the unpaid balance. The interest goes to the issuing bank, making credit cards a very profitable service for them. However, the credit card industry is intensely competitive, highly fragmented, and growing at a rate of 3 to 4 percent per year, making those profits difficult to achieve.

VISA and MasterCard are associations of banks that issue the credit cards. They market their cards, often several different cards, and provide support for the transactions, making networks available to collect and use the data. The most popular credit card has been VISA, with 44.5 percent of the business in 2001, while MasterCard is number two with 31.6 percent. Being very much second to VISA, MasterCard is trying to overtake it. While it had been number two since the beginning, MasterCard began to emerge from "its doldrums" in 1997, according to Robert Selander, MasterCard's CEO. It began to

realize it might really be able to overtake Visa and become number one. To reach that goal, MasterCard needed to present itself so that potential users will choose a MasterCard, rather than a Visa. It also had to spur the bank issuers to promote MasterCard cards, rather than those of their competition.

In 1998, when MasterCard had only 28.8 percent of the credit card charge volume, while VISA's was over 50 percent, MasterCard decided it needed a new computer centre, partially to handle all of the data as the company's business expanded as a result of its drive to overtake VISA. It also foresaw growth as a result of its change in strategy. The company's new strategy required a system that would be able to keep a record of every transaction of every customer for three years. The strategy included ways MasterCard and its member banks could use those data to increase their credit card business. MasterCard wanted to increase its daily volume of 30 million transactions in 1997. At the time, it had three separate computer centres on four floors in the suburbs of St. Louis, Missouri, and it wanted to consolidate the computer centres while enlarging the new centre so that it would be able to handle both the current volume and the planned volume as it expanded. At that time, MasterCard stored nearly 50 terabytes (50 trillion numbers and letters) of data, including the dollar amount, merchant, location, and card number. MasterCard also planned to add other data fields, such as ZIP codes, to make the data more useful. However, to protect MasterCard users, it did decide not to include demographic data, such as income and age. Nonetheless, "The credit card business lives and dies by data," said Ted Iacobuzio, director of consumer credit research for the consulting and research firm, TowerGroup.

While both VISA and MasterCard had already been warehousing so much data, they were both moving toward providing reports to their member banks. MasterCard's goal was to give its members (the banks) direct access to their customers' data as well as tools to analyze all of these data, all in order to persuade the banks to choose MasterCard over VISA. For example, if banks could use MasterCard tools to improve their analysis of the profitability of the cards in their portfolios or to gain more customers and transactions to process, they would be inclined to push MasterCard more often. This analysis could help banks determine the types of customers who were most profitable or find ways to appeal to more potential MasterCard customers. Many banks issue both VISA cards and MasterCard cards (sometimes several of each), and if the banks can use this information from MasterCard while VISA does not have or make available this information, the MasterCard company can gain a strategic advantage. For example, in 2001, MasterCard persuaded Citigroup, the largest issuer of credit cards, to push MasterCard over VISA so that 85 percent of its credit cards came from MasterCard versus only 15 percent from VISA. J.P. Morgan Chase likewise was convinced to use MasterCard for 80 percent of the cards it issued.

MasterCard hoped it could persuade banks to use these data if they could see value (increased profit) in the process. Joseph Caro, MasterCard's vice-president of Internet technology services, said that "little percentages" can be very profitable to banks. In one case, a bank required its merchants to verify the whole process by using the telephone to call in one transaction out of 50 for approval (rather than using a telecommunications method), while most banks required only one transaction in 500. Because call-ins cost about $3 each, that bank could save US $300 000 a year by switching over to the one-in-500 method. Another bank was turning down one transaction out of five because so many call-ins were timing out. The bank was able to discover that most of the customers turned down were actually creditworthy. By changing its setup, the bank would be able to eliminate thousands of unnecessary lost transactions.

About 28 000 banks and financial service companies issue MasterCard credit cards. To draw these customers into using its credit card transaction data, MasterCard needed not only to make each bank's data available to them, but it also needed to make available appropriate analytic software. MasterCard assigned 35 full-time developers to the task of identifying and creating software tools to accomplish this task. Drawing on Business Objects' WebIntelligence software in 2001, these developers created and programmed 27 tools for the banks to use.

(These tools are not free, and they are not available to merchants.) One of MasterCard's new tools, called Business Performance Intelligence, is for operational reporting and includes a suite of 70 standard reports that banks can use to analyze their daily, weekly, or monthly transactions. The banks can then compare the results from one market (such as a Canadian province or region or a single country) with that of another market. MasterCard also works with individual banks to create its own custom reports, enabling it to concentrate on its own issues and concerns. Subscribing banks access the MasterCard business intelligence system via a secure extranet.

The developers also created MarketScope, which are applications that have the goal of helping banks and merchants work together to generate more purchases from the merchants if they are paid for by MasterCard. One example they give is to enable Wal-Mart stores to determine how many MasterCard holders spend $25 or more on sporting goods in January and February. Then, MasterCard's vice-president of systems development, Andrew Clyne, suggested that Wal-Mart could send these cardholders the right to obtain tickets to their closest major league baseball team on the basis of future sporting goods purchases above a certain dollar minimum. Iacobuzio said that such a strategy should appeal to state and regional banks. However, he believes it is likely that national and international banks would have already developed and been using their own analytical software. But even they would have a use for MasterCard's software as a kind of benchmark against which to measure the effectiveness of their own systems.

MasterCard's new data storage site, which was opened in May 2002, is also in St. Louis, in a single building of 48 770 square metres. The complex, which was built on open land, cost MasterCard US $135 million. The changeover to the new site happened over a weekend with almost no problems, despite the purchases of about US $4 billion each day. Moreover, despite the increasing volume, the processing was much faster. As Caro said, "If we can do things faster, little percentages start moving in our direction."

VISA, however, is not sitting still and is managing about 100 trillion terabytes of data for its clients. Until recently, it mainly supplied the data online or on disks to its bank customers, who used their own software and computers to analyze the data. Recently, VISA started to run analyses for the banks on its own computers. In May 2002, VISA also introduced a Web service called Resolve Online to help banks deal with disputed payments and is working on providing banks with online analytic tools. "If MasterCard is ahead of the game in any of this," says Iacobuzio, "VISA will have it in six months."

Sources: Tom Steinert Threlkeld, "MasterCard Tools up Data Handling," *Baseline*, June 17, 2002; Rick Whiting, "Extranets Go the Extra Mile," *InformationWeek*, May 20, 2002; and Kenneth N. Gilpin, "Market Insight: One Rule of Plastic: Recovery Has a Dark Side," *New York Times*, February 24, 2002.

CASE STUDY QUESTIONS

1. Analyze MasterCard using the competitive forces and value chain models. Briefly summarize the problems that MasterCard was facing before 1998 that caused it to change its business strategy.
2. Describe the new business strategy MasterCard developed. What is the role of information systems in its new strategy?

3. What kind of decision support systems did MasterCard develop? How are they related to its business strategy? How do they provide value for MasterCard and its clients?
4. Has MasterCard's strategy been successful? Can MasterCard hold on to its strategic advantage? Explain your answer.

KNOWLEDGE-BASED INFORMATION SYSTEMS

14
CHAPTER

As a manager, you will want to know how your firm can benefit from information systems for knowledge management. After completing this chapter, you should be able to answer the following questions:

1. *Why do businesses today need knowledge management programs and systems for knowledge management?*

2. *Which information systems applications are most useful for distributing, creating, and sharing knowledge in the firm?*

3. *What are the business benefits of using artificial intelligence technology for knowledge management?*

4. *How can businesses use expert systems and case-based reasoning to capture knowledge?*

5. *How can organizations benefit from using neural networks and other intelligent techniques?*

Hill and Knowlton Canada Limited

Hill and Knowlton Canada (H&K) is the nation's leading strategic communications consultancy, with a successful track record of providing high-quality public relations support to companies, agencies, government ministries, and organizations. As a multi-specialty firm, H&K offers in-depth expertise in a variety of areas, including technology communications, corporate communications, health and pharmaceuticals, marketing communications, financial communications, crisis communications, and public affairs.

H&K communicates globally across a network that encompasses 69 offices in 34 countries. H&K knew it needed significant improvements when it came to sharing knowledge and information internally and with clients. On the basis of this need, the company helped develop a knowledge management technology tool, called HK.Net, based on the Microsoft platform.

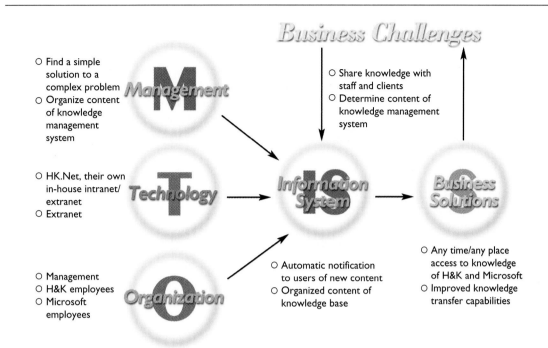

One of H&K's largest accounts is Microsoft Canada Co. (Microsoft), based in Mississauga. Microsoft is one of the leading software providers in Canada. Based on their close relationship, there is a constant stream of strategic counselling, planning, new product announcements, and ongoing media activities between Microsoft and H&K, which make effective knowledge management critical. To add value to the level of service that H&K offers to Microsoft, H&K devised a way to adapt the strategy behind HK.Net and transform it into a useable solution that Microsoft could take advantage of—a private and secure Hill and Knowlton/Microsoft extranet.

An extranet between Microsoft and H&K held the promise of more efficient administration that would allow for the sharing of large documents, saving e-mail histories, storing group files, and approval of documents. The extranet model enables unprecedented ease, efficiency, and simplicity in accessing, sharing and distributing information. The extranet would also offer employees the ability to collaborate anytime and anywhere, share value-added information, budgets, plans, press releases, and more.

On any given day, Microsoft and H&K exchange a substantial amount of information through e-mail. H&K employees send and receive nearly 500 Mb of e-mail every week. In order to stay within storage parameters, employees regularly delete e-mails with attachments to free up space. As a result, important knowledge is often lost.

While e-mail functions primarily as a correspondence vehicle at both H&K and Microsoft, there is also a large amount of file transferring between the two companies' e-mail servers. With the number of file transfers taking place, excessive memory waste on servers and personal computers (PCs) means that files are duplicated and, in some cases, accidentally deleted, in an effort to free up server memory.

The actual process of creating an extranet with Microsoft was reasonably simple for H&K since the initial infrastructure was already in place through HK.Net. And the proposition itself was straightforward: If it worked on a worldwide basis for Hill and Knowlton, why would it not work on a "local" basis when the two companies were merely kilometres away?

H&K called on its internal knowledge management experts to undertake the task of setting up the strategy that would work best for Microsoft. H&K knew that it could have a solution set up in a matter of days; the difficult part was organizing and customizing the extranet in such a way that it would be easy for both H&K and Microsoft to use, store, and navigate through shared information. The HK.Net team began what would be a two-month dialogue with key Microsoft representatives to discuss exactly how the shared extranet should be organized for the optimum benefit of both parties.

"The most challenging part in getting the H&K–Microsoft extranet up and running was the organization of the actual information that would reside on it," said Ted Graham, Hill and Knowlton worldwide director of knowledge management. "Microsoft is a large company, and as such, there is a lot of information that needs to be shared and exchanged. Ensuring that it all resided on the extranet in some semblance of order was critical."

Graham visited Microsoft to present an initial framework to the product and marketing managers who would be the actual users of the extranet. Through this process, it was determined that the site would be organized into four main folders, including Canadian online media links, general Hill and Knowlton, general Microsoft, and individual product group folders.

The Canadian online media links folder was designed to provide key links to publications with an online presence. The links folder was established to allow both sides to stay up to date on current happenings in the technology industry as well as to search for relevant stories that were mentioned in discussion. When new content is added to these Web sites, users are automatically notified; this ensures that everyone has access to the most up-to-date industry information.

The general Hill and Knowlton folder contains information about H&K that would be of relevance to Microsoft team members from team contacts, public relations toolkits, service offerings, best practices, and key learnings. Having this information housed in one centralized repository should help ensure that both parties are aware of who is responsible for what and how best to contact those individuals.

The general Microsoft folder offers a wealth of information to Hill and Knowlton staff, outlining Microsoft staff biographies and pictures, contact lists, organizational charts, and communications and product information that affect all groups.

The group folders section contained a number of sub-areas pertaining to specific Microsoft product and solution groups, where marketing and product managers along with their Hill and Knowlton counterparts could exchange information related directly to projects and day-to-day activities.

The implementation process, which included the population of the four key folders, lasted approximately two months, as both Microsoft and H&K had a large amount of information to add to the extranet. As well, user names and passwords had to be assigned to the Microsoft employees who would be accessing the site on a regular basis.

Through the implementation of the extranet, both sides have recognized numerous key benefits. Employees at both companies can access and work on shared information and documentation—such as press materials, program plans, and presentations—any time, from anywhere.

This type of knowledge management solution provides a more efficient and effective method of knowledge transfer between H&K and Microsoft, resulting in an increase in productivity at both companies. As well, since intellectual capital is now archived, new personnel on both sides can get up to speed more quickly and easily.

"Though the initial process of creating the HK.Net extranet was fairly simple, the challenge was deciding how to best serve everyone involved," said Graham. "The end result is a very robust and functional extranet that has proven to be an invaluable resource for both H&K and Microsoft. But the work isn't finished; this tool continues to evolve, much like our business relationship."

Sources: "Hill and Knowlton Canada Limited: A Microsoft Case Study," available www. Microsoft.com/Canada/casestudies/HandK.asp, accessed May 26, 2003; "Hill and Knowlton and Intraspect Win 2002 World Class Solution Award from DM Review," available http://www.intraspect.com/newsevents/releases/jun3_02.html, June 3, 2002, accessed May 26, 2003.

MANAGEMENT CHALLENGES

Hill and Knowlton's HK.Net is one example of how systems can be used to leverage organizational knowledge by making it more easily available. Collaborating and communicating with practitioners and experts and sharing ideas and information have become essential requirements in business, science, and government. In an information economy, capturing and distributing intelligence and knowledge and enhancing group collaboration have become critical to organizational innovation and survival. Special systems can be used for managing organizational knowledge, but they raise the following management challenges:

1. **Designing knowledge systems that genuinely enhance organizational performance.** Managers have encountered problems when attempting to transform their firms through knowledge management programs (Gold, Malhotra, and Segars, 2001). Information systems that truly enhance the productivity of knowledge workers may be difficult to build because the manner in which information technology can enhance higher-level tasks, such as those performed by managers and professionals, is not always clearly understood. Some aspects of organizational knowledge cannot be captured easily or codified, or the information that organizations finally manage to capture may become outdated as environments change. It is very difficult to integrate knowledge management programs with business strategy. Processes and interactions between information technology and social elements in organizations must be carefully managed (Davenport, Thomas, and Cantrell, 2002; Grover and Davenport, 2001).

2. **Identifying and implementing appropriate organizational applications for artificial intelligence.** Only certain kinds of information problems are appropriate for artificial intelligence (AI) applications. AI tools work best with complex, repetitive information-based activities. Many AI applications improve performance through trial and error and may not be reliable enough for mission-critical problems (Booth and Boluswar, 2002). Expert systems are expensive and time consuming to maintain because their rules must be reprogrammed every time there is a change in the organizational environment. Many thousands of businesses have undertaken experimental projects in expert systems, but only a small percentage have created expert systems that actually can be used on a production basis. Organizations need to determine exactly how they can benefit from AI and whether the benefits are realistic.

This chapter examines information system applications specifically designed to help organizations create, capture, distribute, and apply knowledge and information. First, we examine information systems for supporting information and knowledge work. Then, we look at the ways that organizations can use artificial intelligence technologies for capturing, storing, and using knowledge and expertise.

14.1 KNOWLEDGE MANAGEMENT IN THE ORGANIZATION

Chapter 1 described the emergence of the information economy and the digital firm in which the major source of wealth and prosperity is the production and distribution of information and knowledge, and firms increasingly rely on digital technology to enable business processes. For example, 55 percent of the Canadian labour force consists of knowledge and information workers, and 60 percent of the gross domestic product of the Canada comes from the knowledge and information sectors, such as finance and publishing.

In an information economy, knowledge-based core competencies—the two or three things that an organization does best—are key organizational assets. Producing unique products or services or producing them at a lower cost than competitors is based on superior knowledge of the production process and superior design. Knowing how to do things effectively and efficiently in ways that other organizations cannot duplicate is a primary source of value and is a factor in production that cannot be purchased in external markets. Some management theorists believe that these **knowledge assets** are at least as important as physical and financial assets for competitive advantage and survival.

As knowledge becomes a central productive and strategic asset, organizational success increasingly depends on the firm's ability to produce, gather, store, and disseminate knowledge. With knowledge, firms become more efficient and effective in their use of scarce resources. Without knowledge, firms become less efficient and effective in their use of resources and ultimately fail.

ORGANIZATIONAL LEARNING AND KNOWLEDGE MANAGEMENT

How do firms obtain knowledge? Like humans, organizations create and gather knowledge through a variety of **organizational learning** mechanisms. Through trial and error, careful measurement of planned activities, and feedback from customers and the environment in general, organizations create new standard operating procedures and business processes that reflect their experience. This is called "organizational learning." Arguably, organizations that can sense and respond to their environments rapidly will survive longer than organizations that have poor learning mechanisms.

Knowledge management increases the ability of the organization to learn from its environment and to incorporate knowledge into its business processes. **Knowledge management** refers to the set of processes developed in an organization to create, gather, store, transfer, and apply knowledge. Information technology plays an important role in knowledge management by supporting these business processes for creating, identifying, and leveraging knowledge throughout the organization. Developing procedures and routines—business processes—to optimize the creation, flow, learning, protection, and sharing of knowledge in the firm is now a core management responsibility.

Companies cannot take advantage of their knowledge resources if they have inefficient processes for capturing and distributing knowledge or if they fail to appreciate the value of the knowledge they already possess (Davenport and Prusak, 1998). Some corporations have created explicit knowledge management programs for protecting and distributing knowledge resources that they have identified and for discovering new sources of knowledge. These programs are often headed by a **chief knowledge officer (CKO)**. The chief knowledge officer is a senior executive who is responsible for the firm's knowledge management program. The CKO helps design programs and systems to find new sources of knowledge or to make better use of existing knowledge in organizational and management processes (Flash, 2001; Earl and Scott, 1999).

SYSTEMS AND INFRASTRUCTURE FOR KNOWLEDGE MANAGEMENT

All the major types of information systems described in this text facilitate the flow of information and the management of a firm's knowledge. Earlier chapters described systems that help firms understand and respond to their environments more effectively, notably enterprise

---

knowledge assets

Organizational knowledge regarding how to efficiently and effectively perform business processes and create new products and services that enable the business to create value.

organizational learning

Creation of new standard operating procedures and business processes that reflect organizations' experience.

knowledge management

The set of processes developed in an organization to create, gather, store, maintain, and apply the firm's knowledge.

chief knowledge officer (CKO)

Senior executive in charge of the organization's knowledge management program.

systems, external and internal networks, databases, datamining, and communication-based applications. The concept of a "digital firm" refers to a firm with substantial use of information technology to enhance its ability to sense and respond to its environment. We also discussed systems that help managers and others to analyze their environments in order to make decisions.

Although all the information systems we have described help an organization sense and respond to its environment, some technologies uniquely and directly address the organizational learning and knowledge management task. Office systems, knowledge work systems (KWS), group collaboration systems, and AI applications are especially useful for knowledge management because they focus on supporting information and knowledge work and on defining and capturing the organization's knowledge base. A knowledge base may include (1) structured internal knowledge (explicit knowledge), such as product manuals or research reports; (2) external knowledge of competitors, products, and markets, including competitive intelligence; and (3) informal internal knowledge, often called **tacit knowledge**, which resides in the minds of individual employees but has not been documented in structured form (Davenport, DeLong, and Beers, 1998).

Information systems can promote organizational learning by identifying, capturing, codifying, and distributing both explicit and tacit knowledge. Once information has been collected and organized in a system, it can be leveraged and reused many times. Companies can use information systems to codify their best practices and make knowledge of these practices more widely available to employees. **Best practices** are the most successful solutions or problem solving methods that have been developed by a specific organization or industry. In addition to improving existing work practices, knowledge can be preserved as organizational memory to train future employees or to help them with decision making. **Organizational memory** is the stored learning from an organization's history that can be used for decision making and other purposes. Information systems can also provide *knowledge networks* for linking people so that individuals with special areas of expertise can be easily identified and tacit knowledge can be shared.

Figure 14.1 illustrates the information systems and information technology (IT) infrastructure for supporting knowledge management. Knowledge work systems support the activities of highly skilled knowledge workers and professionals as they create new knowledge and try to integrate it into the firm. Group collaboration and support systems support the creation, identification, and sharing of knowledge among people working in groups. Office systems help

tacit knowledge

Expertise and experience of organizational members that has not been formally documented.

best practices

The most successful solutions or problem solving methods that have been developed by a specific organization or industry.

organizational memory

The stored learning from an organization's history that can be used for decision making and other purposes.

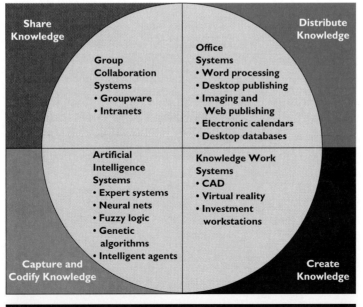

Figure 14.1 Knowledge management requires an information technology (IT) infrastructure that facilitates the collection and sharing of knowledge as well as software for distributing information and making it more meaningful. The information systems illustrated here give easily accessible support to information workers at many levels in the organization.

disseminate and coordinate the flow of information in the organization. AI systems capture new knowledge and provide organizations and managers with codified knowledge that can be reused by others in the organization. These systems require an IT infrastructure that makes heavy use of powerful processors, networks, databases, and Internet tools.

14.2 INFORMATION AND KNOWLEDGE WORK SYSTEMS

information work

Work that primarily consists of creating or processing information.

Information work is work that consists primarily of creating or processing information. It is carried out by information workers who usually are divided into two subcategories: **data workers**, who primarily process and disseminate information; and **knowledge workers**, who primarily create knowledge and information.

data workers

Personnel, such as secretaries or bookkeepers, who process and disseminate the organization's information and paperwork.

Examples of data workers include secretaries, sales personnel, bookkeepers, and draftspeople. Researchers, designers, architects, writers, and judges are examples of knowledge workers. Data workers usually can be distinguished from knowledge workers because knowledge workers usually have higher levels of education and memberships in professional organizations. In addition, knowledge workers exercise independent judgment as a routine aspect of their work. Data and knowledge workers have different information requirements and different systems to support them.

knowledge workers

Professionals, such as engineers, scientists, or architects, who design products or services or create knowledge for the organization.

DISTRIBUTING KNOWLEDGE: OFFICE AND DOCUMENT MANAGEMENT SYSTEMS

Most data work and a great deal of knowledge work takes place in offices, including most of the work done by managers. The office plays a major role in coordinating the flow of information throughout the organization. An office has three basic functions (see Figure 14.2):

■ Managing and coordinating the work of data and knowledge workers

■ Connecting the work of local information workers with all levels and functions of the organization

■ Connecting the organization to the external world, including customers, suppliers, government regulators, and external auditors

Office workers span a very broad range: professionals, managers, sales, and clerical workers working alone or in groups. Their major activities include the following:

■ Managing documents, including document creation, storage, retrieval, and dissemination

■ Scheduling for individuals and groups

■ Communicating, including initiating, receiving, and managing voice, digital, and document-based communications for individuals and groups

■ Managing data, such as data about employees, customers, and vendors

office systems

Computer systems, such as word processing, voice mail, and imaging, that are designed to increase the productivity of information workers in the office.

These activities can be supported by office systems (see Table 14.1). **Office systems** are any application of information technology whose purpose is to increase productivity of

Figure 14.2 Offices perform three major roles. (1) They coordinate the work of local professionals and information workers. (2) They coordinate work in the organization across levels and functions. (3) They connect the organization to the external environment.

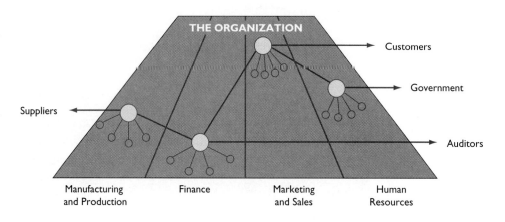

TABLE 14.1	TYPICAL OFFICE SYSTEMS

Office Activity	Technology
Managing documents	Word processing, desktop publishing, document imaging, Web publishing, workflow managers
Scheduling	Electronic calendars, groupware, intranets
Communicating	E-mail, voice mail, digital answering systems, groupware, intranets
Managing data	Desktop databases, spreadsheets, user-friendly interfaces to mainframe databases

information workers in the office. Fifteen years ago, office systems handled only the creation, processing, and management of documents. Today, professional knowledge and information work remains highly document centred. However, digital image processing—words and documents—is also at the core of systems as are high-speed digital communications services. Because office work involves many people jointly engaged in projects, contemporary office systems have powerful group assistance tools, such as networked digital calendars. An ideal office environment would be based on a seamless network of digital machines linking professional, clerical, and managerial work groups and running a variety of types of software.

Although word processing and desktop publishing address the creation and presentation of documents, they only exacerbate the existing paper avalanche problem. Workflow problems arising from paper handling are enormous. It has been estimated that up to 85 percent of corporate information is stored on paper. Locating and updating information in that format is a great source of organizational inefficiency.

One way to reduce problems stemming from paper workflow is to employ document imaging systems. *Document imaging systems* (which we defined in Chapter 2) are systems that convert paper documents and images into digital form so that they can be stored and accessed by a computer. These systems store, retrieve, and manipulate a digitized image of a document, allowing the document itself to be discarded. Once the document has been stored electronically, it can be immediately retrieved or shared with others. The system must contain a scanner that converts the document image into a digitized image, storing that image as a graphic. If the document is not in active use, it usually is stored on an optical disk system that may use a *jukebox* device for storing and retrieving many optical disks.

An imaging system also requires indexes that allow users to identify and retrieve a document when needed. Index data are entered so that a document can be retrieved in a variety of ways, depending upon the application. For example, the index may contain the document scan date, the customer name and number, the document type, and some subject information. Finally, the system must include retrieval equipment, primarily workstations capable of handling graphics, although printers usually are included. Figure 14.3 illustrates the components of a typical imaging system.

Traditional document management systems can be expensive, requiring proprietary client-server networks, special client software, and storage capabilities. Intranets provide a low-cost and universally available platform for basic document publishing, and many companies are using them for this purpose. Employees can publish information using Web page authoring tools and post it to an intranet Web server, where it can be shared and accessed throughout the company with standard Web browsers. These Web-like "documents" can be multimedia objects combining text, graphics, audio, and video along with hyperlinks. After a document has been posted to the server, it can be indexed for quicker access and linked to other documents (see Figure 14.4). For more sophisticated document management functions, such as controlling changes to documents, maintaining histories of activity and changes in the managed documents, and the ability to search documents on either content or index terms, commercial Web-based systems, such as those from IntraNet Solutions or Open Text, are available.

Figure 14.3 Components of an imaging system. A typical imaging system stores and processes digitized images of documents, using scanners, an optical disk system, an index server, workstations, and printers. A midrange or small mainframe computer may be required to control the activities of a large imaging system.

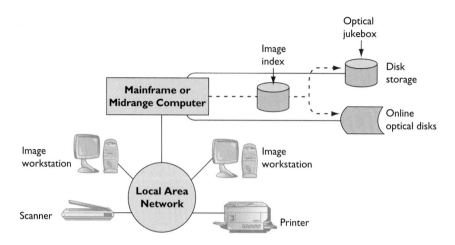

knowledge repository

Collection of documented internal and external knowledge in a single location for more efficient management and utilization by the organization.

In addition to streamlining workflow, Web-based and traditional document management systems provide tools for creating knowledge repositories to help organizations consolidate and leverage their knowledge. A **knowledge repository** is a collection of internal and external knowledge in a single location for more efficient management and utilization by the organization. Using these tools, knowledge from many different sources that can be documented in the form of memos, reports, presentations, and articles can be digitized and placed in a central location for easy storage and retrieval. Organizational knowledge repositories may also include tools for accessing information from corporate databases.

The Window on Management describes the benefits of Web-based systems for workflow management, document control, and project management in the architectural, engineering, and construction industries.

CREATING KNOWLEDGE: KNOWLEDGE WORK SYSTEMS

Knowledge work is that portion of information work that creates new knowledge and information. For example, knowledge workers create new products or find ways to improve existing ones. Knowledge work is segmented into many highly specialized fields, and each field has a different collection of **knowledge work systems (KWS)** to support workers in that field. Knowledge workers perform three key roles that are critical to the organization and to the managers who work within the organization:

knowledge work systems (KWS)

Information systems that aid knowledge workers in the creation and integration of new knowledge in the organization.

1. Keeping the organization up to date in knowledge as it develops in the external world—in technology, science, social thought, and the arts.
2. Serving as internal consultants in the areas of their knowledge, including the changes taking place and opportunities within their areas.
3. Acting as change agents, evaluating, initiating, and promoting change projects.

Knowledge and data workers have somewhat different information systems support needs. Most knowledge workers rely on such office systems as word processors, voice mail, and calendars, but they also require more specialized knowledge work systems. Knowledge work systems are specifically designed to promote the creation of knowledge and to ensure that new knowledge and technical expertise are properly integrated into the business.

Figure 14.4 Web publishing and document management. An author can post information on an intranet Web server, where it can be accessed through a variety of mechanisms.

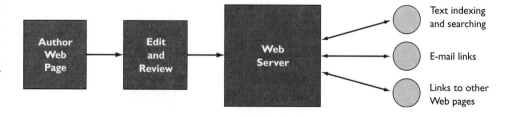

MANAGING CONSTRUCTION PROJECTS WITH THE INTERNET

Many people think that the most widely used tool in a construction project is a hammer, but it is probably a filing cabinet or fax machine. The $5.1-trillion American construction industry is highly paper intensive. A complex project, such as a large building, requires the coordination of many different groups and hundreds of architectural drawings and design documents, which can change daily. Costly delays because of misplaced documents could make or break a company in an industry with razor-thin profit margins of 1 to 2 percent.

Web technology is starting to address this problem. New Web-based construction project management systems enable project managers to exchange documents and work online wherever they have access to a Web browser. Autodesk Building Collaboration Services (formerly Buzzsaw.com), for example, offers customers a shared central space where project managers can exchange documents with engineers and architects, bid for subcontractor services, track scheduling and performance, and hold online meetings.

Toys 'R' Us used Autodesk's services to better manage and speed up construction while reducing costs. In one project, it remodelled two dilapidated theatres in New York's Times Square into the largest toy store in the world. The Times Square project, headed by Tracy LeBlanc, involved weekly meetings of 15 project consultants, partly to decide on design changes. Once finished, agreements on changes were sent to the architects to integrate them into the plans, which were returned to the consultants, who then made more detailed documents and passed them to the general construction contractor.

In the past, all plans were hand drawn and then sent by mail or overnight express to the next person involved, who would have to have new plans drawn. The same process would be repeated until the final detailed documents were in the hands of the general contractor. This took a great deal of time and labour. Now, changes can be uploaded to the Autodesk Building Collaboration Services Web site for instant communication and immediate revision. Depending on the size of the project and the distance between the various individuals, using the Internet can save days or weeks and reduce the number of errors made in manual redrawing. Toys 'R' Us claimed the service would save $150 000 a year in messaging, printing, and photo processing costs alone. Figure 14.5 illustrates how the business processes for construction projects changed as a result of this system.

Even more significant savings resulted from using the service to keep a complicated project, such as the Toys 'R' Us building, on time and within budget. For example, LeBlanc used the system to monitor progress at the Times Square site from two Web cameras installed at the construction site, controlling the rotation of the cameras from his computer keyboard. He and other members of the architectural, design, and construction team also used the Building Collaboration Services Web site to view digital photos of the building.

To Think About: What are the management benefits of using Web-based construction management software? How do these tools provide value? What are the possible drawbacks?

Sources: Donna Fuscaldo, "Building a Market," *Wall Street Journal*, April 15, 2002; Tony Kontzer, "Buzzsaw Gets the Job Done," *InternetWorld*, December 16, 2002; and Mark Roberti, "Cutting Construction Chaos," *The Industry Standard*, June 11, 2001.

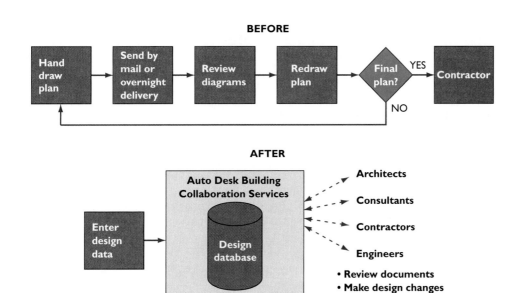

Figure 14.5 Changes in the construction project management process. Toys 'R' Us replaced its multistep paper-based process for generating and revising construction design plans with a much simpler process using Web-based project management tools for the construction industry.

Figure 14.6 Requirements of knowledge work systems. Knowledge work systems require strong links to external knowledge bases in addition to specialized hardware and software.

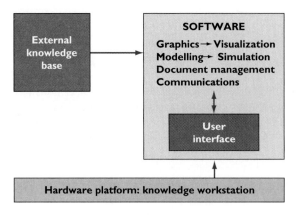

Requirements of Knowledge Work Systems

Knowledge work systems have characteristics that reflect the special needs of knowledge workers. First, knowledge work systems must give knowledge workers the specialized tools they need, such as powerful graphics, analytical tools, and communications and document management tools. These systems require great computing power in order to rapidly handle the sophisticated graphics or complex calculations necessary to knowledge workers, such as scientific researchers, product designers, and financial analysts. Because knowledge workers are so focused on knowledge in the external world, these systems also must give the worker quick and easy access to external databases.

A user-friendly interface is very important to a knowledge worker's system. User-friendly interfaces save time by allowing the user to perform needed tasks and get the required information without having to spend a lot of time learning how to use the computer. Saving time is more important for knowledge workers than for most other employees because knowledge workers are highly paid—wasting a knowledge worker's time is simply too expensive—and knowledge workers can easily fall prey to information overload (Farhoomand and Drury, 2002). Figure 14.6 summarizes the requirements for knowledge work systems.

Knowledge workstations often are designed and optimized for the specific tasks to be performed, so a design engineer will require a workstation different from that of a financial analyst. Design engineers need graphics with enough power to handle three-dimensional computer-aided design (CAD) systems. However, financial analysts are more interested in having access to myriad external databases and in optical disk technology for efficiently storing and accessing massive amounts of financial data.

Examples of Knowledge Work Systems

computer-aided design (CAD)

Information system that automates the creation and revision of designs using sophisticated graphics software.

Major knowledge work applications include CAD systems, virtual reality systems for simulation and modelling, and financial workstations. **Computer-aided design (CAD)** automates the creation and revision of designs, using computers and sophisticated graphics software. Using a more traditional physical design methodology, each design modification requires a mould to be made and a prototype to be physically tested. That process must be repeated many times, which is very expensive and time consuming. Using a CAD workstation, the designer only needs to make a physical prototype toward the end of the design process because the design can be easily tested and changed on the computer. The ability of CAD software to provide design specifications for the tooling and manufacturing processes also saves a great deal of time and money while producing a manufacturing process with far fewer problems. The architect Frank Gehry used CATIA computer-aided design software to create the flowing curves on the innovative Guggenheim Museum in Bilbao, Spain. Drafting this design alone with traditional paper and pencil tools could have taken decades. Hawkes Ocean Technology used Autodesk's Inventor three-dimensional design and engineering program to create and manipulate flowing shapes when designing the revolutionary Deep Flight Aviator submarine for the U.S. Navy. The software allowed Hawkes to create and manipulate flowing shapes, test their stress points, and refine them without ever having to touch a lathe or mould. The system also enabled Hawkes to cut design costs by one-third, reduce engineering staff from 10 to three, and bypass the prototyping stage when developing new products (Salkever, 2002).

virtual reality systems

Interactive graphics software and hardware that create computer-generated simulations that provide sensations that emulate real-world activities.

Virtual reality systems have visualization, rendering, and simulation capabilities that go far beyond those of conventional CAD systems. They use interactive graphics software to create computer-generated simulations that are so close to reality that users almost believe they are participating in a real-world situation. In many virtual reality systems, the user dons special clothing, headgear, and equipment, depending on the application. The clothing contains sensors that record the user's movements and immediately transmit that information back to the computer. For instance, to walk through a virtual reality simulation of a house, you would need garb that monitors the movement of your feet, hands, and head. You also would need goggles containing video screens and sometimes audio attachments and "feeling gloves" so that you could be immersed in the computer feedback.

Computer-aided design (CAD) systems improve the quality and precision of product design by performing much of the design and testing work on the computer.

Virtual reality is just starting to provide benefits in educational, scientific, and business work. For example, Royal LePage real estate firm with offices throughout Canada uses virtual reality to host online tours of properties they list. A visitor to the Royal LePage Web site can take an online tour of various rooms in houses they may wish to consider purchasing—without visiting the property.

Virtual reality applications are being developed for the Web using a standard called **Virtual Reality Modeling Language (VRML)**. VRML is a set of specifications for interactive, three-dimensional modelling on the World Wide Web that can organize multiple media types, including animation, images, and audio to put users in a simulated real-world environment. VRML is platform independent, operates over a desktop computer, and requires little bandwidth. Users can download a three-dimensional virtual world designed using VRML from a server over the Internet using their Web browser.

DuPont, the Wilmington, Delaware, chemical company, created a VRML application called HyperPlant, which allows users to access three-dimensional data over the Internet with a Web browser. Engineers can go through three-dimensional models as if they were physically walking through a plant, viewing objects at eye level. This level of detail reduces the number of mistakes they make during construction of oil rigs, oil plants, and other structures. (See Figure 14.7.)

The financial industry is using specialized **investment workstations** to leverage the knowledge and time of its brokers, traders, and portfolio managers. Some firms, such as Assante, have installed investment workstations that integrate a wide range of data from both

Virtual Reality Modeling Language (VRML)

A set of specifications for interactive three-dimensional modelling on the World Wide Web.

investment workstation

Powerful desktop computer for financial specialists, which is optimized to access and manipulate massive amounts of financial data.

Figure 14.7 Women can create a VRML "virtual model" that approximates their physical proportions to help them visualize how they will look in clothing sold in the Lands' End Web site. The digitized image can be rotated to show how the outfits will look from all angles and users can click to change the clothes' colours.

TABLE 14.2	EXAMPLES OF KNOWLEDGE WORK SYSTEMS

Knowledge Work System	Function in Organization
CAD/CAM (Computer-aided design/ computer-aided manufacturing)	Provides engineers, designers, and factory managers with precise control over industrial design and manufacturing
Virtual reality systems	Provide drug designers, architects, engineers, and medical workers with precise, photo-realistic simulations of objects
Investment workstations	High-end PCs used in financial sector to analyze trading situations instantaneously and to facilitate portfolio management

internal and external sources, including contact management data, real-time and historical market data, and research reports. Previously, financial professionals had to spend considerable time accessing data from separate systems and piecing together the information they needed. By providing one-stop information faster and with fewer errors, the workstations streamline the entire investment process from stock selection to updating client records. Table 14.2 summarizes the major types of knowledge work systems.

SHARING KNOWLEDGE: GROUP COLLABORATION SYSTEMS AND ENTERPRISE KNOWLEDGE ENVIRONMENTS

Although many knowledge and information work applications have been designed for individuals working alone, organizations have an increasing need to support people working in groups. These groups include not only formal work groups but, increasingly, informal communities of practice that are important sources of organizational expertise. A **community of practice** is an informal group of people in an organization with a common professional interest, such as a group in an international bank with a special interest in lending activities in southeast Asia or a Linux user's group in a corporation. Its members may live or work in many different locations. In contrast to project teams, communities of practice often do not have responsibility for the production of a specific deliverable within a given time span and set their own agendas, such as education sessions, conferences, or assisting other members with problems they encounter in their work.

Groupware and Web Collaboration Tools

Chapters 6, 8, and 9 introduced the key technologies for group coordination and collaboration: e-mail, teleconferencing, dataconferencing, videoconferencing, and groupware. *Groupware* (which we introduced in Chapter 6) has been a primary tool for creating collaborative work environments. Groupware is built around three key principles: communication, collaboration, and coordination. It allows groups to work together on documents, schedule meetings, route electronic forms, access shared folders, participate in electronic discussions, develop shared databases, and send e-mail. Information-intensive companies, such as consulting firms, law firms, and financial management companies, have found groupware to be an especially powerful tool for leveraging their knowledge assets.

Internet tools for e-mail, newsgroup discussions, group scheduling, Web publishing, and point-to-point conferencing offer low-cost alternatives to proprietary groupware for collaborative work. These tools are best suited for simple tasks in small and medium businesses. Commercial software tools called teamware make intranets more useful for working in teams. **Teamware** consists of intranet-based applications for building a work team, sharing ideas and documents, brainstorming, scheduling, tracking the status of tasks and projects, and archiving decisions made or rejected by project team members for future use. Teamware is similar to groupware, although its application development capabilities are not as powerful as those provided by sophisticated groupware products. However, it lets companies easily

community of practice

Informal group of people who may live or work in many different locations but who share a common professional interest; an important source of expertise for organizations.

teamware

Group collaboration software that is customized for teamwork.

implement collaboration applications that can be accessed using a Web browser. eRoom Technology's eRoom and Lotus Quickplace are examples of commercial teamware products.

Proprietary groupware remains a key tool for applications requiring extensive coordination, frequent updating and document tracking, and a high-level of security. Lotus Notes, OpenText Livelink, and other conventional groupware products have been enhanced so they can be integrated with the Internet or private intranets and used for collaborative commerce and supply chain management. Groove Networks provides a peer-to-peer collaboration platform that enables workers on the fly to collaborate and share data without going through a central Web server. The basic Groove interface lets users create shared workspaces or join existing workspaces that can be customized with tools for instant messaging, chat, streaming voice and video communication, a notepad, a calendar, shared file repositories, and a shared browser that allows multiple users to jointly surf the Web. Members of groups defined by Groove can be limited to specific applications, files, and discussions.

A growing number of companies are using Web conferencing tools to stage meetings, conferences, and presentations online. Web conferencing and collaboration software provides a "virtual" conference table, where participants can view and modify documents and slides and share their thoughts and comments using chat, telephone, or video. The current generation of these tools from Lotus, Microsoft, PlaceWare, and WebEx work through a standard Web browser. Participants from many different locations can use these Web conferencing tools, which include a virtual whiteboard, to annotate, edit, or view documents, slides, video, and Web pages as part of a presentation. Salespeople might use these tools for offering online product demonstrations, while senior executives might use them to analyze a contract proposal or to stage a presentation for hundreds of investors.

INTRANETS AND ENTERPRISE KNOWLEDGE ENVIRONMENTS

Chapters 4 and 9 described how some organizations are using intranets and Internet technologies for group collaboration and coordination. Some of these intranets provide the foundation for enterprise knowledge environments in which information from a variety of sources and media, including text, sound, video, and digital slides, can be shared, displayed, and accessed across an enterprise through a simple common interface. If properly designed, these knowledge environments can serve as organizational **knowledge maps**. Knowledge maps are tools for identifying and locating the organization's knowledge resources, and they can point to people as sources of knowledge as well as pointing to documents and databases. Examples of enterprise knowledge environments can be found in Table 14.3. These comprehensive intranets can transform decades-old processes, allowing people to inventory and disseminate information, share best practices, communicate, conduct research, and collaborate in ways that were never before possible.

knowledge map

Tool for identifying and locating the organization's knowledge resources.

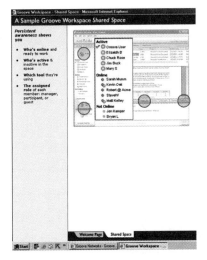
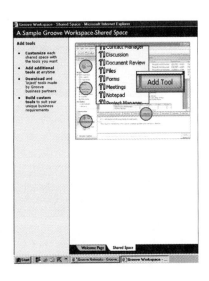

Figure 14.8 Groove Networks provides peer-to-peer desktop collaboration software enabling users to work online or offline in virtual workspaces they create and control. Illustrated here is a sample Groove shared space, which can show who is active or inactive in a space, which tool they are using, and the assigned role of each group member. Each shared space can be customized with the tools selected by users.

| TABLE 14.3 | EXAMPLES OF ENTERPRISE KNOWLEDGE ENVIRONMENTS |

Organization	Knowledge Management Capabilities
Roche Laboratories	Global Healthcare Intelligence Platform integrates documents from multiple sources to provide its professional services group with up-to-date information and expertise relating to new Hoffman-La Roche pharmaceutical products. The system gathers relevant information from global news sources, specialty publishers, healthcare Web sites, government sources, and the firm's proprietary internal information systems, indexing, organizing, linking, and updating the information as it moves through the system. Users can search multiple sources and drill down through layers of detail to see relationships among pieces of data.
Shell Oil Company	Knowledge Management System (KMS) provides a communications and collaboration environment where employees can learn about and share information about best practices. Includes information from internal sources and from external sources, such as universities, consultants, other companies, and research literature. A Lotus Domino groupware application allows employees to carry on dialogues through the company intranet. The author of a best practice in the repository might use this tool to talk with colleagues about his or her experiences.
Booz Allen Hamilton	Knowledge Online intranet provides an online repository of consultants' knowledge and experience, including a searchable database organized around the firm's best specialties and best practices; other intellectual capital, such as research reports, presentations, graphs, images, and interactive training material; and links to résumés and job histories.

enterprise information portal

Application that enables companies to provide users with a single gateway to internal and external sources of information.

Enterprise knowledge environments are so rich and vast that many organizations have built specialized corporate portals to help individuals navigate through various knowledge resources. These **enterprise information portals**, also known as *enterprise knowledge portals,* direct individuals to digital knowledge objects and information system applications, helping them make sense of the volume of information that is available and also showing how organizational knowledge resources are interconnected. Figure 14.9 illustrates what an enterprise information portal might look like. It might include access to external sources of information, such as news feeds and research, as well as internal knowledge resources and capabilities for e-mail, chat (including instant messaging), discussion groups, and videoconferencing. Commercial software tools are available to build and personalize these portals, providing users with a single point of access to multiple types of information from wireless as well as wired devices. Many of these tools include capabilities for categorizing, indexing, and searching content and for linking to business applications, such as enterprise and customer relationship management systems.

A corporate portal can enhance employee productivity by presenting a seamless single point of access to all of the information resources that employees need to do their jobs.

Figure 14.9 An enterprise information portal. The portal provides a single point of access to the firm's knowledge resources and helps the firm coordinate information and people to make decisions and take action.

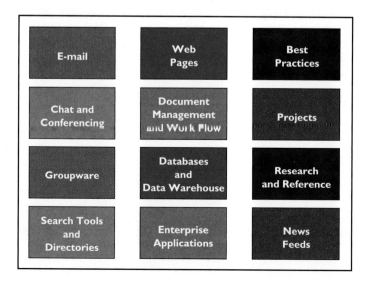

Portals or portions of portals extended to customers, suppliers, and business partners can help these groups understand the company's business or unique value proposition. The Window on Organizations describes some of the benefits of a knowledge portal for a law firm. The Manager's Toolkit describes the business issues that must be addressed when developing a portal.

Another application for knowledge intranets is to provide a platform for *e-learning*, which we introduced in Chapter 8. For example, Bell Canada Enterprises (BCE) faced major training challenges for their 65 000 employees. BCE launched Click and Learn, a training program that covers a wide variety of courses, such as desktop applications, information technology certifications, management topics, safety, legal topics, and customer service.

Window on Organizations
MIS In Action

A KNOWLEDGE PORTAL BECOMES DEACONS' COMPETITIVE WEAPON

Deacons is a 150-year law firm with offices in Hong Kong, the People's Republic of China, Thailand, Vietnam, Indonesia, Singapore, Taiwan, and Australia. It provides the services of lawyers fluent in the host country's language who also have local contacts and expertise. Deacons is one of Hong Kong's largest legal practices. Its Hong Kong office has 180 lawyers and has recently encountered mounting competition from London law firms as well as other firms in Hong Kong. Chief Information Officer (CIO) Philip Scorgie concluded that one way to be more competitive would be to install an information system that would help the company preserve and share its knowledge.

Deacons modelled its system after such portals as Yahoo!, where millions of documents are indexed and powerful search engines help users locate what they want. Deacons began its knowledge portal project in 1999 when search engines had been vastly improved and could now rapidly search through millions of documents. However, because quality indexing, Chinese text searching, and other requisite portal technology were not yet easily available, the firm decided to develop these capabilities in-house. The company turned to Microsoft and Oracle to develop the software and purchased Sun and Compaq hardware.

Eliciting the cooperation of Deacons' lawyers was the tougher challenge. Deacons wanted to load and search over two million documents just to start with, with many more to be added later. The firm hired a special knowledge management team of six nonpractising lawyers to index each existing document in its computer systems and organize the documents into folders where they could be much more easily located and accessed. This allowed the system to demonstrate its usefulness without requiring the cooperation of practising lawyers. Staff usage of the system was logged to determine what information was most frequently requested, and the search engines were tuned so they would more easily locate the information that people most wanted.

Deacons credited contributors of materials. Many younger lawyers were willing to share their work as a way to achieve some recognition in the firm. However, many experienced lawyers opposed sharing their work, such as contracts for the purchase or financing of ships, because they viewed it as proprietary. The firm considered these documents valuable corporate assets because they could serve as templates that could be modified for others to use. These lawyers had to be convinced to allow their work to be seen by others. When other features were added, many of the less eager lawyers were intrigued, and that also helped. By 2002, contributions from lawyers were increasing at a rate of 25 percent per year.

Deacons' knowledge portal was linked to Deacons' other systems so that, for example, one could obtain human resources information about other internal staff members, organization charts, and floor plans. The portal was also connected to other information on the corporate computers, such as company financial data and information on case management. It enabled newly hired lawyers to be trained more quickly, partly because the information needed to do their jobs was immediately available. Almost no training is required to use the system's standardized Web interface. The system is personalized for each user's position in the organization, and when individuals change jobs, the kind of information they can access changes automatically.

The company made the system into a free-of-charge extranet for clients to access documents, issue new instructions, and check the status of cases online. Deacons initially made its extranet available only to a few of its largest clients but has been gradually giving access to others. Soon, the clients will be given customized portals that enable each to access the work being done for them. By adding even more value to company knowledge for its employees and clients, Deacons' portal has enhanced the firm's image in the marketplace.

To Think About: How did Deacons obtain value from using a knowledge portal? How did this system change the way the company conducted business? What management, organization, and technology issues had to be addressed to use this portal successfully?

Sources: Ann Toh, "They've Got Knowledge," *CIO-ASIA*, January 2002; and Deacons' Web site at **www.deaconslaw.com**.

MIS IN ACTION: Manager's Toolkit

ESTABLISHING THE BUSINESS REQUIREMENTS OF AN ENTERPRISE INFORMATION PORTAL

Portals can be viewed as electronic doorways into a company. They help users access essential information and collaborate with each other. Portals can enhance business performance if they are carefully thought out. When designing a portal, here are some key questions business managers should ask:

1. *Content:* What information should the portal point to? How is this information used in the organization's business processes? Which sources of this information are internal? Which are external? Should the external sources be provided by a content aggregation service or gathered by the organization itself? Does any of this content have to be edited or repackaged to be used effectively?
2. *Users:* Who are the users of the portal? All employees or specific groups of employees? Should the portal or parts of the portal be accessible to people outside the organization?
3. *Personalization:* Does the portal page need to be personalized for specific users or groups in the organization? How much customization is required?

4. *Collaboration support:* Should the portal provide capabilities for communication and collaboration, such as e-mail, newsgroups, chat, or groupware?
5. *Ease of use:* How can the portal be designed so that it is easy to use and to navigate from one source of information to another? Do users need special search engines or knowledge maps to help them find information?
6. *Updating and editing:* How often does the information feeding the portal need to be updated? Which individuals in the organization will be responsible for updating this information or editing content?
7. *Management and administration:* Who is responsible for administering the portal and for approving and reviewing content? Who is responsible for editing the content if this is required?
8. *Benefits and costs:* What are the business benefits to be provided by the portal? Can they be quantified? Can these benefits justify the cost of building and maintaining the portal? (See the discussion of information system costs and benefits in Chapter 12.)

Courses are offered at no charge to employees with very low chargeback rates to their departments. In the six months following the launch of Click and Learn, e-learning registrations grew to more than 54 000. BCE estimates it has saved about $12 million during that time. APL Inc., the international subsidiary of the giant transportation firm NOL Group of Singapore, implemented a Web-based platform to train over 1500 sales representatives in more than 126 countries in Siebel System's customer relationship management software along with other key sales and financial software.

Group collaboration and knowledge-sharing technologies alone cannot promote information sharing if team members do not believe it is in their interests to share, especially in organizations that encourage competition among employees. This technology can best enhance the work of a group if the applications are properly designed to fit the organization's needs and work practices and if management encourages a collaborative atmosphere. Successful knowledge sharing requires an appropriate knowledge sharing environment (Pan, Hsieh, and Chen, 2001).

14.3 Artificial Intelligence

Organizations are using artificial intelligence technology to capture individual and collective knowledge and to codify and extend their knowledge base.

What Is Artificial Intelligence?

artificial intelligence (AI)

The effort to develop computer-based systems that can behave like humans, with the ability to learn languages, accomplish physical tasks, use a perceptual apparatus, and emulate human expertise and decision making.

Artificial intelligence (AI) is the effort to develop computer-based systems (both hardware and software) that behave like humans. These systems would be able to learn natural languages, accomplish coordinated physical tasks (robotics), use a perceptual apparatus that informs their physical behaviour and language (visual and oral perception systems), and emulate human expertise and decision making (expert systems). These systems would also exhibit logic, reasoning, intuition, and the just-plain-common-sense qualities that we associate with human beings. Figure 14.10 illustrates the elements of the artificial intelligence family. Another important element is intelligent machines, the physical hardware that performs these tasks.

Successful AI systems are based on human expertise, knowledge, and selected reasoning patterns, but they do not exhibit the intelligence of human beings. Existing AI systems do not come up with new and novel solutions to problems. Existing systems extend the powers

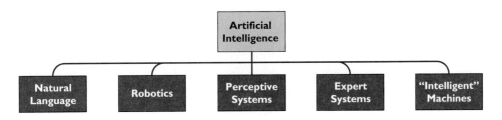

Figure 14.10 The artificial intelligence family. The field of AI currently includes many initiatives: natural language, robotics, perception systems, expert systems, and intelligent machines.

of experts but in no way substitute for them or capture much of their intelligence. Briefly, existing systems lack the common sense and generality of naturally intelligent human beings.

Human intelligence is vastly complex and much broader than computer intelligence. A key factor that distinguishes human beings from other animals is their ability to develop associations and to use metaphors and analogies, such as *like* and *as*. Using metaphor and analogy, humans create new rules, apply old rules to new situations, and, at times, act intuitively and/or instinctively without rules. Much of what we call common sense or generality in humans resides in the ability to create metaphor and analogy.

Human intelligence also includes a unique ability to impose a conceptual apparatus on the surrounding world. Such metaconcepts as cause-and-effect and time, and concepts of a lower order, such as breakfast, dinner, and lunch, are all imposed by human beings on the world around them. Thinking in terms of these concepts and acting on them are central characteristics of intelligent human behaviour.

WHY BUSINESS IS INTERESTED IN ARTIFICIAL INTELLIGENCE

Although artificial intelligence applications are much more limited than human intelligence, they are of great interest to business for the following reasons:

- To store information in an active form as organizational memory, creating an organizational knowledge base that many employees can examine and preserving expertise that might be lost when an acknowledged expert leaves the firm.

- To create a mechanism that is not subject to human feelings, such as fatigue and worry. This may be especially useful when jobs may be environmentally, physically, or mentally dangerous to humans. These systems also may be useful advisers in times of crisis.

- To eliminate routine and unsatisfying jobs held by people.

- To enhance the organization's knowledge base by generating solutions to specific problems that are too massive and complex to be analyzed by human beings in a short period of time.

CAPTURING KNOWLEDGE: EXPERT SYSTEMS

In limited areas of expertise, such as diagnosing a car's ignition system or classifying biological specimens, the rules of thumb used by real-world experts can be understood, codified, and placed in a machine. Information systems that solve problems by capturing knowledge for a very specific and limited domain of human expertise are called **expert systems.** Expert systems capture the knowledge of skilled employees in the form of a set of rules. The set of rules in the expert system adds to the memory or stored learning of the firm. An expert system can assist decision making by asking relevant questions and explaining the reasons for adopting certain actions.

expert system

Knowledge-intensive computer program that captures the expertise of a human in limited domains of knowledge.

Expert systems lack the breadth of knowledge and the understanding of fundamental principles of a human expert. They are quite narrow, shallow, and brittle. They typically perform very limited tasks that can be performed by professionals in a few minutes or hours. Problems that cannot be solved by human experts in the same short period of time are far too difficult for an expert system. However, by capturing human expertise in limited areas, expert systems can provide benefits, helping organizations make high-quality decisions with fewer people.

How Expert Systems Work

Human knowledge must be modelled or represented in a way that a computer can process. The model of human knowledge used by expert systems is called the **knowledge base**. A standard structured programming construct (see Chapter 11) is the selection or IF–THEN construct, in which a condition is evaluated. If the condition is true, an action is taken. For instance,

IF INCOME > $45 000 (condition)
THEN PRINT NAME AND ADDRESS (action)

A series of these rules can be a knowledge base. Any reader who has written computer programs knows that virtually all traditional computer programs contain IF–THEN statements. The difference between a traditional program and a **rule-based expert system** program is one of degree and magnitude. AI programs can easily have 200 to 10 000 rules, far more than traditional programs, which may have 50 to 100 IF–THEN statements. Moreover, in an AI program, the rules tend to be interconnected and nested to a far greater degree than in traditional programs, as shown in Figure 14.11. Hence the complexity of the rules in a rule-based expert system is considerable.

Could you represent the knowledge in the Encyclopedia Britannica this way? Probably not, because the **rule base** would be too large, and not all the knowledge in the encyclopedia can be represented in the form of IF–THEN rules. In general, expert systems can be efficiently used only in those situations in which the domain of knowledge is highly restricted (such as in granting credit) and involves no more than a few thousand rules.

The **AI shell** is the programming environment of an expert system. In the early years of expert systems, computer scientists used specialized AI programming languages, such as LISP or Prolog, that could process lists of rules efficiently. Today, a growing number of expert systems use AI shells that are user-friendly development environments. AI shells can quickly generate user-interface screens, capture the knowledge base, and manage the strategies for searching the rule base.

The strategy used to search through the rule base is called the **inference engine**. Two strategies are commonly used: forward chaining and backward chaining (see Figure 14.12).

knowledge base
Model of human knowledge that is used by expert systems.

rule-based expert system
An AI program that has a large number of interconnected and nested IF–THEN statements or rules that are the basis for the knowledge in the system.

rule base
The collection of knowledge in an AI system that is represented in the form of IF–THEN rules.

AI shell
The programming environment of an expert system.

inference engine
The strategy used to search through the rule base in an expert system; can be forward or backward chaining.

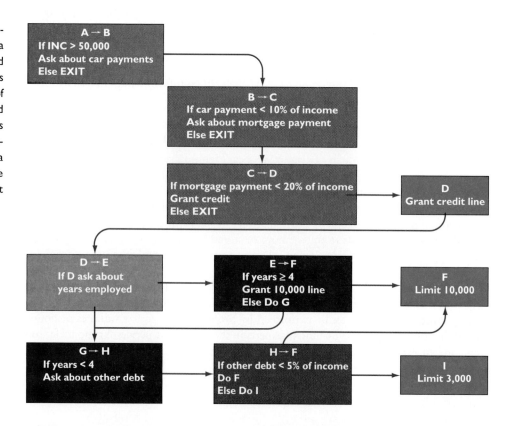

Figure 14.11 Rules in an AI program. An expert system contains a number of rules to be followed when used. The rules themselves are interconnected; the number of outcomes is known in advance and is limited; there are multiple paths to the same outcome; and the system can consider multiple rules at a single time. The rules illustrated are for simple credit-granting expert systems.

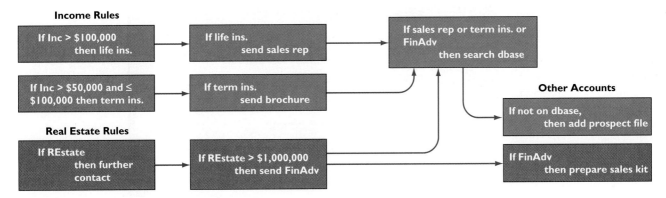

Figure 14.12 Inference engines in expert systems. An inference engine works by searching through the rules and "firing" those rules that are triggered by facts gathered and entered by the user.

In **forward chaining**, the inference engine begins with the information entered by the user and searches the rule base to arrive at a conclusion. The strategy is to fire, or carry out, the action of the rule when a condition is true. In Figure 14.12, beginning on the left, if the user enters a client with income greater than $100 000, the engine will fire all rules in sequence from left to right. If the user then enters information indicating that the same client owns real estate, another pass of the rule base will occur, and more rules will fire. Processing continues until no more rules can be fired.

In **backward chaining**, the strategy for searching the rule base starts with a hypothesis and proceeds by asking the user questions about selected facts until the hypothesis is either confirmed or disproved. In our example, in Figure 14.12, ask the question, "Should we add this person to the prospect database?" Begin on the right of the diagram and work toward the left. You can see that the person should be added to the database if a sales representative is sent, term insurance is granted, or a financial advisor visits the client.

An AI development team is composed of one or more experts, who have a thorough command of the knowledge base, and one or more knowledge engineers, who can translate the knowledge (as described by the expert) into a set of rules. A **knowledge engineer** is similar to a traditional systems analyst but has special expertise in eliciting information and expertise from other professionals.

The team members must select a problem appropriate for an expert system. The project will balance potential savings from the proposed system against the cost. The team members will develop a prototype system to test assumptions about how to encode the knowledge of experts. Next, they will develop a full-scale system, focusing mainly on the addition of a very large number of rules. The complexity of the entire system grows with the number of rules, so the comprehensibility of the system may be threatened. Generally, the system will be pruned to achieve simplicity and power. The system is tested by a range of experts within the organization against the performance criteria established earlier. Once tested, the system will be integrated into the data flow and work patterns of the organization.

Examples of Successful Expert Systems

The following are examples of expert systems that provide organizations with an array of benefits, including reduced errors, reduced costs, reduced training time, improved decisions, and improved quality and service.

The Learning Edge, a Toronto-based company, developed the IBM AS/400 Development Software Advisor as a marketing aid to help IBM's prospective customers better understand their application development needs and options. First, the expert system gathers environmental and business process information; then, it analyzes the data and recommends a programming language.

Countrywide Funding Corp. in Pasadena, California, is a loan-underwriting firm with about 400 underwriters in 150 offices around the country. The company developed a PC-based expert system in 1992 to make preliminary creditworthiness decisions on loan requests. The company had experienced rapid, continuing growth and wanted the system to help

forward chaining

A strategy for searching the rule base in an expert system that begins with the information entered by the user and searches the rule base to arrive at a conclusion.

backward chaining

A strategy for searching the rule base in an expert system that acts like a problem solver by beginning with a hypothesis and seeking out more information until the hypothesis is either proved or disproved.

knowledge engineer

A specialist who elicits information and expertise from other professionals and translates them into a set of rules for an expert system.

Figure 14.13 Countrywide Funding Corporation developed an expert system called CLUES to evaluate the creditworthiness of loan applicants. Countrywide is using the rules in this system to answer inquiries from visitors to its Web site who want to know if they qualify for a loan.

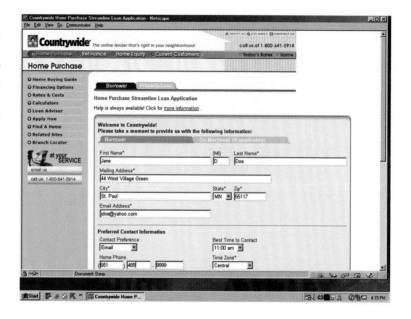

ensure consistent, high-quality loan decisions. CLUES (Countrywide's Loan Underwriting Expert System) has about 400 rules. Countrywide tested the system by sending every loan application handled by a human underwriter to CLUES as well. The system was refined until it agreed with the underwriters in 95 percent of the cases. (See Figure 14.13.)

Countrywide will not rely on CLUES to reject loans because the expert system cannot be programmed to handle exceptional situations, such as those involving a self-employed person or complex financial schemes. An underwriter will review all rejected loans and will make the final decision. CLUES has other benefits. Traditionally, an underwriter could handle six or seven applications a day. Using CLUES, the same underwriter can evaluate at least 16 per day. Countrywide now is using the rules in its expert system to answer e-mail inquiries from visitors to its Web site who want to know if they qualify for a loan.

Galeria Kaufhof, a German superstore chain, uses a rule-based system to help it manage over 110 000 deliveries of goods that it receives each day, ranging from clothing to complex electronics and fine china. Inspecting each delivery is time consuming and expensive, but the company wants to make sure that it is receiving goods that are not damaged or defective. Kaufhof implemented a rule-based system that identifies high-risk deliveries and passes along lower-risk ones automatically. The system scans delivery labels and identifies each delivery in terms of its size, type of product, whether the product is a new product, and the supplier's past history of deliveries to Kaufhof. Deliveries of large numbers of complex products that are new or that have suppliers with unfavourable delivery histories are carefully inspected, while other deliveries are passed on without inspection (Booth and Buluswar, 2002).

The investment banking firm Goldman Sachs uses a rule-based expert system to keep unwanted stocks out of individual portfolios. Almost all of its client portfolios have restrictions, specified by owners, on which stocks or even entire industry sectors to exclude. Goldman wanted to make sure that its global network of financial advisers respected these restrictions so that they did not make any purchases that clients did not want. Goldman's business managers, compliance officers, and private wealth managers all play roles in deciding which stocks to purchase for a portfolio. The company developed a rule-based system that maintains rules for keeping a particular stock from entering a client's portfolio. By creating a centralized portfolio filtering system, Goldman is better able to catch mistakes before erroneous trades go through (Guerra, 2001).

Although expert systems lack the robust and general intelligence of human beings, they can provide benefits to organizations if their limitations are well understood. Only certain classes of problems can be solved using expert systems. Virtually all successful expert systems deal with problems of classification in which there are relatively few alternative outcomes and in which these possible outcomes are all known in advance. Many expert systems require large, lengthy, and expensive development efforts. Hiring or training more experts may be less expensive than building an expert system. Typically, the environment in which an expert system operates is continually changing so that the expert system must also continually change. Some expert systems, especially large ones, are so complex that the maintenance costs equal or surpass the development costs in a few years.

The knowledge base of expert systems is fragile and brittle; they cannot learn or change over time. In fast-moving fields, such as medicine or computer science, keeping the knowledge base up to date is a critical problem. For example, Digital Equipment Corporation stopped using its XCON expert system for configuring VAX computers because its product line was constantly changing and it was too difficult to keep updating the system to capture these changes. Expert systems can only represent limited forms of knowledge. IF–THEN knowledge exists primarily in textbooks. There are no adequate representations for deep causal models or temporal trends. No expert system, for instance, can write a textbook on information systems or engage in other creative activities not explicitly foreseen by system designers. Many experts cannot express their knowledge using an IF–THEN format. Expert systems cannot yet replicate knowledge that is intuitive, based on analogy and on a sense of things.

Contrary to early promises, expert systems are most effective in automating lower-level clerical functions. They can provide electronic checklists for lower-level employees in service bureaucracies, such as banking, insurance, sales, and welfare agencies. The applicability of expert systems to managerial problems is very limited. Managerial problems generally involve drawing facts and interpretations from divergent sources, evaluating the facts, and comparing one interpretation of the facts with another; they are not limited to simple classification. Expert systems based on the prior knowledge of a few known alternatives are unsuitable to the problems managers face on a daily basis.

ORGANIZATIONAL INTELLIGENCE: CASE-BASED REASONING

Expert systems primarily capture the knowledge of individual experts, but organizations also have collective knowledge and expertise that they have built up over the years. This organizational knowledge can be captured and stored using case-based reasoning. In **case-based reasoning (CBR)**, descriptions of past experiences of human specialists, represented as cases, are stored in a database for retrieval later when the user encounters a new case with similar parameters. The system searches for stored cases with problem characteristics similar to the new one, finds the closest fit, and applies the solutions of the old case to the new case. Successful solutions are tagged to the new case and both are stored together with the other cases in the knowledge base. Unsuccessful solutions also are appended to the case database along with explanations as to why the solutions did not work (see Figure 14.14).

Expert systems work by applying a set of IF–THEN–ELSE rules against a knowledge base, both of which are extracted from human experts. CBR, in contrast, represents knowledge as a series of cases, and this knowledge base is continuously expanded and refined by users.

Compaq Computer of Houston, Texas, gave purchasers of its Pagemarq printer CBR software to help reduce customer service costs. The software knowledge base is a series of several hundred actual cases of Pagemarq printer problems—actual stories about smudged copies, printer memory problems, and jammed printers—all the typical problems people face with laser printers. Trained CBR staff entered case descriptions in textual format into the CBR system. They entered key words necessary to categorize the problem, such as smudge, smear, lines, streaks, and paper jam. They also entered a series of questions that might be needed to allow the software to further narrow the problem. Finally, solutions were attached to each case.

With the Compaq-supplied CBR system running on their computer, owners seldom need to call Compaq's service department. Instead, they run the software and describe the problem to the software. The system swiftly searches actual cases, discarding unrelated ones, selecting related ones. If necessary to further narrow the search results, the software will ask the user for more information. In the end, one or more cases relevant to the specific problem are displayed, along with their solutions. Now, customers can solve most of their own problems quickly without a telephone call, and Compaq has saved $15 million to $30 million annually in customer-support costs.

case-based reasoning (CBR)

Artificial intelligence technology that represents knowledge as a database of cases and solutions.

Figure 14.14 How case-based reasoning works. Case-based reasoning represents knowledge as a database of past cases and their solutions. The system uses a six-step process to generate solutions to new problems encountered by the user.

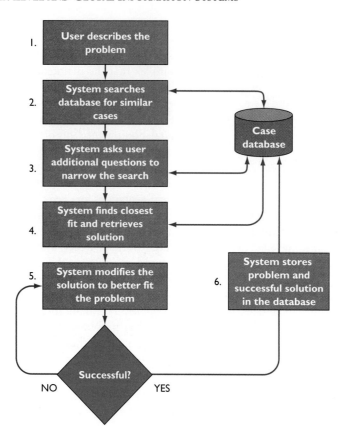

14.4 OTHER INTELLIGENT TECHNIQUES

Organizations are using other intelligent computing techniques to extend their knowledge base by providing solutions to problems that are too massive or complex to be handled by people with limited resources. Neural networks, fuzzy logic, genetic algorithms, and intelligent agents are developing into promising business applications.

NEURAL NETWORKS

Neural networks are designed to imitate the physical thought process of the biological brain. Figure 14.15 shows two neurons from a leech's brain. The soma, or nerve cell, at the centre acts like a switch, stimulating other neurons and being stimulated in turn. Emanating from the neuron is an axon, which is an electrically active link to the dendrites of other neurons. Axons and dendrites are the "wires" that electrically connect neurons to one another. The junction of the two is called a synapse. This simple biological model is the analogy for the

Figure 14.15 Biological neurons of a leech. Simple biological models, like the neurons of a leech, have influenced the development of artificial or computational neural networks in which the biological cells are replaced by transistors or entire processors.
Source: Defense Advance Research Projects Agency (DARPA), 1988. Unclassified.

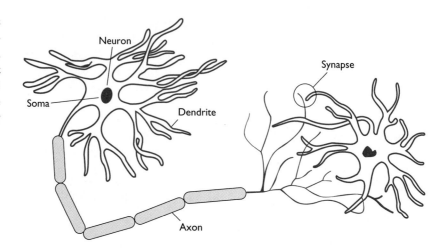

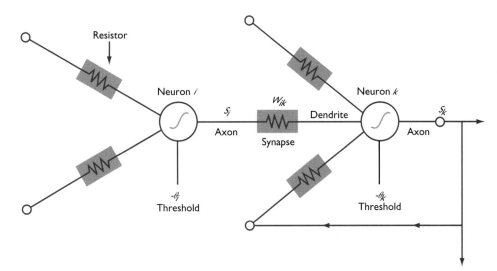

Figure 14.16 Artificial neural network with two neurons. In artificial neurons, the biological neurons become processing elements (switches), the axons and dendrites become wires, and the synapses become variable resistors that carry weighted inputs (currents) that represent data. *Source:* DARPA, 1988. Unclassified.

development of neural networks. A **neural network** consists of hardware or software that attempts to emulate the processing patterns of the biological brain.

Figure 14.16 shows an artificial neural network with two neurons. The resistors in the circuits are variable and can be used to teach the network. When the network makes a mistake (i.e., chooses the wrong pathway through the network and arrives at a false conclusion), resistance can be raised on some circuits, forcing other neurons to fire. If this learning process continues for thousands of cycles, the machine learns the correct response. The neurons are highly interconnected and operate in parallel, as does the human brain, allowing the neural network to process very large amounts of data efficiently.

A neural network has a large number of sensing and processing nodes that continuously interact with each other. Figure 14.17 represents one type of neural network comprising an input layer, an output layer, and a hidden processing layer. Humans "train" the network by feeding it a set of training data for which the inputs produce a known set of outputs or conclusions. This helps the computer learn the correct solution by example. As the computer is fed more data, each case is compared with the known outcome. If it differs, a correction is calculated and applied to the nodes in the hidden processing layer. These steps are repeated until a condition, such as corrections being less than a certain amount, is reached. The neural network in Figure 14.17 has "learned" how to identify a good credit risk. There are also self-organizing neural networks that can be "trained" by exposing them to large amounts of data and allowing them to discover the patterns and relationships in the data.

neural network

Hardware or software that attempts to emulate the processing patterns of the biological brain.

The Difference between Neural Networks and Expert Systems

What is different about neural networks? Expert systems seek to emulate or model a human expert's way of solving problems, but neural network designers claim that they do not model

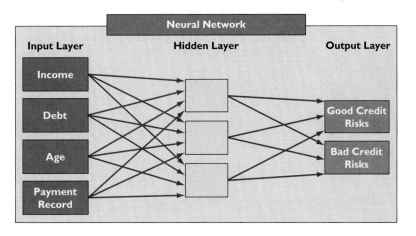

Figure 14.17 A neural network uses rules it "learns" from patterns in data to construct a hidden layer of logic. The hidden layer then processes inputs, classifying them on the basis of the experience of the model. *Source:* Herb Edelstein, "Technology How-To: Mining Data Warehouses," *InformationWeek,* January 8, 1996. Copyright © 1996 CMP Media, Inc., 600 Community Drive, Manhasset, NY 11430. Reprinted with permission.

human intelligence, do not program solutions, and do not aim to solve specific problems per se. Instead, neural network designers seek to put intelligence into the hardware in the form of a generalized capability to learn. In contrast, the expert system is highly specific to a given problem and cannot be easily retrained.

Neural network applications are emerging in medicine, science, and business to address problems in pattern classification, prediction and financial analysis, and control and optimization. Papnet is a neural net-based system that distinguishes between normal and abnormal cells when examining Pap smears for diagnosis of cervical cancer and has far greater accuracy than visual examinations by technicians. The computer cannot make a final decision, so a technician will review any selected abnormal cells. Using Papnet, a technician requires one-fifth the time to review a smear while attaining perhaps 10 times the accuracy of the manual method.

Neural networks are being used by the financial industry to discern patterns in vast pools of data that might help investment firms predict the performance of equities, corporate bond ratings, or corporate bankruptcies. Visa International Inc. is using a neural network to help detect credit card fraud by monitoring all Visa transactions for sudden changes in the buying patterns of cardholders. (See Figure 14.18.)

Unlike expert systems, which typically provide explanations for their solutions, neural networks cannot always explain why they arrived at a particular solution. Moreover, they cannot always guarantee a completely certain solution, arrive at the same solution again with the same input data, or always guarantee the best solution (Trippi and Turban, 1989–1990). They are very sensitive and may not perform well if their training covers too little or too much data. In most current applications, neural networks are best used as aids to human decision makers instead of substitutes for them.

FUZZY LOGIC

Traditional computer programs require precision: on–off, yes–no, right–wrong. However, human beings do not experience the world this way. We might all agree that +40 degrees is hot and -40 degrees is cold; but is +22 degrees hot, warm, comfortable, or cool? The answer depends on many factors: the wind, the humidity, the individual experiencing the temperature, clothing, and expectations. Many of our activities also are inexact. Tractor-trailer drivers would find it nearly impossible to back their rigs into spaces precisely specified to less than an inch on all sides.

fuzzy logic

Rule-based AI that tolerates imprecision by using nonspecific terms called membership functions to solve problems.

Fuzzy logic is a rule-based technology that tolerates imprecision and even uses it to solve problems we could not have solved before. Fuzzy logic consists of a variety of concepts and techniques for representing and inferring knowledge that is imprecise, uncertain, or

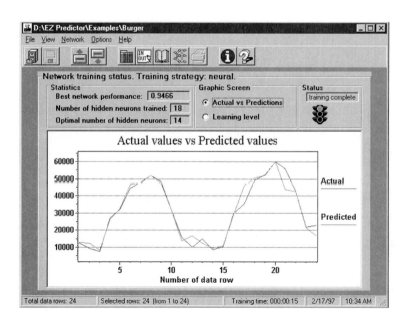

Figure 14.18 Ward Systems' NeuroShell Predictor uses neural network technology to make predictions by "learning" patterns in the user's data file. The Predictor allows users to select columns from their data file which will be used as inputs to the model and to select the output column which contains the values they are trying to predict.

unreliable. Fuzzy logic can create rules that use approximate or subjective values and incomplete or ambiguous data. By expressing logic with some carefully defined imprecision, fuzzy logic is closer to the way people actually think than are traditional IF–THEN rules.

Ford Motor Co. developed a fuzzy logic application that backs a simulated tractor-trailer into a parking space. The application uses the following three rules:

IF the truck is *near* jackknifing, THEN *reduce* the steering angle.

IF the truck is *far away* from the dock, THEN steer *toward* the dock.

IF the truck is *near* the dock, THEN point the trailer *directly* at the dock.

This logic makes sense to us as human beings, for it represents how we think as we back that truck into its berth.

How does the computer make sense of this programming? The answer is relatively simple. The terms (known as membership functions) are imprecisely defined so that, for example, in Figure 14.19, cool is between 50 degrees and 70 degrees Fahrenheit, although the temperature is most clearly cool between about 60 degrees and 67 degrees Fahrenheit. Note that cool is overlapped by cold or norm. To control the room environment using this logic, the programmer would develop similarly imprecise definitions for humidity and other factors, such as outdoor wind and temperature. The rules might include one that says: "If the temperature is cool or cold and the humidity is low while the outdoor wind is high and the outdoor temperature is low, raise the heat and humidity in the room." The computer would combine the membership function readings in a weighted manner and, using all the rules, raise or lower the temperature and humidity.

Fuzzy logic is widely used in Japan and is gaining popularity in the United States. Its popularity has occurred partially because managers find they can use it to reduce costs and shorten development time. Fuzzy logic code requires fewer IF–THEN rules, making it simpler than traditional code. The rules required in the previous trucking example, plus its term definitions, might require hundreds of IF–THEN statements to implement in traditional logic. Compact code requires less computer capacity, allowing, for example, Sanyo Fisher USA to implement camcorder controls without adding expensive memory to their product. In Canada, a proposal has been made to the Meteorological Service of Canada to use fuzzy logic to ingest and intelligently combine orthogonal "interest fields," such as observations, climatology, classification-system-based predictors, and radar, satellite, and lightning data.

Fuzzy logic also allows us to solve problems not previously solvable, thus improving product quality. In Japan, Sendai's subway system uses fuzzy logic controls to accelerate so smoothly that standing passengers need not hold on. Mitsubishi Heavy Industries in Tokyo has been able to reduce the power consumption of its air conditioners by 20 percent by

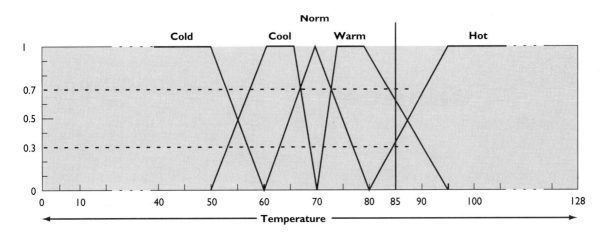

Figure 14.19 Implementing fuzzy logic rules in hardware. The membership functions for the input called temperature are in the logic of the thermostat to control the room temperature. Membership functions help translate linguistic expressions, such as "warm" into numbers that the computer can manipulate.

Source: James M. Sibigtroth, "Implementing Fuzzy Expert Rules in Hardware," *AI Expert*, April 1992 © 1992 Miller Freeman, Inc. Reprinted with permission.

implementing control programs in fuzzy logic. The autofocus device in cameras is only possible because of fuzzy logic. Williams-Sonoma sells an "intelligent" steamer made in Japan that uses fuzzy logic. A variable heat setting detects the amount of grain, cooks it at the preferred temperature, and keeps the food warm up to 12 hours.

Management also has found fuzzy logic useful for decision making and organizational control. A Wall Street firm had a system developed that selects companies for potential acquisition, using the language stock traders understand. Recently, a system has been developed to detect possible fraud in medical claims submitted by healthcare providers anywhere in the United States.

GENETIC ALGORITHMS

genetic algorithms

Problem-solving methods that promote the evolution of solutions to specified problems using the model of living organisms adapting to their environment.

Genetic algorithms (also referred to as adaptive computation) refer to a variety of problem-solving techniques that are conceptually based on the method that living organisms use to adapt to their environments—the process of evolution. They are programmed to work the way populations solve problems—by changing and reorganizing their component parts using such processes as reproduction, mutation, and natural selection. Thus, genetic algorithms promote the evolution of solutions to particular problems, controlling the generation, variation, adaptation, and selection of possible solutions using genetically based processes. As solutions alter and combine, the worst ones are discarded and the better ones survive to go on to produce even better solutions. Genetic algorithms breed programs that solve problems even when no person can fully understand their structure (Holland, 1992).

A genetic algorithm works by representing information as a string of 0s and 1s. A possible solution can be represented by a long string of these digits. The genetic algorithm provides methods of searching all possible combinations of digits to identify the right string representing the best possible structure for the problem.

In one method, the programmer first randomly generates a population of strings consisting of combinations of binary digits (see Figure 14.20). Each string corresponds to one of the variables in the problem. One applies a test for fitness, ranking the strings in the population according to their level of desirability as possible solutions. After the initial population is evaluated for fitness, the algorithm then produces the next generation of strings, consisting of strings that survived the fitness test plus offspring strings produced from mating pairs of strings, and tests their fitness. The process continues until a solution is reached.

Solutions to certain types of problems in areas of optimization, product design, and the monitoring of industrial systems are especially appropriate for genetic algorithms. Many business problems require optimization because they deal with such issues as minimization of

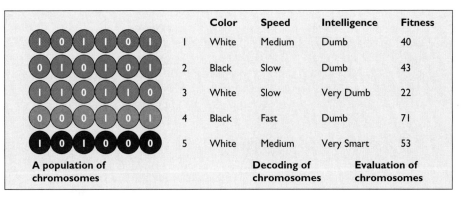

		Color	Speed	Intelligence	Fitness
① ⓪ ① ① ① ①	1	White	Medium	Dumb	40
⓪ ① ⓪ ① ⓪ ①	2	Black	Slow	Dumb	43
① ① ⓪ ① ① ⓪	3	White	Slow	Very Dumb	22
⓪ ⓪ ⓪ ① ⓪ ①	4	Black	Fast	Dumb	71
① ⓪ ① ⓪ ⓪ ⓪	5	White	Medium	Very Smart	53
A population of chromosomes			**Decoding of chromosomes**	**Evaluation of chromosomes**	

Figure 14.20 The components of a genetic algorithm. This example illustrates an initial population of "chromosomes," each representing a different solution. The genetic algorithm uses an iterative process to refine the initial solutions so that the better ones, those with the higher fitness, are more likely to emerge as the best solution.

Source: From Intelligent Decision Support Methods by Vasant Dhar and Roger Stein, p. 65 © 1997. Reprinted by permission of Prentice Hall, Upper Saddle River, N.J.

costs, maximization of profits, efficient scheduling, and use of resources. If these situations are very dynamic and complex, involving hundreds or thousands of variables or formulas, genetic algorithms can expedite the solution because they can evaluate many different solution alternatives quickly to find the best one. For example, the Institute for Aerospace Research developed a specialized genetic algorithm for the design of transonic airfoils. General Electric engineers used genetic algorithms to help optimize the design for jet turbine aircraft engines, where each design change required changes in up to 140 variables. The supply chain management software from i2 Technologies uses genetic algorithms to optimize production scheduling models incorporating hundreds of thousands of details about customer orders, material and resource availability, manufacturing and distribution capability, and delivery dates. International Truck and Engine used this software to iron out snags in production, reducing costly schedule disruptions by 90 percent in five of its plants (Wakefield, 2001; Burtka, 1993).

Hybrid AI Systems

Genetic algorithms, fuzzy logic, neural networks, and expert systems can be integrated into a single application to take advantage of the best features of these technologies. These systems are called **hybrid AI systems.** Hybrid applications in business are growing. In Japan, Hitachi, Mitsubishi, Ricoh, Sanyo, and others are starting to incorporate hybrid AI in products, such as home appliances, factory machinery, and office equipment. Matsushita has developed a "neurofuzzy" washing machine that combines fuzzy logic with neural networks. Nikko Securities has been working on a neurofuzzy system to forecast convertible-bond ratings.

hybrid AI systems
Integration of multiple AI technologies into a single application to take advantage of the best features of these technologies.

INTELLIGENT AGENTS

Intelligent agents are software programs that work in the background without direct human intervention to carry out specific, repetitive, and predictable tasks for an individual user, business process, or software application. The agent uses a built-in or learned knowledge base to accomplish tasks or make decisions on the user's behalf. Intelligent agents can be programmed to make decisions based on the user's personal preferences—for example, to delete junk e-mail, schedule appointments, or travel over interconnected networks to find the cheapest airfare to California. The agent can be likened to a personal digital assistant collaborating with the user in the same work environment. It can help the user by performing tasks on the user's behalf, training or teaching the user, hiding the complexity of difficult tasks, helping the user collaborate with other users, or monitoring events and procedures.

intelligent agent
Software program that uses a built-in or learned knowledge base to carry out specific, repetitive, and predictable tasks for an individual user, business process, or software application.

There are many intelligent agent applications today in operating systems, application software, e-mail systems, mobile computing software, and network tools. For example, the Wizards found in Microsoft Office software tools have built-in capabilities to show users how to accomplish various tasks, such as formatting documents or creating graphs, and to anticipate when users need assistance. Of special interest to business are intelligent agents for cruising networks, including the Internet, in search of information. Chapter 9 described how these *shopping bots* can help consumers find products they want and assist them in comparing prices and other features. Because these mobile agents are personalized, semi-autonomous, and continuously running, they can help automate several of the most time-consuming stages of the buying process and, thus, reduce transaction costs.

Figure 14.21 illustrates the use of intelligent agents in an *autonomous execution system,* which runs continuously, monitors information as it arrives from multiple distributed locations, and executes specific tasks in response to what they find. Arrow Electronics, a $15-billion components distributor uses such a system to match orders from 200 000 customers with data on the availability of components from 600 suppliers. The system uses XML (eXtensible Markup Language) to exchange data using the RosettaNet standard for the electronics industry and handles 14 million transactions around the world each day. By automatically notifying suppliers about orders and customers about the availability and shipment of parts, the system has reduced Arrow's order times by 50 to 75 percent.

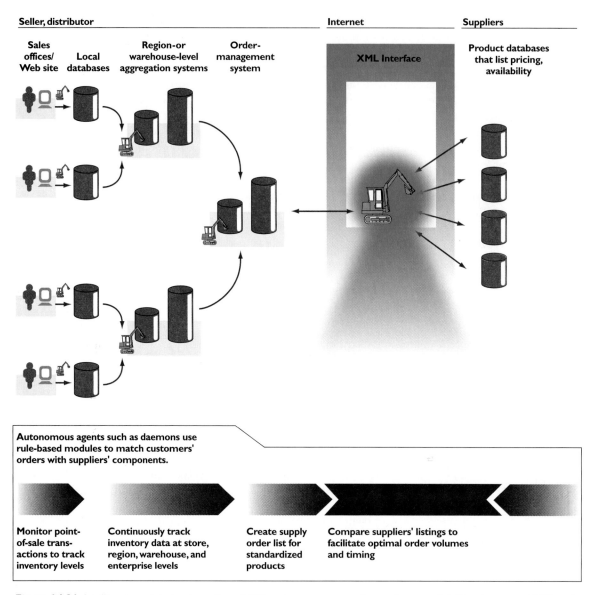

Figure 14.21 Intelligent agent technology at work. This autonomous execution system uses intelligent agent and XML technology to automate the process of matching orders with data on the availability of components. Daemons are computer programs that lie dormant until activated to perform specified operations at predefined times or in response to certain events.
Source: Corey Booth and Sashi Buluswar, "The Return of Artificial Intelligence," *The McKinsey Quarterly*, 2002, No. 2.

MANAGEMENT WRAP-UP

Leveraging and managing organizational knowledge have become core management responsibilities. Managers need to identify the knowledge assets of their organizations and make sure that appropriate systems and processes are in place to maximize their use.

Systems for knowledge and information work and AI can enhance organizational processes in a number of ways. They can facilitate communication, collaboration, and coordination; bring more analytical power to bear in the development of solutions; or reduce the amount of human intervention in organizational processes.

An array of technologies is available to support knowledge management, including AI technologies and tools for knowledge and information work and group collaboration. Managers should understand the costs, benefits, and capabilities of each technology, and the knowledge management problem for which each is best suited.

For Discussion

1. Knowledge management is a business process, not a technology. Discuss.
2. How much can the use of AI change the management process?

SUMMARY

1. *Why do businesses today need knowledge management programs and systems for knowledge management?* Businesses need knowledge management programs because knowledge has become a central productive and strategic asset in today's information economy and a potential source of strategic advantage. Knowledge management is a set of processes for systematically and actively managing and leveraging the stores of knowledge in an organization. Information systems can play a valuable role in knowledge management, helping the organization create, store, disseminate, and apply knowledge and capture and use its knowledge base. Knowledge management systems include support for knowledge repositories, knowledge networks, and communities of practice. Office systems, knowledge work systems (KWS), group collaboration systems, and AI applications are especially useful for knowledge management because they focus on supporting information and knowledge work and on defining and codifying the organization's knowledge base.

2. *Which information system applications are most useful for distributing, creating, and sharing knowledge in the firm?* Offices coordinate information work in the organization, link the work of diverse groups in the organization, and connect the organization to its external environment. Office systems support these functions by automating document management, communications, scheduling, and data management. Word processing, desktop publishing, Web publishing, and digital imaging systems support document management activities. Electronic-mail systems and groupware support communications activities. Electronic calendar applications and groupware support scheduling activities. Desktop data management systems support data management activities.

   Knowledge work systems (KWS) support the creation of knowledge and its integration into the organization. KWS often run on workstations that are customized for the work they must perform. Computer-aided design (CAD) systems and virtual reality systems that create interactive simulations that behave like the real world require graphics and powerful modelling capabilities. KWS for financial professionals provide access to external databases and the ability to analyze massive amounts of financial data very quickly.

   Groupware is special software to support information-intensive activities in which people work collaboratively in groups. Intranets can perform many group collaboration and support functions and allow organizations to use Web publishing capabilities for document management.

3. *What are the business benefits of using artificial intelligence technology for knowledge management?* AI is the development of computer-based systems that behave like humans. There are five members of the AI family tree: natural language, robotics, perceptive systems, expert systems, and intelligent machines. AI lacks the flexibility, breadth, and generality of human intelligence, but it can be used to capture and codify organizational knowledge. Businesses can use AI to help them create an organizational knowledge base to preserve expertise; to perform routine, unsatisfying, or dangerous jobs; and to generate solutions to specific problems that are too massive and complex to be analyzed by human beings in a short period of time.

4. *How can businesses use expert systems and case-based reasoning to capture knowledge?* Expert systems are knowledge-intensive computer programs that solve problems that so far have required human expertise. The systems capture a limited domain of human knowledge using rules. The strategy to search through the knowledge base, called the *inference engine*, can use either forward or backward chaining. Expert systems are most useful for problems of classification or diagnosis. CBR represents organizational knowledge as a database of cases that can be continually expanded and refined. When the user encounters a new case, the system searches for similar cases, finds the closest fit, and applies the solutions of the old case to the new case. The new case is stored with successful solutions in the case database.

5. *How can organizations benefit from using neural networks and other intelligent techniques?* Neural networks consist of hardware and software that attempt to mimic the thought processes of the human brain. Neural networks are notable for their ability to learn without programming and to recognize patterns that cannot be easily described by humans. They are being used in science, medicine, and business primarily to discern patterns in massive amounts of data.

Fuzzy logic expresses logic with some carefully defined imprecision so that it is closer to the way people actually think than are traditional IF–THEN rules. Fuzzy logic has been used for controlling physical devices and is starting to be used for limited decision making applications.

Genetic algorithms develop solutions to particular problems using genetically based processes, such as fitness, crossover, and mutation. Genetic algorithms are beginning to be applied to problems involving optimization, product design, and monitoring industrial systems, where many alternatives or variables must be evaluated to generate an optimal solution.

Intelligent agents are software programs with built-in or learned knowledge bases that carry out specific, repetitive, and predictable tasks for an individual user, business process, or software application. Intelligent agents can be programmed to search for information or conduct transactions on networks, including the Internet.

KEY TERMS

AI shell,   478

Artificial intelligence (AI),   476

Backward chaining,   479

Best practices,   465

Case-based reasoning (CBR),   481

Chief knowledge officer (CKO),   464

Community of practice,   472

Computer-aided design (CAD),   470

Data workers,   466

Enterprise information portal,   474

Expert system,   477

Forward chaining,   479

Fuzzy logic,   484

Genetic algorithms,   486

Hybrid AI systems,   487

Inference engine,   478

Information work,   466

Intelligent agent,   487

Investment workstation,   471

Knowledge assets,   464

Knowledge base,   478

Knowledge engineer,   479

Knowledge management,   464

Knowledge map,   473

Knowledge repository,   468

Knowledge work systems (KWS),   468

Knowledge workers,   466

Neural network,   483

Office systems,   466

Organizational learning,   464

Organizational memory,   465

Rule base,   478

Rule-based expert system,   478

Tacit knowledge,   465

Teamware,   472

Virtual Reality Modeling Language (VRML),   471

Virtual reality systems,   470

REVIEW QUESTIONS

1. What is knowledge management? List and briefly describe the information systems that support it and the kind of information technology (IT) infrastructure it requires.

2. How does knowledge management promote organizational learning? How do knowledge management systems support knowledge networks, knowledge repositories, and communities of practice?

3. Describe the roles of the office in organizations. What are the major activities that take place in offices?

4. What are the principal types of information systems that support information worker activities in the office?

5. What are the generic requirements of knowledge work systems? Why?

6. Describe how the following systems support knowledge work: computer-aided design (CAD), virtual reality, and investment workstations.

7. How does groupware support information work? Describe its capabilities and Internet and intranet capabilities for collaborative work.

8. What is artificial intelligence? Why is it of interest to businesses?

9. What is the difference between artificial intelligence and natural or human intelligence?

10. Define an expert system and describe how it can help organizations use their knowledge assets.

11. Define and describe the role of the following in expert systems: rule base, AI shell, and inference engine.

12. What is case-based reasoning? How does it differ from an expert system?

13. Describe three problems of expert systems.

14. Describe a neural network. For what kinds of tasks would a neural network be appropriate?

15. Define and describe fuzzy logic. For what kinds of applications is it suited?

16. What are genetic algorithms? How can they help organizations solve problems? For what kinds of problems are they suited?

17. What are intelligent agents? How can they be used to benefit businesses?

APPLICATION SOFTWARE EXERCISE

EXPERT SYSTEM EXERCISE: BUILDING A SIMPLE EXPERT SYSTEM FOR RETIREMENT PLANNING

When employees at your company retire, they are given cash bonuses. These cash bonuses are based on the length of employment and the retiree's age. In order to receive a bonus, an employee must be at least 50 years of age and have worked for the company for five years. The following table summarizes the criteria for determining bonuses.

Using the information provided, build a simple expert system. Find a demonstration copy of an expert system software tool on the Web that you can download (see the recommendations at the Companion Website for Chapter 14). Alternatively, use your spreadsheet software to build the expert system.

Length of Employment	Bonus
5 years	No bonus
6–10 years	20 percent of current annual salary
11–15 years	30 percent of current annual salary
16–20 years	40 percent of current annual salary
20–25 years	50 percent of current annual salary
26 or more years	100 percent of current annual salary

GROUP PROJECT

With a group of three or four classmates, select two groupware products, such as Lotus Notes, OpenText LiveLink, and Groove, and compare their features and capabilities. To prepare your analysis, use articles from computer magazines and the Web sites for the groupware vendors. If possible, use electronic presentation software to present your findings to the class.

 # INTERNET TOOLS

COMPANION WEBSITE

The Companion Website for this chapter will take you to the National Aeronautics and Space Administration (NASA) Web site, where you can complete an exercise showing how this Web site can be used by knowledge workers.

At www.pearsoned.ca/laudon, you will find valuable tool to facilitate and enhance your learning of this chapter as well as opportunities to apply your knowledge to realistic situations:

- An Interactive Study Guide of self-test questions that will provide you with immediate feedback.
- Application exercises.
- An Electronic Commerce Project for this chapter will direct you to Web sites where you can compare the capabilities of two shopping bots for the Web.
- A Management Decision Problem on measuring productivity from a knowledge intranet.
- Updates of material in the chapter.

ADDITIONAL SITES OF INTEREST

There are many interesting Web sites to enhance your learning about knowledge management, artificial intelligence, and expert systems. You can search the Web yourself, or just try the following sites to add to what you have already learned.

Fuzzy Clips

http://ai.iit.nrc.ca/IR_public/fuzzy/fuzzyClips/fuzzyCLIPSIndex.html

Describes the evolution of fuzzy clips and links to freeware download of fuzzy clips (easy to use fuzzy logic modules developed by the National Research Council of Canada and the U.S. National Space and Aeronautics Administration

Open Text's LiveLink

www.opentext.com/products/

Web-based enterprise knowledge management and collaboration software

CompInfo's AI Index

www.compinfo-center.com/tpai-t.htm

Links to interesting AI Web sites

CASE STUDY: *Can Boeing Keep Flying High?*

The Boeing Company has been critically important to the United States for over 60 years in both war and peace. During World War II, it produced the B17 and B29 bombers that were the heart of the military bombing campaign against the Axis powers. In 1958, the 707, Boeing's first successful civilian passenger plane, began commercial operation and was so successful that 348 of that model are still flying today. In 1969, when Boeing came out with its long-range 747 jumbo jet, the company became the largest exporter of any corporation in the United States. During the 1990s, the company underwent rapid expansion, acquiring Rockwell International, a major aerospace and defence company in 1996, competing aircraft manufacturer McDonnell Douglas in 1997, and Hughes Aircraft, a leading space and communications company in 2000. Today, with over 180 000 employees, Boeing is a giant producer of passenger planes, business jets, fighter planes, helicopters, flight instruments, and even satellites and missiles.

Although Boeing is a major force in the aerospace, defence, and communications industries as well as the commercial airline industry, its path to growth and prosperity has become clouded. In its commercial airline business, it faces a formidable competitor. Airbus Industrie was founded in 1971 by the British and French governments and was immediately subsidized by these governments. In 1996, Airbus decided to challenge Boeing for the jumbo jet market, then ruled exclusively by Boeing with its 416-seat long-distance 747-400. Airbus predicts air travel will expand rapidly during the next decade, requiring many giant jumbo jets. Its Airbus A380 seats 555 passengers and is the world's largest jetliner. It features a full double-deck, rather than the 747's shorter second story "hump," and later versions could eventually be stretched to accommodate over 650 seats. The A380's major benefit would be that by carrying more passengers, it will not require additional landing slots at the overcrowded hub airports. Moreover, Airbus claims that the operating costs for its A380 will be 17 percent lower than those for the Boeing 747. Airbus, as a newer company, could also build more modern technology into its planes. Its cockpit designs are similar in all of its jets, so pilots need only a few days of extra training to fly another model. Airbus has been steadily taking market share away from Boeing. By 1999, it had surpassed Boeing in the number of planes sold.

At first, Boeing decided to compete with Airbus in the giant jumbo jetliner market by "stretching" its existing 747 at a development cost of only $3 to $4 billion, far lower than the $12 billion price tag for developing the Airbus A380. In March 2001, however, Boeing withdrew from the competition. Its management developed a very different vision of the market for jumbo jets. Boeing's management foresees a turn to smaller planes that will fly close to the speed of sound, enabling passengers to fly nonstop from departure to destination, bypassing the overcrowded hubs. This would stimulate the growth of smaller regional airlines and reduce the need for huge jumbo jets. Boeing announced it was designing a new 230- to 250-passenger aircraft, dubbed the Sonic Cruiser. It will fly fast enough to cut one hour out of each 4827 kilometres of flight, enabling many more direct flights, greatly reducing the need for flight transfers at the large hubs. Moreover, while the current coast-to-coast and overseas jumbo jet flights enable a plane to make one round-trip daily, Boeing claims its faster new plane will fly two round trips daily, making it a valuable investment. Further, Boeing's management claims that these planes will especially attract the profitable first- and business-class passengers. For airlines struggling with lower-cost competitors, Boeing is also considering an ultra-efficient 250-seat airplane built from lightweight materials that travels at the same speed as existing jetliners but would be 20 percent cheaper to operate. All in all, Boeing foresees a strong expansion of smaller jet sales, rather than jumbo jet sales.

In addition to competition from Airbus, Boeing has been facing difficult conditions because the market for commercial airplanes has been shrinking due to airline mergers and the downturn in air travel after the September 11, 2001, terrorist attacks. Boeing's CEO Phil Condit is pushing Boeing into the lucrative services area: maintenance, modifications, financing, and pilot training. He is also looking beyond aircraft and related services to steer Boeing into a variety of high-technology businesses, including airborne Internet services and digital movie distribution. This diversification is one reason why Boeing moved its global headquarters from Seattle, Washington, to Chicago, Illinois.

Boeing now sees its military and space business as its biggest growth area as it switches from commercial airplane production to newer businesses based on information and communications technologies. In July 2002, it announced it was merging its satellite and communications businesses with its military manufacturing unit, creating an operation equal in size to its commercial airplane division. Boeing is a contractor for the United States government's National Missile Defense project. The company is also working on projects related to "network-centric warfare," in which the United States would use a global information grid to orchestrate all of its missiles, planes, tanks, and ships in battle from a central command post. Boeing makes satellites, AWACS (Airborne Warning and Control System) airplanes, unmanned surveillance aircraft, guided missiles, and Global Positioning System (GPS)–equipped handheld radios. The company is developing broadband technology and standards that could network all of these "smart" devices and every element of warfare so that they could be visually displayed on the "data wall" at a command-and-control centre. If Boeing's proposed military infrastructure becomes adopted, the company could see $30 to $45 billion in defence business opportunities over the next 10 years. Analysts warn, however, that the United States government may not like depending on Boeing alone to construct such systems.

Another Boeing initiative is in air traffic management. Boeing set up a separate business unit to overhaul the way air traffic is controlled. It would like to see the United States' air traffic controller system transformed from ground-based traffic control to air-based traffic control relying on the GPS. Navigation computers would be required on all jetliners, enabling every airplane continually to transmit its exact position, direction, and speed to nearby aircraft. This method would permit planes to fly shorter distances on each flight while also reducing the long waits for takeoffs. Some air traffic controllers would still be needed, particularly at larger airports. Inexpensive computer and GPS technologies already exist, and both Boeing and Airbus airplanes are already equipped for flying without using ground-based systems.

Using these new initiatives and its commercial airplane business, Boeing's management is trying to lower costs by using technology to reform inefficient business processes. Boeing's airplane production process was paper intensive, with a final design of the Boeing 747 consisting of approximately 75 000 paper engineering drawings. Boeing designers realized long ago that they would save much production time if they reused existing designs, rather than designing each aircraft from scratch. The process of design customization was manual and took more than 1000 engineers a year of full-time work to complete. For every customization choice on every airplane built, hundreds of pages of detailed drawings needed to be drawn manually. To reuse old paper aircraft configurations and parts designs, the engineers first needed to search through an immense number of paper drawings to find appropriate designs to reuse for a specific configuration. They then laboriously copied the old designs to use for the new plane. Inevitably, errors crept into the new designs—large numbers of errors given the large numbers of design sheets—because of unavoidable copying mistakes.

It used to take 800 computers to manage the coordination of engineering and manufacturing, and many of these did not communicate directly with each other. The list of parts produced by engineering for a given airplane was configured differently from the lists used by manufacturing and customer service. Ultimately, the parts list had to be broken down, converted, and recomputed up to 13 times during the production of a single plane.

Another problem with manual design was that the staff needed to create life-size mockups in plywood and plastic to ensure that everything fitted and that the pipes and wires that ran through the plane were placed properly and did not interfere with other necessary equipment. The mockups were also needed to verify the accuracy of part specifications. Building mockups was a slow, expensive, laborious process. At production time, errors would again occur when part numbers of specifications were manually copied and at times miscopied onto order sheets, resulting in many wrong or mis-sized parts arriving.

Engineers worked in separate fiefdoms based on fields of specialization. Some engineers designed the plane's parts, others assembled them, and others designed the parts' packing crates. They rarely compared notes. If production engineers discovered a part that did not fit, they sent a complaint back to the designers located in another plant. The designers then pulled out their drawings, reconfigured the part to make it match the drawings of the surrounding parts, and sent the new design back to the plant. Warehouses were filled with paper.

In the early 1990s, Boeing began switching to a "paperless design" model, which it used to computerize the design and production of its 777 aircraft. The 777 aircraft carries 300 to 440 passengers and has lower operating, maintenance, and fuel costs because it uses lighter materials and can fly with only two pilots and two engines. The "paperless design" system employs nine IBM mainframes, a Cray supercomputer, and 2200 workstations, storing 3500 billion bits of information. It enables engineers to call up any of the 777's millions of parts, modify them, fit them into the surrounding structure, and put them back into the plane's "electronic box" so that other engineers can make their own adjustments. Boeing assembled a single parts list that could be used by every division without modification and without tabbing. In addition, management established design–production teams that brought together designers and fabricators from a range of specialties throughout the whole process. Ultimately, the airplane was designed entirely on the computer screen and was initially assembled without expensive mockups. The company cut overall engineering design errors by 50 percent while designing and building a 777 in 14 months.

Boeing has been using systems to address its massive supply chain problem. Five to six million parts are required for its large twin-aisle airplanes alone. In the past, inventory of these parts was handled manually, and the production sites became infamous for the large piles of parts not being used. Not surprisingly, Boeing inventory turned over only two to three times per year compared with 12 times a year in an efficient manufacturing operation. Needed parts often arrived late. Boeing had to assign about 300 materials planners in different plants just to find the needed parts on the shop floor.

In 1994, Boeing launched a process improvement program known as Define and Control Airplane Configuration/Manufacturing Resource Management (DCAC/MRM) to streamline and simplify the processes of configuring and assembling airplanes. Boeing had been using 400 software programs, each with its own independent database, to support production. The management team decided to replace these 400 programs with four interconnected, off-the-shelf software packages, one each for configuration, manufacturing, purchasing, and inventory control. This would enable everyone to work from the same database, offering data integrity and coordination. Each airplane was assigned its own unique identification number that could be used to identify all the parts required for that plane. Each airplane would have only one parts list, and the list would be updated electronically during the production cycle. Management estimated that the project would cost $1.5 billion and would require more than 1000 employees but would pay for itself within two years.

Boeing decided to purchase enterprise resource planning (ERP) software from Baan Co., of Putten, Netherlands, because this software could be used to control the flow of parts and was considered particularly well suited for companies with multi-site hybrid manufacturing processes, such as Boeing. The software also includes EDI links with external suppliers and database links for internal suppliers. "As soon as our ERP system determines we don't have enough of a certain part in the assembly line to satisfy an airplane," explained one production manager, "we can identify which supplier we need and where that supplier's part needs to be delivered." Boeing's goal was that 45 000 employees would use the system at 70 plants to coordinate commercial airplane manufacturing. Rollout completion was targeted for the end of 1997. In addition to Baan's software, Boeing selected forecasting software from i2 Technologies, factory floor process planning software from CimLinc, product data management software from Structural Dynamics Research, and a product configuration system from Trilogy.

This project encountered serious problems, nearly causing a "manufacturing nervous breakdown." Parts shortages, defective parts, rework, and overtime approached all-time highs. Managers calculated that Boeing's production system was more than $1 billion over initial cost projections. The company was forced to make late deliveries, jeopardizing Boeing's standing with clients and its financial performance.

Eventually, these problems were solved, and Boeing went on to make other process improvements. At "moonshine shops," mechanics and assemblers are experimenting on innovations to improve efficiency, such as redesigning parts so that they are easier to assemble and load. Management is also working to standardize designs, to design units that require fewer parts, and to emphasize just-in-time parts delivery. Overall, Boeing has already been able to decrease its 777 assembly time from 71 days to 31 days.

Boeing is trying to use Internet technology to reduce procurement costs by making all of its purchases online, reducing the number of suppliers to 18 000, and eliminating EDI. Boeing's old procurement processes were excessively paper driven, with about 90 percent of all transactions, such as purchase orders, contracts, invoices, requests for proposal (RFP), and shipping notices, involving paper. Just removing the reliance on paper could potentially save Boeing 20 to 27 percent of its internal costs. As a result of Boeing's recent corporate acquisitions, Boeing absorbed a number of different divisional order processing systems, many of which were left unchanged. This meant that Boeing now had 18 separate EDI connections for each of its many suppliers.

Boeing launched its Commercial Aviation Web portal called myboeingfleet.com in May 2000. Boeing has 850 customers, including airlines, governments, and leasing companies. The new portal is a customer source of tools, parts, and information about specific planes. Customers can access 1.5 million engineering drawings, 70 000 maintenance manuals, official service bulletins, and even a Web page where customers can discuss their problems with Boeing engineers. Prior to the portal, customers had to go to different sites for different functions, such as parts purchases. Using the unified Web site reduced the cost and the amount of paper needed in each transaction. Boeing now involves only nine people in each transaction, rather than the 38 previously needed. The portal has reduced the amount of paper exchanged between Boeing and its airplane customers and has improved customer relations, but it has not inspired new customer service programs that might create additional revenue.

Boeing's next B2B step was joining BAE Systems, Lockheed Martin, Raytheon Company, and Rolls-Royce to launch Exostar, a global Net marketplace for the aerospace and defence industry in September 2000. The founders had all been building their own electronic commerce supply chain Web sites, investing millions of dollars, and they realized it would be cheaper and easier to join together to create a global electronic marketplace

for their industry, much as COVISINT does for the automobile industry. While these companies are intense rivals for supplies and for commercial military aircraft and space contracts, they are also suppliers to and customers of each other. Their goal is to reduce costs while making their supply chains more efficient. In the past, manually processing a purchase order cost Boeing about $225. Today, the standardized and automated contracts cost around $2.25 each.

Very soon, more than 8000 suppliers joined Exostar out of the approximately 37 000 industry suppliers worldwide. Exostar gave suppliers a single connection point, improving their relationship with their buyers. Exostar uses the XML language, making it much easier for all suppliers and purchasers to join and use. It also enables Boeing and its suppliers to keep their internal systems, including Boeing's 18 legacy purchasing systems. Its suppliers now never have to deal with multiple systems. Moreover, it is now much easier for Boeing to know how much business the whole company is doing with its major suppliers. It also means future merger and acquisition integrations will be much easier. Exostar also includes a facility for suppliers and producers to work together in real time to plan schedules and to design or redesign products. Finally, Exostar is a much cheaper and easier system to use than EDI.

Boeing hopes Exostar will eventually wean all its suppliers off EDI. However, small suppliers have been reluctant to switch to Exostar because they do not have the technical sophistication or financial incentive to change their business processes and systems to work with an online marketplace. Industry analysts also point out that using an industry consortium Net marketplace may not work to Boeing's competitive advantage. Boeing has unique products and has used its status as a major industry player to set procurement standards that were in its best interests. While working on common solutions, each Exostar partner will try to protect its supply chain practices. The four companies compete for business, and the question is whether they will be able to separate their individual interests from their common goals for Exostar. To date, the bulk of Exostar purchases have been for indirect maintenance, repair, and operation goods.

Boeing also hopes to gain efficiencies from stepped-up use of knowledge management systems. Its Commercial Airplanes division, for example, must provide maintenance and support for a wide range of equipment with long life spans. The company's global field workforce needs to refer 50 percent of its questions to Boeing's service engineers. It would cost Boeing up to thousands of dollars each time an engineer had to answer a query because they were spending hours retrieving data and records. About half the queries engineers receive each day have been previously answered, sometimes several times over. But unless the engineer remembered that a query had been previously answered, he or she would treat the inquiry as an entirely new investigation. Boeing implemented software from Primus Knowledge Solutions that includes an electronic repository of answers to a specified set of questions. This system can capture engineers' knowledge more easily, putting documents, messages, and drawings into folders that can be accessed with a sophisticated search engine. This saves engineers as much as several hours per day, since they no longer have to manually organize and coordinate information gathering. Every time a field service person answers a question, it can be funnelled to the knowledge management system and indexed for future users.

In the summer of 2001, Boeing started rolling out an employee portal, starting first with 2000 finance and engineering employees. All employees can access the portal, including nearly 50 000 factory employees given access through factory floor kiosks. For software, the company turned to Plumtree Software's Corporate Portal system. One problem that Boeing hoped this portal would solve was that 172 000 employees were already connected, but to literally hundreds of intranets. The new portal links common data from Boeing's four big divisions, enabling the divisions to share significant data and applications over the Web. The company's plan is to identify the best-of-breed products in use in various units and standardize the company's software on them. The portal gives employees access to large amounts of information, including technical information, such as design data; personalized tools, such as calendars; human resources information, such as retirement systems; and library items, such as a glossary of aerospace industry acronyms. In addition, it gives employees, such as aircraft designers, an easy way to collaborate with other Boeing designers at home or abroad. The Boeing designers will also be able to collaborate with supplier designers when Boeing links its employee portal up with Exostar.

Overall, Boeing's aircraft production costs are still higher than those of the competition, and the company is trying to reduce its American workforce so that it can outsource more of its parts production work with components suppliers in China, Malaysia, and other countries. Jerry Calhoun, Boeing's lead labour negotiator stated that "... even with our efficiencies, even with our abilities to squeeze cost out of our product, we're still not cost effective." According to Calhoun, Boeing would never win a sales campaign strictly on price.

CIO Scott Griffin has said, "The interesting issue for a big company is that when you're big, it is very hard to be fast.... We want to be big and fast." While Boeing has made many changes, the question remains whether these changes will make Boeing a strong yet nimble competitor in its traditional as well as new lines of business. Can Boeing go fast enough to keep on flying?

Sources: Edward Wong, "For Jet Rivals, Caution Here, Swagger There," *New York Times*, July 28, 2002; "Airbus Claims Lead over Boeing Despite Lost Orders," Ananova Web site January 17, 2002, www.ananova.com accessed August 5, 2003; Demir Barias, "Exostar Appoints CEO," *Line56*, January 8, 2002; Stanley Holmes and Mike France, "Boeing's Secret," *BusinessWeek*, May 20, 2002; Steven Greenhouse, "Mediator Joins Stalled Talks by Boeing Co. and Its Unions," *New York Times*, August 17, 2002; Pimm Fox, "Making Support Pay," *Computerworld*, March 11, 2002;

"Boeing Shows How XML Can Help Business," *ITworld.com*, March 12, 2001; J. Lynn Lunsford, "Boeing's Planned Sonic Cruiser Is Buzz of Aerospace Industry," *Wall Street Journal*, February 27, 2002; "Boeing Explores Plan 'B,'" *Wall Street Journal*, June 11, 2002; "Lean Times: With Airbus on Its Tail, Boeing Is Rethinking How It Builds Planes," *Wall Street Journal*, September 5, 2001; "Boeing Plan to Unsnarl Air Traffic: Cede Ground Control to Satellites," *Wall Street Journal*, May 17, 2001; Dominic Gates, "Boeing's Big Move," *The Industry Standard*, April 2, 2001; Tom Kaneshige, "Exostar Unwraps 4.0," *Line56*, November 29, 2001; Richard Karpinski, "Web Supply Chains Revised," *InternetWeek.com*, September 28, 2001; Stephanie Sanborn and Heather Harreld, "U.S. Recovery: Airline Industry Exchanges Adopt 'Wait and See' Approach," *InfoWorld*, September 21, 2001; David Lewis, "Boeing Portal to Serve Employees, Partners," *InternetWeek*, July 30, 2001; Sandra Swanson, "Boeing: Design Anywhere, Build Anywhere, Share Freely," *InformationWeek*, December 14, 2001; J. Lynn Lunsford, Daniel Michaels, and Andy Pasztor, "Industry Focus: At Paris Air Show, Boeing-Airbus Duel Has New Twist," *Wall Street Journal*, June 15, 2001; Stanley Holmes, "Boeing Goes Lean," *BusinessWeek online*, June 4, 2001, www.businessweek.com, accessed August 5, 2003; Daniel Michaels, "New Approach: Airbus Revamp Brings Sense to Consortium, Fuels Boeing Rivalry," *Wall Street Journal*, April 30, 2001; David Gauthier-Villars, Andy Pasztor, Anne Marie Squeo, and Scott McCartney, "Flight Plan: Boeing Revamp Cuts Ties to Seattle, Puts Focus on News Services," *Wall Street Journal*, March 22, 2001; Stuart F. Brown, "How to Build a Really, Really, Really Big Plane," *Fortune*, March 5, 2001; Amy Helen Johnson, "Boeing's Flight Plan," *Line56*, January 15, 2001; Jeff Cole, "Wing Commander: At Boeing, an Old Hand Provides New Tricks to Battle with Airbus," *Wall Street Journal*, January 14, 2001; Phillip L. Zweig, "Can Exostar Transform the Aerospace Industry?" *Outlook 2001*, 2, January 2001.

CASE STUDY QUESTIONS

1. Analyze Boeing and its business strategy using the value chain and competitive forces models.
2. Summarize the business and technology conditions that caused Boeing to change its business strategy. What management, organization, and technology problems prompted this change?
3. How did Boeing change its business processes and information systems to support its new strategy? How do Boeing's information systems provide value?
4. What is the relationship of knowledge management to Boeing's business strategy? How is Boeing using knowledge management to execute its business model and business strategy?
5. Evaluate Boeing's new business strategy. What management, organization, and technology issues will Boeing face as it attempts to implement the strategy? How successful will Boeing be in pursuing that strategy?

MANAGING INTERNATIONAL INFORMATION SYSTEMS

CHAPTER 15

As a manager, you will want to know what special issues must be addressed when developing and managing international information systems. After completing this chapter, you should be able to answer the following questions:

1. *What are the major factors driving the internationalization of business?*
2. *What strategies are available for developing international businesses?*
3. *How can information systems support the various international business strategies?*
4. *What issues should managers address when developing international information systems?*
5. *What technical alternatives are available for developing global systems?*

Paul Hartmann AG Internationalizes with Global Systems

International operations now generate more than half the revenue at Paul Hartmann AG, a German surgical and hygiene products supplier with subsidiaries in over 25 countries. As the company rapidly expanded into North America and Asia, its management realized that it could lower the total cost of ownership of its technology assets if it had a centralized information systems function with common systems worldwide. It implemented SAP R/3 enterprise system modules in its subsidiaries that supported 3000 users by the end of 2002.

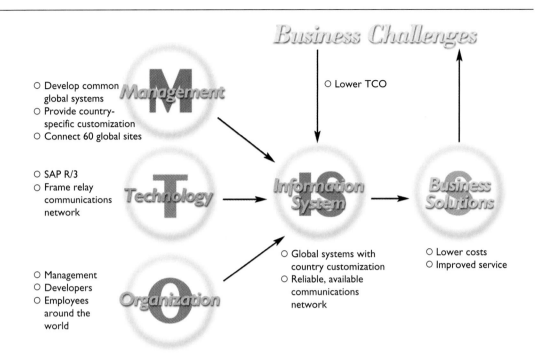

The company wanted a global system that could standardize and integrate some business processes globally while allowing subsidiaries to serve the specific needs of individual countries. It had used earlier versions of SAP software in its general accounting department in its German headquarters and gradually rolled out the software to its European subsidiaries. Forty members of Paul Hartmann's information systems department worked on implementing the new SAP system. The new SAP system is operated and supported from corporate headquarters in Heidenheim, Germany.

The company needed a reliable and available communications network to achieve optimum performance from the SAP software and to facilitate global implementation of the system. A team led by Eugen Grossegesse, Paul Hartmann's Manager of International Networks, selected Infonet Services Corporation's international frame-relay network service. Infonet had good connections with local communications providers in various countries and was able to guarantee a response time of four hours in the event of a line problem. Paul Hartmann operates and monitors the network, which links 60 sites, from Heidenheim.

The company's next goal is to implement more SAP applications at its subsidiaries, including customer relationship management, human resources, and logistics. In the long term, Paul Hartmann would like to set up regionalized systems for Central Europe, North America, and Asia to manage time zone differences using hardware and software operated in Heidenheim.

Sources: Ann Toh, "Under Control, Globally," *CIO Asia*, May 2002; Hartmann corporate Web site, accessed June 23, 2002, www.hartmann-online.de; "SAP BW Takes the Leading Role at Paul Hartmann AG," IBM Corporation, 2000.

Management Challenges

Paul Hartmann AG is one of many business firms moving toward global forms of organization that transcend national boundaries. Paul Hartmann could not make this move unless it reorganized its information systems and standardized some of its business processes so that the same information could be used by disparate business units in different countries. The opening vignette shows some of the issues that must be addressed when making these changes and raises the following management challenges:

1. **Lines of business and global strategy.** Firms must decide whether some or all of their lines of business should be managed on a global basis. There are some lines of business in which locale variations are slight, and the possibility exists to reap large rewards by organizing globally. PCs and power tools may fit this pattern, as well as industrial raw materials. Other consumer goods may be quite different by country or region. It is likely that firms with many lines of business will have to maintain a very mixed organizational structure.

2. **The difficulties of managing change in a multicultural firm.** Although engineering change in a single corporation in a single nation can be difficult, costly, and long term, bringing about significant change in very large-scale global corporations can be daunting. Both the agreement on "core business processes" in a transnational context and the decision on common systems require either extraordinary insight, a lengthy process of consensus building, or the exercise of sheer power.

The changes Paul Hartmann seeks are some of the changes in international information systems architecture—the basic systems needed to coordinate worldwide trade and other activities—that organizations need to consider if they want to operate across the globe. This chapter explores how to organize, manage, and control the development of international information systems as firms become more digital.

15.1 The Growth of International Information Systems

We already have described two powerful worldwide changes driven by advances in information technology that have transformed the business environment and posed new challenges for management. One is the transformation of industrial economies and societies into knowledge- and information-based economies. The other is the emergence of a global economy and global world order.

The new world order will sweep away many national corporations, national industries, and national economies controlled by domestic politicians. Much of the Fortune 500—the 500 largest American corporations—will disappear in the next 50 years, mirroring past behaviour of large firms since 1900. Many firms will be replaced by fast-moving networked corporations that transcend national boundaries. The growth of international trade has radically altered domestic economies around the globe. About $1 trillion worth of goods, services, and financial instruments—roughly the equivalent of Canada's gross national product—changes hands each day in global trade.

Consider a laptop computer as an example: The central processing unit (CPU) is likely to have been designed and manufactured in the United States; the DRAM (or dynamic random access memory, which makes up the majority of primary storage in a computer) was designed in the United States but manufactured in Malaysia; the screen was designed and assembled in Japan, using American patents; the keyboard is from Taiwan; and it was all assembled in Japan, where the case was also made. Management of the project, located in Silicon Valley, California, along with marketing, sales, and finance, coordinated all of the activities from financing and production to shipping and sales efforts. Finally, the company has a major Canadian subsidiary to handle Canadian sales and servicing. None of this would be possible without powerful international information and telecommunication systems—an international information systems architecture.

To be effective, managers need a global perspective on business and an understanding of the support systems needed to conduct business on an international scale.

DEVELOPING AN INTERNATIONAL INFORMATION SYSTEMS ARCHITECTURE

This chapter describes how to go about building an international information systems architecture suitable for your international strategy. An **international information systems architecture** consists of the basic information systems required by organizations to coordinate worldwide trade and other activities. Figure 15.1 illustrates the reasoning we will follow throughout the chapter and depicts the major dimensions of an international information systems architecture.

The basic strategy to follow when building an international system is to understand the global environment in which your firm is operating. This means understanding the overall market forces or business drivers that are pushing your industry toward global competition. A **business driver** is a force in the environment to which businesses must respond and that influences the direction of the business. Likewise, examine carefully the inhibitors or negative factors that create *management challenges*—factors that could scuttle the development of a global business. Once you have examined the global environment, you will need to consider a corporate strategy for competing in that environment. How will your firm respond? You could ignore the global market and focus on domestic competition only, sell to the globe from a domestic base, or organize production and distribution around the globe. There are many in-between choices.

After you have developed a strategy, it is time to consider how to structure your organization so it can pursue the strategy. How will you accomplish a division of labour across a global environment? Where will production, administration, accounting, marketing, and human resource functions be located? Who will handle the systems function?

Next, you must consider the management issues in implementing your strategy and making the organization design come alive. Key here will be the design of business procedures. How can you discover and manage user requirements? How can you induce change in local units to conform to international requirements? How can you re-engineer on a global scale, and how can you coordinate systems development?

The last issue to consider is the technology platform. Although changing technology is a key driving factor leading toward global markets, you need to have a corporate strategy and structure before you can rationally choose the right technology.

After you have completed this process of reasoning, you will be well on your way toward an appropriate international information systems architecture capable of achieving your corporate goals. Let us begin by looking at the overall global environment.

international information systems architecture

The basic information systems required by organizations to coordinate worldwide trade and other activities.

business driver

A force in the environment to which businesses must respond and that influences the direction of business.

Figure 15.1 International information systems architecture. The major dimensions for developing an international information systems architecture are the global environment, the corporate global strategies, the structure of the organization, the management and business processes, and the technology platform.

International Information Systems Architecture

THE GLOBAL ENVIRONMENT: BUSINESS DRIVERS AND CHALLENGES

Table 15.1 illustrates the business drivers in the global environment that are leading all industries toward global markets and competition.

Global business drivers can be divided into two groups: general cultural factors and specific business factors. There are easily recognized general cultural factors driving internationalization since World War II. Information, communication, and transportation technologies have created a *global village,* in which communication (by telephone, television, radio, or computer network) around the globe is no more difficult and not much more expensive than communication down the block. Moving goods and services to and from geographically dispersed locations has fallen dramatically in cost.

The development of global communications has created a global village in a second sense: There is now a **global culture** created by television and other globally shared media, such as movies, that permits different cultures and peoples to develop common expectations about such concepts as right and wrong, desirable and undesirable, heroic and cowardly. The collapse of the Eastern bloc has enormously accelerated the growth of a world culture, increased support for capitalism and business, and reduced the level of cultural conflict considerably.

A last factor to consider is the growth of a global knowledge base. At the end of World War II, knowledge, education, science, and industrial skills were highly concentrated in North America, western Europe, and Japan, with the rest of the world euphemistically called the *Third World.* This is no longer true. Latin America, China, southern Asia, and eastern Europe have developed powerful educational, industrial, and scientific centres, resulting in a much more democratically and widely dispersed knowledge base.

These general cultural factors leading toward internationalization result in specific business globalization factors that affect most industries. The growth of powerful communications technologies and the emergence of world cultures create the condition for *global markets*—global consumers interested in consuming similar products that are culturally approved. Coca-Cola, American sneakers (made in Korea but designed in Los Angeles), and CNN Live (a television show) can now be sold in Latin America, Africa, and Asia.

Responding to this demand, global production and operations have emerged with precise online coordination between far-flung production facilities and central headquarters thousands of miles away. At Sealand Transportation, a major global shipping company based in Newark, New Jersey, shipping managers online can watch the loading of ships in Rotterdam, check trim and ballast, and trace packages to specific ship locations, as each activity proceeds. This is all possible through an international satellite link.

global culture

The development of common expectations, shared artifacts, and social norms among different cultures and peoples.

TABLE 15.1	**THE GLOBAL BUSINESS DRIVERS**

General Cultural Factors

Global communication and transportation technologies

Development of global culture

Emergence of global social norms

Political stability

Global knowledge base

Specific Business Factors

Global markets

Global production and operations

Global coordination

Global workforce

Global economies of scale

The new global markets and the pressure toward global production and operation have called forth whole new capabilities for global coordination of all factors of production. Not only production but also accounting, marketing and sales, human resources, and systems development (all the major business functions) can be coordinated on a global scale. Frito Lay, for instance, can develop a marketing sales force automation system in the United States and, once provided, may try the same techniques and technologies in Spain. Micromarketing—mar-

Businesses need an international information systems architecture to coordinate the activities of their sales, manufacturing, and warehouse units worldwide.

keting to very small geographic and social units—no longer means marketing to neighbourhoods in the United States but to neighbourhoods throughout the world! These new levels of global coordination permit for the first time in history the location of business activity according to comparative advantage. Design should be located where it is best accomplished, as should marketing, production, and finance.

Finally, global markets, production, and administration create the conditions for powerful, sustained global economies of scale. Production driven by worldwide global demand can be concentrated where it can be best accomplished, fixed resources can be allocated over larger production runs, and production runs in larger plants can be scheduled more efficiently and estimated more precisely. Lower cost factors of production can be exploited wherever they emerge. The result is a powerful strategic advantage to firms that can organize globally. These general and specific business drivers have greatly enlarged world trade and commerce.

Not all industries are similarly affected by these trends. Clearly, manufacturing has been much more affected than services that still tend to be domestic and highly inefficient. However, the localism of services is breaking down in telecommunications, entertainment, transportation, financial services, and general business services, including legal services. Clearly, those firms within an industry that can understand the internationalization of the industry and respond appropriately will reap enormous gains in productivity and stability.

Business Challenges

Although the possibilities of globalization for business success are significant, fundamental forces are operating to inhibit a global economy and to disrupt international business. Table 15.2 lists the most common and powerful challenges to the development of global systems.

TABLE 15.2	CHALLENGES AND OBSTACLES TO GLOBAL BUSINESS SYSTEMS

General

Cultural particularism: regionalism, nationalism, language differences

Social expectations: brand-name expectations; work hours

Political laws: transborder data and privacy laws, commercial regulations

Specific

Standards: different EDI (electronic data interchange), e-mail (electronic mail), telecommunications standards

Reliability: phone networks not uniformly reliable

Speed: different data transfer speeds differ, many slower than United States

Personnel: shortages of skilled consultants

particularism

Making judgments and taking actions on the basis of narrow or personal characteristics.

At a cultural level, **particularism**, making judgments and taking action on the basis of narrow or personal characteristics, in all its forms (religious, nationalistic, ethnic, regionalism, geopolitical position) rejects the very concept of a shared global culture and rejects the penetration of domestic markets by foreign goods and services. Differences among cultures produce differences in social expectations, politics, and, ultimately, legal rules. In certain countries, such as the United States, consumers expect domestic name-brand products to be manufactured domestically and are disappointed to learn that much of what they thought of as domestically produced is, in fact, foreign made.

Different cultures produce different political regimes. Among the many different countries of the world, there are different laws governing the movement of information, information privacy, origins of software and hardware, and radio and satellite telecommunications. Even the hours of business and the terms of business trade vary greatly across political cultures. These different legal regimes complicate global business and must be considered when building global systems.

transborder data flow

The movement of information across international boundaries in any form.

For instance, European countries have very strict laws concerning transborder data flow and privacy. **Transborder data flow** is defined as the movement of information across international boundaries in any form. Some European countries prohibit the processing of financial information outside their boundaries or the movement of personal information to foreign countries. The European Directive on Data Protection, which went into effect in October 1998, restricts the flow of any information to countries (such as Canada) that do not meet strict European information laws on personal information. Financial services, travel, and healthcare companies could be directly affected. In response, most multinational firms develop information systems within each European country to avoid the cost and uncertainty of moving information across national boundaries.

Cultural and political differences profoundly affect organizations' standard operating procedures. A host of specific barriers arise from the general cultural differences, everything from different reliability of phone networks to the shortage of skilled consultants (see Steinbart and Nath, 1992).

National laws and traditions have created disparate accounting practices in various countries, which impact the ways profits and losses are analyzed. German companies generally do not recognize the profit from a venture until the project is completely finished and they have been paid. Conversely, British firms begin posting profits before a project is completed, when they are reasonably certain they will get the money.

These accounting practices are tightly intertwined with each country's legal system, business philosophy, and tax code. British, Canadian, and American firms share a predominantly Anglo-Saxon outlook that separates tax calculations from reports to shareholders to focus on showing shareholders how fast their profits are growing. Continental European accounting practices are less oriented toward impressing investors, focusing rather on demonstrating compliance with strict rules and minimizing tax liabilities. These diverging accounting practices make it difficult for large international companies with units in different countries to evaluate their performance.

Cultural differences can also affect the way organizations use information technology. For example, Japanese firms fax extensively but have been reluctant to take advantage of the capabilities of e-mail. One explanation is that the Japanese view e-mail as poorly suited for much intragroup communication and for depiction of the complex symbols used in the Japanese written language (Straub, 1994).

Language remains a significant barrier. Although English has become, to a certain extent, the standard business language, this is true more at the higher levels of companies than throughout the middle and lower ranks. Software may have to be developed with local language interfaces before a new information system can be successfully implemented.

Currency fluctuations can play havoc with planning models and projections. A product that appears profitable in Mexico or Japan may actually produce a loss due to changes in foreign exchange rates. Some of these problems will diminish in parts of the world where the euro becomes more widely used.

These inhibiting factors must be taken into account when designing and developing international systems for business. For example, companies trying to implement "lean production" systems spanning national boundaries typically underestimate the time, expense, and logistical difficulties of making goods and information flow freely across different countries' borders (Levy, 1997).

STATE OF THE ART

Given the opportunities for achieving competitive advantages as outlined previously and the interest in future applications, one might think that most international companies have rationally developed marvellous international systems architectures. Nothing could be further from the truth. Most companies have inherited patchwork international systems from the distant past, often based on concepts of information processing developed in the 1960s—batch-oriented reporting from independent foreign divisions to corporate headquarters, with little online control and communication. Corporations in this situation increasingly will face powerful competitive challenges in the marketplace from firms that have rationally designed truly international systems. Still other companies have recently developed technology platforms for international systems but do not get anywhere using these platforms because they lack a global strategy.

As it turns out, there are significant difficulties in building appropriate international architectures. The difficulties involve planning a system appropriate to the firm's global strategy, structuring the organization of systems and business units, solving implementation issues, and choosing the right technical platform. Let us examine these problems in greater detail.

15.2 ORGANIZING INTERNATIONAL INFORMATION SYSTEMS

There are three organizational issues facing corporations seeking a global position: choosing a strategy, organizing the business, and organizing the systems management area. The first two are closely connected, so we will discuss them together.

GLOBAL STRATEGIES AND BUSINESS ORGANIZATION

Four main global strategies form the basis for the organizational structures of global firms. These are domestic exporter, multinational, franchiser, and transnational. Each of these strategies is pursued with a specific business organizational structure (see Table 15.3). For simplicity's sake, we describe three kinds of organizational structure or governance: centralized (in the home country), decentralized (to local foreign units), and coordinated (all units participate as equals). There are other types of governance patterns observed in specific companies (e.g., authoritarian dominance by one unit, a confederacy of equals, a federal structure balancing power among strategic units, and so forth; see Keen, 1991).

The **domestic exporter** strategy is characterized by heavy centralization of corporate activities in the home country of origin. Nearly all international companies begin this way, and some move on to other forms. Production, finance/accounting, sales/marketing, human resources, and strategic management are set up to optimize resources in the home country. International sales are sometimes dispersed using agency agreements or subsidiaries, but even

domestic exporter

A strategy characterized by heavy centralization of corporate activities in the home country of origin.

TABLE 15.3	GLOBAL BUSINESS STRATEGY AND STRUCTURE			
Business Function	Domestic Exporter	Multinational	Franchiser	Transnational
Production	Centralized	Dispersed	Coordinated	Coordinated
Finance/Accounting	Centralized	Centralized	Centralized	Coordinated
Sales/Marketing	Mixed	Dispersed	Coordinated	Coordinated
Human Resources	Centralized	Centralized	Coordinated	Coordinated
Strategic Management	Centralized	Centralized	Centralized	Coordinated

here, foreign marketing is totally reliant on the domestic home base for marketing themes and strategies. Toromont Corporation and other heavy capital-equipment manufacturers fall into this category of firm.

multinational

A global strategy that concentrates financial management and control out of a central home base while decentralizing production, sales, and marketing operations to units in other countries.

The **multinational** strategy concentrates financial management and control out of a central home base while decentralizing production, sales, and marketing operations to units in other countries. The products and services on sale in different countries are adapted to suit local market conditions. The organization becomes a far-flung confederation of production and marketing facilities in different countries. Many financial service firms, such as HSBC Holdings Ltd. or TD (Toronto-Dominion) Canada Trust, along with a host of manufacturers, such as General Motors, Chrysler, and Intel, fit this pattern.

franchiser

A firm where a product is created, designed, financed, and initially produced in the home country but, for product-specific reasons, must rely heavily on foreign personnel for further production, marketing, and human resources.

Franchisers are an interesting mix of old and new. On the one hand, the product is created, designed, financed, and initially produced in the home country but, for product-specific reasons, must rely heavily on foreign personnel for further production, marketing, and human resources. Food franchisers, such as McDonald's, Mrs. Fields Cookies, and Kentucky Fried Chicken (KFC), fit this pattern. McDonald's created a new form of fast-food chain in the United States and continues to rely largely on the United States for inspiration of new products, strategic management, and financing. Nevertheless, because the product must be produced locally—as it is perishable—extensive coordination and dispersal of production, local marketing, and local recruitment of personnel are required. Generally, foreign franchisees are clones of the mother country units, but fully coordinated worldwide production that could optimize factors of production is not possible. For instance, potatoes and beef can generally not be bought where they are cheapest on world markets but must be produced or obtained from producers reasonably close to the area of consumption.

transnational

Truly globally managed firms that have no national headquarters; value-added activities are managed from a global perspective without reference to national borders, optimizing sources of supply and demand and taking advantage of any local competitive advantage.

Transnational firms are the stateless, truly globally managed firms that may represent a larger part of international business in the future. Transnational firms have no single national headquarters but, instead, have many regional headquarters and perhaps a world headquarters. In a **transnational** strategy, nearly all the value-adding activities are managed from a global perspective without reference to national borders, optimizing sources of supply and demand wherever they appear, and taking advantage of any local competitive advantages. Transnational firms take the globe, not the home country, as their management frame of reference. The governance of these firms has been likened to a federal structure in which there is a strong central management core of decision making, but considerable dispersal of power and financial muscle throughout the global divisions. Few companies have actually attained transnational status, but Citicorp, Sony, Ford, and others are attempting this transition.

Information technology and improvements in global telecommunications are giving international firms more flexibility to shape their global strategies. Protectionism and a need to serve local markets better encourage companies to disperse production facilities and at least become multinational. At the same time, the drive to achieve economies of scale and take advantage of short-term local advantage moves transnationals toward a global management perspective and a concentration of power and authority. Hence, there are forces of decentralization and dispersal, as well as forces of centralization and global coordination (Ives and Jarvenpaa, 1991).

GLOBAL SYSTEMS TO FIT THE STRATEGY

Information technology and improvements in global telecommunications are giving international firms more flexibility to shape their global strategies. The configuration, management, and development of systems tend to follow the global strategy chosen (Roche, 1992; Ives and Jarvenpaa, 1991). Figure 15.2 depicts the typical arrangements. By *systems*, we mean the full range of activities involved in developing information systems: conception and alignment with the strategic business plan, systems development, and ongoing operation. For the sake of simplicity, we consider four types of systems configuration. *Centralized systems* are those in which systems development and operation occur totally at the domestic home base. *Duplicated systems* are those in which development occurs at the home base, but operations are handed over to autonomous units in foreign locations. *Decentralized systems* are those in which each foreign unit designs its own unique solutions and systems. *Networked systems* are those in which systems development and operations occur in an integrated and coordinated fashion across all units.

SYSTEM CONFIGURATION	Strategy			
	Domestic Exporter	Multinational	Franchiser	Transnational
Centralized	X			
Duplicated			X	
Decentralized	x	X	x	
Networked		x		X

Figure 15.2 Global strategy and systems configurations. The large Xs show the dominant patterns, and the small Xs show the emerging patterns. For instance, domestic exporters rely predominantly on centralized systems, but there is continual pressure and some development of decentralized systems in local marketing regions.

As can be seen in Figure 15.2, domestic exporters tend to have highly centralized systems in which a single domestic systems development group develops worldwide applications. Multinationals offer a direct and striking contrast: Here foreign units devise their own systems solutions based on local needs with few, if any, applications in common with headquarters (the exceptions being financial reporting and some telecommunications applications). Franchisers have the simplest systems structure: Like the products they sell, franchisers develop a single system usually at the home base and then replicate it around the world. Each unit, no matter where it is located, has identical applications. Last, the most ambitious form of systems development is found in the transnational: Networked systems are those in which there is a solid, singular global environment for developing and operating systems. This usually presupposes a powerful telecommunications backbone, a culture of shared applications development, and a shared management culture that crosses cultural barriers. The networked systems structure is the most visible in financial services, where the homogeneity of the product—money and money instruments—seems to overcome cultural barriers.

REORGANIZING THE BUSINESS

How should a firm organize itself for doing business on an international scale? To develop a global company and information systems support structure, a firm needs to follow these principles:

1. Organize value-adding activities along lines of comparative advantage. For instance, marketing/sales functions should be located where they can best be performed, for least cost and maximum impact; the same is true of production, finance, human resources, and information systems.

2. Develop and operate systems units at each level of corporate activity—regional, national, and international. To serve local needs, there should be *host country systems units* of some magnitude. *Regional systems units* should handle telecommunications and systems development across national boundaries that take place within major geographic regions (European, Asian, American). *Transnational systems units* should be established to create the linkages across major regional areas and coordinate the development and operation of international telecommunications and systems development (Roche, 1992).

3. Establish at world headquarters a single office responsible for the development of international systems and a global chief information officer (CIO) position.

Many successful companies have devised organizational systems structures along these principles. The success of these companies relies not only on the proper organization of activities but also on a key ingredient—a management team that can understand the risks and benefits of international systems and that can devise strategies for overcoming the risks. We turn to these management topics next.

15.3 MANAGING GLOBAL SYSTEMS

Table 15.4 lists the principal management problems encountered while developing international systems. It is interesting to note that these problems are the chief difficulties managers experience in developing ordinary domestic systems as well! But these are enormously complicated in the international environment.

TABLE 15.4	MANAGEMENT CHALLENGES IN DEVELOPING GLOBAL SYSTEMS

Agreeing on common user requirements

Introducing changes in business processes

Coordinating applications development

Coordinating software releases

Encouraging local users to support global systems

A TYPICAL SCENARIO: DISORGANIZATION ON A GLOBAL SCALE

Let us look at a common scenario. A traditional multinational consumer-goods company based in Canada and operating in Europe would like to expand into Asian markets and knows that it must develop a transnational strategy and a supportive information systems structure. Like most multinationals, it has dispersed production and marketing to regional and national centres while maintaining its world headquarters and strategic management in Canada. Historically, it has allowed each of the subsidiary foreign divisions to develop its own systems. The only centrally coordinated system is financial controls and reporting. The central systems group in Canada focuses only on domestic functions and production. The result is a hodgepodge of hardware, software, and telecommunications. The e-mail systems between Europe and Canada are incompatible. Each production facility uses a different manufacturing resources planning system (or a different version with local variations), and different marketing, sales, and human resource systems. The technology platforms are wildly different: Europe is using mostly UNIX-based file servers and IBM personal computer (PC) clones on desktops. Communications between different sites are poor, given the high cost and low quality of European intercountry communications. The Canadian group is moving from an IBM mainframe environment centralized at headquarters to a highly distributed network architecture, with local sites developing their own local area networks (LANs). The central systems group at headquarters recently was decimated and dispersed to the Canadian local sites in the hope of serving local needs better and reducing costs.

What do you recommend to the senior management leaders of this company, who now want to pursue a transnational strategy and develop an information systems architecture to support a highly coordinated global systems environment? Consider the problems you face by re-examining Table 15.4. The foreign divisions will resist efforts to agree on common user requirements; they have never thought beyond their own units' needs. The systems groups in Canadian local sites, which have been enlarged recently and told to focus on local needs, will not easily accept guidance from anyone recommending a transnational strategy. It will be difficult to convince local managers anywhere in the world that they should change their business procedures to align with other units in the world, especially if this might interfere with their local performance. After all, local managers are rewarded in this company for meeting local objectives of their division or plant. Finally, it will be difficult to coordinate development of projects around the world in the absence of a powerful telecommunications network and, therefore, difficult to encourage local users to take on ownership in the systems developed.

STRATEGY: DIVIDE, CONQUER, APPEASE

core systems

Systems that support functions that are absolutely critical to the organization.

Figure 15.3 lays out the main dimensions of a solution. First, consider that not all systems should be coordinated on a transnational basis; only some core systems are truly worth sharing from a cost and feasibility point of view. **Core systems** are systems that support functions that are absolutely critical to the organization. Other systems should be partially coordinated because they share key elements, but they do not have to be totally uniform across national boundaries. For such systems, a good deal of local variation is possible and desirable. A final group of systems are peripheral and truly provincial and are needed to satisfy local requirements.

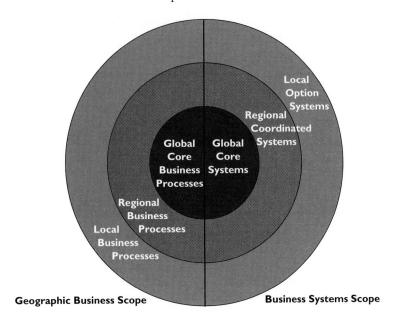

Geographic Business Scope   **Business Systems Scope**

Figure 15.3 Agency and other coordination costs increase as the firm moves from local option systems toward regional and global systems. However, transaction costs of participating in global markets probably decrease as firms develop global systems. A sensible strategy is to reduce agency costs by developing only a few core global systems that are vital for global operations, leaving other systems in the hands of regional and local units.

Source: From *Managing Information Technology in Multinational Corporations* by Edward M. Roche, © 1992. Adapted by permission of Prentice Hall, Inc., Upper Saddle River, NJ.

Define the Core Business Processes

How do you identify *core systems?* The first step is to define a short list of critical core business processes. Business processes were defined in Chapters 1 and 2, which you should review now. Briefly, business processes are sets of logically related tasks, such as shipping out correct orders to customers or delivering innovative products to the market. Each business process typically involves many functional areas, communicating and coordinating work, information, and knowledge.

The way to identify these core business processes is to conduct a workflow analysis. How are customer orders taken, what happens to them once they are taken, who fills the orders, how are they shipped to the customers? What about suppliers? Do they have access to manufacturing resource planning systems so that supply is automatic? You should be able to identify and set priorities in a short list of 10 business processes that are absolutely critical for the firm.

Next, can you identify centres of excellence for these processes? Is customer order fulfillment in Canada, manufacturing process control in Germany, or human resources in Asia superior? You should be able to identify some areas of the company, for some lines of business, where a division or unit stands out in the performance of one or several business functions.

When you understand the business processes of a firm, you can rank-order them. You can then decide which processes should be core applications, centrally coordinated, designed, and implemented around the globe, and which should be regional and local. At the same time, by identifying the critical business processes—the really important ones—you have gone a long way to defining a vision of the future that you should be working toward.

Identify the Core Systems to Coordinate Centrally

By identifying the critical core business processes, you begin to see opportunities for transnational systems. The second strategic step is to conquer the core systems and define these systems as truly transnational. The financial and political costs of defining and implementing transnational systems are extremely high. Therefore, keep the list to an absolute minimum, letting experience be the guide and erring on the side of minimalism. By dividing off a small group of systems as absolutely critical, you divide opposition to a transnational strategy. At the same time, you can appease those who oppose the central worldwide coordination implied by transnational systems by permitting peripheral systems development to progress unabated, with the exception of some technical platform requirements.

Choose an Approach: Incremental, Grand Design, Evolutionary

A third step is to choose an approach. Avoid piecemeal approaches. These surely will fail for lack of visibility, opposition from all who stand to lose from transnational development, and lack of power to convince senior management that the transnational systems are worth it. Likewise, avoid grand design approaches that try to do everything at once. These also tend to fail due to an inability to focus resources. Nothing gets done properly, and opposition to organizational change is needlessly strengthened because the effort requires huge resources. An alternative approach is to evolve transnational applications from existing applications with a precise and clear vision of the transnational capabilities the organization should have in five years.

Make the Benefits Clear

What is in it for the company? One of the worst situations that should be avoided is to develop global systems for the sake of developing global systems. From the beginning, it is crucial that senior management at headquarters and foreign division managers clearly understand the benefits that will come to the company as well as to individual units. Although each system offers unique benefits to a particular budget, the overall contribution of global systems lies in four areas.

Global systems—truly integrated, distributed, and transnational systems—contribute to superior management and coordination. A simple price tag cannot be put on the value of this contribution, and the benefit will not show up in any capital budgeting model. It is the ability to switch suppliers on a moment's notice from one region to another in a crisis, to move production in response to natural disasters, and to use excess capacity in one region to meet raging demand in another.

A second major contribution is vast improvement in production, operation, and supply and distribution. Imagine a global value chain, with global suppliers and a global distribution network. For the first time, senior managers can locate value-adding activities in regions where they are most economically performed.

Third, global systems mean global customers and global marketing. Fixed costs around the world can be amortized over a much larger customer base. This will unleash new economies of scale at production facilities.

Last, global systems mean the ability to optimize the use of corporate funds over a much larger capital base. This means, for instance, that capital in a surplus region can be moved efficiently to expand production of capital-starved regions; that cash can be managed more effectively within the company and put to use more effectively.

These strategies will not by themselves create global systems. You will have to implement what you strategize, and this is a whole new challenge.

IMPLEMENTATION TACTICS: COOPTATION

The overall tactic for dealing with resistant local units in a transnational company is cooptation. **Cooptation** is defined as bringing the opposition into the process of designing and implementing the solution without giving up control over the direction and nature of the change. As much as possible, raw power should be avoided. Minimally, however, local units must agree on a short list of transnational systems, and raw power may be required to solidify the idea that transnational systems of some sort are truly required.

How should cooptation proceed? Several alternatives are possible. One alternative is to permit each national unit the opportunity to develop one transnational application first in its home territory and then throughout the world. In this manner, each major national systems group is given a piece of the action in developing a transnational system, and local units feel a sense of ownership in the transnational effort. On the downside, this assumes the ability to develop high-quality systems is widely distributed and that, say, the German team can successfully implement the new systems in France and Italy. This will not always be the case. Also, the transnational effort will have low visibility.

A second tactic is to develop new transnational centres of excellence, or a single centre of excellence. There may be several centres around the globe that focus on specific business processes. These centres draw heavily from local national units, are based on multinational teams, and must report to worldwide management—their first line of responsibility is to the core applications. Centres of excellence perform the initial identification and specification of the business process, define the information requirements, perform the business and systems analysis, and accomplish all design and testing. Implementation, however, and pilot testing

cooptation

Bringing the opposition into the process of designing and implementing the solution without giving up control over the direction and nature of the change.

occur in world pilot regions, where new applications are installed and tested first. Later, they are rolled out to other parts of the globe. This phased rollout strategy is precisely how national applications are successfully developed.

The Window on Management shows how GN Netcom addressed these issues as it implemented enterprise and customer relationship management systems in 24 different countries.

THE MANAGEMENT SOLUTION

We now can reconsider how to handle the most vexing problems (described in Table 15.4) faced by managers developing transnational information system architectures.

Agreeing on Common User Requirements

Establishing a short list of the core business processes and core support systems will begin a process of rational comparison across the many divisions of the company, develop a common language for discussing the business, and naturally lead to an understanding of common elements (as well as the unique qualities that must remain local).

GN NETCOM'S GLOBAL SYSTEMS CHALLENGE

Denmark-based GN Netcom A/S is a leading supplier of wireless headsets for corporate call centres and hands-free products for mobile phones. As the company expanded into 24 countries in Europe, Canada, the United States, Australia, and Asia, it faced the difficult task of trying to standardize its information systems while making sure that these systems had the flexibility to adapt to local market business requirements.

The company decided it needed centrally run production, supply chain, distribution, finance, and customer relationship management systems. One of the company's first steps was to consolidate its finished goods manufacturing and assembly operations from several plants in Europe and the United States to a plant in Xiamen, China. The lower cost of the Chinese workforce would have seemed to be the obvious reason. But GN Netcom only made the change because of the Chinese workers' skill and willingness to learn. The move worked so well that the 170-person staff in Xiamen is now managing GN Netcom's global supply chain, inventory, and distribution logistics, none of which had been centralized in the past.

GN Netcom next began to install global enterprise resource planning (ERP) and customer relationship management (CRM) software to work with its already installed global chart of accounts. Netcom's Chief Information Officer (CIO) Michael Young explained that the overall system "will provide the vehicle to easily and consistently capture the critical profit and loss numbers, analyze them, and share the business metrics locally and globally." Managers at corporate headquarters will be able to view data by individual countries, sum of countries, or region.

The problems of installing these systems were complex. For example, the tax structures differ greatly in the various countries, and the software had to handle such diversity. GN Netcom selected Navision Attain as the core of its CRM and ERP systems, partly because the software encompasses financials, order entry, inventory management, shipping, receiving and returns, customer services, and CRM. However, central to GN Netcom's requirements was that the software also had versions for local languages and countries. The company also selected Hyperion Solution's data warehousing and financial reporting systems, which together enable headquarters and local offices to see sales trends and business performances.

To face global installation problems, Young established a corporate implementation team with a development manager who spent four months just to plan the rollout for each region and country. He established a single development methodology for the whole process so that all the countries would be working the same way. Young named "a champion" in each country, and said "[I] learn from that person. I ask him [or her] how to communicate [with] and respect [her countrymen]." He continued "It's about listening, and culturally, not to be seen as an arrogant, know-it-all team." Young concluded, "As soon as we show that we respect [our co-workers] as equals, it's amazing the speed at which people move." Young made sure that managers in each country were well trained and well informed about the details of the project.

Young points out that installing the same hardware and software environments in each country has resulted in the ability of GN Netcom to move employees anywhere in the world where they are needed. He also claims the new global systems are reducing the headcounts in finance, administration, and inventory management while keeping the sales and marketing staffs the same size despite the rapidly growing business volume.

To Think About: What were the management, technology, and organization problems that GN Netcom had to face when implementing its global systems? How well did GN Netcom deal with these problems?

Source: Ann Toh, "Attack of the Vikings," *CIO Asia*, March 2002; GN Netcom corporate Web site, **www.gnnetcom.com**, accessed June 25, 2002.

Introducing Changes in Business Processes

Your success as a change agent will depend on your legitimacy, your actual raw power, and your ability to involve users in the change design process. **Legitimacy** is defined as the extent to which your authority is accepted on grounds of competence, vision, or other qualities. The selection of a viable change strategy, which we have defined as evolutionary but with a vision, should assist you in convincing others that the change is feasible and desirable. Involving people in the change, assuring them that it is in the best interests of the company and their local units is a key tactic.

Coordinating Applications Development

Choice of change strategy is critical for tackling this problem. At the global level, there is far too much complexity to attempt a grand design strategy of change. It is far easier to coordinate change by making small incremental steps toward a larger vision. Imagine a five-year plan of action, rather than a two-year plan of action, and reduce the set of transnational systems to a bare minimum to reduce coordination costs.

Coordinating Software Releases

Firms can institute procedures to ensure that all operating units convert to new software updates at the same time so that everyone's software is compatible.

Encouraging Local Users to Support Global Systems

The key here is to involve users in the design without giving up control over the development of the project to parochial interests. Recruiting a wide range of local individuals to transnational centres of excellence helps send the message that all significant groups are involved in the design and will have an influence.

Even with the proper organizational structure and appropriate management choices, it is still possible to stumble over technological issues. Choices of technology, platforms, networks, hardware, and software are the final elements in building transnational information system infrastructures.

15.4 TECHNOLOGY ISSUES AND OPPORTUNITIES FOR GLOBAL VALUE CHAINS

Information technology is itself a powerful business driver for encouraging the development of global systems and global value chains, where firms can coordinate commercial transactions and production with other firms across many different locations throughout the world. Companies pursuing electronic business on a global scale and digital integration with their customers and value partners face many challenges (Farhoomand, Tuunainen, and Yee, 2000). The Manager's Toolkit on How to Develop a Global Electronic Commerce Strategy can help managers determine how to face these challenges.

MAIN TECHNICAL ISSUES

Hardware, software, and telecommunications pose special technical challenges in an international setting. The major hardware challenge is finding some way to standardize the firm's computer hardware platform when there is so much variation from operating unit to operating unit and from country to country. Managers need to think carefully about where to locate the firm's computer centres and how to select hardware suppliers. The major global software challenge is finding applications that are user friendly and that truly enhance the productivity of international work teams. The major telecommunications challenge is making data flow seamlessly across networks shaped by disparate national standards. Overcoming these challenges requires systems integration and connectivity on a global basis.

Hardware and Systems Integration

The development of global systems based on the concept of core systems raises questions about how the new core systems will fit in with the existing suite of applications developed around the globe by different divisions, different people, and for different kinds of computing hardware. The goal is to develop global, distributed, and integrated systems where business processes spanning national boundaries have become highly digital. Briefly, these are the same problems faced by any large domestic systems development effort. However, the problems are more complex because of the international environment. For instance, in Canada, IBM operating systems have played the predominant role in developing core systems for large organizations, while in Europe, UNIX was much more commonly used for large systems. How can the two be integrated in a common transnational system?

The correct solution often will depend on the history of the company's systems and the extent of commitment to proprietary systems. For instance, finance and insurance firms typically have relied almost exclusively on IBM proprietary equipment and architectures, and it would be extremely difficult and cost ineffective to abandon that equipment and software. Newer firms and manufacturing firms generally find it much easier to adopt open UNIX systems for international systems. As pointed out in previous chapters, open UNIX-based systems are far more cost effective in the long run, provide more power at a cheaper price, and preserve options for future expansion.

After a hardware platform is chosen, the question of standards must be addressed. Just because all sites use the same hardware does not guarantee common, integrated systems. Some central authority in the firm must establish data and other technical standards that sites must comply with. For instance, technical accounting terms, such as the beginning and end of the fiscal year, must be standardized (review our earlier discussion of the cultural challenges to building global businesses), as well as the acceptable interfaces among systems, communication speeds and architectures, and network software.

Connectivity

The heart of the international systems challenge is telecommunications—linking together the systems and people of a global firm into a single integrated network, just like the phone system but capable of voice, data, and image transmissions. However, integrated global networks are extremely difficult to create (Lai and Chung, 2002). For example, many countries cannot fulfill basic business telecommunications needs, such as obtaining reliable circuits, coordinating among different carriers and the regional telecommunications authority, obtaining bills in a common currency standard, and obtaining standard agreements for the level of telecommunications service provided. Table 15.5 lists the major challenges posed by international networks.

Despite moves toward economic unity, Europe remains a hodgepodge of disparate national technical standards and service levels. Although most circuits leased by multinational corporations are fault-free more than 99.8 percent of the time, line quality and service vary widely from the north to the south of Europe. Network service is much more unreliable in southern Europe.

Existing European standards for networking and EDI (electronic data interchange) are very industry specific and country specific. Most European banks use the SWIFT (Society for Worldwide Interbank Financial Telecommunications) protocol for international funds transfer, while automobile companies and food producers often use industry- or country-specific

TABLE 15.5	PROBLEMS OF INTERNATIONAL NETWORKS

Costs and tariffs

Network management

Installation delays

Poor quality of international service

Regulatory constraints

Changing user requirements

Disparate standards

Network capacity

versions of standard protocols for EDI. Complicating matters further, the North American standard for EDI is ANSI (American National Standards Institute) X.12. The Open Systems Interconnect (OSI) reference model for linking networks is more popular in Europe than it is in North America. Even standards for cellular phone systems vary from country to country.

Firms have several options for providing international connectivity: build their own international private network, rely on a network service based on the public switched networks throughout the world, or use the Internet and intranets.

One possibility is for the firm to put together its own private network based on leased lines from each country's PTT (post, telegraph, and telephone authorities). Each country, however, has different restrictions on data exchange, technical standards, and acceptable vendors of equipment. These problems are magnified in certain parts of the world. Despite these limitations, in Europe and North America, reliance on PTTs still makes sense while these public networks expand services to compete with private providers.

The major alternative to building one's own network is to use one of several expanding network services. With deregulation of telecommunications around the globe, private providers have sprung up to service business customers' data needs, along with some voice and image communication.

Already common in North America, IVANS (International Value-Added Network Services) are expanding in Europe and Asia. These private firms offer value-added telecommunications capacity, usually rented from local PTTs or international satellite authorities, and then resell it to corporate users. IVANs add value by providing protocol conversion, operating mailboxes and mail systems, and offering integrated billing that permits a firm to track its data communications costs. Currently, these systems are limited to data transmissions, but in the future, they will expand to voice and image.

The third alternative, which is becoming increasingly attractive, is to create global intranets to use the Internet for international communication. However, the Internet is not yet a worldwide tool because many countries lack the communications infrastructure for extensive Internet use. These countries face high costs, government control, or government monitoring. Many of them also do not have the speedy and reliable postal and package delivery services that are essential for electronic commerce (DePalma, 2000).

Western Europe faces both high transmission costs and lack of common technology because it is not politically unified and because European telecommunications systems are still in the process of shedding their government monopolies. The lack of infrastructure and the high costs of installing one are even more prevalent in the rest of the world. The International Telecommunications Union estimated that only 500 million of the world's 1.5 billion households have basic telephone services (Wysocki, 2000). Low penetration of PCs and widespread illiteracy limit the demand for Internet service in India (Burkhardt, Goodman, Mehta, and Press, 1999). When an infrastructure does exixt in a less-developed country, it is often outdated, lacks digital circuits, and has very noisy lines. The purchasing power of most people in the developing countries makes access to Internet services very expensive (Petrazzini and Kibati, 1999).

Governments of many countries, including China and Singapore, monitor Internet traffic and block access to Web sites considered morally or politically offensive. Corporations may be discouraged from using this medium. Companies planning international operations through the Internet still will have many hurdles.

Software

Compatible hardware and communications provide a platform but not the total solution. Also critical to global core infrastructure is software. The development of core systems poses unique challenges for software: How will the old systems interface with the new? Entirely new interfaces must be developed and tested if old systems are kept in local areas (which is common). These interfaces can be costly and messy to develop. If new software must be created, another challenge is to develop software that can be realistically used by multiple business units from different countries, given that these business units are accustomed to their unique business processes and definitions of data.

Besides integrating the new with the old systems, there are problems of human interface design and functionality of systems. For instance, to be truly useful for enhancing the productivity of a global workforce, software interfaces must be understood easily and mastered quickly. Graphical user interfaces are ideal for this but presuppose knowledge of a common language—often English. When international systems involve knowledge workers only, English may be the assumed international standard. But as international systems penetrate deeper into management and clerical groups, a common language may not be assumed, and human interfaces must be developed to accommodate different languages and even conventions.

What are the most important software applications? Many international systems focus on basic transaction and MIS reporting systems. Increasingly, such firms as CIBA Vision, described in the Window on Technology, are turning to supply chain management and enterprise systems to standardize their business processes on a global basis and to create coordinated global supply chains. However, these cross-functional systems are not always compatible with differences in languages, cultural heritages, and business processes in other countries (Davison, 2002; Soh, Kien, and Tay-Yap, 2000). Company units in countries that are not technically sophisticated may also encounter problems trying to manage the technical complexities of supply chain management and enterprise software.

CIBA VISION BRINGS WORLDWIDE INVENTORY INTO CLEAR SIGHT

CIBA Vision, headquartered in Atlanta, Georgia, is a division of Swiss pharmaceutical giant Novartis AG and was established in 1980. While it has become one of the largest suppliers of contact lenses in the world, growth has presented major problems. In the last 10 years, the contact lens business has been transformed as contact lens users have changed from using one pair of lenses each year to using disposable lenses once or even twice a day. At the same time, the company expanded into a global company and now sells massive numbers of lenses worldwide. The company currently makes and keeps track of about 120 000 different types of lenses because they vary in both power and colour. Supplying and satisfying customers became a nightmare, partly because, as a global company, only 40 percent of its inventory was even visible at headquarters. Unni Makkuni, CIBA Vision's supply chain manager, claims he (and others reporting to him) "used to spend pretty much 70 percent of our time trying to chase down supply chain information." The reason, according to Makkuni, was that the company was "a highly decentralized operation in terms of supply chain... We didn't maximize the efficiencies of our inventories. We had excess inventories in one place and a lack of inventory in other places." CIBA Vision needed to make its item-level forecasts more accurate in every country, a very complex requirement.

The company realized it had to turn to more advanced supply chain software. CIBA Vision's goal was to achieve 99.9 percent product availability and simultaneously reduce its inventory. Makkuni wanted to "maximize the efficiencies of our inventories," thereby reducing inventory size and costs. After carefully assessing major supply chain vendors, such as SAP and Manugistics, CIBA Vision settled on 12 Technologies of Dallas, Texas, because its software appeared to closely match CIBA Vision's business requirements. Implementation of the new systems was a multi-

million-dollar project, which began in 2000 and still was not quite fully completed as of mid-2002.

i2's Active Data Warehouse (ASW) software is a repository for all forecasting and planning data. It accepts daily data feeds from 46 systems worldwide, including the company's distribution centres and bulk warehouses. Key to CIBA Vision's needs is that the system cleans up and standardizes the data from the company's various sites around the world. The ASW is the data source for the daily planning systems. Supply chain information, including inventories, back orders, pending orders, and allocated orders, is immediately available. Using these data, the Demand Planner (DP) provides item-specific forecasts based on each country's specific historical usage patterns. These software systems have raised the global inventory visibility to over 90 percent. i2's Inventory Planner (IP) models these variations in different systems around the world to determine an appropriate inventory target and calculates the optimal level in inventory at the various supply points in the supply chain. Looking at the value of i2's software, Makkuni said, "We have been able to have significantly improved the item forecast at a country level."

The i2 system has improved coordination between manufacturing, distribution, and supply chain management, helping CIBA Vision reduce the cycle time for introducing new products by almost 50 percent. CIBA Vision has now achieved 99.5 percent product availability worldwide while realizing a considerable reduction in inventories and inventory costs.

To Think About: How did a new supply chain management system help CIBA Vision's supply chain problems? What value did it provide for the company? What difficulties do you think CIBA may have encountered in implementing this system?

Sources: Peter A Buxbaum, "Ciba Vision Keeps Eye on Supply Chain with i2 Tools," *SearchEBusiness.com,* May 28, 2002; i2 Technologies, "Bringing Vision into the Supply Chain at CIBA Vision," www.i2.com, accessed June 19, 2002.

MIS IN ACTION: MANAGER'S TOOLKIT

HOW TO DEVELOP A GLOBAL ELECTRONIC COMMERCE STRATEGY

Developing a successful global electronic commerce strategy requires a careful assessment of costs and benefits as well as knowledge of global markets and business practices. Here are some basic questions that must be answered:

1. *What is the opportunity?* Do you have a product or service that travels well? Can your product be sold "as-is" outside your domestic market, or does it require some modification for other countries?

2. *What are the impediments to sales?* What are the national laws, business regulations, tariffs, and privacy policies that might apply to your product? Is there a good infrastructure in place for transporting your product to customers?

3. *Can people actually buy what you are selling?* Is there a large enough online population in your target market? Do online consumers have enough disposable income to buy what you want to sell? Do these consumers have the means to pay for purchases online?

4. *What is the nature of the competition?* Are there other companies selling a product or service that directly competes with yours abroad? Can you deliver your product or service with a better value proposition for international customers?

5. *What are the costs and benefits of selling internationally online?* How much will it cost to develop an electronic commerce Web site for international sales? Are special language support, currency conversion, or personalization capabilities required? How do these costs compare to the revenue you could generate from international electronic commerce sales?

EDI (electronic data interchange) is a common global transaction processing application used by manufacturing and distribution firms to connect units of the same company, as well as customers and suppliers on a global basis. Groupware systems, e-mail, and videoconferencing, are especially important worldwide collaboration tools for knowledge- and data-based firms, such as advertising firms, research-based firms in medicine and engineering, and graphics and publishing firms. The Internet will be increasingly employed for these purposes. (See Figure 15.4.)

NEW TECHNICAL OPPORTUNITIES AND THE INTERNET

Technical advances described in Chapter 8, such as wireless and digital subscriber line (DSL) services, should continue to fall in price and gain in power, facilitating the creation and operation of global networks. *Communicate and compute anytime, anywhere* networks based on satellite systems, digital cell phones, and personal communications services will make it even easier to coordinate work and information in many parts of the globe that cannot be reached by existing ground-based systems. Thus, a salesperson in China could send an order-confirmation request to the home office in Vancouver effortlessly and expect an instant reply. (See Figure 15.5.)

Figure 15.4 This Web page from the Prentice Hall Web site, the U.S. counterpart to the publisher for this text, was translated into Spanish using AltaVista's translation tools. Web sites and software interfaces for global systems may have to be translated to accommodate users in other parts of the world.

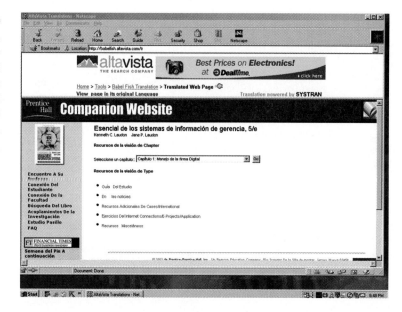

Figure 15.5 Asian Sources is a portal for promoting business in East Asia. It includes a directory of businesses and search capabilities for locating businesses and products of interest to users.

Companies are using Internet technology to construct virtual private networks (VPNs) to reduce wide area networking (WAN) costs and staffing requirements. Instead of using private, leased telephone lines or frame-relay connections, the company outsources the VPN to an Internet service provider. The VPN comprises WAN links, security products, and routers, providing a secure and encrypted connection between two points across the Internet to transmit corporate data. VPNs from Internet service providers can provide many features of a private network to firms operating internationally.

However, VPNs may not provide the same level of quick and predictable response as private networks, especially during times of the day when Internet traffic is very congested. Also, VPNs may not be able to support large numbers of remote users.

MANAGEMENT WRAP-UP

Managers are responsible for devising an appropriate organizational and technology infrastructure for international business. Choosing a global business strategy, identifying core business processes, organizing the firm to conduct business on an international scale, and developing an international information systems architecture are key management decisions.

Cultural, political, and language diversities magnify the differences in organizational cultures and standard operating procedures when companies operate internationally. These differences create barriers to the development of global information systems that transcend national boundaries.

The main technology decision in developing international systems is finding a set of workable standards in hardware, software, and networking for the firm's international IT infrastructure and architecture. The Internet and intranets will increasingly be used to provide global connectivity and to serve as a foundation for global systems, but many companies will still need proprietary systems for certain functions.

For Discussion

1. If you were a manager in a company that operates in many countries, what criteria would you use to determine whether an application should be developed as a global application or as a local application?

2. Describe ways the Internet can be used in international information systems.

SUMMARY

1. *What are the major factors driving the internationalization of business?* There are general cultural factors and specific business factors to consider. The growth of cheap international communication and transportation has created a world culture with stable expectations or norms. Political stability and a growing global knowledge base that is widely shared contribute also to the world culture. These general factors create the conditions for global markets, global production, coordination, distribution, and global economies of scale.

2. *What strategies are available for developing international businesses?* There are four basic international strategies: domestic exporter, multinational, franchiser, and transnational. In a transnational strategy, all factors of production are coordinated on a global scale. However, the choice of strategy is a function of the type of business and product.

3. *How can information systems support the various international business strategies?* There is a connection between firm strategy and information systems design. Domestic exporters typically are centralized in domestic headquarters with some decentralized operations permitted. Multinationals typically rely on decentralized independence among foreign units with some movement toward development of networks. Franchisers almost always duplicate systems across many countries and use centralized financial controls. Transnational firms must develop networked system configurations and permit considerable decentralization of development and operations.

4. *What issues should managers address when developing international information systems?* Implementing a global system requires an implementation strategy. Typically, global systems have evolved without a conscious plan. The remedy is to define a small subset of core business processes and focus on developing systems that could support these processes. Tactically, you will have to coopt widely dispersed foreign units to participate in the development and operation of these systems, being careful to maintain overall control.

5. *What technical alternatives are available for developing global systems?* The main hardware and telecommunications issues are systems integration and connectivity. The choices for integration are to go with either a proprietary architecture or an open systems technology, such as UNIX. Global networks are extremely difficult to develop and operate. Some measure of connectivity may be achieved by relying on local PTT (post, telephone, and telegraph) authorities to provide connections, building a system oneself, relying on private providers to supply communications capacity, or using the Internet and intranets. Companies can use Internet services to create virtual private networks (VPNs) as low-cost alternatives to global private networks. The main software issue concerns developing interfaces to existing systems and providing much needed group support software.

KEY TERMS

Business driver, 499	Franchiser, 504	Legitimacy, 510	Transborder data flow,
Cooptation, 508	Global culture, 500	Multinational, 504	502
Core systems, 506	International information	Particularism, 502	Transnational, 504
Domestic exporter, 503	systems architecture, 499		

REVIEW QUESTIONS

1. What are the five major factors to consider when building an international information systems portfolio?

2. Describe the five general cultural factors leading toward growth in global business and the four specific business factors. Describe the interconnection among these factors.

3. What is meant by a *global culture?*

4. What are the major challenges to the development of global systems?

5. Why have firms not planned for the development of international systems?

6. Describe the four main strategies for global business and organizational structure.

7. Describe the four different system configurations that can be used to support different global strategies.

8. What are the major management issues in developing international systems?

9. What are the three principles to follow when organizing a firm for global business?

10. What are the three steps of a management strategy for developing and implementing global systems?

11. What is meant by *cooptation,* and how can it be used in building global systems?

12. Describe the main technical issues facing global systems.

13. Describe the three new technologies that can help firms develop global systems.

APPLICATION SOFTWARE EXERCISE

DATABASE AND WEB PAGE DEVELOPMENT TOOL EXERCISE: BUILDING A JOB DATABASE AND WEB PAGE FOR AN INTERNATIONAL CONSULTING FIRM

KTP Consulting operates in various locations around the world. KTP specializes in designing, developing, and implementing enterprise systems for medium to large-sized companies. KTP offers its employees opportunities to travel, live, and work in various locations throughout Canada, Europe, and Asia. The firm's human resources department has a simple database that enables its staff to track job vacancies. When an employee is interested in relocating, she or he contacts the human resources department for a list of KTP job vacancies. KTP also posts its employment opportunities on the company Web site.

What type of data should be included in the KTP job vacancies database? What information should not be included in this database? On the basis of your answers to these questions, build a job vacancies database for KTP. Populate the database with at least 20 records. You should also build a simple Web page that incorporates job vacancy data from your newly created database. Submit a disk containing a copy of the KTP database and Web page to your professor.

GROUP PROJECT

In a group of three or four students, identify an area of information technology, and explore how this technology might be useful for supporting global business strategies. For instance, you might choose such an area as digital telecommunications (e.g., e-mail, wireless communications), enterprise systems, collaborative work group software, or the Internet. It will be necessary to choose a business scenario to discuss the technology. You might choose, for instance, an automobile parts franchise or a financial institution, such as TD Trust. What applications would you make global, what core business processes would you choose, and how would the technology be helpful? If possible, use electronic presentation software to present your findings to the class.

 ## INTERNET TOOLS

COMPANION WEBSITE

The Companion Website for this chapter will take you to a series of Web sites where you can complete an exercise to evaluate the capabilities of various global package tracking and delivery services.

At **www.pearsoned.ca/laudon**, you will find valuable tools to facilitate and enhance your learning of this chapter as well as opportunities to apply your knowledge to realistic situations:

- An Interactive Study Guide of self-test questions that will provide you with immediate feedback.
- Application exercises.
- An Electronic Commerce Project that uses the interactive software at a series of Web sites for international marketing and pricing.
- A Management Decision Problem on planning a global Web site.
- Updates of material in the chapter.

ADDITIONAL SITES OF INTEREST

There are many interesting Web sites to enhance your learning about managing international information systems. You can search the Web yourself, or just try the following sites to add to what you have already learned.

International Systems Security Association
> **www.issa.org/**
>
> This not-for-profit, international organization of information security professionals and practitioners has 66 chapters in 10 countries, including Canada

Global Information Technology Management Association
> **www.gitma.org**
>
> The Global Information Technology Management Association's mission is to promote the careful examination and dissemination of information technology management issues in all parts of the world

Journal of Global IT Management
> **http://www.uncg.edu/bae/people/palvia/jgitm.htm**
>
> An academic journal on the topic that contains interesting articles about real-world scenarios from around the globe

CASE STUDY: *Nestlé Struggles with Enterprise Systems*

Nestlé SA is a giant food and pharmaceuticals company that operates virtually all over the world. Headquartered in Vevey, Switzerland, in 1999, the company had revenues of $70 billion and more than 230 000 employees at 500 facilities in 80 countries. Best known for its chocolate, coffee (it invented instant coffee), and milk products, Nestlé sells thousands of other items, most of which are adapted to fit local markets and cultures.

Traditionally, this huge firm has allowed each local organization to conduct business as it saw fit, taking into account the local conditions and business cultures. To support this decentralized strategy, it has had 80 different information technology units that run nearly 900 IBM AS/400 midrange computers, 15 mainframes, and 200 UNIX systems, enabling observers to describe its infrastructure as a veritable Tower of Babel. Interestingly, despite its size, the company has had no corporate computer centre.

However, Nestlé's management has found that allowing these local differences created inefficiencies and extra costs that could prevent the company from competing effectively in electronic commerce. For example, the lack of standard business processes prevented Nestlé from leveraging its worldwide buying power to obtain lower prices for its raw materials. Even though each factory uses the same global suppliers, each negotiated its own deals and prices.

Several years ago, Nestlé embarked on a program to standardize and coordinate its information systems and business processes. The company initially installed SAP's R/3 enterprise resource planning (ERP) software to integrate material, distribution, and accounting applications in the United States, Europe, and Canada.

Nestlé is working on extending its enterprise systems to all of its facilities to make its 500 facilities act as a unified electronic business. Once this project is completed, Nestlé will be able to use sales information from retailers on a global basis to measure the effectiveness of its promotional activities and to reduce overstocking and spoilage caused by having products sit too long on grocery shelves.

The experience of Nestlé USA illustrates some of the challenges Nestlé had to face in implementing enterprise systems. In 2001, Nestlé USA, an $8.1-billion subsidiary, was organized as a series of brands, each operating independently. So, for example, the Stouffer's and Carnation units were separate companies, each owned by Nestlé SA, the Swiss-based parent, but reporting to Nestlé USA. In 1991, Nestlé USA reorganized itself, and the different brands were brought under the parent American control. However, the Nestlé division headquarters were still dispersed, and each division was still free to make its own business decisions, although each one within the United States did report to Nestlé headquarters in Glendale, California. The situation did not really begin to change until the spring of 1997 with the arrival of Jeri Dunn as Vice-President and CIO of the American company.

Dunn actually knew Nestlé technology unusually well because of her long history with the company. In 1991, as Associate Director for Application Systems at Nestlé-owned Stouffer's Hotels, she was sent to Switzerland to participate in an effort to establish a common worldwide methodology for Nestlé

projects. In 1995, she was promoted to Assistant Vice-President of Technology and Standards for Nestlé SA and, while in Switzerland, came to understand and agree with the value of establishing common systems throughout global Nestlé because such a change would enable group buying which, in turn, would reduce costs. Dunn also realized that common systems would facilitate data sharing among subsidiaries. When she was moved to Nestlé USA in 1997 at age 42, she found that her earlier recommendations from Vevey had been mostly ignored. "My team could name the standards," Dunn said, "but the implementation rollout was at the whim of the businesses."

When she arrived, Dunn found that Joe Weller, Chairman and CEO of Nestlé USA, wanted to integrate the company, although he was not an information technology specialist. Dunn joined with the executives in charge of finance, supply chain, distribution, and purchasing to create a team to study the company's strengths and weaknesses. They found many problems including the revelation that the company was paying 29 different prices for vanilla from the same vendor. Dunn's explanation was, "Every plant would buy vanilla from the vendor, and the vendor would just get whatever it thought it could get." She also realized that every division and every factory had assigned different names to the same product so that the company could not even check on the products. "We had no way of comparing," she said. When their studies were completed, they were given only two hours to present their findings to Weller and the rest of the executives. Some of those reporting were upset with the time limit, and in the end, they were given the whole day. Speaking later about the meeting, Dunn said, "[The executives] didn't know how ugly it was. We had nine different general ledgers and 28 points of customer entry. We had multiple purchasing systems. We had no clue how much volume we were doing with a particular vendor because every factory set up their own vendor masters and purchased on their own."

Soon after this meeting, the members of the team offered a three- to five-year plan for the necessary improvements. Central to the plan was the recommendation that the company install SAP, an ERP (enterprise resource planning) system. The team members expected the changeover to take three to five years. Dunn knew it was more than a software change, and she later said, "We made it very clear that this would be a business process reorganization and that you couldn't do it without changing the way you did business." The long time period was the result of Dunn's expectation that "there was going to be pain involved, it was going to be a slow process, and this was not a software project." By October, Nestlé had established a project team of 50 top business executives and 10 senior information systems professionals. They developed a set of best practices to become common work procedures for manufacturing, purchasing, accounting, and sales. A smaller technical team was set up that took 18 months to examine all the data for every item in all the divisions and set up a common data structure for the whole company.

At first, the project group decided not to use SAP's supply chain software because that module was brand new and appeared to be risky. It turned instead to Manugistics for its supply chain module. The team did decide to use SAP's purchasing, financials, sales, and distribution modules. All of these modules would be installed throughout every Nestlé USA division. The plan was completed by March 1998, and development work began in July 1998. The project was called BEST for "Business Excellence through Systems Technology."

In June 2000, Nestlé SA followed the lead of Nestlé USA and contracted with SAP to purchase and deploy the new version of their software called mySAP.com. The new system would not only standardize and coordinate the whole company's information systems and business processes, but it also would extend SAP's enterprise software to the Web. The new system would allow each Nestlé employee to start work from a personalized Web page linked to his or her job function. The employee's job was structured to conform to the "best practices" defined by SAP for 300 work roles. According to Jean Claud Dispaux, senior Nestlé Vice-President for Group Information Systems, "It is an exceptionally simple way to make sure that everyone does the same job in the same way." Nestlé will also create up to five computer centres around the world to run mySAP.com enterprise financial, accounts payable, accounts receivable, planning, production management, supply chain management, and business intelligence software. Nestlé publicity announced that the SAP contract would cost $300 million, plus Nestlé would add an additional $120 million for installing all the systems for the global company. However, a year after the announcement of the project, Anne Alexandre, an HSBC Holdings Ltd. Securities analyst in London who covers Nestlé, downgraded her Nestlé recommendation. Her reason was her doubts about the success of the project. "It touches the corporate culture, which is decentralized," she said, "and tries to centralize it." She added, "That's risky. It's always a risk when you touch the corporate culture." Jeri Dunn agreed after her experience with Best.

The major problem that Best faced in the United States was that both Weller and most of the key stakeholders failed to realize how much the project would change their business processes. Dunn later said, "They still thought it was just about software." The project had set a deadline for the first four modules (including Manugistics) of January 1, 2000, the date that the Year 2000 (Y2K) changes must be operating. They met this deadline, but it soon was clear that they had created as many problems as they had solved. In fact, a rebellion had already taken place when the team moved to install the Manugistics module.

The problem began during the early planning stage of the project when the staffs that would be directly affected by changes were not included in the key stakeholders' team. Dunn summed up the results, saying, "We were always surprising [the heads of sales and the divisions] because we would bring something up to the executive steering committee that they weren't privy to." By the beginning of 2000, it was clear that nobody wanted to learn the new processes; nobody wanted to make the changes. The lower-level workers did not understand how to use the new system and also did not understand the changes. Nobody had been prepared for the new ways of doing things, and their only hope was to call the project help desk. Dunn said the help desk reached a phenomenal 300 calls a day. The workers did not want to learn the changes. Even the divisional executives were confused and angry. No one

seemed willing to take the extra step to learn what to do. Turnover among the employees who were to use the Manugistics software to forecast product demand reached 77 percent. Those who remained found it easier to use their familiar spreadsheets.

The simultaneous installation of the Y2K changes also caused them problems. In the rush to be done on time, the team had failed to integrate the various modules. Therefore, for example, while the purchasing departments used the appropriate systems and data names, their systems were not integrated with the financial, planning, and sales software. As a result, when a salesperson gave a valued customer a special discount rate, it would be entered in the new system, but the accounts receivable department would not know about it and would think the customer did not fully pay its bill.

The team finally called a halt to the project in June 2000. Nestlé removed the project co-leader, and Dunn took over as the sole project leader. In October, Dunn held a three-day offsite retreat with the key stakeholders and the business executives. It became clear that the Y2K deadline of January 1, 2000, had put too much pressure on the project, and as a result, the members of the project team had lost sight of the bigger picture. They just focused on the technology. They now needed to integrate the existing components and to complete the work on the sales and distribution modules. Dunn also decided she now wanted to switch the supply chain module to the new SAP system because it had been improved since her rejection of it in 1998. By the time the retreat was ended, the team decided to start the whole project over again. It would first determine the business requirements and then decide on a new completion date, abandoning the earlier date. They also agreed to educate all employees affected so that they would know not only what changes were taking place but also why, how, and when those changes would happen.

The project team created a detailed design and project road map by April 2001. Nestlé also assigned one person, Tom James, to be Best's director of process change, giving him complete responsibility for liaison between the divisions and the Best project. The team also began taking repeated surveys of the effect of the project on employees and how they were dealing with it. James and Dunn began holding more meetings with the division heads. As a result of the information gathered in this way, James and Dunn determined the manufacturing users were not ready for the many changes, and so the rollout of that package was delayed for six months.

The new project was planned to be completed in the first quarter of 2003, late but successful. Already all of Nestlé USA are using the same software and data. The company not only has been able to produce better sales forecasts, but Dunn said the factories are following these better numbers. Altogether, the company says it already saved $325 million by spring 2002. And Nestlé SA has learned from that project and expects to have an easier success with its project. And that, Dunn says, is despite the fact that she only had to deal with eight or nine autonomous divisions, whereas the global headquarters was dealing with 80 autonomous countries to accomplish the same thing. She concluded by saying, "They're just taking it up a notch. If they go in with an attitude that there's not going to be resistance and pain, they're going to be disappointed."

Sources: Ben Worthen, "Nestlé's ERP Odyssey," *CIO Magazine*, May 15, 2002;William Echikson, "Nestlé: An Elephant Dances," *Business Week Online*, December 11, 2000, www.businessweek.com, accessed August 5, 2003; Steve Konicki, "Nestlé Taps SAP for E-Business," *InformationWeek*, June 26, 2000; and Candee Wilde, "SAP Customers Update Their ERP Applications," *InformationWeek*, June 12, 2000.

CASE STUDY QUESTIONS

1. Evaluate Nestlé SA and Nestlé USA by using the competitive forces and value chain models.

2. What were the problems and issues that Nestlé SA faced that caused the company to be so decentralized?

3. Do you think it was appropriate for Nestlé to distribute decision making so widely? Explain your answer.

4. Why did Nestlé's initial enterprise system project encounter so many problems? What management, organization, and technology factors contributed to those problems?

5. If you had been in charge of the Nestlé enterprise system project, what could you have done to prevent these problems?

Make IT Your Business

Decision Making in a Digital Age
Finance and Accounting

Many decision support systems (DSS) are based on financial models for breakeven analysis, profitability analysis, capital budgeting, and financial forecasting. Retail financial service firms depend on model-based DSS for client portfolio analysis and investment recommendations. Executive support systems (ESS) often provide overviews of firm-wide financial performance, including activity-based costing and financial measures for balanced scorecard reporting. Reporting monthly or yearly cash flows and balances is a typical management information system (MIS) for the finance and accounting function.

Many expert system, neural network, and hybrid artificial intelligence (AI) applications as well as knowledge work systems have been developed for the finance and accounting function. Rule-based expert systems have been widely used tools for evaluating the credit risk of loan applicants and for investment portfolio selection. A number of financial services firms use neural networks for stock and bond trading strategies, commodity trading, and detecting credit card fraud. Financial professionals use investment workstations that integrate a wide range of financial data from internal and external sources to support their research and analysis. The most widespread use of international systems is to allow for the flow of funds between corporate headquarters and operating units and to facilitate purchases in different countries. You can find examples of finance and accounting applications on pages 453, 454, 496–497, and 509.

Human Resources

The human resources function uses model-based decision support systems for analysis of labour contract costs or alternative compensation plans for nonunion employees. Executive information systems are used for human resources planning to project the firm's long-term labour force requirements. Comparing employee salaries to budgeted compensation amounts is a typical MIS for human resources. The human resources function uses Web publishing tools and intranets for knowledge dissemination to communicate company policies to employees and to provide online directories to human resource policies and training programs. Human resources systems may be used to identify employees with the requisite language and other skills to serve as leaders in international system projects or to work on assignments outside of their home country. You can find examples of human resources applications on page 475.

Manufacturing and Production

The manufacturing and production function requires many decisions about the optimization of production, logistics, and maintenance that must evaluate many interrelated variables. Model-based DSS have been guiding decisions about supply chain management, including the development of optimal production plans, delivery schedules, and inventory allocations. Recommending optimal plans for dispatching and routing vehicles and for facilities management are popular geographic information systems (GIS) applications. ESS can provide overviews of the firm's production resources. Comparing actual production amounts to targeted amounts for a monthly or yearly period is a typical MIS for manufacturing and production.

The manufacturing and production function is replete with knowledge system applications. Many companies are using intranets and group collaboration tools for sharing product design and manufacturing specifications among team members in many different locations and for project management. Robotic equipment now performs manufacturing tasks, such as welding or lifting heavy parts, that are too difficult or tedious for humans. Expert systems have been used to guide the configuration of orders when products with many different parts or features are being assembled. Both expert systems and case-based reasoning systems are used for assisting diagnostic and repair work on malfunctioning products and equipment. Fuzzy logic helps improve the performance of such products as camcorders, air conditioners, washing machines, and subway cars. Genetic algorithms have generated solutions for problems in optimizing scheduling or design.

Companies aspiring to some form of global business organization are installing standard supply chain management software or enterprise software for this purpose. Extranets can also be used to develop private industrial networks for this purpose. You can find examples of manufacturing and production applications on pages 442–443, 451, 453, 469, 492–495, 509, 513, and 518–520.

Sales and Marketing

DSS applications abound in sales and marketing. Model-driven DSS support decisions about product pricing, sales forecasting, and advertising and promotional campaigns. Companies increasingly use data-driven DSS for customer relationship management (CRM) to analyze customer purchasing patterns, detect customer retention problems, identify profitable customers, and develop targeted marketing campaigns. Some of these DSS for CRM combine customer data from Web transactions with customer transaction data from offline sources. ESS can be used for competitor analysis and identification of opportunities for new products or sales channels. Listing the best- and worst-performing sales territories for a monthly or yearly period is a typical MIS for sales and marketing.

Specialized corporate portals and knowledge repositories have been created for sales and marketing staff to help them access and share information about customers, sales leads, competitors, and changes in product pricing and specifications. Virtual reality and Virtual Reality Modeling Language (VRML) simulations can help customers experience the "look and feel" of products and even tailor some of these products more precisely to their needs. Case-based reasoning systems have been widely used for customer service and support. Many online intelligent agent tools and services have been developed to search the Web for products and services specified by users and to assist them in comparing prices and features. Large-scale global electronic commerce initiatives may require country-specific Web sites and large expenditures for customization and ongoing management. You can find examples of sales and marketing applications on pages 432–434, 439, 443–444, 452, 457–459, and 460–463.

CBC

CANADA POST DELIVERS TO CONSUMERS AND TRANSFORMS ITSELF WITH SAP

Canada Post delivers mail and packages across five time zones in the world's second largest country. With 66 000 employees, Canada Post is the country's seventh largest employer and 46th largest business, on the basis of revenues, delivering more than 10 billion pieces of mail annually: that is almost a piece of mail per day per person!

Canada Post also has more than 24 000 retail sales points for its products and services. Canada Post has increased its annual mail volumes by 51 percent since 1982–1983, expanding by more than 170 000 addresses over a year. Canada Post delivers mail and packages on 15 000 letter carrier routes in Canada and has more than 550 planned domestic flights carrying mail every business day. In addition, 13 million kilograms of mail are sent to foreign countries every year, with more than 200 planned flights entering and leaving Canada carrying mail every business day.

Canada Post's fleet numbers 60 000 vehicles of various types that log more than 77 million kilometres during the year. Including street letter-box sites, community mail box sites, retail outlets, rural lot-line boxes, and others, there are more than 900 000 possible points of access to Canada's postal system. Canada Post's major competitors are such companies as Federal Express, United Parcel Service, and DHL.

Canada Post was established as a crown corporation in 1981 and is the publicly owned agency that collects, processes, and delivers mail to Canada's 30 million residential customers and nearly one million organizations. Canada Post's vision, "From anywhere to anyone," is a daunting mandate and responsibility.

The Canada Post Group is composed of a number of separate entities that work together to deliver mail, parcels, and related services to Canadians. These entities include Canada Post International Limited, Purolator Courier Ltd., Progistix Solutions, Inc., Intelcom Courier Canada Inc., epost (which is jointly owned by Canada Post, the Bank of Montreal, and TELUS Corporation), and Innovapost (jointly owned by Canada Post and CGI of Montreal).

Canada Post International Limited (CPIL) markets Canada Post's technologies and expertise to postal administrations around the world. Since its creation in 1990, CPIL has carried out 140 projects in 55 countries on every inhabited continent. Canada Post Corporation owns 96 percent of Purolator Courier Limited. As Canada's leading courier company, Purolator

Courier Ltd. (Purolator) of Mississauga, Ontario, offers automated solutions to around-the-clock pickup and delivery to get their shipments across town or around the world.

Canada Post continues to extend its presence in the electronic services market. Launched in November 1999, epost is a Web-based service that allows consumers and businesses to send and receive their mail, pay their bills, and access information online. It currently has over 60 mailers online. In 2000, TELUS Corporation committed to investing $30 million for a minimum 5 percent equity participation in epost. Epost, the world's first electronic post office box, is a secure Internet-based messaging service that allows Canada Post to deliver bills, statements, forms, government services, and targeted advertising electronically. The service is free to all Canadian consumers and helps businesses reduce distribution costs while allowing consumers to control the types of mail they receive electronically. Epost also allows users to pay bills and record transactions online with just a few clicks.

Today, Canada Post's Web site, **www.canadapost.ca**, is Canada's most visited directory Web site. Canada Post's Web site receives more than 40 500 visits per day, ahead of Sears and FutureShop. The site has more than 12 500 users, 2056 configurations, 66 user exits, 29 extensions, and 454 programs, creating 656 daily batch jobs.

Innovapost provides information systems/technology services and electronic business solutions for the Canada Post Group, its customers, and postal administrations worldwide. It is jointly owned with Canada Post Corporation as the majority owner with 51 percent, while CGI owns 49 percent. Canada Post Corporation has also acquired a majority interest in Progistix-Solutions Inc. (Progistix), formerly a wholly owned, third-party logistics subsidiary of Bell Canada. It has also purchased an interest in Intelcom Courier Canada Inc. (Intelcom), a Montreal-based, same-day delivery and logistics company. These strategic initiatives will enable Canada Post to move quickly into the promising and competitive integrated third-party logistics business, offering Canadian businesses supply chain management services that were previously unavailable. This is part of a global trend for distribution, transportation, and logistics companies to consolidate—often with postal administrations—to provide greater scale, reach, and seamless end-to-end service offerings.

Canada Post, partnered with France's La Poste, continued to develop and market PosteCS, a Web-based secure document delivery and electronic messaging service that helps businesses communicate privately and confidentially over the Internet. It allows customized applications to be built and integrated with existing corporate electronic business systems and legacy applications. PosteCS combines high-speed transmission with robust encryption, password protection, and real-time tracking to deliver large files and sensitive or confidential documents. This service helps businesses minimize printing and paper costs while staying connected with business partners.

eParcel solutions make online retailing easy and accessible to startup and existing companies. eParcel services include all of the building blocks needed to create an online store. At the core of each service is Canada Post's unique eParcel Shipping Module to give consumers control over speed and cost of delivery by choosing the shipping service that best meets their needs and budget. Yet another Canada Post service, Volume Electronic Mail (VEM) allows customers in government and industry to send files electronically to be printed or to send preprinted materials for distribution. Customers' electronic files are processed at the VEM hub in Ottawa and sent to printers in Halifax, Montreal, Toronto, Winnipeg, and Vancouver.

Together with 20 other major postal administrations, Canada Post Corporation is also a shareholder in the International Post Corporation (IPC) based in Brussels, Belgium. The IPC's objective is to actively promote the development and improvement of international postal services.

You can easily see the vast scope and differing character of the various components of the Canada Post Group. For larger organizations, it is particularly challenging to change their culture, processes—basically the way people within the organization think and innovate. Yet, Canada Post has been able to do just that. With the advent of the Internet and the World Wide Web, Canada Post transformed itself into a process-based, customer-focused organization with innovative services by re-engineering its traditional postal services and replacing outdated technology.

Cal Hart, Vice-President of Product Management and Business Transformation for Canada Post, led this effort. According to Hart, "Every process must add value for the customer, the employee, or the corporation." Canada Post needed to make changes that could cover the full range of needs throughout the company. The corporation realized that outside help would be necessary to create an IT infrastructure that was platform-independent, scalable, flexible, secure, and reliable. According to Hart, "We needed to be able to share information and data across all our companies. We also needed an infrastructure that would not only grow with us, but also reduce our overall cost of ownership."

The heart of this project was a full-scale ERP system, allowing real-time management of the corporation's needs. Canada Post contracted with Sun Microsystems for hardware and Unix-based operating systems and with SAP, the world's leading provider of ERP systems. Canada Post also contracted with Sun Microsystems and Accenture, one of the leading consulting groups, to develop custom applications that would provide unique business services, such as epost. The Java 2 Platform, Enterprise Edition (J2EE), was chosen as it was compatible with existing systems and applications.

Using a combination of customer relationship management (CRM) and supply chain management (SCM) software from SAP, Canada Post has realized savings through tighter controls on shipping, parcel tracking, and customer documentation. They are continuing to work on the way package shipments are consolidated on various carriers. Hart said that Canada Post expects to realize 20 to 25 percent return on investment (ROI) on these SCM projects.

Using the J2EE base allowed the company to modernize its CRM applications and add Internet-based sales capabilities. The J2EE platform made the cost of development cheaper, which allowed connectivity with other thin-client applications such as PDAs. The mySAP CRM application is the foundation of the new CRM strategy, and the J2EE platform hosts this application.

Why the mySAP CRM solution? To support these significant aspects of CRM.

■ Contact Centres—Canada Post has eight contact centres handing around six million calls a year. MySAP CRM allowed Canada Post to offer its service agents customer transaction details on a single screen. This was a significant improvement from the six sources previously used. SAP phone supports queuing customer queries, automatic screen "pop-ups" for customer service agents, and fax-, e-mail-, and voice-back options for customers. And workflow management routes cases to delivery depots or employees.

■ Internet Sales and Service—By combining the mySAP CRM processes with the Online Store at www.canadapost.ca, customers are provided with better access to the company's services, including package tracking, rate calculations, locating nearby postal locations, viewing accounts online, and so on. Details of customer transactions (e.g., inquiries, complaints, claims, orders) are made available to customer service agents and delivery supervisors online.

■ Electronic Shipping Tools—These tools are intended for large commercial customers and are meant to improve shipping efficiency. In desktop or Internet versions, they allow ordering and shipping documentation online. An estimated 5000 to 6000 companies will use these applications to speed up data capture and reduce error rates.

With the implementation of mySAP, Canada Post can now see a single view of a customer, and the customer has a single view/interface of Canada Post. Canada Post is determined to find the most appropriate service mix for each customer. With its CRM capabilities, Canada Post can now develop finer segmentations of its customer base and tie customer segments to very specific customer service tiers.

In 2002, Canada Post was awarded the prestigious Gartner Customer Relationship Management Award of Excellence for demonstrating excellence in their CRM initiatives based on the eight building block criteria the Gartner Group defined for CRM. The eight categories on which companies are judged comprise vision, strategy, customer experience, organization, metrics, processes, information, and technology. Canada Post was recognized for transforming its business methodology to be customer focused and embracing the Internet while introducing new business channels for its customers. To date, by using mySAP CRM, 60 legacy applications have been replaced with one integrated electronic business platform. Canada Post has seen a significant increase in its customer satisfaction rating over the last two years with increases in net income as well.

What financial benefits did the CRM solution provide? *The ROI Report* estimates that mySAP CRM has saved Canada Post $25 million in revenue leakage due to the implementation of an integrated order-to-cash process and resulting improvements in customer data accuracy at time of receipt. In addition, Canada Post expects a $5-million margin increase through improved billing and contract management processes and an increase in sales time from reduced administrative burden for the sales force. Annually, the company expects to save $50 million from reduced administration and hopes to gain $10 million in incremental margin. Other benefits include an annual $4-million reduction in data entry and maintenance costs from integrating legacy systems and a savings of $3 million annually from an increase of general process efficiencies. According to *The ROI Report*, Canada Post's CRM return on its initial investment of $100 million is estimated at 26 percent over two years.

In addition to SCM and CRM projects, Canada Post found it necessary to revamp their payroll application as well. Canada Post chose TimeLink to provide a technology platform to automate the collection of time and labour data for all of its employees, wherever they worked. One of the major reasons TimeLink was chosen was its ability to integrate with mySAP.

Time Link developed Synapps, a flexible data integration technology platform, to end errors in manual data entry processes for clients with ERP systems. The data path to ERP systems is fully digital and works with a variety of data collection options including biometrics, mobile handhelds, touch-screen kiosks, badge-based devices, and telephony/IVR (interactive voice response). This will permit Canada Post to change the technology through which payroll data is reported without changing the actual application. No matter the size of the organization, eliminating paper processes and streamlining the data entry process creates significant ROI.

Implementing the TimeLink Synapps system entailed an enterprise-wide rollout including wireless RF-based (radio-frequency based) data collection and integration. Employee data from 231 wireless devices is sent and integrated with SAP HR in real-time. While in the future the system will be able to handle transactions for 30 000 employees, at present turnover is 100 000 transactions daily for its 12 000 mail-processing employees.

Where does Canada Post go from here?

Canada Post is still learning the "core processes" that SAP R/3 and CRM can deliver. "We are still learning how to leverage

what has been implemented," explained Jacques Côté, Canada Post's Chief Financial Officer (CFO). According to David Roy, General Manager of the Business Sales Centre, "Exploiting finer customer segmentation is at the top of the list. We see a tremendous opportunity to differentiate our customers by value, rather than by volume. In addition, we'll be able to use multiple contacts so that we don't contact an accounts payable person with a promotional offer, for example."

It is also important to develop and implement key performance indicators (KPI) throughout the organization. Andy Buxton, Director of the Business Transformation Program, explained: "The corporation uses a set of KPIs to manage the business at the executive level. We continuously track earnings before interest and taxes (EBIT), customer satisfaction, employee satisfaction, and service performance. Additionally, we develop performance metrics for each of the 700 subprocesses that were re-engineered. What we want to do now is to link together the subprocesses metrics and executive KPIs with a mid-level organizational scorecard."

Canada Post is now also revisiting its business processes to gain further optimization. The corporation plans to leverage more the capabilities of mySAP CRM, particularly for marketing analytics, campaign management, mobile sales and service, and telesales. Using its postal outlet locator technology, Canada Post can offer this service to other large organizations with multiple outlets, such as banks and chain stores. Another potential revenue source is using customer data to advance philatelic merchandising globally.

Canada Post has yet to implement SAP's SCM solution, but it may do so. The company is exploring the possibility of integrating it with its CRM functionality to better serve its consumers.

We have focused on Canada Post's successful implementation of mySAP CRM and other systems. But not all SAP implementations are successful.

Sobey's, the large Canadian supermarket chain, implemented SAP retail software at a cost of almost $90 million, incurring a five-day database and systems shutdown in December 2001 that severely affected company operations. Both Sobey's and SAP blamed each other for the problems. (For more discussion of this, check the Web, at www.chainstoreage.com.)

Yet many Canadian businesses—and government organizations—have successfully implemented SAP. These successful SAP implementations include Shoppers Drug Mart, Chevron Canada, Canadian National Railway, and Bayer Canada.

CASE STUDY QUESTIONS

1. How does the integration and easy access to customer data assist Canada Post managers in making decisions? What kind of decisions can they now make more easily than before?

2. How will integration of mySAP CRM with SAP's SCM module further Canada Post's mission? Apply your answer to knowledge management concepts you have learned so far.

3. In looking at the various services and products offered by Canada Post in which information technology plays a key role, can you identify the types of systems that are used, their

characteristics, and the benefits that each type of system provides? The primary types of systems involved would include transaction processing systems (TPS), management information systems (MIS), decision support systems (DSS), knowledge management systems, and expert systems.

4. How does the use of an enterprise-wide system assist Canada Post in achieving its mandate? Be specific, referring to materials learned earlier on enterprise-wide systems.

5. Why can't Canada Post simply stop its transformation? Do the job titles of some of its managers help you see how it views business transformation?

6. What kind of data in the CRM data bank can be used for customer segmentation at Canada Post? What kind of segments do you think could be identified using the mySAP CRM solution?

7. Many companies in Canada and abroad have failed to achieve success in implementing SAP and other enterprise-wide systems. Why do you think Canada Post was successful?

SOURCES

Lou Hirsh, "A Tale of Three Supply Chain Rollouts," *CRM Daily*, July 1, 2002, available www.crmbuyer.com, accessed July 16, 2003; "Sun Microsystems Helps Deliver Big Change to a Big Operation," Sun Microsystems, available http://ca.sun.com/en/aboutsun/success-stories/docs/canadapost.pdf, accessed July 16, 2003; Canada Post Web Site, www.canadapost.ca, accessed July 16, 2003; "Canada Post Implements Time Link Wireless Solution for Delivering Payroll," available www.timelink.com/CPC.shtml, accessed July 16, 2003; "Canada Post Wins CRM Award of Excellence," SAP Canada Press Release, available www.sap.com/canada/en/press/press.asp?pressID=1161, accessed July 16, 2003; "SAP Customers Report Significant Return on Investment from mySAP CRM," SAP Canada Press Release, available www.sap.com/canada/en/press/press.asp?pressID=1325, accessed July 16, 2003; "Canada Post Powers Business Transformation with mySAP Customer Relationship Management, Projected to Deliver 26% ROI," *THE ROI Report*, June 2002, available http://196.30.226.221/sections/crm/include/Canada%20Post.pdf, accessed July 16, 2003; Matt Nannery, "The Blame Game: Sobey's Disses SAP, but There's Blame to Go around," *Chain Store Age*, April 2001, available www.chainstoreage.com, accessed July 16, 2003.

VIDEO RESOURCE

"In Tech We Trust," *UNDERcurrents* 113 (October 31, 1999).

References

"A Look at Kmart's History." *The Miami Herald* (January 14, 2003).

Abdel-Hamid, Tarek K. Kishore Sengupta, and **Clint Swett.** "The Impact of Goals on Software Project Management: An Experimental Investigation." *MIS Quarterly* 23, no. 4 (December 1999).

"About Our Company." Family Insurance Solutions Inc., available www.familyins.com/ (accessed May 4, 2003).

"About Wellnet." Alberta Wellnet, available www.albertawellnet.org/ (accessed January 21, 2003).

Ackerman, Mark S., and **Christine A. Halverson.** "Reexamining Organizational Memory." *Communications of the ACM* 43, no. 1 (January 2000).

Ackoff, R. L. "Management Misinformation System." *Management Science* 14, no. 4 (December 1967): B140–B116.

Acona, Deborah, Henrik Breaman, and **Katrin Kaufer.** "The Comparative Advantage of X-Teams," *Sloan Management Review* 43, no. 3 (Spring 2002).

Agarwal, P. K. "Building India's National Internet Backbone." *Communications of the ACM* 42, no. 6 (June 1999).

Agarwal, Ritu, and **Viswanath Venkatesh.** "Assessing a Firm's Web Presence: A Heuristic Evaluation Procedure for the Measurement of Usability." *Information Systems Research* 13, no.3 (September 2002).

Agarwal, Ritu, Jayesh Prasad, Mohan Tanniru, and **John Lynch.** "Risks of Rapid Application Development." *Communications of the ACM 43,* no. 11 (November 2000).

Agarwal, Ritu, Prabudda De, Atish P. Sinha, and **Mohan Tanniru.** "On the Usability of OO Representations." *Comunications of the ACM* 43, no. 10 (October 2000).

Ahituv, Niv, and **Seev Neumann.** "A Flexible Approach to Information System Development." *MIS Quarterly* (June 1984).

Akcura, M. Tolga, and **Kemal Altinkemer.** "Diffusion Models for B2B, B2C and P2P Exchanges and E-Speak." *Journal of Organizational Computing and Electronic Commerce* 12, no. 3 (2002)

Aladwani, Adel M. "An Integrated Performance Model of Information Systems Projects." *Journal of Management Information Systems* 19, no.1 (Summer 2002).

Alavi, Maryam, and **Dorothy E. Leidner.** "Knowledge Management and Knowledge Management Systems." *MIS Quarterly* 25, no. 1 (March 2001).

Alavi, Maryam, and **Dorothy Leidner.** "Knowledge Management Systems: Issues, Challenges, and Benefits." *Communications of the Association for Information Systems* 1 (February 1999).

Alavi, Maryam, and **Erich A. Joachimsthaler.** "Revisiting DSS Implementation Research: A Meta-Analysis of the Literature and Suggestions for Researchers." *MIS Quarterly* 16, no. 1 (March 1992).

Alavi, Maryam, R. Ryan Nelson, and **Ira R. Weiss.** "Strategies for End-User Computing: An Integrative Framework." *Journal of Management Information Systems* 4, no. 3 (Winter 1987–1988).

Alavi, Maryam. "An Assessment of the Prototyping Approach to Information System Development." *Communications of the ACM* 27 (June 1984).

Alberts, David S. "The Economics of Software Quality Assurance." Washington, DC: National Computer Conference, 1976 Proceedings.

Alleman, James. "Real Options Real Opportunities." *Optimize Magazine* (January 2002).

Allen, Bradley P. "CASE-Based Reasoning: Business Applications." *Communications of the ACM* 37, no. 3 (March 1994).

Allen, Brandt R., and **Andrew C. Boynton.** "Information Architecture: In Search of Efficient Flexibility." *MIS Quarterly* 15, no. 4 (December 1991).

Allison, Graham T. *Essence of Decision-Explaining the Cuban Missile Crisis.* Boston, MA: Little Brown (1971).

Alter, Steven, and **Michael Ginzberg.** "Managing Uncertainty in MIS Implementation." *Sloan Management Review* 20, no. 1 (Fall 1978).

Amor, Daniel. *The E-Business Revolution,* 2nd ed. Upper Saddle River, NJ: Prentice Hall (2002).

Anandarajan, Murugan, "Profiling Web Usage in the Workplace: A Behavior-Based Artificial Intelligence Approach." *Journal of Management Information Systems* 19, no. 1 (Summer 2002).

Anderson, Evan A. "Choice Models for the Evaluation and Selection of Software Packages." *Journal of Management Information Systems* 6, no. 4 (Spring 1990).

Anderson, Philip, and **Erin Anderson.** "The New E-Commerce Intermediaries." *Sloan Management Review* 43, no. 4 (Summer 2002)

Andres, Howard P., and **Robert W. Zmud.** "A Contingency Approach to Software Project Coordination." *Journal of Management Information Systems* 18, no. 3 (Winter 2001–2002).

Andrew, James P., Andy Blackburn, and **Harold L. Sirkin.** "The Business-to-Business Opportunity." Boston, MA: Boston Consulting Group (October 2000).

"Anne McLellan Announces Funding for Primary Care Telemedicine and Distance Nursing Network," Health Canada (February 4, 2002), available www.hc-sc.gc.ca/english/media/releases/2002/2002_05.htm (accessed July 21, 2003).

Anthony, R. N. *Planning and Control Systems: A Framework for Analysis.* Cambridge, MA: Harvard University Press (1965).

Aponovich, David. "No Medal, But IT Integrator Still Scores at Salt Lake Games." *CIO Update* (February 27, 2002), available www.cioupdate.com/news/article.php/10493_981721 (accessed June 8, 2003).

Apte, Chidanand, Bing Liu, Edwin P. D. Pednault, and **Padhraic Smuth.** "Business Applications of Data Mining." *Communications of the ACM* 45, no. 8 (August 2002).

Aries, James A., Subhankar Banerjee, Marc S. Brittan, Eric Dillon, Janusz S. Kowalik, and **John P. Lixvar.** "Capacity and Performance Analysis of Distributed Enterprise Systems." *Communications of the ACM* 45, no. 6 (June 2002).

Armstrong, Arthur, and **John Hagel, III.** "The Real Value of Online Communities." *Harvard Business Review* (May–June 1996).

Armstrong, Curtis P., and **V. Sambamurthy.** "Information Technology Assimilation in Firms: The Influence of Senior Leadership and IT Infrastructures." *Information Systems Research* 10, no. 4 (December 1999).

Associated Press. "Global Software Piracy Figures Jump for Second Straight Year." *Wall Street Journal* (June 10, 2002).

Association of Computing Machinery. "ACM's Code of Ethics and Professional Conduct." *Communications of the ACM* 36, no. 12 (December 1993).

Attewell, Paul, and **James Rule.** "Computing and Organizations: What We Know and What We Don't Know." *Communications of the ACM* 27, no. 12 (December 1984).

Attewell, Paul. "Technology Diffusion and Organizational Learning: The Case of Business Computing." *Organization Science,* no. 3 (1992).

Backus, John. "Funding the Computing Revolution's Third Wave." *Communications of the ACM* 44, no. 11 (November 2001).

Badler, Norman I., Martha S. Palmer, and **Rama Bindiganavale.** "Animation Control for Real-time Virtual Humans." *Communications of the ACM 42,* no. 8 (August 1999).

Baglole, Joel. "Canada's New Automated System Simplifies Transoceanic Air Traffic." *The Wall Street Journal* (May 9, 2002).

Bakos, J. Yannis, and **Michael E. Treacy.** "Information Technology and Corporate Strategy: A Research Perspective." *MIS Quarterly* (June 1986).

Bakos, J. Yannis. "The Emerging Role of Electronic Marketplaces on the Internet." *Communications of the ACM* 41, no. 8 (August 1998).

Balasubramanian, V., and **Alf Bashian.** "Document Management and Web Technologies: Alice Marries the Mad Hatter." *Communications of the ACM* 41, no. 7 (July 1998).

Ball, Kirstie S. "Situating Workplace Surveillance: Ethics and Computer-based Performance Monitoring." *Ethics and Information Technology* 3, no. 3 (2001).

Banerjee, Snehamay, and **Ram L. Kumar.** "Managing Electronic Interchange of Business Documents." *Communications of the ACM* 45, no. 7 (July 2002).

Banker, Rajiv D., and **Chris F. Kemerer.** "Performance Evaluation Metrics in Information Systems Development: A Principal-Agent Model." *Information Systems Research* 3, no. 4 (December 1992).

Banker, Rajiv D., Robert J. Kaufmann, and **Rachna Kumar.** "An Empirical Test of Object-Based Output Measurement Metrics in a Computer-Aided Software Engineering (CASE) Environment." *Journal of Management Information Systems* 8, no. 3 (Winter 1991–1992).

Banker, Rajiv D., Srikant M. Datar, Chris F. Kemerer, and **Dani Zweig.** "Software Complexity and Maintenance Costs." *Communications of the ACM* 36, no. 11 (November 1993).

Banker, Rajiv. "Value Implications of Relative Investments in Information Technology." Dallas, TX: Department of Information Systems and Center for Digital Economy Research, University of Texas at Dallas (January 23, 2001).

Bargeron, David, Jonathan Grudin, Anoop Gupta, Elizabeth Sanocki, Francis Li, and **Scott Le Tiernan.** "Asynchronous Collaboration around Multimedia Applied to On-Demand Education." *Journal of Management Information Systems* 18, no. 4 (Spring 2002).

Barker, Virginia E., and **Dennis E. O'Connor.** "Expert Systems for Configuration at Digital: XCON and Beyond." *Communications of the ACM* (March 1989).

Barkhi, Reza. "The Effects of Decision Guidance and Problem Modeling on Group Decision Making." *Journal of Management Information Systems* 18, no. 3 (Winter 2001–2002).

Barki, Henri, and **Jon Hartwick.** "Interpersonal Conflict and Its Management in Information Systems Development." *MIS Quarterly* 25, no.2 (June 2001).

Barki, Henri, Suzanne Rivard, and **Jean Talbot.** "An Integrative Contingency Model of Software Project Risk Management." *Journal of Management Information Systems* 17, no. 4 (Spring 2001).

Baron, John B, Michael J. Shaw, and **Andrew D. Bailey, Jr.** "Web Based E-Catalog Systems in B2B Procurement." *Communications of the ACM* 43, no.5 (May 2000).

Barrett, Stephanie S. "Strategic Alternatives and Interorganizational System Implementations: An Overview." *Journal of Management Information System s* (Winter 1986–1987).

Barthelemy, Jerome. "The Hidden Costs of IT Outsourcing." *Sloan Management Review* (Spring 2001).

Barua, Anitesh, Prabhudev Konana, Andrew B. Whinston, and **Fang Yin,** "Driving E-Business Excellence." *Sloan Management Review* 43, no. 1 (Fall 2001).

Barua, Anitesh, Sophie C. H. Lee, and **Andrew B. Whinston.** "The Calculus of Reengineering." *Information Systems Research* 7, no. 4 (December 1996).

Barua, Anitesh, Sury Ravindran, and **Andrew B. Whinston.** "Efficient Selection of Suppliers over the Internet." *Journal of Management Information Systems* 13, no. 4 (Spring 1997).

Baskerville, Richard L., and **Jan Stage.** "Controlling Prototype Development through Risk Analysis." *MIS Quarterly* 20, no. 4 (December 1996).

Baskerville, Richard L., and **Michael D. Myers.** "Information Systems as a Reference Discipline." *MIS Quarterly* 26, no. 1 (March 2002).

Beath, Cynthia Mathis, and **Wanda J. Orlikowski.** "The Contradictory Structure of Systems Development Methodologies: Deconstructing the IS-User Relationship in Information Engineering." *Information Systems Research* 5, no. 4 (December 1994).

Becerra-Fernandez, Irma and **Rajiv Sabherwal.** "Organizational Knowledge Management: A Contingency Perspective." *Journal of Management Information Systems* 18, no. 1 (Summer 2001).

Beer, Michael, Russell A. Eisenstat, and **Bert Spector.** "Why Change Programs Don't Produce Change." *Harvard Business Review* (November–December 1990).

Beer, Randall D., Roger D. Quinn, Hillel J. Chiel, and **Roy E. Ritzman.** "Biologically Inspired Approaches to Robots." *Communications of the ACM* 40, no. 3 (March 1997).

"Bell Canada Makes Enterprise Transition to e-Learning." Thomson Learning, available http://thomson.com/cms/assets/pdfs/learning/BellCanada_NETg_final.pdf (accessed July 21, 2003).

Bell, Gordon, and **Jim Gray.** "What's Next in High-Performance Computing?" *Communications of the ACM* 45, no. 1 (January 2002).

Bellman, Steven, Eric J. Johnson, and **Gerald L. Lohse.** "To Opt-in or Opt-out? It Depends on the Question." *Communications of the ACM* 44, no. 2 (February 2001).

Benamati, John, and **Albert L. Lederer.** "Coping with Rapid Changes in IT." *Communications of the ACM* 44, no. 8 (August 2001).

Benaroch, Michel, and **Robert J. Kauffman.** "Justifying Electronic Banking Network Expansion Using Real Options Analysis." *MIS Quarterly* 24, no. 2 (June 2000).

Benaroch, Michel. "Managing Information Technology Investment Risk: A Real Options Perspective." *Journal of Management Information Systems* 19, no. 2 (Fall 2002).

Benjamin, Robert, and **Rolf Wigand.** "Electronic Markets and Virtual Value Chains on the Information Superhighway." *Sloan Management Review* (Winter 1995).

Bennett, Colin J. "Cookies, Web Bugs, Webcams, and Cue Cats: Patterns of Surveillance on the World Wide Web." *Ethics and Information Technology* 3, no. 3 (2001).

Bensaou, M. "Portfolios of Buyer-Supplier Relationships," *Sloan Management Review* 40, no. 4 (Summer 1999).

Berdichevsky, Daniel, and **Erik Neunschwander.** "Toward an Ethics of Persuasive Technology." *Communications of the ACM* 42, no. 5 (May 1999).

Berners-Lee, Tim, Robert Cailliau, Ari Luotonen, Henrik Frystyk Nielsen, and **Arthur Secret.** "The World Wide Web." *Communications of the ACM* 37, no. 8 (August 1994).

Berry, Leonard L., and **A. Parasuraman.** "Listening to the Customer—the Concept of a Service-Quality Information System." *Sloan Management Review* (Spring 1997).

Berry, Victoria. "Governing Online Services." *ComputerWorld Canada* (June 14, 2002), available www.itworldcanada.com (accessed June 7, 2003).

Bertin, Michael. "The New Security Threats." *Smart Business Magazine* (February 2001).

Bertino, Elisa, Elena Pagani, Gian Paolo Rossi, and **Pierangela Samarati.** "Protecting Information on the Web." *Communications of the ACM* 43, no.11 (November 2000).

Bharadwaj, Anandhi. "A Resource-Based Perspective on Information Technology Capability and Firm Performance." *MIS Quarterly* 24, no. 1 (March 2000).

Bhattacharjee, Sudip, and **R. Ramesh.** "Enterprise Computing Environments and Cost Assessment." *Communications of the ACM* 43, no. 10 (October 2000).

Bhattacharjee, Yudhijit. "A Swarm of Little Notes." *Time* (September 16, 2002).

Bhattacherjee, Anoi. "Understanding Information Systems Continuance: An Expectation-Confirmation Model." *MIS Quarterly* 25, no.3 (September 2001).

Bhattacherjee, Anol. "Individual Trust in Online Firms: Scale Development and Initial Test." *Journal of Management Information Systems* 19, no. 1 (Summer 2002).

Bieer, Michael, Douglas Englebart Richard Furuta, Starr Roxanne Hiltz, John Noll, Jennifer Preece, Edward A. Stohr, Murray Turoff, and **Bartel Van de Walle.** "Toward Virtual Community Knowledge Evolution." *Journal of Management Information Systems* 18, no. 4 (Spring 2002).

Bikson, T. K., and **J. D. Eveland.** "Integrating New Tools into Information Work." The Rand Corporation (1992). RAND/RP-106.

Bikson, Tora K., Cathleen Stasz, and **Donald A. Monkin.** "Computer-Mediated Work: Individual and Organizational Impact on One Corporate Headquarters." Rand Corporation (1985).

Billsus, Daniel, Clifford A. Brunk, Craig Evans, Brian Gladish, and **Michael Pazzani.** "Adaptive Interfaces for Ubiquitous Web Access." *Communications of the ACM* 45, no. 5 (May 2002).

Birkinshaw, Julian, and **Tony Sheehan.** "Managing the Knowledge Life Cycle." *MIT Sloan Management Review* 44, no. 1 (Fall 2002).

Blackburn, Joseph, Gary Scudder, and **Luk N. Van Wassenhove.** "Concurrent Software Development." *Communications of the ACM* 43, no. 11 (November 2000).

Blanning, Robert W. "Establishing a Corporate Presence on the Internet in Singapore." *Journal of Organizational Computing and Electronic Commerce* 9, no. 1 (1999).

Blanning, Robert W., David R. King, James R. Marsden, and **Ann C. Seror.** "Intelligent Models of Human Organizations: The State of the Art." *Journal of Organizational Computing* 2, no. 2 (1992).

Blau, Peter, and **W. Richard Scott.** *Formal Organizations.* San Francisco, CA: Chandler Press (1962).

Boehm, Barry W. "Understanding and Controlling Software Costs." *IEEE Transactions on Software Engineering* 14, no. 10 (October 1988).

Boer, F. Peter. "Real Options: The IT Investment Risk Buster." *Optimize Magazine* (July 2002).

Bonham-Carter, Rupert. "Cognos Shows Its Intelligence With DB2 Data Management Software." *IBM Canada* (May 2002).

Booth, Corey, and **Shashi Buluswar.** "The Return of Artificial Intelligence," *The McKinsey Quarterl y* no. 2 (2002).

Borriello, Gaetano, and **Roy Want.** "Embedded Computation Meets the World Wide Web." *Communications of the ACM* 43, no. 5 (May 2000).

Boston Consulting Group. "Mobile Commerce: Winning the On-Air Consumer" (November 2000).

Bostrom, R. P., and **J. S. Heinen.** "MIS Problems and Failures: A Socio-Technical Perspective. Part I: The Causes." *MIS Quarterly* 1 (September 1977); "Part II: The Application of Socio-Technical Theory." *MIS Quarterly* 1 (December 1977).

Bowen, Jonathan. "The Ethics of Safety-Critical Systems." *Communications of the ACM* 43, no. 3 (April 2000).

"BP Canada Energy Marketing Corp." Microsoft Case Study (November 6, 2001) available www.microsoft.com/resources/casestudies/CaseStudy.asp?CaseStudyID=11601 (accessed April 10, 2003).

Brachman, Ronald J., Tom Khabaza, Willi Kloesgen, Gregory Piatetsky-Shapiro, and **Evangelos Simoudis.** "Mining Business Databases." *Communications of the ACM* 39, no. 11 (November 1996).

Brancheau, James C., Brian D. Janz, and **James C. Wetherbe.** "Key Issues in Information Systems Management: 1994–1995 SIM Delphi Results." *MIS Quarterly* 20, no. 2 (June 1996).

Brier, Tom, Jerry Luftman, and **Raymond Papp.** "Enablers and Inhibitors of Business—IT Alignment." *Communications of the Association for Information Systems* 1 (March 1999).

British Petroleum Canada Energy Company home page. BP Canada Energy Company, available www.bp.com/in_your_area/transition_page.asp?id=13 (accessed April 10, 2003).

Broadbent, Marianne, Peter Weill, and **Don St. Clair.** "The Implications of Information Technology Infrastructure for Business Process Redesign." *MIS Quarterly* 23, no. 2 (June 1999).

Brod, Craig. *Techno Stress—The Human Cost of the Computer Revolution.* Reading MA: Addison-Wesley (1982).

Brooks, Frederick P. "The Mythical Man-Month." *Datamation* (December 1974).

Brown Bag Software vs. Symantec Corp. 960 F2D 1465 (Ninth Circuit, 1992).

Brown, Jennifer. "Sears Says In-House Portal Key to Call Center Success." *ITBusiness* (April 15, 2003).

Brown, Rodney. "Cognos Called up by U.S. Army Reserve Command to Monitor Operational Readiness." *Mass High Tech (The Journal of New England Technology)* (March 18, 2003).

Brunner, Marcus, Bernhard Plattner, and **Rolf Stadler.** "Service Creation and Management in Active Telecom Networks." *Communications of the ACM* 44, no. 4 (April 2001).

Brutzman, Don. "The Virtual Reality Modeling Language and Java." *Communications of the ACM* 41, no. 6 (June 1998).

Brynjolfsson, E. T., T. W. Malone, V. Gurbaxani, and **A. Kambil.** "Does Information Technology Lead to Smaller Firms?" *Management Science* 40, no. 12 (1994).

Brynjolfsson, Erik, and **Lorin M. Hitt.** "Beyond the Productivity Paradox." *Communications of the ACM* 41, no. 8 (August 1998).

Brynjolfsson, Erik, and **Lorin M. Hitt.** "Information Technology and Organizational Design: Evidence from Micro Data." (January 1998).

Brynjolfsson, Erik, and **Lorin M. Hitt.** "New Evidence on the Returns to Information Systems." Cambridge, MA: MIT Sloan School of Management (October 1993).

Brynjolfsson, Erik, and **S. Yang.** "Intangible Assets: How the Interaction of Computers and Organizational Structure Affects Stock Markets." Cambridge, MA: MIT Sloan School of Management (2000).

Brynjolfsson, Erik. "The Contribution of Information Technology to Consumer Welfare." *Information Systems Research* 7, no. 3 (September 1996).

Brynjolfsson, Erik. "The Productivity Paradox of Information Technology." *Communications of the ACM* 36, no. 12 (December 1993).

Buckler, Grant., "Getting a Grip on CRM." *CIO Canada* (January 1, 2003).

"Building the Future for you Today." D.H. Neill Network Cabling Design Services, available www.dhneill.com/ (accessed March 30, 2003).

Bullen, Christine, and **John F. Rockart.** "A Primer on Critical Success Factors." Cambridge, MA: Center for Information Systems Research, Sloan School of Management (1981).

Burk, Dan L. "Copyrightable Functions and Patentable Speech." *Communications of the ACM* 44, no. 2 (February 2001).

Burkhardt, Grey E., Seymour E. Goodman, Arun Mehta, and **Larry Press.** "The Internet in India: Better Times Ahead?" *Communications of the ACM* 41, no. 11 (November 1998).

Burtka, Michael. "Generic Algorithms." *The Stern Information Systems Review* 1, no. 1 (Spring 1993).

Busch, Elizabeth, Matti Hamalainen, Clyde W. Holsapple, Yongmoo Suh, and **Andrew B. Whinston.** "Issues and

Obstacles in the Development of Team Support Systems." *Journal of Organizational Computing* 1, no. 2 (April–June 1991).

Buss, Martin D. J. "How to Rank Computer Projects." *Harvard Business Review* (January 1983).

Byrd, Terry Anthony. "Measuring the Flexibility of Information Technology Infrastructure: Exploratory Analysis of a Construct." *Journal of Management Information Systems* 17, no. 1 (Summer 2000).

Camuffo, Arnaldo, Pietro Romano, and **Andrea Vinellie.** "Benetton Transforms Its Global Network." *Sloan Management Review* 43, no. 1 (Fall 2001)

"Canada Health Infostructure Partnerships Program." Health Canada. (July 31, 2002), available www.hc-sc.gc.ca/ohih-bsi/about_ apropos/chipp-ppics/chippics-intro_e.html (accessed July 21, 2003).

"Canadian Pacific Looks to ASP Management Tool." ASP.net, available www.asp.net (accessed March 9, 2003).

"Canadian Pacific Railway Speeds Information across Continent with Leading Edge Microsoft Technology Strategy." Microsoft case study (June 2002), available www.microsoft.com/canada/ casestudies/Canadian+Pacific+Railway.asp (accessed July 21, 2003).

"Canada's Oldest Retailer Establishes Zellers Headquarters in Brampton." *BramFacts,* available www.city.brampton.on.ca (accessed June 4, 2003).

Caouette, Margarette J., and **Bridget N. O'Connor.** "The Impact of Group Support Systems on Corporate Teams' Stages of Development." *Journal of Organizational Computing and Electronic Commerce* 8, no. 1 (1998).

Carey, David. "Putting Web Services to Work." *CIO Canada* (December 1, 2002).

Carr, Jim. "The Forgotten Networks." *mBusiness* (June 2001).

Cash, J. I., and **Benn R. Konsynski.** "IS Redraws Competitive Boundaries." *Harvard Business Review* (March–April 1985).

Cavazos, Edward A. "The Legal Risks of Setting up Shop in Cyberspace." *Journal of Organizational Computing* 6, no. 1 (1996).

"Ceridian Canada and Epost Sign Agreement to Enable Employers." Press Release (December 16, 2002), available www.nati.net/ files/03022003_CeridianCanadaEpost.PDF (accessed July 21, 2003).

"Ceridian Canada: IBM and Siebel Deliver A Leading Edge CRM Solution." IDC Case Study, available www-3.ibm.com/ software/success/cssdb.nsf/CS/AKLR-54F57G?OpenDocument &Site=default (accessed July 21, 2003).

"Ceridian Canada takes Customer Service to a New Level." Ceridian Canada, available www.ceridian.ca/en/index.html (accessed July 21, 2003).

Chabrow, Eric. "Supply Chains Go Global." *InformationWeek* (April 3, 2000).

Champy, James A. *X-Engineering the Corporation: Reinventing Your Business in the Digital Age.* New York, NY: Warner Books (2002).

Chan, Yolande E. "Why Haven't We Mastered Alignment? The Importance of the IT Informal Organizational Structure." *MIS Quarterly Executive* 1, no. 2 (2002).

Chan, Yolande E., Sid L. Huff, Donald W. Barclay, and **Duncan G. Copeland.** "Business Strategic Orientation, Information Systems Strategic Orientation, and Strategic Alignment." *Information Systems Research* 8, no. 2 (June 1997).

Chang, Shih-Fu, John R. Amith, Mandis Beigi, and **Ana Benitez.** "Visual Information Retrieval from Large Distributed Online Repositories." *Communications of the ACM* 40, no. 12 (December 1997).

Chanley, Kristen. "Hot Wired Hotels." *IQ Magazine* (July/August 2002).

Chapman, Siobhan. "Data Mining to Stem Insurance Fraud Down Under." *IT World Canada* (March 28, 2002), available www.itworldcanada.com (accessed April 7, 2003).

Chatfield, Akemi Takeoka, and **Philip Yetton.** "Strategic Payoff from EDI as a Function of EDI Embeddedness." *Journal of Management Information Systems* 16, no. 4 (Spring 2000).

Chatterjee, Debabroto, Carl Pacini, and **V. Sambamurthy.** "The Shareholder-Wealth and Trading Volume Effects of Information Technology Infrastructure Investments." *Journal of Management Information Systems* 19, no. 2 (Fall 2002).

Chatterjee, Samir, and **Suzanne Pawlowski.** "All-Optical Networks." *Communications of the ACM* 42, no. 6 (June 1999).

Chatterjee, Samir, Suzanne Pawlowski, and **Il-Horn Hann.** "Rosenbluth International: Strategic Transformation." *Journal of Management Information Systems* 16, no. 2 (Fall 1999).

Chaudhury, Abhijit, Debasish Mallick, and **H. Raghav Rao.** "Web Channels in E-Commerce." *Communications of the ACM* 44, No. 1 (January 2001).

Chen, Pei-Yu (Sharon), and **Lorin M. Hitt.** "Measuring Switching Costs and the Determinants of Customer Retention in Internet-Enabled Businesses: A Study of the Online Brokerage Industry." *Information Systems Research* 13, no.3 (September 2002).

Cheng, Hsing K., Ronald R. Sims, and **Hildy Teegen.** "To Purchase or to Pirate Software: An Empirical Study." *Journal of Management Information Systems* 13, no. 4 (Spring 1997).

Cheyne, Tanya L., and **Frank E. Ritter.** "Targeting Audiences on the Internet." *Communications of the ACM* 44, no. 4 (April 2001).

Chidambaram, Laku. "Relational Development in Computer-Supported Groups." *MIS Quarterly* 20, no. 2 (June 1996).

Chin, Shu-Kai. "High-Confidence Design for Security." *Communications of the ACM* 42, no. 7 (July 1999).

Chismar, William G., and **Laku Chidambaram.** "Telecommunications and the Structuring of U.S. Multinational Corporations." *International Information Systems* 1, no. 4 (October 1992).

Cho, Sungzoon, Chigeun Han, Dae Hee Han, and **Hyung-Il Kim.** "Web-Based Keystroke Dynamics Identity Verification Using Neural Network." *Journal of Organizational Computing and Electronic Commerce* 10, no. 4 (2000).

Choy, Manhoi, Hong Va Leong, and **Man Hon Wong.** "Disaster Recovery Techniques for Database Systems." *Communications of the ACM* 43, no. 11 (November 2000).

Christensen, Clayton M. *The Innovator's Dilemma.* New York, NY: HarperCollins (2000).

Christensen, Clayton. "The Past and Future of Competitive Advantage." *Sloan Management Review* 42, no. 2 (Winter 2001).

Churchland, Paul M., and **Patricia Smith Churchland.** "Could a Machine Think?" *Scientific American* (January 1990).

Clarke, Roger. "Internet Privacy Concerns Confirm the Case for Intervention." *Communications of the ACM* 42, no. 2 (February 1999).

Clement, Andrew, and **Peter Van den Besselaar.** "A Retrospective Look at PD Projects." *Communications of the ACM* 36, no. 4 (June 1993).

Clemons, Eric K. "Evaluation of Strategic Investments in Information Technology." *Communications of the ACM* (January 1991).

Clemons, Eric K., and **Bruce W. Weber.** "Segmentation, Differentiation, and Flexible Pricing: Experience with Information Technology and Segment-Tailored Strategies." *Journal of Management Information Systems* 11, no. 2 (Fall 1994).

Clemons, Eric K., and **Michael Row.** "Limits to Interfirm Coordination through IT." *Journal of Management Information Systems* 10, no. 1 (Summer 1993).

Clemons, Eric K., and **Michael Row.** "McKesson Drug Co.: Case Study of a Strategic Information System." *Journal of Management Information Systems* (Summer 1988).

Clemons, Eric K., and **Michael Row.** "Sustaining IT Advantage: The Role of Structural Differences." *MIS Quarterly* 15, no. 3 (September 1991).

Clifford, James, Albert Croker, and **Alex Tuzhilin.** "On Data Representation and Use in a Temporal Relational DBMS." *Information Systems Research* 7, no. 3 (September 1996).

Cline, Marshall, and **Mike Girou.** "Enduring Business Themes." *Communications of the ACM* 43, no. 5 (May 2000).

Coase, Ronald H. "The Nature of the Firm."(1937) in Putterman, Louis, and Randall Kroszner, *The Economic Nature of the Firm: A Reader,* New York, NY: Cambridge University Press (1995).

"Cognos Technology." Cognos Web site, available www.cognos.com/company/success/ss_manu_electronics.html (accessed July 21, 2003).

Cohen, Michael, James March, and Johan Olsen. "A Garbage Can Model of Organizational Choice." *Administrative Science Quarterly* 17 (1972).

Cole, Kevin, Olivier Fischer, and Phyllis Saltzman. "Just-in-Time Knowledge Delivery." *Communications of the ACM* 40, no. 7 (July 1997).

Collins, W. Robert, Keith W. Miller, Bethany J. Spielman, and Phillip Wherry. "How Good Is Good Enough? An Ethical Analysis of Software Construction and Use." *Communications of the ACM* 37, no. 1 (January 1994).

Coltman, Tim, Timothy M. Devinney, Alopi S. Latukefu, and David D. Midgley. "Keeping E-Business in Perspective." *Communications of the ACM* 46, no. 8 (August 2002).

"Companies Struggle with ERP Implementations." *IntelligentERP News* (June 29, 2001).

Computer Systems Policy Project. "Perspectives on the National Information Infrastructure." (January 12, 1993).

Concours Group. "Delivering Large-Scale System Projects." (2000).

Concours Group. "ESII: Capitalizing on Interprise Systems and Infrastructure." (1999).

Concours Group. "Managing and Exploiting Corporate Intranets" (1999).

Conrath, Chris. "Hacking from the Inside." *Network World Canada,* available www.itworldcanada.com (accessed June 8, 2003).

Conrath, Chris. "Are We Ready for the Big One?" *CIO Canada* (October 1, 2002), available www.itworldcanada.com (accessed June 8, 2003).

Cooper, Brian L., Hugh J. Watson, Barbara H. Wixom, and Dale L. Goodhue. "Data Warehousing Supports Corporate Strategy at First American Corporation." *MIS Quarterly* (December 2000).

Cooper, Randolph B. "Information Technology Development Creativity: A Case Study of Attempted Radical Change." *MIS Quarterly* 24, no. 2 (June 2000).

Copeland, Duncan G., and James L. McKenney. "Airline Reservations Systems: Lessons from History." *MIS Quarterly* 12, no. 3 (September 1988).

Corbato, Fernando J. "On Building Systems that Will Fail." *Communications of the ACM* 34, no. 9 (September 1991).

Cottingham, Robert. "Wireless Web Accesses Wellsite Scada." *Oil & Gas Journal* (December 19, 2001).

Couto, Bernice. "Mark's Sizes Up Linux POS." *Computing Canada* 29, no. 2 (2003).

Cox, Butler. *Globalization: The IT Challenge.* Sunnyvale, CA: Amdahl Executive Institute (1991).

Cranor, Lorrie Faith, and Brian A. LaMacchia. "Spam!" *Communications of the ACM* 41, no. 8 (August 1998).

Crombie, Annie, and Alexandra Katseva. "Deconstructing the Stovepipe Mentality." *CIO Canada* (November 1, 2002).

Cross, Rob, and Lloyd Baird. "Technology is Not Enough: Improving Performance by Building Organizational Memory." *Sloan Management Review* 41, no. 3 (Spring 2000).

Cross, Rob, Nitin Nohria, and Andrew Parker. "Six Myths about Informal Networks and How to Overcome Them." *Sloan Management Review* 43, no. 3 (Spring 2002).

"CSO Norway Awards Contract to C-Core." Press Release (July 24, 2002), available www.nati.net/files/07242002_CCORE.pdf (accessed July 21, 2003).

Culnan, Mary J. "Transaction Processing Applications as Organizational Message Systems: Implications for the Intelligent Organization." Working paper no. 88–10, Twenty-second Hawaii International Conference on Systems Sciences (January 1989).

Damsgaard Jan, and Kalle Lyytinen. "Building Electronic Trading Infrastructures: A Public or Private Responsibility?" *Journal of Organizational Computing and Electronic Commerce* 11, no. 2 (2001).

Dash, Julekha. "Cost Cutting May Spur IT Outsourcing Deals." *Computerworld* (April 16, 2001).

Davamanirajan, Prabu, Tridas Mukhopadhyay, and Charles Kriebel. "Assessing the Business Value of Information Technology in Global Wholesale Banking: The Case of Trade Services." *Journal of Organizational Computing and Electronic Commerce* 12, no. 1 (2002).

Davenport, Thomas H. *Mission Critical: Realizing the Promise of Enterprise Systems.* Boston, MA: Harvard Business School Press (2000).

Davenport, Thomas H., and James E. Short. "The New Industrial Engineering: Information Technology and Business Process Redesign." *Sloan Management Review* 31, no. 4 (Summer 1990).

Davenport, Thomas H., and Keri Pearlson. "Two Cheers for the Virtual Office." *Sloan Management Review* 39, no. 4 (Summer 1998).

Davenport, Thomas H., Keri Pearlson, Jeanne G. Harris, and Ajay K. Kohli, "How Do They Know Their Customers So Well?" *Sloan Management Review* 42, no. 2 (Winter 2001).

Davenport, Thomas H., and Lawrence Prusak. *Working Knowledge: How Organizations Manage What They Know.* Boston, MA: Harvard Business School Press (1997).

Davenport, Thomas H., David W. DeLong, and Michael C. Beers. "Successful Knowledge Management Projects." *Sloan Management Review* 39, no. 2 (Winter 1998).

Davenport, Thomas H., Robert J. Thomas and Susan Cantrell. "The Mysterious Art and Science of Knowledge-Worker Performance." *MIT Sloan Management Review* 44, no. 1 (Fall 2002).

Davenport, Tom. "Putting the Enterprise into Enterprise Systems." *Harvard Business Review* (July–August 1998).

Davenport, Tom. *Mission Critical: Realizing the Promise of Enterprise Systems.* Boston, MA: Harvard Business School Press (2000).

Davern, Michael J. and Robert J. Kauffman. "Discovering Potential and Realizing Value form Information Technology Investments." *Journal of Management Information Systems* 16, no. 4 (Spring 2000).

David, Julie Smith, David Schuff, and Robert St. Louis. "Managing Your IT Total Cost of Ownership." *Communications of the ACM* 45, no. 1 (January 2002).

Davidson, W. H. "Beyond Engineering: The Three Phases of Business Transformation." *IBM Systems Journal* 32, no. 1 (1993).

Davis, Fred R. "Perceived Usefulness, Ease of Use, and User Acceptance of Information Technology." *MIS Quarterly* 13, no. 3 (September 1989).

Davis, Gordon B. "Determining Management Information Needs: A Comparison of Methods." *MIS Quarterly* 1 (June 1977).

Davis, Gordon B. "Information Analysis for Information System Development." In *Systems Analysis and Design: A Foundation for the 1980's,* edited by W.W. Cotterman.

Davis, Gordon B. "Strategies for Information Requirements Determination." *IBM Systems Journal* 1 (1982).

Davis, Gordon B., and Margrethe H. Olson. *Management Information Systems: Conceptual Foundations, Structure, and Development,* 2nd ed. New York, NY: McGraw-Hill (1985).

Davis, Randall. "The Digital Dilemma." *Communications of the ACM* 44, no. 2 (February 2001).

Davison, Robert. "Cultural Complications of ERP." *Communications of the ACM* 45, no. 7 (July 2002).

De Berranger, Pascal, David Tucker, and Laurie Jones. "Internet Diffusion in Creative Micro-Businesses: Identifying Change Agent Characteristics as Critical Success Factors." *Journal of Organizational Computing and Electronic Commerce* 11, no. 3 (2001).

De Meyer, Arnoud, Christoph H. Loch, and Michael T. Pich. "Managing Project Uncertainty: From Variation to Chaos." *Sloan Management Review* 43, no.2 (Winter 2002).

De, Prabudda, and **Thomas W. Ferrat.** "An Information System Involving Competing Organizations." *Communications of the ACM* 41, no. 12 (December 1998).

Deans, Candace P., and **Michael J. Kane.** *International Dimensions of Information Systems and Technology.* Boston, MA: PWS-Kent (1992).

Deans, Candace P., Kirk R. Karwan, Martin D. Goslar, David A. Ricks, and **Brian Toyne.** "Key International Issues in U.S.-Based Multinational Corporations." *Journal of Management Information Systems* 7, no. 4 (Spring 1991).

"Desjardins Expands Relationship with CGI." Bell Canada Enterprises. (December 13, 2002), available www.bce.ca/en/news/releases/cgi/2002/12/13/69616.html (accessed July 21, 2003).

Dejoie, Roy, George Fowler, and **David Paradice,** eds. *Ethical Issues in Information Systems.* Boston,MA: Boyd & Fraser (1991).

Dekleva, Sasa M. "The Influence of Information Systems Development Approach on Maintenance." *MIS Quarterly* 16, no. 3 (September 1992).

Del Rosario, Elise. "Logistical Nightmare." *OR/MS Today* (April 1999).

DeMarco, Tom. *Structured Analysis and System Specification.* New York, NY: Yourdon Press (1978).

Dempsey, Bert J., Debra Weiss, Paul Jones, and **Jane Greenberg.** "What Is an Open Source Software Developer?" *Communications of the ACM* 45, no. 1 (January 2001).

Dempsey, Jed, Robert E. Dvorak, Endre Holen, David Mark, and **William F. Meehan III.** "A Hard and Soft Look at IT Investments." *The McKinsey Quarterl y,* no. 1 (1998).

Denning, Dorothy E., et al. "To Tap or Not to Tap." *Communications of the ACM* 36, no. 3 (March 1993).

Dennis, Alan R. "Information Exchange and Use in Group Decision Making: You Can Lead a Group to Information, but You Can't Make It Think." *MIS Quarterly* 20, no. 4 (December 1996).

Dennis, Alan R., and **Barbara H. Wixom,** "Investigating the Moderators of the Group Support Systems Use with Meta-Analysis." *Journal of Management Information Systems* 18, no. 3 (Winter 2001–2002).

Dennis, Alan R., Barbara H. Wixom, and **Robert J. Vandenberg.** "Understanding Fit and Appropriation Effects in Group Support Systems Via Meta-Analysis." *MIS Quarterly* 25, no. 2 (June 2001).

Dennis, Alan R., Craig K. Tyran, Douglas R. Vogel, and **Jay Nunamaker, Jr.** "Group Support Systems for Strategic Planning." *Journal of Management Information Systems* 14, no. 1 (Summer 1997).

Dennis, Alan R., Jay E. Aronson, William G. Henriger, and **Edward D. Walker III.** "Structuring Time and Task in Electronic Brainstorming." *MIS Quarterly* 23, no. 1 (March 1999).

Dennis, Alan R., Jay F. Nunamaker, Jr., and **Douglas R. Vogel.** "A Comparison of Laboratory and Field Research in the Study of Electronic Meeting Systems." *Journal of Management Information Systems* 7, no. 3 (Winter 1990–1991).

Dennis, Alan R., Joey F. George, Len M. Jessup, Jay F. Nunamaker, and **Douglas R. Vogel.** "Information Technology to Support Electronic Meetings." *MIS Quarterly* 12, no. 4 (December 1988).

Dennis, Alan R., Sridar K. Pootheri, and **Vijaya L. Natarajan.** "Lessons from Early Adopters of Web Groupware." *Journal of Management Information Systems* 14, no. 4 (Spring 1998).

DePalma, Anthony. "Getting There is Challenge for Latin American E-Tailing." *New York Times* (August 17, 2000).

DeSanctis, Geraldine, and **R. Brent Gallupe.** "A Foundation for the Study of Group Decision Support Systems." *Management Science* 33, no. 5 (May 1987).

Desmarais, Michel C., Richard Leclair, Jean-Yves Fiset, and **Hichem Talbi.** "Cost-Justifying Electronic Performance Support Systems." *Communications of the ACM* 40, no. 7 (July 1997).

Deutsch, Claudia. "Six Sigma Enlightenment." *New York Times* (December 7, 1998).

Devaraj, Sarv, Ming Fan, and **Rajiv Kohli.** "Antecedents of B2C Channel Satisfaction and Preference: Validating E-Commerce Metrics." *Information Systems Research* 13, no.3 (September 2002).

Dhar, Vasant, and **Roger Stein.** *Intelligent Decision Support Methods: The Science of Knowledge Work.* Upper Saddle River, NJ: Prentice Hall (1997).

Dhar, Vasant. "Plausibility and Scope of Expert Systems in Management." *Journal of Management Information Systems* (Summer 1987).

Dietrich, Brenda, Nick Donofrio, Grace Lin, and **Jane Snowdon.** "Big Benefits for Big Blue." *OR/MS Today* (June 2000).

Dijkstra, E. "Structured Programming." In *Classics in Software Engineering,* edited by Edward Nash Yourdon. New York, NY: Yourdon Press (1979).

"Direct Wines Limited." Hoovers Online, available www.hoovers.com/free/co/factsheet.xhtml?ID=102549 (accessed July 21, 2003).

"Direct Wines." SPSS Inc, available www.spss.com/success/template_view.cfm?Story_ID=66 (accessed July 21, 2003).

"Direct Wines – A Case Study." QAS UK Customer Case Studies, available www.qas.com/uk/customers/casestudy.asp?Organisation=DirectWines (accessed July 21, 2003).

Doll, William J. "Avenues for Top Management Involvement in Successful MIS Development." *MIS Quarterly* (March 1985).

Domges, Rolf, and **Klaus Pohl.** "Adapting Traceability Environments to Project-Specific Needs." *Communications of the ACM* 41, no. 12 (December 1998).

Dos Santos, Brian. "Justifying Investments in New Information Technologies." *Journal of Management Information Systems* 7, no. 4 (Spring 1991).

Downes, Larry, and **Chunka Mui.** *Unleashing the Killer App: Digital Strategies for Market Dominance.* Boston, MA: Harvard Business School Press (1998).

Drucker, Peter. "The Coming of the New Organization." *Harvard Business Review* (January–February 1988).

Dubowski, Stefan. "Comdex Attendees Ask: Whither Web Services?." *Daily IT Wire* (July 15, 2002), available www.itworldcanada.com (accessed April 8, 2003).

Duchessi, Peter, and **InduShobha Chengalur-Smith.** "Client/Server Benefits, Problems, Best Practices." *Communications of the ACM* 41, no. 5 (May 1998).

Durst, Robert, Terrence Champion, Brian Witten, Eric Miller, and **Luigi Spagnuolo.** "Testing and Evaluating Computer Intrusion Detection Systems." *Communications of the ACM* 42, no. 7 (July 1999).

Dutta, Amitava. "Telecommunications and Economic Activity: An Analysis of Granger Causality," *Journal of Management Information Systems* 17, no. 4 (Spring 2001).

Dutta, Amitava. "Telecommunications Infrastructure in Developing Nations." *International Information Systems* 1, no. 3 (July 1992).

Dutta, Soumitra, Berend Wierenga, and **Arco Dalebout.** "Designing Management Support Systems Using an Integrative Perspective." *Communications of the ACM* 40, no. 6 (June 1997).

Dutta, Soumitra, Luk N. Van Wassenhove, and **Selvan Kulandaiswamy.** "Benchmarking European Software Management Practices." *Communications of the ACM* 41, no. 6 (June 1998).

Eardley, Alan, David Avison, and **Philip Powell.** "Developing Information Systems to Support Flexible Strategy." *Journal of Organizational Computing and Electronic Commerce* 7, no. 1 (1997).

Earl, Michael J., and **Ian A. Scott.** "What Is a Chief Knowledge Officer?" *Sloan Management Review* 40, no. 2 (Winter 1999).

Earl, Michael J., and **Jeffrey L. Sampler.** "Market Management to Transform the IT Organization." *Sloan Management Review* 39, no. 4 (Summer 1998).

Earl, Michael, and **Bushra Khan.** "E-Commerce Is Changing the Face of IT." *Sloan Management Review,* (Fall 2001)

Earl, Michael. "Knowledge Management Strategies: Toward a Taxonomy." *Journal of Management Information Systems* 18, no. 1 (Summer 2001).

"Eastman is Keen on E-Commerce." *Information Week* (August 2, 2000).

Ebner, Manuel, Arthur Hu, Daniel Levitt, and **Jim McCrory.** "How to Rescue CRM." *McKinsey Quarterly* 4 (2002).

Eckholm, Erik. "... And Click Here for China." *New York Times* (August 4, 2002).

Edelstein, Herb. "Technology How To: Mining Data Warehouses." *Information Week* (January 8, 1996).

Ein Dor, Philip, and **Eli Segev.** "Strategic Planning for Management Information Systems." *Management Science* 24, no. 15 (1978).

Ein-Dor, Philip, and **Eli Segev.** "Organizational Context and the Success of Management Information Systems." *Management Science* 24 (June 1978).

Ein-Dor, Philip, Seymour E. Goodman, and **Peter Wolcott.** "From Via Maris to Electronic Highway: The Internet in Canaan." *Communications of the ACM* 43, no. 7 (July 2000).

Eisenhardt, Kathleen M. "Has Strategy Changed?" *Sloan Management Review* 43, no.2 (Winter 2002).

El Najdawi, M. K., and **Anthony C. Stylianou.** "Expert Support Systems: Integrating AI Technologies." *Communications of the ACM* 36, no. 12 (December 1993).

El Sawy, Omar A. "Implementation by Cultural Infusion: An Approach for Managing the Introduction of Information Technologies." *MIS Quarterly* (June 1985).

El Sawy, Omar, and **Burt Nanus.** "Toward the Design of Robust Information Systems." *Journal of Management Information Systems* 5, no. 4 (Spring 1989).

El Sawy, Omar. "Personal Information Systems for Strategic Scanning in Turbulent Environments." *MIS Quarterly* 9, no. 1 (March 1985).

El Sherif, Hisham, and **Omar A. El Sawy.** "Issue-Based Decision Support Systems for the Egyptian Cabinet." *MIS Quarterly* 12, no. 4 (December 1988).

"Electronic Commerce and Technology." *The Daily* (April 2, 2003), available www.statcan.ca/Daily/English/030402/d030402a.htm (accessed June 7, 2003).

Emery, James C. "Cost/Benefit Analysis of Information Systems." Chicago, IL: Society for Management Information Systems Workshop Report No. 1 (1971).

Eng, Paul. "Mega-Data Stored in Mini-Spaces." *ABC News* (January 10, 2003), available http://abcnews.go.com (accessed July 11, 2003).

"Enterprise Application Development: Canadian Pacific Railway Ltd." Quadrus Development Inc. (March 9, 2003), available www.quadrus.com/clients/spotlights/cp+rail+ead.htm (accessed July 21, 2003).

Etzioni, Amitai. *A Comparative Analysis of Complex Organizations.* New York, NY: Free Press (1975).

Evans, Philip and **Thomas S. Wurster.** "Getting Real about Virtual Commerce." *Harvard Business Review* (November–December 1999).

Evans, Philip and **Thomas S. Wurster.** "Strategy and the New Economics of Information." *Harvard Business Review* (September–October 1997).

Evans, Philip, and **Thomas S. Wurster.** *Blown to Bits: How the New Economics of Information Transforms Strategy.* Boston, MA: Harvard Business School Press (2000).

Farhoomand, Ali, and **Don H. Drury.** "Managerial Information Overload." *Communications of the ACM* 45, no. 10 (October 2002).

Farhoomand, Ali, Pauline S. P Ng, and **Justin K. H. Yue.** "The Building of a New Business Ecosystem: Sustaining National Competitive Advantage through Electronic Commerce." *Journal of Organizational Computing and Electronic Commerce* 11, no. 4 (2001)

Farhoomand, Ali, Virpi Kristiina Tuunainen, and **Lester W. Yee.** "Barrier to Global Electronic Commerce: A Cross-Country Study of Hong Kong and Finland." *Journal of Organizational Computing and Electronic Commerce* 10, no. 1 (2000).

Farhoomand, Ali, with **Peter Lovelock.** *Global E-Commerce.* Singapore: Pearson Education Asia (2001).

"Fast Forward 3.0: Maintaining the Momentum." *Report of the Canadian E-Business Opportunities Roundtable* (March 2002), available www.ebusinessroundtable.ca (accessed June 7, 2003).

Favela, Jesus. "Capture and Dissemination of Specialized Knowledge in Network Organizations." *Journal of Organizational Computing and Electronic Commerce* 7, nos. 2 and 3 (1997).

Fayad, Mohamed, and **Marshall P. Cline.** "Aspects of Software Adaptability." *Communications of the ACM* 39, no. 10 (October 1996).

Fayol, Henri. *Administration Industrielle et Generale.* Paris, France: Dunods (1950, first published in 1916).

Fayyad, Usama, Gregory Pitatetsky-Shapiro, and **Padhraic Smyth.** "The KDD Process of Extracting Useful Knowledge from Data." *Communications of the ACM* 39, no. 11 (November 1996).

Fayyad, Usama, Ramasamy Ramakrishnan, and **Ramakrisnan Srikant.** "Evolving Data Mining into Solutions for Insights." *Communications of the ACM* 45, no.8 (August 2002).

Fazlollahi, Bijan, and **Rustam Vahidov.** "A Method for Generation of Alternatives by Decision Support Systems." *Journal of Management Information Systems* 18, no. 2 (Fall 2001).

Feeny, David E., and **Blake Ives.** "In Search of Sustainability: Reaping Long-Term Advantage from Investments in Information Technology." *Journal of Management Information Systems* (Summer 1990).

Feeny, David E., and **Leslie P. Willcocks.** "Core IS Capabilities for Exploiting Information Technology." *Sloan Management Review* 39, no. 3 (Spring 1998).

Feeny, David. "Making Business Sense of the E-Opportunity." *Sloan Management Review* 42, no. 2 (Winter 2001).

Feigenbaum, Edward A. "The Art of Artificial Intelligence: Themes and Case Studies in Knowledge Engineering." *Proceedings of the IJCAI* (1977).

Fichman, Robert G. "The Role of Aggregation in the Measurement of IT-Related Organizational Innovation." *MIS Quarterly* 25, no. 4 (December 2001).

Fichman, Robert G., and **Scott A. Moses.** "An Incremental Process for Software Implementation." *Sloan Management Review* 40, no. 2 (Winter 1999).

Fine, Charles H., Roger Vardan, Robert Pethick, and **Jamal E-Hout.** "Rapid-Response Capability in Value-Chain Design." *Sloan Management Review* 43, no.2 (Winter 2002).

Fingar, Peter. "Component-Based Frameworks for E-Commerce." *Communications of the ACM* 43, no. 10 (October 2000).

Fiori, Rich. "The Information Warehouse." *Relational Database Journal* (January–February 1995).

Fisher, Dennis. "Avril Lavigne Virus Hits the Web." *eWeek* (January 8, 2003).

Fisher, Marshall L., Ananth Raman, and **Anne Sheen McClelland.** "Rocket Science Retailing Is Almost Here: Are You Ready?" *Harvard Business Review* (July-August 2000).

Fitzmaurice, George W., Rvain Balakrishnan, and **Gordon Kurtenbach.** "Sampling, Synthesis, and Input Devices." *Communications of the ACM* 42, no. 8 (August 1999).

Fjermestad, Jerry, and **Starr Roxanne Hiltz.** "An Assessment of Group Support Systems Experimental Research: Methodology, and Results." *Journal of Management Information Systems* 15, no. 3 (Winter, 1998–1999).

Fjermestad, Jerry, and **Starr Roxanne Hiltz.** "Group Support Systems: A Descriptive Evaluation of Case and Field Studies." *Journal of Management Information Systems* 17, no. 3 (Winter 2000–2001).

Fjermestad, Jerry. "An Integrated Framework for Group Support Systems." *Journal of Organizational Computing and Electronic Commerce* 8, no. 2 (1998).

Flash, Cynthia. "Who is the CKO?" *Knowledge Management* (May 2001).

Forgionne, Guiseppe. "Management Support System Effectiveness: Further Empirical Evidence." *Journal of the Association for Information Systems* 1 (May 2000).

Forrest, Stephanie, Steven A. Hofmeyr, and **Anil Somayaji.** "Computer Immunology." *Communications of the ACM* 40, no. 10 (October 1997).

Frank, Robert, and **Robin Sidel.** "Firms that Lived by the Deal in '90s Now Sink by the Dozens." *Wall Street Journal* (June 6, 2002).

Franz, Charles, and **Daniel Robey.** "An Investigation of User-Led System Design: Rational and Political Perspectives." *Communications of the ACM* 27 (December 1984).

Fraser, Martin D., and **Vijay K. Vaishnavi.** "A Formal Specifications Maturity Model." *Communications of the ACM* 40, no. 12 (December 1997).

Freeman, John, Glenn R. Carroll, and **Michael T. Hannan.** "The Liability of Newness: Age Dependence in Organizational Death Rates." *American Sociological Review* 48 (1983).

Friedman, Batya, Peter H. Kahn, Jr. and **Daniel C. Howek.** "Trust Online." *Communications of the ACM* 43, no. 12 (December 2000).

Fritz, Mary Beth Watson, Sridhar Narasimhan, and **Hyeun-Suk Rhee.** "Communication and Coordination in the Virtual Office." *Journal of Management Information Systems* 14, no. 4 (Spring 1998).

Froomkin, A. Michael. "The Collision of Trademarks, Domain Names, and Due Process in Cyberspace." *Communications of the ACM* 44, no. 2 (February 2001).

Fry, Jason. "The Music Man." *Wall Street Journal* (September 16, 2002).

Fulk, Janet, and **Geraldine DeSanctis.** "Electronic Communication and Changing Organizational Forms." *Organization Science* 6, no. 4 (July–August 1995).

Fuller, Mary K., and **E. Burton Swanson.** "Information Centers as Organizational Innovation." *Journal of Management Information Systems* 9, no. 1 (Summer 1992).

Fyfe, Toby. "E-Government on the Inside... Looks a Lot Like the Outside." *CIO Governments Review* (April 1, 2002), available www.itworldcanada.com (accessed June 7, 2003).

Gallagher, Julie. "Proximity, Cultural Similarity, and Inexpensive Labor Are a Few Benefits." *Informationweek* (September 9, 2002).

Gallaugher, John M. "E-Commerce and the Undulating Distribution Channel." *Communications of the ACM* 45, no. 7 (July 2002).

Gallupe, R. Brent, Geraldine DeSanctis, and **Gary W. Dickson.** "Computer-Based Support for Group Problem-Finding: An Experimental Investigation." *MIS Quarterly* 12, no. 2 (June 1988).

Gallupe, R. Brent. "Images of Information Systems in the Early 21st Century." *Communications of the Association for Information Systems* 3, no. 3 (February 2000).

Gane, Chris, and **Trish Sarson.** *Structured Systems Analysis: Tools and Techniques.* Englewood Cliffs, NJ: Prentice Hall (1979).

Gardner, Scott. "ROADS Helps Police Ontario Streets." *Daily IT Wire* (January 16, 2002), available www.itworldcanada.com (accessed July 11, 2003).

Gardner, Stephen R. "Building the Data Warehouse." *Communications of the ACM* 41, no. 9 (September 1998).

Garner, Rochelle. "Internet2... and Counting." *CIO Magazine* (September 1, 2000).

Garvin, David A. "The Processes of Organization and Management." *Sloan Management Review* 39, no. 4 (Summer 1998).

Gattiker, Urs E., and **Helen Kelley.** "Morality and Computers: Attitudes and Differences in Judgments." *Information Systems Research* 10, no. 3 (September 1999).

Gefen, David, and **Catherine M. Ridings.** "Implementation Team Responsiveness and User Evaluation of Customer Relationship Management: A Quasi-Experimental Design Study of Social Exchange Theory." *Journal of Management Information Systems* 19, no. 1 (Summer 2002).

Gefen, David, and **Detmar W. Straub.** "Gender Differences in the Perception and Use of E-Mail: An Extension to the Technology Acceptance Model." *MIS Quarterly* 21, no. 4 (December 1997).

Gelernter, David. "The Metamorphosis of Information Management." *Scientific American* (August 1989).

George, Joey. "Organizational Decision Support Systems." *Journal of Management Information Systems* 8, no. 3 (Winter 1991–1992).

Gerlach, James, Bruce Neumann, Edwin Moldauer, Martha Argo, and **Daniel Frisby.** "Determining the Cost of IT Services." *Communications of the ACM* 45, no. 9 (September 2002).

Ghosh, Anup K., and **Jeffrey M. Voas.** "Inoculating Software for Survivability." *Communications of the ACM* 42, no. 7 (July 1999).

Ghosh, Anup K., and **Tara M. Swaminatha.** "Software Security and Privacy Risks in Mobile E-Commerce." *Communications of the ACM* 44, no. 2 (February 2001).

Ghosh, Shikhar. "Making Business Sense of the Internet." *Harvard Business Review* (March–April 1998).

Giaglis, George. "Focus Issue on Legacy Information Systems and Business Process Change: On the Integrated Design and Evaluation of Business Processes and Information Systems." *Communications of the AIS* 2 (July 1999).

Gibson, Garth A., and **Rodney Van Meter.** "Network Attached Storage Architecture." *Communications of the ACM* 43, no. 11 (November 2000).

Gilbert, Clark, and **Joseph L. Bower.** "Disruptive Change." *Harvard Business Review* (May 2002).

Gill Philip. "Flower Power." *Oracle Profit Magazine* (August 1998).

Ginzberg, Michael J. "Early Diagnosis of MIS Implementation Failure: Promising Results and Unanswered Questions." *Management Science* 27 (April 1981).

Ginzberg, Michael J., W. R. Reitman, and **E. A. Stohr,** eds. *Decision Support Systems.* New York, NY: North Holland Publishing Co. (1982).

Glezer, Chanan, and **Surya B. Yadav.** "A Conceptual Model of an Intelligent Catalog Search System." *Journal of Organizational Computing and Electronic Commerce* 11, no. 1 (2001).

"Global Internet Statistics (by Language)." available www.global-reach.biz/globstats/index.php3 (accessed June 7, 2003).

Glover, Eric J., Steve Lawrence, Michael D. Gordon, William P. Birmingham, and **C. Lee Giles.** "Web Search—Your Way." *Communications of the ACM* 44, no. 12 (December 2001).

Glushko, Robert J., Jay M. Tenenbaum, and **Bart Meltzer.** "An XML Framework for Agent-Based E-Commerce." *Communications of the ACM* 42, no. 3 (March 1999).

Goan, Terrance. "A Cop on the Beat: Collecting and Appraising Intrusion Evidence." *Communications of the ACM* 42, no. 7 (July 1999).

Gogan, Janis L., Jane Fedorowicz, and **Ashok Rao.** "Assessing Risks in Two Projects: A Strategic Opportunity and a Necessary Evil." *Communications of the Association for Information Systems* 1 (May 1999).

Gold, Andrew H., Arvind Malhotra, and **Albert H. Segars.** "Knowledge Management: An Organizational Capabilities Perspective." *Journal of Management Information Systems* 18, no. 1 (Summer 2001).

Goldberg, David E. "Genetic and Evolutionary Algorithms Come of Age." *Communications of the ACM* 37, no. 3 (March 1994).

Goldstein, R. C., and **J. B. McCririck.** "What Do Data Administrators Really Do?" *Datamation* 26 (August 1980).

Goodhue, Dale L., Barbara H. Wixom, and **Hugh J. Watson.** "Realizing Business Benefits through CRM: Hitting the Right Target in the Right Way." *MIS Quarterly Executive* 1, no. 2 (June 2002).

Goodhue, Dale L., Judith A. Quillard, and John F. Rockart. "Managing the Data Resource: A Contingency Perspective." *MIS Quarterly* (September 1988).

Goodhue, Dale L., Laurie J. Kirsch, Judith A. Quillard, and Michael D. Wybo. "Strategic Data Planning: Lessons from the Field." *MIS Quarterly* 16, no. 1 (March 1992).

Goodhue, Dale L., Michael D. Wybo, and Laurie J. Kirsch. "The Impact of Data Integration on the Costs and Benefits of Information Systems." *MIS Quarterly* 16, no. 3 (September 1992).

Gopal, Ram D., and G. Lawrence Sanders. "Global Software Piracy: You Can't Get Blood out of a Turnip." *Communications of the ACM* 43, no. 9 (September 2000).

Gopal, Ram D., and G. Lawrence Sanders. "Preventive and Deterrent Controls for Software Piracy." *Journal of Management Information Systems* 13, no. 4 (Spring 1997).

Gopal, Ram D., Zhiping Walter, and Arvind K. Tripathi. "Amediation: New Horizons in Effective Email Advertising," *Communications of the ACM* 44, no. 12 (December 2001).

Gordon, Graeme. "Following the Leader." *CIO Governments Review* (June 1, 2002), available www.itworldcanada.com (accessed June 7, 2003).

Gorry, G. Anthony, and Michael S. Scott Morton. "A Framework for Management Information Systems." *Sloan Management Review* 13, no. 1 (Fall 1971).

Graham, Robert L. "The Legal Protection of Computer Software." *Communications of the ACM* (May 1984).

Grant, Delvin. "A Wider View of Business Process Engineering." *Communications of the ACM* 45, no. 2 (February 2002).

Grant, Robert M. "Prospering in Dynamically—Competitive Environments: Organizational Capability as Knowledge Integration." *Organization Science* 7, no. 4 (July–August 1996).

Green, R. H. *The Ethical Manager*. New York, NY: Macmillan (1994).

Gregor, Shirley, and Izak Benbasat. "Explanations from Intelligent Systems: Theoretical Foundations and Implications for Practice." *MIS Quarterly* 23, no. 4 (December 1999).

Grobowski, Ron, Chris McGoff, Doug Vogel, Ben Martz, and Jay Nunamaker. "Implementing Electronic Meeting Systems at IBM: Lessons Learned and Success Factors." *MIS Quarterly* 14, no. 4 (December 1990).

Grosky, William I. "Managing Multimedia Information in Database Systems." *Communications of the ACM* 40, no. 12 (December 1997).

Grote, Brigitte, Thomas Rose, and Gerhard Peter. "Filter and Broker: An Integrated Architecture for Information Mediation of Dynamic Sources." *Journal of Organizational Computing and Electronic Commerce* 12, no. 2 (2002).

Grover, Varun, and James Teng. "How Effective Is Data Resource Management?" *Journal of Information Systems Management* (Summer 1991).

Grover, Varun, and Martin D. Goslar. "Initiation, Adoption, and Implementation of Telecommunications Technologies in U.S. Organizations." *Journal of Management Information Systems* 10, no. 1 (Summer 1993).

Grover, Varun, and Pradipkumar Ramanlal. "Six Myths of Information and Markets: Information Technology Networks, Electronic Commerce, and the Battle for Consumer Surplus." *MIS Quarterly* 23, no. 4 (December 1999).

Grover, Varun, and Pradipkumar Ramanlal, and James T.C. Teng. "E-Commerce and the Information Market." *Communications of the ACM* 44, no. 4 (April 2001).

Grover, Varun, and Thomas H. Davenport. "General Perspectives on Knowledge Management: Fostering a Research Agenda." *Journal of Management Information Systems* 18, no. 1 (Summer 2001).

Grover, Varun. "IS Investment Priorities in Contemporary Organizations." *Communications of the ACM* 41, no. 2 (February 1998).

Guerra, Anthony. "Goldman Sachs Embraces Rules-Based Solution." *Wall Street and Technology* (May 2001).

Gulati, Ranjay, and Jason Garino. "Get the Right Mix of Bricks and Clicks." *Harvard Business Review* (May–June 2000).

Gupta, Amarnath, and Ranesh Jain. "Visual Information Retrieval." *Communications of the ACM* 40, no. 5 (May 1997).

Gurbaxani, V., and S. Whang. "The Impact of Information Systems on Organizations and Markets." *Communications of the ACM* 34, no. 1 (Jan. 1991).

Hacki, Remo, and Julian Lighton, "The Future of the Networked Company," *McKinsey Quarerly* 3 (2001).

Hadoulis, John. "Fixing Games Glitches before They Happen." *Athens News* (April 4, 2003), available www.invgr.com/olympics_schlumbergersema_glitches.htm (accessed June 8, 2003).

Hagel III, John, and John Seeley Brown. "Your Next IT Strategy." *Harvard Business Review* (October, 2001).

Hagel, John III, and Marc Singer. "Unbundling the Corporation." *Harvard Business Review* (March–April 1999).

Hagel, John III, and Marc Singer. *Net Worth*. Boston, MA: Harvard Business School Press (1999).

Hamilton, Tyler. "7,000 Visa Clients Exposed to Hacker, Bank Says." *The Winnipeg Free Pres s* (February 20, 2003).

Hammer, Michael, and James Champy. *Reengineering the Corporation*. New York,NY: HarperCollins Publishers (1993).

Hammer, Michael, and Steven A. Stanton. *The Reengineering Revolution*. New York, NY: HarperCollins (1995).

Hammer, Michael. "Process Management and the Future of Six Sigma." *Sloan Management Review* 43, no. 2 (Winter 2002).

Hammer, Michael. "Reengineering Work: Don't Automate, Obliterate." *Harvard Business Review* (July–August 1990).

Handfield, Robert B., and Ernest L. Nichols, Jr. *Introduction to Supply Chain Management*. Upper Saddle River, NJ: Prentice Hall (1999).

Hansen, Morton T., Nitin Nohria, and Thomas Tierney. "What's Your Strategy for Knowledge Management?" *Harvard Business Review* (March–April 1999).

Hansen, Morton, and Bolko von Oetinger. "Introducing T-Shaped Managers: Knowledge Management's Next Generation." *Harvard Business Review* (March 2001).

Hardaway, Don, and Richard P. Will. "Digital Multimedia Offers Key to Educational Reform." *Communications of the ACM* 40, no. 4 (April 1997).

Harmon, Amy. "Software that Tracks E-Mail is Raising Privacy Concerns." *New York Times* (November 22, 2000).

Harrington, Susan J. "The Effect of Codes of Ethics and Personal Denial of Responsibility on Computer Abuse Judgments and Intentions." *MIS Quarterly* 20, no. 2 (September 1996).

Hart, Paul J., and Carol Stoak Saunders. "Emerging Electronic Partnerships: Antecedents and Dimensions of EDI Use from the Supplier's Perspective." *Journal of Management Information Systems* 14, no. 4 (Spring 1998).

Hartman, Amir. "Why Tech Falls Short of Expectations." *Optimize Magazine* (July 2002).

Hayes, Frank. "Don't Shrug Off Bugs." *Computerworld* (July 1, 2002).

Hayes-Roth, Frederick, and Neil Jacobstein. "The State of Knowledge-Based Systems." *Communications of the ACM* 37, no. 3 (March 1994).

Hearst, Marti, Arne Elliott, Jennifer English, Rashmi Sinha, Kirsten Swearinge, and Ka-Ping Yee. "Finding the Flow in Web Search." *Communications of the ACM* 45, no. 9 (Septeber 2002).

Hender, Jillian M., Douglas L. Dean, Thomas L. Rodgers, and Jay F. Nunamaker Jr. "An Examination of the Impact of Stimuli Type and GSS Structure on Creativity." *Journal of Management Information Systems* 18, No. 4 (Spring 2002).

Henderson, John C., and David A. Schilling. "Design and Implementation of Decision Support Systems in the Public Sector." *MIS Quarterly* (June 1985).

"Hill and Knowlton and Intraspect Win 2002 World Class Solution Award." Intraspect Press Release. (June 3, 2002), available www.intraspect.com/newsevents/releases/jun3_02.html (accessed July 21, 2003).

"Hill and Knowlton Canada Limited: Knowledge Management Solution Helps Promote Strategic Communications Offerings." Microsoft Case Study, available www.microsoft.com/canada/casestudies/HandK.asp (accessed July 21, 2003).

Hilson, Gary. "CGI Scores IT Hat Trick with Three Insurance Firms." *IT Business* (February, 5, 2002).

Hilson, Gary. "Composing POS in the Key of C#." *Computing Canada* 29, no. 8 (May 2, 2003).

Hilmer, Kelly M., and Alan R. Dennis. "Stimulating Thinking: Cultivating Better Decisions with Groupware Through Categorization." *Journal of Management Information Systems* 17, no. 3 (Winter 2000–2001).

Hinds, Pamela, and Sara Kiesler. "Communication across Boundaries: Work, Structure, and Use of Communication Technologies in a Large Organization." *Organization Science* 6, no. 4 (July–August 1995).

Hinton, Gregory. "How Neural Networks Learn from Experience." *Scientific American* (September 1992).

Hirji, Karim K. "Exploring Data Mining Implementation." *Communications of the ACM* 44, no. 7 (July 2001).

Hirscheim, Rudy, and Mary Lacity. "The Myths and Realities of Information Technology Insourcing." *Communications of the ACM* 43, no. 2 (February 2000).

Hitt, Lorin M. "Information Technology and Firm Boundaries: Evidence from Panel Data." *Information Systems Research* 10, no. 2 (June 1999).

Hitt, Lorin M., and Erik Brynjolfsson. "Information Technology and Internal Firm Organization: An Exploratory Analysis." *Journal of Management Information Systems* 14, no. 2 (Fall 1997).

Hitt, Lorin, D.J. Wu, and Xiaoge Zhou. "Investment in Enterprise Resource Planning: Business Impact and Productivity Measures." *Journal of Management Information Systems* 19, no. 1 (Summer 2002).

Hoffer, Jeffrey, Joey George, and Joseph Valacich. *Modern Systems Analysis and Design,* 3rd ed. Upper Saddle River, NJ: Prentice Hall (2002).

Hogue, Jack T. "A Framework for the Examination of Management Involvement in Decision Support Systems." *Journal of Management Information Systems* 4, no. 1 (Summer 1987).

Hogue, Jack T. "Decision Support Systems and the Traditional Computer Information System Function: An Examination of Relationships during DSS Application Development." *Journal of Management Information Systems* (Summer 1985).

Holland, John H. "Genetic Algorithms." *Scientific American* (July 1992).

Holweg, Matthias, and Frits K. Pil. "Successful Build-to-Order Strategies Start with the Customer." *Sloan Management Review* 43, no. 1 (Fall 2001).

Hopkins, Jon. "Component Primer." *Communications of the ACM* 43, no. 10 (October 2000).

Hopper, Max. "Rattling SABRE—New Ways to Compete on Information." *Harvard Business Review* (May–June 1990).

Houdeshel, George, and Hugh J. Watson. "The Management Information and Decision Support (MIDS) System at Lockheed Georgia." *MIS Quarterly* 11, no. 1 (March 1987).

Houdeshel, George, and Hugh J. Watson. "The Management Information and Decision Support (MIDS) System at Lockheed, Georgia." *MIS Quarterly* 11, no. 2 (March 1987).

Housel, Thomas J., Omar El Sawy, Jianfang J. Zhong, and Waymond Rodgers. "Measuring the Return on E-Business Initiatives at the Process Level: The Knowledge Value-Added Approach." *ICIS* (2001).

Housel, Tom, and Arthur A. Bell. *Measuring and Managing Knowledge.* New York, NY: McGraw-Hill (2001).

Housel, Tom, and Eric Skopec. *Global Telecommunication Revolution: The Business Perspective.* New York, NY: McGraw-Hill (2001).

Huber, George P. "Cognitive Style as a Basis for MIS and DSS Designs: Much Ado about Nothing?" *Management Science* 29 (May 1983).

Huber, George P. "Organizational Information Systems: Determinants of Their Performance and Behavior." *Management Science* 28, no. 2 (1984).

Huber, George. "Organizational Learning: The Contributing Processes and Literature." *Organization Science* 2 (1991): 88–115.

Huber, George. "The Nature and Design of Post-Industrial Organizations." *Management Science* 30, no. 8 (August 1984).

Huff, Chuck, and C. Dianne Martin. "Computing Consequences: A Framework for Teaching Ethical Computing." *Communications of the ACM* 38, no. 12 (December 1995).

Huff, Sid, Malcolm C. Munro, and Barbara H. Martin. "Growth Stages of End User Computing." *Communications of the ACM* (May 1988).

Hui, Kai Lung, and Patrick Y.K. Chau. "Classifying Digital Products." *Communications of the ACM* 45, no.6 (June 2002).

Huizing, Ard, Esther Koster, and Wim Bouman. "Balance in Business Process Reengineering: An Empirical Study of Fit and Performance." *Journal of Management Information Systems* 14, no. 1 (Summer 1997).

Hunton, James E., and Beeler, Jesse D., "Effects of User Participation in Systems Development: A Longitudinal Field Study." *MIS Quarterly* 21, no. 4 (December 1997).

"IBM Canada Announces $900 Million Outsourcing Agreement with Scotiabank." IBM Canada (March 26, 2001), available www.ibm.com/news/ca/032601_Scotiabank.html (accessed July 21, 2003).

"IBM Names NexInnovations Top Corporate Reseller for PCD Americas." Press Release, available www.canadanewswire.ca/releases/February2003/24/c3363.html (accessed July 21, 2003).

Imielinski, Tomasz, and B. R. Badrinath. "Mobile Wireless Computing: Challenges in Data Management." *Communications of the ACM* 37, no. 10 (October 1994).

"Industry-Leading Technology Vendors Endorse Cognos Metrics Manager." *Cognos* (October 7, 2002), available www.cognos.com/news/releases/2002/1007_2.html (accessed July 21, 2003).

Inman, W. H. "The Data Warehouse and Data Mining." *Communications of the ACM* 39, no. 11 (November 1996).

"Investor Group Acquires Kmart Canada: New President and CEO Appointed." Kmart Press Release (June 16, 1997), available www.kmart.com/corp/story/pressrelease/ (accessed June 5, 2003).

Irani, Zahir, and Peter E.D. Love. "The Propagation of Technology Management Taxonomies for Evaluating Investments in Information Systems." *Journal of Management Information Systems* 17, no.3 (Winter 2000–2001).

Irwin, Gretchen. "The Role of Similarity in the Reuse of Object-Oriented Analysis Models." *Journal of Management Information Systems* 19, no. 2 (Fall 2002).

Isakowitz, Tomas, Michael Bieber, and Fabio Vitali. "Web Information Systems." *Communications of the ACM* 41, no. 7 (July 1998).

Isenberg, Daniel J. "How Senior Managers Think." *Harvard Business Review* (November–December 1984).

Ivari, Juhani, Rudy Hirscheim, and Heinz K. Klein. "A Dynamic Framework for Classifying Information Systems Development Methodologies and Approaches." *Journal of Management Information Systems* 17, no. 3 (Winter 2000–2001).

Ives, Blake, and Sirkka Jarvenpaa. "Applications of Global Information Technology: Key Issues for Management." *MIS Quarterly* 15, no. 1 (March 1991).

Ives, Blake, and Sirkka Jarvenpaa. "Global Business Drivers: Aligning Information Technology to Global Business Strategy." *IBM Systems Journal* 32, no. 1 (1993).

Ives, Blake, and Sirkka Jarvenpaa. "Global Information Technology: Some Lessons from Practice." *International Information Systems* 1, no. 3 (July 1992).

J. D. Cougar, N. L. Enger, and F. Harold. New York, NY: Wiley (1981).

Jajoda, Sushil, Catherine D. McCollum, and Paul Ammann. "Trusted Recovery." *Communications of the ACM* 42, no. 7 (July 1999).

Jarvenpaa, Sirkka L., and **D. Sandy Staples.** "Exploring Perceptions of Organizational Ownership of Information and Expertise." *Journal of Management Information Systems* 18, no. 1 (Summer 2001).

Jarvenpaa, Sirkka L., Kathleen Knoll, and **Dorothy Leidner.** "Is Anybody out There? Antecedents of Trust in Global Virtual Teams." *Journal of Management Information Systems* 14, no. 4 (Spring 1998).

Jarzabek, Stan, and **Riri Huang.** "The Case for User-Centered CASE Tools." *Communications of the ACM* 41, no. 8 (August 1998).

Jensen, M. C., and **W. H. Meckling.** "Specific and General Knowledge and Organizational Science." In L. Wetin and J. Wijkander. *Contract Economics,* ed., Oxford, UK Basil Blackwell (1992).

Jensen, Michael C., and **William H. Meckling.** "Theory of the Firm: Managerial Behavior, Agency Costs, and Ownership Structure." *Journal of Financial Economics* 3 (1976).

Joes, Kathryn. "EDS Set to Restore Cash-Machine Network." *New York Times* (March 26, 1993).

Johnson, Bradford C. "Retail: The Wal-Mart Effect." *The McKinsey Quarterly* (2002 no. 1).

Johnson, Deborah G. "Ethics Online." *Communications of the ACM* 40, no. 1 (January 1997).

Johnson, Deborah G., and **John M. Mulvey.** "Accountability and Computer Decision Systems." *Communications of the ACM* 38, no. 12 (December 1995).

Johnson, Philip M. "Reengineering Inspection." *Communications of the ACM* 41, no. 2 (February 1998).

Johnson, Richard A. "The Ups and Downs of Object-Oriented Systems Development." *Communications of the ACM* 43, no.10 (October 2000).

Johnston, Russell, and **Michael J. Vitale.** "Creating Competitive Advantage with Interorganizational Information Systems." *MIS Quarterly* 12, no. 2 (June 1988).

Jones, Sara, Marc Wilikens, Philip Morris, and **Marcelo Masera.** "Trust Requirements in E-Business." *Communications of the ACM* 43, no. 12 (December 2000).

Joshi, James B.D., Walid G. Aref, Arif Ghafoor, and **Eugene H. Spafford.** "Security Models for Web-Based Applications." *Communications of the ACM* 44, no. 2 (February 2001).

Joshi, Kailash. "A Model of Users' Perspective on Change: The Case of Information Systems Technology Implementation." *MIS Quarterly* 15, no. 2 (June 1991).

Joy, Bill. "Design for the Digital Revolution." *Fortune* (March 6, 2000).

Jukic, Boris, Nenad Jukic, and **Manoj Parameswaran.** "Data Models for Information Sharing in E-Partnerships: Analysis, Improvements, and Relevance." *Journal of Organizational Computing and Electronic Commerce* 12, no. 2 (2002).

Kahn, Beverly K. "Some Realities of Data Administration." *Communications of the ACM* 26 (October 1983).

Kalakota, Ravi, and **Marcia Robinson.** *E-Business 2.0: Roadmap for Success.* Reading, MA: Addison-Wesley (2001).

Kalakota, Ravi, Jan Stallaert, and **Andrew B. Whinston.** "Worldwide Real-Time Decision Support Systems for Electronic Commerce Applications." *Journal of Organizational Computing and Electronic Commerce* 6, no. 1 (1996).

Kambil, Ajit, and **James E. Short.** "Electronic Integration and Business Network Redesign: A Roles-Linkage Perspective." *Journal of Management Information Systems* 10, no. 4 (Spring 1994).

Kanan, P. K., Ai-Mei Chang, and **Andrew B. Whinston.** "Marketing Information on the I-Way." *Communications of the ACM* 41, no. 3 (March 1998).

Kanter, Rosabeth Moss. "The New Managerial Work." *Harvard Business Review* (November–December 1989).

Kanter, Rosabeth Moss. "The Ten Deadly Mistakes of Wanna-Dots." *Harvard Business Review* (January 2001).

Kaplan, David, Ramayya Krishnan, Rema Padman, and **James Peters.** "Assessing Data Quality in Accounting Information Systems." *Communications of the ACM* 41, no. 2 (February 1998).

Kaplan, Steven, and **Mohanbir Sawhney.** "E-Hubs: The New B2B Marketplaces." *Harvard Business Review* (May–June 2000).

Karahanna, Elena, and **Moez Limayem.** "E-Mail and V-Mail Usage: Generalizing across Technologies." *Journal of Organizational Computing and Electronic Commerce* 10, no. 1 (2000).

Karat, John. "Evolving the Scope of User-Centered Design." *Communications of the ACM* 40, no. 7 (July 1997).

Karin, Jahangir, and **Benn R. Konsynski.** "Globalization and Information Management Strategies." *Journal of Management Information Systems* 7 (Spring 1991).

Kauffman, Robert J. and **Yu-Ming Wang.** "The Network Externalities Hypothesis and Competitive Network Growth." *Journal of Organizational Computing and Electronic Commerce* 12, no. 1 (2002).

Kauffman, Robert J., and **Bin Wang.** "New Buyers' Arrival under Dynamic Pricing Market Microstructure: The Case of Group-Buying Discounts on the Internet, *Journal of Management Information Systems* 18, no. 2 (Fall 2001).

Kautz, Henry, Bart Selman, and **Mehul Shah.** "ReferralWeb: Combining Social Networks and Collaborative Filtering." *Communications of the ACM* 40, no. 3 (March 1997).

Keen, Peter G. W. *Competing in Time: Using Telecommunications for Competitive Advantage.* Cambridge, MA: Ballinger Publishing Company (1986).

Keen, Peter G. W. *Shaping the Future: Business Design through Information Technology.* Cambridge, MA: Harvard Business School Press (1991).

Keen, Peter G. W. *The Process Edge.* Boston, MA: Harvard Business School Press (1997).

Keen, Peter G. W., and **M. S. Morton.** *Decision Support Systems: An Organizational Perspective.* Reading, MA: Addison-Wesley (1978).

Keen, Peter G. W., and **M. S. Scott Morton.** *Decision Support Systems: An Organizational Perspective.* 2nd ed. Reading, MA: Addison-Wesley (1982).

Keen, Peter G.W. "Information Systems and Organizational Change." *Communications of the ACM* 24, no. 1 (January 1981).

Keen, Peter. "Ready for the 'New' B2B?" *Computerworld* (September 11, 2000).

Keen, Peter. *Shaping the Future.* Cambridge, MA: Harvard Business School Press (1991).

Keil, Mark, and **Daniel Robey.** "Blowing the Whistle on Troubled Software Projects." *Communications of the ACM* 44, no. 4 (April 2001).

Keil, Mark, and **Ramiro Montealegre.** "Cutting Your Losses: Extricating Your Organization When a Big Project Goes Awry." *Sloan Management Review* 41, no. 3 (Spring 2000).

Keil, Mark, Bernard C. Y. Tan, Kwok-Kee Wei, Timo Saarinen, Virpi Tuunainen, and **Arjen Waassenaar.** "A Cross-Cultural Study on Escalation of Commitment Behavior in Software Projects." *MIS Quarterly* 24, no. 2 (June 2000).

Keil, Mark, Joan Mann, and **Arun Rai.** "Why Software Projects Escalate: An Empirical Analysis and Test of Four Theoretical Models." *MIS Quarterly* 24, no. 4 (December 2000).

Keil, Mark, Paul E. Cule, Kalle Lyytinen, and **Roy C. Schmidt.** "A Framework for Identifying Software Project Risks." *Communications of the ACM* 41, 11 (November 1998).

Keil, Mark, Richard Mixon, Timo Saarinen, and **Virpi Tuunairen.** "Understanding Runaway IT Projects." *Journal of Management Information Systems* 11, no. 3 (Winter 1994–95).

Kelly, Sue, Nicola Gibson, Christopher P. Holland, and **Ben Light.** "Focus Issue on Legacy Information Systems and Business Process Change: A Business Perspective of Legacy Information Systems." *Communications of the AIS* 2 (July 1999).

Kemerer, Chris F. "Progress, Obstacles, and Opportunities in Software Engineering Economics." *Communications of the ACM* 41, no. 8 (August 1998).

Kendall, Kenneth E., and **Julie E. Kendall.** "Information Delivery Systems: An Exploration of Web Push and Pull Technologies." *Communications of the Association for Information Systems* 1 (April 1999).

Kendall, Kenneth E., and **Julie E. Kendall.** *Systems Analysis and Design,* 5th ed. Upper Saddle River, NJ: Prentice Hall (2002).

Kenny, David and **John F. Marshall.** "Contextual Marketing." *Harvard Business Review* (November–December 2000).

Kern, Thomas, Leslie P. Willcocks, and **Mary C. Lacity.** "Application Service Provision: Risk Assessment and Mitigation." *MIS Quarterly Executive* 1, no. 2 (2002).

Kettinger, William J., and **Choong C. Lee.** "Understanding the IS–User Divide in IT Innovation." *Communications of the ACM* 45, no.2 (February 2002).

Kettinger, William J., Varun Grover, Subashish Guhan, and **Albert H. Segors.** "Strategic Information Systems Revisited: A Study in Sustainability and Performance." *MIS Quarterly* 18, no. 1 (March 1994).

Khanna, Poonam. "Mounties Claim Cybercrime Up 65 Percent This Year." *ComputerWorld Canada* (November 15, 2002), available www.itworldcanadacom (accessed June 8, 2003).

Kibati, Mugo, and **Donyaprueth Krairit.** "Building India's National Internet Backbone." *Communications of the ACM* 42, no. 6 (June 1999).

Kim, B. G., and **P. Wang.** "ATM Network: Goals and Challenges." *Communications of the ACM* 38, no. 2 (February 1995).

Kim, Yongbeom, and **Edward A. Stohr.** "Software Reuse." *Journal of Management Information Systems* 14, no. 4 (Spring 1998).

King, J. L., V. Gurbaxani, K. L. Kraemer, F. W. McFarlan, K. S. Raman, and **C. S. Yap.** "Institutional Factors in Information Technology Innovation." *Information Systems Research* 5, no. 2 (June 1994).

King, John L., and **Kenneth Kraemer.** "Information Resource Management Cannot Work." *Information and Management* (1988).

King, John. "Centralized vs. Decentralized Computing: Organizational Considerations and Management Options." *Computing Surveys* (October 1984).

King, Julia. "It's CYA Time." *Computerworld* (March 30, 1992).

King, W. R. "Creating a Strategic Capabilities Architecture." *Information Systems Management* 12, no. 1 (Winter 1995).

King, William R., and **Vikram Sethi.** "An Empirical Analysis of the Organization of Transnational Information Systems." *Journal of Management Information Systems* 15, no. 4 (Spring 1999).

Klein, Barbara D., Dale L. Goodhue, and **Gordon B. Davis.** "Can Humans Detect Errors in Data?" *MIS Quarterly* 21, no. 2 (June 1997).

Klein, Gary, James J. Jiang, and **Debbie B. Tesch.** "Wanted: Project Teams with a Blend of IS Professional Orientations." *Communications of the ACM* 45, no. 6 (June 2002).

Kling, Rob, and **William H. Dutton.** "The Computer Package: Dynamic Complexity." In *Computers and Politics,* edited by James Danzinger, William Dutton, Rob Cling, and Kenneth Kraemer. New York, NY: Columbia University Press (1982).

Kling, Rob. "Social Analyses of Computing: Theoretical Perspectives in Recent Empirical Research." *Computing Survey* 12, no. 1 (March 1980).

Kling, Rob. "When Organizations Are Perpetrators: The Conditions of Computer Abuse and Computer Crime." In *Computerization & Controversy. Value Conflicts & Social Choices,* edited by Charles Dunlop and Rob Kling. New York, NY: Academic Press (1991).

Kohavi, Ron, Neal J. Rothleder, and **Evangelos Simoudis.** "Emerging Trends in Business Analytics." *Communications of the ACM* 45, no. 8 (August 2002).

Kolb, D. A., and **A. L. Frohman.** "An Organization Development Approach to Consulting." *Sloan Management Review* 12, no. 1 (Fall 1970).

Konicki, Steve. "Lockheed Martin Jet Fighter Win Ushers in New Era of Real Time Project Management." *InformationWeek* (November 12, 2001).

Konsynski, Benn R., and **F. Warren McFarlan.** "Information Partnerships—Shared Data, Shared Scale." *Harvard Business Review* (September–October 1990).

Kontzer, Tony. "More Than an In-Box." *InformationWeek* (May 6, 2002).

Kotter, John T. "What Effective General Managers Really Do." *Harvard Business Review* (November–December 1982).

Koufaris, Marios. "Applying the Technology Acceptance Model and Flow Theory to Online Consumer Behavior." *Information Systems Research* 13, no. 2 (2002).

Kraemer, Kenneth, John King, Debora Dunkle, and **Joe Lane.** *Managing Information Systems.* Los Angeles, CA: Jossey-Bass (1989).

Kraut, Robert, Charles Steinfield, Alice P Chan, Brian Butler, and **Anne Hoag.** "Coordination and Virtualization: The Role of Electronic Networks and Personal Relationships." *Organization Science* 10, no. 6 (November–December 1999).

Kreie, Jennifer, and **Timothy Paul Cronan.** "Making Ethical Decisions." *Communications of the ACM* 43, no. 12 (December 2000).

Krill, Paul. "Boosting Access to Customer Data." *InfoWorld* (January 1, 2002).

Kroenke, David. *Database Processing: Fundamentals, Design, and Implementation,* 8th ed. Upper Saddle River, NJ: Prentice Hall (2002).

Kumar, Kuldeep, and **Jos Van Hillegersberg.** "ERP Experiences and Revolution." *Communications of the ACM* 43, no. 4 (April 2000).

Kumar, Kuldeep."Technology for Supporting Supply Chain Management." *Communications of the ACM* 44, no. 6 (June 2001).

Kuo, Geng-Sheng, and **Jing-Pei Lin.** "New Design Concepts for an Intelligent Internet." *Communications of the ACM* 41, no. 11 (November 1998).

Lai, Vincent S. "Intraorganizational Communication with Intranets," *Communications of the ACM* 44, no. 7 (July 2001).

Lai, Vincent S., and **Wingyan Chung.** "Managing International Data Communication." *Communications of the ACM* 45, no.3 (March 2002).

Lais, Sami. "The Power of Location." *Computerworld* (April 15, 2002).

Lange, Danny B. "An Object-Oriented Design Approach for Developing Hypermedia Information Systems." *Journal of Organizational Computing and Electronic Commerce* 6, no. 2 (1996).

Lassila, Kathy S., and **James C. Brancheau.** "Adoption and Utilization of Commercial Software Packages: Exploring Utilization Equilibria, Transitions, Triggers, and Tracks." *Journal of Management Information Systems* 16, no. 2 (Fall 1999).

Laudon, Kenneth C. "A General Model of the Relationship between Information Technology and Organizations." New York, NY: Center for Research on Information Systems, New York University. Working paper, National Science Foundation (1989).

Laudon, Kenneth C. "CIOs Beware: Very Large Scale Systems." New York, NY: Center for Research on Information Systems, New York University Stern School of Business, working paper (1989).

Laudon, Kenneth C. "Data Quality and Due Process in Large Interorganizational Record Systems." *Communications of the ACM* 29 (January 1986a).

Laudon, Kenneth C. "Environmental and Institutional Models of Systems Development." *Communications of the ACM* 28, no. 7 (July 1985).

Laudon, Kenneth C. "Ethical Concepts and Information Technology." *Communications of the ACM* 38, no. 12 (December 1995).

Laudon, Kenneth C. "The Promise and Potential of Enterprise Systems and Industrial Networks." Working paper, The Concours Group. Copyright Kenneth C. Laudon (1999).

Laudon, Kenneth C. and **Carol Guercio Traver.** *E-Commerce: Business, Technology, Society.* Boston, MA: Addison-Wesley (2002).

Laudon, Kenneth C. *Computers and Bureaucratic Reform.* New York, NY: Wiley (1974).

Laudon, Kenneth C. *Dossier Society: Value Choices in the Design of National Information Systems.* New York, NY: Columbia University Press (1986).

Laudon, Kenneth C. *Dossier Society: Value Choices in the Design of National Information Systems.* New York, NY: Columbia University Press (1986b).

Lawrence, Paul, and **Jay Lorsch.** *Organization and Environment.* Cambridge, MA: Harvard University Press (1969).

Leavitt, Harold J. "Applying Organizational Change in Industry: Structural, Technological, and Humanistic Approaches." In *Handbook of Organizations,* edited by James G. March. Chicago, IL: Rand McNally (1965).

Leavitt, Harold J., and **Thomas L. Whisler.** "Management in the 1980s." *Harvard Business Review* (November–December 1958).

Lee, Hau L., and **Seungin Whang.** "Winning the Last Mile of E-Commerce." *Sloan Management Review* 42, no. 4 (Summer 2001).

Lee, Hau, L., V. Padmanabhan, and **Seugin Whang.** "The Bullwhip Effect in Supply Chains." *Sloan Management Review* (Spring 1997).

Lee, Heeseok, and **Woojong Suh.** "A Workflow-Based Methodology for Developing Hypermedia Information Systems." *Journal of Organizational Computing and Electronic Commerce* 11, no. 2 (2001)

Lee, Ho Geun, and **Theodore H. Clark.** "Market Process Reengineering through Electronic Market Systems: Opportunities and Challenges." *Journal of Management Information Systems* 13, no. 3 (Winter 1997).

Lee, Ho Geun, Theodore Clark, and **Kar Yan Tam.** "Research Report: Can EDI Benefit Adopters?" *Information Systems Research* 10, no. 2 (June 1999).

Lee, Ho Geun. "Do Electronic Marketplaces Lower the Price of Goods?" *Communications of the ACM* 41, no. 1 (January 1998).

Lee, Jae Nam, and **Young-Gul Kim.** "Effect of Partnership Quality on IS Outsourcing Success." *Journal of Management Information Systems* 15, no. 4 (Spring 1999).

Lee, Soonchul. "The Impact of Office Information Systems on Power and Influence." *Journal of Management Information Systems* 8, no. 2 (Fall 1991).

Leidner, Dorothy E., and **Joyce Elam.** "Executive Information Systems: Their Impact on Executive Decision Making." *Journal of Management Information Systems* (Winter 1993–1994).

Leidner, Dorothy E., and **Joyce Elam.** "The Impact of Executive Information Systems on Organizational Design, Intelligence, and Decision Making." *Organization Science* 6, no. 6 (November–December 1995).

Leonard-Barton, Dorothy, and **John J. Sviokla.** "Putting Expert Systems to Work." *Harvard Business Review* (March–April 1988).

Leonard-Barton, Dorothy. *Wellsprings of Knowledge.* Boston, MA: Harvard Business School Press (1995).

Lett, Dan. "Hacker Breaches Provincial Web Site." *The Winnipeg Free Press* (November 2002).

Levecq, Hugues, and **Bruce W. Weber.** "Electronic Trading Systems: Strategic Implication of Market Design Choices." *Journal of Organizational Computing and Electronic Commerce* 12, no. 1 (2002).

Levinson, Meredith. "They Know What You'll Buy Next Summer (They Hope)." *CIO Magazine* (May 1, 2002).

Levy, David. "Lean Production in an International Supply Chain." *Sloan Management Review* (Winter 1997).

Lewe, Henrik, and **Helmut Krcmar.** "A Computer-Supported Cooperative Work Research Laboratory." *Journal of Management Information Systems* 8, no. 3 (Winter 1991–1992).

Lewis, P. R. "Direct Wines: Case Study Content." *IT CaseStudies.com* (February 25, 2003), available www.itcasestudies.com (accessed April 8, 2003).

Lieberman, Henry, Christopher Fry, and **Louis Weitzman.** "Exploring the Web with Reconnaissance Agents." *Communications of the ACM* 44, no. 8 (August 2001).

Lientz, Bennett P., and **E. Burton Swanson.** *Software Maintenance Management.* Reading, MA: Addison-Wesley (1980).

Liker, Jeffrey K., David B. Roitman, and **Ethel Roskies.** "Changing Everything All at Once: Work Life and Technological Change." *Sloan Management Review* (Summer 1987).

Lim, Kai H., and **Izak Benbasat.** "The Influence of Multimedia on Improving the Comprehension of Organizational Information," *Journal of Management Information Systems* 19, no. 1 (Summer 2002).

Lindblom, C. E. "The Science of Muddling Through." *Public Administration Review* 19 (1959).

Linthicum, David S. "EAI Application Integration Exposed." *Software Magazine* (February/March 2000).

Lipin, Steven, and **Nikhil Deogun.** "Big Mergers of 90s Prove Disappointing to Shareholders." *Wall Street Journal* (October 30, 2000).

Littlewood, Bev, and **Lorenzo Strigini.** "The Risks of Software." *Scientific American* 267, no. 5 (November 1992).

Littlewood, Bev, and **Lorenzo Strigini.** "Validation of Ultra-high Dependability for Software-Based Systems." *Communications of the ACM* 36, no. 11 (November 1993).

Liu, Ziming, and **David G. Stork.** "Is Paperless Really More?" *Communications of the ACM* 43, no. 11 (November 2000).

"Local College Takes the Lead with Advancements in E-Learning." Press Release (January 29, 2003), available www.nati.net/files/01292003_graduatecentre.PDF (accessed July 21, 2003).

Lohse, Gerald L., and **Peter Spiller.** "Internet Retail Store Design: How the User Interface Influences Traffic and Sales." *Journal of Computer-Mediated Communication* 5, no. 2 (December 1999).

Looney, Clayton A., and **Debabroto Chatterjee.** "Web-Enabled Transformation of the Brokerage Industry." *Communications of the ACM* 45, no. 8 (August 2002)

Lou, Hao, and **Richard W. Scannell.** "Acceptance of Groupware: The Relationships among Use, Satisfaction, and Outcomes." *Journal of Organizational Computing and Electronic Commerce* 6, no. 2 (1996).

Lucas, Henry C., Jr. *Implementation: The Key to Successful Information Systems.* New York, NY: Columbia University Press (1981).

MAC Call Center March Marketing Ltd. Web site, available www.maccallcenter.com/ (accessed. July 21, 2003).

Machlup, Fritz. *The Production and Distribution of Knowledge in the United States.* Princeton, NJ: Princeton University Press (1962).

Maclean, Susan. "HBC Captures the CRM Value of Its Data." *IT Focus* (February 14, 2003), available www.itworldcanada.com (accessed July 11, 2003).

Maclean, Susan. "Shoppers Welcome Innovation." *IT Focus* (November 1, 2002), available www.itworldcanada.com (accessed July 11, 2003).

Maclean, Susan. "Desjardins Delegates Its Data Processing." *IT Focus* (March 1, 2002), available www.itworldcanada.com (accessed July 11, 2003).

MacMillan, Michael. "Integration Help Has Arrived, says IBM." *ComputerWorld Canada* (March 28, 2003).

MacMillan, Michael. "For Linux, It's Only Begun." *ComputerWorld Canada* (January 24, 2003).

Maes, Patti, Robert H. Guttman, and **Alexandros G. Moukas.** "Agents that Buy and Sell." *Communications of the ACM* 42, no. 3 (March 1999).

Maes, Patti. "Agents that Reduce Work and Information Overload." *Communications of the ACM* 38, no. 7 (July 1994).

Magretta, Joan. "Why Business Models Matter." *Harvard Business Review* (May 2002).

Mahmood, Mo Adam, Laura Hall, and **Daniel Leonard Swanberg,** "Factors Affecting Information Technology Usage: A Meta-Analysis of the Empirical Literature." *Journal of Organizational Computing and Electronic Commerce* 11, no. 2 (November 2, 2001)

Maier, Jerry L., R. Kelly Rainer, Jr., and **Charles A. Snyder.** "Environmental Scanning for Information Technology: An Empirical Investigation." *Journal of Management Information Systems* 14, no. 2 (Fall 1997).

Main, Thomas J., and **James E. Short.** "Managing the Merger: Building Partnership Through IT Planning at the New Baxter." *MIS Quarterly* 13, no. 4 (December 1989).

Malhotra, Arvind, Ann Majchrzak, Robert Carman, and **Vern Lott.** "Radical Innovation without Collocation: A Case Study at Boeing Rocketdyne." *MIS Quarterly* 25, no. 2 (June 2001).

Malone, Thomas M., Kevin Crowston, Jintae Lee, and **Brian Pentland.** "Tools for Inventing Organizations: Toward a Handbook of Organizational Processes." *Management Science* 45, no. 3 (March 1999).

Malone, Thomas W. "Is Empowerment Just a Fad? Control, Decision Making, and IT." *Sloan Management Review* (Winter 1997).

Malone, Thomas W., JoAnne Yates, and **Robert I. Benjamin.** "Electronic Markets and Electronic Hierarchies." *Communications of the ACM* (June 1987).

Malone, Thomas W., JoAnne Yates, and **Robert I. Benjamin.** "The Logic of Electronic Markets." *Harvard Business Review* (May–June 1989).

Maltz, Elliott, and **Vincent Chiappetta.** "Maximizing Value in the Digital World." *Sloan Management Review* 43, no. 3 (Spring 2002).

Mannheim, Marvin L. "Global Information Technology: Issues and Strategic Opportunities." *International Information Systems* 1, no. 1 (January 1992).

March, James G., and **G. Sevon.** "Gossip, Information, and Decision Making." In *Advances in Information Processing in Organizations,* edited by Lee S. Sproull and J. P. Crecine. Vol. 1. Hillsdale, NJ: Erlbaum (1984).

March, James G., and **Herbert A. Simon.** *Organizations.* New York, NY: Wiley (1958).

March, Salvatore T., and **Young-Gul Kim.** "Information Resource Management: A Metadata Perspective." *Journal of Management Information Systems* 5, no. 3 (Winter 1988–1989).

Marer, Eva, and **Patrick Thibodeau.** "Companies Confront Rising Network Threats." *Datamation* (July 2, 2001).

Mariano, Gwendolyn. "Music Industry Sounds Off on CD Burning." *CNET* (June 11, 2002).

Markus, M. L. "Power, Politics, and MIS Implementation." *Communications of the ACM* 26, no. 6 (June 1983).

Markus, M. Lynne, and **Mark Keil.** "If We Build It, They Will Come: Designing Information Systems That People Want to Use." *Sloan Management Review* (Summer 1994).

Markus, M. Lynne, and **Robert I. Benjamin.** "Change Agentry—The Next IS Frontier." *MIS Quarterly* 20, no. 4 (December 1996).

Markus, M. Lynne, and **Robert I. Benjamin.** "The Magic Bullet Theory of IT-Enabled Transformation." *Sloan Management Review* (Winter 1997).

Markus, M. Lynne, Conelis Tanis, and **Paul C. van Fenema.** "Multisite ERP Implementations." *Communications of the ACM* 43, no. 3 (April 2000).

Markus, M. Lynne. "Toward a Theory of Knowledge Reuse: Types of Knowledge Reuse Situations and Factors in Reuse Success." *Journal of Management Information Systems* 18, no. 1 (Summer 2001).

Martin, J., and **C. McClure.** "Buying Software Off the Rack." *Harvard Business Review* (November–December 1983).

Martin, James. "PC World's Mobile Computing." *PC World* (January 16, 2003).

Martin, James. *Application Development without Programmers.* Englewood Cliffs, NJ: Prentice Hall (1982).

Martin, James, and **Carma McClure.** *Structured Techniques: The Basis of CASE.* Englewood Cliffs, NJ: Prentice Hall (1988).

Martin, Jr. David M., Richard M. Smith, Michael Brittain, Ivan Fetch, and **Hailin Wu.** "The Privacy Practices of Web Browser Extensions." *Communications of the ACM* 44, no. 2 (February 2001).

Mason, Richard O. "Applying Ethics to Information Technology Issues." *Communications of the ACM* 38, no. 12 (December 1995).

Mason, Richard O. "Four Ethical Issues in the Information Age." *MIS Quarterly* 10, no. 1 (March 1986).

Matlin, Gerald. "What Is the Value of Investment in Information Systems?" *MIS Quarterly* 13, no. 3 (September 1989).

Mazzucchelli, Louis. "Structured Analysis Can Streamline Software Design." *Computerworld* (December 9, 1985).

McKnight, D. Harrison, Vivek Choudhury, and **Charlea Kacmar.** "Developing and Validating Trust Measures for E-Commerce: An Integrative Typology." *Information Systems Research* 13, no.3 (September 2002).

McAfee, Andrew, and **Francois-Xavier Oliveau.** "Confronting the Limits of Networks." *Sloan Management Review* 43, no.4 (Summer 2002).

McCarthy, John. "Generality in Artificial Intelligence." *Communications of the ACM* (December 1987).

McCarthy, John. "Phenomenal Data Mining." *Communications of the ACM* 43, no. 8 (August 2000).

McCullagh, Declan, and **Paul Festa.** "Doctors Log on to Fight SARS Outbreak." *CNet News,* available www.news.com.com/ 2102-1025-997045.html (accessed June 5, 2003).

McCune, Jenny C. "Measuring Value." *Beyond Computing* (July/August 2000).

McDonnell, Sharon. "Putting CRM To Work." *Computerworld* (March 12, 2001).

McDougall, Paul, et al. "Decoding Web Services." *InformationWeek* (October 1, 2001).

McFadden, Fred R., Jeffrey A. Hoffer, and **Mary B. Prescott.** *Modern Database Management,* 6th ed. Upper Saddle River, NJ: Prentice Hall (2002).

McFarlan, F. Warren, James L. McKenney, and **Philip Pyburn.** "Governing the New World." *Harvard Business Review* (July–August 1983).

McFarlan, F. Warren, James L. McKenney, and **Philip Pyburn.** "The Information Archipelago—Plotting a Course." *Harvard Business Review* (January–February 1983).

McFarlan, F. Warren. "Information Technology Changes the Way You Compete." *Harvard Business Review* (May–June 1984).

McFarlan, F. Warren. "Portfolio Approach to Information Systems." *Harvard Business Review* (September–October 1981).

McGrath, Rita Gunther, and **Ian C.McMillan.** "Assessing Technology Projects Using Real Options Reasoning." *Industrial Research Institute* (2000).

McKeen, James D., and **Tor Guimaraes.** "Successful Strategies for User Participation in Systems Development." *Journal of Management Information Systems* 14, no. 2 (Fall 1997).

McKenney, James L., and **F. Warren McFarlan.** "The Information Archipelago—Maps and Bridges." *Harvard Business Review* (September–October 1982).

McKenney, James L., and **Peter G. W. Keen.** "How Managers' Minds Work." *Harvard Business Review* (May–June 1974).

McKinney, Vicki, Kanghyun Yoon, and **Fatemeh "Mariam" Zahedi.** "The Measurement of Web-Customer Satisfaction: An Expectation and Disconfirmation Approach." *Information Systems Research* 13, no.3 (September 2002).

McNeill, Murray. "Outsourcing Helps Firms Stay Competitive." *The Winnipeg Free Press* (February 10, 2003).

McWilliam, Gil. "Building Stronger Brands through Online Communities." *Sloan Management Review* 41, no. 3 (Spring 2000).

Mears, Rena, and **Jason Salzetti.** "The New Wireless Enterprise." *InformationWeek* (September 18, 2000).

"Media Touch Technologies Signs Canadian Coast Guard College." Press Release (January 29, 2003), available www.nati.net/ files/01292003_mediatouch.PDF (accessed July 21, 2003).

Meehan, Michael. "No Pain, No Gain." *Computerworld* (March 11, 2002).

Meister, Frank, Jeetu Patel, and **Joe Fenner.** "E-Commerce Platforms Mature." *InformationWeek* (October 23, 2000).

Memon, Nasir, and **Ping Wah Wong.** "Protecting Digital Media Content." *Communications of the ACM* 41, no. 7 (July 1998).

Mendelson, Haim, and **Ravindra R. Pillai.** "Clock Speed and Informational Response: Evidence from the Information Technology Industry." *Information Systems Research* 9, no. 4 (December 1998).

Messina, Paul, David Culler, Wayne Pfeiffer, William Martin, J. Tinsley Oden, and **Gary Smith.** "Architecture." *Communications of the ACM* 41, no. 11 (November 1998).

Metz, Cade. "Athens Apps Up and Running." *PC Magazine* (December 23, 2002), available http://www.pcmag.com/print_article/0,3048,a=35110,00.asp (accessed June 8, 2003).

Metz, Cade. "Olympian Technology Powers the Games." *PC Magazine* (February 22, 2002), available http://www.pcmag.com/print_article/0,3048,a=23111,00.asp (accessed June 8, 2003).

Milberg, Sandra J., Sandra J. Burke, H. Jeff Smith, and **Ernest A. Kallman.** "Values, Personal Information Privacy, and Regulatory Approaches." *Communications of the ACM* 38, no. 12 (December 1995).

Mintzberg, Henry, and **Frances Westley.** "Decision Making: It's Not What You Think." *Sloan Management Review* (Spring 2001).

Mintzberg, Henry. "Managerial Work: Analysis from Observation." *Management Science* 18 (October 1971).

Mintzberg, Henry. *The Nature of Managerial Work.* New York, NY: Harper & Row (1973).

Mintzberg, Henry. *The Structuring of Organizations.* Englewood Cliffs, NJ: Prentice Hall (1979).

Miranda, Shaila M., and **Robert P. Bostrum.** "Meeting Facilitation: Process versus Content Interventions." *Journal of Management Information Systems* 15, no. 4 (Spring 1999).

Miranda, Shaila M., and **Robert P. Bostrum.** "The Impact of Group Support Systems on Group Conflict and Conflict Management." *Journal of Management Information Systems* 10, no. 3 (Winter 1993–1994).

Moore, Paula. "Kmart Owners Couldn't Pass Up a Deal." *Denver Business Journal* (February 23, 1998).

Moores, Trevor, and **Gurpreet Dhillon.** "Software Piracy: A View from Hong Kong." *Communications of the ACM* 43, no. 12, (December 2000).

Morrison, Mike, Joline Morrison, and **Anthony Keys.** "Integrating Web Sites and Databases." *Communications of the ACM* 45, no.9 (September 2002).

Mougayar, Walid. *Opening Digital Markets,* 2nd ed. New York, NY: McGraw-Hill (1998).

Moulton, Donalee. "Surgeons in Halifax, Patient in Saint John." *Canadian Medical Association Journal* 167, no. 11 (November 26, 2002).

Mueller, Milton. "Universal Service and the Telecommunications Act: Myth Made Law." *Communications of the ACM* 40, no. 3 (March 1997).

Mumford, Enid, and **Mary Weir.** *Computer Systems in Work Design: The ETHICS Method.* New York, NY: John Wiley (1979).

Munakata, Toshinori, and **Yashvant Jani.** "Fuzzy Systems: An Overview." *Communications of the ACM* 37, no. 3 (March 1994).

Mykytyn, Kathleen, Peter P. Mykytyn, Jr., and **Craig W. Slinkman.** "Expert Systems: A Question of Liability." *MIS Quarterly* 14, no. 1 (March 1990).

Nakamura, Kiyoh, Toshihiro Ide, and **Yukio Kiyokane.** "Roles of Multimedia Technology in Telework." *Journal of Organizational Computing and Electronic Commerce* 6, no. 4 (1996).

Nambisan, Satish, and **Yu-Ming Wang.** "Web Technology Adoption and Knowledge Barriers." *Journal of Organizational Computing and Electronic Commerce* 10, no. 2 (2000).

National Telecommunications & Information Administration, U.S. Department of Commerce. "Falling Through the Net: Defining the Digital Divide." (July 8, 1999).

"Nav Canada's Striking Success." *Frontier Centre for Public Policy* (September 18, 2002), available www.fcpp.org/publication_detail.php?PubID=97 (accessed July 21, 2003).

Nedda, Gabriela G. Olazabal. "Banking: The IT Paradox." *The McKinsey Quarterly,* no. 1 (2002).

Needham, Roger M. "Denial of Service: An Example." *Communications of the ACM* 37, no. 11 (November 1994).

Nerson, Jean-Marc. "Applying Object-Oriented Analysis and Design." *Communications of the ACM* 35, no. 9 (September 1992).

Neumann, Peter G. "Risks Considered Global(ly)." *Communications of the ACM* 35, no. 1 (January 1993).

Neumann, Seev. "Issues and Opportunities in International Information Systems." *International Information Systems* 1, no. 4 (October 1992).

"New Instrument Landing System Now Operational at Kelowna International Airport." *Press Release* (February 17, 2003), available www.newswire.ca/releases/February2003/17/c0936.html (accessed July 21, 2003).

"NexInnovations Wins Gold IBM Thomas J. Watson Award." *Press Release* (January 14, 2003), available www.nexinnovations.com/news/press_release_view.asp?PR_ID=24 (accessed July 21, 2003).

Ngwenyama, Ojelanki, and **Allen S. Lee.** "Communication Richness in Electronic Mail: Critical Social Theory and the Contextuality of Meaning." *MIS Quarterly* 21, no. 2 (June 1997).

Nidumolu, Sarma R., Mani Subramani, and **Alan Aldrich.** "Situated Learning and the Situated Knowledge Web: Exploring the Ground Beneath Knowledge Management." *Journal of Management Information Systems* 18, no. 1 (Summer 2001).

Nidumolu, Sarma R., Seymour E. Goodman, Douglas R. Vogel, and **Ann K. Danowitz.** "Information Technology for Local Administration Support: The Governorates Project in Egypt." *MIS Quarterly* 20, no. 2 (June 1996).

Niederman, Fred, Catherine M. Beise, and **Peggy M. Beranek.** "Issues and Concerns about Computer-Supported Meetings: The Facilitator's Perspective." *MIS Quarterly* 20, no. 1 (March 1996).

Nissen, Mark E. "Redesigning Reengineering through Measurement-Driven Inference," *MIS Quarterly* 22, no. 4 (December 1998).

Nissenbaum, Helen. "Computing and Accountability." *Communications of the ACM* 37, no. 1 (January 1994).

Nobel, Carmen. "McDonald's Adds WLAN Access to Its Menu." *eWeek* (March 11, 2003).

Noffsinger, W. B., Robert Niedbalski, Michael Blanks, and **Niall Emmart.** "Legacy Object Modeling Speeds Software Integration." *Communications of the ACM* 41, no. 12 (December 1998).

Nolan, Richard. "Managing Information Systems by Committee." *Harvard Business Review* (July–August 1982).

Nunamaker, J. F., Alan R. Dennis, Joseph S. Valacich, Douglas R. Vogel, and **Joey F. George.** "Electronic Meeting Systems to Support Group Work." *Communications of the ACM* 34, no. 7 (July 1991).

Nunamaker, Jay, Robert O. Briggs, Daniel D. Mittleman, Douglas R. Vogel, and **Pierre A. Balthazard.** "Lessons from a Dozen Years of Group Support Systems Research: A Discussion of Lab and Field Findings." *Journal of Management Information Systems* 13, no. 3 (Winter 1997).

O'Keefe, Robert M., and **Tim McEachern.** "Web-based Customer Decision Support Systems." *Communications of the ACM* 41, no. 3 (March 1998).

O'Leary, Daniel E. *Enterprise Resource Planning Systems: Systems Life Cycle, Electronic Commerce, and Risk.* New York, NY: Cambridge University Press (2000).

O'Leary, Daniel E., Daniel Koukka, and **Robert Plant.** "Artificial Intelligence and Virtual Organizations." *Communications of the ACM* 40, no. 1 (January 1997).

O'Leary, Daniel, and **Peter Selfridge.** "Knowledge management for Best Practices." *Communications of the ACM* 43, no. 11(November 2000).

O'Rourke, Maureen A. "Is Virtual Trespass an Apt Analogy?" *Communications of the ACM* 44, no. 2 (February 2001).

Okerson, Ann. "Who Owns Digital Works?" *Scientific American* (July 1996).

"Olympics Testing Labs Opened." *eWeek* (November 11, 2002), available www.eweek.com/ (accessed June 8, 2003).

Oppliger, Rolf. "Internet Security, Firewalls, and Beyond." *Communications of the ACM* 40, no.7 (May 1997).

Orlikowski, Wanda J. "Knowing in Practice: Enacting a Collective Capability in Distributed Organizing." *Organization Science* 13, no. 3 (May-June 2002).

Orlikowski, Wanda J. "Learning from Notes: Organizational Issues in Groupware Implementation." Sloan Working Paper, no. 3428. Cambridge, MA: Sloan School of Management, Massachusetts Institute of Technology.

Orlikowski, Wanda J., and Daniel Robey. "Information Technology and the Structuring of Organizations." *Information Systems Research* 2, no. 2 (June 1991).

Orlikowski, Wanda J., and J. Debra Hofman. "An Improvisational Change Model for Change Management: The Case of Groupware Technologies." *Sloan Management Review* (Winter 1997).

Orlikowski, Wanda J., and Jack J. Baroudi. "Studying Information Technology in Organizations: Research Approaches and Assumptions." *Information Systems Research* 2, no. 1 (March 1991).

Orlikowski, Wanda J., and Stephen R. Bailey. "Technology and Institutions: What Can Research on Information Technology and Research on Organizations Learn from Each Other?" *MIS Quarterly* 25, no. 2 (June 2001)

Orr, Kenneth. "Data Quality and Systems Theory." *Communications of the ACM* 41, no. 2 (February 1998).

Ottawa Business Journal Staff. "Cognos Teams with Giuliani Group." *Ottawa Business Journal* (March 10, 2003).

Oz, Effy. "Ethical Standards for Information Systems Professionals," *MIS Quarterly* 16, no. 4 (December 1992).

Oz, Effy. "When Professional Standards are Lax: The CONFIRM Failure and Its Lessons." *Communications of the ACM* 37, no. 10 (October 1994).

Oz, Effy. *Ethics for the Information Age*. Dubuque, IA: W. C. Brown (1994).

Palaniswamy, Rajagopal, and Tyler Frank. "Enhancing Manufacturing Performance with ERP Systems." *Information Systems Management* (Summer 2000).

Palen, Leysia. "Mobile Telephony in a Connected Life." *Communications of the ACM* 45, no. 3 (March 2002).

Palmer, Jonathan W. "Web Site Usability, Design and Performance Metrics." *Information Systems Research* 13, no.3 (September 2002).

Palmer, Jonathan W., and David A. Griffith. "An Emerging Model of Web Site Design for Marketing." *Communications of the ACM* 41, no. 3 (March 1998).

Palvia, Shailendra, Prashant Palvia, and Ronald Zigli, eds. *The Global Issues of Information Technology Management*. Harrisburg, PA: Idea Group Publishing (1992).

Pancake, Cherri M. "The Promise and the Cost of Object Technology: A Five-Year Forecast." *Communications of the ACM* 38, no. 10 (October 1995).

Pancake, Cherri M., and Christian Lengauer. "High-Performance Java." *Communications of the ACM* 44, no. 10 (October 2001).

Panko, Raymond R. "Is Office Productivity Stagnant?" *MIS Quarterly* 15, no. 2 (June 1991).

Papazoglou, Mike P. "Agent-Oriented Technology in Support of E-Business." *Communications of the ACM* 44, no. 4 (April 2001).

Parker, M. M. "Enterprise Information Analysis: Cost-Benefit Analysis and the Data-Managed System." *IBM Systems Journal* 21 (1982).

Parsons, Jeffrey, and Yair Wand. "Using Objects for Systems Analysis." *Communications of the ACM* 40, no. 12 (December 1997).

Passmore, David. "Scaling Large E-Commerce Infrastructures." *Packet Magazine* (Third Quarter 1999).

Patel, Samir, and Suneel Saigal. "When Computers Learn to Talk: A Web Services Primer," *The McKinsey Quarterly*, no. 1 (2002).

Patrick, Ryan B. "Sun, Beonix Open Linux facility." *Daily IT Wire* (February 25, 2003), available www.itworldcanada.com (accessed July 11, 2003).

Patrick, Ryan B. "Portals Key To E-Commerce Growth: Report." *ComputerWorld Canada* (June 28, 2002).

Patton, Susannah. "The Truth About CRM." *CIO Magazine* (May 1, 2001).

Paul, Lauren Gibbons. "What Price Ownership?" *Datamation* (December/January 1998).

Peffers, Ken and Timo Saarinen. "Measuring the Business Value of IT Investments: Inferences from a Study of Senior Bank Executives." *Journal of Organizational Computing and Electronic Commerce* 12, no. 1 (2002).

PeopleSoft. "Spotlight on Performance at Detroit Edison." available *www.peoplesoft.com* (accessed November 3, 2002).

Petrazzini, Ben, and Mugo Kibati. "The Internet in Developing Countries." *Communications of the ACM* 42, no. 6 (June 1999).

"Pfizer Canada Sales and Marketing Empowereed with Pharmaceutical Sales Intelligence Factory including Brio Intelligence Interactive Dashboards." *Brio Software* (November 2002), available www.brio.com/pdfs/getpdf.php?file=Pfizer.pdf (accessed July 11, 2003).

"Pharmaceutical Information Network "Optimizing Quality And Utilization Of Health Services."Press Release (July 30, 2002), available www.albertawellnet.org/pin/calherald_073001.html (accessed January 23, 2003).

"Pharmacy/PIN." Western Health Information Collaborative, available www.whic.org/public/profiles/pin.html (accessed July 21, 2003).

Phillips, Charles. "Stemming the Software Spending Spree." *Optimize Magazine* (April 2002).

Phillips, James, and Dan Foody. "Building a Foundation for Web Services." *EAI Journal* (March 2002).

"Physicians Improve Patient Care With ASP solution." Microsoft Case Study, available www.microsoft.com/canada/casestudies/alberta+wellnet.asp (accessed May 4, 2003).

Piccoli, Gabriele, Rami Ahmad, and Blake Ives. "Web-Based Virtual Learning Environments: A Research Framework and a Preliminary Assessment of Effectiveness in Basic IT Skills Training." *MIS Quarterly* 25, no. 4 (December 2001).

Pindyck, Robert S., and Daniel L. Rubinfeld. *Microeconomics,* 5th ed. Upper Saddle River, NJ: Prentice Hall (2001).

Pinker, Edieal, Abraham Seidmann, and Riginald C. Foster. "Strategies for Transitioning 'Old Economy' Firms to E-Business." *Communications of the ACM* 45, no. 5 (May 2002).

Pinsonneault, Alain, and Kenneth L. Kraemer. "Exploring the Role of Information Technology in Organizational Downsizing: A Tale of Two American Cities." *Organization Science* 13, no. 2 (March–April 2002).

Pinsonneault, Alain, Henri Barki, R. Brent Gallupe, and Norberto Hoppen. "Electronic Brainstorming: The Illusion of Productivity." *Information Systems Research* 10, no. 2 (July 1999).

Pitkow, James, Hinrich Schutze, Todd Cass, Rob Cooley, Don Turnbull, Andy Edmonds, Eytan Adar, and Thomas Breuel. "Personalized Search." *Communications of the ACM* 45, no. 9 (September 2002).

Pomerol, Jean-Charles, Patrick Brezillon, and Laurent Pasquier. "Operational Knowledge Representation for Practical Decision Making." *Journal of Management Information Systems* 18, No. 4 (Spring 2002).

Porter, Michael E., and Scott Stern. "Location Matters." *Sloan Management Review* 42, no. 4 (Summer 2001).

Porter, Michael. "How Information Can Help You Compete." *Harvard Business Review* (August–September 1985a).

Porter, Michael. "Strategy and the Internet." *Harvard Business Review* (March 2001).

Porter, Michael. *Competitive Strategy.* New York, NY: Free Press (1980).

Porter, Michael. *Competitive Advantage.* New York, NY: Free Press (1985).

Pottie, G. J., and **W. J. Kaiser.** "Wireless Integrated Network Sensors." *Communications of the ACM* 43, no. 5 (May 2000).

Poulin, Jeffrey S. "Reuse: Been There, Done That." *Communications of the ACM* 42, no. 5 (May 1999).

Prahalad, C. K., and **M.S.. Krishnan.** "Synchronizing Strategy and Information Technology." *Sloan Management Review* 43, no. 4 (Summer 2002).

Prahalad, C.K., and **M.S. Krishnan.** "The New Meaning of Quality in the Information Age." *Harvard Business Review* (September–October 1999).

Prahalad, C.K., and **Venkatram Ramaswamy.** "Coopting Consumer Competence." *Harvard Business Review* (January–February 2000).

Premkumar, G., K. Ramamurthy, and **Sree Nilakanta.** "Implementation of Electronic Data Interchange: An Innovation Diffusion Perspective." *Journal of Management Information Systems* 11, no. 2 (Fall 1994).

Pryma, Kristy. "Alberta Electric Company Standardizes for ROI." *ITBusiness* (May 15, 2003), available www.itbusiness.ca (accessed July 11, 2003).

Quelch, John A., and **Lisa R. Klein.** "The Internet and International Marketing." *Sloan Management Review* (Spring 1996).

Quenneville, Jean-Guy. "Matching Technology with Business Objectives." ITX Awards Submission (April 4, 2000), available www.mohawk.ca (accessed June 7, 2003).

Quinn, James Brian. "Strategic Outsourcing: Leveraging Knowledge Capabilities." *Sloan Management Review* 40, no. 4 (Summer 1999).

Rabson, Mia. "Stolen Financial Data Retrieved." *The Winnipeg Free Press* (February 5, 2003).

Radding, Alan. "Analyze Your Customers." *Datamation* (September 25, 2000).

Rai, Arun, Ravi Patnayakuni, and **Nainika Patnayakuni.** "Technology Investment and Business Performance." *Communications of the ACM* 40, no. 7 (July 1997).

Rai, Arun, Sandra S. Lang, and **Robert B. Welker.** "Assessing the Validity of IS Success Models: An Empirical Test and Theoretical Analysis." *Information Systems Research* 13, no. 1 (March 2002).

Rainer, Rex Kelley, Jr., Charles A. Snyder, and **Houston H. Carr.** "Risk Analysis for Information Technology." *Journal of Management Information Systems* 8, no. 1 (Summer 1991).

Rainie, Lee, and **Dan Packel.** "More Online, Doing More." The Pew Internet and American Life Project (Febuary 18, 2001).

Randall, Dave, John Hughes, Jon O'Brien, Tom Rodden, Mark Rouncefield, Ian Sommerville, and **Peter Tolmie.** "Focus Issue on Legacy Information Systems and Business Process Change: Banking on the Old Technology: Understanding the Organisational Context of 'Legacy' Issues." *Communications of the AIS* 2, (July 1999).

Ranft, Annette L., and **Michael D. Lord.** "Acquiring New Technologies and Capabilities: A Grounded Model of Acquisition Implementation." *Organization Science* 13, no. 4 (July–August 2002).

Ravichandran, T., and **Arun Rai.** "Total Quality Management in Information Systems Development." *Journal of Management Information Systems* 16, no. 3 (Winter 1999–2000).

Ray, Randy. "Web Expands Recruiting Role." *The Globe and Mail* (November 10, 2000).

Raymond, Louis, and **Francois Bergeron.** "EDI Success in Small- and Medium-sized Enterprises: A Field Study." *Journal of Organizational Computing and Electronic Commerce* 6, no. 2 (1996).

Rayport, J. F., and **J. J. Sviokla.** "Managing in the Marketspace." *Harvard Business Review* (November–December 1994).

Reagle, Joseph, and **Lorrie Faith Cranor.** "The Platform for Privacy Preferences." *Communications of the ACM* 42, no. 2 (February 1999).

Redman, Thomas C. "The Impact of Poor Data Quality on the Typical Enterprise." *Communications of the ACM* 41, no. 2 (February 1998).

Regan, Keith. "U.S. E-Commerce Shatters Non-Holiday Record." *Ecommerce Times* (May 23, 2003), available www.ecommercetimes.com/perl/story/21586.html (accessed June 7, 2003).

Reich, Blaize Horner, and **Izak Benbasat.** "Factors that Influence the Social Dimension of Alignment between Business and Information Technology Objectives." *MIS Quarterly* 24, no. 1 (March 2000).

Reichheld, Frederick E., and **Phil Schefter.** "E-Loyalty: Your Secret Weapon on the Web." *Harvard Business Review* (July–August 2000).

Reinartz, Werner, and **V. Kumar.** "The Mismanagement of Customer Loyalty." *Harvard Business Review* (July 2002).

Ricadela, Aaron. "Living on the Grid." *InformationWeek* (June 17, 2002).

Rifkin, Glenn, and **Joel Kurtzman.** "Is Your E-Business Plan Radical Enough?" *Sloan Management Review* 43, no. 3 (Spring 2002).

Rifkin, Jeremy. "Watch Out for Trickle-Down Technology." *New York Times* (March 16, 1993).

Rigdon, Joan E. "Frequent Glitches in New Software Bug Users." *Wall Street Journal* (January 18, 1995).

Rivard, Suzanne, and **Sid L. Huff.** "Factors of Success for End-User Computing." *Communications of the ACM* 31, no. 5 (May 1988).

Roach, Stephen S. "Industrialization of the Information Economy." New York, NY: Morgan Stanley and Co. (1984).

Roach, Stephen S. "Making Technology Work." New York, NY: Morgan Stanley and Co. (1993).

Roach, Stephen S. "Services Under Siege—The Restructuring Imperative." *Harvard Business Review* (September–October 1991).

Roach, Stephen S. "Technology and the Service Sector." *Technological Forecasting and Social Change* 34, no. 4 (December 1988).

Roach, Stephen S. "The Hollow Ring of the Productivity Revival." *Harvard Business Review* (November–December 1996).

Robey, Daniel, and **M. Lynne Markus.** "Rituals in Information System Design." *MIS Quarterly* (March 1984).

Robey, Daniel, and **Marie-Claude Boudreau.** "Accounting for the Contradictory Organizational Consequences of Information Technology: Theoretical Directions and Methodological Implications." *Information Systems Research* 10, no. 42 (June1999).

Robey, Daniel, Jeanne W. Ross, and **Marie-Claude Boudreau.** "Learning to Implement Enterprise Systems: An Exploratory Study of the Dialectics of Change." *Journal of Management Information Systems* 19, no. 1 (Summer 2002).

Robinson, Teri. "NASDAQ Is Bullish on Technology." *InformationWeek* (May 22,2000).

Roche, Edward M. "Planning for Competitive Use of Information Technology in Multinational Corporations." AIB UK Region, Brighton Polytechnic, Brighton, UK: Conference Paper (March 1992). Edward M. Roche, W. Paul Stillman School of Business, Seton Hall University.

Roche, Edward M. *Managing Information Technology in Multinational Corporations.* New York, NY: Macmillan (1992).

Rockart, John F. "Chief Executives Define Their Own Data Needs." *Harvard Business Review* (March–April 1979).

Rockart, John F., and **David W. DeLong.** *Executive Support Systems: The Emergence of Top Management Computer Use.* Homewood, IL: Dow-Jones Irwin (1988).

Rockart, John F., and **James E. Short.** "IT in the 1990s: Managing Organizational Interdependence." *Sloan Management Review* 30, no. 2 (Winter 1989).

Rockart, John F., and **Lauren S. Flannery.** "The Management of End-User Computing." *Communications of the ACM* 26, no. 10 (October 1983).

Rockart, John F., and **Michael E. Treacy.** "The CEO Goes Online." *Harvard Business Review* (January–February 1982).

Ross, Jeanne W. and **Cynthia M. Beath.** "Beyond the Business Case: New Approaches to IT Investment." *Sloan Management Review* 43, no.2 (Winter 2002).

Ross, Jeanne W., and **Peter Weill.** "Six IT Decisions Your IT People Shouldn't Make." *Harvard Business Review* (November 2002).

Rotenberg, Marc. "Communications Privacy: Implications for Network Design." *Communications of the ACM* 36, no. 8 (August 1993).

Ruhleder, Karen, and **John Leslie King.** "Computer Support for Work Across Space, Time, and Social Worlds." *Journal of Organizational Computing* 1, no. 4 (1991).

Rumelhart, David E., Bernard Widrow, and **Michael A. Lehr.** "The Basic Ideas in Neural Networks." *Communications of the ACM* 37, no. 3 (March 1994).

Rundensteiner, Elke A., Andreas Koeller, and **Xin Zhang.** "Maintaining Data Warehouses over Changing Information Sources." *Communications of the ACM* 43, no. 6 (June 2000).

Rupley, Sebastian. "Next-Generation Internet Protocol is in Play." *PC Magazine* (June 5, 2003).

Ruttan, Susan. "Patient Medication Records To Go Online For Doctors: Plan Part Of Electronic Health Record." *The Edmonton Journal* (March 3, 2003).

Ryan, Sherry D. and **David A. Harrison.** "Considering Social Subsystem Costs and Benefits in Information Technology Investment Decisions: A View from the Field on Anticipated Payoffs." *Journal of Management Information Systems* 16, no. 4 (Spring 2000).

Ryan, Sherry D., David A. Harrison, and **Lawrence L Schkade.** "Information Technology Investment Decisions: When Do Cost and Benefits in the Social Subsystem Matter?" *Journal of Management Information Systems* 19, no. 2 (Fall 2002).

"Saab/ICAN Team Wins AIS Infrastructure Contract in the St. Lawrence Seaway." Press Release (May 3, 2002), available www.ican.nf.net/news/StLawrenceSeaway.htm (accessed July 21, 2003).

Sabherwahl, Rajiv. "The Role of Trust in IS Outsourcing Development Projects." *Communications of the ACM* 42, no. 2 (February 1999).

Salisbury, J. Kenneth, Jr. "Making Graphics Physically Tangible." *Communications of the ACM* 42, no. 8 (August 1999).

Salkever, Alex. "Cybersecurity's Leaky Dikes." *BusinessWeek* (July 2, 2002), available *www.businessweek.com.*

Sambamurthy, V., and **Robert W. Zmud.** "Research Commentary: The Organizing Logic for an Enterprise's IT Activities in the Digital Era—A Prognosis of Practice and a Call to Research." *Information Systems Research* 11, No. 2 (June 2000).

Samuelson, Pamela. "Computer Programs and Copyright's Fair Use Doctrine." *Communications of the ACM* 36, no. 9 (September 1993).

Samuelson, Pamela. "Copyright's Fair Use Doctrine and Digital Data." *Communications of the ACM* 37, no. 1 (January 1994).

Samuelson, Pamela. "Liability for Defective Electronic Information." *Communications of the ACM* 36, no. 1 (January 1993).

Samuelson, Pamela. "Self Plagiarism or Fair Use?" *Communications of the ACM* 37, no. 8 (August 1994).

Samuelson, Pamela. "The Ups and Downs of Look and Feel." *Communications of the ACM* 36, no. 4 (April 1993).

Sarkar, Pushpak. "A Paragon of Quality." *Intelligent Enterprise* (October 2002).

"SARS: The Unknown Threat." *BBC News/Health,* available news.bbc.co.uk/1/low/health/2886195.stm (accessed June 5, 2003).

Sauer, Chris, and **Leslie P. Willcocks,** "The Evolution of the Organizational Architect." *Sloan Management Review* 43, no. 3 (Spring 2002).

Sauter, Vicki L. "Intuitive Decision Making." *Communications of the ACM* 42, no 6 (June 1999)

Scheer, August-Wilhelm, and **Frank Habermann.** "Making ERP a Success." *Communications of the ACM* 43, no. 3 (April 2000).

Schein, Edgar H. *Organizational Culture and Leadership.* San Francisco, CA: Jossey-Bass (1985).

Schmidt, Douglas C., and **Mohamed E. Fayad.** "Lessons Learned Building Reusable OO Frameworks for Distributed Software." *Communications of the ACM* 40, no. 10 (October 1997).

Schmidt, Roy, Kalle Lyytinen, Mark Keil, and **Paul Cule.** "Identifying Software Project Risks: An International Delphi Study." *Journal of Management Information Systems* 17, no. 4 (Spring 2001)

Schneiderman, Ben. "Universal Usability." *Communications of the ACM* 43, no. 5 (May 2000).

Schoder, Detlef, and **Pai-ling Yin.** "Building Firm Trust Online." *Communications of the ACM* 43, no. 12 (December 2000).

Schuff, David, and **Robert St. Louis.** "Centralization vs. Decentralization of Application Software." *Communications of the ACM* 44, no. 6 (June 2001).

Schultze, Ulrike, and **Betty Vandenbosch.** "Information Overload in a Groupware Environment: Now You See It, Now You Don't." *Journal of Organizational Computing and Electronic Commerce* 8, no. 2 (1998).

Schwabe, Gerhard. "Providing for Organizational Memory in Computer-Supported Meetings." *Journal of Organizational Computing and Electronic Commerce* 9, nos. 2 and 3 (1999).

Schwenk, C. R. "Cognitive Simplification Processes in Strategic Decision Making." *Strategic Management Journal* 5 (1984).

"Scotiabank Selects Sanchez Banking Solution." Press Release (July 15, 2002), available www.canadanewswire.ca/releases/July2002/15/c4843.html (accessed July 21, 2003).

Scott Morton, Michael, ed. *The Corporation in the 1990s.* New York, NY: Oxford University Press (1991).

Scott, Judy E., and **Iris Vessey.** "Managing Risks in Enterprise Systems Implementations." *Communications of the ACM* 45, no. 4 (April 2002).

Scott, Louise, Levente Horvath, and **Donald Day.** "Characterizing CASE Constraints." *Communications of the ACM* 43, no. 11 (November 2000).

Segars, Albert H., and **Varun Grover.** "Profiles of Strategic Information Systems Planning." *Information Systems Research* 10, no. 3 (September 1999).

Segev, Arie, Janna Porra, and **Malu Roldan.** "Internet Security and the Case of Bank of America." *Communications of the ACM* 41, no. 10 (October 1998).

Selker, Ted. "Coach: A Teaching Agent that Learns." *Communications of the ACM* 37, no. 7 (July 1994).

Sewell, Graham, and **James R. Barker.** "Neither Good, nor Bad, but Dangerous: Surveillance as an Ethical Paradox." *Ethics and Information Technology* 3, no. 3 (2001).

Seybold, Patricia B. "Get Inside the Lives of Your Customers." *Harvard Business Review* (May 2001).

Shan L. Pan, Ming-Huei Hsieh, and **Helen Chen.** "Knowledge Sharing through Intranet-Based Learning." *Journal of Organizational Computing and Electronic Commerce* 11, no. 3 (2001).

Shand, Dawne. "Making It Up as You Go." *Knowledge Management* (April 2000).

Shank, Michael E., Andrew C. Boynton, and **Robert W. Zmud.** "Critical Success Factor Analysis as a Methodology for MIS Planning." *MIS Quarterly* (June 1985).

Shapiro, Carl, and **Hal R. Varian.** *Information Rules.* Boston, MA: Harvard Business School Press (1999).

Sharda, Nalin. "Multimedia Networks: Fundamentals and Future Directions." *Communications of the Association for Information Systems* (February 1999).

Sharda, Ramesh, and **David M. Steiger.** "Inductive Model Analysis Systems: Enhancing Model Analysis in Decision Support Systems." *Information Systems Research* 7, no. 3 (September 1996).

Sharma, Srinarayan, and **Arun Rai.** "CASE Deployment in IS Organizations." *Communications of the ACM* 43, no. 1 (January 2000).

Sheetz, Steven D., Gretchen Irwin, David P. Tegarden, H. James Nelson, and **David E. Monarchi.** "Exploring the Difficulties of Learning Object-Oriented Techniques." *Journal of Management Information Systems* 14, no. 2 (Fall 1997).

Shelfer, Katherine M., and **J. Drew Procaccino.** "Smart Card Evolution." *Communications of the ACM* 45, no. 7 (July 2002).

Shore, Edwin B. "Reshaping the IS Organization." *MIS Quarterly* (December 1983).

Short, James E., and **N. Venkatraman.** "Beyond Business Process Redesign: Redefining Baxter's Business Network." *Sloan Management Review* (Fall 1992).

Shulgan, Christopher. "Brain Power." *Time Canada* (March 18, 2002).

Sia, Siew Kien, and **Boon Siong Neo.** "Reengineering Effectiveness and the Redesign of Organizational Control: A Case Study of the Inland Revenue Authority in Singapore." *Journal of Management Information Systems* 14, no. 1 (Summer 1997).

Sibigtroth, James M. "Implementing Fuzzy Expert Rules in Hardware." *AI Expert* (April 1992).

Silver, Mark S. "Decision Support Systems: Directed and Nondirected Change." *Information Systems Research* 1, no. 1 (March 1990).

Simon, H. A. *The New Science of Management Decision.* New York, NY: Harper & Row (1960).

Simon, Herbert A. "Applying Information Technology to Organization Design." *Public Administration Review* (May–June 1973).

Singh, Surendra N., and **Nikunj P. Dalal.** "Web Home Pages as Advertisements." *Communications of the ACM* 42, no. 8 (August 1999).

Sipior, Janice C., and **Burke T. Ward.** "The Dark Side of Employee E-mail." *Communications of the ACM* 42, no.7 (July 1999).

Sipior, Janice C., and **Burke T. Ward.** "The Ethical and Legal Quandary of E-mail Privacy." *Communications of the ACM* 38, no. 12 (December 1995).

Sircar, Sumit, Joe L. Turnbow, and **Bijoy Bordoloi.** "A Framework for Assessing the Relationship between Information Technology Investments and Firm Performance." *Journal of Management Information Systems* 16, no. 4 (Spring 2000).

Sircar, Sumit, Sridhar P. Nerur, and **Radhakanta Mahapatra.** "Revolution or Evolution? A Comparison of Object-Oriented and Structured Systems Development Methods." *MIS Quarterly* 25, no. 4 (December 2001).

Slaughter, Sandra A., Donald E. Harter, and **Mayuram S. Krishnan.** "Evaluating the Cost of Software Quality." *Communications of the ACM* 41, no. 8 (August 1998).

Slywotzky, Adrian J., and **David J. Morrison.** *How Digital Is Your Business?* New York, NY: Crown Business (2001).

Slywotzky, Adrian J., and **Richard Wise.** "The Growth Crisis, and How to Escape It." *Harvard Business Review* (July 2002).

"Smart Decisions, Smart Government: Real-Life Stories." Cognos Web site, available www.cognos.com/solutions/ca/success_ca_en.html (accessed March 29, 2003).

Smith, Craig S. "Ambivalence in China on Expanding Net Access." *New York Times* (August 11, 2000).

Smith, H. Jeff, and **John Hasnas.** "Ethics and Information Systems: The Corporate Domain." *MIS Quarterly* 23, no. 1 (March 1999).

Smith, H. Jeff, Mark Keil, and **Gordon Depledge.** "Keeping Mum as the Project Goes under." *Journal of Management Information Systems* 18, no. 2 (Fall 2001).

Smith, H. Jeff, Sandra J. Milberg, and **Sandra J. Burke.** "Information Privacy: Measuring Individuals' Concerns about Organizational Practices." *MIS Quarterly* 20, no. 2 (June 1996).

Smith, H. Jeff. "Privacy Policies and Practices: Inside the Organizational Maze." *Communications of the ACM* 36, no. 12, (December 1993).

Smith, Michael D., Joseph Bailey, and **Erik Brynjolfsson.** "Understanding Digital Markets: Review and Assessment." In *Understanding the Digital Economy,* edited by Erik Brynjolfsson and Brian Kahin. Cambridge, MA: MIT Press (1999).

Sniezek, Janet, David C. Wilkins, Patrick L. Wadlington, and **Michael R. Baumann.** "Training for Crisis Decision Making: Psychological Issues and Computer-Based Solutions." *Journal of Management Information Systems* 18, No. 4 (Spring 2002).

Soh, Christina, Sia Siew Kien, and **Joanne Tay-Yap.** "Cultural Fits and Misfits: Is ERP a Universal Solution?" *Communications of the ACM* 43, no. 3 (April 2000).

Songini, Mark L. "Setting the Price Right." *Computerworld* (June 3, 2002).

Soong-Yong, Choi, and **Andrew B. Whinston,** "Communities of Collaboration." *IQ Magazine* (July/August 2001).

Sprague, R. H., and **E. D. Carlson.** *Building Effective Decision Support Systems.* Englewood Cliffs, NJ: Prentice Hall (1982).

Sproull, Lee, and **Sara Kiesler.** *Connections: New Ways of Working in the Networked Organization.* Cambridge, MA: MIT Press (1992).

Stadler, Kevin. "ECR: Leveling the Playing Field." *Food Logistics* (September 2002).

Staples, D. Sandy, John S. Hulland, and **Christopher A. Higgins.** "A Self-Efficacy Theory Explanation for the Management of Remote Workers in Virtual Organizations." *Organization Science* 10, no. 6 (November–December 1999).

Starbuck, William H. "Learning by Knowledge-Intensive Firms." *Journal of Management Studies* 29, no. 6 (November 1992).

Starbuck, William H. "Organizations as Action Generators." *American Sociological Review* 48 (1983).

Starbuck, William H., and **Frances J. Milliken.** "Executives' Perceptual Filters: What They Notice and How They Make Sense." In *The Executive Effect: Concepts and Methods for Studying Top Managers,* edited by D. C. Hambrick. Greenwich, CT: JAI Press (1988).

Steinbart, Paul John, and **Ravinder Nath.** "Problems and Issues in the Management of International Data Networks." *MIS Quarterly* 16, no. 1 (March 1992).

Stillerman, Matthew, Carla Marceau, and **Maureen Stillman.** "Intrusion Detection for Distributed Applications." *Communications of the ACM* 42, no. 7 (July 1999).

Storey, Veda C., and **Robert C. Goldstein.** "Knowledge-Based Approaches to Database Design," *MIS Quarterly* 17, no. 1 (March 1993).

Strapagiel, Ed. "In the Year 5 A.W.: 5 Years after Wal-Mart." available www.kubas.com (accessed June 4, 2003).

Straub, Detmar W. "The Effect of Culture on IT Diffusion: E-Mail and FAX in Japan and the U.S." *Information Systems Research* 5, no. 1 (March 1994).

Straub, Detmar W., and **Richard J. Welke.** "Coping with Systems Risk: Security Planning Models for Management Decision Making." *MIS Quarterly* 22, no. 4 (December 1998).

Straub, Detmar W., Jr., and **Rosann Webb Collins.** "Key Information Liability Issues Facing Managers: Software Piracy, Proprietary Databases, and Individual Rights to Privacy." *MIS Quarterly* 14, no. 2 (June 1990).

Straub, Detmar W., Jr., and **William D. Nance.** "Discovering and Disciplining Computer Abuse in Organizations: A Field Study." *MIS Quarterly* 14, no. 1 (March 1990).

Strong, Diane M., Yang W. Lee, and **Richard Y. Wang.** "Data Quality in Context." *Communications of the ACM* 40, no. 5 (May 1997).

"Study: Canadians Utilizing E-Government." *CIO Governments Review* (December 1, 2002), available www.itworld.ca (accessed June 7, 2003).

Stylianou, Anthony C., Gregory R. Madey, and **Robert D. Smith.** "Selection Criteria for Expert System Shells: A Socio-Technical Framework." *Communications of the ACM* 35, no. 10 (October 1992).

Subramanian, Rangan, and **Ron Adner.** "Profits and the Internet: Seven Misconceptions." *Sloan Management Review* 42, no. 4 (Summer 2001).

"Success Stories: Nikon Optical Canada Inc.; Allowing Web-based Sales Analysis for Senior Management, Marketing Analysts, and Sales Representatives." Microstrategy.com, available www.microstrategy.com/Customers/Successes/nikon_optical.asp (accessed. July 21, 2003).

"Success Story: Bank of Montreal: The Bank of Montreal Minds Its Business Microstrategy-Style." Microstrategy Case Study, available www.microstrategy.com/Customers/Successes/bankofmontreal.asp (accessed July 21, 2003).

Sukhatme, Gaurav S., and Maja J. Mataric. "Embedding Robots into the Internet." *Communications of the ACM* 43, no. 5 (May 2000).

Sullivan, Brian. "IT Worker Pleads Guilty to Sabotaging Computers." *Computerworld* (March 26, 2001).

Suppa, Carly. "Wired Warriors Get To Work." *Network World Canada* (March 8, 2002).

Sviokla, John J. "An Examination of the Impact of Expert Systems on the Firm: The Case of XCON." *MIS Quarterly* 14, no. 5 (June 1990).

Sviokla, John J. "Expert Systems and Their Impact on the Firm: The Effects of PlanPower Use on the Information Processing Capacity of the Financial Collaborative." *Journal of Management Information Systems* 6, no. 3 (Winter 1989–1990).

Swanson, E. Burton, and Enrique Dans. "System Life Expectancy and the Maintenance Effort: Exploring their Equilibration." *MIS Quarterly* 24, no. 2 (June 2000).

Swanson, E. Burton. *Information System Implementation*. Homewood, IL: Richard D. Irwin (1988).

Swanson, Kent, Dave McComb, Jill Smith, and Don McCubbrey. "The Application Software Factory: Applying Total Quality Techniques to Systems Development." *MIS Quarterly* 15, no. 4 (December 1991).

Sweeney, Terry. "Voice Over IP Builds Momentum." *InformationWeek* (November 20, 2000).

Tallon, Paul P, Kenneth L. Kraemer, and Vijay Gurbaxani. "Executives' Perceptions of the Business Value of Information Technology: A Process-Oriented Approach." *Journal of Management Information Systems* 16, no. 4 (Spring 2000).

Tam, Kar Yan, and Kai Lung Hui. "A Choice Model for the Selection of Computer Vendors and Its Empirical Estimation" *Journal of Management Information Systems* 17, no. 4 (Spring 2001).

Tan, Zixiang (Alex), Milton Mueller, and Will Foster. "China's New Internet Regulations: Two Steps Forward, One Step Backward." *Communications of the ACM* 40, no. 12 (December 1997).

Tan, Zixiang, William Foster, and Seymour Goodman. "China's State-Coordinated Internet Infrastructure." *Communications of the ACM* 42, no. 6 (June 1999).

Taudes, Alfred, Markus Feurstein, and Andreas Mild. "Options Analysis of Software Platform Decisions: A Case Study." *MIS Quarterly* 24, no. 2 (June 2000).

Tayi, Giri Kumar, and Donald P. Ballou. "Examining Data Quality." *Communications of the ACM* 41, no. 2 (February 1998).

"Technology and Innovation Solutions." Navigation Canada Web site, available www.navcanada.ca/contentEN/technologySolutions/Solutions.pdf (accessed July 21, 2003).

Teng, James T. C., Seung Ryul Jeong, and Varun Grover. "Profiling Successful Reengineering Projects." *Communications of the ACM* 41, no. 6 (June 1998).

Tennenhouse, David. "Proactive Computing." *Communications of the ACM* 43, no. 5 (May 2000).

Teo, Hock-Hai, Bernard C. Y. Tan, and Kwok-Kee Wei. "Organizational Transformation Using Electronic Data Interchange: The Case of TradeNet in Singapore." *Journal of Management Information Systems* 13, no. 4 (Spring 1997).

Thatcher, Matt E., and Jim R. Oliver. "The Impact of Technology Investments on a Firm's Production Efficiency, Product Quality, and Productivity." *Journal of Management Information Systems* 18, no. 2 (Fall 2001).

"The Canadian Interface." National Law Enforcement Telecomunciations Systems, available www.nlets.org/canada.htm (accessed March 28, 2003).

"The New Role for 'Executive Information Systems." *I/S Analyzer* (January 1992).

The Telecommunications Policy Roundtable. "Renewing the Commitment to a Public Interest Telecommunications Policy." *Communications of the ACM* 37, no. 1 (January 1994).

Thomke, Stefan, and Eric von Hippel. "Customers as Innovators." *Harvard Business Review* (April 2002).

Thompson, Marjorie Sarbough, and Martha S. Feldman. "Electronic Mail and Organizational Communication." *Organization Science* 9, no. 6 (November–December 1998).

Thong, James Y. L., and Chee-Sing Yap. "Testing an Ethical Decision-Making Theory." *Journal of Management Information Systems* 15, no. 1 (Summer 1998).

Thong, James Y.L., Chee-Sing Yap, and Kin-Lee Seah. "Business Process Reengineering in the Public Sector: The Case of the Housing Development Board in Singapore." *Journal of Management Information Systems* 17, no. 1 (Summer 2000).

Thorne, Susan. "U.S. Retail Execs Migrate to Canada." Available icsc.org/srch/sct/ (accessed June 5, 2003).

Tischelle, George, and Sandra Swanson. "Not Just Kid Stuff." *InformationWeek* (September 3, 2001).

Todd, Peter, and Izak Benbasat. "Evaluating the Impact of DSS, Cognitive Effort, and Incentives on Strategy Selection. *Information Systems Research* 10, no. 4 (December 1999).

Torkzadeh, Gholamreza, and Gurpreet Dhillon. "Measuring Factors that Influence the Success of Internet Commerce." *Information Systems Research* 13, no. 2 (June 2002).

Tornatsky, Louis G., J. D. Eveland, and David Wessel. "NASA Explores Future of Software." *The Process of Technological Innovation: Reviewing the Literature*. Washington, DC: National Science Foundation (1983).

Tractinsky, Noam, and Sirkka L. Jarvenpaa. "Information Systems Design Decisions in a Global Versus Domestic Context." *MIS Quarterly* 19, no. 4 (December 1995).

"TransAlta Reports Profits by mySAP Human Resources." *SAP & Partner News* (May 15, 2003), available www.sap.info/index.php4?ACTION=noframe&url=http://www.sap.info/public/en/news.php4/Category-28893c613963f405e/page/0/article/Article-122613ec3725372384/en (accessed July 21, 2003).

Trippi, Robert, and Efraim Turban. "The Impact of Parallel and Neural Computing on Managerial Decision Making." *Journal of Management Information Systems* 6, no. 3 (Winter 1989–1990).

Truex, Duane P., Richard Baskerville, and Heinz Klein. "Growing Systems in Emergent Organizations." *Communications of the ACM* 42, no. 8 (August 1999).

Truman, Gregory E. "Integration in Electronic Exchange Environments." *Journal of Management Information Systems* 17, no. 1 (Summer 2000).

Tse, Daniel, and Louis Chan. "Multi-Point Design of Airfoils by a Genetic Algorithm." Institute for Aerospace Research, National Research Council Canada, Abstract, available www.cerca.umontreal.ca/cfd2ke/abstracts/130.pdf (accessed July 21, 2003).

Tuomi, Ilkka. "Data Is More Than Knowledge." *Journal of Management Information Systems* 16, no. 3 (Winter 1999–2000).

Turban, Efraim, and Jay E. Aronson. *Decision Support Systems and Intelligent Systems*, 6th ed. Upper Saddle River, NJ: Prentice Hall (2000).

Turner, Jon A. "Computer Mediated Work: The Interplay between Technology and Structured Jobs." *Communications of the ACM* 27, no. 12 (December 1984).

Turner, Jon A., and Robert A. Karasek, Jr. "Software Ergonomics: Effects of Computer Application Design Parameters on Operator Task Performance and Health." *Ergonomics* 27, no. 6 (1984).

Tushman, Michael L., and Philip Anderson. "Technological Discontinuities and Organizational Environments." *Administrative Science Quarterly* 31 (September 1986).

Tuttle, Brad, Adrian Harrell, and **Paul Harrison.** "Moral Hazard, Ethical Considerations, and the Decision to Implement an Information System." *Journal of Management Information Systems* 13, no. 4 (Spring 1997).

Tversky, A., and **D. Kahneman.** "The Framing of Decisions and the Psychology of Choice." *Science* 211 (January 1981).

Tyran, Craig K. and **Joey F. George.** "Improving Software Inspections with Group Process Support." *Communications of the ACM* 45, no. 9 (September 2002).

Tyran, Craig K., Alan R. Dennis, Douglas R. Vogel, and **J. F. Nunamaker, Jr.** "The Application of Electronic Meeting Technology to Support Senior Management." *MIS Quarterly* 16, no. 3 (September 1992).

Tyran, Craig K., and **Joey F. George.** "Improving Software Inspections with Group Process Support." *Communications of the ACM* 45, no. 9 (September 2002).

United States Department of Health, Education, and **Welfare.** *Records, Computers, and the Rights of Citizens.* Cambridge, MA: MIT Press (1973).

Urbaczewski, Andrew, and **Leonard M. Jessup.** "Does Electronic Monitoring of Employee Internet Usage Work?" *Communications of the ACM* 45, no. 1 (January 2002).

Urbaczewski, Andrew, Leonard M. Jessup, and **Bradley Wheeler.** "Electronic Commerce Research: A Taxonomy and Synthesis." *Journal of Organizational Computing and Electronic Commerce* 12, no. 2 (2002).

Valera, Francisco, Jorge E. López de Vergara, José I. Moreno, Víctor A. Villagrá, and **Julio Berrocal.** "Communication Management Experiences in E-commerce." *Communications of the ACM* 44, no. 4 (April 2001).

Vandenbosch, Betty, and **Michael J. Ginzberg.** "Lotus Notes and Collaboration: Plus ca change..." *Journal of Management Information Systems* 13, no. 3 (Winter 1997).

Vandenbosch, Mark, and **Niraj Dawar.** "Beyond Better Products: Capturing Value in Customer Interactions." *Sloan Management Review* 43, no. 4 (Summer 2002).

Varshney, Upkar, and **Ron Vetter.** "Emerging Mobile and Wireless Networks." *Communications of the ACM* 42, no. 6 (June 2000).

Varshney, Upkar, Andy Snow, Matt McGivern, and **Christi Howard.** "Voice Over IP." *Communications of the ACM* 45, no. 1 (January 2002).

Varshney, Upkar. "Networking Support for Mobile Computing." *Communications of the Association for Information Systems* 1 (January 1999).

Vedder, Richard G., Michael T. Vanacek, C. Stephen Guynes, and **James J. Cappel.** "CEO and CIO Perspectives on Competitive Intelligence." *Communications of the ACM* 42, no. 8 (August 1999).

Venkatraman, N. "Beyond Outsourcing: Managing IT Resources as a Value Center." *Sloan Management Review* (Spring 1997).

Venkatraman, N. "Five Steps to a Dot-Com Strategy: How to Find Your Footing on the Web." *Sloan Management Review* 41, no. 3 (Spring 2000).

Vessey, Iris, and **Sue A. Conger.** "Requirements Specification: Learning Object, Process, and Data Methodologies." *Communications of the ACM* 37, no. 5 (May 1994).

Vessey, Iris, and **Sue Conger.** "Learning to Specify Information Requirements: The Relationship between Application and Methodology." *Journal of Management Information Systems* 10, no. 2 (Fall 1993).

Vetter, Ron. "The Wireless Web." *Communications of the ACM* 44, no. 3 (March 2001).

Vetter, Ronald J. "ATM Concepts, Architectures, and Protocols." *Communications of the ACM* 38, no. 2 (February 1995).

Viega, John, Tadayoshi Koho, and **Bruce Potter.** "Trust (and Mistrust) in Secure Applications." *Communications of the ACM* 44, no. 2 (February 2001).

Vijayan, Jaikumar. "The Outsourcing Boom." *Computerworld* 36, no. 12 (March 18, 2002).

Volokh, Eugene. "Personalization and Privacy." *Communications of the ACM* 43, no. 8 (August 2000).

Volonino, Linda, and **Hugh J. Watson.** "The Strategic Business Objectives Method for EIS Development." *Journal of Management Information Systems* 7, no. 3 (Winter 1990–1991).

Von Hippel, Eric. "Learning from Open-Source Software." *Sloan Management Review* 42, no. 4 (Summer 2001).

Wagner, Christine, and **Efraim Turban.** "Are Intelligent E-Commerce Agents Partners or Predators?" *Communications of the ACM* 45, no.5 (May 2002).

Wakefield, Julie. "Complexity's Business Model." *Scientific American* (January 2001).

Walczak, Stephen. "An Empirical Analysis of Data Requirements for Financial Forecasting with Neural Networks." *Journal of Management Information Systems* 17, no. 4 (Spring 2001).

Walczak, Steven. "Gaining Competitive Advantage for Trading in Emerging Capital Markets with Neural Networks." *Journal of Management Information Systems* 16, no. 2 (Fall 1999).

Walls, Joseph G., George R. Widmeyer, and **Omar A. El Sawy.** "Building an Information System Design Theory for Vigilant EIS." *Information Systems Research* 3, no. 1 (March 1992).

Walsham, Geoffrey, and **Sundeys Sahay.** "GIS and District Level Administration in India: Problems and Opportunities." *MIS Quarterly* 23, no. 1 (March 1999).

Wand, Yair, and **Richard Y. Wang.** "Anchoring Data Quality Dimensions in Ontological Foundations." *Communications of the ACM* 39, no. 11 (November 1996).

Wang, Huaiqing, John Mylopoulos, and **Stephen Liao.** "Intelligent Agents and Financial Risk Monitoring Systems." *Communications of the ACM* 45, no. 3 (March 2002).

Wang, Huaiqing, Matthew K. O. Lee, and **Chen Wang.** "Consumer Privacy Concerns about Internet Marketing." *Communications of the ACM* 41, no. 3 (March 1998).

Wang, Richard Y., Yang W. Lee, Leo L. Pipino, and **Diane M. Strong.** "Manage Your Information as a Product." *Sloan Management Review* 39, no. 4 (Summer 1998).

Wang, Richard. "A Product Perspective on Total Data Quality Management." *Communications of the ACM* 41, no. 2 (February 1998).

Wareham, Jonathan, and **Armando Levy.** "Who Will Be the Adopters of 3G Mobile Computing Devices? A Probit Estimation of Mobile Telecom Diffusion." *Journal of Organizational Computing and Electronic Commerce* 12, no. 2 (2002).

Wastell, David G. "Learning Dysfunctions in Information Systems Development: Overcoming the Social Defenses with Transitional Objects." *MIS Quarterly* 23, no. 1 (December 1999).

Watad, Mahmoud M., and **Frank J. DiSanzo.** "Case Study: The Synergism of Telecommuting and Office Automation." *Sloan Management Review* 41, no. 2 (Winter 2000).

Watson, Hugh J., and **Barbara J. Haley.** "Managerial Considerations." *Communications of the ACM* 41, no. 9 (September 1998).

Watson, Hugh J., Astrid Lipp, Pamela Z. Jackson, Abdelhafid Dahmani, and **William B. Fredenberger.** "Organizational Support for Decision Support Systems." *Journal of Management Information Systems* 5, no. 4 (Spring 1989).

Watson, Hugh J., R. Kelly Rainer, Jr., and **Chang E. Koh.** "Executive Information Systems: A Framework for Development and a Survey of Current Practices." *MIS Quarterly* 15, no. 1 (March 1991).

Watson, Richard T., Gigi G. Kelly, Robert D. Galliers, and **James C. Brancheau.** "Key Issues in Information Systems Management: An International Perspective." *Journal of Management Information Systems* 13, no. 4 (Spring 1997).

Watson, Richard T., Teck-Hua Ho, and **K. S. Raman.** "Culture: A Fourth Dimension of Group Support Systems." *Communications of the ACM* 37, no. 10 (October 1994).

"Web Content by Language." *eMarketer*, available www. global-reach.biz/globstats/refs.php3 (accessed June 7, 2003).

Weber, Max. *The Theory of Social and Economic Organization.* Translated by Talcott Parsons. New York, NY: Free Press (1947).

Weber, Ron. *Information Systems Control and Audit.* New York, NY: McGraw-Hill (1999).

Weil, Nancy. "Scotiabank Hires IBM in Major Outsourcing Deal." *ComputerWorld Canada* (March 27, 2001).

Weil, Nancy. "Scotiabank Picks IBM Canada for $578 Million Outsourcing Deal." *Computerworld Canada* (March 27, 2001).

Weill, Peter, and **Marianne Broadbent.** "Management by Maxim: How Business and IT Managers Can Create IT Infrastructures," *Sloan Management Review* (Spring 1997).

Weill, Peter, and **Marianne Broadbent.** *Leveraging the New Infrastructure.* Cambridge, MA: Harvard Business School Press (1998).

Weill, Peter, Mani Subramani, and **Marianne Broadbent.** "Building IT Infrastructure for Strategic Agility." *Sloan Management Review* 44, no. 1 (Fall 2002).

Weiser, Mark. "What Ever Happened to the Next-Generation Internet?" *Communications of the ACM* 44, no. 9 (September 2001).

Weitzel, John R., and **Larry Kerschberg.** "Developing Knowledge Based Systems: Reorganizing the System Development Life Cycle." *Communications of the ACM* (April 1989).

Wellman, Barry. "Designing the Internet for a Networked Society." *Communications of the ACM* 45, no. 5 (May 2002).

Welty, Bill, and **Irma Becerra-Fernandez.** "Managing Trust and Commitment in Supply Chain Relationships." *Communications of the ACM* 44, no. 6 (June 2001).

Werbach, Kevin. "Syndication: The Emerging Model for Business in the Internet Era." *Harvard Business Review* (May–June 2000).

Wessel, David. "NASA Explores Future of Software." *Wall Street Journal* (April 26, 2001.)

Westin, Alan F., Heather A. Schweder, Michael A. Baker, and **Sheila Lehman.** *The Changing Workplace.* New York, NY: Knowledge Industries (1995).

Westland, J. Christopher. "Preference Ordering Cash, Near-Cash and Electronic Cash." *Journal of Organizational Computing and Electronic Commerce* 12, no. 3 (2002).

Whiting, Rick. "Companies Boost Sales Efforts with Predictive Analysis." *InformationWeek* (February 25, 2002).

Whiting, Rick. "Cognos Metrics Manager Now in Series 7." *Asia Computer Weekly* (October 21, 2002).

Whitman, Michael E., Anthony M. Townsend, and **Robert J. Aalberts.** "Considerations for Effective Telecommunications-Use Policy." *Communications of the ACM* 42, no. 6 (June 1999).

Widrow, Bernard, David E. Rumelhart, and **Michael A. Lehr.** "Neural Networks: Applications in Industry, Business, and Science." *Communications of the ACM* 37, no. 3 (March 1994).

Wigand, Rolf T., and **Robert Benjamin.** "Electronic Commerce: Effects on Electronic Markets." *JCMC* 1, no. 3 (December 1995).

Wijnhoven, Fons. "Designing Organizational Memories: Concept and Method." *Journal of Organizational Computing and Electronic Commerce* 8, no. 1 (1998).

Willcocks, Leslie, and **Robert Plant.** "Pathways to E-Business Leadership," *Sloan Management Review* (Spring 2001).

Williamson, Oliver E. *The Economic Institutions of Capitalism.* New York, NY: Free Press (1985).

Willis, T. Hillman, and **Debbie B. Tesch.** "An Assessment of Systems Development Methodologies." *Journal of Information Technology Management* 2, no. 2 (1991).

Wilson, E. Vance. "E-mail Winners and Losers." *Communications of the ACM* 45, no. 10 (October 2002).

Wilson, Jeff. "Canada Must Improve to Remain on Top." *CIO Governments' Review* (October 1, 2002).

Wilson, Jeff. "Canada Must Improve to Remain Connectedness Leader." *Daily IT Wire* (August 9, 2002), available www. itworldcanada.com (accessed July 11, 2003).

Wilson, Meredith. "Slices of Life." *CIO Magazine* (August 15, 2000).

Wingfield, Nick. "An eBay Merchant Disappears, Failing to Deliver the Goods." *Wall Street Journal* (February 22, 2002).

Wintrob, Suzanne. "Operating Under a Shadow World in Crisis: Handle Both Data and Human Resources with Care." *The National Post* (February 17, 2003).

Wise, Richard, and **David Morrison.** "Beyond the Exchange: The Future of B2B." *Harvard Business Review* (November-December 2000).

Wiseman, Charles. *Strategic Information Systems.* Homewood, IL: Richard D. Irwin (1988).

Wong, David, Noemi Paciorek, and **Dana Moore.** "Java-Based Mobile Agents." *Communications of the ACM* 42, no. 3 (March 1999).

Wong, Poh-Kam. "Leveraging the Global Information Revolution for Economic Development: Singapore's Evolving Information Industry Strategy." *Information Systems Research* 9, no. 4 (December 1998).

"Worldwide E-Commerce Growth." Forrester Research, available www.glreach.com/eng/ed/art/2004.ecommerce.php3 (accessed June 7, 2003).

Wrapp, H. Edward. "Good Managers Don't Make Policy Decisions." *Harvard Business Review* (July–August 1984).

Wysocki, Bernard. "The Big Bang." *Wall Street Journal* (January 1, 2000).

Ye, Nong, Joseph Giordano, and **John Feldman.** "A Process Control Approach to Cyber Attack Detection." *Communications of the ACM* 44, no. 8 (August 2001).

Yin, Robert K. "Life Histories of Innovations: How New Practices Become Routinized." *Public Administration Review* (January–February 1981).

Yoffie, David B. and **Michael A. Cusumano.** "Judo Strategy: The Competitive Dynamics of Internet Time." *Harvard Business Review* (January 1999).

Youngjin, Yoo, and **Maryam Alavi.** "Media and Group Cohesion: Relative Influences on Social Presence, Task Participation, and Group Consensus." *MIS Quarterly* 25, no. 3 (September 2001).

Yourdon, Edward, and **L. L. Constantine.** *Structured Design.* New York, NY: Yourdon Press (1978).

Yu, Larry. "Successful Customer Relationship Management." *Sloan Management Review* 42, no. 4 (Summer 2001).

Zachman, J. A. "Business Systems Planning and Business Information Control Study: A Comparison." *IBM Systems Journal* 21 (1982).

Zadeh, Lotfi A. "Fuzzy Logic, Neural Networks, and Soft Computing." *Communications of the ACM* 37, no. 3 (March 1994).

Zadeh, Lotfi A. "The Calculus of Fuzzy If/Then Rules." *AI Expert* (March 1992).

Zhao, J. Leon, Akhil Kumar, and **Edward W. Stohr.** "Workflow-Centric Information Distribution through E-Mail." *Journal of Management Information Systems* 17, no. 3 (Winter 2000–2001).

Zhao, J. Leon, and **Vincent H. Resh.** "Internet Publishing and Transformation of Knowledge Processes." *Communications of the ACM* 44, no. 12 (December 2001).

Zhou, Jianying. "Achieving Fair Nonrepudiation in Electronic Transactions." *Journal of Organizational Computing and Electronic Commerce* 11, no. 4 (2001).

Zhu, Kevin, and **Kenneth L. Kraemer.** "E-Commerce Metrics for Net-Enhanced Organizations: Assessing the Value of e-Commerce to Firm Performance in the Manufacturing Sector." *Information Systems Research* 13, no.3 (September 2002).

Zipkin, Paul. "The Limits of Mass Customization." *Sloan Management Review* (Spring 2001).

Zviran, Moshe and **William J. Haga.** "Password Security: An Empirical Study." *Journal of Management Information Systems* 15, no. 4 (Spring 1999).

Name index

ORGANIZATION INDEX

SUBJECT INDEX

CREDITS